BENCHMARK SERIES

MICROSOFT® EXCEL® 2013

LEVELS 1 & 2

NITA RUTKOSKY
Pierce College at Puyallup
Puyallup, Washington

DENISE SEQUIN
Fanshawe College
London, Ontario

JAN DAVIDSON
Lambton College
Sarnia, Ontario

AUDREY ROGGENKAMP
Pierce College at Puyallup
Puyallup, Washington

IAN RUTKOSKY
Pierce College at Puyallup
Puyallup, Washington

Paradigm PUBLISHING
St. Paul

Director of Editorial	Christine Hurney
Director of Production	Timothy W. Larson
Production Editor	Sarah Kearin
Copy Editor	Communicáto, Ltd.; Nan Brooks, Abshier House
Cover Designer	Leslie Anderson
Text Designers	Leslie Anderson, Jaana Bykonich
Desktop Production	Jaana Bykonich, Julie Johnston, Valerie King, Timothy W. Larson, Jack Ross, Sara Schmidt Boldon
Proofreader	Katherine Lee
Indexer	Terry Casey
VP & Director of Digital Projects	Chuck Bratton
Digital Projects Manager	Tom Modl

Acknowledgements: The authors, editors, and publisher thank the following instructors for their helpful suggestions during the planning and development of the books in the Benchmark Office 2013 Series: Olugbemiga Adekunle, Blue Ridge Community College, Harrisonburg, VA; Letty Barnes, Lake WA Institute of Technology, Kirkland, WA; Erika Nadas, Wilbur Wright College, Chicago, IL; Carolyn Walker, Greenville Technical College, Greenville, SC; Carla Anderson, National College, Lynchburg, VA; Judy A. McLaney, Lurleen B. Wallace Community College, Opp, AL; Sue Canter, Guilford Technical Community College, Jamestown, NC; Reuel Sample, National College, Knoxville, TN; Regina Young, Wiregrass Georgia Technical College, Valdosta, GA; William Roxbury, National College, Stow, OH; Charles Adams, II, Danville Community College, Danville, VA; Karen Spray, Northeast Community College, Norfolk, NE; Deborah Miller, Augusta Technical College, Augusta, GA; Wanda Stuparits, Lanier Technical College, Cumming, GA; Gale Wilson, Brookhaven College, Farmers Branch, TX; Jocelyn S. Pinkard, Arlington Career Institute, Grand Prairie, TX; Ann Blackman, Parkland College, Champaign, IL; Fathia Williams, Fletcher Technical Community College, Houma, LA; Leslie Martin, Gaston College, Dallas, NC; Tom Rose, Kellogg Community College, Battle Creek, MI; Casey Thompson, Wiregrass Georgia Technical College, Douglas, GA; Larry Bush, University of Cincinnati, Clermont College, Amelia, OH; Tim Ellis, Schoolcraft College, Liconia, MI; Miles Cannon, Lanier Technical College, Oakwood, GA; Irvin LaFleur, Lanier Technical College, Cumming, GA; Patricia Partyka, Schoolcraft College, Prudenville, MI.

The authors and publishing team also thanks the following individuals for their contributions to this project: checking the accuracy of the instruction and exercises—Brienna McWade, Traci Post, and Janet Blum, Fanshawe College, London, Ontario; creating annotated model answers and developing lesson plans—Ann Mills, Ivy Tech Community College, Evansville, Indiana; developing rubrics—Marjory Wooten, Laneir Techncial College, Cumming, Georgia.

ISBN 978-0-76385-346-4 (Text)
ISBN 978-0-76385-389-1 (Text + CD)

875 Montreal Way
St. Paul, MN 55102
Email: educate@emcp.com
Website: www.emcp.com

Printed in the United States of America

22 21 20 19 18 17 16 15 14 13 1 2 3 4 5 6 7 8 9 10

Contents

Preface vii
Getting Started in Office 2013 1
Using Windows 8 13
Browsing the Internet Using Internet Explorer 10 41

Microsoft Excel 2013 Level 1

Unit 1 Preparing and Formatting Worksheets 1

Chapter 1 Preparing an Excel Workbook 3
Model Answers 4
Creating a Worksheet 5
Saving a Workbook 8
Editing Data in a Cell 10
Printing a Workbook 11
Closing a Workbook 12
Closing Excel 13
Using Automatic Entering Features 13
Using AutoComplete 13
Using AutoCorrect 13
Using AutoFill 15
Opening a Workbook 16
Opening a Workbook from the Recent Workbooks List 16
Pinning a Workbook to the Recent Workbooks List 16
Inserting Formulas 18
Using the AutoSum Button to Add Numbers 18
Using the AutoSum Button to Average Numbers 19
Using the Fill Handle to Copy a Formula 19
Selecting Cells 20
Selecting Cells Using the Mouse 20
Selecting Cells Using the Keyboard 20
Selecting Data within Cells 20
Applying Basic Formatting 21
Changing Column Width 21
Merging and Centering Cells 21
Formatting Numbers 23
Using Help 25
Getting Help on a Button 26
Getting Help in a Dialog Box or Backstage Area 27
Chapter Summary, Commands Review, Concepts Check, Skills Check, Visual Benchmark, Case Study 28

Chapter 2 Inserting Formulas in a Worksheet 35
Model Answers 36
Writing Formulas with Mathematical Operators 37
Copying a Formula with Relative Cell References 38
Checking Cell References in a Formula 39
Writing a Formula by Pointing 40
Determining the Order of Operations 40
Using the Trace Error Button 41
Identifying Common Formula/Function Errors in Excel 41
Inserting Formulas with Functions 43
Writing Formulas with Statistical Functions 45
Writing Formulas with the NOW and TODAY Functions 49
Displaying Formulas 49
Using Absolute and Mixed Cell References in Formulas 50
Using an Absolute Cell Reference in a Formula 50
Using a Mixed Cell Reference in a Formula 52
Chapter Summary, Commands Review, Concepts Check, Skills Check, Visual Benchmark, Case Study 53

Chapter 3 Formatting an Excel Worksheet 61
Model Answers 62
Changing Column Width 63
Changing Column Width Using Column Boundaries 63
Changing Column Width at the Column Width Dialog Box 64
Changing Row Height 65
Inserting and Deleting Cells, Rows, and Columns 66
Inserting Rows 66
Inserting Columns 67
Deleting Cells, Rows, or Columns 68
Clearing Data in Cells 69
Applying Formatting 69
Applying Font Formatting 70
Formatting with the Mini Toolbar 70
Applying Alignment Formatting 70
Applying a Theme 73
Formatting Numbers 74
Formatting Numbers Using Number Group Buttons 74
Formatting Numbers Using the Format Cells Dialog Box 76
Formatting Cells Using the Format Cells Dialog Box 78
Aligning and Indenting Data 78
Changing the Font at the Format Cells Dialog Box 80
Adding Borders to Cells 82
Adding Fill and Shading to Cells 84
Repeating the Last Action 84
Formatting with Format Painter 86
Hiding and Unhiding Columns and Rows 86
Chapter Summary, Commands Review, Concepts Check, Skills Check, Visual Benchmark, Case Study 88

Chapter 4 Enhancing a Worksheet 99
Model Answers 100
Formatting a Worksheet Page 101
Changing Margins 101
Centering a Worksheet Horizontally and/or Vertically 102
Changing Page Orientation 104
Changing the Page Size 104
Inserting and Removing Page Breaks 104
Printing Column and Row Titles on Multiple Pages 107
Scaling Data 108
Inserting a Background Picture 109
Printing Gridlines and Row and Column Headings 110
Printing a Specific Area of a Worksheet 110
Inserting Headers and Footers 112
Customizing Print Jobs 117
Completing a Spelling Check 118
Using Undo and Redo 118
Finding and Replacing Data and Cell Formatting in a Worksheet 120
Sorting Data 125
Completing a Custom Sort 125
Sorting More Than One Column 127
Filtering Data 127

Chapter Summary, Commands Review, Concepts Check, Skills Check, Visual Benchmark, Case Study 130
Unit 1 Performance Assessment 141

Unit 2 Enhancing the Display of Workbooks 147

Chapter 5 Moving Data within and between Workbooks 149
Model Answers 150
Creating a Workbook with Multiple Worksheets 153
Inserting a New Worksheet 153
Deleting a Worksheet 153
Selecting Multiple Worksheets 153
Copying, Cutting, and Pasting Cells 154
Copying and Pasting Selected Cells 154
Using Paste Options 155
Moving Selected Cells 156
Copying and Pasting with the Clipboard Task Pane 157
Pasting Values Only 159
Managing Worksheets 160
Hiding a Worksheet in a Workbook 162
Printing a Workbook Containing Multiple Worksheets 163
Using Zoom 164
Splitting a Worksheet into Windows and Freezing and Unfreezing Panes 165
Working with Ranges 167
Working with Windows 168
Opening Multiple Workbooks 169
Arranging Workbooks 169
Hiding/Unhiding Workbooks 171
Sizing and Moving Workbooks 172
Moving, Linking, Copying, and Pasting Data 172
Moving and Copying Data 173
Linking Data 174
Copying and Pasting Data between Programs 175
Chapter Summary, Commands Review, Concepts Check, Skills Check, Visual Benchmark, Case Study 176

Chapter 6 Maintaining Workbooks 187
Model Answers 188
Maintaining Workbooks 190
Creating a Folder 191
Renaming a Folder 192
Selecting Workbooks 192
Deleting Workbooks and Folders 193
Deleting to the Recycle Bin 193
Copying Workbooks 194
Sending Workbooks to a Different Drive or Folder 195
Cutting and Pasting a Workbook 195
Renaming Workbooks 196
Deleting a Folder and Its Contents 197
Managing the Recent Workbooks List 197
Pinning a Workbook 198
Recovering an Unsaved Workbook 198
Clearing the Recent Workbooks List and the Recent List 199
Managing Worksheets 200
Copying a Worksheet to Another Workbook 200
Moving a Worksheet to Another Workbook 201
Formatting with Cell Styles 204
Applying a Style 204
Defining a Cell Style 205
Modifying a Style 209
Copying Styles to Another Workbook 210
Removing a Style 211
Deleting a Style 211
Inserting Hyperlinks 212
Linking to an Existing Web Page or File 212
Navigating Using Hyperlinks 213
Linking to a Place in the Workbook 214
Linking to a New Workbook 214
Linking Using a Graphic 215
Linking to an Email Address 215
Modifying, Editing, and Removing a Hyperlink 216
Using Excel Templates 217
Chapter Summary, Commands Review, Concepts Check, Skills Check, Visual Benchmark, Case Study 220

Chapter 7 Creating Charts and Inserting Formulas 229
Model Answers 230
Creating a Chart 232
Sizing and Moving a Chart 233
Editing Data and Adding a Data Series 233
Formatting with Chart Buttons 236
Printing a Chart 238
Changing the Chart Design 239
Changing the Chart Style 240
Switching Rows and Columns 240
Changing Chart Layout and Colors 241
Changing the Chart Location 242
Adding, Moving, and Deleting Chart Elements 242
Changing Chart Formatting 245
Formatting a Selection 245
Inserting Shapes 246
Applying Formatting at a Task Pane 248
Changing Chart Height and Width Measurements 248
Deleting a Chart 249
Writing Formulas with Financial Functions 252
Finding the Periodic Payments for a Loan 253
Finding the Future Value of a Series of Payments 255
Writing Formulas with the IF Logical Function 256
Writing Formulas with an IF Function Using the Function Arguments Palette 257
Writing IF Formulas Containing Text 259
Chapter Summary, Commands Review, Concepts Check, Skills Check, Visual Benchmark, Case Study 260

Chapter 8 Adding Visual Interest to Workbooks 271
Model Answers 272
Inserting Symbols and Special Characters 273
Inserting Images 275
Customizing and Formatting an Image 276
Sizing and Moving an Image 276
Formatting an Image at the Format Picture Task Pane 278
Inserting an Image from Office.com 278
Creating and Inserting Screenshots 280
Inserting and Copying Shapes 281
Drawing and Formatting Text Boxes 284

Inserting a Picture as a Watermark 286
Inserting SmartArt Graphics 288
Entering Data in a SmartArt Graphic 288
Sizing, Moving, and Deleting a SmartArt Graphic 289
Changing the SmartArt Graphic Design 290
Changing the SmartArt Graphic Formatting 291
Creating, Sizing, and Moving WordArt 293
Chapter Summary, Commands Review, Concepts Check, Skills Check, Visual Benchmark, Case Study 294
Unit 2 Performance Assessment 305
Excel Level 1 Index 313

Microsoft Excel 2013 Level 2

Unit 1 Advanced Formatting, Formulas, and Data Management 1
Chapter 1 Advanced Formatting Techniques 3
Model Answers 4
Applying Conditional Formatting 6
Creating a New Formatting Rule 8
Editing and Deleting Conditional Formatting Rules 10
Applying Conditional Formatting Using an Icon Set 12
Applying Conditional Formatting Using Data Bars and Color Scales 14
Applying Conditional Formatting Using a Formula 15
Applying Fraction and Scientific Formatting 16
Applying Special Number Formats 18
Creating Custom Number Formats 20
Wrapping Text and Shrinking Text to Fit within Cells 22
Using Text Functions 23
Filtering a Worksheet Using a Custom AutoFilter 27
Filtering and Sorting Data Using Conditional Formatting or Cell Attributes 29
Chapter Summary, Commands Review, Concepts Check, Skills Check, Visual Benchmark, Case Study 31
Chapter 2 Advanced Functions and Formulas 39
Model Answers 40
Creating Name Ranges 41
Using Statistical Functions 42
Using the COUNTA Function 42
Using the COUNTIF and COUNTIFS Functions 43
Using the AVERAGEIF and AVERAGEIFS Functions 46
Using Math and Trigonometry Functions: SUMIF and SUMIFS 49
Managing Range Names 51
Using Lookup Functions 52
Using the VLOOKUP Function 52
Using the HLOOKUP Function 55
Using Financial Functions: PPMT and IPMT 56
Using Logical Functions 58
Creating Nested Functions 58
Using the AND and OR Functions 59
Chapter Summary, Commands Review, Concepts Check, Skills Check, Visual Benchmark, Case Study 62
Chapter 3 Working with Tables and Data Features 71
Model Answers 72
Creating Tables 74
Modifying a Table 75
Applying Table Styles and Table Style Options 76
Sorting and Filtering Tables 78
Working with Data Tools 80
Populating Data Using Flash Fill 81
Removing Duplicate Records 82
Validating and Restricting Data Entry 84
Converting a Table to a Normal Range 89
Subtotaling Related Data 89
Grouping and Ungrouping Data 93
Chapter Summary, Commands Review, Concepts Check, Skills Check, Visual Benchmark, Case Study 95
Chapter 4 Summarizing and Consolidating Data 103
Model Answers 104
Summarizing Data in Multiple Worksheets Using Range Names and 3-D References 106
Summarizing Data by Linking to Ranges in Other Worksheets or Workbooks 110
Maintaining External References 111
Summarizing Data Using the Consolidate Feature 114
Creating PivotTables 116
Filtering a PivotTable Using Slicers 122
Filtering a PivotTable Using Timelines 124
Changing the Summary Function 126
Creating PivotCharts 127
Summarizing Data with Sparklines 130
Creating a Sparkline 130
Customizing Sparklines 132
Chapter Summary, Commands Review, Concepts Check, Skills Check, Visual Benchmark, Case Study 134
Unit 1 Performance Assessment 143
Unit 2 Managing and Integrating Data and the Excel Environment 151
Chapter 5 Using Data Analysis Features 153
Model Answers 154
Pasting Data Using Paste Special Options 155
Transposing Data 156
Performing a Mathematical Operation While Pasting 158
Selecting Other Paste Special Options 159
Using Goal Seek to Populate Cells 159
Creating Assumptions for What-If Analysis
Using the Scenario Manager 161
Applying a Scenario 163
Editing a Scenario 163
Deleting a Scenario 164
Compiling a Scenario Summary Report 165
Performing What-If Analysis Using Data Tables 166
Creating a One-Variable Data Table 166
Creating a Two-Variable Data Table 168
Using Auditing Tools 169
Tracing Precedent and Dependent Cells 170
Troubleshooting Formulas 171
Circling Invalid Data 174
Watching a Formula Cell 174

Chapter Summary, Commands Review, Concepts Check, Skills Check, Visual Benchmark, Case Study 176
Chapter 6 Protecting and Sharing Workbooks **185**
Model Answers 186
Adding Workbook Properties 187
Managing Comments 189
Inserting a Comment 189
Viewing a Comment 189
Printing a Comment 190
Editing and Deleting a Comment 190
Copying and Pasting Comments 190
Sharing Workbooks 192
Changing the User Name 194
Opening Multiple Instances of Excel 194
Resolving Conflicts in a Shared Workbook 196
Printing a History Sheet and Removing Shared Workbook Access 198
Sharing a Workbook on Windows SkyDrive 199
Sending a Workbook via Email 203
Protecting and Unprotecting Worksheets 204
Protecting and Unprotecting the Structure of a Workbook 207
Unprotecting a Workbook 208
Adding and Removing a Password in a Workbook 208
Tracking Changes to a Workbook 211
Accepting and Rejecting Tracked Changes 212
Turning Off Track Changes 215
Chapter Summary, Commands Review, Concepts Check, Skills Check, Visual Benchmark, Case Study 215
Chapter 7 Automating Repetitive Tasks and Customizing Excel **225**
Model Answers 226
Automating Tasks Using Macros 227
Saving Workbooks Containing Macros 228
Running a Macro 230
Assigning a Macro to a Shortcut Key 231
Editing a Macro 233
Deleting a Macro 235
Managing Macros 235
Pinning Workbooks to the Recent Workbooks List 236
Changing Display Options to Customize the Work Area 237
Minimizing the Ribbon 238
Customizing Ribbons and the Quick Access Toolbar 240
Customizing the Ribbon 240
Customizing the Quick Access Toolbar 245
Resetting the Ribbons and Quick Access Toolbar 247
Creating and Applying a Custom View 248
Saving a Workbook as a Template 250
Using a Custom Template 252
Deleting a Custom Template 253
Customizing Save Options 253
Chapter Summary, Commands Review, Concepts Check, Skills Check, Visual Benchmark, Case Study 256
Chapter 8 Importing, Exporting, and Distributing Data **267**
Model Answers 268
Importing Data into Excel 270
Importing Data from Access 271
Importing Data from a Website 272
Importing Data from a Text File 275
Exporting Data from Excel 278
Copying and Pasting Worksheet Data to an Access Table 278
Copying and Pasting Worksheet Data to a Word Document 280
Breaking a Link to an Excel Object 283
Copying and Pasting Worksheet Data to a PowerPoint Presentation 284
Exporting Excel Data as a Text File 286
Preparing a Workbook for Distribution 288
Removing Information from a Workbook before Distributing 289
Marking a Workbook as Final 292
Using the Compatibility Checker 294
Viewing Trust Center Settings for Excel 296
Distributing Workbooks 298
Publishing a Workbook as a PDF Document 298
Publishing a Workbook as an XPS Document 300
Publishing a Worksheet as a Web Page 302
Chapter Summary, Commands Review, Concepts Check, Skills Check, Visual Benchmark, Case Study 304
Unit 2 Performance Assessment **313**
Excel Level 2 Index **321**

Preface

Benchmark Series Microsoft Excel 2013 is designed for students who want to learn how to use this powerful spreadsheet program to manipulate numerical data in resolving issues related to finances or other numbers-based information. No prior knowledge of spreadsheets is required. After successfully completing a course using this textbook, students will be able to

- Create and edit spreadsheets of varying complexity
- Format cells, columns, and rows as well as entire workbooks in a uniform, attractive style
- Analyze numerical data and project outcomes to make informed decisions
- Plan, research, create, revise, and publish worksheets and workbooks to meet specific communication needs
- Given a workplace scenario requiring a numbers-based solution, assess the information requirements and then prepare the materials that achieve the goal efficiently and effectively

In addition to mastering Excel skills, students will learn the essential features and functions of computer hardware, the Windows 8 operating system, and Internet Explorer 10. Upon completing the text, they can expect to be proficient in using Excel to organize, analyze, and present information.

Well-designed textbook pedagogy is important, but students learn technology skills from practice and problem solving. Technology provides opportunities for interactive learning as well as excellent ways to quickly and accurately assess student performance. To this end, this textbook is supported with SNAP, Paradigm Publishing's web-based training and assessment learning management system. Details about SNAP as well as additional student courseware and instructor resources can be found on page xiv.

Achieving Proficiency in Excel 2013

Since its inception several Office versions ago, the Benchmark Series has served as a standard of excellence in software instruction. Elements of the book function individually and collectively to create an inviting, comprehensive learning environment that produces successful computer users. The following visual tour highlights the text's features.

MICROSOFT® EXCEL® Level 1

Unit 1 ■ Preparing and Formatting Worksheets

Chapter 1 ■ Preparing an Excel Workbook
Chapter 2 ■ Inserting Formulas in a Worksheet
Chapter 3 ■ Formatting an Excel Worksheet
Chapter 4 ■ Enhancing a Worksheet

1

UNIT OPENERS display the unit's four chapter titles. Each level has two units, which conclude with a comprehensive unit performance assessment.

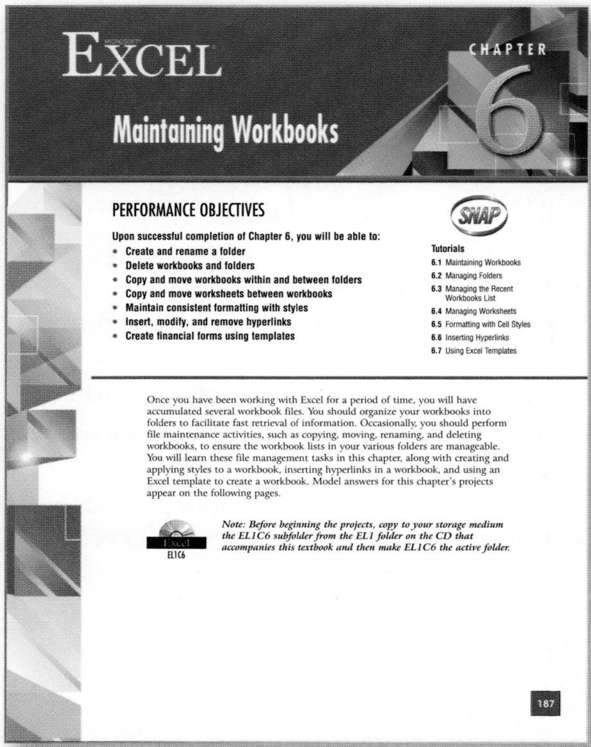

EXCEL

CHAPTER 6

Maintaining Workbooks

PERFORMANCE OBJECTIVES

Upon successful completion of Chapter 6, you will be able to:

- **Create and rename a folder**
- **Delete workbooks and folders**
- **Copy and move workbooks within and between folders**
- **Copy and move worksheets between workbooks**
- **Maintain consistent formatting with styles**
- **Insert, modify, and remove hyperlinks**
- **Create financial forms using templates**

SNAP

Tutorials

6.1 Maintaining Workbooks
6.2 Managing Folders
6.3 Managing the Recent Workbooks List
6.4 Managing Worksheets
6.5 Formatting with Cell Styles
6.6 Inserting Hyperlinks
6.7 Using Excel Templates

Once you have been working with Excel for a period of time, you will have accumulated several workbook files. You should organize your workbooks into folders to facilitate fast retrieval of information. Occasionally, you should perform file maintenance activities, such as copying, moving, renaming, and deleting workbooks, to ensure the workbook lists in your various folders are manageable. You will learn these file management tasks in this chapter, along with creating and applying styles to a workbook, inserting hyperlinks in a workbook, and using an Excel template to create a workbook. Model answers for this chapter's projects appear on the following pages.

Excel
EL1C6

Note: Before beginning the projects, copy to your storage medium the EL1C6 subfolder from the EL1 folder on the CD that accompanies this textbook and then make EL1C6 the active folder.

187

CHAPTER OPENERS present the performance objectives and an overview of the skills taught.

SNAP interactive tutorials are available to support chapter-specific skills at snap2013.emcp.com.

DATA FILES are provided for each chapter. A prominent note reminds students to copy the appropriate chapter data folder and make it active.

PROJECT APPROACH: Builds Skill Mastery within Realistic Context

MODEL ANSWERS provide a preview of the finished chapter projects and allow students to confirm they have created the materials accurately.

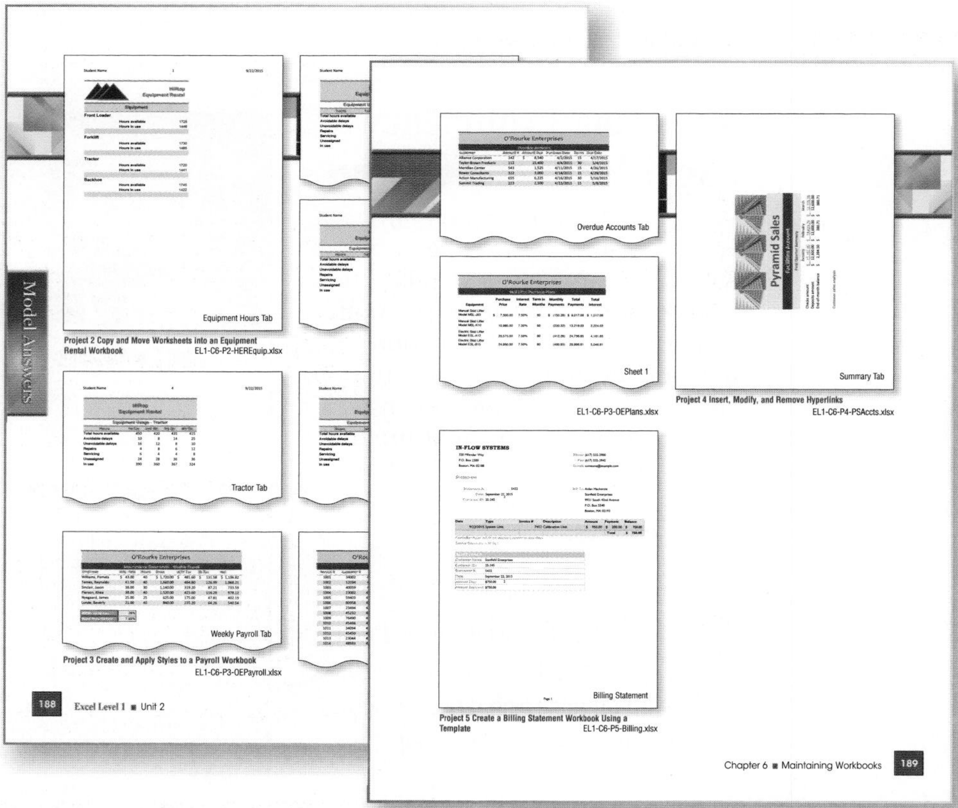

Model Answers

Equipment Hours Tab

Project 2 Copy and Move Worksheets into an Equipment Rental Workbook EL1-C6-P2-HEREquip.xlsx

Tractor Tab

Weekly Payroll Tab

Project 3 Create and Apply Styles to a Payroll Workbook EL1-C6-P3-OEPayroll.xlsx

188 Excel Level 1 ■ Unit 2

O'Rourke Enterprises

Overdue Accounts Tab

Sheet 1

EL1-C6-P3-OEPlans.xlsx

Pyramid Sales

Summary Tab

Project 4 Insert, Modify, and Remove Hyperlinks EL1-C6-P4-PSAccts.xlsx

IN-FLOW SYSTEMS

Billing Statement

Project 5 Create a Billing Statement Workbook Using a Template EL1-C6-P5-Billing.xlsx

Chapter 6 ■ Maintaining Workbooks 189

Project 1 Format a Product Pricing Worksheet 7 Parts

You will open a workbook containing a worksheet with product pricing data and then format the worksheet by changing column widths and row heights, inserting and deleting rows and columns, and clearing data in cells. You will also apply font and alignment formatting to data in cells.

Changing Column Width

Columns in a worksheet are the same width by default. In some worksheets, you may want to change column widths to accommodate more or less data. Change column width using the mouse on column boundaries or at a dialog box.

Changing Column Width Using Column Boundaries

As you learned in Chapter 1, you can adjust the width of a column by dragging the column boundary line or adjust a column width to the longest entry by double-clicking the boundary line. When you drag a column boundary, the column width displays in a box above the mouse pointer. The column width number that displays represents the average number of characters in the standard font that can fit in a cell.

You can change the width of selected adjacent columns at the same time. To do this, select the columns and then drag one of the column boundaries within the selected columns. As you drag the boundary, the column width changes for all selected columns. To select adjacent columns, position the cell pointer on the first desired column header (the mouse pointer turns into a black, down-pointing arrow), hold down the left mouse button, drag the cell pointer to the last desired column header, and then release the mouse button.

HINT To change the width of all columns in a worksheet, click the Select All button and then drag a column boundary to the desired position.

Project 1a Changing Column Width Using a Column Boundary Part 1 of 7

1. Open **CMProducts.xlsx**.
2. Save the workbook with Save As and name it **EL1-C3-P1-CMProducts**.
3. Insert a formula in cell D2 that multiplies the price in cell B2 with the number in cell C2. Copy the formula in cell D2 down to cells D3 through D14.
4. Change the width of column D by completing the following steps:
   a. Position the mouse pointer on the column boundary in the column header between columns D and E until it turns into a double-headed arrow pointing left and right.
   b. Hold down the left mouse button, drag the column boundary to the right until *Width: 11.00 (106 pixels)* displays in the box, and then release the mouse button.

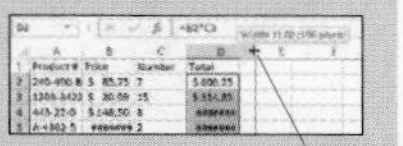

Step 4b

5. Make cell D15 active and then insert the sum of cells D2 through D14.
6. Change the width of columns A and B by completing the following steps:
   a. Select columns A and B. To do this, position the cell pointer on the column A header, hold down the left mouse button, drag the cell pointer to the column B header, and then release the mouse button.

MULTIPART PROJECTS provide a framework for the instruction and practice on software features. A project overview identifies tasks to accomplish and key features to use in completing the work.

STEP-BY-STEP INSTRUCTIONS guide students to the desired outcome for each project part. Screen captures illustrate what the student's screen should look like at key points.

   b. Position the cell pointer on the column boundary between columns A and B until it turns into a double-headed arrow pointing left and right.
   c. Hold down the left mouse button, drag the column boundary to the right until *Width: 10.33 (100 pixels)* displays in the box, and then release the mouse button.
7. Adjust the width of column C to accommodate the longest entry by double-clicking on the column boundary between columns C and D.
8. Save **EL1-C3-P1-CMProducts.xlsx**.

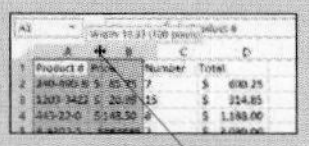

Step 6c

Between project parts, the text presents instruction on the features and skills necessary to accomplish the next section of the project.

Changing Column Width at the Column Width Dialog Box

Quick Steps
Change Column Width
Drag column boundary line.
OR
Double-click column boundary.
OR
1. Click Format button.
2. Click *Column Width* at drop-down list.
3. Type desired width.
4. Click OK.

Format

At the Column Width dialog box, shown in Figure 3.1, you can specify a column width number. Increase the column width number to make the column wider or decrease the column width number to make the column narrower.

To display the Column Width dialog box, click the Format button in the Cells group on the HOME tab and then click *Column Width* at the drop-down list. At the Column Width dialog box, type the number representing the average number of characters in the standard font that you want to fit in the column and then press Enter or click OK.

Figure 3.1 Column Width Dialog Box

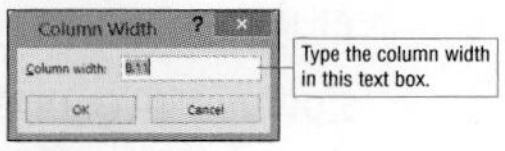

Project 1b Changing Column Width at the Column Width Dialog Box Part 2 of 7

1. With **EL1-C3-P1-CMProducts.xlsx** open, change the width of column A by completing the following steps:
   a. Make any cell in column A active.
   b. Click the Format button in the Cells group on the HOME tab and then click *Column Width* at the drop-down list.
   c. At the Column Width dialog box, type 12.7 in the *Column width* text box.
   d. Click OK to close the dialog box.
2. Make any cell in column B active and then change the width of column B to *12.5* by completing steps similar to those in Step 1.
3. Make any cell in column C active and then change the width of column C to *8* by completing steps similar to those in Step 1.
4. Save **EL1-C3-P1-CMProducts.xlsx**.

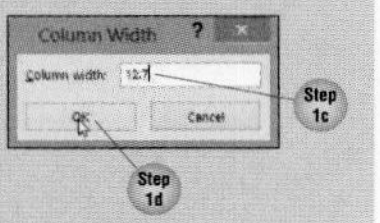

Typically, a file remains open throughout all parts of the project. Students save their work incrementally.

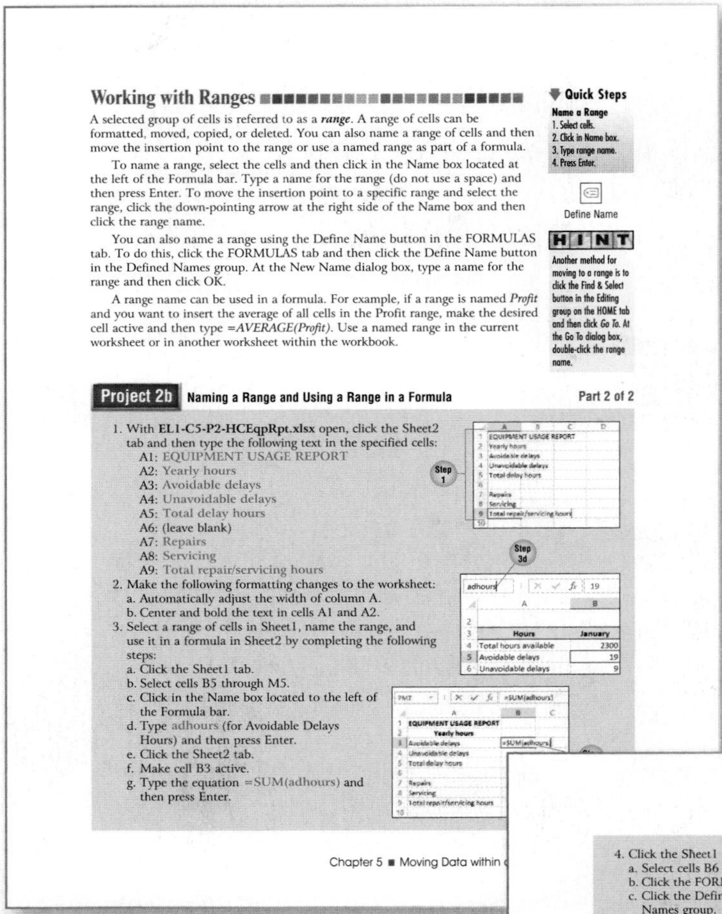

Working with Ranges

A selected group of cells is referred to as a ***range***. A range of cells can be formatted, moved, copied, or deleted. You can also name a range of cells and then move the insertion point to the range or use a named range as part of a formula.

To name a range, select the cells and then click in the Name box located at the left of the Formula bar. Type a name for the range (do not use a space) and then press Enter. To move the insertion point to a specific range and select the range, click the down-pointing arrow at the right side of the Name box and then click the range name.

You can also name a range using the Define Name button in the FORMULAS tab. To do this, click the FORMULAS tab and then click the Define Name button in the Defined Names group. At the New Name dialog box, type a name for the range and then click OK.

A range name can be used in a formula. For example, if a range is named *Profit* and you want to insert the average of all cells in the Profit range, make the desired cell active and then type *=AVERAGE(Profit)*. Use a named range in the current worksheet or in another worksheet within the workbook.

Quick Steps
Name a Range
1. Select cells.
2. Click in Name box.
3. Type range name.
4. Press Enter.

Define Name

HINT
Another method for moving to a range is to click the Find & Select button in the Editing group on the HOME tab and then click *Go To*. At the Go To dialog box, double-click the range name.

Project 2b Naming a Range and Using a Range in a Formula — Part 2 of 2

1. With **EL1-C5-P2-HCEqpRpt.xlsx** open, click the Sheet2 tab and then type the following text in the specified cells:
   A1: EQUIPMENT USAGE REPORT
   A2: Yearly hours
   A3: Avoidable delays
   A4: Unavoidable delays
   A5: Total delay hours
   A6: (leave blank)
   A7: Repairs
   A8: Servicing
   A9: Total repair/servicing hours
2. Make the following formatting changes to the worksheet:
   a. Automatically adjust the width of column A.
   b. Center and bold the text in cells A1 and A2.
3. Select a range of cells in Sheet1, name the range, and use it in a formula in Sheet2 by completing the following steps:
   a. Click the Sheet1 tab.
   b. Select cells B5 through M5.
   c. Click in the Name box located to the left of the Formula bar.
   d. Type adhours (for Avoidable Delays Hours) and then press Enter.
   e. Click the Sheet2 tab.
   f. Make cell B3 active.
   g. Type the equation =SUM(adhours) and then press Enter.

Chapter 5 ■ Moving Data within

QUICK STEPS provide feature summaries for reference and review.

HINTS provide useful tips on how to use features efficiently and effectively.

MAGENTA TEXT identifies material to type.

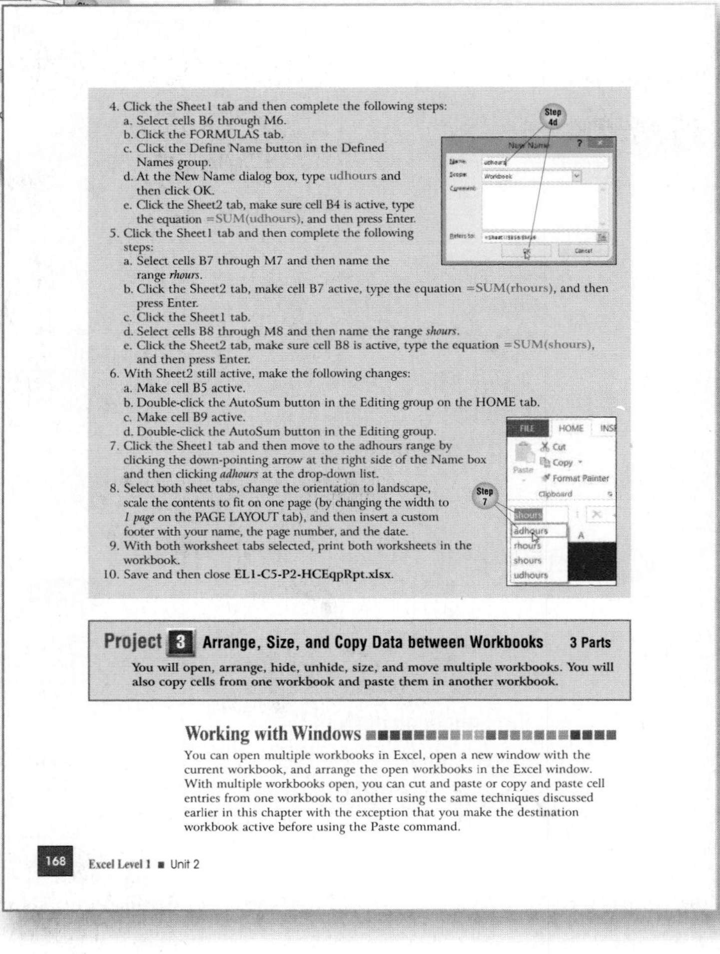

4. Click the Sheet1 tab and then complete the following steps:
   a. Select cells B6 through M6.
   b. Click the FORMULAS tab.
   c. Click the Define Name button in the Defined Names group.
   d. At the New Name dialog box, type udhours and then click OK.
   e. Click the Sheet2 tab, make sure cell B4 is active, type the equation =SUM(udhours), and then press Enter.
5. Click the Sheet1 tab and then complete the following steps:
   a. Select cells B7 through M7 and then name the range *rhours*.
   b. Click the Sheet2 tab, make cell B7 active, type the equation =SUM(rhours), and then press Enter.
   c. Click the Sheet1 tab.
   d. Select cells B8 through M8 and then name the range *shours*.
   e. Click the Sheet2 tab, make sure cell B8 is active, type the equation =SUM(shours), and then press Enter.
6. With Sheet2 still active, make the following changes:
   a. Make cell B5 active.
   b. Double-click the AutoSum button in the Editing group on the HOME tab.
   c. Make cell B9 active.
   d. Double-click the AutoSum button in the Editing group.
7. Click the Sheet1 tab and then move to the adhours range by clicking the down-pointing arrow at the right side of the Name box and then clicking *adhours* at the drop-down list.
8. Select both sheet tabs, change the orientation to landscape, scale the contents to fit on one page (by changing the width to *1 page* on the PAGE LAYOUT tab), and then insert a custom footer with your name, the page number, and the date.
9. With both worksheet tabs selected, print both worksheets in the workbook.
10. Save and then close **EL1-C5-P2-HCEqpRpt.xlsx**.

Project 3 Arrange, Size, and Copy Data between Workbooks — 3 Parts

You will open, arrange, hide, unhide, size, and move multiple workbooks. You will also copy cells from one workbook and paste them in another workbook.

Working with Windows

You can open multiple workbooks in Excel, open a new window with the current workbook, and arrange the open workbooks in the Excel window. With multiple workbooks open, you can cut and paste or copy and paste cell entries from one workbook to another using the same techniques discussed earlier in this chapter with the exception that you make the destination workbook active before using the Paste command.

168 Excel Level 1 ■ Unit 2

At the end of the project, students save, print, and then close the file.

CHAPTER REVIEW ACTIVITIES: A Hierarchy of Learning Assessments

Chapter Summary

- The Page Setup group on the PAGE LAYOUT tab contains buttons for changing the margins and page orientation and size, as well as buttons for establishing the print area, inserting a page break, applying a picture background, and printing titles.
- The default left and right margins are 0.7 inch and the default top and bottom margins are 0.75 inch. Change these default margins with the Margins button in the Page Setup group on the PAGE LAYOUT tab.
- Display the Page Setup dialog box with the Margins tab selected by clicking the Margins button in the Page Setup group on the PAGE LAYOUT tab and then clicking *Custom Margins* at the drop-down list.
- Center a worksheet on the page with the *Horizontally* and *Vertically* options at the Page Setup dialog box with the Margins tab selected.
- Click the Orientation button in the Page Setup group on the PAGE LAYOUT tab to display the two orientation choices: *Portrait* and *Landscape*.
- Insert a page break by selecting the column or row, clicking the Breaks button in the Page Setup group on the PAGE LAYOUT tab, and then clicking *Insert Page Break* at the drop-down list.
- To insert both horizontal and vertical page breaks at the same time, make a cell active, click the Br… down list.
- Preview the page break… button in the view area… clicking the Page Break…
- Use options at the Page… printing column and/or… the Print Titles button i…
- Use options in the Sca… to fit on a specific num…
- Use the Background bu… to insert a worksheet b… screen but does not pri…
- Use options in the She… whether to view and/or…
- Specify the print area b… button in the Page Setu… *Set Print Area* at the dr… desired cells, clicking t… at the drop-down list.
- Create a header and/or… group on the INSERT… Setup dialog box with…
- Customize a print job…
- To check spelling in a w… Spelling button.

CHAPTER SUMMARY captures the purpose and execution of key features.

- Click the Undo button on the Quick Access toolbar to reverse the most recent action and click the Redo button to redo a previously reversed action.
- Use options at the Find and Replace dialog box with the Find tab selected to find specific data and/or formatting in a worksheet.
- Use options at the Find and Replace dialog box with the Replace tab selected to find specific data and/or formatting and replace it with other data and/or formatting.
- Sort data in a worksheet with options from the Sort & Filter button in the Editing group on the HOME tab.
- Create a custom sort with options at the Sort dialog box. Display this dialog box by clicking the Sort & Filter button and then clicking *Custom Sort* at the drop-down list.
- Use filtering to temporarily isolate specific data. Turn on the filter feature by clicking the Sort & Filter button in the Editing group on the HOME tab and then clicking *Filter* at the drop-down list. This inserts filter arrows with each column label. Click a filter arrow and then use options at the drop-down list that displays to specify the filter data.

Commands Review

FEATURE	RIBBON TAB, GROUP	BUTTON, OPTION	KEYBOARD SHORTCUT
background picture	PAGE LAYOUT, Page Setup		
filter data	HOME, Editi…		
Find and Replace dialog box with Find tab selected	HOME, Editi…		
Find and Replace dialog box with Replace tab selected	HOME, Editi…		
header and footer	INSERT, Tex…		
insert page break	PAGE LAYOU…		
margins	PAGE LAYOU…		
orientation	PAGE LAYOU…		
Page Layout view	VIEW, Work…		
Page Setup dialog box with Margins tab selected	PAGE LAYOU…		
Page Setup dialog box with Sheet tab selected	PAGE LAYOU…		
preview page break	VIEW, Work…		

COMMANDS REVIEW summarizes visually the major features and alternative methods of access.

FEATURE	RIBBON TAB, GROUP	BUTTON, OPTION	KEYBOARD SHORTCUT
print area	PAGE LAYOUT, Page Setup		
remove page break	PAGE LAYOUT, Page Setup	*Remove Page Break*	
scale height	PAGE LAYOUT, Scale to Fit		
scale to fit	PAGE LAYOUT, Scale to Fit		
scale width	PAGE LAYOUT, Scale to Fit		
size	PAGE LAYOUT, Page Setup		
sort data	HOME, Editing		
spelling checker	REVIEW, Proofing		F7

Concepts Check Test Your Knowledge SNAP

Completion: In the space provided at the right, indicate the correct term, symbol, or command.

1. This is the default left and right margin measurement. ____________
2. This is the default top and bottom margin measurement. ____________
3. The Margins button is located on this tab. ____________
4. By default, a worksheet prints in this orientation on a page. ____________
5. Click the Print Titles button in the Page Setup group on the PAGE LAYOUT tab and the Page Setup dialog box displays with this tab selected. ____________
6. Use options in this group on the PAGE LAYOUT tab to adjust the printed output by a percentage to fit the number of pages specified. ____________
7. Use this button in the Page Setup group on the PAGE LAYOUT tab to select and print specific areas in a worksheet. ____________
8. Click the Header & Footer button in the Text group on the INSERT tab and the worksheet displays in this view. ____________
9. This tab contains options for formatting and customizing a header and/or footer. ____________

CONCEPTS CHECK questions assess knowledge recall. Students enrolled in SNAP can complete the Concepts Check online. SNAP automatically scores student work.

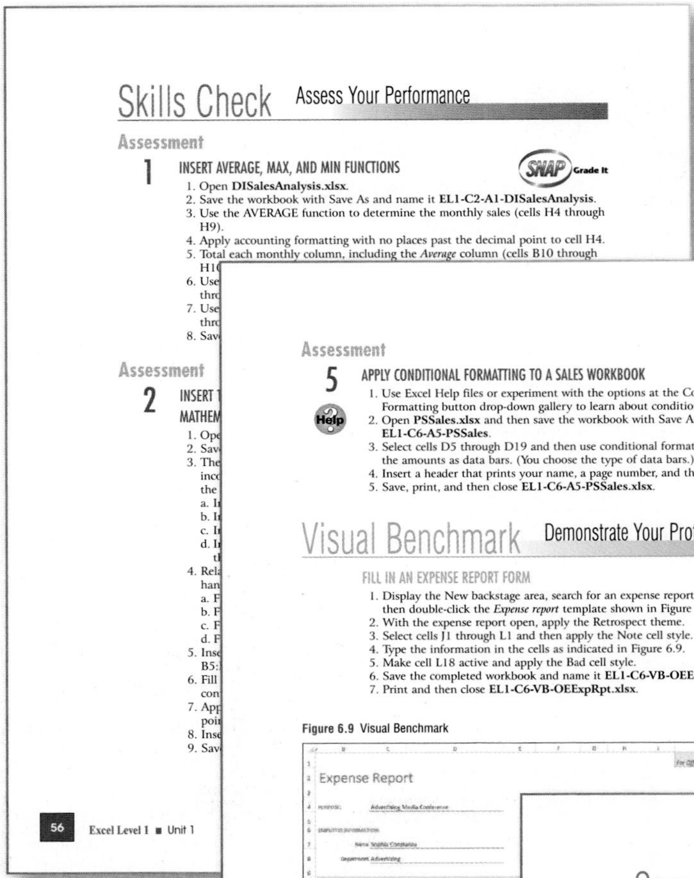

Skills Check Assess Your Performance

Assessment

1 INSERT AVERAGE, MAX, AND MIN FUNCTIONS

SNAP Grade It

1. Open **DISalesAnalysis.xlsx**.
2. Save the workbook with Save As and name it **EL1-C2-A1-DISalesAnalysis**.
3. Use the AVERAGE function to determine the monthly sales (cells H4 through H9).
4. Apply accounting formatting with no places past the decimal point to cell H4.
5. Total each monthly column, including the *Average* column (cells B10 through H1
6. Use thr
7. Use thr
8. Sav

Assessment

2 INSERT T MATHEM

1. Op
2. Sav
3. The inc the
   a. I
   b. I
   c. I
   d. I t
4. Rel han
   a. F
   b. F
   c. F
   d. F
5. Ins B5:
6. Fill con
7. Ap poi
8. Ins
9. Sav

56 Excel Level 1 ■ Unit 1

SKILLS CHECK exercises ask students to create a variety of documents using multiple features without how-to directions. Versions of the activities marked with a SNAP Grade It icon are available for automatic scoring in SNAP.

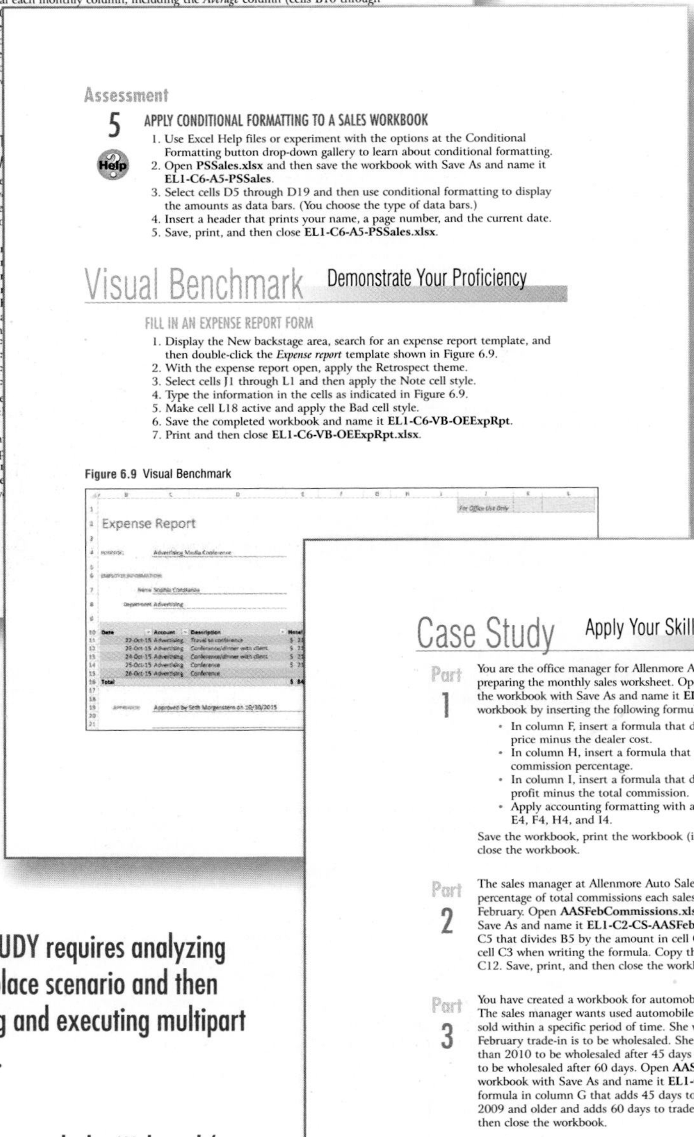

Assessment

5 APPLY CONDITIONAL FORMATTING TO A SALES WORKBOOK

Help

1. Use Excel Help files or experiment with the options at the Conditional Formatting button drop-down gallery to learn about conditional formatting.
2. Open **PSSales.xlsx** and then save the workbook with Save As and name it **EL1-C6-A5-PSSales**.
3. Select cells D5 through D19 and then use conditional formatting to display the amounts as data bars. (You choose the type of data bars.)
4. Insert a header that prints your name, a page number, and the current date.
5. Save, print, and then close **EL1-C6-A5-PSSales.xlsx**.

Visual Benchmark Demonstrate Your Proficiency

FILL IN AN EXPENSE REPORT FORM

1. Display the New backstage area, search for an expense report template, and then double-click the *Expense report* template shown in Figure 6.9.
2. With the expense report open, apply the Retrospect theme.
3. Select cells J1 through L1 and then apply the Note cell style.
4. Type the information in the cells as indicated in Figure 6.9.
5. Make cell L18 active and apply the Bad cell style.
6. Save the completed workbook and name it **EL1-C6-VB-OEExpRpt**.
7. Print and then close **EL1-C6-VB-OEExpRpt.xlsx**.

Figure 6.9 Visual Benchmark

VISUAL BENCHMARK assessments test students' problem-solving skills and mastery of program features.

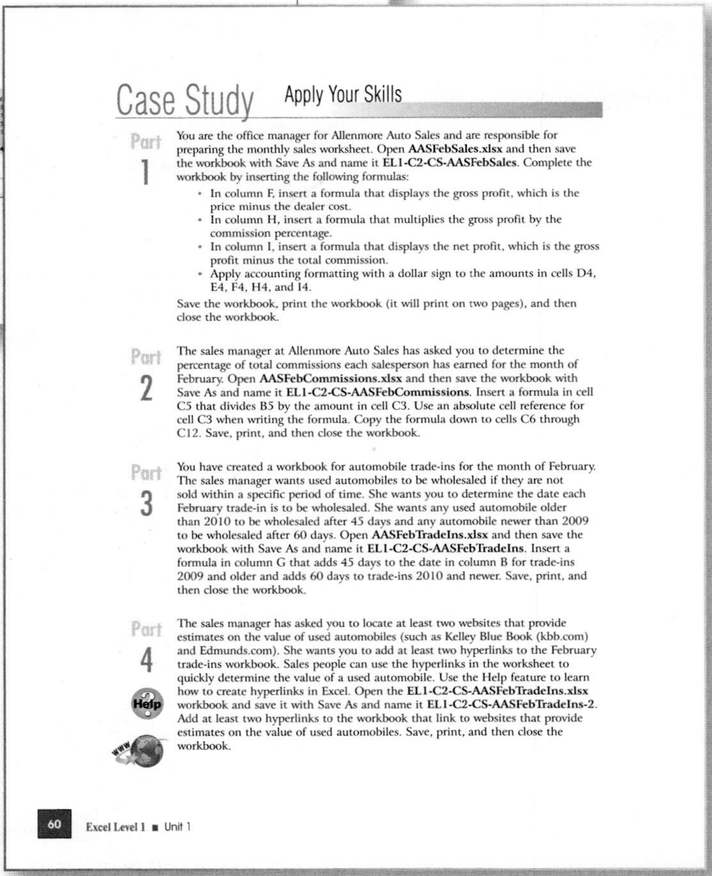

Case Study Apply Your Skills

Part 1

You are the office manager for Allenmore Auto Sales and are responsible for preparing the monthly sales worksheet. Open **AASFebSales.xlsx** and then save the workbook with Save As and name it **EL1-C2-CS-AASFebSales**. Complete the workbook by inserting the following formulas:

- In column F, insert a formula that displays the gross profit, which is the price minus the dealer cost.
- In column H, insert a formula that multiplies the gross profit by the commission percentage.
- In column I, insert a formula that displays the net profit, which is the gross profit minus the total commission.
- Apply accounting formatting with a dollar sign to the amounts in cells D4, E4, F4, H4, and I4.

Save the workbook, print the workbook (it will print on two pages), and then close the workbook.

Part 2

The sales manager at Allenmore Auto Sales has asked you to determine the percentage of total commissions each salesperson has earned for the month of February. Open **AASFebCommissions.xlsx** and then save the workbook with Save As and name it **EL1-C2-CS-AASFebCommissions**. Insert a formula in cell C5 that divides B5 by the amount in cell C3. Use an absolute cell reference for cell C3 when writing the formula. Copy the formula down to cells C6 through C12. Save, print, and then close the workbook.

Part 3

You have created a workbook for automobile trade-ins for the month of February. The sales manager wants used automobiles to be wholesaled if they are not sold within a specific period of time. She wants you to determine the date each February trade-in is to be wholesaled. She wants any used automobile older than 2010 to be wholesaled after 45 days and any automobile newer than 2009 to be wholesaled after 60 days. Open **AASFebTradeIns.xlsx** and then save the workbook with Save As and name it **EL1-C2-CS-AASFebTradeIns**. Insert a formula in column G that adds 45 days to the date in column B for trade-ins 2009 and older and adds 60 days to trade-ins 2010 and newer. Save, print, and then close the workbook.

Part 4

Help

The sales manager has asked you to locate at least two websites that provide estimates on the value of used automobiles (such as Kelley Blue Book (kbb.com) and Edmunds.com). She wants you to add at least two hyperlinks to the February trade-ins workbook. Sales people can use the hyperlinks in the worksheet to quickly determine the value of a used automobile. Use the Help feature to learn how to create hyperlinks in Excel. Open the **EL1-C2-CS-AASFebTradeIns.xlsx** workbook and save it with Save As and name it **EL1-C2-CS-AASFebTradeIns-2**. Add at least two hyperlinks to the workbook that link to websites that provide estimates on the value of used automobiles. Save, print, and then close the workbook.

60 Excel Level 1 ■ Unit 1

CASE STUDY requires analyzing a workplace scenario and then planning and executing multipart projects.

Students search the Web and/or use the program's Help feature to locate additional information required to complete the Case Study.

UNIT PERFORMANCE ASSESSMENT: Cross-Disciplinary, Comprehensive Evaluation

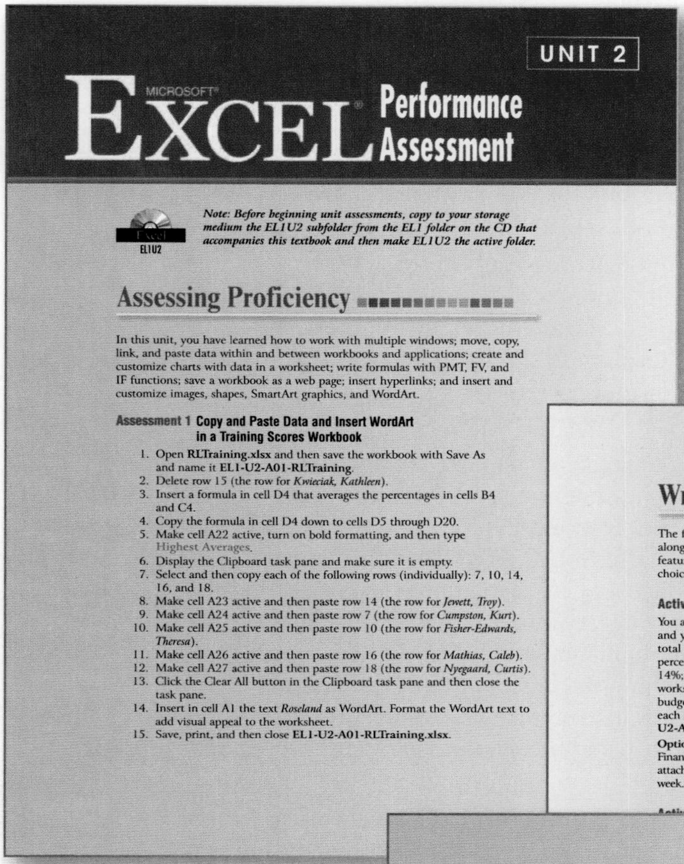

UNIT 2

MICROSOFT® EXCEL® Performance Assessment

Excel EL1U2

Note: Before beginning unit assessments, copy to your storage medium the EL1U2 subfolder from the EL1 folder on the CD that accompanies this textbook and then make EL1U2 the active folder.

Assessing Proficiency

In this unit, you have learned how to work with multiple windows; move, copy, link, and paste data within and between workbooks and applications; create and customize charts with data in a worksheet; write formulas with PMT, FV, and IF functions; save a workbook as a web page; insert hyperlinks; and insert and customize images, shapes, SmartArt graphics, and WordArt.

Assessment 1 Copy and Paste Data and Insert WordArt in a Training Scores Workbook

1. Open **RLTraining.xlsx** and then save the workbook with Save As and name it **EL1-U2-A01-RLTraining**.
2. Delete row 15 (the row for *Kwieciak, Kathleen*).
3. Insert a formula in cell D4 that averages the percentages in cells B4 and C4.
4. Copy the formula in cell D4 down to cells D5 through D20.
5. Make cell A22 active, turn on bold formatting, and then type Highest Averages.
6. Display the Clipboard task pane and make sure it is empty.
7. Select and then copy each of the following rows (individually): 7, 10, 14, 16, and 18.
8. Make cell A23 active and then paste row 14 (the row for *Jewett, Troy*).
9. Make cell A24 active and then paste row 7 (the row for *Cumpston, Kurt*).
10. Make cell A25 active and then paste row 10 (the row for *Fisher-Edwards, Theresa*).
11. Make cell A26 active and then paste row 16 (the row for *Mathias, Caleb*).
12. Make cell A27 active and then paste row 18 (the row for *Nyegaard, Curtis*).
13. Click the Clear All button in the Clipboard task pane and then close the task pane.
14. Insert in cell A1 the text *Roseland* as WordArt. Format the WordArt text to add visual appeal to the worksheet.
15. Save, print, and then close **EL1-U2-A01-RLTraining.xlsx**.

ASSESSING PROFICIENCY checks mastery of features.

WRITING ACTIVITIES involve applying program skills in a communication context.

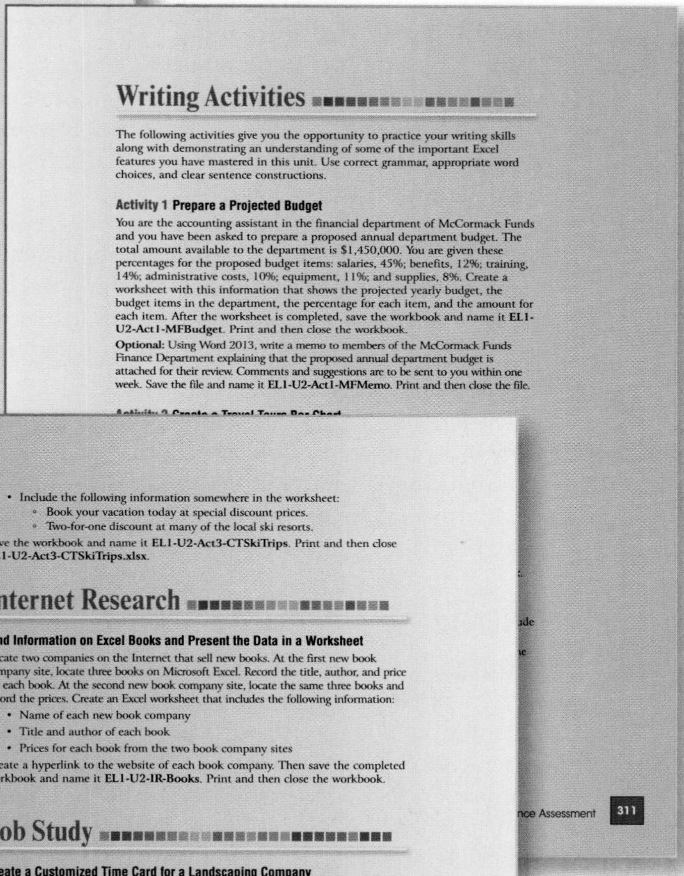

Writing Activities

The following activities give you the opportunity to practice your writing skills along with demonstrating an understanding of some of the important Excel features you have mastered in this unit. Use correct grammar, appropriate word choices, and clear sentence constructions.

Activity 1 Prepare a Projected Budget

You are the accounting assistant in the financial department of McCormack Funds and you have been asked to prepare a proposed annual department budget. The total amount available to the department is $1,450,000. You are given these percentages for the proposed budget items: salaries, 45%; benefits, 12%; training, 14%; administrative costs, 10%; equipment, 11%; and supplies, 8%. Create a worksheet with this information that shows the projected yearly budget, the budget items in the department, the percentage for each item, and the amount for each item. After the worksheet is completed, save the workbook and name it **EL1-U2-Act1-MFBudget**. Print and then close the workbook.

Optional: Using Word 2013, write a memo to members of the McCormack Funds Finance Department explaining that the proposed annual department budget is attached for their review. Comments and suggestions are to be sent to you within one week. Save the file and name it **EL1-U2-Act1-MFMemo**. Print and then close the file.

...nce Assessment 311

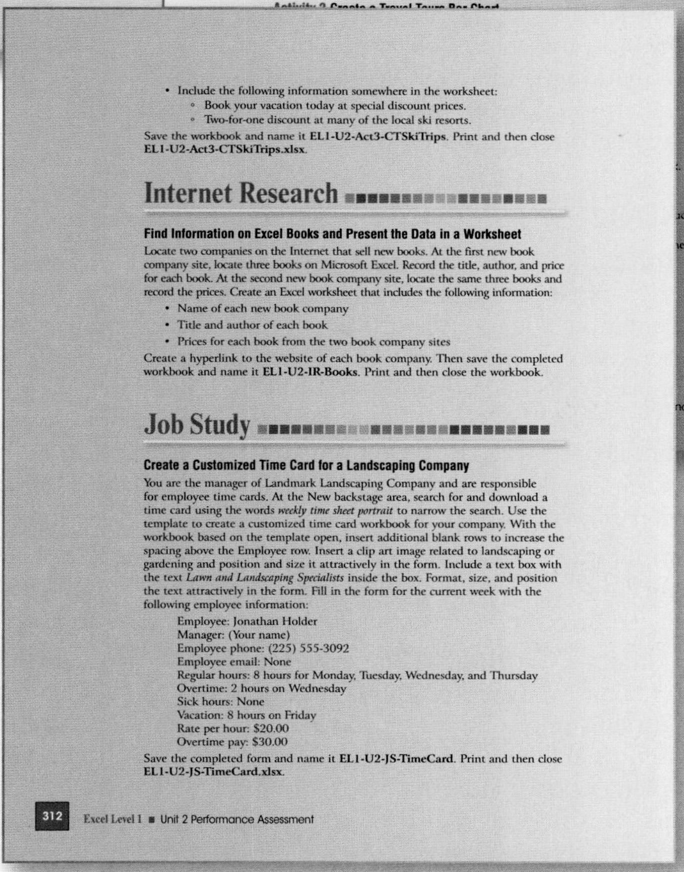

- Include the following information somewhere in the worksheet:
  - Book your vacation today at special discount prices.
  - Two-for-one discount at many of the local ski resorts.

Save the workbook and name it **EL1-U2-Act3-CTSkiTrips**. Print and then close **EL1-U2-Act3-CTSkiTrips.xlsx**.

Internet Research

Find Information on Excel Books and Present the Data in a Worksheet

Locate two companies on the Internet that sell new books. At the first new book company site, locate three books on Microsoft Excel. Record the title, author, and price for each book. At the second new book company site, locate the same three books and record the prices. Create an Excel worksheet that includes the following information:

- Name of each new book company
- Title and author of each book
- Prices for each book from the two book company sites

Create a hyperlink to the website of each book company. Then save the completed workbook and name it **EL1-U2-IR-Books**. Print and then close the workbook.

Job Study

Create a Customized Time Card for a Landscaping Company

You are the manager of Landmark Landscaping Company and are responsible for employee time cards. At the New backstage area, search for and download a time card using the words *weekly time sheet portrait* to narrow the search. Use the template to create a customized time card workbook for your company. With the workbook based on the template open, insert additional blank rows to increase the spacing above the Employee row. Insert a clip art image related to landscaping or gardening and position and size it attractively in the form. Include a text box with the text *Lawn and Landscaping Specialists* inside the box. Format, size, and position the text attractively in the form. Fill in the form for the current week with the following employee information:

Employee: Jonathan Holder
Manager: (Your name)
Employee phone: (225) 555-3092
Employee email: None
Regular hours: 8 hours for Monday, Tuesday, Wednesday, and Thursday
Overtime: 2 hours on Wednesday
Sick hours: None
Vacation: 8 hours on Friday
Rate per hour: $20.00
Overtime pay: $30.00

Save the completed form and name it **EL1-U2-JS-TimeCard**. Print and then close **EL1-U2-JS-TimeCard.xlsx**.

312 Excel Level 1 ■ Unit 2 Performance Assessment

INTERNET RESEARCH project reinforces research and word processing skills.

JOB STUDY at the end of Unit 2 presents a capstone assessment requiring critical thinking and problem solving.

Student Courseware

Student Resources CD Each Benchmark Series textbook is packaged with a Student Resources CD containing the data files required for completing the projects and assessments. A CD icon and folder name displayed on the opening page of chapters reminds students to copy a folder of files from the CD to the desired storage medium before beginning the project exercises. Directions for copying folders are printed on the inside back cover.

Internet Resource Center Additional learning tools and reference materials are available at the book-specific website at www.paradigmcollege.net/BenchmarkExcel13. Students can access the same files that are on the Student Resources CD along with study aids, web links, and tips for using computers effectively in academic and workplace settings.

SNAP Training and Assessment Available at snap2013.emcp.com, SNAP is a web-based program offering an interactive venue for learning Microsoft Office 2013, Windows 8, and Internet Explorer 10. Along with a web-based learning management system, SNAP provides multimedia tutorials, performance skill items, Concepts Check matching activities, Grade It Skills Check Assessment activities, comprehensive performance evaluations, a concepts test bank, an online grade book, and a set of course planning tools. A CD of tutorials teaching the basics of Office, Windows, and Internet Explorer is also available if instructors wish to assign additional SNAP tutorial work without using the web-based SNAP program.

eBook For students who prefer studying with an eBook, the texts in the Benchmark Series are available in an electronic form. The web-based, password-protected eBooks feature dynamic navigation tools, including bookmarking, a linked table of contents, and the ability to jump to a specific page. The eBook format also supports helpful study tools, such as highlighting and note taking.

Instructor Resources

Instructor's Guide and Disc Instructor support for the Benchmark Series includes an *Instructor's Guide and Instructor Resources Disc* package. This resource includes planning information, such as Lesson Blueprints, teaching hints, and sample course syllabi; presentation resources, such as PowerPoint slide shows with lecture notes and audio support; and assessment resources, including an overview of available assessment venues, live model answers for chapter activities, and live and PDF model answers for end-of-chapter exercises. Contents of the *Instructor's Guide and Instructor Resources Disc* package are also available on the password-protected section of the Internet Resource Center for this title at www.paradigmcollege.net/BenchmarkExcel13.

Computerized Test Generator Instructors can use the ExamView® Assessment Suite and test banks of multiple-choice items to create customized web-based or print tests.

Blackboard Cartridge This set of files allows instructors to create a personalized Blackboard website for their course and provides course content, tests, and the mechanisms for establishing communication via e-discussions and online group conferences. Available content includes a syllabus, test banks, PowerPoint presentations with audio support, and supplementary course materials. Upon request, the files can be available within 24–48 hours. Hosting the site is the responsibility of the educational institution.

System Requirements

This text is designed for the student to complete projects and assessments on a computer running a standard installation of Microsoft Office Professional Plus 2013 and the Microsoft Windows 8 operating system. To effectively run this suite and operating system, your computer should be outfitted with the following:

- 1 gigahertz (GHz) processor or higher; 1 gigabyte (GB) of RAM (32 bit) or 2 GB of RAM (64 bit)
- 3 GB of available hard-disk space
- .NET version 3.5, 4.0, or 4.5
- DirectX 10 graphics card
- Minimum 1024 × 576 resolution (or 1366 × 768 to use Windows Snap feature)
- Computer mouse, multi-touch device, or other compatible pointing device

Office 2013 will also operate on computers running the Windows 7 operating system.

Screen captures in this book were created using a screen resolution display setting of 1600 × 900. Refer to the *Customizing Settings* section of *Getting Started in Office 2013* following this preface for instructions on changing your monitor's resolution. Figure G.9 on page 10 shows the Microsoft Office Word ribbon at three resolutions for comparison purposes. Choose the resolution that best matches your computer; however, be aware that using a resolution other than 1600 × 900 means that your screens may not match the illustrations in this book.

About the Authors

Nita Rutkosky began teaching business education courses at Pierce College in Puyallup, Washington, in 1978. Since then she has taught a variety of software applications to students in postsecondary Information Technology certificate and degree programs. In addition to *Benchmark Office 2013*, she has co-authored *Marquee Series: Microsoft Office 2013, 2010, 2007,* and *2003*; *Signature Series: Microsoft Word 2013, 2010, 2007,* and *2003*; *Using Computers in the Medical Office: Microsoft Word, Excel, and PowerPoint 2010, 2007* and *2003*; and *Computer and Internet Essentials: Preparing for IC3*. She has also authored textbooks on keyboarding, WordPerfect, desktop publishing, and voice recognition for Paradigm Publishing, Inc.

Denise Seguin has served in the Faculty of Business at Fanshawe College of Applied Arts and Technology in London, Ontario, since 1986. She has developed curriculum and taught a variety of office technology, software applications, and accounting courses to students in postsecondary Information Technology diploma programs and in Continuing Education courses. Seguin has served as Program Coordinator for Computer Systems Technician, Computer Systems Technology, Office Administration, and Law Clerk programs and was acting Chair of the School of Information Technology in 2001. In addition to co-authoring the Level 2 *Access 2013* and *Excel 2013* books in the Benchmark Series, she has authored *Computer Concepts and Applications for Microsoft Office 2013* and *Microsoft Outlook 2013, 2010, 2007, 2003, 2002,* and *2000*. She has also co-authored *Our Digital World* first and second editions; *Marquee Series: Microsoft Office 2013, 2010, 2007,* and *2003*; *Office 2003*; *Office XP*; and *Using Computers in the Medical Office: Microsoft Word, Excel, and PowerPoint 2010, 2007,* and *2003* for Paradigm Publishing, Inc.

Jan Davidson started her teaching career in 1997 as a corporate trainer and postsecondary instructor. Since 2001, she has been a faculty member of the School of Business and Information Technology at Lambton College of Applied Arts and Technology in Sarnia, Ontario. In this role, she has developed curriculum and taught a variety of office technology, software applications, and office administration courses to domestic and international students in postsecondary Office Administration Executive, General, and Medical; Human Resources; and Fashion Business programs. In addition to co-authoring the Level 2 *Access 2013* and *Excel 2013* books in the Benchmark Series, she has written instructor resources and SNAP content for Paradigm Publishing, Inc. since 2006.

Audrey Roggenkamp has been teaching courses in the Business Information Technology department at Pierce College in Puyallup since 2005. Her courses have included keyboarding, skill building, and Microsoft Office programs. In addition to this title, she has co-authored *Marquee Series: Microsoft Office 2013, 2010,* and *2007*; *Signature Series: Microsoft Word 2013, 2010,* and *2007*; *Using Computers in the Medical Office: Microsoft Word, Excel, and PowerPoint 2010, 2007,* and *2003*; and *Computer and Internet Essentials: Preparing for IC3* for Paradigm Publishing, Inc.

Ian Rutkosky teaches Business Technology courses at Pierce College in Puyallup, Washington. In addition to this title, he has coauthored *Computer and Internet Essentials: Preparing for IC3*, *Marquee Series: Microsoft Office 2013*, and *Using Computers in the Medical Office: Microsoft Word, Excel, and PowerPoint 2010*. He is also a co-author and consultant for Paradigm's SNAP training and assessment software.

Getting Started in Office 2013

In this textbook, you will learn to operate several computer programs that combine to make the Microsoft Office 2013 application suite. The programs you will learn are known as ***software***, and they contain instructions that tell the computer what to do. Some of the application programs in the suite include Word, a word processing program; Excel, a spreadsheet program; Access, a database program; and PowerPoint, a presentation program.

Identifying Computer Hardware

The computer equipment you will use to operate the Microsoft Office suite is referred to as ***hardware***. You will need access to a computer system that includes a CPU, monitor, keyboard, printer, drives, and mouse. If you are not sure what equipment you will be operating, check with your instructor. The computer system shown in Figure G.1 consists of six components. Each component is discussed separately in the material that follows.

Figure G.1 Computer System

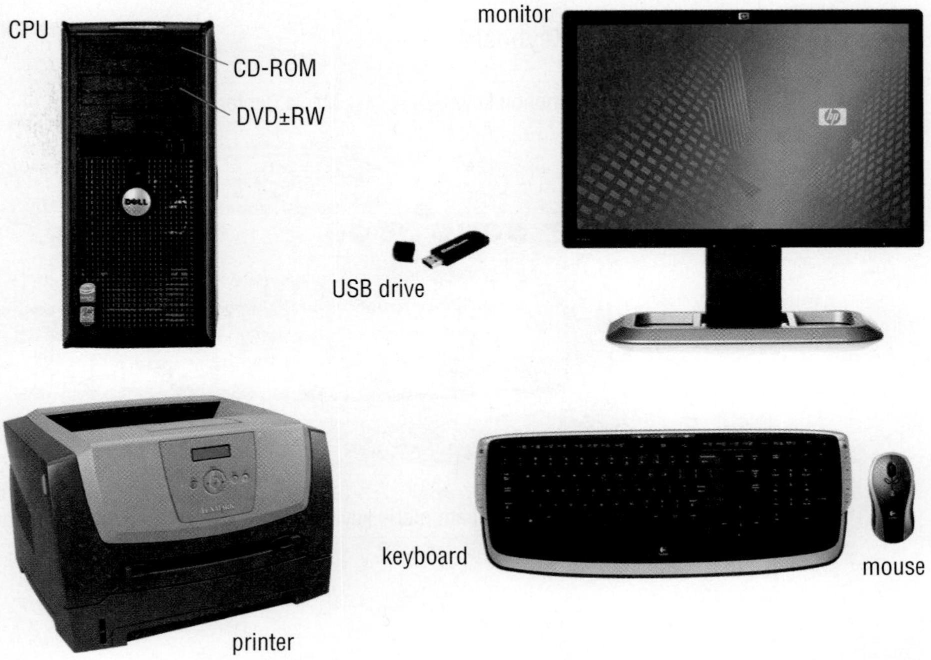

CPU

The ***central processing unit (CPU)*** is the brain of the computer and is where all processing occurs. Silicon chips, which contain miniaturized circuitry, are placed on boards that are plugged into slots within the CPU. Whenever an instruction is given to the computer, it is processed through the circuitry in the CPU.

Monitor

A computer ***monitor*** looks like a television screen. It displays the information in a program and the text you input using the keyboard. The quality of display for monitors varies depending on the type of monitor and the level of resolution. Monitors can also vary in size—generally from 13 inches to 26 inches or larger.

Keyboard

The ***keyboard*** is used to input information into the computer. The number and location of the keys on a keyboard can vary. In addition to letters, numbers, and symbols, most computer keyboards contain function keys, arrow keys, and a numeric keypad. Figure G.2 shows an enhanced keyboard.

The 12 keys at the top of the keyboard, labeled with the letter F followed by a number, are called ***function keys***. Use these keys to perform functions within each of the Office programs. To the right of the regular keys is a group of ***special*** or ***dedicated keys***. These keys are labeled with specific functions that will be performed when you press the key. Below the special keys are arrow keys. Use these keys to move the insertion point in the document screen.

Some keyboards include mode indicator lights. When you select certain modes, a light appears on the keyboard. For example, if you press the Caps Lock key, which disables the lowercase alphabet, a light appears next to Caps Lock. Similarly, pressing the Num Lock key will disable the special functions on the numeric keypad, which is located at the right side of the keyboard.

Figure G.2 Keyboard

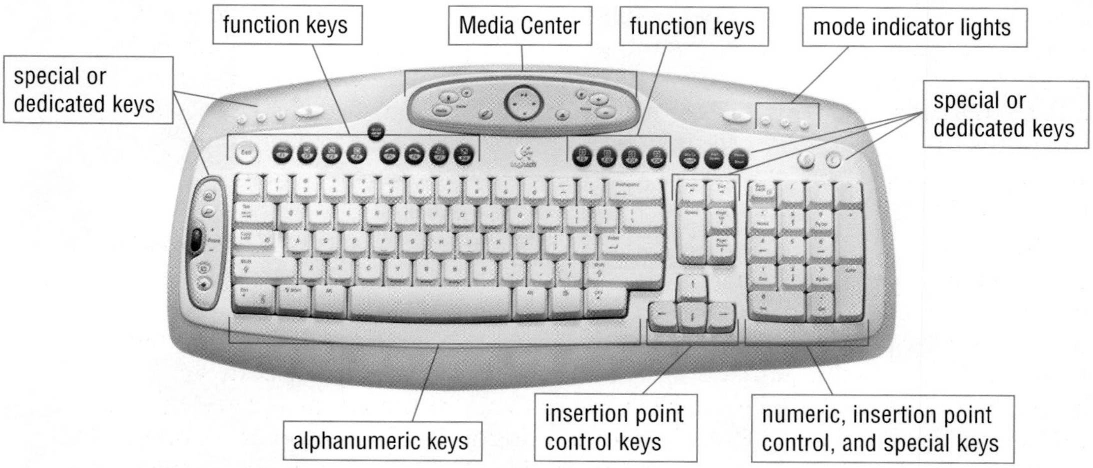

Drives and Ports

Depending on the computer system you are using, Microsoft Office 2013 is installed on a hard drive or as part of a network system. Either way, you will need to have a CD or DVD drive to complete the projects and assessments in this book. If you plan to use a USB drive as your storage medium, you will also need a USB port. You will insert the CD that accompanies this textbook into the CD or DVD drive and then copy folders from the disc to your storage medium. You will also save documents you create to folders on your storage medium.

Printer

An electronic version of a file is known as a ***soft copy***. If you want to create a ***hard copy*** of a file, you need to print it. To print documents you will need to access a printer, which will probably be either a laser printer or an ink-jet printer. A ***laser printer*** uses a laser beam combined with heat and pressure to print documents, while an ***ink-jet printer*** prints a document by spraying a fine mist of ink on the page.

Mouse or Touchpad

Most functions and commands in the Microsoft Office suite are designed to be performed using a mouse or a similar pointing device. A ***mouse*** is an input device that sits on a flat surface next to the computer. You can operate a mouse with your left or right hand. Moving the mouse on the flat surface causes a corresponding pointer to move on the screen, and clicking the left or right mouse buttons allows you to select various objects and commands. Figure G.1 contains an image of a mouse.

If you are working on a laptop computer, you may use a touchpad instead of a mouse. A ***touchpad*** allows you to move the mouse pointer by moving your finger across a surface at the base of the keyboard. You click by using your thumb to press the button located at the bottom of the touchpad.

Using the Mouse

The programs in the Microsoft Office suite can be operated with the keyboard and a mouse. The mouse generally has two buttons on top, which you press to execute specific functions and commands. A mouse may also contain a wheel, which can be used to scroll in a window or as a third button. To use the mouse, rest it on a flat surface or a mouse pad. Put your hand over it with your palm resting on top of the mouse, your wrist resting on the table surface, and your index finger resting on the left mouse button. As you move your hand, and thus the mouse, a corresponding pointer moves on the screen.

When using the mouse, you should understand four terms — point, click, double-click, and drag. When operating the mouse, you may need to point to a specific command, button, or icon. To ***point*** means to position the mouse pointer on the desired item. With the mouse pointer positioned on the desired item, you may need to click a button on the mouse to select the item. To ***click*** means to quickly tap a button on the mouse once. To complete two steps at one time, such as choosing and then executing a function, double-click the mouse button. To ***double-click*** means to tap the left mouse button twice in quick succession. The term ***drag*** means to press and hold the left mouse button, move the mouse pointer to a specific location, and then release the button.

Using the Mouse Pointer

The mouse pointer will look different depending on where you have positioned it and what function you are performing. The following are some of the ways the mouse pointer can appear when you are working in the Office suite:

- The mouse pointer appears as an I-beam (called the ***I-beam pointer***) when you are inserting text in a file. The I-beam pointer can be used to move the insertion point or to select text.

- The mouse pointer appears as an arrow pointing up and to the left (called the ***arrow pointer***) when it is moved to the Title bar, Quick Access toolbar, ribbon, or an option in a dialog box, among other locations.

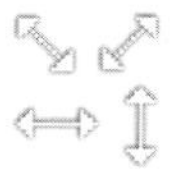

- The mouse pointer becomes a double-headed arrow (either pointing left and right, pointing up and down, or pointing diagonally) when you perform certain functions such as changing the size of an object.

- In certain situations, such as when you move an object or image, the mouse pointer displays with a four-headed arrow attached. The four-headed arrow means that you can move the object left, right, up, or down.

- When a request is being processed or when a program is being loaded, the mouse pointer may appear as a moving circle. The moving circle means "please wait." When the process is completed, the circle is replaced with a normal arrow pointer.

- When the mouse pointer displays as a hand with a pointing index finger, it indicates that more information is available about an item. The mouse pointer also displays as a hand with a pointing index finger when you hover the mouse over a hyperlink.

Choosing Commands

Once a program is open, you can use several methods in the program to choose commands. A ***command*** is an instruction that tells the program to do something. You can choose a command using the mouse or the keyboard. When a program such as Word or PowerPoint is open, the ribbon contains buttons and options for completing tasks, as well as tabs you can click to display additional buttons and options. To choose a button on the Quick Access toolbar or on the ribbon, position the tip of the mouse arrow pointer on the button and then click the left mouse button.

The Office suite provides ***accelerator keys*** you can press to use a command in a program. Press the Alt key on the keyboard to display KeyTips that identify the accelerator key you can press to execute a command. For example, if you press the Alt key in a Word document with the HOME tab active, KeyTips display as shown in Figure G.3. Continue pressing accelerator keys until you execute the desired command. For example, to begin spell checking a document, press the Alt key, press the R key on the keyboard to display the REVIEW tab, and then press the letter S on the keyboard.

Figure G.3 Word HOME Tab KeyTips

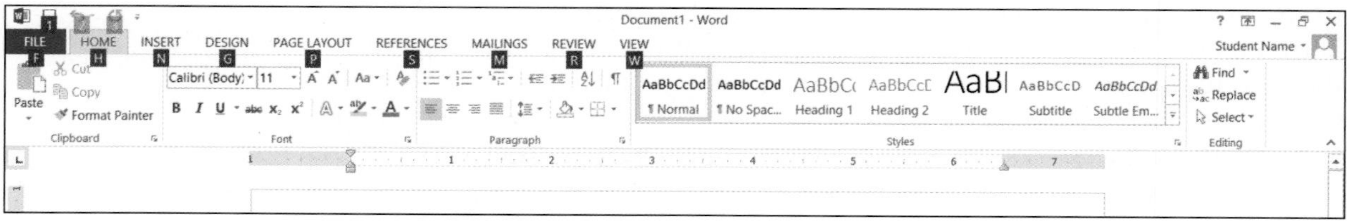

Choosing Commands from Drop-Down Lists

To choose a command from a drop-down list with the mouse, position the mouse pointer on the desired option and then click the left mouse button. To make a selection from a drop-down list with the keyboard, type the underlined letter in the desired option.

Some options at a drop-down list may appear in gray (dimmed), indicating that the option is currently unavailable. If an option at a drop-down list displays preceded by a check mark, it means the option is currently active. If an option at a drop-down list displays followed by an ellipsis (...), clicking that option will display a dialog box.

Choosing Options from a Dialog Box

A ***dialog box*** contains options for applying formatting or otherwise modifying a file or data within a file. Some dialog boxes display with tabs along the top that provide additional options. For example, the Font dialog box shown in Figure G.4 contains two tabs — the Font tab and the Advanced tab. The tab that displays in the front is the active tab. To make a tab active using the mouse, position the arrow pointer on the desired tab and then click the left mouse button. If you are using the keyboard, press Ctrl + Tab or press Alt + the underlined letter on the desired tab.

Figure G.4 Word Font Dialog Box

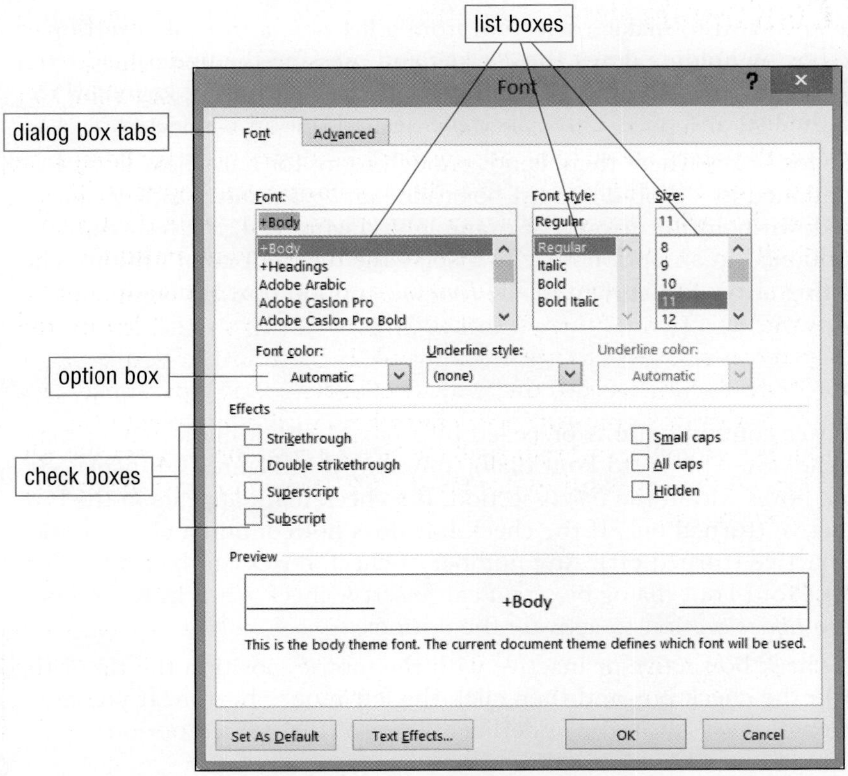

To choose options from a dialog box with the mouse, position the arrow pointer on the desired option and then click the left mouse button. If you are using the keyboard, press the Tab key to move the insertion point forward from option to option. Press Shift + Tab to move the insertion point backward from option to option. You can also hold down the Alt key and then press the underlined letter of the desired option. When an option is selected, it displays with a blue background or surrounded by a dashed box called a ***marquee***. A dialog box contains one or more of the following elements: list boxes, option boxes, check boxes, text boxes, option buttons, measurement boxes, and command buttons.

List Boxes and Option Boxes

The fonts below the *Font* option in the Font dialog box in Figure G.4 are contained in a ***list box***. To make a selection from a list box with the mouse, move the arrow pointer to the desired option and then click the left mouse button.

Some list boxes may contain a scroll bar. This scroll bar will display at the right side of the list box (a vertical scroll bar) or at the bottom of the list box (a horizontal scroll bar). Use a vertical scroll bar or a horizontal scroll bar to move through the list if the list is longer (or wider) than the box. To move down a list using a vertical scroll bar, position the arrow pointer on the down-pointing arrow and hold down the left mouse button. To scroll up through the list, position the arrow pointer on the up-pointing arrow and hold down the left mouse button. You can also move the arrow pointer above the scroll box and click the left mouse button to scroll up the list or move the arrow pointer below the scroll box and click the left mouse button to move down the list. To navigate a list with a horizontal scroll bar, click the left-pointing arrow to scroll to the left of the list or click the right-pointing arrow to scroll to the right of the list.

To use the keyboard to make a selection from a list box, move the insertion point into the box by holding down the Alt key and pressing the underlined letter of the desired option. Press the Up and/or Down Arrow keys on the keyboard to move through the list, and press Enter once the desired option is selected.

In some dialog boxes where there is not enough room for a list box, lists of options are contained in a drop-down list box called an ***option box***. Option boxes display with a down-pointing arrow. For example, in Figure G.4, the font color options are contained in an option box. To display the different color options, click the down-pointing arrow at the right of the *Font color* option box. If you are using the keyboard, press Alt + C.

Check Boxes

Some dialog boxes contain options preceded by a box. A check mark may or may not appear in the box. The Word Font dialog box shown in Figure G.4 displays a variety of check boxes within the *Effects* section. If a check mark appears in the box, the option is active (turned on). If the check box does not contain a check mark, the option is inactive (turned off). Any number of check boxes can be active. For example, in the Word Font dialog box, you can insert a check mark in several of the boxes in the *Effects* section to activate the options.

To make a check box active or inactive with the mouse, position the tip of the arrow pointer in the check box and then click the left mouse button. If you are using the keyboard, press Alt + the underlined letter of the desired option.

Text Boxes

Some options in a dialog box require you to enter text. For example, the boxes below the *Find what* and *Replace with* options at the Excel Find and Replace dialog box shown in Figure G.5 are text boxes. In a text box, you type text or edit existing text. Edit text in a text box in the same manner as normal text. Use the Left and Right Arrow keys on the keyboard to move the insertion point without deleting text and use the Delete key or Backspace key to delete text.

Option Buttons

The Word Insert Table dialog box shown in Figure G.6 contains options in the *AutoFit behavior* section preceded by ***option button**s*. Only one option button can be selected at any time. When an option button is selected, a blue or black circle displays in the button. To select an option button with the mouse, position the tip of the arrow pointer inside the option button or on the option and then click the left mouse button. To make a selection with the keyboard, hold down the Alt key and then press the underlined letter of the desired option.

Measurement Boxes

Some options in a dialog box contain measurements or amounts you can increase or decrease. These options are generally located in a ***measurement box***. For example, the Word Insert Table dialog box shown in Figure G.6 contains the *Number of columns* and *Number of rows* measurement boxes. To increase a number in a measurement box, position the tip of the arrow pointer on the up-pointing arrow at the right of the desired option and then click the left mouse button. To decrease the number, click the down-pointing arrow. If you are using the keyboard, press and hold down Alt + the underlined letter of the desired option and then press the Up Arrow key to increase the number or the Down Arrow key to decrease the number.

Command Buttons

The buttons at the bottom of the Excel Find and Replace dialog box shown in Figure G.5 are called ***command buttons***. Use a command button to execute or cancel a command. Some command buttons display with an ellipsis (...), which means another dialog box will open if you click that button. To choose a command button with the mouse, position the arrow pointer on the desired button and then click the left mouse button. To choose a command button with the keyboard, press the Tab key until the desired command button is surrounded by a marquee and then press the Enter key.

Figure G.5 Excel Find and Replace Dialog Box

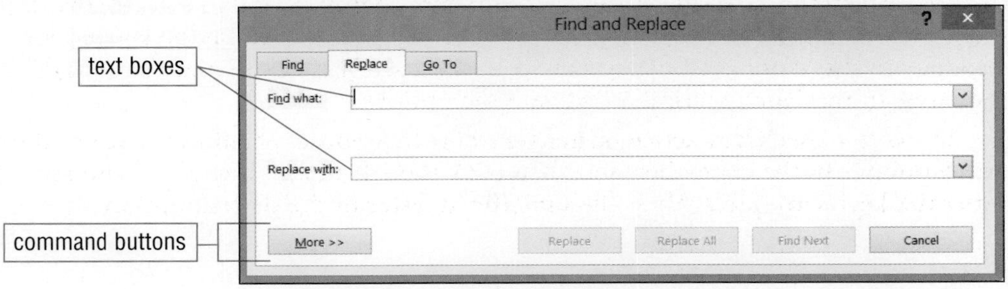

Choosing Commands with Keyboard Shortcuts

Applications in the Office suite offer a variety of keyboard shortcuts you can use to execute specific commands. Keyboard shortcuts generally require two or more keys. For example, the keyboard shortcut to display the Open dialog box in an application is Ctrl + F12. To use this keyboard shortcut, hold down the Ctrl key, press the F12 function on the keyboard, and then release the Ctrl key. For a list of keyboard shortcuts, refer to the Help files.

Choosing Commands with Shortcut Menus

The software programs in the Office suite include shortcut menus that contain commands related to different items. To display a shortcut menu, position the mouse pointer over the item for which you want to view more options, and then click the right mouse button or press Shift + F10. The shortcut menu will appear wherever the insertion point is positioned. For example, if the insertion point is positioned in a paragraph of text in a Word document, clicking the right mouse button or pressing Shift + F10 will cause the shortcut menu shown in Figure G.7 to display in the document screen (along with the Mini toolbar).

To select an option from a shortcut menu with the mouse, click the desired option. If you are using the keyboard, press the Up or Down Arrow key until the desired option is selected and then press the Enter key. To close a shortcut menu without choosing an option, click anywhere outside the shortcut menu or press the Esc key.

Figure G.6 Word Insert Table Dialog Box

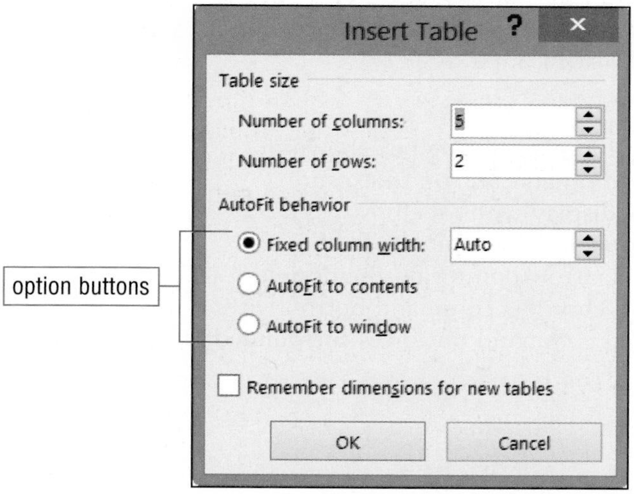

Figure G.7 Word Shortcut Menu

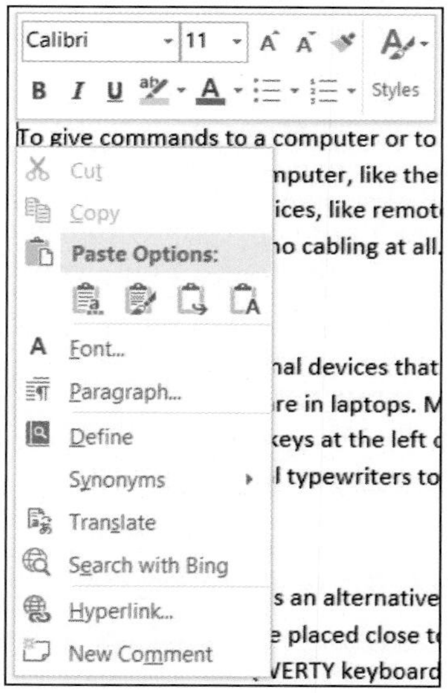

Working with Multiple Programs

As you learn the various programs in the Microsoft Office suite, you will notice many similarities between them. For example, the steps to save, close, and print are virtually the same whether you are working in Word, Excel, or PowerPoint. This consistency between programs greatly enhances a user's ability to transfer knowledge learned in one program to another within the suite. Another benefit to using Microsoft Office is the ability to have more than one program open at the same time and to integrate content from one program with another. For example, you can open Word and create a document, open Excel and create a spreadsheet, and then copy the Excel spreadsheet into Word.

When you open a program, a button containing an icon representing the program displays on the Taskbar. If you open another program, a button containing an icon representing that program displays to the right of the first program button on the Taskbar. Figure G.8 on the next page, shows the Taskbar with Word, Excel, Access, and PowerPoint open. To move from one program to another, click the Taskbar button representing the desired program.

Figure G.8 Taskbar with Word, Excel, Access, and PowerPoint Open

Customizing Settings

Before beginning computer projects in this textbook, you may need to customize your monitor's settings and turn on the display of file extensions. Projects in the chapters in this textbook assume that the monitor display is set at 1600 x 900 pixels and that the display of file extensions is turned on.

Before you begin learning the applications in the Microsoft Office 2013 suite, take a moment to check the display settings on the computer you are using. Your monitor's display settings are important because the ribbon in the Microsoft Office suite adjusts to the screen resolution setting of your computer monitor. A computer monitor set at a high resolution will have the ability to show more buttons in the ribbon than will a monitor set to a low resolution. The illustrations in this textbook were created with a screen resolution display set at 1600 × 900 pixels. In Figure G.9 on the next page, the Word ribbon is shown three ways: at a lower screen resolution (1366 × 768 pixels), at the screen resolution featured throughout this textbook, and at a higher screen resolution (1920 × 1080 pixels). Note the variances in the ribbon in all three examples. If possible, set your display to 1600 × 900 pixels to match the illustrations you will see in this textbook.

Figure G.9 Monitor Resolution

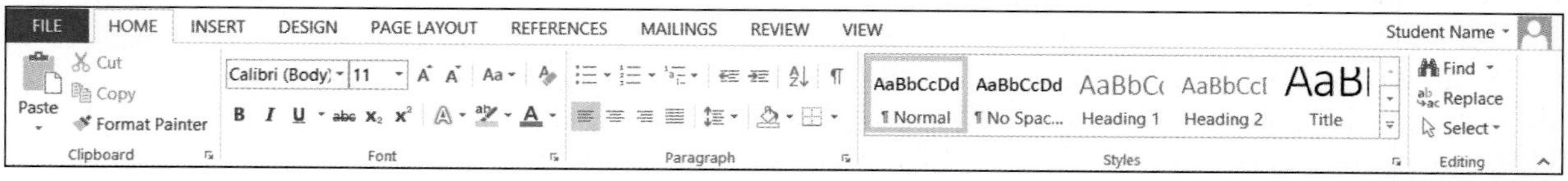

1366 × 768 screen resolution

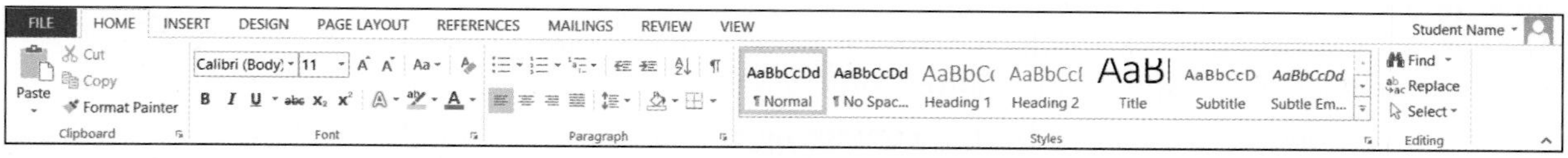

1600 × 900 screen resolution

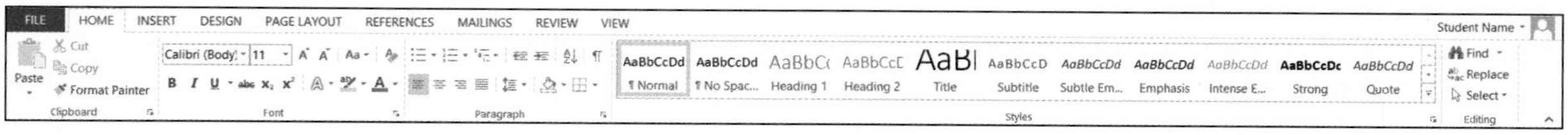

1920 × 1080 screen resolution

Project 1 Setting Monitor Display to 1600 by 900

1. At the Windows 8 desktop, right-click a blank area of the screen.
2. At the shortcut menu, click the *Screen resolution* option.
3. At the Screen Resolution window, click the *Resolution* option box. (This displays a slider bar. Your slider bar may display differently than what you see in the image at the right.)
4. Drag the button on the slider bar until *1600 × 900* displays to the right of the slider bar.
5. Click in the Screen Resolution window to remove the slider bar.
6. Click the Apply button.
7. Click the Keep Changes button.
8. Click the OK button.

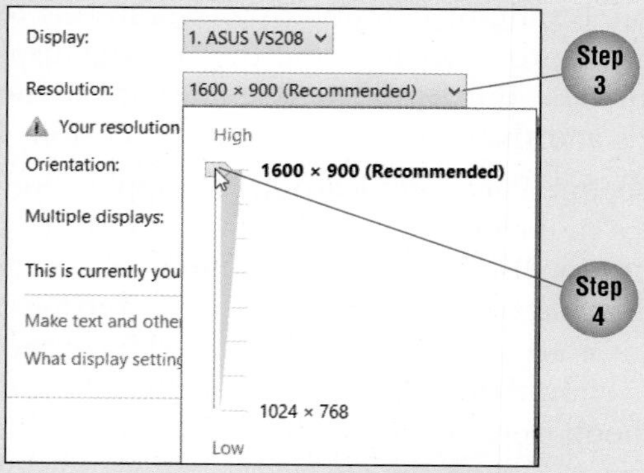

Project 2 Displaying File Extensions

1. At the Windows 8 desktop, position the mouse pointer in the lower left corner of the Taskbar until the Start screen thumbnail displays and then click the right mouse button.
2. At the pop-up list, click the *File Explorer* option.
3. At the Computer window, click the View tab on the ribbon and then click the *File name extensions* check box in the Show/hide group to insert a check mark.
4. Close the Computer window.

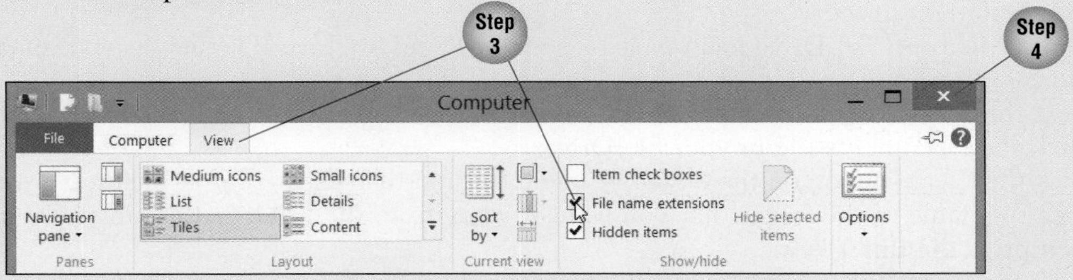

Completing Computer Projects

Some projects in this textbook require that you open an existing file. Project files are saved on the Student Resources CD in individual chapter folders. Before beginning a chapter, copy the necessary folder from the CD to your storage medium (such as a USB flash drive or your SkyDrive) using the Computer window. To maximize storage capacity, delete previous chapter folders before copying a new chapter folder onto your storage medium.

Project 3 Copying a Folder from the Student Resources CD to a USB Flash Drive

1. Insert the CD that accompanies this textbook into your computer's CD/DVD drive.
2. Insert your USB flash drive into an available USB port.
3. At the Windows 8 Start screen, click the Desktop tile.
4. Open File Explorer by clicking the File Explorer button on the Taskbar.
5. Click *Computer* in the Navigation pane at the left side of the File Explorer window.
6. Double-click the CD/DVD drive that displays with the name *BM13StudentResources* preceded by the drive letter.
7. Double-click ***StudentDataFiles*** in the Content pane.
8. Double-click the desired program folder name (and level number, if appropriate) in the Content pane.
9. Click once on the desired chapter (or unit performance assessment) folder name to select it.
10. Click the Home tab and then click the Copy button in the Clipboard group.
11. Click your USB flash drive that displays in the Navigation pane at the left side of the window.
12. Click the Home tab and then click the Paste button in the Clipboard group.
13. Close the File Explorer window by clicking the Close button located in the upper right corner of the window.

Project 4 Copying a Folder from the Student Resources CD to your SkyDrive Account

Note: SkyDrive is updated periodically, so the steps to create folders and upload files may vary from the steps below.

1. Insert the CD that accompanies this textbook into your computer's CD/DVD drive.
2. At the Windows 8 Start screen, click the Desktop tile.
3. Open Internet Explorer by clicking the Internet Explorer button on the Taskbar.
4. At the Internet Explorer home page, click in the Address bar, type **www.skydrive.com**, and then press Enter.
5. At the Microsoft SkyDrive login page, type your Windows Live ID (such as your email address).
6. Press the Tab key, type your password, and then press Enter.
7. Click the Documents tile in your SkyDrive.
8. Click the Create option on the SkyDrive menu bar and then click *Folder* at the drop-down list.
9. Type the name of the folder that you want to copy from the Student Resources CD and then press the Enter key.
10. Click the folder tile you created in the previous step.
11. Click the Upload option on the menu bar.
12. Click the CD/DVD drive that displays in the Navigation pane at the left side of the Choose File to Upload dialog box.
13. Open the chapter folder on the CD that contains the required student data files.
14. Select all of the files in the folder by pressing Ctrl + A and then click the Open button.

Project 5 Deleting a Folder

Note: Check with your instructor before deleting a folder.

1. Insert your storage medium (such as a USB flash drive) into your computer's USB port.
2. At the Windows desktop, open File Explorer by right-clicking the Start screen thumbnail and then clicking *File Explorer* at the shortcut menu.
3. Double-click the drive letter for your storage medium (the drive containing your USB flash drive, such as *Removable Disk (F:)*).
4. Click the chapter folder in the Content pane.
5. Click the Home tab and then click the Delete button in the Organize group.
6. At the message asking if you want to delete the folder, click the Yes button.
7. Close the Computer window by clicking the Close button located in the upper right corner of the window.

Using Windows 8

A computer requires an operating system to provide necessary instructions on a multitude of processes including loading programs, managing data, directing the flow of information to peripheral equipment, and displaying information. Windows 8 is an operating system that provides functions of this type (along with much more) in a graphical environment. Windows is referred to as a ***graphical user interface*** (GUI—pronounced *gooey*) that provides a visual display of information with features such as icons (pictures) and buttons. In this introduction, you will learn these basic features of Windows 8:

- Use the Start screen to launch programs
- Use desktop icons and the Taskbar to launch programs and open files or folders
- Organize and manage data, including copying, moving, creating, and deleting files and folders; and create a shortcut
- Explore the Control Panel and personalize the desktop
- Use the Windows Help and Support features
- Use search tools
- Customize monitor settings

Before using the software programs in the Microsoft Office suite, you will need to start the Windows 8 operating system. To do this, turn on the computer. Depending on your computer equipment configuration, you may also need to turn on the monitor and printer. If you are using a computer that is part of a network system or if your computer is set up for multiple users, a screen will display showing the user accounts defined for your computer system. At this screen, click your user account name; if necessary, type your password; and then press the Enter key. The Windows 8 operating system will start and, after a few moments, the Windows 8 Start screen will display as shown in Figure W.1. (Your Windows 8 Start screen may vary from what you see in Figure W.1.)

Exploring the Start Screen and Desktop

When Windows is loaded, the Windows 8 Start screen displays. This screen contains tiles that open various applications. Open an application by clicking an application's tile or display the Windows 8 desktop by clicking the Desktop tile. Click the Desktop tile and the screen displays as shown in Figure W.2. Think of the desktop in Windows as the top of a desk in an office. A businessperson places necessary tools—such as pencils, pens, paper, files, calculator—on the desktop to perform functions. Like the tools that are located on a desk, the Windows 8 desktop contains tools for operating the computer. These tools are logically grouped and placed in dialog boxes or panels that you can display using icons on the desktop. The desktop contains a variety of features for using your computer and applications installed on the computer.

Figure W.1 Windows 8 Start Screen

Figure W.2 Windows 8 Desktop

Using Icons

Icons are visual symbols that represent programs, files, or folders. Figure W.2 identifies the Recycle Bin icon on the Windows desktop. The Windows desktop on your computer may contain additional icons. Applications that have been installed on your computer may be represented by an icon on the desktop. Icons that represent files or folders may also display on your desktop. Double-click an icon and the application, file, or folder it represents opens on the desktop.

Using the Taskbar

The bar that displays at the bottom of the desktop (see Figure W.2) is called the ***Taskbar***. The Taskbar, shown in Figure W.3, contains the Start screen area (a spot where you point to access the Start screen), pinned items, a section that displays task buttons representing active tasks, the notification area, and the Show desktop button.

Position the mouse pointer in the lower left corner of the Taskbar to display the Start screen thumbnail. When the Start screen thumbnail displays, click the left mouse button to access the Windows 8 Start screen, shown in Figure W.1. (Your Start screen may look different.) You can also display the Start screen by pressing the Windows key on your keyboard or by pressing Ctrl + Esc. The left side of the Start menu contains tiles you can click to access the most frequently used applications. The name of the active user (the person who is currently logged on) displays in the upper right corner of the Start screen.

To open an application from the Start screen, drag the arrow pointer to the desired tile (referred to as ***pointing***) and then click the left mouse button. When a program is open, a task button representing the program appears on the Taskbar. If multiple programs are open, each program will appear as a task button on the Taskbar (a few specialized tools may not).

Figure W.3 Windows 8 Taskbar

Manipulating Windows

When you open a program, a defined work area known as a ***window*** displays on the screen. A Title bar displays at the top of the window and contains buttons at the right side for minimizing, maximizing, and restoring the size of the window, as well as for closing it. You can open more than one window at a time and the open windows can be cascaded or stacked. Windows 8 contains a Snap feature that causes a window to "stick" to the edge of the screen when the window is moved to the left or right side of the screen. Move a window to the top of the screen and the window is automatically maximized. If you drag down a maximized window, the window is automatically restored down (returned to its previous smaller size).

In addition to moving and sizing a window, you can change the display of all open windows. To do this, position the mouse pointer on the Taskbar and then click the right mouse button. At the pop-up menu that displays, you can choose to cascade all open windows, stack all open windows, or display all open windows side by side.

Project 1 Opening Programs, Switching between Programs, and Manipulating Windows

1. Open Windows 8. (To do this, turn on the computer and, if necessary, turn on the monitor and/or printer. If you are using a computer that is part of a network system or if your computer is set up for multiple users, you may need to click your user account name, type your password, and then press the Enter key. Check with your instructor to determine if you need to complete any additional steps.)
2. When the Windows 8 Start screen displays, open Microsoft Word by positioning the mouse pointer on the *Word 2013* tile and then clicking the left mouse button. (You may need to scroll to the right to display the Word 2013 tile.)
3. When the Microsoft Word program is open, notice that a task button representing Word displays on the Taskbar.
4. Open Microsoft Excel by completing the following steps:
   a. Position the arrow pointer in the lower left corner of the Taskbar until the Start screen thumbnail displays and then click the left mouse button.
   b. At the Start screen, position the mouse pointer on the *Excel 2013* tile and then click the left mouse button.
5. When the Microsoft Excel program is open, notice that a task button representing Excel displays on the Taskbar to the right of the task button representing Word.
6. Switch to the Word program by clicking the Word task button on the Taskbar.
7. Switch to the Excel program by clicking the Excel task button on the Taskbar.
8. Restore down the Excel window by clicking the Restore Down button that displays immediately left of the Close button in the upper right corner of the screen. (This reduces the Excel window so it displays along the bottom half of the screen.)
9. Restore down the Word window by clicking the Restore Down button located immediately left of the Close button in the upper right corner of the screen.

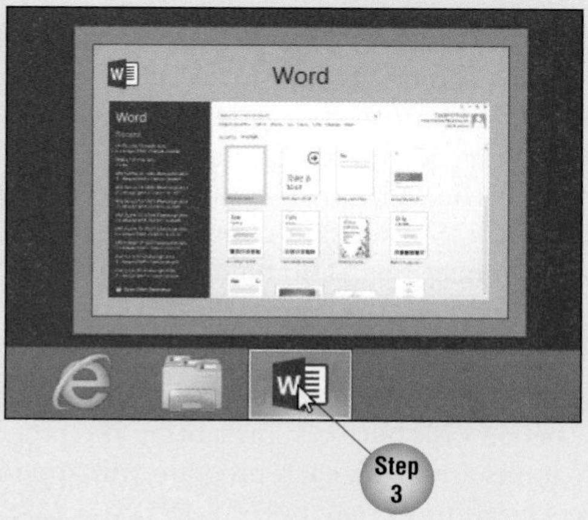

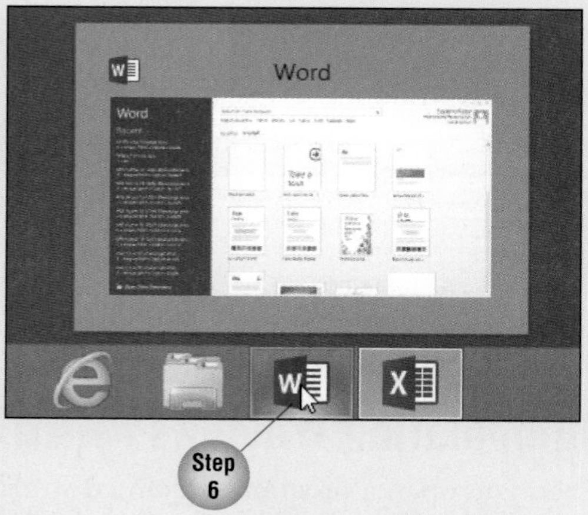

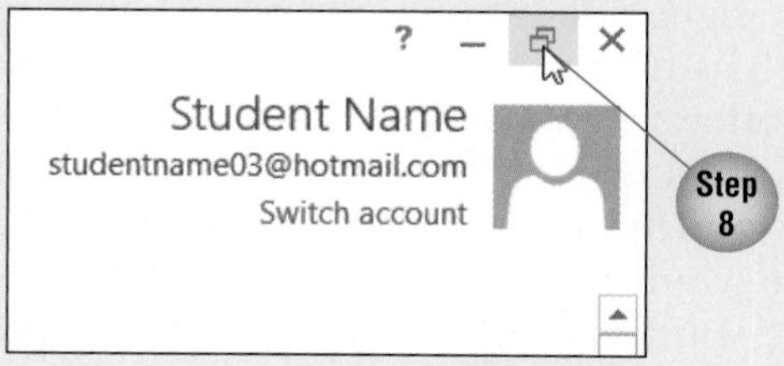

10. Position the mouse pointer at the top of the Word window screen, hold down the left mouse button, drag to the left side of the screen until an outline of the window displays in the left half of the screen, and then release the mouse button. (This "sticks" the window to the left side of the screen.)
11. Position the mouse pointer at the top of the Excel window screen, hold down the left mouse button, drag to the right until an outline of the window displays in the right half of the screen, and then release the mouse button.
12. Minimize the Excel window by clicking the Minimize button that displays in the upper right corner of the Excel window screen.

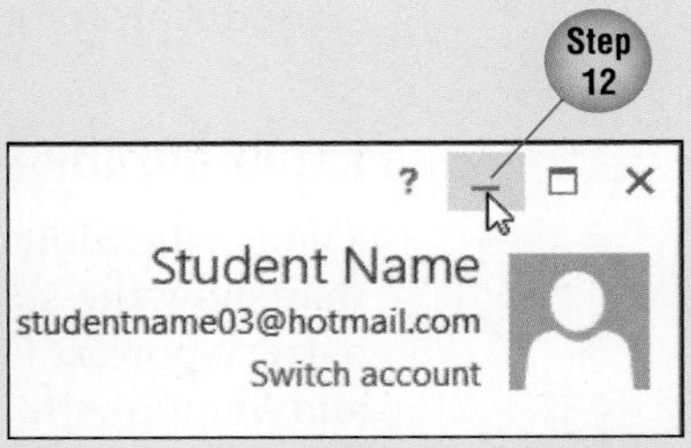

13. Hover your mouse over the Excel button on the Taskbar and then click the Excel window thumbnail that displays. (This displays the Excel window at the right side of the screen.)

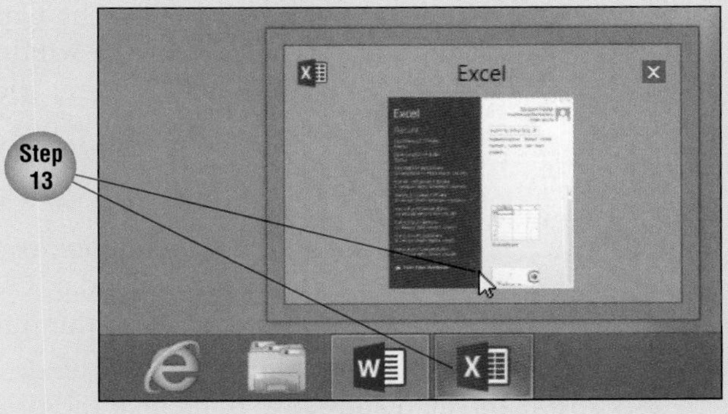

14. Cascade the Word and Excel windows by positioning the arrow pointer in an empty area of the Taskbar, clicking the right mouse button, and then clicking *Cascade windows* at the shortcut menu.

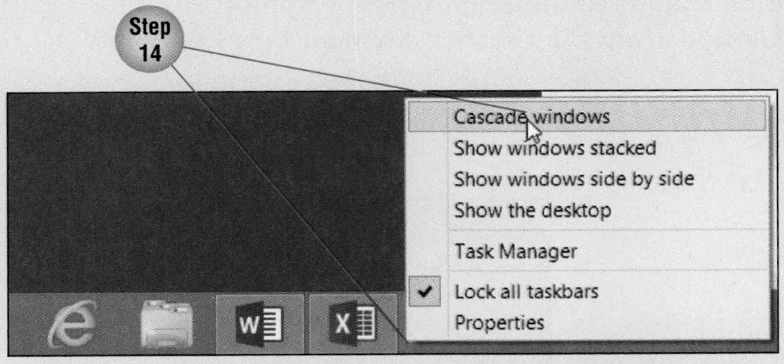

15. After viewing the windows cascaded, display them stacked by right-clicking an empty area of the Taskbar and then clicking *Show windows stacked* at the shortcut menu.
16. Display the desktop by right-clicking an empty area of the Taskbar and then clicking *Show the desktop* at the shortcut menu.
17. Display the windows stacked by right-clicking an empty area of the Taskbar and then clicking *Show open windows* at the shortcut menu.
18. Position the mouse pointer at the top of the Word window screen, hold down the left mouse button, drag the window to the top of the screen, and then release the mouse button. This maximizes the Word window so it fills the screen.
19. Close the Word window by clicking the Close button located in the upper right corner of the window.
20. At the Excel window, click the Maximize button located immediately left of the Close button in the upper right corner of the Excel window.
21. Close the Excel window by clicking the Close button located in the upper right corner of the window.

Using the Pinned Area

The icons that display immediately right of the Start screen area represent ***pinned applications***. Clicking an icon opens the application associated with the icon. Click the first icon to open the Internet Explorer web browser and click the second icon to open a File Explorer window containing Libraries.

Exploring the Notification Area

The notification area is located at the right side of the Taskbar and contains icons that show the status of certain system functions such as a network connection or battery power. The notification area contains icons for managing certain programs and Windows 8 features, as well as the system clock and date. Click the time or date in the notification area and a window displays with a clock and a calendar of the current month. Click the Change date and time settings hyperlink that displays at the bottom of the window and the Date and Time dialog box displays. To change the date and/or time, click the Change date and time button and the Date and Time Settings dialog box displays, similar to the dialog box shown in Figure W.4. (If a dialog box displays telling you that Windows needs your permission to continue, click the Continue button.)

Change the month and year by clicking the left-pointing or right-pointing arrow at the top of the calendar. Click the left-pointing arrow to display the previous month(s) and click the right-pointing arrow to display the next month(s).

To change the day, click the desired day in the monthly calendar that displays in the dialog box. To change the time, double-click either the hour, minute, or seconds number and then type the appropriate time or use the up- and down-pointing arrows in the measurement boxes to adjust the time.

Figure W.4 Date and Time Settings Dialog Box

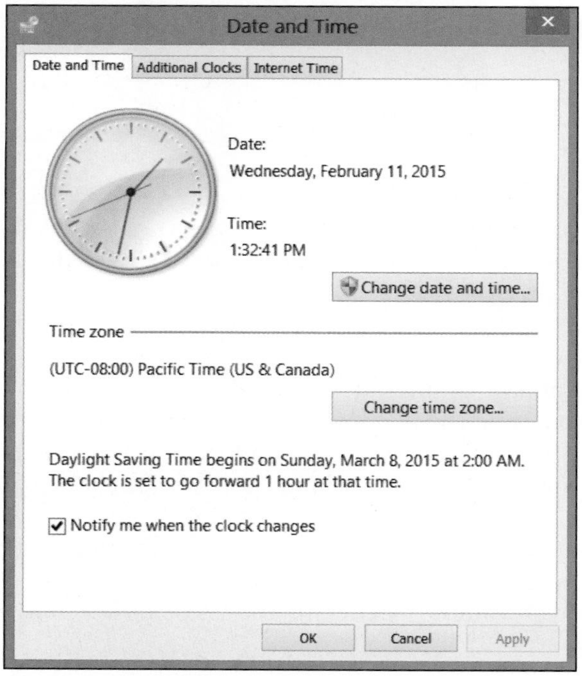

Some applications, when installed, will add an icon to the notification area of the Taskbar. To determine the name of an icon, position the mouse pointer on the icon and, after approximately one second, its label will display. If more icons have been inserted in the notification area than can be viewed at one time, an up-pointing arrow button displays at the left side of the notification area. Click this up-pointing arrow to display the remaining icons.

Setting Taskbar Properties

Customize the Taskbar with options at the Taskbar shortcut menu. Display this menu by right-clicking in an empty portion of the Taskbar. The Taskbar shortcut menu contains options for turning on or off the display of specific toolbars, specifying the display of multiple windows, displaying the Start Task Manager dialog box, locking or unlocking the Taskbar, and displaying the Taskbar Properties dialog box.

With options in the Taskbar Properties dialog box, shown in Figure W.5, you can change settings for the Taskbar. Display this dialog box by right-clicking an empty area on the Taskbar and then clicking *Properties* at the shortcut menu.

Each Taskbar property is controlled by a check box or an option box. If a property's check box contains a check mark, that property is active. Click the check box to remove the check mark and make the option inactive. If an option is inactive, clicking the check box will insert a check mark and turn on the option (make it active). A property option box displays the name of the currently active option. Click the option box to select a different option from the drop-down list.

Figure W.5 Taskbar Properties Dialog Box

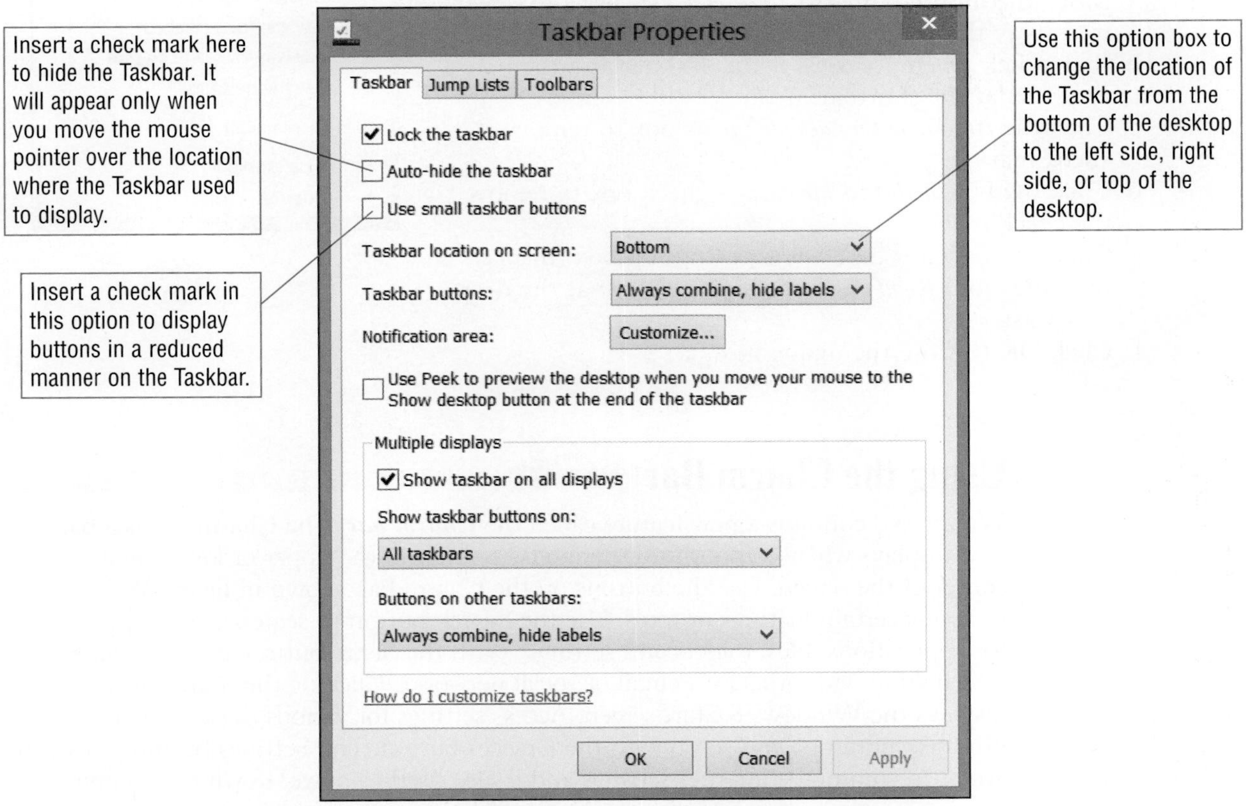

Project 2 Changing Taskbar Properties

1. Make sure the Windows 8 desktop displays.
2. Change the Taskbar properties by completing the following steps:
   a. Position the arrow pointer in an empty area of the Taskbar and then click the right mouse button.
   b. At the shortcut menu that displays, click *Properties*.
   c. At the Taskbar Properties dialog box, click the *Auto-hide the taskbar* check box to insert a check mark.
   d. Click the *Use small taskbar buttons* check box to insert a check mark.
   e. Click the option box (contains the word *Bottom*) that displays at the right side of the *Taskbar location on screen:* option and then click *Right* at the drop-down list.
   f. Click OK to close the dialog box.

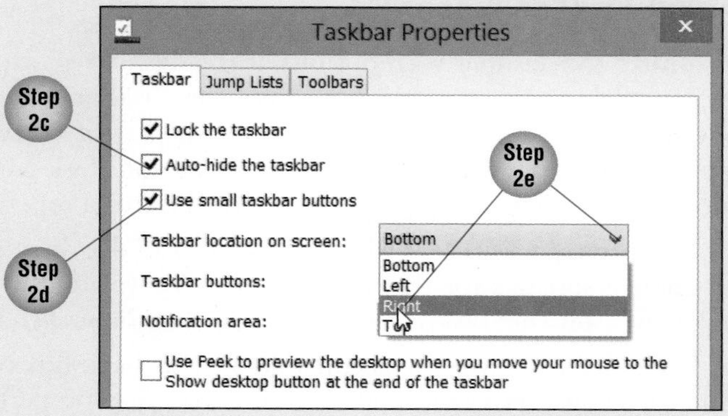

3. Since the *Auto-hide the taskbar* check box contains a check mark, the Taskbar does not display. Display the Taskbar by moving the mouse pointer to the right side of the screen. Notice that the buttons on the Taskbar are smaller than they were before.
4. Return to the default Taskbar properties by completing the following steps:
   a. Move the mouse pointer to the right side of the screen to display the Taskbar.
   b. Right-click an empty area of the Taskbar and then click *Properties* at the shortcut menu.
   c. Click the *Auto-hide the taskbar* check box to remove the check mark.
   d. Click the *Use small taskbar buttons* check box to remove the check mark.
   e. Click the *Taskbar location on screen* option box (displays with the word *Right*) and then click *Bottom* at the drop-down list.
   f. Click OK to close the dialog box.

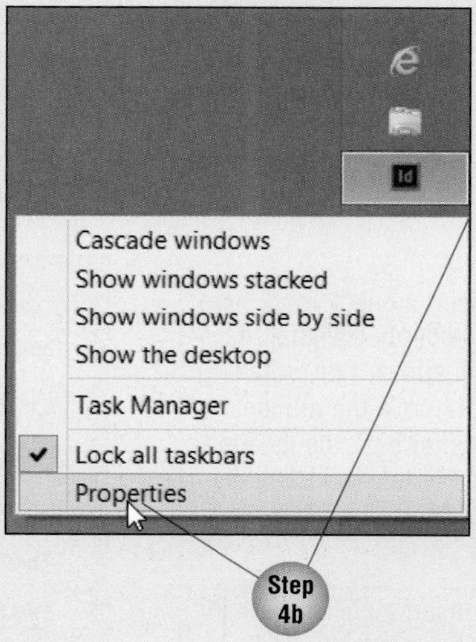

Using the Charm Bar

Windows 8 contains a new feature called the ***Charm bar***. The Charm bar is a bar that displays when you position the mouse pointer in the upper or lower right corner of the screen. Use the buttons on the Charm bar, shown in Figure W.6, to access certain features or tools. Use the Search button to search the computer for applications, files, folders and settings. With the Share button, you can share information with others via email or social networks. Clicking the Start button displays the Windows 8 Start screen. Access settings for various devices such as printers, monitors, and so on with the Devices button. The Settings button gives you access to common computer settings and is also used to power down the computer.

Figure W.6 Charm Bar

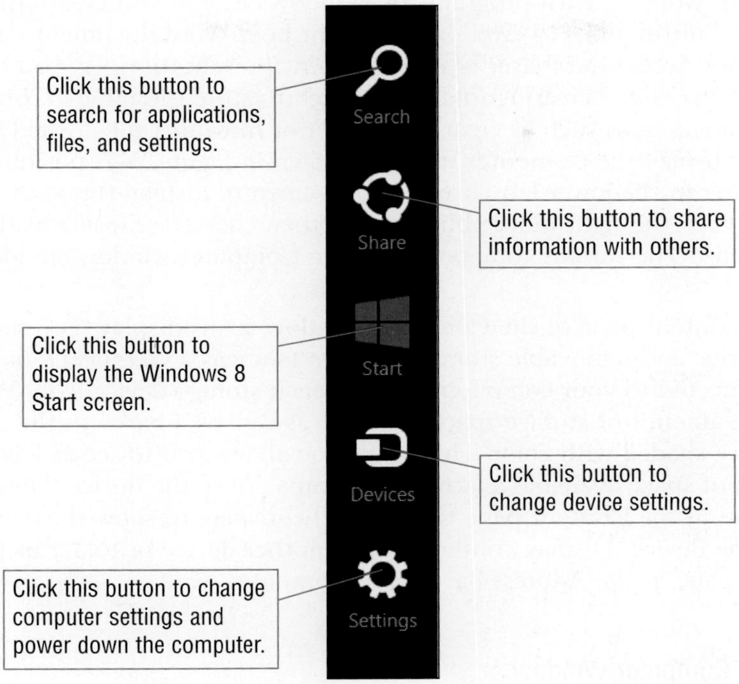

Powering Down the Computer

If you want to shut down Windows, first close any open programs and then display the Charm bar. Click the Settings button on the Charm bar, click the Power tile, and then click the *Shut down* option. The Power tile also contains options for restarting the computer or putting the computer to sleep. Restarting the computer may be useful when installing new applications or if Windows 8 stops working properly. In sleep mode, Windows saves files and information about applications and then powers down the computer to a low-power state. To "wake up" the computer, press the computer's power button.

In a multi-user environment, you can sign out of or lock your account so that no one can tamper with your work. To access these features, display the Windows 8 Start screen and then click your user account tile in the upper right corner. This displays a shortcut menu with three options. The *Lock* option locks the computer, which means that it is still powered on but requires a user password in order to access any applications or files that were previously opened. (To unlock the computer, click the icon on the login screen representing your account, type your password, and then press Enter.) Use the *Sign out* option to sign out of your user account while still keeping the computer turned on so that others may log on to it. Click the *Change account picture* option if you want to change the picture associated with your user account.

Managing Files and Folders

As you begin working with programs in Windows 8, you will create files in which data (information) is saved. A file might be a Word document, an Excel workbook, an Access database, or a PowerPoint presentation. As you begin creating files, consider creating folders in which to store these files. Complete file management tasks such as creating a folder or moving a file at the Computer window. To display the Computer window, shown in Figure W.7, position your mouse pointer in the lower left corner of the screen to display the Start screen thumbnail, click the right mouse button, and then click *File Explorer* at the shortcut menu. The various components of the Computer window are identified in Figure W.7.

In the Content pane of the Computer window, icons display representing each hard disk drive and removable storage medium (such as a CD, DVD, or USB device) connected to your computer. Next to each storage device icon, Windows displays the amount of storage space available as well as a bar with the amount of used space shaded with color. This visual cue allows you to see at a glance the amount of space available relative to the capacity of the device. Double-click a device icon in the Content pane to change the display to show the contents stored on the device. Display contents from another device or folder using the Navigation pane or the Address bar on the Computer window.

Figure W.7 Computer Window

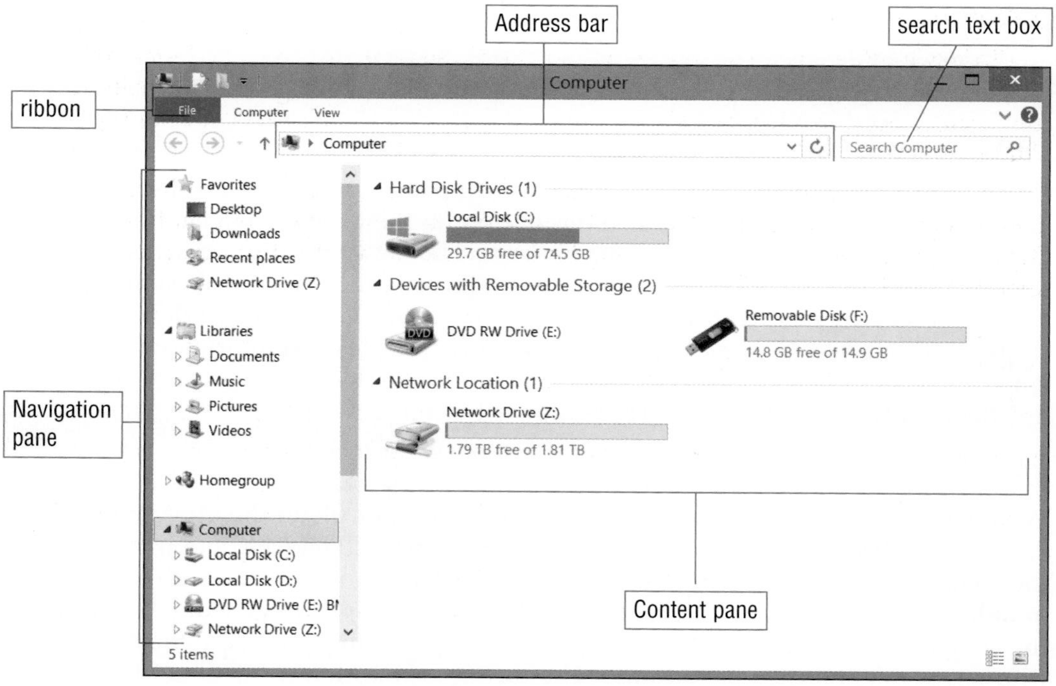

Copying, Moving, and Deleting Files and Folders

File and folder management activities include copying and moving files and folders from one folder or drive to another, as well as deleting files and folders. The Computer window offers a variety of methods for performing these actions. This section will provide you with steps for copying, moving, and deleting files and folders using options from the Home tab (shown in Figure W.8) and the shortcut menu (shown in Figure W.9).

To copy a file to another folder or drive, first display the file in the Content pane. If the file is located in the Documents folder, click the *Documents* folder in the *Libraries* section of the Navigation pane and then, in the Content pane, click the name of the file you want to copy. Click the Home tab on the ribbon and then click the Copy button in the Clipboard group. Use the Navigation pane to navigate to the location where you want to paste the file. Click the Home tab and then click the Paste button at the drop-down list. Complete similar steps to copy and paste a folder to another location.

If the desired file is located on a storage medium such as a CD, DVD, or USB device, double-click the device in the section of the Content pane labeled *Devices with Removable Storage*. (Each removable device is assigned an alphabetic drive letter by Windows, usually starting at E or F and continuing through the alphabet depending on the number of removable devices that are currently in use.) After double-clicking the storage medium in the Content pane, navigate to the desired folder and then click the file to select it. Click the Home tab on the ribbon and then click the Copy button in the Clipboard group. Navigate to the desired folder, click the Home tab, and then click the Paste button in the Clipboard group.

To move a file, click the desired file in the Content pane, click the Home tab on the ribbon, and then click the Cut button in the Clipboard group. Navigate to the desired location, click the Home tab, and then click the Paste button in the Clipboard group.

To delete a file or folder, click the file or folder in the Content pane in the Computer window. Click the Home tab and then click the Delete button in the Organize group. At the message asking if you want to move the file or folder to the Recycle Bin, click the Yes button.

Figure W.8 File Explorer Home tab

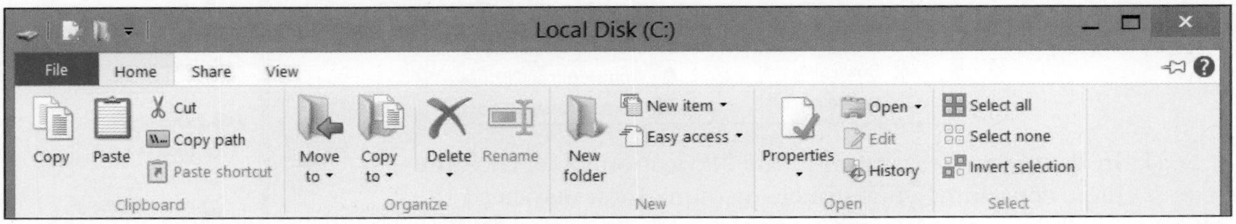

Figure W.9 Shortcut Menu

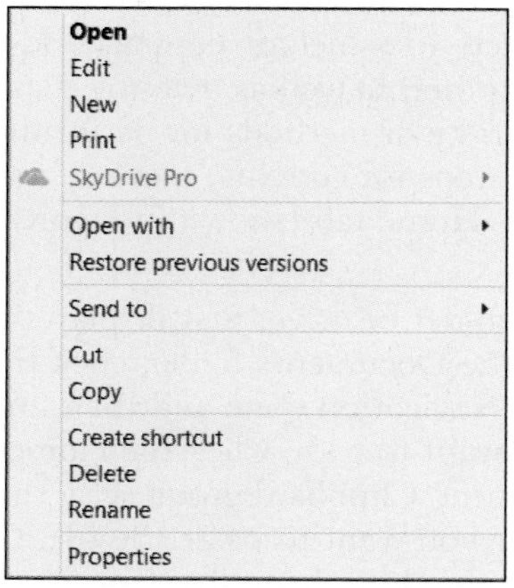

Project 4 Copying a File and Folder and Deleting a File

1. Insert the CD that accompanies this textbook into the appropriate drive.
2. Insert your storage medium (such as a USB flash drive) into the appropriate drive.
3. At the Windows 8 desktop, position the mouse pointer in the lower left corner of the Taskbar to display the Start screen thumbnail, click the right mouse button, and then click *File Explorer* at the shortcut menu.
4. Copy a file from the CD that accompanies this textbook to the drive containing your storage medium by completing the following steps:
   a. In the Content pane, double-click the drive into which you inserted the CD that accompanies this textbook.
   b. Double-click the *StudentDataFiles* folder in the Content pane.
   c. Double-click the *Windows8* folder in the Content pane.
   d. Click ***WordDocument01.docx*** in the Content pane.
   e. Click the Home tab and then click *Copy* in the Clipboard group.

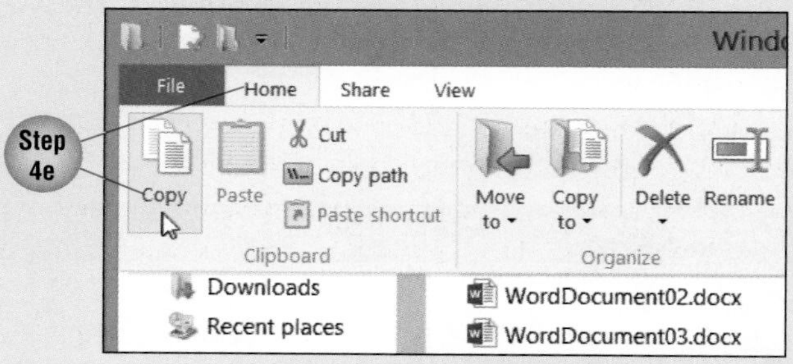

   f. In the Computer section in the Navigation pane, click the drive containing your storage medium. (You may need to scroll down the Navigation pane.)
   g. Click the Home tab and then click the Paste button in the Clipboard group.

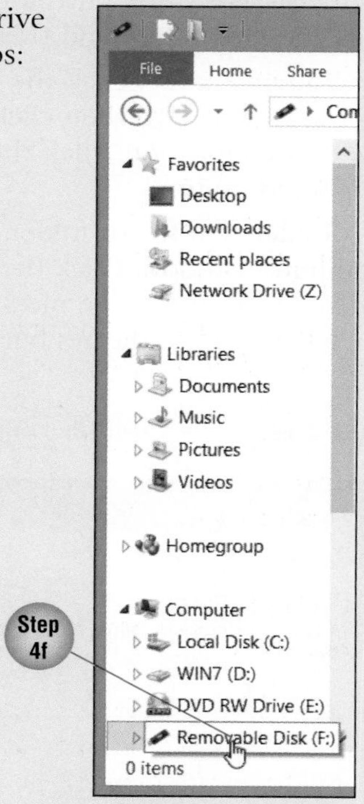

5. Delete ***WordDocument01.docx*** from your storage medium by completing the following steps:
   a. Make sure the contents of your storage medium display in the Content pane in the Computer window.

b. Click ***WordDocument01.docx*** in the Content pane to select it.
c. Click the Home tab and then click the Delete button in the Organize group.
d. At the message asking if you want to permanently delete the file, click the Yes button.
6. Copy the Windows8 folder from the CD to your storage medium by completing the following steps:
   a. With the Computer window open, click the drive in the *Computer* section in the Navigation pane that contains the CD that accompanies this book.
   b. Double-click *StudentDataFiles* in the Content pane.
   c. Click the *Windows8* folder in the Content pane.
   d. Click the Home tab and then click the Copy button in the Clipboard group.
   e. In the *Computer* section in the Navigation pane, click the drive containing your storage medium.
   f. Click the Home tab and then click the Paste button in the Clipboard group.
7. Close the Computer window by clicking the Close button located in the upper right corner of the window.

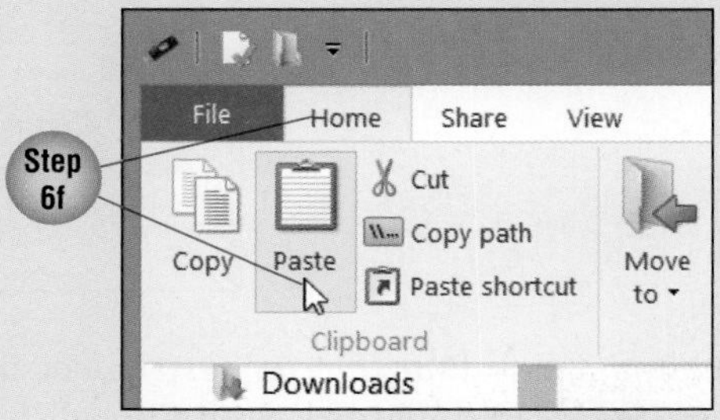

In addition to options on the Home tab, you can use options in a shortcut menu to copy, move, and delete files or folders. To use a shortcut menu, select the desired file(s) or folder(s), position the mouse pointer on the selected item, and then click the right mouse button. At the shortcut menu that displays, click the desired option, such as *Copy*, *Cut*, or *Delete*.

Selecting Files and Folders

You can move, copy, or delete more than one file or folder at the same time. Before moving, copying, or deleting files or folders, select the desired files or folders. To make selecting easier, consider displaying the files in the Content pane in a list or detailed list format. To change the display, click the View tab on the ribbon and then click *List* or *Details* in the Layout group.

To select adjacent files or folders, click the first file or folder, hold down the Shift key, and then click the last file or folder. To select nonadjacent files or folders, click the first file or folder, hold down the Ctrl key, and then click the other files or folders you wish to select.

Project 5 Copying and Deleting Files

1. At the Windows 8 desktop, position the mouse pointer in the lower left corner of the Taskbar to display the Start screen thumbnail, click the right mouse button, and then click *File Explorer* at the shortcut menu.
2. Copy files from the CD that accompanies this textbook to the drive containing your storage medium by completing the following steps:
   a. Make sure the CD that accompanies this textbook and your storage medium are inserted in the appropriate drives.
   b. Double-click the CD drive in the Content pane in the Computer window.

c. Double-click the *StudentDataFiles* folder in the Content pane.
d. Double-click the *Windows8* folder in the Content pane.
e. Change the display to List by clicking the View tab and then clicking *List* in the Layout group list box.

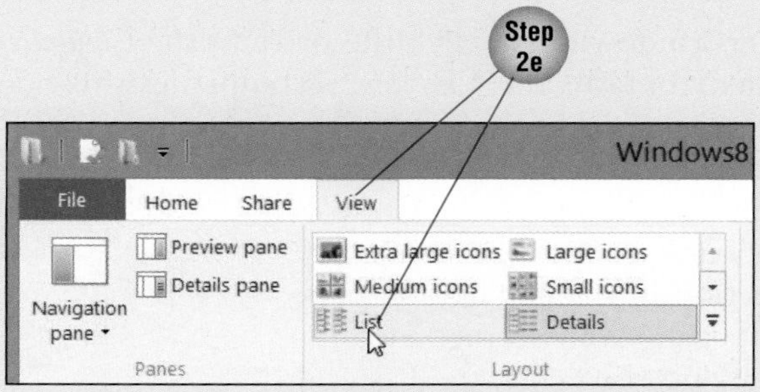

f. Click ***WordDocument01.docx*** in the Content pane.
g. Hold down the Shift key, click ***WordDocument05.docx***, and then release the Shift key. (This selects five documents.)

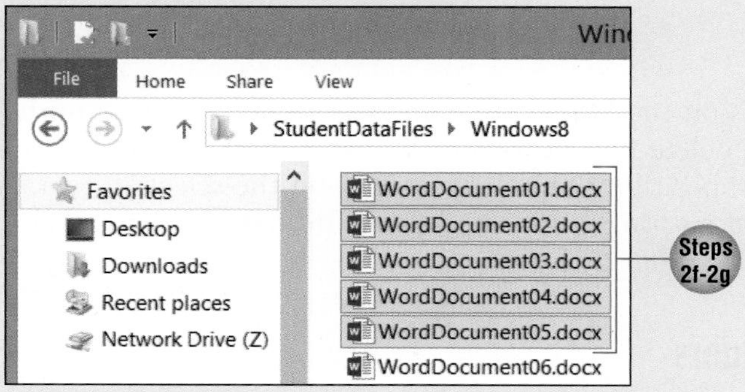

h. Click the Home tab and then click the Copy button in the Clipboard group.
i. In the *Computer* section of the Navigation pane, click the drive containing your storage medium.
j. Click the Home tab and then click the Paste button in the Clipboard group.
3. Delete the files you just copied to your storage medium by completing the following steps:
   a. Change the display by clicking the View tab and then clicking *List* in the Layout group.
   b. Click ***WordDocument01.docx*** in the Content pane.
   c. Hold down the Shift key, click ***WordDocument05.docx***, and then release the Shift key.
   d. Position the mouse pointer on any selected file, click the right mouse button, and then click *Delete* at the shortcut menu.
   e. At the message asking if you are sure you want to permanently delete the files, click Yes.

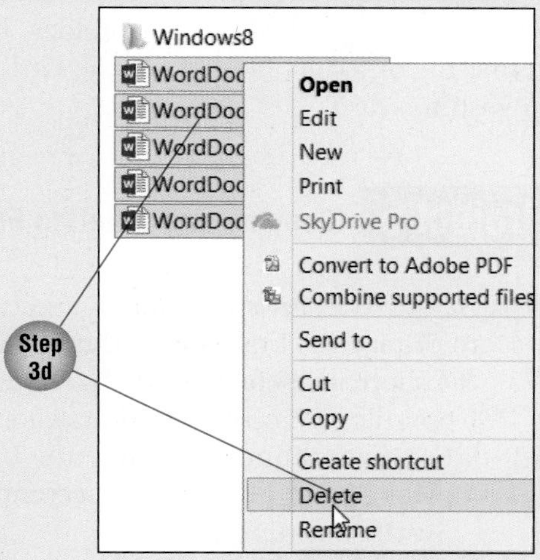

4. Close the Computer window by clicking the Close button located in the upper right corner of the window.

Manipulating and Creating Folders

As you begin working with and creating multiple files, consider creating folders in which you can logically group and store the files. To create a folder, display the Computer window and then display the drive or folder where you want to create the folder in the Content pane. To create the new folder, click the New folder button in the New group on the Home tab; click the New folder button on the Quick Access toolbar; or click in a blank area in the Content pane, click the right mouse button, point to *New* in the shortcut menu, and then click *Folder* at the side menu. Any of the three methods inserts a folder icon in the Content pane and names the folder *New folder*. Type the desired name for the new folder and then press Enter.

Project 6 Creating a New Folder

1. At the Windows 8 desktop, open the Computer window.
2. Create a new folder by completing the following steps:
   a. In the Content pane, double-click the drive that contains your storage medium.
   b. Double-click the *Windows8* folder in the Content pane. (This opens the folder.)
   c. Click the View tab and then click *List* in the Layout group.
   d. Click the Home tab and then click the New folder button in the New group.
   e. Type SpellCheckFiles and then press Enter. (This changes the name from *New folder* to *SpellCheckFiles*.)

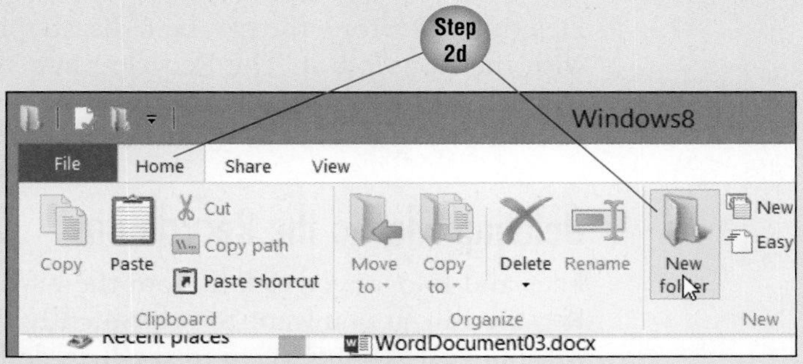

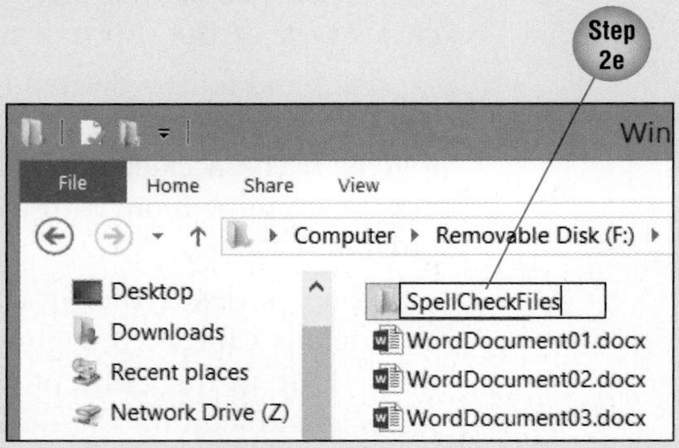

3. Copy **WordSpellCheck01.docx**, **WordSpellCheck02.docx**, and **WordSpellCheck03.docx** into the SpellCheckFiles folder you just created by completing the following steps:
   a. Click the View tab and then click *List* in the Layout group. (Skip this step if *List* is already selected.)
   b. Click ***WordSpellCheck01.docx*** in the Content pane.
   c. Hold down the Shift key, click ***WordSpellCheck03.docx***, and then release the Shift key. (This selects three documents.)
   d. Click the Home tab and then click the Copy button in the Clipboard group.
   e. Double-click the *SpellCheckFiles* folder in the Content pane.
   f. Click the Home tab and then click the Paste button in the Clipboard group.

4. Delete the SpellCheckFiles folder and its contents by completing the following steps:
   a. Click the Back button (contains a left-pointing arrow) located at the left side of the Address bar.
   b. With the SpellCheckFiles folder selected in the Content pane, click the Home tab and then click the Delete button in the Organize group.
   c. At the message asking you to confirm the deletion, click Yes.
5. Close the window by clicking the Close button located in the upper right corner of the window.

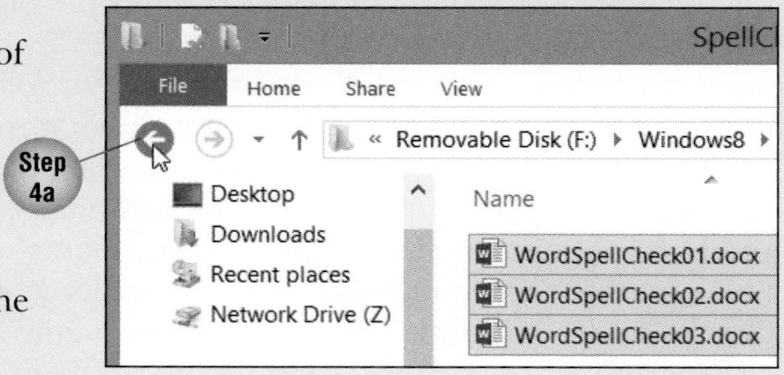

Using the Recycle Bin

Deleting the wrong file can be a disaster, but Windows 8 helps protect your work with the ***Recycle Bin***. The Recycle Bin acts just like an office wastepaper basket; you can "throw away" (delete) unwanted files, but you can also "reach in" to the Recycle Bin and take out (restore) a file if you threw it away by accident.

Deleting Files to the Recycle Bin

Files and folders you delete from the hard drive are sent automatically to the Recycle Bin. If you want to permanently delete files or folders from the hard drive without first sending them to the Recycle Bin, select the desired file(s) or folder(s), right-click one of the selected files or folders, hold down the Shift key, and then click *Delete* at the shortcut menu.

Files and folders deleted from a USB flash drive or disc are deleted permanently. (Recovery programs are available, however, that will help you recover deleted files or folders. If you accidentally delete a file or folder from a USB flash drive or disc, do not do anything more with the USB flash drive or disc until you can run a recovery program.)

You can delete files in the manner described earlier in this section and you can also delete a file by dragging the file icon to the Recycle Bin. To do this, click the desired file in the Content pane in the Computer window, drag the file icon to the Recycle Bin icon on the desktop until the text *Move to Recycle Bin* displays, and then release the mouse button.

Restoring Files from the Recycle Bin

To restore a file from the Recycle Bin, double-click the Recycle Bin icon on the desktop. This opens the Recycle Bin window, shown in Figure W.10. (The contents of the Recycle Bin will vary.) To restore a file, click the file you want restored, click the Recycle Bin Tools Manage tab and then click the Restore the selected items button in the Restore group. This removes the file from the Recycle Bin and returns it to its original location. You can also restore a file by positioning the mouse pointer on the file, clicking the right mouse button, and then clicking *Restore* at the shortcut menu.

Figure W.10 Recycle Bin Window

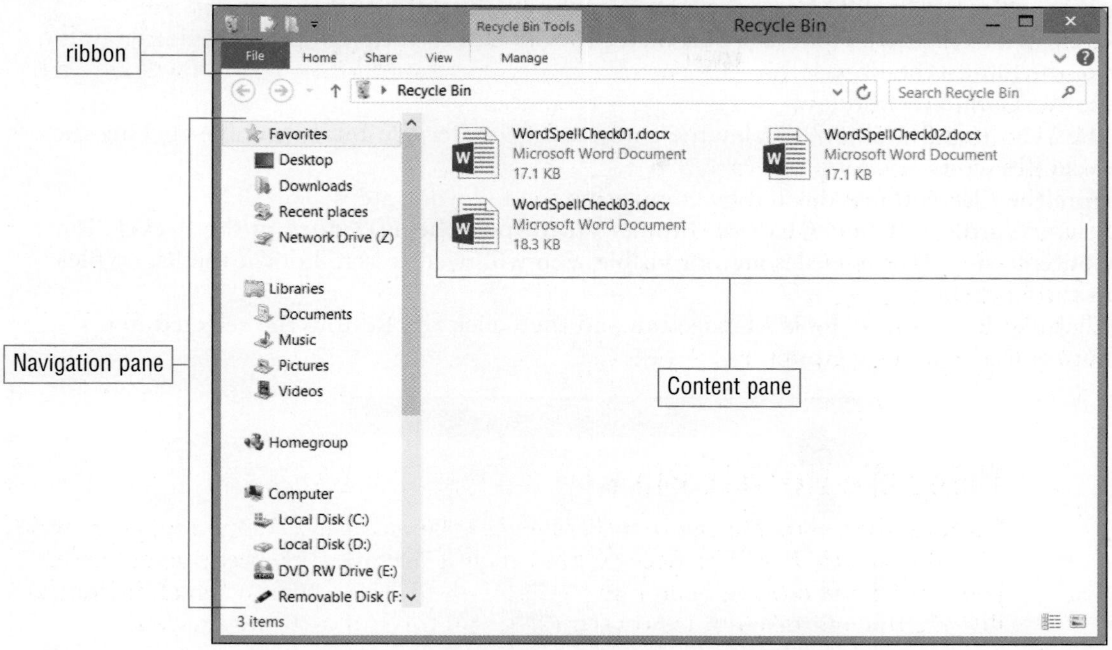

Project 7 Deleting Files to and Restoring Files from the Recycle Bin

Before beginning this project, check with your instructor to determine if you can copy files to the hard drive.

1. At the Windows 8 desktop, open the Computer window.
2. Copy files from your storage medium to the Documents folder on your hard drive by completing the following steps:
   a. In the Content pane, double-click the drive containing your storage medium.
   b. Double-click the *Windows8* folder in the Content pane.
   c. Click the View tab and then click *List* in the Layout group. (Skip this step if *List* is already selected.)
   d. Click ***WordSpellCheck01.docx*** in the Content pane.
   e. Hold down the Shift key, click ***WordSpellCheck03.docx***, and then release the Shift key.
   f. Click the Home tab and then click the Copy button in the Clipboard group.
   g. Click the *Documents* folder in the *Libraries* section of the Navigation pane.
   h. Click the Home tab and then click the Paste button in the Clipboard group.

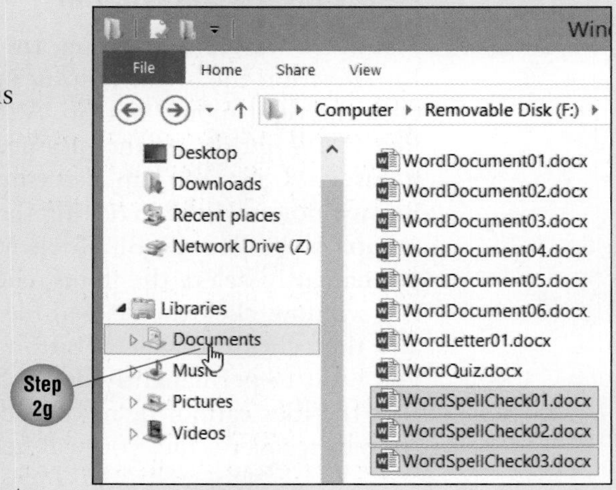

3. With **WordSpellCheck01.docx** through **WordSpellCheck03.docx** selected in the Content pane, click the Home tab and then click the Delete button in the Organize group to delete the files to the Recycle Bin.
4. Close the Computer window.
5. At the Windows 8 desktop, display the contents of the Recycle Bin by double-clicking the Recycle Bin icon.
6. Restore the files you just deleted by completing the following steps:
   a. Select **WordSpellCheck01.docx** through **WordSpellCheck03.docx** in the Recycle Bin Content pane. (If these files are not visible, you will need to scroll down the list of files in the Content pane.)
   b. Click the Recycle Bin Tools Manage tab and then click the Restore the selected items button in the Restore group.

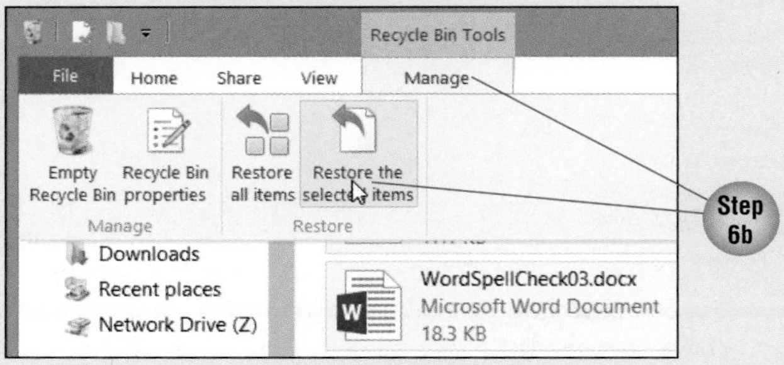

7. Close the Recycle Bin by clicking the Close button located in the upper right corner of the window.
8. Display the Computer window.
9. Click the *Documents* folder in the *Libraries* section of the Navigation pane.
10. Delete the files you restored.
11. Close the Computer window.

Emptying the Recycle Bin

Just like a wastepaper basket, the Recycle Bin can get full. To empty the Recycle Bin, position the arrow pointer on the Recycle Bin icon on the desktop and then click the right mouse button. At the shortcut menu that displays, click the *Empty Recycle Bin* option. At the message asking if you want to permanently delete the items, click Yes. You can also empty the Recycle Bin by displaying the Recycle Bin window and then clicking the Empty Recycle Bin button in the Manage group on the Recycle Bin Tools Manage tab. At the message asking if you want to permanently delete the items, click Yes. To delete a specific file from the Recycle Bin window, click the desired file in the Recycle Bin window, click the Home tab, and then click the Delete button in the Organize group. At the message asking if you want to permanently delete the file, click Yes. When you empty the Recycle Bin, the files cannot be recovered by the Recycle Bin or by Windows 8. If you have to recover a file, you will need to use a file recovery program.

Project 8 Emptying the Recycle Bin

Note: Before beginning this project, check with your instructor to determine if you can delete files/folders from the Recycle Bin.

1. At the Windows 8 desktop, double-click the Recycle Bin icon.
2. At the Recycle Bin window, empty the contents by clicking the Empty Recycle Bin button in the Manage group on the Recycle Bin Tools Manage tab.
3. At the message asking you if you want to permanently delete the items, click Yes.
4. Close the Recycle Bin by clicking the Close button located in the upper right corner of the window.

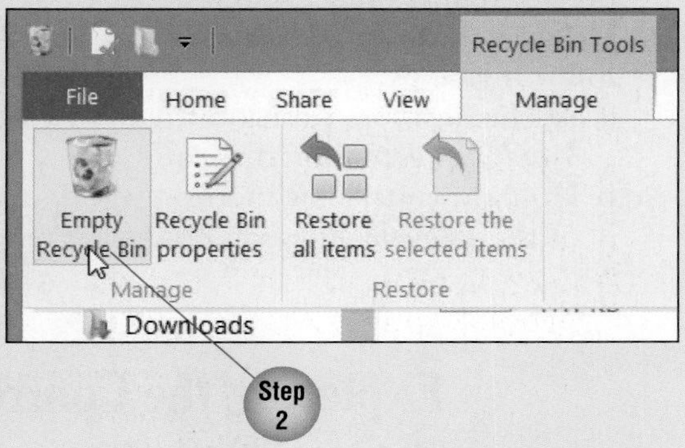

Creating a Shortcut

If you use a file or application on a consistent basis, consider creating a shortcut to the file or application. A ***shortcut*** is a specialized icon that points the operating system to an actual file, folder, or application. If you create a shortcut to a Word document, the shortcut icon is not the actual document but a very small file that contains the path to the document. Double-click the shortcut icon and Windows 8 opens the document in Word.

One method for creating a shortcut is to display the Computer window and then make active the drive or folder where the file is located. Right-click the desired file, point to *Send to*, and then click *Desktop (create shortcut)*. You can easily delete a shortcut icon from the desktop by dragging the shortcut icon to the Recycle Bin icon. This deletes the shortcut icon but does not delete the file to which the shortcut pointed.

Project 9 Creating a Shortcut

1. At the Windows 8 desktop, display the Computer window.
2. Double-click the drive containing your storage medium.
3. Double-click the *Windows8* folder in the Content pane.
4. Change the display of files to a list by clicking the View tab and then clicking *List* in the Layout group. (Skip this step if *List* is already selected.)
5. Create a shortcut to the file named **WordQuiz.docx** by right-clicking ***WordQuiz.docx***, pointing to *Send to*, and then clicking *Desktop (create shortcut)*.
6. Close the Computer window.

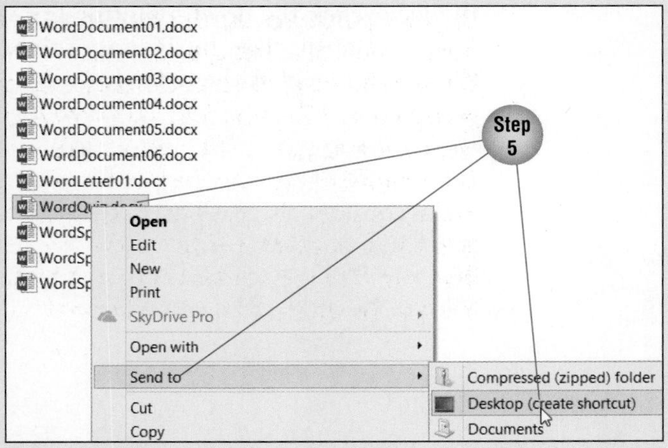

7. Open Word and **WordQuiz.docx** by double-clicking the *WordQuiz.docx* shortcut icon on the desktop.
8. After viewing the file in Word, close Word by clicking the Close button that displays in the upper right corner of the window.
9. Delete the *WordQuiz.docx* shortcut icon by completing the following steps:
   a. At the desktop, position the mouse pointer on the *WordQuiz.docx* shortcut icon.
   b. Hold down the left mouse button, drag the icon on top of the Recycle Bin icon, and then release the mouse button.

Exploring the Control Panel

The Control Panel, shown in Figure W.11, contains a variety of icons for customizing the appearance and functionality of your computer as well as accessing and changing system settings. Display the Control Panel by right-clicking the Start screen thumbnail and then clicking *Control Panel* at the shortcut menu. The Control Panel organizes settings into categories to make them easier to find. Click a category icon and the Control Panel displays lower-level categories and tasks within each of them.

Hover your mouse over a category icon in the Control Panel and a ScreenTip displays with an explanation of what options are available. For example, if you hover the mouse over the Appearance and Personalization icon, a ScreenTip displays with information about the tasks available in the category, such as changing the appearance of desktop items, applying a theme or screen saver to your computer, or customizing the Taskbar.

If you click a category icon in the Control Panel, the Control Panel displays all of the available subcategories and tasks in the category. Also, the categories display in text form at the left side of the Control Panel. For example, if you click the Appearance and Personalization icon, the Control Panel displays as shown in Figure W.12. Notice how the Control Panel categories display at the left side of the Control Panel and options for changing the appearance and personalizing your computer display in the middle of the Control Panel.

By default, the Control Panel displays categories of tasks in what is called *Category* view. You can change this view to display large or small icons. To change the view, click the down-pointing arrow that displays at the right side of the text *View by* that displays in the upper right corner of the Control Panel, and then click the desired view at the drop-down list (see Figure W.11).

Figure W.11 The Control Panel

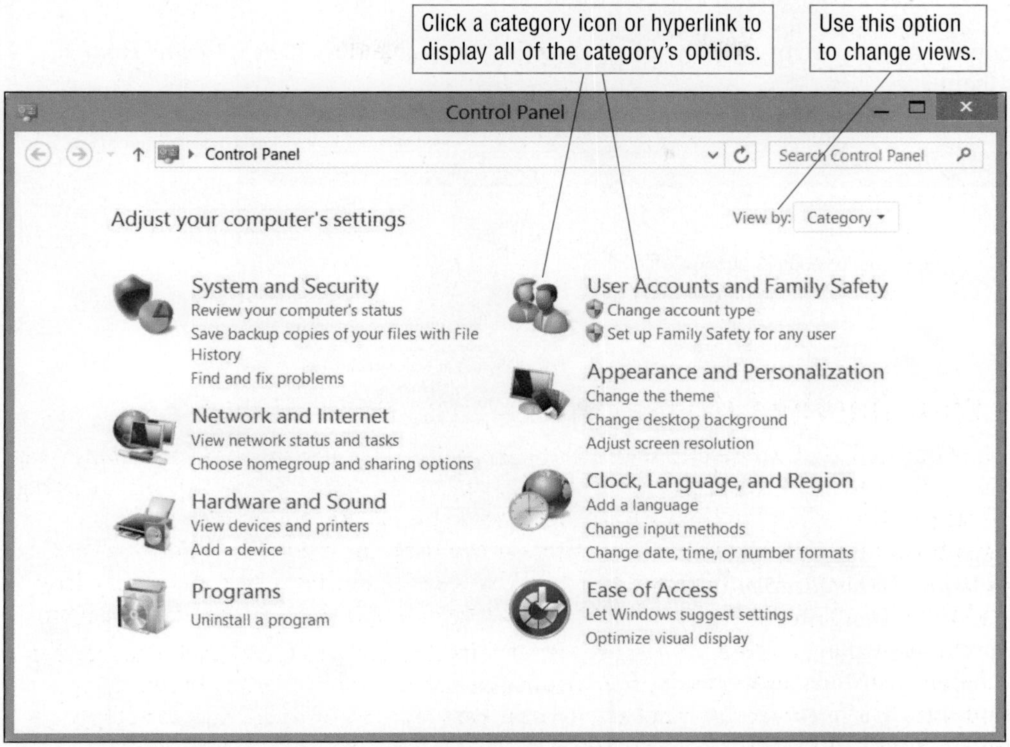

Figure W.12 Appearance and Personalization Window

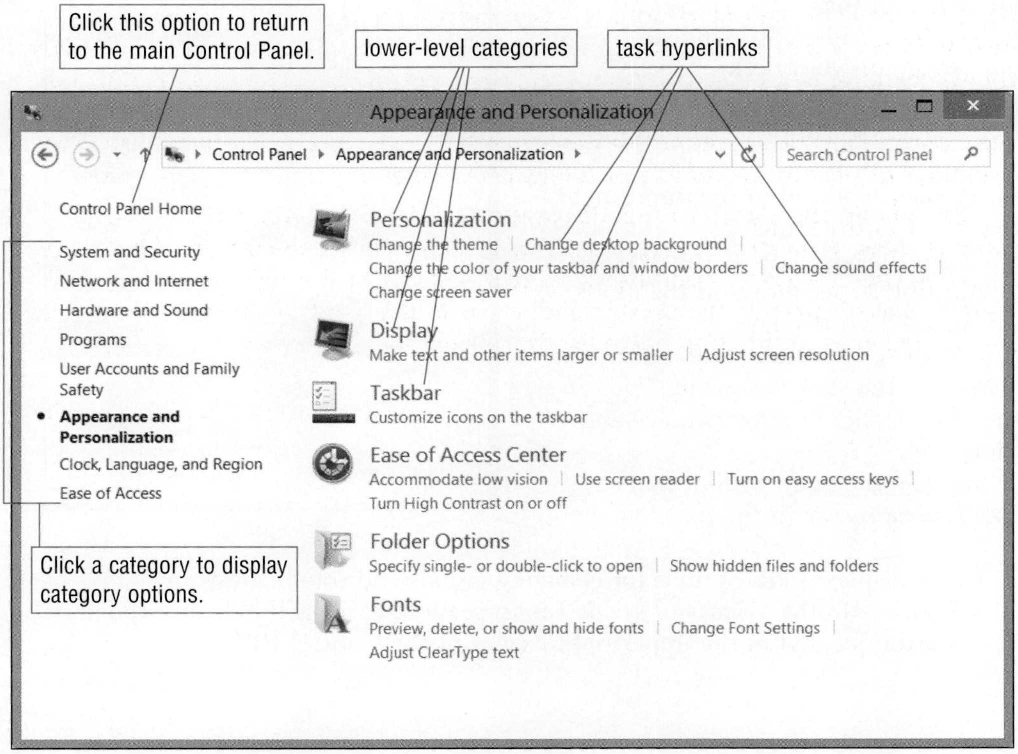

Project 10 Changing the Desktop Theme

1. At the Windows 8 desktop, right-click the Start screen thumbnail and then click *Control Panel* at the shortcut menu.
2. At the Control Panel, click the Appearance and Personalization icon.

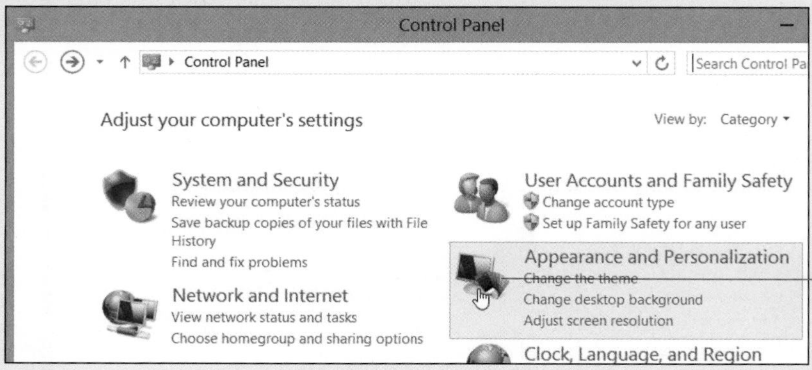

3. Click the Change the theme hyperlink that displays below *Personalization* in the panel at the right in the Control Panel.
4. At the window that displays with options for changing visuals and sounds on your computer, click *Earth* in the *Windows Default Themes* section.

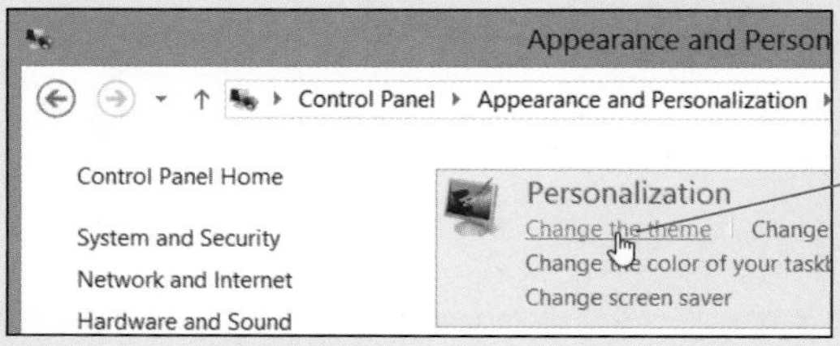

5. Click the Desktop Background hyperlink that displays in the lower left corner of the panel.
6. Click the button that displays below the text *Change picture every* and then click *10 Seconds* at the drop-down list. (This tells Windows to change the picture on your desktop every 10 seconds.)
7. Click the Save changes button that displays in the lower right corner of the Control Panel.
8. Click the Close button located in the upper right corner to close the Control Panel.
9. Look at the picture that displays as the desktop background. Wait for 10 seconds and then look at the second picture that displays.
10. Right-click the Start screen thumbnail and then click *Control Panel* at the shortcut menu.
11. At the Control Panel, click the Appearance and Personalization icon.
12. Click the Change the theme hyperlink that displays below *Personalization* in the panel at the right.

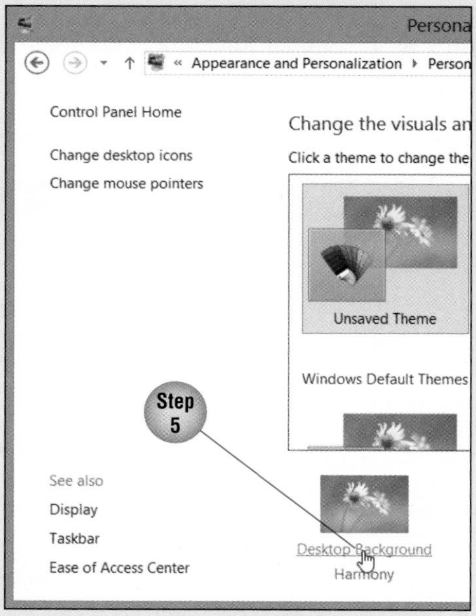

13. At the window that displays with options for changing visuals and sounds on your computer, click *Windows* in the *Windows Default Themes* section. (This is the default theme.)
14. Click the Close button located in the upper right corner of the Control Panel.

Searching in the Control Panel

The Control Panel contains a large number of options for customizing the appearance and functionality of your computer. If you want to customize a feature and are not sure where the options for the feature are located, search for the feature. To do this, display the Control Panel and then type the name of the desired feature. By default, the insertion point is positioned in the *Search Control Panel* text box. When you type the feature name in the text box, options related to the feature display in the Control Panel.

Project 11 **Customizing the Mouse**

1. Right-click the Start screen thumbnail and then click *Control Panel.*
2. At the Control Panel, type **mouse**. (The insertion point is automatically located in the *Search Control Panel* text box when you open the Control Panel. When you type *mouse,* features for customizing the mouse display in the Control Panel.)

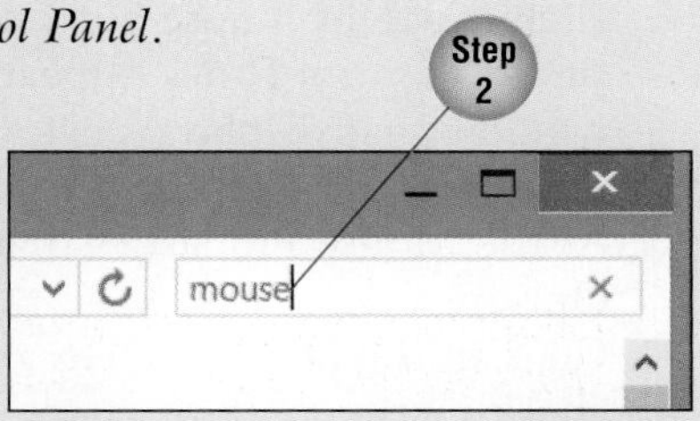

3. Click the Mouse icon that displays in the Control Panel.
4. At the Mouse Properties dialog box, notice the options that display. (The *Switch primary and secondary buttons* option might be useful, for example, if you are left-handed and want to switch the buttons on the mouse.)
5. Click the Cancel button to close the dialog box.
6. At the Control Panel, click the Change the mouse pointer display or speed hyperlink.

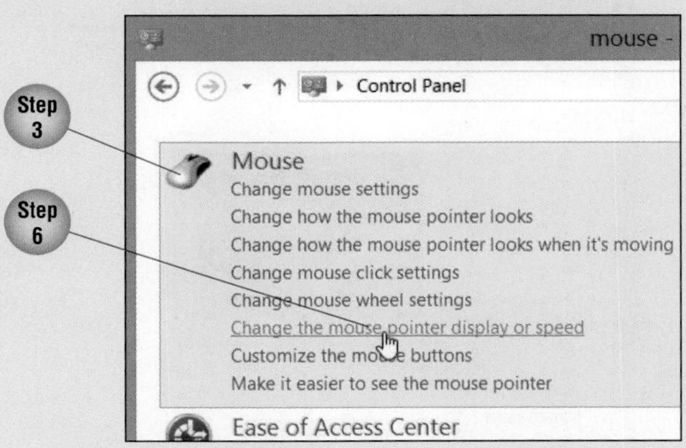

7. At the Mouse Properties dialog box with the Pointer Options tab selected, click the *Display pointer trails* check box in the *Visibility* section to insert a check mark.
8. Drag the button on the slider bar (located below the *Display pointer trails* check box) approximately to the middle of the bar.
9. Click OK to close the dialog box.
10. Close the Control Panel.
11. Move the mouse pointer around the screen to see the pointer trails.

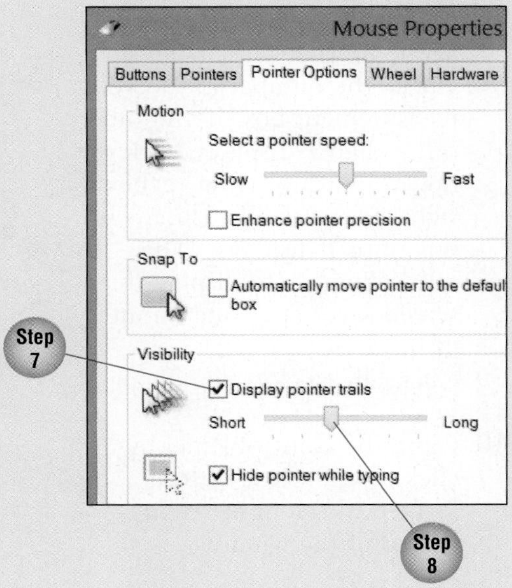

Displaying Personalize Options with a Shortcut Command

In addition to the Control Panel, display customization options with a command from a shortcut menu. Display a shortcut menu by positioning the mouse pointer in the desired position and then clicking the right mouse button. For example, display a shortcut menu with options for customizing the desktop by positioning the mouse pointer in an empty area of the desktop and then clicking the right mouse button. At the shortcut menu that displays, click the desired shortcut command.

Project 12 Customizing with a Shortcut Command

1. At the Windows 8 desktop, position the mouse pointer in an empty area on the desktop, click the right mouse button, and then click *Personalize* at the shortcut menu.
2. At the Control Panel Appearance and Personalization window that displays, click the Change mouse pointers hyperlink that displays at the left side of the window.
3. At the Mouse Properties dialog box, click the Pointer Options tab.
4. Click in the *Display pointer trails* check box to remove the check mark.
5. Click OK to close the dialog box.
6. At the Control Panel Appearance and Personalization window, click the Screen Saver hyperlink that displays in the lower right corner of the window.
7. At the Screen Saver Settings dialog box, click the option button below the *Screen saver* option and then click *Ribbons* at the drop-down list.
8. Check the number in the *Wait* measurement box. If a number other than *1* displays, click the down-pointing arrow at the right side of the measurement box until *1* displays. (This tells Windows to display the screen saver after one minute of inactivity.)
9. Click OK to close the dialog box.
10. Close the Control Panel by clicking the Close button located in the upper right corner of the window.

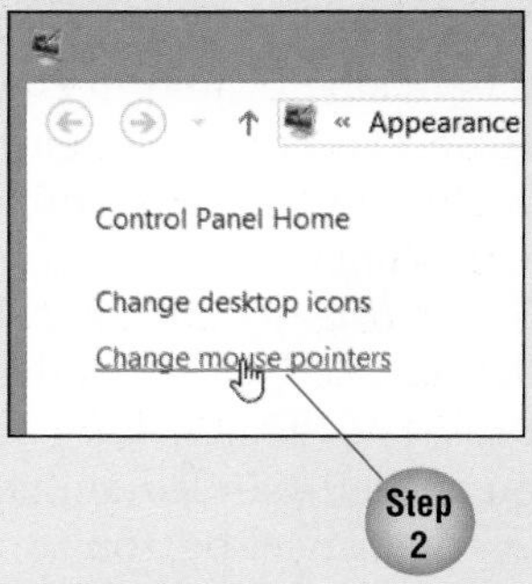

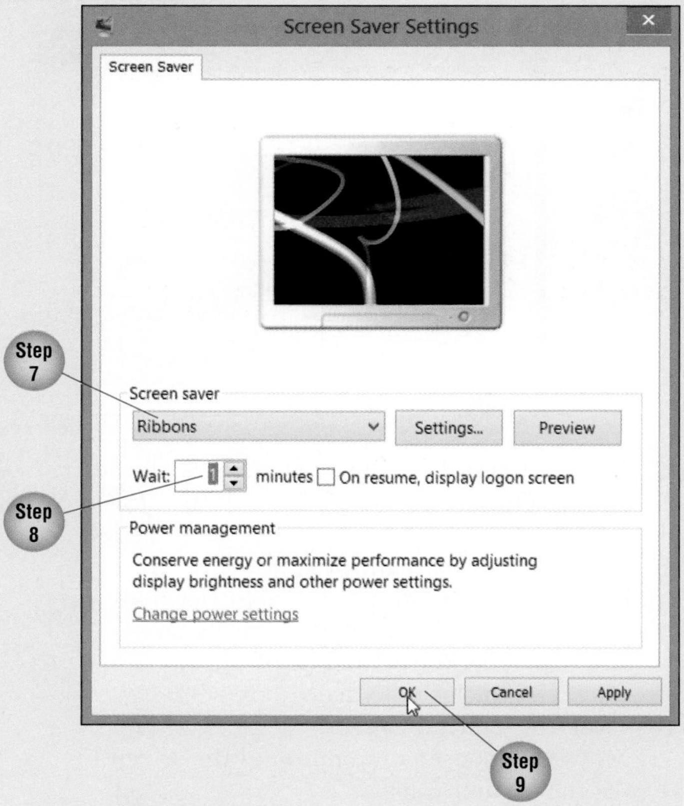

11. Do not touch the mouse or keyboard and wait over one minute for the screen saver to display. After watching the screen saver, move the mouse. (This redisplays the desktop.)
12. Right-click in an empty area of the desktop and then click *Personalize* at the shortcut menu.
13. At the Control Panel Appearance and Personalization window, click the Screen Saver hyperlink.
14. At the Screen Saver Settings dialog box, click the option button below the *Screen saver* option and then click *(None)* at the drop-down list.
15. Click OK to close the dialog box.
16. Close the Control Panel Appearance and Personalization window.

Exploring Windows Help and Support

Windows 8 includes an on-screen reference guide providing information, explanations, and interactive help on learning Windows features. Get help at the Windows Help and Support window, shown in Figure W.13. Display this window by clicking the Start screen thumbnail to display the Windows 8 Start screen. Right-click a blank area of the Start screen, click the All apps button, and then click the *Help and Support* tile in the Windows System group. Use options in the Windows Help and Support window to search for help on a specific feature; display the opening Windows Help and Support window; print the current information; and display information on getting started with Windows 8, setting up a network, and protecting your computer.

Figure W.13 Windows Help and Support Window

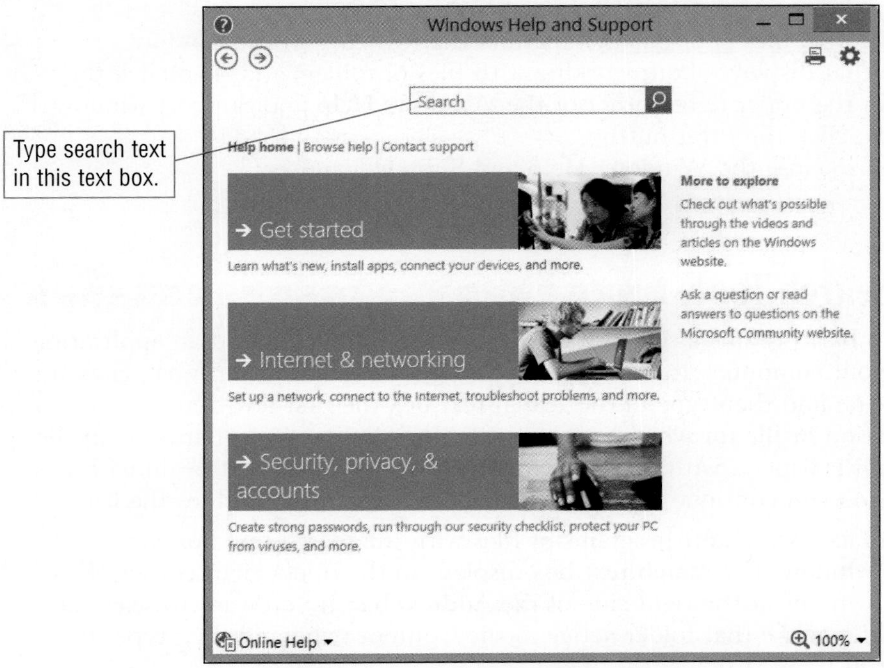

Project 13 Getting Help

1. Display the Windows 8 Help and Support window by following these steps:
   a. At the Windows 8 desktop, position the mouse pointer in the lower left corner of the screen and then click the Start screen thumbnail.
   b. Position the mouse in a blank area of the Windows 8 Start screen and then click the right mouse button.
   c. Click the All apps button that appears in the lower right corner of the Start screen and then scroll to the right of the Start screen.
   d. Click the *Help and Support* tile located in the *Windows System* category.
2. At the Windows Help and Support window, click the Get started hyperlink.
3. Click a hyperlink that interests you, read the information, and then click the Back button. (The Back button is located in the upper left corner of the window.)
4. Click another hyperlink that interests you and then read the information.
5. Click the Help home hyperlink that displays below the search text box. (This returns you to the opening Windows Help and Support window.)
6. Click in the search text box, type **delete files**, and then press Enter.
7. Click the How to work with files and folders hyperlink that displays in the window.
8. Read the information that displays about working with files or folders and then click the Print button located in the upper right corner of the Windows Help and Support window.
9. At the Print dialog box, click the Print button.
10. Click the Close button to close the Windows Help and Support window.

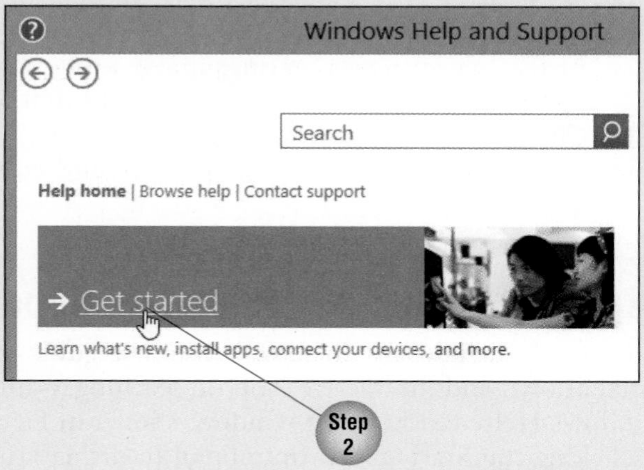

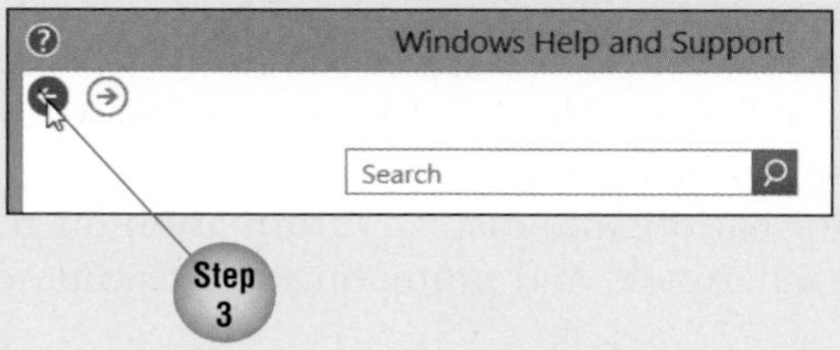

Using Search Tools

The Charm bar contains a search tool you can use to quickly find an application or file on your computer. To use the search tool, display the Charm bar, click the Search button and then type in the search text box the first few characters of the application or file for which you are searching. As you type characters in the text box, a list displays with application names or file names that begin with the characters. As you continue typing characters, the search tool refines the list.

You can also search for programs or files with the search text box in the Computer window. The search text box displays in the upper right corner of the Computer window at the right side of the Address bar. If you want to search a specific folder, make that folder active in the Content pane and then type the search text in the text box.

When conducting a search, you can use the asterisk (*) as a wildcard character in place of any letters, numbers, or symbols within a file name. For example, in the following project you will search for file names containing *check* by typing ***check** in the search text box. The asterisk indicates that the file name can start with any letter but it must contain the letters *check* somewhere in the file name.

Project 14 Searching for Programs and Files

1. At the Windows 8 desktop, display the Charm bar and then click the Search button.
2. With the insertion point positioned in the search text box, type **paint**. (Notice as you type the letters that Windows displays applications that begin with the same letters you are typing or that are associated with the same letters in a keyword. Notice that the Paint program displays below the heading *Apps* at the top of the list. Depending on the contents stored in the computer you are using, additional items may display below Paint.)

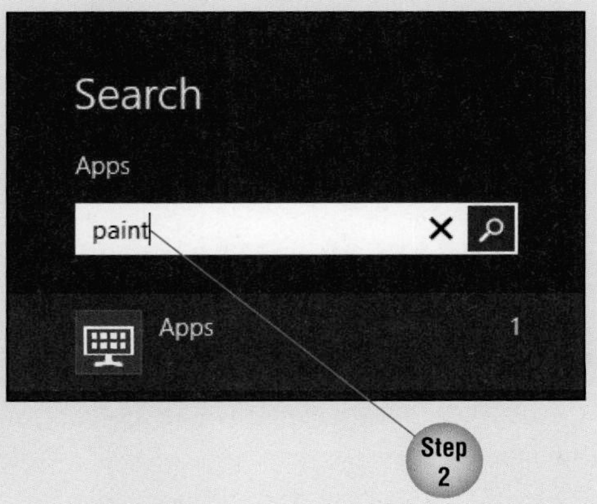

3. Click *Paint* that displays below the *Apps* heading.
4. Close the Paint window.
5. Right-click the Start screen thumbnail and then click *File Explorer*.
6. At the Computer window, double-click the icon representing your storage medium.
7. Double-click the *Windows8* folder.
8. Click in the search text box located at the right of the Address bar and then type **document**. (As you begin typing the letters, Windows filters the list of files in the Content pane to those that contain the letters you type. Notice that the Address bar displays *Search Results in Windows8* to indicate that the files that display matching your criteria are limited to the current folder.)

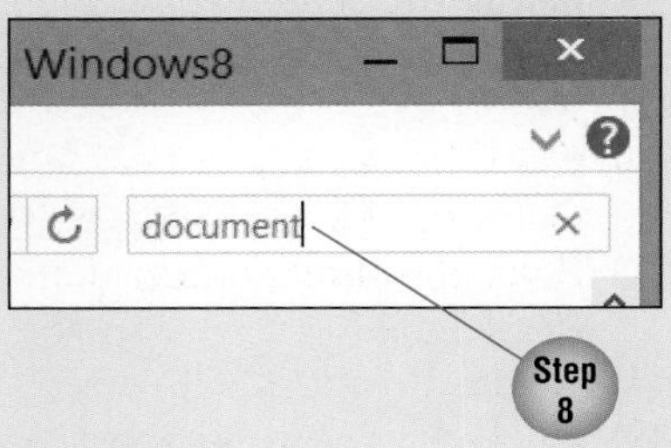

9. Select the text *document* that displays in the search text box and then type ***check**. (Notice that the Content pane displays file names containing the letters *check* no matter how the file name begins.)
10. Double-click ***WordSpellCheck02.docx*** to open the document in Word.
11. Close the document and then close Word by clicking the Close button located in the upper right corner of the window.
12. Close the Computer window.

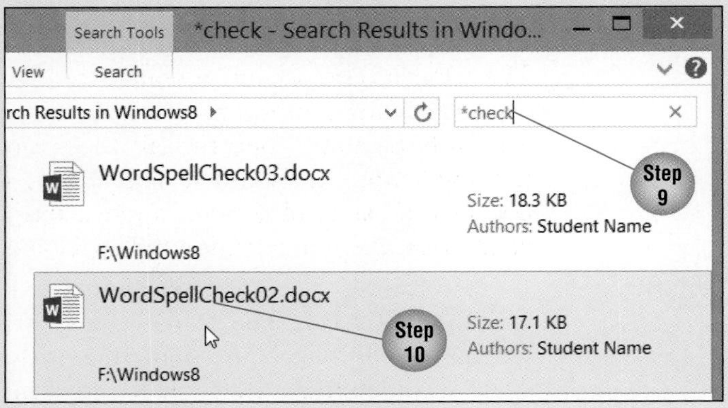

Browsing the Internet Using Internet Explorer 10

Microsoft Internet Explorer 10 is a web browser with options and features for displaying sites as well as navigating and searching for information on the Internet. The ***Internet*** is a network of computers connected around the world. Users access the Internet for several purposes: to communicate using instant messaging and/or email, to subscribe to newsgroups, to transfer files, to socialize with other users around the globe on social websites, and to access virtually any kind of information imaginable.

Using the Internet, people can find a phenomenal amount of information for private or public use. To use the Internet, three things are generally required: an ***Internet Service Provider (ISP)***, software to browse the Web (called a ***web browser***), and a ***search engine***. In this section, you will learn how to:

- Navigate the Internet using URLs and hyperlinks
- Use search engines to locate information
- Download web pages and images

You will use the Microsoft Internet Explorer web browser to locate information on the Internet. A ***Uniform Resource Locator***, referred to as a ***URL***, identifies a location on the Internet. The steps for browsing the Internet vary but generally include opening Internet Explorer, typing the URL for the desired site, navigating the various pages of the site, navigating to other sites using links, and then closing Internet Explorer.

To launch Internet Explorer 10, click the Internet Explorer icon on the Taskbar at the Windows desktop. Figure IE.1 identifies the elements of the Internet Explorer 10 window. The web page that displays in your Internet Explorer window may vary from what you see in Figure IE.1.

If you know the URL for a desired website, click in the Address bar, type the URL, and then press Enter. The website's home page displays in a tab within the Internet Explorer window. The format of a URL is *http://server-name.path*. The first part of the URL, *http*, stands for HyperText Transfer Protocol, which is the protocol or language used to transfer data within the World Wide Web. The colon and slashes separate the protocol from the server name. The server name is the second component of the URL. For example, in the URL http://www.microsoft.com, the server name is *microsoft*. The last part of the URL specifies the domain to which the server belongs. For example, *.com* refers to "commercial" and establishes that the URL is a commercial company. Examples of other domains include *.edu* for "educational," *.gov* for "government," and *.mil* for "military."

Internet Explorer 10 has been streamlined to provide users with more browsing space and reduced clutter. By default, Microsoft has turned off many features in Internet Explorer 10 such as the Menu bar, Command bar, and Status bar. You can turn these features on by right-clicking the empty space above the Address bar and to the right of the new tab button (see Figure IE.1) and then clicking the desired option at the drop-down list that displays. For example, if you want to turn on the Menu bar (the bar that contains File, Edit, and so on), right-click the empty space above the Address bar and then click *Menu bar* at the drop-down list. (This inserts a check mark next to *Menu bar*.)

Figure IE.1 Internet Explorer Window

Project 1 Browsing the Internet Using URLs

1. Make sure you are connected to the Internet through an Internet Service Provider and that the Windows 8 desktop displays. (Check with your instructor to determine if you need to complete steps for accessing the Internet such as typing a user name and password to log on.)
2. Launch Microsoft Internet Explorer by clicking the Internet Explorer icon located at the left side of the Windows Taskbar, which is located at the bottom of the Windows desktop.
3. Turn on the Command bar by right-clicking the empty space above the Address bar or to the right of the new tab button (see Figure IE.1) and then clicking *Command bar* at the drop-down list.

4. At the Internet Explorer window, explore the website for Yosemite National Park by completing the following steps:
   a. Click in the Address bar, type **www.nps.gov/yose**, and then press Enter.
   b. Scroll down the home page for Yosemite National Park by clicking the down-pointing arrow on the vertical scroll bar located at the right side of the Internet Explorer window.

c. Print the home page by clicking the Print button located on the Command bar. (Note that some websites have a printer-friendly button you can click to print the page.)

5. Explore the website for Glacier National Park by completing the following steps:
   a. Click in the Address bar, type **www.nps.gov/glac**, and then press Enter.
   b. Print the home page by clicking the Print button located on the Command bar.

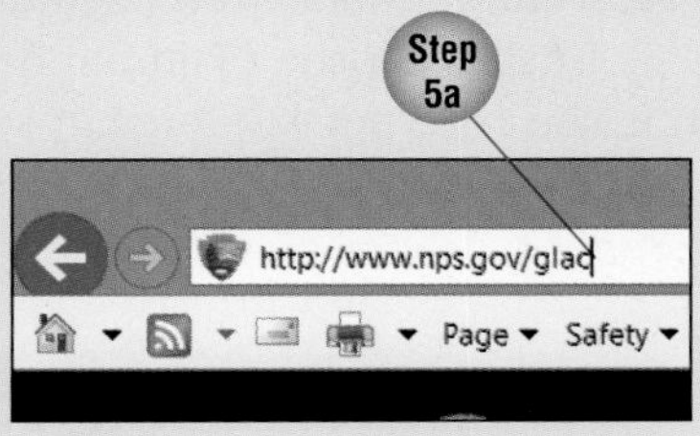

6. Close Internet Explorer by clicking the Close button (contains an X) located in the upper right corner of the Internet Explorer window.

Navigating Using Hyperlinks

Most web pages contain ***hyperlinks*** that you click to connect to another page within the website or to another site on the Internet. Hyperlinks may display in a web page as underlined text in a specific color or as images or icons. To use a hyperlink, position the mouse pointer on the desired hyperlink until the mouse pointer turns into a hand and then click the left mouse button. Use hyperlinks to navigate within and between sites on the Internet. The Internet Explorer window contains a Back button (see Figure IE.1) that, when clicked, takes you to the previous web page viewed. If you click the Back button and then want to return to the previous page, click the Forward button. You can continue clicking the Back button to back your way out of several linked pages in reverse order since Internet Explorer maintains a history of the websites you visit.

Project 2 Navigating Using Hyperlinks

1. Make sure you are connected to the Internet and then click the Internet Explorer icon on the Windows Taskbar.
2. At the Internet Explorer window, display the White House web page and navigate in the page by completing the following steps:
   a. Click in the Address bar, type **whitehouse.gov**, and then press Enter.
   b. At the White House home page, position the mouse pointer on a hyperlink that interests you until the pointer turns into a hand and then click the left mouse button.
   c. At the linked web page, click the Back button. (This returns you to the White House home page.)
   d. At the White House home page, click the Forward button to return to the previous web page viewed.
   e. Print the web page by clicking the Print button on the Command bar.

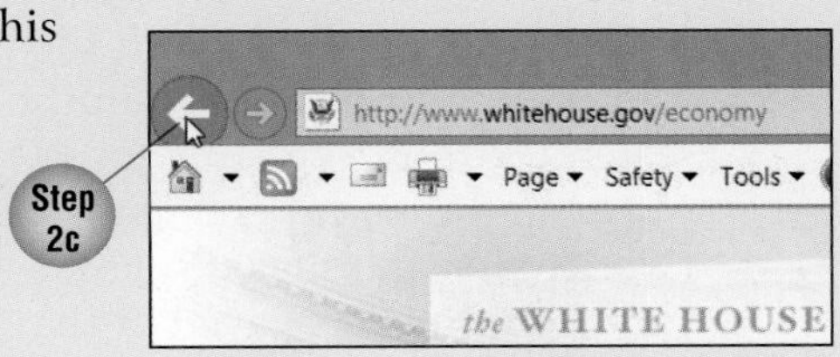

3. Display the website for Amazon.com and navigate in the site by completing the following steps:
   a. Click in the Address bar, type **www.amazon.com**, and then press Enter.
   b. At the Amazon.com home page, click a hyperlink related to books.
   c. When a book web page displays, click the Print button on the Command bar.

4. Close Internet Explorer by clicking the Close button (contains an X) located in the upper right corner of the Internet Explorer window.

Searching for Specific Sites

If you do not know the URL for a specific site or you want to find information on the Internet but do not know what site to visit, complete a search with a search engine. A ***search engine*** is software created to search quickly and easily for desired information. A variety of search engines are available on the Internet, each offering the opportunity to search for specific information. One method for searching for information is to click in the Address bar, type a keyword or phrase related to your search, and then press Enter. Another method for completing a search is to visit the website for a search engine and use options at the site.

Bing is Microsoft's online search portal and is the default search engine used by Internet Explorer. Bing organizes search results by topic category and provides related search suggestions.

Project 3 Searching for Information by Topic

1. Start Internet Explorer.
2. At the Internet Explorer window, search for sites on bluegrass music by completing the following steps:
   a. Click in the Address bar.
   b. Type **bluegrass music** and then press Enter.
   c. When a list of sites displays in the Bing results window, click a site that interests you.
   d. When the page displays, click the Print button.

3. Use the Yahoo! search engine to find sites on bluegrass music by completing the following steps:
   a. Click in the Address bar, type **www.yahoo.com**, and then press Enter.
   b. At the Yahoo! website, with the insertion point positioned in the search text box, type **bluegrass music** and then press Enter. (Notice that the sites displayed vary from sites displayed in the earlier search.)

c. Click hyperlinks until a website displays that interests you.
d. Print the page.
4. Use the Google search engine to find sites on jazz music by completing the following steps:
   a. Click in the Address bar, type www.google.com, and then press Enter.
   b. At the Google website, with the insertion point positioned in the search text box, type jazz music and then press Enter.
   c. Click a site that interests you.
   d. Print the page.
5. Close Internet Explorer.

Using a Metasearch Engine

Bing, Yahoo!, and Google are search engines that search the Web for content and display search results. In addition to individual search engines, you can use a metasearch engine, such as Dogpile, that sends your search text to other search engines and then compiles the results in one list. With a metasearch engine, you type the search text once and then access results from a wider group of search engines. The Dogpile metasearch engine provides search results from Google, Yahoo!, and Yandex.

Project 4 Searching with a Metasearch Search Engine

1. Start Internet Explorer.
2. Click in the Address bar.
3. Type www.dogpile.com and then press Enter.
4. At the Dogpile website, type jazz music in the search text box and then press Enter.
5. Click a hyperlink that interests you.
6. Close the Internet Explorer window. If a message displays asking if you want to close all tabs, click the Close all tabs button.

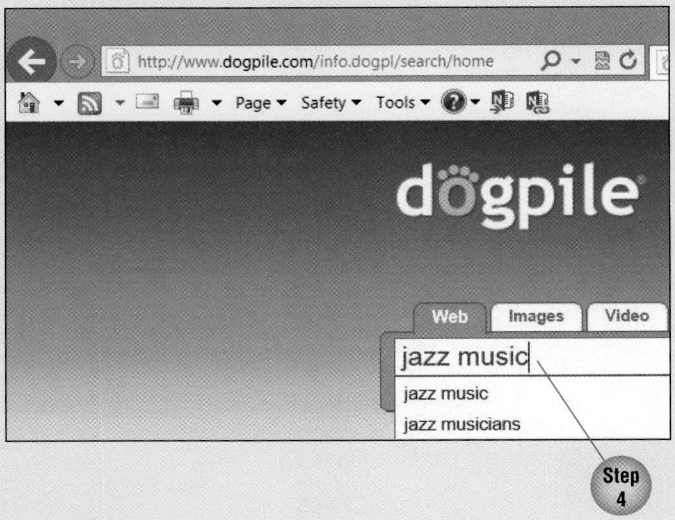

Completing Advanced Searches for Specific Sites

The Internet contains an enormous amount of information. Depending on what you are searching for on the Internet and the search engine you use, some searches can result in several thousand "hits" (sites). Wading through a large number of sites can be very time-consuming and counterproductive. Narrowing a search to very specific criteria can greatly reduce the number of hits for a search. To narrow a search, use the advanced search options offered by the search engine.

Project 5 Narrowing a Search

1. Start Internet Explorer.
2. Search for sites on skydiving in Oregon by completing the following steps:
   a. Click in the Address bar, type **www.yahoo.com**, and then press Enter.
   b. At the Yahoo! home page, click the Search button next to the search text box.
   c. Click the More hyperlink located above the search text box and then click *Advanced Search* at the drop-down list.
   d. At the Advanced Web Search page, click in the search text box next to *all of these words*.
   e. Type **skydiving Oregon tandem static line**. (This limits the search to web pages containing all of the words typed in the search text box.)
   f. Click the Yahoo! Search button.
   g. When the list of websites displays, click a hyperlink that interests you.
   h. Click the Back button until the Yahoo! Advanced Web Search page displays.
   i. Click in the *the exact phrase* text box and then type **skydiving in Oregon**.
   j. Click the *Only .com domains* option in the *Site/Domain* section.
   k. Click the Yahoo! Search button.
   l. When the list of websites displays, click a hyperlink that interests you.
   m. Print the page.
3. Close Internet Explorer.

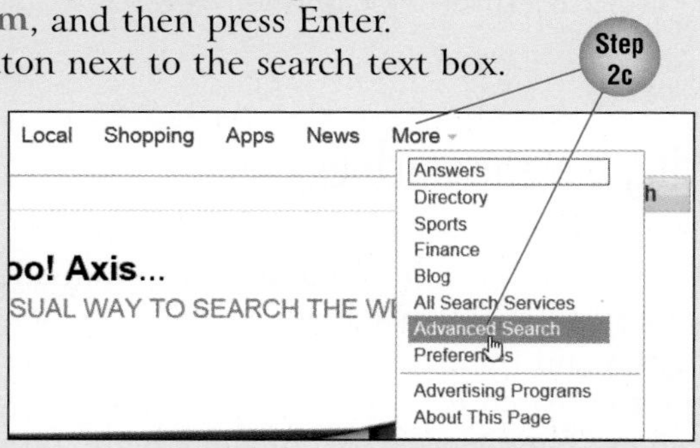

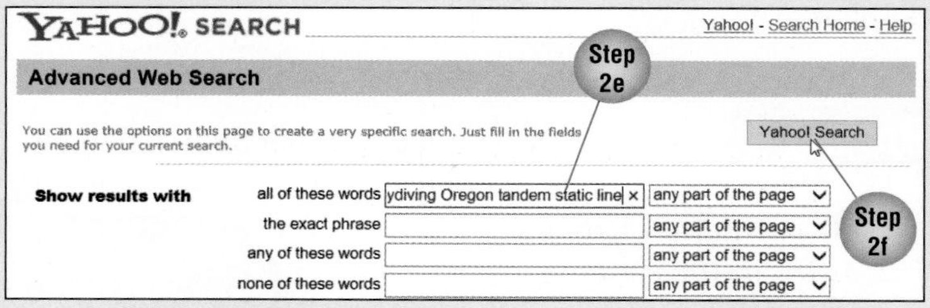

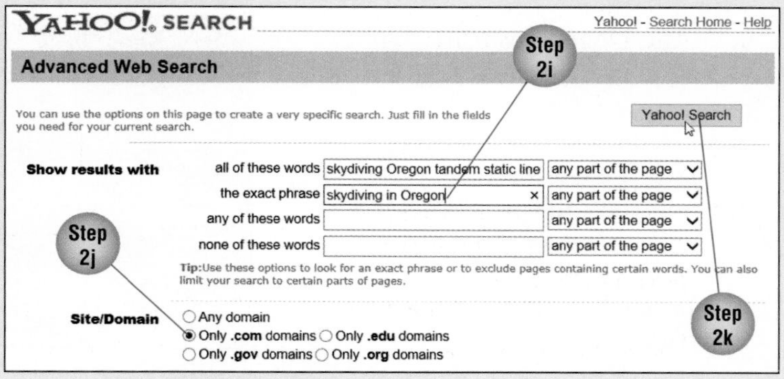

Downloading Images, Text, and Web Pages from the Internet

The image(s) and/or text that display when you open a web page, as well as the web page itself, can be saved as a separate file. This separate file can be viewed, printed, or inserted in another file. The information you want to save in a separate file is downloaded from the Internet by Internet Explorer and saved in a folder of your choosing with the name you specify. Copyright laws protect much of the information on the Internet. Before using information downloaded from the Internet, check the site for restrictions. If you do use information, make sure you properly cite the source.

Project 6 **Downloading Images and Web Pages**

1. Start Internet Explorer.
2. Download a web page and image from Banff National Park by completing the following steps:
   a. Search for websites related to Banff National Park.
   b. From the list of sites that displays, choose a site that contains information about Banff National Park and at least one image of the park.
   c. Make sure the Command bar is turned on. (If the Command bar is turned off, turn it on by right-clicking the empty space above the Address bar or to the right of the new tab button and then clicking *Command bar* at the drop-down list.)

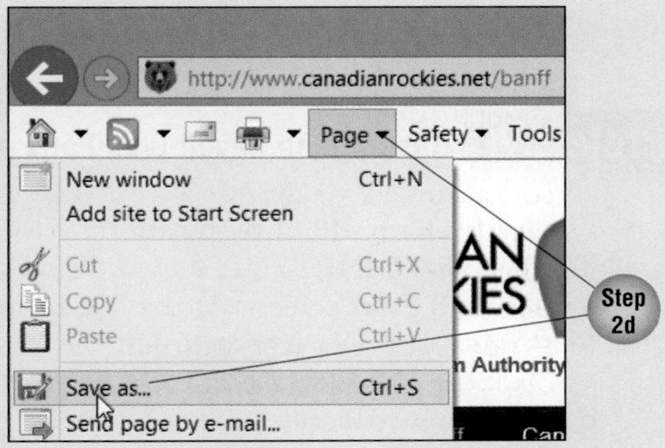

   d. Save the web page as a separate file by clicking the Page button on the Command bar and then clicking *Save as* at the drop-down list.
   e. At the Save Webpage dialog box, type **BanffWebPage**.
   f. Click the down-pointing arrow for the *Save as type* option and then click *Web Archive, single file (*.mht)*.
   g. Navigate to the drive containing your storage medium and then click the Save button.

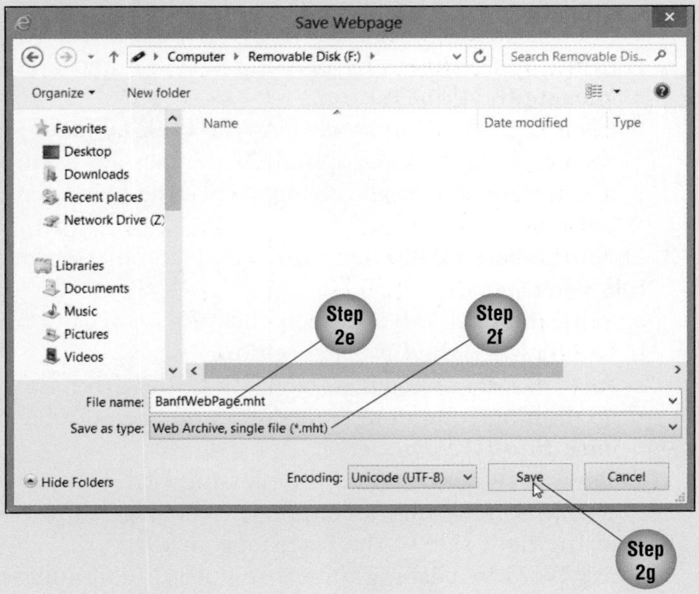

3. Save an image file by completing the following steps:
   a. Right-click an image that displays at the website.
   b. At the shortcut menu that displays, click *Save picture as*.

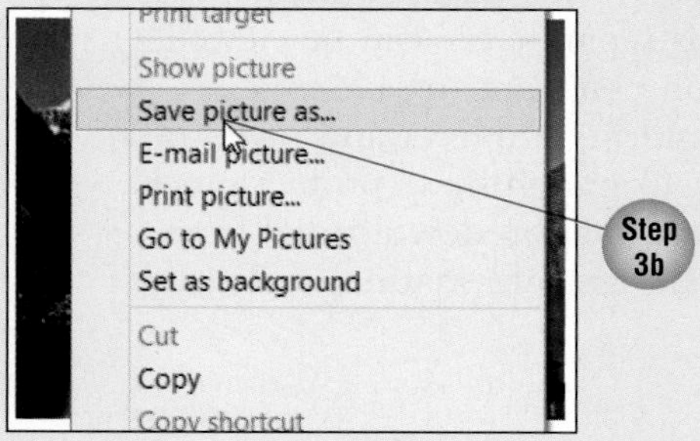

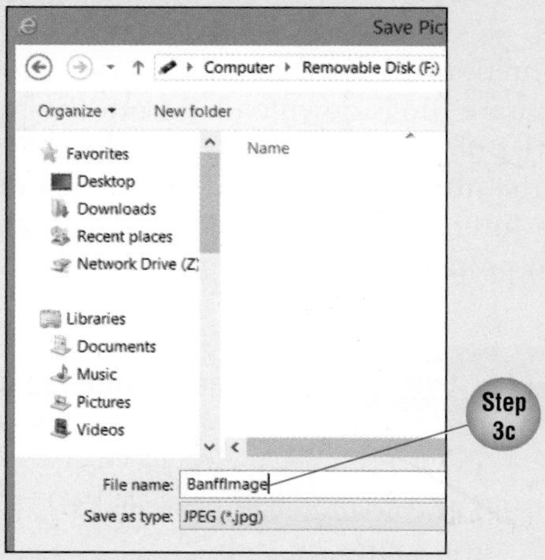

   c. At the Save Picture dialog box, type **BanffImage** in the *File name* text box.
   d. Navigate to the drive containing your storage medium and then click the Save button.
4. Close Internet Explorer.

Project 7 Opening the Saved Web Page and Image in a Word Document

1. Open Microsoft Word by positioning the mouse pointer in the lower left corner of the Taskbar, clicking the Start screen thumbnail, and then clicking the *Word 2013* tile in the Windows 8 Start screen. At the Word opening screen, click the *Blank document* template.
2. With Microsoft Word open, insert the image in a document by completing the following steps:
   a. Click the INSERT tab and then click the Pictures button in the Illustrations group.
   b. At the Insert Picture dialog box, navigate to the drive containing your storage medium and then double-click ***BanffImage.jpg***.
   c. When the image displays in the Word document, print the document by pressing Ctrl + P and then clicking the Print button.
   d. Close the document by clicking the FILE tab and then clicking the *Close* option. At the message asking if you want to save the changes, click the Don't Save button.

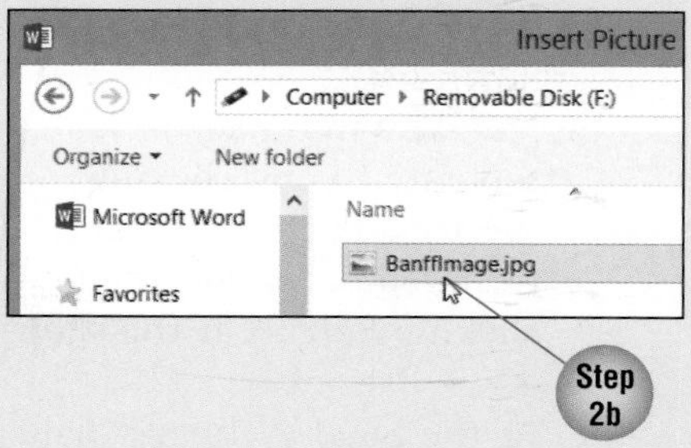

3. Open the **BanffWebPage.mht** file by completing the following steps:
   a. Click the FILE tab and then click the *Open* option.
   b. Double-click the *Computer* option.
   c. At the Open dialog box, navigate to the drive containing your storage medium and then double-click ***BanffWebPage.mht***.
   d. Preview the web page(s) by pressing Ctrl + P. At the Print backstage area, preview the page shown at the right side of the backstage area.

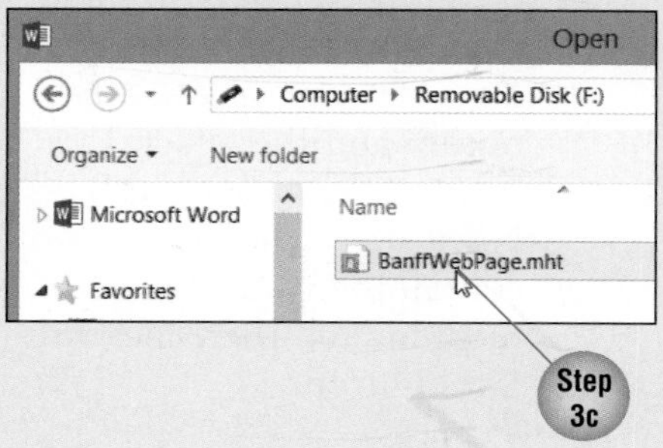

4. Close Word by clicking the Close button (contains an X) that displays in the upper right corner of the screen.

MICROSOFT® EXCEL®

Level 1

Unit 1 ■ Preparing and Formatting Worksheets

Chapter 1 ■ Preparing an Excel Workbook

Chapter 2 ■ Inserting Formulas in a Worksheet

Chapter 3 ■ Formatting an Excel Worksheet

Chapter 4 ■ Enhancing a Worksheet

MICROSOFT® EXCEL®

CHAPTER 1

Preparing an Excel Workbook

PERFORMANCE OBJECTIVES

Upon successful completion of Chapter 1, you will be able to:

- **Identify the various elements of an Excel workbook**
- **Create, save, and print a workbook**
- **Enter data in a workbook**
- **Edit data in a workbook**
- **Insert a formula using the AutoSum button**
- **Apply basic formatting to cells in a workbook**
- **Use the Help feature**

SNAP

Tutorials

1.1 Opening, Saving, and Closing an Excel Workbook

1.2 Entering Data in Cells and Saving a Workbook with a New Name

1.3 Editing Cells and Using Proofing Tools

1.4 Printing a Worksheet

1.5 Performing Calculations Using the AutoSum Button

1.6 Navigating and Scrolling in a Worksheet

1.7 Applying Basic Formatting

1.8 Applying Number Formatting

1.9 Getting Help at the Excel Help Window

Many companies use spreadsheets to organize numerical and financial data and to analyze and evaluate information. An Excel spreadsheet can be used for such activities as creating financial statements, preparing budgets, managing inventory, and analyzing cash flow. In addition, numbers and values can be easily manipulated to create "What if?" situations. For example, using a spreadsheet, a person in a company can ask questions such as "What if the value in this category is decreased? How would that change affect the department budget?" Questions like these can be easily answered using the information in an Excel spreadsheet. Change the value in a category and Excel will recalculate formulas for the other values. In this way, a spreadsheet can be used not only for creating financial statements or budgets, but also as a planning tool. Model answers for this chapter's projects appear on the following page.

Excel
EL1C1

Note: Before beginning the projects, copy to your storage medium the EL1C1 subfolder from the EL1 folder on the CD that accompanies this textbook. Steps on how to copy a folder are presented on the inside of the back cover of this textbook. Do this every time you start a chapter's projects.

Team Net®

Employee	Location	Classification
Avery	West	Hourly
Bryant	North	Salaried
Estrada	West	Salaried
Juergens	West	Salaried
Mickulich	North	Hourly
Talbot	West	Hourly

Project 1 Prepare a Worksheet with Employee Information

EL1-C1-P1-EmpBene.xlsx

	January	February	March	April	May	June
Year 1	**100**	100	100	100	125	125
Year 3	**150**	150	150	150	175	175
Year 5	**200**	200	200	150	150	150
Year 7	**250**	250	250	250	250	250
Total	700	700	700	650	700	700

Qtr 1	$5,500	$6,250	$7,000	$8,500	$5,500	$4,500
Qtr 2	$6,000	$7,250	$6,500	$9,000	$4,000	$5,000
Qtr 3	$4,500	$8,000	$6,000	$7,500	$6,000	$5,000
Qtr 4	$6,500	$8,500	$7,000	$8,000	$5,500	$6,000
Average	$5,625	$7,500	$6,625	$8,250	$5,250	$5,125

Project 2 Open and Format a Workbook and Insert Formulas

EL1-C1-P2-FillCells.xlsx

Monthly Expenses
January, 2015

Expense	Budget	Actual
Accounting Services	$ 500	$ 423
Advertising	3,200	3,475
Utilities	2,700	3,045
Estimated Taxes	25,000	25,000
Health Insurance	9,420	9,595
Inventory Purchases	4,200	2,155
Equipment Repair	500	214
Loan Payment	5,586	5,586
Office Supplies	225	415
Total	$ 51,331	$ 49,908

Budget Percentages

Department	Percentage
Personnel	26%
Development	22%
Sales	18%
Production	13%
Maintenance	8%
Accounting	7%
Administration	6%

Project 3 Format a Worksheet

EL1-C1-P3-MoExps.xlsx

Project 1 Prepare a Worksheet with Employee Information 3 Parts

You will create a worksheet containing employee information, edit the contents, and then save and close the workbook.

Creating a Worksheet

Open Excel by clicking the Excel 2013 tile at the Windows Start screen. (Depending on your operating system, these steps may vary.) At the Excel 2013 opening screen that displays, click the *Blank workbook* template. This displays a workbook with a blank worksheet, as shown in Figure 1.1. The elements of a blank Excel worksheet are described in Table 1.1.

A file created in Excel is referred to as a ***workbook***. An Excel workbook consists of an individual worksheet (or *sheet*) by default, but it can contain multiple worksheets, like the sheets of paper in a notebook. Notice the tab named *Sheet1*, located toward the bottom of the Excel window. The area containing the gridlines in the Excel window is called the ***worksheet area***. Figure 1.2 identifies the elements of the worksheet area. Create a worksheet in the worksheet area that will be saved as part of a workbook. Columns in a worksheet are labeled with letters of the alphabet and rows are numbered.

Figure 1.1 Blank Excel Worksheet

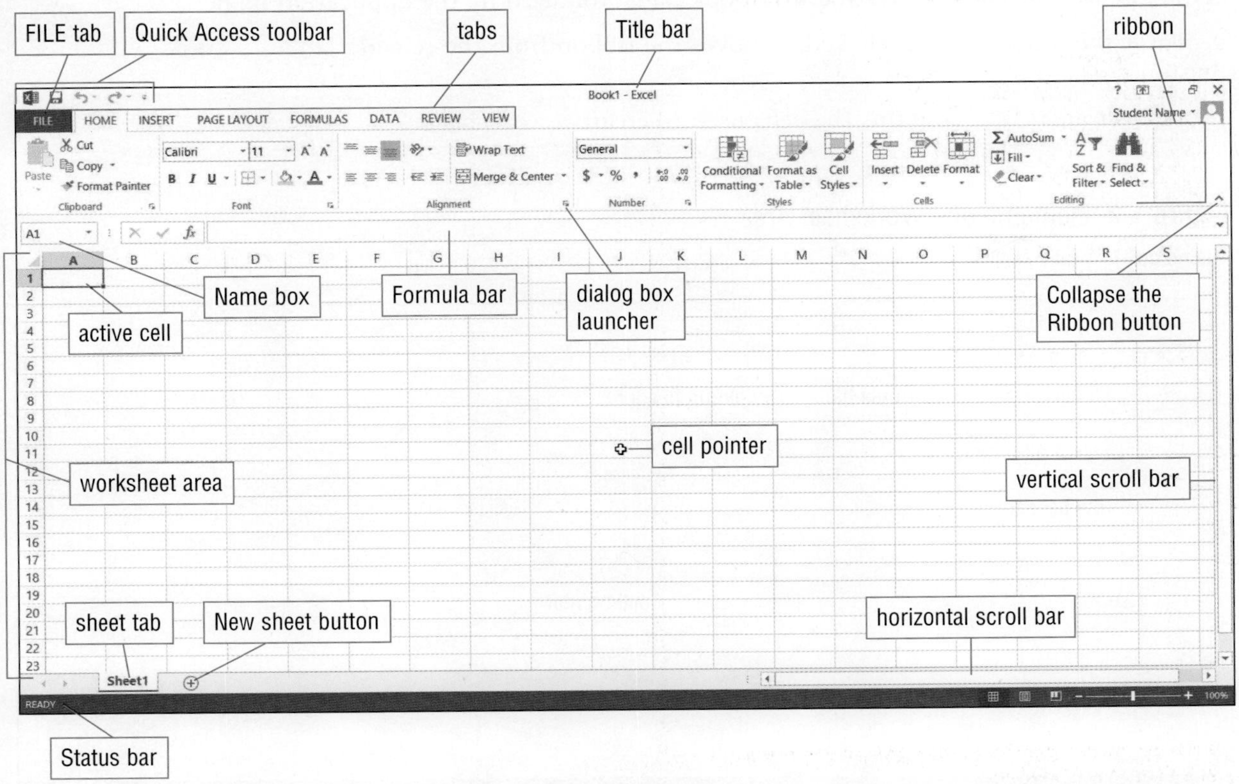

Table 1.1 Elements of an Excel Worksheet

Feature	Description
active cell	location in the worksheet that will display typed data or that will be affected by a command
cell pointer	when this icon appears, select cells by clicking or dragging the mouse
dialog box launcher	click to open a dialog box with more options for that group
FILE tab	displays the backstage area that contains options for working with and managing files
Formula bar	displays the contents stored in the active cell
horizontal and vertical scroll bars	used to view various parts of the worksheet beyond the current screen
Name box	displays the active cell address or name assigned to the active cell
New sheet button	click to insert a new worksheet in the workbook
Quick Access toolbar	contains buttons for commonly used commands that can be executed with a single mouse click
ribbon	area containing the tabs with commands and buttons
sheet tab	identifies the current worksheet in the workbook
Status bar	displays the current mode, action messages, view buttons, and Zoom slider bar
tab	contains commands and buttons organized into groups
Title bar	displays the workbook name followed by the application name
Collapse the Ribbon button	when clicked, removes the ribbon from the screen
worksheet area	contains the cells used to create a worksheet

Figure 1.2 Elements of a Worksheet Area

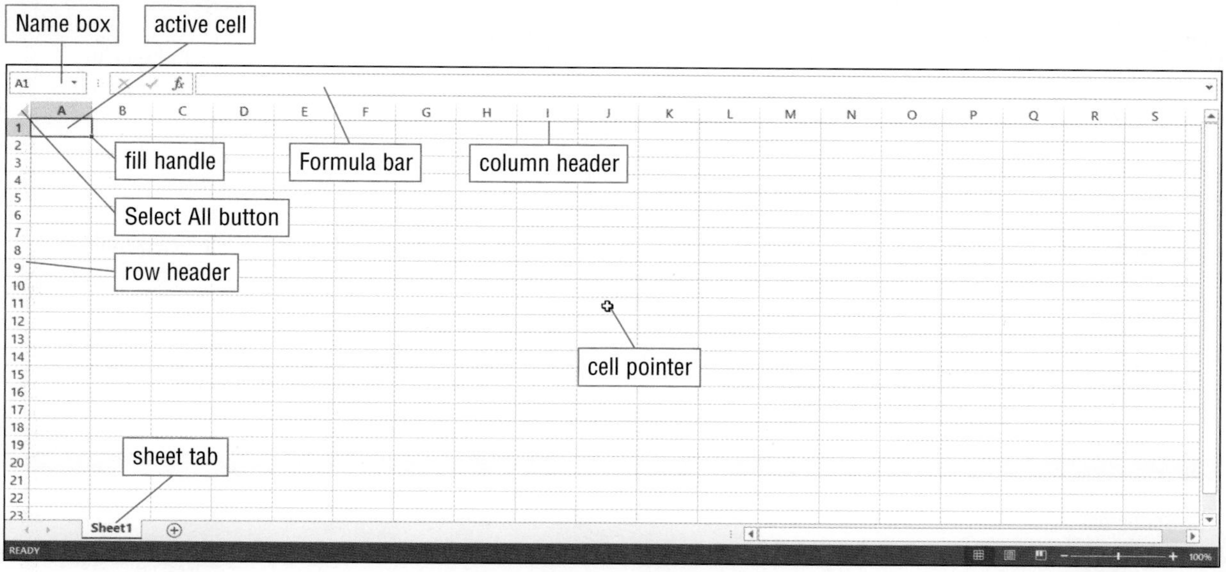

The horizontal and vertical lines that define the cells in the worksheet area are called ***gridlines***. When a cell is active (displays with a green border), the ***cell address***, also called the ***cell reference***, displays in the ***Name box***. The cell reference includes the column letter and row number. For example, if the first cell of the worksheet is active, the cell reference *A1* displays in the Name box. A green border surrounds the active cell.

HINT
To make a cell active, position the cell pointer in the cell and then click the left mouse button.

Enter data such as text, a number, or a value in a cell. To enter data in a cell, make the desired cell active and then type the data. To make the next cell active, press the Tab key. Table 1.2 displays additional commands for making a specific cell active.

Another method for making a specific cell active is to use the Go To feature. To use this feature, click the Find & Select button in the Editing group on the HOME tab and then click *Go To*. At the Go To dialog box, type the cell reference in the *Reference* text box and then click OK.

Find & Select

HINT
Ctrl + G is the keyboard shortcut to display the Go To dialog box.

When you are ready to type data into the active cell, check the Status bar. The word *Ready* should display at the left side. As you type data, the word *Ready* changes to *Enter*. Data you type in a cell displays in the cell as well as in the Formula bar. If the data you type is longer than the cell can accommodate, the data overlaps the next cell to the right. (It does not become a part of the next cell—it simply overlaps it.) You will learn how to change column widths to accommodate data later in this chapter.

Table 1.2 Commands for Making a Specific Cell Active

To make this cell active	*Press*
cell below current cell	Enter
cell above current cell	Shift + Enter
next cell	Tab
previous cell	Shift + Tab
cell at beginning of row	Home
next cell in direction of arrow	Up, Down, Left, or Right Arrow keys
last cell in worksheet	Ctrl + End
first cell in worksheet	Ctrl + Home
cell in next window	Page Down
cell in previous window	Page Up
cell in window to right	Alt + Page Down
cell in window to left	Alt + Page Up

If the data you enter in a cell consists of text and the text does not fit into the cell, it overlaps the next cell. If, however, you enter a number in a cell, specify it as a number (rather than text), and the number is too long to fit in the cell, Excel changes the display of the number to number symbols *(###)*. This change is made because Excel does not want you to be misled by a number when you see only a portion of it in the cell.

Along with the keyboard, the mouse can be used to make a specific cell active. To make a specific cell active with the mouse, position the mouse pointer, which displays as a white plus sign (called the ***cell pointer***), on the desired cell and then click the left mouse button. The cell pointer displays as a white plus sign when positioned in a cell in the worksheet and displays as an arrow pointer when positioned on other elements of the Excel window, such as options on tabs or scroll bars.

Scroll through a worksheet using the horizontal and/or vertical scroll bars. Scrolling shifts the display of cells in the worksheet area but does not change the active cell. Scroll through a worksheet until the desired cell is visible and then click the desired cell.

Saving a Workbook

Quick Steps

Save a Workbook

1. Click Save button on Quick Access toolbar.
2. At Save As backstage area, click desired location.
3. Click Browse button.
4. At Save As dialog box, navigate to desired folder.
5. Type workbook name.
6. Press Enter.

Save

HINT

Ctrl + S is the keyboard shortcut to save a workbook.

Save an Excel workbook, which consists of one or more worksheets, by clicking the Save button on the Quick Access toolbar or by clicking the FILE tab and then clicking the *Save As* option at the backstage area. At the Save As backstage area, click the location where you want to save the workbook. For example, click the SkyDrive option preceded by your name if you are saving to your SkyDrive or click the *Computer* option if you are saving to a USB flash drive (or other location on your computer). After specifying the place, click the Browse button and the Save As dialog box displays. If you are saving the workbook to your computer or a flash drive, you can double-click the *Computer* option at the Save As backstage area to display the Save As dialog box. At the Save As dialog box, type a name for the workbook in the *File name* text box and then press Enter or click the Save button. You can bypass the Save As backstage area and go directly to the Save As dialog box by using the keyboard shortcut F12.

When you click your SkyDrive or the *Computer* option at the Save As backstage area, the names of the most recently accessed folders display below the Recent Folders heading in the *Computer* section. Open a folder by clicking the folder name.

A workbook file name can contain up to 255 characters, including the drive letter and any folder names, and can include spaces. You cannot give a workbook the same name in first uppercase and then lowercase letters. Also, some symbols cannot be used in a file name, such as:

forward slash (/)	question mark (?)
backslash (\)	quotation mark (“)
greater-than symbol (>)	colon (:)
less-than symbol (<)	semicolon (;)
asterisk (*)	pipe symbol (|)

To save an Excel workbook in the EL1C1 folder on your storage medium, display the Save As dialog box, click the drive representing your storage medium in the Navigation pane, and then double-click *EL1C1* in the Content pane.

Project 1a Creating and Saving a Document

Part 1 of 3

1. Open Excel by clicking the Excel 2013 tile at the Windows Start screen. (Depending on your operating system, these steps may vary.)
2. At the Excel 2013 opening screen, click the *Blank workbook* template. (This opens a workbook with a blank worksheet.)
3. At the blank Excel worksheet that displays, create the worksheet shown in Figure 1.3 by completing the following steps:
   a. Press the Enter key once to make cell A2 the active cell.
   b. Type **Employee** in cell A2 .
   c. Press the Tab key. (This makes cell B2 active.)
   d. Type **Location** and then press the Tab key. (This makes cell C2 active.)
   e. Type **Benefits** and then press the Enter key to move the insertion point to cell A3.
   f. Type **Avery** (a name) in cell A3.
   g. Continue typing the data shown in Figure 1.3. (For commands that make specific cells active, refer to Table 1.2.)
4. After typing the data shown in the cells in Figure 1.3, save the workbook by completing the following steps:
   a. Click the Save button on the Quick Access toolbar.
   b. At the Save As backstage area, click the desired location, such as your SkyDrive or *Computer,* and then click the Browse button.
   c. At the Save As dialog box, navigate to the EL1C1 folder in the Navigation pane and then double-click the *EL1C1* folder that displays in the Content pane.
   d. Select the text in the *File name* text box and then type **EL1-C1-P1-EmpBene** (for Excel Level 1, Chapter 1, Project 1, and the workbook that contains information about employee benefits).
   e. Press the Enter key or click the Save button.

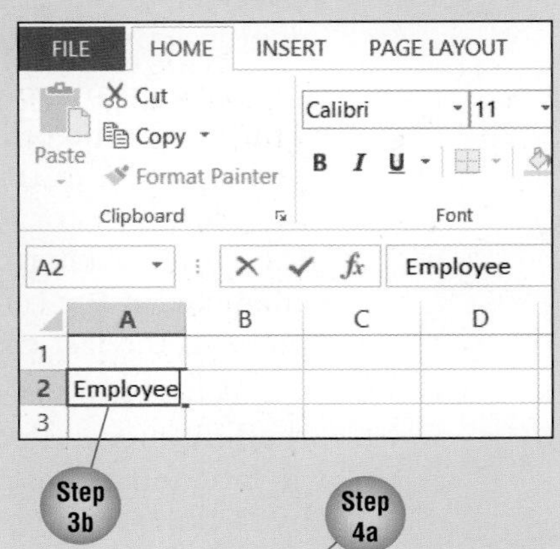

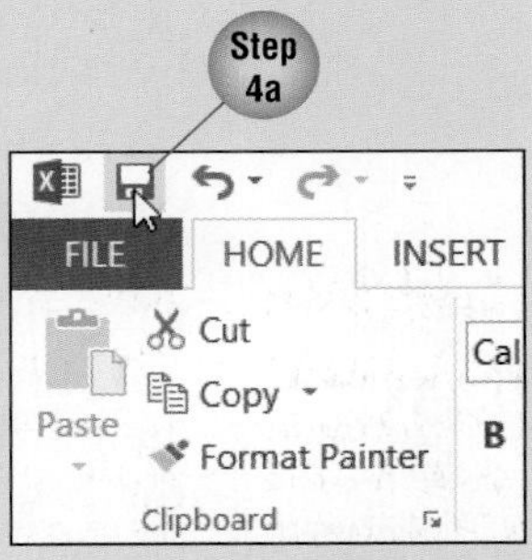

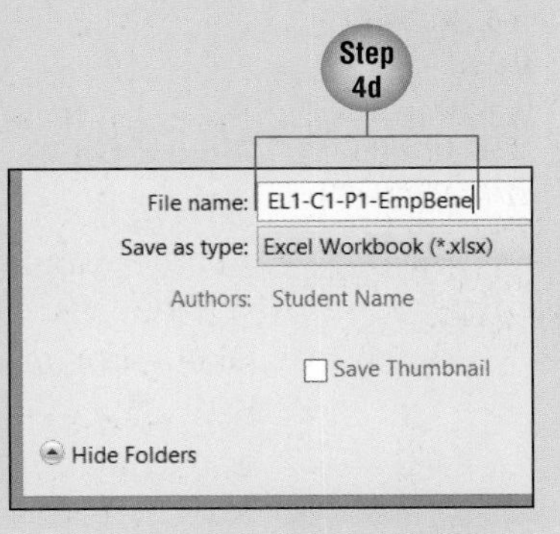

Figure 1.3 Project 1a

	A	B	C	D
1				
2	Employee	Location	Benefits	
3	Avery			
4	Connors			
5	Estrada			
6	Juergens			
7	Mikulich			
8	Talbot			
9				

Editing Data in a Cell

Edit data being typed in a cell by pressing the Backspace key to delete the character to the left of the insertion point or pressing the Delete key to delete the character to the right of the insertion point. To change the data in a cell, click the cell once to make it active and then type the new data. When a cell containing data is active, anything typed will take the place of the existing data.

If you want to edit only a portion of the data in a cell, double-click in the cell. This makes the cell active, moves the insertion point inside the cell, and displays the word *Edit* at the left side of the Status bar. Move the insertion point using the arrow keys or the mouse and then make the needed corrections. If you are using the keyboard, press the Home key to move the insertion point to the first character in the cell or Formula bar or press the End key to move the insertion point to the last character.

When you are finished editing the data in the cell, be sure to change out of the Edit mode. To do this, make another cell active by pressing Enter, Tab, or Shift + Tab. You can also change out of the Edit mode and return to the Ready mode by clicking another cell or clicking the Enter button on the Formula bar.

Cancel

Enter

If the active cell does not contain data, the Formula bar displays only the cell reference (by column letter and row number). As you type data, two buttons display on the Formula bar to the right of the Name box, as shown in Figure 1.4. Click the Cancel button to delete the current cell entry. You can also delete the cell entry by pressing the Delete key. Click the Enter button to indicate that you are finished typing or editing the cell entry. When you click the Enter button on the Formula bar, the word *Enter* (or *Edit*) located at the left side of the Status bar changes to *Ready*.

Figure 1.4 Buttons on the Formula Bar

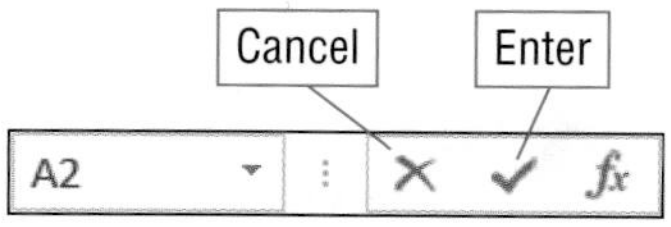

Project 1b **Editing Data in a Cell** **Part 2 of 3**

1. With **EL1-C1-P1-EmpBene.xlsx** open, double-click in cell A7 (contains *Mikulich*).
2. Move the insertion point immediately left of the *k* and then type **c**. (This changes the spelling to *Mickulich*.)
3. Click once in cell A4 (contains *Connors*), type **Bryant**, and then press the Tab key. (Clicking only once allows you to type over the existing data.)
4. Edit cell C2 by completing the following steps:
   a. Click the Find & Select button in the Editing group on the HOME tab and then click *Go To* at the drop-down list.

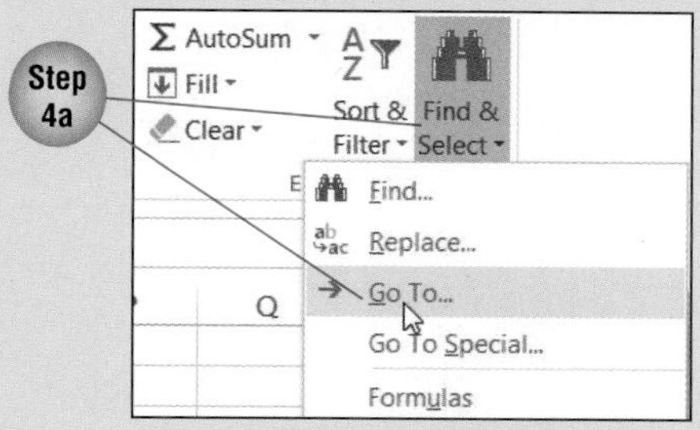

b. At the Go To dialog box, type **C2** in the *Reference* text box and then click OK.
c. Type **Classification** (over *Benefits*).
5. Click once in any other cell.
6. Click the Save button on the Quick Access toolbar to save the workbook again.

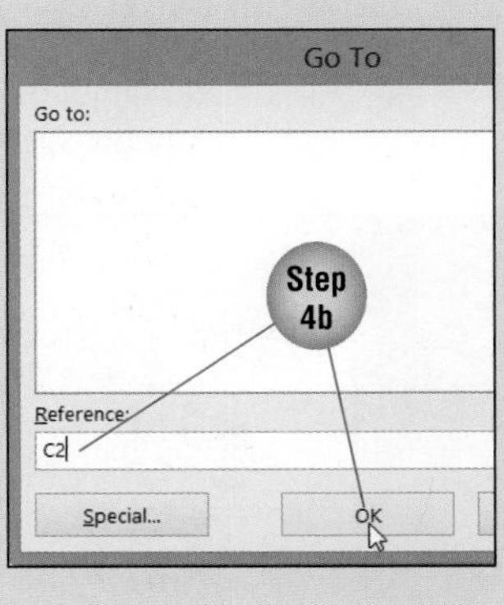

Printing a Workbook

With a workbook open, click the FILE tab and the Info backstage area displays, as shown in Figure 1.5. Use buttons and options at the backstage area to perform functions such as opening, closing, saving, and printing a workbook. If you want to exit the backstage area without completing an action, click the Back button (located in the upper left corner of the backstage area) or press the Esc key on your keyboard.

Many of the computer projects you create will need to be printed. Print a workbook from the Print backstage area, as shown in Figure 1.6. To display this backstage area, click the FILE tab and then click the *Print* option. You can also display the Print backstage area with the keyboard shortcut Ctrl + P.

HINT

Ctrl + P is the keyboard shortcut to display the Print backstage area.

Figure 1.5 Info Backstage Area

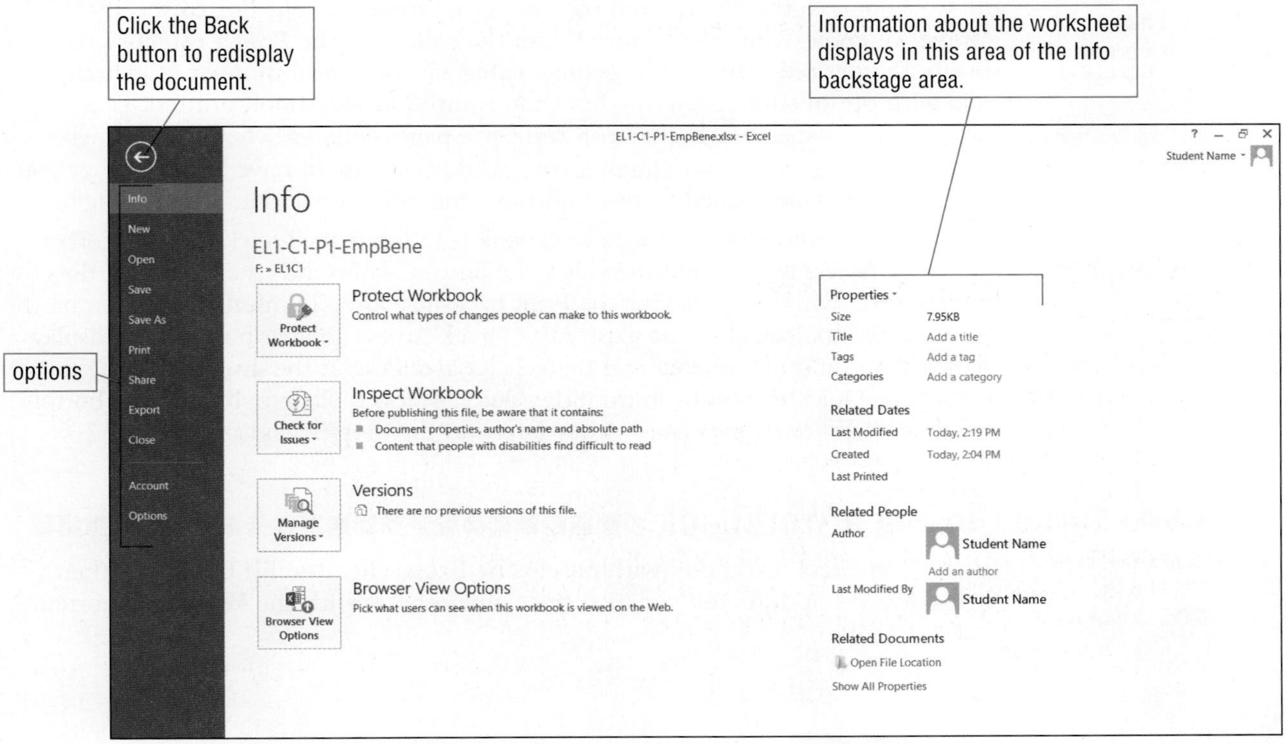

Figure 1.6 Print Backstage Area

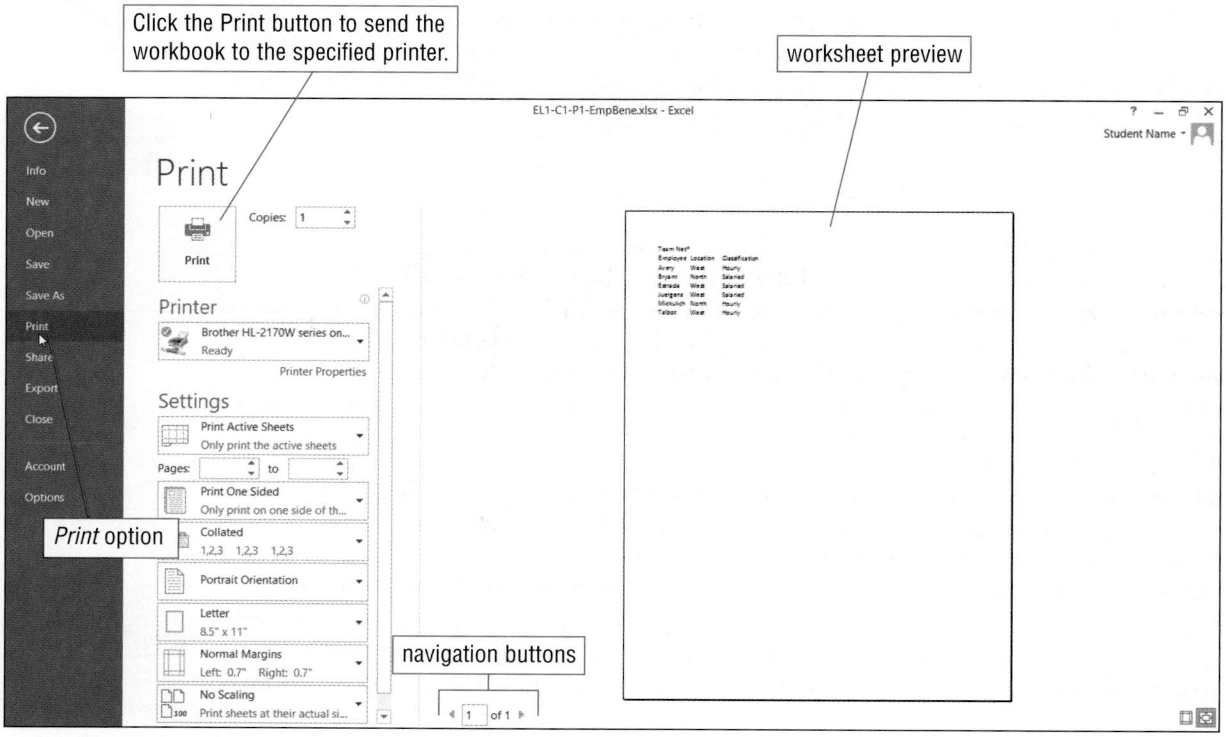

Quick Steps

Print a Workbook
1. Click FILE tab.
2. Click *Print* option.
3. Click Print button.
OR
Click Quick Print button on Quick Access toolbar.

The left side of the Print backstage area displays three categories: *Print, Printer*, and *Settings*. Click the Print button in the Print backstage area to send the workbook to the printer and use the *Copies* measurement box to specify the number of copies you want printed. Use the gallery in the *Printer* category to specify the desired printer. The *Settings* category contains a number of galleries, each with options for specifying how you want your workbook printed. Use the galleries to specify whether you want the pages collated when printed; what orientation, page size, and margins your workbook should have; and whether you want the worksheet scaled to print all rows and columns of data on one page.

Another method for printing a workbook is to insert the Quick Print button on the Quick Access toolbar and then click the button. This sends the workbook directly to the printer without displaying the Print backstage area. To insert this button on the Quick Access toolbar, click the Customize Quick Access Toolbar button that displays at the right side of the toolbar and then click *Quick Print* at the drop-down list. To remove the Quick Print button from the Quick Access toolbar, right-click the button and then click *Remove from Quick Access Toolbar* at the drop-down list.

Quick Steps

Close a Workbook
1. Click FILE tab.
2. Click *Close* option.

Closing a Workbook

To close an Excel workbook without closing Excel, click the FILE tab and then click the *Close* option. You can also close a workbook with the keyboard shortcut Ctrl + F4.

Closing Excel

To close Excel, click the Close button that displays in the upper right corner of the screen. The Close button contains an X, and if you position the mouse pointer on the button, a ScreenTip displays with the name *Close*. You can also close Excel with the keyboard shortcut Alt + F4.

Quick Steps

Close Excel
Click Close button.

Close

Using Automatic Entering Features

Excel contains several features that help you enter data into cells quickly and efficiently. These features include ***AutoComplete***, which automatically inserts data in a cell that begins the same as a previous entry; ***AutoCorrect***, which automatically corrects many common typographical errors; and ***AutoFill***, which automatically inserts words, numbers, or formulas in a series.

Using AutoComplete

The AutoComplete feature automatically inserts data in a cell that begins the same as a previous entry. If the data inserted by AutoComplete is the data you want in the cell, press the Tab key or the Enter key. If it is not the desired data, simply continue typing the correct data. This feature can be very useful in a worksheet that contains repetitive data entries. For example, consider a worksheet that repeats the word *Payroll*. The second and subsequent times this word is to be inserted in a cell, simply typing the letter *P* will cause AutoComplete to insert the entire word.

Using AutoCorrect

The AutoCorrect feature automatically corrects many common typing errors. To see what symbols and words are in the AutoCorrect feature, click the FILE tab and then click *Options*. At the Excel Options dialog box, click *Proofing* in the left panel and then click the AutoCorrect Options button located in the right panel. This displays the AutoCorrect dialog box with the AutoCorrect tab selected, as shown in Figure 1.7, with a list box containing the replacement data.

Figure 1.7 AutoCorrect Dialog Box with AutoCorrect Tab Selected

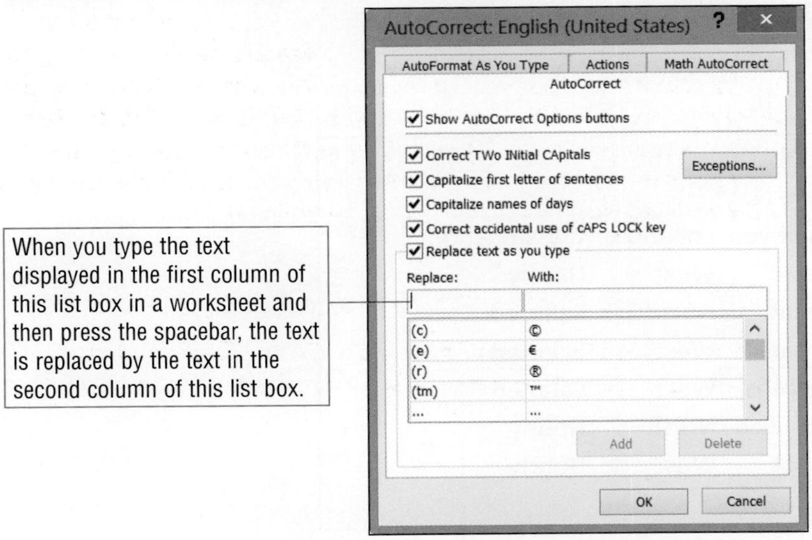

At the AutoCorrect dialog box, type the text shown in the first column in the list box and the text in the second column is inserted in the cell. Along with symbols, the AutoCorrect dialog box contains commonly misspelled words and common typographical errors.

Project 1c Inserting Data in Cells with AutoComplete — Part 3 of 3

1. With **EL1-C1-P1-EmpBene.xlsx** open, make cell A1 active.
2. Type the text in cell A1, as shown in Figure 1.8. Insert the ® symbol by typing (r) and then pressing Enter. (AutoCorrect will change (r) to ®.)
3. Type the remaining text in the cells. When you type the W in *West* in cell B5, the AutoComplete feature will insert *West*. Accept this by pressing the Tab key. (Pressing the Tab key accepts *West* and also makes the cell to the right active.) Use the AutoComplete feature to enter *West* in cells B6 and B8 and *North* in cell B7. Use AutoComplete to enter the second and subsequent occurrences of *Salaried* and *Hourly*.
4. Click the Save button on the Quick Access toolbar.
5. Print **EL1-C1-P1-EmpBene.xlsx** by clicking the FILE tab, clicking the *Print* option, and then clicking the Print button at the Print backstage area. (The gridlines will not print.)

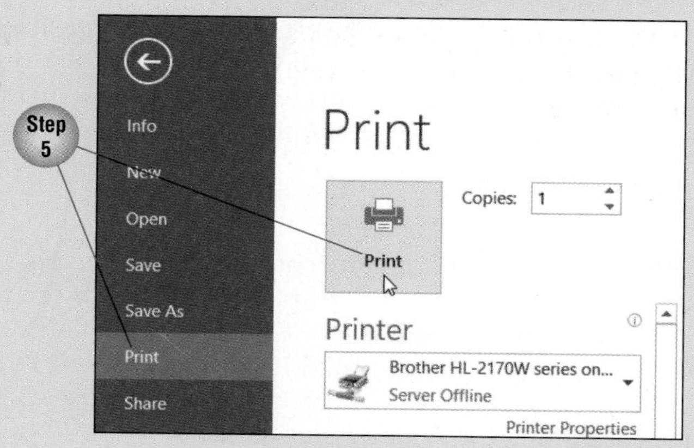

6. Close the workbook by clicking the FILE tab and then clicking the *Close* option at the backstage area.

Figure 1.8 Project 1c

	A	B	C	D
1	Team Net®			
2	Employee	Location	Classification	
3	Avery	West	Hourly	
4	Bryant	North	Salaried	
5	Estrada	West	Salaried	
6	Juergens	West	Salaried	
7	Mickulich	North	Hourly	
8	Talbot	West	Hourly	
9				

Project 2 Open and Format a Workbook and Insert Formulas 3 Parts

You will open an existing workbook and insert formulas to find the sums and averages of numbers.

Using AutoFill

When a cell is active, a thick, green border surrounds it and a small, green square displays in the bottom right corner of the border. This green square is called the AutoFill ***fill handle*** (see Figure 1.2 on page 6). With the fill handle, you can quickly fill a range of cells with the same data or with consecutive data. For example, suppose you need to insert the year 2015 in a row or column of cells. To do this quickly, type *2015* in the first cell, position the mouse pointer on the fill handle, hold down the left mouse button, drag across the cells in which you want the year inserted, and then release the mouse button.

You can also use the fill handle to insert a series in a row or column of cells. For example, suppose you are creating a worksheet with data for all of the months in the year. Type *January* in the first cell, position the mouse pointer on the fill handle, hold down the left mouse button, drag down or across to 11 more cells, and then release the mouse button. Excel automatically inserts the other 11 months in the year in the proper order. When using the fill handle, the cells must be adjacent. Table 1.3 identifies the sequences inserted in cells by Excel when specific types of data are entered.

Certain sequences, such as *2, 4* and *Jan 12, Jan 13,* require that both cells be selected before using the fill handle. If only the cell containing *2* is active, the fill handle will insert *2*s in the selected cells. The list in Table 1.3 is only a sampling of what the fill handle can do. You may find a variety of other sequences that can be inserted in a worksheet using the fill handle.

An Auto Fill Options button displays when you fill cells with the fill handle. Click this button and a list of options displays for filling the cells. By default, data and formatting are filled in each cell. You can choose to fill only the formatting in the cells or fill only the data without the formatting. You can also choose to copy data into the selected cells or fill the data as a series.

HINT

When filling cells with the fill handle, hold down the Ctrl key if you want to copy the same data instead of displaying the next instance in the series.

Auto Fill Options

Table 1.3 AutoFill Fill Handle Series

Enter this data *(commas represent data in separate cells)*	***And the fill handle will insert this sequence in adjacent cells***
January	February, March, April, and so on
Jan	Feb, Mar, Apr, and so on
Jan 12, Jan 13	14-Jan, 15-Jan, 16-Jan, and so on
Monday	Tuesday, Wednesday, Thursday, and so on
Product 1	Product 2, Product 3, Product 4, and so on
Qtr 1	Qtr 2, Qtr 3, Qtr 4
2, 4	6, 8, 10, and so on

Opening a Workbook

Quick Steps

Open a Workbook
1. Click FILE tab.
2. Click *Open* option.
3. Click the desired location (your SkyDrive or *Computer*).
4. Click the Browse button.
5. Display desired folder.
6. Double-click workbook name.

Open an Excel workbook at the Open dialog box. To display this dialog box, click the FILE tab and then click the *Open* option. This displays the Open backstage area. You can also display the Open backstage area with the keyboard shortcut Ctrl + O or by inserting an Open button on the Quick Access toolbar. At the Open backstage area, click the desired location, such as your SkyDrive or *Computer*, and then click the Browse button. (If you are opening a workbook from your computer or USB flash drive, you can double-click the *Computer* option.) At the Open dialog box, navigate to the desired folder and then double-click the desired workbook name in the Content pane. You can bypass the Open backstage area and go directly to the Open dialog box by using the keyboard shortcut Ctrl + F12.

When you click your SkyDrive or the *Computer* option at the Open backstage area, a list of the most recently accessed folders displays below the *Recent Folders* heading in the *Computer* section. Open a folder by clicking the folder name.

Opening a Workbook from the Recent Workbooks List

Click the *Recent Workbooks* option in the middle panel at the Open backstage area and a list of the most recently opened workbooks displays below the Recent Workbooks heading at the right side of the backstage area. Up to twenty-five workbook names display in the list by default. Open a workbook from this list by clicking the workbook name.

Pinning a Workbook to the Recent Workbooks List

If you want a workbook to remain in the Recent Workbooks list at the Open backstage area, "pin" the workbook to the list. To do this, position the mouse pointer over the desired workbook name and then click the small, left-pointing stick pin that displays at the right side of the workbook name. This changes it to a down-pointing stick pin. The next time you display the Open backstage area, the workbook you pinned displays at the top of the Recent Workbooks list. You can also pin a workbook to the Recent list at the Excel 2013 opening screen. When you pin a workbook here, it will display in the Recent Workbooks list at the Open backstage area as well. To "unpin" the workbook, click the stick pin to change it from a down-pointing pin to a left-pointing pin. You can pin more than one workbook to the list.

Project 2a **Inserting Data in Cells with the Fill Handle** **Part 1 of 3**

1. Open **FillCells.xlsx**. (This workbook is located in the EL1C1 folder on your storage medium.)
2. Save the workbook with Save As and name it **EL1-C1-P2-FillCells**.
3. Add data to cells as shown in Figure 1.9. Begin by making cell B1 active and then typing January.
4. Position the mouse pointer on the fill handle for cell B1, hold down the left mouse button, drag across to cell G1, and then release the mouse button.

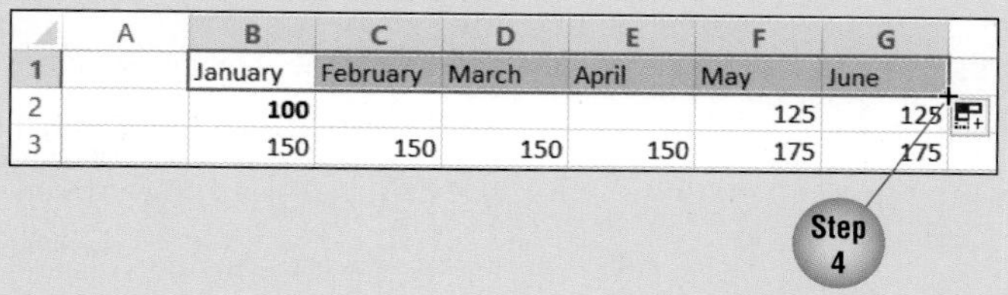

5. Type a sequence and then use the fill handle to fill the remaining cells by completing the following steps:
   a. Make cell A2 active and then type **Year 1**.
   b. Make cell A3 active and then type **Year 3**.
   c. Select cells A2 and A3 by positioning the mouse pointer in cell A2, holding down the left mouse button, dragging down to cell A3, and then releasing the mouse button.
   d. Drag the fill handle for cell A3 to cell A5. (This inserts *Year 5* in cell A4 and *Year 7* in cell A5.)
6. Use the fill handle to fill adjacent cells with a number but not the formatting by completing the following steps:
   a. Make cell B2 active. (This cell contains *100* with bold formatting.)
   b. Drag the fill handle for cell B2 to cell E2. (This inserts **100** in cells C2, D2, and E2.)
   c. Click the Auto Fill Options button that displays at the bottom right of the selected cells.
   d. Click the *Fill Without Formatting* option at the drop-down list.

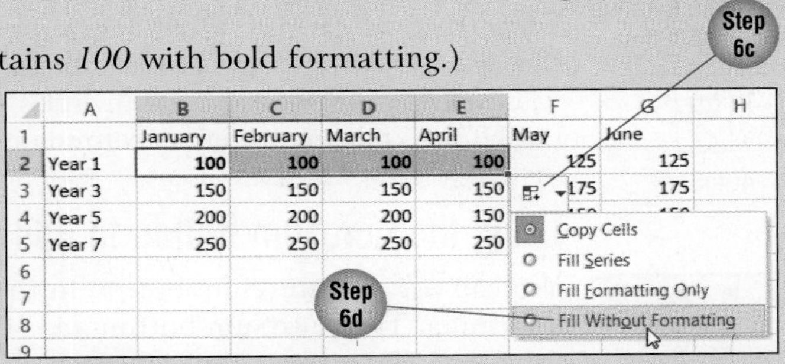

7. Use the fill handle to apply formatting only by completing the following steps:
   a. Make cell B2 active.
   b. Drag the fill handle to cell B5.
   c. Click the Auto Fill Options button and then click *Fill Formatting Only* at the drop-down list.
8. Make cell A10 active and then type **Qtr 1**.
9. Drag the fill handle for cell A10 to cell A13.
10. Save **EL1-C1-P2-FillCells.xlsx**.

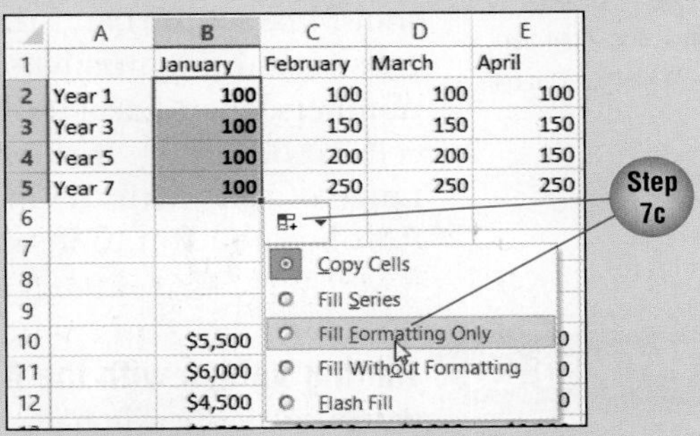

Figure 1.9 Project 2a

	A	B	C	D	E	F	G	H
1		January	February	March	April	May	June	
2	Year 1	**100**	100	100	100	125	125	
3	Year 3	**150**	150	150	150	175	175	
4	Year 5	**200**	200	200	150	150	150	
5	Year 7	**250**	250	250	250	250	250	
6								
7								
8								
9								
10	Qtr 1	$5,500	$6,250	$7,000	$8,500	$5,500	$4,500	
11	Qtr 2	$6,000	$7,250	$6,500	$9,000	$4,000	$5,000	
12	Qtr 3	$4,500	$8,000	$6,000	$7,500	$6,000	$5,000	
13	Qtr 4	$6,500	$8,500	$7,000	$8,000	$5,500	$6,000	
14								

Inserting Formulas

Quick Steps

Insert a Formula Using the AutoSum button

1. Click in desired cell.
2. Click AutoSum button.
3. Check range identified and make changes if necessary.
4. Press Enter.

Σ AutoSum

Excel is a powerful decision-making tool you can use to manipulate data to answer questions in "What if?" situations. Insert a formula in a worksheet and then manipulate the data to make projections, answer specific questions, and plan for the future. For example, the manager of a department might use an Excel worksheet to prepare a department budget and then determine the impact on the budget of hiring a new employee or increasing the volume of production.

Insert a ***formula*** in a worksheet to perform calculations on values. A formula contains a mathematical operator, value, cell reference, cell range, and function. Formulas can be written that add, subtract, multiply, and/or divide values. Formulas can also be written that calculate averages, percentages, minimum and maximum values, and much more. Excel includes an AutoSum button in the Editing group on the HOME tab that inserts a formula to calculate the total of a range of cells.

Using the AutoSum Button to Add Numbers

HINT You can use the keyboard shortcut Alt + = to insert the SUM function in a cell.

You can use the AutoSum button in the Editing group on the HOME tab to insert a formula. The AutoSum button adds numbers automatically with the SUM function. Make active the cell in which you want to insert the formula (this cell should be empty) and then click the AutoSum button. Excel looks for a range of cells containing numbers that are above the active cell. If no cell above contains numbers, then Excel looks to the left of the active cell. Excel suggests the range of cells to be added. If the suggested range is not correct, drag through the desired range of cells with the mouse and then press Enter. You can also double-click the AutoSum button to insert the SUM function with the range Excel chooses.

Project 2b **Adding Values with the AutoSum Button** **Part 2 of 3**

1. With **EL1-C1-P2-FillCells.xlsx** open, make cell A6 active and then type Total.
2. Make cell B6 active and then calculate the sum of the cells by clicking the AutoSum button in the Editing group on the HOME tab.
3. Excel inserts the formula *=SUM(B2:B5)* in cell B6. This is the correct range of cells, so press Enter.

Step 2

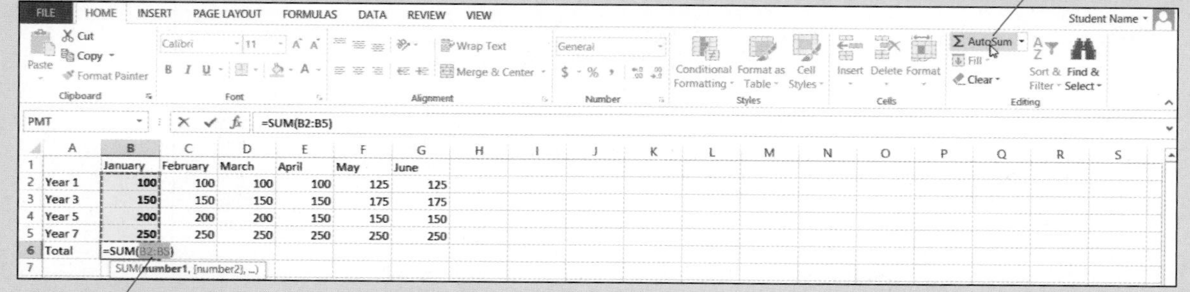

Step 3

4. Make cell C6 active and then click the AutoSum button in the Editing group.
5. Excel inserts the formula *=SUM(C2:C5)* in cell C6. This is the correct range of cells, so press Enter.

6. Make cell D6 active.
7. Double-click the AutoSum button. This inserts the formula *=SUM(D2:D5)* in cell D6 and inserts the sum *700*.
8. Insert the sum in cells E6, F6, and G6.
9. Save **EL1-C1-P2-FillCells.xlsx**.

Using the AutoSum Button to Average Numbers

A common function in a formula is the AVERAGE function. With this function, a range of cells is added together and then divided by the number of cell entries. The AVERAGE function is available on the AutoSum button. Click the AutoSum button arrow and a drop-down list displays with a number of common functions.

Quick Steps

Insert an Average Formula Using the AutoSum Button
1. Click in desired cell.
2. Click AutoSum button arrow.
3. Click *Average*.
4. Specify range.
5. Press Enter.

Copy a Formula Using the Fill Handle
1. Insert formula in cell.
2. Make active cell containing formula.
3. Using fill handle, drag through cells you want to contain formula.

Using the Fill Handle to Copy a Formula

In a worksheet, you may want to insert the same basic formula in other cells. In a situation where a formula is copied to other locations in a worksheet, use a ***relative cell reference***. Copy a formula containing relative cell references and the cell references change. For example, if you enter the formula *=SUM(A2:C2)* in cell D2 and then copy it relatively to cell D3, the formula in cell D3 displays as *=SUM(A3:C3)*. You can use the fill handle to copy a formula relatively in a worksheet. To do this, position the mouse pointer on the fill handle until the mouse pointer turns into a thin, black cross; hold down the left mouse button; drag and select the desired cells; and then release the mouse button.

Project 2c Inserting the AVERAGE Function and Copying a Formula Relatively — Part 3 of 3

1. With **EL1-C1-P2-FillCells.xlsx** open, make cell A14 active and then type Average.
2. Insert the average of cells B10 through B13 by completing the following steps:
   a. Make cell B14 active.
   b. Click the AutoSum button arrow in the Editing group and then click *Average* at the drop-down list.
   c. Excel inserts the formula *=AVERAGE(B10:B13)* in cell B14. This is the correct range of cells, so press Enter.

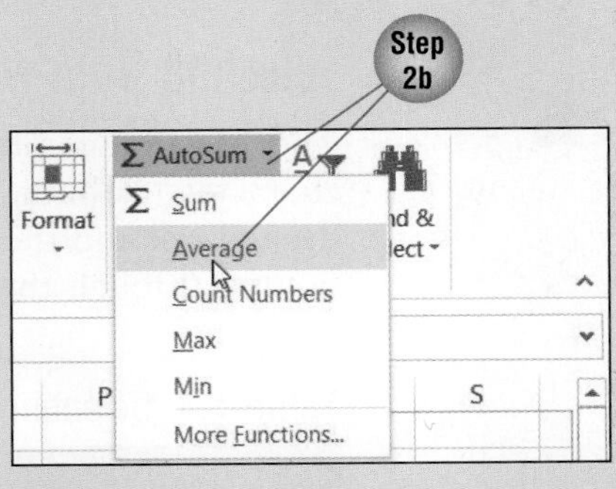

3. Copy the formula relatively to cells C14 through G14 by completing the following steps:
   a. Make cell B14 active.
   b. Position the mouse pointer on the fill handle, hold down the left mouse button, drag across to cell G14, and then release the mouse button.

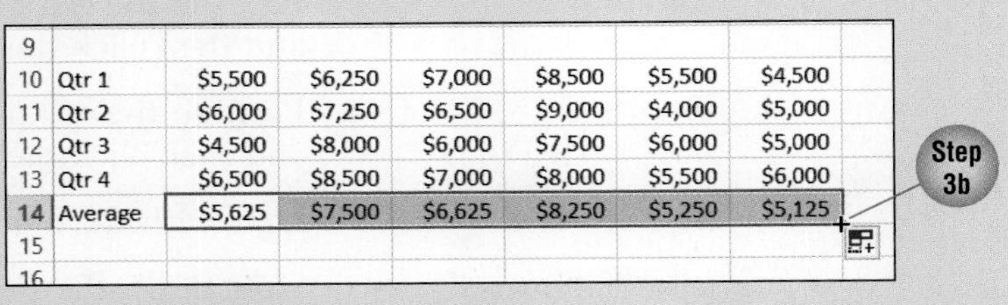

4. Save, print, and then close **EL1-C1-P2-FillCells.xlsx**.

Project 3 Format a Worksheet — 2 Parts

You will open a monthly expenses workbook and then change column width, merge and center cells, and apply number formatting to numbers in cells.

Selecting Cells

You can use a variety of methods for formatting cells in a worksheet. For example, you can change the alignment of data in cells or rows or add character formatting. To identify the cells that are to be affected by the formatting, select the specific cells.

Selecting Cells Using the Mouse

Select specific cells in a worksheet using the mouse or select columns or rows. Table 1.4 displays the methods for selecting cells using the mouse.

HINT

The first cell in a range displays with a white background and is the active cell.

Selected cells, except the active cell, display with a gray background (this may vary) rather than a white background. The active cell is the first cell in the selection block and displays in the normal manner (white background with black data). Selected cells remain selected until you click a cell with the mouse or press an arrow key on the keyboard.

Selecting Cells Using the Keyboard

You can use the keyboard to select specific cells within a worksheet. Table 1.5 displays the commands for selecting specific cells. If a worksheet contains data, Ctrl + A selects the cells containing data. If the worksheet contains groups of data separated by empty cells, Ctrl + A or Ctrl + Shift + spacebar will select a group of cells rather than all of the cells.

Selecting Data within Cells

The selection commands presented select the entire cell. You can also select specific characters within a cell. To do this with the mouse, position the cell pointer in the desired cell and then double-click the left mouse button. Drag with the I-beam pointer through the data you want selected. Data selected within a cell displays in

Table 1.4 Selecting with the Mouse

To select this	*Do this*
column	Position the cell pointer on the column header (a letter) and then click the left mouse button.
row	Position the cell pointer on the row header (a number) and then click the left mouse button.
adjacent cells	Drag with the mouse to select specific cells.
nonadjacent cells	Hold down the Ctrl key while clicking the column header, row header, or specific cells.
all cells in worksheet	Click Select All button. (Refer to Figure 1.2 on page 6.)

Table 1.5 Selecting Cells Using the Keyboard

To select	*Press*
cells in direction of arrow key	Shift + arrow key
from active cell to beginning of row	Shift + Home
from active cell to beginning of worksheet	Shift + Ctrl + Home
from active cell to last cell in worksheet containing data	Shift + Ctrl + End
entire column	Ctrl + spacebar
entire row	Shift + spacebar
cells containing data	Ctrl + A
groups of data separated by empty cells	Ctrl + Shift + spacebar

black with a gray background. If you are using the keyboard to select data in a cell, hold down the Shift key and then press the arrow key that moves the insertion point in the desired direction. All data the insertion point passes through will be selected. You can also press F8 to turn on the Extend Selection mode, move the insertion point in the desired direction to select the data, and then press F8 to turn off the Extend Selection mode. When the Extend Selection mode is on, the words *EXTEND SELECTION* display toward the left side of the Status bar.

HINT

Select nonadjacent columns or rows by holding down the Ctrl key while selecting cells.

Applying Basic Formatting

Excel provides a wide range of formatting options you can apply to cells in a worksheet. Some basic formatting options that are helpful when creating a worksheet include changing column width, merging and centering cells, and formatting numbers.

Changing Column Width

If data such as text or numbers overlaps in a cell, you can increase the width of the column to accommodate the data. To do this, position the mouse pointer on the gray boundary line between columns in the column header (Figure 1.2 identifies the column header) until the pointer turns into a left-and-right-pointing arrow and then drag the boundary to the desired location. If the column contains data, double-click the column boundary at the right side of the column to automatically adjust the width of the column to accommodate the longest entry.

Quick Steps

Change the Column Width
Drag column boundary line.
OR
Double-click column boundary.

Merge and Center Cells
1. Select cells.
2. Click Merge & Center button on HOME tab.

Merge & Center

Merging and Centering Cells

As you learned earlier in this chapter, if the text you type is longer than the cell can accommodate, the text overlaps the next cell to the right (unless you are typing numbers). You can merge cells to accommodate the text and also center the text within the merged cells. To merge cells and center the text, select the desired cells and then click the Merge & Center button located in the Alignment group on the HOME tab.

Project 3a Changing Column Width and Merging and Centering Cells Part 1 of 2

1. Open **MoExps.xlsx** from the EL1C1 folder on your storage medium.
2. Save the workbook with Save As and name it **EL1-C1-P3-MoExps**.
3. Change the column width by completing the following steps:
   a. Position the mouse pointer in the column header on the boundary line between columns A and B until the pointer turns into a double-headed arrow pointing left and right.

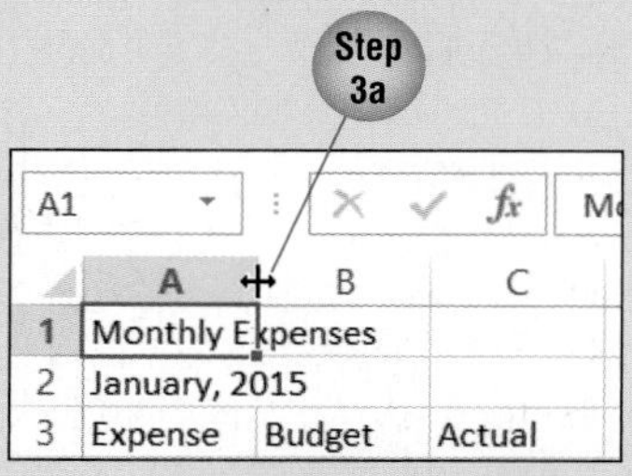

   b. Double-click the left mouse button.
   c. Position the mouse pointer in the column header on the boundary line between columns E and F and then double-click the left mouse button.
   d. Position the mouse pointer in the column header on the boundary line between columns F and G and then double-click the left mouse button.
4. Merge and center cells by completing the following steps:
   a. Select cells A1 through C1.
   b. Click the Merge & Center button in the Alignment group on the HOME tab.

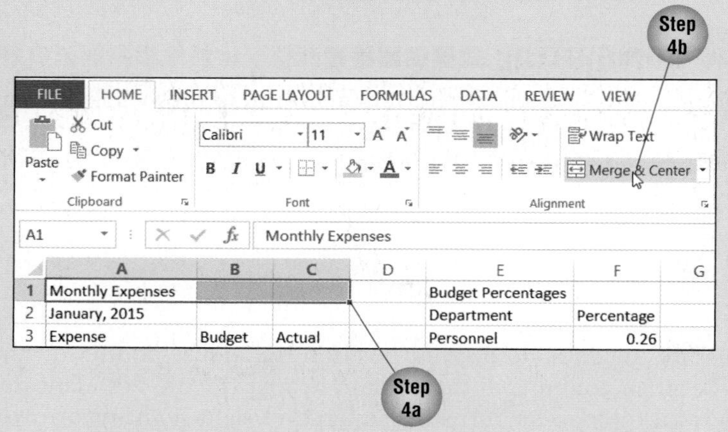

   c. Select cells A2 through C2.
   d. Click the Merge & Center button.
   e. Select cells E1 and F1 and then click the Merge & Center button.
5. Save **EL1-C1-P3-MoExps.xlsx**.

Formatting Numbers

Numbers in a cell, by default, are aligned at the right and decimals and commas do not display unless they are typed in the cell. Change the format of numbers with buttons in the Number group on the HOME tab. Symbols you can use to format numbers include a percent sign (%), a comma (,), and a dollar sign ($). For example, if you type the number *$45.50* in a cell, Excel automatically applies the Currency format to the number. If you type *45%*, Excel automatically applies the Percent format to the number. The Number group on the HOME tab contains five buttons you can use to format numbers in cells. The five buttons are shown and described in Table 1.6.

Specify the formatting for numbers in cells in a worksheet before typing the numbers or format existing numbers in a worksheet. The Increase Decimal and Decrease Decimal buttons in the Number group on the HOME tab will change decimal places for existing numbers only. The Number group on the HOME tab also contains the Number Format button. Click the Number Format button arrow and a drop-down list displays of common number formats. Click the desired format at the drop-down list to apply the number formatting to the cell or selected cells.

A general guideline in accounting is to insert a dollar sign before the first number amount in a column and before the total number amount but not before the number amounts in between. You can format a worksheet following this guideline by applying accounting formatting to the first amount and total amount (using the Accounting Number Format button) and applying comma formatting to the number amounts in between (using the Comma Style button).

Table 1.6 Number Formatting Buttons

Click this button		*To do this*
$ ▾	Accounting Number Format	Add a dollar sign, any necessary commas, and a decimal point followed by two decimal digits, if none are typed; right-align the number in the cell.
%	Percent Style	Multiply the cell value by 100 and display the result with a percent symbol; right-align the number in the cell.
,	Comma Style	Add any necessary commas and a decimal point followed by two decimal digits, if none are typed; right-align the number in the cell.
←.0 .00	Increase Decimal	Increase the number of decimal places displayed after the decimal point in the selected cell.
.00 →.0	Decrease Decimal	Decrease the number of decimal places displayed after the decimal point in the selected cell.

Project 3b Formatting Numbers

1. With **EL1-C1-P3-MoExps.xlsx** open, make cell B13 active and then double-click the AutoSum button. (This inserts the total of the numbers in cells B4 through B12.)
2. Make cell C13 active and then double-click the AutoSum button.
3. Apply accounting formatting to cells by completing the following steps:
   a. Select cells B4 and C4.
   b. Click the accounting Number Format button in the Number group on the HOME tab.
   c. Decrease the decimals by clicking twice on the Decrease Decimal button in the Number group.

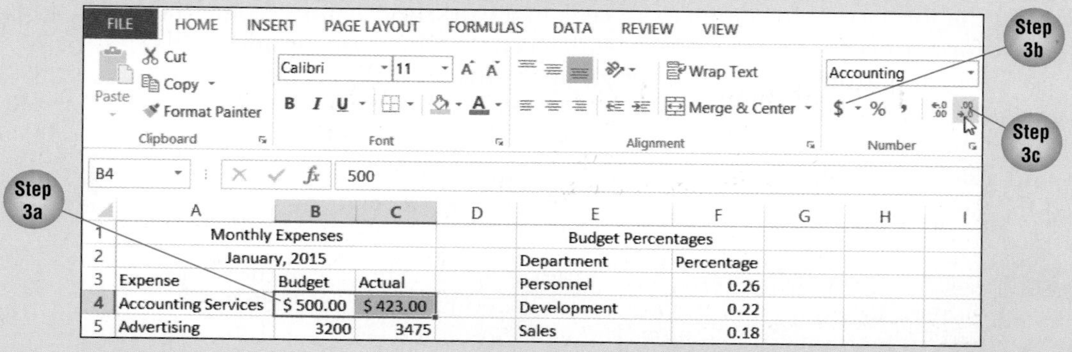

   d. Select cells B13 and C13.
   e. Click the Accounting Number Format button.
   f. Click twice on the Decrease Decimal button.
4. Apply comma formatting to numbers by completing the following steps:
   a. Select cells B5 through C12.
   b. Click the Comma Style button in the Number group.
   c. Click twice on the Decrease Decimal button.

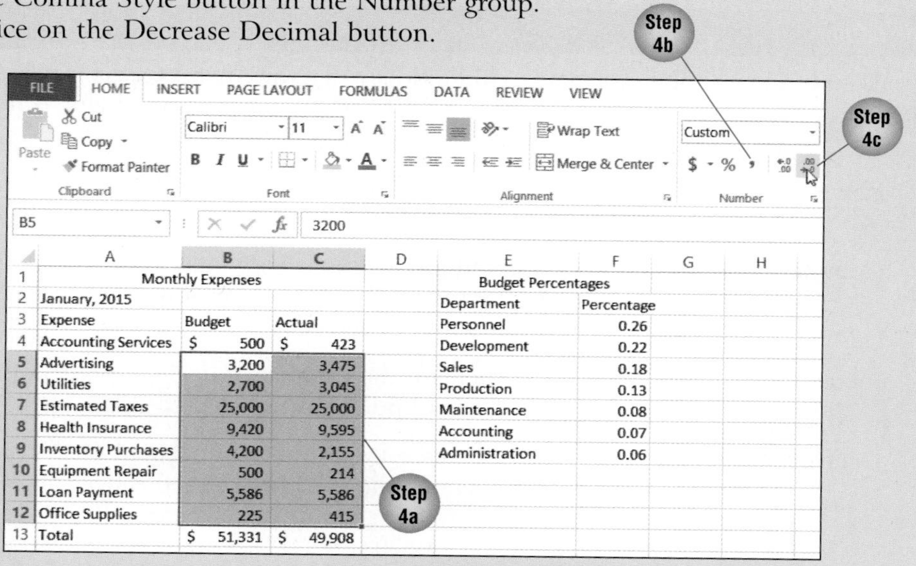

5. Apply percent formatting to numbers by completing the following steps:
   a. Select cells F3 through F9.
   b. Click the Percent Style button in the Number group on the HOME tab.
6. Click in cell A1.
7. Save, print, and then close **EL1-C1-P3-MoExps.xlsx**.

Project 4 Use the Help Feature

2 Parts

You will use the Help feature to learn more about entering data in cells and saving a workbook and use the ScreenTip to display information about a specific button.

Using Help

Microsoft Excel includes a Help feature that contains information about Excel features and commands. This on-screen reference manual is similar to Windows Help and the Help features in Word, PowerPoint, and Access. Click the Microsoft Excel Help button (the question mark) located in the upper right corner of the screen or press the keyboard shortcut F1 to display the Excel Help window, as shown in Figure 1.10. In this window, type a topic, feature, or question in the search text box and then press the Enter key or click the Search help button. Topics related to the search text display in the Excel Help window. Click a topic that interests you. If the topic window contains a Show All hyperlink in the upper right corner, click this hyperlink and the topic options expand to show additional information related to the topic. When you click the Show All hyperlink, it becomes the Hide All hyperlink.

The Excel Help window contains five buttons that display to the left of the search text box as identified in Figure 1.10. Use the Back and Forward buttons to navigate in the window. Click the Home button to return to the Excel Help window opening screen. If you want to print information on a topic or feature,

Quick Steps

Use the Help Feature

1. Click Microsoft Excel Help button.
2. Type topic or feature.
3. Press Enter.
4. Click desired topic.

Help

Figure 1.10 Excel Help Window

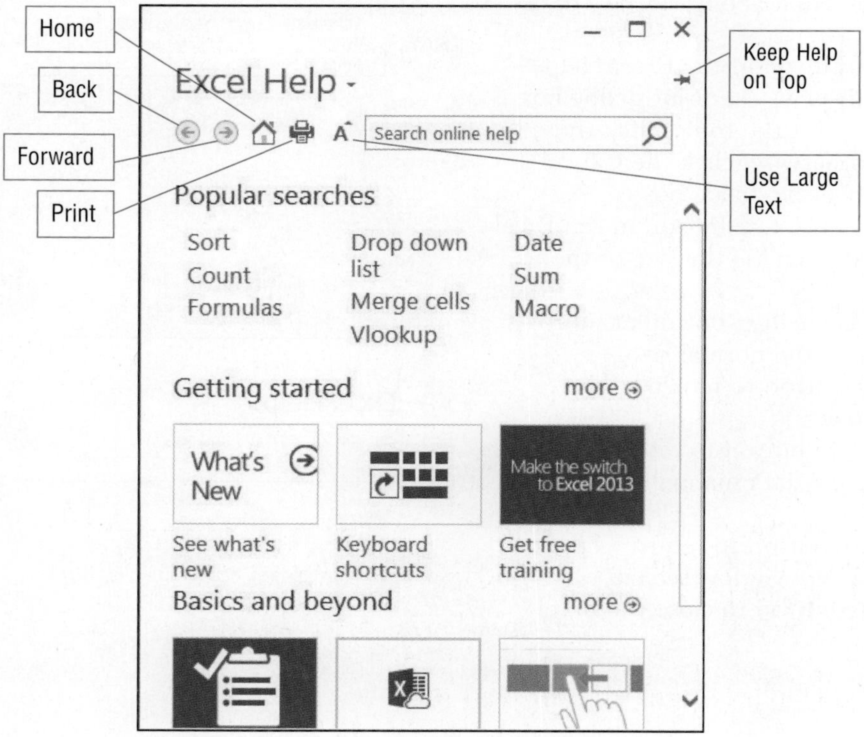

click the Print button and then click the Print button at the Print dialog box. Make the text in the Excel Help window larger by clicking the Use Large Text button. In addition to these five buttons, the Excel Help window contains a Keep Help on Top button located near the upper right corner of the window. Click this button and the Excel Help window remains on the screen (pinned to the screen) even when you work in a worksheet. Click the button again to remove the window from the screen.

Getting Help on a Button

When you position the mouse pointer on a button, a ScreenTip displays with information about the button. Some button ScreenTips display with a Help icon and the hyperlinked text Tell me more. Click this hyperlinked text or press F1 and the Excel Help window opens with information about the button feature.

Project 4a **Using the Help Feature** New Blank Doc **Part 1 of 2**

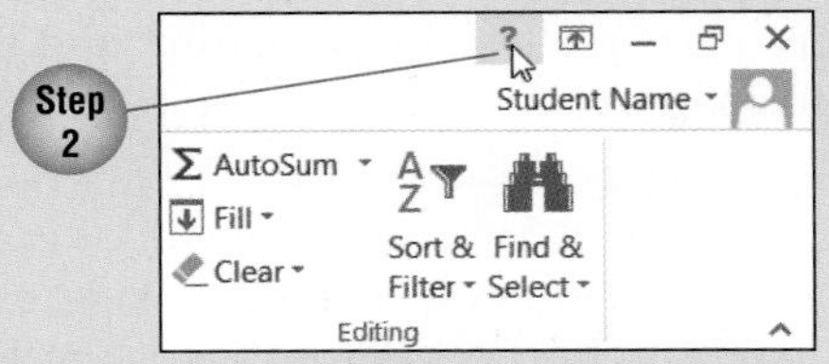

1. At the blank screen, press Ctrl + N to display a blank workbook. (Ctrl + N is the keyboard shortcut to open a blank workbook.)
2. Click the Microsoft Excel Help button located in the upper right corner of the screen.
3. At the Excel Help window, type **enter data** in the search text box and then press the Enter key.
4. When the list of topics displays, click the Enter data manually in worksheet cells hyperlink.
5. Read the information about entering data in cells.
6. Click the Print button in the Excel Help window. This displays the Print dialog box. If you want to print the topic, click the Print button; otherwise, click the Cancel button to remove the dialog box.
7. Click the Use Large Text button in the Excel Help window to increase the size of the text.
8. Click the Use Large Text button again to return the text to the normal size.
9. Click the Back button to return to the previous window.
10. Click the Forward button to return to the article on entering data manually in worksheet cells.
11. Click the Home button to return to the original Excel Help window screen.
12. Click the Close button to close the Excel Help window.

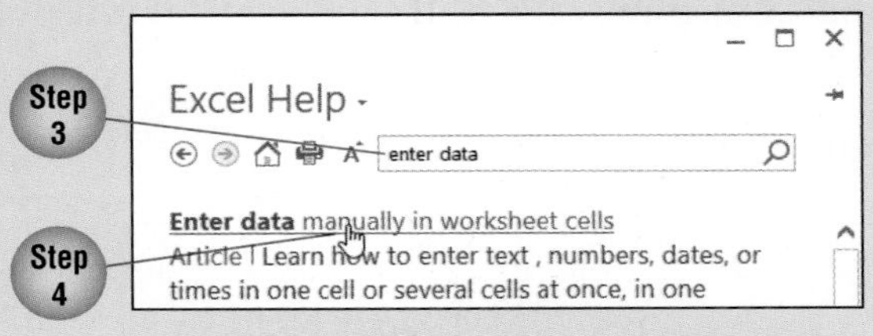

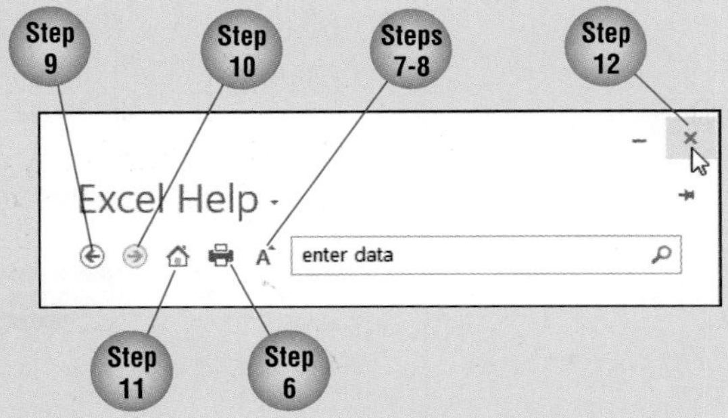

13. Hover the mouse pointer over the Wrap Text button in the Alignment group on the HOME tab until the ScreenTip displays and then click the hyperlinked text Tell me more that displays at the bottom of the ScreenTip.
14. At the Excel Help window, read the information that displays and then close the window.

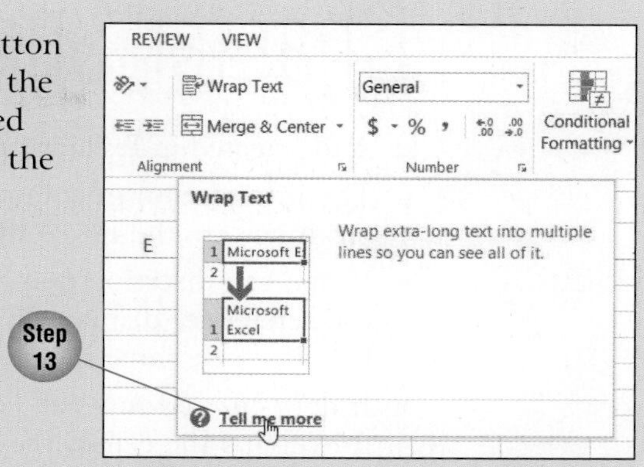

Getting Help in a Dialog Box or Backstage Area

Some dialog boxes and backstage areas contain a help button you can click to display the Excel Help window with specific information about the dialog box or backstage area. After reading and/or printing the information, close the dialog box by clicking the Close button located in the upper right corner of the dialog box or close the backstage area by clicking the Back button or pressing the Esc key.

Project 4b Getting Help in a Dialog Box or Backstage Area Part 2 of 2

1. At the blank workbook, click the FILE tab and then click the *Print* option.
2. At the Print backstage area, click the Microsoft Excel Help button that displays in the upper right corner.
3. At the Excel Help window that displays, click the hyperlink to an article on printing that interests you. Read the article and then close the Excel Help window.
4. Click the Back button to return to the blank workbook.
5. At the blank workbook, click the Number group dialog box launcher.
6. At the Format Cells dialog box with the Number tab selected, click the Help button that displays in the upper right corner of the dialog box.

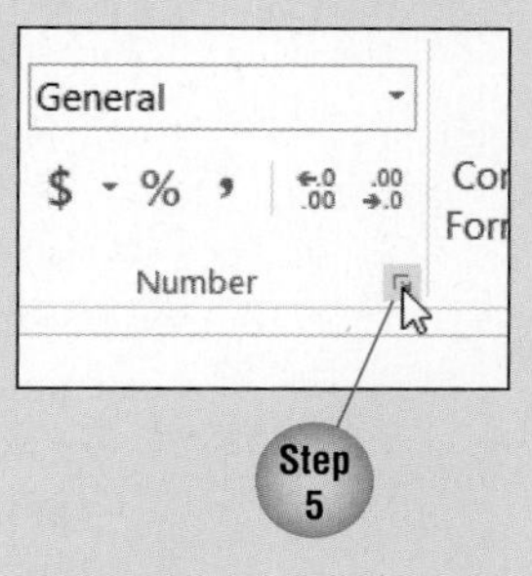

7. Click the hyperlink to the article on available number formats.
8. Read the article, close the Excel Help window and then close the Format Cells dialog box.

Chapter Summary

- A file created in Excel is called a workbook and it consists of individual worksheets.
- The intersection of columns and rows in a worksheet is referred to as a cell. Gridlines are the horizontal and vertical lines that define cells.
- When the insertion point is positioned in a cell, the cell name (also called the cell reference) displays in the Name box located at the left side of the Formula bar. The cell name includes the column letter and row number.
- If data entered in a cell consists of text (letters) and does not fit into the cell, it overlaps the cell to the right. If the data consists of numbers and does not fit into the cell, the numbers are changed to number symbols (###).
- Save a workbook by clicking the Save button on the Quick Access toolbar or by clicking the FILE tab and then clicking the *Save As* option. At the Save As backstage area, click the desired location and then click the Browse button. At the Save As dialog box, navigate to the desired folder, type the workbook name in the *File name* text box, and then press Enter.
- To replace data in a cell, click the cell once and then type the new data. To edit data within a cell, double-click the cell and then make necessary changes.
- Print a workbook by clicking the FILE tab, clicking the *Print* option, and then clicking the Print button.
- Close a workbook by clicking the FILE tab and then clicking the *Close* option or by using the keyboard shortcut Ctrl + F4.
- Close Excel by clicking the Close button located in the upper right corner of the screen or with the keyboard shortcut Alt + F4.
- The AutoComplete feature automatically inserts a previous entry if the character or characters being typed in a cell match a previous entry. The AutoCorrect feature corrects many common typographical errors. The AutoFill fill handle fills a range of cells with the same or consecutive data.
- Open a workbook by clicking the FILE tab and then clicking the *Open* option. At the Open backstage area, click the desired location and then click the Browse button. At the Open dialog box, double-click the desired workbook.
- Use the AutoSum button in the Editing group on the HOME tab to find the total or average of data in columns or rows.
- Select all cells in a column by clicking the column header. Select all cells in a row by clicking the row header. Select all cells in a worksheet by clicking the Select All button located immediately to the left of the column headers.
- Change column width by dragging or double-clicking the column boundary.
- Merge and center cells by selecting the desired cells and then clicking the Merge & Center button in the Alignment group on the HOME tab.
- Format numbers in cells with buttons in the Number group on the HOME tab.
- Click the Microsoft Excel Help button or press F1 to display the Excel Help window. At this window, type a topic in the search text box and then press Enter.
- The ScreenTip for some buttons displays with the hyperlinked text Tell me more. Click this hyperlink (or press F1) and the Excel Help window opens with information about the button feature.
- Some dialog boxes and backstage areas contain a help button you can click to display information specific to the dialog box or backstage area.

Commands Review

FEATURE	RIBBON TAB, GROUP/OPTION	BUTTON	KEYBOARD SHORTCUT
Accounting format	HOME, Number	$ ▾	
AutoSum	HOME, Editing	Σ	Alt + =
close Excel		×	Alt + F4
close workbook	FILE, *Close*		Ctrl + F4
Comma format	HOME, Number	,	
decrease decimal places	HOME, Number	.00 →.0	
Excel Help window		?	F1
Go To dialog box	HOME, Editing		Ctrl + G
increase decimal places	HOME, Number	←.0 .00	
merge and center cells	HOME, Alignment		
Open backstage area	FILE, *Open*		Ctrl + O
Percent format	HOME, Number	%	Ctrl + Shift + %
Print backstage area	FILE, *Print*		Ctrl + P
Save As backstage area	FILE, *Save As*		Ctrl + S

Concepts Check

Test Your Knowledge

Completion: In the space provided at the right, indicate the correct term, symbol, or command.

1. The horizontal and vertical lines that define the cells in a worksheet area are referred to as this. Gridlines
2. Columns in a worksheet are labeled with these. letters
3. Rows in a worksheet are labeled with these. numbers
4. Press this key on the keyboard to move the insertion point to the next cell. Enter

5. Press these keys on the keyboard to move the insertion point to the previous cell. Shift + Tab
6. Data being typed in a cell displays in the cell as well as here. formula bar
7. If a number entered in a cell is too long to fit inside the cell, the number is changed to this. ###
8. This feature automatically inserts words, numbers, or formulas in a series. Auto Fill
9. This is the name of the small black square that displays in the bottom right corner of the active cell. fill handle
10. Use this button in the Editing group on the HOME tab to insert a formula in a cell. AutoSum
11. With this function, a range of cells are added together and then divided by the number of cell entries. Average
12. To select nonadjacent columns using the mouse, hold down this key on the keyboard while clicking the column headers. Ctl
13. Click this button to merge selected cells and center data within the merged cells. Merge & Center
14. The Accounting Number Format button is located in this group on the HOME tab. Number
15. Press this function key to display the Excel Help window. F1

Skills Check Assess Your Performance

Assessment 1

CREATE A WORKSHEET USING AUTOCOMPLETE

SNAP Grade It

1. Create the worksheet shown in Figure 1.12 with the following specifications:
   a. To create the © symbol in cell A1, type (c).
   b. Type the misspelled words as shown and let the AutoCorrect feature correct them. Use the AutoComplete feature to insert the second occurrence of *Category, Available,* and *Balance*.
   c. Merge and center cells A1 and B1.
2. Save the workbook and name it **EL1-C1-A1-Plan**.
3. Print and then close **EL1-C1-A1-Plan.xlsx**.

Figure 1.12 Assessment 1

	A	B	C
1	Premiere Plan©		
2	Plan A	Catagory	
3		Availalbe	
4		Balence	
5	Plan B	Category	
6		Available	
7		Balance	
8			

Assessment 2

CREATE AND FORMAT A WORKSHEET

SNAP Grade It

1. Create the worksheet shown in Figure 1.13 with the following specifications:
   a. Merge and center cells A1 through C1.
   b. After typing the data, automatically adjust the width of column A.
   c. Insert in cell B8 the sum of cells B3 through B7 and insert in cell C8 the sum of cells C3 through C7.
   d. Apply accounting formatting and decrease the decimal point by two positions to cells B3, C3, B8, and C8.
   e. Apply comma formatting and decrease the decimal point by two positions to cells B4 through C7.
   f. If any of the number amounts display as number symbols (###), automatically adjust the width of the appropriate columns.
2. Save the workbook and name it **EL1-C1-A2-Exp**.
3. Print and then close **EL1-C1-A2-Exp.xlsx**.

Figure 1.13 Assessment 2

	A	B	C	D
1	Construction Project			
2	Expense	Original	Current	
3	Material	129000	153000	
4	Labor	97000	98500	
5	Equipment rental	14500	11750	
6	Permits	1200	1350	
7	Tax	1950	2145	
8	Total			
9				

Assessment

3 CREATE A WORKSHEET USING THE FILL HANDLE

SNAP Grade It

1. Type the worksheet data shown in Figure 1.14 with the following specifications:
   a. Type **Monday** in cell B2 and then use the fill handle to fill in the remaining days of the week.
   b. Type **350** in cell B3 and then use the fill handle to fill in the remaining numbers in the row.
   c. Merge and center cells A1 through G1.
2. Insert in cell G3 the sum of cells B3 through F3 and insert in cell G4 the sum of cells B4 through F4.
3. After typing the data, select cells B3 through G4 and then apply accounting formatting with two places past the decimal point.
4. If necessary, adjust column widths.
5. Save the workbook and name it **EL1-C1-A3-Invest**.
6. Print and then close **EL1-C1-A3-Invest.xlsx**.

Figure 1.14 Assessment 3

	A	B	C	D	E	F	G	H
1	CAPITAL INVESTMENTS							
2		Monday	Tuesday	Wednesday	Thursday	Friday	Total	
3	Budget	350	350	350	350	350		
4	Actual	310	425	290	375	400		
5								

Assessment

4 INSERT FORMULAS IN A WORKSHEET

SNAP Grade It

1. Open **DIAnalysis.xlsx** and then save the workbook with Save As and name it **EL1-C1-A4-DIAnalysis**.
2. Insert a formula in cell B15 that totals the amounts in cells B4 through B14.
3. Use the fill handle to copy relatively the formula in cell B15 to cell C15.
4. Insert a formula in cell D4 that finds the average of the amounts in cells B4 and C4.
5. Use the fill handle to copy relatively the formula in cell D4 down to cells D5 through D14.
6. Select cells D5 through D14 and then apply comma formatting with no places past the decimal point.
7. Save, print, and then close **EL1-C1-A4-DIAnalysis.xlsx**.

Visual Benchmark Demonstrate Your Proficiency

CREATE, FORMAT, AND INSERT FORMULAS IN A WORKSHEET

1. At a blank workbook, create the worksheet shown in Figure 1.15 with the following specifications:
   a. Type the data in cells, as shown in the figure. Use the fill handle when appropriate, merge and center the text *Personal Expenses - July through December*, and automatically adjust column widths.

b. Insert formulas to determine averages and totals.
c. Apply accounting formatting with no places past the decimal point to the amounts in cells B4 through H4 and cells B12 through H12.
d. Apply comma formatting with no places past the decimal point to the amounts in cells B5 through H11.
2. Save the workbook and name it **EL1-C1-VB-PersExps**.
3. Print and then close **EL1-C1-VB-PersExps.xlsx**.

Figure 1.15 Visual Benchmark

	A	B	C	D	E	F	G	H	I
1									
2	Personal Expenses - July through December								
3	Expense	July	August	September	October	November	December	Average	
4	Rent	850	850	850	850	850	850		
5	Rental insurance	55	55	55	55	55	55		
6	Health insurance	120	120	120	120	120	120		
7	Electricity	129	135	110	151	168	173		
8	Utilities	53	62	49	32	55	61		
9	Telephone	73	81	67	80	82	75		
10	Groceries	143	137	126	150	147	173		
11	Gasoline	89	101	86	99	76	116		
12	Total								
13									

Case Study Apply Your Skills

Part 1

You are the office manager for Deering Industries. One of your responsibilities is to create a monthly calendar containing information on staff meetings, training, and due dates for time cards. Open **DICalendar.xlsx** and then insert the following information:

- Type the text **November, 2015** in cell A2.
- Insert the days of the week (*Sunday*, *Monday*, *Tuesday*, *Wednesday*, *Thursday*, *Friday*, and *Saturday*) in cells A3 through G3. (Use the fill handle to fill in the days of the week and fill without formatting.)
- Insert the numbers *1* through *7* in cells A4 through G4.
- Insert in the calendar the remaining numbers of the days (numbers *8* through *14* in cells A6 through G6, numbers *15* through *21* in cells A8 through G8, numbers *22* through *28* in cells A10 through G10, and numbers *29* and *30* in cells A12 and B12. If you use the fill handle, fill without formatting.
- Excel training will be held Thursday, November 5, from 9:00 to 11:00 a.m. Insert this information in cell E5. (Insert the text on two lines by typing **Excel Training**, pressing Alt + Enter to move the insertion point to the next line, and then typing **9-11 a.m.**)
- A staff meeting is held the second and fourth Monday of each month from 9:00 to 10:00 a.m. Insert this information in cell B7 and cell B11.

- Time cards are due the first and third Fridays of the month. Insert in cells F5 and F9 information indicating that time cards are due.
- A production team meeting is scheduled for Tuesday, November 24, from 1:00 to 3:00 p.m. Insert this information in cell C11.

Save the workbook and name it **EL1-C1-CS-DICalendar**. Print and then close the workbook.

Part 2

The manager of the purchasing department has asked you to prepare a worksheet containing information on quarterly purchases. Open **DIExpenditures.xlsx** and then insert the data as shown in Figure 1.16. After typing the data, insert in the appropriate cells formulas to calculate averages and totals. Apply comma formatting to cells F5 through F8. Save the workbook and name it **EL1-C1-CS-DIExpenditures**. Print and then close the workbook.

Figure 1.16 Case Study, Part 2

	A	B	C	D	E	F	G
1	DEERING INDUSTRIES						
2	PURCHASING DEPARTMENT - EXPENDITURES						
3	*Category*					*Average*	
4	**Supplies**	$ 645.75	$ 756.25	$ 534.78	$ 78,950.00		
5	**Equipment**	4,520.55	10,789.35	3,825.00	12,890.72		
6	**Furniture**	458.94	2,490.72	851.75	743.20		
7	**Training**	1,000.00	250.00	1,200.00	800.00		
8	**Software**	249.00	1,574.30	155.45	3,458.70		
9	**Total**						
10							

Part 3

The manager of the purchasing department has asked you to prepare a note to the finances coordinator, Jennifer Strauss. In Word, type a note to Jennifer Strauss explaining that you have prepared an Excel worksheet with the purchasing department expenditures. You are including the cells from the worksheet containing the expenditure information. In Excel, open **EL1-C1-CS-DIExpenditures.xlsx**, copy cells A3 through F9, and then paste them in the Word document. Make any corrections to the table so the information is readable. Save the document and name it **EL1-C1-CS-DINotetoJS**. Print and then close the document. Close **EL1-C1-CS-DIExpenditures.xlsx**.

Part 4

You will be ordering copy machines for several departments in the company and have decided to research prices. Using the Internet, find three companies that sell copiers and write down information on different copier models. Open **DICopiers.xlsx** and then type the company, model number, and price in the designated cells. Save the completed workbook and name it **EL1-C1-CS-DICopiers**. Print and then close **EL1-C1-CS-DICopiers.xlsx**.

MICROSOFT® EXCEL®

CHAPTER 2

Inserting Formulas in a Worksheet

PERFORMANCE OBJECTIVES

Upon successful completion of Chapter 2, you will be able to:

- **Write formulas with mathematical operators**
- **Type a formula in the Formula bar**
- **Copy a formula**
- **Use the Insert Function feature to insert a formula in a cell**
- **Write formulas with the AVERAGE, MAX, MIN, COUNT, NOW, and TODAY functions**
- **Create absolute and mixed cell references**

SNAP

Tutorials

2.1 Performing Calculations Using Formulas

2.2 Copying and Testing Formulas

2.3 Using Statistical Functions

2.4 Writing Formulas with Date Functions and Dates

2.5 Displaying Formulas in a Worksheet

2.6 Creating Formulas with Absolute Addressing

Excel is a powerful decision-making tool containing data that can be manipulated to answer "What if?" situations. Insert a formula in a worksheet and then manipulate the data to make projections, answer specific questions, and plan for the future. For example, the owner of a company might prepare a worksheet on production costs and then determine the impact on company revenues if production is increased or decreased. Insert a formula in a worksheet to perform calculations on values. A formula contains a mathematical operator, value, cell reference, cell range, and function. Formulas can be written that add, subtract, multiply, and/or divide values. Formulas can also be written that calculate averages, percentages, minimum and maximum values, and much more. As you learned in Chapter 1, Excel includes an AutoSum button in the Editing group on the HOME tab that inserts a formula to calculate the total of a range of cells and also includes some commonly used formulas. Along with the AutoSum button, Excel includes a FORMULAS tab that offers a variety of functions to create formulas. Model answers for this chapter's projects appear on the following pages.

Excel
EL1C2

Note: Before beginning the projects, copy to your storage medium the EL1C2 subfolder from the EL1 folder on the CD that accompanies this textbook and make EL1C2 the active folder.

Highland Construction

Customer	Actual	Planned	Difference
Sellar Corporation	$ 30,349	$ 34,109	$ 3,760
Main Street Photos	46,425	48,100	1,675
Sunset Automotive	34,192	32,885	(1,307)
Linstrom Enterprises	63,293	60,000	(3,293)
Morcos Media	29,400	30,500	1,100
Green Valley Optics	57,415	58,394	979
Detailed Designs	14,115	13,100	(1,015)
Arrowstar Company	87,534	86,905	(629)

Name	Hours	Rate	Salary
Carolyn Bentley	35	$ 23.15	$ 810.25
Lindon Cassini	28	19.00	532.00
Michelle DeFord	40	19.10	764.00
Javier Farias	24	16.45	394.80
Deborah Gould	24	11.50	276.00
William Jarman	15	11.50	172.50

Expense	Actual	Budget	% of Actual
Salaries	$ 126,000	$ 124,000	98%
Commissions	58,000	54,500	94%
Media space	8,250	10,100	122%
Travel expenses	6,350	6,000	94%
Dealer display	4,140	4,500	109%
Payroll taxes	2,430	2,200	91%
Telephone	1,450	1,500	103%

EQUIPMENT USAGE REPORT						
Hours	January	February	March	April	May	June
Total hours available	2,300	2,430	2,530	2,400	2,440	2,240
Avoidable delays	19	12	16	20	14	15
Unavoidable delays	9	8	6	12	9	10
Repairs	5	7	12	9	10	6
Servicing	6	13	7	6	4	5
Unassigned	128	95	85	135	95	75
In use	2,040	2,105	2,320	2,180	2,050	1,995
% of down time	11%	13%	8%	9%	16%	11%
Jan - March hours	7,260					
April - June hours	7,080					

Project 1 Insert Formulas in a Worksheet

EL1-C2-P1-HCReports.xlsx

Dollar Wise Financial Services

Technical Support Department

Employee	Test 1	Test 2	Test 3	Average
Arnson, Patrick	91%	87%	82%	87%
Barclay, Jeanine	76%	74%	72%	74%
Calahan, Jack	67%	71%	65%	68%
Cumpston, Kurt	86%	91%	90%	89%
Donovan, Nancy	85%	89%	78%	84%
Fisher-Edwards, Teri	70%	70%	70%	70%
Flanery, Stephanie	70%	70%	72%	71%
Herbertson, Wynn	91%	80%	85%	85%
Jewett, Troy	97%	94%	92%	94%
Leibrand, Maxine	72%	63%	65%	67%
Markovits, Claude	68%	93%	70%	77%
Nyegaard, Curtis	90%	89%	88%	89%
Pherson, Douglas	72%	82%	55%	70%

Highest Test Average	94%
Lowest Test Average	67%
Average of All Tests	79%
Test 2 Completed	13
Test 3 Completed	13

Prepared by:
Student Name
9/18/2015 14:05

Project 2 Insert Formulas with Statistical Functions

EL1-C2-P2-DWTests.xlsx

Dollar Wise Financial Services

Technical Support Department

Employee	Test 1	Test 2
Arnson, Patrick	0.91	0.87
Barclay, Jeanine	0.76	0.74
Calahan, Jack	0.67	0.71
Cumpston, Kurt	0.86	0.91
Donovan, Nancy	0.85	0.89
Fisher-Edwards, Teri	0.7	0.7
Flanery, Stephanie	0.7	0.7
Herbertson, Wynn	0.91	0.8
Jewett, Troy	0.97	0.94
Leibrand, Maxine	0.72	0.63
Markovits, Claude	0.68	0.93
Nyegaard, Curtis	0.9	0.89
Pherson, Douglas	0.72	0.82

Highest Test Average	=MAX(E4:E16)
Lowest Test Average	=MIN(E4:E16)
Average of All Tests	=AVERAGE(E4:E16)
Test 2 Completed	=COUNT(C4:C16)
Test 3 Completed	=COUNT(D4:D16)

Prepared by:
Student Name
=NOW()

Page 1

Test 3	Average
0.82	=AVERAGE(B4:D4)
0.72	=AVERAGE(B5:D5)
0.65	=AVERAGE(B6:D6)
0.9	=AVERAGE(B7:D7)
0.78	=AVERAGE(B8:D8)
0.7	=AVERAGE(B9:D9)
0.72	=AVERAGE(B10:D10)
0.85	=AVERAGE(B11:D11)
0.92	=AVERAGE(B12:D12)
0.65	=AVERAGE(B13:D13)
0.7	=AVERAGE(B14:D14)
0.88	=AVERAGE(B15:D15)
0.55	=AVERAGE(B16:D16)

Page 2

EL1-C2-P2-DWTests.xlsx, Formulas

Cedarview Construction

Customer	Planned	Actual
Sellar Corporation	$ 34,109	$ 40,931
Main Street Photos	48,100	57,720
Sunset Automotive	32,885	39,462
Linstrom Enterprises	61,220	73,464
Morcos Media	30,500	36,600
Green Valley Optics	58,394	70,073
Detailed Designs	13,100	15,720
Arrowstar Company	86,905	104,286
% Increase/Decrease	1.2	

Employee Training				
Name	Plumbing	Electrical	Carpentry	Weighted Average
Allesandro	76%	80%	84%	80%
Ellington	66%	72%	64%	67%
Goodman	90%	88%	94%	91%
Huntington	76%	82%	88%	83%
Kaplan-Downing	90%	84%	92%	89%
Larimore	58%	62%	60%	60%
Training Averages	76%	78%	80%	
Training Weights	30%	30%	40%	

Weekly Payroll							
Employee	Hrly. Wage	Hours	Overtime	Gross	W/H Tax	SS Tax	Net
Allesandro	$ 55.00	40	2	$ 2,365.00	$ 662.20	$ 180.92	$ 1,521.88
Ellington	52.50	40	0	2,100.00	588.00	160.65	1,351.35
Goodman	45.00	30	4	1,620.00	453.60	123.93	1,042.47
Huntington	34.00	40	0	1,360.00	380.80	104.04	875.16
Kaplan-Downing	23.50	25	5	763.75	213.85	58.43	491.47
Larimore	19.00	40	0	760.00	212.80	58.14	489.06
Overtime	1.5		W/H Rate	28%		SS Rate	7.65%

SIMPLE INTEREST LOAN TABLE					
	$ 1,000	$ 2,000	$ 3,000	$ 4,000	$ 5,000
5%	$ 50	$ 100	$ 150	$ 200	$ 250
6%	$ 60	$ 120	$ 180	$ 240	$ 300
7%	$ 70	$ 140	$ 210	$ 280	$ 350
8%	$ 80	$ 160	$ 240	$ 320	$ 400

Page 1

9%	$ 90	$ 180	$ 270	$ 360	$ 450
10%	$ 100	$ 200	$ 300	$ 400	$ 500
11%	$ 110	$ 220	$ 330	$ 440	$ 550
12%	$ 120	$ 240	$ 360	$ 480	$ 600
13%	$ 130	$ 260	$ 390	$ 520	$ 650
14%	$ 140	$ 280	$ 420	$ 560	$ 700
15%	$ 150	$ 300	$ 450	$ 600	$ 750

Page 2

Project 3 Insert Formulas Using Absolute and Mixed Cell References EL1-C2-P3-CCReports.xlsx

Project 1 Insert Formulas in a Worksheet — 4 Parts

You will open a worksheet containing data and then insert formulas to calculate differences, salaries, and percentages of budgets.

Writing Formulas with Mathematical Operators

As you learned in Chapter 1, the AutoSum button in the Editing group on the HOME tab creates the formula for you. You can also write your own formulas using ***mathematical operators***. Commonly used mathematical operators and their functions are displayed in Table 2.1. When writing your own formula, begin the formula with the equals sign (=). For example, to create a formula that divides the contents of cell B2 by the contents of cell C2 and inserts the result in cell D2, you would make D2 the active cell and then type *=B2/C2*.

HINT

After typing a formula in a cell, press the Enter key, the Tab key, Shift + Tab, or click Formula bar.

Table 2.1 Mathematical Operators

Operator	*Function*	*Operator*	*Function*
+	addition	/	division
-	subtraction	%	percentage
*	multiplication	^	exponentiation

Copying a Formula with Relative Cell References

Quick Steps

Copy a Formula Relatively
1. Insert formula in cell.
2. Select cell containing formula and all cells you want to contain formula.
3. Click Fill button.
4. Click desired direction.

Fill

In many worksheets, the same basic formula is used repetitively. In a situation where a formula is copied to other locations in a worksheet, use a ***relative cell reference***. Copy a formula containing relative cell references and the cell references change. For example, if you enter the formula *=SUM(A2:C2)* in cell D2 and then copy it relatively to cell D3, the formula in cell D3 displays as *=SUM(A3:C3)*. (Additional information on cell references is discussed later in this chapter in the "Using an Absolute Cell Reference in a Formula" section.)

To copy a formula relatively in a worksheet, use the Fill button or the fill handle. (You used the fill handle to copy a formula in Chapter 1.) To use the Fill button, select the cell containing the formula as well as the cells to which you want the formula copied and then click the Fill button in the Editing group on the HOME tab. At the Fill button drop-down list, click the desired direction. For example, if you are copying the formula down cells, click the *Down* option.

Project 1a **Finding Differences by Inserting and Copying a Formula** **Part 1 of 4**

1. Open **HCReports.xlsx**.
2. Save the workbook with Save As and name it **EL1-C2-P1-HCReports**.
3. Insert a formula by completing the following steps:
   a. Make cell D3 active.
   b. Type the formula =C3-B3.
   c. Press Enter.
4. Copy the formula to cells D4 through D10 by completing the following steps:
   a. Select cells D3 through D10.
   b. Click the Fill button in the Editing group on the HOME tab and then click *Down* at the drop-down list.
5. Save **EL1-C2-P1-HCReports.xlsx**.
6. With the worksheet open, make the following changes to cell contents:
   B4: Change *48,290* to *46425*
   C6: Change *61,220* to *60000*
   B8: Change *55,309* to *57415*
   B9: Change *12,398* to *14115*
7. Make cell D3 active, apply Accounting formatting, and then decrease the places past the decimal point to none.
8. Save **EL1-C2-P1-HCReports.xlsx**.

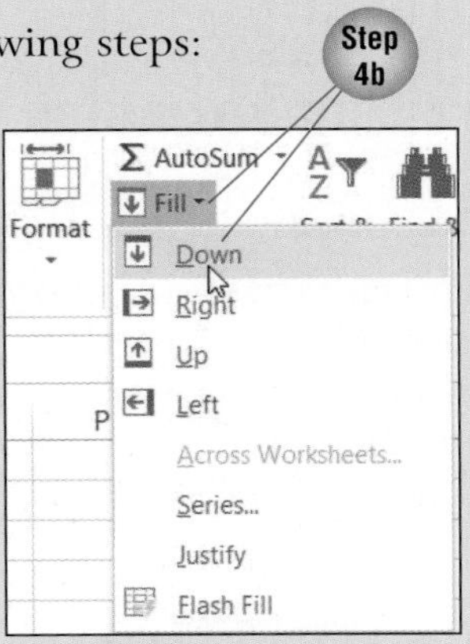

As you learned in Chapter 1, you can use the fill handle to copy a formula up, down, left, or right within a worksheet. To use the fill handle, insert the desired data in the cell (text, value, formula, etc.). With the cell active, position the mouse pointer on the fill handle until the mouse pointer turns into a thin, black cross. Hold down the left mouse button, drag and select the desired cells, and then release the mouse button. If you are dragging a cell containing a formula, a relative version of the formula is copied to the selected cells.

HINT
Use the fill handle to copy a relative version of a formula.

Checking Cell References in a Formula

To verify if a formula is using the correct cell references, double-click in a cell containing a formula and the cells referenced in the formula display with a colored border and shading in the worksheet. This feature makes identifying which cells are being referenced in a formula easy and is helpful when trying to identify errors that may occur in a formula.

Project 1b **Calculating Salary by Inserting and Copying a Formula with the Fill Handle** **Part 2 of 4**

1. With **EL1-C2-P1-HCReports.xlsx** open, insert a formula by completing the following steps:
   a. Make cell D15 active.
   b. Click in the Formula bar text box and then type =C15*B15.
   c. Click the Enter button on the Formula bar.
2. Copy the formula to cells D16 through D20 by completing the following steps:
   a. Make sure cell D15 is still the active cell.
   b. Position the mouse pointer on the fill handle that displays at the lower right corner of cell D15 until the pointer turns into a thin, black cross.
   c. Hold down the left mouse button, drag down to cell D20, and then release the mouse button.
3. Save **EL1-C2-P1-HCReports.xlsx**.
4. Double-click in cell D20 to display the formula with cell references color coded to ensure the formula was copied relatively.
5. Make the following changes to cell contents in the worksheet:
   B16: Change *20* to *28*
   C17: Change *18.75* to *19.10*
   B19: Change *15* to *24*
6. Select cells D16 through D20 and then apply Comma formatting.
7. Save **EL1-C2-P1-HCReports.xlsx**.

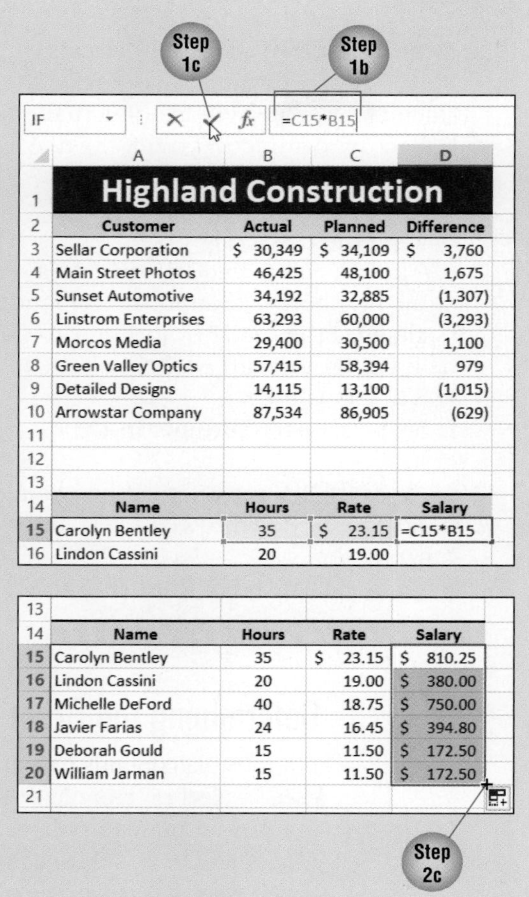

Writing a Formula by Pointing

Quick Steps

Write a Formula by Pointing
1. Click cell that will contain formula.
2. Type equals sign.
3. Click cell you want to reference in formula.
4. Type desired mathematical operator.
5. Click next cell reference.
6. Press Enter.

In Project 1a and Project 1b, you wrote formulas using cell references such as *=C3-B3*. Another method for writing a formula is to "point" to the specific cells that are to be part of the formula. Creating a formula by pointing is more accurate than typing the cell reference since a mistake can happen when typing the cell reference.

To write a formula by pointing, click in the cell that will contain the formula, type the equals sign to begin the formula, and then click in the cell you want to reference in the formula. This inserts a moving border around the cell and also changes the mode from Enter to Point. (The word *Point* displays at the left side of the Status bar.) Type the desired mathematical operator and then click the next cell reference. Continue in this manner until all cell references are specified and then press the Enter key. This ends the formula and inserts the result of the calculation of the formula in the active cell. When writing a formula by pointing, you can also select a range of cells you want included in the formula.

Project 1c **Writing a Formula by Pointing that Calculates Percentage of Actual Budget** **Part 3 of 4**

1. With **EL1-C2-P1-HCReports.xlsx** open, enter a formula by pointing that calculates the percentage of actual budget by completing the following steps:
   a. Make cell D25 active.
   b. Type the equals sign (=).
   c. Click in cell C25. (This inserts a moving border around the cell and changes the mode from Enter to Point.)
   d. Type the forward slash symbol (/).
   e. Click in cell B25.
   f. Make sure the formula in D25 is *=C25/B25* and then press Enter.
2. Make cell D25 active, position the mouse pointer on the fill handle, drag down to cell D31, and then release the mouse button.
3. Save **EL1-C2-P1-HCReports.xlsx**.

	A	B	C	D
23				
24	Expense	Actual	Budget	% of Actual
25	Salaries	$ 126,000	$ 124,000	=C25/B25
26	Commissions	58,000	54,500	
27	Media space	8,250	10,100	
28	Travel expenses	6,350	6,000	
29	Dealer display	4,140	4,500	
30	Payroll taxes	2,430	2,200	
31	Telephone	1,450	1,500	

Steps 1a-1e

C	D
Budget	% of Actual
$ 124,000	98%
54,500	94%
10,100	122%
6,000	94%
4,500	109%
2,200	91%
1,500	103%

Step 2

Determining the Order of Operations

If a formula contains two or more operators, Excel uses the same ***order of operations*** used in algebra. From left to right in a formula, this order is negations (negative number—a number preceded by -) first, then percentages (%), then exponentiations (^), followed by multiplications (*), divisions (/), additions (+), and subtractions (-). If you want to change the order of operations, use parentheses around the part of the formula you want calculated first. For example, suppose you want to create a formula using cells A1, B1, and C1, and each cell contains the value *5*. If the formula is written as *=A1+B1*C1*, the result would be 30 (because 5*5=25 and 5+25=30). However, if you place parentheses around the first two cell references so the formula displays as *=(A1+B1)*C1*, the result would be 50 (because 5+5=10 and 10*5=50).

Excel requires each left parenthesis to be paired with a right parenthesis. If a formula is missing a left or right parenthesis, a message box will display explaining that an error exists in the formula and providing a possible correction, which you can accept or decline. This feature is useful when creating a formula that contains multiple layers of parentheses (called ***nested parentheses***) because it will identify any missing left or right parentheses in the formula. Parentheses can also be used in various functions to further determine the order of operations in the function.

Using the Trace Error Button

As you are working in a worksheet, you may occasionally notice a button pop up near the active cell. The general term for this button is ***smart tag***. The display of the smart tag button varies depending on the action performed. In Project 1d, you will insert a formula that will cause a smart tag button, named the Trace Error button, to appear. When the Trace Error button appears, a small, dark green triangle also displays in the upper left corner of the cell. Click the Trace Error button and a drop-down list displays with options for updating the formula to include specific cells, getting help with the error, ignoring the error, editing the error in the Formula bar, and completing an error check. In Project 1d, two of the formulas you insert return the desired results. You will click the Trace Error button, read information on what Excel perceives as the error, and then tell Excel to ignore the error.

Trace Error

Identifying Common Formula/Function Errors in Excel

Excel is a sophisticated program that requires data input and formula creation to follow strict guidelines in order to function properly. When guidelines that specify how data or formulas are entered are not followed, Excel will display one of many ***error codes***. When an error is identified with a code, determining and then fixing the problem is easier than if no information is provided. Table 2.2 lists some common error codes.

Most errors in Excel are the result of the user incorrectly inputting data into a worksheet. However, most error messages will not display until the data is used in a formula or function. Common mistakes made while inputting data include placing text in a cell that requires a number, entering data in the wrong location, and entering numbers in an incorrect format. Other errors are the result of entering a formula or function improperly. A formula will often display an error message if it is trying to divide a number by zero or it contains a circular reference (that is, when a formula within a cell uses the results of that formula in the same cell). Functions tend to display error messages if the arguments of a particular function are not correctly defined or if a function name is typed incorrectly.

Table 2.2 Common Error Codes

Error Code	*Meaning*
#DIV/0	A formula is attempting to divide a number by zero.
#N/A	An argument parameter has been left out of a function.
#NAME?	A function name is not entered correctly.
#NUM!	An argument parameter does not meet a function's requirements.
#REF!	A referenced cell no longer exists within a worksheet.
#VALUE	The data entered is the wrong type (for example, text instead of numbers).

Project 1d Writing a Formula by Pointing That Calculates Percentage of Down Time

Part 4 of 4

1. With **EL1-C2-P1-HCReports.xlsx** open, enter a formula by pointing that computes the percentage of equipment down time by completing the following steps:
   a. Make cell B45 active.
   b. Type the equals sign followed by the left parenthesis (=().
   c. Click in cell B37. (This inserts a moving border around the cell and changes the mode from Enter to Point.)
   d. Type the minus symbol (-).
   e. Click in cell B43.
   f. Type the right parenthesis followed by the forward slash ()/).
   g. Click in cell B37.
   h. Make sure the formula in cell B45 is *=(B37-B43)/B37* and then press Enter.

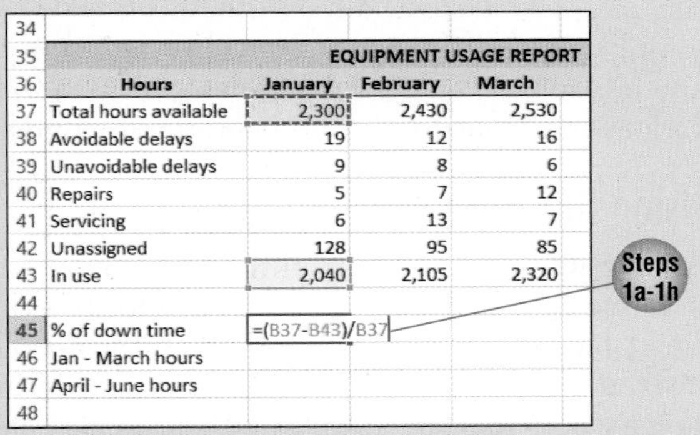

2. Make cell B45 active, position the mouse pointer on the fill handle, drag across to cell G45, and then release the mouse button.
3. Enter a formula by dragging through a range of cells by completing the following steps:
   a. Click in cell B46 and then click the AutoSum button in the Editing group on the HOME tab.
   b. Select cells B37 through D37.
   c. Click the Enter button on the Formula bar. (This inserts *7,260* in cell B46.)

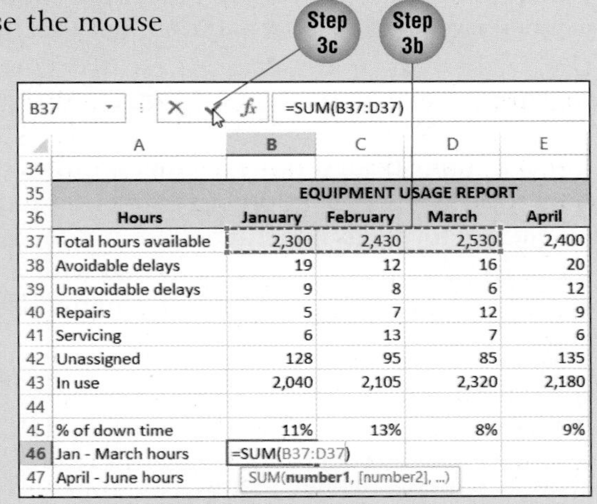

4. Click in cell B47 and then complete steps similar to those in Step 3 to create a formula that totals hours available from April through June (cells E37 through G37). (This inserts *7,080* in cell B47.)
5. Click in cell B46 and notice the Trace Error button that displays. Complete the following steps to read about the error and then tell Excel to ignore the error:
   a. Click the Trace Error button.
   b. At the drop-down list that displays, click the *Help on this error* option.
   c. Read the information that displays in the Excel Help window and then close the window.
   d. Click the Trace Error button again and then click *Ignore Error* at the drop-down list.

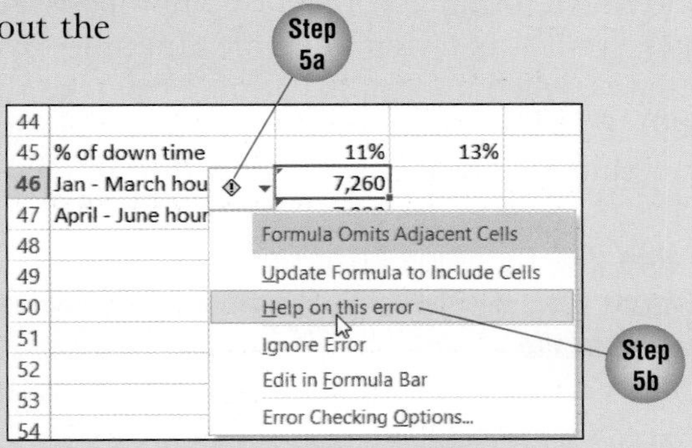

6. Remove the dark green triangle from cell B47 by completing the following steps:
   a. Click in cell B47.
   b. Click the Trace Error button and then click *Ignore Error* at the drop-down list.
7. Save, print, and then close **EL1-C2-P1-HCReports.xlsx**.

Project 2 Insert Formulas with Statistical Functions **4 Parts**

You will use the AVERAGE function to determine average test scores, use the MINIMUM and MAXIMUM functions to determine lowest and highest averages, use the COUNT function to count the number of students taking a test, and display a formula in a cell rather than the result of the formula.

Inserting Formulas with Functions

In Project 2b in Chapter 1, you used the AutoSum button to insert the formula *=SUM(B2:B5)* in a cell. The beginning section of the formula, *=SUM*, is called a ***function***, and it is a built-in formula. Using a function takes fewer keystrokes when creating a formula. For example, using the *=SUM* function saved you from having to type each cell to be included in the formula with the plus (+) symbol between cell entries.

Excel provides other functions for writing formulas. A function operates on what is referred to as an ***argument***. An argument may consist of a constant, a cell reference, or another function. In the formula *=SUM(B2:B5)*, the cell range *(B2:B5)* is an example of a cell reference argument. An argument may also contain a ***constant***. A constant is a value entered directly into the formula. For example, if you enter the formula *=SUM(B3:B9,100)*, the cell range *B3:B9* is a cell reference argument and *100* is a constant. In this formula, 100 is always added to the sum of the cells.

When a value calculated by the formula is inserted in a cell, this process is referred to as ***returning the result***. The term *returning* refers to the process of calculating the formula and the term *result* refers to inserting the value in the cell.

You can type a function in a cell in a worksheet or you can use the Insert Function button on the Formula bar or on the FORMULAS tab to help you write the formula. Figure 2.1 displays the FORMULAS tab, which provides the Insert Function button as well as other buttons for inserting functions in a worksheet. The Function Library group on the FORMULAS tab contains a number of buttons for inserting functions from a variety of categories, such as *Financial*, *Logical*, *Text*, and *Date & Time*.

fx Insert Function

Click the Insert Function button on the Formula bar or on the FORMULAS tab and the Insert Function dialog box displays, as shown in Figure 2.2. At the Insert Function dialog box, the most recently used functions display in the *Select a function* list box. Choose a function category by clicking the down-pointing arrow

Figure 2.1 FORMULAS Tab

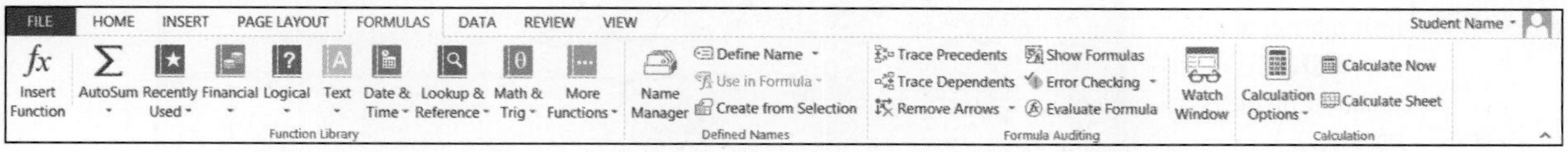

Figure 2.2 Insert Function Dialog Box

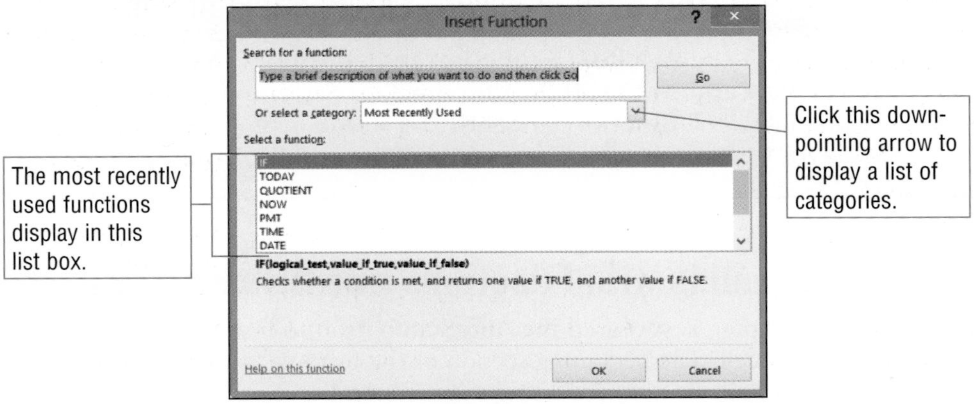

HINT

You can also display the Insert Function dialog box by clicking the down-pointing arrow at the right side of the AutoSum button and then clicking *More Functions*.

HINT

Click the AutoSum button arrow on the FORMULAS tab and common functions display in a drop-down list.

at the right side of the *Or select a category* option box and then clicking the desired category at the drop-down list. Use the *Search for a function* search box to locate a specific function.

With the desired function category selected, choose a function in the *Select a function* list box and then click OK. This displays a Function Arguments palette like the one shown in Figure 2.3. At this palette, enter in the *Number1* text box the range of cells you want included in the formula, any constants that are to be included as part of the formula, or another function. You can either type a cell reference or a range of cells in an argument text box or you can point to a cell or select a range of cells with the mouse pointer. Pointing to cells or selecting a range of cells using the mouse pointer is the preferred method of entering data into an argument text box because there is less chance of making errors. After entering a range of cells, a constant, or another function, click the OK button. You can include more than one argument in a function. If the function you are creating contains more than one argument, press the Tab key to move the insertion point to the *Number2* text box and then enter the second argument. If you need to display a specific cell or cells behind the function palette, move the palette by clicking and dragging it.

Figure 2.3 Example of a Function Arguments Palette

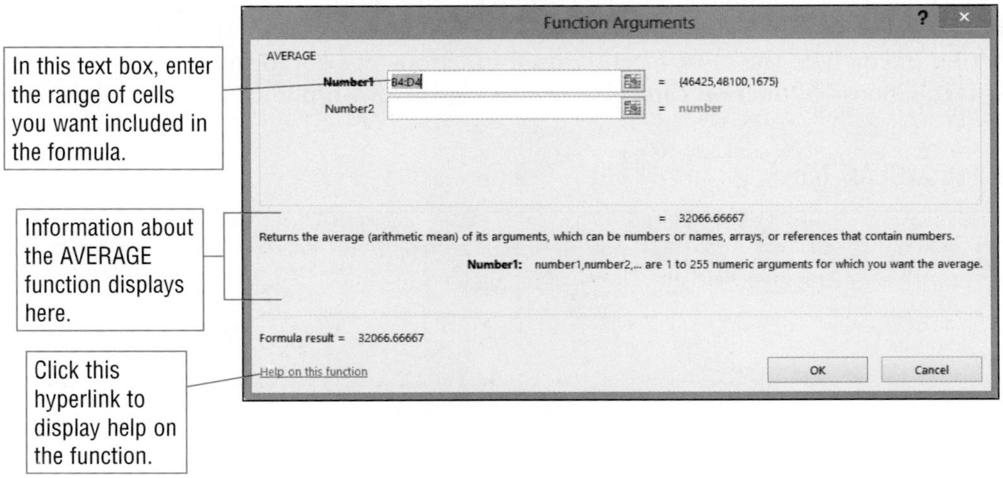

Excel performs over 300 functions that are divided into these 13 categories: *Financial*, *Date & Time*, *Math & Trig*, *Statistical*, *Lookup & Reference*, *Database*, *Text*, *Logical*, *Information*, *Engineering*, *Cube*, *Compatibility*, and *Web*. Clicking the AutoSum button in the Function Library group on the FORMULAS tab or the Editing group on the HOME tab automatically adds numbers with the SUM function. The SUM function is included in the *Math & Trig* category. In some projects in this chapter, you will write formulas with functions in other categories, including *Statistical* and *Date & Time*.

Excel includes the Formula AutoComplete feature that displays a drop-down list of functions. To use this feature, click in the desired cell or click in the Formula bar text box, type the equals sign (=), and then type the first letter of the desired function. This displays a drop-down list with functions that begin with the letter. Double-click the desired function, enter the cell references, and then press Enter.

Writing Formulas with Statistical Functions

In this section, you will learn to write formulas with the statistical functions AVERAGE, MAX, MIN, and COUNT. The AVERAGE function returns the average (arithmetic mean) of the arguments. The MAX function returns the largest value in a set of values, and the MIN function returns the smallest value in a set of values. Use the COUNT function to count the number of cells that contain numbers within the list of arguments.

Finding Averages

A common function in a formula is the ***AVERAGE function***. With this function, a range of cells is added together and then divided by the number of cell entries. In Project 2a, you will use the AVERAGE function, which will add all of the test scores for a student and then divide that number by the total number of tests. You will use the Insert Function button to simplify the creation of the formula containing an AVERAGE function.

One of the advantages to using formulas in a worksheet is that you can easily manipulate data to answer certain questions. In Project 2a, you will learn the impact of retaking certain tests on the final average score.

Project 2a **Averaging Test Scores in a Worksheet** **Part 1 of 4**

1. Open **DWTests.xlsx**.
2. Save the workbook with Save As and name it **EL1-C2-P2-DWTests**.
3. Use the Insert Function button to find the average of test scores by completing the following steps:
   a. Make cell E4 active.
   b. Click the Insert Function button on the Formula bar.

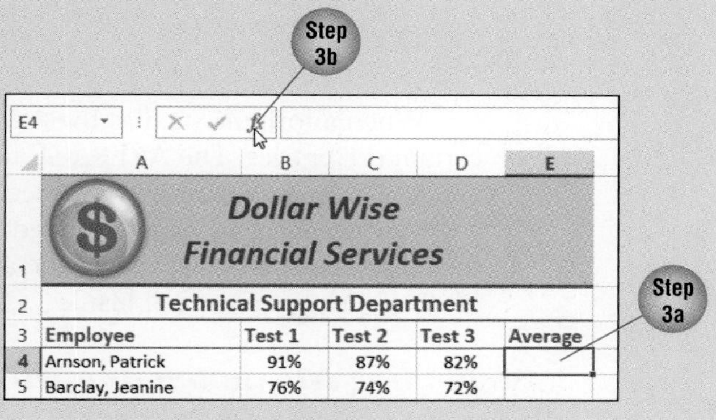

c. At the Insert Function dialog box, click the down-pointing arrow at the right side of the *Or select a category* option box and then click *Statistical* at the drop-down list.

d. Click *AVERAGE* in the *Select a function* list box.

e. Click OK.

f. At the Function Arguments palette, make sure *B4:D4* displays in the *Number1* text box. (If not, type **B4:D4** in the *Number1* text box.)

g. Click OK.

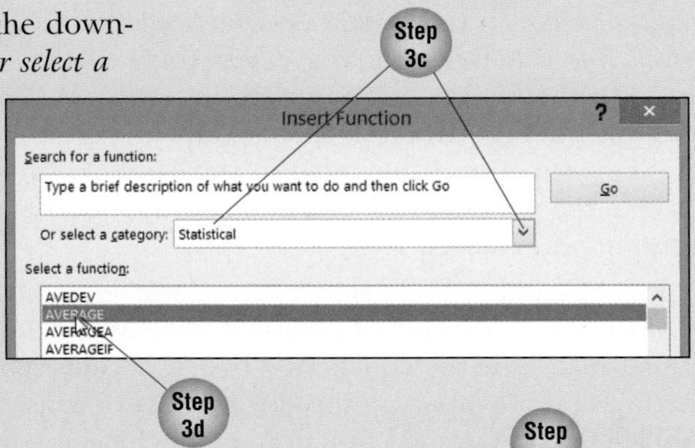

4. Copy the formula by completing the following steps:
   a. Make sure cell E4 is still active.
   b. Position the mouse pointer on the fill handle until the pointer turns into a thin black cross.
   c. Hold down the left mouse button, drag down to cell E16, and then release the mouse button.

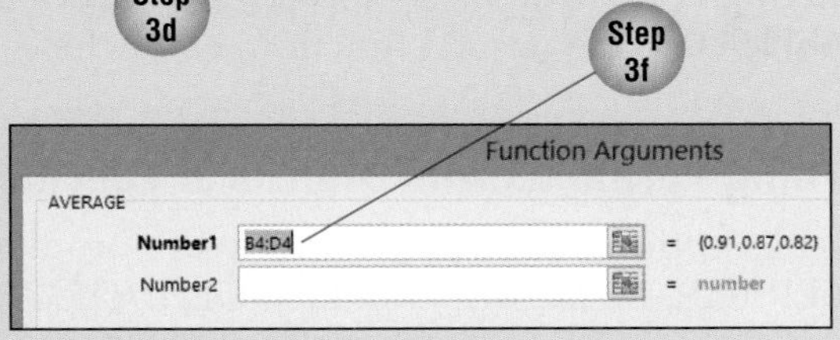

5. Save and then print **EL1-C2-P2-DWTests.xlsx**.
6. After viewing the averages of test scores, you notice that a couple of students have low averages. You decide to see what happens to these average scores if students make up the tests on which they scored the lowest. You decide that a student can score a maximum of 70% on a retake of the test. Make the following changes to test scores to see how the changes will affect the test averages:

   B9: Change *50* to *70*
   C9: Change *52* to *70*
   D9: Change *60* to *70*
   B10: Change *62* to *70*
   B14: Change *0* to *70*
   D14: Change *0* to *70*
   D16: Change *0* to *70*

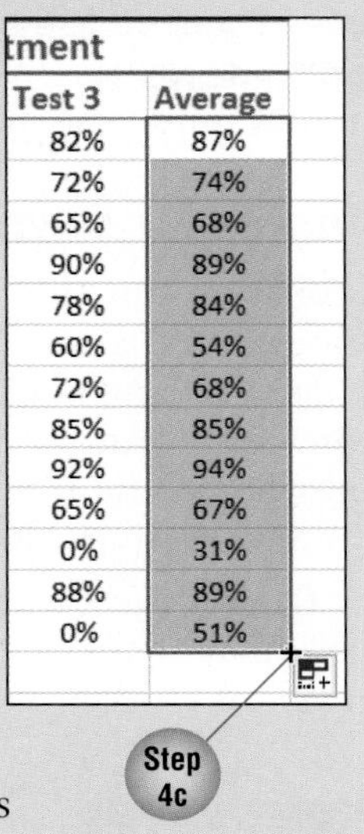

7. Save and then print **EL1-C2-P2-DWTests.xlsx**. (Compare the test averages of Teri Fisher-Edwards, Stephanie Flanery, Claude Markovits, and Douglas Pherson to see how retaking the tests affected their final test averages.)

When a formula such as the AVERAGE formula calculates cell entries, it ignores certain cell entries. The AVERAGE function will ignore text in cells and blank cells (not zeros). For example, in the worksheet containing test scores, a couple of cells contained a *0%* entry. This entry was included in the averaging of the test scores. To prevent including that particular test in the average, enter text in the cell such as *N/A* (for *not applicable*) or leave the cell blank.

Finding Maximum and Minimum Values

The ***MAX function*** in a formula returns the maximum value in a cell range and the ***MIN function*** returns the minimum value in a cell range. As an example, you could use the MAX and MIN functions in a worksheet containing employee hours to determine which employee worked the most number of hours and which worked the least. In a worksheet containing sales commissions, you could use the MAX and MIN functions to determine the salesperson who earned the most commission dollars and the one who earned the least.

Insert a MAX or a MIN function into a formula in the same manner as an AVERAGE function. In Project 2b, you will use the Formula AutoComplete feature to insert the MAX function in cells to determine the highest test score average and the Insert Function button to insert the MIN function to determine the lowest test score average.

Project 2b Finding Maximum and Minimum Values in a Worksheet — Part 2 of 4

1. With **EL1-C2-P2-DWTests.xlsx** open, type the following in the specified cells:
   A19: Highest Test Average
   A20: Lowest Test Average
   A21: Average of All Tests

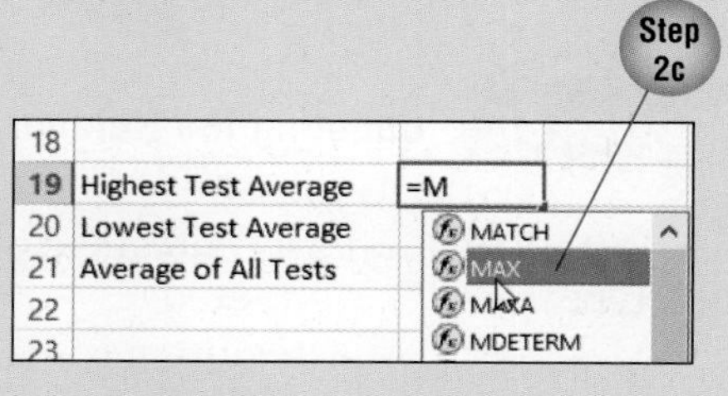

2. Insert a formula to identify the highest test score average by completing the following steps:
   a. Make cell B19 active.
   b. Type =M. (This displays the Formula AutoComplete list.)
   c. Double-click *MAX* in the Formula AutoComplete list.
   d. Type E4:E16) and then press Enter.

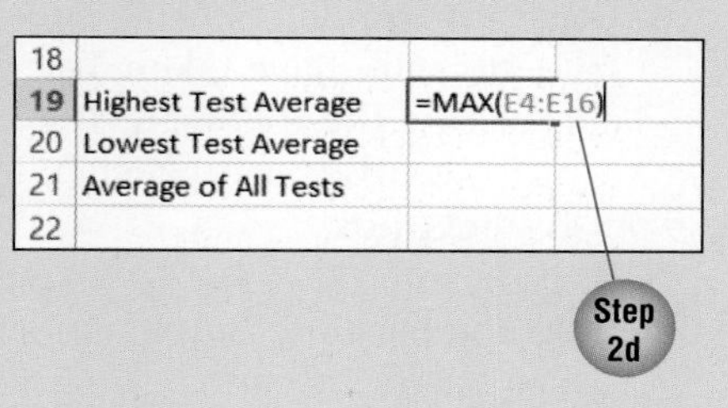

3. Insert a formula to identify the lowest test score average by completing the following steps:
   a. Make sure cell B20 is active.
   b. Click the Insert Function button on the Formula bar.
   c. At the Insert Function dialog box, make sure *Statistical* is selected in the *Or select a category* option box, and then click *MIN* in the *Select a function* list box. (You will need to scroll down the list to display *MIN*.)
   d. Click OK.
   e. At the Function Arguments palette, type E4:E16 in the *Number1* text box.
   f. Click OK.

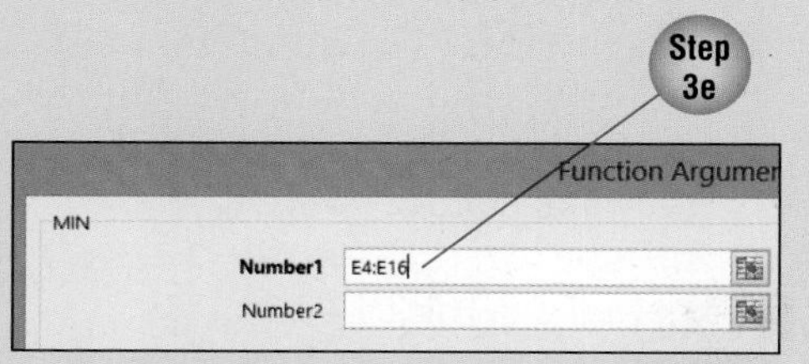

4. Insert a formula to determine the average of all test scores by completing the following steps:
   a. Make cell B21 active.
   b. Click the FORMULAS tab.
   c. Click the Insert Function button in the Function Library group.
   d. At the Insert Function dialog box, make sure *Statistical* is selected in the *Or select a category* option box and then click *AVERAGE* in the *Select a function* list box.
   e. Click OK.
   f. At the Function Arguments palette, make sure the insertion point is positioned in the *Number1* text box with existing text selected, use the mouse pointer to select the range E4:E16 in the worksheet, (you may need to move the palette to display the cells) and then click OK.

5. Save and then print **EL1-C2-P2-DWTests.xlsx**.
6. Change the *70%* values (which were previously *0%*) in cells B14, D14, and D16 to *N/A*. (This will cause the average test scores for Claude Markovits and Douglas Pherson to increase and will change the minimum number and average of all test scores.)
7. Save and then print **EL1-C2-P2-DWTests.xlsx**.

Counting Numbers in a Range

Use the ***COUNT function*** to count the numeric values in a range. For example, in a range of cells containing cells with text and cells with numbers, you can count how many cells in the range contain numbers. In Project 2c, you will use the COUNT function to specify the number of students taking Test 2 and Test 3. In the worksheet, the cells containing the text N/A are not counted by the COUNT function.

Project 2c Counting the Number of Students Taking Tests — Part 3 of 4

1. With **EL1-C2-P2-DWTests.xlsx** open, make cell A22 active.
2. Type Test 2 Completed.
3. Make cell B22 active.
4. Insert a formula counting the number of students who have taken Test 2 by completing the following steps:
   a. With cell B22 active, click in the Formula bar text box.
   b. Type =C.
   c. At the Formula AutoComplete list that displays, scroll down the list until *COUNT* displays and then double-click *COUNT*.
   d. Type C4:C16) and then press Enter.

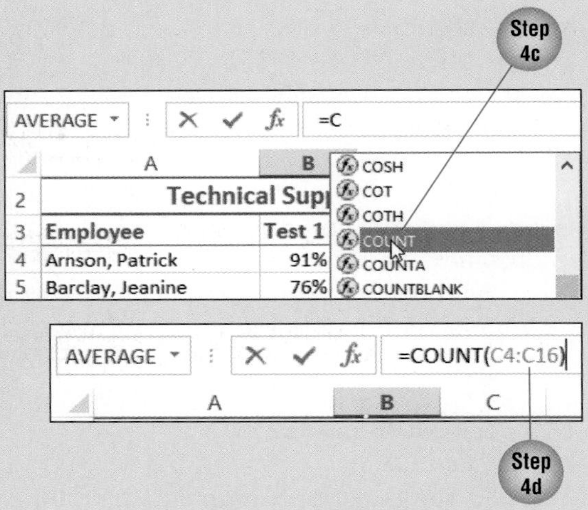

5. Count the number of students who have taken Test 3 by completing the following steps:
   a. Make cell A23 active.
   b. Type Test 3 Completed.
   c. Make cell B23 active.
   d. Click the Insert Function button on the Formula bar.
   e. At the Insert Function dialog box, make sure *Statistical* is selected in the *Or select a category* option box.
   f. Scroll down the list of functions in the *Select a function* list box until *COUNT* is visible and then double-click *COUNT*.
   g. At the formula palette, type D4:D16 in the *Value1* text box and then click OK.
6. Save and then print **EL1-C2-P2-DWTests.xlsx**.
7. Add the test scores by completing the following steps:
   a. Make cell B14 active and then type 68.
   b. Make cell D14 active and then type 70.
   c. Make cell D16 active and then type 55.
   d. Press Enter.
8. Save and then print **EL1-C2-P2-DWTests.xlsx**.

Writing Formulas with the NOW and TODAY Functions

The NOW and TODAY functions are part of the *Date & Time* category of functions. The ***NOW function*** returns the current date and time in a date and time format. The ***TODAY function*** returns the current date in a date format. Both the NOW and TODAY functions automatically update when a workbook is opened. To access the NOW and TODAY functions, click the Date & Time button in the Function Library group on the FORMULAS tab. You can also access these functions at the Insert Function dialog box.

Date & Time

The NOW and TODAY functions can also be updated without closing and then reopening the workbook. To update a workbook that contains a NOW or TODAY function, click the Calculate Now button in the Calculation group on the FORMULAS tab or press the F9 function key.

Calculate Now

Displaying Formulas

In some situations, you may need to display the formulas in a worksheet rather than the results of the formula. For instance, you may want to turn on formulas for auditing purposes or to check formulas for accuracy. Display all formulas in a worksheet, rather than the results, by clicking the FORMULAS tab and then clicking the Show Formulas button in the Formula Auditing group. You can also turn on the display of formulas with the keyboard shortcut Ctrl + `. (This is the grave accent, generally located to the left of the 1 key on the keyboard.) Press Ctrl + ` to turn off the display of formulas or click the Show Formulas button on the FORMULAS tab.

HINT

Press Ctrl + ` to display formulas in a worksheet rather than the results.

Show Formulas

Project 2d Using a NOW Function and Displaying Formulas — Part 4 of 4

1. With **EL1-C2-P2-DWTests.xlsx** open, make cell A26 active and then type Prepared by:.
2. Make cell A27 active and then type your first and last names.
3. Insert the current date and time by completing the following steps:
   a. Make cell A28 active.
   b. Click the Date & Time button in the Function Library group on the FORMULAS tab and then click *NOW* at the drop-down list.
   c. At the Function Arguments palette telling you that the function takes no argument, click OK.
4. Update the time in cell A28 by completing the following steps:
   a. Wait for 1 minute.
   b. Click the Calculate Now button in the Calculations group on the FORMULAS tab.
5. Click the Show Formulas button in the Formula Auditing group to turn on the display of formulas.
6. Print the worksheet with the formulas. (The worksheet will print on two pages.)
7. Press Ctrl + ` to turn off the display of formulas.
8. Save, print, and then close **EL1-C2-P2-DWTests.xlsx**.

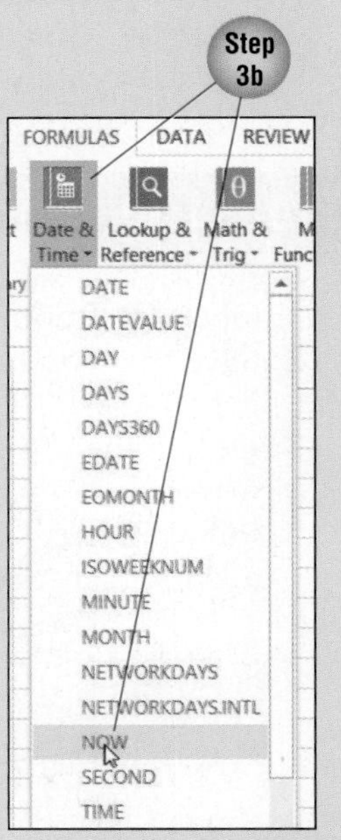

Project 3 Insert Formulas Using Absolute and Mixed Cell References — 4 Parts

You will insert a formula containing an absolute cell reference that determines the effect on earnings with specific increases, insert a formula with multiple absolute cell references that determine the weighted average of scores, and use mixed cell references to determine simple interest.

Using Absolute and Mixed Cell References in Formulas

A reference identifies a cell or a range of cells in a worksheet and can be relative, absolute, or mixed. A ***relative cell reference*** refers to a cell relative to a position in a formula. An ***absolute cell reference*** refers to a cell in a specific location. When a formula is copied, a relative cell reference adjusts while an absolute cell reference remains constant. A ***mixed cell reference*** does both: either the column remains absolute and the row is relative or the column is relative and the row remains absolute. Distinguish among relative, absolute, and mixed cell references using the dollar sign ($). Type a dollar sign before the column and/or row cell reference in a formula to specify that the column or row is an absolute cell reference.

Using an Absolute Cell Reference in a Formula

In this chapter, you have learned to copy a relative formula. For example, if the formula *=SUM(A2:C2)* in cell D2 is copied relatively to cell D3, the formula changes to *=SUM(A3:C3)*. In some situations, you may want a formula to contain an absolute cell reference, which always refers to a cell in a specific location. In Project 3a, you will add a column for projected job earnings and then perform "What if?" situations using a formula with an absolute cell reference. To identify an absolute cell reference, insert a $ sign before the row and the column. For example, the absolute cell reference C12 would be typed as *$C$12* in a formula.

Project 3a Inserting and Copying a Formula with an Absolute Cell Reference — Part 1 of 4

1. Open **CCReports.xlsx**.
2. Save the workbook with Save As and name it **EL1-C2-P3-CCReports**.
3. Determine the effect on actual job earnings with a 10% increase by completing the following steps:
   a. Make cell C3 active, type the formula =B3*$B$12, and then press Enter.
   b. Make cell C3 active and then use the fill handle to copy the formula to cells C4 through C10.
   c. Make cell C3 active, click the Accounting Number Format button on the HOME tab, and then click the Decrease Decimal button twice.

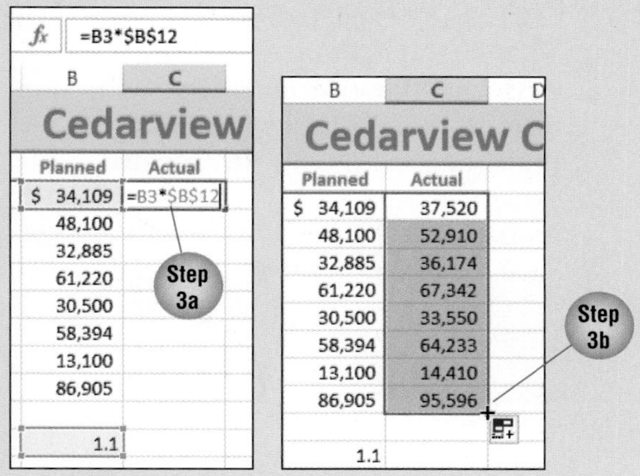

4. Save and then print **EL1-C2-P3-CCReports.xlsx**.
5. With the worksheet still open, determine the effect on actual job earnings with a 10% decrease by completing the following steps:
   a. Make cell B12 active.
   b. Type 0.9 and then press Enter.
6. Save and then print the **EL1-C2-P3-CCReports.xlsx**.
7. Determine the effects on actual job earnings with a 20% increase. (To do this, type 1.2 in cell B12 and then press Enter.)
8. Save and then print **EL1-C2-P3-CCReports.xlsx**.

B	C
Cedarview	
Planned	Actual
$ 34,109	$ 30,698
48,100	43,290
32,885	29,597
61,220	55,098
30,500	27,450
58,394	52,555
13,100	11,790
86,905	78,215
0.9	

Step 5b

In Project 3a, you created a formula with one absolute cell reference. You can also create a formula with multiple absolute cell references. For example, in Project 3b. you will create a formula that contains both relative and absolute cell references to determine the average of training scores based on specific weight percentages. In a weighted average, some scores have more value (weight) than others. For example, in project 3b, you will create a formula that determines the weighted average of training scores that gives more weight to the Carpentry percentages then the Plumbing or Electrical percentages.

Project 3b Inserting and Copying a Formula with Multiple Absolute Cell References

Part 2 of 4

1. With **EL1-C2-P3-CCReports.xlsx** open, insert the following formulas:
   a. Insert a formula in cell B23 that averages the percentages in cells B17 through B22.
   b. Copy the formula in cell B23 to the right to cells C23 and D23.
2. Insert a formula that determines the weighted average of training scores by completing the following steps:
   a. Make cell E17 active.
   b. Type the following formula:
      =$B$24*B17+$C$24*C17+$D$24*D17
   c. Press the Enter key.
   d. Copy the formula in cell E17 down to cells E18 through E22.
   e. With cells E17 through E22 selected, click the Decrease Decimal button three times.
3. Save and then print **EL1-C2-P3-CCReports.xlsx**.
4. With the worksheet still open, determine the effect on weighted training scores if the weighted values change by completing the following steps:
   a. Make cell B24 active, type 30, and then press Enter.
   b. Make cell D24 active, type 40, and then press Enter.
5. Save and then print **EL1-C2-P3-CCReports.xlsx**.

Employee Training				
Name	Plumbing	Electrical	Carpentry	Weighted Average
Allesandro	76%	80%	84%	80%
Ellington	66%	72%	64%	67%
Goodman	90%	88%	94%	91%
Huntington	76%	82%	88%	83%
Kaplan-Downing	90%	84%	92%	89%
Larimore	58%	62%	60%	60%
Training Averages	76%	78%	80%	
Training Weights	30%	30%	40%	

Step 4a

Step 4b

Using a Mixed Cell Reference in a Formula

The formula you created in Step 3a in Project 3a contained a relative cell reference (B3) and an absolute cell reference ($B$12). A formula can also contain a mixed cell reference. As stated earlier, in a mixed cell reference, either the column remains absolute and the row is relative or the column is relative and the row remains absolute. In Project 3c, you will insert a number of formulas—two of which will contain mixed cell references. You will insert the formula *=E29*E$26* to calculate withholding tax and *=E29*H$36* to calculate social security tax. The dollar sign before each row indicates that the row is an absolute cell reference.

Project 3c **Determining Payroll Using Formulas with Absolute and Mixed Cell References** **Part 3 of 4**

1. With **EL1-C2-P3-CCReports.xlsx** open, make cell E29 active and then type the following formula that calculates the gross pay, including overtime (press Enter after typing each of the formulas):
   =(B29*C29+(B29*$B$36*D29))
2. Copy the formula in cell E29 down to cells E30 through E34.
3. Make cell F29 active and then type the following formula that calculates the amount of withholding tax:
   =E29*E$36
4. Copy the formula in cell F29 down to cells F30 through F34.
5. Make cell G29 active and then type the following formula that calculates the amount of social security tax:
   =E29*H$36
6. Copy the formula in cell G29 down to cells G30 through G34.
7. Make cell H29 active and then type the following formula that calculates net pay:
   =E29-(F29+G29)
8. Copy the formula in cell H29 down to cells H30 through H34.
9. Select cells E29 through H29 and then click the Accounting Number Format button.
10. Save **EL1-C2-P3-CCReports.xlsx**.

As you learned in Project 3c, a formula can contain a mixed cell reference. In Project 3d, you will create the formula *=$A41*B$40*. In the first cell reference in the formula, *$A41*, the column is absolute and the row is relative. In the second cell reference, *B$40*, the column is relative and the row is absolute. The formula containing the mixed cell reference allows you to fill in the column and row data using only one formula.

Identify an absolute or mixed cell reference by typing a dollar sign before the column and/or row reference or press the F4 function key to cycle through the various cell references. For example, type *=A41* in a cell, press F4, and the cell reference changes to *=$A$41*. Press F4 again and the cell reference changes to *=A$41*. The next time you press F4, the cell reference changes to *=$A41* and if you press it again, the cell reference changes back to *=A41*.

Project 3d Determining Simple Interest Using a Formula with Mixed Cell References **Part 4 of 4**

1. With **EL1-C2-P3-CCReports.xlsx** open, make cell B41 the active cell and then insert a formula containing mixed cell references by completing the following steps:
   a. Type =A41 and then press the F4 function key three times. (This changes the cell reference to *$A41*.)
   b. Type *B40 and then press the F4 function key twice. (This changes the cell reference to *B$40*.)
   c. Make sure the formula displays as *=$A41*B$40* and then press Enter.

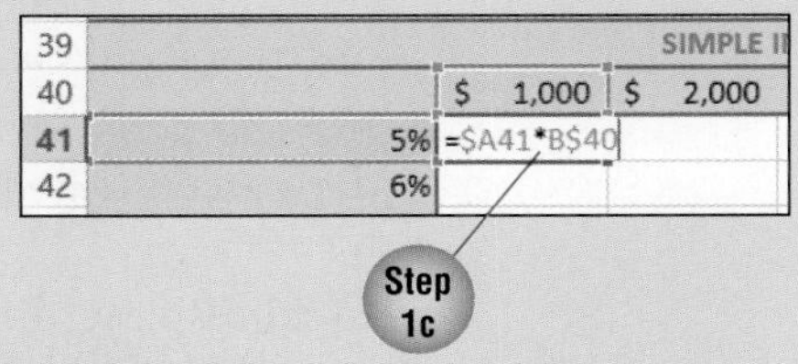

2. Copy the formula to the right by completing the following steps:
   a. Make cell B41 active and then use the fill handle to copy the formula right to cell F41.
   b. With cells B41 through F41 selected, use the fill handle to copy the formula down to cell F51.

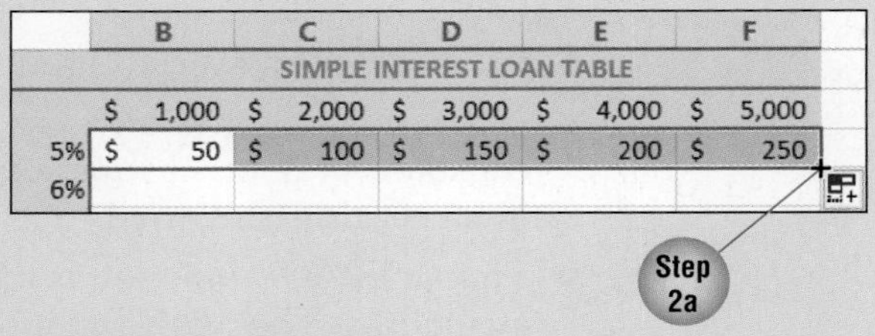

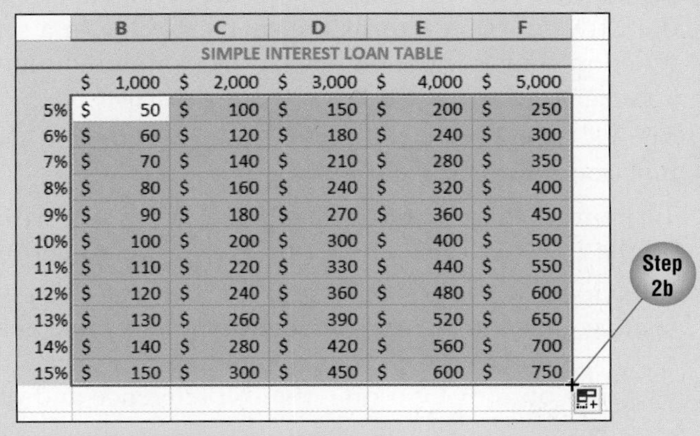

	B	C	D	E	F
	SIMPLE INTEREST LOAN TABLE				
	$ 1,000	$ 2,000	$ 3,000	$ 4,000	$ 5,000
5%	$ 50	$ 100	$ 150	$ 200	$ 250
6%	$ 60	$ 120	$ 180	$ 240	$ 300
7%	$ 70	$ 140	$ 210	$ 280	$ 350
8%	$ 80	$ 160	$ 240	$ 320	$ 400
9%	$ 90	$ 180	$ 270	$ 360	$ 450
10%	$ 100	$ 200	$ 300	$ 400	$ 500
11%	$ 110	$ 220	$ 330	$ 440	$ 550
12%	$ 120	$ 240	$ 360	$ 480	$ 600
13%	$ 130	$ 260	$ 390	$ 520	$ 650
14%	$ 140	$ 280	$ 420	$ 560	$ 700
15%	$ 150	$ 300	$ 450	$ 600	$ 750

3. Save, print, and then close **EL1-C2-P3-CCReports.xlsx**.

Chapter Summary

- Type a formula in a cell and the formula displays in the cell as well as in the Formula bar. If cell entries are changed, a formula automatically recalculates the values and inserts the result in the cell.
- Create your own formula with commonly used operators, such as addition (+), subtraction (-), multiplication (*), division (/), percentage (%), and exponentiation (^). When writing a formula, begin with the equals sign (=).
- Excel uses the same order of operations as algebra and that order can be modified by adding parentheses around certain parts of a formula.

- Copy a formula to other cells in a row or column with the Fill button in the Editing group on the HOME tab or with the fill handle that displays in the bottom right corner of the active cell.
- Double-click in a cell containing a formula and the cell references will display with a colored border and cell shading.
- Another method for writing a formula is to point to specific cells that are part of the formula as the formula is being built.
- If Excel detects an error in a formula, a Trace Error button appears and a dark green triangle displays in the upper left corner of the cell containing the formula.
- Excel displays different error codes for different formula errors. An error code helps identify an error in a formula by providing information on the specific issue.
- Excel performs over 300 functions that are divided into 13 categories.
- A function operates on an argument, which may consist of a cell reference, a constant, or another function. When a value calculated by a formula is inserted in a cell, this is referred to as returning the result.
- The AVERAGE function returns the average (arithmetic mean) of the arguments. The MAX function returns the largest value in a set of values and the MIN function returns the smallest value in a set of values. The COUNT function counts the number of cells containing numbers within the list of arguments.
- The NOW function returns the current date and time and the TODAY function returns the current date.
- Turn on the display of formulas in a worksheet with the Show Formulas button on the FORMULAS tab or with the keyboard shortcut Ctrl + ` (grave accent).
- A reference identifies a cell or a range of cells in a worksheet and can be relative, absolute, or mixed. Identify an absolute cell reference by inserting a dollar sign ($) before the column and row. Cycle through the various cell reference options by typing the cell reference and then pressing F4.

Commands Review

FEATURE	RIBBON TAB, GROUP	BUTTON	KEYBOARD SHORTCUT
display formulas	FORMULAS, Formula Auditing		Ctrl + `
cycle through cell references			F4
Insert Function dialog box	FORMULAS, Function Library	fx	Shift + F3
SUM function	HOME, Editing OR FORMULAS, Function Library	Σ	Alt + =
update formulas	FORMULAS, Calculation		F9

Concepts Check Test Your Knowledge SNAP

Completion: In the space provided at the right, indicate the correct term, symbol, or command.

1. When typing a formula, begin the formula with this sign. equals
2. This is the operator for division that is used when writing a formula. ____________
3. This is the operator for multiplication that is used when writing a formula. ____________
4. As an alternative to the fill handle, use this button to copy a formula relatively in a worksheet. ____________
5. To display cell references for a formula, perform this action on a cell containing a formula. ____________
6. A formula's order of operations can be modified with these. ____________
7. Excel inserts this symbol in a cell that may contain a possible error. ____________
8. A function operates on this, which may consist of a constant, a cell reference, or another function. ____________
9. This function returns the largest value in a set of values. ____________
10. This is the keyboard shortcut to display formulas in a worksheet. ____________
11. This function returns the current date and time. ____________
12. To identify an absolute cell reference, type this symbol before the column and row. ____________

Skills Check Assess Your Performance

Assessment 1

INSERT AVERAGE, MAX, AND MIN FUNCTIONS

SNAP Grade It

1. Open **DISalesAnalysis.xlsx**.
2. Save the workbook with Save As and name it **EL1-C2-A1-DISalesAnalysis**.
3. Use the AVERAGE function to determine the monthly sales (cells H4 through H9).
4. Apply accounting formatting with no places past the decimal point to cell H4.
5. Total each monthly column, including the *Average* column (cells B10 through H10).
6. Use the MAX function to determine the highest monthly total (for cells B10 through G10) and insert the amount in cell B11.
7. Use the MIN function to determine the lowest monthly total (for cells B10 through G10) and insert the amount in cell B12.
8. Save, print, and then close **EL1-C2-A1-DISalesAnalysis.xlsx**.

Assessment 2

INSERT THE SUM FUNCTION AND ENTER FORMULAS WITH MATHEMATICAL OPERATORS

SNAP Grade It

1. Open **CMQrtlyIncome.xlsx**.
2. Save the workbook with Save As and name it **EL1-C2-A2-CMQrtlyIncome**.
3. The manager of Capstan Marine needs a condensed quarterly statement of income for the third quarter. Insert each of the following formulas by typing the formula, using the pointing method, or using the AutoSum button.
   a. In cell B7, subtract cost of goods sold from sales by entering =B5-B6.
   b. In cell B12, add the three expenses by entering =SUM(B9:B11).
   c. In cell B14, subtract total expenses from gross margin by entering =B7-B12.
   d. In cell B15, multiply net income before taxes by 22% and then subtract that value from net income before taxes by entering =B14-(B14*22%).
4. Relatively copy the formulas in column B to columns C and D using the fill handle as follows.
   a. Fill the formula in cell B7 to cells C7 and D7 .
   b. Fill the formula in cell B12 to cells C12 and D12.
   c. Fill the formula in cell B14 to C14 and D14.
   d. Fill the formula in cell B15 to C15 and D15.
5. Insert the total in cell E5 by using the AutoSum button to add the range B5:D5.
6. Fill the SUM function in cell E5 to the range E6:E15. (Cells E8 and E13 will contain hyphens.)
7. Apply accounting formatting with a dollar sign and one place past the decimal point to cells B5 through E5.
8. Insert a TODAY function in cell A18.
9. Save, print, and then close **EL1-C2-A2-CMQrtlyIncome.xlsx**.

Assessment 3

WRITE FORMULAS WITH ABSOLUTE CELL REFERENCES

SNAP Grade It

1. Open **CCQuotas.xlsx**.
2. Save the workbook with Save As and name it **EL1-C2-A3-CCQuotas**.
3. Make the following changes to the worksheet:
   a. Insert a formula using an absolute reference to determine the projected quotas with a 10% increase from the current quota.
   b. Save and then print **EL1-C2-A3-CCQuotas.xlsx**.
   c. Determine the projected quotas with a 15% increase from the current quota by changing cell A15 to *15% Increase* and cell B15 to *1.15*.
   d. Save and then print **EL1-C2-A3-CCQuotas.xlsx**.
   e. Determine the projected quotas with a 20% increase from the current quota.
4. Apply accounting formatting with no places after the decimal point to cell C4.
5. Save, print, and then close **EL1-C2-A3-CCQuotas.xlsx**.

Assessment 4

WRITE FORMULAS WITH MIXED CELL REFERENCES

SNAP Grade It

1. Open **AASMileageChart.xlsx**.
2. Save the workbook with Save As and name it **EL1-C2-A4-AASMileageChart**.
3. Determine the mileage range of vehicles that have differing miles per gallon and fuel tank capacites by following these steps:
   a. In cell C5, multiply vehicle fuel tank capacity by vehicle miles per gallon rating by entering **=B5*C4**.
   b. Change the cell references in the formula so when it is copied, it will multiply the correct values in the chart. Either type dollar signs in the formula or press the F4 function key until the correct mixed cell references display. ***Hint: Refer to Project 3d for assistance.***
   c. Use the fill handle to complete the chart (fill without formatting).
4. Save, print, and then close **EL1-C2-A4-AASMileageChart.xlsx**.

Assessment 5

USE HELP TO LEARN ABOUT EXCEL OPTIONS

Help

1. Learn more about using parentheses within formulas by completing the following steps:
   a. At a blank workbook, display the Excel Help window, click in the search text box, type **overview of formulas**, and then press Enter.
   b. Click the Overview of formulas article hyperlink and then scroll down approximately one-third of the article to the heading *Use of parentheses*.
   c. Read the information about using parentheses in formulas.
   d. Close the Excel Help window.
2. Open **ParenFormulas.xlsx**.
3. Save the workbook with Save As and name it **EL1-C2-A5-ParenFormulas**.
4. Change the results of the formulas individually (do not use the fill handle) in the range B6:B10 by editing the formulas to include parentheses. Consider writing the formulas on paper before inserting them in the cells. ***Note: The last formula will require nested parentheses.***

5. Once the formulas have been edited, compare the new results to the values in column C.
6. Make sure that YES displays in column D for each formula.
7. Turn on the display of formulas.
8. Save, print, and then close **EL1-C2-A5-ParenFormulas.xlsx**.

Visual Benchmark Demonstrate Your Proficiency

CREATE A WORKSHEET AND INSERT FORMULAS

1. At a blank workbook, type the data in the cells indicated in Figure 2.4 but **do not** type the data in the following cells. Instead, insert the formulas as indicated:
   - Cells D3 through D9: Insert a formula that calculates the salary.
   - Cells D14 through D19: Insert a formula that calculates the differences.
   - Cells B29 through D29: Insert a formula that calculates the averages.
   - Cells E24 through E28: Insert a formula that calculates the weighted average of test scores. ***Hint: Refer to Project 3b, Step 2, for assistance on writing a formula with weighted averages.***

   The results of your formulas should match the results you see in the figure.
2. Apply any other formatting so your worksheet looks similar to the worksheet shown in Figure 2.4.
3. Save the workbook and name it **EL1-C2-VB-Formulas**.
4. Print **EL1-C2-VB-Formulas.xlsx**.
5. Press Ctrl + ` to turn on the display of formulas and then print the worksheet again.
6. Turn off the display of formulas and then close the workbook.

Figure 2.4 Visual Benchmark

	A	B	C	D	E	F
1	Weekly Payroll					
2	Employee	Hours	Rate	Salary		
3	Alvarez, Rita	40	$ 22.50	$ 900.00		
4	Campbell, Owen	15	22.50	337.50		
5	Heitmann, Luanne	25	19.00	475.00		
6	Malina, Susan	40	18.75	750.00		
7	Parker, Kenneth	40	18.75	750.00		
8	Reitz, Collette	20	15.00	300.00		
9	Shepard, Gregory	15	12.00	180.00		
10						
11						
12	Construction Projects					
13	Project	Projected	Actual	Difference		
14	South Cascade	$145,000	$ 141,597	$ (3,403)		
15	Rogue River Park	120,000	124,670	4,670		
16	Meridian	120,500	99,450	(21,050)		
17	Lowell Ridge	95,250	98,455	3,205		
18	Walker Canyon	70,000	68,420	(1,580)		
19	Nettleson Creek	52,000	49,517	(2,483)		
20						
21						
22	Test Scores					
23	Employee	Test No. 1	Test No. 2	Test No. 3	Wgt. Avg.	
24	Coffey, Annette	62%	64%	76%	70%	
25	Halverson, Ted	88%	96%	90%	91%	
26	Kohler, Jeremy	80%	76%	82%	80%	
27	McKnight, Carol	68%	72%	78%	74%	
28	Parkhurst, Jody	98%	96%	98%	98%	
29	Test Averages	79%	81%	85%		
30	Test Weights	25%	25%	50%		
31						

Case Study Apply Your Skills

Part 1

You are the office manager for Allenmore Auto Sales and are responsible for preparing the monthly sales worksheet. Open **AASFebSales.xlsx** and then save the workbook with Save As and name it **EL1-C2-CS-AASFebSales**. Complete the workbook by inserting the following formulas:

- In column F, insert a formula that displays the gross profit, which is the price minus the dealer cost.
- In column H, insert a formula that multiplies the gross profit by the commission percentage.
- In column I, insert a formula that displays the net profit, which is the gross profit minus the total commission.
- Apply accounting formatting with a dollar sign to the amounts in cells D4, E4, F4, H4, and I4.

Save the workbook, print the workbook (it will print on two pages), and then close the workbook.

Part 2

The sales manager at Allenmore Auto Sales has asked you to determine the percentage of total commissions each salesperson has earned for the month of February. Open **AASFebCommissions.xlsx** and then save the workbook with Save As and name it **EL1-C2-CS-AASFebCommissions**. Insert a formula in cell C5 that divides B5 by the amount in cell C3. Use an absolute cell reference for cell C3 when writing the formula. Copy the formula down to cells C6 through C12. Save, print, and then close the workbook.

Part 3

You have created a workbook for automobile trade-ins for the month of February. The sales manager wants used automobiles to be wholesaled if they are not sold within a specific period of time. She wants you to determine the date each February trade-in is to be wholesaled. She wants any used automobile older than 2010 to be wholesaled after 45 days and any automobile newer than 2009 to be wholesaled after 60 days. Open **AASFebTradeIns.xlsx** and then save the workbook with Save As and name it **EL1-C2-CS-AASFebTradeIns**. Insert a formula in column G that adds 45 days to the date in column B for trade-ins 2009 and older and adds 60 days to trade-ins 2010 and newer. Save, print, and then close the workbook.

Part 4

Help

The sales manager has asked you to locate at least two websites that provide estimates on the value of used automobiles (such as Kelley Blue Book (kbb.com) and Edmunds.com). She wants you to add at least two hyperlinks to the February trade-ins workbook. Sales people can use the hyperlinks in the worksheet to quickly determine the value of a used automobile. Use the Help feature to learn how to create hyperlinks in Excel. Open the **EL1-C2-CS-AASFebTradeIns.xlsx** workbook and save it with Save As and name it **EL1-C2-CS-AASFebTradeIns-2**. Add at least two hyperlinks to the workbook that link to websites that provide estimates on the value of used automobiles. Save, print, and then close the workbook.

MICROSOFT® EXCEL®

CHAPTER 3

Formatting an Excel Worksheet

PERFORMANCE OBJECTIVES

Upon successful completion of Chapter 3, you will be able to:

- **Change column widths**
- **Change row heights**
- **Insert rows and columns in a worksheet**
- **Delete cells, rows, and columns in a worksheet**
- **Clear data in cells**
- **Apply formatting to data in cells**
- **Apply formatting to selected data using the Mini toolbar**
- **Apply a theme and customize the theme font and color**
- **Format numbers**
- **Repeat the last action**
- **Automate formatting with Format Painter**
- **Hide and unhide rows and columns**

SNAP

Tutorials

3.1 Adjusting Column Width and Row Height

3.2 Inserting and Deleting Columns and Rows

3.3 Applying Font Formatting

3.4 Applying Alignment Formatting

3.5 Applying Cell Styles and Themes

3.6 Formatting Numbers

3.7 Adding Borders and Shading to Cells

3.8 Using Format Painter and the Repeat Command

3.9 Hiding and Unhiding Columns and/or Rows

The appearance of a worksheet on the screen and how it looks when printed is called the ***format***. In Chapter 1, you learned how to apply basic formatting to cells in a worksheet. Additional types of formatting you may want to apply to a worksheet include changing column width and row height; applying character formatting such as bold, italic, and underlining; specifying number formatting; inserting and deleting rows and columns; and applying borders, shading, and patterns to cells. You can also apply formatting to a worksheet with a theme. A theme is a set of formatting choices that include colors and fonts. Model answers for this chapter's projects appear on the following page.

Excel
EL1C3

Note: Before beginning the projects, copy to your storage medium the EL1C3 subfolder from the EL1 folder on the CD that accompanies this textbook and then make EL1C3 the active folder.

Model Answers

Capstan Marine Products				
Purchasing Department				
Company	***Product #***	***Price***	***Number***	***Total***
RD Manufacturing	240-490-B	$ 85.75	7	$ 600.25
	443-22-0	148.50	8	1,188.00
	855-495	42.75	5	213.75
Ray Enterprises	S894-T	4.99	30	149.70
	B-3448	25.50	12	306.00
	43-GB-39	45.00	20	900.00
Sunrise Corporation	341-453	19.99	8	159.92
	CT-342	304.75	5	1,523.75
	83-492	9.75	35	341.25
	L-756-M	95.40	4	381.60
Geneva Systems	340-19	15.99	20	319.80
	T-3491-S	450.50	5	2,252.50
	900-599	35.95	15	539.25
	43-49CE	120.00	5	600.00
	Total			$9,475.77

Project 1 Format a Product Pricing Worksheet

EL1-C3-P1-CMProducts.xlsx

Stanton & Barnett Associates							
Weekly Payroll							
Employee	Hrly. Rate	Hours	Overtime	Gross	W/H Tax	SS Tax	Net
Lowell	$ 40.00	40	1	$ 1,660.00	$ 464.80	$ 126.99	$ 1,068.21
McIntyre	$ 40.00	40	3	$ 1,780.00	$ 498.40	$ 136.17	$ 1,145.43
Rawlings	$ 37.50	30	0	$ 1,125.00	$ 315.00	$ 86.06	$ 723.94
Fratzke	$ 32.00	40	2	$ 1,376.00	$ 385.28	$ 105.26	$ 885.46
Singleton	$ 25.00	25	0	$ 625.00	$ 175.00	$ 47.81	$ 402.19
Gleason	$ 22.00	40	1	$ 913.00	$ 255.64	$ 69.84	$ 587.52
Overtime	1.5		W/H Rate	28%		SS Rate	7.65%

Project 2 Apply a Theme to a Payroll Worksheet

EL1-C3-P2-SBAPayroll.xlsx

REAL PHOTOGRAPHY					
Invoices					
Invoice #	Client #	Service	Amount	Tax	Amount Due
2930	03-392	Family Portraits	$ 450.00	8.5%	$ 488.25
2942	02-498	Wedding Portraits	$ 1,075.00	8.8%	$ 1,169.60
2002	11-279	Development	$ 225.00	0.0%	$ 225.00
2007	04-325	Sports Portraits	$ 750.00	8.5%	$ 813.75
2376	03-392	Senior Portraits	$ 850.00	8.5%	$ 922.25
2129	11-279	Development	$ 350.00	0.0%	$ 350.00
2048	11-325	Wedding Portraits	$ 875.00	8.5%	$ 949.38
2054	04-325	Sports Portraits	$ 750.00	8.5%	$ 813.75
2064	05-665	Family Portraits	$ 560.00	8.8%	$ 609.28
2077	11-279	Development	$ 400.00	0.0%	$ 400.00
2079	04-325	Sports Portraits	$ 600.00	8.5%	$ 651.00
2908	55-340	Senior Portraits	$ 725.00	8.8%	$ 788.80
3001	11-279	Development	$ 310.00	8.8%	$ 337.28

Project 3 Format an Invoices Worksheet

EL1-C3-P3-RPInvoices.xlsx

Harris & Briggs Construction				
Preferred Customer	Job #	Projected	Actual	Difference
Sellar Corporation	2130	$ 34,109	$ 30,349	$ (3,760)
Main Street Photos	1201	$ 48,100	$ 48,290	$ 190
Sunset Automotive	318	$ 32,885	$ 34,192	$ 1,307
Linstrom Enterprises	1009	$ 61,220	$ 63,293	$ 2,073
Morcos Media	676	$ 30,500	$ 29,400	$ (1,100)
Green Valley Optics	2117	$ 52,394	$ 55,309	$ 2,915
Detailed Designs	983	$ 13,100	$ 12,398	$ (702)
Summit Services	899	$ 12,000	$ 11,734	$ (266)
Arrowstar Company	786	$ 88,905	$ 87,534	$ (1,371)

Project 4 Format a Company Budget Worksheet

EL1-C3-P4-HBCJobs.xlsx

Project 1 Format a Product Pricing Worksheet — 7 Parts

You will open a workbook containing a worksheet with product pricing data and then format the worksheet by changing column widths and row heights, inserting and deleting rows and columns, and clearing data in cells. You will also apply font and alignment formatting to data in cells.

Changing Column Width

Columns in a worksheet are the same width by default. In some worksheets, you may want to change column widths to accommodate more or less data. Change column width using the mouse on column boundaries or at a dialog box.

Changing Column Width Using Column Boundaries

As you learned in Chapter 1, you can adjust the width of a column by dragging the column boundary line or adjust a column width to the longest entry by double-clicking the boundary line. When you drag a column boundary, the column width displays in a box above the mouse pointer. The column width number that displays represents the average number of characters in the standard font that can fit in a cell.

You can change the width of selected adjacent columns at the same time. To do this, select the columns and then drag one of the column boundaries within the selected columns. As you drag the boundary, the column width changes for all selected columns. To select adjacent columns, position the cell pointer on the first desired column header (the mouse pointer turns into a black, down-pointing arrow), hold down the left mouse button, drag the cell pointer to the last desired column header, and then release the mouse button.

HINT

To change the width of all columns in a worksheet, click the Select All button and then drag a column boundary to the desired position.

Project 1a Changing Column Width Using a Column Boundary — Part 1 of 7

1. Open **CMProducts.xlsx**.
2. Save the workbook with Save As and name it **EL1-C3-P1-CMProducts**.
3. Insert a formula in cell D2 that multiplies the price in cell B2 with the number in cell C2. Copy the formula in cell D2 down to cells D3 through D14.
4. Change the width of column D by completing the following steps:
   a. Position the mouse pointer on the column boundary in the column header between columns D and E until it turns into a double-headed arrow pointing left and right.
   b. Hold down the left mouse button, drag the column boundary to the right until *Width: 11.00 (106 pixels)* displays in the box, and then release the mouse button.

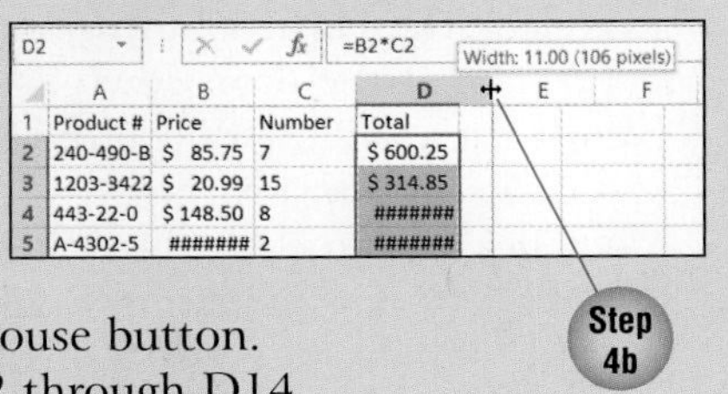

5. Make cell D15 active and then insert the sum of cells D2 through D14.
6. Change the width of columns A and B by completing the following steps:
   a. Select columns A and B. To do this, position the cell pointer on the column A header, hold down the left mouse button, drag the cell pointer to the column B header, and then release the mouse button.

b. Position the cell pointer on the column boundary between columns A and B until it turns into a double-headed arrow pointing left and right.

c. Hold down the left mouse button, drag the column boundary to the right until *Width: 10.33 (100 pixels)* displays in the box, and then release the mouse button.

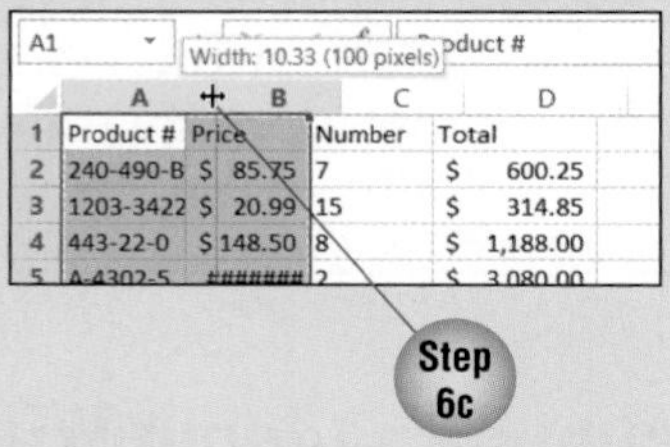

7. Adjust the width of column C to accommodate the longest entry by double-clicking on the column boundary between columns C and D.
8. Save **EL1-C3-P1-CMProducts.xlsx**.

Changing Column Width at the Column Width Dialog Box

Quick Steps

Change Column Width

Drag column boundary line.

OR

Double-click column boundary.

OR

1. Click Format button.
2. Click *Column Width* at drop-down list.
3. Type desired width.
4. Click OK.

Format

At the Column Width dialog box, shown in Figure 3.1, you can specify a column width number. Increase the column width number to make the column wider or decrease the column width number to make the column narrower.

To display the Column Width dialog box, click the Format button in the Cells group on the HOME tab and then click *Column Width* at the drop-down list. At the Column Width dialog box, type the number representing the average number of characters in the standard font that you want to fit in the column and then press Enter or click OK.

Figure 3.1 Column Width Dialog Box

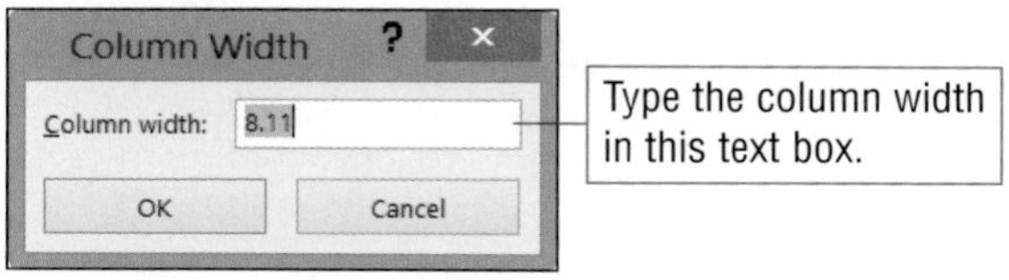

Project 1b **Changing Column Width at the Column Width Dialog Box** **Part 2 of 7**

1. With **EL1-C3-P1-CMProducts.xlsx** open, change the width of column A by completing the following steps:
   a. Make any cell in column A active.
   b. Click the Format button in the Cells group on the HOME tab and then click *Column Width* at the drop-down list.
   c. At the Column Width dialog box, type 12.7 in the *Column width* text box.
   d. Click OK to close the dialog box.

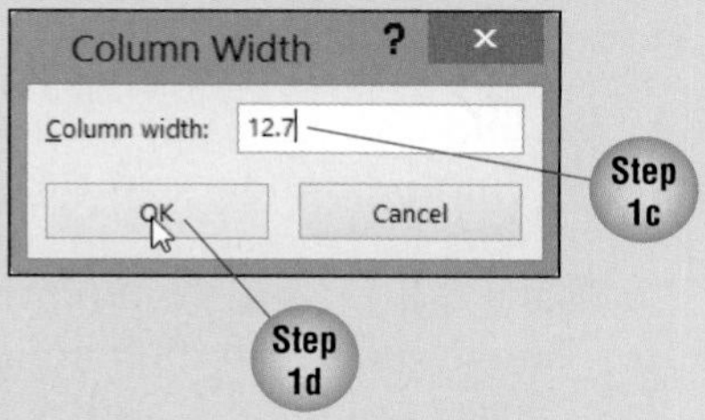

2. Make any cell in column B active and then change the width of column B to *12.5* by completing steps similar to those in Step 1.
3. Make any cell in column C active and then change the width of column C to *8* by completing steps similar to those in Step 1.
4. Save **EL1-C3-P1-CMProducts.xlsx**.

Changing Row Height

Row height can be changed in much the same manner as column width. For example, you can change the row height using the mouse on a row boundary or at the Row Height dialog box. Change row height using a row boundary in the same manner as you learned to change column width. To do this, position the cell pointer on the boundary between rows in the row header until it turns into a double-headed arrow pointing up and down, hold down the left mouse button, drag up or down until the row is the desired height, and then release the mouse button.

The height of selected rows that are adjacent can be changed at the same time. (The height of nonadjacent rows will not all change at the same time.) To do this, select the rows and then drag one of the row boundaries within the selected rows. As the boundary is being dragged, the row height changes for all selected rows.

As a row boundary is being dragged, the row height displays in a box above the mouse pointer. The row height number that displays represents a point measurement. A vertical inch contains approximately 72 points. Increase the point size to increase the row height; decrease the point size to decrease the row height.

At the Row Height dialog box, shown in Figure 3.2, you can specify a row height number. To display the Row Height dialog box, click the Format button in the Cells group on the HOME tab and then click *Row Height* at the drop-down list.

Quick Steps

Change Row Height

Drag row boundary line.

OR

1. Click Format button.
2. Click *Row Height* at drop-down list.
3. Type desired height.
4. Click OK.

HINT

To change the height of all rows in a worksheet, click the Select All button and then drag a row boundary to the desired position.

HINT

Excel measures row height in points and column width in characters.

Figure 3.2 Row Height Dialog Box

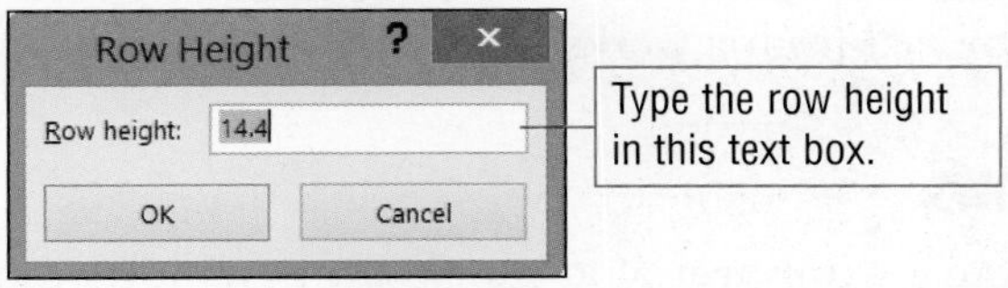

Project 1c **Changing Row Height** **Part 3 of 7**

1. With **EL1-C3-P1-CMProducts.xlsx** open, change the height of row 1 by completing the following steps:
   a. Position the cell pointer in the row header on the row boundary between rows 1 and 2 until it turns into a double-headed arrow pointing up and down.
   b. Hold down the left mouse button, drag the row boundary down until *Height: 19.80 (33 pixels)* displays in the box, and then release the mouse button.

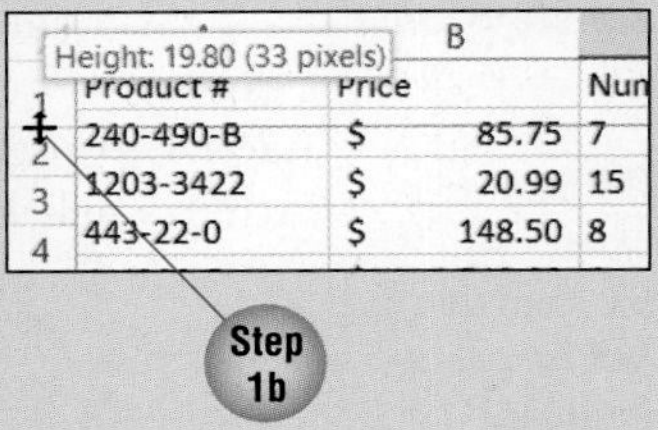

2. Change the height of rows 2 through 14 by completing the following steps:
   a. Select rows 2 through 14. To do this, position the cell pointer on the number 2 in the row header, hold down the left mouse button, drag the cell pointer to the number 14 in the row header, and then release the mouse button.
   b. Position the cell pointer on the row boundary between rows 2 and 3 until it turns into a double-headed arrow pointing up and down.

c. Hold down the left mouse button, drag the row boundary down until *Height: 16.80 (28 pixels)* displays in the box, and then release the mouse button.

3. Change the height of row 15 by completing the following steps:
   a. Make cell A15 active.
   b. Click the Format button in the Cells group on the HOME tab and then click *Row Height* at the drop-down list.
   c. At the Row Height dialog box, type 20 in the *Row height* text box and then click OK.

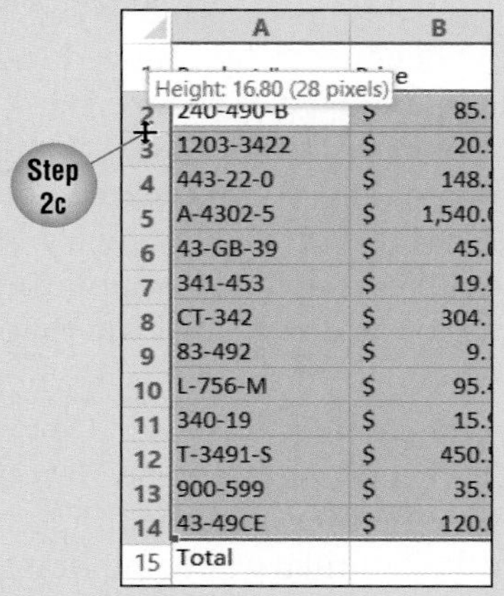

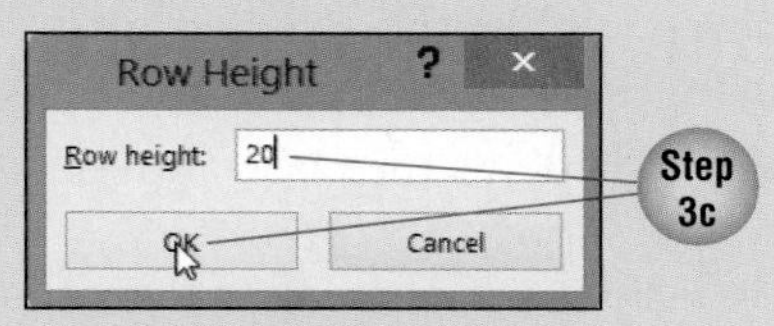

4. Save **EL1-C3-P1-CMProducts.xlsx**.

HINT

When you insert cells, rows, or columns in a worksheet, all references affected by the insertion are automatically adjusted.

Inserting and Deleting Cells, Rows, and Columns

New data may need to be included in an existing worksheet. For example, a row or several rows of new data may need to be inserted into a worksheet or data may need to be removed from a worksheet.

Inserting Rows

Quick Steps

Insert a Row
Click Insert button.
OR
1. Click Insert button arrow.
2. Click *Insert Sheet Rows* at drop-down list.

OR
1. Click Insert button arrow.
2. Click *Insert Cells*.
3. Click *Entire row* in dialog box.
4. Click OK.

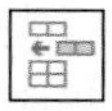

Insert

After you create a worksheet, you can add (insert) rows to the worksheet. Insert a row with the Insert button in the Cells group on the HOME tab or with options at the Insert dialog box. By default, a row is inserted above the row containing the active cell. To insert a row in a worksheet, select the row below where the row is to be inserted and then click the Insert button. If you want to insert more than one row, select the number of rows in the worksheet that you want inserted and then click the Insert button.

You can also insert a row by making a cell active in the row below where the row is to be inserted, clicking the Insert button arrow, and then clicking *Insert Sheet Rows*. Another method for inserting a row is to click the Insert button arrow and then click *Insert Cells*. This displays the Insert dialog box, as shown in Figure 3.3. At the Insert dialog box, click *Entire row*. This inserts a row above the active cell.

Figure 3.3 Insert Dialog Box

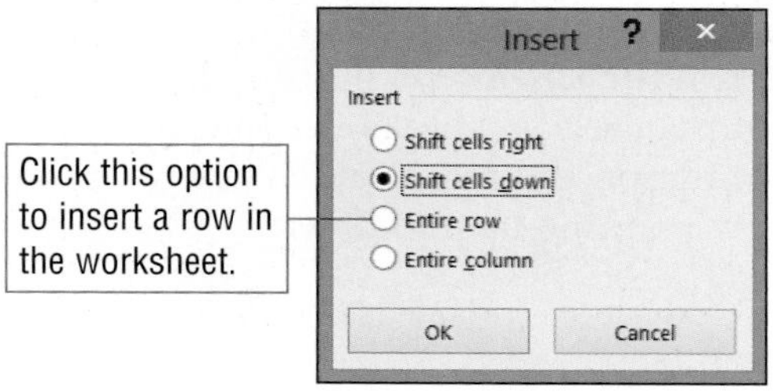

Project 1d Inserting Rows

Part 4 of 7

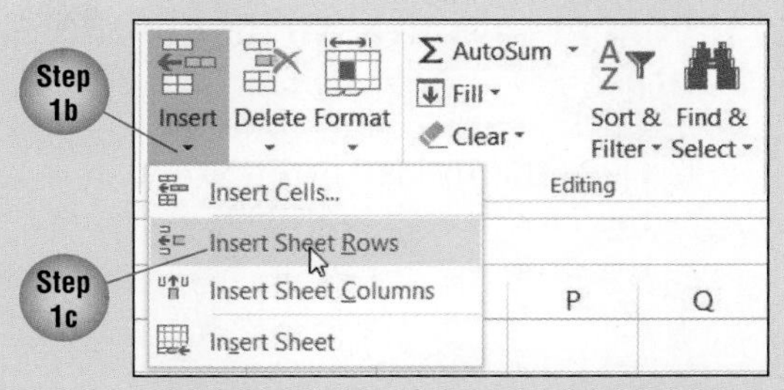

1. With **EL1-C3-P1-CMProducts.xlsx** open, insert two rows at the beginning of the worksheet by completing the following steps:
   a. Make cell A1 active.
   b. Click the Insert button arrow in the Cells group on the HOME tab.
   c. At the drop-down list that displays, click *Insert Sheet Rows*.
   d. With cell A1 active, click the Insert button arrow and then click *Insert Sheet Rows* at the drop-down list.
2. Type the text **Capstan Marine Products** in cell A1.
3. Make cell A2 active and then type **Purchasing Department**.
4. Change the height of row 1 to *42.00 (70 pixels)*.
5. Change the height of row 2 to *21.00 (35 pixels)*.
6. Insert two rows by completing the following steps:
   a. Select rows 7 and 8 in the worksheet.
   b. Click the Insert button in the Cells group on the HOME tab.

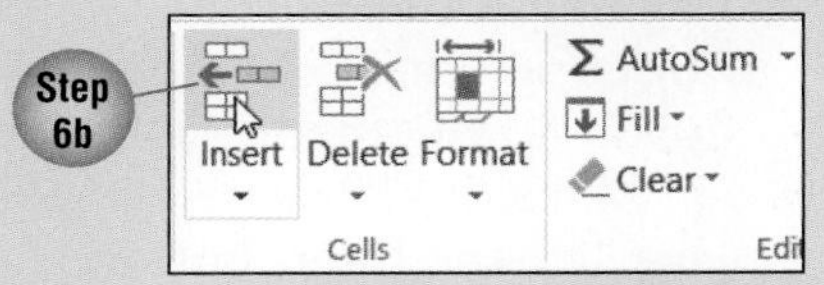

7. Type the following data in the specified cells. For the cells that contain money amounts, you do not need to type the dollar sign:
   A7: 855-495
   B7: 42.75
   C7: 5
   A8: ST039
   B8: 12.99
   C8: 25
8. Make cell D6 active and then use the fill handle to copy the formula down to cells D7 and D8.
9. Save **EL1-C3-P1-CMProducts.xlsx**.

Inserting Columns

Insert columns in a worksheet in much the same way as rows. Insert a column with options from the Insert button drop-down list or with options at the Insert dialog box. By default, a column is inserted immediately to the left of the column containing the active cell. To insert a column in a worksheet, make a cell active in the column immediately to the right of where the new column is to be inserted, click the Insert button arrow, and then click *Insert Sheet Columns* at the drop-down list. If you want to insert more than one column, select the number of columns in the worksheet that you want inserted, click the Insert button arrow, and then click *Insert Sheet Columns*.

You also can insert a column by making a cell active in the column immediately to the right of where the new column is to be inserted, clicking the Insert button arrow, and then clicking *Insert Cells* at the drop-down list. At the Insert dialog box that displays, click *Entire column*. This inserts an entire column immediately to the left of the active cell.

Excel includes an especially helpful and time-saving feature related to inserting columns. When you insert columns in a worksheet, all references affected by the insertion are automatically adjusted.

Quick Steps

Insert a Column
Click Insert button.
OR
1. Click Insert button arrow.
2. Click *Insert Sheet Columns* at drop-down list.

OR
1. Click Insert button arrow.
2. Click *Insert Cells*.
3. Click *Entire column*.
4. Click OK.

Project 1e Inserting a Column   Part 5 of 7

1. With **EL1-C3-P1-CMProducts.xlsx** open, insert a column by completing the following steps:
   a. Click in any cell in column A.
   b. Click the Insert button arrow in the Cells group on the HOME tab and then click *Insert Sheet Columns* at the drop-down list.
2. Type the following data in the specified cell:
   A3: Company
   A4: RD Manufacturing
   A8: Smithco, Inc.
   A11: Sunrise Corporation
   A15: Geneva Systems
3. Make cell A1 active and then adjust the width of column A to accommodate the longest entry.
4. Insert another column by completing the following steps:
   a. Make cell B1 active.
   b. Click the Insert button arrow and then click *Insert Cells* at the drop-down list.
   c. At the Insert dialog box, click *Entire column*.
   d. Click OK.
5. Type Date in cell B3 and then press Enter.
6. Save **EL1-C3-P1-CMProducts.xlsx**.

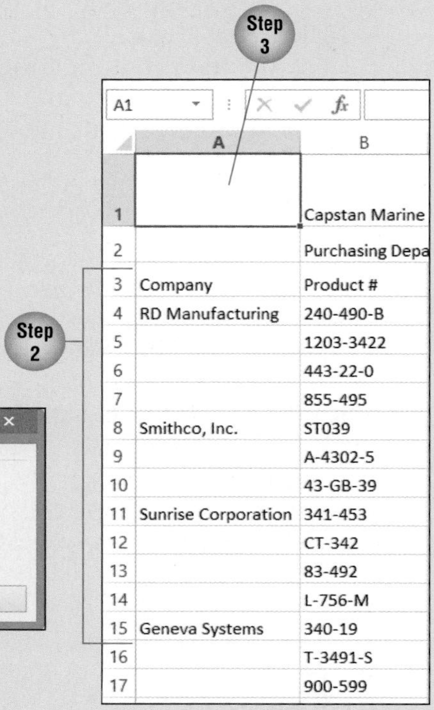

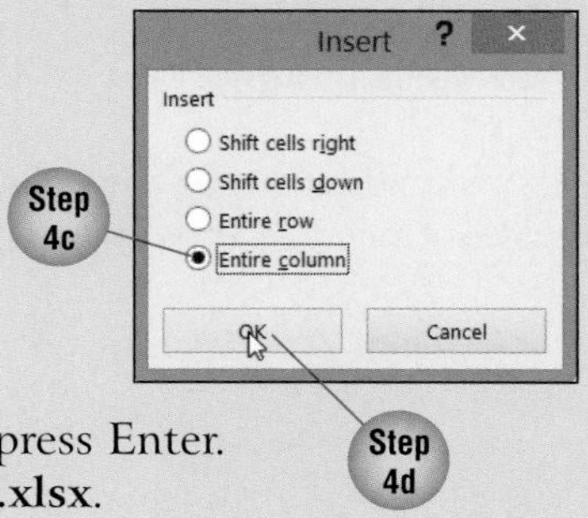

Deleting Cells, Rows, or Columns

Delete

HINT

Display the Delete dialog box by positioning the cell pointer in the worksheet, clicking the right mouse button, and then clicking *Delete* at the shortcut menu.

You can delete specific cells in a worksheet or rows or columns in a worksheet. To delete a row, select the row and then click the Delete button in the Cells group on the HOME tab. To delete a column, select the column and then click the Delete button. Delete a specific cell by making the cell active, clicking the Delete button arrow, and then clicking *Delete Cells* at the drop-down list. This displays the Delete dialog box, shown in Figure 3.4. At the Delete dialog box, specify what you want deleted and then click OK. You can also delete adjacent cells by selecting the cells and then displaying the Delete dialog box.

Figure 3.4 Delete Dialog Box

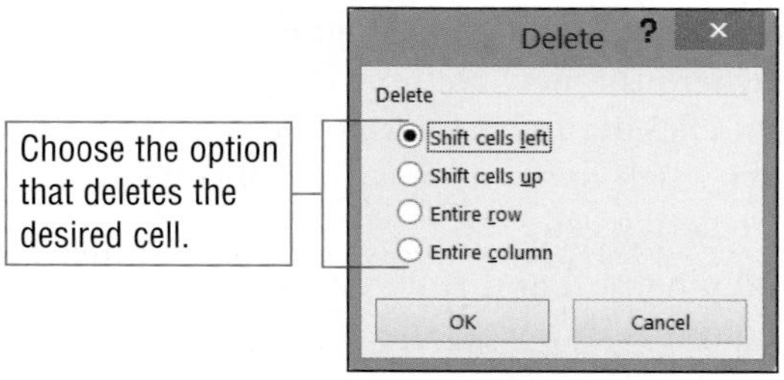

Clearing Data in Cells

If you want to delete the cell contents but not the cell, make the cell active or select desired cells and then press the Delete key. A quick method for clearing the contents of a cell is to right-click in the cell and then click *Clear Contents* at the shortcut menu. Another method for deleting cell content is to make the cell active or select desired cells, click the Clear button in the Editing group on the HOME tab, and then click *Clear Contents* at the drop-down list.

With the options at the Clear button drop-down list, you can clear the contents of the cell or selected cells as well as the formatting and comments. Click the *Clear Formats* option to remove formatting from cells or selected cells while leaving the data. You can also click the *Clear All* option to clear the contents of the cell or selected cells as well as the formatting.

Quick Steps

Clear Data in Cells
1. Select desired cells.
2. Press Delete key.

OR
1. Select desired cells.
2. Click Clear button.
3. Click *Clear Contents* at drop-down list.

Clear

Project 1f **Deleting and Clearing Rows in a Worksheet** **Part 6 of 7**

1. With **EL1-C3-P1-CMProducts.xlsx** open, delete column B in the worksheet by completing the following steps:
   a. Click in any cell in column B.
   b. Click the Delete button arrow in the Cells group on the HOME tab and then click *Delete Sheet Columns* at the drop-down list.
2. Delete row 5 by completing the following steps:
   a. Select row 5.
   b. Click the Delete button in the Cells group.
3. Clear row contents by completing the following steps:
   a. Select rows 7 and 8.
   b. Click the Clear button in the Editing group on the HOME tab and then click *Clear Contents* at the drop-down list.
4. Type the following data in the specified cell:
   A7: Ray Enterprises
   B7: S894-T
   C7: 4.99
   D7: 30
   B8: B-3448
   C8: 25.50
   D8: 12
5. Make cell E6 active and then copy the formula down to cells E7 and E8.
6. Save **EL1-C3-P1-CMProducts.xlsx**.

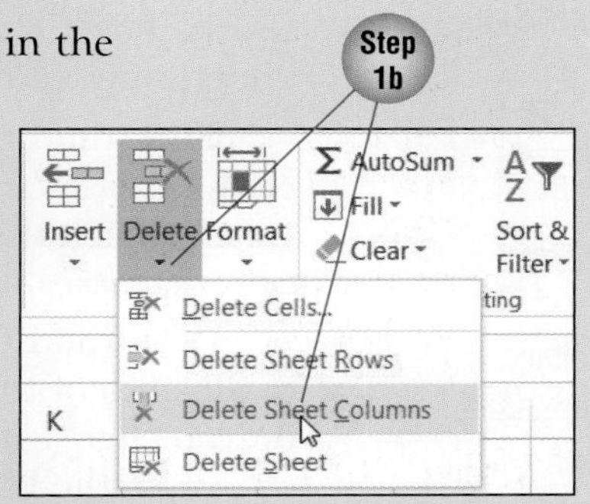

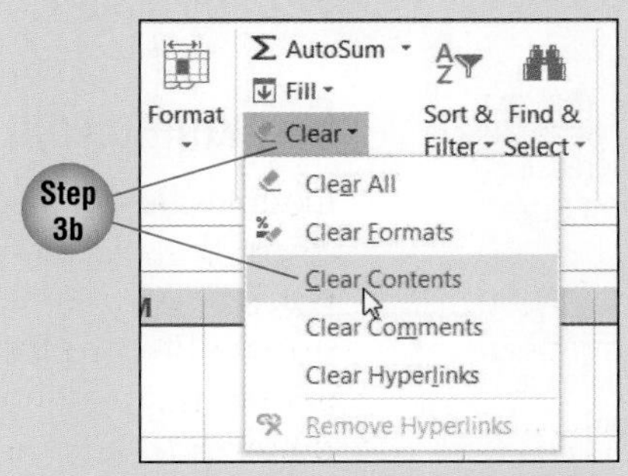

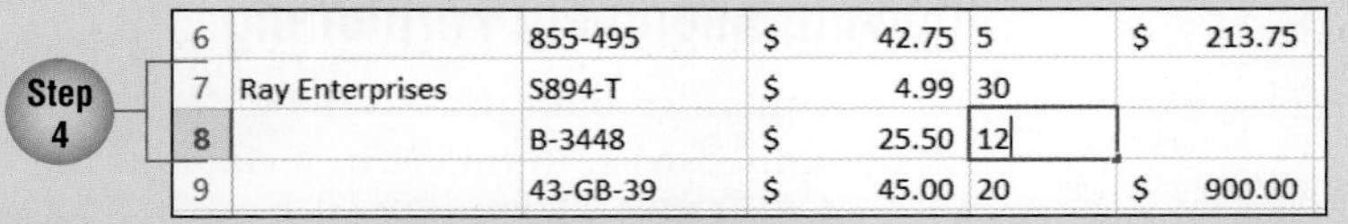

Applying Formatting

With many of the groups on the HOME tab, you can apply formatting to text in the active cell or selected cells. Use buttons in the Font group to apply font formatting to text and use buttons in the Alignment group to apply alignment formatting to text.

Figure 3.5 Font Group

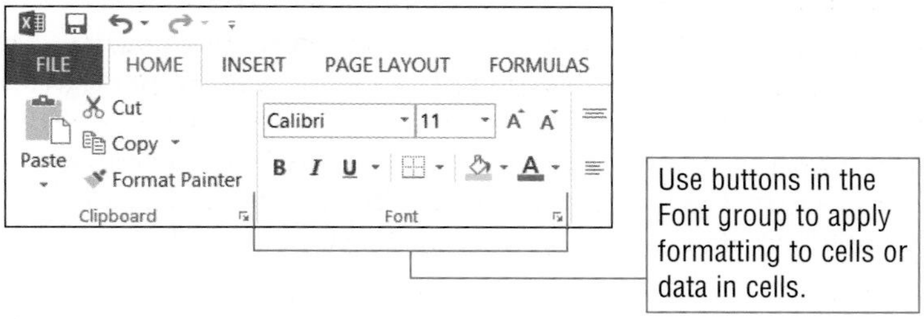

Applying Font Formatting

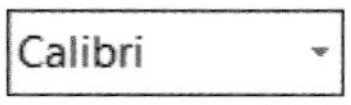

Font

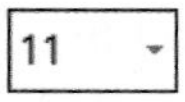

Font Size

Bold

Italic

Underline

Increase Font Size

Decrease Font Size

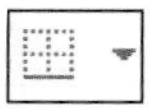

Borders

Fill Color

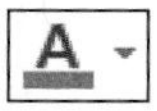

Font Color

Merge & Center

Apply a variety of formatting to cells in a worksheet with buttons in the Font group on the HOME tab. With buttons in the Font group, shown in Figure 3.5, you can change the font, font size, and font color; bold, italicize, and underline data in cells; change the text color; and apply a border or add fill to cells.

Use the Font button in the Font group to change the font of text in a cell and use the Font Size button to specify the size for the text. Apply bold formatting to text in a cell with the Bold button, italic formatting with the Italic button, and underlining with the Underline button.

Click the Increase Font Size button and the text in the active cell or selected cells increases to the next font size in the Font Size button arrow drop-down gallery. Click the Decrease Font Size button and text in the active cell or selected cells decreases in point size.

With the Borders button in the Font group, you can insert a border on any or all sides of the active cell or any or all sides of selected cells. The name of the button changes depending on the most recent border applied to a cell or selected cells. Use the Fill Color button to insert color in the active cell or in selected cells. With the Font Color button, you can change the color of text within a cell.

Formatting with the Mini Toolbar

Double-click in a cell and then select data within the cell and the Mini toolbar displays above the selected data. The Mini toolbar also displays when you right-click in any cell. The Mini toolbar contains buttons for applying font formatting such as font, font size, and font color, as well as bold and italic formatting. Click a button on the Mini toolbar to apply formatting to selected text.

Applying Alignment Formatting

The alignment of data in cells depends on the type of data entered. Enter words or text combined with numbers in a cell and the text is aligned at the left edge of the cell. Enter numbers in a cell and the numbers are aligned at the right side of the cell. Use options in the Alignment group to align text at the left, center, or right side of the cell; align text at the top, center, or bottom of the cell; increase and/or decrease the indent of text; and change the orientation of text in a cell.

As you learned in Chapter 1, you can merge selected cells by clicking the Merge & Center button. If you merged cells, you can split the merged cell into the original cells by selecting the cell and then clicking the Merge & Center button. If you click the Merge & Center button arrow, a drop-down list of options displays. Click the *Merge & Center* option to merge all of the selected cells and change to center cell alignment. Click the *Merge Across* option to merge each row of the selected cells. For example, if you select three cells and two rows, clicking the *Merge Across* option will merge the three cells in the first row and merge the three cells in the second row so you end up with two cells. Click the *Merge Cells* option to merge all selected cells but not change to center cell alignment. Use the last option, *Unmerge Cells* to split cells that were previously merged. If you select and merge cells containing data, only the data in the upper left cell will remain. Data in any other cells in the merged cells is deleted.

Orientation

Wrap Text

Click the Orientation button to rotate data in a cell. Click the Orientation button and a drop-down list displays with options for rotating text in a cell. If data typed in a cell is longer than the cell, it overlaps the next cell to the right. If you want data to remain in a cell and wrap to the next line within the same cell, click the Wrap Text button in the Alignment group.

Project 1g Applying Font and Alignment Formatting — Part 7 of 7

1. With **EL1-C3-P1-CMProducts.xlsx** open, make cell B1 active and then click the Wrap Text button in the Alignment group on the HOME tab. (This wraps the company name within the cell.)
2. Select cells B1 through C2, click the Merge & Center button arrow in the Alignment group on the HOME tab, and then click *Merge Across* at the drop-down list.
3. After looking at the merged cells, you decide to merge additional cells and horizontally and vertically center text in the cells by completing the following steps:
   a. With cells B1 through C2 selected, click the Merge & Center button arrow and then click *Unmerge Cells* at the drop-down list.
   b. Select cells A1 through E2.
   c. Click the Merge & Center button arrow and then click the *Merge Across* option at the drop-down list.
   d. Click the Middle Align button in the Alignment group and then click the Center button.

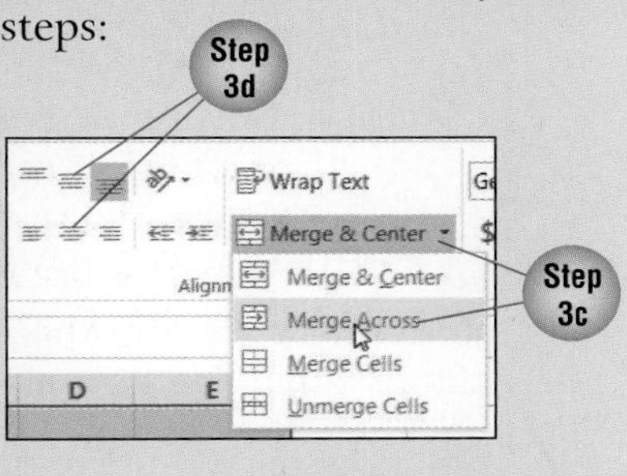

4. Rotate text in the third row by completing the following steps:
   a. Select cells A3 through E3.
   b. Click the Orientation button in the Alignment group and then click *Angle Counterclockwise* at the drop-down list.
   c. After looking at the rotated text, you decide to return the orientation back to horizontal by clicking the Undo button on the Quick Access toolbar.

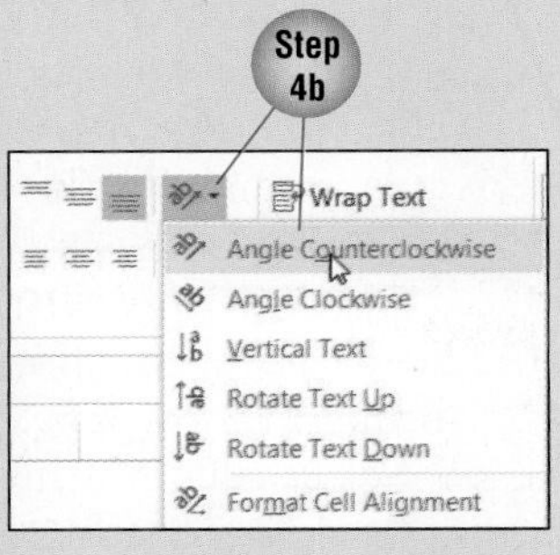

5. Change the font, font size, and font color for text in specific cells by completing the following steps:
   a. Make cell A1 active.
   b. Click the Font button arrow in the Font group, scroll down the drop-down gallery, and then click *Bookman Old Style*.
   c. Click the Font Size button arrow in the Font group and then click *22* at the drop-down gallery.

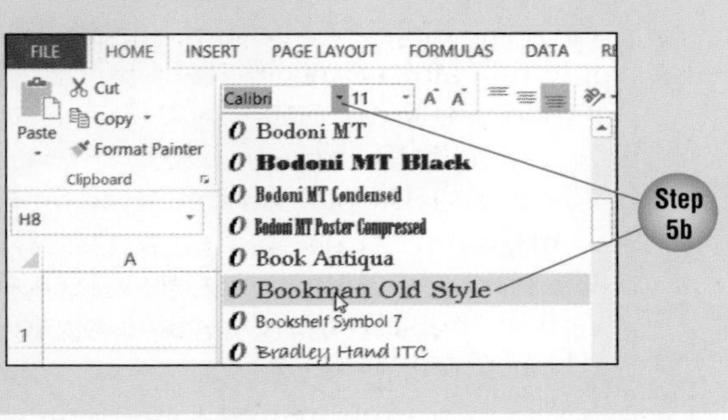

d. Click the Font Color button arrow and then click the *Dark Blue* option (ninth option in the *Standard Colors* section).

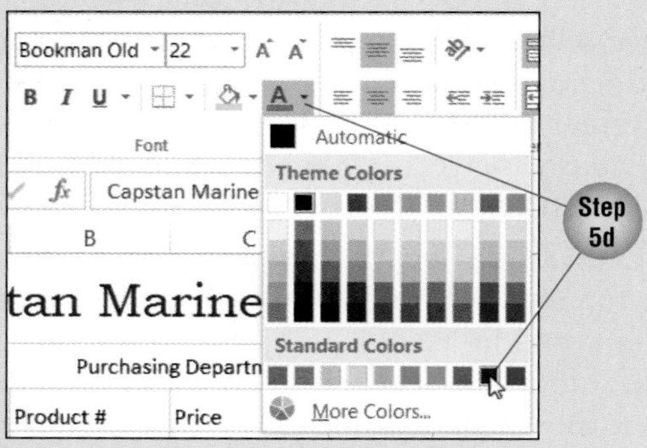

6. Make cell A2 active and then complete steps similar to those in Step 5 to change the font to Bookman Old Style, the font size to 16 points, and the font color to Dark Blue.
7. Select cells A3 through E3 and then click the Center button in the Alignment group.
8. With cells A3 through E3 still selected, click the Bold button in the Font group and then click the Italic button.
9. Select cells A3 through E18 and then change the font to Bookman Old Style.
10. Use the Mini toolbar to apply formatting to selected data by completing the following steps:

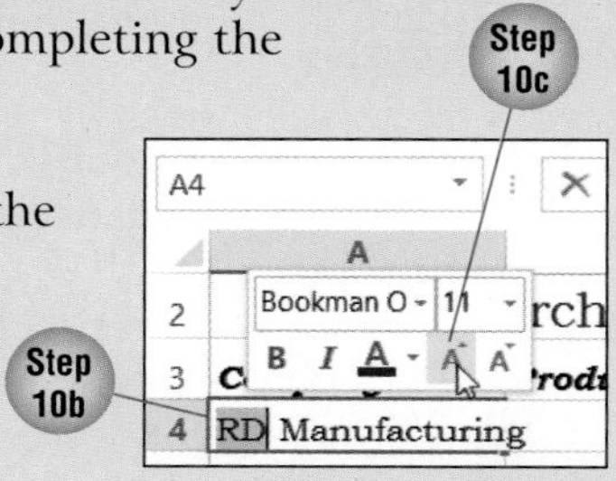

   a. Double-click in cell A4.
   b. Select the letters *RD*. (This displays the Mini toolbar above the selected word.)
   c. Click the Increase Font Size button on the Mini toolbar.
   d. Double-click in cell A14.
   e. Select the word *Geneva* and then click the Italic button on the Mini toolbar.
11. Adjust columns A through E to accommodate the longest entry in each column. To do this, select columns A through E and then double-click any selected column boundary.

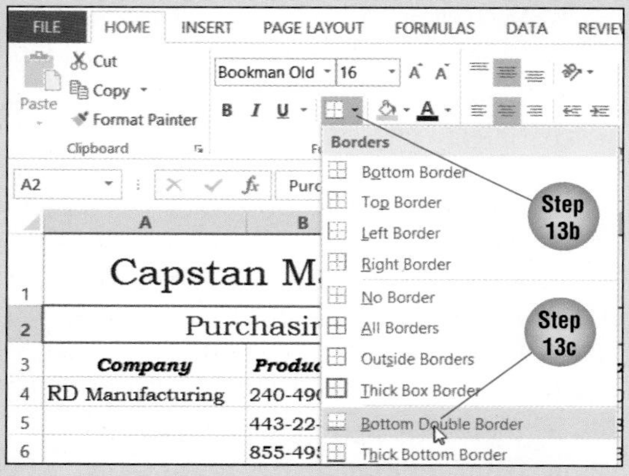

12. Select cells D4 through D17 and then click the Center button in the Alignment group.
13. Add a double-line bottom border to cell A2 by completing the following steps:
   a. Make cell A2 active.
   b. Click the Borders button arrow in the Font group. (The name of this button varies depending on the last option selected.)
   c. Click the *Bottom Double Border* option at the drop-down list.
14. Add a single-line bottom border to cells A3 through E3 by completing the following steps:

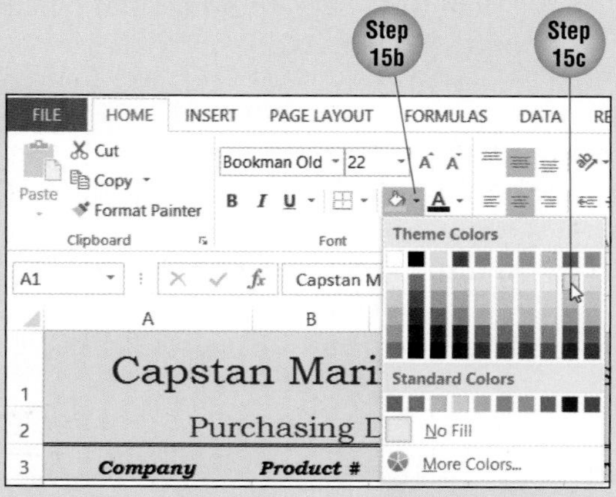

   a. Select cells A3 through E3.
   b. Click the Borders button arrow and then click the *Bottom Border* option.
15. Apply fill color to specific cells by completing the following steps:
   a. Select cells A1 through E3.
   b. Click the Fill Color button arrow in the Font group.
   c. Click the *Blue, Accent 5, Lighter 80%* color option (ninth column, second row in the *Theme Colors* section).
16. Select cells C5 through C17 and then click the Comma Style button.
17. Select cells E5 through E17 and then click the Comma Style button.
18. Save, print, and then close **EL1-C3-P1-CMProducts.xlsx**.

Project 2 Apply a Theme to a Payroll Worksheet — 1 Part

You will open a workbook containing a worksheet with payroll information and then insert text, apply formatting to cells and cell contents, apply a theme, and then change the theme font and colors.

Applying a Theme

Excel provides a number of themes you can use to format text and cells in a worksheet. A ***theme*** is a set of formatting choices that includes a color theme (a set of colors), a font theme (a set of heading and body text fonts), and an effects theme (a set of lines and fill effects). To apply a theme, click the PAGE LAYOUT tab and then click the Themes button in the Themes group. At the drop-down gallery that displays, click the desired theme. Position the mouse pointer over a theme and the ***live preview*** feature will display the worksheet with the theme formatting applied. With the live preview feature, you can see how the theme formatting affects your worksheet before you make your final choice.

HINT
Apply a theme to give your worksheet a professional look.

Themes

Project 2 Applying a Theme — Part 1 of 1

1. Open **SBAPayroll.xlsx** and then save it with Save As and name it **EL1-C3-P2-SBAPayroll**.
2. Make cell G4 active and then insert a formula that calculates the amount of social security tax. (Multiply the gross pay amount in cell E4 with the social security rate in cell H11; you will need to use the mixed cell reference H$11 when writing the formula.)
3. Copy the formula in cell G4 down to cells G5 through G9.
4. Make H4 the active cell and then insert a formula that calculates the net pay (gross pay minus withholding and social security tax).
5. Copy the formula in cell H4 down to cells H5 through H9.
6. Increase the height of row 1 to 36.00 points.
7. Make cell A1 active, click the Middle Align button in the Alignment group, click the Font Size button arrow, click *18* at the drop-down list, and then click the Bold button.
8. Type **Stanton & Barnett Associates** in cell A1.
9. Select cells A2 through H3 and then click the Bold button in the Font group.
10. Apply a theme and customize the font and colors by completing the following steps:
    a. Make cell A1 active.
    b. Click the PAGE LAYOUT tab.
    c. Click the Themes button in the Themes group and then click *Wisp* at the drop-down gallery. (You might want to point the mouse to individual themes to see how each theme's formatting affects the worksheet.)

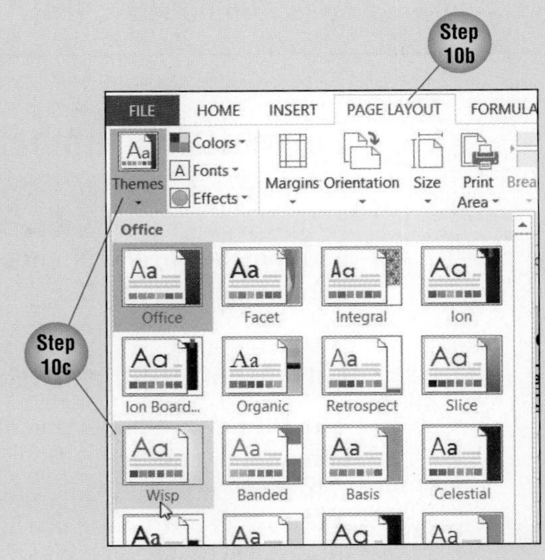

d. Click the Colors button in the Themes group and then click *Red Orange* at the drop-down gallery.
e. Click the Fonts button in the Themes group, scroll down the drop-down gallery, and then click *TrebuchetMS*.

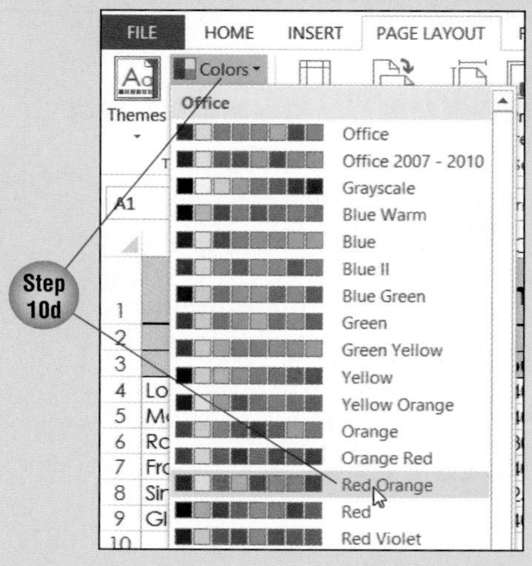

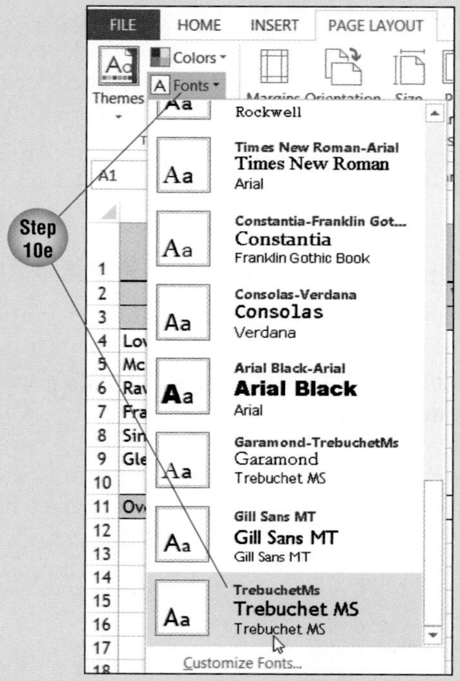

11. Select columns A through H and adjust the width of the columns to accommodate the longest entries.
12. Save, print, and then close **EL1-C3-P2-SBAPayroll.xlsx**.

Project 3 Format an Invoices Worksheet — 2 Parts

You will open a workbook containing an invoice worksheet and apply number formatting to numbers in cells.

Formatting Numbers

Numbers in a cell, by default, are aligned at the right and decimals and commas do not display unless they are typed in the cell. Change the format of numbers with buttons in the Number group on the HOME tab or with options at the Format Cells dialog box with the Number tab selected.

Formatting Numbers Using Number Group Buttons

The format symbols you can use to format numbers include a percent sign (%), comma (,), and dollar sign ($). For example, if you type the number *$45.50* in a cell, Excel automatically applies currency formatting to the number. If you type *45%*, Excel automatically applies percent formatting to the number. The Number group on the HOME tab contains five buttons you can use to format numbers in cells. You learned about these buttons in Chapter 1.

Specify the formatting for numbers in cells in a worksheet before typing the numbers or format existing numbers in a worksheet. The Increase Decimal and Decrease Decimal buttons in the Number group on the HOME tab will change the number of places after the decimal point for existing numbers only.

The Number group on the HOME tab also contains the Number Format button. Click the Number Format button arrow and a drop-down list displays of common number formats. Click the desired format at the drop-down list to apply the number formatting to the cell or selected cells.

Number Format

Project 3a Formatting Numbers with Buttons in the Number Group — Part 1 of 2

1. Open **RPInvoices.xlsx**.
2. Save the workbook with Save As and name it **EL1-C3-P3-RPInvoices**.
3. Make the following changes to column widths:
   a. Change the width of column C to 17.00 characters.
   b. Change the width of column D to 10.00 characters.
   c. Change the width of column E to 7.00 characters.
   d. Change the width of column F to 12.00 characters.
4. Select row 1 and then click the Insert button in the Cells group on the HOME tab.
5. Change the height of row 1 to 42.00 points.
6. Select cells A1 through F1 and then make the following changes:
   a. Click the Merge & Center button in the Alignment group on the HOME tab.
   b. With cell A1 active, change the font size to 24 points.
   c. Click the Fill Color button arrow in the Font group and then click *Green, Accent 6, Lighter 80%* (last column, second row in the *Theme Colors* section).
   d. Click the Borders button arrow in the Font group and then click the *Top and Thick Bottom Border* option.
   e. With cell A1 active, type **REAL PHOTOGRAPHY** and then press Enter.
7. Change the height of row 2 to 24.00 points.
8. Select cells A2 through F2 and then make the following changes:
   a. Click the Merge & Center button in the Alignment group.
   b. With cell A2 active, change the font size to 18 points.
   c. Click the Fill Color button in the Font group. (This will fill the cell with green color.)
   d. Click the Borders button arrow in the Font group and then click the *Bottom Border* option.
9. Make the following changes to row 3:
   a. Change the height of row 3 to 18.00 points.
   b. Select cells A3 through F3, click the Bold button in the Font group, and then click the Center button in the Alignment group.
   c. With the cells still selected, click the Borders button arrow and then click the *Bottom Border* option.

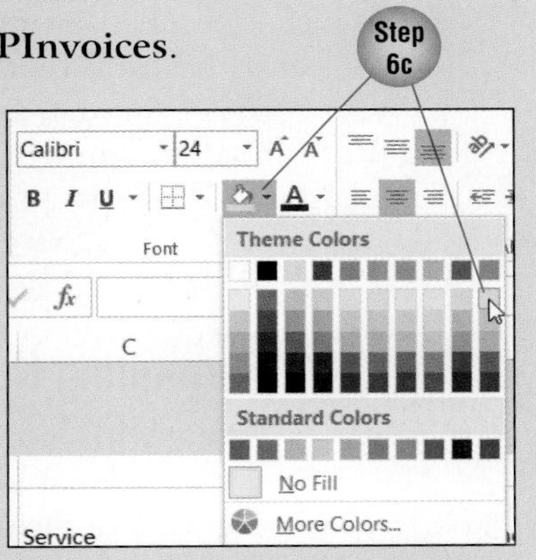

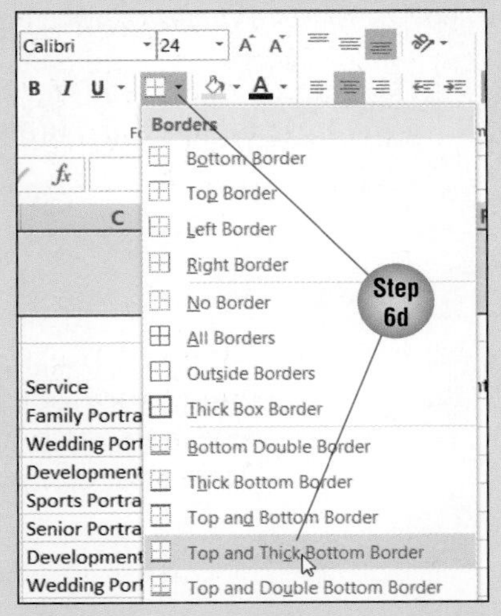

10. Make the following number formatting changes:
    a. Select cells E4 through E16 and then click the Percent Style button in the Number group on the HOME tab.
    b. With the cells still selected, click once on the Increase Decimal button in the Number group. (The percentages should include one place after the decimal point.)

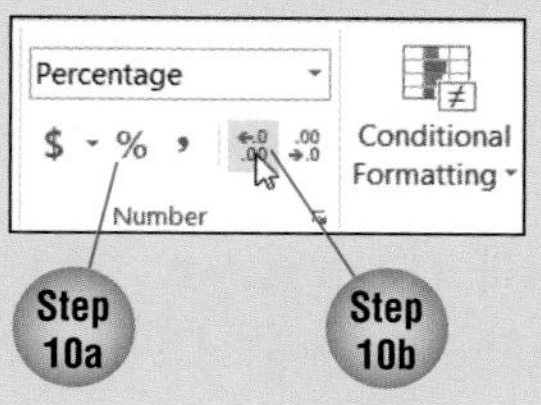

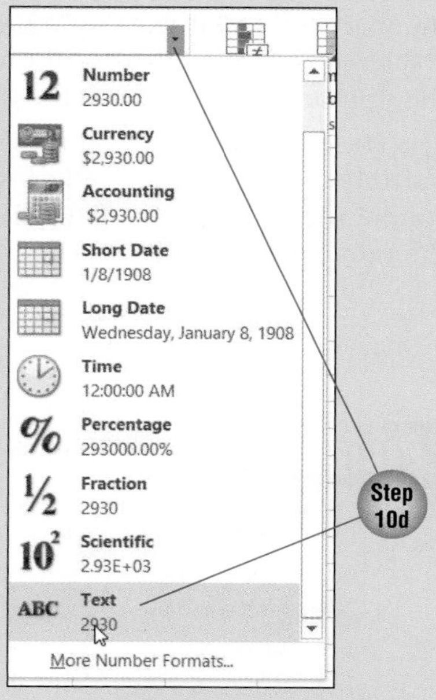

    c. Select cells A4 through B16.
    d. Click the Number Format button arrow, scroll down the drop-down list, and then click *Text*.
    e. With cells A4 through B16 still selected, click the Center button in the Alignment group.
11. Save **EL1-C3-P3-RPInvoices.xlsx**.

Formatting Numbers Using the Format Cells Dialog Box

Along with buttons in the Number group, you can format numbers with options at the Format Cells dialog box with the Number tab selected, as shown in Figure 3.6. Display this dialog box by clicking the Number group dialog box launcher or by clicking the Number Format button arrow and then clicking *More Number Formats* at the drop-down list. The left side of the dialog box displays

Figure 3.6 Format Cells Dialog Box with Number Tab Selected

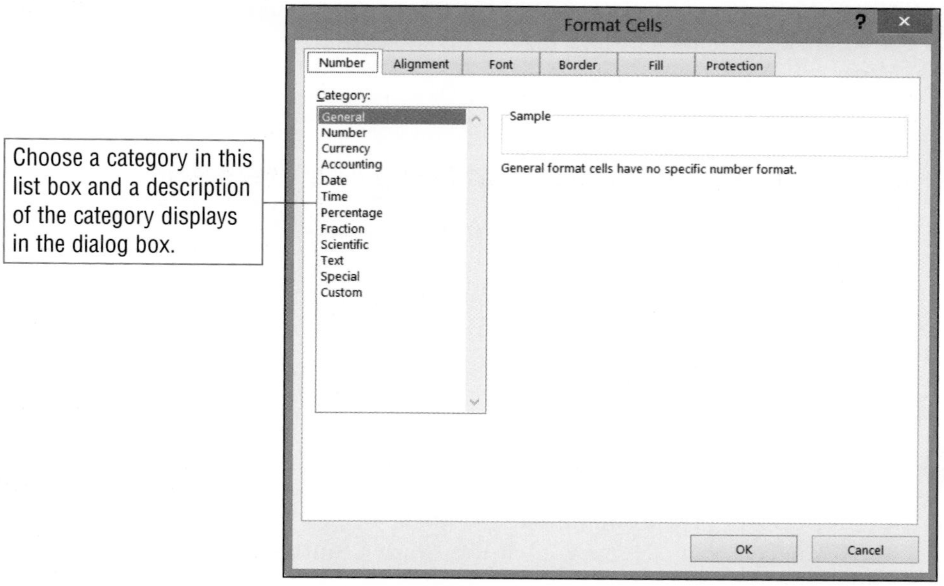

number categories with a default category of *General*. At this setting, no specific formatting is applied to numbers except right alignment in the cells. The other number categories are described in Table 3.1.

Table 3.1 Number Categories at the Format Cells Dialog Box

Click this category	*To apply this number formatting*
Number	Specify the number of places after the decimal point and whether a thousand separator should be used; choose the display of negative numbers; right-align numbers in the cell.
Currency	Apply general monetary values; add a dollar sign as well as commas and decimal points, if needed; right-align numbers in the cell.
Accounting	Line up the currency symbols and decimal points in a column; add a dollar sign and two places after the decimal point; right-align numbers in the cell.
Date	Display the date as a date value; specify the type of formatting desired by clicking an option in the *Type* list box; right-align the date in the cell.
Time	Display the time as a time value; specify the type of formatting desired by clicking an option in the *Type* list box; right-align the time in the cell.
Percentage	Multiply the cell value by 100 and display the result with a percent symbol; add a decimal point followed by two places by default; change the number of digits with the *Decimal places* option; right-align numbers in the cell.
Fraction	Specify how a fraction displays in the cell by clicking an option in the *Type* list box; right-align a fraction in the cell.
Scientific	Use for very large or very small numbers; use the letter *E* to tell Excel to move the decimal point a specified number of places.
Text	Treat a number in the cell as text; the number is displayed in the cell exactly as typed.
Special	Choose a number type, such as *Zip Code*, *Phone Number*, or *Social Security Number*, in the *Type* option list box; useful for tracking list and database values.
Custom	Specify a numbering type by choosing an option in the *Type* list box.

Project 3b **Formatting Numbers at the Format Cells Dialog Box** **Part 2 of 2**

1. With **EL1-C3-P3-PRInvoices.xlsx** open, make cell F4 active, insert the formula =(D4*E4)+D4, and then press Enter.
2. Make cell F4 active and then copy the formula down to cells F5 through F16.
3. Apply accounting formatting by completing the following steps:
   a. Select cells D4 through D16.
   b. Click the Number group dialog box launcher.

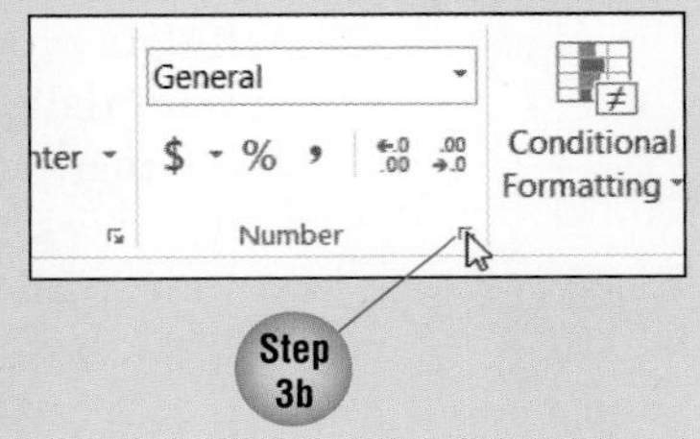

c. At the Format Cells dialog box with the Number tab selected, click *Accounting* in the *Category* list box.
d. Make sure a *2* displays in the *Decimal places* option box and a *$* (dollar sign) displays in the *Symbol* option box.
e. Click OK.

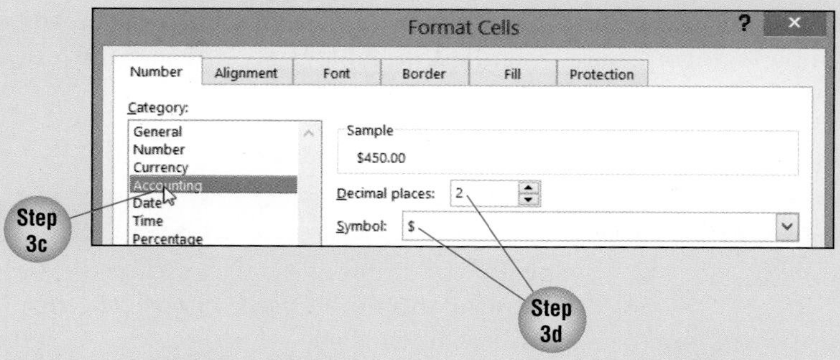

4. Apply accounting formatting to cells F4 through F16 by completing actions similar to those in Step 3.
5. Save, print, and then close **EL1-C3-P3-RPInvoices.xlsx**.

Project 4 Format a Company Budget Worksheet — 6 Parts

You will open a workbook containing a company budget worksheet and then apply formatting to cells with options at the Format Cells dialog box, use the Format Painter to apply formatting, and hide and unhide rows and columns in the worksheet.

Formatting Cells Using the Format Cells Dialog Box

In the previous section, you learned how to format numbers with options at the Format Cells dialog box with the Number tab selected. This dialog box also contains a number of other tabs you can select to format cells.

Aligning and Indenting Data

Align and indent data in cells using buttons in the Alignment group on the HOME tab or with options at the Format Cells dialog box with the Alignment tab selected, as shown in Figure 3.7. Display this dialog box by clicking the Alignment group dialog box launcher.

In the *Orientation* section, you can choose to rotate data. A portion of the *Orientation* section shows points on an arc. Click a point on the arc to rotate the text along that point. You can also type a rotation degree in the *Degrees* measurement box. Type a positive number to rotate selected text from the lower left to the upper right of the cell. Type a negative number to rotate selected text from the upper left to the lower right of the cell.

If data typed in a cell is longer than the cell, it overlaps the next cell to the right. If you want data to remain in a cell and wrap to the next line within the same cell, insert a check mark in the *Wrap text* check box in the *Text control* section of the dialog box. Insert a check mark in the *Shrink to fit* check box if you want to reduce the size of the text font so all selected data fits within the column. Insert a check mark in the *Merge cells* check box to combine two or more selected cells into a single cell.

If you want to enter data on more than one line within a cell, enter the data on the first line and then press Alt + Enter. Pressing Alt + Enter moves the insertion point to the next line within the same cell.

Figure 3.7 Format Cells Dialog Box with Alignment Tab Selected

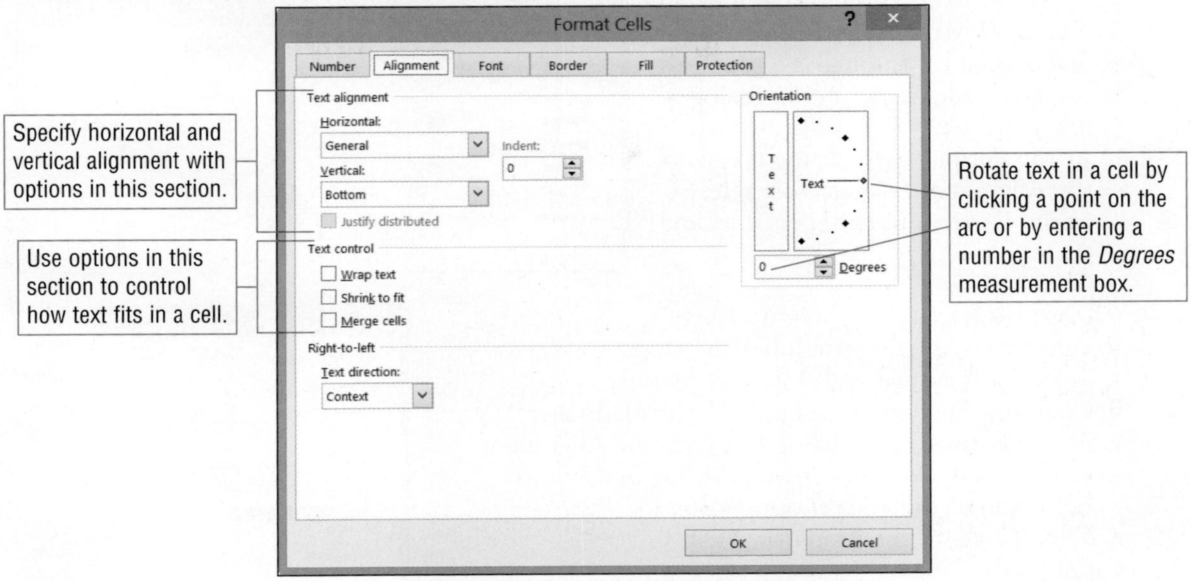

Project 4a Aligning and Rotating Data in Cells — Part 1 of 6

1. Open **HBCJobs.xlsx**.
2. Save the workbook with Save As and name it **EL1-C3-P4-HBCJobs**.
3. Make the following changes to the worksheet:
   a. Insert a new row at the beginning of the worksheet.
   b. Change the height of row 1 to 66.00 points.
   c. Merge and center cells A1 through E1.
   d. Type Harris & Briggs in cell A1 and then press Alt + Enter. (This moves the insertion point down to the next line in the same cell.)
   e. Type Construction and then press Enter.
   f. With cell A2 active, type Preferred, press Alt + Enter, type Customer, and then press Enter.
   g. Change the width of column A to 22.00 characters.
   h. Change the width of column B to 7.00 characters.
   i. Change the widths of columns C, D, and E to 10.00 characters.
4. Change number formatting for specific cells by completing the following steps:
   a. Select cells C3 through E11.
   b. Click the Number group dialog box launcher.
   c. At the Format Cells dialog box with the Number tab selected, click *Accounting* in the *Category* list box.
   d. Click the down-pointing arrow at the right side of the *Decimal places* measurement box until *0* displays.
   e. Make sure a *$* (dollar sign) displays in the *Symbol* option box.
   f. Click OK.

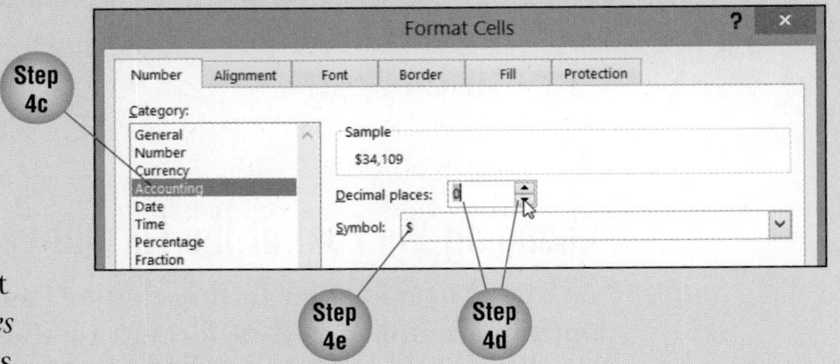

5. Make cell E3 active and then insert the formula =D3-C3. Copy this formula down to cells E4 through E11.

6. Change the orientation of data in cells by completing the following steps:
   a. Select cells B2 through E2.
   b. Click the Alignment group dialog box launcher.
   c. At the Format Cells dialog box with the Alignment tab selected, select *0* in the *Degrees* measurement box and then type 45.
   d. Click OK.

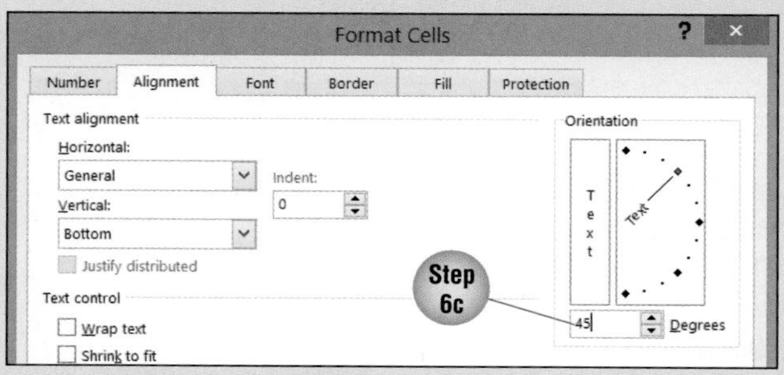

7. Change the vertical alignment of text in cells by completing the following steps:
   a. Select cells A1 through E2.
   b. Click the Alignment group dialog box launcher.
   c. At the Format Cells dialog box with the Alignment tab selected, click the down-pointing arrow at the right side of the *Vertical* option box.
   d. Click *Center* at the drop-down list.
   e. Click OK.

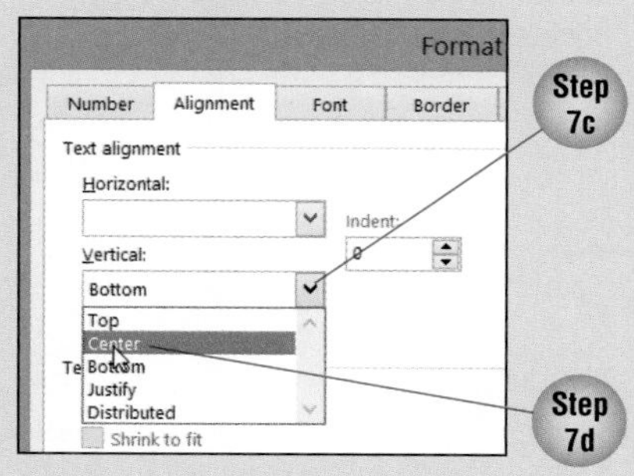

8. Change the horizontal alignment of text in cells by completing the following steps:
   a. Select cells A2 through E2.
   b. Click the Alignment group dialog box launcher.
   c. At the Format Cells dialog box with the Alignment tab selected, click the down-pointing arrow at the right side of the *Horizontal* option box.
   d. Click *Center* at the drop-down list.
   e. Click OK.

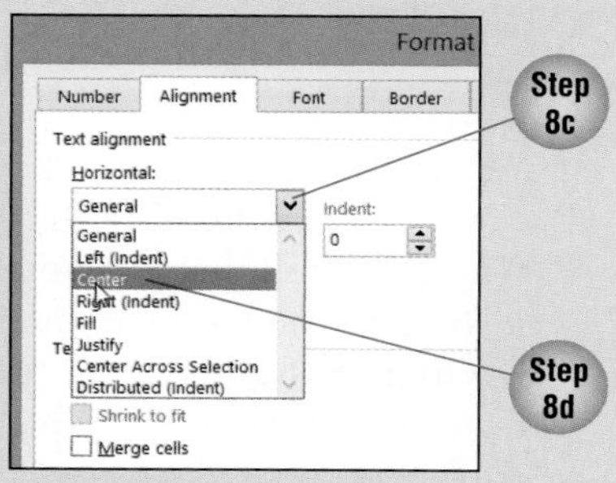

9. Change the horizontal alignment and indent of text in cells by completing the following steps:
   a. Select cells B3 through B11.
   b. Click the Alignment group dialog box launcher.
   c. At the Format Cells dialog box with the Alignment tab selected, click the down-pointing arrow at the right side of the *Horizontal* option box and then click *Right (Indent)* at the drop-down list.
   d. Click once on the up-pointing arrow at the right side of the *Indent* measurement box. (This displays *1*.)
   e. Click OK.

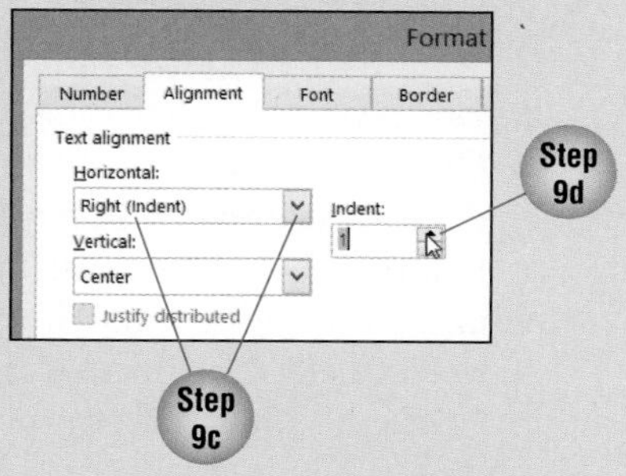

10. Save **EL1-C3-P4-HBCJobs.xlsx**.

Changing the Font at the Format Cells Dialog Box

As you learned earlier in this chapter, the Font group on the HOME tab contains buttons for applying font formatting to data in cells. You can also change the font for data in cells with options at the Format Cells dialog box with the Font tab selected, as shown in Figure 3.8. At the Format Cells dialog box with the Font tab selected, you can change the font, font style, font size, and font color. You can also change the underlining method and add effects such as superscript and subscript. Click the Font group dialog box launcher to display this dialog box.

Figure 3.8 Format Cells Dialog Box with Font Tab Selected

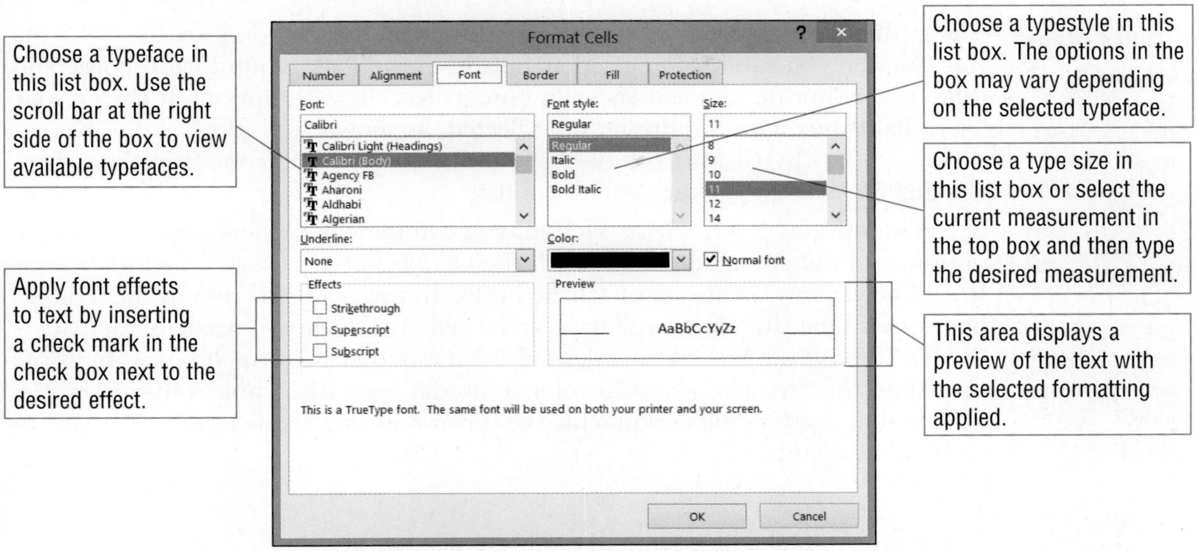

Project 4b Applying Font Formatting at the Format Cells Dialog Box **Part 2 of 6**

1. With **EL1-C3-P4-HBCJobs.xlsx** open, change the font and font color by completing the following steps:
   a. Select cells A1 through E11.
   b. Click the Font group dialog box launcher.
   c. At the Format Cells dialog box with the Font tab selected, click *Garamond* in the *Font* list box. (You will need to scroll down the list to make this font visible.)
   d. Click *12* in the *Size* list box.
   e. Click the down-pointing arrow at the right of the *Color* option box.
   f. At the palette of color choices that displays, click the *Dark Red* color (first option in the *Standard Colors* section).
   g. Click OK to close the dialog box.
2. Make cell A1 active and then change the font to 24-point Garamond and apply bold formatting.
3. Select cells A2 through E2 and then apply bold formatting.
4. Save and then print **EL1-C3-P4-HBCJobs.xlsx**.

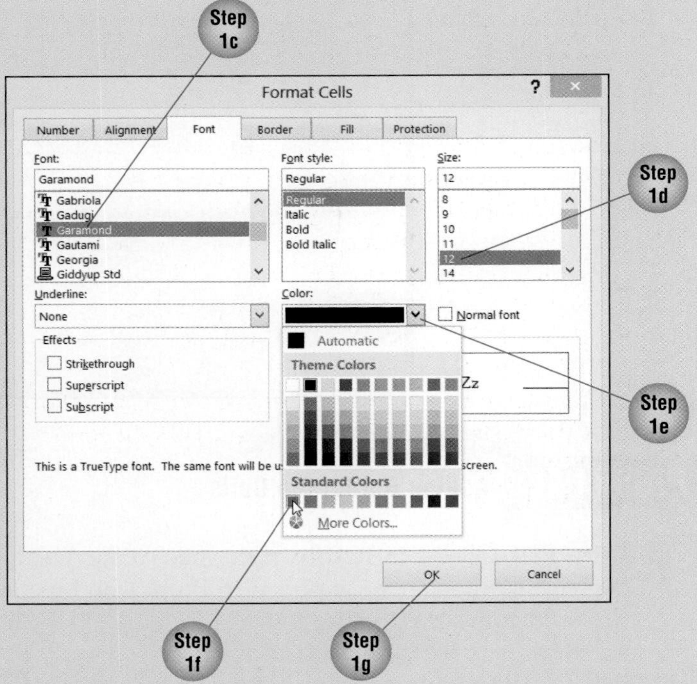

Adding Borders to Cells

Quick Steps

Add Borders to Cells
1. Select cells.
2. Click Borders button arrow.
3. Click desired border.

OR

1. Select cells.
2. Click Borders button arrow.
3. Click *More Borders*.
4. Use options in dialog box to apply desired border.
5. Click OK.

The gridlines that display in a worksheet do not print. As you learned earlier in this chapter, you can use the Borders button in the Font group to add borders to cells that will print. You can also add borders to cells with options at the Format Cells dialog box with the Border tab selected, as shown in Figure 3.9. Display this dialog box by clicking the Borders button arrow in the Font group and then clicking *More Borders* at the drop-down list.

With options in the *Presets* section, you can remove borders with the *None* option, add only outside borders with the *Outline* option, or click the *Inside* option to add borders to the inside of selected cells. In the *Border* section of the dialog box, specify the side of the cell or selected cells to which you want to apply a border. Choose the style of line desired for the border with the options that display in the *Style* list box. Add color to border lines with choices from the color palette that displays when you click the down-pointing arrow at the right side of the *Color* option box.

Figure 3.9 Format Cells Dialog Box with Border Tab Selected

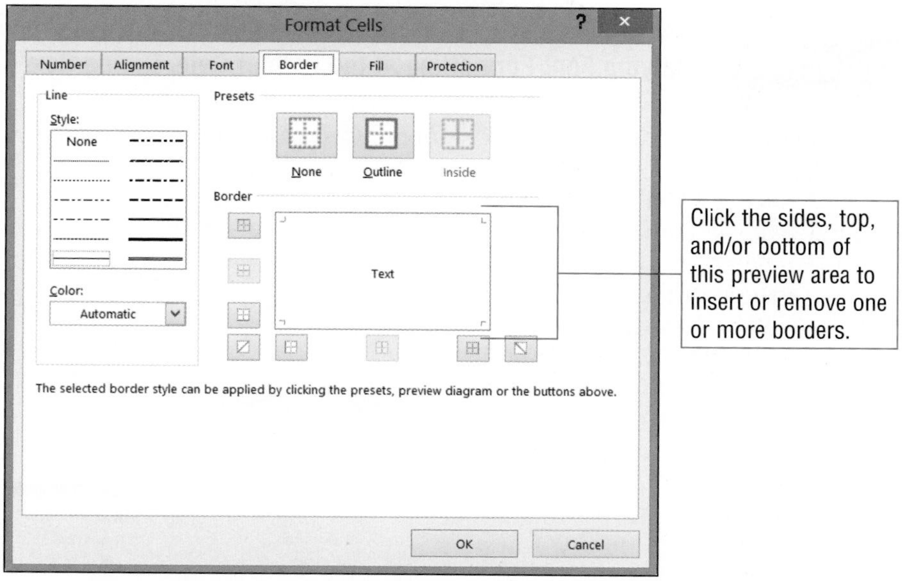

Project 4c **Adding Borders to Cells** **Part 3 of 6**

1. With **EL1-C3-P4-HBCJobs.xlsx** open, remove the 45 degrees orientation you applied in Project 4a by completing the following steps:
   a. Select cells B2 through E2.
   b. Click the Alignment group dialog box launcher.
   c. At the Format Cells dialog box with the Alignment tab selected, select *45* in the *Degrees* measurement box and then type 0.
   d. Click OK.
2. Change the height of row 2 to 33.00 points.

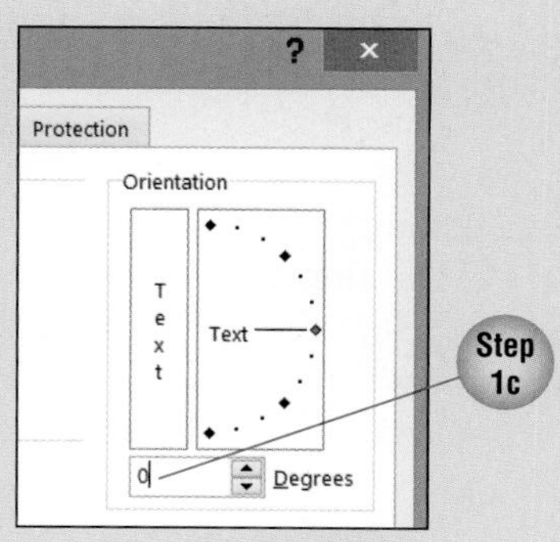

3. Add a thick, Dark Red border line to cells by completing the following steps:
   a. Select cells A1 through E11 (cells containing data).
   b. Click the Borders button arrow in the Font group and then click the *More Borders* option at the drop-down list.
   c. At the Format Cells dialog box with the Border tab selected, click the down-pointing arrow at the right side of the *Color* option box and then click the *Dark Red* color (first option in the *Standard Colors* section).
   d. Click the thick, single-line option in the *Style* list box in the *Line* section (sixth option in the second column).
   e. Click the *Outline* option in the *Presets* section.
   f. Click OK.

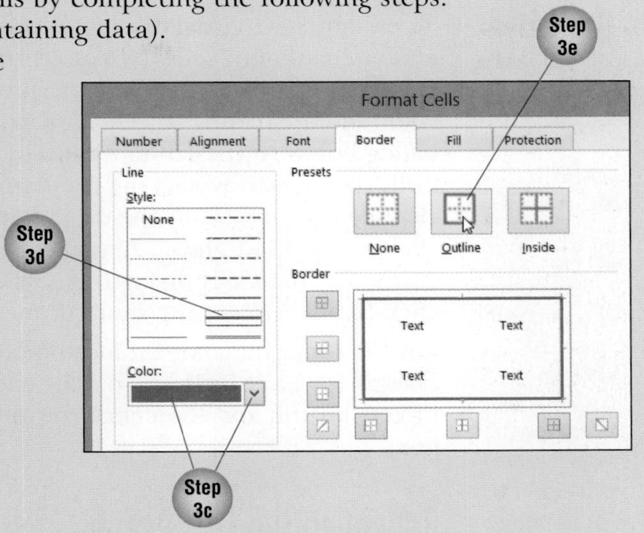

4. Add borders above and below cells by completing the following steps:
   a. Select cells A2 through E2.
   b. Click the Borders button arrow in the Font group and then click *More Borders* at the drop-down list.
   c. At the Format Cells dialog box with the Border tab selected, make sure the color is still Dark Red.
   d. Make sure the thick, single-line option is still selected in the *Style* list box in the *Line* section.
   e. Click the top border of the sample cell in the *Border* section of the dialog box.
   f. Click the double-line option in the *Style* list box (last option in the second column).
   g. Click the bottom border of the sample cell in the *Border* section of the dialog box.
   h. Click OK.

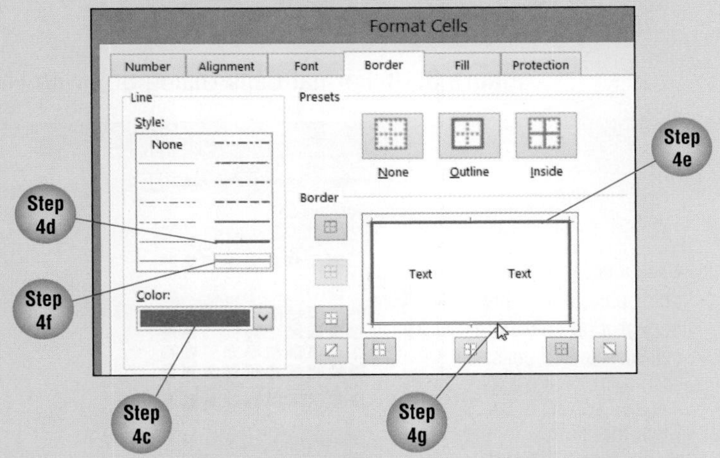

5. Save **EL1-C3-P4-HBCJobs.xlsx**.

Adding Fill and Shading to Cells

Quick Steps

Add Fill and Shading to Cells
1. Select cells.
2. Click Fill Color button arrow.
3. Click desired color.

OR
1. Select cells.
2. Click Format button.
3. Click *Format Cells* at drop-down list.
4. Click Fill tab.
5. Use options in dialog box to apply desired shading.
6. Click OK.

Repeat Last Action
1. Apply formatting.
2. Move to desired location.
3. Press F4 or Ctrl + Y.

To enhance the visual display of cells and data within cells, consider adding fill and/or shading to cells. As you learned earlier in this chapter, you can add fill color to cells with the Fill Color button in the Font group. You can also add fill color and/or shading to cells in a worksheet with options at the Format Cells dialog box with the Fill tab selected, as shown in Figure 3.10. Display the Format Cells dialog box by clicking the Format button in the Cells group and then clicking *Format Cells* at the drop-down list. You can also display the dialog box by clicking the Font group, Alignment group, or Number group dialog box launcher. At the Format Cells dialog box, click the Fill tab or right-click in a cell and then click *Format Cells* at the shortcut menu.

Choose a fill color for a cell or selected cells by clicking a color choice in the *Background Color* section. To add shading to a cell or selected cells, click the Fill Effects button and then click the desired shading style at the Fill Effects dialog box.

Repeating the Last Action

If you want to apply other types of formatting, such as number, border, or shading formatting to other cells in a worksheet, use the Repeat command by pressing F4 or Ctrl + Y. The Repeat command repeats the last action performed.

Figure 3.10 Format Cells Dialog Box with Fill Tab Selected

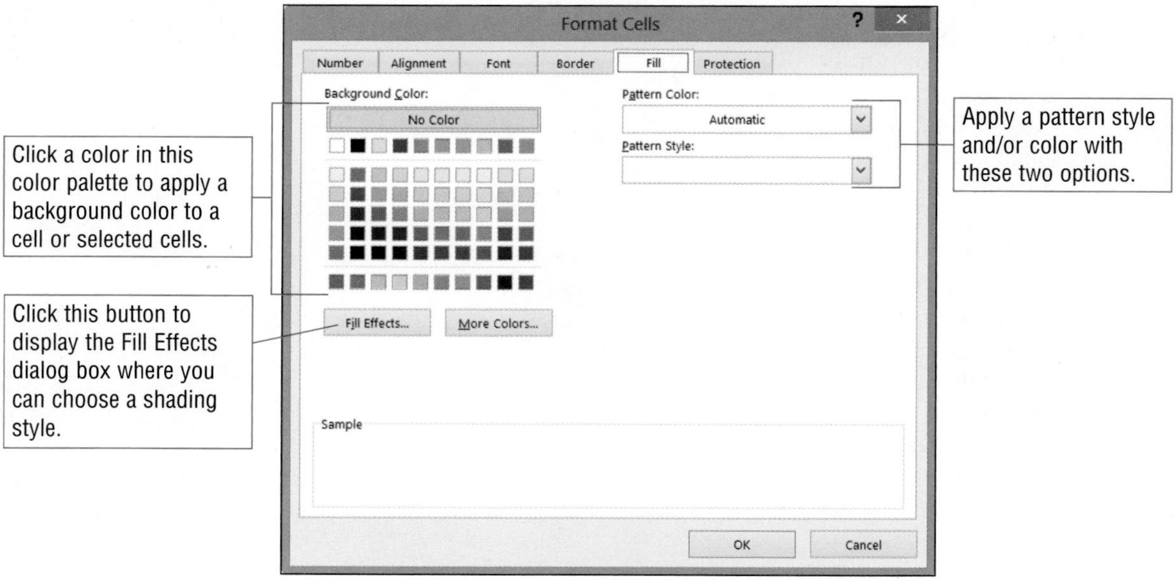

Project 4d Adding Fill Color and Shading to Cells Part 4 of 6

1. With **EL1-C3-P4-HBCJobs.xlsx** open, add fill color to cell A1 and repeat the formatting by completing the following steps:
   a. Make cell A1 active.
   b. Click the Format button in the Cells group and then click *Format Cells* at the drop-down list.
   c. At the Format Cells dialog box, click the Fill tab.
   d. Click the light gold color in the *Background Color* section (eighth column, second row—see image below).

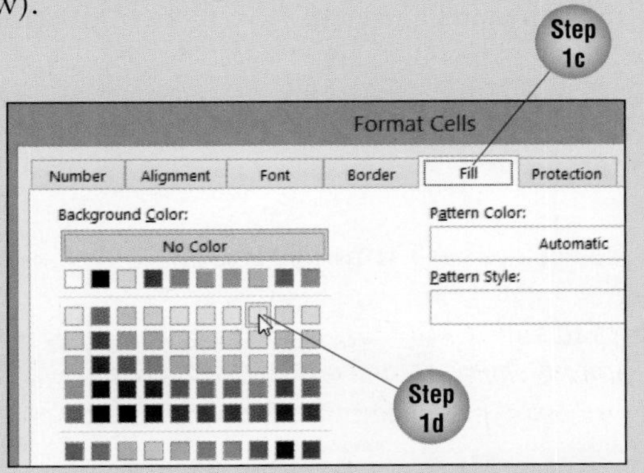

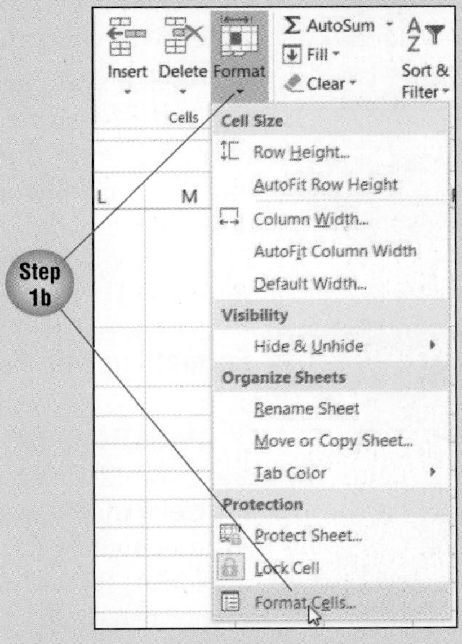

   e. Click OK.
   f. Select cells A2 through E2 and then press the F4 function key. (This repeats the light gold fill.)
2. Select row 2, insert a new row, and then change the height of the new row to 12.00 points.
3. Add shading to cells by completing the following steps:
   a. Select cells A2 through E2.
   b. Click the Format button in the Cells group and then click *Format Cells* at the drop-down list.
   c. At the Format Cells dialog box, if necessary, click the Fill tab.
   d. Click the Fill Effects button.
   e. At the Fill Effects dialog box, click the down-pointing arrow at the right side of the *Color 2* option box and then click *Gold, Accent 4* in the *Theme Colors* section (eighth column, top row).
   f. Click OK to close the Fill Effects dialog box.
   g. Click OK to close the Format Cells dialog box.
4. Save **EL1-C3-P4-HBCJobs.xlsx**.

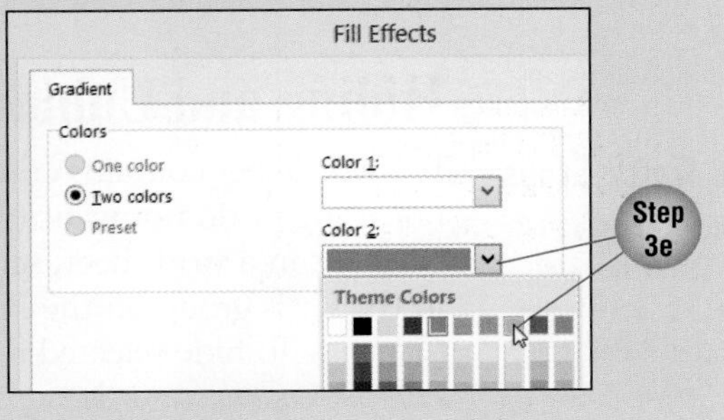

Formatting with Format Painter

Quick Steps

Format with Format Painter
1. Select cells with desired formatting.
2. Double-click Format Painter button.
3. Select desired cells.
4. Click Format Painter button.

Format Painter

Use the Format Painter button in the Clipboard group on the HOME tab to copy formatting to different locations in the worksheet. To use the Format Painter button, make active a cell or selected cells that contain the desired formatting, click the Format Painter button, and then click in the cell or selected cells to which you want the formatting applied.

When you click the Format Painter button, the mouse pointer displays with a paintbrush attached. If you want to apply formatting a single time, click the Format Painter button once. If you want to apply the formatting in more than one location in the worksheet, double-click the Format Painter button, selected the desired cells, and then click the Format Painter button to turn off the feature.

Project 4e **Formatting with Format Painter** **Part 5 of 6**

1. With **EL1-C3-P4-HBCJobs.xlsx** open, select cells A5 through E5.
2. Click the Font group dialog box launcher.
3. At the Format Cells dialog box, click the Fill tab.
4. Click the light green color in the *Background Color* section (last column, second row).
5. Click OK to close the dialog box.
6. Use Format Painter to "paint" formatting to rows by completing the following steps:
   a. With cells A5 through E5 selected, double-click the Format Painter button in the Clipboard group.
   b. Select cells A7 through E7.
   c. Select cells A9 through E9.
   d. Select cells A11 through E11.
   e. Turn off Format Painter by clicking the Format Painter button.
7. Save and then print **EL1-C3-P4-HBCJobs.xlsx**.

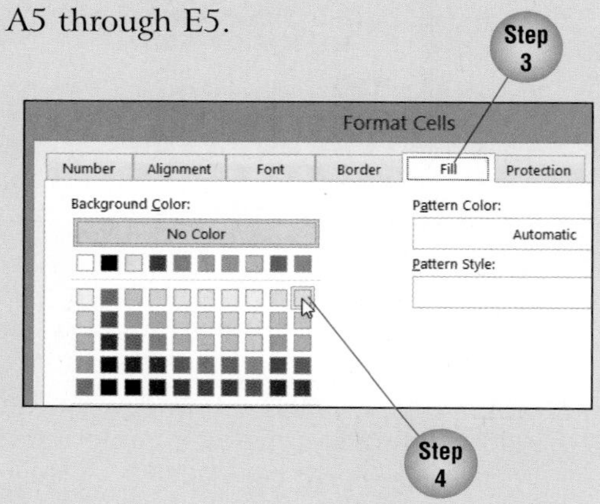

Hiding and Unhiding Columns and Rows

Quick Steps

Hide Columns
1. Select columns.
2. Click Format button.
3. Point to *Hide & Unhide*.
4. Click *Hide Columns*.

Hide Rows
1. Select rows.
2. Click Format button.
3. Point to *Hide & Unhide*.
4. Click *Hide Rows*.

If a worksheet contains columns and/or rows of sensitive data or data that you are not using or do not want to view, consider hiding the columns and/or rows. To hide columns in a worksheet, select the columns to be hidden, click the Format button in the Cells group on the HOME tab, point to *Hide & Unhide*, and then click *Hide Columns*. To hide selected rows, click the Format button in the Cells group, point to *Hide & Unhide*, and then click *Hide Rows*. To make a hidden column visible, select the column to the left and the column to the right of the hidden column, click the Format button in the Cells group, point to *Hide & Unhide*, and then click *Unhide Columns*. To make a hidden row visible, select the row above and the row below the hidden row, click the Format button in the Cells group, point to *Hide & Unhide*, and then click *Unhide Rows*.

If the first row or column is hidden, use the Go To feature to make the row or column visible. To do this, click the Find & Select button in the Editing group on the HOME tab and then click *Go To* at the drop-down list. At the Go To dialog box, type *A1* in the *Reference* text box and then click OK. At the worksheet, click the Format button in the Cells group, point to *Hide & Unhide*, and then click *Unhide Columns* or click *Unhide Rows*.

You can also unhide columns or rows using the mouse. If a column or row is hidden, the light gray boundary line in the column or row header displays as a slightly thicker gray line. To unhide a column, position the mouse pointer on the slightly thicker gray line that displays in the column header until the mouse pointer changes into a left-and-right-pointing arrow with a double line in the middle. (Make sure the mouse pointer displays with two lines between the arrows. If a single line displays, you will simply change the size of the visible column.) Hold down the left mouse button, drag to the right until the column displays at the desired width, and then release the mouse button. Unhide a row in a similar manner. Position the mouse pointer on the slightly thicker gray line in the row header until the mouse pointer changes into an up-and-down-pointing arrow with a double line in the middle. Drag down to display the row and then release the mouse button. If two or more adjacent columns or rows are hidden, you will need to unhide each column or row separately.

HINT

Set the column width to zero and the column is hidden. Set the row height to zero and the row is hidden.

Project 4f Hiding and Unhiding Columns and Rows

Part 6 of 6

1. With **EL1-C3-P4-HBCJobs.xlsx** open, hide the row for Linstrom Enterprises and the row for Summit Services by completing the following steps:
   a. Click the row 7 header to select the entire row.
   b. Hold down the Ctrl key and then click the row 11 header to select the entire row.
   c. Click the Format button in the Cells group on the HOME tab, point to *Hide & Unhide*, and then click *Hide Rows*.

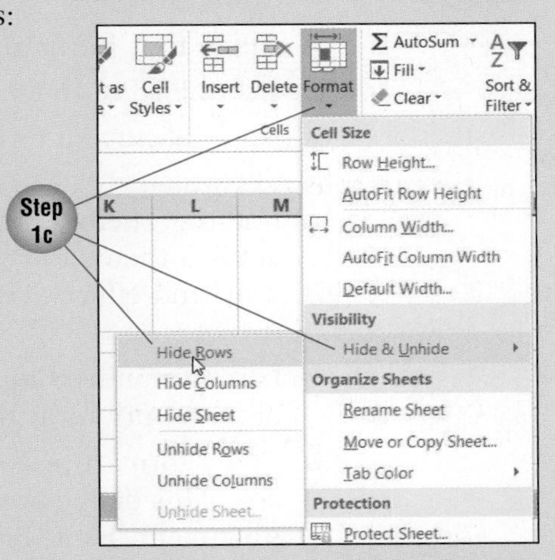

2. Hide the column containing the actual amounts by completing the following steps:
   a. Click in cell D3 to make it the active cell.
   b. Click the Format button in the Cells group, point to *Hide & Unhide*, and then click *Hide Columns*.
3. Save and then print **EL1-C3-P4-HBCJobs.xlsx**.
4. Unhide the rows by completing the following steps:
   a. Select rows 6 through 12.
   b. Click the Format button in the Cells group, point to *Hide & Unhide*, and then click *Unhide Rows*.
   c. Click in cell A4.
5. Unhide column D by completing the following steps:
   a. Position the mouse pointer on the thicker gray line that displays between columns C and E in the column header until the pointer turns into a left-and-right-pointing arrow with a double line in the middle.
   b. Hold down the left mouse button, drag to the right until *Width: 9.56 (93 pixels)* displays in a box above the mouse pointer, and then release the mouse button.

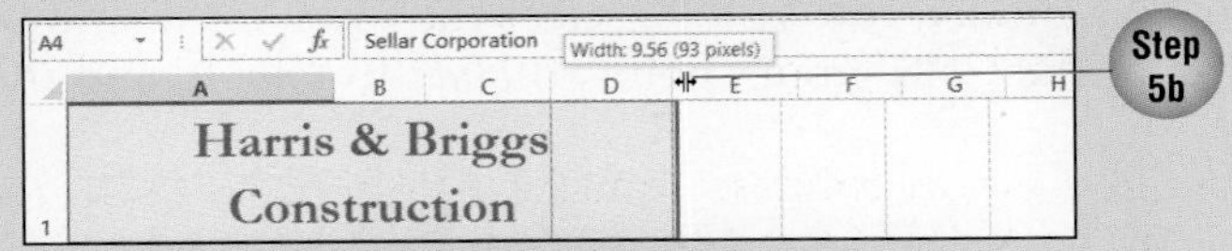

6. Save, print, and then close **EL1-C3-P4-HBCJobs.xlsx**.

Chapter Summary

- Change column width using the mouse on column boundaries or with options at the Column Width dialog box.
- Change row height using the mouse on row boundaries or with options at the Row Height dialog box.
- Insert a row in a worksheet with the Insert button in the Cells group on the HOME tab or with options at the Insert dialog box.
- Insert a column in a worksheet with the Insert button in the Cells group or with options at the Insert dialog box.
- Delete a specific cell by clicking the Delete button arrow and then clicking *Delete Cells* at the drop-down list. At the Delete dialog box, specify if you want to delete just the cell or an entire row or column.
- Delete a selected row(s) or column(s) by clicking the Delete button in the Cells group.
- Delete cell contents by pressing the Delete key or clicking the Clear button in the Editing group on the HOME tab and then clicking *Clear Contents* at the drop-down list.
- Apply font formatting with buttons in the Font group on the HOME tab.
- Use the Mini toolbar to apply font formatting to selected data in a cell.
- Apply alignment formatting with buttons in the Alignment group on the HOME tab.
- Use the Themes button in the Themes group on the PAGE LAYOUT tab to apply a theme to cells in a worksheet that applies formatting such as color, font, and effects. Use the other buttons in the Themes group to customize the theme.
- Format numbers in cells with buttons in the Number group on the HOME tab or with options at the Format Cells dialog box with the Number tab selected.
- Apply formatting to cells in a worksheet with options at the Format Cells dialog box. This dialog box includes the following tabs for formatting cells: Number, Alignment, Font, Border, and Fill.
- Press F4 or Ctrl + Y to repeat the last action performed.
- Use the Format Painter button in the Clipboard group on the HOME tab to apply formatting to different locations in a worksheet.
- Hide selected columns or rows in a worksheet by clicking the Format button in the Cells group on the HOME tab, pointing to *Hide & Unhide*, and then clicking *Hide Columns* or *Hide Rows*.
- To make a hidden column visible, select the columns to the left and right, click the Format button in the Cells group, point to *Hide & Unhide*, and then click *Unhide Columns*.
- To make a hidden row visible, select the rows above and below, click the Format button in the Cells group, point to *Hide & Unhide*, and then click *Unhide Rows*.

Commands Review

FEATURE	RIBBON TAB, GROUP	BUTTON	KEYBOARD SHORTCUT
bold text	HOME, Font	B	Ctrl + B
borders	HOME, Font		
bottom-align (in row)	HOME, Alignment		
center-align (in column)	HOME, Alignment		
clear cell or cell contents	HOME, Editing		
decrease font size	HOME, Font		
decrease indent	HOME, Alignment		Ctrl + Alt + Shift + Tab
delete cells, rows, or columns	HOME, Cells		
fill color	Home, Font		
font	HOME, Font	Calibri	
font color	Home, Font		
font size	HOME, Font	11	
format	HOME, Cells		
Format Painter	HOME, Clipboard		
increase font size	HOME, Font		
increase indent	HOME, Alignment		Ctrl + Alt + Tab
insert cells, rows, or columns	HOME, Cells		
italicize text	HOME, Font	I	Ctrl + I
left-align (in column)	HOME, Alignment		
merge and center cells	HOME, Alignment		
middle-align (in row)	HOME, Alignment		
number format	HOME, Number	General	
orientation	HOME, Alignment		
repeat last action			F4 or Ctrl + Y
right-align (in column)	HOME, Alignment		
themes	PAGE LAYOUT, Themes		

FEATURE	RIBBON TAB, GROUP	BUTTON	KEYBOARD SHORTCUT
top-align (in row)	HOME, Alignment		
underline text	HOME, Font	U	Ctrl + U
wrap text	HOME, Alignment		

Concepts Check Test Your Knowledge SNAP

Completion: In the space provided at the right, indicate the correct term, symbol, or command.

1. By default, a column is inserted on this side of the column containing the active cell. (1 word) — left
2. To delete a row, select the row and then click the Delete button in this group on the HOME tab. (1) — cells
3. Use the options at this button's drop-down list to clear the contents of the cell or selected cells. (1) Clear — ~~clear~~ button in ~~Home tab,~~ Editing group
4. Use this button to insert color in the active cell or selected cells. (2) — Fill Color
5. Select data in a cell and this displays above the selected text. (2) — mini toolbar
6. By default, numbers are aligned at this side of a cell. (1) — right
7. Click this button in the Alignment group on the HOME tab to rotate data in a cell. (1) — Orientation
8. The Themes button is located on this tab. (2) — Page Layout
9. If you type a number with a dollar sign, such as *$50.25*, Excel automatically applies this formatting to the number. (1) — Currency
10. If you type a number with a percent sign, such as *25%*, Excel automatically applies this formatting to the number. (1) — Percent
11. Align and indent data in cells using buttons in the Alignment group on the HOME tab or with options at this dialog box with the Alignment tab selected. (2) — Format Cells ~~Dialog box~~
12. You can repeat the last action performed by pressing Ctrl + Y or this function key. (1) — F4
13. The Format Painter button is located in this group on the HOME tab. (1) — Clipboard
14. To hide a column, select the column, click this button in the Cells group on the HOME tab, point to *Hide & Unhide*, and then click *Hide Columns*. (1) — Format ~~button~~

Skills Check Assess Your Performance

Assessment 1

FORMAT A SALES AND BONUSES WORKSHEET

SNAP Grade It

1. Open **NSPSales.xlsx**.
2. Save the workbook with Save As and name it **EL1-C3-A1-NSPSales**.
3. Change the width of columns as follows:
   Column A: 14.00
   Columns B–E: 10.00
4. Select row 2 and then insert a new row.
5. Merge and center cells A2 through E2.
6. Type **Sales Department** in cell A2 and then press Enter.
7. Increase the height of row 1 to 33.00 points.
8. Increase the height of row 2 to 21.00 points.
9. Increase the height of row 3 to 18.00 points.
10. Make the following formatting changes to the worksheet:
    a. Make cell A1 active, change the font size to 18 points, and turn on bold formatting.
    b. Make cell A2 active, change the font size to 14 points, and turn on bold formatting.
    c. Select cells A3 through E3, click the Bold button in the Font group, and then click the Center button in the Alignment group.
    d. Select cells A1 through E3 and change the vertical alignment to *Middle Align*.
11. Insert the following formulas in the worksheet:
    a. Insert a formula in cell D4 that adds the amounts in cells B4 and C4. Copy the formula down to cells D5 through D11.
    b. Insert a formula in cell E4 that averages the amounts in cells B4 and C4. Copy the formula down to cells E5 through E11.
12. Make the following changes to the worksheet:
    a. Select cells B4 through E4 and then apply accounting formatting with a dollar sign and no places past the decimal point.
    b. Select cells B5 through E11 and then apply comma formatting and change the number of places past the decimal point to zero.
    c. Apply the Facet theme to the worksheet.
    d. Add a double-line border outline around cells A1 through E11.
    e. Select cells A1 and A2 and then apply Blue-Gray, Text 2, Lighter 80% fill color (fourth column, second row in the *Theme Colors* section).
    f. Select cells A3 through E3 and then apply Blue-Gray, Text 2, Lighter 60% fill color (fourth column, third row in the *Theme Colors* section).
13. Save, print, and then close **EL1-C3-A1-NSPSales.xlsx**.

Assessment 2

FORMAT AN OVERDUE ACCOUNTS WORKSHEET

SNAP Grade It

1. Open **CCorpAccts.xlsx**.
2. Save the workbook with Save As and name it **EL1-C3-A2-CCorpAccts**.
3. Change the width of columns as follows:
   - Column A: 21.00 characters
   - Column B: 10.00 characters
   - Column C: 12.00 characters
   - Column D: 13.00 characters
   - Column E: 7.00 characters
   - Column F: 12.00 characters
4. Make cell A1 active and then insert a new row.
5. Merge and center cells A1 through F1.
6. Type **Compass Corporation** in cell A1 and then press Enter.
7. Increase the height of row 1 to 42.00 points.
8. Increase the height of row 2 to 24.00 points.
9. Make the following formatting changes to the worksheet:
   a. Select cells A1 through F11 and then change the font to 10-point Cambria.
   b. Make cell A1 active, change the font size to 24 points, and turn on bold formatting.
   c. Make cell A2 active, change the font size to 18 points, and turn on bold formatting.
   d. Select cells A3 through F3, click the Bold button in the Font group, and then click the Center button in the Alignment group.
   e. Select cell A1 and then click the Middle Align button in the Alignment group.
   f. Select cells B4 through B11 and then click the Center button in the Alignment group.
   g. Select cells E4 through E11 and then click the Center button in the Alignment group.
10. Enter a formula in cell F4 that inserts the due date (the purchase date plus the number of days in the *Terms* column). Copy the formula down to cells F5 through F11.
11. Apply the following borders and fill color:
    a. Add a thick line outline border around cells A1 through F11.
    b. Make cell A2 active and then add a double-line border at the top and the bottom of the cell.
    c. Select cells A3 through F3 and then add a single line border to the bottom of the cells.
    d. Select cells A1 and A2 and then apply Blue, Accent 1, Lighter 80% fill color (fifth column, second row in the *Theme Colors* section).
12. Save, print, and then close **EL1-C3-A2-CCorpAccts.xlsx**.

Assessment 3

FORMAT A SUPPLIES AND EQUIPMENT WORKSHEET

SNAP Grade It

1. Open **OEBudget.xlsx**.
2. Save the workbook with Save As and name it **EL1-C3-A3-OEBudget**.
3. Select and then merge across cells A1 through D2. ***Hint: Use the* Merge Across *option at the Merge & Center button drop-down list.***

4. With cells A1 and A2 selected, click the Middle Align button in the Alignment group and then click the Center button.
5. Make cell A1 active and then change the font size to 22 points and turn on bold formatting.
6. Make cell A2 active and then change the font size to 12 points and turn on bold formatting.
7. Change the height of row 1 to 36.00 points.
8. Change the height of row 2 to 21.00 points.
9. Change the width of column A to 15.00 characters.
10. Select cells A3 through A17, turn on bold, and then click the Wrap Text button in the Alignment group.
11. Make cell B3 active and then apply currency formatting with no places past the decimal point.
12. Select cells C6 through C19 and then apply percentage formatting with one place past the decimal point.
13. Make cell D6 active and then type a formula that multiplies the absolute cell reference $B$3 with the percentage in cell C6. Copy the formula down to cells D7 through D19.
14. With cells D6 through D19 selected, apply currency formatting with no places past the decimal point.
15. Make cell D8 active and then clear the cell contents. Use the Repeat command, F4, to clear the contents from cells D11, D14, and D17.
16. Select cells A1 through D19, change the font to Constantia, and then change the font color to Dark Blue (in the *Standard Colors* section).
17. Add Green, Accent 6, Lighter 80% green fill color (last column, second row in the *Theme Colors* section) to the following cells: A1, A2, A5–D5, A8–D8, A11–D11, A14–D14, and A17–D17.
18. Automatically adjust the width of column B.
19. Save, print, and then close **EL1-C3-A3-OEBudget.xlsx**.

Assessment 4

FORMAT A FINANCIAL ANALYSIS WORKSHEET

1. At a blank workbook, display the Format Cells dialog box with the Alignment tab selected and then experiment with the options in the *Text control* section.
2. Open **FinAnalysis.xlsx**.
3. Save the workbook with Save As and name it **EL1-C3-A4-FinAnalysis**.
4. Make cell B9 active and then insert a formula that averages the percentages in cells B3 through B8. Copy the formula to the right to cells C9 and D9.
5. Select cells B3 through D9, display the Format Cells dialog box with the Alignment tab selected, change the horizontal alignment to *Right (Indent)* and the indent to *2*, and then close the dialog box.
6. Select cells A1 through D9 and then change the font size to 14 points.
7. Select cells B2 through D2 and then change the orientation to 45 degrees.
8. Save, print, and then close **EL1-C3-A4-FinAnalysis.xlsx**.

Visual Benchmark Demonstrate Your Proficiency

CREATE A WORKSHEET AND INSERT FORMULAS

1. At a blank workbook, type the data in the cells indicated in Figure 3.11 but **do not** type the data in the following cells: B8:D8, B14:D14, B20:D20, B22:D22, and B25:D25. For these cells, enter the appropriate formulas so your results match what you see in the figure.
2. Apply formatting so your worksheet looks similar to the worksheet shown in Figure 3.11.
3. Save the workbook and name it **EL1-C3-VB-BTBookings**.
4. Print **EL1-C3-VB-BTBookings.xlsx**.
5. Press Ctrl + ` to turn on the display of formulas and then print the worksheet again.
6. Turn off the display of formulas and then close the workbook.

Figure 3.11 Visual Benchmark

	A	B	C	D	E
1	**Bayside Travel**				
2	**First Quarter Booking Totals**				
3		**January**	**February**	**March**	
4	**Los Angeles**				
5	Tours	$ 65,395	$ 62,103	$ 58,450	
6	Cruises	48,525	43,218	54,055	
7	Other	29,329	26,398	30,391	
8	**Total**	143,249	131,719	142,896	
9					
10	**San Francisco**				
11	Tours	41,438	39,493	56,461	
12	Cruises	23,147	18,530	40,530	
13	Other	18,642	14,320	17,305	
14	**Total**	83,227	72,343	114,296	
15					
16	**Toronto**				
17	Tours	50,229	42,519	52,403	
18	Cruises	49,260	41,490	39,230	
19	Other	31,322	21,579	27,430	
20	**Total**	130,811	105,588	119,063	
21					
22	TOTAL	$357,287	$309,650	$376,255	
23					
24	**Gross Profit Factor**	26%			
25	**Estimated Gross Profit**	$ 92,895	$ 80,509	$ 97,826	

Case Study Apply Your Skills

Part 1

You are the office manager for HealthWise Fitness Center and decide to prepare an Excel worksheet that displays the various plans offered by the health club. In this worksheet, you want to include yearly dues for each plan as well as quarterly and monthly payments. Open the **HFCDues.xlsx** workbook and then save it with Save As and name it **EL1-C3-CS-HFCDues-1**. Make the following changes to the worksheet:

- Select cells B3 through D8 and then apply accounting formatting with two places past the decimal point and without dollar signs.
- Make cell B3 active and then insert *500.00*.
- Make cell B4 active and then insert a formula that adds the amount in cell B3 with the product (multiplication) of cell B3 multiplied by 10%. (The formula should look like this: **=B3+(B3*10%)**. The Economy plan is the base plan and each additional plan costs 10% more than the previous plan.)
- Copy the formula in cell B4 down to cells B5 through B8.
- Insert a formula in cell C3 that divides the amount in cell B3 by 4 and then copy the formula down to cells C4 through C8.
- Insert a formula in cell D3 that divides the amount in cell B3 by 12 and then copy the formula down to cells D4 through D8.
- Apply formatting to enhance the visual display of the worksheet.

Save and print the completed worksheet.

With **EL1-C3-CS-HFCDues-1.xlsx** open, save the workbook with Save As and name it **EL1-C3-CS-HFCDues-2** and then make the following changes:

- You have been informed that the base rate for yearly dues has increased from $500.00 to $600.00. Change this amount in cell B3 of the worksheet.
- If clients are late with their quarterly or monthly dues payments, a late fee is charged. You decide to add the late fee information to the worksheet. Insert a new column to the right of column C. Type **Late Fees** in cell D2 and also in cell F2.
- Insert a formula in cell D3 that multiplies the amount in C3 by 5%. Copy this formula down to cells D4 through D8.
- Insert a formula in cell F3 that multiplies the amount in cell E3 by 7%. Copy this formula down to cells F4 through F8. If necessary, apply accounting formatting to cells F3 through F8 with two places after the decimal point and without dollar signs.
- Select cells B3 through F3 and change the accounting formatting to include dollar signs.
- Select cells B8 through F8 and change the accounting formatting to include dollar signs.
- Apply formatting to enhance the visual display of the worksheet.

Save, print, and then close **EL1-C3-CS-HFCDues-2.xlsx**.

Part 2

Prepare a payroll sheet for the employees of the fitness center using the information in Figure 3.12, and include the following information:

Insert a formula in the *Overtime Pay* column that multiples the hourly wage by the overtime rate, which is 1.5, and then multiple that amount by the number of overtime hours. (Make sure you include parentheses around the first part of the formula.)

Insert a formula in the *Weekly Salary* column that multiplies the hourly wage by the number of hours plus the overtime pay. (Make sure you include parentheses in the first part of the formula.)

Apply formatting to enhance the visual display of the worksheet. Save the workbook and name it **EL1-C3-CS-HFCPayroll**. Press Ctrl + ` to turn on the display of formulas, print the worksheet, and then turn off the display of formulas.

Make the following changes to the worksheet:

- Change the hourly wage for Amanda Turney to *$22.00*.
- Increase the hours for Daniel Joyner to *20*.
- Remove the row for Grant Baker.
- Insert a row between Jean Overmeyer and Bonnie Haddon and then type the following information in the cells in the new row: *Employee:* McGuire, Tonya; *Hourly Wage:* $17.50; *Hours:* 15; *Overtime Hours:* 0.

Save and then print **EL1-C3-CS-HFCPayroll.xlsx**. Press Ctrl + ` to turn on the display of formulas, print the worksheet again, and then turn off the display of formulas. Save and close **EL1-C3-CS-HFCPayroll.xlsx**.

Figure 3.12 Case Study Part 2

HealthWise Fitness Center
Weekly Payroll

Employee	Hourly Wage	Hours	Overtime Hours	Overtime Pay	Weekly Salary
Heaton, Kelly	$26.50	40	2		
Severson, Joel	$25.00	40	0		
Turney, Amanda	$20.00	15	0		
Walters, Leslie	$19.65	30	0		
Overmeyer, Jean	$18.00	20	0		
Haddon, Bonnie	$16.00	40	3		
Baker, Grant	$15.00	40	0		
Calveri, Shannon	$12.00	15	0		
Dugan, Emily	$10.50	40	4		
Joyner, Daniel	$10.50	10	0		
Lee, Alexander	$10.50	10	0		

Part 3

Your boss is interested in ordering new equipment for the health club. She is interested in ordering three elliptical machines, three recumbent bikes, and three upright bikes. She has asked you to use the Internet to research models and prices for this new equipment. She then wants you to prepare a worksheet with the information. Using the Internet, search for information about the following equipment:

- Search for elliptical machines for sale. Locate two different models and, if possible, find at least two companies that sell each model. Make a note of the company names, model numbers, and prices.
- Search for recumbent bikes for sale. Locate two different models and, if possible, find at least two companies that sell each model. Make a note of the company names, model numbers, and prices.
- Search for upright bikes for sale. Locate two different models and, if possible, find at least two companies that sell each model. Make a note of the company names, model numbers, and prices.

Using the information you found on the Internet, prepare an Excel worksheet with the following information:

- Company name
- Equipment name
- Equipment model
- Price
- A column that multiplies the price by the number required (which is 3)

Include the fitness center name, HealthWise Fitness Center, and any other information you think is necessary to the worksheet. Apply formatting to enhance the visual display of the worksheet. Save the workbook and name it **EL1-C3-CS-HFCEquip**. Print and then close **EL1-C3-CS-HFCEquip.xlsx**.

Part 4

When a prospective client contacts HealthWise about joining, you send a letter containing information about the fitness center, the plans offered, and the dues amounts. Use a letter template in Word to create a letter to send to a prospective client. (You determine the client's name and address). Copy the cells in **EL1-C3-CS-HFCDues-02.xlsx** containing data and paste them into the body of the letter. Make formatting changes to make the data readable. Save the document and name it **HFCLetter**. Print and then close **HFCLetter.docx**.

MICROSOFT® EXCEL®

CHAPTER 4

Enhancing a Worksheet

PERFORMANCE OBJECTIVES

Upon successful completion of Chapter 4, you will be able to:

- **Change worksheet margins**
- **Center a worksheet horizontally and vertically on the page**
- **Insert a page break in a worksheet**
- **Print gridlines and row and column headings**
- **Set and clear a print area**
- **Insert headers and footers**
- **Customize print jobs**
- **Complete a spelling check on a worksheet**
- **Find and replace data and cell formatting in a worksheet**
- **Sort data in cells in ascending and descending order**
- **Filter a list using AutoFilter**

SNAP

Tutorials

4.1 Changing Page Margins and Layout Options
4.2 Formatting a Worksheet Page for Printing
4.3 Using Page Break Preview
4.4 Inserting Headers and Footers
4.5 Formatting and Printing Multiple Worksheets
4.6 Completing a Spelling Check
4.7 Using Undo and Redo
4.8 Using Find and Replace
4.9 Finding and Replacing Text and Formatting
4.10 Sorting Data
4.11 Filtering Data Using a Custom AutoFilter

Excel contains features you can use to enhance and control the formatting of a worksheet. In this chapter, you will learn how to change worksheet margins, orientation, size, and scale; print column and row titles; print gridlines; and center a worksheet horizontally and vertically on the page. You will also learn how to complete a spelling check on text in a worksheet, find and replace specific data and formatting in a worksheet, sort and filter data, and plan and create a worksheet. Model answers for this chapter's projects appear on the following pages.

Excel
EL1C4

Note: Before beginning the projects, copy to your storage medium the EL1C4 subfolder from the EL1 folder on the CD that accompanies this textbook and make EL1C4 the active folder.

1

Real P

Y

	January	February	March	April
Income				
Sublet Rent	$ 1,100	$ 1,100	$ 1,100	$ 1,100
Archway Systems Contract	235	235	235	235
Lowell-Briggs Contract	750	750	525	525
Wedding Portraits	4,500	2,000	1,500	2,800
Senior Portraits	2,250	1,500	4,500	5,000
Catalog Pictures	-	-	-	-
Total Income	$ 8,835	$ 5,585	$ 7,860	$ 9,660
Expenses				
Mortgage	$ 4,230	$ 4,230	$ 4,230	$ 4,230
Utilities	625	550	600	425
Insurance	375	375	375	375
Equipment Purchases	525	1,250	950	3,500
Supplies	750	750	1,500	1,250
Equipment Leases	825	825	825	825
Total Expenses	7,330	7,980	8,480	10,605
Profit	1,505	(2,395)	(620)	(945)

Yearly Budget 2

Photography

early Budget

May	June	July	August	September	October
$ 1,100	$ 1,100	$ 1,100	$ 1,100	$ 1,100	$ 1,100
235	235	235	235	235	235
-	-	450	450	450	575
4,000	8,250	7,500	6,850	4,500	3,500
3,250	1,000	300	500	650	650
500	500	500	500	500	-
$ 9,085	$ 11,085	$ 10,085	$ 9,635	$ 7,435	$ 6,060
$ 4,230	$ 4,230	$ 4,230	$ 4,230	$ 4,230	$ 4,230
400	500	650	700	700	500
375	375	375	375	375	375
-	-	-	-	-	-
1,500	2,500	2,250	1,750	950	850
825	825	825	825	825	825
7,330	8,430	8,330	7,880	7,080	6,780
1,755	2,655	1,755	1,755	355	(720)

Student Name

Yearly Budget 3

November	December	Total
$ 1,100	$ 1,100	$ 13,200
235	235	2,820
575	575	5,625
3,500	7,000	55,900
400	400	20,400
-	-	2,500
$ 5,810	$ 9,310	$100,445
$ 4,230	$ 4,230	$ 50,760
550	650	6,850
375	375	4,500
-	-	6,225
850	2,000	16,900
825	825	9,900
6,830	8,080	95,135
(1,020)	1,230	5,310

Student Name

Project 1 Format a Yearly Budget Worksheet

EL1-C4-P1-RPBudget.xlsx

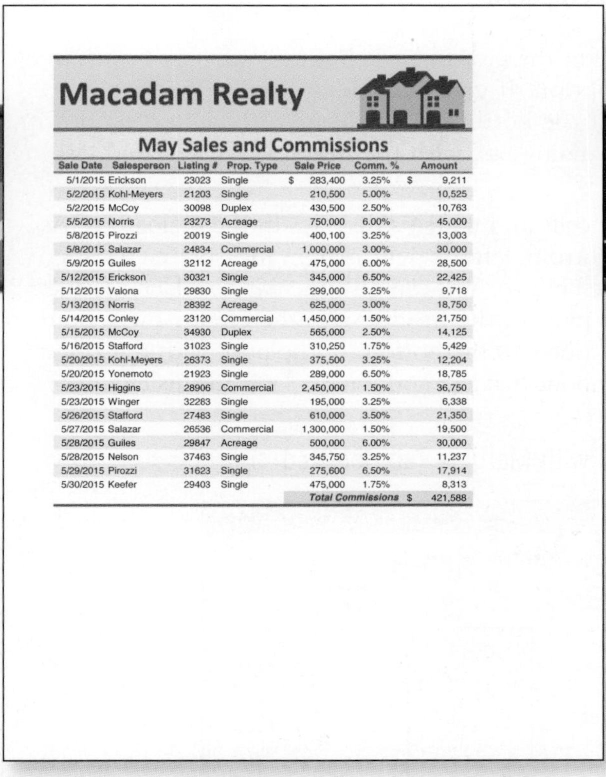

Macadam Realty

May Sales and Commissions

Sale Date	Salesperson	Listing #	Prop. Type	Sale Price	Comm. %	Amount
5/1/2015	Erickson	23023	Single	$ 283,400	3.25%	$ 9,211
5/2/2015	Kohl-Meyers	21203	Single	210,500	5.00%	10,525
5/2/2015	McCoy	30098	Duplex	430,500	2.50%	10,763
5/5/2015	Norris	23273	Acreage	750,000	6.00%	45,000
5/8/2015	Pirozzi	20019	Single	400,100	3.25%	13,003
5/8/2015	Salazar	24834	Commercial	1,000,000	3.00%	30,000
5/9/2015	Guiles	32112	Acreage	475,000	6.00%	28,500
5/12/2015	Erickson	30321	Single	345,000	6.50%	22,425
5/12/2015	Valona	29830	Single	299,000	3.25%	9,718
5/13/2015	Norris	28392	Acreage	625,000	3.00%	18,750
5/14/2015	Conley	23120	Commercial	1,450,000	1.50%	21,750
5/15/2015	McCoy	34930	Duplex	565,000	2.50%	14,125
5/16/2015	Stafford	31023	Single	310,250	1.75%	5,429
5/20/2015	Kohl-Meyers	26373	Single	375,500	3.25%	12,204
5/20/2015	Yonemoto	21923	Single	289,000	6.50%	18,785
5/23/2015	Higgins	28906	Commercial	2,450,000	1.50%	36,750
5/23/2015	Winger	32283	Single	195,000	3.25%	6,338
5/26/2015	Stafford	27483	Single	610,000	3.50%	21,350
5/27/2015	Salazar	26536	Commercial	1,300,000	1.50%	19,500
5/28/2015	Guiles	29847	Acreage	500,000	6.00%	30,000
5/28/2015	Nelson	37463	Single	345,750	3.25%	11,237
5/29/2015	Pirozzi	31623	Single	275,600	6.50%	17,914
5/30/2015	Keefer	29403	Single	475,000	1.75%	8,313
					Total Commissions	$ 421,588

Project 2 Format a May Sales and Commissions Worksheet

EL1-C4-P2-MRSales.xlsx

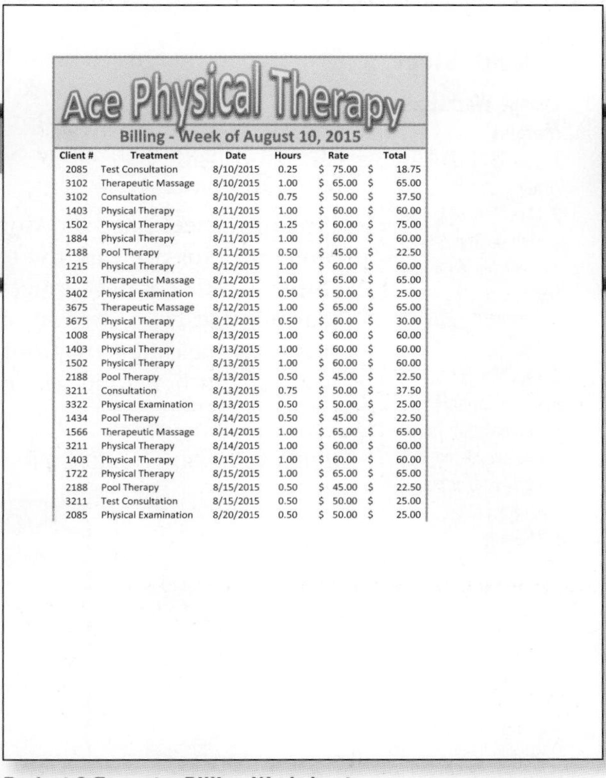

Ace Physical Therapy

Billing - Week of August 10, 2015

Client #	Treatment	Date	Hours	Rate	Total
2085	Test Consultation	8/10/2015	0.25	$ 75.00	$ 18.75
3102	Therapeutic Massage	8/10/2015	1.00	$ 65.00	$ 65.00
3102	Consultation	8/10/2015	0.75	$ 50.00	$ 37.50
1403	Physical Therapy	8/11/2015	1.00	$ 60.00	$ 60.00
1502	Physical Therapy	8/11/2015	1.25	$ 60.00	$ 75.00
1884	Physical Therapy	8/11/2015	1.00	$ 60.00	$ 60.00
2188	Pool Therapy	8/11/2015	0.50	$ 45.00	$ 22.50
1215	Physical Therapy	8/12/2015	1.00	$ 60.00	$ 60.00
3102	Therapeutic Massage	8/12/2015	1.00	$ 65.00	$ 65.00
3402	Physical Examination	8/12/2015	0.50	$ 50.00	$ 25.00
3675	Therapeutic Massage	8/12/2015	1.00	$ 65.00	$ 65.00
3675	Physical Therapy	8/12/2015	0.50	$ 60.00	$ 30.00
1008	Physical Therapy	8/13/2015	1.00	$ 60.00	$ 60.00
1403	Physical Therapy	8/13/2015	1.00	$ 60.00	$ 60.00
1502	Physical Therapy	8/13/2015	1.00	$ 60.00	$ 60.00
2188	Pool Therapy	8/13/2015	0.50	$ 45.00	$ 22.50
3211	Consultation	8/13/2015	0.75	$ 50.00	$ 37.50
3322	Physical Examination	8/13/2015	0.50	$ 50.00	$ 25.00
1434	Pool Therapy	8/14/2015	0.50	$ 45.00	$ 22.50
1566	Therapeutic Massage	8/14/2015	1.00	$ 65.00	$ 65.00
3211	Physical Therapy	8/14/2015	1.00	$ 60.00	$ 60.00
1403	Physical Therapy	8/15/2015	1.00	$ 60.00	$ 60.00
1722	Physical Therapy	8/15/2015	1.00	$ 65.00	$ 65.00
2188	Pool Therapy	8/15/2015	0.50	$ 45.00	$ 22.50
3211	Test Consultation	8/15/2015	0.50	$ 50.00	$ 25.00
2085	Physical Examination	8/20/2015	0.50	$ 50.00	$ 25.00

Project 3 Format a Billing Worksheet

EL1-C4-P3-APTBilling.xlsx

Project 1 Format a Yearly Budget Worksheet — 12 Parts

You will format a yearly budget worksheet by inserting formulas; changing margins, page orientation, and page size; inserting a page break; printing column headings on multiple pages; scaling data to print on one page; inserting a background picture; inserting headers and footers; and identifying a print area and customizing a print job.

Formatting a Worksheet Page

An Excel worksheet contains default page formatting. For example, a worksheet contains left and right margins of 0.7 inch and top and bottom margins of 0.75 inch. In addition, a worksheet prints in portrait orientation and the worksheet page size is 8.5 inches by 11 inches. These defaults, along with additional settings, can be changed and/or controlled with options on the PAGE LAYOUT tab.

Changing Margins

The Page Setup group on the PAGE LAYOUT tab contains buttons for changing the margins and the page orientation and size, as well as buttons for establishing a print area, inserting a page break, applying a picture background, and printing titles.

Margins

Change the worksheet margins by clicking the Margins button in the Page Setup group on the PAGE LAYOUT tab. This displays a drop-down list of

> **Quick Steps**
>
> **Change Worksheet Margins**
> 1. Click PAGE LAYOUT tab.
> 2. Click Margins button.
> 3. Click desired predesigned margin.
>
> OR
> 1. Click PAGE LAYOUT tab.
> 2. Click Margins button.
> 3. Click *Custom Margins* at drop-down list.
> 4. Change the top, left, right, and/or bottom measurements.
> 5. Click OK.

predesigned margin choices. If one of the predesigned choices is what you want to apply to the worksheet, click the option. If you want to customize the margins, click the *Custom Margins* option at the bottom of the Margins button drop-down list. This displays the Page Setup dialog box with the Margins tab selected, as shown in Figure 4.1.

A worksheet page showing the cells and margins displays in the dialog box. As you increase or decrease the top, bottom, left, or right margin measurements, the sample worksheet page reflects the change. You can also increase or decrease the measurement from the top of the page to the header with the *Header* measurement box or the measurement from the footer to the bottom of the page with the *Footer* measurement box. (You will learn about headers and footers later in this chapter.)

Figure 4.1 Page Setup Dialog Box with Margins Tab Selected

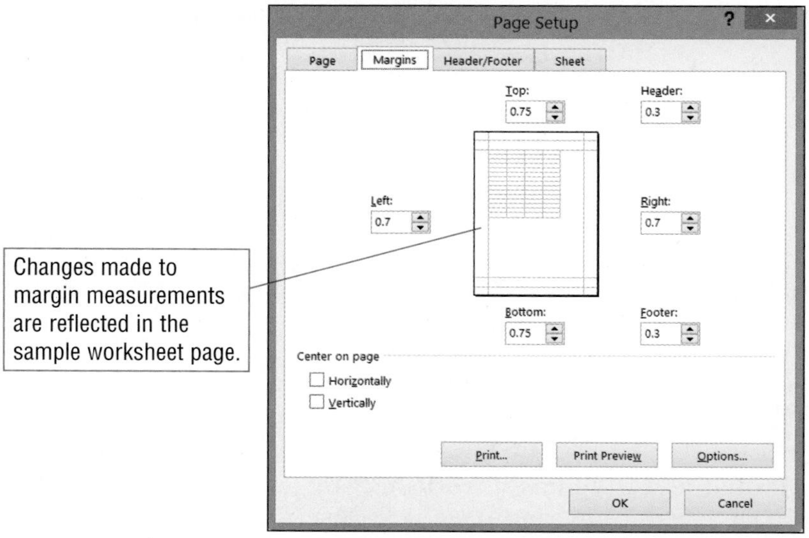

> **Quick Steps**
>
> **Center a Worksheet Horizontally and/or Vertically**
> 1. Click PAGE LAYOUT tab.
> 2. Click Margins button.
> 3. Click *Custom Margins* at drop-down list.
> 4. Click *Horizontally* option and/or click *Vertically* option.
> 5. Click OK.

Centering a Worksheet Horizontally and/or Vertically

By default, a worksheet prints in the upper left corner of the page. You can center a worksheet on the page by changing the margins. However, an easier method for centering a worksheet is to use the *Horizontally* and/or *Vertically* options that display in the Page Setup dialog box with the Margins tab selected. If you choose one or both of these options, the worksheet page in the preview section displays how the worksheet will print on the page.

Project 1a Changing Margins and Horizontally and Vertically Centering a Worksheet — Part 1 of 12

1. Open **RPBudget.xlsx**.
2. Save the workbook with Save As and name it **EL1-C4-P1-RPBudget**.
3. Insert the following formulas in the worksheet:
   a. Insert formulas in column N, rows 5 through 10 that sum the totals for each income item.
   b. Insert formulas in row 11, columns B through N that sum the income as well as the total for all income items.

c. Insert formulas in column N, rows 14 through 19 that sum the totals for each expense item.
d. Insert formulas in row 20, columns B through N that sum the expenses as well as the total of expenses.
e. Insert formulas in row 21, columns B through N that subtract the total expenses from the income. (To begin the formula, make cell B21 active and then type the formula =B11-B20. Copy this formula to columns C through N.)
f. Apply the Accounting format with no places past the decimal point to cells N5 and N14.

4. Click the PAGE LAYOUT tab.
5. Click the Margins button in the Page Setup group and then click *Custom Margins* at the drop-down list.
6. At the Page Setup dialog box with the Margins tab selected, click the up-pointing arrow at the right side of the *Top* measurement box until *3.5* displays.
7. Click the up-pointing arrow at the right side of the *Bottom* measurement box until *1.5* displays.
8. Preview the worksheet by clicking the Print Preview button located toward the bottom of the Page Setup dialog box. The worksheet appears to be a little low on the page so you decide to horizontally and vertically center it by completing the following steps:
   a. Click the Page Setup hyperlink that displays below the galleries in the *Settings* category in the Print backstage area.
   b. Click the Margins tab at the Page Setup dialog box.
   c. Change the *Top* and *Bottom* measurements to *1*.
   d. Click the *Horizontally* check box.
   e. Click the *Vertically* check box.
   f. Click OK to close the dialog box.
   g. Look at the preview of the worksheet and then click the Back button to return to the worksheet.
9. Save **EL1-C4-P1-RPBudget.xlsx**.

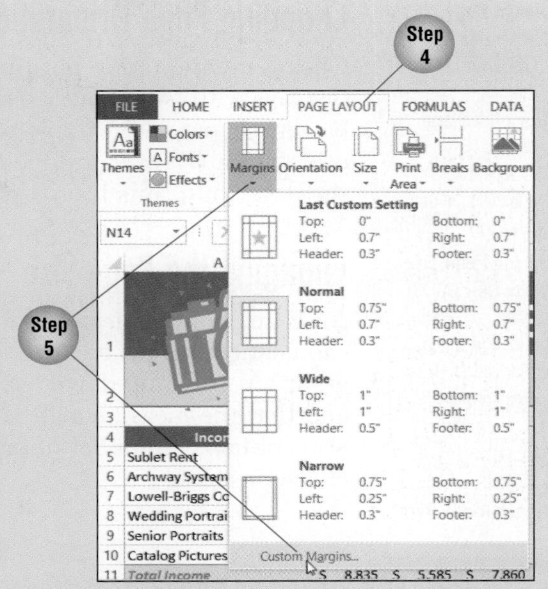

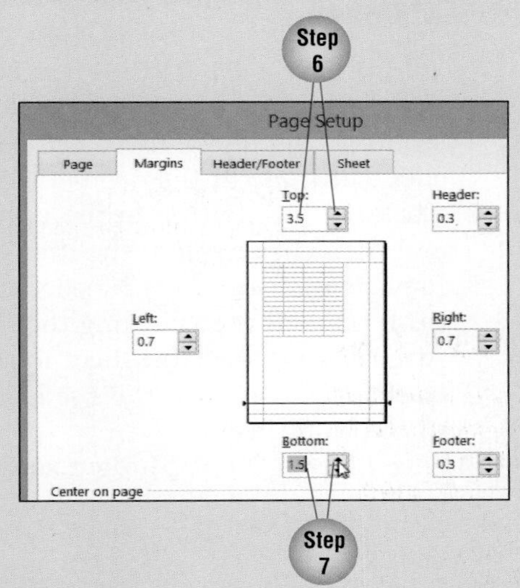

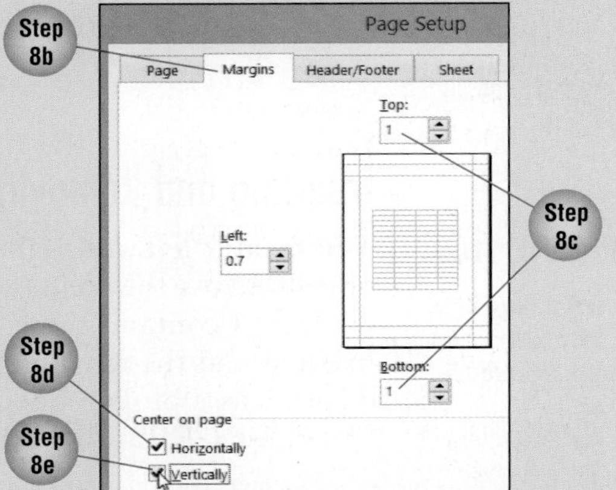

Quick Steps

Change Page Orientation
1. Click PAGE LAYOUT tab.
2. Click Orientation button.
3. Click desired orientation at drop-down list.

Change Page Size
1. Click PAGE LAYOUT tab.
2. Click Size button.
3. Click desired size at drop-down list.

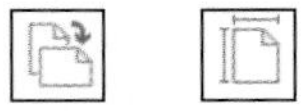

Orientation Size

Changing Page Orientation

Click the Orientation button in the Page Setup group and a drop-down list displays with two choices: *Portrait* and *Landscape*. The two choices are represented by sample pages. A sample page that is taller than it is wide shows how the default orientation (*Portrait*) prints data on the page. The other choice, *Landscape*, rotates the data and prints it on a page that is wider than it is tall.

Changing the Page Size

An Excel worksheet page size, by default, is set at 8.5 inches × 11 inches. You can change this default page size by clicking the Size button in the Page Setup group. At the drop-down list that displays, notice that the default setting is *Letter* and that the measurement *8.5"× 11"* displays below *Letter*. This drop-down list also contains a number of page sizes, such as *Executive* and *Legal*, and a number of envelope sizes.

Project 1b Changing Page Orientation and Size — Part 2 of 12

1. With **EL1-C4-P1-RPBudget.xlsx** open, click the Orientation button in the Page Setup group on the PAGE LAYOUT tab and then click *Landscape* at the drop-down list.
2. Click the Size button in the Page Setup group and then click *Legal* at the drop-down list.
3. Preview the worksheet by clicking the FILE tab and then clicking the *Print* option. After viewing the worksheet in the Print backstage area, press the Esc key to return to the worksheet.
4. Save **EL1-C4-P1-RPBudget.xlsx**.

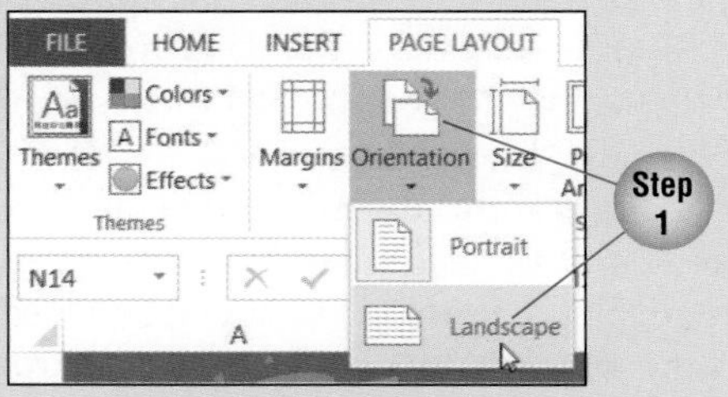

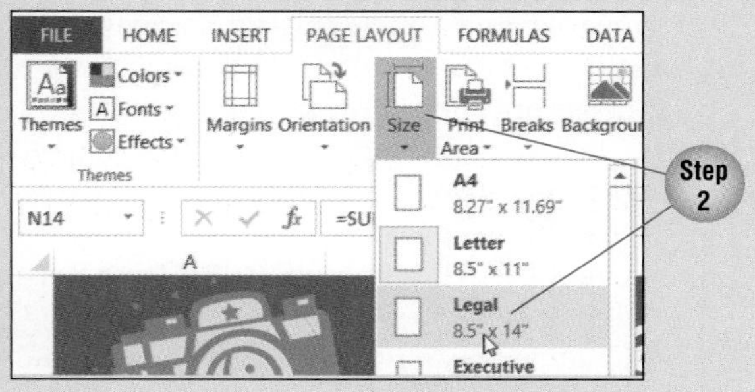

Inserting and Removing Page Breaks

Quick Steps

Insert a Page Break
1. Select column or row.
2. Click PAGE LAYOUT tab.
3. Click Breaks button.
4. Click *Insert Page Break* at drop-down list.

The default left and right margins of 0.7 inch allow approximately 7 inches of cells across the page (8.5 inches minus 1.4 inches equals 7.1 inches). If a worksheet contains more than 7 inches of cells across the page, a page break is inserted and the remaining columns are moved to the next page. A page break displays as a broken line along cell borders. Figure 4.2 shows the page break in **EL1-C4-P1-RPBudget.xlsx** when the paper size is set to *Letter*.

A page break also displays horizontally in a worksheet. By default, a worksheet can contain approximately 9.5 inches of cells vertically down the page. This is because the paper size is set by default at 11 inches. With the default top and bottom margins of 0.75 inch, this allows 9.5 inches of cells to print on one page.

Figure 4.2 Page Break

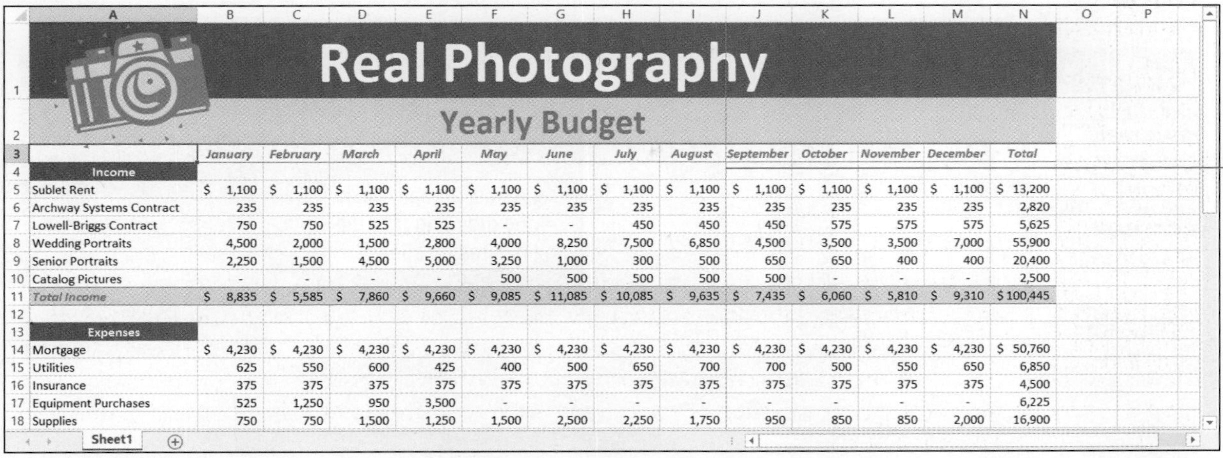

Real Photography

Yearly Budget

	A	B	C	D	E	F	G	H	I	J	K	L	M	N
3		January	February	March	April	May	June	July	August	September	October	November	December	Total
4	Income													
5	Sublet Rent	$ 1,100	$ 1,100	$ 1,100	$ 1,100	$ 1,100	$ 1,100	$ 1,100	$ 1,100	$ 1,100	$ 1,100	$ 1,100	$ 1,100	$ 13,200
6	Archway Systems Contract	235	235	235	235	235	235	235	235	235	235	235	235	2,820
7	Lowell-Briggs Contract	750	750	525	525	-	-	450	450	450	575	575	575	5,625
8	Wedding Portraits	4,500	2,000	1,500	2,800	4,000	8,250	7,500	6,850	4,500	3,500	3,500	7,000	55,900
9	Senior Portraits	2,250	1,500	4,500	5,000	3,250	1,000	300	500	650	650	400	400	20,400
10	Catalog Pictures	-	-	-	-	500	500	500	500	500	-	-	-	2,500
11	*Total Income*	$ 8,835	$ 5,585	$ 7,860	$ 9,660	$ 9,085	$ 11,085	$ 10,085	$ 9,635	$ 7,435	$ 6,060	$ 5,810	$ 9,310	$ 100,445
12														
13	Expenses													
14	Mortgage	$ 4,230	$ 4,230	$ 4,230	$ 4,230	$ 4,230	$ 4,230	$ 4,230	$ 4,230	$ 4,230	$ 4,230	$ 4,230	$ 4,230	$ 50,760
15	Utilities	625	550	600	425	400	500	650	700	700	500	550	650	6,850
16	Insurance	375	375	375	375	375	375	375	375	375	375	375	375	4,500
17	Equipment Purchases	525	1,250	950	3,500	-	-	-	-	-	-	-	-	6,225
18	Supplies	750	750	1,500	1,250	1,500	2,500	2,250	1,750	950	850	850	2,000	16,900

Excel automatically inserts page breaks in a worksheet. Insert your own page break if you would like more control over what cells print on a page. To insert your own page break, select the column or row, click the Breaks button in the Page Setup group on the PAGE LAYOUT tab, and then click *Insert Page Break* at the drop-down list. A page break is inserted immediately left of the selected column or immediately above the selected row.

Breaks

If you want to insert both horizontal and vertical page breaks at the same time, make a cell active, click the Breaks button in the Page Setup group, and then click *Insert Page Break*. This causes a horizontal page break to be inserted immediately above the active cell and a vertical page break to be inserted at the left side of the active cell. To remove a page break, select the column or row or make the desired cell active, click the Breaks button in the Page Setup group, and then click *Remove Page Break* at the drop-down list.

A page break automatically inserted by Excel may not be visible initially in a worksheet. One way to display the page break is to display the worksheet in the Print backstage area. When you return to the worksheet, the page break will display in the worksheet.

Excel provides a page break view that displays worksheet pages and page breaks. To display this view, click the Page Break Preview button located in the view area at the right side of the Status bar or click the VIEW tab and then click the Page Break Preview button in the Workbook Views group. This causes the worksheet to display similar to the worksheet shown in Figure 4.3. The word *Page* along with the page number displays in gray behind the cells in the worksheet. A dashed blue line indicates a page break inserted by Excel and a solid blue line indicates a page break inserted manually.

Page Break Preview

HINT

You can edit a worksheet in Page Break Preview.

Move a page break by positioning the arrow pointer on the blue line, holding down the left mouse button, dragging the line to the desired location, and then releasing the mouse button. To return to the Normal view, click the Normal button in the view area on the Status bar or click the VIEW tab and then click the Normal button in the Workbook Views group.

Normal

Figure 4.3 Worksheet in Page Break Preview

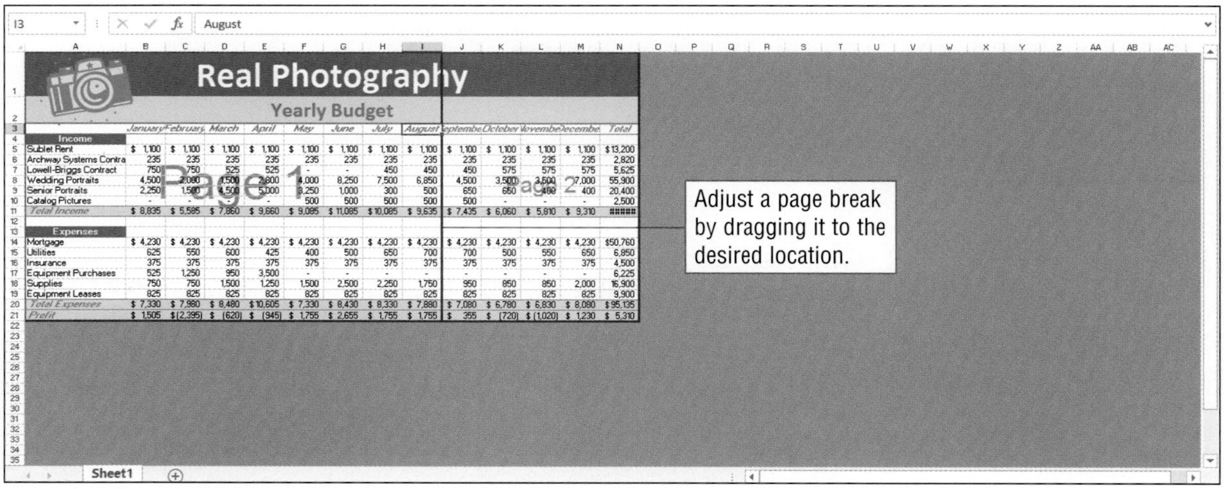

Project 1c Inserting a Page Break in a Worksheet

Part 3 of 12

1. With **EL1-C4-P1-RPBudget.xlsx** open, click the Size button in the Page Setup group on the PAGE LAYOUT tab and then click *Letter* at the drop-down list.
2. Click the Margins button and then click *Custom Margins* at the drop-down list.
3. At the Page Setup dialog box with the Margins tab selected, click in the *Horizontally* check box to remove the check mark, click in the *Vertically* check box to remove the check mark, and then click OK to close the dialog box.
4. Insert a page break between columns I and J by completing the following steps:
   a. Select column J.
   b. Click the Breaks button in the Page Setup group and then click *Insert Page Break* at the drop-down list. Click in any cell in column I.

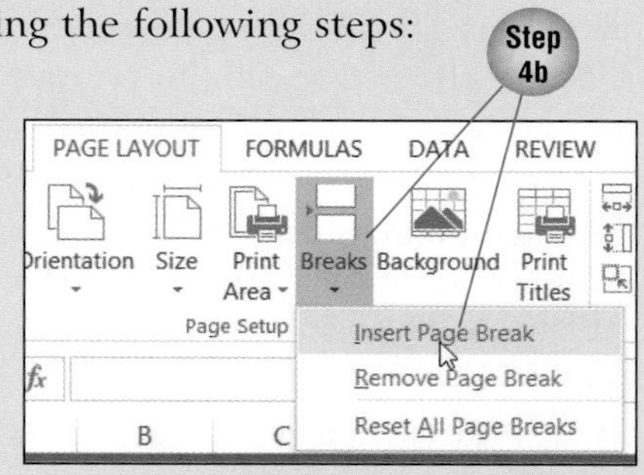

5. View the worksheet in Page Break Preview by completing the following steps:
   a. Click the Page Break Preview button located in the view area on the Status bar.
   b. View the pages and page breaks in the worksheet.
   c. You decide to include the first six months of the year on one page. To do this, position the arrow pointer on the vertical blue line until the arrow pointer displays as a left-and-right-pointing arrow, hold down the left mouse button, drag the line to the left so it is between columns G and H, and then release the mouse button.

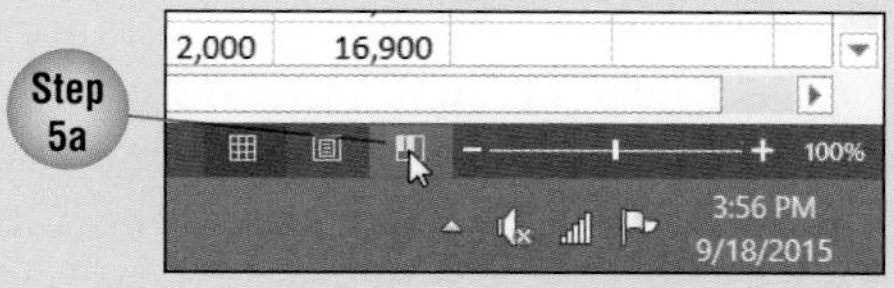

d. Click the Normal button located in the view area on the Status bar.

6. Save **EL1-C4-P1-RPBudget.xlsx**.

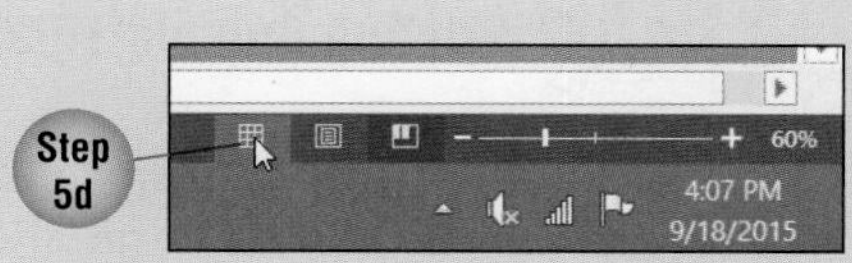

Printing Column and Row Titles on Multiple Pages

The columns and rows in a worksheet are usually titled. For example, in **EL1-C4-P1-RPBudget.xlsx**, the column titles include *Income*, *Expenses*, *January*, *February*, *March*, and so on. The row titles include the income and expenses categories. If a worksheet prints on more than one page, having column and/or row titles printing on each page can be useful. To do this, click the Print Titles button in the Page Setup group on the PAGE LAYOUT tab. This displays the Page Setup dialog box with the Sheet tab selected, as shown in Figure 4.4.

At the Page Setup dialog box with the Sheet tab selected, specify the range of row cells you want to print on every page in the *Rows to repeat at top* text box. Type a cell range using a colon. For example, if you want cells A1 through J1 to print on every page, type *A1:J1* in the *Rows to repeat at top* text box. Type the range of column cells you want to print on every page in the *Columns to repeat at left* text box. To make rows and columns easier to identify on the printed page, specify that row and/or column headings print on each page.

Quick Steps

Print Column and Row Titles

1. Click PAGE LAYOUT tab.
2. Click Print Titles button.
3. Type row range in *Rows to repeat at top* option.
4. Type column range in *Columns to repeat at left* option.
5. Click OK.

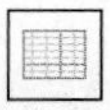

Print Titles

Figure 4.4 Page Setup Dialog Box with Sheet Tab Selected

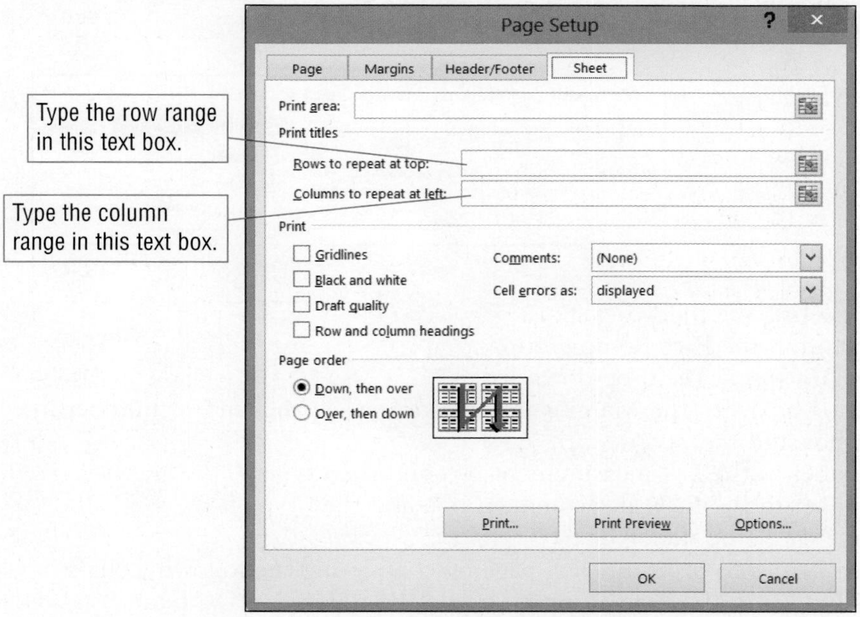

Project 1d Printing Column Titles on Each Page of a Worksheet Part 4 of 12

1. With **EL1-C4-P1-RPBudget.xlsx** open, click the PAGE LAYOUT tab and then click the Print Titles button in the Page Setup group.
2. At the Page Setup dialog box with the Sheet tab selected, click in the *Columns to repeat at left* text box.
3. Type A1:A21.
4. Click OK to close the dialog box.
5. Save and then print **EL1-C4-P1-RPBudget.xlsx**.

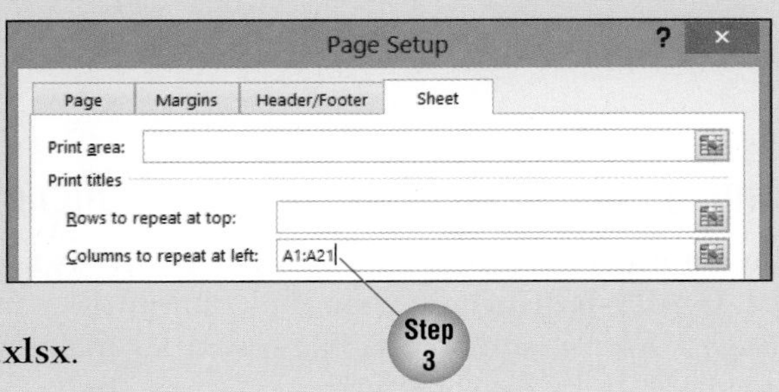

Scaling Data

Width

Using buttons in the Scale to Fit group on the PAGE LAYOUT tab, you can adjust the printed output by a percentage to fit the number of pages specified. For example, if a worksheet contains too many columns to print on one page, click the down-pointing arrow at the right side of the *Width* option box in the Scale to Fit group on the PAGE LAYOUT tab and then click *1 page*. This causes the data to shrink so all columns display and print on one page.

Project 1e Scaling Data to Fit on One Page and Printing Row Titles on Each Page Part 5 of 12

1. With **EL1-C4-P1-RPBudget.xlsx** open, click the down-pointing arrow at the right side of the *Width* option box in the Scale to Fit group on the PAGE LAYOUT tab.
2. At the drop-down list that displays, click the *1 page* option.
3. Display the Print backstage area, notice that all cells containing data display on one page in the worksheet, and then return to the worksheet.
4. Change margins by completing the following steps:
   a. Click the Margins button in the Page Setup group and then click *Custom Margins* at the drop-down list.
   b. At the Page Setup dialog box with the Margins tab selected, select the current number in the *Top* measurement box and then type 3.5.
   c. Select the current number in the *Left* measurement box and then type 0.3.
   d. Select the current number in the *Right* measurement box and then type 0.3.
   e. Click OK to close the Page Setup dialog box.
5. Specify that you want row titles to print on each page by completing the following steps:
   a. Click the Print Titles button in the Page Setup group on the PAGE LAYOUT tab.
   b. At the Page Setup dialog box with the Sheet tab selected, select and then delete the text that displays in the *Columns to repeat at left* text box.

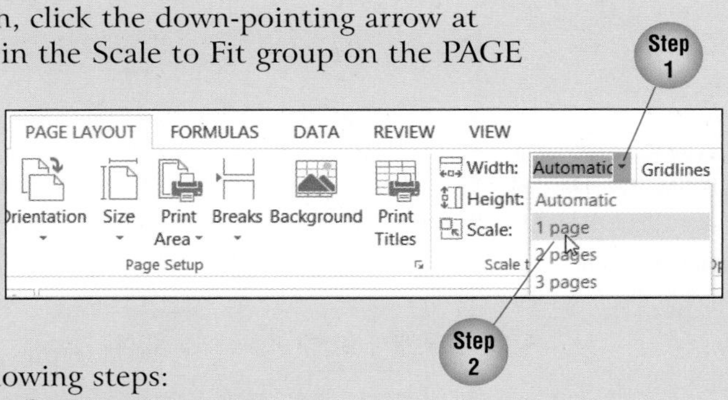

c. Click in the *Rows to repeat at top* text box and then type A3:N3.
d. Click OK to close the dialog box.

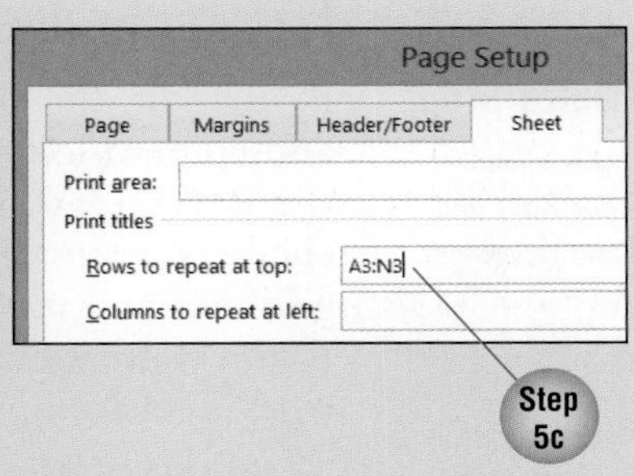

6. Save and then print **EL1-C4-P1-RPBudget.xlsx**. (The worksheet will print on two pages with the row titles repeated on the second page.)
7. At the worksheet, return to the default margins by clicking the PAGE LAYOUT tab, clicking the Margins button, and then clicking the *Normal* option at the drop-down list.
8. Prevent titles from printing on second and subsequent pages by completing the following steps:
   a. Click the Print Titles button in the Page Setup group.
   b. At the Page Setup dialog box with the Sheet tab selected, select and then delete the text that displays in the *Rows to repeat at top* text box.
   c. Click OK to close the dialog box.
9. Change the scaling back to the default by completing the following steps:
   a. Click the down-pointing arrow at the right side of the *Width* option box in the Scale to Fit group and then click *Automatic* at the drop-down list.
   b. Click the up-pointing arrow at the right side of the *Scale* measurement box until *100%* displays in the box.

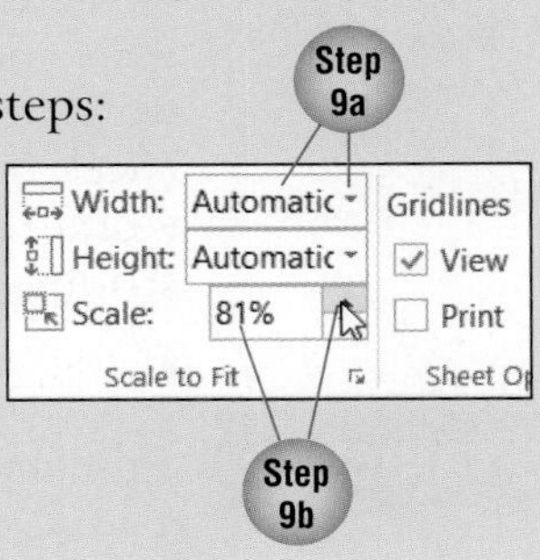

10. Save **EL1-C4-P1-RPBudget.xlsx**.

Inserting a Background Picture

Using the Background button in the Page Setup group on the PAGE LAYOUT tab, you can insert a picture as a background to the worksheet. The picture displays only on the screen and does not print. To insert a picture, click the Background button in the Page Setup group and then click the Browse button at the Insert Pictures window. At the Sheet Background dialog box, navigate to the folder containing the desired picture and then double-click the picture. To remove the picture from the worksheet, click the Delete Background button.

Quick Steps

Insert a Background Picture
1. Click PAGE LAYOUT tab.
2. Click Background button.
3. Navigate to desired picture and double-click picture.

Background

Project 1f Inserting a Background Picture Part 6 of 12

1. With **EL1-C4-P1-RPBudget.xlsx** open, insert a background picture by completing the following steps:
   a. Click the Background button in the Page Setup group on the PAGE LAYOUT tab.
   b. At the Insert Pictures window, click the Browse button.
   c. At the Sheet Background dialog box, navigate to the EL1C4 folder and then double-click ***Ship.jpg***.
   d. Scroll down the worksheet to display the ship.

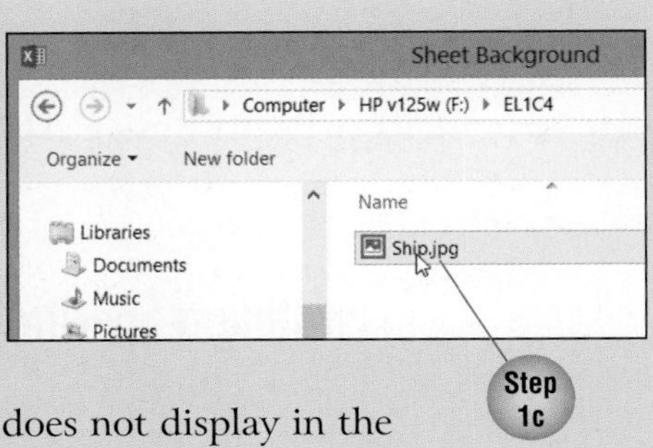

2. Display the Print backstage area, notice that the picture does not display in the preview worksheet, and then return to the worksheet.
3. Remove the picture by clicking the Delete Background button in the Page Setup group on the PAGE LAYOUT tab.
4. Save **EL1-C4-P1-RPBudget.xlsx**.

Printing Gridlines and Row and Column Headings

Quick Steps

Print Gridlines and/or Row and Column Headings
1. Click PAGE LAYOUT tab.
2. Click *Print* check boxes in *Gridlines* and/or *Headings* section in Sheet Options group.

OR
1. Click PAGE LAYOUT tab.
2. Click Sheet Options dialog box launcher.
3. Click *Gridlines* and/or *Row and column headings* check boxes.
4. Click OK.

By default, the gridlines that create the cells in a worksheet and the row numbers and column letters that label the cells do not print. The Sheet Options group on the PAGE LAYOUT tab contain check boxes for gridlines and headings. The *View* check boxes for gridlines and headings contain check marks. At these settings, gridlines and row and column headings display on the screen but do not print. If you want them to print, insert check marks in the *Print* check boxes. Complex worksheets may be easier to read with the gridlines printed.

You can also control the display and printing of gridlines and headings with options at the Page Setup dialog box with the Sheet tab selected. Display this dialog box by clicking the Sheet Options dialog box launcher. To print gridlines and headings, insert check marks in the check boxes located in the *Print* section of the dialog box. The *Print* section contains two additional options: *Black and white* and *Draft quality*. If you are printing with a color printer, you can print the worksheet in black and white by inserting a check mark in the *Black and white* check box. Insert a check mark in the *Draft quality* option if you want to print a draft of the worksheet. With this option checked, some formatting, such as shading and fill, does not print.

Project 1g **Printing Gridlines and Row and Column Headings** **Part 7 of 12**

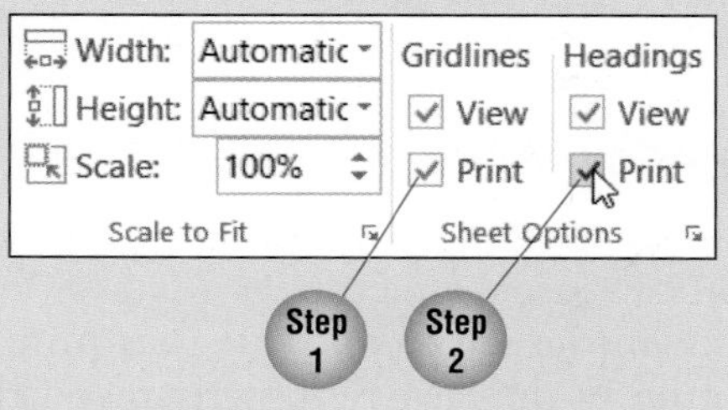

1. With **EL1-C4-P1-RPBudget.xlsx** open, click in the *Print* check box below *Gridlines* in the Sheet Options group on the PAGE LAYOUT tab to insert a check mark.
2. Click in the *Print* check box below *Headings* in the Sheet Options group to insert a check mark.
3. Click the Margins button in the Page Setup group and then click *Custom Margins* at the drop-down list.
4. At the Page Setup dialog box with the Margins tab selected, click in the *Horizontally* check box to insert a check mark.
5. Click in the *Vertically* check box to insert a check mark.
6. Click OK to close the dialog box.
7. Save and then print **EL1-C4-P1-RPBudget.xlsx**.
8. Click in the *Print* check box below *Headings* in the Sheet Options group to remove the check mark.
9. Click in the *Print* check box below *Gridlines* in the Sheet Options group to remove the check mark.
10. Save **EL1-C4-P1-RPBudget.xlsx**.

Printing a Specific Area of a Worksheet

Print Area

Use the Print Area button in the Page Setup group on the PAGE LAYOUT tab to select and print specific areas in a worksheet. To do this, select the cells you want to print, click the Print Area button in the Page Setup group, and then click *Set Print Area* at the drop-down list. This inserts a border around the selected cells. Display the Print backstage area and click the Print button and the cells within the border are printed.

You can specify more than one print area in a worksheet. To do this, select the first group of cells, click the Print Area button in the Page Setup group, and then click *Set Print Area*. Select the next group of cells, click the Print Area button, and then click *Add to Print Area*. Clear a print area by clicking the Print Area button in the Page Setup group and then clicking *Clear Print Area* at the drop-down list.

Each area specified as a print area will print on a separate page. If you want nonadjacent print areas to print on the same page, consider hiding columns and/or rows in the worksheet to bring the areas together.

Project 1h Printing Specific Areas

Part 8 of 12

1. With **EL1-C4-P1-RPBudget.xlsx** open, print the first half of the year's income and expenses by completing the following steps:
   a. Select cells A3 through G21.
   b. Click the Print Area button in the Page Setup group on the PAGE LAYOUT tab and then click *Set Print Area* at the drop-down list.
   c. With the border surrounding the cells A3 through G21, click the FILE tab, click the *Print* option, and then click the Print button at the Print backstage area.
   d. Clear the print area by clicking the Print Area button in the Page Setup group and then clicking *Clear Print Area* at the drop-down list.

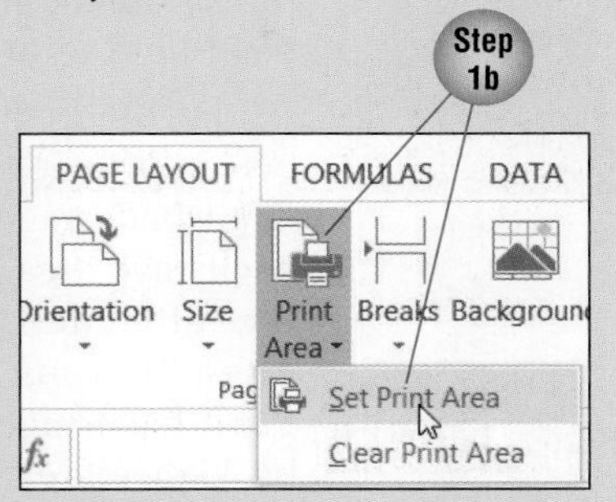

2. Suppose you want to print the income and expenses information as well as the totals for the month of April. To do this, hide columns and select a print area by completing the following steps:
   a. Select columns B through D.
   b. Click the HOME tab.
   c. Click the Format button in the Cells group, point to *Hide & Unhide*, and then click *Hide Columns*.
   d. Click the PAGE LAYOUT tab.
   e. Select cells A3 through E21. (Columns A and E are now adjacent.)
   f. Click the Print Area button in the Page Setup group and then click *Set Print Area* at the drop-down list.
3. Click the FILE tab, click the *Print* option, and then click the Print button.
4. Clear the print area by ensuring cells A3 through E21 are selected, clicking the Print Area button in the Page Setup group, and then clicking *Clear Print Area* at the drop-down list.
5. Unhide the columns by completing the following steps:
   a. Click the HOME tab.
   b. Select columns A and E. (These columns are adjacent.)
   c. Click the Format button in the Cells group, point to *Hide & Unhide*, and then click *Unhide Columns*.
   d. Deselect the text by clicking in any cell containing data in the worksheet.
6. Save **EL1-C4-P1-RPBudget.xlsx**.

Inserting Headers and Footers

Quick Steps

Insert a Header or Footer
1. Click INSERT tab.
2. Click Header & Footer button.
3. Click Header button and then click predesigned header or click Footer button and then click predesigned footer.

OR
1. Click INSERT tab.
2. Click Header & Footer button.
3. Click desired header or footer elements.

Header & Footer

Text that prints at the top of each worksheet page is called a ***header*** and text that prints at the bottom of each worksheet page is called a ***footer***. Create a header and/or footer with the Header & Footer button in the Text group on the INSERT tab, in Page Layout View, or with options at the Page Setup dialog box with the Header/Footer tab selected.

To create a header with the Header & Footer button, click the INSERT tab and then click the Header & Footer button in the Text group. This displays the worksheet in Page Layout view and displays the HEADER & FOOTER TOOLS DESIGN tab. Use buttons on this tab, shown in Figure 4.5, to insert predesigned headers and/or footers or insert header and footer elements such as page numbers, date, time, path name, and file name. You can also create a different header or footer on the first page of the worksheet or create a header or footer for even pages and another for odd pages.

At the Print backstage area, you can preview your headers and footers before printing. Click the FILE tab and then the *Print* option to display the Print backstage area. A preview of the worksheet displays at the right side of the backstage area. If your worksheet will print on more than one page, you can view the different pages by clicking the Next Page button or the Previous Page button. These buttons are located below and to the left of the preview worksheet at the Print backstage area. Two buttons display in the bottom right corner of the Print backstage area. Click the Zoom to Page button to zoom in or out of the preview of the worksheet. Click the Show Margins button in the Print backstage area and margin guidelines and handles display on the preview page. The handles display as black squares that you can use to increase or decrease the page margins and column widths. To do this, position the mouse pointer on the desired handle, hold down the left mouse button, and then drag to the desired position.

Figure 4.5 HEADER & FOOTER TOOLS DESIGN Tab

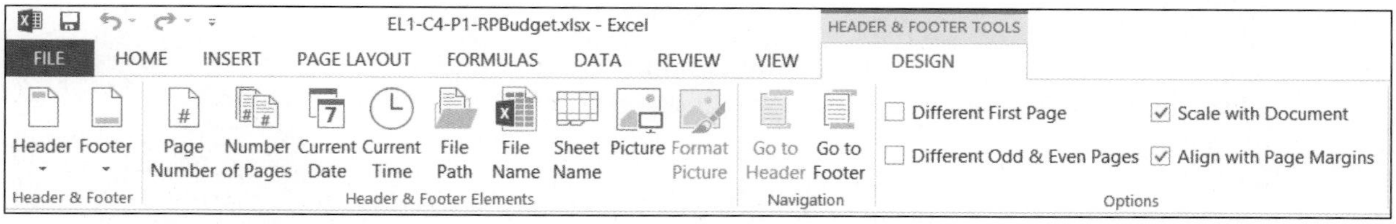

Project 1i **Inserting a Header in a Worksheet** **Part 9 of 12**

1. With **EL1-C4-P1-RPBudget.xlsx** open, create a header by completing the following steps:
   a. Click the INSERT tab.
   b. Click the Header & Footer button in the Text group.

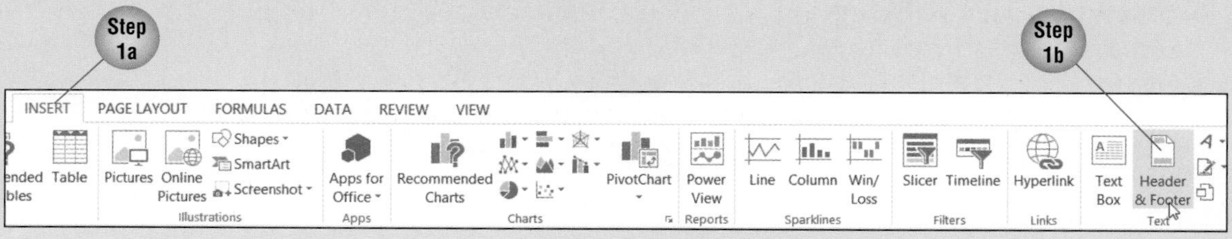

c. Click the Header button located at the left side of the HEADER & FOOTER TOOLS DESIGN tab and then click *Page 1, EL1-C4-P1-RPBudget.xlsx* at the drop-down list. (This inserts the page number in the middle header box and the workbook name in the right header box.)

2. Preview the worksheet by completing the following steps:
   a. Click the FILE tab and then click the *Print* option.
   b. At the Print backstage area, look at the preview worksheet that displays at the right side of the backstage area.
   c. View the next page of the worksheet by clicking the Next Page button that displays below and to the left of the preview worksheet.

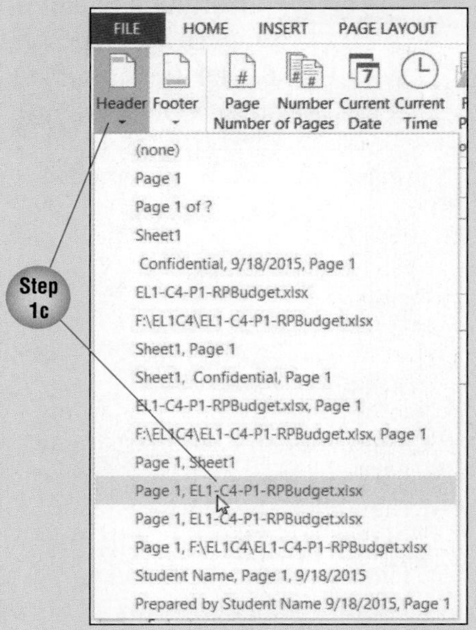

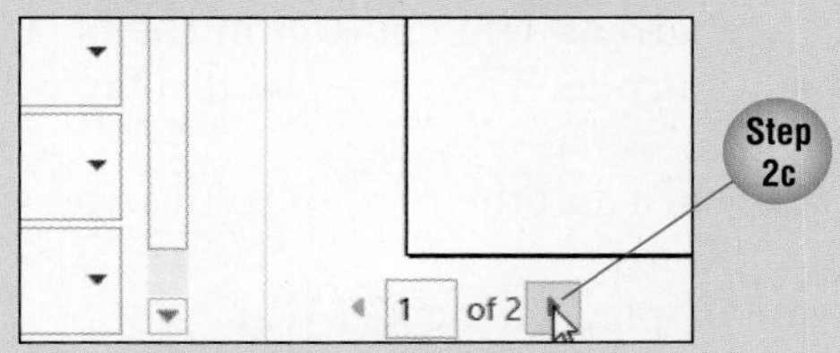

   d. View the first page by clicking the Previous Page button that displays left of the Next Page button.
   e. Click the Zoom to Page button in the lower right corner of the backstage area. (Notice that the preview page has zoomed in on the worksheet.)
   f. Click the Zoom to Page button.
   g. Click the Page Margins button in the lower right corner of the backstage area. (Notice the guidelines and handles that display on the preview page.)
   h. Click the Page Margins button to remove the guidelines and handles.
   i. Click the Back button to return to the workbook.

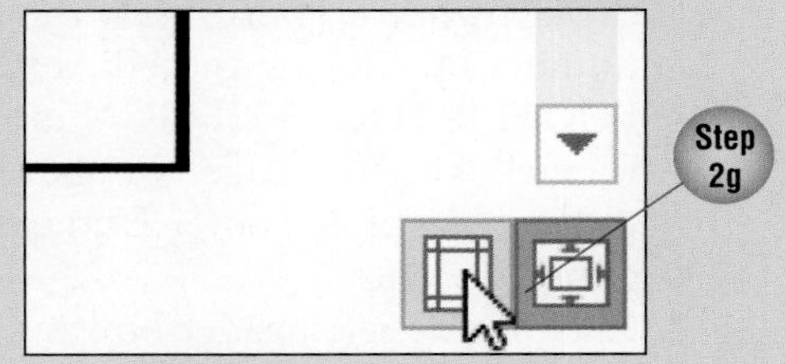

3. Save **EL1-C4-P1-RPBudget.xlsx**.

You also can insert a header and/or footer by switching to Page Layout view. In Page Layout view, the top of the worksheet page displays with the text *Click to add header*. Click this text and the insertion point is positioned in the middle header box. Type the desired header in this box or click in the left box or the right box and then type the header. Create a footer in a similar manner. Scroll down the worksheet until the bottom of the page displays and then click the text *Click to add footer*. Type the footer in the center footer box or click the left or right box and then type the footer.

Project 1j Inserting a Footer and Modifying a Header in a Worksheet Part 10 of 12

1. With **EL1-C4-P1-RPBudget.xlsx** open, make sure the workbook displays in Page Layout view.
2. Scroll down the worksheet until the text *Click to add footer* displays and then click the text.

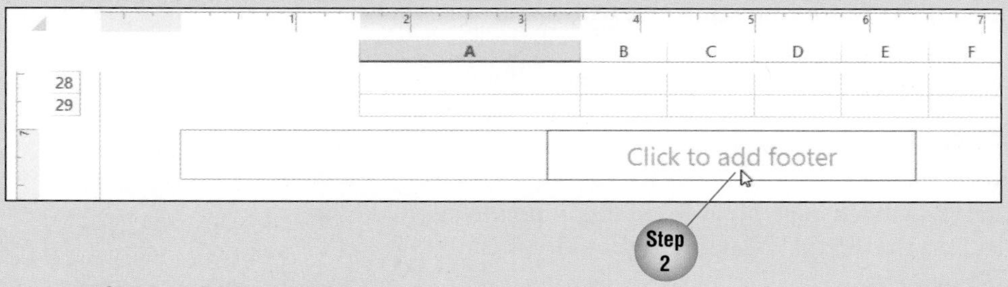

3. Type your first and last names.
4. Click in the left footer box, click the HEADER & FOOTER TOOLS DESIGN tab, and then click the Current Date button in the Header & Footer Elements group. (This inserts a date code. The date will display when you click outside the footer box.)
5. Click in the right footer box and then click the Current Time button in the Header & Footer Elements group. (This inserts the time as a code. The time will display when you click outside the footer box.)
6. View the header and footer at the Print backstage area and then return to the worksheet.
7. Modify the header by completing the following steps:
   a. Scroll to the beginning of the worksheet and display the header text.
   b. Click the page number in the middle header box. (This displays the HEADER & FOOTER TOOLS DESIGN tab, changes the header to a field, and selects the field.)
   c. Press the Delete key to delete the header.
   d. Click the header text that displays in the right header box and then press the Delete key.
   e. With the insertion point positioned in the right header box, insert the page number by clicking the HEADER & FOOTER TOOLS DESIGN tab and then clicking the Page Number button in the Header & Footer Elements group.
   f. Click in the left header box and then click the File Name button in the Header & Footer Elements group.

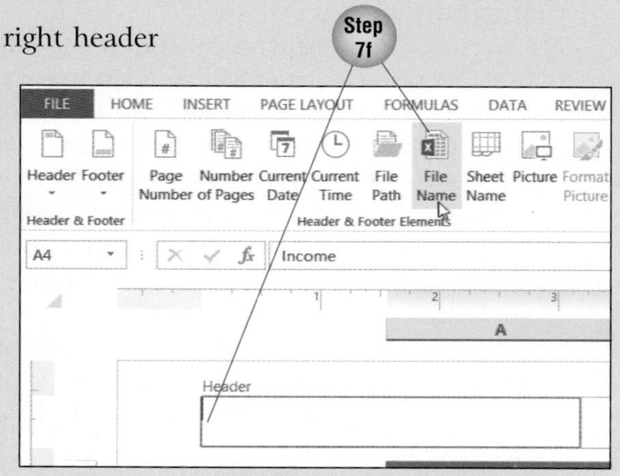

8. Click in any cell in the worksheet that contains data.
9. View the header and footer at the Print backstage area and then return to the worksheet.
10. Save **EL1-C4-P1-RPBudget.xlsx**.

In addition to selecting options on the HEADER & FOOTER TOOLS DESIGN tab, you can insert and customize headers and footers with options at the Page Setup dialog box with the Header/Footer tab selected, as shown in Figure 4.6. Display this dialog box by clicking the PAGE LAYOUT tab and then clicking the Page Setup group dialog box launcher. At the Page Setup dialog box, click the Header/Footer tab. If your worksheet contains headers or footers, they will display in the dialog box. With the check box options that display in

Figure 4.6 Page Setup Dialog Box with Header/Footer Tab Selected

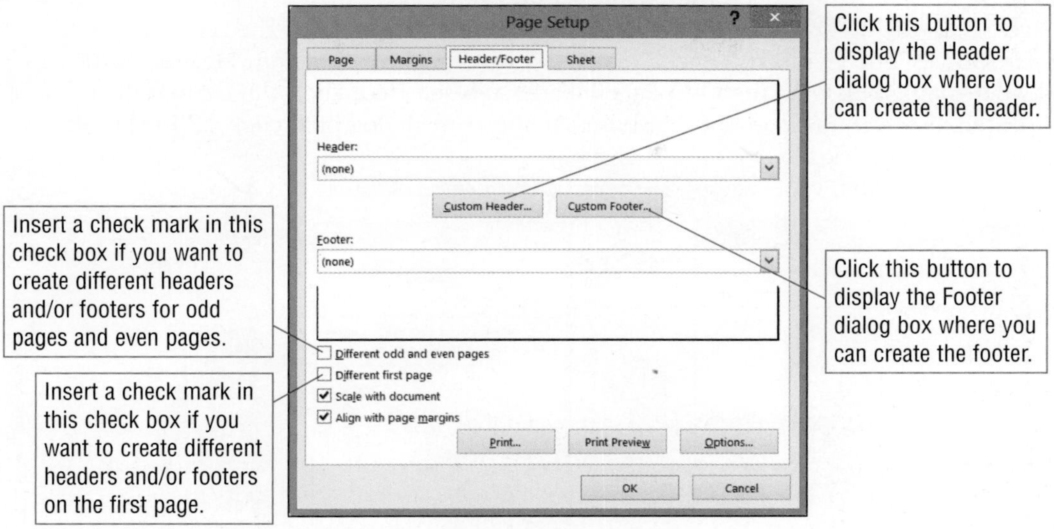

the lower left corner of the dialog box, you can specify that you want to insert different odd and even page headers and/or footers or insert a different first page header and/or footer. The bottom two check box options are active by default. These defaults scale the header and footer text with the worksheet text and align the header and footer with the page margins.

To create different odd and even page headers, click the *Different odd and even pages* check box to insert a check mark and then click the Custom Header button. This displays the Header dialog box with the Odd Page Header tab selected. Type or insert the desired odd page header data in the *Left section*, *Center section*, or *Right section* text box and then click the Even Page Header tab. Type or insert the desired even page header data in the desired section text box and then click OK. Use the buttons that display above the section boxes to format the header text and insert information such as the page number, current date, current time, file name, worksheet name, and so on. Complete similar steps to create different odd and even page footers and a different first page header or footer.

Project 1k Creating Different Odd and Even Page Headers and Footers and a Different First Page Header and Footer

Part 11 of 12

1. With **EL1-C4-P1-RPBudget.xlsx** open, remove the page break by clicking the PAGE LAYOUT tab, clicking the Breaks button in the Page Setup group, and then clicking *Reset All Page Breaks* at the drop-down list.
2. Change the margins by completing the following steps:
   a. Click the Margins button in the Page Setup group on the PAGE LAYOUT tab and then click *Custom Margins* at the drop-down list.
   b. At the Page Setup dialog box with the Margins tab selected, select the current number in the *Left* measurement box and then type 3.
   c. Select the current number in the *Right* measurement box and then type 3.
   d. Click OK to close the dialog box.
3. Click the Page Setup group dialog box launcher on the PAGE LAYOUT tab.

4. At the Page Setup dialog box, click the Header/Footer tab.
5. At the Page Setup dialog box with the Header/Footer tab selected, click the *Different odd and even pages* check box to insert a check mark and then click the Custom Header button.
6. At the Header dialog box with the Odd Page Header tab selected, click the Format Text button (located above the *Left section* text box). At the Font dialog box, click *12* in the *Size* list box box and then click OK.
7. At the Header dialog box, type **Yearly Budget** in the *Left section* text box.

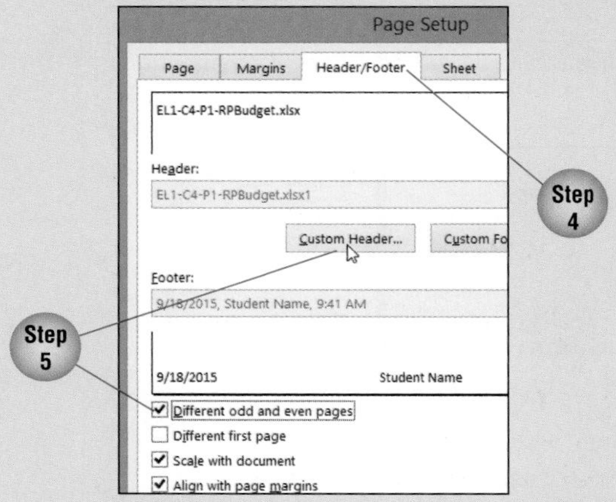

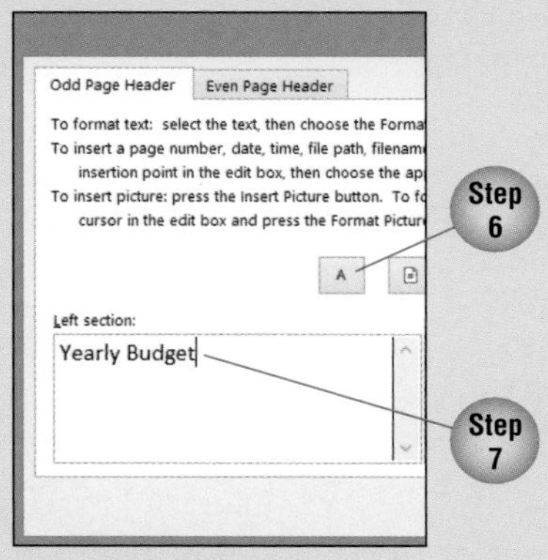

8. Click the Even Page Header tab, click in the *Left section* text box, and then click the Insert Page Number button.
9. Click in the *Right section* text box and then type **Yearly Budget**.
10. Select the text *Yearly Budget*, click the Format Text button, click *12* in the *Size* list box box, and then click OK.
11. Click OK to close the Header dialog box.
12. Click the Custom Footer button and at the Footer dialog box with the Odd Page Footer tab selected, delete the data in the *Left section* text box and select and delete the data in the *Right section* text box. (The footer should contain only your name.)

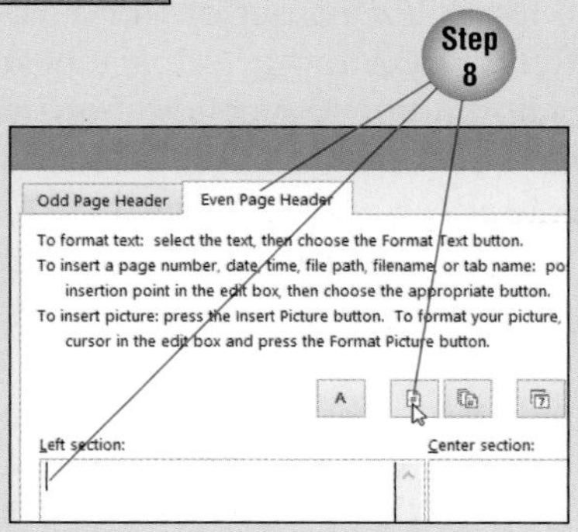

13. Select your name, click the Format Text button, click *12* in the *Size* list box box, and then click OK.
14. Click the Even Page Footer tab, type your name in the *Center section* text box, select your name, and then change the font size to 12 points.
15. Click OK to close the Footer dialog box and then click OK to close the Page Setup dialog box. (View the header and footer in the Print backstage area and then return to the worksheet.)
16. Click the Page Setup group dialog box launcher on the PAGE LAYOUT tab.
17. At the Page Setup dialog box, click the Header/Footer tab.
18. At the Page Setup dialog box with the Header/Footer tab selected, click the *Different odd and even pages* check box to remove the check mark.
19. Click the *Different first page* check box to insert a check mark and then click the Custom Header button.
20. At the Header dialog box with the Header tab selected, click the First Page Header tab.
21. Click in the *Right section* text box and then click the Insert Page Number button located above the section boxes.

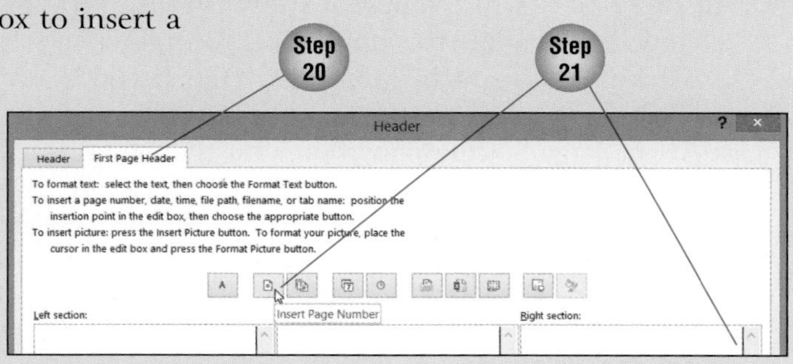

22. Click OK to close the Header dialog box and then click OK to close the Page Setup dialog box.
23. View the header and footer in the Print backstage area and then return to the worksheet.
24. Save **EL1-C4-P1-RPBudget.xlsx**.

Customizing Print Jobs

As you learned earlier in this chapter, you can preview worksheets in the Print backstage area. Use options in the *Settings* category at the Print backstage area, to specify what you want printed. By default, the active worksheet prints. You can change this by clicking the first gallery that displays in the *Settings* category. At the drop-down list that displays, you can specify to print the entire workbook (which is useful when a workbook contains more than one worksheet) or only selected cells. With the other galleries in the *Settings* category, you can specify if you want pages printed on one side or both sides (this is dependent on your printer) and collated. You can also specify the worksheet orientation, size, and margins and whether you want the worksheet scaled to fit all columns or rows on one page.

With the *Pages* text boxes in the *Settings* category, specify the pages of your worksheet you want printed. For example, if you want to print pages 2 and 3 of your active worksheet, type *2* in the measurement box immediately right of the word *Pages* in the *Settings* category and then type *3* in the measurement box immediately right of the word *to*. You can also use the up- and down-pointing arrows to insert page numbers.

Project 1l **Printing Specific Pages of a Worksheet** **Part 12 of 12**

1. With **EL1-C4-P1-RPBudget.xlsx** open, print the first two pages of the worksheet by completing the following steps:
   a. Click the FILE tab and then click the *Print* option.
   b. At the Print backstage area, click in the measurement box immediately right of *Pages* and below the first gallery in the *Settings* category and then type 1.
   c. Click in the measurement box immediately right of *to* in the *Settings* category and then type 2.
   d. Click the Print button.

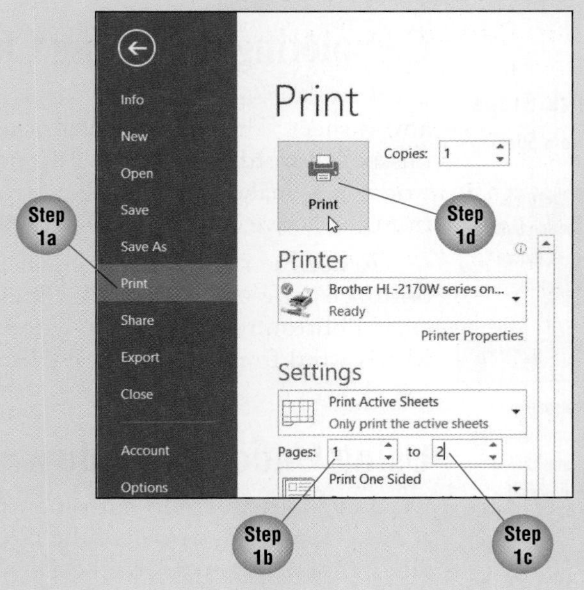

2. Print selected cells by completing the following steps:
   a. Display the worksheet in Normal view.
   b. Select cells A3 through D11.
   c. Click the FILE tab and then the *Print* option.
   d. At the Print backstage area, select and then delete the numbers in the *Pages* measurement boxes. (These are the numbers you inserted in Steps 1b and 1c.)
   e. Click the first gallery in the *Settings* category (displays with *Print Active Sheets*) and then click *Print Selection* at the drop-down list.
   f. Click the Print button.
3. Save and then close **EL1-C4-P1-RPBudget.xlsx**.

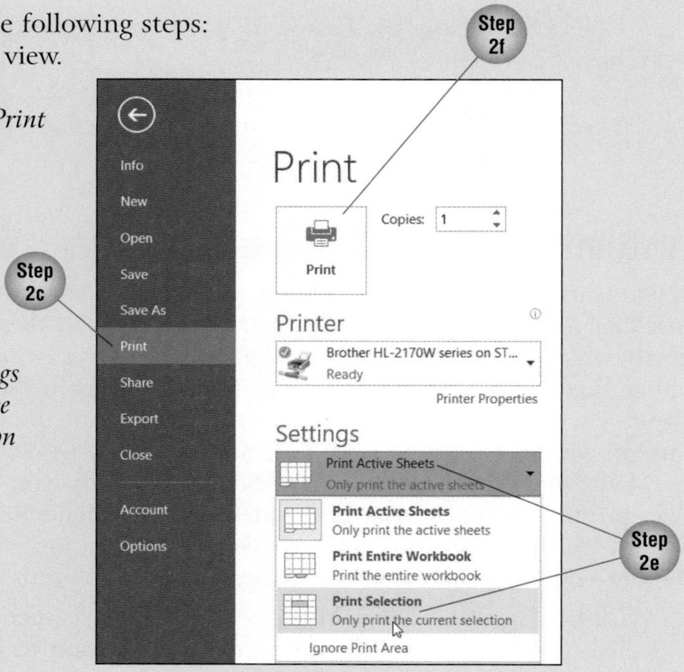

Project 2 Format a May Sales and Commissions Worksheet — 3 Parts

You will format a sales commission worksheet by inserting a formula, completing a spelling check, and finding and replacing data and cell formatting.

Quick Steps

Complete a Spelling Check
1. Click REVIEW tab.
2. Click Spelling button.
3. Replace or ignore selected words.

Spelling

HINT

Customize spell checking options at the Excel Options dialog box with *Proofing* selected.

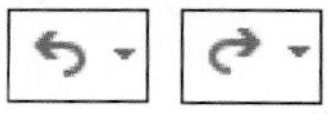
Undo Redo

Completing a Spelling Check

Excel includes a spelling checker you can use to verify the spelling of text in a worksheet. The spelling checker uses an electronic dictionary to identity misspelled words and suggest alternatives. Before checking the spelling in a worksheet, make the first cell active. The spelling checker reviews the worksheet from the active cell to the last cell in the worksheet that contains data.

To use the spelling checker, click the REVIEW tab and then click the Spelling button. Figure 4.7 displays the Spelling dialog box. At this dialog box, you can click a button to tell Excel to ignore a word or you can replace a misspelled word with a word from the *Suggestions* list box.

Using Undo and Redo

Excel includes an Undo button on the Quick Access toolbar that will reverse certain commands or delete the last data typed in a cell. For example, if you apply formatting to selected cells in a worksheet and then decide you want the formatting removed, click the Undo button on the Quick Access toolbar. If you decide you want the formatting back again, click the Redo button on the Quick Access toolbar.

Figure 4.7 Excel Spelling Dialog Box

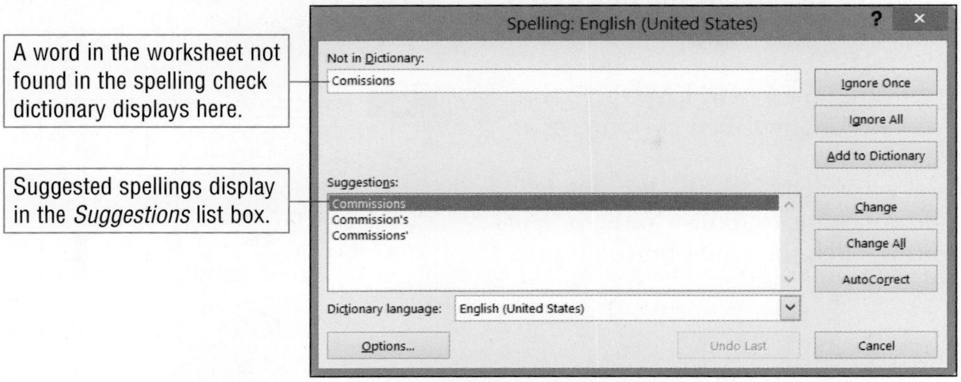

Excel maintains actions in temporary memory. If you want to undo an action, click the down-pointing arrow at the right side of the Undo button and a drop-down list displays containing the actions performed on the worksheet. Click the desired action at the drop-down list. Any actions preceding a chosen action are also undone. You can do the same with the Redo drop-down list. Multiple actions must be undone or redone in sequence.

HINT

Ctrl + Z is the keyboard shortcut to undo a command.

Project 2a Spell Checking and Formatting a Worksheet

Part 1 of 3

1. Open **MRSales.xlsx**.
2. Save the workbook with Save As and name it **EL1-C4-P2-MRSales**.
3. Complete a spelling check on the worksheet by completing the following steps:
   a. Make cell A1 active.
   b. Click the REVIEW tab.
   c. Click the Spelling button in the Proofing group.
   d. Click the Change button as needed to correct misspelled words in the worksheet. (When the spelling check stops at the proper names *Pirozzi* and *Yonemoto*, click the Ignore All button.)
   e. At the message telling you the spelling check is complete, click OK.

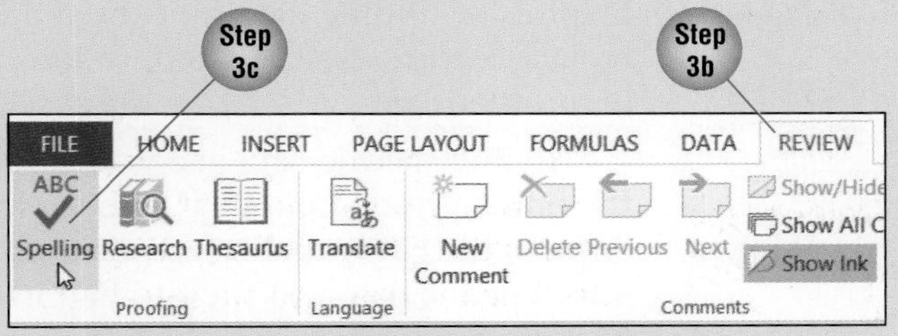

4. Insert a formula and then copy the formula without the formatting by completing the following steps:
   a. Make cell G4 active and then insert a formula that multiplies the sale price by the commission percentage.
   b. Copy the formula down to cells G5 through G26.
   c. Some of the cells contain shading that you do not want removed, so click the Auto Fill Options button that displays at the bottom right of the selected cells and then click the *Fill Without Formatting* option at the drop-down list.

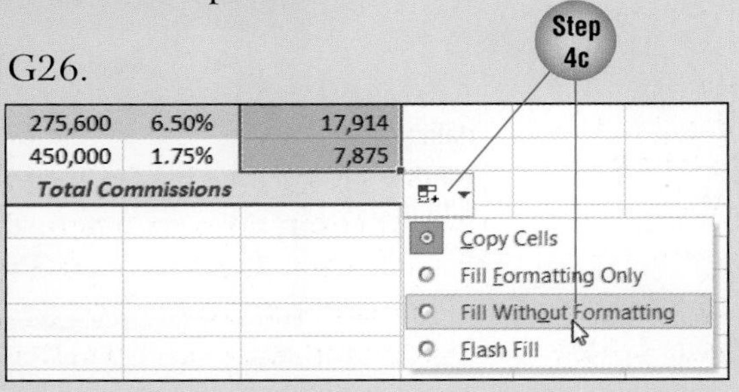

5. Make cell G27 active and then insert the sum of cells G4 through G26.
6. Apply accounting formatting with no places past the decimal point and add a dollar sign to cells G4 and G27.
7. Apply a theme by clicking the PAGE LAYOUT tab, clicking the Themes button, and then clicking *Ion* at the drop-down gallery.
8. After looking at the worksheet with the Ion theme applied, you decide you want to return to the original formatting. To do this, click the Undo button on the Quick Access toolbar.

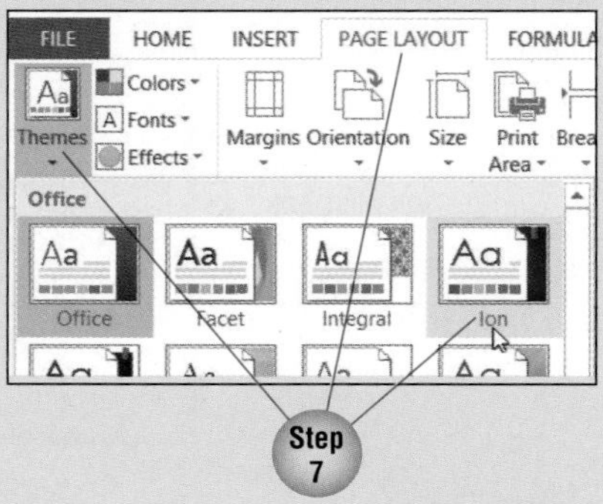

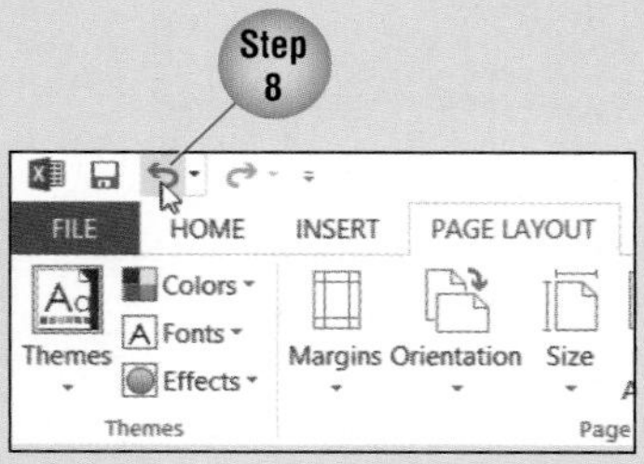

9. Save **EL1-C4-P2-MRSales.xlsx**.

Finding and Replacing Data and Cell Formatting in a Worksheet

Quick Steps

Find Data
1. Click Find & Select button.
2. Click *Find* at drop-down list.
3. Type data in *Find what* text box.
4. Click Find Next button.

Find & Select

Excel provides a Find feature you can use to look for specific data and either replace it with nothing or replace it with other data. This feature is particularly helpful for finding data quickly in a large worksheet. Excel also includes a find and replace feature. Use this tool to look for specific data in a worksheet and replace it with other data.

To find specific data in a worksheet, click the Find & Select button located in the Editing group on the HOME tab and then click *Find* at the drop-down list. This displays the Find and Replace dialog box with the Find tab selected, as shown in Figure 4.8. Type the data you want to find in the *Find what* text box and then click the Find Next button. Continue clicking the Find Next button to move to the next occurrence of the data. If the Find and Replace dialog box obstructs your view of the worksheet, use the mouse pointer on the title bar to drag the dialog box to a different location.

Figure 4.8 Find and Replace Dialog Box with Find Tab Selected

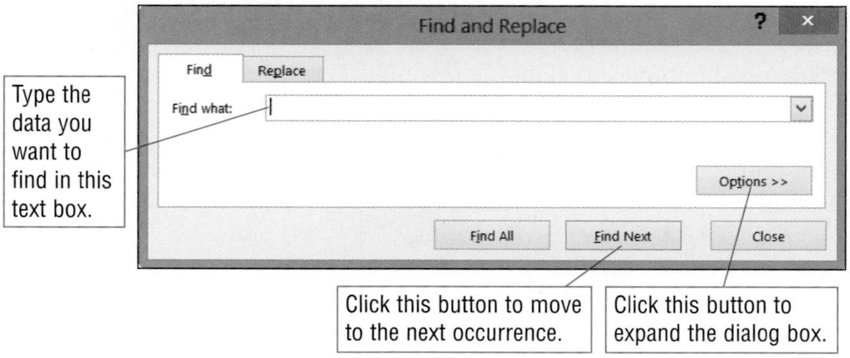

To find specific data in a worksheet and replace it with other data, click the Find & Select button in the Editing group on the HOME tab and then click *Replace* at the drop-down list. This displays the Find and Replace dialog box with the Replace tab selected, as shown in Figure 4.9. Enter the data you want to find in the *Find what* text box. Press the Tab key or click in the *Replace with* text box and then enter the data that is to replace the data in the *Find what* text box.

Click the Find Next button to tell Excel to find the next occurrence of the data. Click the Replace button to replace the data and find the next occurrence. If you know that you want to replace all occurrences of the data in the *Find what* text box with the data in the *Replace with* text box, click the Replace All button. Click the Close button to close the Replace dialog box.

Display additional find and replace options by clicking the Options button. This expands the dialog box, as shown in Figure 4.10. By default, Excel will look for any data that contains the same characters as the data in the *Find what* text box, without concern for the characters before or after the entered data. For example, in Project 2b, you will look for sale prices of $450,000 and replace them with sale prices of $475,000. If you do not specify to Excel that you want to find cells that contain only *450000,* Excel will stop at any cell containing *450000.* In this example, Excel will stop at a cell containing *$1,450,000* and a cell containing *$2,450,000.* To specify that the only data that should be contained in the cell is what is entered in the *Find what* text box, click the Options button to expand the dialog box and then insert a check mark in the *Match entire cell contents* check box.

Quick Steps

Find and Replace Data
1. Click Find & Select button.
2. Click *Replace* at drop-down list.
3. Type data in *Find what* text box.
4. Type data in *Replace with* text box.
5. Click Replace button or Replace All button.

Figure 4.9 Find and Replace Dialog Box with Replace Tab Selected

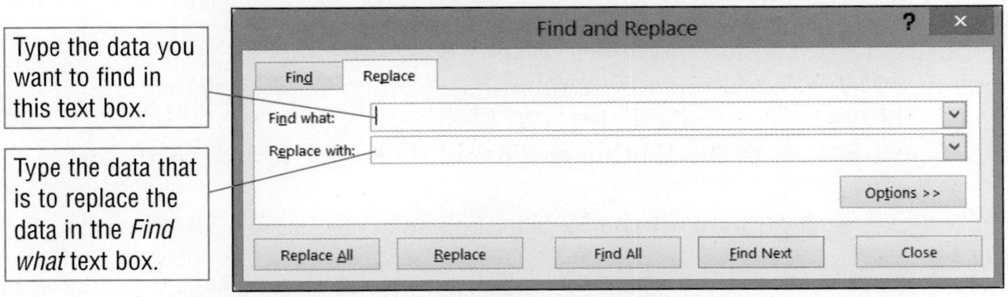

Figure 4.10 Expanded Find and Replace Dialog Box

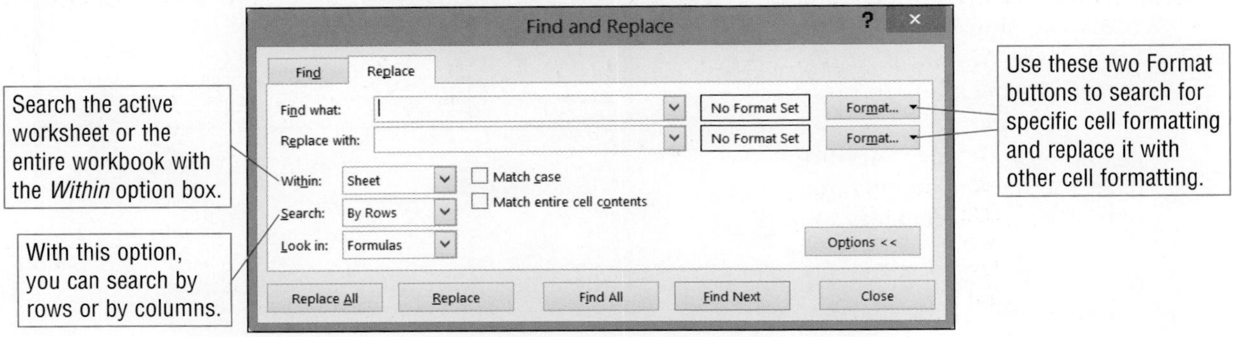

If the *Match case* option is active (contains a check mark), Excel will look for only that data that matches the case of the data entered in the *Find what* text box. Remove the check mark from this check box if you do not want Excel to find exact case matches. Excel will search in the current worksheet. If you want Excel to search an entire workbook, change the *Within* option to *Workbook*. Excel, by default, searches by rows in a worksheet. You can change this to *By Columns* with the *Search* option.

Project 2b Finding and Replacing Data — Part 2 of 3

1. With **EL1-C4-P2-MRSales.xlsx** open, find all occurrences of *Land* in the worksheet and replace with *Acreage* by completing the following steps:
   a. Click the Find & Select button in the Editing group on the HOME tab and then click *Replace* at the drop-down list.
   b. At the Find and Replace dialog box with the Replace tab selected, type **Land** in the *Find what* text box.
   c. Press the Tab key. (This moves the insertion point to the *Replace with* text box.)
   d. Type **Acreage**.
   e. Click the Replace All button.
   f. At the message telling you that four replacements were made, click OK.
   g. Click the Close button to close the Find and Replace dialog box.

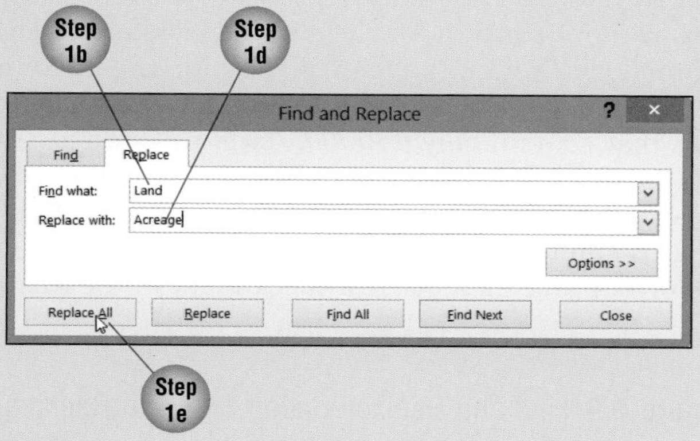

2. Find all occurrences of *$450,000* and replace them with *$475,000* by completing the following steps:
   a. Click the Find & Select button in the Editing group and then click *Replace* at the drop-down list.
   b. At the Find and Replace dialog box with the Replace tab selected, type **450000** in the *Find what* text box.
   c. Press the Tab key.
   d. Type **475000**.
   e. Click the Options button to display additional options. (If additional options already display, skip this step.)
   f. Click the *Match entire cell contents* check box to insert a check mark.
   g. Click the Replace All button.
   h. At the message telling you that two replacements were made, click OK.
   i. At the Find and Replace dialog box, click the *Match entire cell contents* check box to remove the check mark.
   j. Click the Close button to close the Find and Replace dialog box.

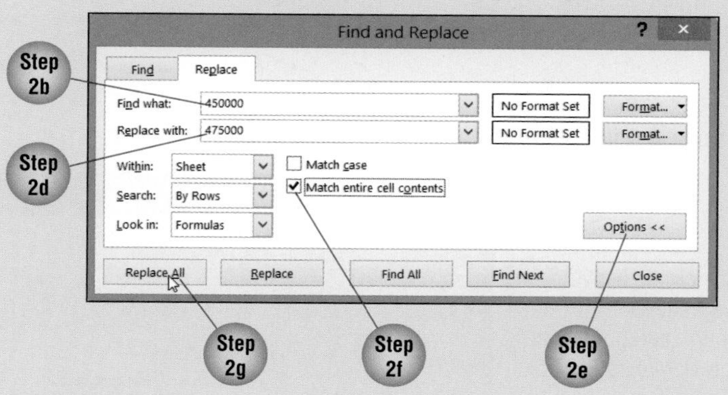

3. Save **EL1-C4-P2-MRSales.xlsx**.

Use the Format buttons at the expanded Find and Replace dialog box (see Figure 4.10) to search for specific cell formatting and replace it with other formatting. Click the down-pointing arrow at the right side of the Format button and a drop-down list displays. Click the *Format* option and the Find Format dialog box displays with the Number, Alignment, Font, Border, Fill, and Protection tabs. Specify formatting at this dialog box. Click the *Choose Format From Cell* option from the Format button drop-down list or click the Choose Format From Cell button in the Find Format dialog box and the mouse pointer displays with a pointer tool attached. Click in the cell containing the desired formatting and the formatting displays in the *Preview* box to the left of the Format button. Click the *Clear Find Format* option at the Find button drop-down list and any formatting in the *Preview* box is removed.

Project 2c Finding and Replacing Cell Formatting — Part 3 of 3

1. With **EL1-C4-P2-MRSales.xlsx** open, search for a light turquoise fill color and replace it with a light green fill color by completing the following steps:

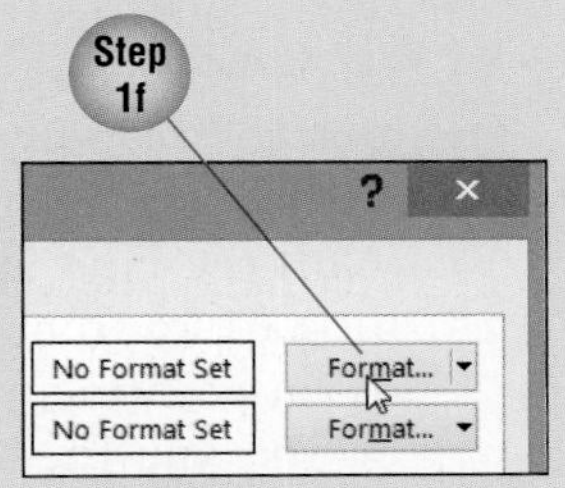

   a. Click the Find & Select button in the Editing group on the HOME tab and then click *Replace* at the drop-down list.
   b. At the Find and Replace dialog box with the Replace tab selected, make sure the dialog box is expanded. (If not, click the Options button.)
   c. Select and then delete any text that displays in the *Find what* text box.
   d. Select and then delete any text that displays in the *Replace with* text box.

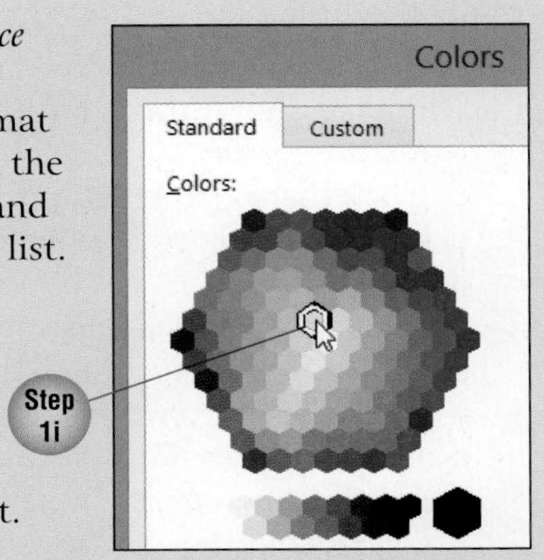

   e. Make sure the boxes immediately preceding the two Format buttons display with the text *No Format Set*. (If not, click the down-pointing arrow at the right of the Format button, and then click the *Clear Find Format* option at the drop-down list. Do this for each Format button.)
   f. Click the top Format button.
   g. At the Find Format dialog box, click the Fill tab.
   h. Click the More Colors button.
   i. At the Colors dialog box with the Standard tab selected, click the light turquoise color shown at the right.
   j. Click OK to close the Colors dialog box.
   k. Click OK to close the Find Format dialog box.

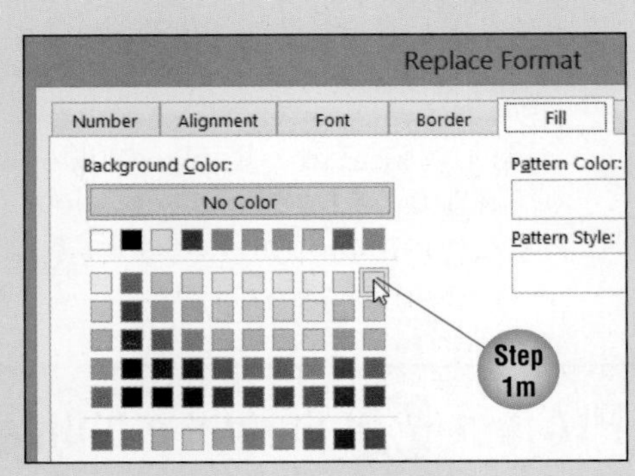

   l. Click the bottom Format button.
   m. At the Replace Format dialog box with the Fill tab selected, click the light green color (last column, second row), as shown at the right.
   n. Click OK to close the dialog box.
   o. At the Find and Replace dialog box, click the Replace All button.
   p. At the message telling you that 10 replacements were made, click OK.

2. Search for a light gray fill color and replace it with a light yellow fill color by completing the following steps:
   a. At the Find and Replace dialog box, click the top Format button.
   b. At the Find Format dialog box with the Fill tab selected, click the light gray color (fourth column, second row), as shown at the right.
   c. Click OK to close the Find Format dialog box.
   d. Click the bottom Format button.
   e. At the Replace Format dialog box with the Fill tab selected, click the yellow color (eighth column, second row), as shown below and to the right.
   f. Click OK to close the dialog box.
   g. At the Find and Replace dialog box, click the Replace All button.
   h. At the message telling you that 78 replacements were made, click OK.

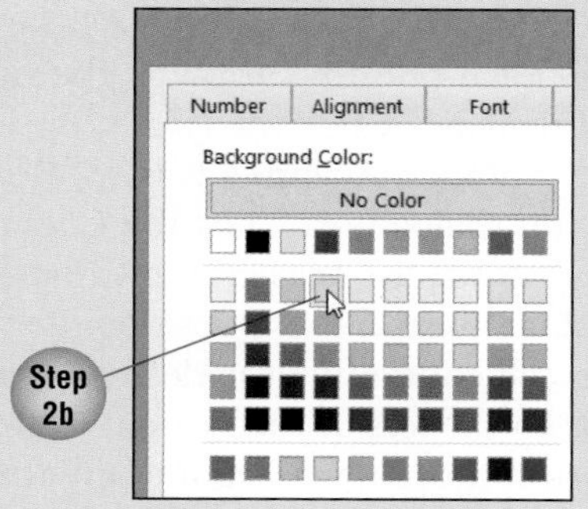

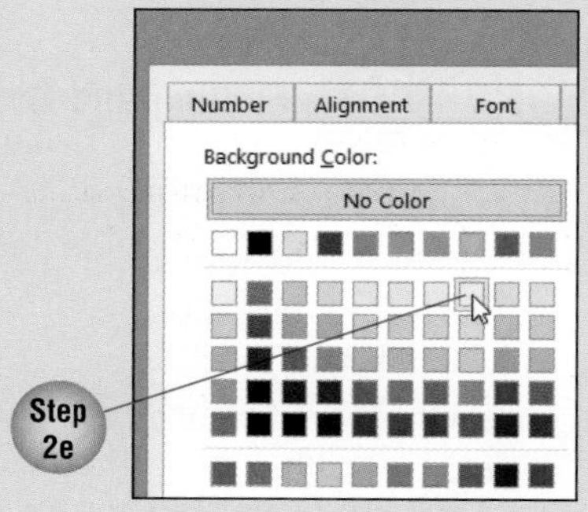

3. Search for 11-point Calibri formatting and replace it with 10-point Arial formatting by completing the following steps:
   a. With the Find and Replace dialog box open, clear formatting from the top Format button by clicking the down-pointing arrow at the right side of the top Format button and then clicking the *Clear Find Format* option at the drop-down list.
   b. Clear formatting from the bottom Format button by clicking the down-pointing arrow at the right side of the bottom Format button and then clicking *Clear Replace Format.*
   c. Click the top Format button.
   d. At the Find Format dialog box, click the Font tab.
   e. Scroll down the *Font* list box and then click *Calibri.*
   f. Click *11* in the *Size* list box.
   g. Click OK to close the dialog box.
   h. Click the bottom Format button.
   i. At the Replace Format dialog box with the Font tab selected, scroll down the *Font* list box and then click *Arial.*
   j. Click *10* in the *Size* list box.
   k. Click OK to close the dialog box.
   l. At the Find and Replace dialog box, click the Replace All button.
   m. At the message telling you that 174 replacements were made, click OK.
   n. At the Find and Replace dialog box, remove formatting from both Format buttons.
   o. Click the Close button to close the Find and Replace dialog box.

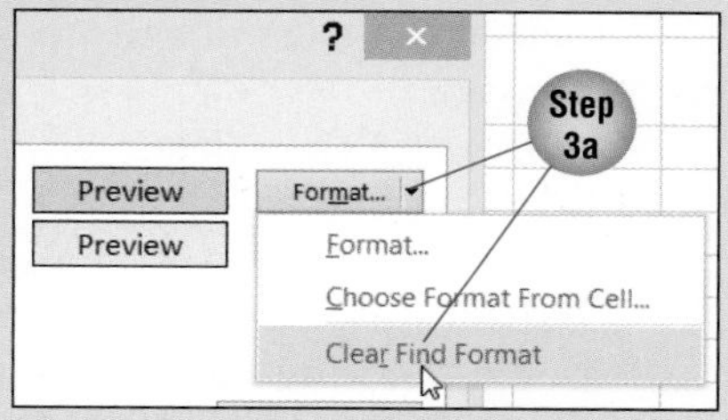

4. Save, print, and then close **EL1-C4-P2-MRSales.xlsx**.

Project 3 Format a Billing Worksheet — 4 Parts

You will insert a formula in a weekly billing worksheet and then sort and filter specific data in the worksheet.

Sorting Data

Excel is primarily a spreadsheet program, but it also includes some basic database functions. With a database program, you can alphabetize information or arrange numbers numerically. Data can even be sorted by columns in a worksheet. To sort data in a worksheet, use the Sort & Filter button in the Editing group on the HOME tab.

To sort data in a worksheet, select the cells containing the data you want to sort, click the Sort & Filter button in the Editing group, and then click the option representing the desired sort. The sort option names vary depending on the data in selected cells. For example, if the first column of selected cells contains text, the sort options in the drop-down list display as *Sort A to Z* and *Sort Z to A*. If the selected cells contain dates, the sort options in the drop-down list display as *Sort Oldest to Newest* and *Sort Newest to Oldest*, and if the cells contain numbers or values, the sort options display as *Sort Smallest to Largest* and *Sort Largest to Smallest*. If you select more than one column in a worksheet, Excel will sort the data in the first selected column.

Quick Steps

Sort Data
1. Select cells.
2. Click Sort & Filter button.
3. Click desired sort option at drop-down list.

Sort & Filter

HINT

If you are not satisfied with the results of the sort, immediately click the Undo button.

Project 3a **Sorting Data** **Part 1 of 4**

1. Open **APTBilling.xlsx** and save it with Save As and name it **EL1-C4-P3-APTBilling**.
2. Insert a formula in cell F4 that multiplies the rate by the hours. Copy the formula down to cells F5 through F29.
3. Sort the data in the first column in descending order by completing the following steps:
   a. Make cell A4 active.
   b. Click the Sort & Filter button in the Editing group on the HOME tab.
   c. Click the *Sort Largest to Smallest* option at the drop-down list.
4. Sort in ascending order by clicking the Sort & Filter button and then clicking *Sort Smallest to Largest* at the drop-down list.
5. Save **EL1-C4-P3-APTBilling.xlsx**.

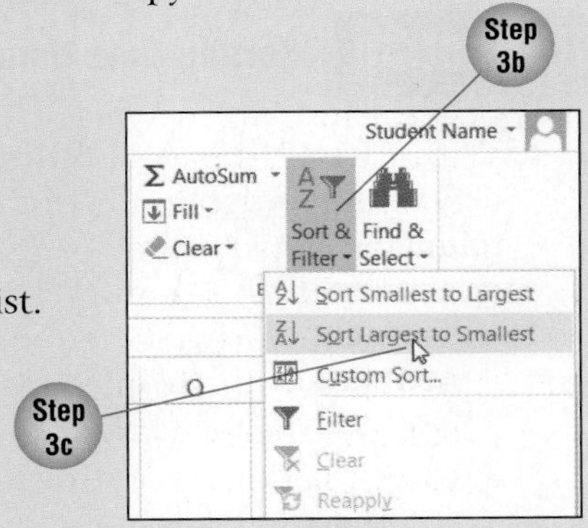

Completing a Custom Sort

If you want to sort data in a column other than the first column, use the Sort dialog box. If you select just one column in a worksheet, click the Sort & Filter button, and then click the desired sort option, only the data in that column is sorted. If this data is related to data to the left or right of the data in the sorted column, that relationship is broken. For example, if you sort cells C4 through C29 in EL1-C4-P3-APTBilling.xlsx, the client number, treatment, hours, and total no longer match the date.

Use the Sort dialog box to sort data and maintain the relationship among all cells. To sort using the Sort dialog box, select the cells you want sorted, click the Sort & Filter button, and then click *Custom Sort*. This displays the Sort dialog box, shown in Figure 4.11.

Quick Steps

Complete a Custom Sort
1. Select cells.
2. Click Sort & Filter button.
3. Click *Custom Sort* at drop-down list.
4. Specify options at Sort dialog box.
5. Click OK.

Figure 4.11 Sort Dialog Box

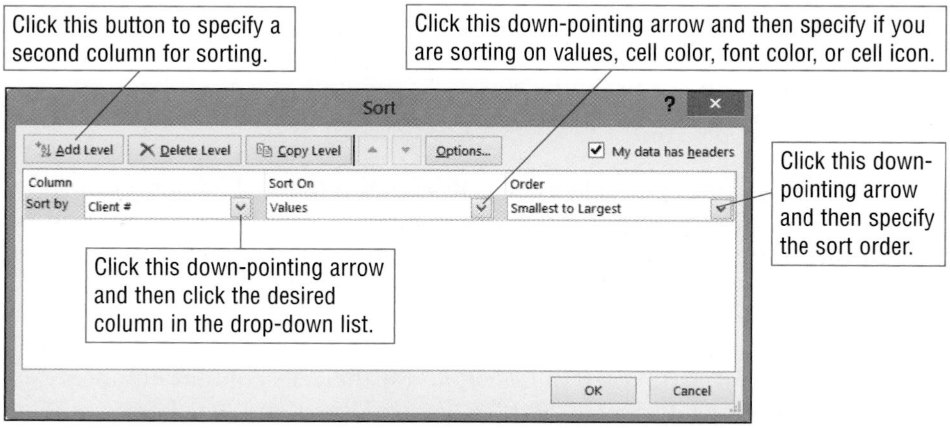

The data displayed in the *Sort by* option box will vary depending on what you have selected. Generally, the data that displays is the title of the first column of selected cells. If the selected cells do not have a title, the data may display as *Column A*. Use this option to specify what column you want sorted. Using the Sort dialog box to sort data in a column maintains the relationship among the data.

Project 3b Sorting Data Using the Sort Dialog Box — Part 2 of 4

1. With **EL1-C4-P3-APTBilling.xlsx** open, sort the rates in cells E4 through E29 in descending order and maintain the relationship to the other data by completing the following steps:
   a. Select cells A3 through F29.
   b. Click the Sort & Filter button and then click *Custom Sort*.
   c. At the Sort dialog box, click the down-pointing arrow at the right of the *Sort by* option box and then click *Rate* at the drop-down list.
   d. Click the down-pointing arrow at the right of the *Order* option box and then click *Largest to Smallest* at the drop-down list.

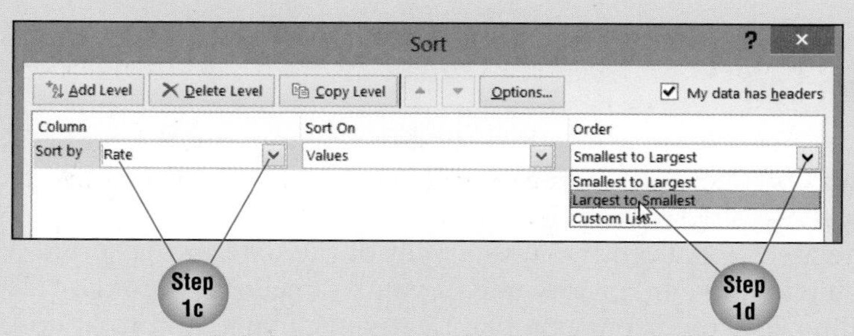

   e. Click OK to close the Sort dialog box.
   f. Deselect the cells.
2. Sort the dates in ascending order (oldest to newest) by completing steps similar to those in Step 1.
3. Save and then print **EL1-C4-P3-APTBilling.xlsx**.

Sorting More Than One Column

When sorting data in cells, you can sort in more than one column. For example, in Project 3c, you will sort the dates from oldest to newest and the client numbers from lowest to highest. In this sort, the dates are sorted first and then the client numbers are sorted in ascending order within the same date.

To sort in more than one column, select all columns in the worksheet that need to remain relative and then display the Sort dialog box. At the Sort dialog box, specify the first column you want sorted in the *Sort by* option box, click the *Add Level* button, and then specify the second column in the first *Then by* option box. In Excel, you can sort on multiple columns. Add additional *Then by* option boxes by clicking the *Add Level* button.

Project 3c **Sorting Data in Two Columns** **Part 3 of 4**

1. With **EL1-C4-P3-APTBilling.xlsx** open, select cells A3 through F29.
2. Click the Sort & Filter button and then click *Custom Sort*.
3. At the Sort dialog box, click the down-pointing arrow at the right side of the *Sort by* option box and then click *Date* in the drop-down list. (Skip this step if *Date* already displays in the *Sort by* option box.)
4. Make sure *Oldest to Newest* displays in the *Order* option box.
5. Click the Add Level button.
6. Click the down-pointing arrow at the right of the *Then by* option box and then click *Client #* in the drop-down list.
7. Click OK to close the dialog box.
8. Deselect the cells.
9. Save and then print **EL1-C4-P3-APTBilling.xlsx**.

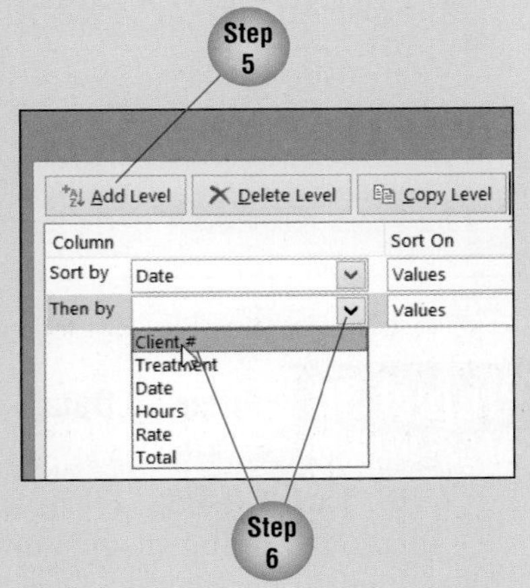

Filtering Data

You can place a restriction, called a ***filter***, on data in a worksheet to temporarily isolate specific data. To turn on filtering, make a cell containing data active, click the Sort & Filter button in the Editing group on the HOME tab, and then click *Filter* at the drop-down list. This turns on filtering and causes a filter arrow to appear with each column label in the worksheet, as shown in Figure 4.12. You do not need to select data before turning on filtering because Excel automatically searches for column labels in a worksheet.

To filter data in a worksheet, click the filter arrow in the heading you want to filter. This causes a drop-down list to display with options to filter all records, create a custom filter, or select an entry that appears in one or more of the cells in the column. When you filter data, the filter arrow changes to a funnel icon. The funnel icon indicates that rows in the worksheet have been filtered. To turn off filtering, click the Sort & Filter button and then click *Filter*.

If a column contains numbers, click the filter arrow and point to *Number Filters* and a side menu displays with options for filtering numbers. For example, you can filter numbers that are equal to, greater than, or less than a number you specify; filter the top ten numbers; and filter numbers that are above or below a specified number.

Quick Steps

Filter a List
1. Select cells.
2. Click Sort & Filter button.
3. Click *Filter* at drop-down list.
4. Click down-pointing arrow of heading to filter.
5. Click desired option at drop-down list.

Figure 4.12 Filtering Data

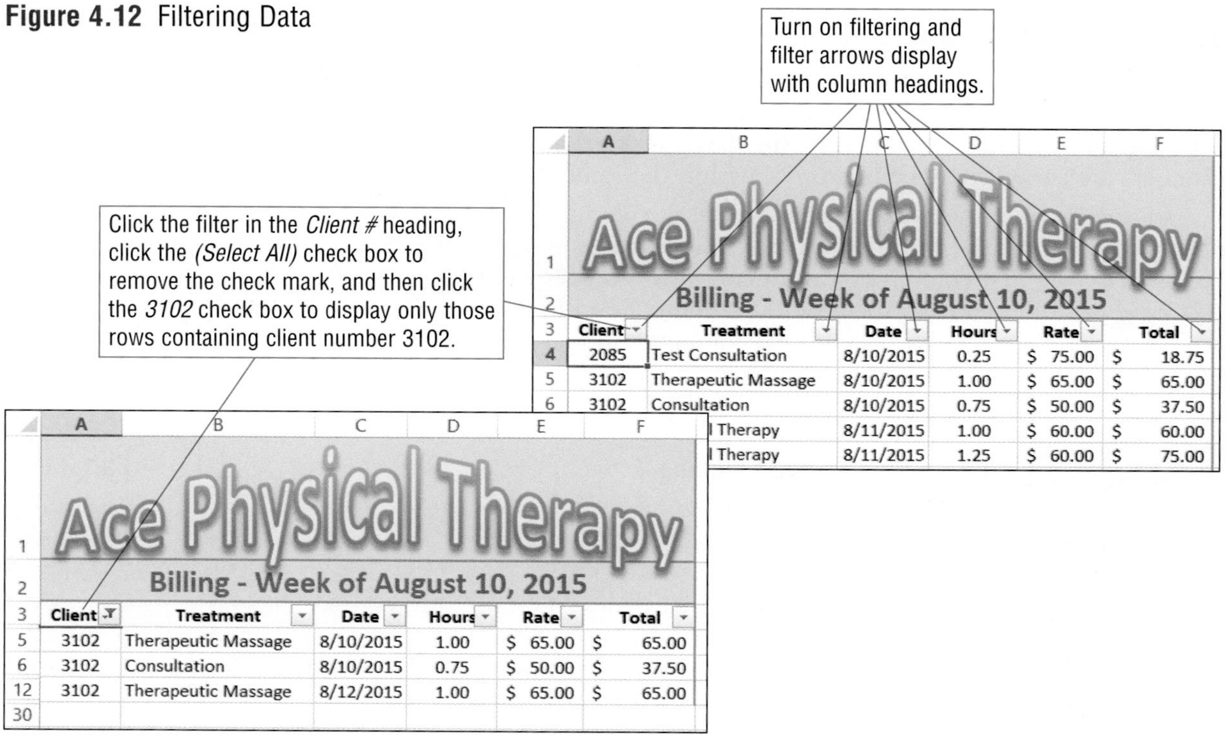

Project 3d Filtering Data

Part 4 of 4

1. With **EL1-C4-P3-APTBilling.xlsx** open, click in cell A4.
2. Turn on filtering by clicking the Sort & Filter button in the Editing group on the HOME tab and then clicking *Filter* at the drop-down list.
3. Filter rows for client number 3102 by completing the following steps:
   a. Click the filter arrow in the *Client #* heading.
   b. Click the *(Select All)* check box to remove the check mark.
   c. Scroll down the list box and then click *3102* to insert a check mark in the check box.
   d. Click OK.
4. Redisplay all rows containing data by completing the following steps:
   a. Click the funnel icon in the *Client #* heading.
   b. Click the *(Select All)* check box to insert a check mark. (This also inserts check marks for all items in the list.)
   c. Click OK.

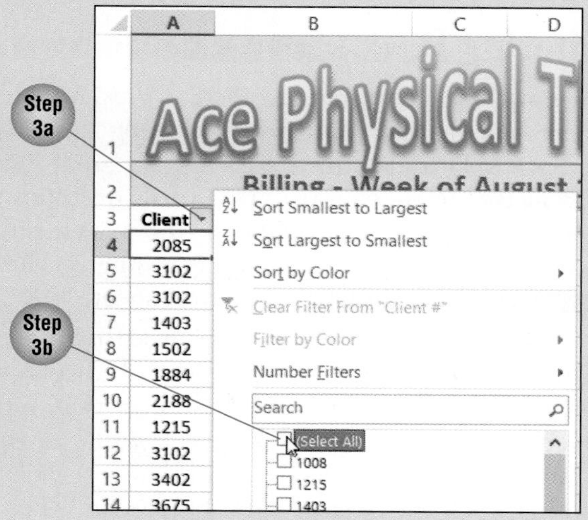

5. Filter a list of clients receiving physical therapy by completing the following steps:
   a. Click the filter arrow in the *Treatment* heading.
   b. Click the *(Select All)* check box.
   c. Click the *Physical Therapy* check box.
   d. Click OK.
6. Redisplay all rows containing data by completing the following steps:
   a. Click the funnel icon in the *Treatment* heading.
   b. Click the *Clear Filter From "Treatment"* option.
7. Display the top two highest rates by completing the following steps:
   a. Click the filter arrow in the *Rate* heading.
   b. Point to *Number Filters* and then click *Top 10* at the side menu.
   c. At the Top 10 AutoFilter dialog box, select the *10* that displays in the middle measurement box and then type 2.
   d. Click OK to close the dialog box.

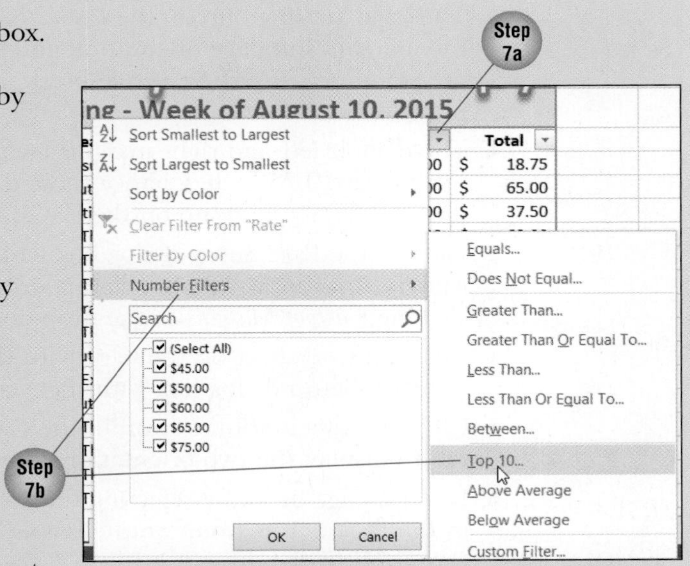

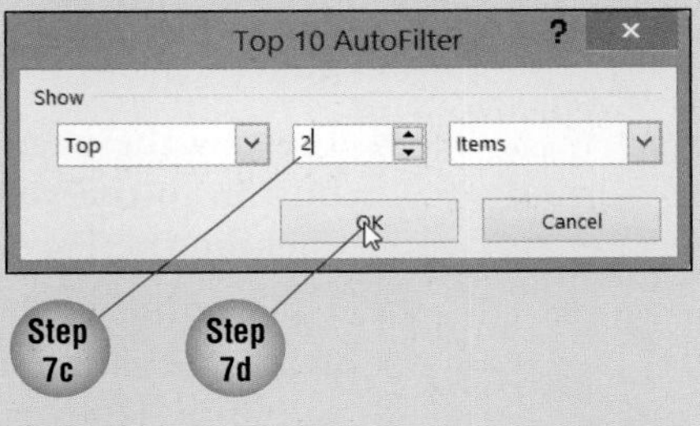

8. Redisplay all rows that contain data by completing the following steps:
   a. Click the funnel icon in the *Rate* heading.
   b. Click the *Clear Filter From "Rate"* option.
9. Display totals greater than $60 by completing the following steps:
   a. Click the filter arrow in the *Total* heading.
   b. Point to *Number Filters* and then click *Greater Than*.
   c. At the Custom AutoFilter dialog box, type 60 and then click OK.
10. Print the worksheet by clicking the FILE tab, clicking the *Print* option, and then clicking the Print button.
11. Turn off the filtering feature by clicking the Sort & Filter button and then clicking *Filter* at the drop-down list.
12. Save, print, and then close **EL1-C4-P3-APTBilling.xlsx**.

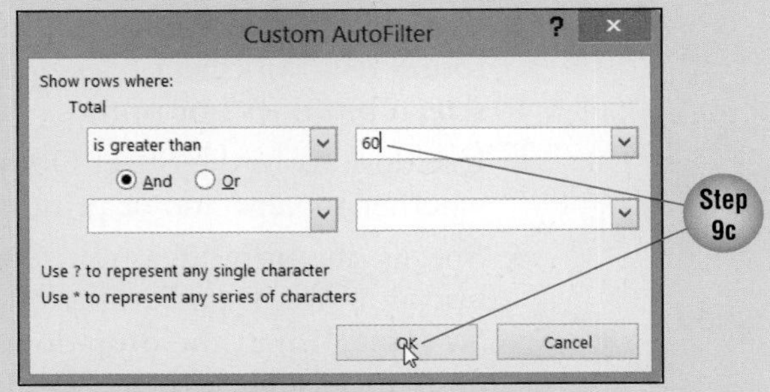

Chapter Summary

- The Page Setup group on the PAGE LAYOUT tab contains buttons for changing the margins and page orientation and size, as well as buttons for establishing the print area, inserting a page break, applying a picture background, and printing titles.
- The default left and right margins are 0.7 inch and the default top and bottom margins are 0.75 inch. Change these default margins with the Margins button in the Page Setup group on the PAGE LAYOUT tab.
- Display the Page Setup dialog box with the Margins tab selected by clicking the Margins button in the Page Setup group on the PAGE LAYOUT tab and then clicking *Custom Margins* at the drop-down list.
- Center a worksheet on the page with the *Horizontally* and *Vertically* options at the Page Setup dialog box with the Margins tab selected.
- Click the Orientation button in the Page Setup group on the PAGE LAYOUT tab to display the two orientation choices: *Portrait* and *Landscape*.
- Insert a page break by selecting the column or row, clicking the Breaks button in the Page Setup group on the PAGE LAYOUT tab, and then clicking *Insert Page Break* at the drop-down list.
- To insert both horizontal and vertical page breaks at the same time, make a cell active, click the Breaks button, and then click *Insert Page Break* at the drop-down list.
- Preview the page breaks in a worksheet by clicking the Page Break Preview button in the view area on the Status bar or clicking the VIEW tab and then clicking the Page Break Preview button in the Workbook Views group.
- Use options at the Page Setup dialog box with the Sheet tab selected to specify printing column and/or row titles on each page. Display this dialog box by clicking the Print Titles button in the Page Setup group on the PAGE LAYOUT tab.
- Use options in the Scale to Fit group on the PAGE LAYOUT tab to scale data to fit on a specific number of pages.
- Use the Background button in the Page Setup group on the PAGE LAYOUT tab to insert a worksheet background picture. A background picture displays on the screen but does not print.
- Use options in the Sheet Options group on the PAGE LAYOUT tab to specify whether to view and/or print gridlines and headings.
- Specify the print area by selecting the desired cells, clicking the Print Area button in the Page Setup group on the PAGE LAYOUT tab, and then clicking *Set Print Area* at the drop-down list. Add another print area by selecting the desired cells, clicking the Print Area button, and then clicking *Add to Print Area* at the drop-down list.
- Create a header and/or footer with the Header & Footer button in the Text group on the INSERT tab, in Page Layout view, or with options at the Page Setup dialog box with the Header/Footer tab selected.
- Customize a print job with options at the Print backstage area.
- To check spelling in a worksheet, click the REVIEW tab and then click the Spelling button.

- Click the Undo button on the Quick Access toolbar to reverse the most recent action and click the Redo button to redo a previously reversed action.
- Use options at the Find and Replace dialog box with the Find tab selected to find specific data and/or formatting in a worksheet.
- Use options at the Find and Replace dialog box with the Replace tab selected to find specific data and/or formatting and replace it with other data and/or formatting.
- Sort data in a worksheet with options from the Sort & Filter button in the Editing group on the HOME tab.
- Create a custom sort with options at the Sort dialog box. Display this dialog box by clicking the Sort & Filter button and then clicking *Custom Sort* at the drop-down list.
- Use filtering to temporarily isolate specific data. Turn on the filter feature by clicking the Sort & Filter button in the Editing group on the HOME tab and then clicking *Filter* at the drop-down list. This inserts filter arrows with each column label. Click a filter arrow and then use options at the drop-down list that displays to specify the filter data.

Commands Review

FEATURE	RIBBON TAB, GROUP	BUTTON, OPTION	KEYBOARD SHORTCUT
background picture	PAGE LAYOUT, Page Setup		
filter data	HOME, Editing		
Find and Replace dialog box with Find tab selected	HOME, Editing	, *Find*	Ctrl + F
Find and Replace dialog box with Replace tab selected	HOME, Editing	, *Replace*	Ctrl + H
header and footer	INSERT, Text		
insert page break	PAGE LAYOUT, Page Setup	, *Insert Page Break*	
margins	PAGE LAYOUT, Page Setup		
orientation	PAGE LAYOUT, Page Setup		
Page Layout view	VIEW, Workbook Views		
Page Setup dialog box with Margins tab selected	PAGE LAYOUT, Page Setup	, *Custom Margins*	
Page Setup dialog box with Sheet tab selected	PAGE LAYOUT, Page Setup		
preview page break	VIEW, Workbook Views		

FEATURE	RIBBON TAB, GROUP	BUTTON, OPTION	KEYBOARD SHORTCUT
print area	PAGE LAYOUT, Page Setup		
remove page break	PAGE LAYOUT, Page Setup	, *Remove Page Break*	
scale height	PAGE LAYOUT, Scale to Fit		
scale to fit	PAGE LAYOUT, Scale to Fit		
scale width	PAGE LAYOUT, Scale to Fit		
size	PAGE LAYOUT, Page Setup		
sort data	HOME, Editing		
spelling checker	REVIEW, Proofing		F7

Concepts Check Test Your Knowledge SNAP

Completion: In the space provided at the right, indicate the correct term, symbol, or command.

1. This is the default left and right margin measurement. .7
2. This is the default top and bottom margin measurement. .75
3. The Margins button is located on this tab. Page Layout
4. By default, a worksheet prints in this orientation on a page. Portrait
5. Click the Print Titles button in the Page Setup group on the PAGE LAYOUT tab and the Page Setup dialog box displays with this tab selected. Sheet
6. Use options in this group on the PAGE LAYOUT tab to adjust the printed output by a percentage to fit the number of pages specified. Scale to Fit
7. Use this button in the Page Setup group on the PAGE LAYOUT tab to select and print specific areas in a worksheet. Print Area
8. Click the Header & Footer button in the Text group on the INSERT tab and the worksheet displays in this view. Page Layout
9. This tab contains options for formatting and customizing a header and/or footer. 5 Words ?! Header & Footer Design Tools

10. Click this tab to display the Spelling button. Review

11. The Undo and Redo buttons are located on this toolbar. Quick Access

12. Click this button in the Find and Replace dialog box to expand the dialog box. Options

13. Use these two buttons at the expanded Find and Replace dialog box to search for specific cell formatting and replace it with other formatting. format

14. Use this button in the Editing group on the HOME tab to sort data in a worksheet. Sort & Filter

15. Use this feature to temporarily isolate specific data in a worksheet. filter

Skills Check Assess Your Performance

Assessment 1

FORMAT A DATA ANALYSIS WORKSHEET

SNAP Grade It

1. Open **DISemiSales.xlsx**.
2. Save the workbook with Save As and name it **EL1-C4-A1-DISemiSales**.
3. Make the following changes to the worksheet:
   a. Insert a formula in cell H4 that averages the amounts in cells B4 through G4.
   b. Copy the formula in cell H4 down to cells H5 through H9.
   c. Insert a formula in cell B10 that adds the amounts in cells B4 through B9.
   d. Copy the formula in cell B10 over to cells C10 through H10. (Click the Auto Fill Options button and then click *Fill Without Formatting* at the drop-down list.)
   e. Apply accounting formatting to cell H4.
   f. Change the orientation of the worksheet to landscape.
   g. Change the top margin to 3 inches and the left margin to 1.5 inches.
4. Save and then print **EL1-C4-A1-DISemiSales.xlsx**.
5. Make the following changes to the worksheet:
   a. Change the orientation back to portrait.
   b. Change the top margin to 1 inch and the left margin to 0.7 inch.
   c. Horizontally and vertically center the worksheet on the page.
   d. Scale the worksheet so it fits on one page.
6. Save, print, and then close **EL1-C4-A1-DISemiSales.xlsx**.

Assessment 2

FORMAT A TEST RESULTS WORKSHEET

SNAP Grade It

1. Open **CMTests.xlsx**.
2. Save the workbook with Save As and name it **EL1-C4-A2-CMTests**.
3. Make the following changes to the worksheet:
   a. Insert a formula in cell N4 that averages the test scores in cells B4 through M4.
   b. Copy the formula in cell N4 down to cells N5 through N21.
   c. Type Average in cell A22.
   d. Insert a formula in cell B22 that averages the test scores in cells B4 through B21.
   e. Copy the formula in cell B22 across to cells C22 through N22.
   f. Insert a page break between columns G and H.
4. View the worksheet using Page Break Preview.
5. Change back to the Normal view.
6. Specify that the column titles (A3 through A22) are to print on each page.
7. Create a header that prints the page number at the right side of the page.
8. Create a footer that prints your name at the left side of the page and the workbook file name at the right side of the page.
9. Display the worksheet in Normal view.
10. Save and then print the worksheet.
11. Set a print area for cells N3 through N22 and then print the cells.
12. Clear the print area.
13. Save and then close **EL1-C4-A2-CMTests.xlsx**.

Assessment 3

FORMAT AN EQUIPMENT RENTAL WORKSHEET

SNAP Grade It

1. Open **HERInvoices.xlsx**.
2. Save the workbook with Save As and name it **EL1-C4-A3-HERInvoices**.
3. Insert a formula in cell H3 that multiplies the rate in cell G3 by the hours in cell F3. Copy the formula in cell H3 down to cells H4 through H16.
4. Insert a formula in cell H17 that sums the amounts in cells H3 through H16.
5. Complete the following find and replaces:
   a. Find all occurrences of cells containing *75* and replace them with *90*.
   b. Find all occurrences of cells containing *55* and replace them with *60*.
   c. Find all occurrences of *Barrier Concrete* and replace them with *Lee Sand and Gravel*.
   d. Find all occurrences of 11-point Calibri and replace them with 10-point Cambria.
   e. After completing the find and replaces, clear all formatting from the Format buttons.
6. Insert a header that prints the date at the left side of the page and the time at the right side of the page.
7. Insert a footer that prints your name at the left side of the page and the workbook file name at the right side of the page.
8. Print the worksheet horizontally and vertically centered on the page.
9. Save and then close **EL1-C4-A3-HERInvoices.xlsx**.

Assessment 4

FORMAT AN INVOICES WORKSHEET

SNAP Grade It

1. Open **RPInvoices.xlsx**.
2. Save the workbook with Save As and name it **EL1-C4-A4-RPInvoices**.
3. Insert a formula in G4 that multiplies the amount in E4 with the percentage in F4 and then adds the product to cell E4. (If you write the formula correctly, the result in G4 will display as *$488.25*.)
4. Copy the formula in cell G4 down to cells G5 through G17, click the Auto Fill Options button, and then click the *Fill Without Formatting* option.
5. Complete a spelling check on the worksheet.
6. Find all occurrences of *Picture* and replace them with *Portrait*. (Do not type a space after *Picture* or *Portrait* because you want to find occurrences that end with an *s*. Make sure the *Match entire cell contents* check box does not contain a check mark.)
7. Sort the records by invoice number in ascending order (smallest to largest).
8. Complete a new sort that sorts the records by client number in ascending order (A to Z).
9. Complete a new sort that sorts by date in ascending order (oldest to newest).
10. Insert a footer in the worksheet that prints your name at the left side of the page and the current date at the right side of the page.
11. Center the worksheet horizontally and vertically on the page.
12. Display the worksheet in Normal view.
13. Save and then print **EL1-C4-A4-RPInvoices.xlsx**.
14. Select cells A3 through G3 and then turn on the filter feature and complete the following filters:
    a. Filter and then print a list of rows containing client number 11-279 and then clear the filter.
    b. Filter and then print a list of rows containing the top three highest amounts due and then clear the filter.
    c. Filter and then print a list of rows containing amounts due that are less than $500 and then clear the filter.
15. Save and then close **EL1-C4-A4-RPInvoices.xlsx**.

Assessment 5

CREATE A WORKSHEET CONTAINING KEYBOARD SHORTCUTS

Help

1. Use Excel's Help feature to learn about keyboard shortcuts in Excel. After reading the information presented, create a worksheet with the following features:
    - Create a title for the worksheet.
    - Include at least 10 keyboard shortcuts along with an explanation of each shortcut.
    - Set the data in cells in a typeface other than Calibri and change the data color.
    - Add borders to the cells. (You determine the border style.)
    - Add a color of shading to cells. (You determine the color; make it complement the data color.)
    - Create a header that prints the date at the right margin and create a footer that prints your name at the left margin and the file name at the right margin.
2. Save the workbook and name it **EL1-C4-A5-KeyboardShortcuts**.
3. Print and then close **EL1-C4-A5-KeyboardShortcuts.xlsx**.

Visual Benchmark Demonstrate Your Proficiency

CREATE AND FORMAT AN EXPENSE WORKSHEET

1. At a blank workbook, type the data in the cells as indicated in Figure 4.13 on the next page, but **do not** type the data in the cells noted below. Instead, insert the formulas as indicated:
   - Cells N3 through N8: Insert a formula that sums the monthly expenses for the year.
   - Cells B9 through N9: Insert a formula that sums the monthly expenses for each month and the entire year.

   (The results of your formulas should match the results you see in the figure.)
2. Change the left and right margins to 0.45 inch and change the top margin to 1.5 inches.
3. Apply formatting so your worksheet looks similar to the worksheet shown in Figure 4.13. (Set the heading in 26-point Cambria and set the remaining data in 10-point Cambria. Apply bold formatting as shown in the figure.)
4. Save the workbook and name it **EL1-C4-VB-HERExpenses**.
5. Look at the printing of the worksheet shown in Figure 4.14 and then make the following changes:
   - Insert a page break between columns G and H.
   - Insert the headers and footer as shown.
   - Specify that the column titles print on the second page, as shown in Figure 4.14.
6. Save and then print **EL1-C4-VB-HERExpenses.xlsx**. (Your worksheet should print on two pages and appear as shown in Figure 4.14 on the next page.)
7. Close **EL1-C4-VB-HERExpenses.xlsx**.

Figure 4.13 Visual Benchmark Data

	A	B	C	D	E	F	G	H	I	J	K	L	M	N
1	Hilltop Equipment Rental													
2	Expenses	January	February	March	April	May	June	July	August	September	October	November	December	*Total*
3	Lease	$ 3,250	$ 3,250	$ 3,250	$ 3,250	$ 3,250	$ 3,250	$ 3,250	$ 3,250	$ 3,250	$ 3,250	$ 3,250	$ 3,250	$ 39,000
4	Utilities	3,209	2,994	2,987	2,500	2,057	1,988	1,845	1,555	1,890	2,451	2,899	3,005	29,380
5	Payroll	10,545	9,533	11,542	10,548	11,499	12,675	13,503	13,258	12,475	10,548	10,122	9,359	135,607
6	Insurance	895	895	895	895	895	895	895	895	895	895	895	895	10,740
7	Maintenance	2,439	1,856	2,455	5,410	3,498	3,110	2,479	3,100	1,870	6,105	4,220	3,544	40,086
8	Supplies	341	580	457	330	675	319	451	550	211	580	433	601	5,528
9	*Total Expenses*	$ 20,679	$ 19,108	$ 21,586	$ 22,933	$ 21,874	$ 22,237	$ 22,423	$ 22,608	$ 20,591	$ 23,829	$ 21,819	$ 20,654	$ 260,341
10														

Figure 4.14 Visual Benchmark Printed Pages

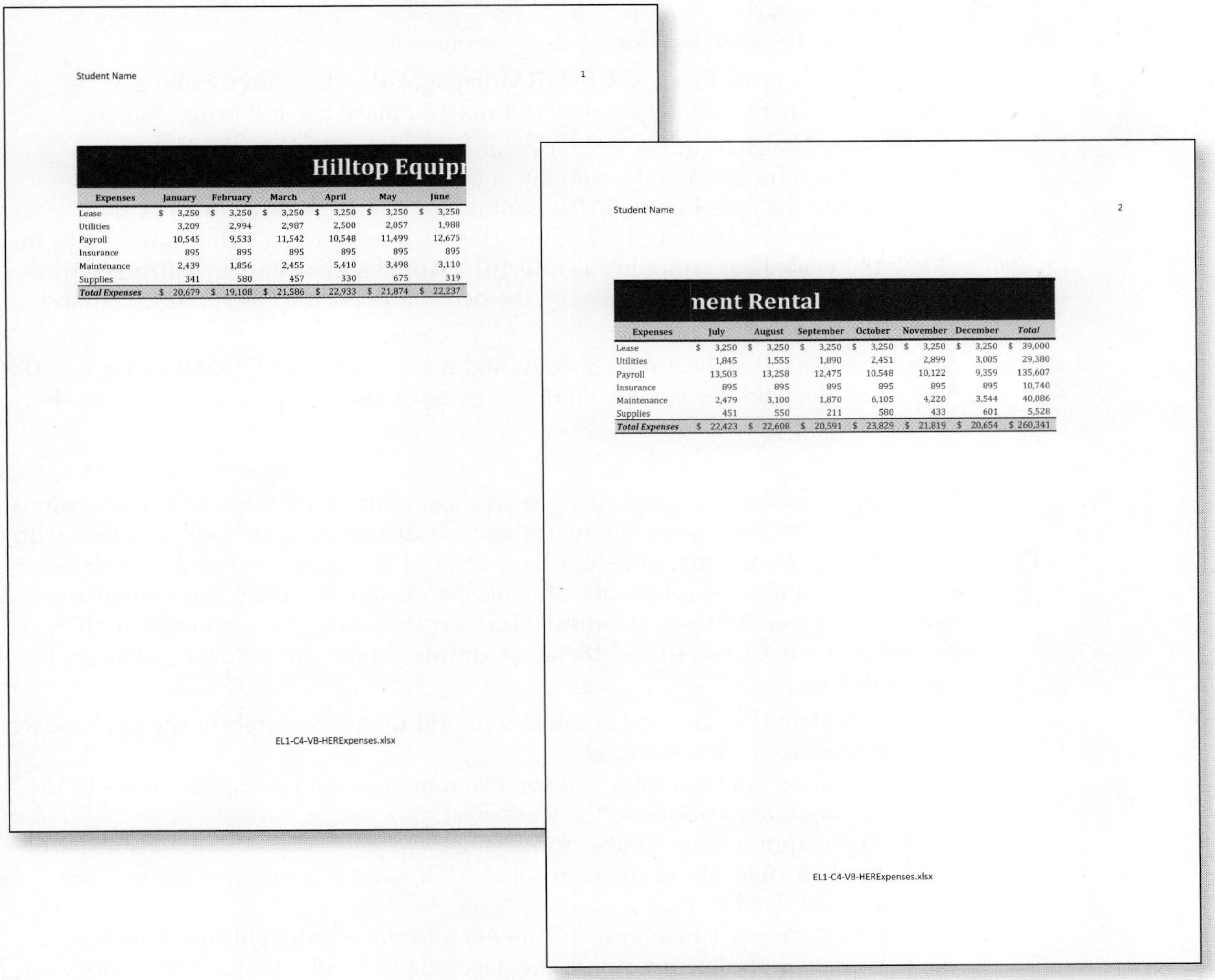

Student Name 1

Hilltop Equipi						
Expenses	January	February	March	April	May	June
Lease	$ 3,250	$ 3,250	$ 3,250	$ 3,250	$ 3,250	$ 3,250
Utilities	3,209	2,994	2,987	2,500	2,057	1,988
Payroll	10,545	9,533	11,542	10,548	11,499	12,675
Insurance	895	895	895	895	895	895
Maintenance	2,439	1,856	2,455	5,410	3,498	3,110
Supplies	341	580	457	330	675	319
Total Expenses	$ 20,679	$ 19,108	$ 21,586	$ 22,933	$ 21,874	$ 22,237

EL1-C4-VB-HERExpenses.xlsx

Student Name 2

nent Rental							
Expenses	July	August	September	October	November	December	*Total*
Lease	$ 3,250	$ 3,250	$ 3,250	$ 3,250	$ 3,250	$ 3,250	$ 39,000
Utilities	1,845	1,555	1,890	2,451	2,899	3,005	29,380
Payroll	13,503	13,258	12,475	10,548	10,122	9,359	135,607
Insurance	895	895	895	895	895	895	10,740
Maintenance	2,479	3,100	1,870	6,105	4,220	3,544	40,086
Supplies	451	550	211	580	433	601	5,528
Total Expenses	$ 22,423	$ 22,608	$ 20,591	$ 23,829	$ 21,819	$ 20,654	$ 260,341

EL1-C4-VB-HERExpenses.xlsx

Case Study Apply Your Skills

Part 1

You are a sales associate for Macadam Realty. Your supervisor has asked you to complete a form that she started containing information on sample mortgages. She wants to display the form in the reception area display rack. She has already inserted a formula (in cell G4) that calculates monthly payments using the PMT function. (You will learn more about this function in Chapter 5.) Open **MRMortgages.xlsx** and then save it with Save As and name it **EL1-C4-CS-MRMortgages-01**. Add the following information and make the following changes:

- In column C, insert a formula that determines the down payment amount.
- In column D, insert a formula that determines the loan amount.
- In column G, drag the formula in cell G4 down to cells G5 through G47.
- Insert the date and time as a header and your name and the workbook name (**EL1-C4-CS-MRMortgages-01.xlsx**) as a footer.
- Find 11-point Calibri formatting and replace it with 11-point Candara formatting.
- Scale the worksheet so it prints on one page.

Save and then print **EL1-C4-CS-MRMortgages-01.xlsx**. After looking at the printed worksheet, you decide that you need to make the following changes:

- Sort the values in the *Price of Home* column from smallest to largest.
- Change the percentage amount in column E from 6% to 7%.
- Shade the cells in row 4 that contain data in the light gold color that matches the fill in cell A2. Copy this shading to every other row of cells in the worksheet (stopping at row 46). *Apply accounting formatting with a dollar sign and no places past the decimal point to cells A4, C4, D4, and G4.

Save the edited worksheet with Save As and name it **EL1-C4-CS-MRMortgages-02**. Make sure the worksheet prints on one page. Save, print, and then close **EL1-C4-CS-MRMortgages-02.xlsx**.

Part 2

You are responsible for preparing a worksheet containing sales and commissions for the year. You will print the worksheet for distribution to staff members who attend an upcoming meeting. You have created the worksheet and included the sales and commission totals and now need to insert formulas and format the worksheet. Open **MRSalesComms.xlsx** and then save the workbook with Save As and name it **EL1-C4-CS-MRSalesComms**. Make the following changes to the worksheet:

- Calculate the sales and commissions and insert the totals in the appropriate locations in the worksheet.
- Calculate the total sales and total commissions and insert the totals in the appropriate locations in the worksheet.
- Apply appropriate number formatting.
- Apply formatting so the worksheet is formatted similar to the worksheet you prepared in Part 1.
- Change the left margin to 1.2 inches and the top margin to 1.5 inches.
- Include a header that prints the page number and a footer that prints your name.

Save the worksheet and then print it so that the row titles (A4:A14) print on both pages. After looking at the worksheet, you decide to make the following changes:

- Remove the header containing the page number.
- Edit the footer so the date prints at the left margin and your name prints at the right margin.
- Change the orientation to landscape.
- Scale the worksheet so it prints on one page.

Print, save, and then close **EL1-C4-CS-MRSalesComms.xlsx**.

Part 3

You have clients living in Canada that are interested in purchasing real estate in the United States. For those clients, you like to keep a dollar conversion worksheet available. Using the Internet, search for a site that converts the US dollar to the Canadian dollar. Determine the current currency exchange rate for the Canadian dollar and then create a worksheet with the following specifications:

- Apply formatting that is similar to the formatting in the worksheets you worked with in the first two parts of the case study.
- Create a column for home prices in US dollars with home amounts that begin with $100,000, increment every $50,000, and end with $1,000,000.
- Create a column for home prices converted to Canadian dollars.
- Apply any other formatting you feel is necessary to improve the worksheet.

Save the completed workbook and name it **EL1-C4-CS-CanadaPrices**. Display formulas and then print the worksheet. Turn off the display of formulas and then save and close the workbook.

MICROSOFT® EXCEL® Performance Assessment

Excel

Excel L1U1

Note: Before beginning unit assessments, copy to your storage medium the EL1U1 subfolder from the EL1U1 folder on the CD that accompanies this textbook and then make EL1U1 the active folder.

Assessing Proficiency

In this unit, you have learned to create, save, print, edit, and format Excel worksheets; create and insert formulas; and enhance worksheets with features such as headers and footers, page numbering, sorting, and filtering.

Assessment 1 Calculate Total, Maximum, Minimum, and Average Yearly Sales

1. Open **DI2015Sales.xlsx** and then save the workbook with Save As and name it **EL1-U1-A1-DI2015Sales**.
2. Insert in cells D4 through D14 the appropriate sales totals.
3. Insert in cells B15, C15, and D15 the appropriate first half, second half, and total sales, respectively. (If you use the fill handle to copy the formula in cell B15 to cells C15 and D15, you will need to fill without formatting so the right border remains in cell D15.)
4. Insert in cell B17 a formula that inserts the maximum total sales amount from cells D4 through D14.
5. Insert in cell B18 a formula that inserts the minimum total sales amount from cells D4 through D14.
6. Insert in cell B19 a formula that inserts the average of total sales in cells D4 through D14.
7. Apply accounting formatting to cell D4 with a dollar sign. (Make sure the places after the decimal point remain set at zero.)
8. Save, print, and then close **EL1-U1-A1-DI2015Sales.xlsx**.

Assessment 2 Create Worksheet with AutoFill and Calculate Hours and Gross Pay

1. Create the Excel worksheet shown in Figure U1.1. Use AutoFill to fill in the days of the week and some of the hours.
2. Insert a formula in cells H4 through H10 that calculates the total hours.
3. Insert a formula in cells J4 through J10 that calculates the gross pay (total hours multiplied by pay rate).
4. Insert a formula in cells B11 through J11 that totals the hours, total hours, pay rate, and gross pay.

5. Apply formatting to the cells as shown in the figure.
6. Change the page orientation to landscape.
7. Save the worksheet and name it **EL1-U1-A2-CPPayroll**.
8. Turn on the display of formulas, print the worksheet (prints on two pages), and then turn off the display of formulas.
9. Save and then close **EL1-U1-A2-CPPayroll.xlsx**.

Figure U1.1 Assessment 2

	A	B	C	D	E	F	G	H	I	J
1	**Capstan Products**									
2	**Payroll - Week Ended: March 14, 2015**									
3	**Employee**	**Monday**	**Tuesday**	**Wednesday**	**Thursday**	**Friday**	**Saturday**	**Total Hours**	**Pay Rate**	**Gross Pay**
4	Loftus, Maureen	8	8	8	8	8	0	40	$ 28.50	$1,140.00
5	Banyai, Robert	3	3	3	3	0	8	20	15.35	307.00
6	Martinez, Michelle	0	8	8	8	8	8	40	19.00	760.00
7	Wilhelm, Marshall	0	5	5	5	5	8	28	13.50	378.00
8	Ziegler, Cathleen	0	0	0	0	4	4	8	22.45	179.60
9	Hope, Trevor	0	0	0	0	4	4	8	13.50	108.00
10	Anthony, Charles	0	4	4	4	4	4	20	13.50	270.00
11	**Total**	11	28	28	28	33	36	164	$ 125.80	$3,142.60

Assessment 3 Sales Bonuses Workbook

1. Create the Excel worksheet shown in Figure U1.2. Format the cells as you see them in the figure.
2. Insert a formula in cells D4 through D11 that calculates the bonus amount (sales times bonus).
3. Insert a formula in cells E4 through E11 that calculates the net sales (sales minus bonus amount).
4. Insert the sum of cells B4 through B11 in cell B12, the sum of cells D4 through D11 in cell D12, and the sum of cells E4 through E11 in cell E12.
5. Apply accounting formatting with no places after the decimal point and no dollar sign to cells B5 through B11 and cells D5 through E11.
6. Apply accounting formatting with a dollar sign and no places after the decimal point to cells B4, D4, E4, B12, D12, and E12.
7. Insert a footer that contains your first and last names and the current date.
8. Print the worksheet horizontally and vertically centered on the page.
9. Save the workbook and name it **EL1-U1-A3-SBASales**.
10. Close **EL1-U1-A3-SBASales.xlsx**.

Figure U1.2 Assessment 3

	A	B	C	D	E	F
1	Stanton & Barnet Associates					
2	Sales Department					
3	Associate	Sales	Bonus	Bonus Amount	Net Sales	
4	Conway, Amanda	$ 101,450	5%			
5	Eckhart, Geneva	94,375	2%			
6	Farris, Edward	73,270	0%			
7	Greenwood, Wayne	110,459	5%			
8	Hagen, Chandra	120,485	5%			
9	Logan, Courtney	97,520	2%			
10	Pena, Geraldo	115,850	5%			
11	Rubin, Alex	76,422	0%			
12	Total					
13						

Assessment 4 Format First-Quarter Sales Workbook

1. Open **CMDeptBudgets.xlsx** and then save the workbook with Save As and name it **EL1-U1-A4-CMDeptBudgets**.
2. Insert a formula using an absolute cell reference to determine the projected budget with an increase of 10% over the current budget. (Use the number *1.1* in cell B3 when writing the formula.)
3. Insert formulas to total the budget amounts and the projected budget amounts.
4. Make cell A15 active and then use the NOW function to insert the current date and time.
5. Save and then print the worksheet.
6. Determine the projected budget with an increase of 5% over the current budget by changing the text in cell A3 to *5% Increase* and the number in cell B3 to *1.05*.
7. Save, print, and then close **EL1-U1-A4-CMDeptBudgets.xlsx**.

Assessment 5 Format Weekly Payroll Workbook

1. Open **CCPayroll.xlsx** and then save the workbook with Save As and name it **EL1-U1-A5-CCPayroll**.
2. Insert a formula in cell E3 that multiplies the hourly rate by the hours and then adds that to the multiplication of the hourly rate by the overtime pay rate (1.5) and then overtime hours. (Use parentheses in the formula and use an absolute cell reference for the overtime pay rate. Refer to Chapter 2, Project 3c.) Copy the formula down to cells E4 through E16.
3. Insert a formula in cell F3 that multiplies the gross pay by the withholding tax rate (W/H Rate). (Use an absolute cell reference for the cell containing the withholding rate. Refer to Chapter 2, Project 3c.) Copy the formula down to cells F4 through F16.

4. Insert a formula in cell G3 that multiplies the gross pay by the social security rate (SS Rate). Use an absolute cell reference for the cell containing the social security rate. (Refer to Chapter 2, Project 3c.) Copy the formula down to cells G4 through G16.
5. Insert a formula in cell H4 that adds together the social security tax and the withholding tax and subtracts that sum from the gross pay. (Refer to Chapter 2, Project 3c.) Copy the formula down to cells H4 through H16.
6. Sort the employee last names alphabetically in ascending order (A to Z).
7. Center the worksheet horizontally and vertically on the page.
8. Insert a footer that prints your name at the left side of the page and the file name at the right side of the page.
9. Save, print, and then close **EL1-U1-A5-CCPayroll.xlsx**.

Assessment 6 Format Customer Sales Analysis Workbook

1. Open **DIAnnualSales.xlsx** and then save the workbook with Save As and name it **EL1-U1-A6-DIAnnualSales**.
2. Insert formulas and drag formulas to complete the worksheet. After dragging the total formula in row 10, specify that you want to fill without formatting. (This retains the right border in cell N10.) Do this with the Auto Fill Options button.
3. Insert in cell B11 the highest total from cells B10 through M10. Insert in cell B12 the lowest total from cells B10 through M10.
4. Change the orientation to landscape.
5. Insert a header that prints the page number at the right side of the page.
6. Insert a footer that prints your name at the right side of the page.
7. Horizontally and vertically center the worksheet on the page.
8. Specify that the column headings in cells A3 through A12 print on both pages.
9. Save, print, and then close **EL1-U1-A6-DIAnnualSales.xlsx**.

Assessment 7 Format Invoices Workbook

1. Open **RPInvoices.xlsx** and then save the workbook with Save As and name it **EL1-U1-A7-RPInvoices**.
2. Insert a formula in cell G4 that multiplies the amount in cell E4 by the percentage in cell F4 and then adds that total to the amount in cell E4. (Use parentheses in this formula.)
3. Copy the formula in cell G4 down to cells G5 through G18.
4. Apply accounting formatting with two places after the decimal point and a dollar sign to cell G4, and then apply comma formatting with two places after the decimal point to cells G5 through G18.
5. Find all occurrences of cells containing *11-279* and replace them with *10-005*.
6. Find all occurrences of cells containing *8.5* and replace them with *9.0*.
7. Search for all occurrences of the Calibri font and replace them with the Candara font. (Do not specify a type size so that Excel replaces all sizes of Calibri with Candara.)
8. Print **EL1-U1-A7-RPInvoices.xlsx**.
9. Filter and then print a list of rows containing only the client number *04-325*. (After printing, return the list to *(Select All)*.)
10. Filter and then print a list of rows containing only the service *Development*. (After printing, return the list to *(Select All)*.)
11. Filter and then print a list of rows containing the three highest totals in the *Amount Due* column. (After printing, turn off the filter feature.)
12. Save and then close **EL1-U1-A7-RPInvoices.xlsx**.

Writing Activities

The following activities give you the opportunity to practice your writing skills along with demonstrating an understanding of some of the important Excel features you have mastered in this unit. Use correct grammar, appropriate word choices, and clear sentence construction.

Activity 1 Plan and Prepare Orders Summary Workbook

Plan and prepare a worksheet with the information shown in Figure U1.3. Apply formatting of your choosing to the worksheet. Save the completed worksheet and name it **EL1-U1-Act1-OrdersSumm**. Print and then close **EL1-U1-Act1-OrdersSumm.xlsx**.

Figure U1.3 Activity 1

Prepare a weekly summary of orders taken that itemizes the products coming into the company and the average order size. The products and average order size include:

Black and gold wall clock: $2,450 worth of orders, average order size of $125
Traveling alarm clock: $1,358 worth of orders, average order size of $195
Waterproof watch: $890 worth of orders, average order size of $90
Dashboard clock: $2,135 worth of orders, average order size of $230
Pyramid clock: $3,050 worth of orders, average order size of $375
Gold chain watch: $755 worth of orders, average order size of $80

In the worksheet, total the amount ordered and also calculate the average weekly order size. Sort the data in the worksheet by the order amount in descending order.

Activity 2 Prepare Depreciation Workbook

Assets within a company, such as equipment, can be depreciated over time. Several methods are available for determining the amount of depreciation, such as the straight-line depreciation method, the fixed-declining balance method, and the double-declining method. Use Excel's Help feature to learn about two depreciation methods: straight-line and double-declining depreciation. (The straight-line depreciation function, SLN, and the double-declining depreciation function, DDB, are located in the *Financial* category.) After reading about the two methods, create an Excel worksheet describing the methods with the following information:

- An appropriate title
- A heading for straight-line depreciation
- The straight-line depreciation function
- The name of and a description for each straight-line depreciation function argument category
- A heading for double-declining depreciation

- The double-declining depreciation function
- The name of and a description for each double-declining depreciation function argument category

Apply formatting of your choosing to the worksheet. Save the completed workbook and name it **EL1-U1-Act2-DepMethods**. Print the worksheet horizontally and vertically centered on the page. Close **EL1-U1-Act2-DepMethods.xlsx**.

Activity 3 Insert Straight-Line Depreciation Formula

Open **RPDepreciation.xlsx** and then save the workbook and name it **EL1-U1-Act3-RPDepreciation**. Insert the function to determine straight-line depreciation in cell E4. Copy the formula down to cells E5 through E9. Print the worksheet horizontally and vertically centered on the page. Save and then close **EL1-U1-Act3-RPDepreciation.xlsx**.

Optional: Briefly research straight-line and double-declining depreciation to find out why businesses depreciate their assets. What purpose does it serve? Locate information about the topics on the Internet or in your school library. Then use Word 2013 to write a half-page, single-spaced report explaining the financial reasons for using depreciation methods. Save the document and name it **EL1-U1-Act3-DepReport**. Print and then close the document.

Internet Research

Create a Travel Planning Worksheet

Search for information on the Internet on traveling to a specific country that interests you. Find sites that provide cost information for airlines, hotels, meals, entertainment, and car rentals. Using the first week of the next month as the travel dates, create a travel planning worksheet for the country that includes the following:

- An appropriate title
- Appropriate headings
- Airline costs
- Hotel costs (off-season and in-season rates if available)
- Estimated meal costs
- Entertainment costs
- Car rental costs

Save the completed workbook and name it **EL1-U1-Act4-TrvlWksht**. Print and then close the workbook.

MICROSOFT®

EXCEL®

Level 1

Unit 2 ■ Enhancing the Display of Workbooks

Chapter 5 ■ Moving Data within and between Workbooks

Chapter 6 ■ Maintaining Workbooks

Chapter 7 ■ Creating Charts and Inserting Formulas

Chapter 8 ■ Adding Visual Interest to Workbooks

MICROSOFT® EXCEL®

CHAPTER 5

Moving Data within and between Workbooks

PERFORMANCE OBJECTIVES

Upon successful completion of Chapter 5, you will be able to:

- **Create a workbook with multiple worksheets**
- **Move, copy, and paste cells within and between worksheets**
- **Split a worksheet into windows and freeze panes**
- **Name a range of cells and use a range in a formula**
- **Open multiple workbooks**
- **Arrange, size, and move workbooks**
- **Copy and paste data between workbooks**
- **Link data between worksheets**

SNAP

Tutorials

5.1 Moving and Copying Cells

5.2 Inserting, Moving, Renaming, and Deleting a Worksheet

5.3 Formatting Multiple Worksheets

5.4 Using Paste Options

5.5 Printing a Workbook Containing Multiple Worksheets

5.6 Freezing Panes and Changing the Zoom

5.7 Splitting a Worksheet into Windows

5.8 Naming and Using a Range

5.9 Working with Windows

5.10 Linking Data between Worksheets

5.11 Copying and Pasting Data between Programs

Up to this point, the workbooks you have been working in have consisted of only single worksheets. In this chapter, you will learn to create a workbook with several worksheets and complete tasks such as copying and pasting data within and between worksheets. Moving and pasting or copying and pasting selected cells in and between worksheets is useful for rearranging data and saving time. You will also work with multiple workbooks and complete tasks such as arranging, sizing, and moving workbooks and opening and closing multiple workbooks. Model answers for this chapter's projects appear on the following pages.

Excel
EL1C5

Note: Before beginning the projects, copy to your storage medium the EL1C5 subfolder from the EL1 folder on the CD that accompanies this textbook and then make EL1C5 the active folder.

Model Answers

Student Name | Page 1 | 9/25/2015

Real Photography			
Facilities Account			
First Quarter Summary 2015			
	January	February	March
Checks amount	$ 6,781.69	$ 6,842.57	$ 6,586.74
Deposit amount	6,600.00	6,600.00	6,600.00
End-of-month balance	714.81	472.24	485.50

Summary Tab

Student Name | Page 2 | 9/25/2015

Real Photography						
Facilities Account						
January 2015						
Date	Check No.	Payee	Description	Amount	Deposit	Balance
1-Jan			Balance from previous month			$ 896.50
1-Jan			Deposit - General Account		$ 5,500.00	6,396.50
2-Jan	501	Cascade Insurance	Facilities insurance	$ 225.00		6,171.50
2-Jan	502	Quality Insurance	Equipment insurance	150.00		6,021.50
5-Jan	503	Stationery Plus	Paper supplies	205.55		5,815.95
6-Jan	504	Firstline Mortgage	Mortgage payment	4,230.00		1,585.95
8-Jan	505	Clear Source	Developer supplies	123.74		1,462.21
9-Jan			Deposit - sublet rent		1,100.00	2,562.21
12-Jan	506	Rainier Suppliers	Camera supplies	119.62		2,442.59
13-Jan	507	A1 Wedding Supplies	Photo albums	323.58		2,119.01
12-Jan	508	General Systems	Developer payment	525.00		1,594.01
14-Jan	509	Randall Machines	Copier lease payment	250.00		1,344.01
16-Jan	510	Hometown Energy	Electric bill payment	413.74		930.27
19-Jan	511	Steward-Holmes Energy	Natural gas bill payment	86.51		843.76
23-Jan	512	Parkland City Services	Water/sewer payment	45.70		798.06
28-Jan	513	New Century Telephones	Telephone bill payment	83.25		714.81
			Total	$ 6,781.69	$ 6,600.00	

January Tab

Project 1 Manage Data in a Multiple-Worksheet Account Workbook EL1-C5-P1-RPFacAccts.xlsx

Student Name | Page 3 | 9/25/2015

Real Photography						
Facilities Account						
February 2015						
Date	Check No.	Payee	Description	Amount	Deposit	Balance
1-Feb			Balance from previous month			$ 714.81
2-Feb			Deposit - General Account		$ 5,500.00	6,214.81
3-Feb	514	Firstline Mortgage	Mortgage payment	$ 4,230.00		1,984.81
5-Feb	515	Cascade Insurance	Facilities insurance	225.00		1,759.81
10-Feb	516	Quality Insurance	Equipment insurance	150.00		1,609.81
11-Feb	517	Stationery Plus	Paper supplies	266.43		1,343.38
12-Feb	518	Clear Source	Developer supplies	123.74		1,219.64
13-Feb			Deposit - sublet rent		1,100.00	2,319.64
16-Feb	519	Rainier Suppliers	Camera supplies	119.62		2,200.02
17-Feb	520	A1 Wedding Supplies	Photo albums	323.58		1,876.44
17-Feb	521	General Systems	Developer payment	525.00		1,351.44
20-Feb	522	Randall Machines	Copier lease payment	250.00		1,101.44
20-Feb	523	Hometown Energy	Electric bill payment	413.74		687.70
23-Feb	524	Steward-Holmes Energy	Natural gas bill payment	86.51		601.19
24-Feb	525	Parkland City Services	Water/sewer payment	45.70		555.49
26-Feb	526	New Century Telephones	Telephone bill payment	83.25		472.24
			Total	$ 6,842.57	$ 6,600.00	

February Tab

Student Name | Page 4 | 9/25/2015

Real Photography						
Facilities Account						
March 2015						
Date	Check No.	Payee	Description	Amount	Deposit	Balance
1-Mar			Balance from previous month			$ 472.24
2-Mar			Deposit - General Account		$ 5,500.00	5,972.24
2-Mar	527		Deposit - sublet rent			5,972.24
4-Mar	528	Firstline Mortgage	Mortgage payment	$ 4,230.00		1,742.24
5-Mar	529	Cascade Insurance	Facilities insurance	225.00		1,517.24
6-Mar	530	Stationery Plus	Paper supplies	113.76		1,403.48
9-Mar	531	Clear Source	Developer supplies	251.90		1,151.58
9-Mar			Deposit - sublet rent		1,100.00	2,251.58
9-Mar	532	Rainier Suppliers	Camera supplies	119.62		2,131.96
9-Mar	533	A1 Wedding Supplies	Photo albums	323.58		1,808.38
12-Mar	534	General Systems	Developer payment	525.00		1,283.38
16-Mar	535	Randall Machines	Copier lease payment	250.00		1,033.38
17-Mar	536	Hometown Energy	Electric bill payment	326.42		706.96
23-Mar	537	Steward-Holmes Energy	Natural gas bill payment	92.51		614.45
24-Mar	538	Parkland City Services	Water/sewer payment	45.70		568.75
27-Mar	539	New Century Telephones	Telephone bill payment	83.25		485.50
			Total	$ 6,586.74	$ 6,600.00	

March Tab

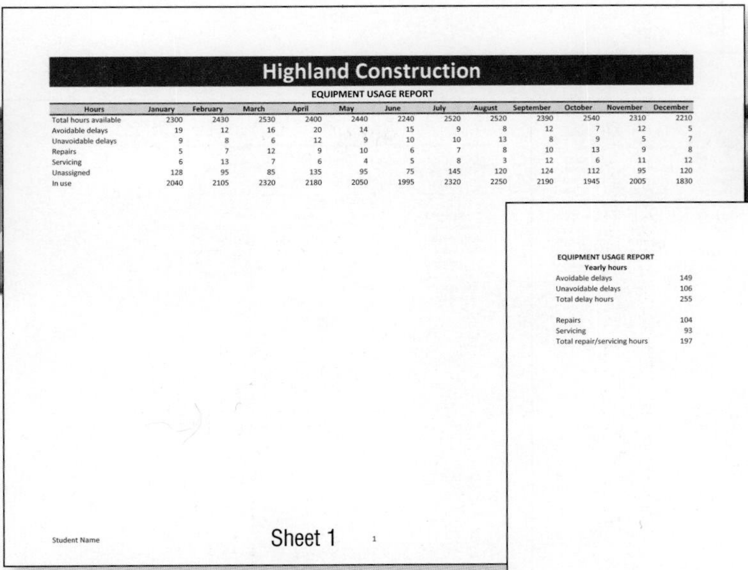

Highland Construction

EQUIPMENT USAGE REPORT

Hours	January	February	March	April	May	June	July	August	September	October	November	December
Total hours available	2300	2430	2530	2400	2440	2240	2520	2520	2390	2540	2310	2210
Avoidable delays	19	12	16	20	14	15	9	8	12	7	12	5
Unavoidable delays	9	8	6	12	9	10	10	13	8	9	5	7
Repairs	5	7	12	9	10	6	7	8	10	13	9	8
Servicing	6	13	7	6	4	5	8	3	12	6	11	12
Unassigned	128	95	85	135	95	75	145	120	124	112	95	120
In use	2040	2105	2320	2180	2050	1995	2320	2250	2190	1945	2005	1830

Student Name

1

Sheet 1

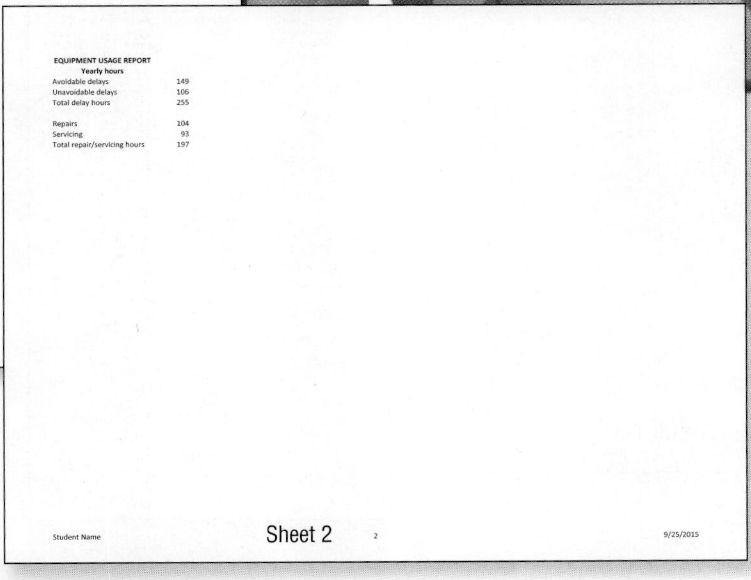

EQUIPMENT USAGE REPORT

Yearly hours

Avoidable delays	149
Unavoidable delays	106
Total delay hours	255
Repairs	104
Servicing	93
Total repair/servicing hours	197

Student Name

2

9/25/2015

Sheet 2

Project 2 Write Formulas Using Ranges in an Equipment Usage Workbook

EL1-C5-P2-HCEqpRpt.xlsx

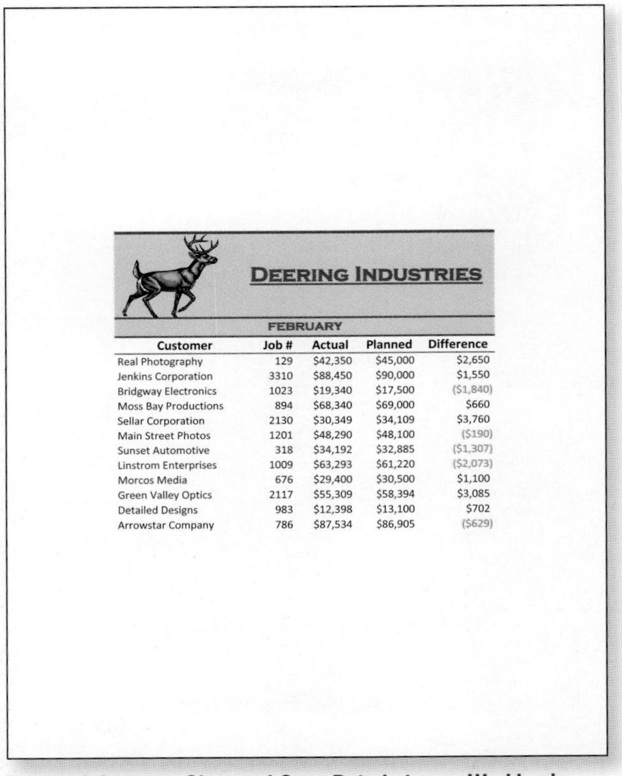

DEERING INDUSTRIES

FEBRUARY

Customer	Job #	Actual	Planned	Difference
Real Photography	129	$42,350	$45,000	$2,650
Jenkins Corporation	3310	$88,450	$90,000	$1,550
Bridgway Electronics	1023	$19,340	$17,500	($1,840)
Moss Bay Productions	894	$68,340	$69,000	$660
Sellar Corporation	2130	$30,349	$34,109	$3,760
Main Street Photos	1201	$48,290	$48,100	($190)
Sunset Automotive	318	$34,192	$32,885	($1,307)
Linstrom Enterprises	1009	$63,293	$61,220	($2,073)
Morcos Media	676	$29,400	$30,500	$1,100
Green Valley Optics	2117	$55,309	$58,394	$3,085
Detailed Designs	983	$12,398	$13,100	$702
Arrowstar Company	786	$87,534	$86,905	($629)

Project 3 Arrange, Size, and Copy Data between Workbooks

EL1-C5-P3-DIFebJobs.xlsx

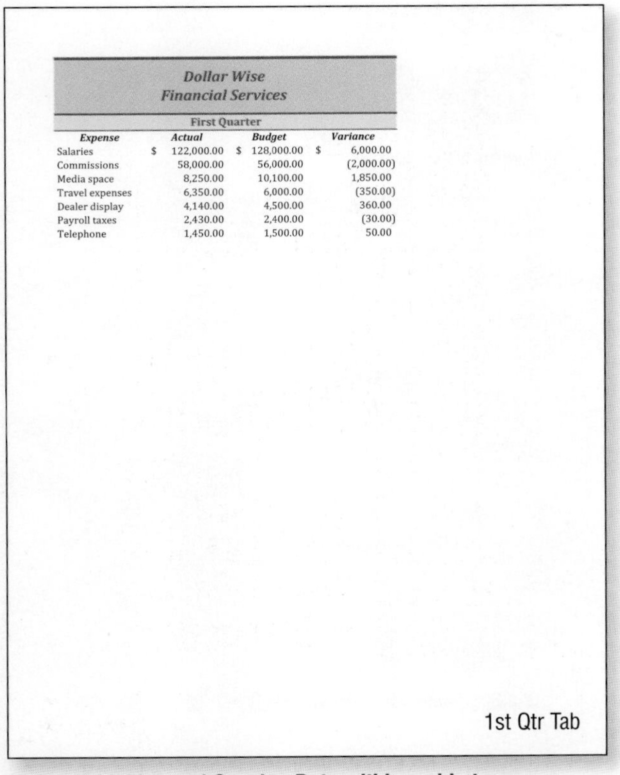

Dollar Wise
Financial Services

First Quarter

Expense	*Actual*	*Budget*	*Variance*
Salaries	$ 122,000.00	$ 128,000.00	$ 6,000.00
Commissions	58,000.00	56,000.00	(2,000.00)
Media space	8,250.00	10,100.00	1,850.00
Travel expenses	6,350.00	6,000.00	(350.00)
Dealer display	4,140.00	4,500.00	360.00
Payroll taxes	2,430.00	2,400.00	(30.00)
Telephone	1,450.00	1,500.00	50.00

1st Qtr Tab

Project 4 Linking and Copying Data within and between Worksheets and Word

EL1-C5-P4-DWQtrlyExp.xlsx

Dollar Wise
Financial Services

Second Quarter			
Expense	***Actual***	***Budget***	***Variance***
Salaries	$ 98,200.00	$ 128,000.00	$ 29,800.00
Commissions	42,300.00	56,000.00	13,700.00
Media space	9,150.00	10,100.00	950.00
Travel expenses	6,350.00	6,000.00	(350.00)
Dealer display	3,140.00	4,500.00	1,360.00
Payroll taxes	1,675.00	2,400.00	725.00
Telephone	1,255.00	1,500.00	245.00

2nd Qtr Tab

Dollar Wise
Financial Services

Third Quarter			
Expense	***Actual***	***Budget***	***Variance***
Salaries	$ 129,000.00	$ 128,000.00	$ (1,000.00)
Commissions	48,000.00	56,000.00	8,000.00
Media space	9,000.00	10,100.00	1,100.00
Travel expenses	5,250.00	6,000.00	750.00
Dealer display	5,140.00	4,500.00	(640.00)
Payroll taxes	2,150.00	2,400.00	250.00
Telephone	1,250.00	1,500.00	250.00

3rd Qtr Tab

Dollar Wise
Financial Services

Fourth Quarter			
Expense	***Actual***	***Budget***	***Variance***
Salaries	$ 125,200.00	$ 128,000.00	$ 2,800.00
Commissions	49,300.00	56,000.00	6,700.00
Media space	9,150.00	10,100.00	950.00
Travel expenses	5,850.00	6,000.00	150.00
Dealer display	3,240.00	4,500.00	1,260.00
Payroll taxes	1,975.00	2,400.00	425.00
Telephone	1,355.00	1,500.00	145.00

4th Qtr Tab

Dollar Wise
Financial Services

Quarterly Expenses

First Quarter			
Expense	***Actual***	***Budget***	***Variance***
Salaries	$ 122,000.00	$ 128,000.00	$ 6,000.00
Commissions	58,000.00	56,000.00	(2,000.00)
Media space	8,250.00	10,100.00	1,850.00
Travel expenses	6,350.00	6,000.00	(350.00)
Dealer display	4,140.00	4,500.00	360.00
Payroll taxes	2,430.00	2,400.00	(30.00)
Telephone	1,450.00	1,500.00	50.00

Second Quarter			
Expense	***Actual***	***Budget***	***Variance***
Salaries	$ 98,200.00	$ 128,000.00	$ 29,800.00
Commissions	42,300.00	56,000.00	13,700.00
Media space	9,150.00	10,100.00	950.00
Travel expenses	6,350.00	6,000.00	(350.00)
Dealer display	3,140.00	4,500.00	1,360.00
Payroll taxes	1,675.00	2,400.00	725.00
Telephone	1,255.00	1,500.00	245.00

Third Quarter			
Expense	***Actual***	***Budget***	***Variance***
Salaries	$ 129,000.00	$ 128,000.00	$ (1,000.00)
Commissions	48,000.00	56,000.00	8,000.00
Media space	9,000.00	10,100.00	1,100.00
Travel expenses	5,250.00	6,000.00	750.00
Dealer display	5,140.00	4,500.00	(640.00)
Payroll taxes	2,150.00	2,400.00	250.00
Telephone	1,250.00	1,500.00	250.00

5005 Tenth Avenue ◆ Omaha, NE 68121 ◆ 1-800-555-5005

Dollar Wise
Financial Services

Fourth Quarter			
Expense	***Actual***	***Budget***	***Variance***
Salaries	$ 125,200.00	$ 128,000.00	$ 2,800.00
Commissions	49,300.00	56,000.00	6,700.00
Media space	9,150.00	10,100.00	950.00
Travel expenses	5,850.00	6,000.00	150.00
Dealer display	3,240.00	4,500.00	1,260.00
Payroll taxes	1,975.00	2,400.00	425.00
Telephone	1,355.00	1,500.00	145.00

5005 Tenth Avenue ◆ Omaha, NE 68121 ◆ 1-800-555-5005

EL1-C5-P4-DWQtrlyRpt.docx

Project 1 Manage Data in a Multiple-Worksheet Account Workbook

7 Parts

You will open an account workbook containing four worksheets and then insert and delete worksheets and move, copy, and paste data between the worksheets. You will also hide and unhide worksheets and format and print multiple worksheets in the workbook.

Creating a Workbook with Multiple Worksheets

An Excel workbook, by default, contains one worksheet, but you can add additional worksheets to it. Add additional worksheets to a workbook to store related data. For example, you might want to create a workbook with a worksheet for the expenses for each salesperson in the company and another worksheet for the monthly payroll for each department within the company. Another example is recording sales statistics for each quarter in individual worksheets within a workbook.

HINT

Creating multiple worksheets within a workbook is helpful for saving related data.

Inserting a New Worksheet

Insert a new worksheet in a workbook by clicking the New sheet button that displays to the right of the Sheet1 tab at the bottom of the worksheet area. You can also insert a new worksheet with the keyboard shortcut Shift + F11. A new worksheet tab is inserted to the right of the active tab. To move between worksheets, click the desired tab. The active worksheet tab displays with a white background and the worksheet name displays in green. Any inactive tabs display with a light gray background and gray text.

Quick Steps

Insert a Worksheet
Click New sheet button.
OR
Press Shift + F11.

New sheet

Deleting a Worksheet

If you no longer need a worksheet in a workbook, delete the worksheet by clicking the desired worksheet tab, clicking the Delete button arrow in the Cells group on the HOME tab, and then clicking *Delete Sheet* at the drop-down list. You can also delete a worksheet by right-clicking the worksheet tab and then clicking *Delete* at the shortcut menu. When you click the Delete button or option, Excel displays a message telling you that you cannot undo deleting sheets. At this message, click the Delete button.

Quick Steps

Delete a Worksheet
1. Click worksheet tab.
2. Click Delete button arrow.
3. Click *Delete Sheet*.
4. Click Delete button.

Selecting Multiple Worksheets

To work with more than one worksheet at a time, select the desired worksheets. You might want to select multiple worksheets to apply the same formatting to cells or to delete multiple worksheets. To select adjacent worksheet tabs, click the first tab, hold down the Shift key, and then click the last tab. To select nonadjacent worksheet tabs, click the first tab, hold down the Ctrl key, and then click any other tabs you want selected.

Copy

Cut

Paste

Copying, Cutting, and Pasting Cells

At times, you may need to copy cells or move cells to a different location within a worksheet or to another worksheet or workbook. You can move or copy cells in a worksheet or between worksheets or workbooks. Perform these actions by selecting cells and then using the Cut, Copy, and/or Paste buttons in the Clipboard group on the HOME tab.

Copying and Pasting Selected Cells

Quick Steps

Copy and Paste Cells
1. Select cells.
2. Click Copy button.
3. Click desired cell.
4. Click Paste button.

HINT

Ctrl + C is the keyboard shortcut to copy selected data.

Copying selected cells can be useful in worksheets that contain repetitive data. To copy cells, select the cells and then click the Copy button in the Clipboard group on the HOME tab. This causes a moving dashed line border (called a ***marquee***) to display around the selected cells. If you are copying cells to another worksheet, click the worksheet tab. Click the cell where you want the first selected cell copied and then click the Paste button in the Clipboard group. Remove the moving marquee from selected cells by pressing the Esc key or double-clicking in any cell.

You can also copy selected cells in the same worksheet using the mouse and the Ctrl key. To do this, select the cells you want to copy and then position the mouse pointer on any border around the selected cells until the pointer turns into an arrow pointer. Hold down the Ctrl key and the left mouse button, drag the outline of the selected cells to the desired location, release the left mouse button, and then release the Ctrl key.

Project 1a **Inserting, Deleting, Selecting, Copying, Pasting, and Formatting Worksheets** **Part 1 of 7**

1. Open **RPFacAccts.xlsx** and then save the workbook with Save As and name it **EL1-C5-P1-RPFacAccts**.
2. Insert a new worksheet in the workbook by completing the following steps:
   a. Click the 2ndHalfSales worksheet tab to make it active.
   b. Click the New sheet button that displays to the right of the 2ndHalfSales worksheet tab. (This inserts a new worksheet to the right of the 2ndHalfSales worksheet with the name Sheet4.)

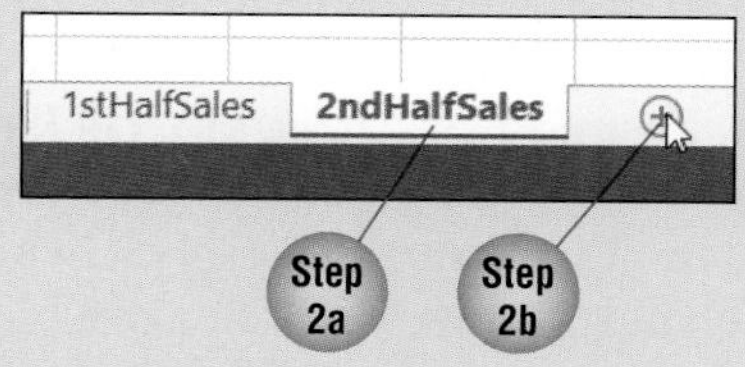

3. Delete two worksheet tabs by completing the following steps:
   a. Click the 1stHalfSales worksheet tab.
   b. Hold down the Shift key and then click the 2ndHalfSales worksheet tab. (These tabs must be adjacent. If they are not, hold down the Ctrl key when clicking the 2ndHalfSales worksheet tab.)
   c. With the two worksheet tabs selected, click the Delete button arrow in the Cells group on the HOME tab and then click *Delete Sheet* at the drop-down list.
   d. At the message that displays telling you that you cannot undo deleting sheets, click the Delete button.

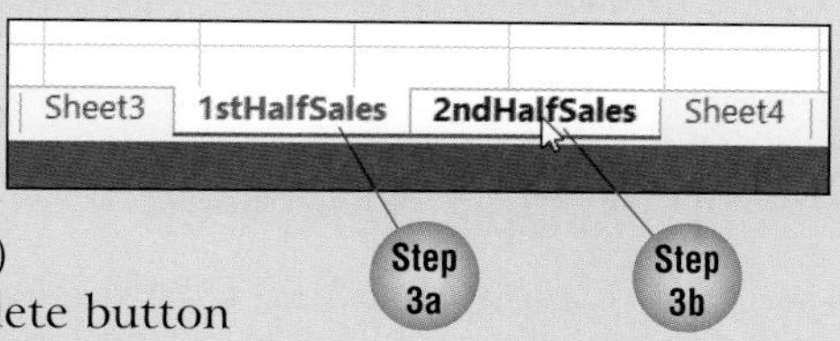

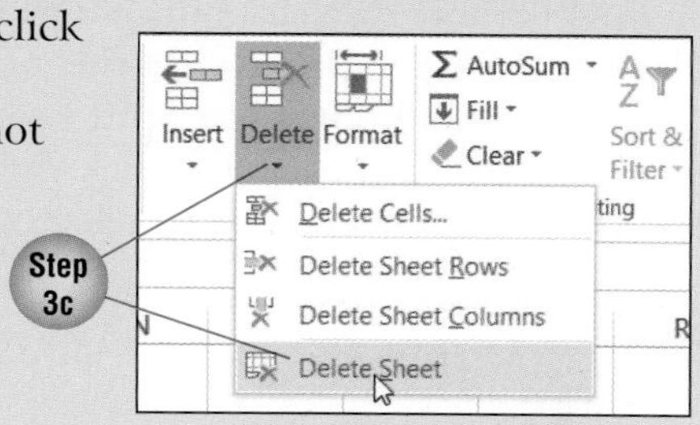

4. Copy cells from Sheet1 to Sheet4 by completing the following steps:
   a. Click the Sheet1 tab to make it the active worksheet.
   b. Select cells A1 through A3 (the first three rows of data).
   c. Click the Copy button in the Clipboard group on the HOME tab.
   d. Click the Sheet4 tab to make it the active tab.
   e. With A1 the active cell, click the Paste button in the Clipboard group on the HOME tab.

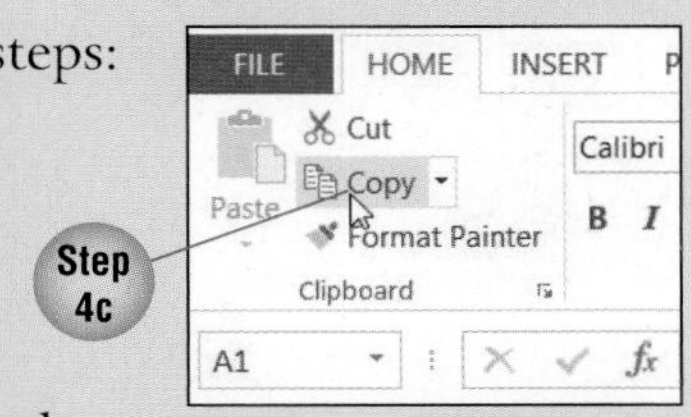

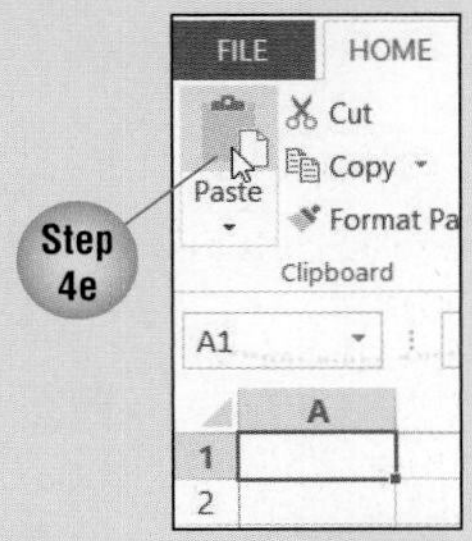

5. Make the following changes to the new worksheet:
   a. Make cell A3 active and then type **First Quarter Summary 2015**.
   b. Change the width of column A to 20.00 characters.
   c. Change the widths of columns B, C, and D to 12.00 characters.
   d. Type the following text in the specified cells:
      B4: **January**
      C4: **February**
      D4: **March**
      A5: **Checks amount**
      A6: **Deposit amount**
      A7: **End-of-month balance**
   e. Select cells B4 through D4, click the Bold button in the Font group on the HOME tab, and then click the Center button in the Alignment group.
   f. Select cells B5 through D7 and then apply accounting formatting without dollar signs and with two places after the decimal point.
6. Apply formatting to cells in all four worksheets by completing the following steps:
   a. Click Sheet1 to make it active and then click in cell A1 to make it the active cell.
   b. Hold down the Shift key and then click Sheet4. (This selects all four worksheets.)
   c. With cell A1 active, change the row height to 51.00 points.
   d. Make cell A3 active.
   e. Change the font size to 14 points.
   f. Click each remaining worksheet tab (Sheet2, Sheet3, and Sheet4) and notice the formatting changes applied to all of the cells.

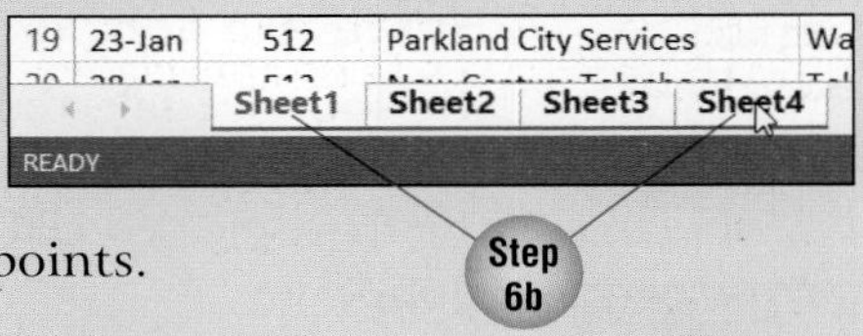

7. Change column widths for the three worksheets by completing the following steps:
   a. Click Sheet1 to make it active.
   b. Hold down the Shift key and then click Sheet3.
   c. Select columns E, F, and G and then change the column width to 10.00 characters.
   d. Click Sheet2 and then click Sheet 3. Notice that the widths of columns E, F, and G have changed to 10.00 characters. Click Sheet4 and notice that the column widths did not change.
8. Save **EL1-C5-P1-RPFacAccts.xlsx**.

Using Paste Options

When you paste cells in a worksheet, you can specify how you want the cells pasted by clicking the Paste button arrow and then clicking the desired paste option button at the drop-down list. You can also click the Paste button (not the button arrow) and a Paste Options button displays in the lower right corner of the pasted cell(s). Display a list of paste options by clicking the button or pressing

Paste Options

Figure 5.1 Paste Option Buttons

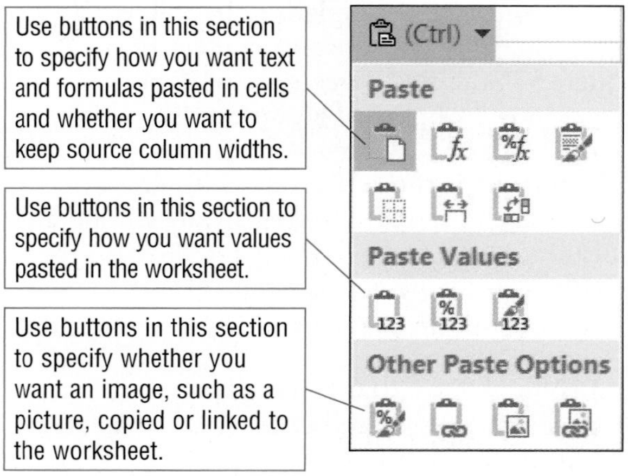

the Ctrl key. This causes a drop-down list to display, as shown in Figure 5.1. The same option buttons display when you click the Paste button arrow. Hover your mouse over a button in the drop-down list and the descriptive name of the button displays along with the keyboard shortcut. Use buttons in this drop-down list to specify what you want pasted.

Moving Selected Cells

Quick Steps

Move and Paste Cells
1. Select cells.
2. Click Cut button.
3. Click desired cell.
4. Click Paste button.

HINT

Ctrl + X is the keyboard shortcut to cut selected data. Ctrl + V is the keyboard shortcut to paste data.

You can move selected cells and cell contents within and between worksheets. Move selected cells with the Cut and Paste buttons in the Clipboard group on the HOME tab or by dragging with the mouse.

To move selected cells with buttons on the HOME tab, select the cells and then click the Cut button in the Clipboard group. Click the cell where you want the first selected cell inserted and then click the Paste button in the Clipboard group.

To move selected cells with the mouse, select the cells and then position the mouse pointer on any border of the selected cells until the pointer turns into an arrow pointer with a four-headed arrow attached. Hold down the left mouse button, drag the outline of the selected cells to the desired location, and then release the mouse button.

Project 1b **Copying and Moving Cells and Pasting Cells Using Paste Options** **Part 2 of 7**

1. With **EL1-C5-P1-RPFacAccts.xlsx** open, copy cells from Sheet2 to Sheet3 using the Paste Options button by completing the following steps:
   a. Click the Sheet2 tab to make it active.
   b. Select cells C7 through E9.
   c. Click the Copy button in the Clipboard group.
   d. Click the Sheet3 tab.
   e. Make cell C7 active.
   f. Click the Paste button in the Clipboard group.

g. Click the Paste Options button that displays in the lower right corner of the pasted cells and then click the Keep Source Column Widths button at the drop-down list.
h. Make Sheet2 active and then press the Esc key to remove the moving marquee.

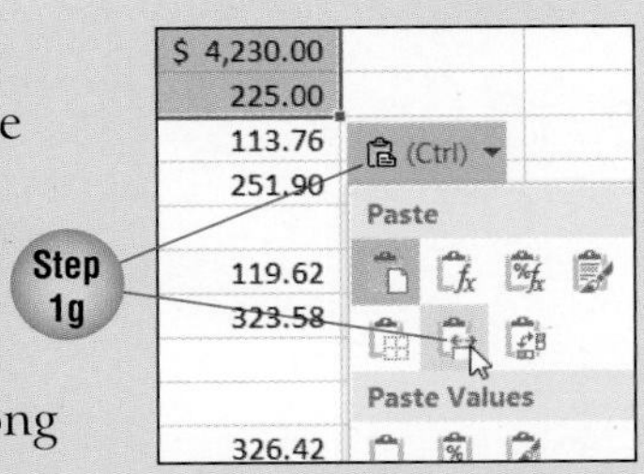

2. Make Sheet1 active.
3. You realize that the sublet rent deposit was recorded on the wrong day. The correct day is January 9. To move the cells containing information on the deposit, complete the following steps:
   a. Make cell A13 active and then insert a row. (The new row should display above the row containing information on *Rainier Suppliers*.)
   b. Select cells A7 through F7.
   c. Click the Cut button in the Clipboard group on the HOME tab.
   d. Click in cell A13 to make it active.
   e. Click the Paste button in the Clipboard group.
   f. Change the date of the deposit from January 1 to January 9.
   g. Select row 7 and then delete it.

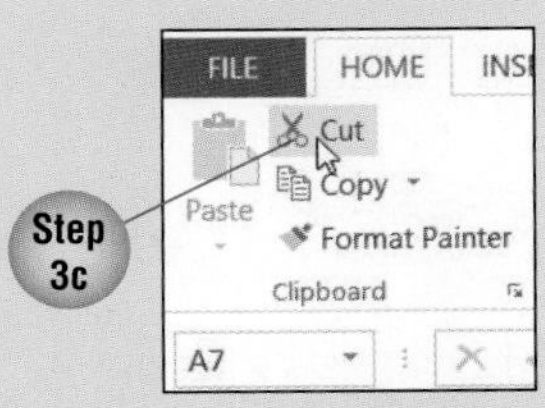

4. Move cells using the mouse by completing the following steps:
   a. Click the Sheet2 tab.
   b. Make cell A13 active and then insert a new row.
   c. Using the mouse, select cells A7 through F7.
   d. Position the mouse pointer on any boundary of the selected cells until it turns into an arrow pointer with a four-headed arrow attached. Hold down the left mouse button, drag the outline of the selected cells to row 13, and then release the mouse button.

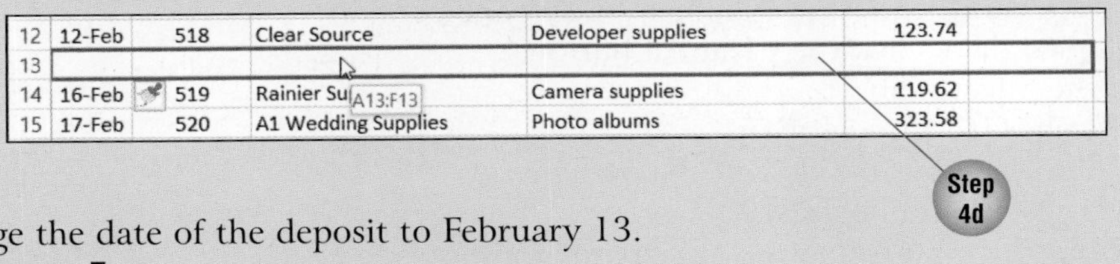

   e. Change the date of the deposit to February 13.
   f. Delete row 7.
5. Save **EL1-C5-P1-RPFacAccts.xlsx**.

Copying and Pasting with the Clipboard Task Pane

Use the Clipboard task pane to copy and paste multiple items. To use the task pane, click the Clipboard task pane launcher. This button is located in the lower right corner of the Clipboard group on the HOME tab. The Clipboard task pane displays at the left side of the screen in a manner similar to what you see in Figure 5.2.

Select data or an object you want to copy and then click the Copy button in the Clipboard group. Continue selecting cells, text, or other items and clicking the Copy button. To paste an item into a worksheet, make the desired cell active and then click the item in the Clipboard task pane. If the copied item is text, the first 50 characters display in the task pane. If you want to paste all of the selected items into a single location, make the desired cell active and then click the Paste All button in the task pane. When all desired items have been pasted into the worksheet, click the Clear All button to remove any remaining items from the task pane.

Quick Steps

Copy and Paste Multiple Items

1. Click Clipboard task pane launcher.
2. Select desired cells.
3. Click Copy button.
4. Repeat Steps 2 and 3 as desired.
5. Make desired cell active.
6. Click item in Clipboard task pane to be inserted in worksheet.
7. Repeat Step 6 as desired.

Figure 5.2 Clipboard Task Pane

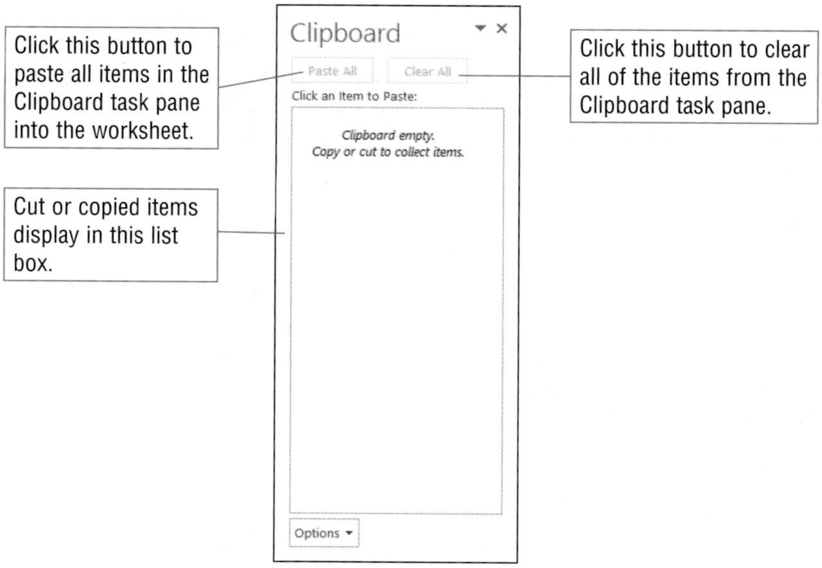

Project 1c Copying and Pasting Cells Using the Clipboard Task Pane

Part 3 of 7

1. With **EL1-C5-P1-RPFacAccts.xlsx** open, select cells for copying by completing the following steps:
   a. Display the Clipboard task pane by clicking the Clipboard task pane launcher. (If the Clipboard task pane contains any copied data, click the Clear All button.)
   b. Click the Sheet1 tab.
   c. Select cells C15 through E16.
   d. Click the Copy button in the Clipboard group.
   e. Select cells C19 through E19.
   f. Click the Copy button in the Clipboard group.

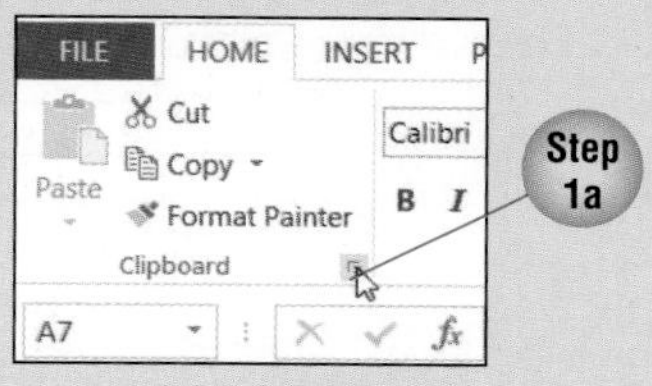

2. Paste the copied cells by completing the following steps:
   a. Click the Sheet2 tab.
   b. Make cell C15 active.
   c. Click the item in the Clipboard task pane representing *General Systems Developer*.
   d. Click the Sheet3 tab.
   e. Make cell C15 active.
   f. Click the item in the Clipboard task pane representing *General Systems Developer*.
   g. Make cell C19 active.
   h. Click the item in the Clipboard task pane representing *Parkland City Services*.

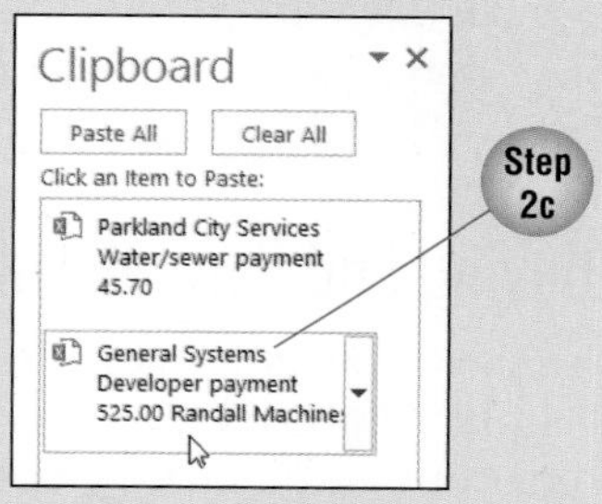

3. Click the Clear All button located toward the top of the Clipboard task pane.
4. Close the Clipboard task pane by clicking the Close button (contains an X) located in the upper right corner of the task pane.
5. Save **EL1-C5-P1-RPFacAccts.xlsx**.

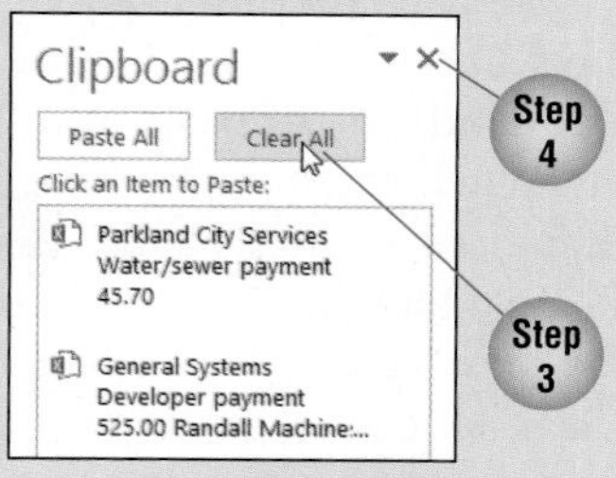

Pasting Values Only

When you paste cells containing a value as well as a formula, use button options from the Paste button or Paste Options button drop-down list to specify what you want pasted. With the buttons in the *Paste Values* section of the drop-down list, you can choose to insert the value only, the value with numbering formatting, or the value with the source formatting.

Project 1d **Copying and Pasting Values** **Part 4 of 7**

1. With **EL1-C5-P1-RPFacAccts.xlsx** open, make Sheet1 the active tab.
2. Make cell G6 active, type the formula **=(F6-E6)+G5**, and then press Enter.
3. Copy the formula in cell G6 down to cells G7 through G20.
4. Copy as a value (and not a formula) the final balance amount from Sheet1 to Sheet2 by completing the following steps:
   a. Make cell G20 active.
   b. Click the Copy button in the Clipboard group.
   c. Click the Sheet2 tab.
   d. Make cell G5 active and then click the Paste button arrow.
   e. At the drop-down list that displays, click the Values button in the *Paste Values* section of the drop-down list. (This inserts the value and not the formula.)
5. Make cell G6 active, insert a formula that determines the balance (see Step 2), and then copy the formula down to cells G7 through G20.

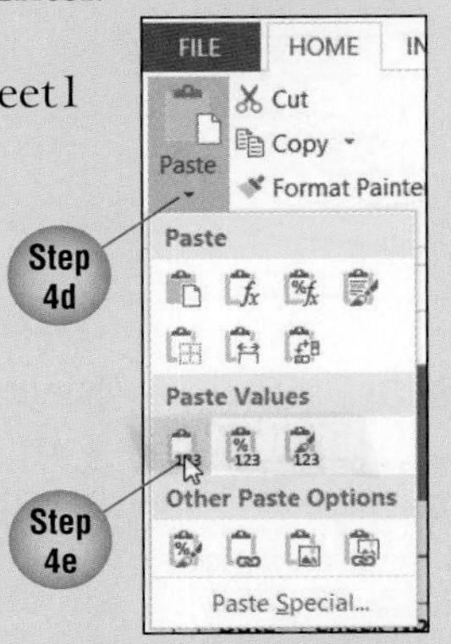

6. Copy the amount in cell G20 and then paste the value only in cell G5 in Sheet3. Apply accounting formatting with a dollar sign and two decimal places to the cell.
7. With Sheet3 active, make cell G6 active, insert a formula that determines the balance (see Step 2), and then copy the formula down to cells G7 through G20.
8. Insert formulas and apply formatting to cells in three worksheets by completing the following steps:
   a. Click Sheet1 to make it active.
   b. Hold down the Shift key and then click Sheet3.
   c. Make cell D21 active, click the Bold button in the Font group on the HOME tab, and then type **Total**.
   d. Make cell E21 active and then click once on the AutoSum button in the Editing group on the HOME tab. (This inserts the formula *=SUM(E13:E20)*.)
   e. Change the formula to *=SUM(E7:E20)* and then press Enter.
   f. Make cell F21 active and then click once on the AutoSum button. (This inserts the formula *=SUM(F12:F20)*.)
   g. Change the formula to *=SUM(F6:F20)* and then press Enter.
   h. Select cells E21 and F21 and then click the Accounting Number Format button. Make cell G5 active and then click the Accounting Number Format button. (Cell G5 in Sheet1 already contains accounting formatting but cells G5 in Sheet2 and Sheet3 do not.)

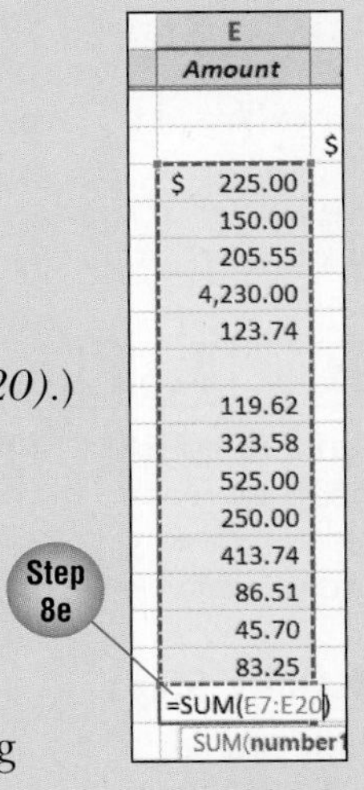

   i. Click the Sheet2 tab and notice the text and formulas inserted in the worksheet, click Sheet3 and notice the text and formulas, and then click Sheet4 (to deselect the tabs).
9. Copy values from Sheet1 to Sheet4 by completing the following steps:
   a. Make Sheet1 active.
   b. Make cell E21 active and then click the Copy button in the Clipboard group.
   c. Make Sheet4 active.
   d. Make cell B5 active and then click the Paste button in the Clipboard group.

e. Click the Paste Options button and then click the Values button in the *Paste Values* section of the drop-down list.
f. Make Sheet1 active.
g. Make cell F21 active and then click the Copy button.
h. Make Sheet4 active.
i. Make cell B6 active, click the Paste button arrow, and then click the Values button at the drop-down list.
j. Make Sheet1 active.
k. Make cell G20 active and then click the Copy button.
l. Make Sheet4 active.
m. Make cell B7 active, click the Paste button arrow, and then click the Values button at the drop-down list.

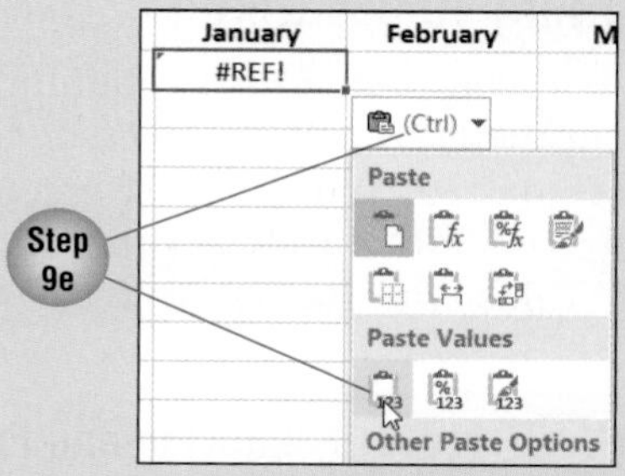

10. Complete steps similar to those in Step 9 to insert amounts and balances for February and March.
11. Select cells B5 through D5 and then click the Accounting Number Format button.
12. Save **EL1-C5-P1-RPFacAccts.xlsx**.

Managing Worksheets

Quick Steps

Move or Copy a Worksheet
1. Right-click sheet tab.
2. Click *Move or Copy*.
3. At Move or Copy dialog box, click desired worksheet name in *Before sheet* list box.
4. Click OK.

OR

Drag worksheet tab to desired position. (To copy, hold down Ctrl key while dragging.)

HINT

Use the tab scroll button to bring into view any worksheet tabs not currently visible.

Quick Steps

Apply Color to a Sheet Tab
1. Right-click sheet tab.
2. Point to *Tab Color*.
3. Click desired color at color palette.

Right-click a sheet tab and a shortcut menu displays, as shown in Figure 5.3, with the options for managing worksheets. For example, remove a worksheet by clicking the *Delete* option. Move or copy a worksheet by clicking the *Move or Copy* option. Clicking this option causes a Move or Copy dialog box to display, in which you specify where you want to move or copy the selected sheet. By default, Excel names worksheets in a workbook *Sheet1, Sheet2, Sheet3,* and so on. To rename a worksheet, click the *Rename* option (which selects the default sheet name) and then type the desired name.

In addition to the shortcut menu options, you can use the mouse to move or copy worksheets. To move a worksheet, position the mouse pointer on the worksheet tab, hold down the left mouse button (a page icon displays next to the mouse pointer), drag the page icon to the desired position, and then release the mouse button. For example, to move the Sheet2 tab after the Sheet3 tab, position the mouse pointer on the Sheet2 tab, hold down the left mouse button, drag the page icon so it is positioned after the Sheet3 tab, and then release the mouse button. To copy a worksheet, hold down the Ctrl key while dragging the sheet tab.

Use the *Tab Color* option at the shortcut menu to apply a color to a worksheet tab. Right-click a worksheet tab, point to *Tab Color* at the shortcut menu, and then click the desired color at the color palette.

Figure 5.3 Sheet Tab Shortcut Menu

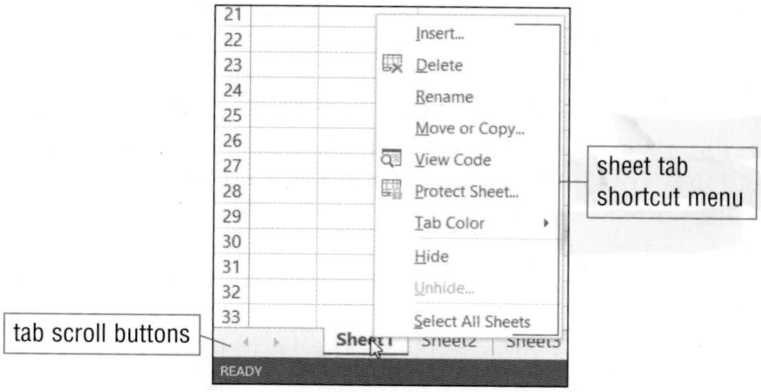

Project 1e Selecting, Moving, Renaming, and Changing the Color of Worksheet Tabs Part 5 of 7

1. With **EL1-C5-P1-RPFacAccts.xlsx** open, move Sheet4 by completing the following steps:
   a. Right-click Sheet4 and then click *Move or Copy* at the shortcut menu.
   b. At the Move or Copy dialog box, make sure *Sheet1* is selected in the *Before sheet* list box, and then click OK.

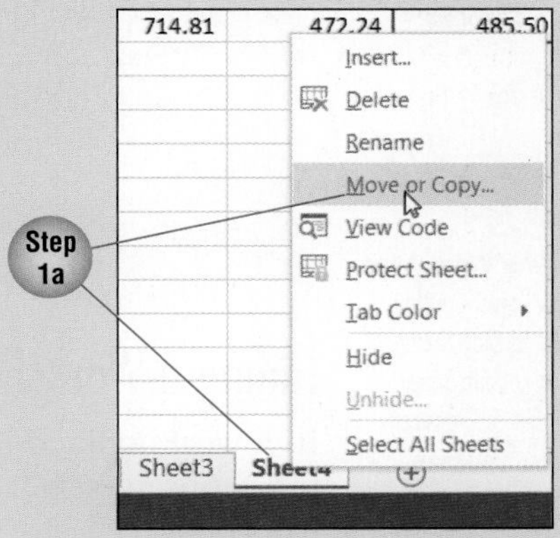

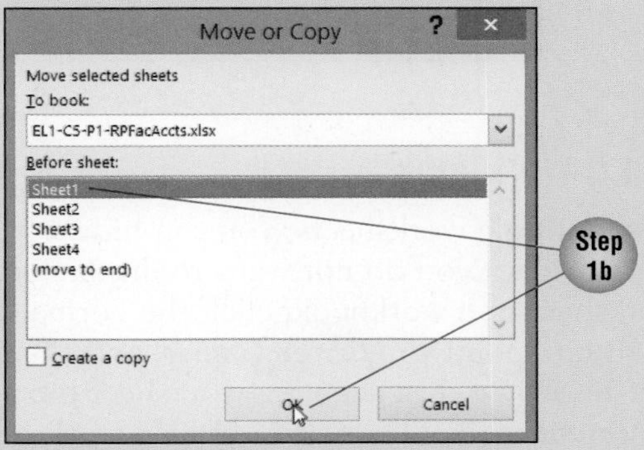

2. Rename Sheet4 by completing the following steps:
   a. Right-click the Sheet4 tab and then click *Rename*.
   b. Type **Summary** and then press Enter.
3. Complete steps similar to those in Step 2 to rename Sheet1 to *January*, Sheet2 to *February*, and Sheet3 to *March*.

4. Change the color of the Summary sheet tab by completing the following steps:
   a. Right-click the Summary sheet tab.
   b. Point to *Tab Color* at the shortcut menu.
   c. Click the *Red* color option in the *Standard Colors* section (second color option).

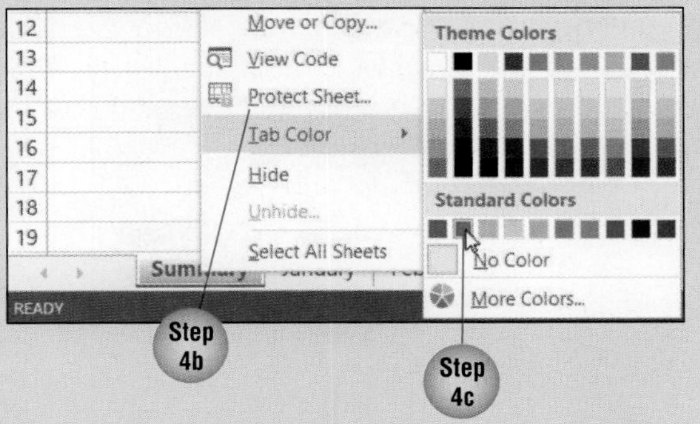

5. Follow steps similar to those in Step 4 to change the January sheet tab to Blue (eighth color option in the *Standard Colors* section), the February sheet tab to Purple (last color option in the *Standard Colors* section), and the March sheet tab to Green (sixth color option in the *Standard Colors* section).
6. Save **EL1-C5-P1-RPFacAccts.xlsx**.

Quick Steps

Hide a Worksheet
1. Click Format button.
2. Point to *Hide & Unhide.*
3. Click *Hide Sheet.*

OR
1. Right-click worksheet tab.
2. Click *Hide* at shortcut menu.

Unhide a Worksheet
1. Click Format button.
2. Point to *Hide & Unhide.*
3. Click *Unhide Sheet.*
4. Double-click desired hidden worksheet in Unhide dialog box.

OR
1. Right-click worksheet tab.
2. Click *Unhide* at shortcut menu.
3. Double-click desired hidden worksheet in Unhide dialog box.

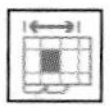

Format

Figure 5.4 Unhide Dialog Box

The names of hidden worksheets display in this list box.

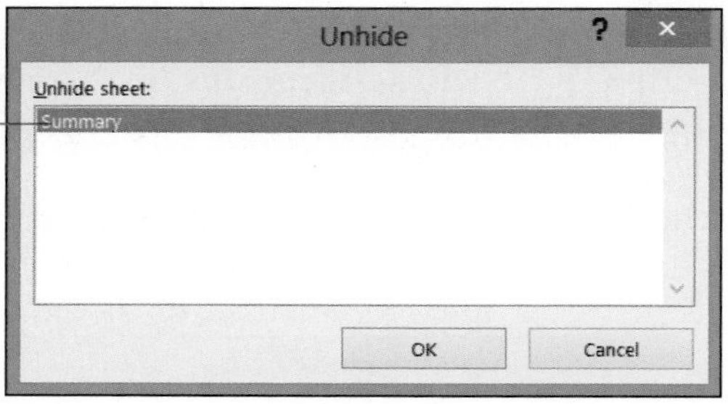

Hiding a Worksheet in a Workbook

In a workbook containing multiple worksheets, you can hide a worksheet that may contain sensitive data or data you do not want to display or print with the workbook. To hide a worksheet in a workbook, click the Format button in the Cells group on the HOME tab, point to *Hide & Unhide,* and then click *Hide Sheet.* You can also hide a worksheet by right-clicking a worksheet tab and then clicking the *Hide* option at the shortcut menu. To make a hidden worksheet visible, click the Format button in the Cells group, point to *Hide & Unhide,* and then click *Unhide Sheet,* or right-click a worksheet tab and then click *Unhide* at the shortcut menu. At the Unhide dialog box, as shown in Figure 5.4, double-click the name of the hidden worksheet you want to display.

Project 1f **Hiding a Worksheet and Formatting Multiple Worksheets** **Part 6 of 7**

1. With **EL1-C5-P1-RPFacAccts.xlsx** open, hide the Summary worksheet by completing the following steps:
   a. Click the Summary tab.
   b. Click the Format button in the Cells group on the HOME tab, point to *Hide & Unhide,* and then click *Hide Sheet.*

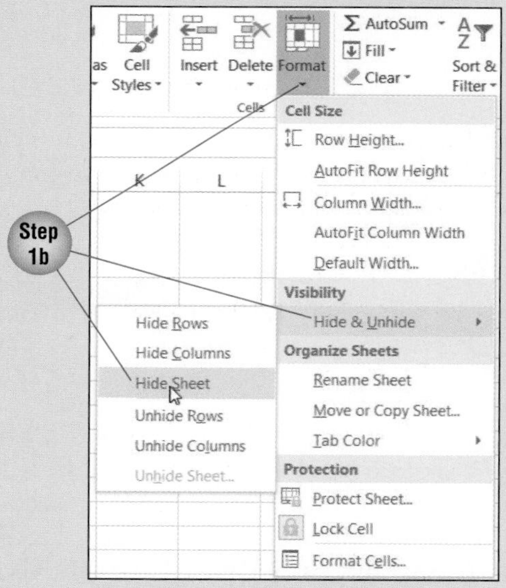

2. Unhide the worksheet by completing the following steps:
   a. Click the Format button in the Cells group, point to *Hide & Unhide*, and then click *Unhide Sheet*.
   b. At the Unhide dialog box, make sure *Summary* is selected and then click OK.

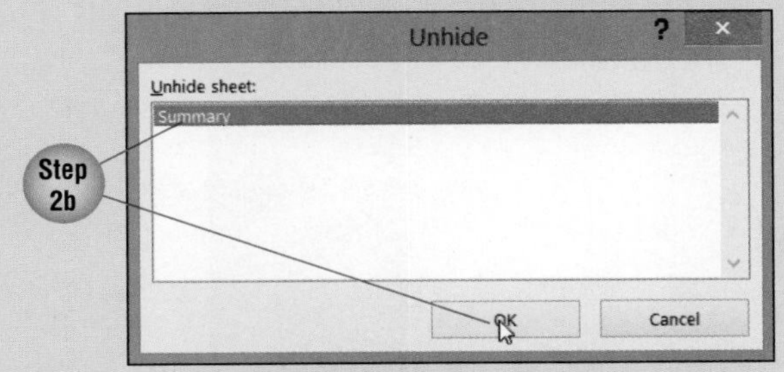

3. Insert a header for each worksheet by completing the following steps:
   a. With the Summary tab active, hold down the Shift key and then click the March tab. (This selects all four tabs.)
   b. Click the INSERT tab.
   c. Click the Header & Footer button in the Text group.
   d. Click the Header button in the Header & Footer group on the HEADER & FOOTER TOOLS DESIGN tab and then click the option at the drop-down list that prints your name at the left side of the page (if a name displays at the left side of the page, select the name and then type your first and last names), the page number in the middle, and the date at the right side.
4. With all the sheet tabs selected, horizontally and vertically center each worksheet on the page. ***Hint: Do this at the Page Setup dialog box with the Margins tab selected.***
5. With all of the sheet tabs still selected, change the page orientation to landscape. ***Hint: Do this with the Orientation button on the PAGE LAYOUT tab.***
6. Save **EL1-C5-P1-RPFacAccts.xlsx**.

Printing a Workbook Containing Multiple Worksheets

By default, Excel prints the currently displayed worksheet. If you want to print all of the worksheets in a workbook, display the Print backstage area, click the first gallery in the *Settings* category, click *Print Entire Workbook* at the drop-down list, and then click the Print button. You can also print specific worksheets in a workbook by selecting the tabs of the worksheets you want printed. With the desired worksheet tabs selected, display the Print backstage area and then click the Print button.

Quick Steps

Print All Worksheets in a Workbook
1. Click FILE tab.
2. Click *Print* option.
3. Click first gallery in *Settings* category.
4. Click *Print Entire Workbook*.
5. Click Print button.

Project 1g Printing All Worksheets in a Workbook — Part 7 of 7

1. With **EL1-C5-P1-RPFacAccts.xlsx** open, click the FILE tab and then click the *Print* option.
2. At the Print backstage area, click the first gallery in the *Settings* category and then click *Print Entire Workbook* at the drop-down list.
3. Click the Print button.
4. Save and then close **EL1-C5-P1-RPFacAccts.xlsx**.

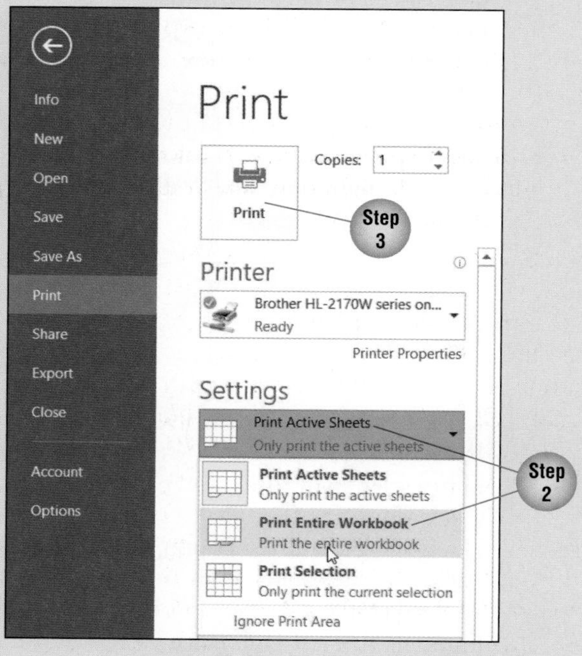

Project 2 Write Formulas Using Ranges in an Equipment Usage Workbook — 2 Parts

You will open an equipment usage workbook, view the document at different zoom percentages, and then split the window and edit cells. You will also name ranges and then use the range names to write formulas in the workbook.

Using Zoom

Zoom

100%

Zoom to Selection

The VIEW tab contains a Zoom group with three buttons to change zoom settings. Click the Zoom button in the Zoom group to open the Zoom dialog box, which contains options for changing the zoom percentage. Click the 100% button in the Zoom group to return the view to 100%, which is the default. Select a range of cells and then click the Zoom to Selection button to cause Excel to scale the zoom setting so that the selected range fills the worksheet area.

Use the zoom slider bar that displays at the right side of the Status bar to change the zoom percentage. Click the Zoom Out button (displays with a minus symbol) to decrease the zoom percentage or click the Zoom In button (displays with a plus symbol) to increase the zoom percentage. Another method for increasing or decreasing zoom percentage is to click and drag the zoom slider bar button on the slider bar.

Splitting a Worksheet into Windows and Freezing and Unfreezing Panes

In some worksheets, not all cells display at one time in the worksheet area (for example, in **EL1-C5-P2-HCEqpRpt.xlsx**). When working in a worksheet with more cells than can display at one time, you may find splitting the worksheet window into panes helpful. Split the worksheet window into panes with the Split button in the Window group on the VIEW tab. When you click the Split button, the worksheet splits into four window panes, as shown in Figure 5.5. The windows are split by thick, light gray lines called ***split lines***. To remove split lines from a worksheet, click the Split button to deactivate it.

Quick Steps

Split a Worksheet
1. Click VIEW tab.
2. Click Split button.

Split

HINT

Remove a split line by double-clicking anywhere on the split line that divides the panes.

A window pane will display the active cell. As the insertion point is moved through the pane, another active cell may display. This additional active cell displays when the insertion point passes over one of the split lines that creates the pane. As you move through a worksheet, you may see both active cells. If you make a change to one active cell, the change is made in the other as well. If you want only one active cell to display, freeze the window panes by clicking the Freeze Panes button in the Window group on the VIEW tab and then clicking *Freeze Panes* at the drop-down list. You can maintain the display of column headings while editing or typing text in cells by clicking the Freeze Panes button and then clicking *Freeze Top Row*. Maintain the display of row headings by clicking the Freeze Panes button and then clicking *Freeze First Column*. Unfreeze window panes by clicking the Freeze Panes button and then clicking *Unfreeze Panes* at the drop-down list.

Freeze Panes

Using the mouse, you can move the split lines that divide the window. To do this, position the mouse pointer on a split line until the pointer turns into a left-and-right-pointing arrow with a double line in the middle. Hold down the left mouse button, drag the outline of the split line to the desired location, and then release the mouse button. If you want to move both the horizontal and vertical split lines at the same time, position the mouse pointer on the intersection of the split lines until the pointer turns into a four-headed arrow. Hold down the left mouse button, drag the split lines to the desired direction, and then release the mouse button.

Figure 5.5 Split Window

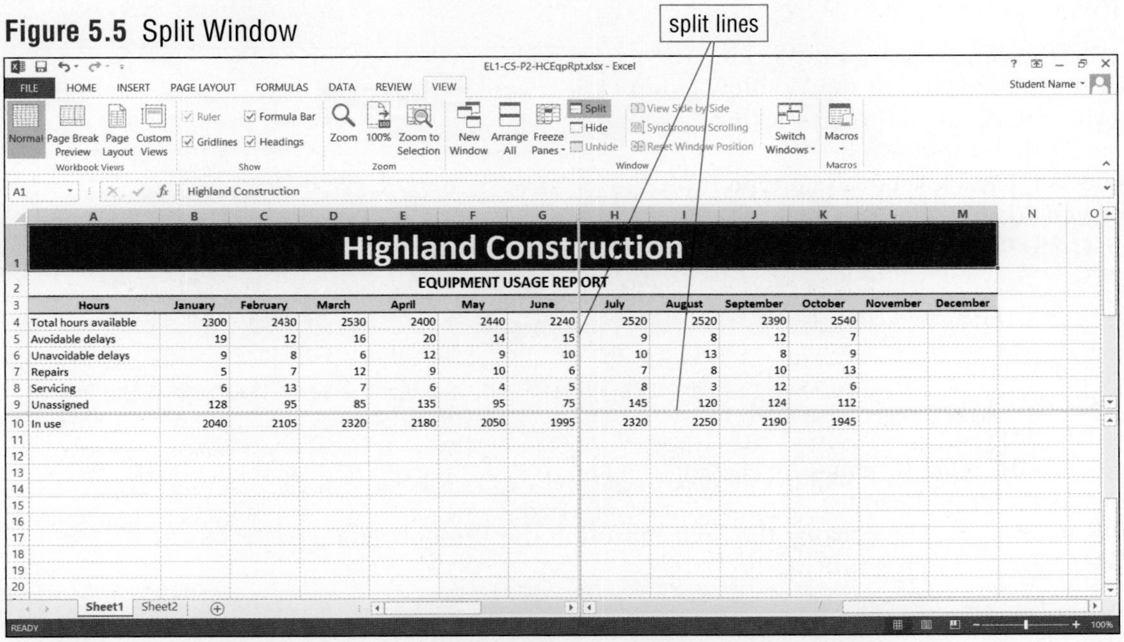

Project 2a Using Zoom, Splitting Windows, and Editing Cells

Part 1 of 2

1. Open **HCEqpRpt.xlsx** and then save the workbook with Save As and name it **EL1-C5-P2-HCEqpRpt**.
2. Increase the Zoom percentage by clicking twice on the Zoom In button at the right side of the zoom slider bar. 120%
3. Select cells G3 through I10, click the VIEW tab, and then click the Zoom to Selection button in the Zoom group.
4. Click the Zoom button in the Zoom group, click the *75%* option at the Zoom dialog box, and then click OK.

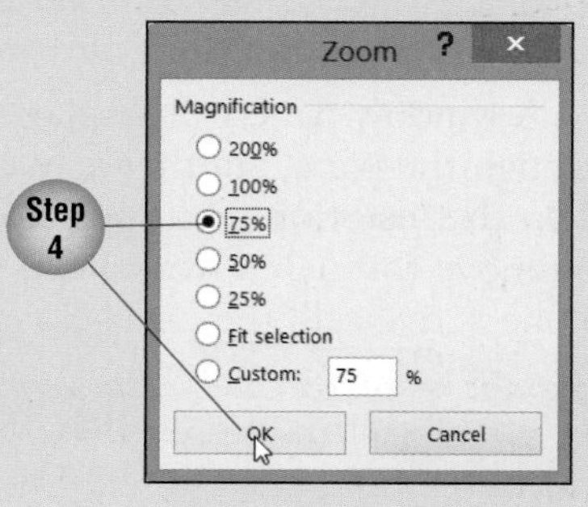

5. Click the 100% button in the Zoom group.
6. Make cell A1 active and then split the window by clicking the Split button in the Window group on the VIEW tab. (This splits the window into four panes.) Ctrl Home
7. Drag the vertical split line by completing the following steps:
   a. Position the mouse pointer on the vertical split line until the pointer turns into a left-and-right-pointing arrow with a double line in the middle.
   b. Hold down the left mouse button, drag to the left until the vertical split line is immediately to the right of the first column, and then release the mouse button.

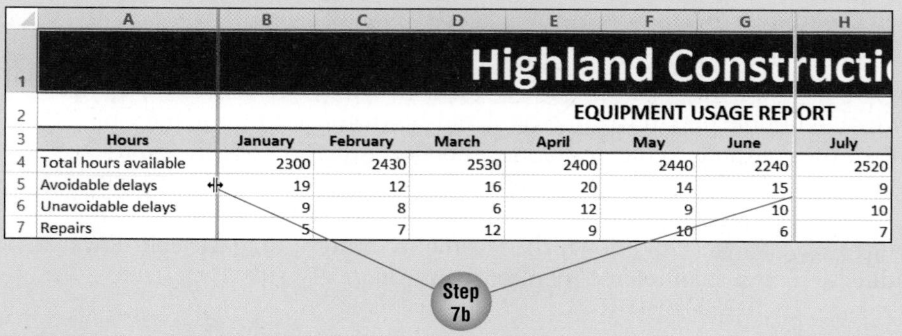

8. Freeze the window panes by clicking the Freeze Panes button in the Window group on the VIEW tab and then clicking *Freeze Panes* at the drop-down list.

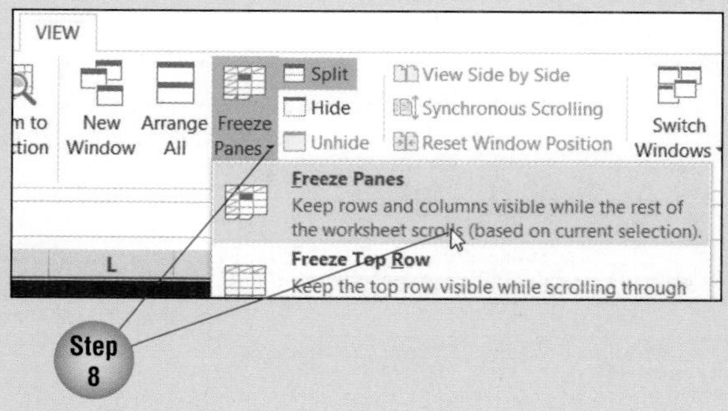

9. Make cell L4 active and then type the following data in the specified cells:

L4: 2310	M4: 2210
L5: 12	M5: 5
L6: 5	M6: 7
L7: 9	M7: 8
L8: 11	M8: 12
L9: 95	M9: 120
L10: 2005	M10: 1830

10. Unfreeze the window panes by clicking the Freeze Panes button and then clicking *Unfreeze Panes* at the drop-down list.
11. Remove the panes by clicking the Split button in the Window group to deactivate it.
12. Save **EL1-C5-P2-HCEqpRpt.xlsx**.

Working with Ranges

A selected group of cells is referred to as a ***range***. A range of cells can be formatted, moved, copied, or deleted. You can also name a range of cells and then move the insertion point to the range or use a named range as part of a formula.

To name a range, select the cells and then click in the Name box located at the left of the Formula bar. Type a name for the range (do not use a space) and then press Enter. To move the insertion point to a specific range and select the range, click the down-pointing arrow at the right side of the Name box and then click the range name.

You can also name a range using the Define Name button in the FORMULAS tab. To do this, click the FORMULAS tab and then click the Define Name button in the Defined Names group. At the New Name dialog box, type a name for the range and then click OK.

A range name can be used in a formula. For example, if a range is named *Profit* and you want to insert the average of all cells in the Profit range, make the desired cell active and then type *=AVERAGE(Profit)*. Use a named range in the current worksheet or in another worksheet within the workbook.

Quick Steps

Name a Range
1. Select cells.
2. Click in Name box.
3. Type range name.
4. Press Enter.

Define Name

HINT

Another method for moving to a range is to click the Find & Select button in the Editing group on the HOME tab and then click *Go To*. At the Go To dialog box, double-click the range name.

Project 2b Naming a Range and Using a Range in a Formula

Part 2 of 2

1. With **EL1-C5-P2-HCEqpRpt.xlsx** open, click the Sheet2 tab and then type the following text in the specified cells:
   A1: EQUIPMENT USAGE REPORT
   A2: Yearly hours
   A3: Avoidable delays
   A4: Unavoidable delays
   A5: Total delay hours
   A6: (leave blank)
   A7: Repairs
   A8: Servicing
   A9: Total repair/servicing hours

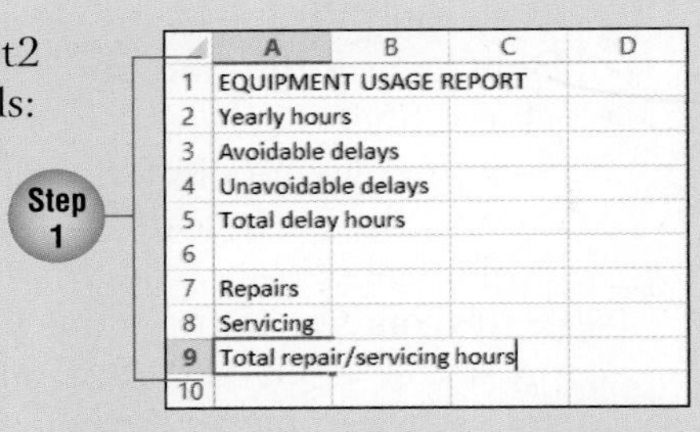

2. Make the following formatting changes to the worksheet:
   a. Automatically adjust the width of column A.
   b. Center and bold the text in cells A1 and A2.
3. Select a range of cells in Sheet1, name the range, and use it in a formula in Sheet2 by completing the following steps:
   a. Click the Sheet1 tab.
   b. Select cells B5 through M5.
   c. Click in the Name box located to the left of the Formula bar.
   d. Type adhours (for Avoidable Delays Hours) and then press Enter.
   e. Click the Sheet2 tab.
   f. Make cell B3 active.
   g. Type the equation =SUM(adhours) and then press Enter.

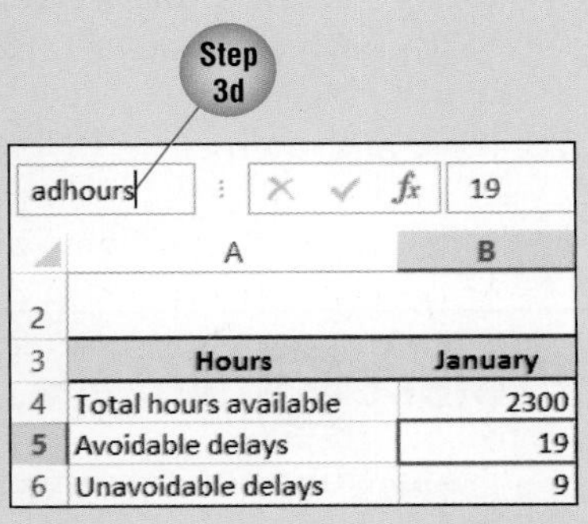

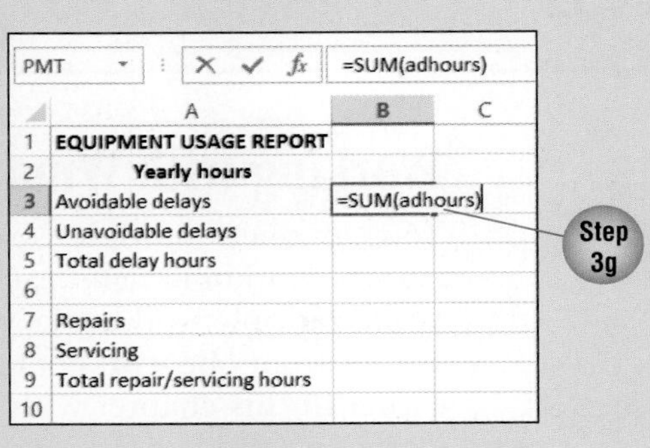

4. Click the Sheet1 tab and then complete the following steps:
   a. Select cells B6 through M6.
   b. Click the FORMULAS tab.
   c. Click the Define Name button in the Defined Names group.
   d. At the New Name dialog box, type udhours and then click OK.
   e. Click the Sheet2 tab, make sure cell B4 is active, type the equation =SUM(udhours), and then press Enter.

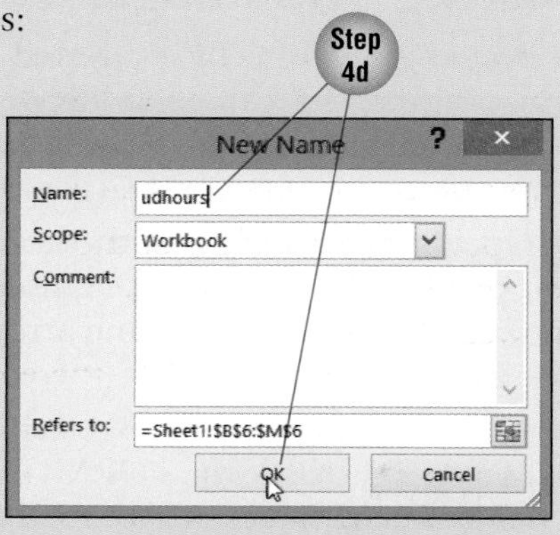

5. Click the Sheet1 tab and then complete the following steps:
   a. Select cells B7 through M7 and then name the range *rhours*.
   b. Click the Sheet2 tab, make cell B7 active, type the equation =SUM(rhours), and then press Enter.
   c. Click the Sheet1 tab.
   d. Select cells B8 through M8 and then name the range *shours*.
   e. Click the Sheet2 tab, make sure cell B8 is active, type the equation =SUM(shours), and then press Enter.
6. With Sheet2 still active, make the following changes:
   a. Make cell B5 active.
   b. Double-click the AutoSum button in the Editing group on the HOME tab.
   c. Make cell B9 active.
   d. Double-click the AutoSum button in the Editing group.
7. Click the Sheet1 tab and then move to the adhours range by clicking the down-pointing arrow at the right side of the Name box and then clicking *adhours* at the drop-down list.
8. Select both sheet tabs, change the orientation to landscape, scale the contents to fit on one page (by changing the width to *1 page* on the PAGE LAYOUT tab), and then insert a custom footer with your name, the page number, and the date.
9. With both worksheet tabs selected, print both worksheets in the workbook.
10. Save and then close **EL1-C5-P2-HCEqpRpt.xlsx**.

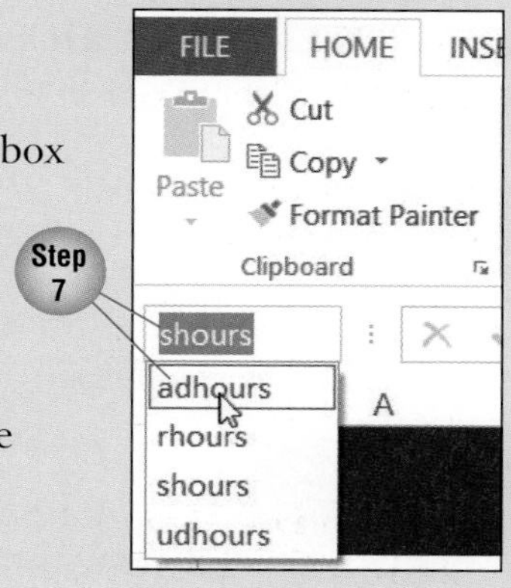

Project 3 Arrange, Size, and Copy Data between Workbooks 3 Parts

You will open, arrange, hide, unhide, size, and move multiple workbooks. You will also copy cells from one workbook and paste them in another workbook.

Working with Windows

You can open multiple workbooks in Excel, open a new window with the current workbook, and arrange the open workbooks in the Excel window. With multiple workbooks open, you can cut and paste or copy and paste cell entries from one workbook to another using the same techniques discussed earlier in this chapter with the exception that you make the destination workbook active before using the Paste command.

Opening Multiple Workbooks

With multiple workbooks open, or more than one version of the current workbook open, you can move or copy information between workbooks and compare the contents of several workbooks. When you open a new workbook or a new window of the current workbook, it is placed on top of the original workbook.

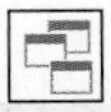
New Window

Open a new window of the current workbook by clicking the VIEW tab and then clicking the New Window button in the Window group. Excel adds a colon followed by the number *2* to the end of the workbook title and adds a colon followed by the number *1* to the end of the originating workbook name.

Open multiple workbooks at one time at the Open dialog box. Select adjacent workbooks by clicking the name of the first workbook to be opened, holding down the Shift key, clicking the name of the last workbook to be opened, and then clicking the Open button. If workbooks are nonadjacent, click the name of the first workbook to be opened, hold down the Ctrl key, and then click the names of any other workbooks you want to open.

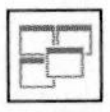
Switch Windows

To see what workbooks are currently open, click the VIEW tab and then click the Switch Windows button in the Window group. The names of the open workbooks display in a drop-down list and the workbook name preceded by a check mark is the active workbook. To make one of the other workbooks active, click the desired workbook name at the drop-down list.

Another method for determining which workbooks are open is to hover your mouse over the Excel icon button that displays on the Taskbar. This causes a thumbnail to display of each open workbook. If you have more than one workbook open, the Excel button on the Taskbar displays additional layers in a cascaded manner. The layer behind the Excel button displays only a portion of the edge at the right side of the button. If you have multiple workbooks open, hovering the mouse over the Excel button on the Taskbar will cause thumbnails of all of the workbooks to display above the button. (This depends on your monitor size.) To change to the desired workbook, click the thumbnail that represents the workbook.

Arranging Workbooks

Quick Steps

Arrange Workbooks
1. Click VIEW tab.
2. Click Arrange All button.
3. At Arrange Windows dialog box, click desired arrangement.
4. Click OK.

Arrange All

If you have more than one workbook open, you can arrange the workbooks at the Arrange Windows dialog box, shown in Figure 5.6. To display this dialog box, open several workbooks and then click the Arrange All button in the Window group on the VIEW tab. At the Arrange Windows dialog box, click *Tiled* to display a portion of each open workbook. Figure 5.7 displays four tiled workbooks.

Figure 5.6 Arrange Windows Dialog Box

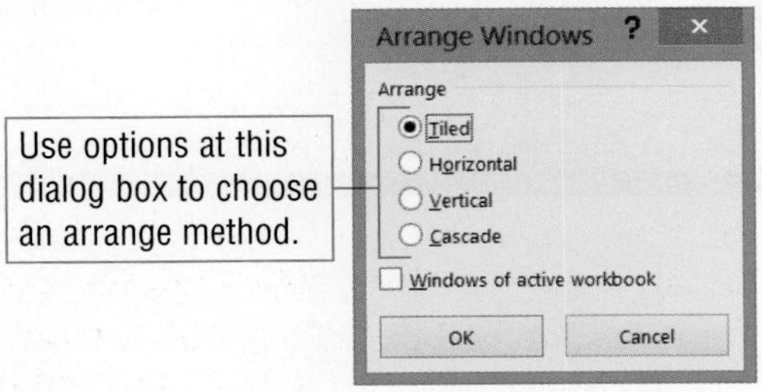

Figure 5.7 Tiled Workbooks

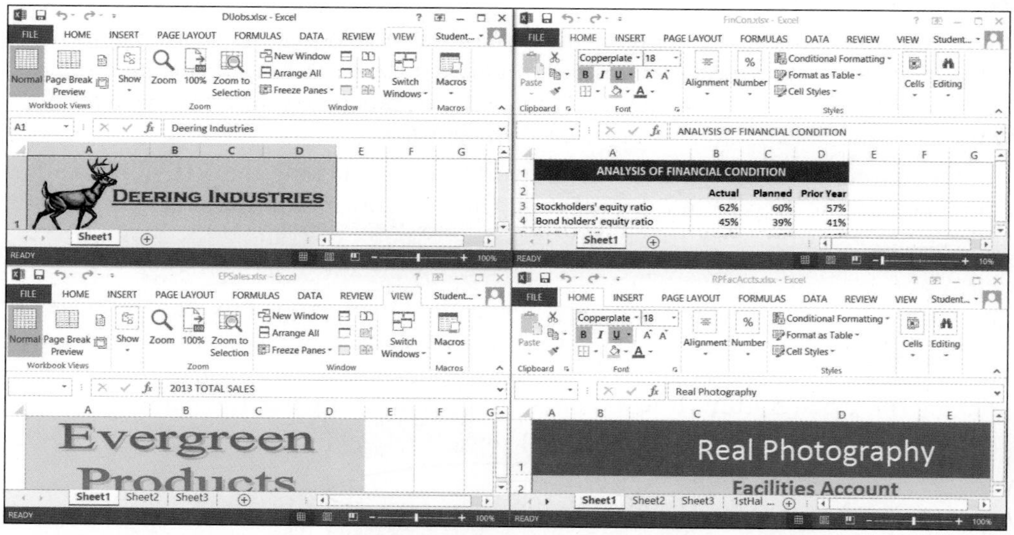

Choose the *Horizontal* option at the Arrange Windows dialog box and the open workbooks display across the screen. The *Vertical* option displays the open workbooks up and down the screen. The last option, *Cascade*, displays the Title bar of each open workbook. Figure 5.8 shows four cascaded workbooks.

The option you select for displaying multiple workbooks depends on which part of the workbooks is most important to view simultaneously. For example, the tiled workbooks in Figure 5.7 allow you to view the company names and the first few rows and columns of each workbook.

Figure 5.8 Cascaded Workbooks

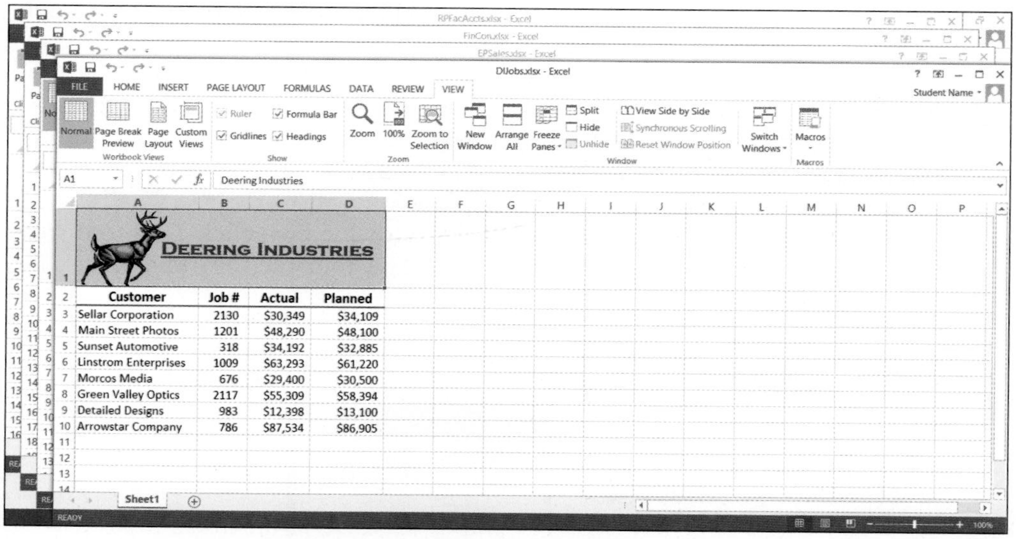

Hiding/Unhiding Workbooks

With the Hide button in the Window group on the VIEW tab, you can hide the active workbook. If a workbook has been hidden, redisplay it by clicking the Unhide button in the Window group. At the Unhide dialog box, make sure the desired workbook is selected in the list box and then click OK.

Hide Unhide

Project 3a **Opening, Arranging, and Hiding/Unhiding Workbooks** **Part 1 of 3**

1. Open several workbooks at the same time by completing the following steps:
   a. Display the Open dialog box with EL1C5 the active folder.
   b. Click the workbook named ***DIJobs.xlsx***.
   c. Hold down the Ctrl key, click ***EPSales.xlsx***, click ***FinCon.xlsx***, and then click ***RPFacAccts.xlsx***.
   d. Release the Ctrl key and then click the Open button in the dialog box.
2. Make **DIJobs.xlsx** the active workbook by clicking the VIEW tab, clicking the Switch Windows button, and then clicking ***DIJobs.xlsx*** at the drop-down list.

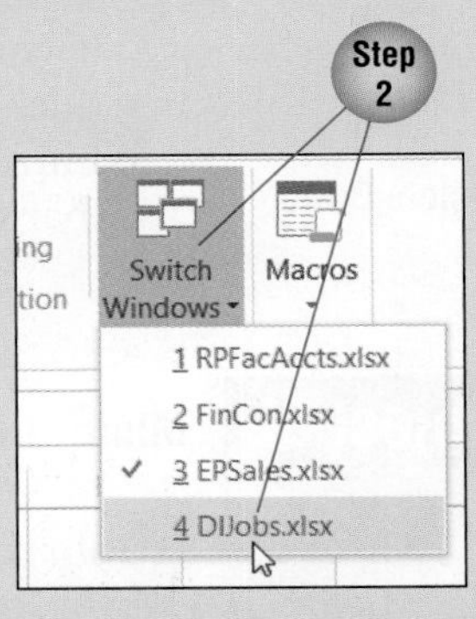

3. Tile the workbooks by completing the following steps:
   a. Click the VIEW tab and then click the Arrange All button in the Window group.
   b. At the Arrange Windows dialog box, make sure *Tiled* is selected and then click OK.

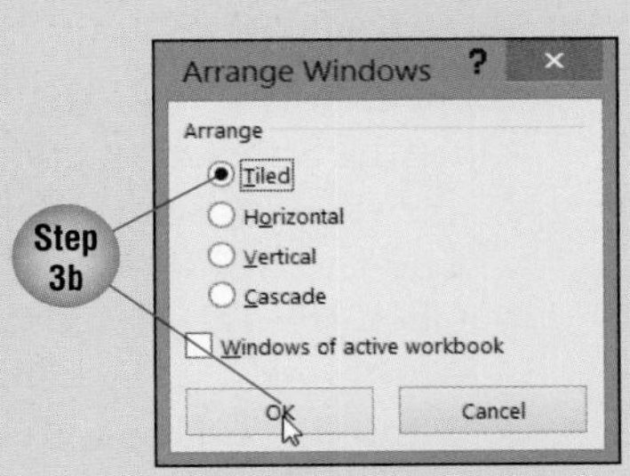

4. Cascade the workbooks by completing the following steps:
   a. Click the Arrange All button in the **DIJobs.xlsx** workbook.
   b. At the Arrange Windows dialog box, click *Cascade* and then click OK.
5. Hide and unhide workbooks by completing the following steps:
   a. Make sure **DIJobs.xlsx** is the active workbook. (The file name displays on top of each workbook file.)
   b. Click the Hide button in the Window group on the VIEW tab.
   c. Make sure **RPFacAccts.xlsx** is the active workbook. (The file name displays at the top of each workbook file.)
   d. Click the VIEW tab and then click the Hide button.
   e. At the active workbook, click the Unhide button.
   f. At the Unhide dialog box, click ***RPFacAccts.xlsx*** in the list box and then click OK.
   g. Click the Unhide button.
   h. At the Unhide dialog box, make sure **DIJobs.xlsx** is selected in the list box and then click OK. (If the workbook is not selected, click the **RPFacAccts.xlsx** title bar to make it active.)

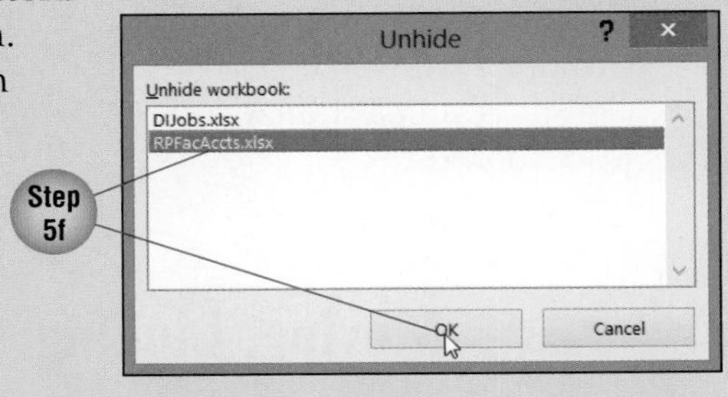

6. Close all of the open workbooks (without saving changes) except **DIJobs.xlsx**.
7. Open a new window with the current workbook by clicking the New Window button in the Window group on the VIEW tab. (Notice that the new window contains the workbook name followed by a colon and the number *2*.)
8. Switch back and forth between the two versions of the workbook.
9. Make **DIJobs.xlsx:2** the active window and then close the workbook.

Sizing and Moving Workbooks

Maximize

Minimize

Close

Restore Down

Use the Maximize and Minimize buttons located in the upper right corner of the active workbook to change the size of the window. The Maximize button is the button in the upper right corner of the active workbook immediately to the left of the Close button. (The Close button is the button containing the *X*.) The Minimize button is located immediately to the left of the Maximize button.

If you arrange all open workbooks and then click the Maximize button in the active workbook, the active workbook expands to fill the screen. In addition, the Maximize button changes to the Restore Down button. To return the active workbook back to its original size, click the Restore Down button.

If you click the Minimize button in the active workbook, the workbook is reduced and displays as a layer behind the Excel button on the Taskbar. To maximize a workbook that has been minimized, click the Excel button on the Taskbar and then click the thumbnail representing the workbook.

Project 3b **Minimizing, Maximizing, and Restoring Workbooks** **Part 2 of 3**

1. Make sure **DIJobs.xlsx** is open.
2. Maximize **DIJobs.xlsx** by clicking the Maximize button located in the upper right corner of the screen immediately left of the Close button.
3. Open **EPSales.xlsx** and **FinCon.xlsx**.
4. Make the following changes to the open workbooks:
   a. Tile the workbooks.
   b. Click the **DIJobs.xlsx** Title bar to make it the active workbook.
   c. Minimize **DIJobs.xlsx** by clicking the Minimize button that displays at the right side of the Title bar.
   d. Make **EPSales.xlsx** the active workbook and then minimize it.
   e. Minimize **FinCon.xlsx**.
5. Click the Excel button on the Taskbar, click the **DIJobs.xlsx** thumbnail, and then close the workbook without saving changes.
6. Complete steps similar to Step 5 to close the other two workbooks.

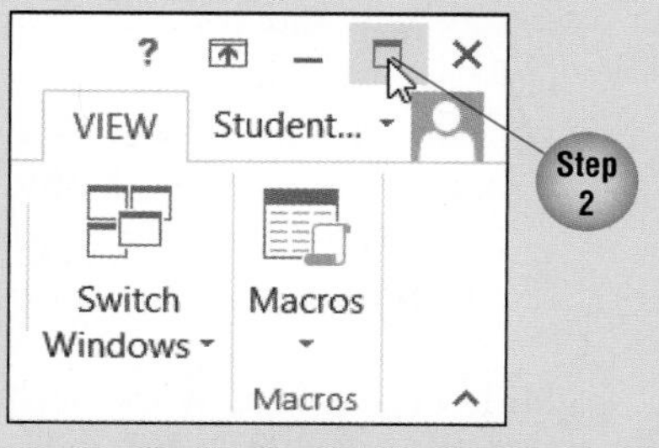

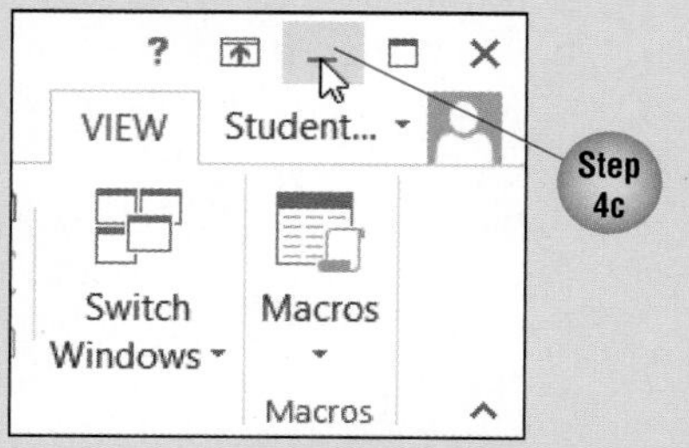

Moving, Linking, Copying, and Pasting Data

With more than one workbook open, you can move, link, copy, and/or paste data from one workbook to another. To move, link, copy, and/or paste data between workbooks, use the cutting and pasting options you learned earlier in this chapter together with the information about windows.

Moving and Copying Data

You can move or copy data within a worksheet, between worksheets, and between workbooks and other programs, such as Word, PowerPoint, and Access. The Paste Options button provides a variety of options for pasting data in a worksheet, another workbook, or another program. In addition to pasting data, you can also link data and paste data as an object or a picture object.

Project 3c Copying Selected Cells from One Open Worksheet to Another — Part 3 of 3

1. Open **DIFebJobs.xlsx**.
2. If you just completed Project 3b, click the Maximize button so the worksheet fills the entire worksheet window.
3. Save the workbook with Save As and name it **EL1-C5-P3-DIFebJobs**.
4. With **EL1-C5-P3-DIFebJobs.xlsx** open, open **DIJobs.xlsx**.
5. Select and then copy text from **DIJobs.xlsx** to **EL1-C5-P3-DIFebJobs.xlsx** by completing the following steps:
   a. With **DIJobs.xlsx** the active workbook, select cells A3 through D10.
   b. Click the Copy button in the Clipboard group on the HOME tab.
   c. Click the Excel button on the Taskbar and then click the **EL1-C5-P3-DIFebJobs.xlsx** thumbnail.

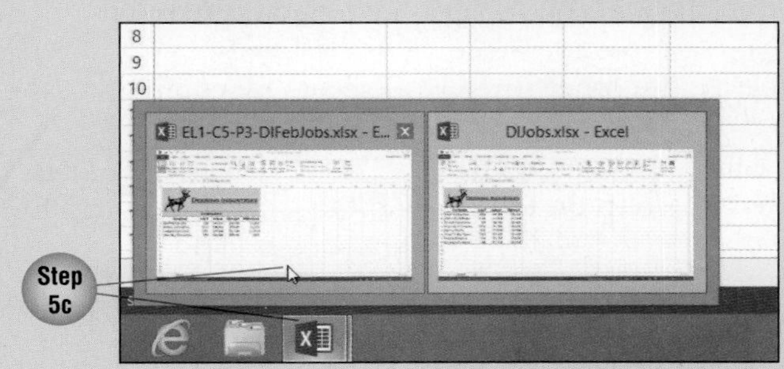

   d. Make cell A8 active and then click the Paste button in the Clipboard group.
   e. Make cell E7 active and then drag the fill handle down to cell E15.
6. Print **EL1-C5-P3-DIFebJobs.xlsx** horizontally and vertically centered on the page.
7. Save and then close **EL1-C5-P3-DIFebJobs.xlsx**.
8. Close **DIJobs.xlsx**.

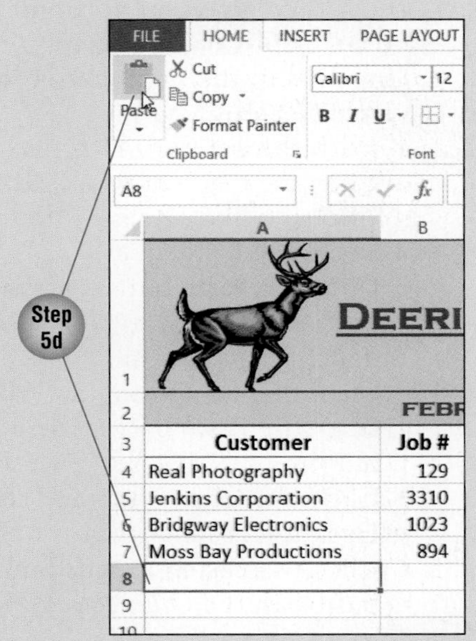

Project 4 Linking and Copying Data within and between Worksheets and Word — 2 Parts

You will open a workbook containing four worksheets with quarterly expenses data, copy and link cells between the worksheets, and then copy and paste the worksheets into Word as picture objects.

Linking Data

> **Quick Steps**
> **Link Data between Worksheets**
> 1. Select cells.
> 2. Click Copy button.
> 3. Click desired worksheet tab.
> 4. Click in desired cell.
> 5. Click Paste button arrow.
> 6. Click *Paste Link* at drop-down list.

In some situations, you may want to copy and link data within or between worksheets or workbooks rather than copy and paste data. Linking data is useful when you need to maintain consistency and control over critical data in worksheets or workbooks. When data is linked, a change made in a linked cell is automatically made to the other cells in the link. You can make links with individual cells or with a range of cells. When linking data, the worksheet that contains the original data is called the ***source worksheet*** and the worksheet relying on the source worksheet for the data in the link is called the ***dependent worksheet***.

To create a link, make active the cell containing the data to be linked (or select the cells) and then click the Copy button in the Clipboard group on the HOME tab. Make active the worksheet where you want to paste the cells, click the Paste button arrow, and then click the Paste Link button located in the *Other Paste Options* section in the drop-down list. You can also create a link by clicking the Paste button, clicking the Paste Options button, and then clicking the Paste Link button in the *Other Paste Options* section in the drop-down list.

Project 4a Linking Cells between Worksheets — Part 1 of 2

1. Open **DWQtrlyExp.xlsx** and then save the workbook with Save As and name it **EL1-C5-P4-DWQtrlyExp**.
2. Link cells in the first quarter worksheet to the other three worksheets by completing the following steps:
   a. With the 1st Qtr tab active, select cells C4 through C10.
   b. Click the Copy button in the Clipboard group on the HOME tab.
   c. Click the 2nd Qtr tab.
   d. Make cell C4 active.
   e. Click the Paste button arrow and then click the Paste Link button located in the *Other Paste Options* section in the drop-down list.
   f. Click the 3rd Qtr tab and then make cell C4 active.
   g. Click the Paste button arrow and then click the Paste Link button.
   h. Click the 4th Qtr tab and then make cell C4 active.
   i. Click the Paste button.
   j. Click the Paste Options button and then click the Paste Link button in the *Other Paste Options* section in the drop-down list.

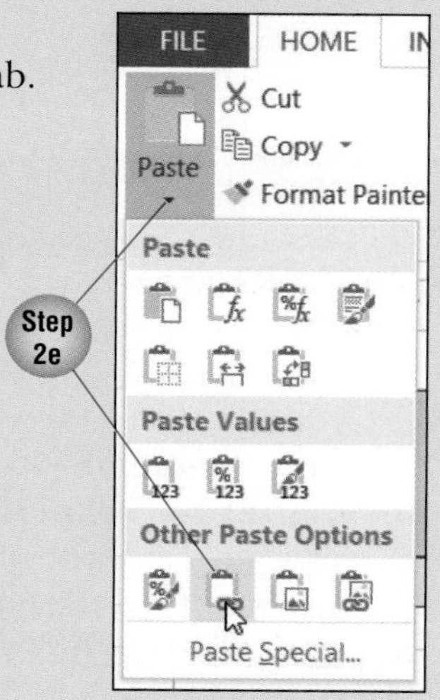

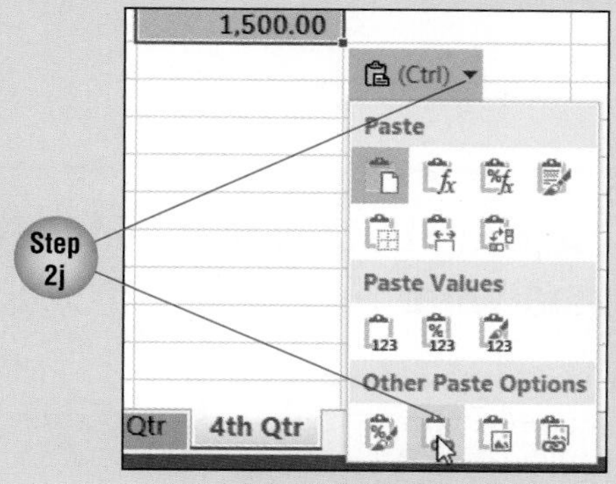

3. Click the 1st Qtr tab and then press the Esc key to remove the moving marquee.
4. Insert a formula in each worksheet that subtracts the budget amount from the variance amount by completing the following steps:
   a. Make sure the first quarter worksheet displays.
   b. Hold down the Shift key and then click the 4th Qtr tab. (This selects all four tabs.)
   c. Make cell D4 active and then type the formula =C4-B4 and press Enter.
   d. Copy the formula in cell D4 down to cells D5 through D10.
   e. Make cell D4 active and then apply accounting formatting with two places after the decimal point and a dollar sign.
   f. Click the 2nd Qtr tab and notice that the formula was inserted and copied in this worksheet.
   g. Click the other worksheet tabs and notice the amounts in column D.
   h. Click the 1st Qtr tab.

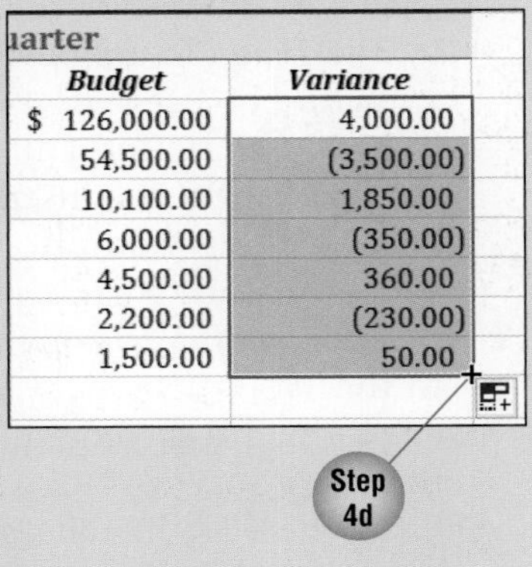

5. With the first quarter worksheet active, make the following changes to some of the linked cells:

   C4: Change *$126,000* to *$128,000*

   C5: Change *54,500* to *56,000*

   C9: Change *2,200* to *2,400*
6. Click the 2nd Qtr tab and notice that the values in cells C4, C5, and C9 automatically changed (because they were linked to the first quarter worksheet).
7. Click the other tabs and notice that the values changed.
8. Save **EL1-C5-P4-DWQtrlyExp.xlsx** and then print all four worksheets in the workbook.

Copying and Pasting Data between Programs

Microsoft Office is a suite that allows ***integration***, which is the combining of data from two or more programs into one file. Integration can occur by copying and pasting data between programs. For example, you can create a worksheet in Excel, select specific data in the worksheet, and then copy it to a Word document. When pasting Excel data in a Word document, you can choose to keep the source formatting, use destination styles, link the data, insert the data as a picture, or keep the text only.

Project 4b Copying and Pasting Excel Data into a Word Document — Part 2 of 2

1. With **EL1-C5-P4-DWQtrlyExp.xlsx** open, open the Word program.
2. In Word, open the document named **DWQtrlyRpt.docx** located in the EL1C5 folder on your storage medium.
3. Save the Word document with Save As and name it **EL1-C5-P4-DWQtrlyRpt**.
4. Click the Excel button on the Taskbar.
5. Copy the first quarter data into the Word document by completing the following steps:
   a. Click the 1st Qtr tab.
   b. Select cells A2 through D10.
   c. Click the Copy button in the Clipboard group on the HOME tab.
   d. Click the Word button on the Taskbar.

e. In the **EL1-C5-P4-DWQtrlyRpt.docx** document, press Ctrl + End to move the insertion point below the heading.

f. Click the Paste button arrow. (This displays a drop-down list of paste option buttons.)

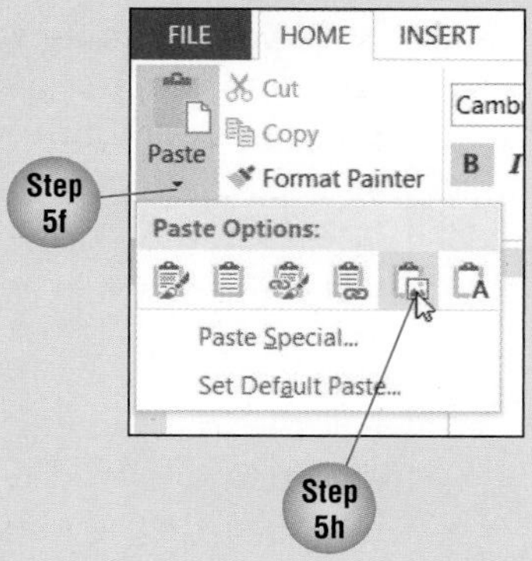

g. Move your mouse over the various buttons in the drop-down list to see how each option will insert the data in the document.

h. Click the Picture button. (This inserts the data as a picture object.)

i. Press Ctrl + End and then press the Enter key twice. (This moves the insertion point below the data.)

j. Click the Excel button on the Taskbar.

6. Click the 2nd Qtr tab and then complete steps similar to those in Step 5 to copy and paste the second quarter data to the Word document.
7. Click the 3rd Qtr tab and then complete steps similar to those in Step 5 to copy and paste the third quarter data to the Word document.
8. Click the 4th Qtr tab and then complete steps similar to those in Step 5 to copy and paste the fourth quarter data to the Word document. (The data will display on two pages.)
9. Print the document by clicking the FILE tab, clicking the *Print* option, and then clicking the Print button at the Print backstage area.
10. Save and close **EL1-C5-P4-DWQtrlyRpt.docx** and then close Word.
11. In Excel, press the Esc key to remove the moving marquee and then make cell A1 active.
12. Save and then close **EL1-C5-P4-DWQtrlyExp.xlsx**.

Chapter Summary

- An Excel workbook, by default, contains one worksheet. Add a new worksheet to a workbook by clicking the New sheet button or with the keyboard shortcut Shift + F11.
- Delete a worksheet with the Delete button in the Cells group on the HOME tab or by right-clicking a worksheet tab and then clicking *Delete* at the shortcut menu.
- Manage more than one worksheet at a time by first selecting the worksheets. Use the mouse together with the Shift key to select adjacent worksheet tabs and use the mouse together with the Ctrl key to select nonadjacent worksheet tabs.
- Copy or move selected cells and cell contents in and between worksheets using the Cut, Copy, and Paste buttons in the Clipboard group on the HOME tab or by dragging with the mouse.
- Move selected cells with the mouse by dragging the outline of the selected cells to the desired position.
- Copy selected cells with the mouse by holding down the Ctrl key while dragging the cells to the desired position.
- When pasting data, specify how you want cells pasted by clicking the Paste button arrow or pasting the cells and then clicking the Paste Options button. Clicking either button causes a drop-down list of paste option buttons to display. Click the desired button in the drop-down list.

- Use the Clipboard task pane to copy and paste data within and between worksheets and workbooks. Display the Clipboard task pane by clicking the Clipboard task pane launcher.
- Perform maintenance activities, such as deleting and renaming, on worksheets within a workbook by clicking the right mouse button on a worksheet tab and then clicking the desired option at the shortcut menu.
- You can use the mouse to move or copy worksheets. To move a worksheet, drag the worksheet tab with the mouse. To copy a worksheet, hold down the Ctrl key and then drag the worksheet tab with the mouse.
- Use the *Tab Color* option at the worksheet tab shortcut menu to apply a color to a worksheet tab.
- Hide and unhide a worksheet by clicking the Format button in the Cells group and then clicking the desired option at the drop-down list or by right-clicking the worksheet tab and then clicking the desired option at the shortcut menu.
- To print all worksheets in a workbook, display the Print backstage area, click the first gallery in the *Settings* category, and then click *Print Entire Workbook* at the drop-down list. You can also print specific worksheets by selecting the tabs of the worksheets you want to print.
- Use buttons in the Zoom group on the VIEW tab or the zoom slider bar located at the right side of the Status bar to change the display zoom percentage.
- Split the worksheet window into panes with the Split button in the Window group on the VIEW tab. To remove a split from a worksheet, click the Split button to deactivate it.
- Freeze window panes by clicking the Freeze Panes button in the Window group on the VIEW tab and then clicking *Freeze Panes* at the drop-down list. Unfreeze window panes by clicking the Freeze Panes button and then clicking *Unfreeze Panes* at the drop-down list.
- A selected group of cells is referred to as a range. A range can be named and used in a formula. Name a range by typing the name in the Name box located to the left of the Formula bar or at the New Name dialog box.
- To open multiple workbooks that are adjacent, display the Open dialog box, click the first workbook, hold down the Shift key, click the last workbook, and then click the Open button. To open workbooks that are nonadjacent, click the first workbook, hold down the Ctrl key, click the desired workbooks, and then click the Open button.
- To see a list of open workbooks, click the VIEW tab and then click the Switch Windows button in the Window group.
- Arrange multiple workbooks in a window with options at the Arrange Windows dialog box.
- Hide the active workbook by clicking the Hide button and unhide a workbook by clicking the Unhide button in the Window group on the VIEW tab.
- Click the Maximize button located in the upper right corner of the active workbook to make the workbook fill the entire window area. Click the Minimize button to shrink the active workbook to a button on the Taskbar. Click the Restore Down button to return the workbook to its previous size.
- You can move, link, copy, and/or paste data between workbooks.

Commands Review

FEATURE	RIBBON TAB, GROUP	BUTTON, OPTION	KEYBOARD SHORTCUT
Arrange Windows dialog box	VIEW, Window		
Clipboard task pane	HOME, Clipboard		
copy selected cells	HOME, Clipboard		Ctrl + C
cut selected cells	HOME, Clipboard		Ctrl + X
freeze window panes	VIEW, Window	, *Freeze Panes*	
hide worksheet	HOME, Cells	, *Hide & Unhide, Hide Sheet*	
insert new worksheet			Shift + F11
maximize window			
minimize window			
New Name dialog box	FORMULAS, Defined Names		
paste selected cells	HOME, Clipboard		Ctrl + V
restore down			
split window into panes	VIEW, Window		
unfreeze window panes	VIEW, Window	, *Unfreeze Panes*	
unhide worksheet	HOME, Cells	, *Hide & Unhide, Unhide Sheet*	

Concepts Check

Test Your Knowledge SNAP

Completion: In the space provided at the right, indicate the correct term, symbol, or command.

1. By default, a workbook contains this number of worksheets. one
2. Click this button to insert a new worksheet in a workbook. ____________
3. To select nonadjacent worksheet tabs, click the first tab, hold down this key, and then click any other tabs you want selected. ____________
4. To select adjacent worksheet tabs, click the first tab, hold down this key, and then click the last tab. ____________

5. The Cut, Copy, and Paste buttons are located in this group on the HOME tab. ______________

6. This button displays in the lower right corner of pasted cells. ______________

7. Use this task pane to copy and paste multiple items. ______________

8. Click this option at the worksheet tab shortcut menu to apply a color to a worksheet tab. ______________

9. To print all of the worksheets in a workbook, display the Print backstage area, click the first gallery in the *Settings* category, and then click this option at the drop-down list. ______________

10. The Split button is located on this tab. ______________

11. Display the Arrange Windows dialog box by clicking this button in the Window group on the VIEW tab. ______________

12. Click this button to make the active workbook expand to fill the screen. ______________

13. Click this button to reduce the active workbook to a layer behind the Excel button on the Taskbar. ______________

14. When linking data between worksheets, the worksheet containing the original data is called this. ______________

Skills Check Assess Your Performance

Assessment 1

COPY AND PASTE DATA BETWEEN WORKSHEETS IN A SALES WORKBOOK

SNAP Grade It

1. Open **EPSales.xlsx** and then save the workbook with Save As and name it **EL1-C5-A1-EPSales**.
2. Turn on the display of the Clipboard task pane, click the Clear All button to clear any content, and then complete the following steps:
   a. Select and copy cells A7 through C7.
   b. Select and copy cells A10 through C10.
   c. Select and copy cells A13 through C13.
   d. Display the second worksheet, make cell A7 active, and then paste the *Avalon Clinic* cells.
   e. Make cell A10 active and then paste the *Stealth Media* cells.
   f. Make A13 active and then paste the *Danmark Contracting* cells.
   g. Make the third worksheet active and then complete similar steps to paste the cells in the same location as in the second worksheet.
   h. Clear the contents of the Clipboard task pane and then close the task pane.

3. Change the name of the Sheet1 tab to *2013 Sales*, the name of the Sheet2 tab to *2014 Sales*, and the name of the Sheet3 tab to *2015 Sales*.
4. Change the color of the 2013 Sales tab to Blue, the color of the 2014 Sales tab to Green, and the color of the 2015 Sales tab to Yellow.
5. Make 2013 Sales the active worksheet, select all three tabs, and then insert a formula in cell D4 that sums the amounts in cells B4 and C4. Copy the formula in cell D4 down to cells D5 through D14.
6. Make cell D15 active and then insert a formula that sums the amounts in cells D4 through D14.
7. Apply accounting formatting with a dollar sign and no places after the decimal point to cell D4 (on all three worksheets).
8. Insert a footer on all three worksheets that prints your name at the left side and the current date at the right.
9. Save **EL1-C5-A1-EPSales.xlsx**.
10. Print all three worksheets and then close **EL1-C5-A1-EPSales.xlsx**.

Assessment 2 COPY, PASTE, AND FORMAT WORKSHEETS IN AN INCOME STATEMENT WORKBOOK

SNAP Grade It

1. Open **CMJanIncome.xlsx** and then save the workbook with Save As and name it **EL1-C5-A2-CMJanIncome**.
2. Copy cells A1 through B17 in Sheet1 and paste them into Sheet2. (Click the Paste Options button and then click the Keep Source Column Widths button at the drop-down list.)
3. Make the following changes to the Sheet2 worksheet:
   a. Adjust the row heights so they match the heights in the Sheet1 worksheet.
   b. Change the month from *January* to *February*.
   c. Change the amount in cell B4 to *97,655*.
   d. Change the amount in cell B5 to *39,558*.
   e. Change the amount in cell B11 to *1,105*.
4. Select both sheet tabs and then insert the following formulas:
   a. Insert a formula in cell B6 that subtracts the cost of sales from the sales revenue (*=B4-B5*).
   b. Insert a formula in cell B16 that sums the amounts in cells B8 through B15.
   c. Insert a formula in cell B17 that subtracts the total expenses from the gross profit (*=B6-B16*).
5. Change the name of the Sheet1 tab to *January* and the name of the Sheet2 tab to *February*.
6. Change the color of the January tab to Blue and the color of the February tab to Red.
7. Insert a custom header on both worksheets that prints your name at the left side, the date in the middle, and the file name at the right side.
8. Save, print, and then close **EL1-C5-A2-CMJanIncome.xlsx**.

Start here

Assessment 3

FREEZE AND UNFREEZE WINDOW PANES IN A TEST SCORES WORKBOOK

SNAP Grade It

1. Open **CMCertTests.xlsx** and then save the workbook with Save As and name it **EL1-C5-A3-CMCertTests**.
2. Make sure cell A1 is active and then split the window by clicking the VIEW tab and then clicking the Split button in the Window group. (This causes the window to split into four panes.)
3. Drag both the horizontal and vertical split lines up and to the left until the horizontal split line is immediately below the second row and the vertical split line is immediately to the right of the first column.
4. Freeze the window panes.
5. Add two rows immediately above row 18 and then type the following text in the specified cells:

A18: **Nauer, Sheryl**	A19: **Nunez, James**
B18: **75**	B19: **98**
C18: **83**	C19: **96**
D18: **85**	D19: **100**
E18: **78**	E19: **90**
F18: **82**	F19: **95**
G18: **80**	G19: **93**
H18: **79**	H19: **88**
I18: **82**	I19: **91**
J18: **92**	J19: **89**
K18: **90**	K19: **100**
L18: **86**	L19: **96**
M18: **84**	M19: **98**

6. Insert a formula in cell N3 that averages the percentages in cells B3 through M3 and then copy the formula down to cells N4 through N22.
7. Unfreeze the window panes.
8. Remove the split.
9. Change the orientation to landscape and then scale the worksheet to print on one page. ***Hint: Do this with the* Width *option in the Scale to Fit group on the PAGE LAYOUT tab.***
10. Save, print, and then close **EL1-C5-A3-CMCertTests.xlsx**.

Assessment 4

CREATE, COPY, PASTE, AND FORMAT CELLS IN AN EQUIPMENT USAGE WORKBOOK

1. Create the worksheet shown in Figure 5.9. (Change the width of column A to 21.00 characters.)
2. Save the workbook and name it **EL1-C5-A4-HCMachRpt**.
3. With **EL1-C5-A4-HCMachRpt.xlsx** open, open **HCEqpRpt.xlsx**.

4. Select and copy the following cells from **HCEqpRpt.xlsx** to **EL1-C5-A4-HCMachRpt.xlsx**:
   a. Copy cells A4 through G4 in **HCEqpRpt.xlsx** and paste them into **EL1-C5-A4-HCMachRpt.xlsx** beginning with cell A12.
   b. Copy cells A10 through G10 in **HCEqpRpt.xlsx** and paste them into **EL1-C5-A4-HCMachRpt.xlsx** beginning with cell A13.
5. With **EL1-C5-A4-HCMachRpt.xlsx** the active workbook, make cell A1 active and then apply the following formatting:
   a. Change the height of row 1 to 25.20 points.
   b. Change the font size of the text in cell A1 to 14 points.
   c. Apply the Blue, Accent 5, Lighter 80% fill color (ninth column, second row in the *Theme Colors* section) to cell A1.
6. Select cells A2 through G2 and apply the Blue, Accent 5, Darker 50% fill color (ninth column, last row in the *Theme Colors* section).
7. Select cells B2 through G2 and apply the White, Background 1 text color (first column, first row in the *Theme Colors* section). (Make sure the text in the cells is right-aligned.)
8. Select and then apply the Blue, Accent 5, Lighter 80% fill color (ninth column, second row in the *Theme Colors* section) to the following cells: A3 through G3, A7 through G7, and A11 through G11.
9. Print the worksheet centered horizontally and vertically on the page.
10. Save and then close **EL1-C5-A4-HCMachRpt.xlsx**.
11. Close **HCEqpRpt.xlsx** without saving the changes.

Figure 5.9 Assessment 4

	A	B	C	D	E	F	G	H
1				**EQUIPMENT USAGE REPORT**				
2		**January**	**February**	**March**	**April**	**May**	**June**	
3	**Machine #12**							
4	Total hours available	2200	2330	2430	2300	2340	2140	
5	In use	1940	2005	2220	2080	1950	1895	
6								
7	**Machine #25**							
8	Total hours available	2100	2240	2450	2105	2390	1950	
9	In use	1800	1935	2110	1750	2215	1645	
10								
11	**Machine #30**							
12								

Assessment 5 COPYING AND LINKING DATA IN A WORD DOCUMENT

1. In this chapter you learned how to link data in cells between worksheets. You can also copy data in an Excel worksheet and then paste and link the data in a file in another program such as Word. Use buttons in the Paste Options button drop-down list to link data or use options at the Paste Special dialog box. Open Word and then open the document named **DWLtr.docx** located in the EL1C5 folder. Save the document with Save As and name it **EL1-C5-A5-DWLtr**.

2. Click the Excel button on the Taskbar, open **DWMortgages.xlsx**, and then save the workbook with Save As and name it **EL1-C5-A5-DWMortgages**.
3. Select cells A2 through G10 and then click the Copy button.
4. Click the Word button on the Taskbar. (This displays **EL1-C5-A5-DWLtr.docx**.)
5. Move the insertion point between the two paragraphs of text.
6. Click the Paste button arrow and then click *Paste Special* at the drop-down list.
7. At the Paste Special dialog box, look at the options available and click the *Paste link* option, click *Microsoft Excel Worksheet Object* in the *As* list box, and then click OK.
8. Save, print, and then close **EL1-C5-A5-DWLtr.docx**.
9. Click the Excel button on the Taskbar.
10. Make cell A3 active and then change the number from *$300,000* to *$400,000*. Copy the number in cell A3 down to cells A4 through A10. (Cells A3 through A10 should now contain the amount *$400,000*.) Select cells A4 through A10 and then apply accounting formatting with no dollars signs and no places after the decimal point.
11. Save, print, and then close **EL1-C5-A5-DWMortgages.xlsx**.
12. Click the Word button on the Taskbar.
13. Open **EL1-C5-A5-DWLtr.docx**. At the message that displays asking if you want to update the data from the linked files, click Yes.
14. Save, print, and then close **EL1-C5-A5-DWLtr.docx**.
15. Close Word.

Visual Benchmark Demonstrate Your Proficiency

CREATE AND FORMAT A SALES WORKSHEET USING FORMULAS

1. At a blank workbook, create the worksheet shown in Figure 5.10 with the following specifications:
   - Do not type the data in cells D4 through D9. Instead, enter a formula that totals the first-half and second-half yearly sales.
   - Apply the formatting shown in the figure, including changing font sizes, column widths, and row heights and inserting shading and border lines.
   - Rename the sheet tab and change the tab color as shown in the figure.
2. Copy cells A1 through D9 and then paste the cells in Sheet2.
3. Edit the cells and apply formatting so your worksheet matches the worksheet shown in Figure 5.11. Rename the sheet tab and change the tab color as shown in the figure.
4. Save the completed workbook and name it **EL1-C5-VB-CMSemiSales**.
5. Print both worksheets.
6. Close **EL1-C5-VB-CMSemiSales.xlsx**.

Figure 5.10 Sales 2014 Worksheet

	A	B	C	D
1	Clearline Manufacturing			
2	SEMIANNUAL SALES - 2014			
3	Customer	1st Half	2nd Half	Total
4	Lakeside Trucking	$ 84,300	$ 73,500	$ 157,800
5	Gresham Machines	33,000	40,500	73,500
6	Real Photography	30,890	35,465	66,355
7	Genesis Productions	72,190	75,390	147,580
8	Landower Company	22,000	15,000	37,000
9	Jewell Enterprises	19,764	50,801	70,565

Sales 2014 | Sales 2015

Figure 5.11 Sales 2015 Worksheet

	A	B	C	D
1	Clearline Manufacturing			
2	SEMIANNUAL SALES - 2015			
3	Customer	1st Half	2nd Half	Total
4	Lakeside Trucking	$ 84,300	$ 73,500	$ 157,800
5	Gresham Machines	33,000	40,500	73,500
6	Real Photography	20,750	15,790	36,540
7	Genesis Productions	51,270	68,195	119,465
8	Landower Company	22,000	15,000	37,000
9	Jewell Enterprises	14,470	33,770	48,240

Sales 2014 | Sales 2015

Case Study Apply Your Skills

Part 1

You are an administrator for Gateway Global, an electronics manufacturing corporation. You are gathering information on money spent on supplies and equipment purchases. You have gathered information for the first quarter of the year and decide to create a workbook containing worksheets for monthly information. To do this, create a worksheet that contains the following information:

- Company name is Gateway Global.
- Create the title *January Expenditures*.
- Create the columns shown in Figure 5.12.

Figure 5.12 Case Study Part 1

Department	Supplies	Equipment	Total
Production	$25,425	$135,500	
Technical Support	$14,500	$65,000	
Finance	$5,790	$22,000	
Sales and Marketing	$35,425	$8,525	
Facilities	$6,000	$1,200	
Total			

- Insert a formula in the *Total* column that sums the amounts in the *Supplies* and *Equipment* columns and insert a formula in the *Total* row that sums the supplies amounts, equipment amounts, and total amounts.
- Apply formatting such as fill color, borders, font color, and shading to enhance the appearance of the worksheet.

After creating and formatting the worksheet, complete the following:

- Insert a new worksheet and then copy the data in Sheet1 to Sheet2.
- Insert a new worksheet and then copy the data in Sheet1 to Sheet3.
- Make the following changes to data in Sheet2:
  - Change *January Expenditures* to *February Expenditures*.
  - Change the Production department supplies amount to *$38,550* and the equipment amount to *$88,500*.
  - Change the Technical Support department equipment amount to *$44,250*.
  - Change the Finance department supplies amount to *$7,500*.
- Make the following changes to data in Sheet3:
  - Change *January Expenditures* to *March Expenditures*.
  - Change the Production department supplies amount to *$65,000* and the equipment amount to *$150,000*.
  - Change the Technical Support department supplies amount to *$21,750* and the equipment amount to *$43,525*.
  - Change the Facilities department equipment amount to *$18,450*.

Create a new worksheet that summarizes the supplies and equipment totals for January, February, and March. Apply the same formatting to the worksheet as you applied to the other three. Change the tab name for Sheet1 to *Jan. Expenditures*, the tab name for Sheet2 to *Feb. Expenditures*, the tab name for Sheet3 to *Mar. Expenditures*, and the tab name for Sheet4 to *Qtr. Summary*. Change the color of each tab. (You determine the colors.)

Insert a header that prints your name at the left side of each worksheet and the current date at the right side of each worksheet. Save the workbook and name it **EL1-C5-CS-GGExp**. Print all the worksheets in the workbook and then close the workbook.

Part 2

Help

Employees of Gateway Global have formed two intramural co-ed softball teams and you have volunteered to keep statistics for the players. Open **GGStats.xlsx** and then make the following changes to both worksheets in the workbook:

- Insert a formula that calculates a player's batting average (Hits / At Bats).
- Insert a formula that calculates a player's on-base percentage: (Walks + Hits) / (At Bats + Walks). Select cells E5 through F15 and then specify that you want to display three places after the decimal point.
- Insert the company name.
- Apply formatting to enhance the appearance of the worksheets.
- Horizontally and vertically center the worksheets.
- Insert a footer that prints on both worksheets and prints your name at the left side of the worksheet and the date at the right of the worksheet.

Use the Help feature to learn about applying cell styles or click the Cells Styles button in the Styles group on the HOME tab and then experiment with applying different styles. Apply the Good cell style to any cell in the *Batting Average* column with an average over .400. Apply this style to cells in both worksheets. Save the workbook and name it **EL1-C5-CS-GGStats**. Print both worksheets and then close **EL1-C5-CS-GGStats.xlsx**.

Part 3

Many of the suppliers for Gateway Global are international and use metric measurements. The purchasing manager has asked you to prepare a worksheet in Excel that converts length measurements..

Use the Internet to locate information on converting the following length measurements:

- 1 inch to centimeters
- 1 foot to centimeters
- 1 yard to meters
- 1 mile to kilometers

Locate a site on the Internet that provides the formula for converting Fahrenheit temperatures to Celsius temperatures and then create another worksheet in the workbook with the following information:

- Insert Fahrenheit temperatures beginning with 0 and continuing to 100 in increments of 5 (for example, 0, 5, 10, 15, and so on).
- Insert a formula that converts the Fahrenheit temperature to a Celsius temperature.

Include the company name, Gateway Global, in both worksheets. Apply additional formatting to improve the appearance of both worksheets. Rename both sheet names and apply a color to each tab. (You determine the names and colors.) Save the workbook and name it **EL1-C5-CS-GGConv**. Print both worksheets centered horizontally and vertically on the page and then close **EL1-C5-CS-GGConv.xlsx**.

Part 4

Open Microsoft Word and then create a letterhead document that contains the company name, *Gateway Global*; the address (you decide the street address, city, state, and ZIP code or street address, city, province, and postal code); and the telephone number (you decide). Apply formatting to improve the appearance of the letterhead. Save the document and name it **EL1-C5-CS-GGLtrhd**. Save the document again and name it **EL1-C5-CS-GGConvLtr**.

In Excel, open **EL1-C5-CS-GGConv.xlsx** (the workbook you created in Part 3). In the Fahrenheit conversion worksheet, copy the cells containing data and then paste the cells in **EL1-C5-CS-GGConvLtr.docx** as a picture object. Center the cells (picture object) between the left and right margins. Save, print, and then close **EL1-C5-CS-GGConvLtr.docx**. Close Microsoft Word and then in Excel close **EL1-C5-CS-GGConv.xlsx**.

MICROSOFT® EXCEL®

CHAPTER 6

Maintaining Workbooks

PERFORMANCE OBJECTIVES

Upon successful completion of Chapter 6, you will be able to:

- **Create and rename a folder**
- **Delete workbooks and folders**
- **Copy and move workbooks within and between folders**
- **Copy and move worksheets between workbooks**
- **Maintain consistent formatting with styles**
- **Insert, modify, and remove hyperlinks**
- **Create financial forms using templates**

SNAP

Tutorials

6.1 Maintaining Workbooks
6.2 Managing Folders
6.3 Managing the Recent Workbooks List
6.4 Managing Worksheets
6.5 Formatting with Cell Styles
6.6 Inserting Hyperlinks
6.7 Using Excel Templates

Once you have been working with Excel for a period of time, you will have accumulated several workbook files. You should organize your workbooks into folders to facilitate fast retrieval of information. Occasionally, you should perform file maintenance activities, such as copying, moving, renaming, and deleting workbooks, to ensure the workbook lists in your various folders are manageable. You will learn these file management tasks in this chapter, along with creating and applying styles to a workbook, inserting hyperlinks in a workbook, and using an Excel template to create a workbook. Model answers for this chapter's projects appear on the following pages.

Excel
EL1C6

Note: Before beginning the projects, copy to your storage medium the EL1C6 subfolder from the EL1 folder on the CD that accompanies this textbook and then make EL1C6 the active folder.

Student Name 1 9/22/2015

Hilltop
Equipment Rental

Equipment		
Front Loader		
	Hours available	1725
	Hours in use	1446
Forklift		
	Hours available	1730
	Hours in use	1485
Tractor		
	Hours available	1720
	Hours in use	1441
Backhoe		
	Hours available	1745
	Hours in use	1422

Equipment Hours Tab

Student Name 2 9/22/2015

Hilltop
Equipment Rental

Equipment Usage - Front Loader

Hours	1st Qtr.	2nd Qtr.	3rd Qtr.	4th Qtr.
Total hours available	434	425	440	426
Avoidable delays	11	9	11	9
Unavoidable delays	8	14	7	11
Repairs	10	4	12	7
Servicing	5	10	8	11
Unassigned	32	24	36	40
In use	368	364	366	348

Front Loader Tab

Student Name 3 9/22/2015

Hilltop
Equipment Rental

Equipment Usage - Forklift

Hours	1st Qtr.	2nd Qtr.	3rd Qtr.	4th Qtr.
Total hours available	436	440	428	426
Avoidable delays	12	8	5	8
Unavoidable delays	7	10	10	5
Repairs	4	9	12	3
Servicing	12	6	12	8
Unassigned	32	21	32	29
In use	369	386	357	373

Forklift Tab

Project 2 Copy and Move Worksheets into an Equipment Rental Workbook EL1-C6-P2-HEREquip.xlsx

Student Name 4 9/22/2015

Hilltop
Equipment Rental

Equipment Usage - Tractor

Hours	1st Qtr.	2nd Qtr.	3rd Qtr.	4th Qtr.
Total hours available	450	420	435	415
Avoidable delays	10	8	14	25
Unavoidable delays	16	12	8	10
Repairs	4	8	6	12
Servicing	6	4	4	8
Unassigned	24	28	36	36
In use	390	360	367	324

Tractor Tab

Student Name 5 9/22/2015

Hilltop
Equipment Rental

Equipment Usage - Backhoe

Hours	1st Qtr.	2nd Qtr.	3rd Qtr.	4th Qtr.
Total hours available	450	435	440	420
Avoidable delays	14	10	8	15
Unavoidable delays	12	8	12	12
Repairs	8	5	14	8
Servicing	10	8	10	4
Unassigned	62	32	26	45
In use	344	372	370	336

Backhoe Tab

O'Rourke Enterprises

Maintenance Department - Weekly Payroll

Employee	Hrly. Rate	Hours	Gross	W/H Tax	SS Tax	Net
Williams, Pamela	$ 43.00	40	$ 1,720.00	$ 481.60	$ 131.58	$ 1,106.82
Ternes, Reynaldo	41.50	40	1,660.00	464.80	126.99	1,068.21
Sinclair, Jason	38.00	30	1,140.00	319.20	87.21	733.59
Pierson, Rhea	38.00	40	1,520.00	425.60	116.28	978.12
Nyegaard, James	25.00	25	625.00	175.00	47.81	402.19
Lunde, Beverly	21.00	40	840.00	235.20	64.26	540.54

Withholding rate	28%
Social Security rate	7.65%

Weekly Payroll Tab

Project 3 Create and Apply Styles to a Payroll Workbook
EL1-C6-P3-OEPayroll.xlsx

O'Rourke Enterprises

Invoices

Invoice #	Customer #	Date	Amount	Tax	Amount Due
1001	34002	4/2/2012	$ 450.00	8.50%	$ 488.25
1002	12034	4/4/2012	1,075.00	8.80%	1,169.60
1003	40059	4/6/2012	225.00	0.00%	225.00
1004	23002	4/10/2012	750.00	8.50%	813.75
1005	59403	4/10/2012	350.00	0.00%	350.00
1006	80958	4/11/2012	875.00	8.50%	949.38
1007	23494	4/13/2012	750.00	8.50%	813.75
1008	45232	4/17/2012	560.00	8.80%	609.28
1009	76490	4/18/2012	400.00	0.00%	400.00
1010	45466	4/19/2012	600.00	8.50%	651.00
1011	34094	4/23/2012	95.00	0.00%	95.00
1012	45450	4/25/2012	2,250.00	8.50%	2,441.25
1013	23044	4/26/2012	225.00	8.80%	244.80
1014	48933	4/30/2012	140.00	0.00%	140.00

Invoices Tab

O'Rourke Enterprises

Overdue Accounts

Customer	Account #	Amount Due	Purchase Date	Terms	Due Date
Alliance Corporation	342	$ 8,540	4/2/2015	15	4/17/2015
Taylor-Brown Products	112	15,400	4/4/2015	30	5/4/2015
Meridian Center	543	1,525	4/11/2015	15	4/26/2015
Bower Consultants	322	3,000	4/14/2015	15	4/29/2015
Action Manufacturing	655	6,225	4/16/2015	30	5/16/2015
Summit Trading	223	2,500	4/23/2015	15	5/8/2015

Overdue Accounts Tab

O'Rourke Enterprises

Skid Lifter Purchase Plans

Equipment	Purchase Price	Interest Rate	Term in Months	Monthly Payments	Total Payments	Total Interest
Manual Skid Lifter Model MSL-J03	$ 7,500.00	7.50%	60	$ (150.28)	$ 9,017.08	$ 1,517.08
Manual Skid Lifter Model MSL-K10	10,995.00	7.50%	60	(220.32)	13,219.03	2,224.03
Electric Skid Lifter Model ESL-A12	20,575.00	7.50%	60	(412.28)	24,736.85	4,161.85
Electric Skid Lifter Model ESL-B15	24,950.00	7.50%	60	(499.95)	29,996.81	5,046.81

Sheet 1

EL1-C6-P3-OEPlans.xlsx

Pyramid Sales

Facilities Account

First Quarter Summary

	January	February	March
Checks amount	$ 15,102.00	$ 14,613.79	$ 12,195.96
Deposits amount	$ 12,600.00	$ 12,600.00	$ 12,600.00
End-of-month balance	$ 2,394.50	$ 380.71	$ 380.71

Customer sales analysis

Summary Tab

Project 4 Insert, Modify, and Remove Hyperlinks

EL1-C6-P4-PSAccts.xlsx

IN-FLOW SYSTEMS

320 Milander Way
P.O. Box 2300
Boston, MA 02188

Phone: (617) 555-3900
Fax: (617) 555-3945
E-mail: someone@example.com

Statement

Statement #: 5432
Date: September 22, 2015 2
Customer ID: 25-345

Bill To: Aidan Mackenzie
Stanfield Enterprises
9921 South 42nd Avenue
P.O. Box 5540
Boston, MA 02193

Date	Type	Invoice #	Description	Amount	Payment	Balance
9/22/2015	System Unit	7452	Calibration Unit	$ 950.00	$ 200.00	$ 750.00
					Total	$ 750.00

Reminder: Please include the statement number on your check.

Terms: Balance due in 30 days.

REMITTANCE	
Customer Name:	Stanfield Enterprises
Customer ID:	25-345
Statement #:	5432
Date:	September 22, 2015
Amount Due:	$750.00 2
Amount Enclosed:	$750.00

Page 1

Billing Statement

Project 5 Create a Billing Statement Workbook Using a Template

EL1-C6-P5-Billing.xlsx

Project 1 Manage Workbooks

8 Parts

You will perform a variety of file management tasks, including creating and renaming a folder; selecting and then deleting, copying, cutting, pasting, and renaming workbooks; deleting a folder; and opening, printing, and closing a workbook.

Maintaining Workbooks

You can complete many workbook management tasks at the Open and Save As dialog boxes. These tasks include copying, moving, printing, and renaming workbooks; opening multiple workbooks; and creating and renaming new folders. Perform some file maintenance tasks, such as creating a folder and deleting files, with options from the Organize button drop-down list or a shortcut menu and navigate to folders using the Address bar. The elements of the Open dialog box are identified in Figure 6.1.

Figure 6.1 Open Dialog Box

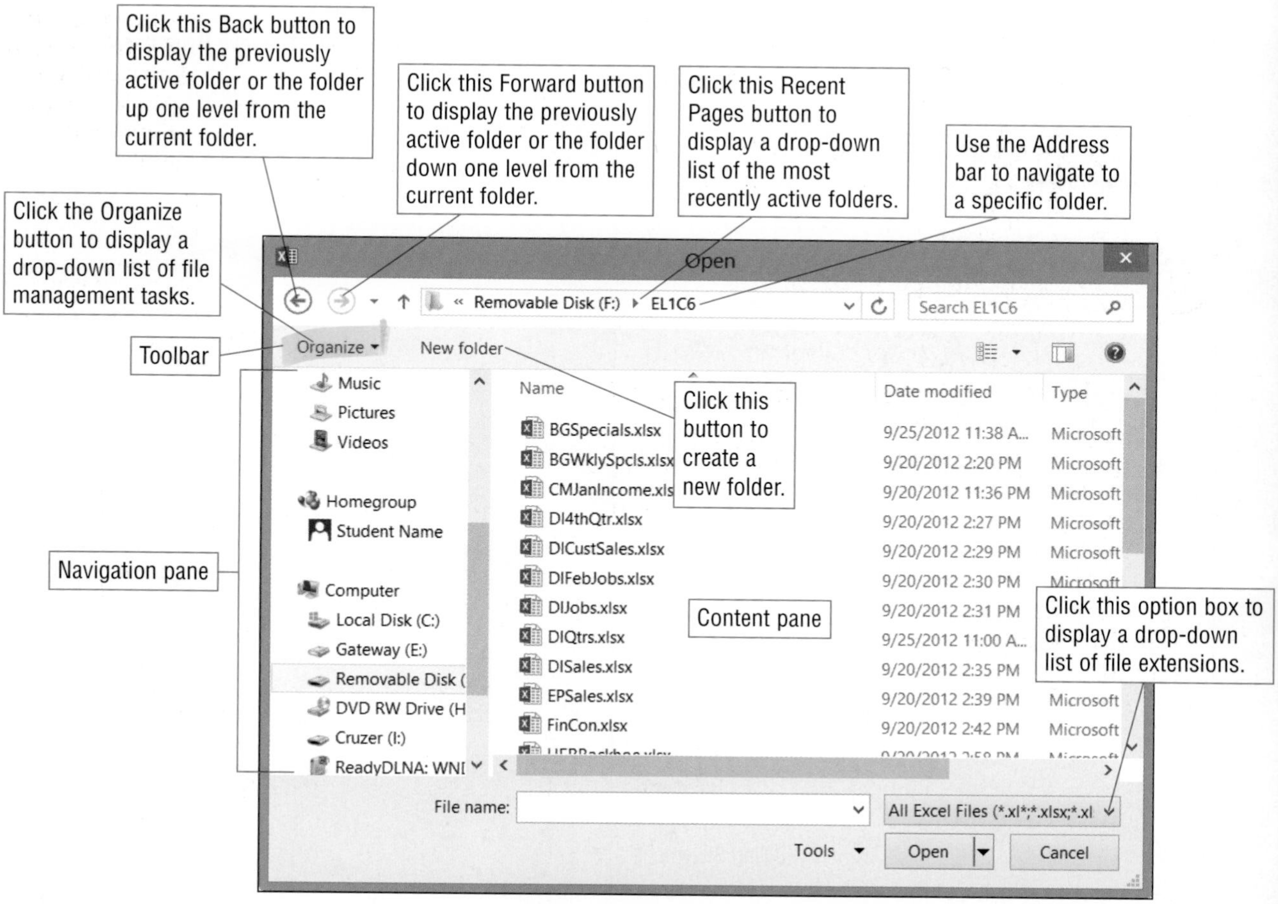

Directions and projects in this chapter assume that you are managing workbooks and folders on a USB flash drive or your computer's hard drive. If you are using your SkyDrive, some of the workbook and folder management tasks may vary.

Creating a Folder

In Excel, you should logically group and store workbooks in ***folders***. For example, you could store all of the workbooks related to one department in one folder with the department name being the folder name. You can also create a folder within a folder (called a ***subfolder***). If you create workbooks for a department by individuals, each individual name could have a subfolder within the department folder. The main folder on a disk or drive is called the root folder. You create additional folders as branches of this root folder.

At the Open dialog box and Save As dialog box, workbook file names display in the Content pane preceded by workbook icons and folder names display preceded by folder icons. Create a new folder by clicking the New folder button located in the toolbar at the Open dialog box or Save As dialog box. This inserts a new folder in the Content pane. Type the name for the folder and then press Enter.

A folder name can contain a maximum of 255 characters. Numbers, spaces, and symbols can be used in the folder name, except those symbols identified in the Saving a Workbook section in Chapter 1.

Quick Steps

Create a Folder
1. Press Ctrl + F12 to display the Open dialog box.
2. Click New folder button.
3. Type folder name.
4. Press Enter.

New folder

HINT

Change the default folder with the *Default local file location* option at the Excel Options dialog box with *Save* selected in the left panel.

Project 1a **Creating a Folder** **Part 1 of 8**

1. With Excel open, create a folder named *Payroll* on your storage medium by completing the following steps:
   a. Press Ctrl + F12 to display the Open dialog box.
   b. At the Open dialog box, navigate to your storage medium.
2. Double-click the *EL1C6* folder name to make it the active folder.
3. Click the New folder button on the toolbar.
4. Type **Payroll** and then press Enter.
5. Close the Open dialog box.

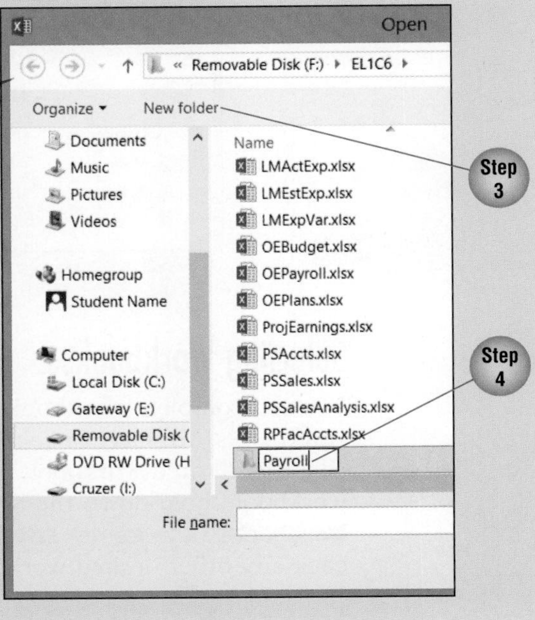

Renaming a Folder

Quick Steps

Rename a Folder

1. Display Open dialog box.
2. Click desired folder.
3. Click Organize button.
4. Click *Rename* at drop-down list.
5. Type new name.
6. Press Enter.

OR

1. Display Open dialog box.
2. Right-click folder name.
3. Click *Rename*.
4. Type new name.
5. Press Enter.

Organize

As you organize your files and folders, you may decide to rename a folder. Rename a folder using the Organize button in the Open dialog box or using a shortcut menu. To rename a folder using the Organize button, display the Open dialog box, click in the Content pane the folder you want to rename, click the Organize button located on the toolbar, and then click *Rename* at the drop-down list. This selects the folder name and inserts a border around the name. Type the new name for the folder and then press Enter. To rename a folder using a shortcut menu, display the Open dialog box, right-click the folder name in the Content pane, and then click *Rename* at the shortcut menu. Type a new name for the folder and then press Enter.

A tip to remember when you are organizing files and folders is to make sure your system is set up to display all of the files in a particular folder and not just the Excel files, for example. You can display all files in a folder in the Open dialog box by clicking the button to the right of the *File name* text box and then clicking *All Files (*.*)* at the drop-down list.

Project 1b **Renaming a Folder** **Part 2 of 8**

1. Press Ctrl + F12 to display the Open dialog box and make sure the EL1C6 folder is the active folder.
2. Right-click the *Payroll* folder name in the Content pane.
3. Click *Rename* at the shortcut menu.
4. Type Finances and then press Enter.

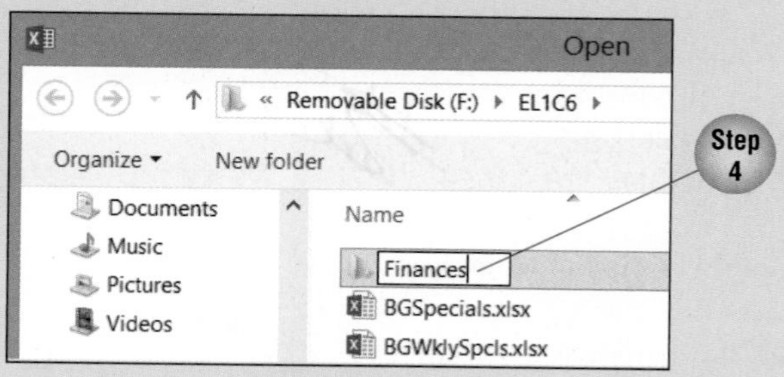

Selecting Workbooks

You can complete workbook management tasks on one workbook or selected workbooks. To select one workbook, display the Open dialog box and then click the desired workbook. To select several adjacent workbooks, click the first workbook, hold down the Shift key, and then click the last workbook. To select workbooks that are not adjacent, click the first workbook, hold down the Ctrl key, click any other desired workbooks, and then release the Ctrl key.

Deleting Workbooks and Folders

At some point, you may want to delete certain workbooks from your storage medium or any other drive or folder in which you may be working. To delete a workbook, display the Open or Save As dialog box, click the workbook in the Content pane, click the Organize button, and then click *Delete* at the drop-down list. If you are deleting a file from a removable storage medium such as a USB drive, a message will display asking you to confirm the deletion. At this message, click the Yes button. To delete a workbook using a shortcut menu, display the Open dialog box, right-click the workbook name in the Content pane, and then click *Delete* at the shortcut menu. If you are deleting a file from a removable storage medium such as a USB flash drive, click Yes at the confirmation dialog box.

Quick Steps

Delete a Workbook or Folder

1. Display Open dialog box.
2. Right-click workbook or folder name.
3. Click *Delete*.
4. If deleting from a removable drive, click Yes.

Deleting to the Recycle Bin

Workbooks deleted from a removable drive are deleted permanently while workbooks deleted from the hard drive are automatically sent to the Windows Recycle Bin. You can easily restore a deleted workbook from the Recycle Bin. To free space on the drive, empty the Recycle Bin on a periodic basis. Restoring a workbook from or emptying the contents of the Recycle Bin is completed at the Windows desktop (not in Excel). To display the Recycle Bin, minimize the Excel window and then double-click the Recycle Bin icon located on the Windows desktop. At the Recycle Bin, you can restore file(s) and empty the Recycle Bin.

Project 1c **Selecting and Deleting Workbooks** **Part 3 of 8**

1. At the Open dialog box, open **RPFacAccts.xlsx** (located in the EL1C6 folder).
2. Save the workbook with Save As and name it **EL1-C6-P1-RPFacAccts**.
3. Close **EL1-C6-P1-RPFacAccts.xlsx**.
4. Delete **EL1-C6-P1-RPFacAccts.xlsx** by completing the following steps:
   a. Display the Open dialog box with the EL1C6 folder the active folder.
   b. Click ***EL1-C6-P1-RPFacAccts.xlsx*** to select it.
   c. Click the Organize button and then click *Delete* at the drop-down list.
   d. If a message displays asking if you are sure you want to delete the worksheet, click Yes.

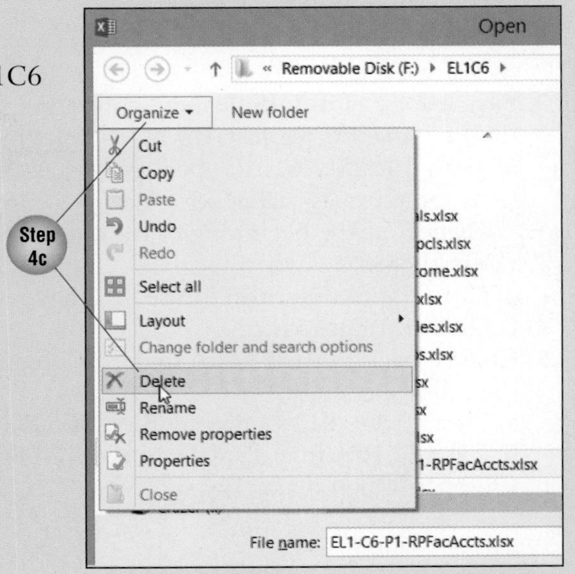

5. Delete selected workbooks by completing the following steps:
   a. Click ***DICustSales.xlsx*** in the Content pane.
   b. Hold down the Shift key and then click ***DIJobs.xlsx***.
   c. Position the mouse pointer on one of the selected workbooks and then click the right mouse button.
   d. At the shortcut menu that displays, click *Delete*.
   e. If a message displays asking if you are sure you want to delete the items, click Yes.
6. Close the Open dialog box.

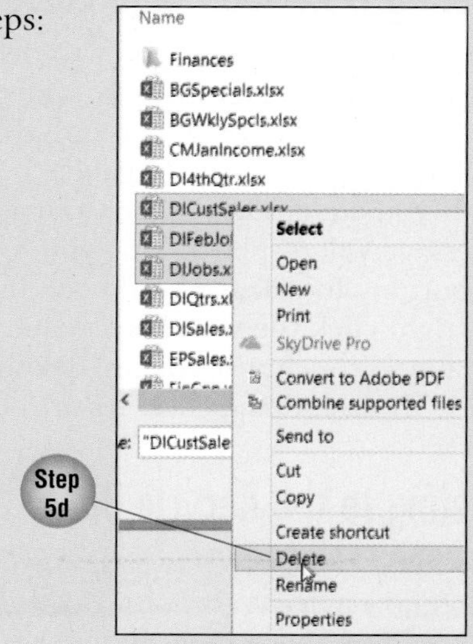

Copying Workbooks

In previous chapters, you have been opening a workbook from your storage medium and saving it with a new name in the same location. This process makes an exact copy of the workbook, preserving the original file on your storage medium. You can also copy a workbook into another folder.

Project 1d **Saving a Copy of an Open Workbook to Another Folder** **Part 4 of 8**

1. Open **EPSales.xlsx**.
2. Save the workbook with Save As and name it **TotalSales**. (Make sure the EL1C6 folder is the active folder.)
3. Save a copy of **TotalSales.xlsx** in the Finances folder you created in Project 1a (and renamed in Project 1b) by completing the following steps:
   a. With **TotalSales.xlsx** open, press F12 to display the Save As dialog box.
   b. At the Save As dialog box, change to the Finances folder. To do this, double-click *Finances* at the beginning of the Content pane. (Folders are listed before workbooks.)
   c. Click the Save button located in the lower right corner of the dialog box.
4. Close **TotalSales.xlsx**.
5. Change back to the EL1C6 folder by completing the following steps:
   a. Press Ctrl + F12 to display the Open dialog box.
   b. Click *EL1C6* that displays in the Address bar.
6. Close the Open dialog box.

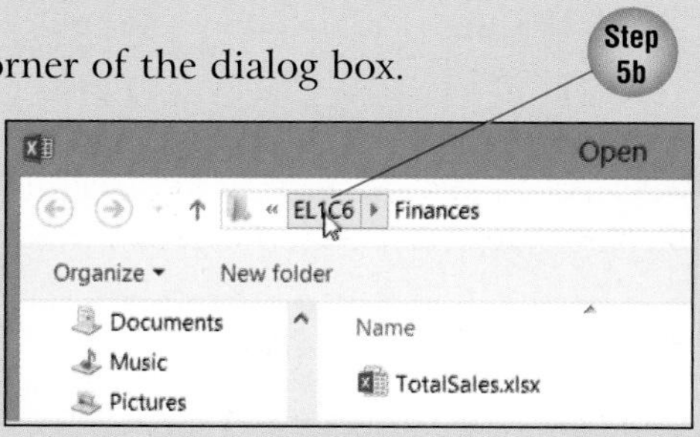

You can copy a workbook to another folder without opening the workbook first. To do this, use the *Copy* and *Paste* options from the shortcut menu at the Open dialog box or the Save As dialog box. You can also copy a workbook or selected workbooks into the same folder. When you do this, Excel adds a hyphen followed by the word *Copy* to the end of the document name.

To move or copy files or folders on your SkyDrive, go to skydrive.com, make sure you are logged in to your account, and then use the skydrive.com toolbar to move a workbook or folder to another location or copy and then move a workbook or folder to another location.

Quick Steps

Copy a Workbook

1. Display Open or Save As dialog box.
2. Right-click workbook name.
3. Click *Copy*.
4. Navigate to desired folder.
5. Right-click blank area in Content pane.
6. Click *Paste*.

Project 1e **Copying a Workbook at the Open Dialog Box** **Part 5 of 8**

Note: If you are using your SkyDrive, the steps for copying, cutting, and pasting workbooks will vary from the steps in Project 1e and 1f. Please check with your instructor.

1. Copy **CMJanIncome.xlsx** to the Finances folder. To begin, display the Open dialog box with the EL1C6 folder active.
2. Position the arrow pointer on **CMJanIncome.xlsx**, click the right mouse button, and then click *Copy* at the shortcut menu.
3. Change to the Finances folder by double-clicking *Finances* at the beginning of the Content pane.
4. Position the arrow pointer in any blank area in the Content pane, click the right mouse button, and then click *Paste* at the shortcut menu.
5. Change back to the EL1C6 folder by clicking *EL1C6* that displays in the Address bar.
6. Close the Open dialog box.

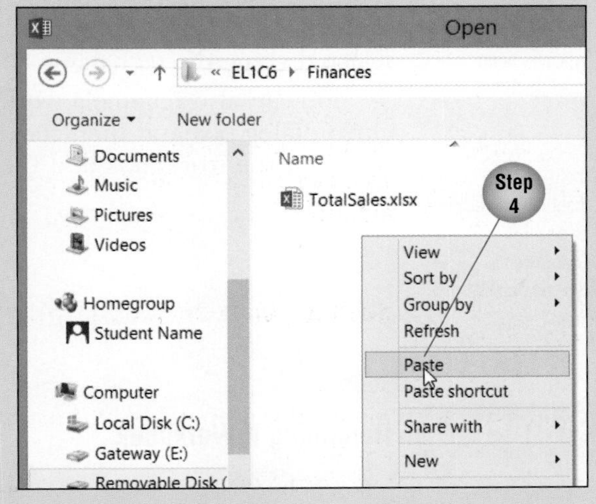

Sending Workbooks to a Different Drive or Folder

You can copy a workbook to another folder or drive without having to navigate to the new location. With the *Send to* option, you can send a copy of a workbook to another drive or folder. To use this option, position the arrow pointer on the workbook you want to copy, click the right mouse button, point to *Send to* (which causes a side menu to display), and then click the desired drive or folder.

Cutting and Pasting a Workbook

You can remove a workbook from one folder and insert it in another folder using the *Cut* and *Paste* options from the shortcut menu at the Open dialog box. To do this, display the Open dialog box, position the arrow pointer on the workbook to be removed (cut), click the right mouse button, and then click *Cut* at the shortcut menu. Change to the desired folder or drive, position the arrow pointer in any blank area in the Content pane, click the right mouse button, and then click *Paste* at the shortcut menu.

Quick Steps

Move a Workbook

1. Display Open dialog box.
2. Right-click workbook name.
3. Click *Cut*.
4. Navigate to desired folder.
5. Right-click blank area in Content pane.
6. Click *Paste*.

Project 1f Cutting and Pasting a Workbook — Part 6 of 8

1. Display the Open dialog box with the EL1C6 folder active.
2. Position the arrow pointer on **FinCon.xlsx**, click the right mouse button, and then click *Cut* at the shortcut menu.
3. Double-click *Finances* to make it the active folder.
4. Position the arrow pointer in any blank area in the Content pane, click the right mouse button, and then click *Paste* at the shortcut menu.
5. Click *EL1C6* that displays in the Address bar.

Quick Steps

Rename a Workbook
1. Display Open dialog box.
2. Click desired workbook.
3. Click Organize button.
4. Click *Rename.*
5. Type new name.
6. Press Enter.

OR
1. Display Open dialog box.
2. Right-click workbook name.
3. Click *Rename.*
4. Type new name.
5. Press Enter.

Renaming Workbooks

At the Open dialog box, use the *Rename* option from the Organize button drop-down list or the shortcut menu to give a workbook a different name. The *Rename* option changes the name of the workbook and keeps it in the same folder. To use *Rename*, display the Open dialog box, click once on the workbook to be renamed, click the Organize button, and then click *Rename* at the drop-down list. This causes a thin black border to surround the workbook name and the name to be selected. Type the new name and then press Enter.

You can also rename a workbook by right-clicking the workbook name at the Open dialog box and then clicking *Rename* at the shortcut menu. Type the new name for the workbook and then press the Enter key.

Project 1g Renaming a Workbook — Part 7 of 8

1. Make sure the Open dialog box displays with the EL1C6 folder the active folder.
2. Double-click *Finances* to make it the active folder.
3. Click once on ***FinCon.xlsx*** to select it.
4. Click the Organize button on the toolbar.
5. Click *Rename* at the drop-down list.
6. Type Analysis and then press the Enter key.

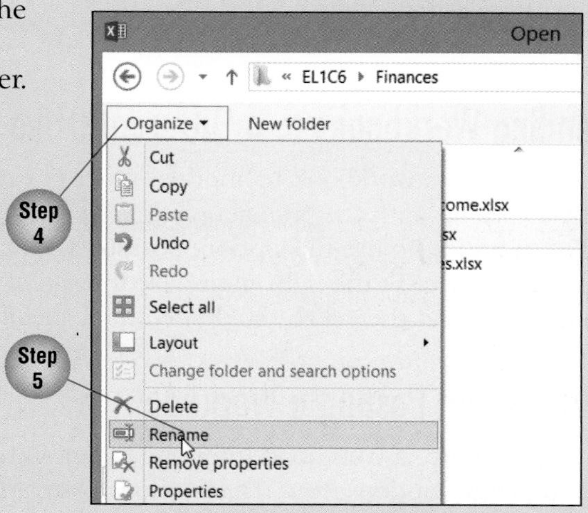

7. Complete steps similar to those in Steps 3 through 6 to rename **CMJanIncome.xlsx** to **CMJanProfits**.
8. Click the Back button (displays as *Back to EL1C6*) at the left side of the Address bar.

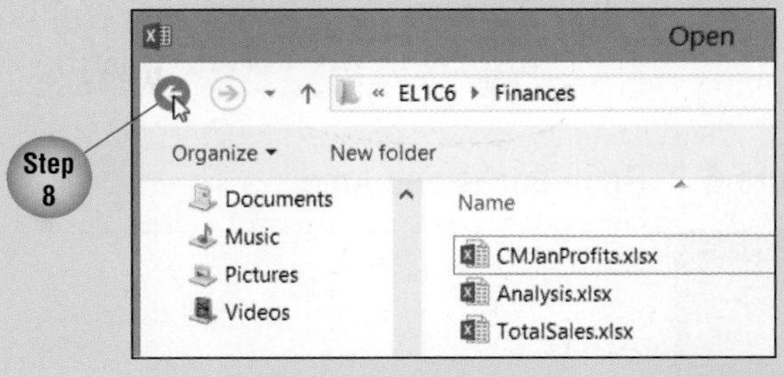

Deleting a Folder and Its Contents

As you learned earlier in this chapter, you can delete a workbook or selected workbooks. In addition to workbooks, you can delete a folder and all of its contents. Delete a folder in the same manner as you delete a workbook.

Project 1h Deleting a Folder and Its Contents — Part 8 of 8

1. Make sure the Open dialog box displays with the EL1C6 folder active.
2. Right-click the *Finances* folder name in the Content pane.
3. Click *Delete* at the shortcut menu.
4. If you are deleting the folder from a removable drive, click Yes at the message that displays asking if you want to delete the folder.
5. Close the Open dialog box.

Project 2 Copy and Move Worksheets into an Equipment Rental Workbook — 3 Parts

You will manage workbooks at the Open backstage area and then open multiple workbooks and copy and move worksheets between the workbooks.

Managing the Recent Workbooks List

When you open and close workbooks, Excel keeps a list of the most recently opened workbooks. To view this list, click the FILE tab and then click the *Open* option. This displays the Open backstage area, similar to what you see in Figure 6.2. (Your workbook names may vary from what you see in the figure.) The most recently opened workbook names display in the Recent Workbooks list, which displays when the *Recent Workbooks* option is selected. The most recently accessed folder names display in the Recent Folders list, which displays when the *Computer* option is selected. Generally, the 25 most recently opened workbook names display in the Recent Workbooks list. To open a workbook, scroll down the list and then click the desired workbook name.

The Excel opening screen contains a Recent list that displays the most recently opened workbooks. The workbook names in the Recent list are the same that display in the Recent Workbooks list at the Open backstage area.

Figure 6.2 Open Backstage Area

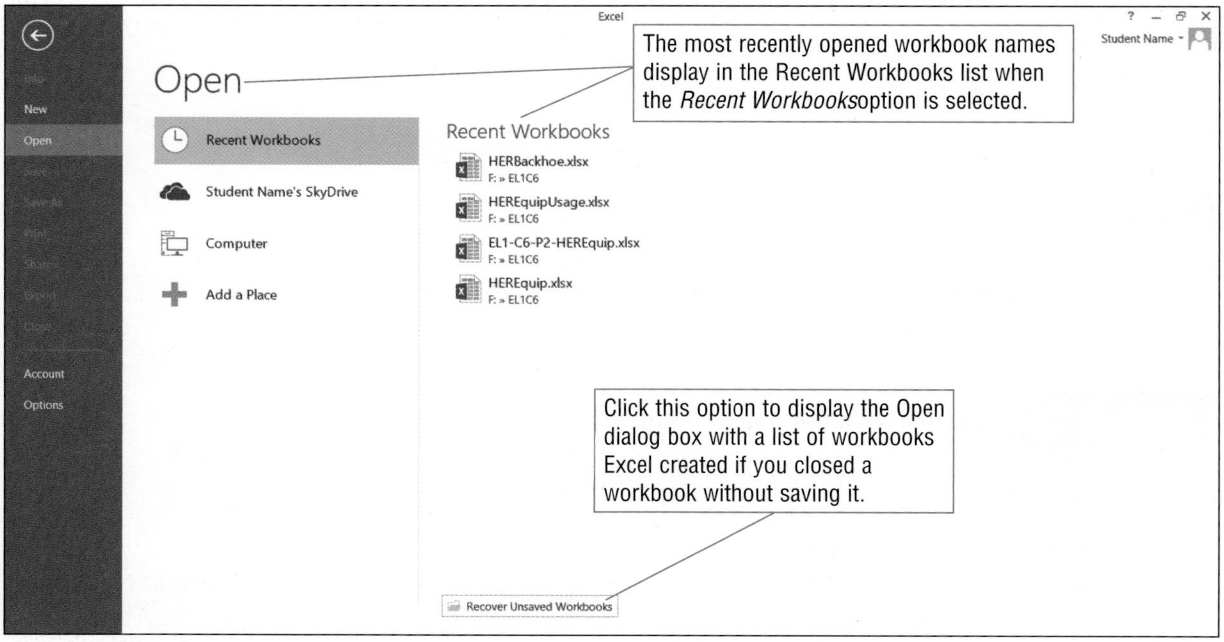

Pinning a Workbook

If you want a workbook name to remain at the top of the Recent Workbooks list, at the Open backstage area or the Recent list at the Excel opening screen "pin" the workbook name. To do this, click the gray pin that displays at the right side of the workbook name. This changes the left-pointing pin to a down-pointing pin. The next time you display the Open backstage area or the Excel opening screen, the workbook name you pinned displays at the top of the list. To "unpin" a workbook name, click the down-pointing pin to change it to a left-pointing pin. You can also pin a workbook name to the Recent Workbooks list or Recent list by right-clicking the workbook name and then clicking *Pin to list* at the shortcut menu. To unpin the workbook name, right-click the workbook name and then click *Unpin from list* at the shortcut menu.

Recovering an Unsaved Workbook

If you close a workbook without saving it, you can recover it with the *Recover Unsaved Workbooks* option located below the Recent Workbooks list. Click this option and the Open dialog box displays with workbook names that Excel automatically saved. At this dialog box, double-click the desired workbook name to open the workbook.

Clearing the Recent Workbooks List and the Recent List

Clear the contents (except pinned workbooks) of the Recent Workbooks list or Recent list by right-clicking a workbook name in the list and then clicking *Clear unpinned Workbooks* at the shortcut menu. At the message asking if you are sure you want to remove the items, click the Yes button. To clear a folder in the Recent Folders list, right-click a folder in the list and then click *Remove from list* at the shortcut menu.

Project 2a **Managing Workbooks at the Open Backstage Area** **Part 1 of 3**

1. Close any open workbooks.
2. Click the FILE tab and then click the *Open* option.
3. Make sure the *Recent Workbooks* option is selected. Notice the workbook names that display in the Recent Workbooks list.
4. Navigate to the EL1C6 folder on your storage medium, open **HEREquip.xlsx**, and then save the workbook with Save As and name it **EL1-C6-P2-HEREquip**.
5. Close **EL1-C6-P2-HEREquip.xlsx**.
6. Open **HEREquipUsage.xlsx** and then close it.
7. Open **HERBackhoe.xlsx** and then close it.
8. Pin the three workbooks to the Recent Workbooks list (you will use them in Project 2b) by completing the following steps:
   a. Click the FILE tab and then make sure the *Open* option is selected. (This displays the Open backstage area with the *Recent Workbooks* option selected.)
   b. Click the left-pointing pin that displays at the right side of **EL1-C6-P2-HEREquip.xlsx**. (This rotates the pin from left pointing to down pointing.)

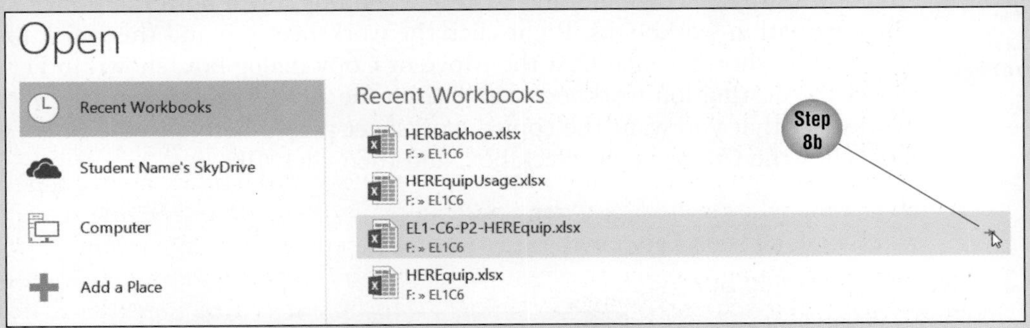

   c. Click the left-pointing pin that displays at the right side of **HEREquipUsage.xlsx**.

d. Right-click **HERBackhoe.xlsx** and then click *Pin to list* at the shortcut menu.
e. Click the Back button to exit the Open backstage area.

9. Open **EL1-C6-P2-HEREquip.xlsx** by clicking the FILE tab and then clicking ***EL1-C6-P2-HEREquip.xlsx*** in the Recent Workbooks list. (After clicking the FILE tab, make sure the *Open* option is selected. This displays the Open backstage area with *Recent Workbooks* selected.)

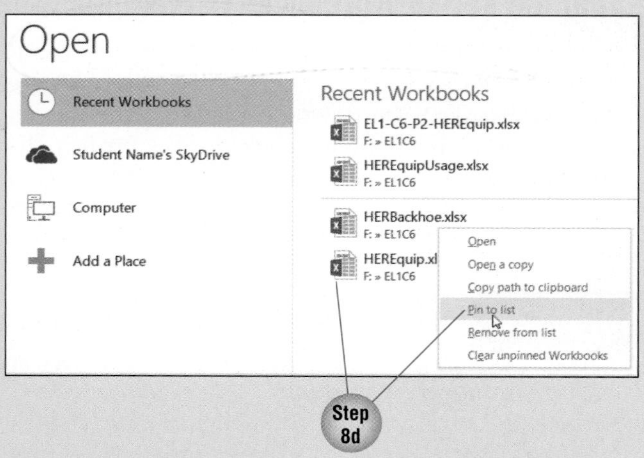

Managing Worksheets

Quick Steps

Copy a Worksheet to Another Workbook
1. Right-click desired sheet tab.
2. Click *Move or Copy*.
3. Select desired destination workbook.
4. Select desired worksheet location.
5. Click *Create a copy* check box.
6. Click OK.

You can move or copy individual worksheets within the same workbook or to another existing workbook. Exercise caution when moving sheets, since calculations or charts based on data in a worksheet might become inaccurate if you move the worksheet. To make a duplicate of a worksheet in the same workbook, hold down the Ctrl key and then drag the worksheet tab to the desired position.

Copying a Worksheet to Another Workbook

To copy a worksheet to another existing workbook, open both the source and the destination workbooks. Right-click the worksheet tab and then click *Move or Copy* at the shortcut menu. At the Move or Copy dialog box, shown in Figure 6.3, select the destination workbook name from the *To book* drop-down list, select the worksheet that you want the copied worksheet placed before in the *Before sheet* list box, click the *Create a copy* check box, and then click OK.

Figure 6.3 Move or Copy Dialog Box

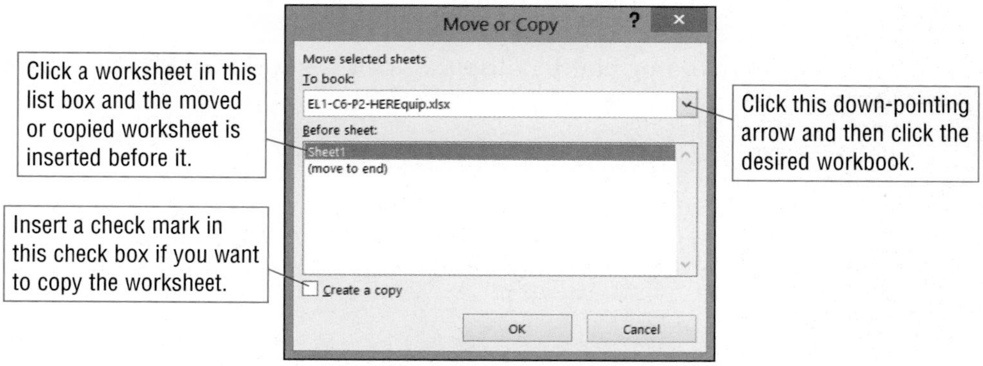

Project 2b Copying a Worksheet to Another Workbook

Part 2 of 3

1. With **EL1-C6-P2-HEREquip.xlsx** open, open **HEREquipUsage.xlsx**.
2. Copy the Front Loader worksheet by completing the following steps:
   a. With **HEREquipUsage.xlsx** the active workbook, right-click the Front Loader tab and then click *Move or Copy* at the shortcut menu.
   b. Click the down-pointing arrow next to the *To book* option box and then click ***EL1-C6-P2-HEREquip.xlsx*** at the drop-down list.
   c. Click *(move to end)* in the *Before sheet* list box.
   d. Click the *Create a copy* check box to insert a check mark.
   e. Click OK. (Excel switches to the **EL1-C6-P2-HEREquip.xlsx** workbook and inserts the copied Front Loader worksheet after Sheet1.)
3. Complete steps similar to those in Step 2 to copy the Tractor worksheet to the **EL1-C6-P2-HEREquip.xlsx** workbook.
4. Complete steps similar to those in Step 2 to copy the Forklift worksheet to the **EL1-C6-P2-HEREquip.xlsx** workbook and insert the Forklift worksheet before the Tractor worksheet.
5. Save **EL1-C6-P2-HEREquip.xlsx**.
6. Make **HEREquipUsage.xlsx** the active workbook and then close it.

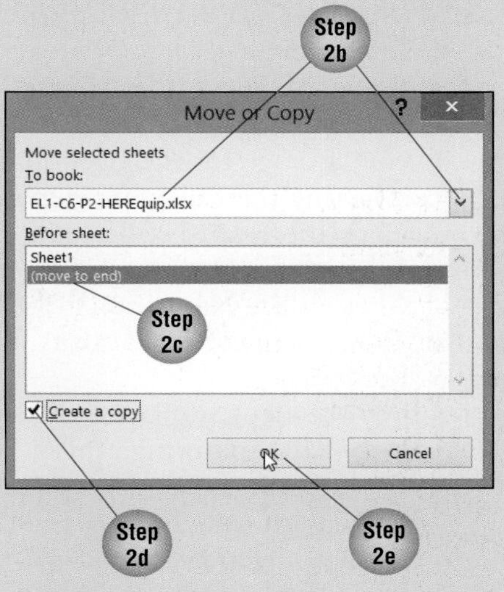

Moving a Worksheet to Another Workbook

To move a worksheet to another existing workbook, open both the source and the destination workbooks. Make active the worksheet you want to move in the source workbook, right-click the worksheet tab, and then click *Move or Copy* at the shortcut menu. At the Move or Copy dialog box, shown in Figure 6.3, select the destination workbook name from the *To book* drop-down list, select the worksheet before which you want the worksheet placed in the *Before sheet* list box, and then click OK. If you need to reposition a worksheet tab, drag the tab to the desired position.

Be careful when moving a worksheet to another workbook file. If formulas exist in the source workbook that depend on the contents of the cells in the worksheet that is moved, they will no longer calculate properly.

Quick Steps

Move a Worksheet to Another Workbook

1. Right-click desired worklsheet tab.
2. Click *Move or Copy*.
3. Select desired destination workbook.
4. Select desired worksheet location.
5. Click OK.

Project 2c Moving a Worksheet to Another Workbook

1. With **EL1-C6-P2-HEREquip.xlsx** open, open **HERBackhoe.xlsx**.
2. Move Sheet1 from **HERBackhoe.xlsx** to **EL1-C6-P2-HEREquip.xlsx** by completing the following steps:
   a. With **HERBackhoe.xlsx** the active workbook, right-click the Sheet1 tab and then click *Move or Copy* at the shortcut menu.
   b. Click the down-pointing arrow next to the *To book* option box and then click ***EL1-C6-P2-HEREquip.xlsx*** at the drop-down list.
   c. Click *(move to end)* in the *Before sheet* list box.
   d. Click OK.

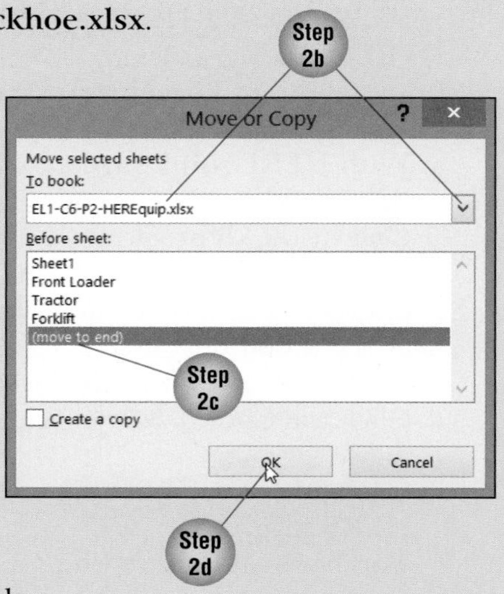

3. With **EL1-C6-P2-HEREquip.xlsx** open, make the following changes:
   a. Rename Sheet1 as *Equipment Hours*.
   b. Rename Sheet1 (2) as *Backhoe*.
4. Create a range for the front loader total hours available by completing the following steps:
   a. Click the Front Loader tab.
   b. Select cells B4 through E4.
   c. Click in the Name box.
   d. Type **FrontLoaderHours**.
   e. Press Enter.

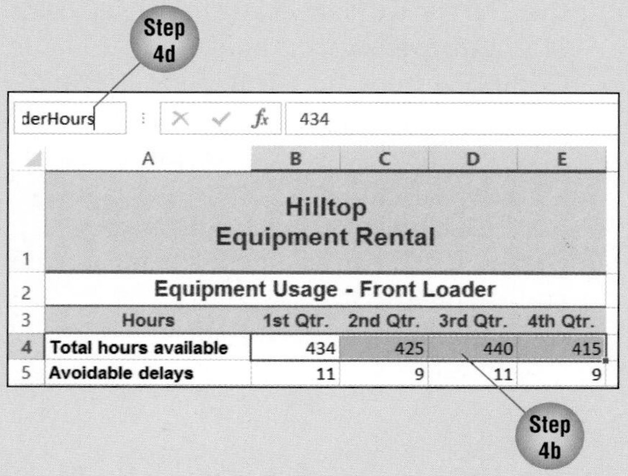

5. Complete steps similar to those in Step 4 to create the following ranges:
   a. In the Front Loader worksheet, create a range with cells B10 through E10 and name it *FrontLoaderHoursInUse*.
   b. Click the Forklift tab and then create a range with cells B4 through E4 and name it *ForkliftHours* and create a range with cells B10 through E10 and name it *ForkliftHoursInUse*.
   c. Click the Tractor tab and then create a range with cells B4 through E4 and name it *TractorHours* and create a range with cells B10 through E10 and name it *TractorHoursInUse*.
   d. Click the Backhoe tab and then create a range with cells B4 through E4 and name it *BackhoeHours* and create a range with cells B10 through E10 and name it *BackhoeHoursInUse*.
6. Click the Equipment Hours tab to make it the active worksheet and then insert a formula that calculates the total hours for the front loader by completing the following steps:
   a. Make cell C4 active.
   b. Type **=SUM(Fr**.
   c. When you type *Fr,* a drop-down list displays with the front loader ranges. Double-click *FrontLoaderHours*.

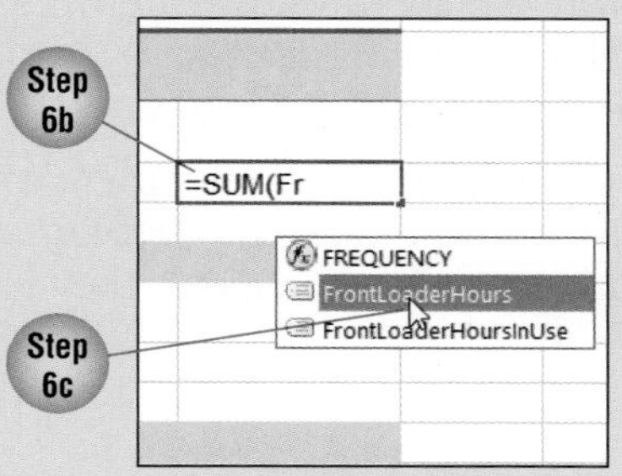

d. Type) (the closing parenthesis).
e. Press Enter.

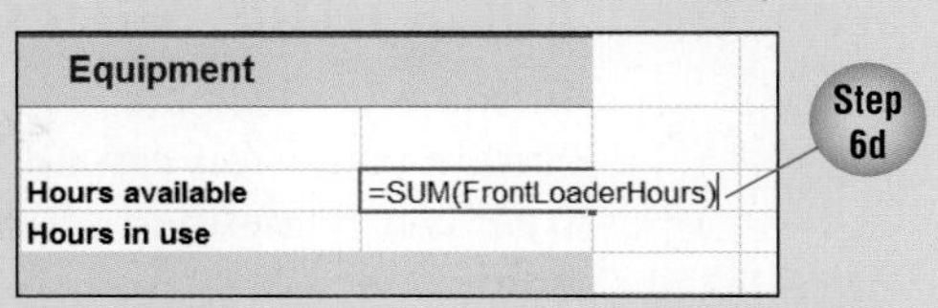

7. Complete steps similar to those in Step 6 to insert ranges in the following cells:
   a. Make cell C5 active and then insert a formula that calculates the total in-use hours for the front loader.
   b. Make cell C8 active and then insert a formula that calculates the total hours available for the forklift.
   c. Make cell C9 active and then insert a formula that calculates the total in-use hours for the forklift.
   d. Make cell C12 active and then insert a formula that calculates the total hours available for the tractor.
   e. Make cell C13 active and then insert a formula that calculates the total in-use hours for the tractor.
   f. Make cell C16 active and then insert a formula that calculates the total hours available for the backhoe.
   g. Make cell C17 active and then insert a formula that calculates the total in-use hours for the backhoe.
8. Make the following changes to specific worksheets:
   a. Click the Front Loader tab and then change the number in cell E4 from *415* to *426* and change the number in cell C6 from *6* to *14*.
   b. Click the Forklift tab and then change the number in cell E4 from *415* to *426* and change the number in cell D8 from *4* to *12*.
9. Select all of the worksheet tabs and then create a header that prints your name at the left side of each worksheet, the page number in the middle, and the current date at the right side.
10. Save and then print all of the worksheets in **EL1-C6-P2-HEREquip.xlsx**.
11. Close the workbook. (Make sure all workbooks are closed.)
12. Make the following changes to the Open backstage area.
    a. Click the FILE tab.
    b. Make sure the *Open* option is selected and *Recent Workbooks* is selected.
    c. Unpin **EL1-C6-P2-HEREquip.xlsx** from the Recent Workbooks list by clicking the down-pointing pin that displays at the right side of **EL1-C6-P2-HEREquip.xlsx**. (This changes the down-pointing pin to a left-pointing pin and moves the file down the list.)
    d. Unpin **HERBackhoe.xlsx** and **HEREquipUsage.xlsx**.
    e. Click the Back button to exit the Open backstage area.

Project 3 Create and Apply Styles to a Payroll Workbook — 5 Parts

You will open a payroll workbook, define and apply styles, and then modify the styles. You will also copy the styles to another workbook and then apply the styles in the new workbook.

Formatting with Cell Styles

In some worksheets, you may want to apply formatting to highlight or accentuate certain cells. You can apply formatting to a cell or selected cells with a cell style. A ***style*** is a predefined set of formatting attributes, such as font, font size, alignment, borders, shading, and so forth. You can use one of the predesigned styles from the Cell Styles drop-down gallery or create your own style.

Quick Steps

Apply a Cell Style
1. Select desired cell(s).
2. Click Cell Styles button.
3. Click desired style.

Cell Styles

Applying a Style

To apply a style, select the desired cell(s), click the Cell Styles button in the Styles group on the HOME tab, and then click the desired option at the drop-down gallery shown in Figure 6.4. If you hover your mouse pointer over a style in the drop-down gallery, the cell or selected cells display with the formatting applied.

Figure 6.4 Cell Styles Drop-Down Gallery

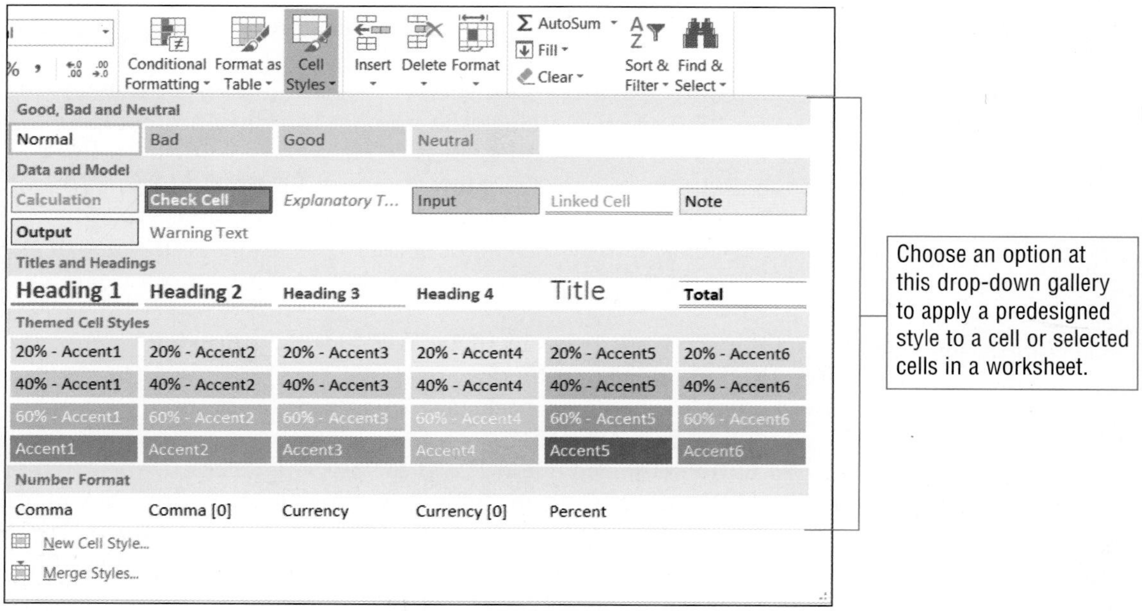

Project 3a **Formatting with Cell Styles** **Part 1 of 5**

1. Open **OEPayroll.xlsx** and then save the workbook with Save As and name it **EL1-C6-P3-OEPayroll**.
2. With Sheet1 the active worksheet, insert the necessary formulas to calculate gross pay, withholding tax amount, social security tax amount, and net pay. ***Hint: Refer to Project 3c in Chapter 2 for assistance.*** Select cells D4 through G4 and then click the Accounting Number Format button to insert dollar signs.
3. Make Sheet2 active and then insert a formula that calculates the amount due. Make cell F4 active and then click the Accounting Number Format button to insert a dollar sign.

4. Make Sheet3 active and then insert a formula in the *Due Date* column that calculates the purchase date plus the number of days in the *Terms* column. ***Hint: The formula in cell F4 will be =D4+E4.***
5. Apply cell styles to cells by completing the following steps:
   a. Make Sheet1 active and then select cells A11 and A12.
   b. Click the Cell Styles button in the Styles group on the HOME tab.
   c. At the drop-down gallery, hover your mouse over styles to see how the style formatting affects the selected cells.
   d. Click the *Check Cell* option in the *Data and Model* section.
6. Select cells B11 and B12, click the Cell Styles button, and then click the *Output* option in the *Data and Model* section (first column, second row in the *Data and Model* section).

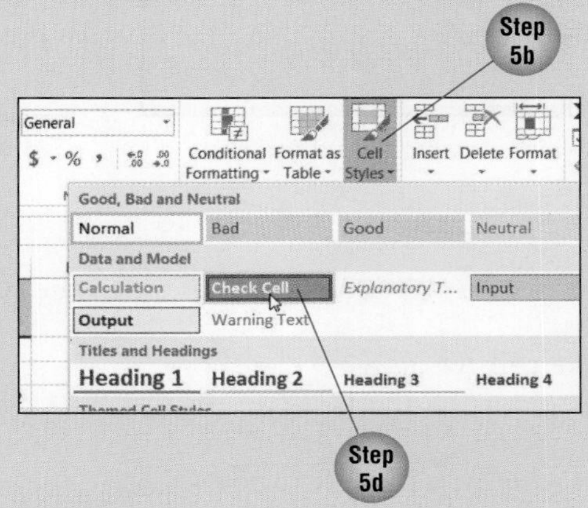

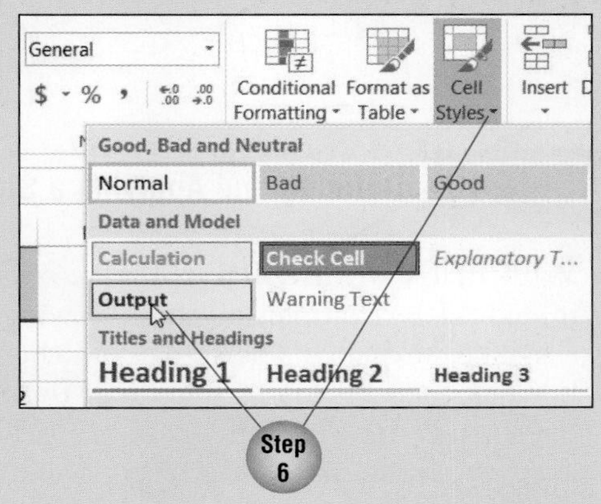

7. Save **EL1-C6-P3-OEPayroll.xlsx**.

Defining a Cell Style

You can apply a style from the Cell Styles drop-down gallery or you can create your own style. Using a style to apply formatting has several advantages. A style helps to ensure consistent formatting from one worksheet to another. Once you define all attributes for a particular style, you do not have to redefine them again. If you need to change the formatting, change the style and all cells formatted with that style automatically reflect the change.

Two basic methods are available for defining your own cell style. You can define a style with formats already applied to a cell or you can display the Style dialog box, click the Format button, and then choose formatting options at the Format Cells dialog box. Styles you create are available only in the workbook in which they are created.

To define a style with existing formatting, select the cell or cells containing the desired formatting, click the Cell Styles button in the Styles group on the HOME tab, and then click the *New Cell Style* option located toward the bottom of the drop-down gallery. At the Style dialog box, shown in Figure 6.5, type a name for the new style in the *Style name* text box and then click OK to close the dialog box. The styles you create display at the top of the drop-down gallery in the *Custom* section when you click the Cell Styles button.

Quick Steps

Define a Cell Style with Existing Formatting
1. Select cell containing formatting.
2. Click Cell Styles button.
3. Click *New Cell Style.*
4. Type name for new style.
5. Click OK.

HINT

Cell styles are based on the workbook theme.

Figure 6.5 Style Dialog Box

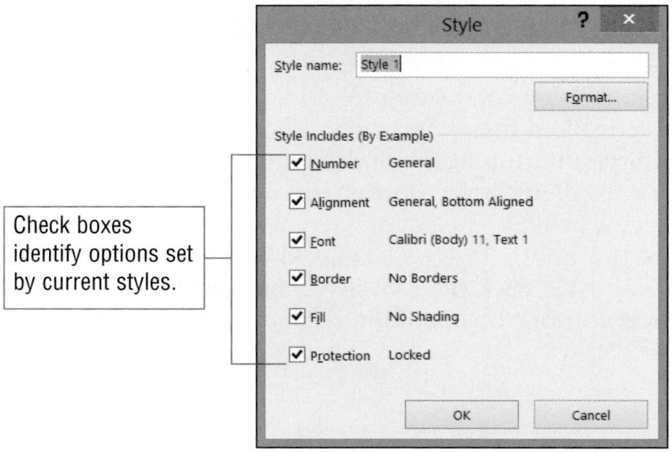

Project 3b Defining and Applying a Style

Part 2 of 5

1. With **EL1-C6-P3-OEPayroll.xlsx** open, define a style named *C06Title* with the formatting in cell A1 by completing the following steps:
   a. Make sure Sheet1 is active and then make cell A1 active.
   b. Click the Cell Styles button in the Styles group on the HOME tab and then click the *New Cell Style* option located toward the bottom of the drop-down gallery.
   c. At the Style dialog box, type C06Title in the *Style name* text box.
   d. Click OK.

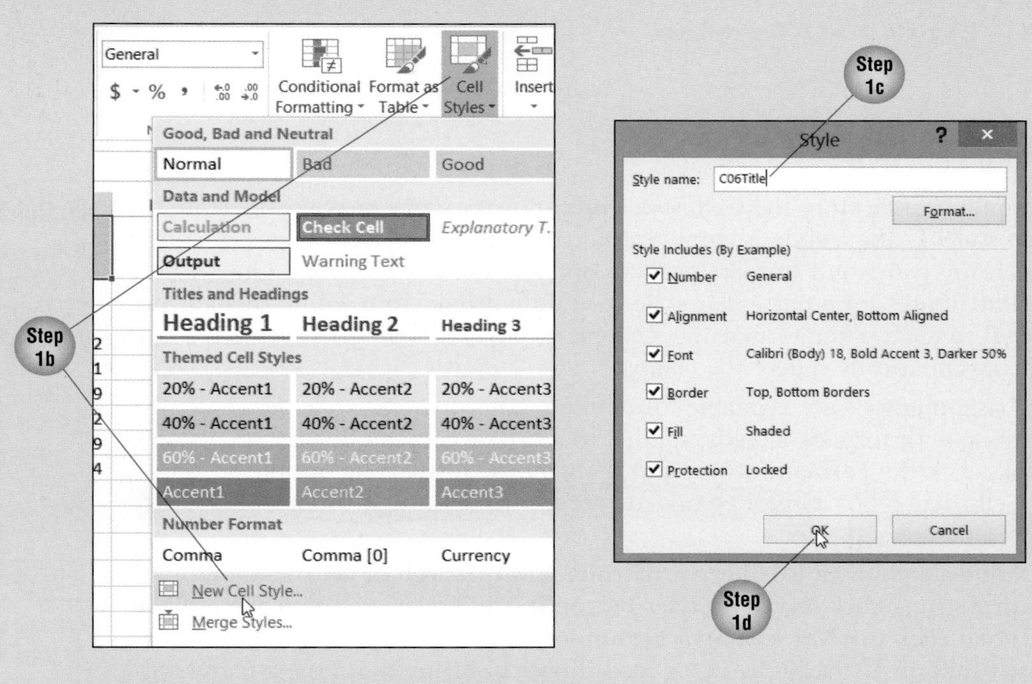

2. Even though cell A1 is already formatted, the style has not been applied to it. (Later, you will modify the style and the style must be applied to the cell for the change to affect it.) Apply the C06Title style to cell A1 by completing the following steps:
   a. Make sure cell A1 is the active cell.

b. Click the Cell Styles button in the Styles group on the HOME tab.
c. Click the *C06Title* style in the *Custom* section located toward the top of the drop-down gallery.

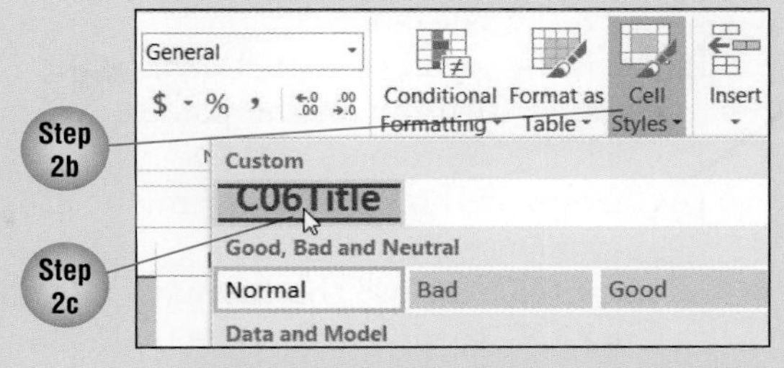

3. Apply the C06Title style to other cells by completing the following steps:
   a. Click the Sheet2 tab.
   b. Make cell A1 active.
   c. Click the Cell Styles button in the Styles group and then click the *C06Title* style at the drop-down gallery. (Notice that the style did not apply the row height formatting. The style applies only cell formatting.)
   d. Click the Sheet3 tab.
   e. Make cell A1 active.
   f. Click the Cell Styles button and then click the *C06Title* style at the drop-down gallery.
   g. Click the Sheet1 tab.
4. Save **EL1-C6-P3-OEPayroll.xlsx**.

In addition to defining a style based on cell formatting, you can also define a new style without first applying the formatting. To do this, you would display the Style dialog box, type a name for the new style, and then click the Format button. At the Format Cells dialog box, apply any desired formatting and then click OK to close the dialog box. At the Style dialog box, remove the check mark from any formatting that you do not want included in the style and then click OK to close the Style dialog box.

Quick Steps

Define a Style
1. Click in blank cell.
2. Click Cell Styles button.
3. Click *New Cell Style*.
4. Type name for style.
5. Click Format button.
6. Choose formatting options.
7. Click OK.
8. Click OK.

Project 3c Defining a Style without First Applying Formatting — Part 3 of 5

1. With **EL1-C6-P3-OEPayroll.xlsx** open, define a new style named *C06Subtitle* without first applying the formatting by completing the following steps:
   a. With Sheet1 active, click in any empty cell.
   b. Click the Cell Styles button in the Styles group and then click *New Cell Style* at the drop-down gallery.
   c. At the Style dialog box, type C06Subtitle in the *Style name* text box.
   d. Click the Format button in the Style dialog box.
   e. At the Format Cells dialog box, click the Font tab.
   f. At the Format Cells dialog box with the Font tab selected, change the font to Candara, the font style to bold, the size to 12 points, and the color to White, Background 1.

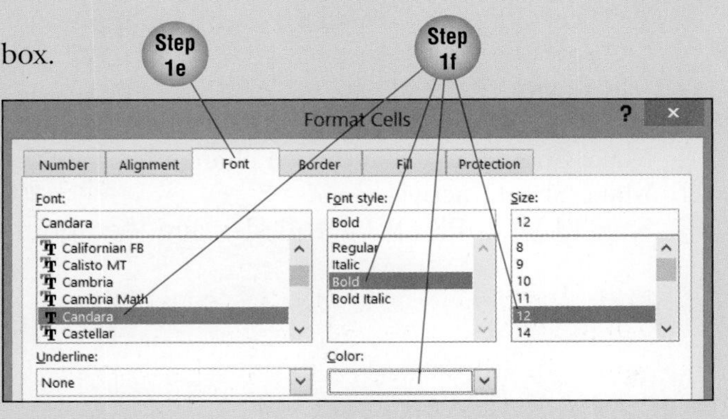

g. Click the Fill tab.
h. Click the green option shown at the right (last column, fifth row in the palette).
i. Click the Alignment tab.
j. Change the horizontal alignment to center alignment.
k. Click OK to close the Format Cells dialog box.
l. Click OK to close the Style dialog box.

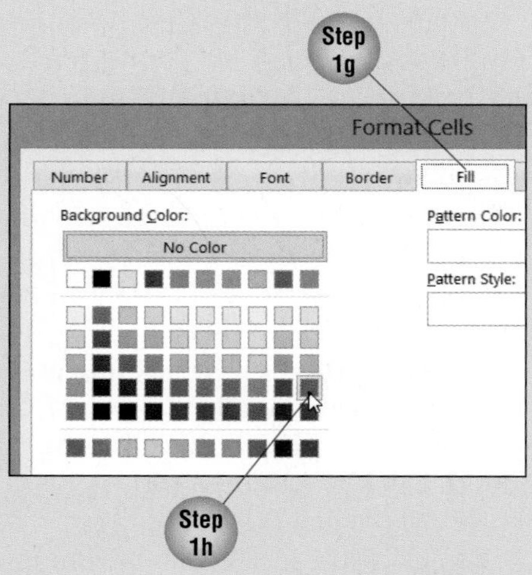

2. Apply the C06Subtitle style by completing the following steps:
   a. Make cell A2 active.
   b. Click the Cell Styles button and then click the *C06Subtitle* style located toward the top of the drop-down gallery in the *Custom* section.
   c. Click the Sheet2 tab.
   d. Make cell A2 active.
   e. Click the Cell Styles button and then click the *C06Subtitle* style.
   f. Click the Sheet3 tab.
   g. Make cell A2 active.
   h. Click the Cell Styles button and then click the *C06Subtitle* style.
   i. Click the Sheet1 tab.
3. Apply the following predesigned cell styles:
   a. Select cells A3 through G3.
   b. Click the Cell Styles button and then click the *Heading 3* style at the drop-down gallery.
   c. Select cells A5 through G5.
   d. Click the Cell Styles button and then click the *20% - Accent3* style.
   e. Apply the 20% - Accent3 style to cells A7 through G7 and cells A9 through G9.

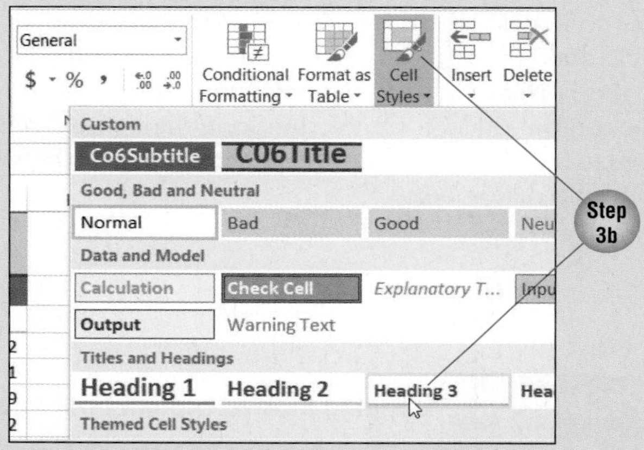

   f. Click the Sheet2 tab.
   g. Select cells A3 through F3 and then apply the Heading 3 style.
   h. Select cells A5 through F5 and then apply the 20% - Accent3 style.
   i. Apply the 20% - Accent3 style to every other row of cells (cells A7 through F7, A9 through F9, and so on, finishing with cells A17 through F17).
   j. Click the Sheet3 tab.
   k. Select cells A3 through F3 and then apply the Heading 3 style.
   l. Apply the 20% - Accent3 style to cells A5 through F5, A7 through F7, and A9 through F9.
4. With Sheet3 active, change the height of row 1 to 36.00 points.
5. Make Sheet2 active and then change the height of row 1 to 36.00 points.
6. Make Sheet1 active.
7. Save **EL1-C6-P3-OEPayroll.xlsx** and then print only the first worksheet.

Modifying a Style

One of the advantages to formatting with a style is that you can modify the formatting of the style and all cells formatted with that style automatically reflect the change. You can modify a style you create or one of the predesigned styles provided by Excel. When you modify a predesigned style, only the style in the current workbook is affected. If you open a blank workbook, the cell styles available are the default styles.

To modify a style, click the Cell Styles button in the Styles group on the HOME tab and then right-click the desired style at the drop-down gallery. At the shortcut menu that displays, click *Modify*. At the Style dialog box, click the Format button. Make the desired formatting changes at the Format Cells dialog box and then click OK. Click OK to close the Style dialog box and any cells formatted with the specific style are automatically updated.

Quick Steps

Modify a Style
1. Click Cell Styles button.
2. Right-click desired style at drop-down gallery.
3. Click *Modify*.
4. Click Format button.
5. Make desired formatting changes.
6. Click OK to close Format Cells dialog box.
7. Click OK to close Style dialog box.

Project 3d **Modifying Styles** **Part 4 of 5**

1. With **EL1-C6-P3-OEPayroll.xlsx** open, modify the C06Title style by completing the following steps:
   a. Click in any empty cell.
   b. Click the Cell Styles button in the Styles group.
   c. At the drop-down gallery, right-click the *C06Title* style located toward the top of the gallery in the *Custom* section and then click *Modify*.
   d. At the Style dialog box, click the Format button.
   e. At the Format Cells dialog box, click the Font tab and then change the font to Candara.
   f. Click the Alignment tab.
   g. Click the down-pointing arrow to the right of the *Vertical* option box and then click *Center* at the drop-down list.
   h. Click the Fill tab.
   i. Click the light blue fill color as shown at the right (fifth column, third row in the palette).
   j. Click OK to close the Format Cells dialog box.
   k. Click OK to close the Style dialog box.

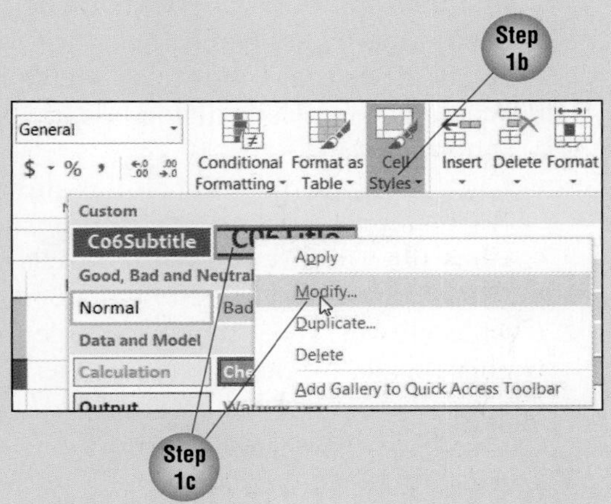

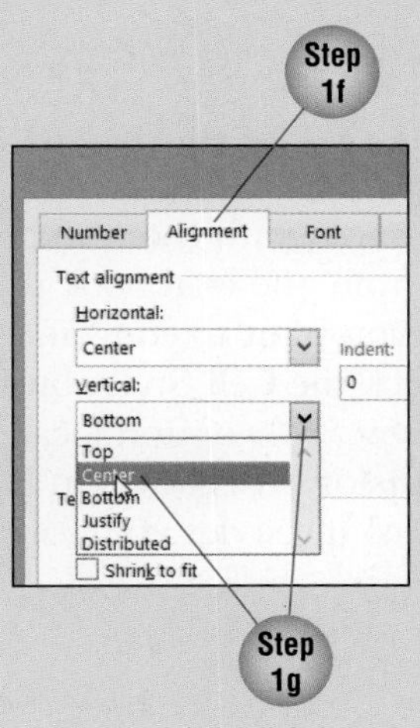

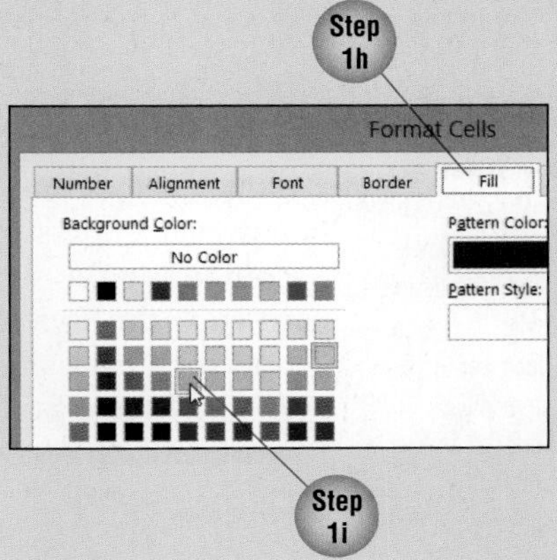

2. Modify the C06Subtitle style by completing the following steps:
   a. Click in any empty cell.
   b. Click the Cell Styles button in the Styles group.
   c. At the drop-down gallery, right-click on the *C06Subtitle* style located toward the top of the gallery in the *Custom* section and then click *Modify*.
   d. At the Style dialog box, click the Format button.
   e. At the Format Cells dialog box, click the Font tab and then change the font to Calibri.
   f. Click the Fill tab.
   g. Click the dark blue fill color as shown at the right (fifth column, sixth row in the palette).
   h. Click OK to close the Format Cells dialog box.
   i. Click OK to close the Style dialog box.

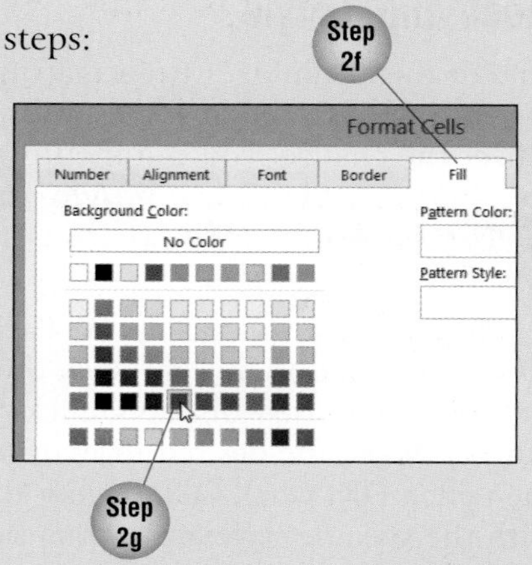

3. Modify the predefined 20% - Accent3 style by completing the following steps:
   a. Click the Cell Styles button in the Styles group.
   b. At the drop-down gallery, right-click on the *20% - Accent3* style and then click *Modify*.
   c. At the Style dialog box, click the Format button.
   d. At the Format Cells dialog box, make sure the Fill tab is active.
   e. Click the light blue fill color as shown at the right (fifth column, second row in the palette).
   f. Click OK to close the Format Cells dialog box.
   g. Click OK to close the Style dialog box.

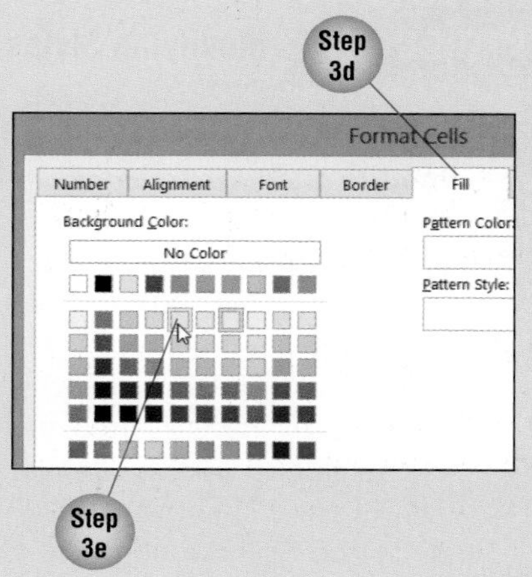

4. Click each worksheet tab and notice the formatting changes made by the modified styles.
5. Change the name of Sheet1 to *Weekly Payroll*, the name of Sheet2 to *Invoices*, and the name of Sheet3 to *Overdue Accounts*.
6. Apply a different color to each of the three worksheet tabs.
7. Save and then print all the worksheets in **EL1-C6-P3-OEPayroll.xlsx**.

Quick Steps

Copy Styles to Another Workbook
1. Open workbook containing desired styles.
2. Open workbook to be modified.
3. Click Cell Styles button.
4. Click *Merge Styles* option.
5. Double-click name of workbook that contains styles.

Copying Styles to Another Workbook

Styles you define are saved with the workbook in which they are created. You can, however, copy styles from one workbook to another. To do this, open the workbook containing the styles you want to copy and open the workbook into which you want to copy the styles. Click the Cell Styles button in the Styles group on the HOME tab and then click the *Merge Styles* option located at the bottom of the drop-down gallery. At the Merge Styles dialog box, shown in Figure 6.6, double-click the name of the workbook that contains the styles you want to copy.

Figure 6.6 Merge Styles Dialog Box

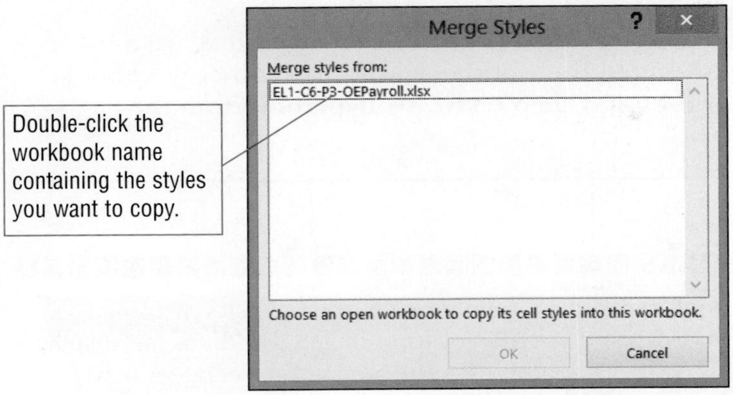

HINT

The Undo command will not reverse the effects of the Merge Styles dialog box.

Quick Steps

Remove a Style
1. Select cells formatted with style to be removed.
2. Click Cell Styles button.
3. Click *Normal* at drop-down gallery.

Delete a Style
1. Click Cell Styles button.
2. Right-click style to be deleted.
3. Click *Delete* at shortcut menu.ç

Removing a Style

If you apply a style to text and then decide you do not want it applied, return the formatting to Normal, which is the default. To do this, select the cells formatted with the style you want to remove, click the Cell Styles button, and then click *Normal* at the drop-down gallery.

Deleting a Style

To delete a style, click the Cell Styles button in the Styles group on the HOME tab. At the drop-down gallery that displays, right-click the style you want to delete and then click *Delete* at the shortcut menu. Formatting applied by the deleted style is removed from cells in the workbook.

HINT

You cannot delete the Normal style.

Project 3e **Copying Styles** **Part 5 of 5**

1. With **EL1-C6-P3-OEPayroll.xlsx** open, open **OEPlans.xlsx**.
2. Save the workbook with Save As and name it **EL1-C6-P3-OEPlans**.
3. Copy the styles in **EL1-C6-P3-Payroll.xlsx** into **EL1-C6-P3-OEPlans.xlsx** by completing the following steps:
   a. Click the Cell Styles button in the Styles group on the HOME tab.
   b. Click the *Merge Styles* option located toward the bottom of the drop-down gallery.
   c. At the Merge Styles dialog box, double-click ***EL1-C6-P3-OEPayroll.xlsx*** in the *Merge styles from* list box.
   d. At the message that displays asking if you want to merge styles that have the same names, click Yes.

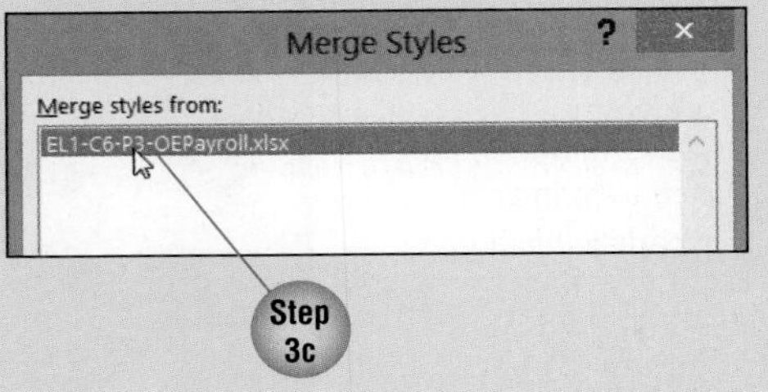

4. Apply the C06Title style to cell A1 and the C06Subtitle style to cell A2.
5. Increase the height of row 1 to 36.00 points.
6. Save, print, and then close **EL1-C6-P3-OEPlans.xlsx**.
7. Close **EL1-C6-P3-OEPayroll.xlsx**.

Project 4 Insert, Modify, and Remove Hyperlinks — 3 Parts

You will open a facilities account workbook and then insert hyperlinks to a website, to cells in other worksheets in the workbook, and to another workbook. You will modify and edit hyperlinks and then remove a hyperlink from the workbook.

Inserting Hyperlinks

Quick Steps

Insert Hyperlink
1. Click INSERT tab.
2. Click Hyperlink button.
3. Make desired changes at Insert Hyperlink dialog box.
4. Click OK.

A hyperlink in a workbook can serve a number of purposes: Click it to navigate to a web page on the Internet or a specific location in the workbook, to display a different workbook, to open a file in a different program, to create a new document, or to link to an email address. Create a customized hyperlink by clicking the desired cell in a workbook, clicking the INSERT tab, and then clicking the Hyperlink button in the Links group. This displays the Insert Hyperlink dialog box, shown in Figure 6.7. At this dialog box, identify what you want to link to and the location of the link. Click the ScreenTip button to customize the hyperlink ScreenTip.

Hyperlink

Linking to an Existing Web Page or File

Link to a web page on the Internet by typing a web address or with the Existing File or Web Page button in the *Link to* section. To link to an existing web page, type the address of the web page, such as *www.emcp.com*. By default, the automatic formatting of hyperlinks is turned on and the web address is formatted as a hyperlink. (The text is underlined and the color is changed to blue.)

You can turn off the automatic formatting of hyperlinks at the AutoCorrect dialog box. Display this dialog box by clicking the FILE tab, clicking *Options*, and then clicking *Proofing* in the left panel of the Excel Options dialog box. Click the AutoCorrect Options button to display the AutoCorrect dialog box. At this dialog

Figure 6.7 Insert Hyperlink Dialog Box

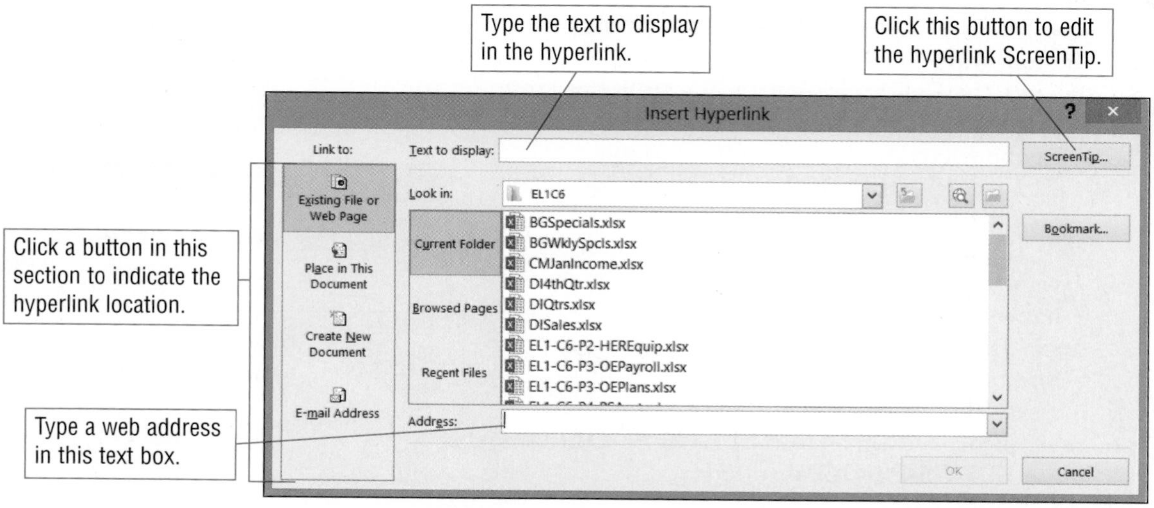

box, click the AutoFormat As You Type tab and then remove the check mark from the *Internet and network paths with hyperlinks* check box. To link to a web page at the Insert Hyperlink dialog box, display the dialog box, click the Existing File or Web Page button in the *Link to* section and then type the web address in the *Address* text box.

In some situations, you may want to provide information to your readers from a variety of sources. For example, you may want to provide additional information in an Excel workbook, a Word document, or a PowerPoint presentation. To link an Excel workbook to a workbook or file in another application, display the Insert Hyperlink dialog box and then click the Existing File or Web Page button in the *Link to* section. Use buttons in the *Look in* section to navigate to the folder containing the desired file and then click the file. Make other changes in the Insert Hyperlink dialog box as needed and then click OK.

Navigating Using Hyperlinks

Navigate to a hyperlinked location by clicking the hyperlink in the worksheet. Hover the mouse over the hyperlink and a ScreenTip displays with the address of the hyperlinked location. If you want specific information to display in the ScreenTip, click the ScreenTip button in the Insert Hyperlink dialog box, type the desired text in the Set Hyperlink ScreenTip dialog box, and then click OK.

Project 4a Linking to a Website and Another Workbook — Part 1 of 3

1. Open **PSAccts.xlsx** and then save the workbook with Save As and name it **EL1-C6-P4-PSAccts**.
2. Insert a hyperlink to information about Pyramid Sales, a fictitious company (the hyperlink will connect to the publishing company website), by completing the following steps:
   a. Make cell A13 active.
   b. Click the INSERT tab and then click the Hyperlink button in the Links group.
   c. At the Insert Hyperlink dialog box, if necessary, click the Existing File or Web Page button in the *Link to* section.
   d. Type www.emcp.com in the *Address* text box.
   e. Select the text that displays in the *Text to display* text box and then type Company information.
   f. Click the ScreenTip button located in the upper right corner of the dialog box.

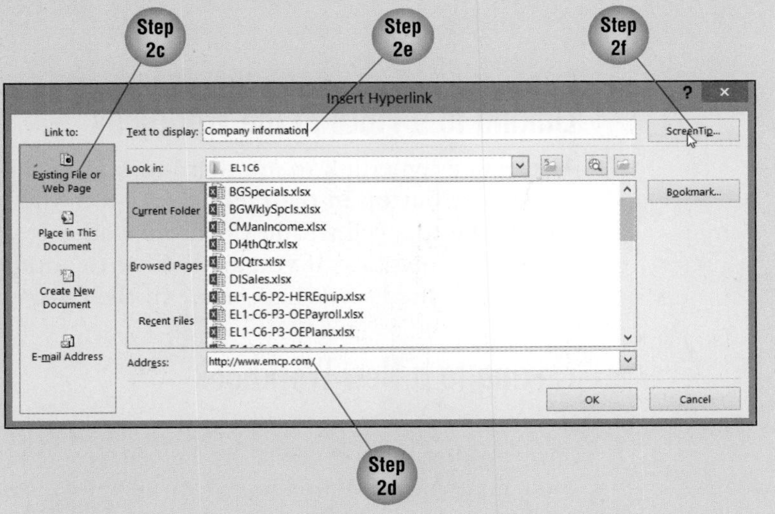

g. At the Set Hyperlink ScreenTip dialog box, type **View the company website.** and then click OK.
h. Click OK to close the Insert Hyperlink dialog box.

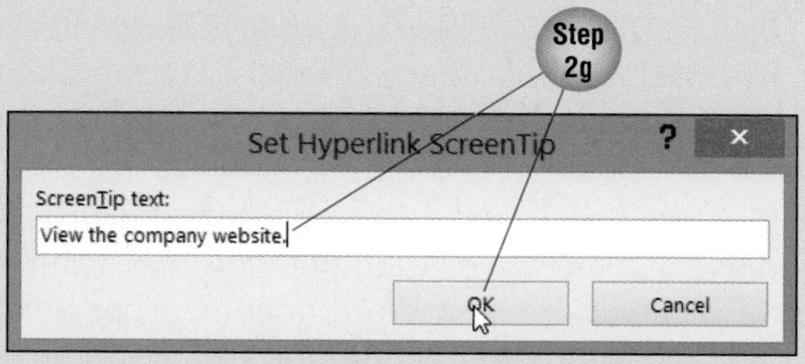

3. Navigate to the company website (in this case, the publishing company website) by clicking the Company information hyperlink in cell A13.
4. Close the Web browser.

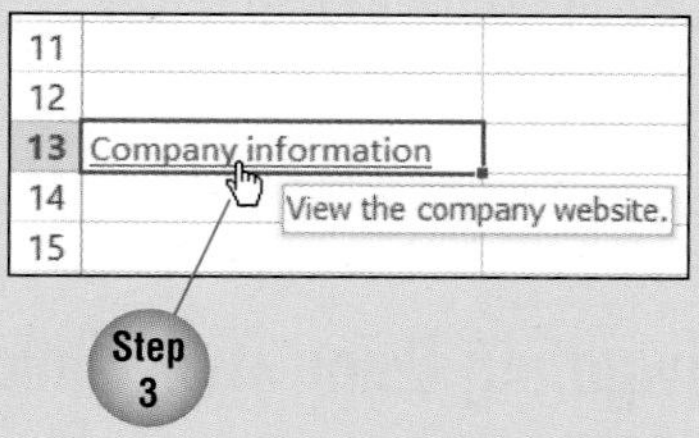

5. Create a link to another workbook by completing the following steps:
   a. Make cell A11 active, type **Semiannual sales**, and then press the Enter key.
   b. Make cell A11 active and then click the Hyperlink button in the Links group on the INSERT tab.
   c. At the Insert Hyperlink dialog box, make sure the Existing File or Web Page button is selected.
   d. If necessary, click the down-pointing arrow at the right side of the *Look in* option box and then navigate to the EL1C6 folder on your storage medium.
   e. Double-click ***PSSalesAnalysis.xlsx***.

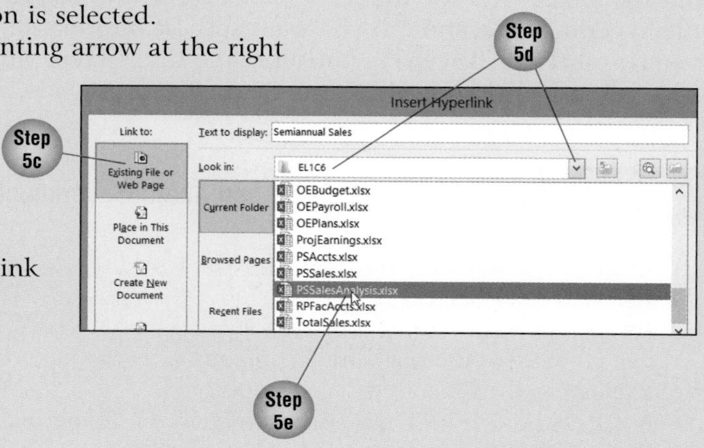

6. Click the Semiannual sales hyperlink to open **PSSalesAnalysis.xlsx**.
7. Look at the information in the workbook and then close it.
8. Save **EL1-C6-P4-PSAccts.xlsx**.

Linking to a Place in the Workbook

To create a hyperlink to another location in the workbook, click the Place in This Document button in the *Link to* section in the Edit Hyperlink dialog box. If you are linking to a cell within the same worksheet, type the cell name in the *Type the cell reference* text box. If you are linking to another worksheet in the workbook, click the desired worksheet name in the *Or select a place in this document* list box.

Linking to a New Workbook

In addition to linking to an existing workbook, you can create a hyperlink to a new workbook. To do this, display the Insert Hyperlink dialog box and then click the Create New Document button in the *Link to* section. Type a name for the new workbook in the *Name of new document* text box and then specify if you want to edit the workbook now or later.

Linking Using a Graphic

You can use a graphic, such as a clip art image, picture, or text box, to hyperlink to a file or website. To hyperlink with a graphic, select the graphic, click the INSERT tab, and then click the Hyperlink button. You can also right-click the graphic and then click *Hyperlink* at the shortcut menu. At the Insert Hyperlink dialog box, specify the location you want to link to and the text you want to display in the hyperlink.

Linking to an Email Address

You can insert a hyperlink to an email address at the Insert Hyperlink dialog box. To do this, click the E-mail Address button in the *Link to* section, type the desired address in the *E-mail address* text box, and then type a subject for the email in the *Subject* text box. Click in the *Text to display* text box and then type the text you want to display in the worksheet.

Project 4b **Linking to a Place in a Workbook, to Another Workbook, and Using a Graphic** **Part 2 of 3**

1. With **EL1-C6-P4-PSAccts.xlsx** open, create a link from the checks amount in cell B6 to the checks amount in cell G20 in the January worksheet by completing the following steps:
   a. Make cell B6 active.
   b. Click the Hyperlink button in the Links group on the INSERT tab.
   c. At the Insert Hyperlink dialog box, click the Place in This Document button in the *Link to* section.
   d. Select the text in the *Type the cell reference* text box and then type **G20**.
   e. Click *January* in the *Or select a place in this document* list box.
   f. Click OK to close the Insert Hyperlink dialog box.

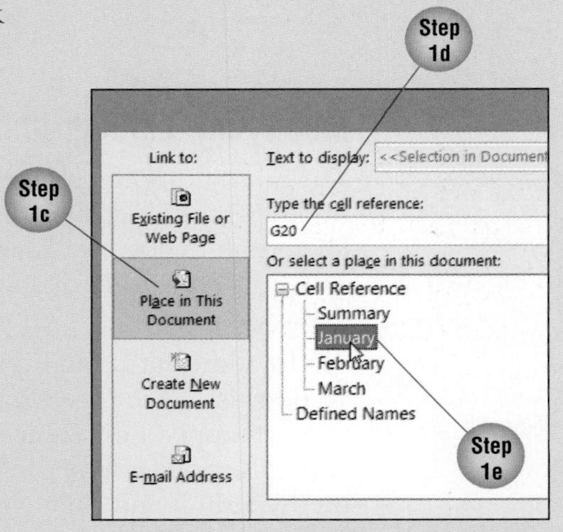

2. Make cell C6 active and then complete steps similar to those in Steps 1b through 1f except click *February* in the *Or select a place in this document* list box.
3. Make cell D6 active and then complete steps similar to those in Steps 1b through 1f except click *March* in the *Or select a place in this document* list box.
4. Click the hyperlinked amount in cell B6. (This makes cell G20 active in the January worksheet.)
5. Click the Summary worksheet tab.
6. Click the hyperlinked amount in cell C6. (This makes cell G20 active in the February worksheet.)
7. Click the Summary worksheet tab.
8. Click the hyperlinked amount in cell D6. (This makes cell G20 active in the March worksheet.)
9. Click the Summary worksheet tab.

10. Use the first pyramid graphic image in cell A1 to create a link to the company web page by completing the following steps:
    a. Right-click the first pyramid graphic image in cell A1 and then click *Hyperlink* at the shortcut menu.
    b. At the Insert Hyperlink dialog box, if necessary, click the Existing File or Web Page button in the *Link to* section.
    c. Type www.emcp.com in the *Address* text box.
    d. Click the ScreenTip button located in the upper right corner of the dialog box.
    e. At the Set Hyperlink ScreenTip dialog box, type View the company website. and then click OK.
    f. Click OK to close the Insert Hyperlink dialog box.

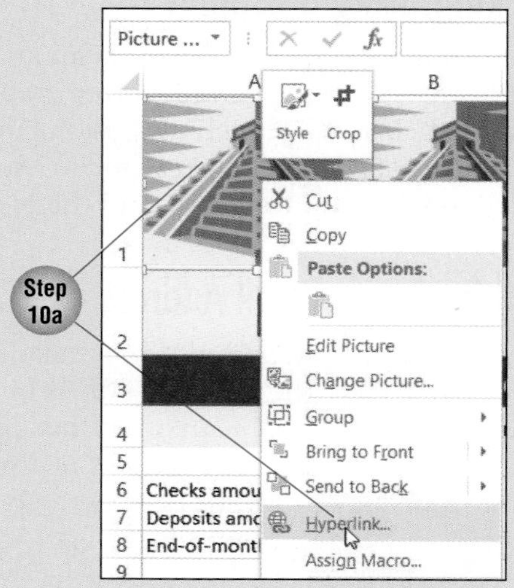

11. Make cell A5 active.
12. Navigate to the company website (the publishing company website) by clicking the first pyramid graphic image.
13. Close the Web browser.
14. Save **EL1-C6-P4-PSAccts.xlsx**.

Modifying, Editing, and Removing a Hyperlink

You can modify or change the hyperlink text or destination. To do this, right-click the hyperlink and then click *Edit Hyperlink* at the shortcut menu. At the Edit Hyperlink dialog box, make any desired changes and then close the dialog box. The Edit Hyperlink dialog box contains the same options as the Insert Hyperlink dialog box.

In addition to modifying the hyperlink, you can edit hyperlink text in a cell. To do this, make the cell active and then make the desired changes. For example, you can apply a different font or font size, change the text color, and apply a text effect. Remove a hyperlink from a workbook by right-clicking the cell containing the hyperlink and then clicking *Remove Hyperlink* at the shortcut menu.

Project 4c **Modifying, Editing, and Removing a Hyperlink** **Part 3 of 3**

1. With **EL1-C6-P4-PSAccts.xlsx** open, modify the Semiannual sales hyperlink by completing the following steps:
    a. Position the mouse pointer on the Semiannual sales hyperlink in cell A11, click the right mouse button, and then click *Edit Hyperlink* at the shortcut menu.
    b. At the Edit Hyperlink dialog box, select the text *Semiannual sales* in the *Text to display* text box and then type Customer sales analysis.

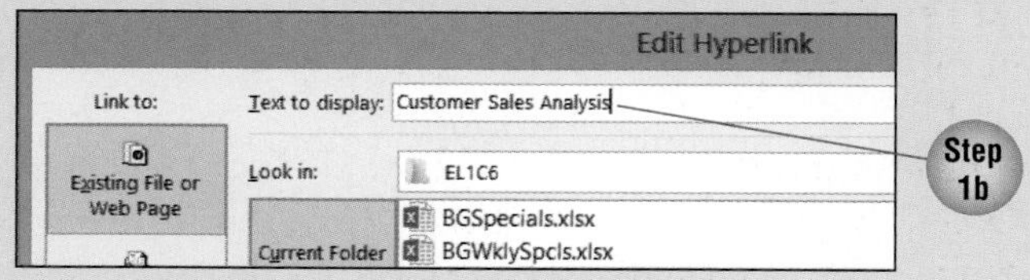

c. Click the ScreenTip button located in the upper right corner of the dialog box.
d. At the Set Hyperlink ScreenTip dialog box, type **Click this hyperlink to display the workbook containing customer sales analysis.**
e. Click OK to close the Set Hyperlink ScreenTip dialog box.
f. Click OK to close the Edit Hyperlink dialog box.
2. Click the Customer sales analysis hyperlink.
3. After looking at the **PSSalesAnalysis.xlsx** workbook, close it.
4. With cell A11 active, edit the Customer sales analysis hyperlink text by completing the following steps:
   a. Click the HOME tab.
   b. Click the Font Color button arrow in the Font group and then click the *Dark Red* color option (first option in the *Standard Colors* section).
   c. Click the Bold button.
   d. Click the Underline button. (This removes underlining from the text.)
5. Remove the Company information hyperlink by right-clicking in cell A13 and then clicking *Remove Hyperlink* at the shortcut menu.
6. Press the Delete key to remove the contents of cell A13.
7. Save, print only the first worksheet (the Summary worksheet), and then close **EL1-C6-P4-PSAccts.xlsx**.

Project 5 Create a Billing Statement Workbook Using a Template — 1 Part

You will open a Billing Statement template provided by Excel, add data, save it as an Excel workbook, and then print the workbook.

Using Excel Templates

Excel provides a number of template worksheet forms formatted for specific uses. With Excel templates, you can create a variety of worksheets with specialized formatting, such as balance sheets, billing statements, loan amortizations, sales invoices, and time cards. Display installed templates by clicking the FILE tab and then clicking the *New* option. This displays the New backstage area, as shown in Figure 6.8.

Quick Steps

Use an Excel Template
1. Click FILE tab.
2. Click *New* option.
3. Double-click desired template.

Click the desired template in the New backstage area and a preview of the template displays in a window. Click the Create button that displays below the template preview and a workbook based on the template opens and displays on the screen. Locations for personalized text display in placeholders in the worksheet. To enter information in the worksheet, position the mouse pointer (white plus sign) in the location you want to type data and then click the left mouse button. After typing the data, click the next location. You can also move the insertion point to another cell using the commands learned in Chapter 1. For example, press the Tab key to make the next cell active or press Shift + Tab to make the previous cell active. If you are connected to the Internet, you can download a number of predesigned templates offered by Microsoft.

Figure 6.8 New Backstage Area

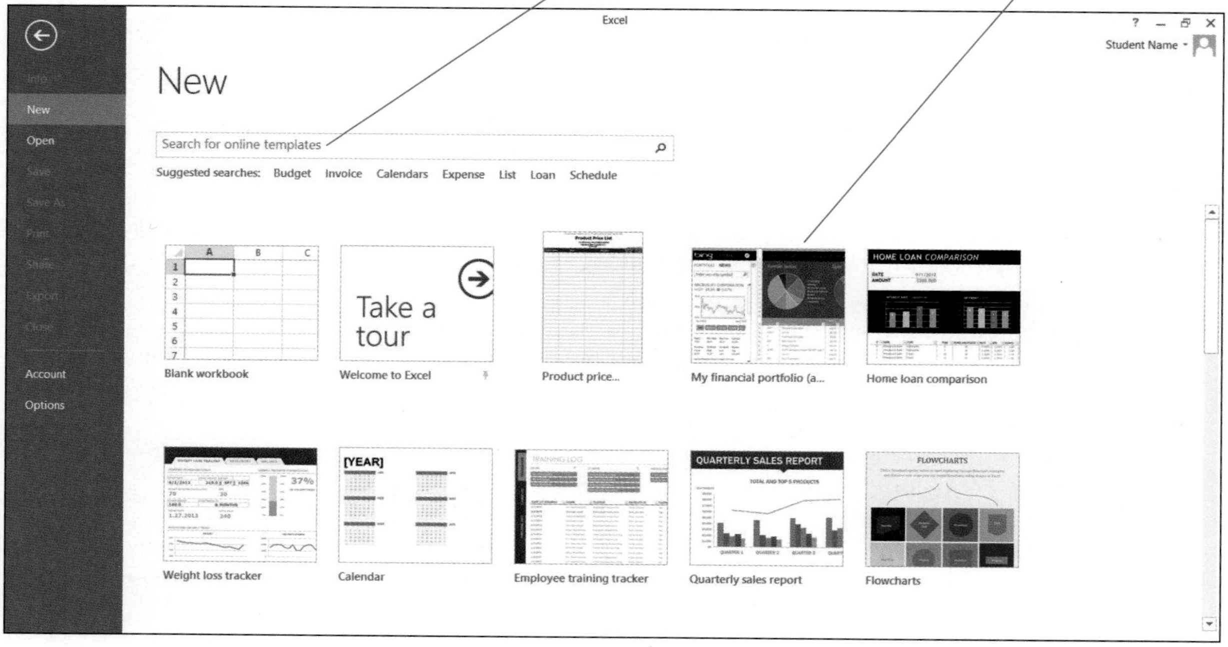

Project 5 Preparing a Billing Statement Using a Template

Part 1 of 1

1. Click the FILE tab and then click the *New* option.
2. At the New backstage area, type **billing statement** in the search text box and then press Enter.
3. Double-click the *Billing statement* template (first row, first column).

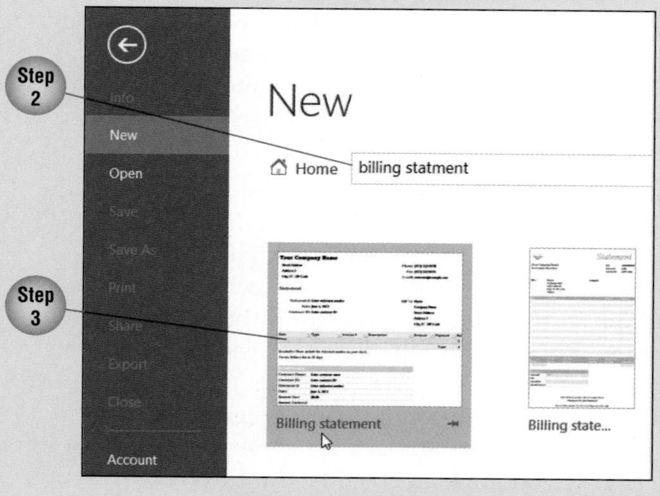

4. Click the Normal button in the view area on the Status bar.

5. With cell B1 active, type **IN-FLOW SYSTEMS**.
6. Click the text *Street Address* (cell B2) and then type **320 Milander Way**.
7. Click in each specified location (cell) and then type the text indicated:
   Address 2 (cell B3): **P.O. Box 2300**
   City, ST ZIP Code (cell B4): **Boston, MA 02188**
   Phone (cell F2): **(617) 555-3900**
   Fax (cell F3): **(617) 555-3945**
   Statement # (cell C8): **5432**
   Customer ID (cell C10): **25-345**
   Name (cell F8): **Aidan Mackenzie**
   Company Name (cell F9): **Stanfield Enterprises**
   Street Address (cell F10): **9921 South 42nd Avenue**
   Address 2 (cell F11): **P.O. Box 5540**
   City, ST ZIP Code (cell F12): **Boston, MA 02193**
   Date (cell B15): (insert current date in numbers as ##/##/#### and if necessary, adjust the width of the column)
   Type (cell C15): **System Unit**
   Invoice # (cell D15): **7452**
   Description (cell E15): **Calibration Unit**
   Amount (cell F15): **950**
   Payment (cell G15): **200**
   Customer Name (cell C21): **Stanfield Enterprises**
   Amount Enclosed (cell C26): **750**

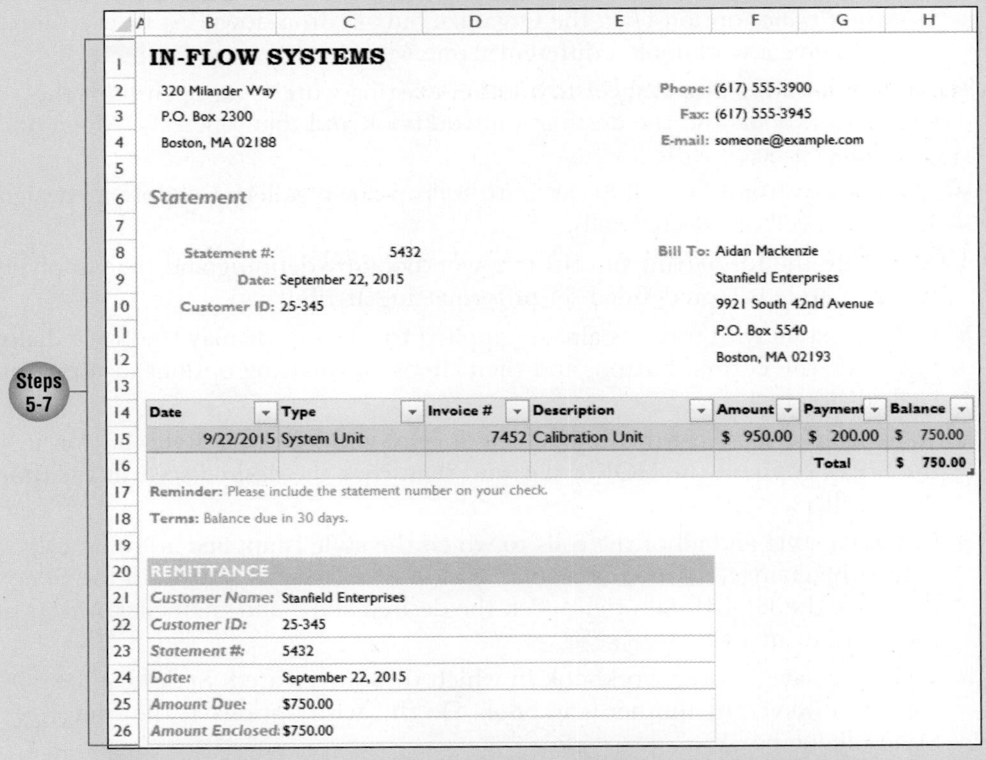

8. Save the completed invoice and name it **EL1-C6-P5-Billing**.
9. Print and then close **EL1-C6-P5-Billing.xlsx**.

Chapter Summary

- Perform file management tasks, such as copying, moving, printing, and renaming workbooks and creating and renaming folders, at the Open dialog box or Save As dialog box.
- Create a new folder by clicking the New folder button located on the toolbar at the Open dialog box or Save As dialog box.
- Rename a folder with the *Rename* option from the Organize button drop-down list or with a shortcut menu.
- Use the Shift key to select adjacent workbooks in the Open dialog box and use the Ctrl key to select nonadjacent workbooks.
- To delete a workbook, use the *Delete* option from the Organize button drop-down list or use a shortcut menu option. Workbooks deleted from the hard drive are automatically sent to the Windows Recycle Bin, where they can be restored or permanently deleted.
- Use the *Copy* and *Paste* options from the shortcut menu at the Open dialog box or Save As dialog box to copy a workbook from one folder to another folder or drive.
- Use the *Send to* option from the shortcut menu to send a copy of a workbook to another drive or folder.
- Remove a workbook from a folder or drive and insert it in another folder or drive using the *Cut* and *Paste* options from the shortcut menu.
- Use the *Rename* option from the Organize button drop-down list or the shortcut menu to give a workbook a different name.
- To move or copy a worksheet to another existing workbook, open both the source workbook and the destination workbook and then open the Move or Copy dialog box.
- Use options from the Cell Styles button drop-down gallery to apply predesigned styles to a cell or selected cells.
- Automate the formatting of cells in a workbook by defining and then applying styles. A style is a predefined set of formatting attributes.
- Define a style with formats already applied to a cell or display the Style dialog box, click the Format button, and then choose formatting options at the Format Cells dialog box.
- To apply a style, select the desired cell or cells, click the Cell Styles button in the Styles group in the HOME tab, and then click the desired style at the drop-down gallery.
- Modify a style and all of the cells to which the style is applied automatically reflect the change. To modify a style, click the Cell Styles button in the Styles group on the HOME tab, right-click the desired style, and then click *Modify* at the shortcut menu.
- Styles are saved in the workbook in which they are created. Styles can be copied, however, to another workbook. Do this with options at the Merge Styles dialog box.
- With options at the Insert Hyperlink dialog box, you can create a hyperlink to a web page, another workbook, a location within a workbook, a new workbook, or an email. You can also create a hyperlink using a graphic.
- You can modify, edit, and remove hyperlinks.

- Excel provides preformatted templates for creating forms. Search for and download templates at the New backstage area.
- Templates contain unique areas where information is entered at the keyboard.

Commands Review

FEATURE	RIBBON TAB, GROUP/OPTION	BUTTON, OPTION	KEYBOARD SHORTCUT
cell styles	HOME, Styles		
Insert Hyperlink dialog box	INSERT, Links		
Merge Styles dialog box	HOME, Styles	, *Merge Styles*	
New backstage area	FILE, *New*		
new folder	FILE, *Open*	New folder	
Open backstage area	FILE, *Open*		Ctrl + O
Open dialog box			Ctrl + F12
Save As backstage area	FILE, *Save As*		Ctrl + S
Save As dialog box			F12
Style dialog box	HOME, Styles	, *New Cell Style*	

Concepts Check

Test Your Knowledge SNAP

Completion: In the space provided at the right, indicate the correct term, symbol, or command.

1. Perform file management tasks, such as copying, moving, and deleting workbooks, with options at the Open dialog box or this dialog box. save as
2. At the Open dialog box, a list of folders and files displays in this pane. content
3. Rename a folder or file at the Open dialog box using a shortcut menu or this button. organize
4. At the Open dialog box, hold down this key while selecting nonadjacent workbooks. control

5. Workbooks deleted from the hard drive are automatically sent to this location. 3 — window recycle bin

6. The most recently opened workbook names display in this list, which displays when the *Recent Workbooks* option is selected at the Open backstage area. 2 — recent workbooks

7. Do this to a workbook name you want to remain at the top of the Recent Workbooks list at the Open backstage area. 2 — pin workbook

8. If you close a workbook without saving it, you can recover it with this option at the Open backstage area. 3 — recover unsaved workbooks

9. The Cell Styles button is located in this group on the HOME tab. — styles

10. Click the *New Cell Style* option at the Cell Styles button drop-down gallery and this dialog box displays. — style

11. A style you create displays in this section of the Cell Styles button drop-down gallery. 1 — custom

12. Copy styles from one workbook to another with options at this dialog box. 2 — merge styles

13. To link a workbook to another workbook, click this button in the *Link to* section of the Insert Hyperlink dialog box. 5 — existing file or web page

14. Templates display at this backstage area. 1 — new

Skills Check Assess Your Performance

Assessment 1

MANAGE WORKBOOKS

1. Display the Open dialog box with the EL1C6 folder the active folder.
2. Create a new folder named *O'Rourke* in the EL1C6 folder.
3. Copy **OEBudget.xlsx**, **OEPayroll.xlsx**, and **OEPlans.xlsx** to the O'Rourke folder.
4. Display the contents of the O'Rourke folder and then rename **OEBudget.xlsx** as **OEEquipBudget.xlsx**.
5. Rename **OEPlans.xlsx** as **OEPurchasePlans.xlsx** in the O'Rourke folder.
6. Change the active folder back to EL1C6.
7. Close the Open dialog box.

Assessment 2

MOVE AND COPY WORKSHEETS BETWEEN SALES ANALYSIS WORKBOOKS

SNAP Grade It

1. Open **DISales.xlsx** and then save the workbook with Save As and name it **EL1-C6-A2-DISales**.
2. Rename Sheet1 as *1st Qtr*.
3. Open **DIQtrs.xlsx**.
4. Rename Sheet1 as *2nd Qtr* and then copy it to **EL1-C6-A2-DISales.xlsx** following the 1st Qtr worksheet. (When copying the worksheet, make sure you insert a check mark in the *Create a copy* check box in the Move or Copy dialog box.)
5. Make **DIQtrs.xlsx** active, rename Sheet2 as *3rd Qtr*, and then copy it to **EL1-C6-A2-DISales.xlsx** following the 2nd Qtr tab. (Make sure you insert a check mark in the *Create a copy* check box.)
6. Make **DIQtrs.xlsx** active and then close it without saving the changes.
7. Open **DI4thQtr.xlsx**.
8. Rename Sheet1 as *4th Qtr* and then move it to **EL1-C6-A2-DISales.xlsx** following the 3rd Qtr worksheet.
9. With **EL1-C6-A2-DISales.xlsx** open, make the following changes to all four quarterly worksheets at the same time:
   a. Make 1st Qtr the active worksheet.
   b. Hold down the Shift key and then click the 4th Qtr tab. (This selects the four quarterly worksheet tabs.)
   c. Insert in cell E4 a formula to calculate the average of cells B4 through D4 and then copy the formula down to cells E5 through E9.
   d. Insert in cell B10 a formula to calculate the sum of cells B4 through B9 and then copy the formula across to cells C10 through E10.
   e. Make cell E4 active and apply accounting formatting with a dollar sign and no places after the decimal point.
10. Insert a footer on all worksheets that prints your name at the left, the page number in the middle, and the current date at the right.
11. Horizontally and vertically center all of the worksheets.
12. Save and then print all four worksheets.
13. Close **EL1-C6-A2-DISales.xlsx**.

Assessment 3

DEFINE AND APPLY STYLES TO A PROJECTED EARNINGS WORKBOOK

SNAP Grade It

1. At a blank worksheet, define a style named *C06Heading* that contains the following formatting:
   a. Font:14-point Cambria bold in dark blue
   b. Horizontal alignment: Center alignment
   c. Borders: Top and bottom in dark blue
   d. Fill: Light yellow (eighth column, second row)
2. Define a style named *C06Subheading* that contains the following formatting:
   a. Font: 12-point Cambria bold in dark blue
   b. Horizontal alignment: Center alignment
   c. Borders: Top and bottom in dark blue
   d. Fill: Light green (last column second row)

3. Define a style named *C06Column* that contains the following formatting:
   a. Number: At the Style dialog box, click the *Number* check box to remove the check mark.
   b. Font: 12-point Cambria in dark blue
   c. Fill: Light green (last column second row)
4. Save the workbook and name it **EL1-C6-A3-Styles**.
5. With **EL1-C6-A3-Styles.xlsx** open, open **ProjEarnings.xlsx**.
6. Save the workbook with Save As and name it **EL1-C6-A3-ProjEarnings**.
7. Make cell C6 active and then insert a formula that multiplies the content of cell B6 by the amount in cell B3. (When writing the formula, identify cell B3 as an absolute reference.) Copy the formula down to cells C7 through C17.
8. Make cell C6 active and then click the Accounting Number Format button.
9. Copy the styles from **EL1-C6-A3-Styles.xlsx** into **EL1-C6-A3-ProjEarnings.xlsx**. ***Hint: Do this at the Merge Styles dialog box.***
10. Apply the following styles:
    a. Select cells A1 and A2 and then apply the C06Heading style.
    b. Select cells A5 through C5 and then apply the C06Subheading style.
    c. Select cells A6 through A17 and then apply the C06Column style.
11. Save the workbook again and then print **EL1-C6-A3-ProjEarnings.xlsx**.
12. With **EL1-C6-A3-ProjEarnings.xlsx** open, modify the following styles:
    a. Modify the C06Heading style so it changes the font color to dark green (last column, sixth row) instead of dark blue, changes the vertical alignment to center alignment, and inserts top and bottom borders in dark green (last column, sixth row) instead of dark blue.
    b. Modify the C06Subheading style so it changes the font color to dark green (last column, sixth row) instead of dark blue and inserts top and bottom borders in dark green (instead of dark blue).
    c. Modify the C06Column style so it changes the font color to dark green (last column, sixth row) instead of dark blue. Do not change any of the other formatting attributes.
13. Save and then print the workbook.
14. Close **EL1-C6-A3-ProjEarnings.xlsx** and then close **EL1-C6-A3-Styles.xlsx** without saving the changes.

Assessment

4 INSERT HYPERLINKS IN A BOOKSTORE WORKBOOK

SNAP Grade It

1. Open **BGSpecials.xlsx** and then save the workbook with Save As and name it **EL1-C6-A4-BGSpecials.xlsx**.
2. Make cell E3 active and then create a hyperlink to www.microsoft.com.
3. Make cell E4 active and then create a hyperlink to www.symantec.com
4. Make cell E5 active and then create a hyperlink to www.nasa.gov.
5. Make cell E6 active and then create a hyperlink to www.cnn.com.
6. Make cell A8 active, type **Weekly specials!**, and then create a hyperlink to the workbook named **BGWklySpcls.xlsx**.
7. Click the hyperlink to the Microsoft website, explore the site, and then close the web browser.
8. Click the hyperlink to the NASA website, explore the site, and then close the web browser.
9. Click the <u>Weekly specials!</u> hyperlink, view the workbook, and then close the workbook.
10. Save, print, and then close **EL1-C6-A4-BGSpecials.xlsx**.

Assessment

5 APPLY CONDITIONAL FORMATTING TO A SALES WORKBOOK

Help

1. Use Excel Help files or experiment with the options at the Conditional Formatting button drop-down gallery to learn about conditional formatting.
2. Open **PSSales.xlsx** and then save the workbook with Save As and name it **EL1-C6-A5-PSSales**.
3. Select cells D5 through D19 and then use conditional formatting to display the amounts as data bars. (You choose the type of data bars.)
4. Insert a header that prints your name, a page number, and the current date.
5. Save, print, and then close **EL1-C6-A5-PSSales.xlsx**.

Visual Benchmark Demonstrate Your Proficiency

FILL IN AN EXPENSE REPORT FORM

1. Display the New backstage area, search for an expense report template, and then double-click the *Expense report* template shown in Figure 6.9.
2. With the expense report open, apply the Retrospect theme.
3. Select cells J1 through L1 and then apply the Note cell style.
4. Type the information in the cells as indicated in Figure 6.9.
5. Make cell L18 active and apply the Bad cell style.
6. Save the completed workbook and name it **EL1-C6-VB-OEExpRpt**.
7. Print and then close **EL1-C6-VB-OEExpRpt.xlsx**.

Figure 6.9 Visual Benchmark

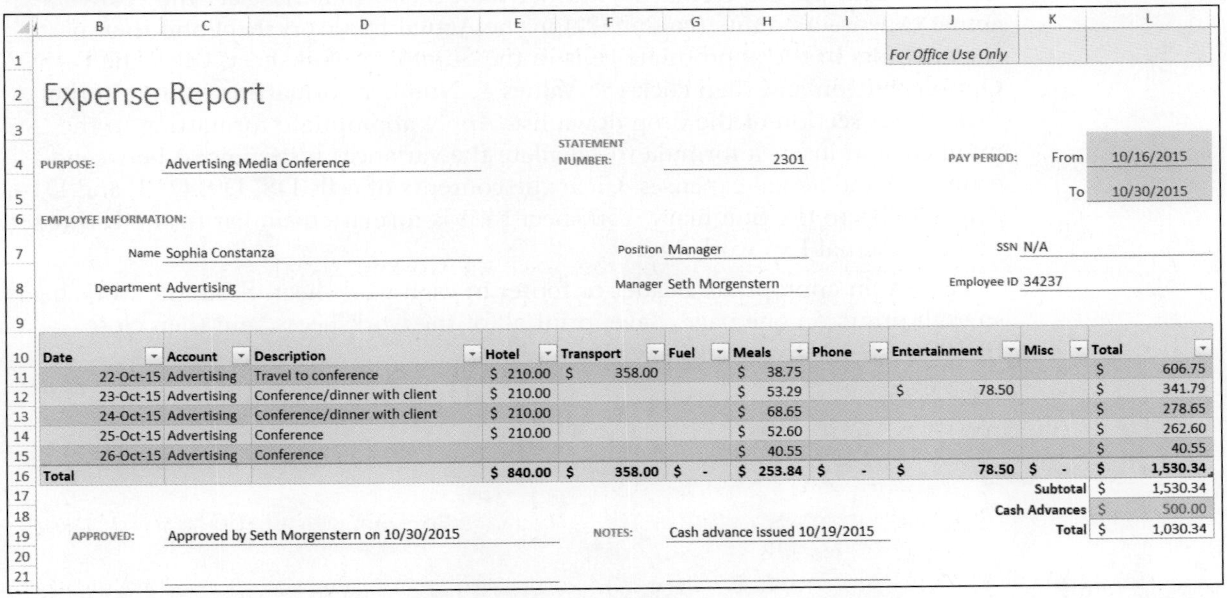

For Office Use Only

Expense Report

PURPOSE: Advertising Media Conference — STATEMENT NUMBER: 2301 — PAY PERIOD: From 10/16/2015 To 10/30/2015

EMPLOYEE INFORMATION:

Name Sophia Constanza — Position Manager — SSN N/A

Department Advertising — Manager Seth Morgenstern — Employee ID 34237

Date	Account	Description	Hotel	Transport	Fuel	Meals	Phone	Entertainment	Misc	Total
22-Oct-15	Advertising	Travel to conference	$ 210.00	$ 358.00		$ 38.75				$ 606.75
23-Oct-15	Advertising	Conference/dinner with client	$ 210.00			$ 53.29		$ 78.50		$ 341.79
24-Oct-15	Advertising	Conference/dinner with client	$ 210.00			$ 68.65				$ 278.65
25-Oct-15	Advertising	Conference	$ 210.00			$ 52.60				$ 262.60
26-Oct-15	Advertising	Conference				$ 40.55				$ 40.55
Total			$ 840.00	$ 358.00	$ -	$ 253.84	$ -	$ 78.50	$ -	$ 1,530.34
									Subtotal	$ 1,530.34
									Cash Advances	$ 500.00
									Total	$ 1,030.34

APPROVED: Approved by Seth Morgenstern on 10/30/2015 — NOTES: Cash advance issued 10/19/2015

Case Study Apply Your Skills

Part 1

You are the office manager for Leeward Marine and you decide to consolidate into one workbook several worksheets containing information on expenses. Open **LMEstExp.xlsx** and then save the workbook and name it **EL1-C6-CS-LMExpSummary**. Open **LMActExp.xlsx**, copy the worksheet into **EL1-C6-CS-LMExpSummary.xlsx**, make **LMActExp.xlsx** the active workbook, and then close it. Apply appropriate formatting to numbers and insert necessary formulas in each worksheet. (Use the Clear button in the HOME tab to clear the contents of cells N8, N9, N13, and N14 in both worksheets.) Include the company name, Leeward Marine, in both worksheets. Create styles and apply the styles to cells in both worksheets to maintain consistent formatting. Automatically adjust the widths of the columns to accommodate the longest entries. Save **EL1-C6-CS-LMExpSummary.xlsx**.

Part 2

You decide that you want to include another worksheet that displays the yearly estimated expenses, actual expenses, and variances (differences) between the two. With **EL1-C6-CS-LMExpSummary.xlsx** open, open **LMExpVar.xlsx**. Copy the worksheet into **EL1-C6-CS-LMExpSummary.xlsx**, make **LMExpVar.xlsx** the active workbook, and then close it. Rename the sheet tab containing the estimated expenses as *Estimated Exp*, rename the sheet tab containing the actual expenses as *Actual Exp*, and rename the sheet tab containing the variances as *Summary*. Recolor the three sheet tabs you just renamed.

Select the yearly estimated expense amounts (column N) in the Estimated Exp worksheet and then paste the amounts in the appropriate cells in the Summary worksheet. Click the Paste Options button and then click the Values & Number Formatting button in the *Paste Values* section of the drop-down list. (This pastes the value and the cell formatting, rather than the formula.) Select the yearly actual expense amounts (column N) in the Actual Exp worksheet and then paste the amounts in the appropriate cells in the Summary worksheet. Click the Paste Options button and then click the Values & Number Formatting button in the *Paste Values* section of the drop-down list. Apply appropriate formatting to the numbers and insert a formula to calculate the variances (differences) between estimated and actual expenses. Clear the contents of cells D8, D9, D13, and D14. Apply styles to the Summary worksheet so it is formatted similar to the Estimated Exp and Actual Exp worksheets.

Insert an appropriate header or footer in each worksheet. Scale the worksheets so each prints on one page. Save, print all of the worksheets, and then close **EL1-C6-CS-LMExpSummary.xlsx**.

Part 3

Based on the summary of the yearly expense variances, your supervisor has created projected expenses for next year and has asked you to format the worksheet. Open **LMProjectedExp.xlsx** and then save it and name it **EL1-C6-CS-LMProjectedExp**. Format the worksheet in a similar manner to the formatting you applied to **EL1-C6-CS-LMExpSummary.xlsx** (use the styles you created). Save and then close **EL1-C6-CS-LMProjectedExp.xlsx**. Open **EL1-C6-CS-LMExpSummary.xlsx**, make the Summary worksheet active and then insert a hyperlink to the **EL1-C6-CS-LMProjectedExp.xlsx** workbook. You determine the cell location and hyperlink text for the hyperlink. Save **EL1-C6-CS-LMExpSummary.xlsx** and then print only the Summary worksheet.

Part 4

You need to print a number of copies of the summary worksheet in the **EL1-C6-CS-LMExpSummary.xlsx** workbook and you want the company letterhead to print at the top of the page. You decide to use the letterhead in a Word document and copy the summary data from Excel into the Word letterhead document. To do this, open Word and then open the document named **LMLtrd.docx** (located in the EL1C6 folder on your storage medium). Press the Enter key two times. Make Excel the active program and with **EL1-C6-CS-LMExpSummary.xlsx** open, make the Summary worksheet active, select and then copy cells containing information on the yearly expense variances, and then paste them into the **LMLtrhd.docx** Word document as a picture object. (Click the Paste Options button and then click the Picture button.) Save the document with Save As and name it **EL1-C6-CS-LMExpSummary**. Print and then close **EL1-C6-CS-LMExpSummary.docx** and then close Word. In Excel, close **EL1-C6-CS-LMExpSummary.xlsx**.

MICROSOFT® EXCEL®

CHAPTER 7

Creating Charts and Inserting Formulas

PERFORMANCE OBJECTIVES

Upon successful completion of Chapter 7, you will be able to:

- **Create a chart with data in an Excel worksheet**
- **Size, move, edit, format, and delete charts**
- **Print a selected chart and print a worksheet containing a chart**
- **Change a chart location**
- **Insert, move, size, and delete chart elements and shapes**
- **Write formulas with the PMT and FV financial functions**
- **Write formulas with the IF logical function**

SNAP

Tutorials

7.1 Creating Charts in Excel
7.2 Editing Chart Data
7.3 Formatting with Chart Buttons
7.4 Printing Charts
7.5 Changing Chart Design
7.6 Changing Chart Formatting
7.7 Inserting and Formatting a Shape
7.8 Moving, Sizing, and Deleting a Chart
7.9 Using Financial Functions
7.10 Using the Logical IF Function

In the previous Excel chapters, you learned to create data in worksheets. While a worksheet does an adequate job of representing data, some data are better represented visually with a chart. A ***chart***, which is sometimes referred to as a ***graph***, is a picture of numeric data. In this chapter, you will learn to create and customize charts in Excel. You will also learn how to write formulas using financial and logical functions. Model answers for this chapter's projects appear on the following pages.

Excel
EL1C7

Note: Before beginning the projects, copy to your storage medium the EL1C7 subfolder from the EL1 folder on the CD that accompanies this textbook and then make EL1C7 the active folder.

Model Answers

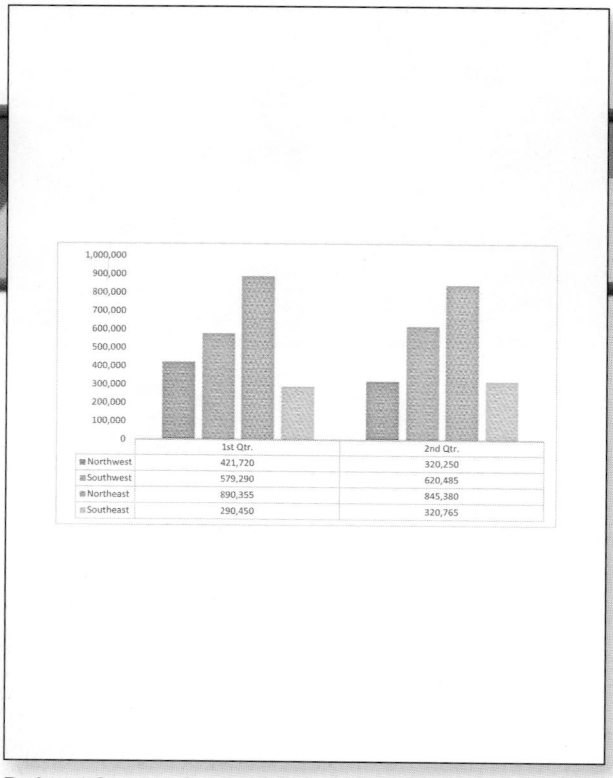

Project 1 Create a Quarterly Sales Column Chart
EL1-C7-P1-SalesChart.xlsx

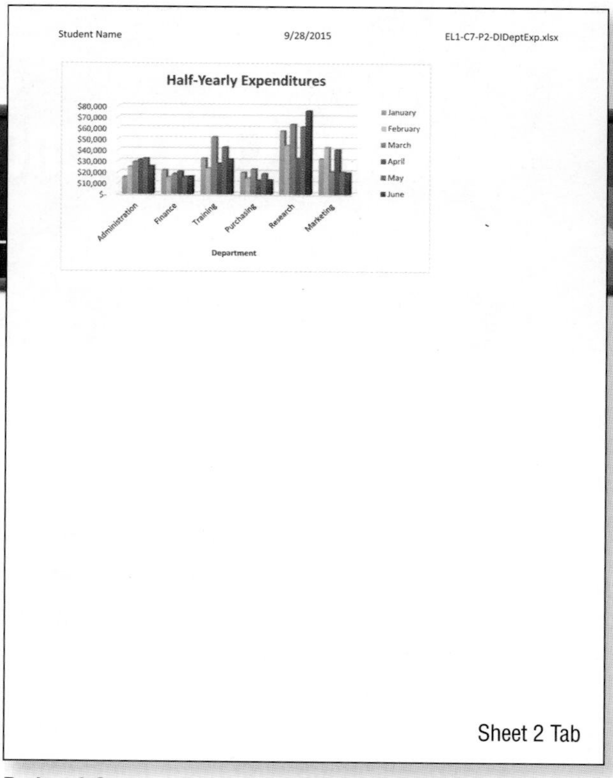

Project 2 Create a Technology Purchases Bar Chart and Column Chart
EL1-C7-P2-DIDeptExp.xlsx

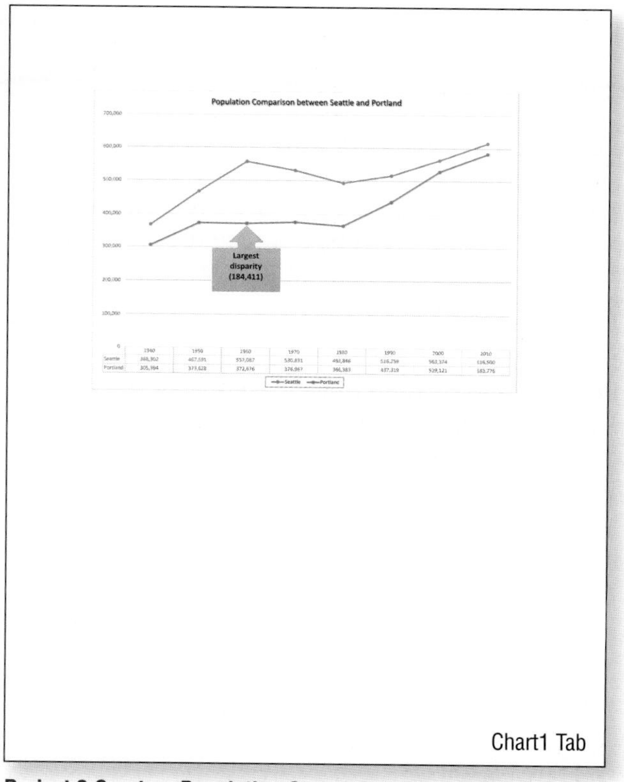

Project 3 Create a Population Comparison Line Chart
EL1-C7-P3-PopComp.xlsx

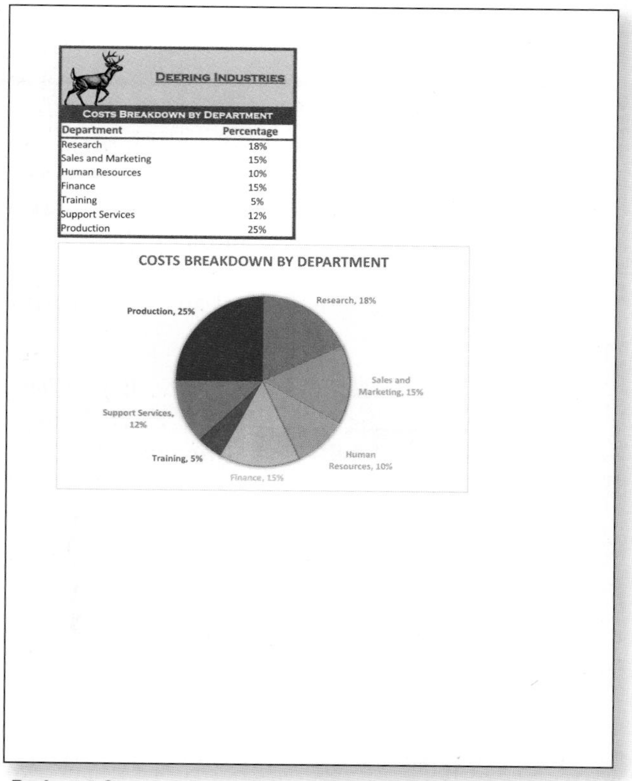

Project 4 Create a Costs Percentage Pie Chart
EL1-C7-P4-DIDeptCosts.xlsx

REAL PHOTOGRAPHY

Equipment Purchase Plans

Equipment	Purchase Price	Interest Rate	Term in Months	Monthly Payments
Developer, Model L10	$ 15,450.00	8.50%	60	($316.98)
Developer, Model S25	29,995.00	8.50%	60	($615.39)
Developer, Model E500	34,700.00	8.50%	60	($711.92)

	Purchase Price	Interest Rate	Term in Months	Monthly Payments
Pre-owned Van	$ 10,000.00	6.25%	36	($305.35)
	15,000.00	6.25%	36	($458.03)
	20,000.00	6.25%	36	($610.71)
	25,000.00	6.25%	36	($763.38)

	Sale Price	Interest Rate	Term in Months	Monthly Income
Camera	$ 6,250.00	4.50%	36	$185.92

REAL PHOTOGRAPHY

Future Value of Investment

Rate	7.50%
Number of Months	24
Monthly Payment	$ (1,200.00)
Future Value	$30,968.07

Project 5 Calculate Payments and the Future Value of an Investment

EL1-C7-P5-RPReports.xlsx

EL1-C7-P5-RPInvest.xlsx

Capstan Marine Products

Sales Department

Salesperson	Quota	Actual Sales	Bonus
Allejandro	$ 95,500.00	$ 103,295.00	$ 20,659.00
Crispin	137,000.00	129,890.00	-
Frankel	124,000.00	133,255.00	26,651.00
Hiesmann	85,500.00	94,350.00	18,870.00
Jarvis	159,000.00	167,410.00	33,482.00
Littleman	110,500.00	109,980.00	-

Sales Department

Product #	Price	Discount Price	Discount
C-2340	$ 1,250.00	$ 1,187.50	YES
C-3215	695.00	660.25	YES
C-4390	475.00	475.00	NO
E-2306	225.00	225.00	NO
E-3420	520.00	520.00	NO
G-2312	2,150.00	2,042.50	YES
G-4393	2,450.00	2,327.50	YES
J-1203	755.00	717.25	YES
J-3288	455.00	455.00	NO
J-4594	1,050.00	997.50	YES
M-2355	890.00	845.50	YES
M-3129	645.00	612.75	YES
M-4392	475.00	475.00	NO

New Employee Orientation

Name	Quiz 1	Quiz 2	Quiz 3	Average	Grade
Angelo	78	69	88	78	FAIL
Cunningham	90	95	86	90	PASS
Elliot	82	88	94	88	PASS
Kennedy	100	98	96	98	PASS
Lipscomb	64	76	62	67	FAIL

Project 6 Insert Formulas with the IF Logical Function

EL1-C7-P6-CMPReports.xlsx

Capstan Marine Products

Sales Department		
Salesperson	**Quota**	**Actual Sales**
Allejandro	95500	103295
Crispin	137000	129890
Frankel	124000	133255
Hiesmann	85500	94350
Jarvis	159000	167410
Littleman	110500	109980

Sales Department		
Product #	**Price**	**Discount Price**
C-2340	1250	=IF(B14>599,B14*0.95,B14)
C-3215	695	=IF(B15>599,B15*0.95,B15)
C-4390	475	=IF(B16>599,B16*0.95,B16)
E-2306	225	=IF(B17>599,B17*0.95,B17)
E-3420	520	=IF(B18>599,B18*0.95,B18)
G-2312	2150	=IF(B19>599,B19*0.95,B19)
G-4393	2450	=IF(B20>599,B20*0.95,B20)
J-1203	755	=IF(B21>599,B21*0.95,B21)
J-3288	455	=IF(B22>599,B22*0.95,B22)
J-4594	1050	=IF(B23>599,B23*0.95,B23)
M-2355	890	=IF(B24>599,B24*0.95,B24)
M-3129	645	=IF(B25>599,B25*0.95,B25)
M-4392	475	=IF(B26>599,B26*0.95,B26)

		New Employee Ori
Name	**Quiz 1**	**Quiz 2**
Angelo	78	69
Cunningham	90	95
Elliot	82	88
Kennedy	100	98
Lipscomb	64	76

Page 1

Bonus
=IF(C4>B4,C4*0.2,0)
=IF(C5>B5,C5*0.2,0)
=IF(C6>B6,C6*0.2,0)
=IF(C7>B7,C7*0.2,0)
=IF(C8>B8,C8*0.2,0)
=IF(C9>B9,C9*0.2,0)

Discount
=IF(B14>599,"YES","NO")
=IF(B15>599,"YES","NO")
=IF(B16>599,"YES","NO")
=IF(B17>599,"YES","NO")
=IF(B18>599,"YES","NO")
=IF(B19>599,"YES","NO")
=IF(B20>599,"YES","NO")
=IF(B21>599,"YES","NO")
=IF(B22>599,"YES","NO")
=IF(B23>599,"YES","NO")
=IF(B24>599,"YES","NO")
=IF(B25>599,"YES","NO")
=IF(B26>599,"YES","NO")

entation		
Quiz 3	**Average**	**Grade**
88	=AVERAGE(B31:D31)	=IF(E31>79,"PASS","FAIL")
86	=AVERAGE(B32:D32)	=IF(E32>79,"PASS","FAIL")
94	=AVERAGE(B33:D33)	=IF(E33>79,"PASS","FAIL")
96	=AVERAGE(B34:D34)	=IF(E34>79,"PASS","FAIL")
62	=AVERAGE(B35:D35)	=IF(E35>79,"PASS","FAIL")

Page 2

EL1-C7-P6-CMReports(Formulas).xlsx

Project 1 Create a Quarterly Sales Column Chart — 3 Parts

You will open a workbook containing quarterly sales data and then use the data to create a column chart. You will decrease the size of the chart, move it to a different location in the worksheet, and then make changes to sales numbers. You will also use buttons to customize and filter chart elements.

Creating a Chart

Quick Steps

Create a Chart
1. Select cells.
2. Click INSERT tab.
3. Click desired chart button.
4. Click desired chart style at drop-down gallery.

Recommended Charts

To provide a visual representation of your data, consider inserting data in a chart. With buttons in the Charts group on the INSERT tab, you can create a variety of charts, such as a column chart, line chart, pie chart, and much more. Excel provides 11 basic chart types, as described in Table 7.1.

To create a chart, select the cells in the worksheet that you want to chart, click the INSERT tab, and then click the desired chart button in the Charts group. At the drop-down gallery that displays, click the desired chart style. If you are not sure what type of chart will best illustrate your data, consider letting Excel recommend a chart. To do this, select the data, click the INSERT tab, and then click the Recommended Charts button. This displays the data in a chart in the Insert Chart dialog box. Customize the recommended chart with options in the left panel of the dialog box. Click the OK button to insert the recommended chart in the worksheet. You can also insert a recommended chart in the worksheet with the keyboard shortcut Alt+ F1.

Table 7.1 Types of Charts

Chart	*Description*
area	Emphasizes the magnitude of change rather than time and the rate of change. Also shows the relationship of the parts to the whole by displaying the sum of the plotted values.
bar	Shows individual figures at a specific time or shows variations between components but not in relationship to the whole.
bubble	Compares sets of three values in a manner similar to a scatter chart, with the third value displayed as the size of the bubble marker.
column	Compares separate (noncontinuous) items as they vary over time.
doughnut	Shows the relationship of the parts to the whole.
line	Shows trends and overall change across time at even intervals. Emphasizes the rate of change across time rather than the magnitude of change.
pie	Shows proportions and the relationship of the parts to the whole.
radar	Emphasizes differences and amounts of change over time and variations and trends. Each category has a value axis radiating from the center point. Lines connect all values in the same series.
stock	Shows four values for a stock: open, high, low, and close.
surface	Shows trends in values across two dimensions in a continuous curve.
xy (scatter)	Shows the relationships among numeric values in several data series or plots the interception points between *x* and *y* values. Shows uneven intervals of data and is commonly used in scientific data.

Sizing and Moving a Chart

When you create a chart, it is inserted in the same worksheet as the selected cells. Figure 7.1 displays the worksheet and chart you will create in Project 1a. The chart is inserted in a box, which you can size and/or move in the worksheet.

Change the size of the chart using the sizing handles (white squares) that display on the chart borders. Drag the top and bottom middle sizing handles to increase or decrease the height of the chart; use the left and right middle sizing handles to increase or decrease the width; and use the corner sizing handles to increase or decrease the height and width at the same time. To increase or decrease the size of the chart but maintain its proportions, hold down the Shift key while dragging one of the chart's corner borders.

To move the chart, make sure the chart is selected (border with sizing handles displays around the chart), position the mouse pointer on a border until the pointer displays with a four-headed arrow attached, hold down the left mouse button, and then drag to the desired position.

Quick Steps

Create a Recommended Chart

1. Select cells.
2. Click INSERT tab.
3. Click Recommended Charts button.
4. Click OK at Insert Chart dialog box.

OR

1. Select cells.
2. Press Alt + F1.

HINT

Hide rows or columns that you do not want to chart.

Editing Data and Adding a Data Series

The cells you select to create the chart are linked to it. If you need to change the data for a chart, edit the data in the desired cell and the corresponding section of the chart will be automatically updated. If you add data to cells within the range

range of cells used for chart

of cells used for the chart, called the source data, the new data will be included in the chart. If you add a data series in cells next to or below the source data, you will need to click in the chart to display the source data with sizing handles and then drag with a sizing handle to include the new data.

Figure 7.1 Project 1a Chart

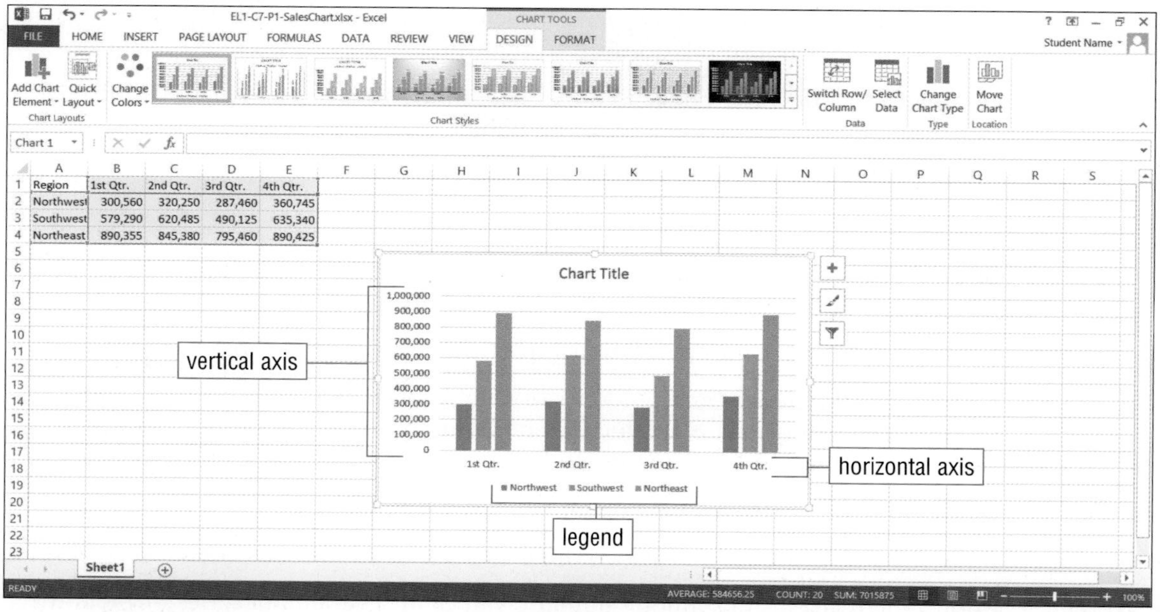

Project 1a Creating a Chart

Part 1 of 3

1. Open **SalesChart.xlsx** and then save the workbook with Save As and name it **EL1-C7-P1-SalesChart.**
2. Select cells A1 through E4.
3. Let Excel recommend a chart type by completing the following steps:
   a. Click the INSERT tab.
   b. Click the Recommended Charts button in the Charts group.

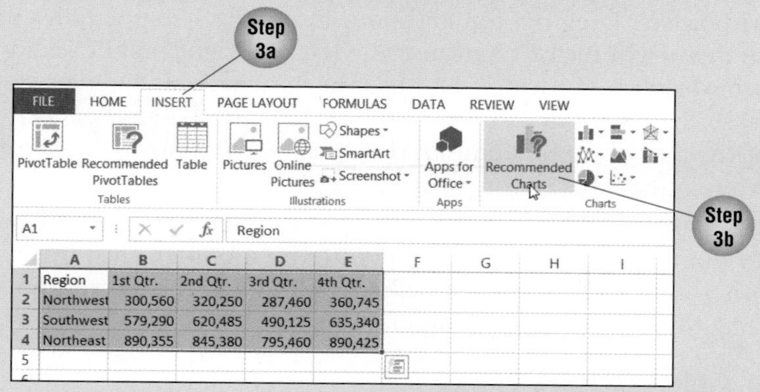

   c. At the Insert Chart dialog box, look at the options that display in the left panel and then click OK.

4. Slightly increase the size of the chart and maintain its proportions by completing the following steps:
   a. Position the mouse pointer on the sizing handle in the lower right corner of the chart border until the pointer turns into a two-headed arrow pointing diagonally.
   b. Hold down the Shift key and then hold down the left mouse button.
   c. Drag out approximately 0.5 inch. Release the mouse button and then release the Shift key.

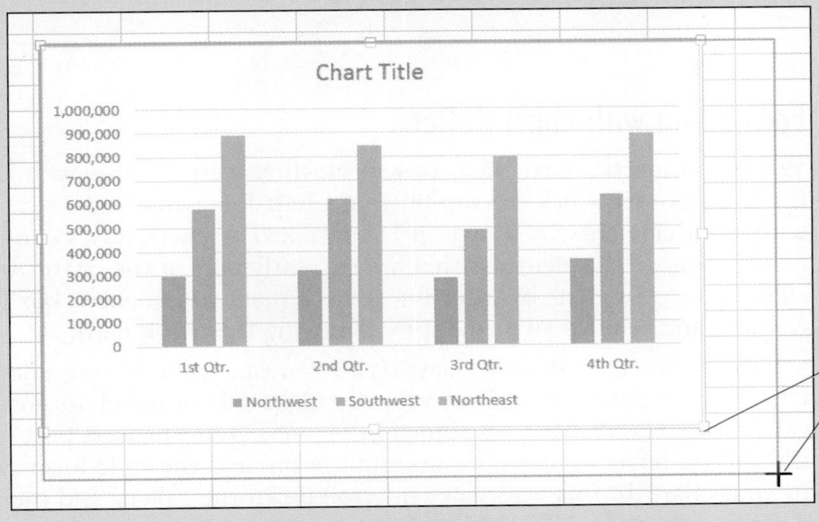

5. Move the chart below the cells containing data by completing the following steps:
   a. Make sure the chart is selected. (When the chart is selected, the border surrounding it displays with sizing handles.)
   b. Position the mouse pointer on the chart border until the pointer displays with a four-headed arrow attached.
   c. Hold down the left mouse button, drag the chart so it is positioned in row 6 below the cells containing data, and then release the mouse button.

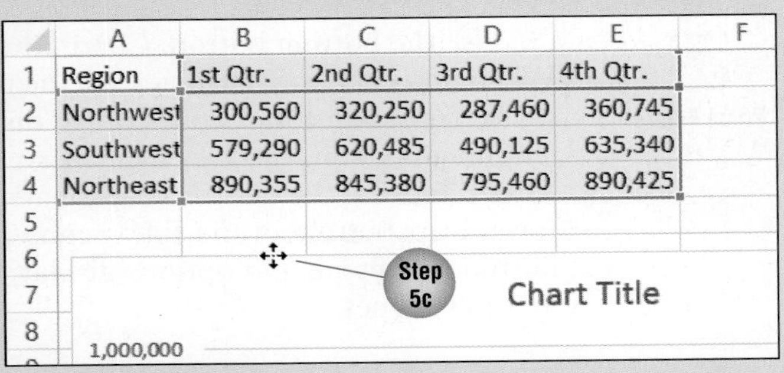

	A	B	C	D	E	F
1	Region	1st Qtr.	2nd Qtr.	3rd Qtr.	4th Qtr.	
2	Northwest	300,560	320,250	287,460	360,745	
3	Southwest	579,290	620,485	490,125	635,340	
4	Northeast	890,355	845,380	795,460	890,425	
5						
6						
7						
8						

6. Make the following changes to the specified cells:
   a. Make cell B2 active and then change *300,560* to *421,720*.
   b. Make cell D2 active and then change *287,460* to *397,460*.
7. Add a new data series by typing data in the following cells:
   A5: Southeast
   B5: 290,450
   C5: 320,765
   D5: 270,450
   E5: 300,455

8. Add the new data series to the chart by completing the following steps:
   a. Click in the chart. (This selects the data source A1 through E4.)
   b. Position the mouse pointer on the sizing handle in the lower right corner of cell E4 until the pointer displays as a two-headed diagonally pointing arrow.
   c. Hold down the left mouse button, drag down to cell E5, and then release the mouse button. (This incorporates the data row E in the chart.)
9. Save **EL1-C7-P1-SalesChart.xlsx**.

Formatting with Chart Buttons

Chart Elements

When you insert a chart in a worksheet, three buttons display at the right side of the chart border. Click the top button, Chart Elements, and a side menu displays with chart elements, as shown in Figure 7.2. The check boxes containing check marks indicate the elements that are currently part of the chart. Add a new element to your chart by inserting a check mark in the check box for the desired element and remove an element by removing the check mark.

Chart Styles

Excel offers a variety of chart styles you can apply to your chart. Click the Chart Styles button that displays at the right side of the chart and a side menu gallery of styles displays, as shown in Figure 7.3 on the next page. Scroll down the gallery, hover your mouse over an option, and the style formatting is applied to your chart. In this way, you can scroll down the gallery and then choose the desired chart style.

In addition to applying a chart style, you can use the Chart Styles button side menu gallery to change the chart colors. Click the Chart Styles button and then click the COLOR tab that displays to the right of the STYLE tab. Click the desired color option at the color palette that displays. Hover your mouse over a color option to view how the color change affects the elements in your chart.

Chart Filters

Use the bottom button, Chart Filters, to isolate specific data in your chart. When you click the button, a side menu displays, as shown in Figure 7.4. Specify the series or categories you want to display in your chart. To do this, remove check marks from those elements that you do not want to appear in your chart. After removing the desired check marks, click the Apply button that displays toward the bottom of the side menu. Click the NAMES tab at the Chart Filters button side menu and options display for turning on/off the display of column and row names.

Figure 7.2 Chart Elements Button Side Menu Gallery

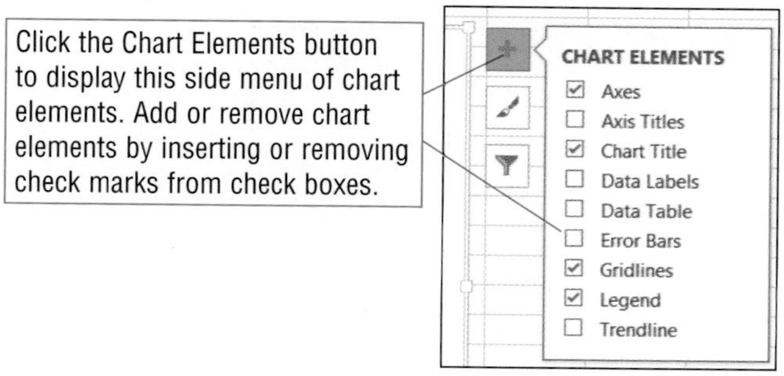

Figure 7.3 Chart Styles Button Side Menu Gallery

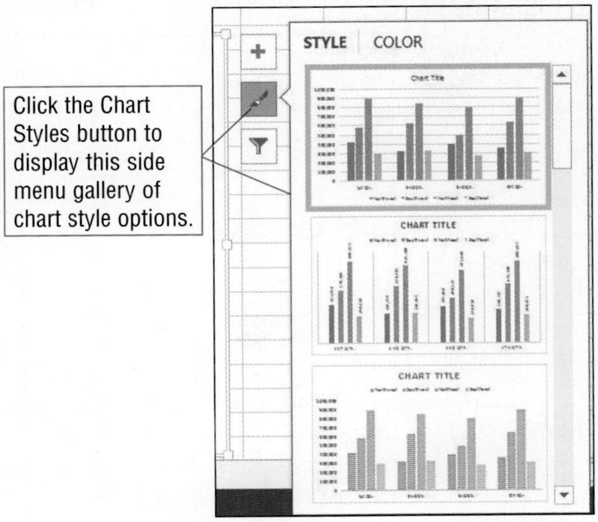

Figure 7.4 Chart Filters Button Side Menu

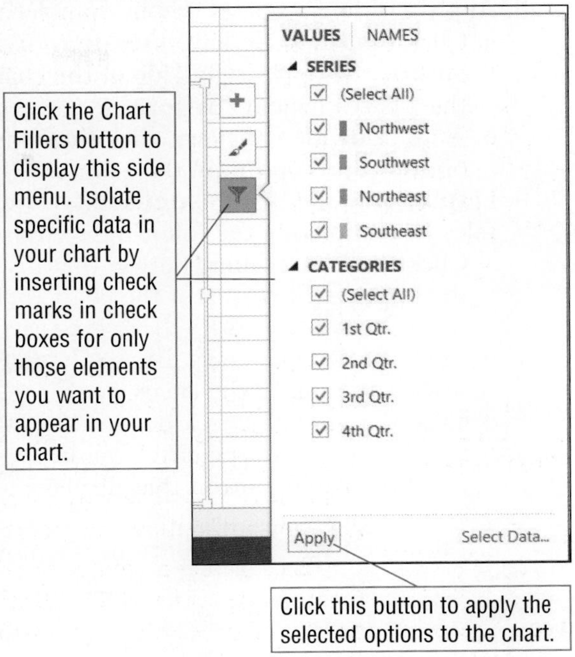

Project 1b Formatting with Chart Buttons

Part 2 of 3

1. With **EL1-C7-P1-SalesChart.xlsx** open, make the chart active by clicking inside the chart but outside any elements.
2. Insert and remove chart elements by completing the following steps:
   a. Click the Chart Elements button that displays outside the upper right side of the chart.
   b. At the side menu that displays, click the *Chart Title* check box to remove the check mark.
   c. Click the *Data Table* check box to insert a check mark.
   d. Hover your mouse over *Gridlines* in the Chart Elements button side menu and then click the right-pointing triangle that displays.
   e. At the side menu that displays, click the *Primary Major Vertical* check box to insert a check mark.
   f. Click the *Legend* check box to remove the check mark.

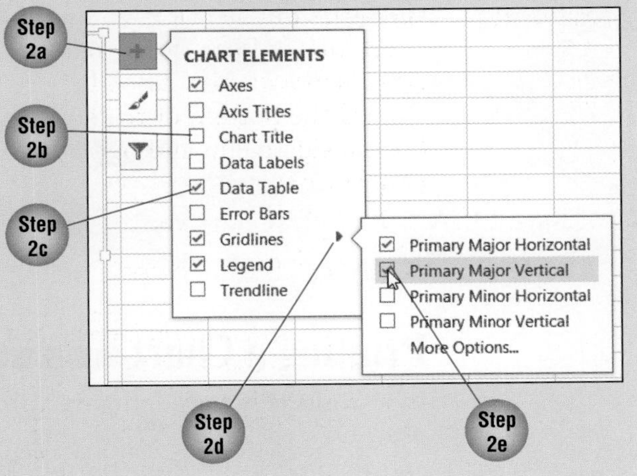

3. Apply a different chart style by completing the following steps:
   a. Click the Chart Styles button that displays outside the upper right side of the chart (below the Chart Elements button).
   b. At the side menu gallery, click the *Style 3* option (third option in the gallery).

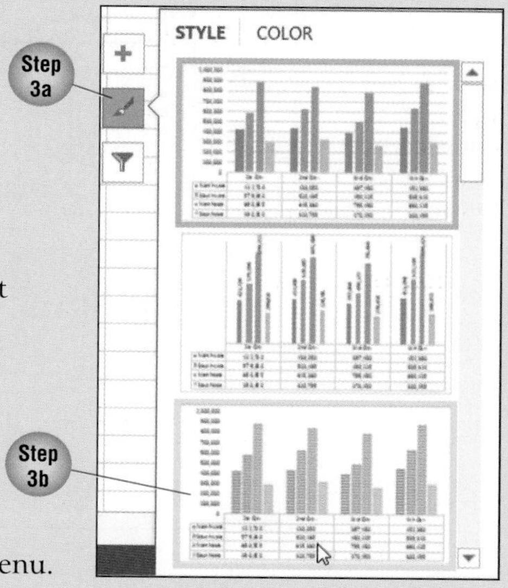

4. Display only the first quarter and second quarter sales by completing the following steps:
   a. Click the Chart Filters button that displays outside the upper right corner of the chart (below the Chart Styles button).
   b. Click the *3rd Qtr.* check box in the *CATEGORIES* section to remove the check mark.
   c. Click the *4th Qtr.* check box in the *CATEGORIES* section to remove the check mark.
   d. Click the Apply button that displays toward the bottom of the side menu.
   e. Click the Chart Filters button to remove the side menu.

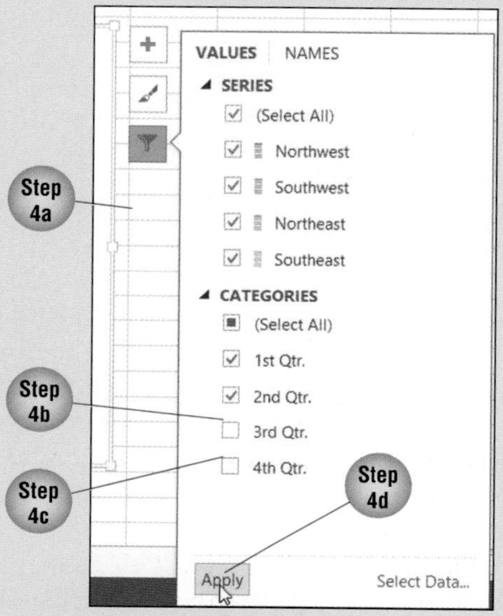

5. Save **EL1-C7-P1-SalesChart.xlsx**.

Printing a Chart

In a worksheet containing data in cells as well as a chart, you have the option to print only the chart. To do this, select the chart, display the Print backstage area, and then click the Print button. With a chart selected, the first gallery in the *Settings* category is automatically changed to *Print Selected Chart*. A preview of the chart displays at the right side of the Print backstage area.

Project 1c Printing a Chart

Part 3 of 3

1. With **EL1-C7-P1-SalesChart.xlsx** open, make sure the chart is selected.
2. Click the FILE tab and then click the *Print* option.
3. At the Print backstage area, look at the preview of the chart that displays at the right side and notice that the first gallery in the *Settings* category is set to *Print Selected Chart*.
4. Click the Print button.
5. Save and then close **EL1-C7-P1-SalesChart.xlsx**.

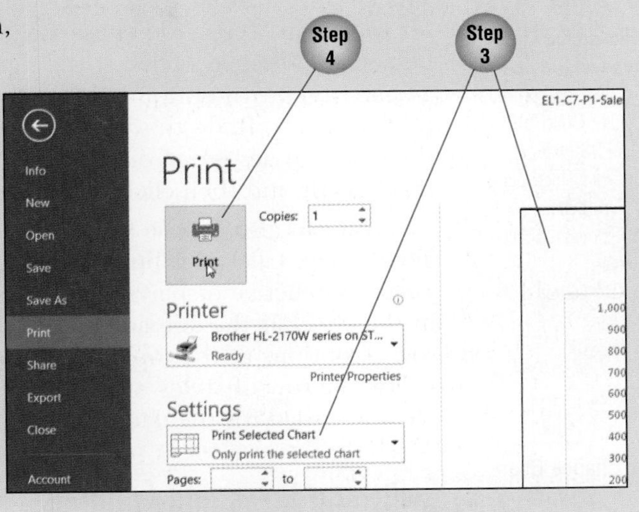

Project 2 Create a Technology Purchases Bar Chart and Column Chart

2 Parts

You will open a workbook containing technology-purchases data by department and then create a bar chart with the data. You will then change the chart type, layout, and style; add chart elements; and move the chart to a new worksheet.

Changing the Chart Design

Along with the buttons that display outside the upper right side of the chart, you can apply formatting to change the chart design with options on the CHART TOOLS DESIGN tab. This tab, shown in Figure 7.5, displays when you insert a chart in a worksheet. Use options on this tab to add chart elements, change the chart type, specify a different layout or style for the chart, and change the location of the chart so it displays in a separate worksheet.

Figure 7.5 CHART TOOLS DESIGN Tab

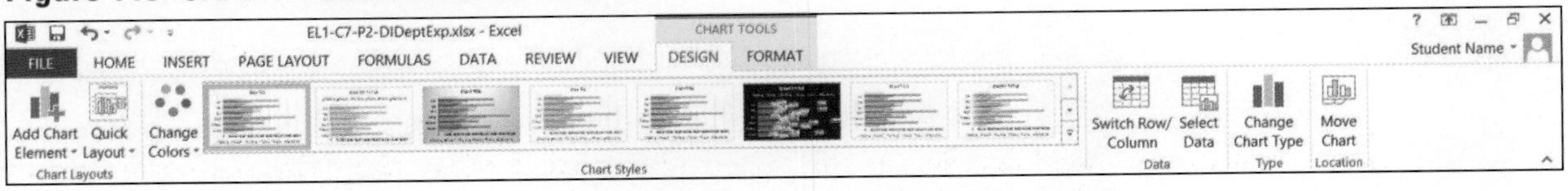

Changing the Chart Style

Quick Steps

Change the Chart Type and Style

1. Make chart active.
2. Click CHART TOOLS DESIGN tab.
3. Click Change Chart Type button.
4. Click desired chart type.
5. Click desired chart style.
6. Click OK.

Change Chart Type

The chart feature offers a variety of preformatted custom charts and varying styles for each chart type. You chose a chart style in Project 1b using the Chart Styles button that displays outside the right border of the chart. You can also choose a chart style with options in the Chart Styles group on the CHART TOOLS DESIGN tab. To do this, click the desired chart style thumbnail that displays in the Chart Styles group or click the More button that displays to the right of the thumbnails and then click the desired chart style thumbnail.

You can also choose a chart style with the Change Chart Type button in the Type group. Click this button and the Change Chart Type dialog box with the All Charts tab active displays, as shown in Figure 7.6. Click the desired chart type in the panel at the left side of the dialog box, click the desired chart style in the row of options at the top at the right, and then click a specific style that displays below the row of styles. Click the Recommended Chart tab to display chart styles recommended for the data by Excel.

Switching Rows and Columns

Quick Steps

Switch Rows and Columns

1. Make chart active.
2. Click CHART TOOLS DESIGN tab.
3. Click Switch Row/ Column button.

Switch Row/Column

When creating a chart, Excel uses row headings for grouping data along the bottom of the chart (the horizontal axis) and uses column headings for the legend. You can change this order by clicking the Switch Row/Column button in the Data group on the CHART TOOLS DESIGN tab. When you click this button, Excel uses the column headings for grouping data along the horizontal axis and uses row headings for the legend.

Figure 7.6 Change Chart Type Dialog Box

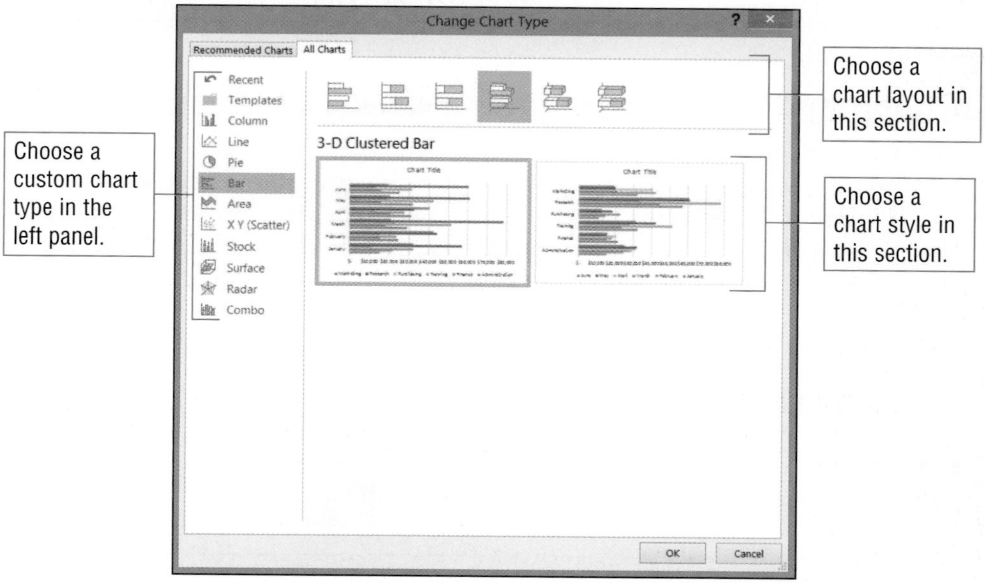

Project 2a Creating a Chart and Changing the Design

Part 1 of 2

1. Open **DIDeptExp.xlsx** and then save the workbook with Save As and name it **EL1-C7-P2-DIDeptExp**.
2. Create a bar chart by completing the following steps:
   a. Select cells A3 through G9.
   b. Click the INSERT tab.
   c. Click the Insert Bar Chart button in the Charts group.
   d. Click the *3-D Clustered Bar* option (first option in the *3-D Bar* section).

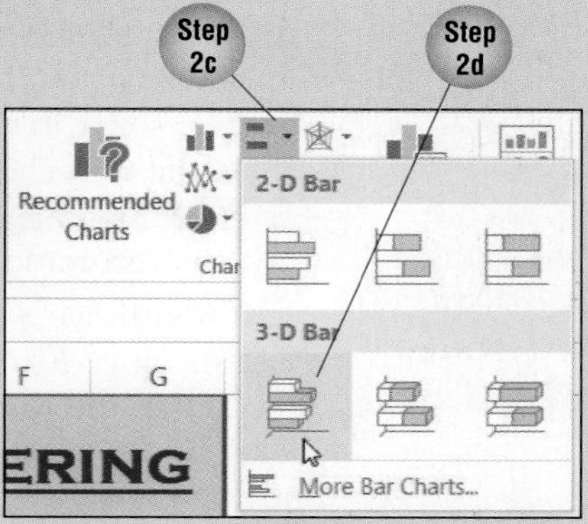

3. With the CHART TOOLS DESIGN tab active, change the chart type by completing the following steps:
   a. Click the Change Chart Type button located in the Type group.
   b. At the Change Chart Type dialog box, click the *Column* option in the left panel.
   c. Click the *3-D Clustered Column* option in the top row (fourth option from left).
   d. Click OK to close the Change Chart Type dialog box.

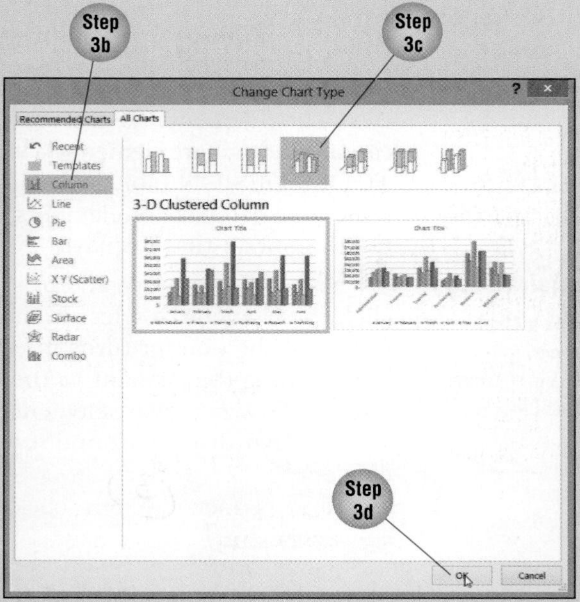

4. With the chart selected and the CHART TOOLS DESIGN tab active, click the Switch Row/Column button located in the Data group.

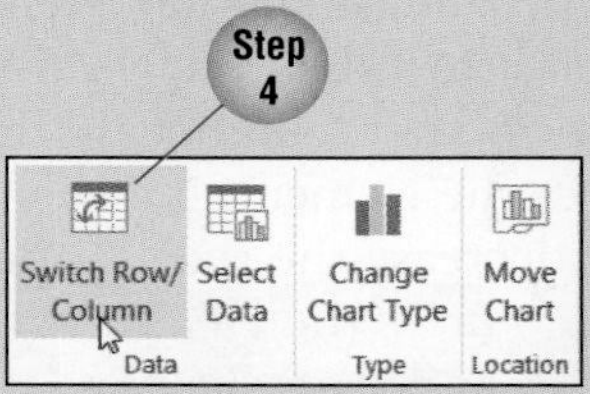

5. Save **EL1-C7-P2-DIDeptExp.xlsx**.

Changing Chart Layout and Colors

The CHART TOOLS DESIGN tab contains options for changing the chart layout and chart colors. Click the Quick Layout button in the Chart Layouts group and a drop-down gallery of layout options displays. Hover the mouse over a layout option at the drop-down gallery and the chart will reflect the layout. Change the colors used in the chart by clicking the Change Colors button in the Chart Styles group and then clicking the desired color at the drop-down gallery.

Quick Layout

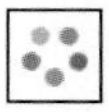

Change Colors

Changing the Chart Location

Quick Steps

Change the Chart Location

1. Make chart active.
2. Click CHART TOOLS DESIGN tab.
3. Click Move Chart button.
4. Click *New Sheet* option.
5. Click OK.

Move Chart

Create a chart and the chart is inserted in the currently open worksheet as an embedded object. Change the location of a chart with the Move Chart button in the Location group on the CHART TOOLS DESIGN tab. Click this button and the Move Chart dialog box displays, as shown in Figure 7.7. To move the chart to a new sheet in the workbook, click the *New sheet* option; Excel automatically names the new sheet *Chart1*. Earlier in this chapter you learned that pressing Alt + F1 will insert a recommended chart in the currently open worksheet. If you want the recommended chart inserted into a separate worksheet, press F11.

If you move a chart to a separate sheet, you can move it back to the original sheet or move it to a different sheet within the workbook. To move a chart to a sheet, click the Move Chart button in the Location group. At the Move Chart dialog box, click the down-pointing arrow at the right side of the *Object in* option and then click the desired sheet at the drop-down list. Click OK and the chart is inserted in the specified sheet as an object that you can move, size, and format.

Adding, Moving, and Deleting Chart Elements

Add Chart Element

As you learned earlier in this chapter, you can add chart elements to a chart with the Chart Elements button that displays at the right side of a selected chart. You can also add chart elements with the Add Chart Element button on the CHART TOOLS DESIGN tab. Click this button to display a drop-down list of elements, point to a category of elements, and then click the element you want to apply at the side menu that displays.

Quick Steps

Delete a Chart Element

1. Click chart element.
2. Press Delete key.

OR

1. Right-click chart element.
2. Click *Delete*.

You can also move and/or size a chart element. To move a chart element, click the element to select it and then move the mouse pointer over the border line until the pointer turns into a four-headed arrow. Hold down the left mouse button, drag the element to the desired location, and then release the mouse button. To size a chart element, click to select the element and then use the sizing handles that display around it to increase or decrease the size. To delete a chart element, click the element to select it and then press the Delete key. You can also delete an element by right-clicking the element and then clicking *Delete* at the shortcut menu.

Figure 7.7 Move Chart Dialog Box

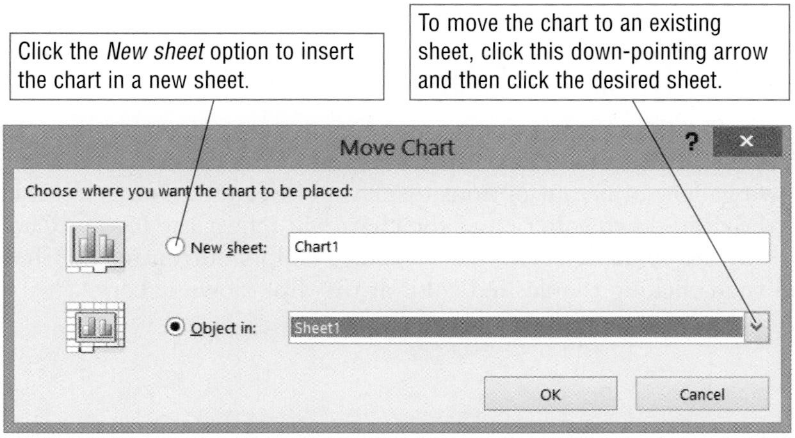

Project 2b Changing Chart Layout and Location and Adding Chart Elements Part 2 of 2

1. With **EL1-C7-P2-DIDeptExp.xlsx** open, make sure the CHART TOOLS DESIGN tab is active. (If it is not, make sure the chart is selected and then click the CHART TOOLS DESIGN tab.)
2. Change the chart style by clicking the *Style 5* thumbnail in the Chart Styles group (fifth option from the left).

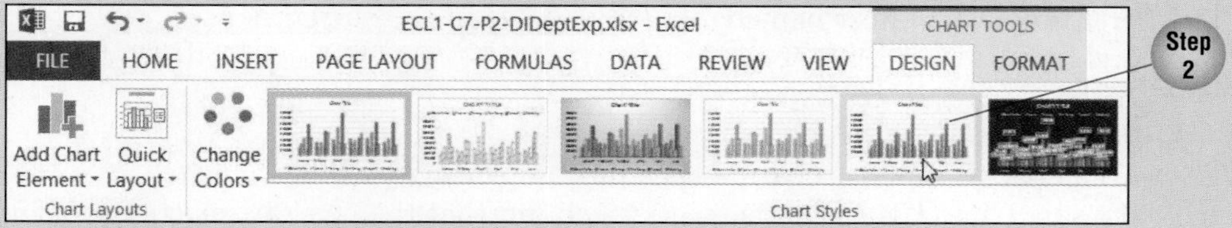

3. Change the chart colors by clicking the Change Colors button in the Chart Styles group and then clicking the *Color 3* option (third row in the *Colorful* group).
4. Change the chart layout by clicking the Quick Layout button in the Chart Layouts group and then clicking the *Layout 1* option (first option in the drop-down gallery).

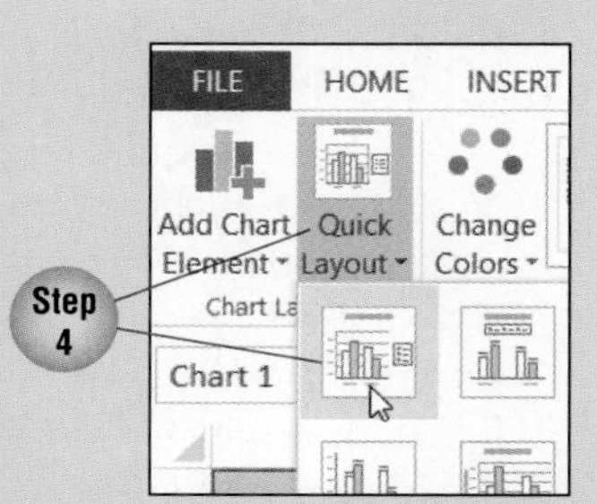

5. Add axis titles by completing the following steps:
   a. Click the Add Chart Element button in the Chart Layouts group on the CHART TOOLS DESIGN tab.
   b. Point to *Axis Titles* and then click *Primary Horizontal* at the side menu.
   c. Type **Department** and then press Enter. (The word *Department* will display in the Formula bar.)
   d. Click the Add Chart Element button, point to *Axis Titles*, and then click *Primary Vertical* at the side menu.
   e. Type **Expenditure Amounts** and then press Enter.

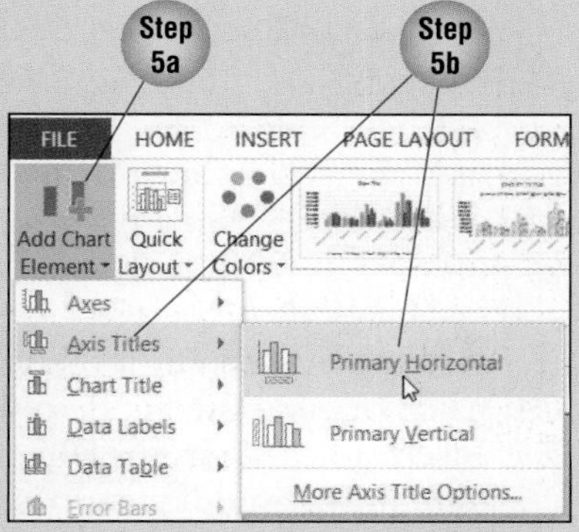

6. Click in the text *Chart Title* that displays toward the top of the chart, type **Half-Yearly Expenditures**, and then press Enter.
7. Delete the *Expenditure Amounts* axis title by clicking on any character in the axis title and then pressing the Delete key.
8. Move the legend by completing the following steps:
   a. Click on any character in the legend to select it.
   b. Move the mouse pointer over the border line until the pointer turns into a four-headed arrow.
   c. Hold down the left mouse button, drag up until the top border of the legend aligns with the top gridline in the chart, and then release the mouse button.

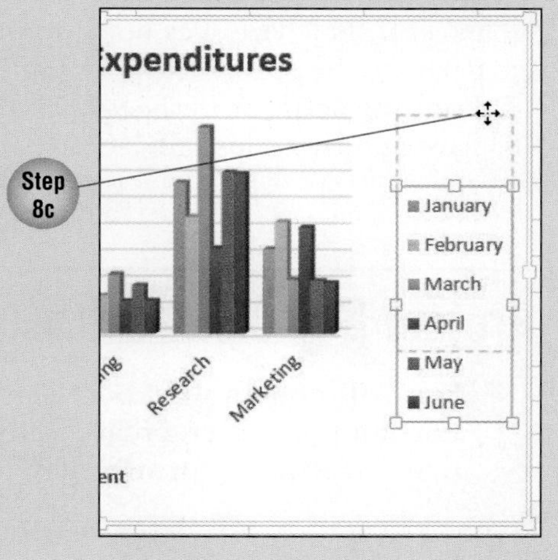

9. Move the chart to a new location by completing the following steps:
   a. Click the Move Chart button in the Location group.
   b. At the Move Chart dialog box, click the *New sheet* option and then click OK. (The chart is inserted in a worksheet named *Chart1*.)

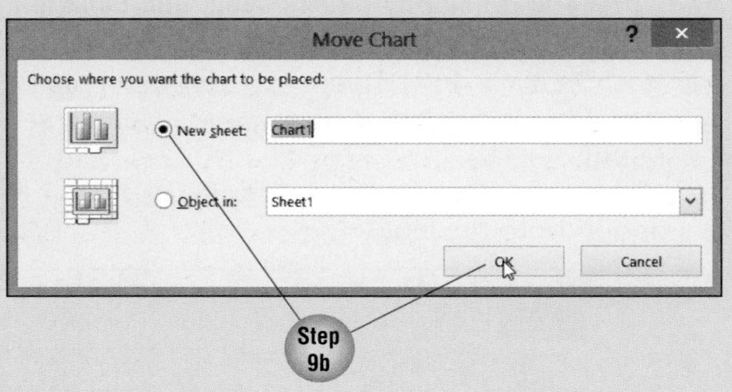

10. Save **EL1-C7-P2-DIDeptExp.xlsx**.
11. Print the Chart1 worksheet.
12. Move the chart from Chart1 to Sheet2 by completing the following steps:
    a. Make sure Chart1 is the active worksheet and that the chart is selected (not just an element in the chart).
    b. Make sure the CHART TOOLS DESIGN tab is active.
    c. Click the Move Chart button in the Location group.
    d. At the Move Chart dialog box, click the down-pointing arrow at the right side of the *Object in* option box and then click *Sheet2* at the drop-down list.
    e. Click OK.

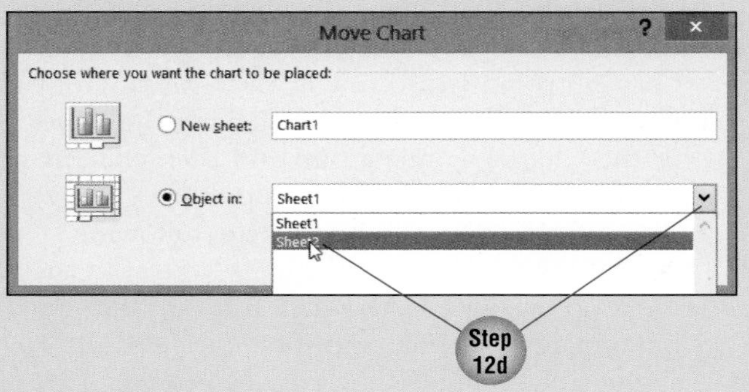

13. Change the amounts in Sheet1 by completing the following steps:
    a. Click Sheet1.
    b. Make cell B7 active and then change the amount from *10,540* to *19,750*.
    c. Make cell D8 active and then change the amount from *78,320* to *63,320*.
    d. Make cell G8 active and then change the amount from *60,570* to *75,570*.
    e. Make cell A2 active.
    f. Click the Sheet2 tab and notice that the chart displays the updated amounts.
14. Click outside the chart to deselect it.
15. Insert a header in the Sheet2 worksheet that prints your name at the left side, the current date in the middle, and the workbook file name at the right side.
16. Display the worksheet at the Print backstage area and make sure it will print on one page. If the chart does not fit on the page, return to the worksheet and then move and/or decrease the size of the chart until it fits on one page.
17. Print the active worksheet (Sheet2).
18. Save and then close **EL1-C7-P2-DIDeptExp.xlsx**.

Project 3 Create a Population Comparison Line Chart — 2 Parts

You will open a workbook containing population comparison data for Seattle and Portland and then create a line chart with the data. You will move the chart to a new worksheet, format chart elements, and insert a shape in the chart.

Changing Chart Formatting

Customize the formatting of a chart and chart elements with options on the CHART TOOLS FORMAT tab, as shown in Figure 7.8. With buttons in the Current Selection group, you can identify specific elements in the chart and then apply formatting. Insert a shape in a chart with options in the Insert Shapes group and format shapes with options in the Shape Styles group. Apply WordArt formatting to data in a chart with options in the WordArt Styles group. Arrange, align, and size a chart with options in the Arrange and Size groups.

Formatting a Selection

Identify a specific element in a chart for formatting by clicking the Chart Elements button arrow in the Current Selection group on the CHART TOOLS FORMAT tab and then clicking the desired element at the drop-down list. This selects the specific element in the chart. Click the Reset to Match Style button to return the formatting of the element back to the original style. Use buttons in the Shapes Styles group to apply formatting to a selected object and use buttons in the WordArt Styles group to apply formatting to selected data.

Chart Elements

Figure 7.8 CHART TOOLS FORMAT Tab

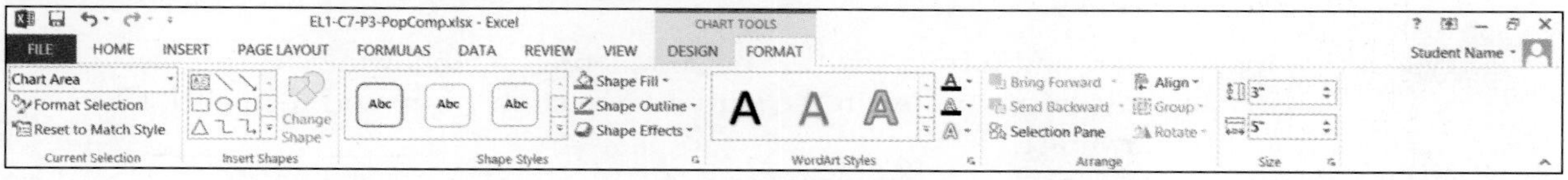

Project 3a **Creating and Formatting a Line Chart** **Part 1 of 2**

1. Open **PopComp.xlsx** and then save the workbook with Save As and name it **EL1-C7-P3-PopComp**.
2. Create a line chart and add a chart element by completing the following steps:
   a. Select cells A2 through I4.
   b. Click the INSERT tab.
   c. Click the Insert Line Chart button in the Charts group.
   d. Click the *Line with Markers* option at the drop-down list (first column, second row in the *2-D Line* section).
   e. Click the Chart Elements button that displays outside the upper right side of the chart.
   f. Hover your mouse over the *Data Table* option at the side menu, click the right-pointing triangle that displays, and then click *No Legend Keys* at the side menu that appears.
   g. Click the Chart Elements button to remove the side menu.
3. Move the chart to a new sheet by completing the following steps:
   a. Click the Move Chart button in the Location group on the CHART TOOLS DESIGN tab.
   b. At the Move Chart dialog box, click the *New sheet* option.
   c. Click OK.

4. Format the *Portland* line by completing the following steps:
   a. Click the CHART TOOLS FORMAT tab.
   b. Click the Chart Elements button arrow in the Current Selection group and then click *Series "Portland"* at the drop-down list.
   c. Click the Shape Fill button arrow in the Shape Styles group and then click the *Green* color at the drop-down color palette (sixth color in the *Standard Colors* section).

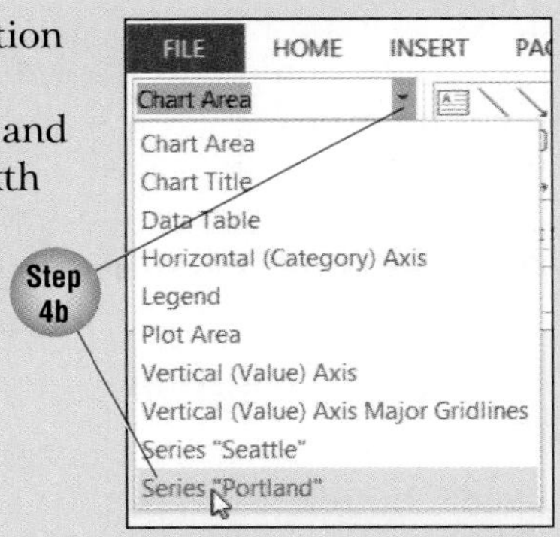

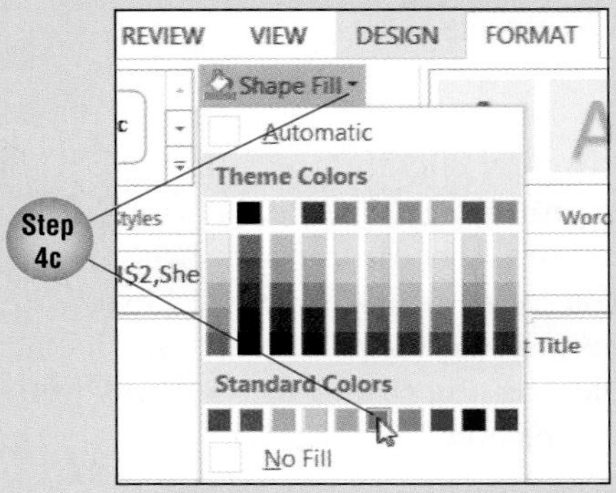

   d. Click the Shape Outline button arrow in the Shape Styles group and then click the *Green* color.
5. Type a title for the chart and format the title by completing the following steps:
   a. Click Chart Elements button arrow in the Current Selection group and then click *Chart Title* at the drop-down list.
   b. Type **Population Comparison between Seattle and Portland** and then press Enter.
   c. Click the *Fill - Black, Text 1, Shadow* WordArt style thumbnail in the WordArt Styles group (first WordArt style thumbnail).

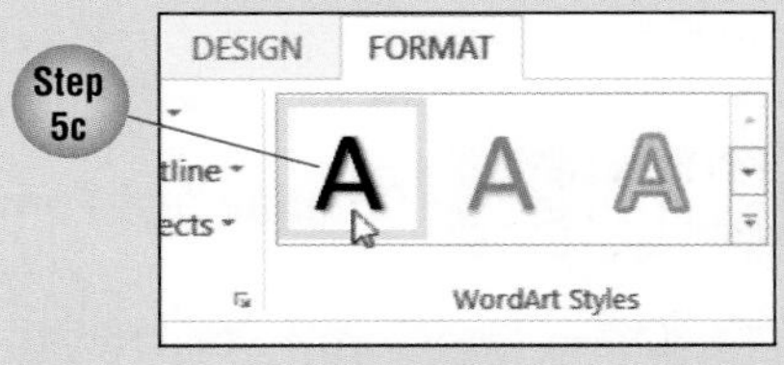

6. Format the legend by completing the following steps:
   a. Click the Chart Elements button arrow in the Current Selection group and then click *Legend* at the drop-down list.
   b. Click the *Colored Outline - Blue, Accent 1* shape style thumbnail in the Shape Styles group (second shape style thumbnail).
7. Save **EL1-C7-P3-PopComp.xlsx**.

Inserting Shapes

Quick Steps

Insert a Shape
1. Make chart active.
2. Click CHART TOOLS FORMAT tab.
3. Click More button at right side of shapes.
4. Click desired shape at drop-down list.
5. Click or drag to create shape in chart.

The Insert Shapes group on the CHART TOOLS FORMAT tab contains options for inserting shapes in a chart. Click a shape option and the mouse pointer turns into a thin, black plus symbol. Click in the chart or drag with the mouse to create the shape in the chart. The shape is inserted in the chart and the DRAWING TOOLS FORMAT tab is active. This tab contains many of the same options as the CHART TOOLS FORMAT tab. For example, you can insert a shape, apply a shape or WordArt style, and arrange and size the shape. Size a shape by clicking the up- or down-pointing arrows that display at the right side of the *Shape Height* or *Shape Width* measurement boxes in the Size group on the DRAWING TOOLS FORMAT tab. You can also select the current measurement and then type a specific measurement.

Project 3b Inserting and Customizing a Shape Part 2 of 2

1. With **EL1-C7-P3-PopComp.xlsx** open, create a shape similar to the one shown in Figure 7.9 on the next page by completing the following steps:
   a. Click the More button at the right side of the shapes in the Insert Shapes group on the CHART TOOLS FORMAT tab.
   b. Click the *Up Arrow Callout* shape in the *Block Arrows* section.

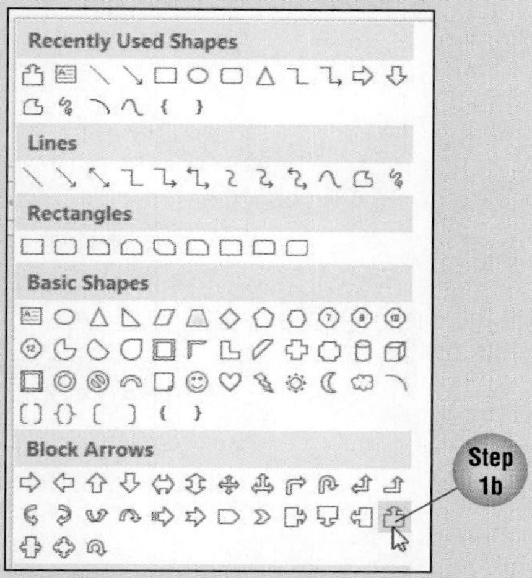

   c. Click in the chart to insert the shape.
   d. Click in the *Shape Height* measurement box in the Size group on the DRAWING TOOLS FORMAT tab, type 1.5, and then press Enter.
   e. Click in the *Shape Width* measurement box, type 1.5, and then press Enter.
   f. Apply a shape style by clicking the More button at the right side of the shape style thumbnails in the Shape Style group and then clicking the *Subtle Effect - Blue, Accent 1* option (second column, fourth row).

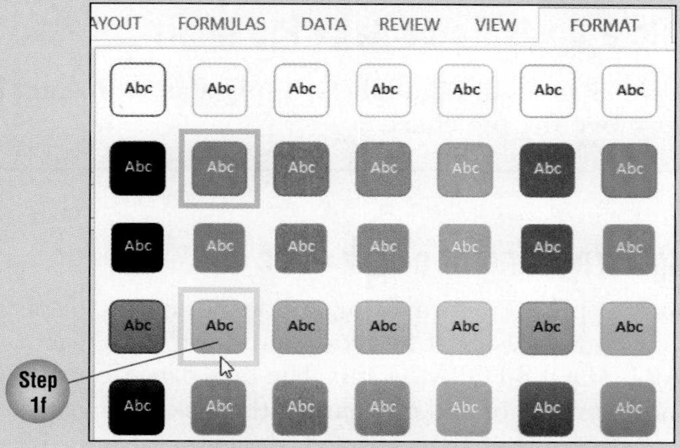

   g. Type **Largest disparity** in the shape, press Enter, and then type **(184,411)**.
   h. Select the text you just typed.
   i. Click the HOME tab.
   j. Click the Bold button in the Font group.
   k. Click the Font Size button arrow and then click *14*.
   l. Click the Center button in the Alignment group.
2. With the shape selected, drag the shape so it is positioned as shown in Figure 7.9.
3. Save **EL1-C7-P3-PopComp.xlsx**, print the Chart1 worksheet, and then close the workbook.

Figure 7.9 Project 3 Chart

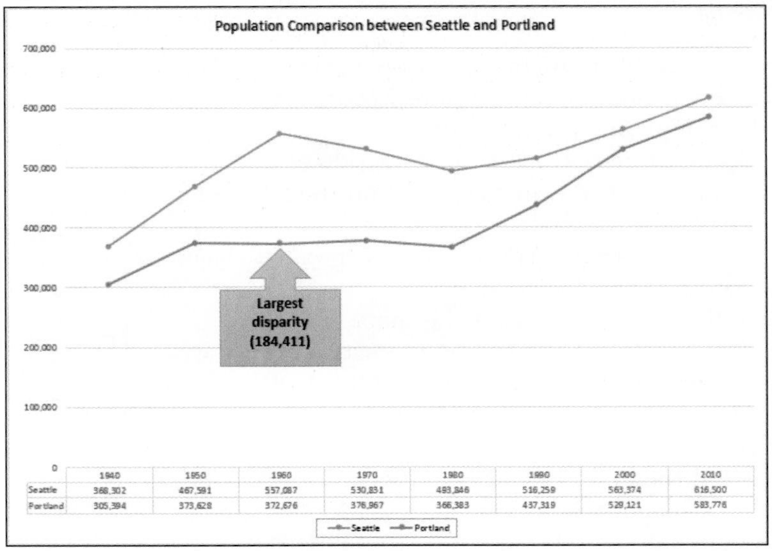

Project 4 Create a Costs Percentage Pie Chart 1 Part

You will create a pie chart, add data labels, apply a style, format chart elements, and then size and move the pie chart.

Quick Steps

Display a Task Pane
1. Select chart or specific element.
2. Click CHART TOOLS FORMAT tab.
3. Click Format Selection button.

Format Selection

Quick Steps

Change Chart Height and/or Width
1. Make chart active.
2. Click CHART TOOLS FORMAT tab.
3. Insert desired height and/or width with *Shape Height* and/or *Shape Width* measurement boxes.

Applying Formatting at a Task Pane

To view and apply more formatting options for charts, display the formatting task pane by clicking the Format Selection button in the Current Selection group on the CHART TOOLS FORMAT tab. The task pane displays at the right side of the screen and the name of and contents in the task pane vary depending on what is selected. If the entire chart is selected, the Format Chart Area task pane displays, as shown in Figure 7.10. Format the chart by clicking the desired formatting options in the task pane. Display additional formatting options by clicking the icons that display toward the top of the task pane. For example, click the Effects icon in the Format Chart Area task pane and options for applying shadow, glow, soft edges, and 3-D formatting display.

Click a chart element and then click the Format Selection button and the task pane name and options change. You can also right-click a chart or chart element and then click the format option at the shortcut menu. The name of the format option varies depending on the selected element.

Changing Chart Height and Width Measurements

As you learned earlier in this chapter, if you insert a chart into the current worksheet (not into a separate, new worksheet), you can size the chart by selecting it and then dragging a sizing handle. You can also size a chart to specific measurements. To do this, display the CHART TOOLS FORMAT tab and then click the up- or down-pointing arrow that displays at the right side of the *Shape*

Figure 7.10 Format Chart Area Task Pane

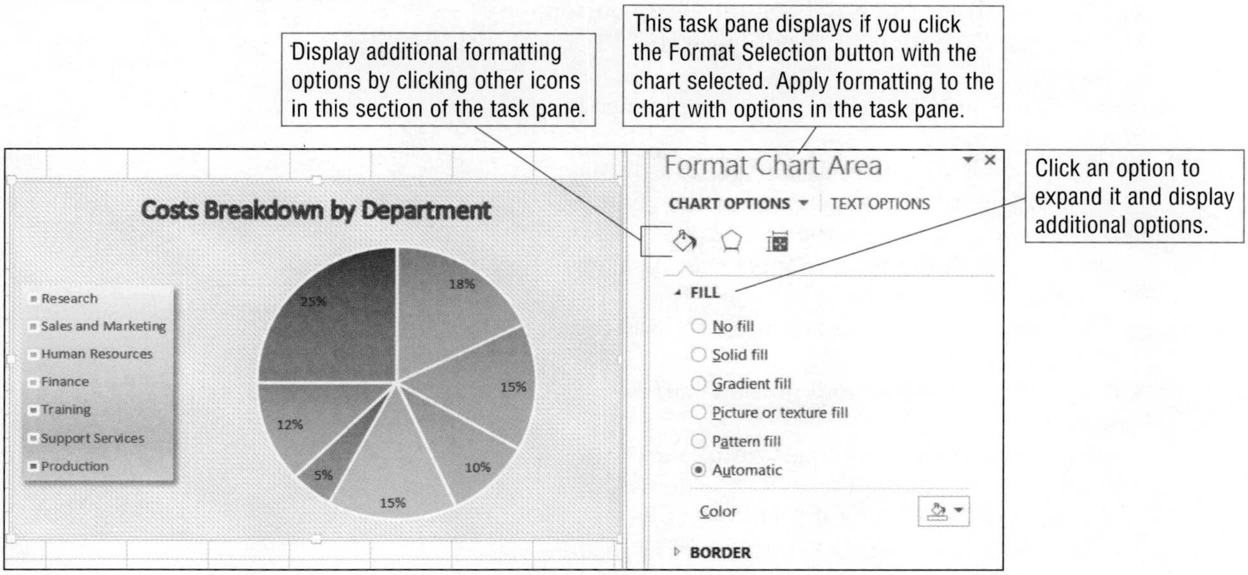

Height or *Shape Width* measurement box or select the current measurement and then type a specific measurement. In addition to using the *Shape Height* and *Shape Width* measurement boxes on the CHART TOOLS FORMAT tab, you can change the chart size with options at the Format Chart Area task pane.

Deleting a Chart

Delete a chart created in Excel by clicking once in the chart to select it and then pressing the Delete key. If you move a chart to a different worksheet in the workbook and then delete the chart, the chart will be deleted but the worksheet will not. To delete the worksheet as well as the chart, position the mouse pointer on the Chart1 tab, click the right mouse button, and then click *Delete* at the shortcut menu. At the message box telling you that selected sheets will be permanently deleted, click Delete.

Quick Steps

Delete a Chart
1. Click once in chart.
2. Press Delete key.
OR
1. Right-click chart tab.
2. Click *Delete*.

Project 4 **Deleting a Chart and Creating and Formatting a Pie Chart** **Part 1 of 1**

1. Open **DIDeptCosts.xlsx** and then save the workbook with Save As and name it **EL1-C7-P4-DIDeptCosts**.
2. Delete the column chart by completing the following steps:
   a. Click the column chart to select the chart. (Make sure the chart is selected and not a specific element in the chart.)
   b. Press the Delete key.
3. Create the pie chart shown in Figure 7.10 by completing the following steps:
   a. Select cells A3 through B10.
   b. Click the INSERT tab.

c. Click the Insert Pie or Doughnut Chart button.
d. Click the *Pie* option (first option in the *2-D Pie* section).

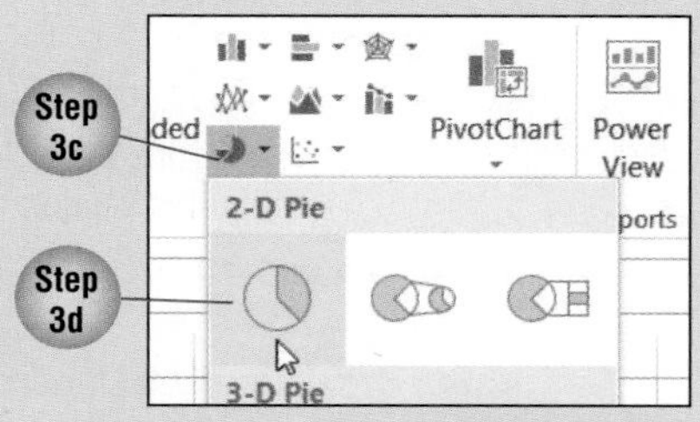

4. Insert data labels in the chart by completing the following steps:
   a. Click the Chart Elements button that displays outside the upper right border of the chart.
   b. Hover the mouse over the *Data Labels* option and click the right-pointing triangle that displays.
   c. Click *Inside End* at the side menu.
   d. Click the Chart Elements button to hide the side menu.

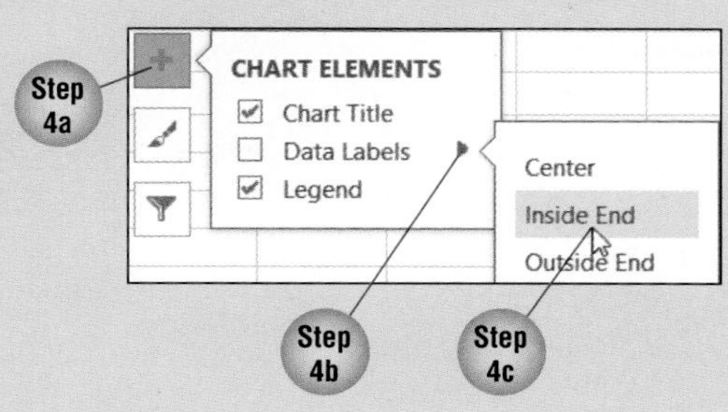

5. Click the *Style 6* thumbnail in the Chart Styles group.
6. Type a title and then apply a WordArt style to the title by completing the following steps:
   a. Click the CHART TOOLS FORMAT tab.
   b. Click the Chart Elements button arrow in the Current Selection group.
   c. Click *Chart Title* at the drop-down list.
   d. Type C and Excel's AutoComplete feature inserts the entire title *Costs Breakdown by Department* in the Formula bar. Accept this name by pressing the Enter key.
   e. Click the More button at the right side of the WordArt style thumbnails in the WordArt Styles group.
   f. Click the *Pattern Fill - Gray-50%, Accent 3, Narrow Horizontal, Inner Shadow* style thumbnail at the drop-down gallery (second column, fourth row).
7. Use the Format Legend task pane to apply formatting to the legend by completing the following steps:
   a. Click the Chart Elements button arrow and then click *Legend* at the drop-down list.
   b. Click the Format Selection button in the Current Selection group.

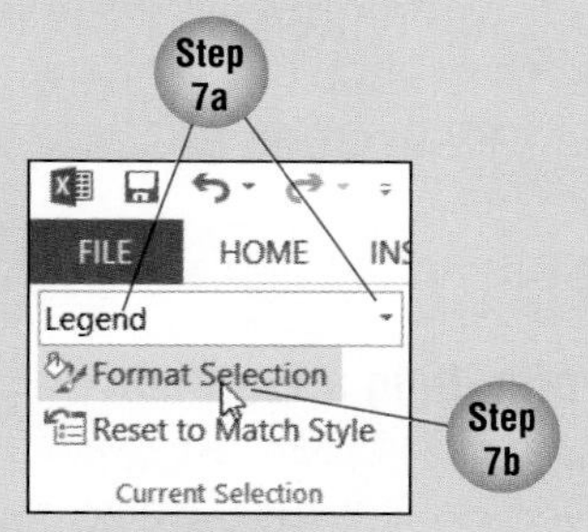

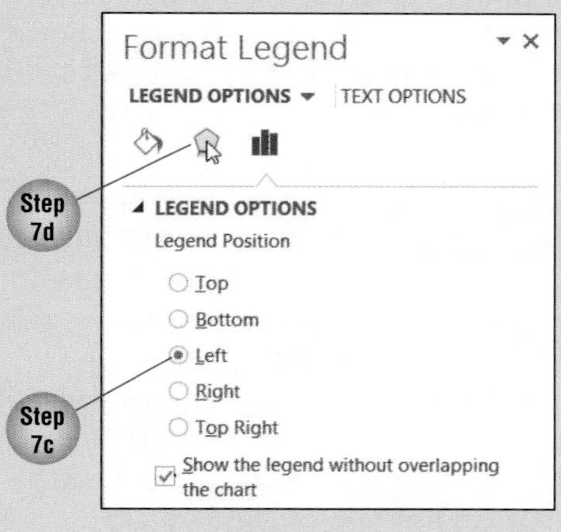

   c. At the Format Legend task pane, click the *Left* option in the *LEGEND OPTIONS* section.
   d. Click the Effects icon in the task pane. (This changes the options in the task pane.)

e. Click the *SHADOW* option. (This displays shadow options in the task pane.)
f. Click the Shadow button that displays to the right of *Presets* and then click the *Offset Diagonal Bottom Right* option (first option in the *Outer* section).
g. Click the Fill & Line icon in the task pane.
h. Click the *FILL* option.
i. Click the *Gradient fill* option.
j. Close the task pane by clicking the Close button located in the upper right corner of the task pane.

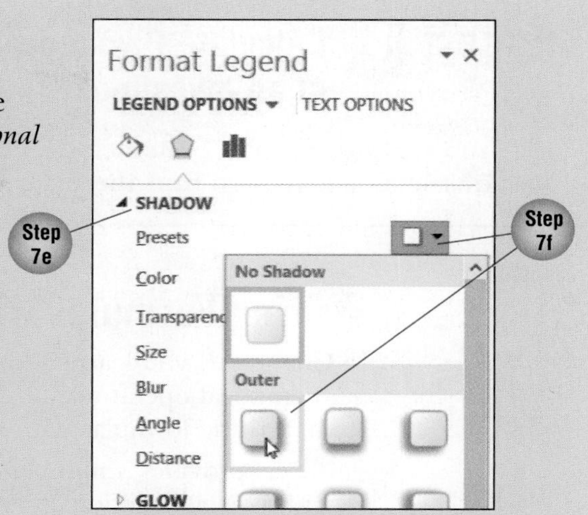

8. Use the Format Chart Area task pane to apply formatting to the chart by completing the following steps:
   a. Click inside the chart but outside any chart elements.
   b. Click the Format Selection button in the Current Selection group.
   c. Make sure the Fill & Line icon in the Format Chart Area task pane is selected. (If not, click the icon.)
   d. Make sure the *FILL* option is expanded. (If not, click the *FILL* option.)
   e. Click the *Gradient fill* option.
   f. Click the Size & Properties icon in the task pane.
   g. Click the *SIZE* option to display size options.
   h. Select the current measurement in the *Height* measurement box, type 4, and then press Enter.
   i. Close the task pane.

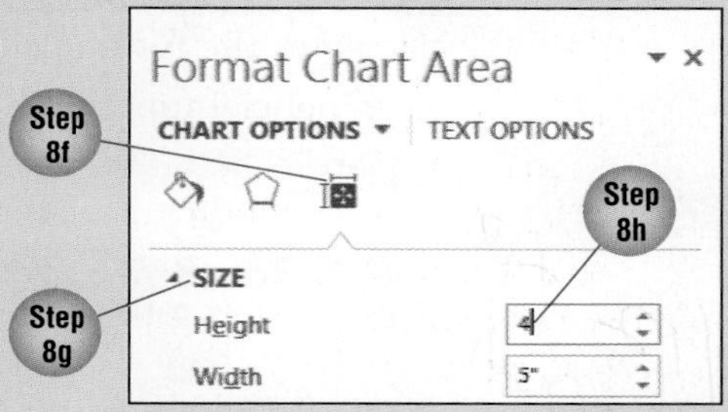

9. Save **EL1-C7-P4-DIDeptCosts.xlsx** and then print only the chart.
10. Change the chart style by completing the following steps:
    a. Click the CHART TOOLS DESIGN tab.
    b. Click the More button at the right side of the chart style thumbnails.
    c. Click the *Style 9* thumbnail at the drop-down gallery.
11. Change the size of the chart by completing the following steps:
    a. Click the CHART TOOLS FORMAT tab.
    b. Click in the *Shape Height* measurement box, type 3.5, and then press Enter.
    c. Click in the *Shape Width* measurement box, type 5.5, and then press Enter.
12. Drag the chart so it is positioned below the cells containing data.
13. Click outside the chart to deselect it.
14. Display the Print backstage area, make sure the chart fits on the page with the data, and then click the Print button.
15. Save **EL1-C7-P4-DIDeptCosts.xlsx** and then close the workbook.

Project 5 Calculate Payments and the Future Value of an Investment

2 Parts

You will use the PMT financial function to calculate payments and the FV financial function to find the future value of an investment.

Writing Formulas with Financial Functions

In Chapter 2, you learned how to insert formulas in a worksheet using mathematical operators and functions. In this section, you will continue learning about writing formulas with functions.

Excel provides a number of financial functions you can use in a formula. With financial functions, you can determine different aspects of a financial loan or investment, such as the payment amount, present value, future value, interest rate, and number of payment periods. Each financial function requires some of the variables listed below in order to return a result. Two such financial functions are the PMT function and FV function. The ***PMT function*** calculates the payment for a loan based on constant payments and a constant interest rate. The ***FV function*** calculates the future value of an investment.

Financial functions use some of the following arguments:

- **Rate:** The rate is the interest rate for a payment period. The rate may need to be modified for the function to display the desired results. For example, most rate values are given as an APR (annual percentage rate), which is the percentage rate for one year, not a payment period. So a percentage rate may be given as 12% APR but if the payment period is a month, then the percentage rate for the function is 1%, not 12%. If your worksheet contains the annual percentage rate, you can enter the cell reference in the function argument and specify that you want it divided by 12 months. For example, if cell B6 contains the annual interest rate, enter *B6/12* as the Rate argument.
- **Nper:** The Nper is the number of payment periods in an investment. The Nper may also need to be modified depending on what information is provided. For example, if a loan duration is expressed in years but the payments are paid each month, the Nper value needs to be adjusted accordingly. A five-year loan has an Nper of 60 (five years times 12 months in each year).
- **Pmt:** The Pmt is the payment amount for each period. This variable describes the payment amount for a period and is commonly expressed as a negative value because it is an outflow of cash. However, the Pmt value can be entered as a positive value if the present value (Pv) or future value (Fv) is entered as a negative value. Whether the Pmt value is positive or negative depends on who created the workbook. For example, a home owner lists the variable as outflow, while the lending institution lists it as inflow.
- **Pv:** The Pv is the present value of an investment, expressed in a lump sum. The Pv variable is generally the initial loan amount. For example, if a person is purchasing a new home, the Pv is the amount of money the buyer borrowed to buy the home. Pv can be expressed as a negative value, which denotes it as an investment instead of a loan. For example, if a bank issues a loan to a home buyer, it enters the Pv value as a negative because it is an outflow of cash for the bank.

- **Fv:** The Fv is the future value of an investment, expressed in a lump sum amount. The Fv variable is generally the loan amount plus the amount of interest paid during the loan. In the example of a home buyer, the Fv is the sum of payments, which includes both the principle and interest paid on the loan. In the example of a bank, the Fv is the total amount received after a loan has been paid off. Fv can also be expressed as either a positive or negative value depending on which side of the transaction you review.

Finding the Periodic Payments for a Loan

The PMT function finds the payment for a loan based on constant payments and a constant interest rate. In Project 5a, you will use the PMT function to determine monthly payments for equipment and a used van as well as monthly income from selling equipment. The formulas you will create with the PMT function in Project 5a will include Rate, Nper, and Pv arguments. The Nper argument is the number of payments that will be made on the loan or investment, Pv is the current value of amounts to be received or paid in the future, and Fv is the value of the loan or investment at the end of all periods.

To write the PMT function, click the FORMULAS tab, click the Financial button in the Function Library group, and then click the PMT function at the drop-down list. This displays the Function Arguments palette with options for inserting cell designations for Rate, Nper, and Pv. (These are the arguments in bold. The palette also contains the Fv and Type functions, which are dimmed.)

Financial

Project 5a **Calculating Payments** **Part 1 of 2**

1. Open **RPReports.xlsx** and then save the workbook with Save As and name it **EL1-C7-P5-RPReports**.
2. The owner of Real Photography is interested in purchasing a new developer and needs to determine monthly payments on three different models. Insert a formula that calculates monthly payments and then copy that formula by completing the following steps:
   a. Make cell E5 active.
   b. Click the FORMULAS tab.
   c. Click the Financial button in the Function Library group, scroll down the drop-down list, and then click *PMT*.

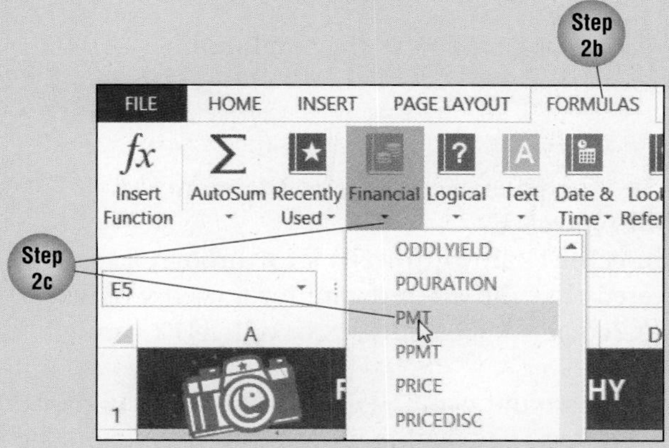

d. At the Function Arguments palette, type C5/12 in the *Rate* text box. (This tells Excel to divide the interest rate by 12 months.)
e. Press the Tab key. (This moves the insertion point to the *Nper* text box).
f. Type D5. (This is the total number of months for the investment.)
g. Press the Tab key. (This moves the insertion point to the *Pv* text box.)
h. Type B5. (This is the purchase price of the developer.)
i. Click OK. (This closes the palette and inserts the monthly payment of *($316.98)* in cell E5. Excel displays the result of the PMT function as a negative number since the loan represents money going out of the company—a negative cash flow.)
j. Copy the formula in cell E5 down to cells E6 and E7.

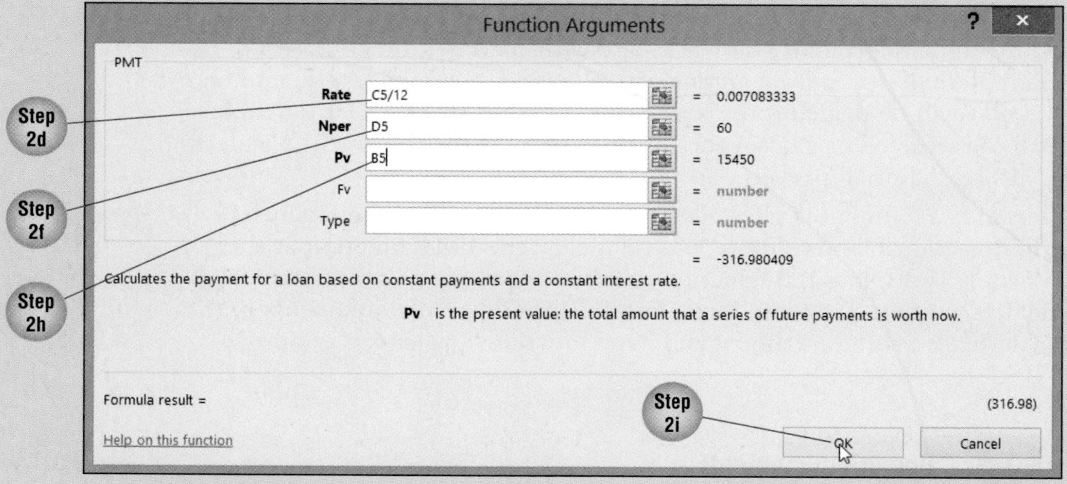

3. The owner is interested in purchasing a used van for the company and wants an idea of what monthly payments would be at various terms and rates. Insert a formula that calculates monthly payments for a three-year loan at 5% interest by completing the following steps:
   a. Make cell E12 active.
   b. Make sure the FORMULAS tab is active
   c. Click the Financial button in the Function Library group, scroll down the drop-down list, and then click *PMT*.
   d. At the Function Arguments palette, type C12/12 in the *Rate* text box. (This tells Excel to divide the interest rate by 12 months.)
   e. Press the Tab key.
   f. Type D12 in the *Nper* text box. (This is the total number of months for the investment.)
   g. Press the Tab key.
   h. Type B12 in the *Pv* text box.
   i. Click OK. (This closes the palette and inserts the monthly payment of *($299.71)* in cell E12.)
   j. Copy the formula in cell E12 down to cells E13 through E15.

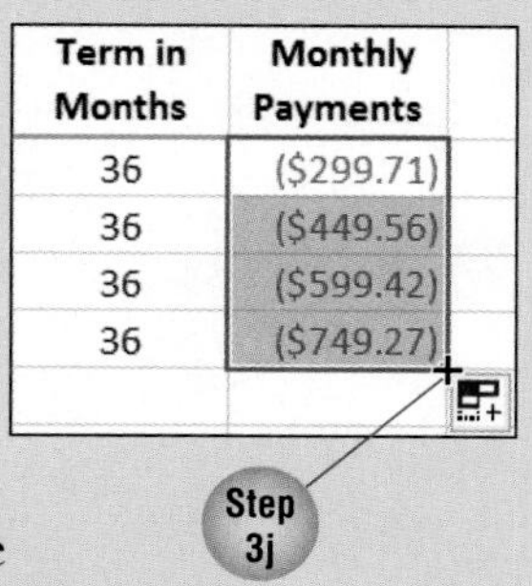

4. The owner has discovered that the interest rate for a used van will be 6.25% instead of 5%. Change the percentages in cells D12 through D15 to 6.25%.
5. The owner is selling a camera and wants you to determine the monthly payments for a two-year loan at 4.5% interest. Determine monthly payments on the camera (income to Real Photography) by completing the following steps:

a. Make cell E20 active.
b. Make sure the FORMULAS tab is active.
c. Click the Financial button in the Function Library group, scroll down the drop-down list, and then click *PMT*.
d. At the Function Arguments palette, type C20/12 in the *Rate* text box.
e. Press the Tab key.
f. Type D20 in the *Nper* text box.
g. Press the Tab key.
h. Type -B20. In the *Pv* text box. (Excel displays the result of the PMT function as a negative number since the loan represents a negative cash flow. The sale of the camera represents a cash outflow because the business is selling the camera in order to receive payments—cash in flow).
i. Click OK. (This closes the palette and inserts the monthly income of *$185.92* in cell E20.)

6. Save, print, and then close **EL1-C7-P5-RPReports.xlsx**.

Sale

Finding the Future Value of a Series of Payments

The FV function calculates the future value of a series of equal payments or an annuity. Use this function to determine information such as how much money can be earned in an investment account with a specific interest rate and over a specific period of time.

Project 5b Finding the Future Value of an Investment Part 2 of 2

1. Open **RPInvest.xlsx** and then save the workbook with Save As and name it **EL1-C7-P5-RPInvest**.
2. The owner of Real Photography has decided to save money to purchase a new developer and wants to compute how much money can be earned by investing the money in an investment account that returns 7.5% annual interest. The owner determines that $1,200 per month can be invested in the account for three years. Complete the following steps to determine the future value of the investment account:
   a. Make cell B6 active.
   b. Make sure the FORMULAS tab is active.
   c. Click the Financial button in the Function Library group.
   d. At the drop-down list that displays, scroll down the list and then click *FV*.
   e. At the Function Arguments palette, type B3/12 in the *Rate* text box.
   f. Press the Tab key.
   g. Type B4 in the *Nper* text box.
   h. Press the Tab key.
   i. Type B5 in the *Pmt* text box.
   j. Click OK. (This closes the palette and also inserts the future value of *$48,277.66* in cell B6.)
3. Save and then print **EL1-C7-P5-RPInvest.xlsx**.
4. The owner decides to determine the future return after two years. To do this, change the amount in cell B4 from *36* to *24* and then press Enter. (This recalculates the future investment amount in cell B6.)
5. Save, print, and then close **EL1-C7-P5-RPInvest.xlsx**.

Project 6 Insert Formulas with the IF Logical Function — 3 Parts

You will use the IF logical function to calculate sales bonuses, determine pass/fail grades based on averages, and identify discounts and discount amounts.

Writing Formulas with the IF Logical Function

A question that can be answered with true or false is considered a ***logical test***. You can use the ***IF function*** to create a logical test that performs a particular action if the answer is true (condition met) and another action if the answer is false (condition not met).

For example, an IF function can be used to write a formula that calculates a salesperson's bonus as 10% if the salesperson sells more than $99,999 worth of product and 0% if he or she does not sell more than $99,999 worth of product. When writing a formula with an IF function, think about the words *if* and *then*. For example, the formula written out for the bonus example would look like this:

> ***If*** the salesperson sells more than $99,999 of product, ***then*** he or she receives a bonus of 10%.
>
> ***If*** the salesperson does not sell more than $99,999 of product, ***then*** he or she receives a bonus of 0%.

When writing a formula with an IF function, commas separate the condition and the action. The formula for the bonus example would look like this: ***=IF(sales>99999,sales*0.1,0)***. The formula contains three parts:

- the condition or logical test: ***IF(sales>99999***
- the action taken if the condition or logical test is true: ***sales*0.1***
- the action taken if the condition or logical test is false: ***0***

In Project 6a, you will write a formula with cell references rather than cell data. In the project, you will write a formula with an IF function that determines the following:

> ***If*** the sales amount is greater than the quota amount, ***then*** the salesperson will receive a 15% bonus.
>
> ***If*** the sales amount is not greater than the quota amount, ***then*** the salesperson will not receive a bonus.

Written with cell references in the project, the formula looks like this: ***=IF(C4>B4,C4*0.15,0)***. In this formula the condition or logical test is whether or not the number in cell C4 is greater than the number in cell B4. If the condition is true and the number is greater, then the number in cell C4 is multiplied by 0.15 (providing a 15% bonus). If the condition is false and the number in cell C4 is less than the number in cell B4, then nothing happens (no bonus). Notice how commas are used to separate the logical test from the action.

Project 6a Writing a Formula with an IF Function **Part 1 of 3**

1. Open **CMPReports.xlsx** and then save it with Save As and name it **EL1-C7-P6-CMPReports**.
2. Write a formula with the IF function that determines if a sales quota has been met and, if it has, inserts the bonus: 15% of actual sales. (If the quota has not been met, the formula will insert a 0.) Write the formula by completing the following steps:
   a. Make cell D4 active.
   b. Type =IF(C4>B4,C4*0.15,0) and then press Enter.

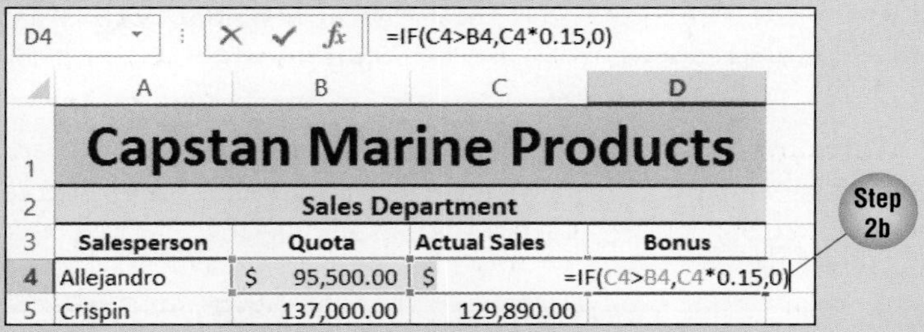

   c. Make cell D4 active and then use the fill handle to copy the formula to cells D5 through D9.
3. Print the worksheet.
4. Revise the formula so it inserts a 20% bonus if the quota has been met by completing the following steps:
   a. Make cell D4 active.
   b. Click in the Formula bar, edit the formula so it displays as *=IF(C4>B4,C4*0.2,0)*, and then click the Enter button on the Formula bar.
   c. Copy the formula in cell D4 down to cells D5 through D9.
   d. Apply accounting formatting with a dollar sign and two places beyond the decimal point.
5. Save **EL1-C7-P6-CMPReports.xlsx**.

Writing Formulas with an IF Function Using the Function Arguments Palette

You can type a formula containing an IF function directly into a cell or you can use the Function Arguments palette to help you write the formula. To use the Function Arguments palette to write a formula with the IF function, click the FORMULAS tab, click the Logical button in the Function Library group, and then click *IF* at the drop-down list. This displays the Function Arguments palette, shown in Figure 7.11. The Function Arguments palette displays the information you will type in the three argument text boxes for Project 6b.

Logical

At the Function Arguments palette, click in the *Logical_test* text box and information about the Logical_test argument displays in the palette. In this text box, type the cell designation followed by what is evaluated. In the figure, the *Logical_test* text box contains *B14>599*, indicating that what is being evaluated is whether or not the amount in cell B14 is greater than $599. The *Value_if_true* text box contains *B14*0.95*, indicating that if the logical test is true, then multiply the amount in cell B14 by 0.95. (The discount for any product price greater than $599

Figure 7.11 Function Arguments Palette

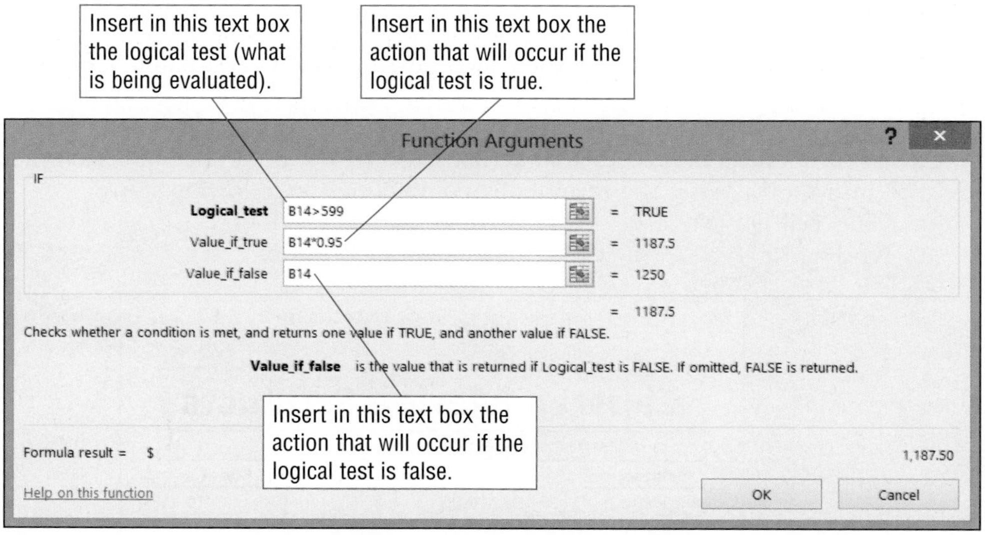

is 5% and multiplying the product price by 0.95 determines the price after the 5% discount is applied.) The *Value_if_false* text box contains *B14*, indicating that if the logical test is false (the product price is not greater than $599), then simply insert the amount from cell B14.

Project 6b Writing a Formula with an IF Function Using the Function Arguments Palette

Part 2 of 3

1. With **EL1-C7-P6-CMPReports.xlsx** open, insert a formula with an IF function using the Function Arguments palette by completing the following steps:
   a. Make cell C14 active.
   b. Click the FORMULAS tab.
   c. Click the Logical button in the Function Library group.
   d. Click *IF* at the drop-down list.
   e. At the Function Arguments palette, type B14>599 in the *Logical_test* text box.
   f. Press the Tab key and then type B14*0.95 in the *Value_if_true* text box.
   g. Press the Tab key and then type B14 in the *Value_if_false* text box.
   h. Click OK to close the Function Arguments palette.

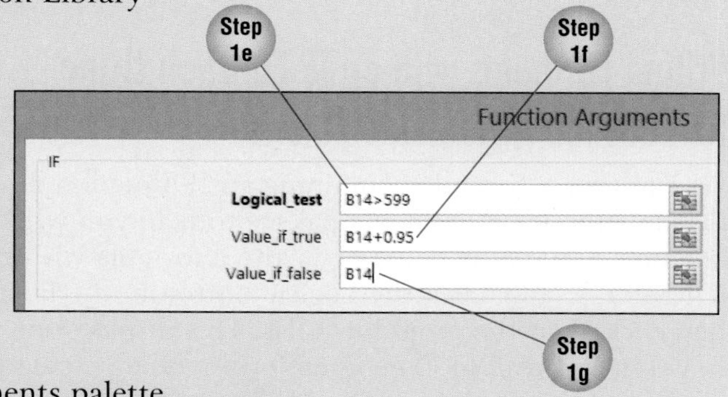

2. Copy the formula in cell C14 down to cells C15 through C26.
3. Apply accounting formatting with a dollar sign and two places after the decimal point to cell C14.
4. Save **EL1-C7-P6-CMPReports.xlsx**.

Writing IF Formulas Containing Text

If you write a formula with an IF function and want text inserted in a cell rather than a value, you must insert quotation marks around the text. For example, in Step 2 of Project 6c, you will write a formula with an IF function that, when written out, looks like this:

> ***If*** the employee averages more than 79 on the quizzes, ***then*** he or she passes.
>
> ***If*** the employee does not average more than 79 on the quizzes, ***then*** he or she fails.

When writing the formula in the project, the word *PASS* is inserted in a cell if the average of the new employee quizzes is greater than 79 and inserts the word *FAIL* if the condition is not met. To write this formula in Project 6c, you will type ***=IF(E31>79, "PASS", "FAIL")***. The quotation marks before and after *PASS* and *FAIL* identify the data as text rather than a value.

You can use the Function Arguments palette to write a formula with an IF function that contains text. For example, in Step 3 of Project 6c, you will write a formula with an IF function using the Function Arguments palette that, when written out, looks like this:

> ***If*** the product price is greater than $599, ***then*** insert *YES*.
>
> ***If*** the product price is not greater than $599, ***then*** insert *NO*.

To create the formula in Step 3 in the Function Arguments palette, display the palette and then type **B14>599** in the *Logical_test* text box, **YES** in the *Value_if_true* text box, and **NO** in the *Value_if_false* text box. When you press Enter after typing YES in the *Value_if_true* text box, Excel automatically inserts quotations marks around the text. Excel will do the same thing for NO in the *Value_if_false* text box.

Project 6c **Writing IF Statements Containing Text** **Part 3 of 3**

1. With **EL1-C7-P6-CMPReports.xlsx** open, insert quiz averages by completing the following steps:
   a. Make cell E31 active and then insert a formula that calculates the average of the test scores in cells B31 through D31.
   b. Copy the formula in cell E31 down to cells E32 through E35.
2. Write a formula with an IF function that inserts the word *PASS* if the quiz average is greater than 79 and inserts the word *FAIL* if the quiz average is not greater than 79. Write the formula by completing the following steps:
   a. Make cell F31 active.
   b. Type =IF(E31>79,"PASS","FAIL") and then press Enter.

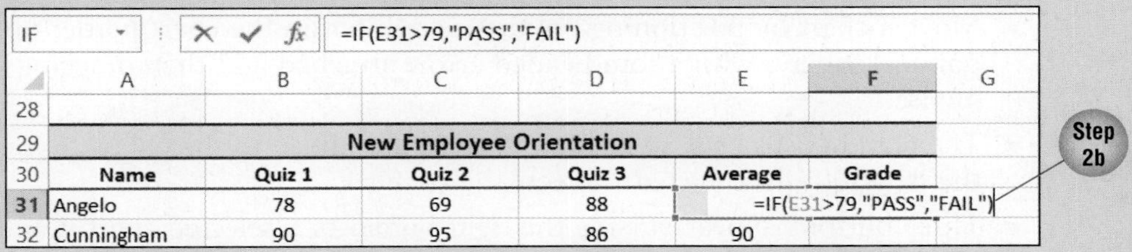

   c. Copy the formula in cell F31 down to cells F32 through F35.

3. Write a formula with an IF function using the Function Arguments palette that inserts the word *YES* in the cell if the product price is greater than $599 and inserts the word *NO* if the price is not greater than $599. Write the formula by completing the following steps:
   a. Make cell D14 active.
   b. Click the FORMULAS tab.
   c. Click the Logical button in the Function Library group.
   d. Click *IF* at the drop-down list.
   e. Type B14>599 in the *Logical_test* text box.
   f. Press the Tab key and then type YES in the *Value_if_true* text box.
   g. Press the Tab key and then type NO in the *Value_if_false* text box.

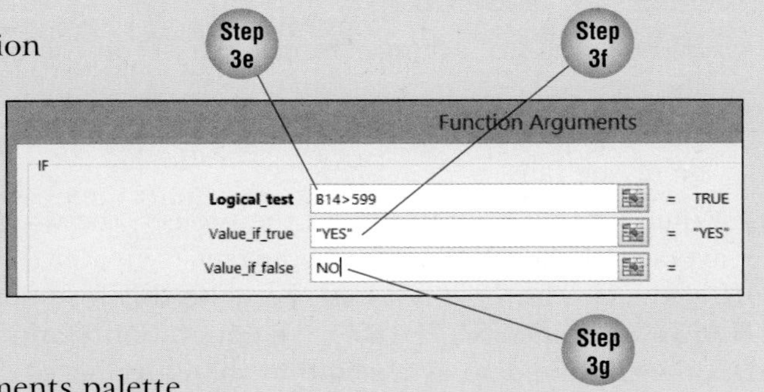

   h. Click OK to close the Function Arguments palette.
   i. Copy the formula in cell D14 down to cells D15 through D26.
4. Save and then print **EL1-C7-P6-CMPReports.xlsx**.
5. Press Ctrl + ` to turn on the display of formulas.
6. Print the worksheet again. (The worksheet will print on two pages.)
7. Press Ctrl + ` to turn off the display of formulas.
8. Save and then close **EL1-C7-P6-CMPReports.xlsx**.

Chapter Summary

- A chart is a visual presentation of data. Excel provides 11 basic chart types: area, bar, bubble, column, doughnut, line, pyramid, radar, stock, surface, and xy (scatter).
- To create a chart, select the cells containing data you want to chart, click the INSERT tab, and then click the desired chart button in the Charts group. Click the Recommended Charts button in the Charts group and Excel will recommend a type of chart for the data.
- A chart you create is inserted in the same worksheet as the selected cells.
- Change the size of a chart using the mouse by dragging one of the sizing handles that display around the border of the chart. When changing the chart size, maintain the proportion of the chart by holding down the Shift key while dragging a sizing handle.
- Move a chart by positioning the mouse pointer on the chart border until the pointer displays with a four-headed arrow attached and then dragging with the mouse.
- The data in cells used to create the chart are linked to the chart. If you change the data in cells, the chart reflects the changes.
- Three buttons appear outside the right border of a selected chart. Use the Chart Elements button to insert or remove chart elements, use the Chart Styles button to apply a chart style, and use the Chart Filters button to isolate specific data in the chart.

- Print a chart by selecting the chart, displaying the Print backstage area, and then clicking the Print button.
- When you insert a chart in a worksheet, the CHART TOOLS DESIGN tab is active. Use options on this tab to add chart elements, change the chart type, specify a different layout or style, and change the location of the chart.
- Choose a chart style with options in the Chart Styles group on the CHART TOOLS DESIGN tab or at the Change Chart Type dialog box.
- Click the Switch Row/Column button in the Data group to change what Excel uses to determine the grouping of data along the horizontal axis and legend.
- Use the Quick Layout button in the Chart Layouts group to change the chart layout.
- Use the Change Colors button to apply different colors to a chart.
- By default, a chart is inserted in the active worksheet. You can move the chart to a new worksheet within the workbook with the *New sheet* option at the Move Chart dialog box.
- Add chart elements with the Add Chart Element button arrow in the Chart Layouts group on the CHART TOOLS DESIGN tab.
- Move a chart element by selecting the element and then dragging it with the mouse. Use the sizing handles that display around a chart element to change the size of the element. Delete a chart element by selecting it and then pressing the Delete key or right-clicking the selected element and then clicking Delete at the shortcut menu.
- Customize the formatting of a chart and chart elements with options on the CHART TOOLS FORMAT tab. With options on the tab, you can identify specific elements in the chart for formatting, insert a shape, apply formatting to a shape, apply WordArt formatting to data in a chart, and arrange, align, and size a chart.
- Insert a shape by clicking the desired shape in the Insert Shapes group on the CHART TOOLS FORMAT tab and then clicking or dragging in the chart.
- Excel provides additional formatting options at a formatting task pane. A formatting task pane displays at the right side of the screen and the name and the contents in the task pane vary depending on whether the entire chart or an element in the chart is selected. Display a task pane by clicking the chart or element in the chart and then clicking the Format Selection button in the Current Selection group on the CHART TOOLS FORMAT tab.
- Change the size of a chart with shape height and width measurement boxes on the CHART TOOLS FORMAT tab or at the Format Chart Area task pane.
- To delete a chart in a worksheet, click the chart to select it and then press the Delete key. To delete a chart created in a separate sheet, position the mouse pointer on the chart tab, click the right mouse button, and then click *Delete*.
- Write a formula with the PMT function to calculate the payment for a loan based on constant payments and a constant interest rate. Write a formula with the FV function to calculate the future value of an investment based on periodic, constant payments and a constant interest rate.
- A logical test is a question that can be answered with true or false. Use the IF function to create a logical test that performs a particular action if the answer is true (condition met) or another action if the answer is false (condition not met).

Commands Review

FEATURE	RIBBON TAB, GROUP	BUTTON, OPTION	KEYBOARD SHORTCUT
Change Chart Type dialog box	CHART TOOLS DESIGN, Type		
chart in separate sheet			F11
chart or chart element task pane	CHART TOOLS FORMAT, Current Selection		
financial functions	FORMULAS, Function Library		
logical functions	FORMULAS, Function Library		
Move Chart dialog box	CHART TOOLS DESIGN, Location		
recommended chart	INSERT, Charts		Alt + F1

Concepts Check

Test Your Knowledge

SNAP

Completion: In the space provided at the right, indicate the correct term, symbol, or command.

2 1. Let Excel determine a chart type for selected data in a worksheet by clicking this button in the Charts group on the INSERT tab. recommended chart

1 2. This type of chart shows proportions and relationships of the parts to the whole. pie

3 or 5 3. When you create a chart, the chart is inserted in this location by default. wrksht containing data

2 4. Size a chart by dragging one of these on the selected chart border. sizing handles

2 5. When a chart is selected, three buttons display at the right side of the chart border: the Chart Elements button, the Chart Styles button, and this button. Chart filters

3 6. Select a chart in a worksheet, display the Print backstage area, and the first gallery in the *Settings* category is automatically changed to this option. Print selected chart

7. The Switch Row/Column button is located in this group on the CHART TOOLS DESIGN tab. data

8. Click this option at the Move Chart dialog box to move the chart to a separate sheet. new sheet

9. Insert a shape in a chart and this tab is active. chart tools format tab

10. Select a chart (not a chart element), click the Format Selection button in the Current Selection group on the CHART TOOLS FORMAT tab, and this task pane displays at the right side of the screen. ____________

11. This function finds the payment for a loan based on constant payments and a constant interest rate. PMT

12. Suppose cell B2 contains the total sales amount. Write a formula that inserts the word *BONUS* in cell C2 if the sales amount is greater than $49,999 and inserts the words *NO BONUS* if the sales amount is not greater than $49,999. ____________

Skills Check Assess Your Performance

Assessment

1 CREATE A NET PROFIT CHART

SNAP Grade It

1. Open **NetProfit.xlsx** and then save the workbook with Save As and name it **EL1-C7-A1-NetProfit**.
2. Select cells A2 through E7 and then create a chart using the Recommended Charts button. (Accept the chart recommended by Excel.)
3. Use the Chart Elements button that displays outside the right border of the chart to insert a data table and remove the legend.
4. Use the Chart Styles button that displays outside the right border of the chart to apply the Style 7 chart style.
5. Use the Chart Filters button that displays outside the right border of the chart to display only New York and Philadelphia net profits in the chart. (Make sure you click the Apply button.)
6. Click the text *Chart Title*, type **Net Profit by Office**, and then press Enter.
7. Move the chart below the cells containing data, deselect the chart, make sure the data and chart fit on one page, and then print the worksheet (data and chart).
8. Save and then close **EL1-C7-A1-NetProfit.xlsx**.

Assessment 2

CREATE A COMPANY SALES COLUMN CHART

SNAP Grade It

1. Open **CMSales.xlsx** and then save the workbook with Save As and name it **EL1-C7-A2-CMSales**.
2. Select cells A3 through C15 and then create a column chart with the following specifications:
   a. Click the *3-D Clustered Column* option at the Insert Column Chart button drop-down list.
   b. At the CHART TOOLS DESIGN tab, click the Quick Layout button and then click the *Layout 3* option at the drop-down gallery.
   c. Apply the Style 11 chart style.
   d. Click the text *Chart Title*, type 2015 Company Sales, and then press Enter.
   e. Move the location of the chart to a new sheet.
3. Print only the worksheet containing the chart.
4. Save and then close **EL1-C7-A2-CMSales.xlsx**.

Assessment 3

CREATE QUARTERLY DOMESTIC AND FOREIGN SALES BAR CHART

SNAP Grade It

1. Open **CMPQtrlySales.xlsx** and then save the workbook with Save As and name it **EL1-C7-A3-CMPQtrlySales**.
2. Select cells A3 through E5 and then create a bar chart with the following specifications:
   a. Click the *3-D Clustered Bar* option at the Insert Bar Chart button drop-down list.
   b. Apply the Layout 2 quick layout. (Use the Quick Layout button.)
   c. Apply the Style 6 chart style.
   d. Type Quarterly Sales as the chart title. (Excel will convert the text to uppercase letters.)
   e. Click in the chart but outside any chart element.
   f. Click the CHART TOOLS FORMAT tab and then apply the Subtle Effect - Gold, Accent 4 shape style (fifth column, fourth row).
   g. Click the Chart Elements button arrow, click *Series "Foreign"* at the drop-down list, and then apply Dark Red shape fill. (Use the Shape Fill button arrow in the Shape Styles group and choose Dark Red in the *Standard Colors* section.)
   h. Select the chart title and then apply the Fill - Black, Text 1, Shadow WordArt style (first column, first row).
   i. Increase the height of the chart to 4 inches and the width to 6 inches.
3. Move the chart below the cells containing data, deselect the chart, make sure the data and chart fit on one page, and then print the worksheet (data and chart).
4. Save and then close **EL1-C7-A3-CMPQtrlySales.xlsx**.

Assessment 4

CREATE A FUND ALLOCATIONS PIE CHART

SNAP Grade It

1. Open **SMFFunds.xlsx** and then save the workbook with Save As and name it **EL1-C7-A4-SMFFunds**.
2. Select cells A3 through B7 and then create a pie chart with the following specifications:
   a. Click the *3-D Pie* option at the Insert Pie or Doughnut Chart button drop-down list.
   b. Apply the Layout 1 quick layout.
   c. Apply the Style 2 chart style.
   d. Change the color to Color 3.
   e Move the pie chart to a new worksheet.
   f. Change the title to *Fund Allocations*.
   g. Click the CHART TOOLS FORMAT tab, make sure the chart is selected and not a chart element, and then click the Format Selection button.
   h. At the Format Chart Area task pane, make sure the Fill & Line icon is active, click the *FILL* option to display additional options, click the *Gradient fill* option, and then close the task pane.
   i. Use the Chart Elements button arrow to select *Series "Allocation" Data Labels*.
   j. With the data labels selected, click the Text Fill button arrow (located in the WordArt Styles group) and then click the *Orange, Accent 2, Darker 50%* option (sixth column, bottom row in the *Theme Colors* section).
   k. With the data labels still selected, click the HOME tab and then change the font size to 18 points.
3. Print only the worksheet containing the chart.
4. Save and then close **EL1-C7-A4-SMFFunds.xlsx**.

Assessment 5

WRITE A FORMULA WITH THE PMT FUNCTION

SNAP Grade It

1. Open **CMRefiPlan.xlsx** and then save the workbook with Save As and name it **EL1-C7-A5-CMRefiPlan**.
2. The manager of Clearline Manufacturing is interested in refinancing a loan for either $125,000 or $300,000 and wants to determine the monthly payments. Make cell E4 active and then insert a formula using the PMT function. (For assistance, refer to Project 5a. The monthly payment amounts will display as negative numbers representing outflows of cash.)
3. Copy the formula in cell E4 down to cells E5 through E7.
4. Save, print, and then close **EL1-C7-A5-CMRefiPlan.xlsx**.

Assessment 6

WRITE A FORMULA WITH THE FV FUNCTION

SNAP Grade It

1. Open **CMInvest.xlsx** and then save the workbook with Save As and name it **EL1-C7-A6-CMInvest**.
2. Make cell B6 active and then use the FV function to insert a formula that calculates the future value of the investment.
3. Save and then print the worksheet.

4. Make the following changes to the worksheet:
   a. Change the percentage in cell B3 from *6.5%* to *8.0%*.
   b. Change the number in cell B4 from *48* to *60*.
   c. Change the amount in cell B5 from *($1,000)* to *-500*.
5. Save, print, and then close **EL1-C7-A6-CMInvest.xlsx**.

Assessment 7

WRITE A FORMULA WITH THE IF FUNCTION

SNAP Grade It

1. Open **DISalesBonuses.xlsx** and then save the workbook with Save As and name it **EL1-C7-A7-DISalesBonuses**.
2. Insert a formula in cell C4 that inserts the word *YES* if the amount in B4 is greater than 99999 and inserts *NO* if the amount is not greater than 99999. Copy the formula in cell C4 down to cells C5 through C14.
3. Make cell D4 active and then insert the formula =IF(C4="YES",B4*0.05,0). If sales are over $99,999, this formula will multiply the sales amount by 5% and then insert the product (result) of the formula in the cell. Copy the formula in cell D4 down to cells D5 through D14.
4. Apply accounting formatting with a dollar sign and no places past the decimal point to cell D4.
5. Save and then print **EL1-C7-A7-DISalesBonuses.xlsx**.
6. Display the formulas in the worksheet and then print the worksheet.
7. Turn off the display of formulas.
8. Save and then close **EL1-C7-A7-DISalesBonuses.xlsx**

Assessment 8

CREATE A STACKED CYLINDER CHART

Help

1. Use Excel's Help feature to learn more about chart types and specifically about 3-D stacked column charts.
2. Open **CMPerSales.xlsx** and then save the workbook with Save As and name it **EL1-C7-A8-CMPerSales**.
3. With the data in the worksheet, create a 3-D 100% stacked column chart in a separate sheet. Create an appropriate title for the chart and apply any other formatting to enhance the appearance of the chart.
4. Print only the worksheet containing the chart.
5. Close **EL1-C7-A8-CMPerSales.xlsx**.

Assessment 9 LEARN ABOUT EXCEL OPTIONS

1. Learn about specific options in the Excel Options dialog box by completing the following steps:
   a. At a blank workbook, display the Excel Options dialog box by clicking the FILE tab and then clicking *Options*.
   b. At the Excel Options dialog box, click the *Advanced* option in the left panel.
   c. Scroll down the dialog box and look for the section *Display options for this workbook* and then read the information in the section. Also read the information in the *Display options for this worksheet* section.
   d. Write down the check box options available in the *Display options for this workbook* section and the *Display options for this worksheet* section and identify whether or not the check box contains a check mark. (Record only check box options and ignore buttons and options preceded by circles.)
2. With the information you wrote down about the options, create an Excel worksheet with the following information:
   a. In column C, type each option you wrote down. (Include an appropriate heading.)
   b. In column B, insert an X in the cell that precedes any option that contains a check mark in the check box. (Include an appropriate heading.)
   c. In column A, write a formula with the IF function that inserts the word *ON* in the cell if the cell in column B contains an X and inserts the word *OFF* if it does not (the cell is blank). (Include an appropriate heading.)
   d. Apply formatting to improve the appearance of the worksheet.
3. Save the workbook and name it **EL1-C7-A9-DisplayOptions**.
4. Turn on the display of formulas.
5. Print the worksheet.
6. Turn off the display of formulas.
7. Save, print, and then close **EL1-C7-A9-DisplayOptions.xlsx**.

Visual Benchmark Demonstrate Your Proficiency

CREATE AND FORMAT A PIE CHART

1. At a blank workbook, enter data and then create a pie chart in a separate sheet, as shown in Figure 7.12. Use the information shown in the pie chart to create the data. Format the pie chart so it appears similar to what you see in Figure 7.12. (Apply the Layout 4 quick style and the Style 8 chart style. Create and format the title as shown in the figure and change the size of the data labels to 12 points.)
2. Save the completed workbook and name it **EL1-C7-VB-CMFebExp**.
3. Print both worksheets in the workbook.
4. Close **EL1-C7-VB-CMFebExp.xlsx.**

Figure 7.12 Visual Benchmark

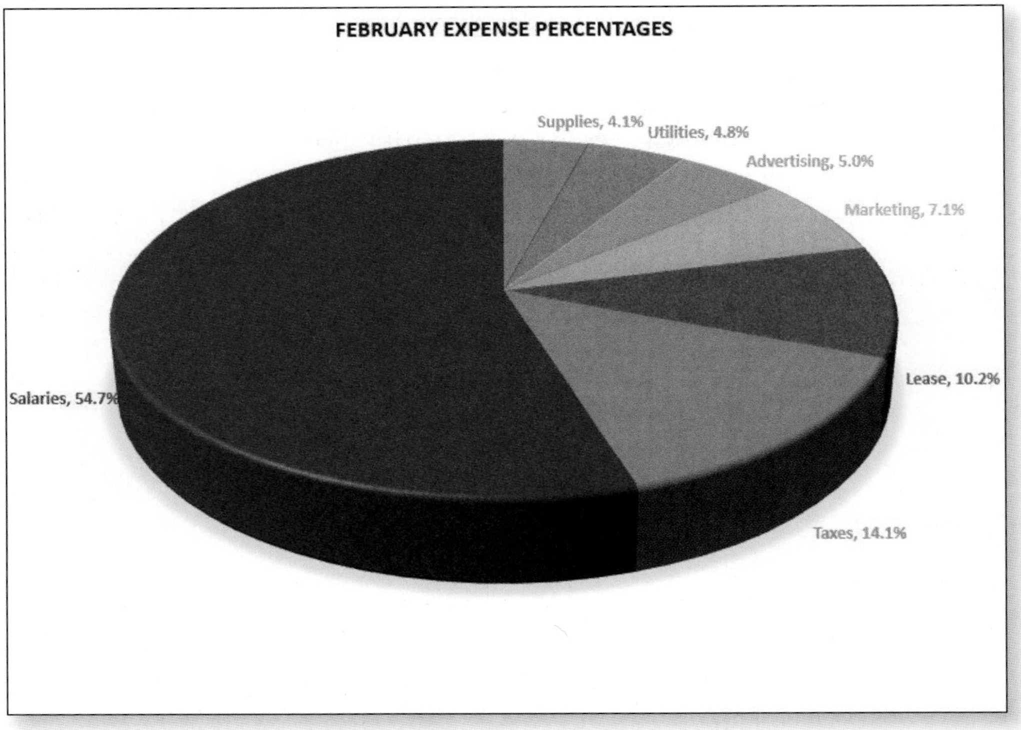

Case Study Apply Your Skills

Part 1

You are an administrator for Dollar Wise Financial Services and need to prepare charts indicating home loan and commercial loan amounts for the past year. Use the information below to prepare a chart in Excel. You determine the type and style of the chart and the layout and formatting of the chart. Insert a shape in the Commercial Loans chart that contains the text *All-time High* and points to the second quarter amount (*$6,785,250*).

Home Loans

1st Qtr.	=	$2,675,025
2nd Qtr.	=	$3,125,750
3rd Qtr.	=	$1,975,425
4th Qtr.	=	$875,650

Commercial Loans

1st Qtr.	=	$5,750,980
2nd Qtr.	=	$6,785,250
3rd Qtr.	=	$4,890,625
4th Qtr.	=	$2,975,900

Save the workbook and name it **EL1-C7-CS-DWQtrSales**. Print only the chart and then close **EL1-C7-CS-DWQtrSales.xlsx**.

Part 2

You need to present information on the budget for the company. You have the dollar amounts and need to convert each amount to a percentage of the entire budget. Use the information below to calculate the percentage of the budget for each item and then create a pie chart with the information. You determine the chart style, layout, and formatting.

Total Budget: $6,000,000

Building Costs	=	$720,000
Salaries	=	$2,340,000
Benefits	=	$480,000
Advertising	=	$840,000
Marketing	=	$600,000
Client Expenses	=	$480,000
Equipment	=	$420,000
Supplies	=	$120,000

Save the workbook containing the pie chart and name it **EL1-C7-CS-DWBudget**. Print only the chart and then close **EL1-C7-CS-DWBudget.xlsx**.

Part 3

The loan officer for Dollar Wise Financial Services has asked you to prepare a sample home mortgage worksheet to show prospective clients. This mortgage worksheet will show the monthly payments on variously priced homes with varying interest rates. Open the **DWMortgageWksht.xlsx** worksheet and then complete the home mortgage worksheet by inserting the following formulas:

- Since many homes in your area sell for at least $400,000, you decide to use that amount in the worksheet with down payments of 5%, 10%, 15%, and 20%. (Insert the amount $400,000 in cells A11 through A14.)
- In column C, insert a formula that determines the down payment amount.
- In column D, insert a formula that determines the loan amount.
- In column G, insert a formula using the PMT function. (The monthly payment will display as a negative number.)

Save the worksheet and name it **EL1-C7-CS-DWMortgageWksht**.

Part 4

If home buyers put down less than 20% of the home's purchase price, mortgage insurance is required. With **EL1-C7-CS-DWMortgageWksht.xlsx** open, insert an IF statement in the cells in column H that inserts the word *NO* if the percentage in column B is equal to or greater than 20% and inserts the word *YES* if the percentage in column B is less than 20%. Save and then print **EL1-C7-CS-DWMortgageWksht.xlsx**.

Part 5

You need to prepare information on mortgage interest rates for a community presentation. You decide to provide the information on mortgage rates in a chart for easy viewing. Use the Internet to search for historical data on the national average for mortgage interest rates. Determine the average mortgage rate for a 30-year FRM (fixed-rate mortgage) for each January and July beginning with the year 2011 and continuing to the current year. Also include the current average interest rate. Use this information to create the chart. Save the workbook and name it **EL1-C7-CS-DWRates**. Print only the chart and then close **EL1-C7-CS-DWRates.xlsx.**

MICROSOFT®
EXCEL®

CHAPTER 8

Adding Visual Interest to Workbooks

PERFORMANCE OBJECTIVES

Upon successful completion of Chapter 8, you will be able to:

- **Insert symbols and special characters**
- **Insert, size, move, and format images**
- **Insert a screenshot**
- **Draw, format, and copy shapes**
- **Insert, format, and type text in a text box**
- **Insert a picture image as a watermark**
- **Insert and format SmartArt graphics**
- **Insert and format WordArt**

SNAP

Tutorials

8.1 Inserting Symbols and Special Characters
8.2 Inserting and Modifying Images
8.3 Inserting and Modifying Clip Art Images
8.4 Creating and Inserting Screenshots
8.5 Inserting and Copying Shapes
8.6 Drawing and Formatting Text Boxes
8.7 Inserting a Picture as a Watermark
8.8 Inserting and Formatting a SmartArt Graphic
8.9 Creating WordArt

Microsoft Excel includes a variety of features that you can use to enhance the appearance of a workbook. Some methods for adding visual appeal that you will learn in this chapter include inserting and modifying pictures and clip art images, screenshots, shapes, text boxes, SmartArt, and WordArt. Model answers for this chapter's projects appear on the following pages.

Excel
EL1C8

Note: Before beginning the projects, copy to your storage medium the EL1C8 subfolder from the EL1 folder on the CD that accompanies this textbook and make EL1C8 the active folder.

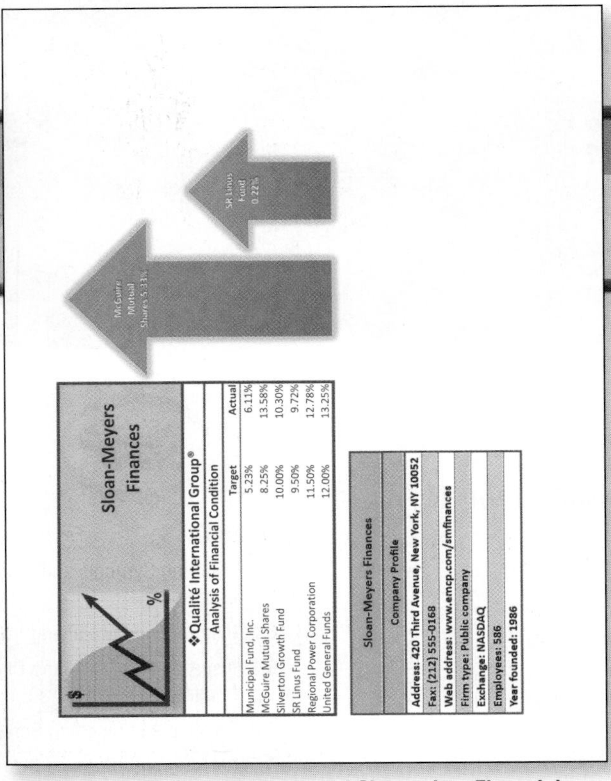

Sloan-Meyers Finances

❖ Qualité International Group®

Analysis of Financial Condition

	Target	Actual
Municipal Fund, Inc.	5.23%	6.11%
McGuire Mutual Shares	8.25%	13.58%
Silverton Growth Fund	10.00%	10.30%
SR Linus Fund	9.50%	9.72%
Regional Power Corporation	11.50%	12.78%
United General Funds	12.00%	13.25%

Sloan-Meyers Finances

Company Profile

Address: 420 Third Avenue, New York, NY 10052
Fax: (212) 555-0168
Web address: www.emcp.com/smfinances
Firm type: Public company
Exchange: NASDAQ
Employees: 586
Year founded: 1986

Project 1 Insert a Clip Art Image and Shapes in a Financial Analysis Workbook EL1-C8-P1-SMFFinCon.xlsx

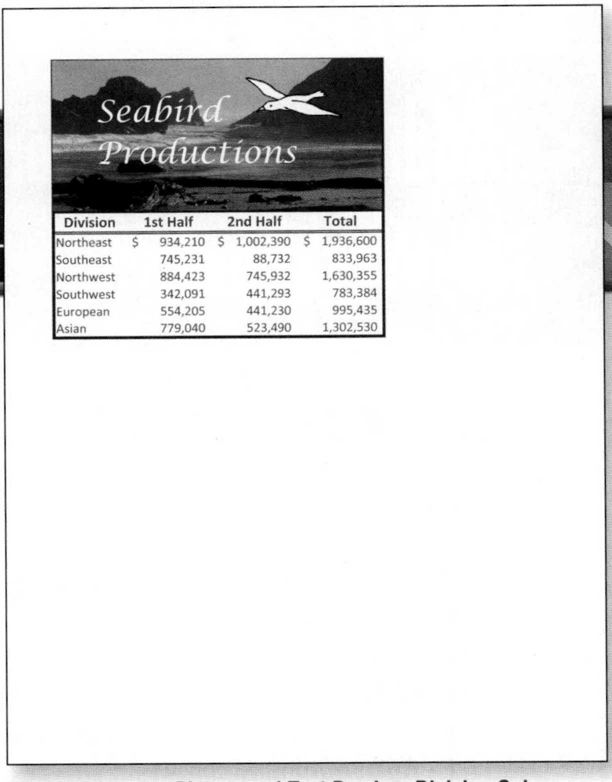

Seabird Productions

Division	1st Half	2nd Half	Total
Northeast	$ 934,210	$ 1,002,390	$ 1,936,600
Southeast	745,231	88,732	833,963
Northwest	884,423	745,932	1,630,355
Southwest	342,091	441,293	783,384
European	554,205	441,230	995,435
Asian	779,040	523,490	1,302,530

Project 2 Insert a Picture and Text Box in a Division Sales Workbook EL1-C8-P2-SPDivSales.xlsx

Highland Constr

EQUIPMENT USAGE REP

Hours	January	February	March	April	May	June
Total hours available	2300	2430	2530	2400	2440	2240
Avoidable delays	19	12	16	20	14	15
Unavoidable delays	9	8	6	12	9	10
Repairs	5	7	12	9	10	6
Servicing	6	13	7	6	4	5
Unassigned	128	95	85	135	95	75
In use	2040	2105	2320	2180	2050	1995

Page 1

uction

ORT

July	August	September	October	November	December
2520	2520	2390	2540	2310	2210
9	8	12	7	12	5
10	13	8	9	5	7
7	8	10	13	9	8
8	3	12	6	11	12
145	120	124	112	95	120
2320	2250	2190	1945	2005	1830

Page 2

Project 3 Insert a Watermark in an Equipment Usage Workbook EL1-C8-P3-HCEqpRpt.xlsx

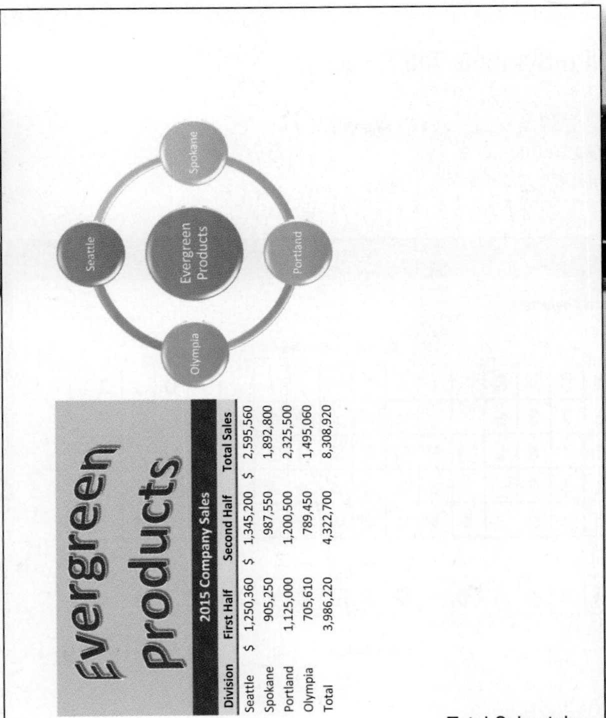

Total Sales tab

Seattle Sales tab

Project 4 Insert and Format SmartArt Graphics in a Company Sales Workbook EL1-C8-P4-EPSales.xlsx

Project 1 Insert a Clip Art Image and Shapes in a Financial Analysis Workbook — 5 Parts

You will open a financial analysis workbook and then insert symbols and move, size, and format an image in the workbook. You will also insert an arrow shape, type and format text in the shape, and then copy the shape.

Inserting Symbols and Special Characters

Use the Symbol button on the INSERT tab to insert special symbols in a worksheet. Click the Symbol button in the Symbols group on the INSERT tab and the Symbol dialog box displays, as shown in Figure 8.1. At the Symbol dialog box, double-click the desired symbol and then click Close or click the desired symbol, click the Insert button, and then click Close. At the Symbol dialog box with the Symbols tab selected, you can change the font at the *Font* option box. When you change the font, different symbols display in the dialog box. Click the Special Characters tab at the Symbol dialog box and a list of special characters displays. Click the desired character, click the Insert button, and then click the Close button.

Quick Steps

Insert a Symbol
1. Click in desired cell.
2. Click INSERT button.
3. Click Symbol button.
4. Double-click desired symbol.
5. Click Close.

Ω

Symbol

Quick Steps

Insert a Special Character

1. Click in desired cell.
2. Click INSERT tab.
3. Click Symbol button.
4. Click Special Characters tab.
5. Double-click desired special character.
6. Click Close.

HINT

You can increase or decrease the size of the Symbol dialog box by positioning the mouse pointer on the lower right corner until the pointer displays as a two-headed arrow and then dragging with the mouse.

Figure 8.1 Symbol Dialog Box with Symbols Tab Selected

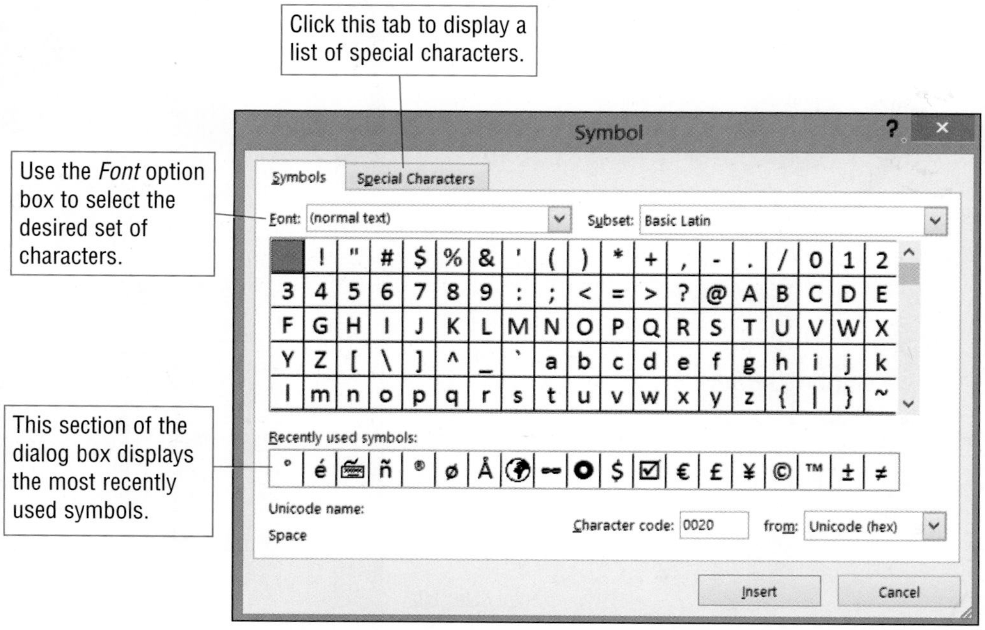

Project 1a Inserting Symbols and Special Characters

Part 1 of 5

1. Open **SMFFinCon.xlsx** and then save the workbook with Save As and name it **EL1-C8-P1-SMFFinCon**.
2. Insert a symbol by completing the following steps:
   a. Double-click in cell A2.
   b. Delete the *e* that displays at the end of *Qualite*.
   c. With the insertion point positioned immediately right of the *t* in *Qualit*, click the INSERT tab.
   d. Click the Symbol button in the Symbols group.
   e. At the Symbol dialog box, scroll down the list box and then click the *é* symbol (located in approximately the ninth through eleventh row).
   f. Click the Insert button and then click the Close button.

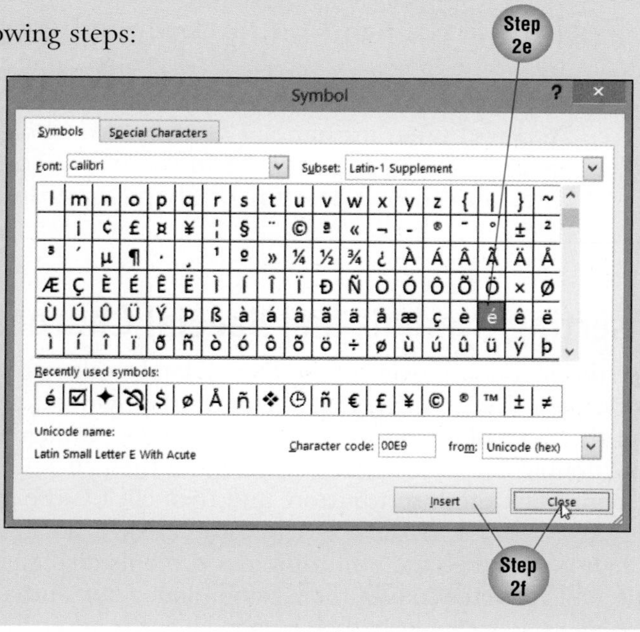

3. Insert a special character by completing the following steps:
   a. With cell A2 selected and in EDIT mode, move the insertion point so it is positioned immediately right of *Group*.
   b. Click the Symbol button in the Symbols group.
   c. At the Symbol dialog box, click the Special Characters tab.
   d. Double-click the ® symbol (tenth option from the top).
   e. Click the Close button.
4. Insert a symbol by completing the following steps:
   a. With cell A2 selected and in EDIT mode, move the insertion point so it is positioned immediately left of the *Q* in *Qualité*.
   b. Click the Symbol button in the Symbols group.
   c. At the Symbol dialog box, click the down-pointing arrow at the right side of the *Font* option box and then click *Wingdings* at the drop-down list. (You will need to scroll down the list to display this option.)
   d. Click the ❖ symbol (located in approximately the fifth or sixth row).
   e. Click the Insert button and then click the Close button.
5. Click in cell A3.
6. Save **EL1-C8-P1-SMFFinCon.xlsx**.

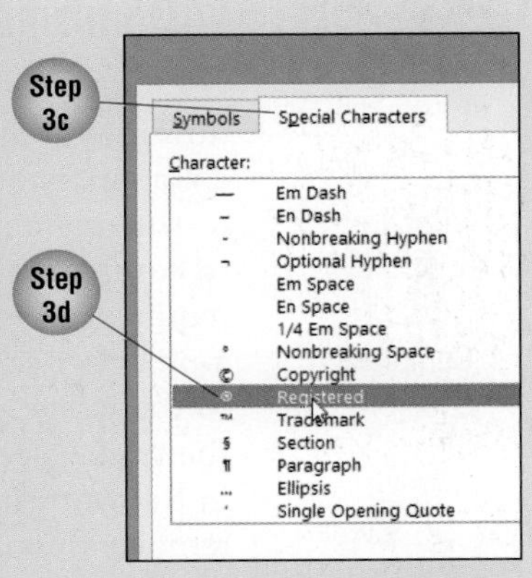

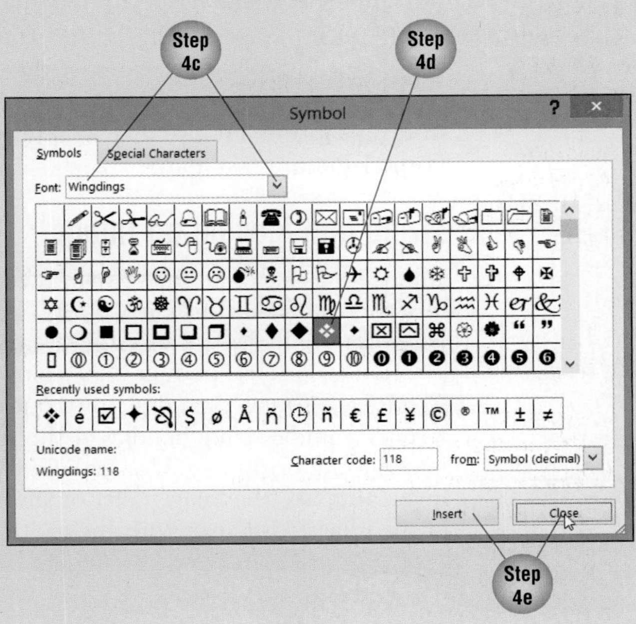

Inserting Images

Insert an image, such as a picture or clip art, in an Excel workbook with buttons in the Illustrations group on the INSERT tab. Click the Pictures button to display the Insert Picture dialog box, where you can specify the desired picture file, or click the Online Pictures button and search for images online. When you insert an image in a worksheet, the PICTURE TOOLS FORMAT tab displays, as shown in Figure 8.2.

Quick Steps

Insert a Picture
1. Click INSERT tab.
2. Click Pictures button.
3. Navigate to desired folder.
4. Double-click desired picture.

Pictures

Figure 8.2 PICTURE TOOLS FORMAT Tab

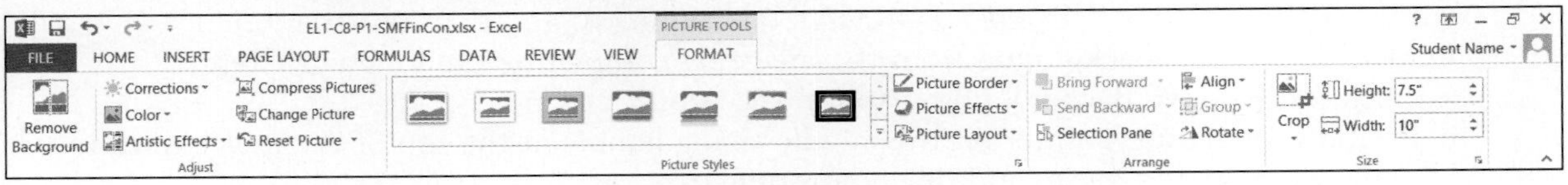

Customizing and Formatting an Image

Use buttons in the Adjust group on the PICTURE TOOLS FORMAT tab to remove unwanted portions of an image, correct the brightness and contrast, change the image color, apply artistic effects, change to a different image, and reset the image back to the original formatting. Use the Compress Pictures button in the Adjust group to compress the size of an image file and reduce the amount of space the image requires on your storage medium. Use buttons in the Picture Styles group to apply a predesigned style to the image, change the image border, or apply other effects to the image. With options in the Arrange group, you can position the image on the page, specify how text will wrap around it, align the image with other elements in the worksheet, and rotate the image. Use the Crop button in the Size group to remove any unnecessary parts of the image and use the *Shape Height* and *Shape Width* measurement boxes to specify the image size.

Compress Pictures

Crop

In addition to the PICTURE TOOLS FORMAT tab, you can customize and format an image with options at the shortcut menu. Display this menu by right-clicking the image. With options at the shortcut menu, you can change the image, insert a caption, choose text wrapping, size and position the image, and display the Format Picture task pane.

Sizing and Moving an Image

Change the size of an image with the *Shape Height* and *Shape Width* measurement boxes in the Size group on the PICTURE TOOLS FORMAT tab or with the sizing handles that display around the selected image. To change size with a sizing handle, position the mouse pointer on a sizing handle until the pointer turns into a double-headed arrow and then drag in or out to decrease or increase the size of the image. Use the middle sizing handles at the left and right sides of the image to make the image wider or thinner. Use the middle sizing handles at the top and bottom of the image to make the image taller or shorter. Use the sizing handles at the corners of the image to change both the width and height at the same time. Hold down the Shift key while dragging a sizing handle to maintain the proportions of the image.

HINT

You can use arrow keys on the keyboard to move a selected image. To move the image in small increments, hold down the Ctrl key while pressing one of the arrow keys.

Move an image by positioning the mouse pointer on the image border until the pointer displays with a four-headed arrow attached and then dragging the image to the desired location. Rotate the image by positioning the mouse pointer on the white, round rotation handle until the pointer displays as a circular arrow. Hold down the left mouse button, drag in the desired direction, and then release the mouse button.

Project 1b **Formatting an Image** **Part 2 of 5**

1. With **EL1-C8-P1-SMFFinCon.xlsx** open, insert a picture by completing the following steps:
   a. Click the INSERT tab and then click the Pictures button in the Illustrations group.
   b. At the Insert Picture dialog box, navigate to the EL1C8 folder on your storage medium and then double-click ***WallStreet.jpg***.
2. Change the size of the image by clicking in the *Shape Height* measurement box in the Size group on the PICTURE TOOLS FORMAT tab, typing 2, and then pressing Enter.
3. Remove the yellow background from the image by completing the following steps:
   a. Click the Remove Background button in the Adjust group.
   b. Position the mouse pointer on the middle sizing handle at the top of the image until the pointer displays as an up-and-down-pointing arrow.

c. Hold down the left mouse button, drag the border up to the top of the image, and then release the mouse.
d. Position the mouse pointer on the middle sizing handle at the bottom of the image until the pointer displays as an up-and-down-pointing arrow.
e. Hold down the left mouse button, drag the border up approximately 0.25 inch, and then release the mouse button.
f. Click the Keep Changes button in the Close group on the BACKGROUND REMOVAL tab.

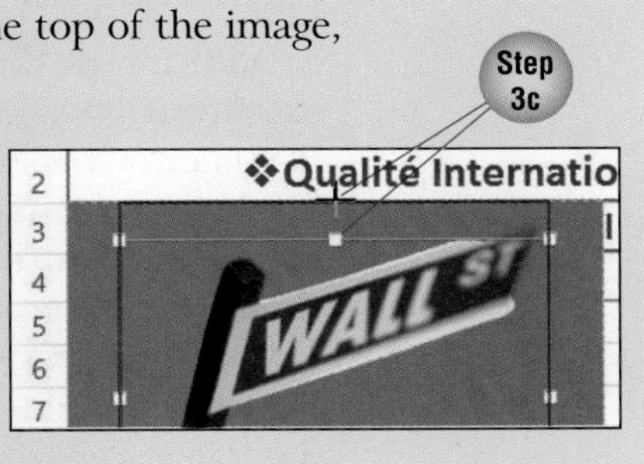

4. Change the color by clicking the Color button in the Adjust group and then clicking the *Blue, Accent color 1 Light* option (second column, third row in the *Recolor* section).
5. Apply a correction by clicking the Corrections button and then clicking the *Brightness: +20% Contrast: +20%* option (fourth column, fourth row in the *Brightness and Contrast* section).

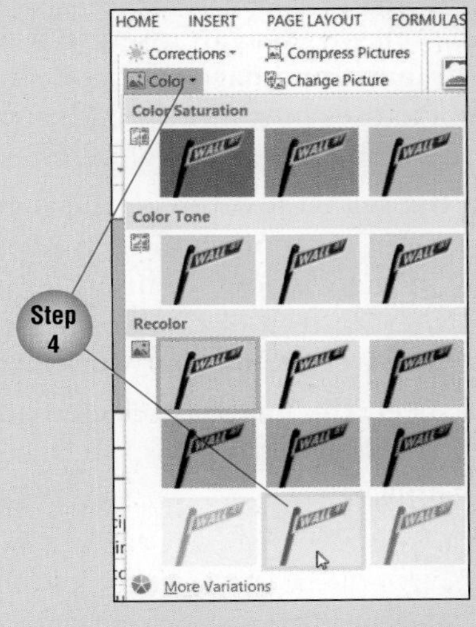

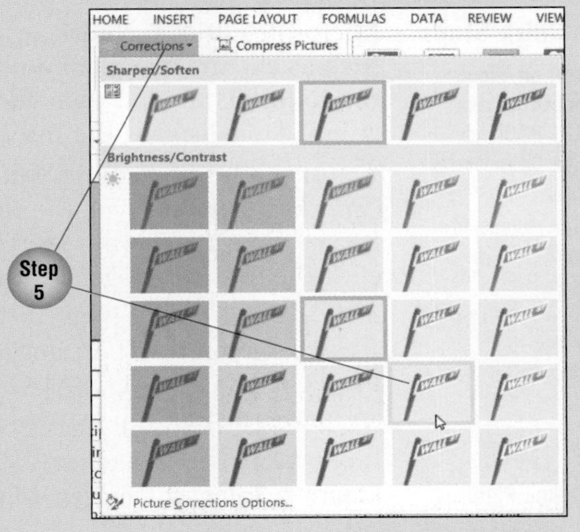

6. Apply an artistic effect by clicking the Artistic Effects button and then clicking the *Glow Edges* option (last option in the drop-down gallery).
7. Move the image by completing the following steps:
a. Position the mouse pointer on the image (displays with a four-headed arrow attached).
b. Hold down the left mouse button, drag the image to the upper left corner of the worksheet, and then release the mouse button.

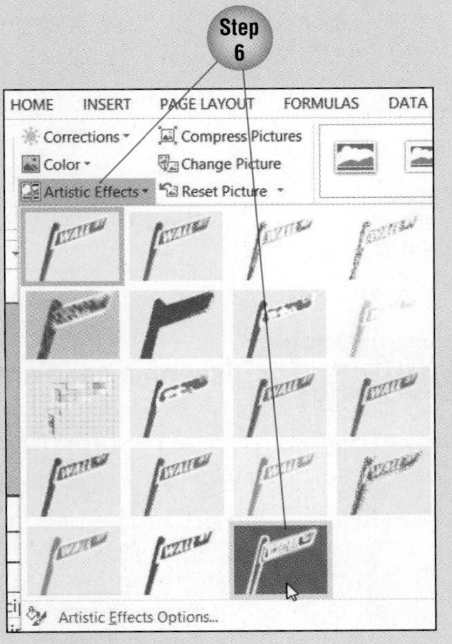

8. Save and then print **EL1-C8-P1-SMFFinCon.xlsx**.

Formatting an Image at the Format Picture Task Pane

In addition to the PICTURES TOOLS FORMAT tab, the Format Picture task pane is available for formatting an image. Click the Picture Styles group task pane launcher or the Size group task pane launcher and the Format Picture task pane displays at the right side of the screen. If you click the Picture Styles group task pane launcher, the task pane displays with the Effects icon selected, and if you click the Size group task pane launcher, the Size & Properties icon is selected. Two other icons are also available in this task pane: the Fill & Line icon and the Picture icon. You may need to display (expand) the formatting options within the icons. For example, click SIZE with the Size & Properties icon selected and options for changing the size of the image display. Close the task pane by clicking the Close button located in the upper right corner of the task pane.

Inserting an Image from Office.com

Quick Steps

Insert an Image from Office.com
1. Click INSERT tab.
2. Click Online Pictures button.
3. Type search word or topic.
4. Press Enter.
5. Double-click desired image.
6. Click desired image.

Online Pictures

Microsoft Office includes a gallery of media images you can insert in a worksheet, such as clip art images and photographs. To insert an image in a worksheet, click the INSERT tab and then click the Online Pictures button in the Illustrations group. This displays the Insert Pictures window, as shown in Figure 8.3.

At the Insert Pictures window, click in the search text box to the right of *Office.com Clip Art*; type the search word(s), term, or topic; and then press Enter. Images that match your search text display in the window. To insert an image, click the desired image and then click the Insert button or double-click the image. This downloads the image from the Office.com website to your worksheet.

When you insert an image in the worksheet, the image is selected and the PICTURE TOOLS FORMAT tab is active. Use buttons on this tab to customize an image, just as you learned to customize a picture.

Figure 8.3 Insert Pictures Window

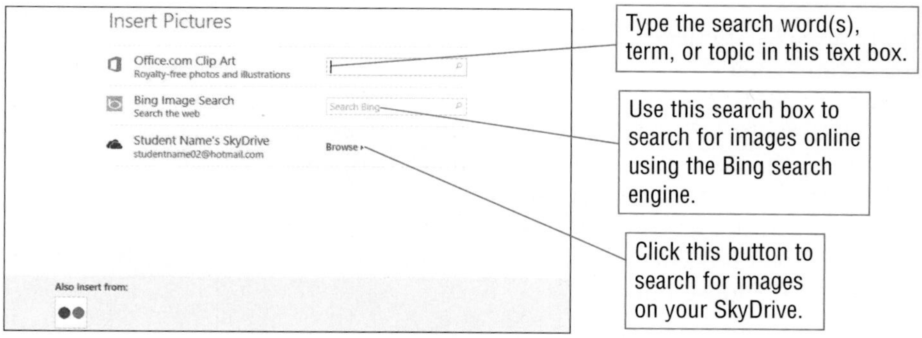

Project 1c **Inserting and Formatting a Clip Art Image** **Part 3 of 5**

1. With **EL1-C8-P1-SMFFinCon.xlsx** open, delete the Wall Street sign image by clicking the image and then pressing the Delete key.
2. Insert a clip art image by completing the following steps:
   a. Make cell A1 active.
   b. Click the INSERT tab and then click the Online Pictures button in the Illustrations group.

any graph going up
Bailouts for Dummies

c. At the Insert Pictures window, type **charts, graphs, stock market** in the search box and then press Enter.
d. Double-click the image shown below and to the right.

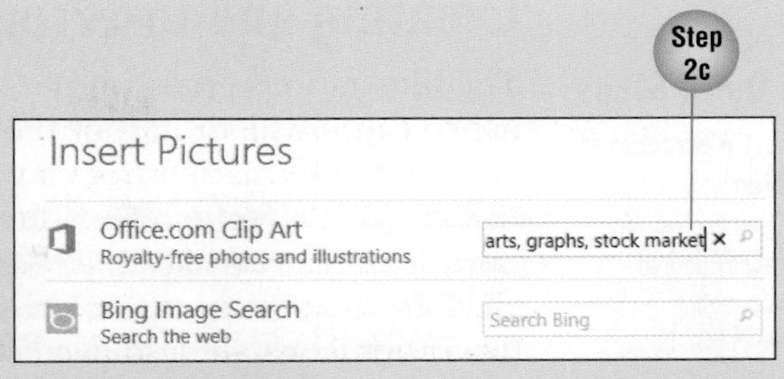

3. Apply a border to the image by clicking the Picture Border button arrow, pointing to *Weight* at the drop-down list, and then clicking *1 pt* at the side menu.
4. Change the image border to a picture style by clicking the *Soft Edge Rectangle* thumbnail in the Picture Styles group (sixth thumbnail).

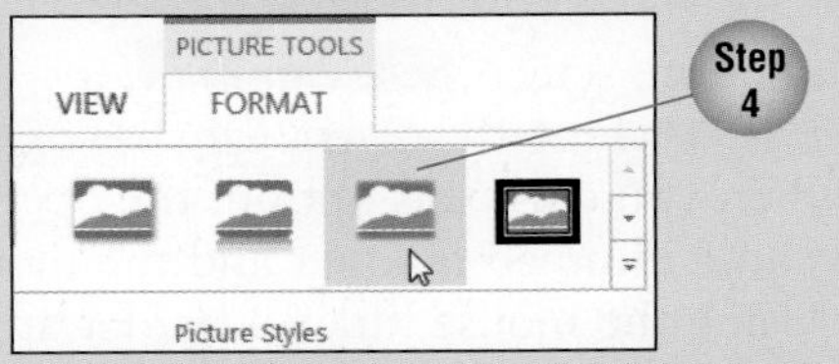

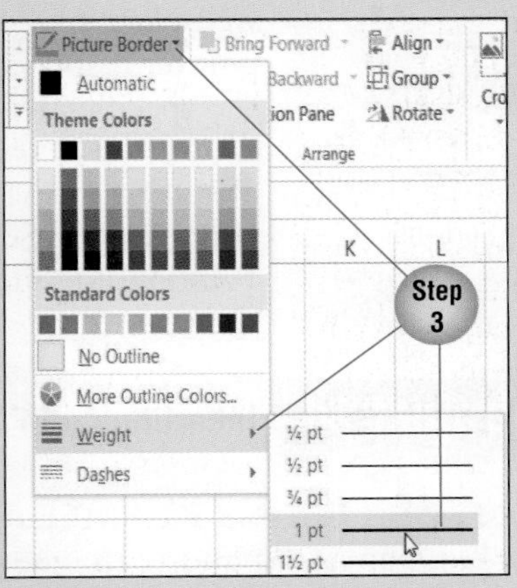

5. Display the Format Picture task pane with the Size & Properties icon selected by clicking the Size group task pane launcher on the PICTURE TOOLS FORMAT tab.
6. If necessary, click *SIZE* in the task pane to display the sizing options.
7. Change the height of the image by selecting the current measurement in the *Height* measurement box, typing **1.7**, and then pressing Enter. (The width automatically changes to maintain the proportions of the image.)
8. Change the properties of the image by clicking PROPERTIES to expand the options and then clicking the *Move and size with cells* option. (With this option selected, if you change the size of the row, the size of the image will also change.)

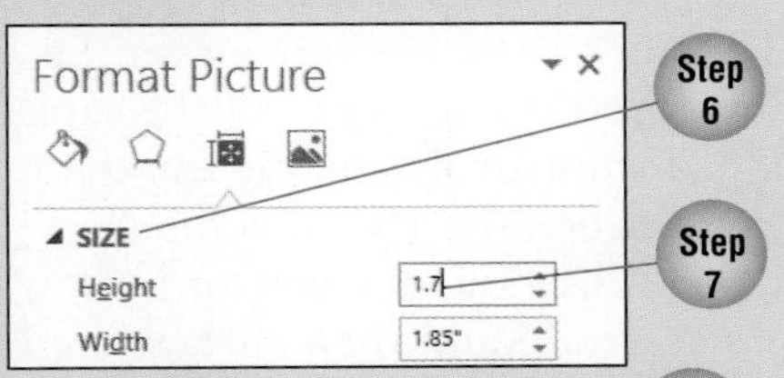

9. Apply a correction to the image by completing the following steps:
   a. Click the Picture icon located toward the top of the task pane.
   b. Click PICTURE CORRECTIONS to expand the options.
   c. Select the current percentage in the *Brightness* text box and then type **-23**.
   d. Select the current percentage in the *Contract* text box, type **45**, and then press Enter.
10. Close the Format Picture task pane by clicking the Close button in the upper right corner of the task pane.
11. Click outside the clip art image to deselect it.
12. Increase the height of row 1 to 126.00 pixels and notice that the image size increases with the row height.
13. Save **EL1-C8-P1-SMFFinCon.xlsx**.

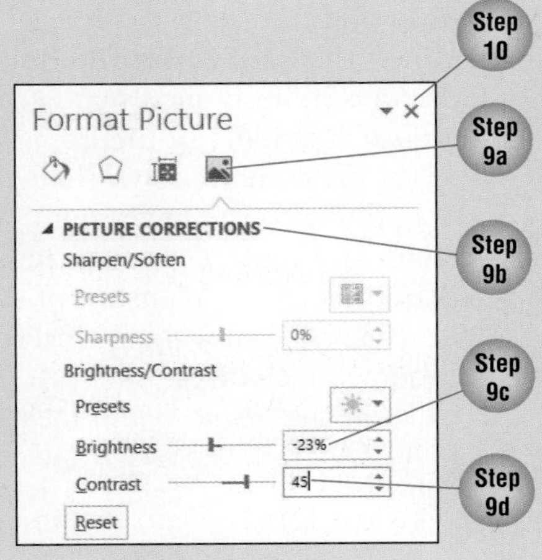

Creating and Inserting Screenshots

Quick Steps

Insert a Screenshot

1. Open workbook.
2. Open another file.
3. Display desired information.
4. Make workbook active.
5. Click INSERT tab.
6. Click Screenshot button.
7. Click desired window at drop-down list.

OR

6. Click Screenshot button and then *Screen Clipping*.
7. Drag to specify capture area.

Screenshot

The Illustrations group on the INSERT tab contains a Screenshot button you can use to capture all or part of the contents of a screen as an image. This is useful for capturing information from a web page or a file in another program. If you want to capture the entire screen, display the desired web page or open the desired file from a program, make Excel active, and then open a workbook or blank workbook. Click the INSERT tab, click the Screenshot button, and then click the desired screen thumbnail at the drop-down list. The currently active worksheet does not display as a thumbnail at the drop-down list—only any other file or program you have open. If you do not have another file or program open, the Windows desktop displays. When you click the desired thumbnail, the screenshot is inserted as an image in the open workbook, the image is selected, and the PICTURE TOOLS FORMAT tab is active. Use buttons on this tab to customize the screenshot image.

In addition to making a screenshot of an entire screen, you can make a screenshot of a specific portion of the screen by clicking the *Screen Clipping* option at the Screenshot button drop-down list. When you click this option, the open web page, file, or Windows desktop displays in a dimmed manner and the mouse pointer displays as crosshairs (a plus sign). Using the mouse, draw a border around the specific area of the screen you want to capture. The specific area you identify is inserted in the workbook as an image, the image is selected, and the PICTURE TOOLS FORMAT tab is active. If you have only one workbook or file open when you click the Screenshot button, clicking the *Screen Clipping* option will cause the Windows desktop to display.

Project 1d Inserting and Formatting a Screenshot — Part 4 of 5

1. With **EL1-C8-P1-SMFFinCon.xlsx** open, make sure that no other programs are open.
2. Open Word and then open the document named **SMFCoProfile.docx** from the EL1C8 folder on your storage medium.
3. Click the Excel button on the Taskbar.
4. Insert a screenshot of the table in the Word document by completing the following steps:
   a. Click the INSERT tab.
   b. Click the Screenshot button in the Illustrations group and then click *Screen Clipping* at the drop-down list.
   c. When the **SMFCoProfile.docx** document displays in a dimmed manner, position the mouse crosshairs in the upper left corner of the table, hold down the left mouse button, drag down to the lower right corner of the table, and then release the mouse button. (This creates a screenshot of the entire table.)

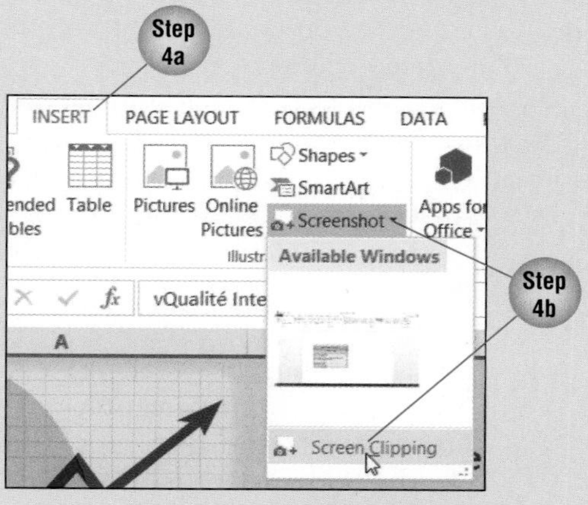

5. With the screenshot image inserted in the **EL1-C8-P1-SMFFinCon.xlsx** workbook, make the following changes:
   a. Click in the *Shape Width* measurement box in the Size group on the PICTURE TOOLS FORMAT tab, type 3.7, and then press Enter.

b. Click the Corrections button and then click the *Sharpen: 25%* option (fourth option in the *Sharpen/Soften* section).
c. Click the Corrections button and then click the *Brightness: 0% (Normal) Contrast: -40%* (third column, first row in the *Brightness/Contrast* section).

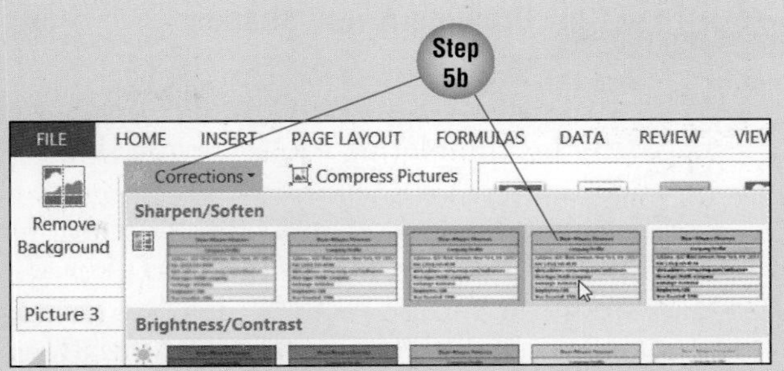

d. Using the mouse, drag the screenshot image one row below the data in row 10.
6. Make cell A4 active.
7. Save **EL1-C8-P1-SMFFinCon.xlsx**.
8. Click the Word button on the Taskbar, close **SMFCoProfile.docx**, and then close Word.

Inserting and Copying Shapes

In Chapter 7, you learned how to insert shapes in a chart. With the Shapes button in the Illustrations group on the INSERT tab, you can also insert shapes in a worksheet. Use the Shapes button to draw shapes in a worksheet, including lines, basic shapes, block arrows, flow chart shapes, callouts, stars, and banners. Click a shape and the mouse pointer displays as crosshairs. Click in the worksheet or position the crosshairs where you want the shape to begin, hold down the left mouse button, drag to create the shape, and then release the mouse button. If you click or drag in the worksheet, the shape is inserted in the worksheet and the DRAWING TOOLS FORMAT tab, shown in Figure 8.4, becomes active. Use the buttons on this tab to change the shape, apply a style to the shape, arrange the shape, and change the size of the shape.

If you choose a shape in the *Lines* section of the Shapes button drop-down list, the shape you draw is considered a line drawing. If you choose an option in the other sections of the drop-down list, the shape you draw is considered an enclosed object. When drawing an enclosed object, you can maintain the proportions of the shape by holding down the Shift key while dragging with the mouse to create the shape. You can type text in an enclosed object and then use buttons in the WordArt Styles group (or options on the HOME tab) to format the text.

Copy a shape in a worksheet by selecting the shape and then clicking the Copy button in the Clipboard group on the HOME tab. Make active the cell where you want to copy the shape and then click the Paste button. You can also copy a selected shape by holding down the Ctrl key while dragging the shape to the desired location.

Quick Steps

Insert a Shape
1. Click INSERT tab.
2. Click Shapes button.
3. Click desired shape at drop-down list.
4. Click or drag in worksheet.

Copy a Shape
1. Select shape.
2. Click Copy button.
3. Position insertion point in desired location.
4. Click Paste button.
OR
1. Select shape.
2. Hold down Ctrl key.
3. Drag shape to desired location.

Shapes

Figure 8.4 DRAWING TOOLS FORMAT Tab

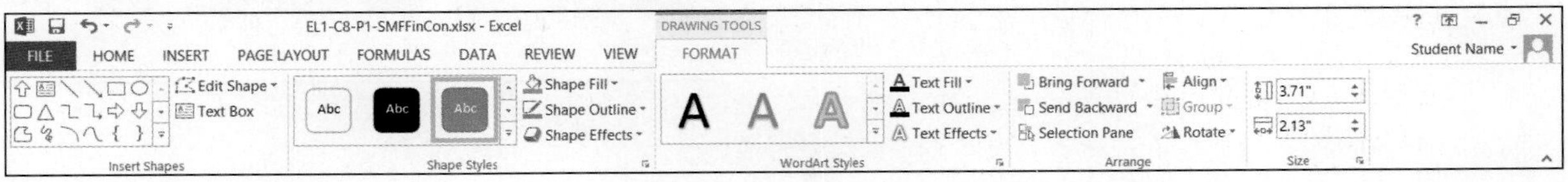

Project 1e Drawing Arrow Shapes Part 5 of 5

1. With **EL1-C8-P1-SMFFinCon.xlsx** open, create the larger arrow shown in Figure 8.5 on page 284 by completing the following steps:
   a. Click the INSERT tab.
   b. Click the Shapes button in the Illustrations group and then click the *Up Arrow* shape (third column, top row in the *Block Arrows* section).
   c. Position the mouse pointer (displays as crosshairs) near the upper left corner of cell D1 and then click the left mouse button. (This inserts the arrow shape in the worksheet.)

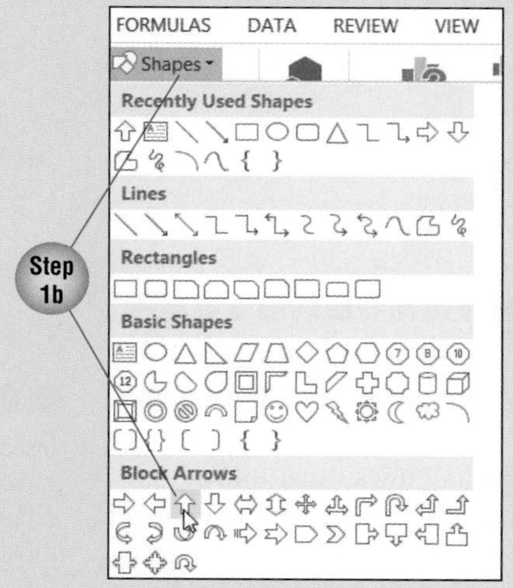

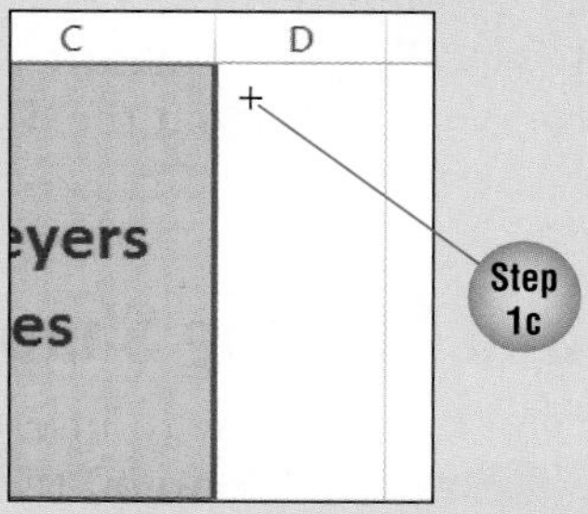

   d. Click in the *Shape Height* measurement box and then type 3.7.
   e. Click in the *Shape Width* measurement box, type 2.1, and then press Enter.
   f. If necessary, drag the arrow so it is positioned as shown in Figure 8.5 on page 284. (To drag the arrow, position the mouse pointer on the border of the selected arrow until the pointer displays with a four-headed arrow attached, hold down the left mouse button, drag the arrow to the desired position, and then release the mouse button.)
   g. Click the More button at the right side of the thumbnails in the Shape Styles group on the DRAWING TOOLS FORMAT tab and then click the *Intense Effect - Blue, Accent 1* option (second column, bottom row).

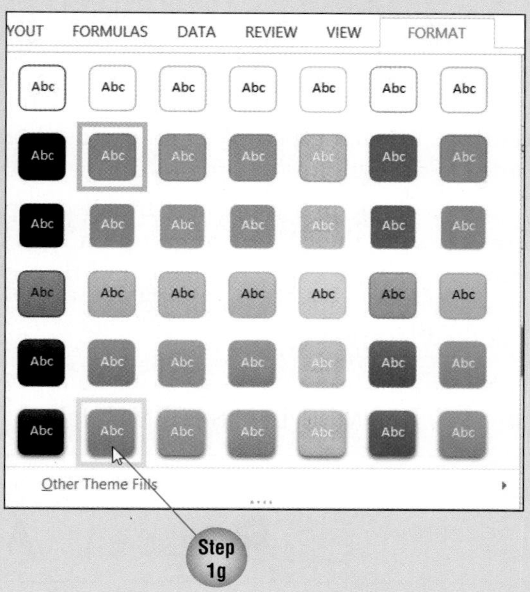

h. Click the Shape Effects button in the Shape Styles group, point to *Glow*, and then click the *Orange, 11 pt glow, Accent color 2* option (second column, third row in the *Glow Variations* section).

2. Insert text in the arrow shape by completing the following steps:
   a. With the arrow shape selected, type McGuire Mutual Shares 5.33%.
   b. Select the text you just typed (*McGuire Mutual Shares 5.33%*).
   c. Click the More button at the right side of the thumbnails in the WordArt Styles group and then click the *Fill - White, Outline - Accent 2, Hard Shadow - Accent 2* option (fourth column, third row).
   d. Press Ctrl + E to center the text.
3. With the arrow selected, copy the arrow by completing the following steps:
   a. Hold down the Ctrl key.
   b. Position the mouse pointer on the arrow border until the pointer displays with a square box and plus symbol attached.
   c. Hold down the left mouse button and drag to the right so the outline of the arrow is positioned at the right side of the existing arrow.
   d. Release the mouse button and then release the Ctrl key.
4. Format the second arrow by completing the following steps:
   a. With the second arrow selected, click in the *Shape Height* measurement box on the DRAWING TOOLS FORMAT tab and then type 2.
   b. Click in the *Shape Width* measurement box, type 1.6, and then press Enter
   c. Select the text *McGuire Mutual Shares 5.33%* and then type SR Linus Fund 0.22%.
   d. Drag the arrow so it is positioned as shown in Figure 8.5.
5. Change the orientation to landscape. (Make sure the cells containing data, the screenshot image, and the arrows will print on the same page.)
6. Save, print, and then close **EL1-C8-P1-SMFFinCon.xlsx**.

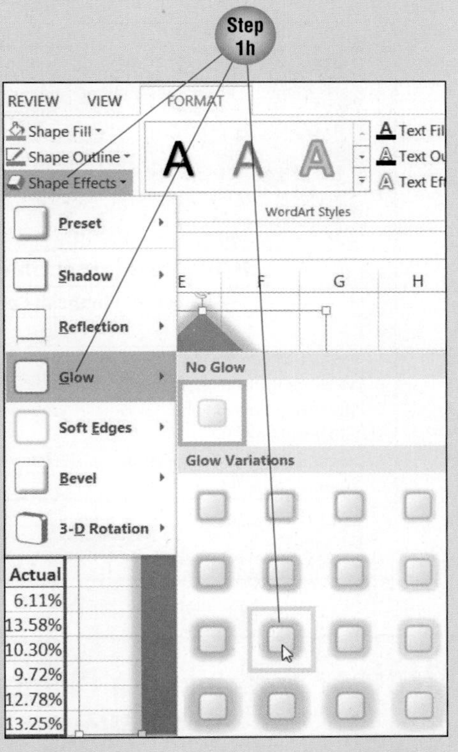

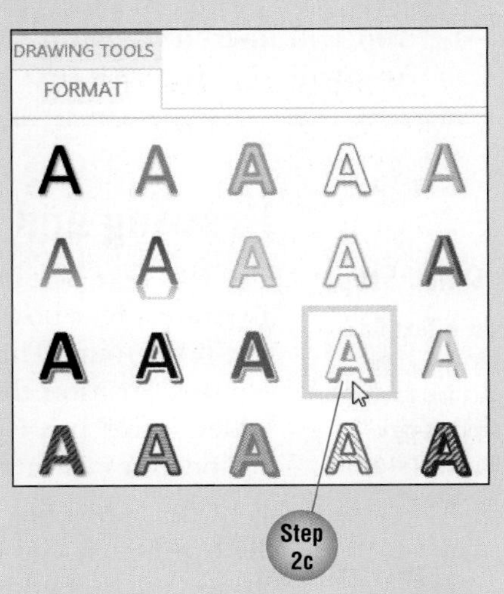

Figure 8.5 Project 1e

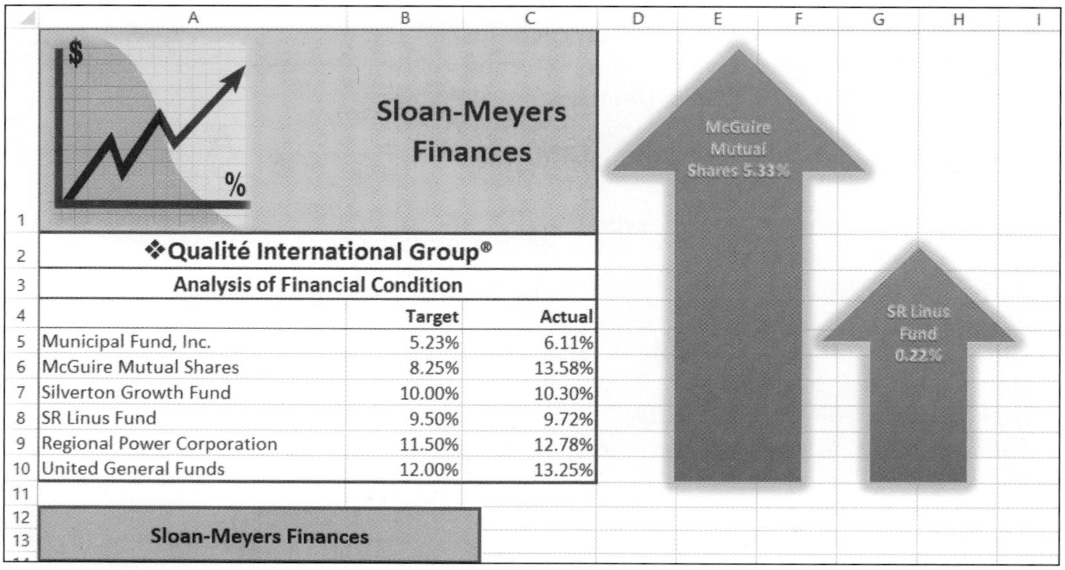

Project 2 Insert a Picture and Text Box in a Division Sales Workbook — 1 Part

You will open a division sales workbook and then insert, move, and size a picture. You will also insert a text box and then format the text.

Drawing and Formatting Text Boxes

Quick Steps

Draw a Text Box
1. Click INSERT tab.
2. Click Text Box button.
3. Click or drag in worksheet to create text box.

Text Box

Use the Text Box button on the INSERT tab to draw a text box in a worksheet. To draw a text box, click the INSERT tab and then click the Text Box button in the Text group. This causes the mouse pointer to display as a long, thin, crosslike pointer. Position the pointer in the worksheet and then drag to create the text box. When a text box is selected, the DRAWING TOOLS FORMAT tab displays with options for customizing the text box.

Click a text box to select it and a dashed border and sizing handles display around the text box. If you want to delete the text box, click the text box border again to change the dashed border lines to solid border lines and then press the Delete key.

Project 2 Inserting and Customizing a Picture and Text Box — Part 1 of 1

1. Open **SPDivSales.xlsx** and then save the workbook with Save As and name it **EL1-C8-P2-SPDivSales**.
2. Make the following changes to the bird clip art image:
   a. Click the bird clip art image to select it.
   b. Click the PICTURE TOOLS FORMAT tab.

c. Click the Rotate button in the Arrange group and then click *Flip Horizontal* at the drop-down list.

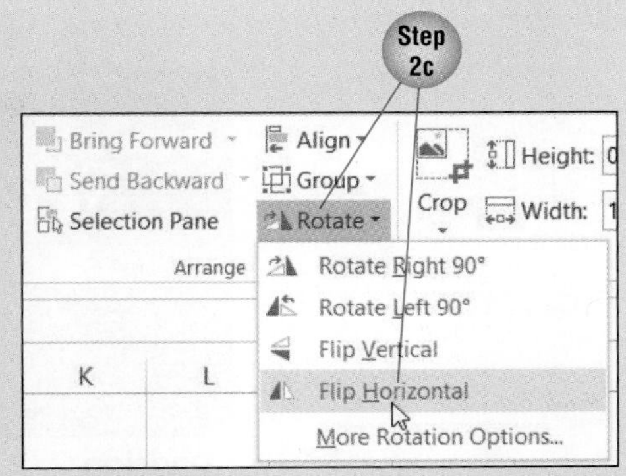

3. Insert and format a picture by completing the following steps:
   a. Click in cell A1 outside the bird image.
   b. Click the INSERT tab.
   c. Click the Pictures button in the Illustrations group.
   d. At the Insert Picture dialog box, navigate to the EL1C8 folder on your storage medium and then double-click ***Ocean.jpg***.
   e. With the picture selected, click the Send Backward button in the Arrange group on the PICTURE TOOLS FORMAT tab.
   f. Use the sizing handles that display around the picture image to move and size it so it fills cell A1, as shown in Figure 8.6.
   g. If necessary, click the bird clip art image and then drag the image so it is positioned as shown in Figure 8.6 on the next page.

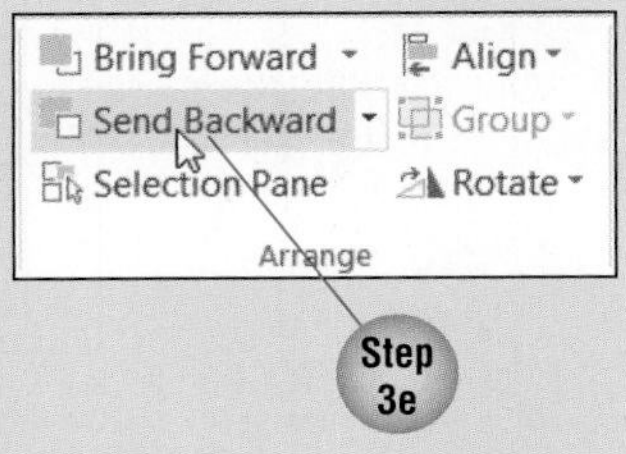

4. Save **EL1-C8-P2-SPDivSales.xlsx**.
5. Draw a text box by completing the following steps:
   a. Click the INSERT tab.
   b. Click the Text Box button in the Text group.
   c. Drag in cell A1 to draw a text box the approximate size and shape shown at the right.

6. Format the text box by completing the following steps:
   a. Click the DRAWING TOOLS FORMAT tab.
   b. Click the Shape Fill button arrow in the Shape Styles group and then click *No Fill* at the drop-down gallery.
   c. Click the Shape Outline button arrow in the Shape Styles group and then click *No Outline* at the drop-down gallery.

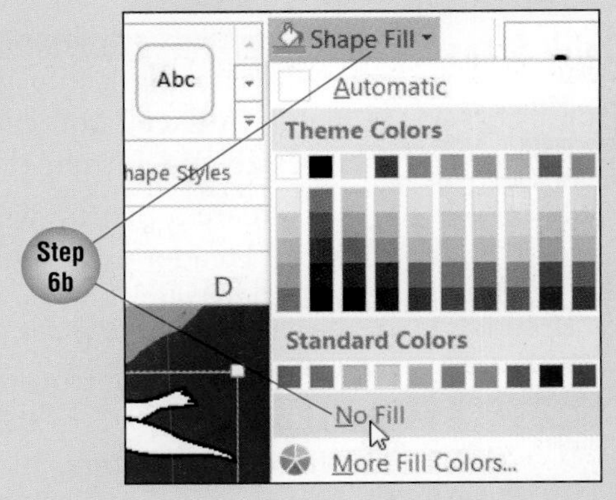

7. Insert text in the text box by completing the following steps:
   a. With the text box selected, click the HOME tab.
   b. Click the Font button arrow and then click *Lucida Calligraphy* at the drop-down gallery. (You will need to scroll down the gallery to display this font.)
   c. Click the Font Size button arrow and then click *32* at the drop-down gallery.
   d. Click the Font Color button arrow and then click *White, Background 1* (first column, first row in the *Theme Colors* section).
   e. Type **Seabird Productions**.
8. Move the text box so the text is positioned in cell A1 as shown in Figure 8.6.
9. Save, print, and then close **EL1-C8-P2-SPDivSales.xlsx**.

Figure 8.6 Project 2

Division	1st Half	2nd Half	Total
Northeast	$ 934,210	$ 1,002,390	$ 1,936,600
Southeast	745,231	88,732	833,963
Northwest	884,423	745,932	1,630,355
Southwest	342,091	441,293	783,384
European	554,205	441,230	995,435
Asian	779,040	523,490	1,302,530

Project 3 Insert a Watermark in an Equipment Usage Workbook — 1 Part

You will open an equipment usage report workbook and then insert a picture as a watermark that prints on both pages of the worksheet.

Inserting a Picture as a Watermark

Quick Steps

Insert a Picture as a Watermark
1. Click INSERT tab.
2. Click Header & Footer button.
3. Click Picture button.
4. Click Browse button.
5. Navigate to desired folder.
6. Double-click desired picture.
7. Click Format Picture button.
8. Change size, brightness, and contrast of image.
9. Click OK.

Format Picture

A ***watermark*** is a lightened image that displays behind data in a file. You can create a watermark in a Word document but the watermark functionality is not available in Excel. You can, however, insert a picture in a header or footer and then resize and format the picture to display behind each page of the worksheet.

To create a picture watermark in a worksheet, click the INSERT tab and then click the Header & Footer button in the Text group. With the worksheet in Print Layout view, click the Picture button in the Header & Footer Elements group on the HEADER & FOOTER TOOLS DESIGN tab. At the Insert Pictures window, click the Browse button to the right of the *From a file* option. At the Insert Picture dialog box, navigate to the desired folder and then double-click the desired picture. This inserts &*[Picture]* in the header. Resize and format the picture by clicking the Format Picture button in the Header & Footer Elements group. Use options at the Format Picture dialog box with the Size tab selected to specify the size of the picture and use options in the dialog box with the Picture tab selected to specify brightness and contrast.

Project 3 Inserting a Picture as a Watermark

Part 1 of 1

1. Open **HCEqpRpt.xlsx** and then save it and name it **EL1-C8-P3-HCEqpRpt**.
2. Insert a picture as a watermark by completing the following steps:
   a. Click the INSERT tab.
   b. Click the Header & Footer button in the Text group.
   c. Click the Picture button in the Header & Footer Elements group on the HEADER & FOOTER TOOLS DESIGN tab.
   d. At the Insert Pictures window, click the Browse button that displays to the right of the *From a file* option.
   e. At the Insert Picture dialog box, navigate to the EL1C8 folder on your storage medium and then double-click ***Olympics.jpg***.
   f. Click the Format Picture button in the Header & Footer Elements group.
   g. At the Format Picture dialog box with the Size tab selected, click the *Lock aspect ratio* check box in the *Scale* section to remove the check mark.
   h. Select the current measurement in the *Height* measurement box in the *Size and rotate* section and then type 10.
   i. Select the current measurement in the *Width* measurement box in the *Size and rotate* section and then type 7.5.
   j. Click the Picture tab.
   k. Select the current percentage in the *Brightness* measurement box in the *Image control* section and then type 75.
   l. Select the current percentage in the *Contrast* measurement box and then type 25.
   m. Click OK to close the Format Picture dialog box.
3. Click in the worksheet.
4. Display the worksheet in the Print backstage area to view how the image will print on page 1 and page 2 and then print the worksheet.
5. Save and then close **EL1-C8-P3-HCEqpRpt.xlsx**.

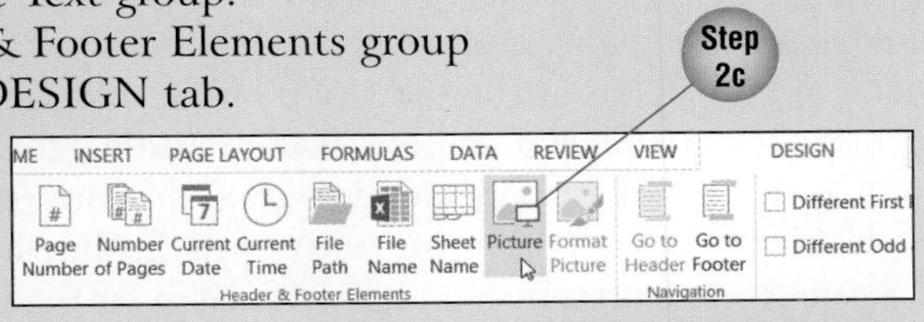

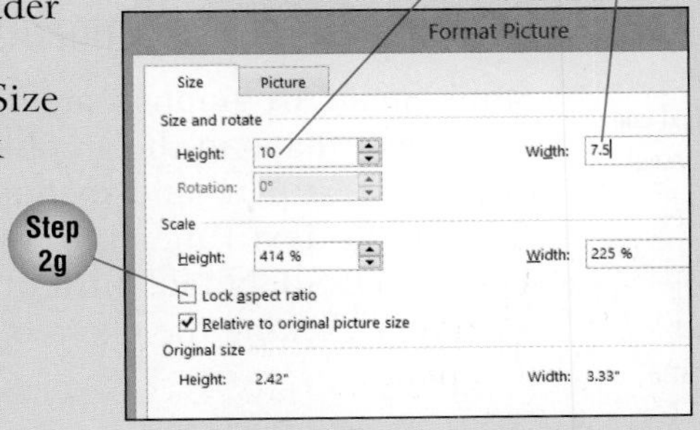

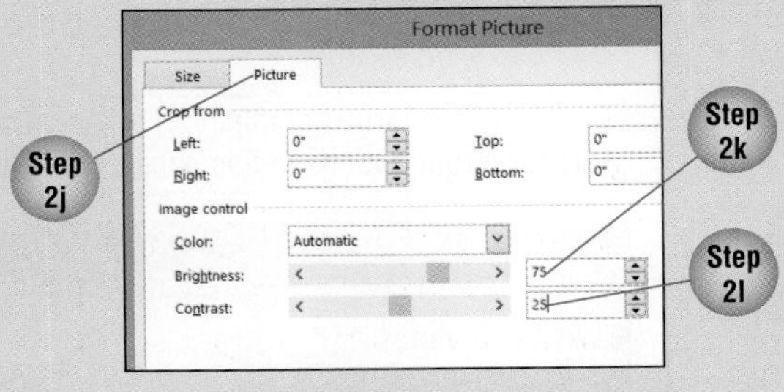

Project 4 Insert and Format SmartArt Graphics in a Company Sales Workbook

4 Parts

You will open a workbook that contains two company sales worksheets. You will insert and format a SmartArt cycle graphic in one worksheet and insert and format a SmartArt relationship graphic in the other. You will also create and format WordArt text.

Inserting SmartArt Graphics

Quick Steps

Insert a SmartArt Graphic
1. Click INSERT tab.
2. Click SmartArt button.
3. Double-click desired graphic.

SmartArt

HINT

Generally, you would use a SmartArt graphic to represent text and a chart to represent numbers.

Text Pane

Use the SmartArt feature included in Excel to insert graphics, such as diagrams and organizational charts, in a worksheet. SmartArt offers a variety of predesigned graphics that are available at the Choose a SmartArt Graphic dialog box, shown in Figure 8.7. Display this dialog box by clicking the INSERT tab and then clicking the SmartArt button in the Illustrations group. At the dialog box, *All* is selected in the left panel and all available predesigned graphics display in the middle panel. Use the scroll bar at the right side of the middle panel to scroll down the list of graphic choices. Click a graphic in the middle panel and the name of the graphic displays in the right panel along with a description of the graphic type. SmartArt includes graphics for presenting a list of data; showing data processes, cycles, and relationships; and presenting data in a matrix or pyramid. Double-click a graphic in the middle panel of the dialog box and the graphic is inserted in the worksheet.

Entering Data in a SmartArt Graphic

Some SmartArt graphics are designed to include text. Type text in a graphic by selecting a shape in the graphic and then typing text in the shape or you can display a text pane and then type text in the pane. Display the text pane by clicking the Text Pane button in the Create Graphic group on the SMARTART TOOLS DESIGN tab. Turn off the display of the pane by clicking the Text Pane button or clicking the Close button that displays in the upper right corner of the text pane.

Figure 8.7 Choose a SmartArt Graphic Dialog Box

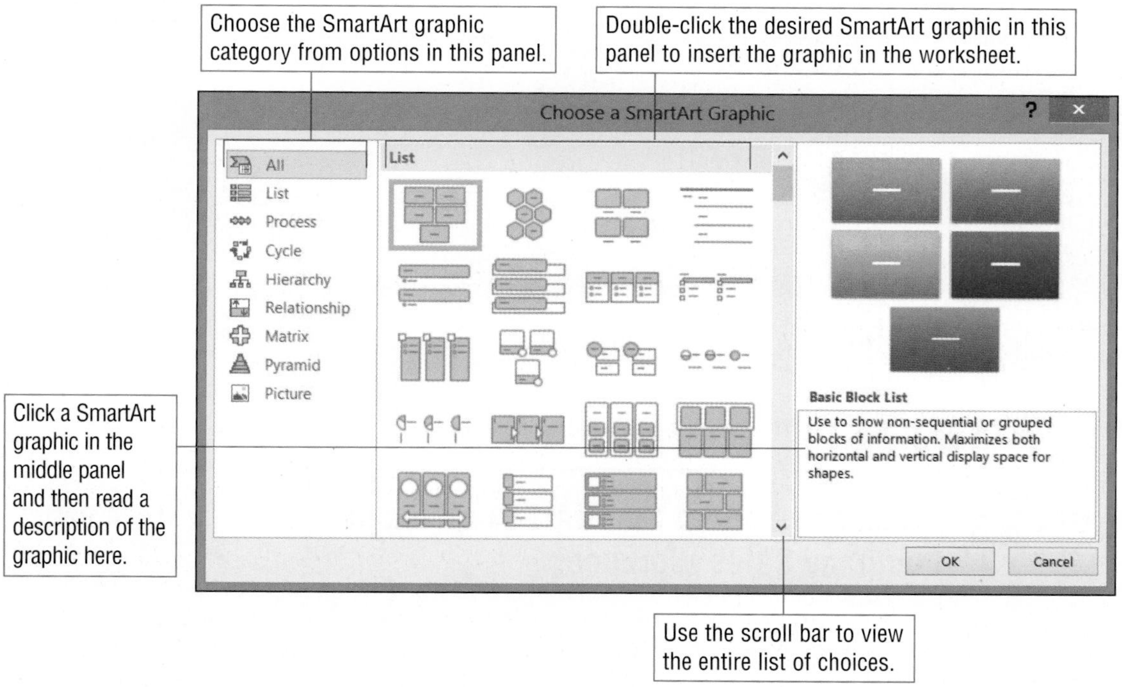

Sizing, Moving, and Deleting a SmartArt Graphic

Increase or decrease the size of a SmartArt graphic by dragging one of the sizing handles that display around the selected graphic. Use the corner sizing handles to increase or decrease the height and width at the same time. Use the middle sizing handles to increase or decrease the height or width of the SmartArt graphic.

To move a SmartArt graphic, select the graphic and then position the mouse pointer on the graphic border until the pointer displays with a four-headed arrow attached. Hold down the left mouse button, drag the graphic to the desired position, and then release the mouse button. Delete a graphic by selecting the graphic and then pressing the Delete key.

Project 4a **Inserting, Moving, and Sizing a SmartArt Graphic in a Worksheet** **Part 1 of 4**

1. Open **EPSales.xlsx** and then save the workbook with Save As and name it **EL1-C8-P4-EPSales**.
2. Create the SmartArt graphic shown in Figure 8.8 on page 291. To begin, click the INSERT tab.
3. Click the SmartArt button in the Illustrations group.
4. At the Choose a SmartArt Graphic dialog box, click *Cycle* in the left panel.
5. Double-click *Radial Cycle* in the middle panel (first column, third row).
6. If the text pane is not open, click the Text Pane button in the Create Graphic group. (The text pane will display at the left side of the SmartArt graphic.)
7. With the insertion point positioned after the top bullet in the text pane, type **Evergreen Products**.
8. Click the *[Text]* placeholder below *Evergreen Products* and then type **Seattle**.
9. Click the next *[Text]* placeholder and then type **Olympia**.
10. Click the next *[Text]* placeholder and then type **Portland**.
11. Click the next *[Text]* placeholder and then type **Spokane**.
12. Click the Text Pane button to turn off the display of the text pane.
13. Drag the SmartArt graphic so it is positioned as shown in Figure 8.8. To drag the graphic, position the mouse pointer on the graphic border until the pointer displays with a four-headed arrow attached. Hold down the left mouse button, drag the graphic to the desired position, and then release the mouse button.
14. Use the sizing handles that display around the SmartArt graphic to increase or decrease the size of the graphic so it displays as shown in Figure 8.8.
15. Save **EL1-C8-P4-EPSales.xlsx**.

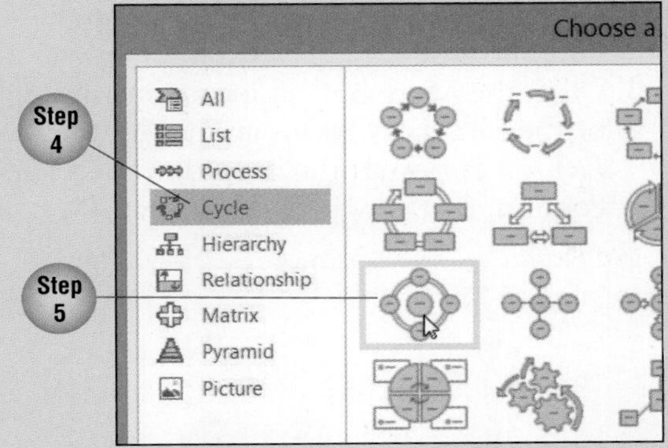

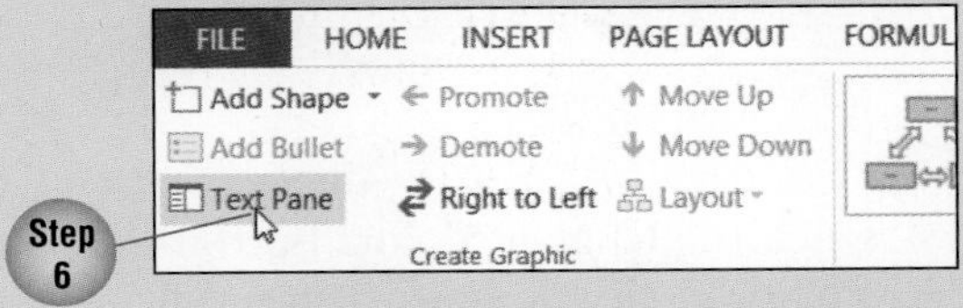

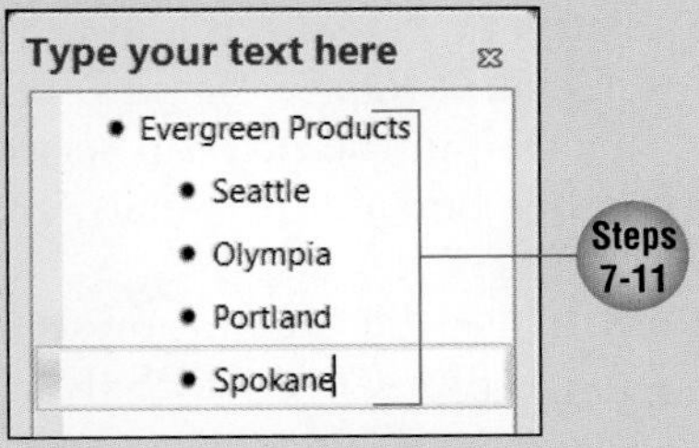

Changing the SmartArt Graphic Design

HINT
To restore the SmartArt default layout and color, click the Reset Graphic button in the Reset group on the SMARTART TOOLS DESIGN tab.

When you double-click a SmartArt graphic at the Choose a SmartArt Graphic dialog box, the graphic is inserted in the worksheet and the SMARTART TOOLS DESIGN tab is active. Use options and buttons on this tab to add objects, change the graphic layout, apply a style to the graphic, and reset the graphic back to the original formatting.

Project 4b **Changing the SmartArt Graphic Design** **Part 2 of 4**

1. With **EL1-C8-P4-EPSales.xlsx** open, make sure the SMARTART TOOLS DESIGN tab is active and then click the *Spokane* circle shape in the graphic to select it.
2. Click the Right to Left button in the Create Graphic group. (This switches *Olympia* and *Spokane*.)
3. Click the More button located at the right side of the SmartArt Styles group and then click the *Polished* option at the drop-down list (first column, first row in the *3-D* section).

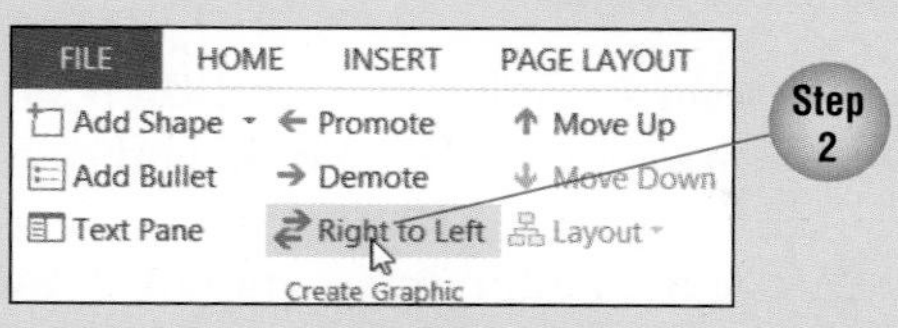

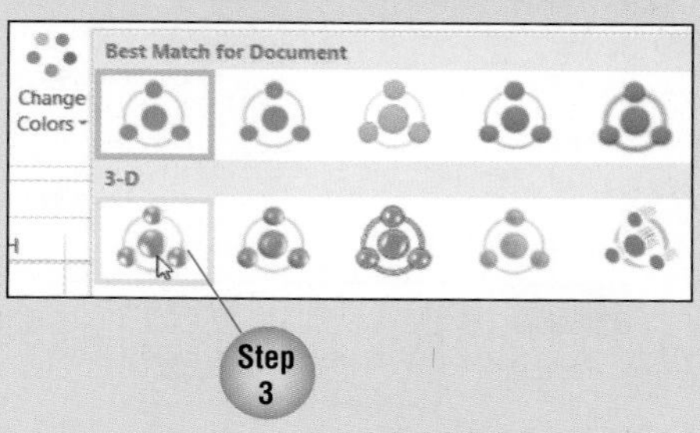

4. Click the Change Colors button in the SmartArt Styles group, scroll down the drop-down gallery, and then click the *Gradient Range - Accent 6* option (third option in the *Accent 6* section).
5. Click outside the SmartArt graphic to deselect it.
6. Change the orientation to landscape. (Make sure the graphic fits on the first page.)
7. Save **EL1-C8-P4-EPSales.xlsx** and then print the Total Sales worksheet.

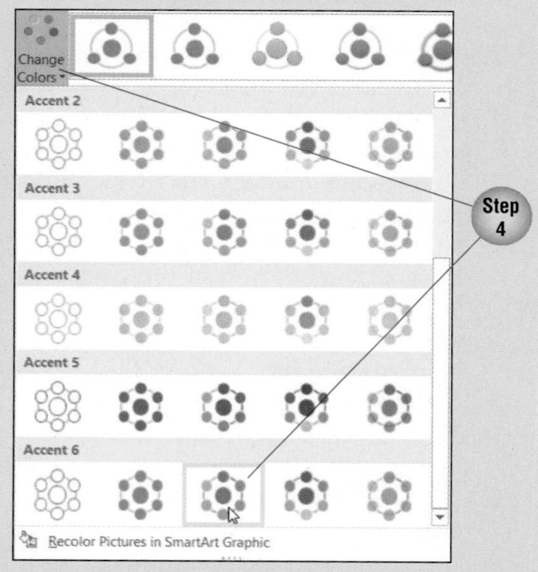

Figure 8.8 Projects 4a and 4b

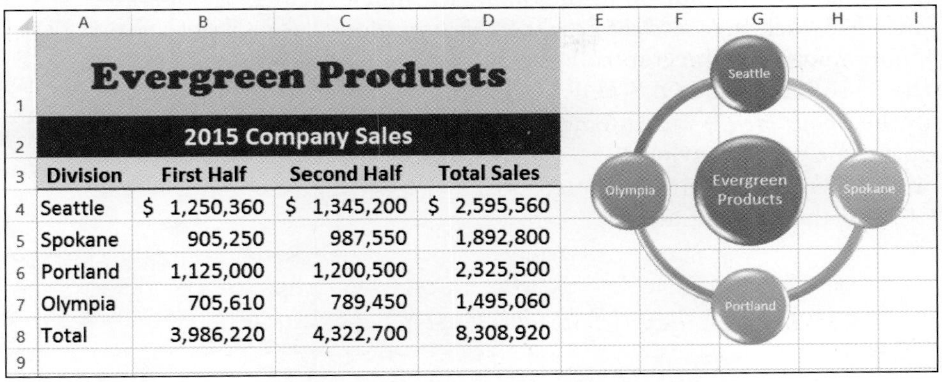

	A	B	C	D
1	**Evergreen Products**			
2	2015 Company Sales			
3	Division	First Half	Second Half	Total Sales
4	Seattle	$ 1,250,360	$ 1,345,200	$ 2,595,560
5	Spokane	905,250	987,550	1,892,800
6	Portland	1,125,000	1,200,500	2,325,500
7	Olympia	705,610	789,450	1,495,060
8	Total	3,986,220	4,322,700	8,308,920
9				

Changing the SmartArt Graphic Formatting

Click the SMARTART TOOLS FORMAT tab and options display for formatting a SmartArt graphic. Use buttons on this tab to insert and customize shapes; apply a shape style; apply WordArt styles; and specify the position, alignment, rotation, wrapping style, height, and width of the graphic.

Project 4c Changing the SmartArt Graphic Formatting

Part 3 of 4

1. With **EL1-C8-P4-EPSales.xlsx** open, click the Seattle Sales worksheet tab.
2. Create the SmartArt graphic shown in Figure 8.9 on the next page. To begin, click the INSERT tab and then click the SmartArt button in the Illustrations group.
3. At the Choose a SmartArt Graphic dialog box, click *Relationship* in the left panel and then double-click *Gear* in the middle panel.

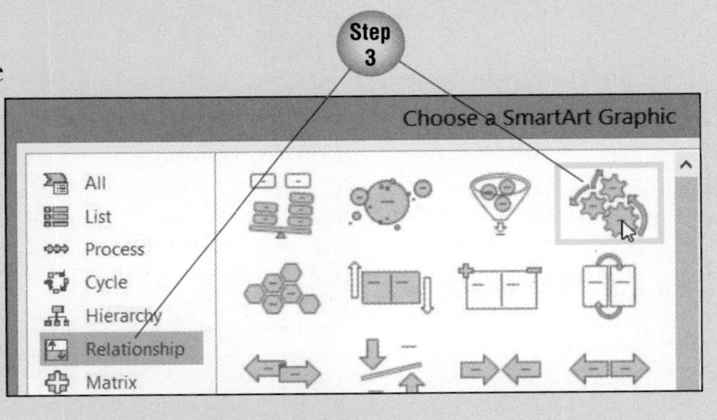

4. Click *[Text]* in the bottom gear and then type **Quality Products**.
5. Click *[Text]* in the left gear and then type **Customized Plans**.
6. Click *[Text]* in the top gear and then type **Exemplary Service**.
7. Click inside the SmartArt graphic border but outside any graphic element.
8. Click the More button that displays at the right side of the SmartArt Styles group and then click the *Inset* option (second column, first row in the *3-D* section).

9. Click the Change Colors button in the SmartArt Styles group and then click the *Gradient Loop - Accent 6* option (fourth option in the *Accent 6* section).
10. Click the SMARTART TOOLS FORMAT tab.
11. Click in the *Shape Height* measurement box in the Size group and then type 4.
12. Click in the *Shape Width* measurement box, type 4.5, and then press Enter.

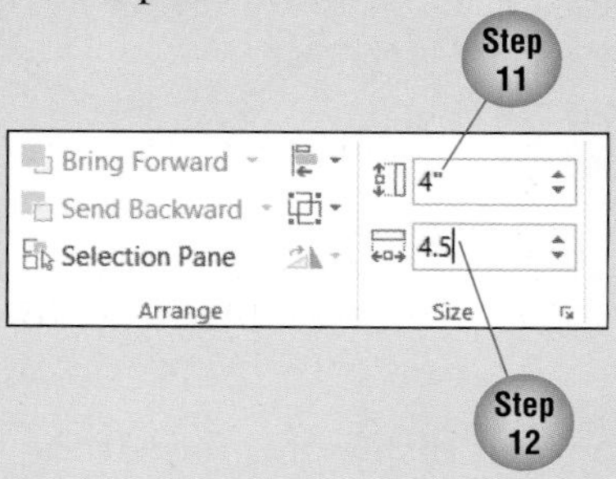

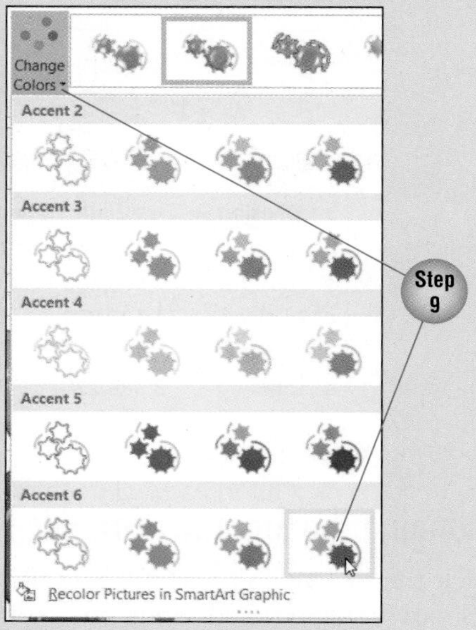

13. Click the bottom gear to select it.
14. Click the Shape Fill button arrow in the Shape Styles group and then click the *Green, Accent 6, Darker 50%* option (last column, last row in the *Theme Colors* section).
15. Click the top gear to select it.
16. Click the Shape Fill button arrow and then click the *Green, Accent 6, Darker 25%* option (last column, fifth row in the *Theme Colors* section).
17. Change the orientation to landscape.
18. Move the SmartArt graphic so it fits on the first page and displays as shown in Figure 8.9.
19. Click outside the chart to deselect it.
20. Save **EL1-C8-P4-EPSales.xlsx** and then print the Seattle Sales worksheet.

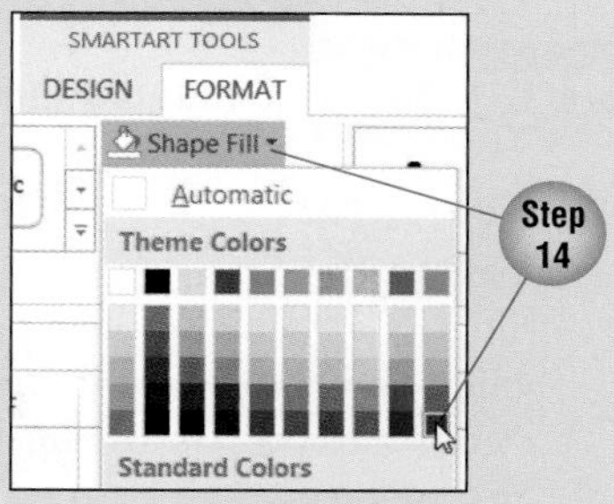

Figure 8.9 Project 4c

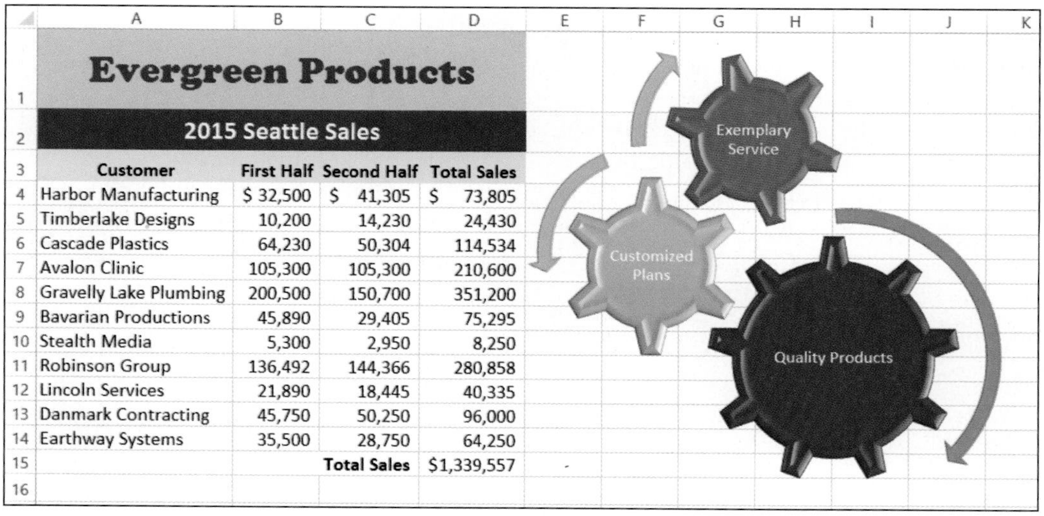

	A	B	C	D
1	Evergreen Products			
2	2015 Seattle Sales			
3	Customer	First Half	Second Half	Total Sales
4	Harbor Manufacturing	$ 32,500	$ 41,305	$ 73,805
5	Timberlake Designs	10,200	14,230	24,430
6	Cascade Plastics	64,230	50,304	114,534
7	Avalon Clinic	105,300	105,300	210,600
8	Gravelly Lake Plumbing	200,500	150,700	351,200
9	Bavarian Productions	45,890	29,405	75,295
10	Stealth Media	5,300	2,950	8,250
11	Robinson Group	136,492	144,366	280,858
12	Lincoln Services	21,890	18,445	40,335
13	Danmark Contracting	45,750	50,250	96,000
14	Earthway Systems	35,500	28,750	64,250
15			Total Sales	$1,339,557
16				

Creating , Sizing, and Moving WordArt

With the WordArt feature, you can distort or modify text to conform to a variety of shapes. This is useful for creating company logos and headings. With WordArt, you can change the font, style, and alignment of text. You can also use different fill patterns and colors, customize border lines, and add shadow and three-dimensional effects.

To insert WordArt in an Excel worksheet, click the INSERT tab, click the Insert WordArt button in the Text group, and then click the desired option at the drop-down list. This inserts the text *Your text here* in the worksheet, formatted in the WordArt option you selected at the drop-down list. Type the desired text and then use the buttons on the DRAWING TOOLS FORMAT tab to format the WordArt.

WordArt text inserted in a worksheet is surrounded by white sizing handles. Use these sizing handles to change the height and width of the WordArt text. To move WordArt text, position the arrow pointer on the border of the WordArt text box until the pointer displays with a four-headed arrow attached and then drag the outline of the WordArt text box to the desired location.

Conform WordArt text to a variety of shapes using the *Transform* option from Text Effects button drop-down list. When you apply a transform shape, the WordArt border displays with a small, purple, square shape. Use this shape to change the slant of the WordArt text.

Quick Steps

Create WordArt
1. Click INSERT tab.
2. Click Insert WordArt button.
3. Click desired WordArt style at drop-down list.
4. Type desired text.

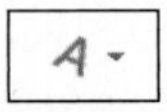

Insert WordArt

HINT

To remove a WordArt style from text and still retain the text, click the More button in the WordArt Styles group on the DRAWING TOOLS FORMAT tab and then click *Clear WordArt.*

Project 4d **Inserting and Formatting WordArt** **Part 4 of 4**

1. With **EL1-C8-P4-EPSales.xlsx** open, click the Total Sales worksheet tab.
2. Make cell A1 active and then press the Delete key. (This removes the text from the cell.)
3. Increase the height of row 1 to 137 points.
4. Click the INSERT tab.
5. Click the Insert WordArt button in the Text group and then click the *Fill - Black, Text 1, Outline - Background 1, Hard Shadow - Background 1* option (first column, third row).
6. Type **Evergreen**, press the Enter key, and then type **Products**.
7. Click the WordArt border to change the border to a solid line (not a dashed line).
8. Click the Text Fill button arrow in the WordArt Styles group and then click the *Green, Accent 6, Darker 50%* option (last column, last row in the *Theme Colors* section).

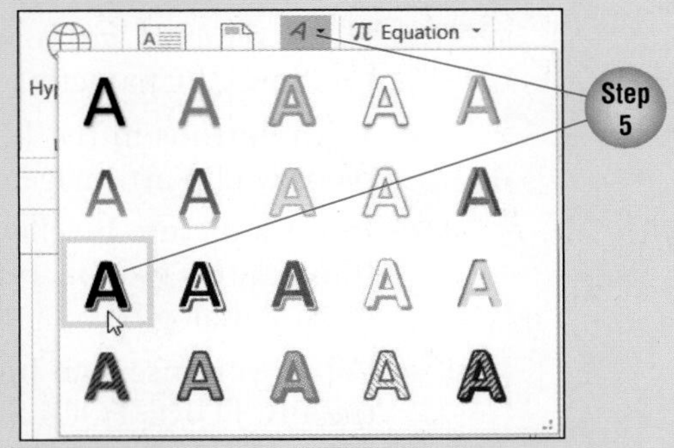

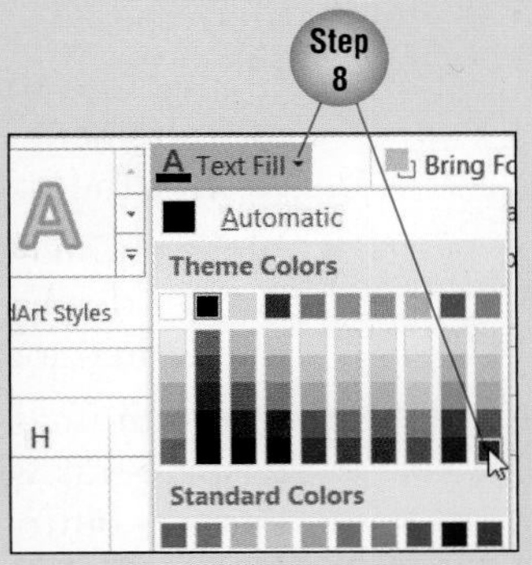

9. Click the Text Effects button in the WordArt Styles group, point to *Transform*, and then click the *Can Up* option (third column, fourth row in the *Warp* section).
10. Position the mouse pointer (turns into a white arrow) on the small, purple square that displays right below the *d* in *Products*, hold down the left mouse button, drag up approximately 0.25 inch, and then release the mouse button. (This changes the slant of the text.)
11. Drag the WordArt text so it is positioned in cell A1.
12. If necessary, resize the SmartArt graphic and position it so it prints on one page with the data.
13. Click the Seattle Sales worksheet tab and then complete steps similar to those in Steps 2 through 11 to insert *Evergreen Products* as WordArt in cell A1.
14. Make sure the SmartArt graphic fits on the page with the data. If necessary, decrease the size of the graphic.
15. Save **EL1-C8-P4-EPSales.xlsx** and then print both worksheets.
16. Close **EL1-C8-P4-EPSales.xlsx**.

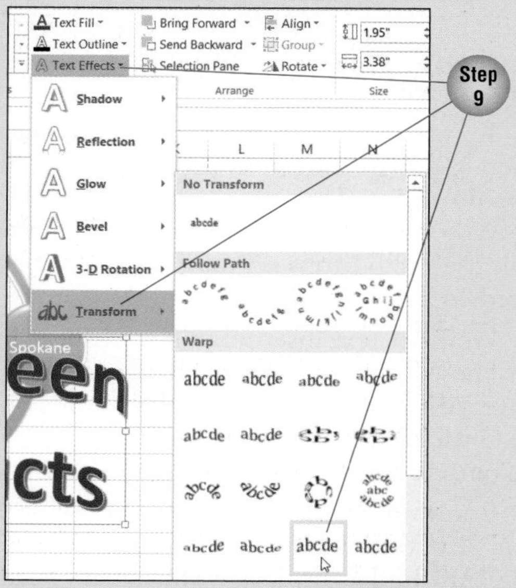

Chapter Summary

- Insert symbols with options at the Symbol dialog box with the Symbols tab or the Special Characters tab selected.
- With buttons in the Illustrations group on the INSERT tab, you can insert a picture, clip art image, screenshot, shape, or SmartArt graphic.
- Insert a picture by clicking the INSERT tab, clicking the Pictures button in the Illustrations group, and then double-clicking the desired picture at the Insert Picture dialog box.
- When you insert an image, such as a picture or clip art image, in a worksheet, the PICTURE TOOLS FORMAT tab is active and includes options for adjusting the image, applying preformatted styles, and arranging and sizing the image.
- Change the size of an image with the *Shape Height* and *Shape Width* measurement boxes in the Size group on the PICTURE TOOLS FORMAT tab or with the sizing handles that display around the selected image.
- Move an image by positioning the mouse pointer on the image border until the pointer displays with a four-headed arrow attached and then drag the image to the desired location.
- Insert an image from Office.com with options at the Insert Pictures window. Display this window by clicking the INSERT tab and then clicking the Online Pictures button in the Illustrations group.

- Use the Screenshot button in the Illustrations group on the INSERT tab to capture all or part of the contents of a screen.
- To draw shapes in a workbook, click the INSERT tab, click the Shapes button in the Illustrations group, and then click the desired shape at the drop-down list. Click or drag in the worksheet to insert the shape. To maintain the proportions of the shape, hold down the Shift key while dragging in the worksheet.
- Copy a shape with the Copy and Paste buttons in the Clipboard group on the HOME tab or by holding down the Ctrl key while dragging the shape.
- Draw a text box in a worksheet by clicking the INSERT tab, clicking the Text Box button in the Text group, and then clicking or dragging in the worksheet. Use options on the DRAWING TOOLS FORMAT tab to format and customize the text box.
- A watermark is a lightened image that displays behind data in a file. Create a picture watermark in a worksheet by inserting a picture in a header or footer and then changing the size and formatting of the picture.
- Insert a SmartArt graphic in a worksheet by clicking the INSERT tab, clicking the SmartArt button in the Illustrations group, and then double-clicking the desired graphic at the Choose a SmartArt Graphic dialog box. Customize a SmartArt graphic with options on the SMARTART TOOLS DESIGN tab and the SMARTART TOOLS FORMAT tab.
- Use WordArt to create, distort, modify, and/or conform text to a variety of shapes. Insert WordArt in a worksheet with the WordArt button in the Text group on the INSERT tab. Customize WordArt text with options on the DRAWING TOOLS FORMAT tab.

Commands Review

FEATURE	RIBBON TAB, GROUP	BUTTON
Choose a SmartArt Graphic dialog box	INSERT, Illustrations	
Insert Picture dialog box	INSERT, Illustrations	
Insert Pictures window	INSERT, Illustrations	
Insert WordArt button drop-down list	INSERT, Text	
screenshot	INSERT, Illustrations	
Shapes button drop-down list	INSERT, Illustrations	
Symbol dialog box	INSERT, Symbols	Ω
text box	INSERT, Text	

Concepts Check Test Your Knowledge SNAP

Completion: In the space provided at the right, indicate the correct term, symbol, or command.

1. The Symbol button is located on this tab. 1 insert
2. The *Font* option is available at the Symbol dialog box with this tab selected. 1 symbols
3. Insert a picture, clip art image, screenshot, shape, or SmartArt graphic with buttons in this group on the INSERT tab. 1 illustrations
4. Display the Insert Pictures window by clicking this button on the INSERT tab. 1 picture
5. When you insert an image, such as a picture or clip art, in a worksheet, this tab is active. 3 pic tools format
6. Maintain the proportions of an image by holding down this key while dragging a sizing handle. 1 shift
7. To move an image, position the mouse pointer on the image border until the mouse pointer displays with this attached and then drag the image to the desired location. 3 four headed arrow
8. To capture a portion of a screen, click the Screenshot button and then click this option at the drop-down list. 2 screen clipping
9. To copy a shape, hold down this key while dragging the shape. 1 control
10. When you draw a text box in a worksheet and then release the mouse button, this tab is active. 3 drawing tools format
11. This term refers to a lightened image that displays behind data in a file. 1 watermark
12. Click the SmartArt button in the Illustrations group on the INSERT tab and this dialog box displays. 4 choose a smartart graphic

Skills Check Assess Your Performance

Assessment

1 INSERT A CLIP ART IMAGE AND WORDART IN AN EQUIPMENT SALES WORKBOOK

SNAP Grade It

1. Open **MSSalesPlans.xlsx** and then save the workbook with Save As and name it **EL1-C8-A1-MSSalesPlans**.
2. Insert a formula in cell E4 using the PMT function that calculates monthly payments. (Type a minus sign before the cell designation in the *Pv* text box at the Function Arguments palette.) ***Hint: For assistance, refer to Chapter 7, Project 5a.***

3. Copy the formula in cell E4 down to cells E5 and E6.
4. Insert a formula in cell F4 that calculates the total amount of the payments.
5. Copy the formula in cell F4 down to cells F5 and F6.
6. Insert a formula in cell G4 that calculates the total amount of interest paid.
7. Copy the formula in cell G4 down to cells G5 and G6.
8. Insert the clip art image shown in Figure 8.10 with the following specifications:
   a. Click the INSERT tab and then click the Online Pictures button. At the Insert Pictures window, search for images related to maple leaves. (The colors of the original clip art image are green and white.)
   b. Apply the Orange, Accent color 2 Dark clip art image color (third column, second row).
   c. Apply the Brightness: -20% Contrast: +20% correction (second column, fourth row).
   d. Apply the Drop Shadow Rectangle picture style (fourth thumbnail).
   e. Size and move the image so it is positioned as shown in Figure 8.10.

use maple leaf color map instead

9. Insert the company name *Maplewood Suppliers* in cell A1 as WordArt with the following specifications:
   a. Click the WordArt button on the INSERT tab and then click the *Fill - White, Outline - Accent 2, Hard Shadow - Accent 2* image color (fourth column, third row).
   b. Apply the Orange, Accent 2, Darker 50% text fill (sixth column, bottom row in the *Theme Colors* section).
   c. Apply the Orange, Accent 2, Lighter 60% text outline (sixth column, third row in the *Theme Colors* section).
   d. Using the Text Effects button, apply the Square transform text effect.
   e. Change the width of the WordArt to 5 inches.
   f. Move the WordArt so it is positioned in cell A1 as shown in Figure 8.10.
10. Change the worksheet orientation to landscape.
11. Save, print, and then close **EL1-C8-A1-MSSalesPlans.xlsx**.

Figure 8.10 Assessment 1

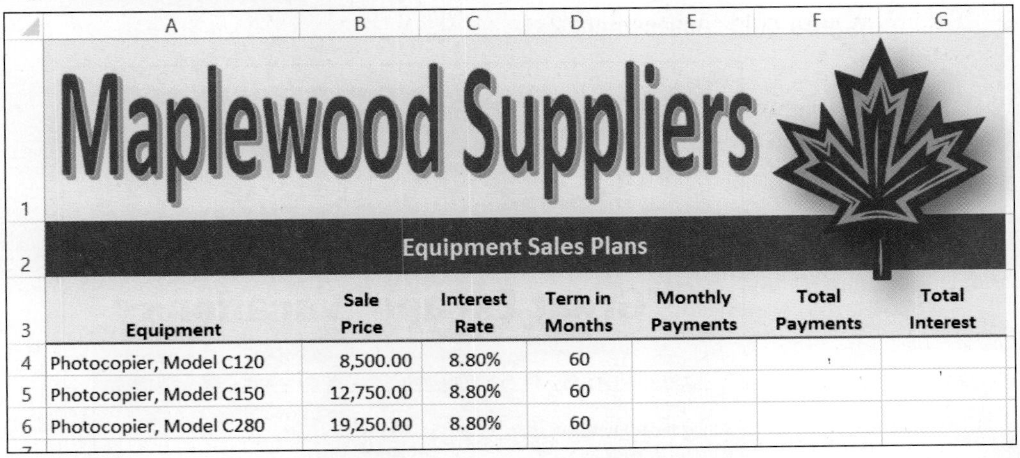

	A	B	C	D	E	F	G
1	Maplewood Suppliers						
2	Equipment Sales Plans						
3	Equipment	Sale Price	Interest Rate	Term in Months	Monthly Payments	Total Payments	Total Interest
4	Photocopier, Model C120	8,500.00	8.80%	60			
5	Photocopier, Model C150	12,750.00	8.80%	60			
6	Photocopier, Model C280	19,250.00	8.80%	60			

Assessment

2 INSERT FORMULAS AND FORMAT A TRAVEL COMPANY WORKBOOK

SNAP Grade It

1. Open **TSGEVacs.xlsx** and then save the workbook with Save As and name it **EL1-C8-A2-TSGEVacs**.
2. Insert appropriate formulas to calculate the prices based on 10% and 20% discounts and apply the appropriate number formatting. ***Hint: For the 10% discount column, multiply the price per person by 0.90 (which determines 90% of the price) and for the 20% discount column, multiply the price per person by 0.80 (which determines 80% of the price).***
3. Format the image of the airplane and position it as shown in Figure 8.11 with the following specifications:
   a. Use the Remove Background button in the Adjust group on the PICTURE TOOLS FORMAT tab to remove a portion of the yellow background so the image displays similar to what you see in the figure.
   b. Rotate the image to flip it horizontally.
   c. Apply the Brightness: +20% Contrast: +20% correction.
   d. Change the height of the image to 1.4 inches and then position the image as shown in the figure.
4. Open Word and then open the document named **TSAirfare.docx** located in the EL1C8 folder on your storage medium. Click the Excel button on the Taskbar and then use the Screenshot button (with the *Screen Clipping* option) to select and then insert the airfare information in **EL1-C8-A2-TSGEVacs.xlsx**. Position the information at the right side of the data in the worksheet.
5. Change the orientation to landscape.
6. Make sure the data and the airfare information display on one page and then print the worksheet.
7. Save and then close **EL1-C8-A2-TSGEVacs.xslx**.
8. Click the Word button on the Taskbar, close **TSAirfare.docx**, and then close Word.

Figure 8.11 Assessment 2

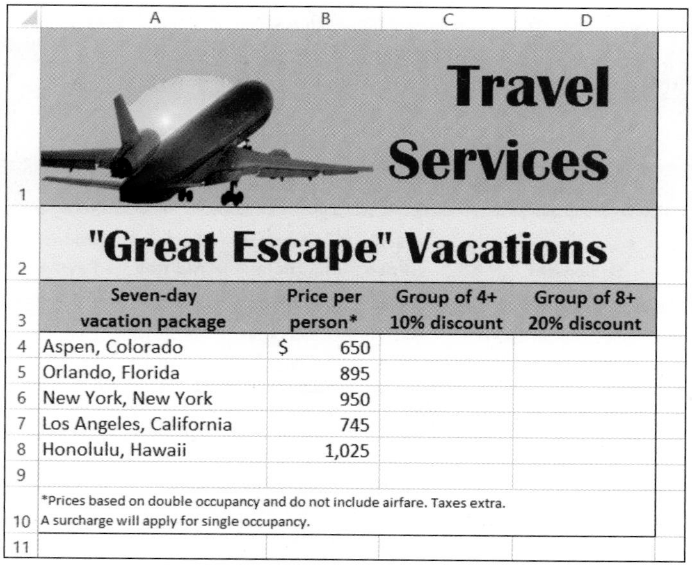

Assessment

3 INSERT AND FORMAT SHAPES IN A COMPANY SALES WORKBOOK

SNAP Grade It

1. Open **MGSales.xlsx** and then save the workbook with Save As and name it **EL1-C8-A3-MGSales**.
2. Use the Isosceles Triangle shape located in the *Basic Shapes* section of the Shapes drop-down palette to draw a triangle as shown in Figure 8.12.
3. Apply Green, Accent 6, Darker 50% shape outline color (last column, last row in the *Theme Colors* section) to the triangle.
4. Apply Green, Accent 6, Darker 25% shape fill (last column, fifth row in the *Theme Colors* section) to the triangle.
5. Copy the triangle three times.
6. Position the triangles as shown in Figure 8.12.
7. Select the second and fourth triangles and then apply the Green, Accent 6, Lighter 80% shape fill (last column, second row in the *Theme Colors* section).
8. Insert the total amounts in cells B10 through D10.
9. Insert an arrow pointing to *$97,549* with the following specifications:
   a. Use the Left Arrow shape to draw the arrow.
   b. Change the height of the arrow to 0.6 inch and the width to 1.2 inches.
   c. Apply Green, Accent 6, Darker 25% shape fill (last column, fifth row in the *Theme Colors* section) to the arrow.
   d. Type the text **Largest Order** in the arrow and then select the text and change the font to 10-point Calibri bold.
   e. Position the arrow as shown in Figure 8.12.
10. Save, print, and then close **EL1-C8-A3-MGSales.xlsx**.

Figure 8.12 Assessment 3

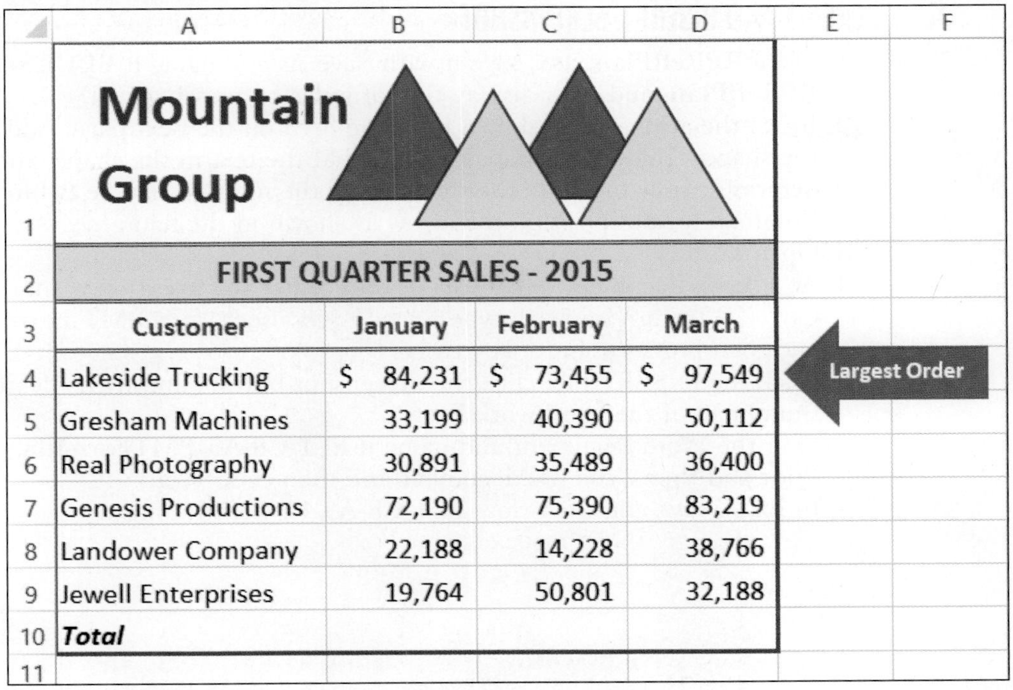

	A	B	C	D	E	F
1	Mountain Group					
2	FIRST QUARTER SALES - 2015					
3	Customer	January	February	March		
4	Lakeside Trucking	$ 84,231	$ 73,455	$ 97,549	Largest Order	
5	Gresham Machines	33,199	40,390	50,112		
6	Real Photography	30,891	35,489	36,400		
7	Genesis Productions	72,190	75,390	83,219		
8	Landower Company	22,188	14,228	38,766		
9	Jewell Enterprises	19,764	50,801	32,188		
10	***Total***					
11						

Assessment 4

INSERT AND FORMAT A SMARTART GRAPHIC IN A SALES WORKBOOK

SNAP Grade It

1. Open **PS2ndQtrSales.xlsx** and then save the workbook with Save As and name it **EL1-C8-A4-PS2ndQtrSales**.
2. Change the orientation to landscape.
3. Insert the Pyramid List SmartArt graphic at the right side of the worksheet data with the following specifications:
   a. Apply the Gradient Loop - Accent 2 color (fourth option in the *Accent 2* section).
   b. Apply the Cartoon SmartArt style (third column, first row in the *3-D* section).
   c. In the bottom text box, type **Red Level**, press Enter, and then type **$25,000 to $49,999**.
   d. In the middle text box, type **Blue Level**, press Enter, and then type **$50,000 to $99,999**.
   e. In the top text box, type **Gold Level**, press Enter, and then type **$100,000+**.
   f. Apply fill color to each text box to match the level color. (Use the Orange fill color for the Gold Level text box.)
4. Size and/or move the SmartArt graphic so it displays attractively at the right side of the worksheet data. (Make sure the entire graphic will print on the same page as the worksheet data.)
5. Save, print, and then close **EL1-C8-A4-PS2ndQtrSales.xlsx**.

Assessment 5

CREATE AND INSERT A SCREENSHOT

1. Open **RPRefiPlan.xlsx**, save it with Save As and name it **EL1-C8-A5-RPRefiPlan**, and then display the formulas by pressing Ctrl + `.
2. Insert the arrow shape shown in Figure 8.13 on the next page. Add fill to the shape, remove the shape outline, bold the text in the shape, and then determine how to rotate the shape using the rotation handle (white circle). Rotate, size, and position the arrow as shown in the figure.
3. Open Word.
4. At a blank document, press Ctrl + E to center the insertion point, press Ctrl + B to turn on bold, type **Excel Worksheet with PMT Formula**, and then press the Enter key twice.
5. Click the INSERT tab, click the Screenshot button, and then click the thumbnail of the Excel worksheet.
6. Save the Word document and name it **EL1-C8-A5-PMTFormula**.
7. Print and then close the document and then close Word.
8. In Excel, save and then close **EL1-C8-A5-RPRefiPlan.xlsx**.

Figure 8.13 Assessment 5

	A	B	C	D	E	F
1	REAL PHOTOGRAPHY					
2	Refinance Plan					
3						
4	Lender	Amount	Interest Rate	Term in Months	Monthly Payments	Total Payments
5	Castle Credit Union	400000	0.065	300	=PMT(C5/12,D5,-B5)	=E5*D5
6	Castle Credit Union	500000	0.062	300	=PMT(C6/12,D6,-B6)	=E6*D6
7	Millstone Bank	400000	0.064	240	=PMT(C7/12,D7,-B7)	=E7*D7
8	Millstone Bank	500000	0.061	240	=PMT(C8/12,D8,-B8)	=E8*D8
9						
10						
11						

PMT Formula

Visual Benchmark Demonstrate Your Proficiency

INSERT FORMULAS, WORDART, AND CLIP ART IN A WORKSHEET

1. Open **TSYrlySales.xlsx** and then save the workbook with Save As and name it **EL1-C8-VB-TSYrlySales**.
2. Insert formulas that will calculate the results shown in the worksheet in Figure 8.14 on the next page. (***Do not*** type the data in the cells. Instead, insert the following formulas. The results of your formulas should match the results you see in the figure.)
    - Cells C4 through C14: Insert a formula with an IF function that inserts *5%* if the amount in the cell in column B is greater than $249,999 and inserts *2%* if the amount is not greater than $249,999.
    - Cells D4 through D14: Insert a formula that multiplies the amount in column B with the amount in column C.
    - Apply accounting formatting with a dollar sign and no places past the decimal point to cell D4.
3. Insert the company name *Target Supplies* as WordArt with the following specifications:
    - Choose the *Fill - Black, Text 1, Outline - Background 1, Hard Shadow - Accent 1* option (second column, third row).
    - To type the WordArt text, press Ctrl + L (which changes to left text alignment), type **Target**, press Enter, and then type **Supplies**.
    - Apply Orange, Accent 2, Darker 50% text fill color (sixth column, bottom row in the *Theme Colors* section).
    - Apply the Orange, Accent 2, Lighter 40% text outline color (sixth column, fourth row in the *Theme Colors* section).
    - Move the WordArt so it is positioned as shown in Figure 8.14.
4. Insert the target clip art image (use the Insert Pictures window and search with the words *archery, arrows, target* to find this clip art image) with the following specifications:
    - Apply the Orange, Accent color 2 light color (third column, third row).
    - Apply the Brightness: -20% Contrast: -20% correction (second column, second row).
    - Size and position the clip art image as shown in the figure.

5. Draw the shape that displays below the data with the following specifications:
    - Use the Bevel shape (located in the *Basic Shapes* section).
    - Type the text in the shape, apply bold formatting, and change to center and middle alignment.
    - Apply the Orange, Accent 2, Darker 50% shape fill color (sixth column, bottom row in the *Theme Colors* section).
    - Apply the Orange, Accent 2 shape outline color (sixth column, top row in the *Theme Colors* section).
6. Save and then print the worksheet.
7. Press Ctrl + ` to turn on the display of formulas and then print the worksheet again.
8. Turn off the display of formulas and then close the workbook.

Figure 8.14 Visual Benchmark

	A	B	C	D
1				
2	ANNUAL CUSTOMER SALES ANALYSIS			
3	***Salesperson***	***Sales***	***Bonus***	***Bonus Amount***
4	Barclay, Richard	$ 350,182	5%	$ 17,509
5	Carolus, Lisa	203,485	2%	4,070
6	Ehrlich, Arnold	150,274	2%	3,005
7	Hale, Rebecca	363,740	5%	18,187
8	Kinyon, Christopher	257,954	5%	12,898
9	Martinez, Michelle	274,655	5%	13,733
10	Oswald, Jeffery	109,485	2%	2,190
11	Parente, Heather	200,455	2%	4,009
12	Rios, Douglas	149,304	2%	2,986
13	Uznay, Grace	302,938	5%	15,147
14	Walden, Albert	177,439	2%	3,549
15				
16				
17				
18				
19				
20				

Top Sales
Rebecca Hale

Case Study Apply Your Skills

Part 1

You are the office manager for Ocean Truck Sales and are responsible for maintaining a spreadsheet of the truck and SUV inventory. Open **OTSales.xlsx** and then save the workbook and name it **EL1-C8-CS-OTSales**. Apply formatting to improve the appearance of the worksheet and insert at least one clip art image (related to a truck or ocean). Save **EL1-C8-CS-OTSales.xlsx** and then print the worksheet.

Part 2

With **EL1-C8-CS-OTSales.xlsx** open, save the workbook with Save As and name it **EL1-C8-CS-OTSalesF&C**. You make the inventory workbook available to each salesperson at the beginning of the week. For easier viewing, you decide to divide the workbook into two worksheets, with one worksheet containing all Ford vehicles and the other worksheet containing all Chevrolet vehicles. Rename the worksheet tabs to reflect the contents. Sort the data in each worksheet by price from most expensive to least expensive.

The owner offers incentives each week to help motivate the sales force. Insert in the first worksheet a SmartArt graphic of your choosing that contains the following information:

Small-sized truck: $200

2WD regular cab: $150

SUV 4x4: $100

Copy the SmartArt graphic in the first worksheet and then paste it into the second worksheet. Change the orientation to landscape and then save, print, and close both worksheets in **EL1-C8-CS-OTSalesF&C.xlsx**.

Part 3

You have been asked to save the inventory worksheet as a web page for viewing online. Open **EL1-C8-CS-OTSales.xlsx**, display the Save As dialog box, click the *Save as type* option, and then determine how to save the workbook as a single-file web page (*.mht, *.mhtml). Save the workbook as a single-file web page with the name **EL1-C8-CS-OTSales-WebPage**. Open your Internet browser and then open the web page. Look at the information in the file and then close the Internet browser.

Part 4

As part of your weekly duties, you post the incentive SmartArt graphic in various locations throughout the company. You decide to insert the graphic in PowerPoint for easy printing. Open **EL1-C8-CS-OTSalesF&C.xlsx** and then open PowerPoint. Change the slide layout in PowerPoint to Blank. Copy the SmartArt graphic in the first worksheet and paste it into the PowerPoint blank slide. Increase and/or move the graphic so it better fills the slide. Print the slide and then close PowerPoint without saving the presentation. Close **EL1-C8-CS-OTSalesF&C.xlsx**.

UNIT 2

MICROSOFT® EXCEL® Performance Assessment

Excel
EL1U2

Note: Before beginning unit assessments, copy to your storage medium the EL1U2 subfolder from the EL1 folder on the CD that accompanies this textbook and then make EL1U2 the active folder.

Assessing Proficiency

In this unit, you have learned how to work with multiple windows; move, copy, link, and paste data within and between workbooks and applications; create and customize charts with data in a worksheet; write formulas with PMT, FV, and IF functions; save a workbook as a web page; insert hyperlinks; and insert and customize images, shapes, SmartArt graphics, and WordArt.

Assessment 1 Copy and Paste Data and Insert WordArt in a Training Scores Workbook

1. Open **RLTraining.xlsx** and then save the workbook with Save As and name it **EL1-U2-A01-RLTraining**.
2. Delete row 15 (the row for *Kwieciak, Kathleen*).
3. Insert a formula in cell D4 that averages the percentages in cells B4 and C4.
4. Copy the formula in cell D4 down to cells D5 through D20.
5. Make cell A22 active, turn on bold formatting, and then type Highest Averages.
6. Display the Clipboard task pane and make sure it is empty.
7. Select and then copy each of the following rows (individually): 7, 10, 14, 16, and 18.
8. Make cell A23 active and then paste row 14 (the row for *Jewett, Troy*).
9. Make cell A24 active and then paste row 7 (the row for *Cumpston, Kurt*).
10. Make cell A25 active and then paste row 10 (the row for *Fisher-Edwards, Theresa*).
11. Make cell A26 active and then paste row 16 (the row for *Mathias, Caleb*).
12. Make cell A27 active and then paste row 18 (the row for *Nyegaard, Curtis*).
13. Click the Clear All button in the Clipboard task pane and then close the task pane.
14. Insert in cell A1 the text *Roseland* as WordArt. Format the WordArt text to add visual appeal to the worksheet.
15. Save, print, and then close **EL1-U2-A01-RLTraining.xlsx**.

Assessment 2 Manage Multiple Worksheets in a Projected Earnings Workbook

1. Open **RLProjEarnings.xlsx** and then save the workbook with Save As and name it **EL1-U2-A02-RLProjEarnings**.
2. Delete *Roseland* in cell A1. Open **EL1-U2-A01-RLTraining.xlsx**, copy the *Roseland* WordArt text, and then paste it into cell A1 in **EL1-U2-A02-RLProjEarnings.xlsx**. If necessary, increase the height of row 1 to accommodate the WordArt text.
3. Close **EL1-U2-A01-RLTraining.xlsx**.
4. Insert a new worksheet in the **EL1-U2-A02-RLProjEarnings.xlsx** workbook.
5. Select cells A1 through C11 in Sheet1 and then copy and paste the cells to Sheet2, keeping the source column widths.
6. With Sheet2 displayed, make the following changes:
   a. Increase the height of row 1 to accommodate the WordArt text.
   b. Delete the contents of cell B2.
   c. Change the contents of the following cells:
      A6: Change *January* to *July*
      A7: Change *February* to *August*
      A8: Change *March* to *September*
      A9: Change *April* to *October*
      A10: Change *May* to *November*
      A11: Change *June* to *December*
      B6: Change *8.30%* to *8.10%*
      B8: Change *9.30%* to *8.70%*
7. Make Sheet1 active, copy cell B2, and then paste link it to cell B2 in Sheet2.
8. Rename Sheet1 *First Half* and rename Sheet2 *Second Half*.
9. Make the First Half worksheet active and then determine the effect on projected monthly earnings if the projected yearly income is increased by 10% by changing the number in cell B2 to *$1,480,380*.
10. Horizontally and vertically center both worksheets in the workbook and insert a custom header that prints your name at the left, the current date in the center, and the sheet name (click the Sheet Name button in the Header & Footer Elements group on the Header & Footer Tools Design tab) at the right.
11. Print both worksheets.
12. Determine the effect on projected monthly earnings if the projected yearly income is increased by 20% by changing the number in cell B2 to *$1,614,960*.
13. Save the workbook again and then print both worksheets.
14. Close **EL1-U2-A02-RLProjEarnings.xlsx**.

Assessment 3 Create Charts in Worksheets in a Sales Totals Workbook

1. Open **EPYrlySales.xlsx** and then save the workbook with Save As and name it **EL1-U2-A03-EPYrlySales**.
2. Rename Sheet1 as *2013 Sales*, rename Sheet2 as *2014 Sales*, and rename Sheet3 as *2015 Sales*.
3. Select all three sheet tabs, make cell A12 active, turn on bold formatting, and then type Total. Make cell B12 active and then insert a formula to total the amounts in cells B4 through B11. Make cell C12 active and then insert a formula to total the amounts in cells C4 through C11.
4. Make the 2013 Sales worksheet active, select cells A3 through C11 (being careful not to select the totals in row 12), and then create a column chart. Click the Switch Row/Column button on the Chart Tools Design tab. Apply formatting to increase the visual appearance of the chart. Drag the chart below the worksheet data. (Make sure the chart fits on one page.)
5. Make the 2014 Sales worksheet active and then create the same type of chart you created in Step 4.
6. Make the 2015 Sales worksheet active and then create the same type of chart you created in Step 4. Filter the records in this chart so that only the following companies display: *Harbor Manufacturing*, *Avalon Clinic*, and *Stealth Media*.
7. Save the workbook and then print the entire workbook.
8. Close **EL1-U2-A03-EPYrlySales.xlsx**.

Assessment 4 Create and Format a Line Chart

1. Open **ProfitCompare.xlsx** and then save the workbook with Save As and name it **EL1-U2-A04-ProfitCompare**.
2. Use the data in the workbook to create a line chart with the following specifications:
   a. Apply the Style 11 chart style.
   b. Include the chart title *NET PROFIT COMPARISON*.
   c. Apply the Green shape fill and shape outline color of the Asia series (in the *Standard Colors* section).
   d. Move the chart to a new worksheet.
3. Save the workbook and then print only the worksheet containing the chart.
4. Close **EL1-U2-A04-ProfitCompare.xlsx**.

Assessment 5 Create and Format a Pie Chart

1. Open **EPProdDept.xlsx** and then save the workbook with Save As and name it **EL1-U2-A05-EPProdDept**.
2. Create a pie chart as a separate worksheet with the data in cells A3 through B10. You determine the type of pie chart. Include an appropriate title for the chart, as well as percentage labels.
3. Print only the worksheet containing the chart.
4. Save and then close **EL1-U2-A05-EPProdDept.xlsx**.

Assessment 6 Use the PMT Function and Apply Formatting to a Workbook

1. Open **HERSalesInfo.xlsx** and then save the workbook with Save As and name it **EL1-U2-A06-HERSalesInfo**.
2. The owner of Hilltop Equipment Rental is interested in selling three tractors owned by the business and needs to determine the possible monthly income from the sales. Using the PMT function, insert a formula in cell E4 that calculates monthly payments. (Type a minus sign before the cell designation in the *Pv* text box at the Function Arguments palette.)
3. Copy the formula in cell E4 down to cells E5 and E6.
4. Insert a formula in cell F4 that multiplies the amount in cell E4 by the amount in cell D4.
5. Copy the formula in cell F4 down to cells F5 and F6.
6. Insert a formula in cell G4 that subtracts the amount in cell B4 from the amount in cell F4. ***Hint: The formula should return a positive number.***
7. Copy the formula in cell G4 down to cells G5 and G6.
8. Save, print, and then close **EL1-U2-A06-HERSalesInfo.xlsx**.

Assessment 7 Use the IF Function and Apply Formatting to a Workbook

1. Open **PSQtrlySales.xlsx** and then save the workbook with Save As and name it **EL1-U2-A07-PSQtrlySales**.
2. Insert an IF statement in cell F4 that inserts *Yes* if cell E4 contains a number greater than 74999 and inserts *No* if the number in cell E4 is not greater than 74999. Copy the formula in cell F4 down to cells F5 through F18. Center align the text in cells F4 through F18.
3. Insert a footer that prints your name at the left, the current date in the middle, and the current time at the right.
4. Turn on the display of formulas, print the worksheet in landscape orientation, and then turn off the display of formulas. (The worksheet will print on two pages.)
5. Save and then close **EL1-U2-A07-PSQtrlySales.xlsx**.

Assessment 8 Insert a Text Box and Hyperlinks in a Travel Workbook

1. Open **TravDest.xlsx** and then save the workbook with Save As and name it **EL1-U2-A08-TravDest**.
2. Insert a text box in the workbook with the following specifications:
   a. Draw the text box at the right side of the clip art image.
   b. Type **Call 1-888-555-1288 for last-minute vacation specials!**
   c. Select the text and then change the font to 24-point Forte and apply the Blue color in the *Standard Colors* section.
   d. Size and position the text box so it appears visually balanced with the travel clip art image.
3. Make sure you are connected to the Internet and then, for each city in the worksheet, search for sites that might be of interest to tourists. Write down the web address of the best web page you find for each city.
4. Create a hyperlink with each city name to the web address you wrote down in Step 3. (Select the hyperlink text in each cell and change the font size to 18 points.)
5. Test each hyperlink to make sure you entered the web address correctly. Click the hyperlink and then close the web browser after the page has loaded.
6. Save, print, and then close **EL1-U2-A08-TravDest.xlsx**.

Assessment 9 Insert an Image and a SmartArt Graphic in a Workbook

1. Open **SalesQuotas.xlsx** and then save the workbook with Save As and name it **EL1-U2-A09-SalesQuotas**.
2. Insert a formula in cell C3 using an absolute reference to determine the projected quotas at a 10% increase of the current quotas.
3. Copy the formula in cell C3 down to cells C4 through C12. Apply the Accounting format with two places past the decimal point and a dollar sign to cell C3.
4. In row 1, insert a clip art image related to money. You determine the size and position of the clip art image. If necessary, increase the height of the row.
5. Insert a SmartArt graphic at the right side of the data that contains three shapes. Insert the following quota ranges in the shapes and apply the specified fill colors:
   $50,000 to $99,999 (apply a green color)
   $100,000 to $149,999 (apply a blue color)
   $150,000 to $200,000 (apply a red color)
6. Apply formatting to the SmartArt graphic to improve the visual appearance.
7. Insert a custom header that prints your name at the left, the current date in the middle, and the file name at the right.
8. Change the orientation to landscape and make sure the graphic fits on the page.
9. Save, print, and then close **EL1-U2-A09-SalesQuotas.xlsx**.

Assessment 10 Insert Symbol, Clip Art, and WordArt in a Sales Workbook

1. Open **CISales.xlsx** and then save the workbook with Save As and name it **EL1-U2-A10-CISales**.
2. Delete the text *Landower Company* in cell A7 and then type **Económico** in the cell. (Use the Symbol dialog box to insert *ó*.)
3. Insert a new row at the beginning of the worksheet.
4. Select and then merge cells A1 through D1.
5. Increase the height of row 1 to approximately 141.00 points.
6. Insert the text *Custom Interiors* as WordArt in cell A1. You determine the formatting of the WordArt. Move and size the WordArt so it fits in cell A1.
7. Open Word and then open **CICustomers.docx** located in the EL1U2 folder on your storage medium. Click the Excel button and with **EL1-U2-A10-CISales.xlsx** open, make a screenshot (using the *Screen Clipping* option) of the customer information in the Word document. Position the screenshot image below the data in the cells.
8. Insert a custom footer that prints your name at the left and the file name at the right.
9. Make sure the data in the cells and the screenshot display on the same page and then print the worksheet.
10. Save and then close **EL1-U2-A10-CISales.xlsx**.
11. Make Word the active program, close **CICustomers.docx**, and then close Word.

Assessment 11 Insert and Format a Shape in a Budget Workbook

1. Open **SEExpenses.xlsx** and then save the workbook with Save As and name it **EL1-U2-A11-SEExpenses**.
2. Make the following changes to the worksheet so it displays as shown in Figure U2.1:
   a. Select and then merge cells A1 through D1.
   b. Add fill to the cells as shown in Figure U2.1. (Use the Green, Accent 6, Lighter 40% fill color.)
   c. Increase the height of row 1 to the approximate size shown in Figure U2.1.
   d. Make cell A1 active, type **SOLAR**, press Alt + Enter, and then type **ENTERPRISES**. Set the text you just typed in 20-point Calibri bold, center and middle aligned, and change the font color to *Green, Accent 6, Darker 25%*.
   e. Insert the sun shape (located in the *Basic Shapes* section of the Shapes button drop-down list). Apply orange shape fill (using the Orange option in the *Standard Colors* section) and change the shape outline to *Green, Accent 6, Darker 25%*. Copy the shape in the cell and then size and position the shapes as shown in the figure.
3. Save, print, and then close **EL1-U2-A11-SEExpenses.xlsx**.

Figure U2.1 Assessment 11

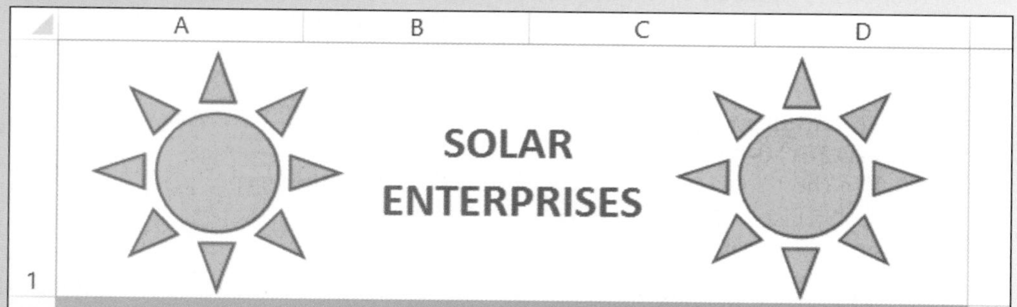

	A	B	C	D
2	*Expense*	*Actual*	*Budget*	*% of Actual*
3	Salaries	$ 126,000.00	$ 124,000.00	98%
4	Benefits	25,345.00	28,000.00	110%
5	Commissions	58,000.00	54,500.00	94%
6	Media space	8,250.00	10,100.00	122%
7	Travel expenses	6,350.00	6,000.00	94%
8	Dealer display	4,140.00	4,500.00	109%
9	Payroll taxes	2,430.00	2,200.00	91%
10	Telephone	1,450.00	1,500.00	103%
11				

Writing Activities

The following activities give you the opportunity to practice your writing skills along with demonstrating an understanding of some of the important Excel features you have mastered in this unit. Use correct grammar, appropriate word choices, and clear sentence constructions.

Activity 1 Prepare a Projected Budget

You are the accounting assistant in the financial department of McCormack Funds and you have been asked to prepare a proposed annual department budget. The total amount available to the department is $1,450,000. You are given these percentages for the proposed budget items: salaries, 45%; benefits, 12%; training, 14%; administrative costs, 10%; equipment, 11%; and supplies, 8%. Create a worksheet with this information that shows the projected yearly budget, the budget items in the department, the percentage for each item, and the amount for each item. After the worksheet is completed, save the workbook and name it **EL1-U2-Act1-MFBudget**. Print and then close the workbook.

Optional: Using Word 2013, write a memo to members of the McCormack Funds Finance Department explaining that the proposed annual department budget is attached for their review. Comments and suggestions are to be sent to you within one week. Save the file and name it **EL1-U2-Act1-MFMemo**. Print and then close the file.

Activity 2 Create a Travel Tours Bar Chart

Prepare a worksheet in Excel for Carefree Travels that includes the following information:

Scandinavian Tours

Country	**Tours Booked**
Norway	52
Sweden	62
Finland	29
Denmark	38

Use the information in the worksheet to create and format a bar chart as a separate sheet. Save the workbook and name it **EL1-U2-Act2-CTTours**. Print only the sheet containing the chart and then close **EL1-U2-Act2-CTTours.xlsx**.

Activity 3 Prepare a Ski Vacation Worksheet

Prepare a worksheet for Carefree Travels that advertises a snow skiing trip. Include the following information in the announcement:

- At the beginning of the worksheet, create a company logo that includes the company name *Carefree Travels* and a clip art image related to travel.
- Include the heading *Whistler Ski Vacation Package* in the worksheet.
- Include the following details below the heading:
  - Round-trip air transportation: $395
  - Seven nights' hotel accommodations: $1,550
  - Four all-day ski passes: $425
  - Compact rental car with unlimited mileage: $250
  - Total price of the ski package: (calculate the total price)

- Include the following information somewhere in the worksheet:
  - Book your vacation today at special discount prices.
  - Two-for-one discount at many of the local ski resorts.

Save the workbook and name it **EL1-U2-Act3-CTSkiTrips**. Print and then close **EL1-U2-Act3-CTSkiTrips.xlsx**.

Internet Research

Find Information on Excel Books and Present the Data in a Worksheet

Locate two companies on the Internet that sell new books. At the first new book company site, locate three books on Microsoft Excel. Record the title, author, and price for each book. At the second new book company site, locate the same three books and record the prices. Create an Excel worksheet that includes the following information:

- Name of each new book company
- Title and author of each book
- Prices for each book from the two book company sites

Create a hyperlink to the website of each book company. Then save the completed workbook and name it **EL1-U2-IR-Books**. Print and then close the workbook.

Job Study

Create a Customized Time Card for a Landscaping Company

You are the manager of Landmark Landscaping Company and are responsible for employee time cards. At the New backstage area, search for and download a time card using the words *weekly time sheet portrait* to narrow the search. Use the template to create a customized time card workbook for your company. With the workbook based on the template open, insert additional blank rows to increase the spacing above the Employee row. Insert a clip art image related to landscaping or gardening and position and size it attractively in the form. Include a text box with the text *Lawn and Landscaping Specialists* inside the box. Format, size, and position the text attractively in the form. Fill in the form for the current week with the following employee information:

Employee: Jonathan Holder
Manager: (Your name)
Employee phone: (225) 555-3092
Employee email: None
Regular hours: 8 hours for Monday, Tuesday, Wednesday, and Thursday
Overtime: 2 hours on Wednesday
Sick hours: None
Vacation: 8 hours on Friday
Rate per hour: $20.00
Overtime pay: $30.00

Save the completed form and name it **EL1-U2-JS-TimeCard**. Print and then close **EL1-U2-JS-TimeCard.xlsx**.

Index

A

absolute cell reference
  defined, 50
  using in formula, 50–51
Accounting, as category in Format Cells dialog box, 77
accounting formatting, 23
Accounting Number Format button, 23
active cell, 5, 6
Add Chart Elements button, 242
addition, AutoSum to add numbers, 19
alignment
  aligning data, 78–80
  applying formatting, 70–72
area chart, 233
argument, defined, 43
Arrange All button, 169
Arrange Windows dialog box, 169
arrow shapes, drawing, 282–284
AutoComplete, 13, 14
AutoCorrect, 13–14
AutoCorrect dialog box, 13–14, 212–213
AutoFill, 15
automatic entering features, 13–15
AutoSum button, 45
  to add numbers, 18–19
  to average numbers, 19
average
  AutoSum to average numbers, 19
  finding, 45–46
AVERAGE function, 19, 45
  writing formulas with, 45–46

B

background picture, inserting, 109
bar chart, 233
billing statement, preparing, using template, 218–219
Bold button, 70
borders, adding, to cells, 82–83
Borders button, 70
Breaks button, 105
bubble chart, 233
budget, calculating percentage of actual, 40

C

Calculate Now button, 49
Cancel button, 10
cascaded workbook, 170
cell address, 7
cell pointer, 5, 6, 8
cell reference, 7
  absolute, 50–51
  checking in formula, 39
  mixed, 50, 52–53
  relative, 50
cells
  active
    keyboard commands for, 7
    mouse for, 8
  clearing data in, 69
  copying and pasting
    cells from one worksheet to another, 173
    with Clipboard task pane, 157–158
    pasting values only, 159–160
    selected cells, 154–155
    using Paste Options button, 155–157
  deleting, 68–69
  editing data in, 10–11
  entering data in
    with fill handle, 15, 16–17
    typing in, 7–8
  formatting
    adding borders to, 82–83
    adding fill and shading to, 84–85
    centering, 21–22
    finding and replacing, 123–124
    with Format Cells dialog box, 78–85
    merging, 21–22
  linking between worksheets, 174–175
  range
    naming, 167
    using in formula, 167–168
  selecting, 20–21
    with keyboard, 20–21
    with mouse, 20
cell styles
  applying, 204, 206–207
  copying to another workbook, 210–211
  defining, 205–208
  deleting, 211
  formatting with, 204–211
  modifying, 209–210
  removing, 211
    Cell Styles button, 204
centering
  cells, 21–22
  worksheet horizontally/vertically, 102–103
Change Chart Type button, 240
Change Chart Type dialog box, 240
Change Colors button, 241
Chart Elements button, 236, 245
Chart Filters button, 236–237
charts
  adding data series, 233–234
  creating, 232–235
  deleting, 249–251
  design changes
    adding, moving and deleting chart elements, 242–244
    chart layout and colors, 241
    chart location, 242
    chart style, 240
    switching rows and columns, 240
  editing data in, 233–234
  formatting
    changing chart height and width measurements, 248–249
    with chart buttons, 236–238
    with CHART TOOLS FORMAT tab, 245–246

Format Chart Area task pane, 248, 249
line chart, 245–246
pie chart, 249–251
inserting and customizing shapes, 246–248
moving, 233
printing, 238–239
sizing, 233
types of, 232–233
Chart Styles button, 236–237
CHART TOOLS DESIGN tab, 239, 240
CHART TOOLS FORMAT tab, 245
Clear button, 69
clip art, inserting and formatting, 278–279
Clipboard task pane, 157–158
Close button, 172
closing
Excel, 13
workbook, 12
Collapse the Ribbon button, 5, 6
color
change colors in charts, 241
change worksheet color, 160–161
font formatting and, 70
column boundary line, changing width with, 63–64
column chart, 233
columns
deleting, 68–69
formatting
row height, 65–66
width, 21–22, 63–64
hiding and unhiding, 86–87
inserting, 67–68
printing column headings, 110
printing titles on multiple pages, 107–108
sorting in more than one, 127
switching in charts, 240
Column Width dialog box, changing column width at, 64–65
comma formatting, 23
Comma Style button, 23
Compress Pictures button, 276
constant, defined, 43
Copy button, 154
copying
cell styles, 210–211
data, 173
between programs, 175–176
formulas
with fill handle, 19
with relative cell references, 38–39
shapes, 281–284
workbook, 194–195
worksheet, 160
to another workbook, 200–201
copying and pasting, cells
with Clipboard task pane, 157–158
pasting values only, 159–160
selected cells, 154–155
using Paste Options button, 155–157
COUNT function, 45
writing formulas with, 48
Crop button, 276
Currency, as category in Format Cells dialog box, 77
Custom, as category in Format Cells dialog box, 77
customizing
images, 276–277
print jobs, 117–118
shapes in charts, 246–248
Cut button, 154
cutting
cells, 154–155
workbooks, 195–196

D

data
aligning, 78–80
clearing, in cells, 69
copying, 173
editing
in cell, 10–11
in chart, 233–234
entering into cells
with fill handle, 15, 16–17
typing in, 7–8
filtering, 127–128
finding and replacing, 120–122
indenting, 78–80
linking, 174–175
moving, 173
rotating, 79–80
scaling, 108–109
selecting within cell
with keyboard, 21
with mouse, 20–21
sorting, 125–127
data series, adding to chart, 233–234
Date, as category in Format Cells dialog box, 77
Date & Time button, 49
Decrease Decimal button, 23, 75
Decrease Font Size button, 70
Define Name button, 167
Delete button, 68
Delete dialog box, 68
Delete key, 69
deleting
cells, 68–69
cell styles, 211
chart element, 242
charts, 249–251
columns, 68–69
data in cell, 10
folder, 193, 197
hyperlink, 216–217
to Recycle Bin, 193
rows, 68–69
SmartArt graphic, 289
workbook, 193
worksheet, 153–155, 160
dependent worksheet, 174
dialog box launder, 5, 6
DIV/O error code, 41
doughnut chart, 233
down time, writing formula to calculate percentage of, 42
drawing
arrow shapes, 282–284
text boxes, 284–286
DRAWING TOOLS FORMAT tab, 281, 284–286

E

editing
  data in cell, 10–11
  data in chart, 233–234
  hyperlinks, 216–217
email address, linking using, 215
Enter button, 10
error codes, common formula and function, 41
Esc key, to escape backstage area, 11
Excel
  closing, 13
  copying and pasting data into Word document, 175–176
  opening, 5

F

FILE tab, 5, 6
fill, adding to cells, 84–85
fill button, copying formula relatively in worksheet, 38
Fill Color button, 70
fill handle
  to copy formula, 19
  copying formula relatively in worksheet, 39
  inserting data in cells with, 15, 16–17
filter, 127
filtering data, 127–128
financial functions, writing formulas with, 252–255
Find and Replace dialog box, 120–121
find and replace feature
  cell formatting, 123–124
  data, 120–122
Find and Select button, 120
folders
  copying workbook into another, 194
  creating, 191
  deleting, 193, 197
  naming, 191
  renaming, 192
  root folder, 191
  sending workbook to different, 195
  subfolder, 191
font
  changing, at Format Cells dialog box, 80–81
  formatting, 70–72
Font button, 70
Font Color button, 70
Font Size button, 70
footers
  inserting, 112–117
  insert picture watermark, 286–287
Format button, 162
Format Cells dialog box
  adding fill and shading, 84–85
  aligning and indenting data, 78–80
  changing fonts, 80–81
  formatting cells with, 78–85
  formatting numbers with, 76–78
Format Chart Area task pane, 248, 249
Format Painter, formatting with, 86
Format Picture button, 286–287
Format Picture task pane, 278
Format Selection button, 248
formatting
  alignment, 70–72, 78–80
  applying theme, 73–74
  cells
    adding borders to, 82–83
    adding fill and shading, 84–85
    centering, 21–22
    finding and replacing, 123–124
    Format Cells dialog box, 79–80
    merging, 21–22
  with cell styles, 204–211
  charts
    changing chart height and width measurements, 248–249
    with chart buttons, 236–238
    with CHART TOOLS FORMAT tab, 245–246
    Format Chart Area task pane, 248, 249
    line chart, 245–246
    pie chart, 249–251
  clearing data in cells, 69
  clip art, 278–279
  column row height, 65–66
  column width, 21–22, 63–64
  deleting cells, rows or columns, 68–69
  font, 70–72, 80–81
  with Format Painter, 86
  images, 276–278
  inserting columns, 67–68
  inserting rows, 66–67
  with Mini toolbar, 70
  numbers, 23–24, 74–78
  repeating last action, 84
  screenshots, 280–281
  text boxes, 284–286
  WordArt, 293–294
  worksheet
    background picture, inserting, 109
    centering horizontally vertically, 102–103
    headers and footers, inserting, 112–117
    margin changes, 101–102
    page breaks, inserting and removing, 104–107
    page orientation changes, 104
    page size changes, 104
    scaling data, 108–109
    undo and redo, 118–119
Formula AutoComplete, 45
Formula bar, 5, 6, 10
formulas
  absolute cell references in, 50–51
  checking cell references in, 39
  copying, with relative cell references, 38–39
  defined, 18
  determining order of operations, 40–41
  displaying, 49
  finding future value of investment, 255
  finding periodic payments for loan, 253–255

identifying common errors, 41
inserting
AutoSum, 18–19
fill handle to copy formula, 19
with functions, 43–49
mixed cell references in, 52–53
ranges in, 167–168
Trace Error button, 41
writing
with AVERAGE, MIN, MAX, COUNT functions, 45–48
with financial functions, 252–255
with IF logical function, 256–260
with mathematical operators, 37–42
with NOW and TODAY function, 49
by pointing, 40, 41
with statistical functions, 45–48
FORMULA tab, 43
Fraction, as category in Format Cells dialog box, 77
Freeze Panes button, 165–166
Function Arguments palette, 44, 257–258
Function Library group, 43
functions
argument, 43
AVERAGE, 45–46
constants, 43
COUNT function, 48
defined, 43
finding future value of investment, 255
finding periodic payments for loan, 253–255
FV function, 252
identifying common errors, 41
inserting formulas with, 43–48
MAX function, 46–48
MIN function, 46–48
NOW function, 49
PMT function, 252
TODAY function, 49
writing formulas
with financial functions, 252–255
with IF logical function, 256–260
writing formulas with statistical functions, 45–48
future value, 253
finding, 255
Fv, in financial functions, 253
FV function, 252

G

Go To feature, 7
graphic, linking using, 215–216
gridlines, 7
printing, 110

H

Header & Footer button, 112
HEADER & FOOTER TOOLS DESIGN tab, 112–113, 286–287
headers
inserting, 112–117
insert picture watermark, 286–287
headings, printing row and column headings, 110
Help feature
in dialog box or backstage area, 27
Help window, 25–26
ScreenTips, 26
Hide button, 171
hiding
columns and rows, 86–87
worksheet, 162–163
horizontal scroll bar, 5, 6, 8
Hyperlink button, 212
hyperlinks
automatic formatting of, 212–213
editing, 216–217
inserting, 212–217
linking
to existing web page or file, 212–213
to new workbook, 214–216
to place in workbook, 214–216
using email address, 215
using graphic, 215–216
modifying, 216–217
navigating using, 213–214
purposes of, 212
removing, 216–217

I

IF function, writing formulas with, 257–260
images
compress and crop, 276
customizing and formatting, 276–277
formatting with Format Picture task pane, 278
inserting, 275–279
inserting and formatting clip art images, 278–279
sizing and moving, 276
Increase Decimal button, 23, 75
Increase Font Size button, 70
indenting, data, 78–80
Info backstage area, 11
Insert button, 66
Insert dialog box, 66
Insert Function button, 43
Insert Function dialog box, 43–44
Insert Hyperlink dialog box, 212
inserting
background picture, 109
clip art, 278–279
columns, 67–68
data in cells with fill handle, 15, 16–17
footers, 112–117
formulas
AutoSum, 18–19
fill handle to copy, 19
with functions, 43–49
headers, 112–117
hyperlinks, 212–217
images, 275–279
new worksheet, 153–155
page breaks, 104–107
picture as watermark, 286–287

rows, 66–67
screenshots, 280–281
shapes, 246–248, 281–284
SmartArt graphic, 288–292
symbols and special characters, 273–275
WordArt, 293–294
Insert WordArt button, 293
integration, 175–176
interest, simple, formula with mixed cell references, 53
Italic button, 70

K

keyboard shortcuts
to activate cells, 7
repeat last action, 84
selecting cell with, 20–21
selecting data within cell, 21

L

landscape orientation, 104
line chart, 233
creating and formatting, 245–246
linking
cells between worksheets, 174–175
data, 174–175
live preview feature, 73
loan, finding periodic payments for, 253–255
logical test, 256

M

margins
changing in worksheet, 101–103
default settings, 101
Margins button, 101
marquee, 154
mathematical operations, writing formulas with, 37–42
MAX function, 45
writing formulas with, 46–48
Maximize button, 172
Merge & Center button, 21, 70–71
Merge Styles dialog box, 210–211
merging, cells, 21–22
MIN function, 45
writing formulas with, 46–48
Minimize button, 172
Mini toolbar, formatting with, 70
mixed cell reference, 50
mouse
to activate cells, 8
moving split lines, 165
selecting cell with, 20
selecting data within cell, 20–21
Move Chart button, 242
Move Chart dialog box, 242
Move or Copy dialog box, 200
moving
chart, 233
chart element, 242
chart location, 242
data, 173
images, 276
SmartArt graphic, 289
split lines, 165
WordArt, 293
workbook, 172
worksheet, 160–161
worksheet to another workbook, 201–203
multiple cell reference, using in formula, 52–53

N

N/A error code, 41
Name box, 5, 6, 7
NAME? error code, 41
navigating, using hyperlinks, 213–214
nested parentheses, 41
New folder button, 191
New sheet button, 5, 6, 153
New Window button, 169
Normal button, 105
NOW function, writing formulas with, 49
Nper, in financial functions, 252
Number, as category in Format Cells dialog box, 77
Number Format button, 23, 75
numbers
AutoSum
to add, 18–19
to average numbers, 19
formatting, 23–24
with Format Cells dialog box, 76–78
with Number group buttons, 74–76
number symbol (###) for exceeding space in cell, 8
NUM! error code, 41

O

Office.com, inserting images from, 278–279
100% button, 164
Online Pictures button, 278
Open dialog box, 16
copying workbook to another folder, 195
creating folder, 191
cutting and pasting workbook, 195–196
deleting workbooks and folders, 193
elements of, 190–191
renaming folder, 192
renaming workbook, 196–197
selecting workbook, 192
opening, workbook
multiple, 169
from Open dialog box, 16
from Recent Workbook list, 16
order of operations, 40–41
Orientation button, 71, 104

P

page break, inserting and removing, 104–107
Page Break Preview button, 105–106
page orientation
changing, 104
default, 101
Page Setup dialog box
centering horizontally/vertically, 102–103
changing margins, 102

inserting headers and footers, 114–117
printing column and row titles on multiple pages, 107–108
printing gridlines and column and row headings, 110
printing specific area of worksheet, 110–111
page size
changing, 104
default, 101
pane, freezing and unfreezing, 165–166
Paste button, 154
Paste Options button, 155–157
pasting
cells, 154–156
data, between programs, 175–176
workbooks, 195–196
payroll, formulas with absolute and mixed cell references, 52–53
Percentage, as category in Format Cells dialog box, 77
Percent Style button, 23
pictures
compress and crop, 276
customizing and formatting, 276
formatting with Format Picture task pane, 278
inserting and customizing picture and text box, 284–286
inserting background picture, 109
sizing and moving, 276
as watermark, 286–287
Pictures button, 275
PICTURE TOOLS FORMAT tab, 275
pie chart, 233
formatting, 249–251
pinning, workbook to Recent Workbooks list, 16, 198
Pmt, in financial functions, 252
PMT function, 252
pointing, writing formula by, 40, 42
portrait orientation, 104
Print Area button, 110–111
Print backstage area, 11–12
printing
charts, 238–239
column and row titles on multiple pages, 107–108
gridlines, 110
row and column headings, 110
specific area of worksheet, 110–111
specific pages of worksheet, 117–118
workbook, 11–12
with multiple worksheets, 163–164
Print Titles button, 107
Pv, in financial functions, 252

Q

Quick Access toolbar, 5, 6
Print button on, 12
Quick Layout button, 241

R

radar chart, 233
range
defined, 167
naming, 167
using in formula, 167–168
rate, in financial functions, 252
Recent Workbooks list
clearing, 199
opening workbook from, 16
pinning workbook to, 16, 198
recovering unsaved workbook, 198
Recommended Charts button, 232
Recycle Bin
deleting workbook to, 193
display contents of, 193
restoring workbooks from, 193
Redo button, 118–119
REF! error code, 41
relative cell reference, 19
copying formulas with, 38–39
defined, 50
removing
cell styles, 211
hyperlink, 216–217
page breaks, 104–107
worksheet, 160
renaming
folder, 192
workbook, 196–197
worksheet, 160–161
Repeat command, 84
Reset to Match Style button, 245
Restore Down button, 172
returning the result, 43
ribbon, 5, 6
root folder, 191
rotating, text, 79–80
Row Height dialog box, 65–66
rows
deleting, 68–69
hiding and unhiding, 86–87
inserting, 66–67
printing row headings, 110
printing titles on multiple pages, 107–108
switching in charts, 240

S

salary, calculating by inserting and copying formula, 39
Save As backstage area, 8
Save As dialog box, creating folder, 191
Save button, 8
saving, workbook, 8–9
scaling data, 108–109
scatter chart, 233
Scientific, as category in Format Cells dialog box, 77
Screenshot button, 280
screenshots, inserting and formatting, 280–281
ScreenTips, 26
scroll bar, 8
horizontal, 5, 6
vertical, 5, 6
selecting
cells, 20–21

multiple worksheets, 153–155
workbook, 192
shading, adding to cells, 84–85
shapes
drawing arrow shapes, 282–284
inserting and copying, 281–284
Shapes button, 281
sheet tab, 5, 6
Sheet Tab shortcut menu, 160–162
Show Formulas button, 49
simple interest, formula with mixed cell references, 53
Size button, 104
sizing
chart, 233
image, 276
SmartArt graphic, 289
WordArt, 293
workbook, 172
SmartArt button, 288
SmartArt graphic
changing design of, 290–291
changing formatting of, 291–293
entering data in, 288
sizing, moving and deleting, 289
SmartArt Graphic dialog box, 288
SMARTART TOOLS DESIGN tab, 288
smart tag, 41
Sort dialog box, 125–127
Sort & Filter button, 125, 127
sorting data, 125–127
custom sort, 125–126
more than one column, 127
source worksheet, 174
Special, as category in Format Cells dialog box, 77
special characters, inserting, 273–275
Spelling button, 118
spelling checker, 118, 119–120
Spelling dialog box, 119
Split button, 165
split lines, 165
statistical functions, writing formulas with, 45–48
Status bar, 5, 6, 7
stock chart, 233
style, 204
Style dialog box, 205–208
subfolder, 191
subtraction, inserting and copying formula, 38
SUM function, 18, 45
surface chart, 233
Switch Row/Column button, 240
Switch Windows button, 169
Symbol button, 273
Symbol dialog box, 274
symbols, inserting, 273–275

T

tab, 5, 6
templates, for worksheets, 217–219
Text, as category in Format Cells dialog box, 77
text, rotating, 79–80
Text Box button, 284
text boxes, drawing and formatting, 284–286
Text Pane button, 288
theme
applying, 73–74
defined, 73
Themes button, 73
tiled workbook, 170
Time, as category in Format Cells dialog box, 77
Title bar, 5, 6
TODAY function, writing formulas with, 49
Trace Error button, 41

U

Underline button, 70
Undo button, 118–119
Unfreeze Panes, 165–166
Unhide button, 171
Unhide dialog box, 162–163
unhiding, columns and rows, 86–87

V

VALUE error code, 41
vertical scroll bar, 5, 6, 8

W

watermark, inserting picture as, 286–287
web page, linking to existing, 212–213
Width option box, 108
windows
arranging workbooks in, 169–170
cascaded workbooks, 170
hiding/unhiding workbooks, 171
opening multiple workbooks, 169
opening new window, 169
sizing and moving workbooks, 172
splitting worksheet into, 165–166
tiled workbooks, 170
WordArt, inserting and formatting, 293–294
Word document, copying and pasting Excel data into, 175–176
workbook
arranging, 169–170
automatic entering features, 13–15
cascaded, 170
closing, 12
copying, 194–195
worksheet to another, 200–201
creating, 5–8
with multiple worksheets, 153–155
cutting and pasting, 195–196
defined, 5
deleting, 193
worksheet in, 153–155
folders to organize, 191–192
hide/unhiding, 171
hide worksheet in, 162–163
inserting new worksheet, 153–155
linking
to new workbook, 214–216
to place in, 214–216
maintaining, 190–197

maximizing, 172
minimizing, 172
moving, 172
moving and copying data between, 173
moving worksheet to another, 201–203
naming, 8
opening, 16
multiple, 169
pinning to Recent Workbook list, 16, 199
printing, 11–12
with multiple worksheets, 163–164
Recent List of, 197–200
recovering unsaved workbook, 198
renaming, 196–197
restoring, 172
saving, 8–9
selecting, 192
sending to different drive or folder, 195
sizing, 172
tiled, 170
worksheet
change color, 160–161
column width changes, 63–66
copying, 160
to another workbook, 200–201
defined, 5
deleting, 153–155, 160
dependent, 174
elements of, 5–8
filtering data, 127–128
finding and replacing data, 120–124
finding averages in, 45–46
finding maximum and minimum values in, 47–48
formatting
background picture, inserting, 109
centering horizontally/vertically, 102–103
headers and footers, inserting, 112–117
margin changes, 101–102
page breaks, inserting and removing, 104–107
page orientation changes, 104
page size changes, 104
scaling data, 108–109
undo and redo, 118–119
freezing and unfreezing panes, 165–166
hiding, 162–163
inserting
columns, 67–68
formulas, 18–19
headers and footers, 112–117
new, 153–155
rows, 66–67
linking cells between, 174–175
managing, 160–166, 200–203
moving, 160–161
to another workbook, 201–203
moving and copying data between, 173
printing
column and row titles on multiple pages, 107–108
gridlines and row and column headings, 110
specific area of, 110–111
specific pages of, 117–118
workbook containing multiple, 163–164
removing, 160
renaming, 160–161
selecting multiple, 153–155
sorting data
custom sort, 125–126
sorting more than one column, 127
source, 174
spelling check, 118, 119–120
splitting into windows, 165–166
templates for, 217–219
worksheet area, 5, 6
Wrap Text button, 71
writing, formulas
with financial functions, 252–255
with IF logical function, 256–260
with mathematical operations, 37–42
by pointing, 40, 41

X

xy (scatter) chart, 233

Z

zoom, using, 164, 166
Zoom button, 164
Zoom to Selection button, 164

MICROSOFT® EXCEL® Level 2

Unit 1 ■ Advanced Formatting, Formulas, and Data Management

Chapter 1 ■ Advanced Formatting Techniques

Chapter 2 ■ Advanced Functions and Formulas

Chapter 3 ■ Working with Tables and Data Features

Chapter 4 ■ Summarizing and Consolidating Data

MICROSOFT® EXCEL®

CHAPTER 1

Advanced Formatting Techniques

PERFORMANCE OBJECTIVES

Upon successful completion of Chapter 1, you will be able to:

- **Apply conditional formatting by entering parameters for a rule**
- **Apply conditional formatting using a predefined rule**
- **Create and apply a new rule for conditional formatting**
- **Edit, delete, and clear conditional formatting rules**
- **Apply conditional formatting using an icon set, data bars, and color scale**
- **Apply conditional formatting using a formula**
- **Apply fraction and scientific formatting**
- **Apply a special format for a number**
- **Create a custom number format**
- **Apply wrap text and shrink to fit text control options**
- **Modify text using the text functions PROPER, UPPER, LOWER, SUBSTITUTE, RIGHT, LEFT, MID and TRIM**
- **Filter a worksheet using a custom AutoFilter**
- **Filter and sort a worksheet using conditional formatting or cell attributes**

SNAP

Tutorials

1.1 Applying Conditional Formatting
1.2 Applying Conditional Formatting Using Icon Sets
1.3 Applying Conditional Formatting Using Data Bars and Color Scales
1.4 Applying Conditional Formatting Using a Formula
1.5 Using Fraction, Scientific, and Special Number Formatting
1.6 Creating a Custom Number Format
1.7 Wrapping and Shrinking Text to Fit within a Cell
1.8 Filtering and Sorting Data Using Conditional Formatting and Cell Attributes
1.9 Using Text Functions
1.10 Filtering a Worksheet Using a Custom AutoFilter

Although many worksheets can be formatted using buttons available in the Font, Alignment, and Number groups on the HOME tab of the ribbon, on the Mini toolbar, or with the new Quick Analysis button, some situations require format categories that are not represented with a button. In other worksheets, you may want to make use of Excel's advanced formatting techniques to format based on a condition. In this chapter, you will learn how to create, edit, and apply advanced formatting and filtering techniques. Model answers for this chapter's projects appear on the following pages.

Excel
EL2C1

Note: Before beginning the projects, copy to your storage medium the EL2C1 subfolder from the EL2 folder on the CD that accompanies this textbook and make EL2C1 the active folder. Steps on how to copy a folder are presented on the inside of the back cover of this textbook. Do this every time you start a chapter's projects.

ViewItVideo
Payroll
Week Ended: October 24, 2015

First Name	Last Name	Sun	Mon	Tue	Wed	Thu	Fri	Sat	Total Hours	Overtime Hours	Pay Rate	Gross Pay
Alexis	Torres	-	5.0	7.0	8.0	8.0	9.0	9.5	46.5	6.5	7.75	385.56
Derrick	MacLean	8.0	-	6.5	8.0	8.0	8.5	9.0	48.0	8.0	7.35	382.20
Priya	Singh	8.0	-	4.0	8.0	8.0	8.5	6.5	43.0	3.0	7.35	327.08
Emil	Fedorov	8.0	8.0	8.0	5.5	8.0	-	8.0	45.5	5.5	7.75	373.94
Leslie	Sparling	-	6.0	7.5	8.0	8.0	-	8.0	37.5	-	8.15	305.63
Irene	O'Rourke	4.0	-	8.0	-	6.5	9.5	7.5	35.5	-	8.15	289.33
Ruthann	Goldstein	5.5	-	8.0	-	4.0	7.5	6.0	31.0	-	7.75	240.25
Stefan	Kominek	-	6.0	8.0	-	8.0	8.5	4.5	35.0	-	7.75	271.25
Alex	Spivak	-	5.0	8.0	8.5	7.5	8.0	8.0	45.0	5.0	7.75	368.13
Erica	Wilkins	-	7.0	-	6.0	-	6.0	6.4	25.4	-	7.35	186.69
Dana	Vanderhoek	8.0	7.0	-	8.0	-	5.5	5.0	33.5	-	7.35	246.23
Ashley	Castillo	4.0	8.0	-	7.5	8.0	4.0	8.5	40.0	-	8.15	326.00
Susan	Anez	-	3.0	5.5	-	-	7.0	7.0	22.5	-	8.15	183.38
Dana	Ivanowski	4.5	4.0	6.0	-	8.5	6.8	-	29.8	-	7.75	230.95
Maria	Alvarez	-	7.0	4.5	-	7.5	7.5	-	26.5	-	7.35	194.78
Xue	Chen	9.0	-	9.0	8.0	7.5	8.0	-	41.5	1.5	7.35	310.54
Annette	Fournier	8.0	-	-	6.5	5.0	7.5	7.0	34.0	-	7.35	249.90
Randy	Brown	6.5	-	-	5.5	4.0	6.0	4.0	26.0	-	7.35	191.10
TOTAL		73.5	66.0	90.0	87.5	106.5	117.8	104.9	646.2	29.5		5,062.90

Project 1 Format Cells Based on Values

EL2-C1-P1-VIVPay-Oct24.xlsx

AllClaims Insurance Brokers
Policy Information

Customer ID	Policy ID	No. of Autos	All Perils Deductible	Liability Limit	No. of Drivers	Rating	Claims	Premium
C-025	6512485	2	500	500,000	3	1	0	1,875.00
C-055	6123584	1	250	500,000	2	1	0	995.00
C-072	6583157	2	775	1,000,000	2	2	1	1,575.00
C-085	6124893	3	1,000	500,000	4	2	1	2,250.00
C-094	3481274	1	500	2,000,000	1	5	3	2,150.00
C-114	4956875	2	250	750,000	2	4	2	2,345.00
C-124	3354867	1	250	1,000,000	2	2	1	1,168.00
C-131	6598642	3	775	500,000	4	5	2	3,247.00
C-148	4668457	3	1,000	1,000,000	3	5	2	2,948.00
C-155	8512475	4	500	2,000,000	6	8	4	4,177.00
C-168	6984563	2	250	675,000	2	5	3	2,110.00
C-171	4856972	1	500	500,000	2	6	3	1,845.00
C-184	5124876	1	500	500,000	2	1	0	995.00
C-190	6845962	1	775	900,000	1	3	2	1,550.00
C-199	8457326	1	1,000	2,000,000	1	5	3	2,150.00
C-201	4968532	2	500	500,000	3	2	1	2,025.00
C-212	2698715	2	500	500,000	2	1	0	1,140.00
				Total Policy Premiums:				$ 34,545.00
				Average Number of Claims:			1.6	

Project 2 Apply Conditional Formatting to Insurance Policy Data

EL2-C1-P2-ACInsce-Autos2+.xlsx

AllClaims Insurance Brokers
Policy Information

Customer ID	Policy ID	No. of Autos	All Perils Deductible	Liability Limit	No. of Drivers	Rating	Claims	Premium
C-025	6512485	2	500	500,000	3	1	0	1,875.00
C-055	6123584	1	250	500,000	2	1	0	995.00
C-072	6583157	2	775	1,000,000	2	2	1	1,575.00
C-085	6124893	3	1,000	500,000	4	2	1	2,250.00
C-094	3481274	1	500	2,000,000	1	5	3	2,150.00
C-114	4956875	2	250	750,000	2	4	2	2,345.00
C-124	3354867	1	250	1,000,000	2	2	1	1,168.00
C-131	6598642	3	775	500,000	4	5	2	3,247.00
C-148	4668457	3	1,000	1,000,000	3	5	2	2,948.00
C-155	8512475	4	500	2,000,000	6	8	4	4,177.00
C-168	6984563	2	250	675,000	2	5	3	2,110.00
C-171	4856972	1	500	500,000	2	6	3	1,845.00
C-184	5124876	1	500	500,000	2	1	0	995.00
C-190	6845962	1	775	900,000	1	3	2	1,550.00
C-199	8457326	1	1,000	2,000,000	1	5	3	2,150.00
C-201	4968532	2	500	500,000	3	2	1	2,025.00
C-212	2698715	2	500	500,000	2	1	0	1,140.00
				Total Policy Premiums:				$ 34,545.00
				Average Number of Claims:			1.6	

EL2-C1-P2-ACInsce.xlsx

Math by Janelle Tutoring Service
Converting Decimals to Fractions Lesson

Background
A fraction expresses a number as a part of a group.

Stated Objective
Students will learn to convert a decimal value into a fraction.

Method
Demonstration followed by guided practice.

Examples	Converted to a Fraction
0.1	1/10
0.2	1/5
0.25	1/4
0.5	1/2
0.75	3/4
1	1
0.6	3/5
0.33	1/3
0.92	23/25

Math by Janelle Tutoring Service
Scientific Notation Lesson

Background
Scientific notation is used by scientists and mathematicians to express very large or very small numbers.

Stated Objective
Students will convert numbers to scientific notation.

Method
Demonstration followed by guided practice.

Examples	Converted to Scientific Notation
1,000,000,000	1.00E+09
100,000,000	1.00E+08
10,000,000	1.00E+07
1,000,000	1.00E+06
100,000	1.00E+05
10,000	1.00E+04
1,000	1.00E+03
100	1.00E+02
10	1.00E+01
1	1.00E+00
0.1	1.00E-01
0.01	1.00E-02
0.001	1.00E-03
0.0001	1.00E-04
0.00001	1.00E-05

Project 3 Use Fraction and Scientific Formatting Options

EL2-C1-P3-JTutor.xlsx, Step 6 and Step 8

Precision Design and Packaging Bulk Container Products *Custom imprinting available for all models*				
Model Number	**Description**	**Dimensions L x W x D in inches**	**Test Weight in pounds**	**Recommended Weight in pounds**
PD-1140	Gaylord with lid	48 x 40 x 36	200 lbs	100 lbs
PD-2185	Premium Gaylord with lid	48 x 40 x 36	200 lbs	125 lbs
PD-3695	Telescoping top and bottom	46 x 38 x 36	200 lbs	70 lbs
PD-4415	"EO" container	30 x 17 x 17	350 lbs	150 lbs
PD-5367	"EH" container	36 x 22 x 22	275 lbs	250 lbs
PD-6418	"E" container	40 x 28 x 24	275 lbs	500 lbs
PD-7459	Economy R.S.C.	36 x 36 x 36	200 lbs	65 lbs
PD-8854	Premium R.S.C.	36 x 36 x 36	200 lbs	100 lbs

Regional Sales Representatives		
North	Jordan Lavoie	(800) 555-3429
South	Pat Gallagher	(800) 555-3439
East	Alonso Rodriguez	(800) 555-3449
West	Karsten Das	(800) 555-3459
Canada	Kelli Olsen	(800) 555-3469
International	Bianca Santini	(800) 555-3479

Minimum order quantity of 25 applies.
Preferred carriers are UPS and DHL.

Project 4 Apply Advanced Formatting Options

EL2-C1-P4-Precision.xlsx

Two-Year Average Median Household Income by State Median Income for 2011		Two-Year Average Median Household Income by State Median Income for 2015	
United States	50,443	UNITED STATES	54,125
Alabama	42,407	ALABAMA	45,503
Alaska	58,552	ALASKA	62,826
Arizona	48,498	ARIZONA	52,038
Arkansas	40,553	ARKANSAS	43,513
California	54,681	CALIFORNIA	58,673
Colorado	60,381	COLORADO	64,789
Connecticut	66,748	CONNECTICUT	71,621
Delaware	55,808	DELAWARE	59,882
District of Columbia	56,988	DISTRICT OF COLUMBIA	61,148
Florida	45,281	FLORIDA	48,587
Georgia	45,741	GEORGIA	49,080
Hawaii	60,232	HAWAII	64,629
Idaho	47,997	IDAHO	51,501
Illinois	51,483	ILLINOIS	55,241
Indiana	46,020	INDIANA	49,379
Iowa	50,391	IOWA	54,070
Kansas	46,827	KANSAS	50,245
Kentucky	41,129	KENTUCKY	44,131
Louisiana	40,599	LOUISIANA	43,563
Maine	49,568	MAINE	53,186
Maryland	67,551	MARYLAND	72,482
Massachusetts	63,085	MASSACHUSETTS	67,690
Michigan	48,308	MICHIGAN	51,834
Minnesota	55,896	MINNESOTA	59,976
Mississippi	40,227	MISSISSIPPI	43,164
Missouri	46,518	MISSOURI	49,914
Montana	41,430	MONTANA	44,454
Nebraska	54,888	NEBRASKA	58,895
Nevada	49,929	NEVADA	53,574
New Hampshire	67,308	NEW HAMPSHIRE	72,221
New Jersey	63,646	NEW JERSEY	68,292
New Mexico	44,270	NEW MEXICO	47,502
New York	50,994	NEW YORK	54,717
North Carolina	45,210	NORTH CAROLINA	48,510
North Dakota	54,488	NORTH DAKOTA	58,466
Ohio	45,991	OHIO	49,348
Oklahoma	46,459	OKLAHOMA	49,851
Oregon	51,862	OREGON	55,648
Pennsylvania	49,874	PENNSYLVANIA	53,515
Rhode Island	51,143	RHODE ISLAND	54,876
South Carolina	41,549	SOUTH CAROLINA	44,582
South Dakota	47,003	SOUTH DAKOTA	50,434
Tennessee	41,044	TENNESSEE	44,040
Texas	48,902	TEXAS	52,472
Utah	56,991	UTAH	61,151
Vermont	54,777	VERMONT	58,776
Virginia	62,444	VIRGINIA	67,002
Washington	57,392	WASHINGTON	61,582
West Virginia	42,974	WEST VIRGINIA	46,111
Wisconsin	51,999	WISCONSIN	55,795
Wyoming	54,178	WYOMING	58,133

Data shown above is the two-year average median for 2010 to 2011. Two-year average median is the sum of two inflation-adjusted single-year medians divided by 2.

Source: U.S. Census Bureau
http://www.census.gov/hhes/www/income/data/statemedian/index.html

Project 5 Convert Text Using Text Functions

EL2-C1-P5-USIncomeStats.xlsx

ViewItVideo Proposed Computer Logins 10/24/2015						
Imported				Codes		
First Name	Last Name	SSN	SSN	First Name	Last Name	SSN
Terri	Burkowski	000 25 548	000 25 548	T	Burk	25
Beatriz	Santiago	000 46 584	000 46 584	B	Sant	46
Aram	Haji	000 78 859	000 78 859	A	Haji	78
Gerri	Kinnear	000 14 014	000 14 014	G	Kinn	14
Sam	Quinn	000 56 567	000 56 567	S	Quin	56
Andrea	Ruiz	000 99 123	000 99 123	A	Ruiz	99
Martina	Tisdale	000 21 321	000 21 321	M	Tisd	21
Carl	Wisenberg	000 54 457	000 54 457	C	Wise	54
Chen	Zhao	000 33 458	000 33 458	C	Zhao	33

Date: 10/24/2015

EL2-C1-P5b-VIVCodes.xlsx

AllClaims Insurance Brokers Policy Information								
Customer ID	Policy ID	No. of Autos	All Perils Deductible	Liability Limit	No. of Drivers	Rating	Claims	Premium
C-114	4956875	2	250	750,000	2	4	2	2,345.00
C-131	6598642	3	775	500,000	4	5	2	3,247.00
C-148	4668457	3	1,000	1,000,000	3	5	2	2,948.00
C-168	6984563	2	250	675,000	2	5	3	2,110.00
C-171	4856972	1	500	500,000	2	6	3	1,845.00
C-190	6845962	1	775	900,000	1	3	2	1,550.00

Project 6 Filter and Sort Data Based on Values, Icon Set, and Font Color

EL2-C1-P6-ACInsce.xlsx

AllClaims Insurance Brokers Policy Information								
Customer ID	Policy ID	No. of Autos	All Perils Deductible	Liability Limit	No. of Drivers	Rating	Claims	Premium
C-055	6123584	● 1	250	500,000	2	1	0	995.00
C-094	3481274	● 1	500	2,000,000	1	5	3	2,150.00
C-124	3354867	● 1	250	1,000,000	2	2	1	1,168.00
C-171	4856972	● 1	500	500,000	2	6	3	1,845.00
C-184	5124876	● 1	500	500,000	2	1	0	995.00
C-190	6845962	● 1	775	900,000	1	3	2	1,550.00
C-199	8457326	● 1	1,000	2,000,000	1	5	3	2,150.00

EL2-C1-P6-ACInsce-1Auto.xlsx

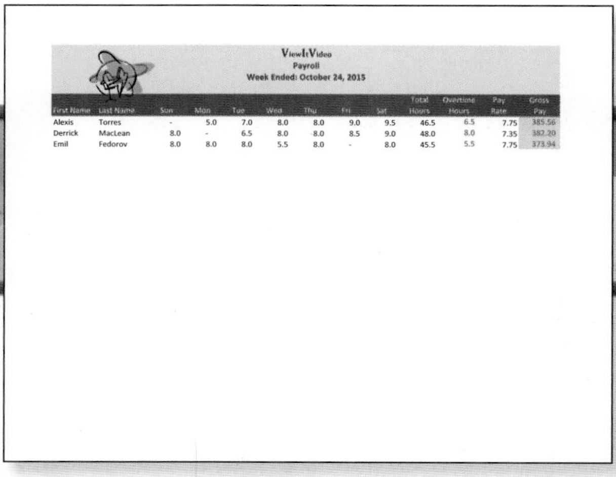

ViewItVideo
Payroll
Week Ended: October 24, 2015

First Name	Last Name	Sun	Mon	Tue	Wed	Thu	Fri	Sat	Total Hours	Overtime Hours	Pay Rate	Gross Pay
Alexis	Torres	-	5.0	7.0	8.0	8.0	9.0	9.5	46.5	6.5	7.75	385.56
Derrick	MacLean	8.0	-	6.5	8.0	8.0	8.5	9.0	48.0	8.0	7.35	382.20
Emil	Fedorov	8.0	8.0	8.0	5.5	8.0	-	8.0	45.5	5.5	7.75	373.94

EL2-C1-P6-VIVPay-Oct24-HighOT.xlsx

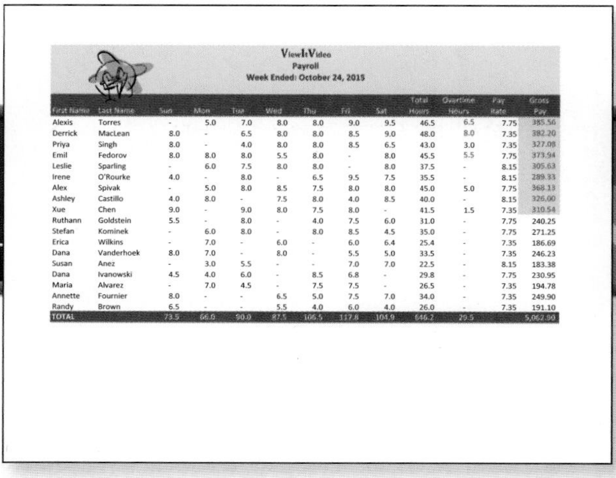

ViewItVideo
Payroll
Week Ended: October 24, 2015

First Name	Last Name	Sun	Mon	Tue	Wed	Thu	Fri	Sat	Total Hours	Overtime Hours	Pay Rate	Gross Pay
Alexis	Torres	-	5.0	7.0	8.0	8.0	9.0	9.5	46.5	6.5	7.75	385.56
Derrick	MacLean	8.0	-	6.5	8.0	8.0	8.5	9.0	48.0	8.0	7.35	382.20
Priya	Singh	8.0	-	4.0	8.0	8.0	8.5	6.5	43.0	3.0	7.35	327.08
Emil	Fedorov	8.0	8.0	8.0	5.5	8.0	-	8.0	45.5	5.5	7.75	373.94
Leslie	Sparling	-	6.0	7.5	8.0	8.0	-	8.0	37.5	-	8.15	305.63
Irene	O'Rourke	4.0	-	8.0	-	6.5	9.5	7.5	35.5	-	8.15	289.33
Alex	Spivak	-	5.0	8.0	8.5	7.5	8.0	8.0	45.0	5.0	7.75	368.13
Ashley	Castillo	4.0	8.0	-	7.5	8.0	4.0	8.5	40.0	-	8.15	326.00
Xue	Chen	9.0	-	9.0	8.0	7.5	8.0	-	41.5	1.5	7.35	310.54
Ruthann	Goldstein	5.5	-	8.0	-	4.0	7.5	6.0	31.0	-	7.75	240.25
Stefan	Kominek	-	6.0	8.0	-	8.0	8.5	4.5	35.0	-	7.75	271.25
Erica	Wilkins	-	7.0	-	6.0	-	6.0	6.4	25.4	-	7.35	186.69
Dana	Vanderhoek	8.0	7.0	-	8.0	-	5.5	5.0	33.5	-	7.35	246.23
Susan	Anez	-	3.0	5.5	-	-	7.0	7.0	22.5	-	8.15	183.38
Dana	Ivanowski	4.5	4.0	6.0	-	8.5	6.8	-	29.8	-	7.75	230.95
Maria	Alvarez	-	7.0	4.5	-	7.5	7.5	-	26.5	-	7.35	194.78
Annette	Fournier	8.0	-	-	6.5	5.0	7.5	7.0	34.0	-	7.35	249.90
Randy	Brown	6.5	-	-	5.5	4.0	6.0	4.0	26.0	-	7.35	191.10
TOTAL		73.5	66.0	90.0	87.5	106.5	117.8	104.9	646.2	29.5		5,062.90

EL2-C1-P6-VIVPay-Oct24-Sorted.xlsx

Model Answers

Project 1 Format Cells Based on Values 2 Parts

Working with a payroll worksheet, you will change the appearance of cells based on criteria related to overtime hours and gross pay.

Applying Conditional Formatting

Quick Steps

Apply Conditional Formatting Using a Predefined Rule

1. Select desired range.
2. Click Conditional Formatting button.
3. Point to desired rule category.
4. Click desired rule.
5. If necessary, enter parameter value.
6. If necessary, change format options.
7. Click OK.

Conditional Formatting

Quick Analysis

Conditional formatting applies special formatting to those cells within a specified range that meet a specific condition. The formatting of the cells that do not meet the condition remains unchanged. Changing the appearance of a cell based on a condition allows you to quickly identify values that are high or low and makes it easier to spot trends. Formatting can be applied based on a specific value or a value that falls within a range, or it can be applied by using a comparison operator, such as equals (=), greater than (>), or less than (<). Conditional formats can also be based on dates, text entries, or duplicated values. Consider using conditional formatting to analyze a question, such as *Which store locations earned sales above their target?* Using a different color to identify those stores that exceeded their target sales makes it easy to quickly identify the top performers.

The Quick Analysis button is a new feature in Excel 2013. When you select data, the Quick Analysis button appears near the fill handle at the bottom right corner of the selection and the options shown in Figure 1.1 are made available. You can use these options to quickly apply conditional formatting, create charts, add totals, create tables or add Sparklines. With predefined conditional formatting rules, Excel can quickly analyze and format your data. If you require more options than the Quick Analysis button provides, you can access the rules from the Conditional Formatting button drop-down list, as shown in Figure 1.2, or you can create your own conditional formatting rules.

Figure 1.1 Quick Analysis Button

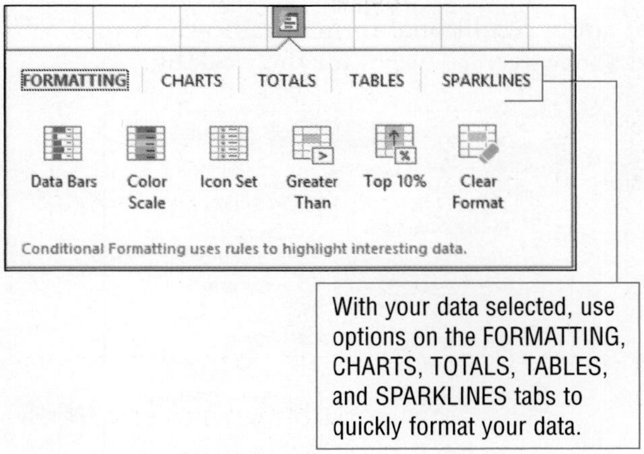

Figure 1.2 Conditional Formatting Button Drop-down List

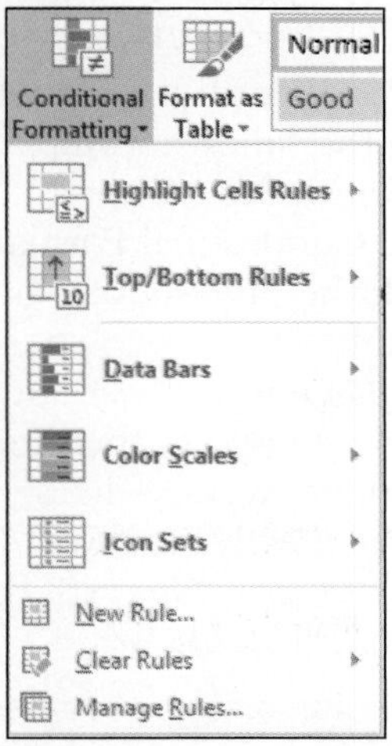

Project 1a Using Quick Analysis to Format Cells Based on a Value Comparison Part 1 of 2

1. Start Excel.
2. Open **VIVPay-Oct24.xlsx**. (This workbook is located in the EL2C1 folder you copied to your storage medium.)
3. Save the workbook and name it **EL2-C1-P1-VIVPay-Oct24**.
4. Apply conditional formatting to highlight overtime hours that exceeded five hours for the week by completing the following steps:
   a. Select K6:K23.
   b. Click the Quick Analysis button located at the bottom right of the selected cells.
   c. Click the Greater Than button on the FORMATTING tab.
   d. At the Greater Than dialog box, with the text already selected in the *Format cells that are GREATER THAN* text box, type 5.

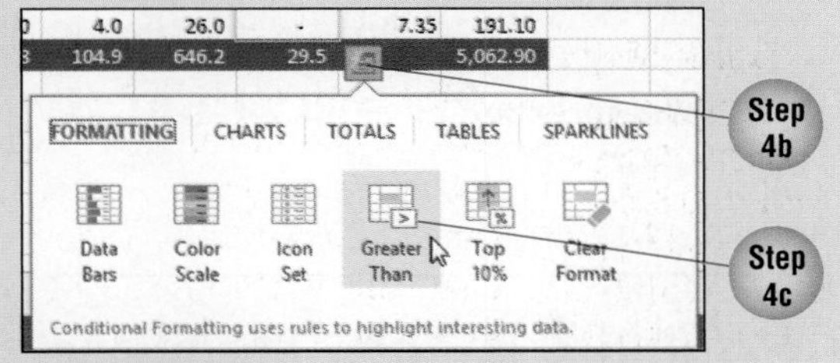

   e. Click the down-pointing arrow next to the option box to the right of *with* (which currently displays *Light Red Fill with Dark Red Text*) and then click *Red Text* at the drop-down list.

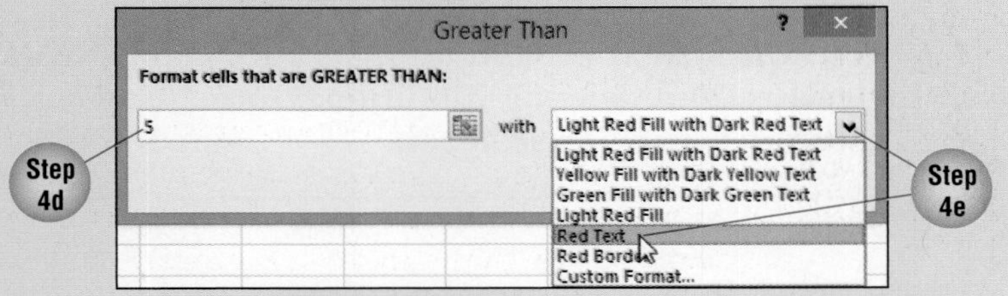

   f. Click OK to close the Greater Than dialog box.
   g. Click in any cell to deselect the range.
   h. Review the cells that have been conditionally formatted. Notice that cells with overtime hours greater than five hours are formatted with red text.
5. Save **EL2-C1-P1-VIVPay-Oct24.xlsx**.

Using the Top/Bottom Rules list, you can elect to highlight cells based on a top 10 or bottom 10 value or percentage, or by above average or below average values.

Project 1b Formatting Cells Based on Top/Bottom Rules

1. With **EL2-C1-P1-VIVPay-Oct24.xlsx** open, apply conditional formatting to the Gross Pay values to identify employees who earned above average wages for the week by completing the following steps:
   a. Select M6:M23.
   b. Click the Conditional Formatting button in the Styles group on the HOME tab.
   c. Point to *Top/Bottom Rules* and then click *Above Average* at the drop-down list.
   d. At the Above Average dialog box, with *Light Red Fill with Dark Red Text* selected in the *Format cells that are ABOVE AVERAGE* option box, click OK.

Step 1b

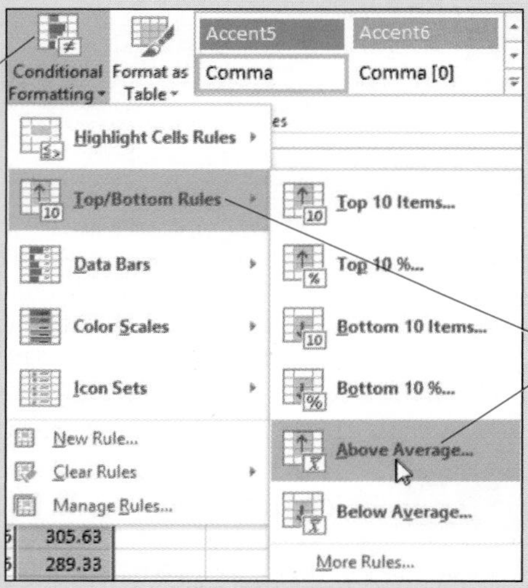

Step 1c

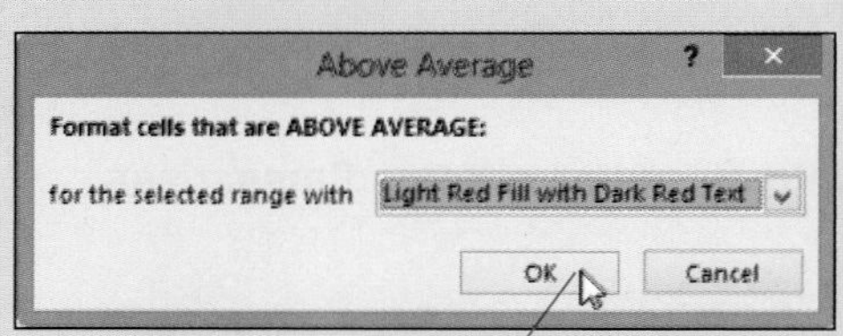

Step 1d

   e. Click in any cell to deselect the range.
   f. Review the cells that have been conditionally formatted.
2. Print the worksheet.
3. Save and then close **EL2-C1-P1-VIVPay-Oct24.xlsx**.

Project 2 Apply Conditional Formatting to Insurance Policy Data

4 Parts

You will format cells in an insurance claims worksheet by creating, editing, clearing, and deleting conditional formatting rules and by classifying data into categories using an icon set.

Creating a New Formatting Rule

HINT
You can create a rule to format cells based on cell values, specific text, dates, blanks, or error values.

Cells are conditionally formatted based on a rule. A rule defines the criterion by which cells are selected for formatting and includes the formatting attributes that are applied to cells that meet the criterion. The predefined rules that you used in Project 1a and Project 1b allowed you to use the feature without having to specify each component in a rule's parameters. At the New Formatting Rule dialog box, shown in Figure 1.3, you can create your own custom conditional formatting rule in which you define all parts of the criterion and the formatting. The *Edit the Rule Description* section of the dialog box varies depending on the active option in the *Select a Rule Type* section.

Figure 1.3 New Formatting Rule Dialog Box

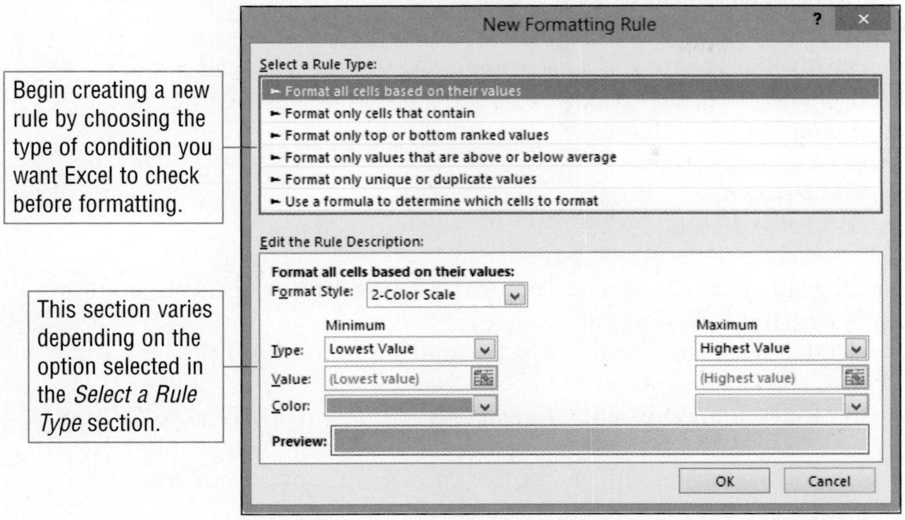

Quick Steps

Create and Apply a New Formatting Rule

1. Select desired range.
2. Click Conditional Formatting button.
3. Click *New Rule.*
4. Click desired rule type.
5. Add criteria as required.
6. Click Format button.
7. Select desired formatting attributes.
8. Click OK to close Format Cells dialog box.
9. Click OK to close New Formatting Rule dialog box.

Project 2a Creating and Applying New Formatting Rules

Part 1 of 4

1. Open **ACInsce.xlsx**.
2. Save the workbook and name it **EL2-C1-P2-ACInsce**.
3. The owner of AllClaims Insurance Brokers is considering changing the discount plan for those customers with no claims or with only one claim. The owner would like to see the two claim criteria formatted in color to provide a reference for how many customers this discount would affect. Create a formatting rule that changes the appearance of cells in the *Claims* column that contain *0* by completing the following steps:
   a. Select H4:H20.
   b. Click the Conditional Formatting button in the Styles group on the HOME tab.
   c. Click *New Rule* at the drop-down list.
   d. At the New Formatting Rule dialog box, click *Format only cells that contain* in the *Select a Rule Type* section.
   e. Click the down-pointing arrow at the right of the second option box from the left (which currently displays *between*) in the *Format only cells with* section and then click *equal to* at the drop-down list.

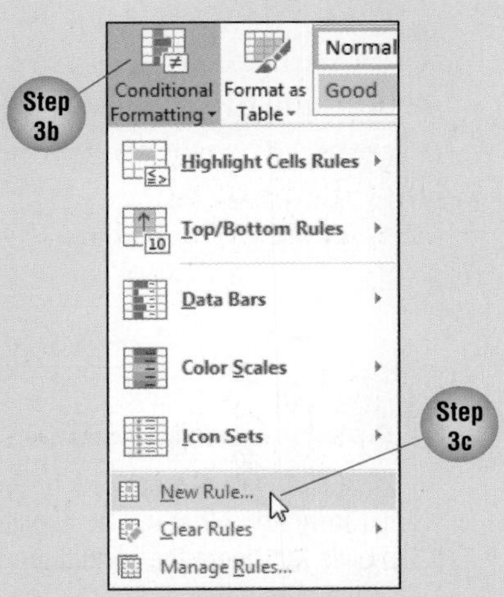

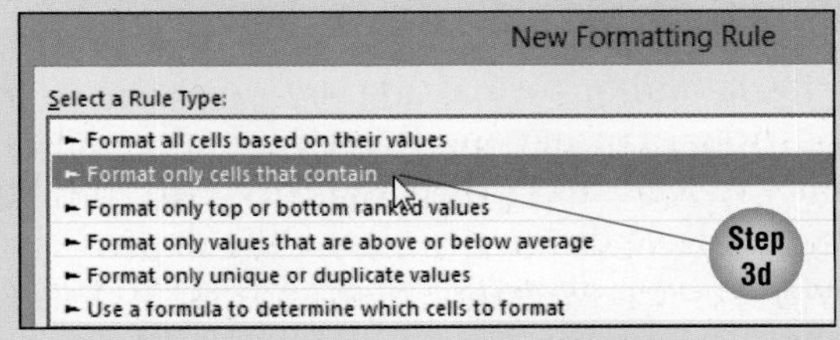

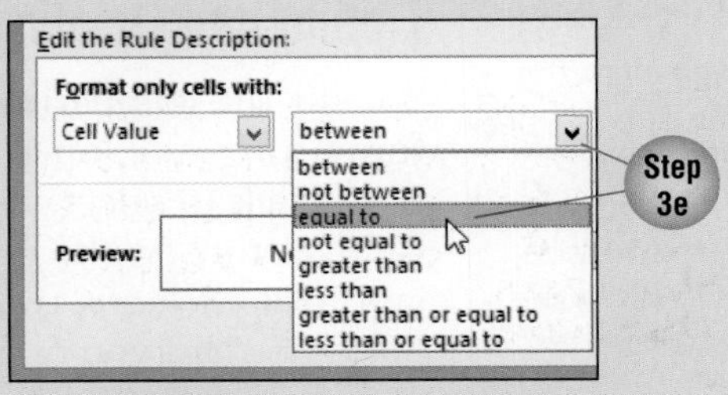

f. Click in the blank text box next to *equal to* and then type 0.

g. Click the Format button in the *Preview* section.

h. At the Format Cells dialog box with the Font tab selected, apply the Dark Red color (in the *Standard Colors* section), turn on bold formatting, and then click OK.

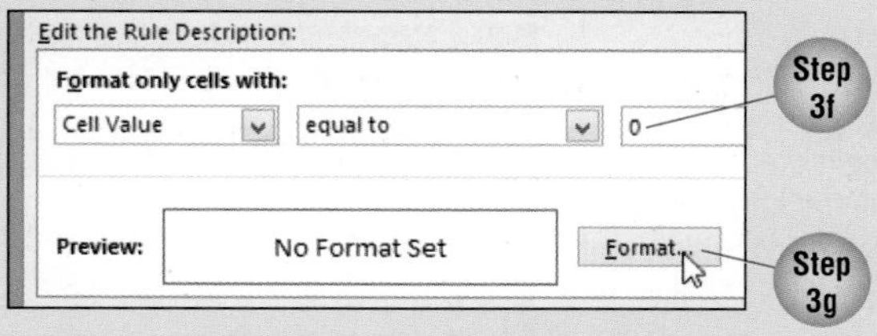

i. Click OK at the New Formatting Rule dialog box.

4. Create a second formatting rule that changes the appearance of cells in the *Claims* column that contain *1* by completing the following steps:
   a. With H4:H20 still selected, click the Conditional Formatting button and then click *New Rule*.
   b. At the New Formatting Rule dialog box, click *Format only cells that contain* in the *Select a Rule Type* section.
   c. Click the down-pointing arrow located at the right of the second option box from the left in the *Format only cells with* section (which currently displays *between*) and then click *equal to* at the drop-down list.
   d. Click in the blank text box next to *equal to* and then type 1.
   e. Click the Format button.
   f. At the Format Cells dialog box with the Font tab selected, apply the Blue color (in the *Standard Colors* section), turn on bold formatting, and then click OK.
   g. Click OK at the New Formatting Rule dialog box.
5. Click in any cell to deselect the range and review the conditionally formatted cells in column H.

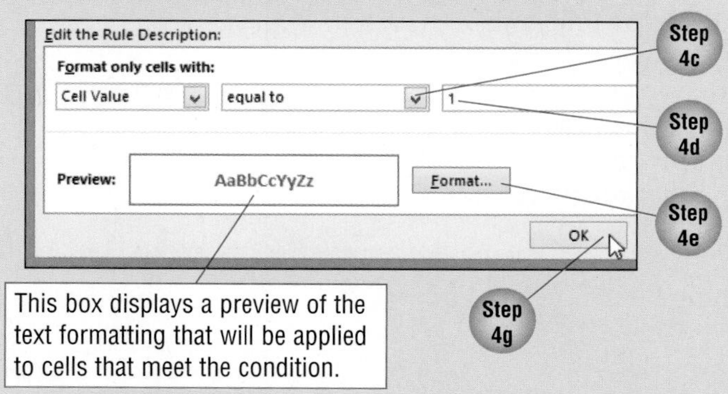

Rating	Claims
1	0
1	0
2	1
2	1
5	3
4	2
2	1
5	2
5	2
8	4
5	3
6	3
1	0
3	2
5	3
2	1
1	0

Step 5

Bold dark red formatting has been applied to cells containing *0* and bold blue formatting has been applied to cells containing *1*.

6. Save **EL2-C1-P2-ACInsce.xlsx**.

Quick Steps

Edit a Formatting Rule

1. Select range.
2. Click Conditional Formatting button.
3. Click *Manage Rules*.
4. Click desired rule.
5. Click Edit Rule button.
6. Make desired changes.
7. Click OK twice.

Editing and Deleting Conditional Formatting Rules

To edit the comparison rule criteria and/or formatting options for a conditional formatting rule, open the Conditional Formatting Rules Manager dialog box. Click to select the rule that you want to change and then click the Edit Rule button. At the Edit Formatting Rule dialog box, make the desired changes and then click OK twice. By default, *Show formatting rules for* is set to *Current Selection* when you open the Conditional Formatting Rules Manager dialog box. If necessary, click the down-pointing arrow at the right of the option box and then select *This Worksheet* to show all of the formatting rules in the current sheet.

To remove conditional formatting from a range, select the range, click the Quick Analysis button, and then click the Clear Format button, or click the Conditional Formatting button in the Styles group on the HOME tab, point to *Clear Rules* at the drop-down list, and then click either *Clear Rules from Selected Cells* or *Clear Rules from Entire Sheet*. You can also delete a custom rule at the Conditional Formatting Rules Manager dialog box. Formatting options applied to the cells by the rule that was deleted will be removed.

Quick Steps

Remove Conditional Formatting

1. Select range.
2. Click Quick Analysis button.
3. Click Clear Format button.

Project 2b Creating, Editing, and Deleting a Formatting Rule — Part 2 of 4

1. With **EL2-C1-P2-ACInsce.xlsx** open, create a new formatting rule to add a fill color to the cells in the *No. of Autos* column for those policies that have more than two cars by completing the following steps:
   a. Select C4:C20.
   b. Click the Conditional Formatting button and then click *New Rule* at the drop-down list.
   c. Click *Format only cells that contain* in the *Select a Rule Type* section of the New Formatting Rule dialog box.
   d. In the *Edit the Rule Description* section, change the rule's parameters to format only cells with a value greater than 2. (If necessary, refer to Project 2a, Steps 3e–3f, for assistance.)
   e. Click the Format button and then click the Fill tab at the Format Cells dialog box.
   f. Click the *Yellow* color (fourth from left in bottom row) in the *Background Color* palette and then click OK.
   g. Click OK to close the New Formatting Rule dialog box.
   h. Deselect the range by clicking any cell.

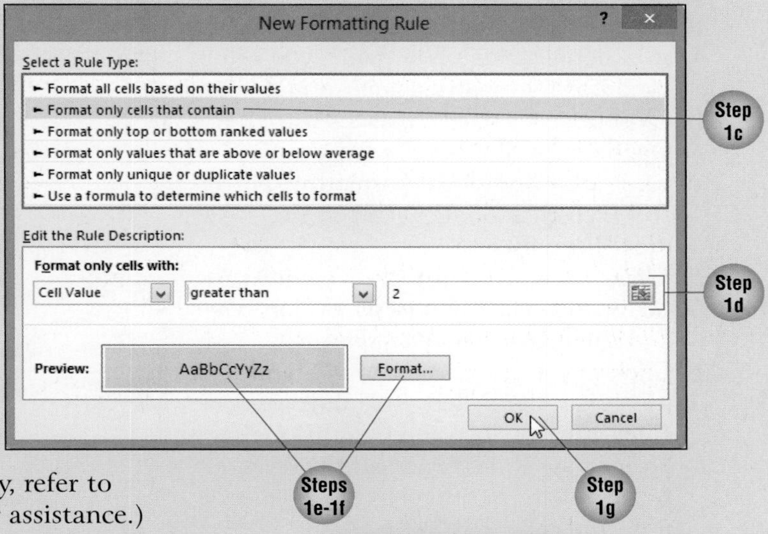

Customer ID	Policy ID	No. of Autos
C-025	6512485	2
C-055	6123584	1
C-072	6583157	2
C-085	6124893	3
C-094	3481274	1
C-114	4956875	2
C-124	3354867	1
C-131	6598642	3
C-148	4668457	3
C-155	8512475	4
C-168	6984563	2
C-171	4856972	1
C-184	5124876	1
C-190	6845962	1
C-199	8457326	1
C-201	4968532	2
C-212	2698715	2

Formatting has applied to cell values greater than 2.

2. After reviewing the formatted cells, you decide that cells should be formatted for all policies with 2 or more cars. Edit the formatting rule by completing the following steps:
   a. Select C4:C20.
   b. Click the Conditional Formatting button and then click *Manage Rules* at the drop-down list.
   c. Click to select *Cell Value > 2* in the Conditional Formatting Rules Manager dialog box and then click the Edit Rule button.

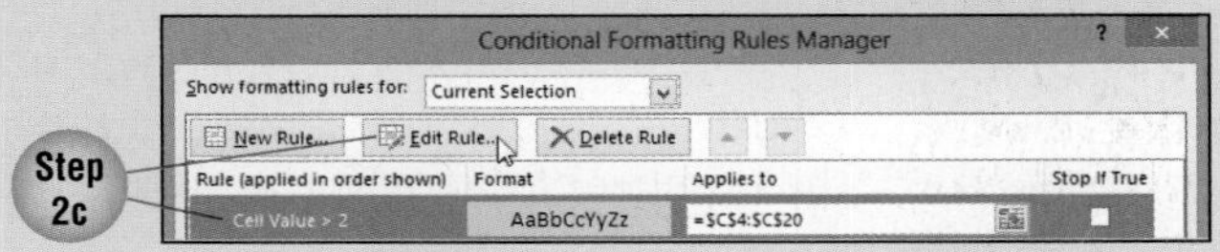

d. Click the down-pointing arrow next to the second option box from the left (which currently displays *greater than*) and then click *greater than or equal to* at the drop-down list.
e. Click OK.
f. Click OK to close the Conditional Formatting Rules Manager dialog box.
g. Deselect the range by clicking any cell.

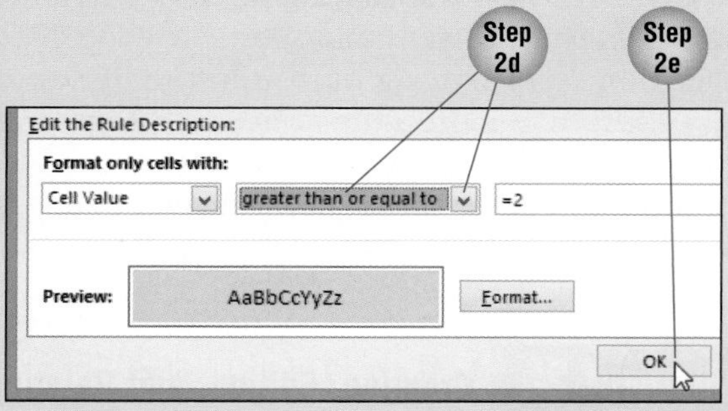

3. Save and print the worksheet.
4. After reviewing the printed copy of the formatted worksheet, you decide to experiment with another method of formatting the data that classifies the policies by the number of cars. You will do this in the next project. In preparation, save the revised worksheet under a new name and then delete the formatting rule in the original worksheet by completing the following steps:
   a. Save the workbook and name it **EL2-C1-P2-ACInsce-Autos2+**. By saving the workbook under a new name, you will be able to keep a copy of the workbook with the conditional formatting applied in this project.
   b. Close **EL2-C1-P2-ACInsce-Autos2+.xlsx**.
   c. Open **EL2-C1-P2-ACInsce.xlsx**.
   d. Click the Conditional Formatting button and then click *Manage Rules* at the drop-down list.
   e. Click the down-pointing arrow next to the *Show formatting rules for* option box and then click *This Worksheet*.
   f. Click to select *Cell Value >= 2* and then click the Delete Rule button.
   g. Click OK to close the Conditional Formatting Rules Manager dialog box. Notice the formatting has been removed from the cells in column C.

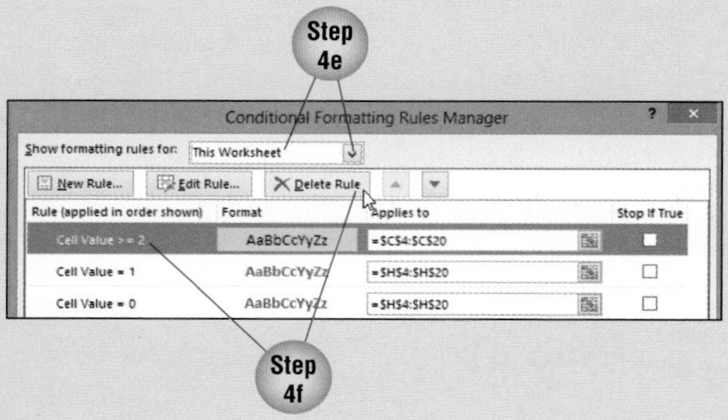

5. Save **EL2-C1-P2-ACInsce.xlsx**.

Applying Conditional Formatting Using an Icon Set

Green Up Arrow

Red Down Arrow

Yellow Sideways Arrow

Format a range of values using an icon set to classify data into three to five categories. Excel places an icon in a cell to visually portray the cell's value relative to the other cell values within the selected range. Using an icon set, you can group similar data to easily identify high points, low points, or other trends. Icons are assigned to cells based on default threshold values for the selected range. For example, if you choose the *3 Arrows (Colored)* icon set, icons are assigned as follows:

- Green up arrow for values greater than or equal to 67%
- Red down arrow for values less than 33%
- Yellow sideways arrow for values between 33% and 67%

The available icon sets, shown in Figure 1.4, are grouped into four sections: *Directional*, *Shapes*, *Indicators*, and *Ratings*. Choose the icon set that best represents the number of different categories within the range and desired symbol type, such as

Figure 1.4 Conditional Formatting Icon Sets Gallery

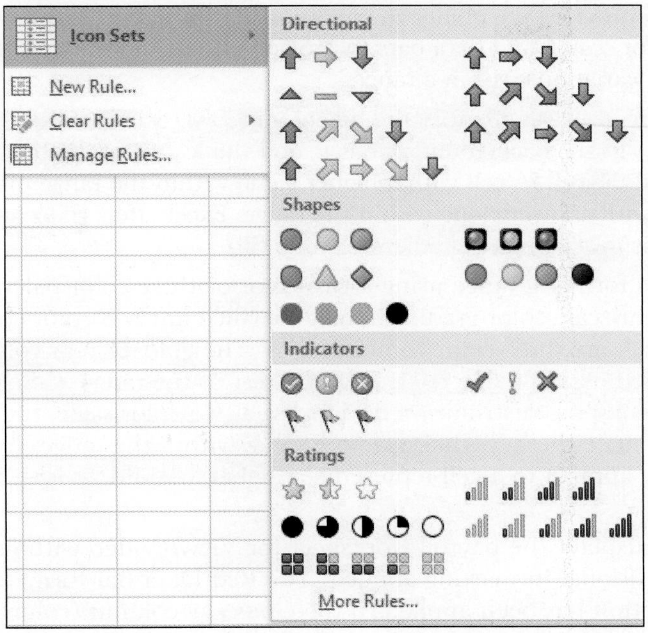

directional colored arrows, traffic light shapes, flag indicators, star ratings, and so on. You can modify the default threshold values or create your own icon set by opening the Manage Rules dialog box and editing an existing rule or creating a new rule.

Quick Steps

Apply Conditional Formatting Using an Icon Set

1. Select desired range.
2. Click Conditional Formatting button.
3. Point to *Icon Sets*.
4. Click desired icon set.
5. Deselect range.

Project 2c Applying Conditional Formatting Using an Icon Set

Part 3 of 4

1. With **EL2-C1-P2-ACInsce.xlsx** open, select C4:C20.
2. Use an icon set to classify the number of automobiles into categories by completing the following steps:
   a. Click the Conditional Formatting button.
   b. Point to *Icon Sets*.
   c. Click *Red To Black* at the Icon Sets drop-down gallery (third icon set in the left column of the *Shapes* section).

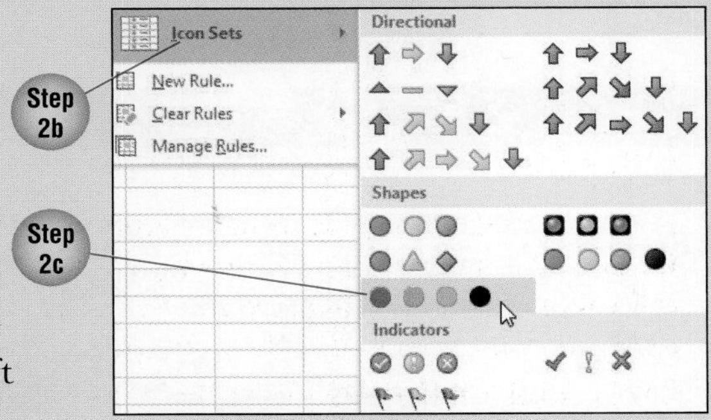

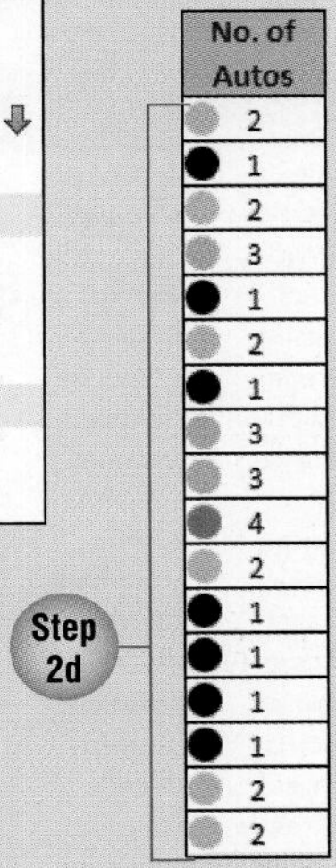

   d. Click in any cell to deselect the range. Notice that Excel assigns an icon to each cell, and that these icons correlate with the cell's value. For example, all cells containing the value *1* have the same icon, all cells containing the value *2* have the same icon, and so on.
3. Save **EL2-C1-P2-ACInsce.xlsx**.

Applying Conditional Formatting Using Data Bars and Color Scales

Excel 2013 also provides the ability to conditionally format cells using two-color scales, three-color scales, and data bars to provide visual guides for identifying distributions or variations within a range.

Use data bars to easily identify the higher and lower values within a range. A data bar appears in the background of a cell, and the length of the bar depends on the value within the cell. A cell with a higher value within the range displays a longer bar than a cell with a lower value within the range. Excel offers six colors for data bars and each color is available in a gradient or solid fill.

Color scales format a range using a two-color or three-color palette. Excel provides 12 color scale color gradients, half of which are two-color combinations and half of which are three-color combinations. The gradation of color applied to a cell illustrates the cell's value relative to the rest of the range. Color scales are useful for reviewing the distribution of data. In a two-color scale, the shade applied to a cell represents either a higher or lower value within the range. In a three-color scale, the shade applied to a cell represents a higher, middle, or lower value within the range.

HINT

Be careful not to use too many icon sets, color scales, and/or data bars. Readers can quickly lose focus when too many items compete for attention.

Figure 1.5 displays the payroll worksheet for ViewItVideo with data bar and color scale conditional formatting applied. The Red Data Bar format from the *Gradient Fill* section has been applied to the *Gross Pay* column (column M). Notice that the lengths of the colored bars in the cells reflect various gross pay amounts, with longer bars representing higher gross pay. In column J, *Total Hours*, the Red-White Color Scale color gradient has been applied to show the distribution of total hours. The cell with the highest value is displayed in red and as the values decrease, the cells become increasingly lighter colored. Notice that the cell with the lowest value is displayed in white.

Figure 1.5 Data Bar and Color Scale Conditional Formatting Applied to a Payroll Worksheet

	A	B	C	D	E	F	G	H	I	J	K	L	M
1						ViewItVideo							
2						Payroll							
3						Week Ended: October 24, 2015							
4													
5	First Name	Last Name	Sun	Mon	Tue	Wed	Thu	Fri	Sat	Total Hours	Overtime Hours	Pay Rate	Gross Pay
6	Alexis	Torres	-	5.0	7.0	8.0	8.0	9.0	9.5	46.5	6.5	7.75	385.56
7	Derrick	MacLean	8.0	-	6.5	8.0	8.0	8.5	9.0	48.0	8.0	7.35	382.20
8	Priya	Singh	8.0	-	4.0	8.0	8.0	8.5	6.5	43.0	3.0	7.35	327.08
9	Emil	Fedorov	8.0	8.0	8.0	5.5	8.0	-	8.0	45.5	5.5	7.75	373.94
10	Leslie	Sparling	-	6.0	7.5	8.0	8.0	-	8.0	37.5	-	8.15	305.63
11	Irene	O'Rourke	4.0	-	8.0	-	6.5	9.5	7.5	35.5	-	8.15	289.33
12	Ruthann	Goldstein	5.5	-	8.0	-	4.0	7.5	6.0	31.0	-	7.75	240.25
13	Stefan	Kominek	-	6.0	8.0	-	8.0	8.5	4.5	35.0	-	7.75	271.25
14	Alex	Spivak	-	5.0	8.0	8.5	7.5	8.0	8.0	45.0	5.0	7.75	368.13
15	Erica	Wilkins	-	7.0	-	6.0	-	6.0	6.4	25.4	-	7.35	186.69
16	Dana	Vanderhoek	8.0	7.0	-	8.0	-	5.5	5.0	33.5	-	7.35	246.23
17	Ashley	Castillo	4.0	8.0	-	7.5	8.0	4.0	8.5	40.0	-	8.15	326.00
18	Susan	Anez	-	3.0	5.5	-	-	7.0	7.0	22.5	-	8.15	183.38
19	Dana	Ivanowski	4.5	4.0	6.0	-	8.5	6.8	-	29.8	-	7.75	230.95
20	Maria	Alvarez	-	7.0	4.5	-	7.5	7.5	-	26.5	-	7.35	194.78
21	Xue	Chen	9.0	-	9.0	8.0	7.5	8.0	-	41.5	1.5	7.35	310.54
22	Annette	Fournier	8.0	-	-	6.5	5.0	7.5	7.0	34.0	-	7.35	249.90
23	Randy	Brown	6.5	-	-	5.5	4.0	6.0	4.0	26.0	-	7.35	191.10
24	TOTAL		73.5	66.0	90.0	87.5	106.5	117.8	104.9	646.2	29.5		5,062.90

Conditional formatting using the Red Data Bar format has been applied to the data in the *Gross Pay* column.

Conditional formatting using the Red - White Color Scale color gradient has been applied to the data in the *Total Hours* column.

Applying Conditional Formatting Using a Formula

Sometimes you may want to format a cell based on the value in another cell or using some logical test. At the New Formatting Rule dialog box, choose *Use a formula to determine which cells to format* in the *Select a Rule Type* section. You can enter a formula, such as an IF statement, that will be used to determine whether a cell will be formatted.

For example, in Project 2d, you will format the premium values in the insurance worksheet in column I based on the rating value for each policy that is stored in column G. In this project, using an IF statement allows you to conditionally format the premiums if the rating value for the policy is greater than 3. The IF function's logical test returns only a true or false result. The value in the rating cell is either greater than 3 (true) or it is not greater than 3 (false). Excel conditionally formats only those cells in the *Premium* column for which the conditional test returns a true result.

The formula that you will enter into the New Formatting Rule dialog box in Project 2d is *=if(g4:g20>3,true,false)*. Excel treats any formula entered for conditional formatting as an ***array formula***, which means you only need to add one rule for the range G4:G20. In the first cell in the selected range (cell I4), Excel will perform the following test: *Is the value in G4 greater than 3?* In the first row, this test returns a false result, so Excel will not conditionally format the value in cell I4. Excel will apply bold formatting and the Red font color to those cells in column I for which the test returns a true result based on the corresponding cell in column G.

Project 2d **Applying Conditional Formatting Using a Formula** **Part 4 of 4**

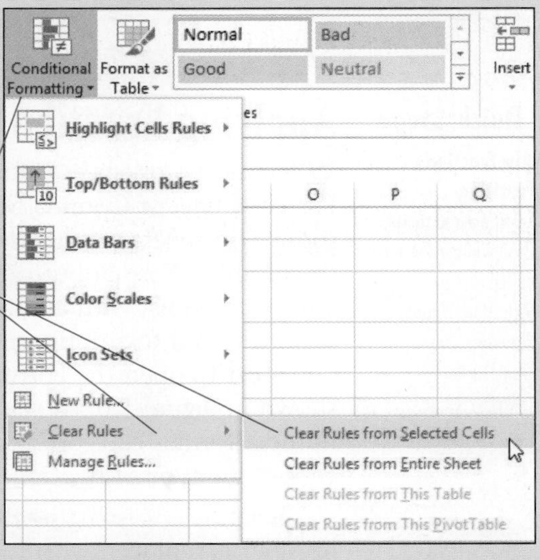

1. With **EL2-C1-P2-ACInsce.xlsx** open, clear the conditional formatting applied in the *Claims* column by completing the following steps:
   a. Select H4:H20.
   b. Click the Conditional Formatting button, point to *Clear Rules*, and then click *Clear Rules from Selected Cells*.
   c. Click in any cell to deselect the range.
2. The owner of AllClaims Insurance Brokers would like the premiums for those clients who have a rating higher than 3 to stand out. You decide to conditionally format the premiums in column I using a formula that checks the ratings in column G by completing the following steps:
   a. Select I4:I20 and then click the Conditional Formatting button.
   b. Click *New Rule* at the drop-down list.

c. At the New Formatting Rule dialog box, click *Use a formula to determine which cells to format* in the *Select a Rule Type* section.
d. Click in the *Format values where this formula is true* text box in the *Edit the Rule Description* section of the New Formatting Rule dialog box and then type =if(g4:g20>3,true,false).
e. Click the Format button.
f. At the Format Cells dialog box, click the Font tab and apply the Red font color (in the *Standard Colors* section), apply bold formatting, and then click OK.
g. Click OK to close the New Formatting Rule dialog box and apply the rule to the selected cells.
h. Click in any cell to deselect the range. Notice that the cells in column I that have bold formatting and the Red font color applied are those for which the corresponding rating value in column G is greater than 3.

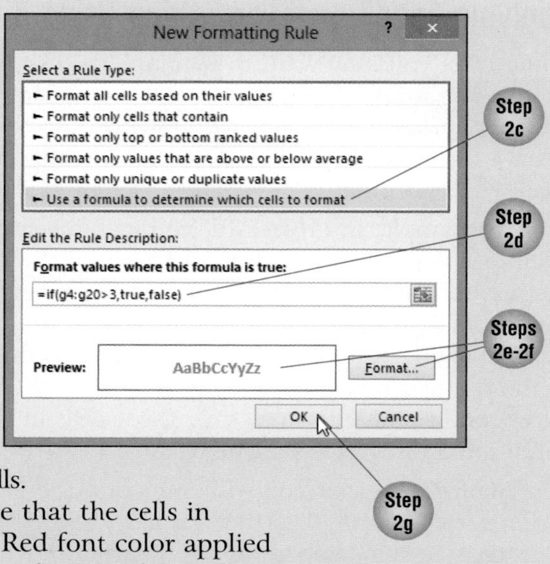

3. Save, print, and then close **EL2-C1-P2-ACInsce.xlsx**.

Project 3 Use Fraction and Scientific Formatting Options 1 Part

Using two lesson plan worksheets for a math tutor, you will format cells in a solution column to the appropriate format to display the answers for the tutor.

Quick Steps

Apply Fraction Formatting
1. Select desired range.
2. Click Number Format button arrow.
3. Click *More Number Formats*.
4. Click *Fraction* in *Category* list box.
5. Click desired option in *Type* list box.
6. Click OK.
7. Deselect range.

Apply Scientific Formatting
1. Select desired range.
2. Click Number Format button arrow.
3. Click *Scientific*.
4. Deselect range.

Applying Fraction and Scientific Formatting

While most worksheet values are formatted using the Accounting Number Format, Percent Style, or Comma Style buttons in the Number group on the HOME tab, some worksheets contain values that require other number formats. When clicked, the Number Format button arrow in the Number group on the HOME tab displays a drop-down list with additional format options, including date, time, fraction, scientific, and text options. Click *More Number Formats* at the Number Format drop-down list to open the Format Cells dialog box with the Number tab selected, as shown in Figure 1.6. At this dialog box, you can specify additional parameters for the number format categories. For example, with the *Fraction* category selected, you can choose the type of fraction you want displayed.

Scientific formatting converts a number to exponential notation. Part of the number is replaced with E+*n*, where *E* means "exponent" and *n* represents the power. For example, the number *1,500,000.00* formatted in scientific number format displays as *1.50E+06*. In this example, *+06* means "Add six zeros to the right of the number left of E and then move the decimal point six positions to the right." Scientists, mathematicians, engineers, and statisticians often use exponential notation to write very large numbers and very small numbers in a more manageable way.

Figure 1.6 Format Cells Dialog Box with the Number Tab Selected and *Fraction* Category Active

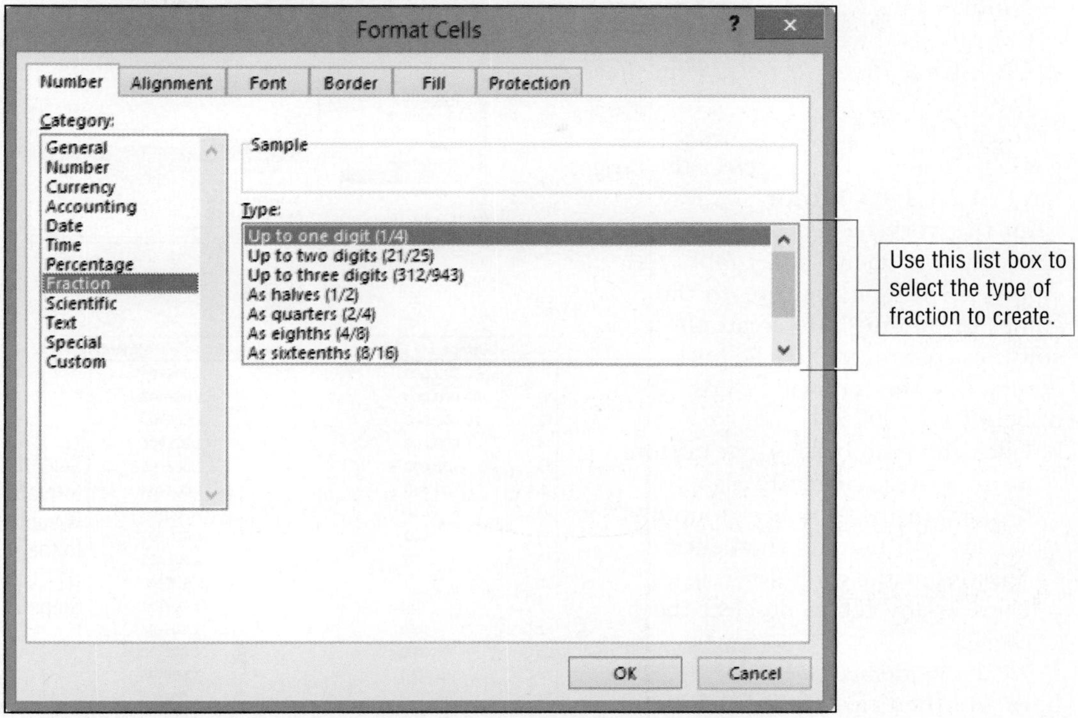

Project 3 Applying Fraction and Scientific Formatting

Part 1 of 1

1. Open **JTutor.xlsx**.
2. Save the workbook and name it **EL2-C1-P3-JTutor**.
3. Make Fractions the active worksheet by clicking the Fractions sheet tab located at the bottom of the worksheet area just above the Status bar.
4. Apply fraction formatting to the values in column D to create the solution column for the tutor, Janelle, by completing the following steps:
   a. Select D11:D20.
   b. Click the Number Format button arrow (which currently displays *General*) in the Number group on the HOME tab.
   c. Click *More Number Formats* at the drop-down list.

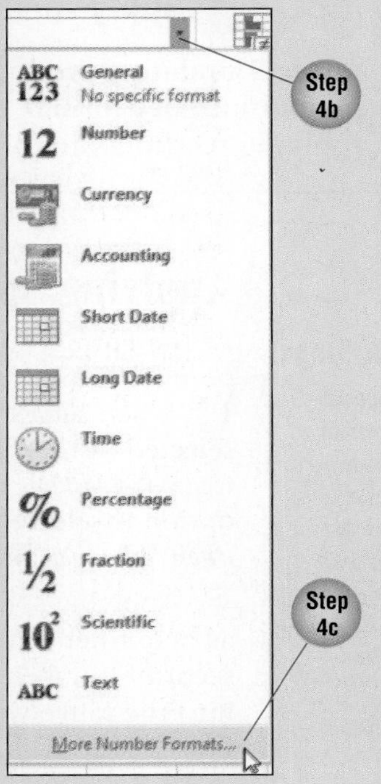

d. At the Format Cells dialog box with the Number tab selected, click *Fraction* in the *Category* list box.
e. Click *Up to two digits (21/25)* in the *Type* list box.
f. Click OK.
g. Click in any cell to deselect the range.
5. Save **EL2-C1-P3-JTutor**.
6. Print the worksheet.
7. Click the Exponents sheet tab.
8. Apply scientific formatting to the values in column D to create the solution column for Janelle by completing the following steps:
a. Select D11:D25.
b. Click the Number Format button arrow (which currently displays *Custom*) in the Number group on the HOME tab and then click *Scientific* at the drop-down list.
c. Click in any cell to deselect the range.
8. Print the worksheet.
9. Save and then close **EL2-C1-P3-JTutor.xlsx**.

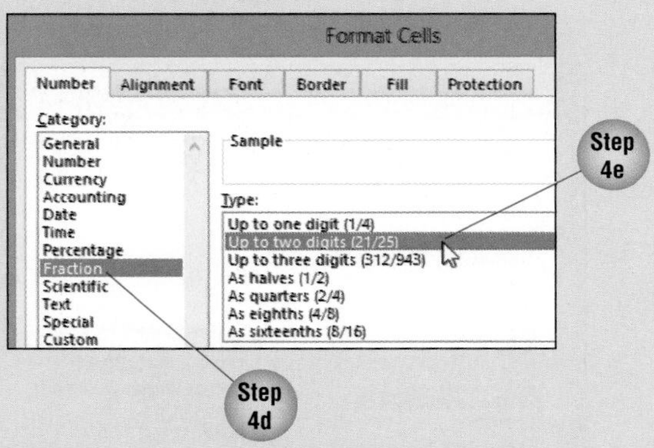

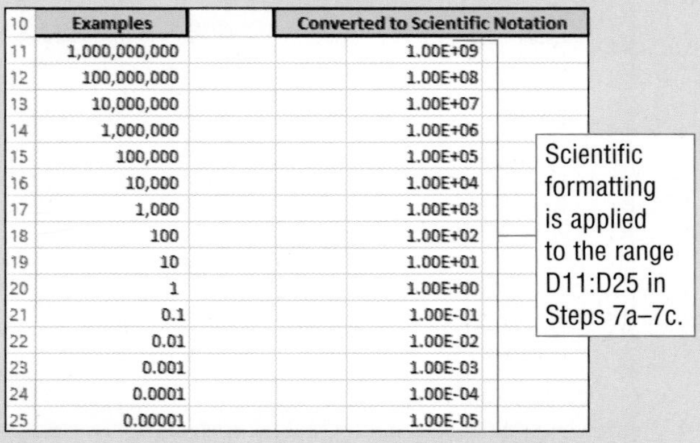

Project 4 Apply Advanced Formatting Options — 3 Parts

You will update a product worksheet by formatting telephone numbers, creating a custom number format to add descriptive characters before and after a value, and applying text alignment options for long labels.

Applying Special Number Formats

Quick Steps
Apply a Special Number Format
1. Select desired range.
2. Click Number group dialog box launcher.
3. Click *Special* in *Category* list box.
4. Click desired option in *Type* list box.
5. Click OK.
6. Deselect range.

At the Format Cells dialog box with the Number tab active, Excel provides special number formats that are specific to a country and language. As shown in Figure 1.7, when *Special* is selected in the *Category* list box and *English (United States)* is selected in the *Locale (location)* option box, the *Type* list box includes *Zip Code, Zip Code + 4, Phone Number,* and *Social Security Number*. When the *English (Canadian)* option is selected in the *Locale (location)* option box, the *Type* list box includes *Phone Number* and *Social Insurance Number*.

Applying special number formatting can save you time and keystrokes, as well as help to ensure consistent formatting. For example, if you apply special social security number formatting to a range, you can type the social security numbers into the range without hyphens and Excel will add the hyphens for you. Typing 000223456 will enter 000-22-3456 in the cell with special formatting applied.

Figure 1.7 Format Cells Dialog Box with the Number Tab Selected and the *Special* Category Active

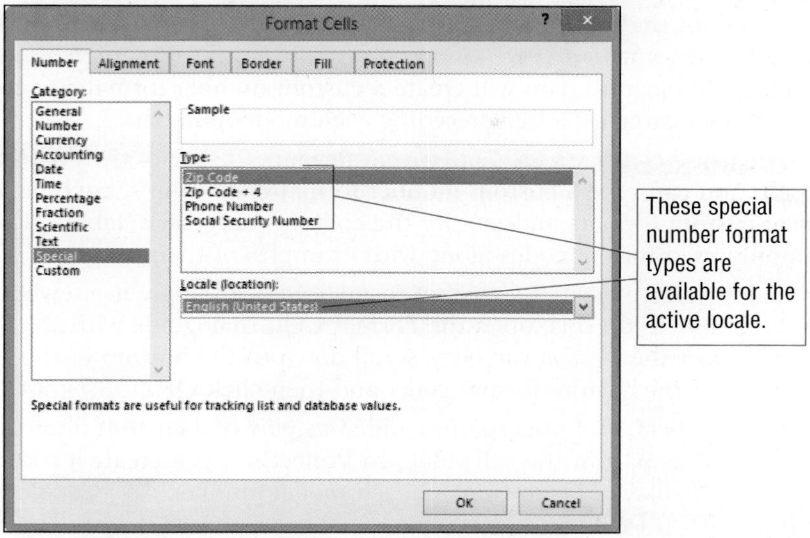

Project 4a Applying Special Formatting

Part 1 of 3

1. Open **Precision.xlsx**.
2. Save the workbook and name it **EL2-C1-P4-Precision**.
3. Format the range that will contain telephone numbers to include brackets around the area code and a hyphen between the first three and last four digits of the number by completing the following steps:
   a. Select C15:C20.
   b. Click the Number group dialog box launcher located at the bottom right of the Number group on the HOME tab.
   c. At the Format Cells dialog box with the Number tab selected, click *Special* in the *Category* list box.
   d. Click *Phone Number* in the *Type* list box and make sure the *Locale (location)* option box is set to *English (United States)*.
   e. Click OK.
   f. Click in cell C15 to deselect the range and make the first cell to contain a telephone number the active cell.

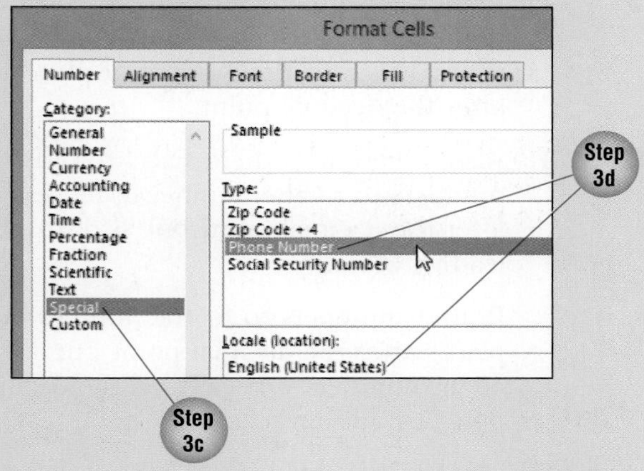

4. Type the telephone numbers for the sales representatives as follows:
   C15: 8005553429
   C16: 8005553439
   C17: 8005553449
   C18: 8005553459
   C19: 8005553469
   C20: 8005553479

5. Save **EL2-C1-P4-Precision.xlsx**.

Quick Steps

Create a Custom Number Format

1. Select desired range.
2. Click Number group dialog box launcher.
3. Click *Custom* in *Category* list box.
4. Select *General* in *Type* text box.
5. Press Delete.
6. Type desired custom format codes.
7. Click OK.
8. Deselect range.

HINT

Custom number formats are stored in the workbook in which they are created.

Creating Custom Number Formats

You can create a custom number format for a worksheet into which you want to enter values that do not conform to predefined number formats or for values for which you want to add punctuation, text, or formatting, such as color. For example, in Project 4b, you will create a custom number format to automatically add a product category letter preceding each model number.

Formatting codes are used in custom formats to specify the type of formatting to apply. You can type a custom number format code from scratch or select from a list of custom formats and modify the codes as necessary. Table 1.1 displays commonly used format codes along with examples of their usage.

Once you have created a custom format, you can apply it elsewhere within the workbook. To do this, open the Format Cells dialog box with the Number tab selected, select the *Custom* category, scroll down to the bottom of the *Type* list box, click to select the custom format code, and then click OK.

Text, numbers, and punctuation added as part of a custom number format are not saved as part of the cell value. In Project 4b, you create a custom number format that displays *PD-* in front of each model number. The value in cell A5 displays as *PD-1140*, but *1140* is the actual value that is stored. This is important to remember when you search for or filter data.

Table 1.1 Custom Number Format Code Examples

Format Code	Description	Custom Number Format Example	Display Result
#	Represents a digit; type one for each number. Excel rounds numbers if necessary to fit the number of places after the decimal point.	####.###	Typing *145.0068* displays *145.007*.
0	Also represents a digit. Excel rounds numbers to fit the number of places after the decimal point but also fills in leading zeros.	000.00	Typing *50.45* displays *050.45*.
?	Rounds numbers to fit the number of places after the decimal point but also aligns numbers vertically on the decimal point by adding spaces.	???.???	Typing *123.5*, *.8*, and *55.356* one below the other in a column aligns the numbers vertically on the decimal point.
"text"	Adds the characters between the quotation marks to the entry.	"Model No." ##	Typing *58* displays *Model No. 58*.
[color]	Applies the font color specified in square brackets to the cell entry.	[Blue]##.##	Typing *55.346* displays *55.35*.
;	Separates the positive value format from the negative value format.	[Blue];[Red]	Typing *25* displays as *25* and typing *-25* displays as *25*.

Project 4b Creating a Custom Number Format

Part 2 of 3

1. With **EL2-C1-P4-Precision.xlsx** open, select A5:A12.
2. Create a custom number format to insert *PD-* in front of each model number by completing the following steps:
   a. Click the Number group dialog box launcher located at the bottom right of the Number group on the HOME tab.
   b. Click *Custom* in the *Category* list box in the Format Cells dialog box with the Number tab selected.
   c. Scroll down the list of custom formats in the *Type* list box, noticing the various combinations of format codes for numbers, dates, and times.
   d. Select *General* in the *Type* text box, press Delete, and then type "PD-"####.
   e. Click OK.
   f. With A5:A12 still selected, click the Center button in the Alignment group on the HOME tab.
   g. Deselect the range.

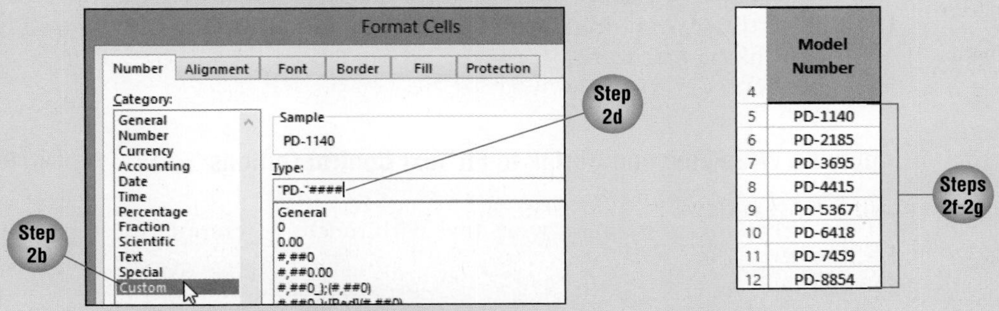

3. Create a custom number format to insert *lbs* after the weights in columns D and E by completing the following steps:
   a. Select D5:E12.
   b. Click the Number group dialog box launcher.
   c. Click *Custom* in the *Category* list box.
   d. Select *General* in the *Type* text box, press Delete, and then type ### "lbs". Make sure to include one space after ###.
   e. Click OK.
   f. Deselect the range.

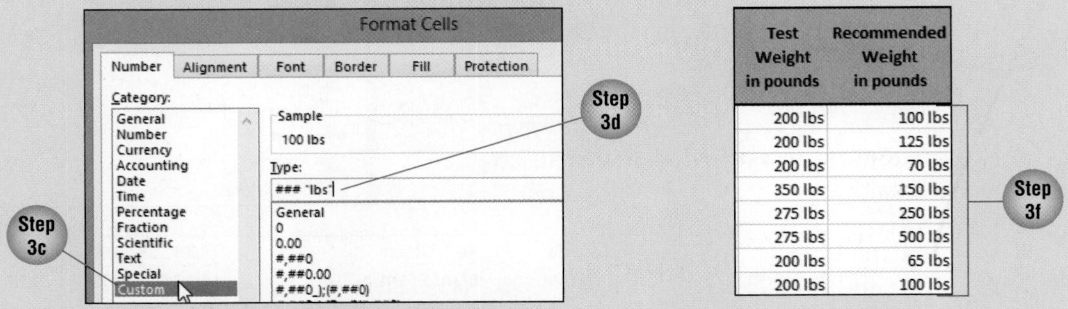

4. Save **EL2-C1-P4-Precision.xlsx**.

To delete a custom number format, open the workbook in which you created the custom format code, open the Format Cells dialog box with the Number tab selected, click *Custom* in the *Category* list box, scroll down the list of custom formats in the *Type* list box to the bottom of the list, click the custom format code that you created, and then click the Delete button. Deleting the formatting code also removes the custom formatting from any cells to which it was applied.

Quick Steps

Wrap Text in a Cell
1. Select desired cell(s).
2. Click Wrap Text button.
3. Deselect cell(s).

Shrink Text to Fit within a Cell
1. Select desired cell(s).
2. Click Aligment group dialog box launcher.
3. Click *Shrink to fit* in *Text control* section.
4. Click OK.
5. Deselect cell(s).

Wrap Text

Wrapping Text and Shrinking Text to Fit within Cells

You have several options for formatting long labels that do not fit within the column width. You can expand column width, reduce the font to a smaller size, merge a group of cells, or allow the text to spill over into adjacent unused columns. Additional options available in the *Text Control* section of the Format Cells dialog box with the Alignment tab selected include *Wrap text* and *Shrink to fit*. Text wrapping within a cell causes the row height to automatically increase to accommodate the number of lines needed. Alternatively, shrinking the text to fit within the cell causes the font size to automatically scale down to the size required to fit all of the text on one line. Consider widening the column before wrapping text or shrinking text to fit.

Project 4c **Applying Wrap Text and Shrink to Fit Text Control Options** **Part 3 of 3**

1. With **EL2-C1-P4-Precision.xlsx** open, wrap text within cells by completing the following steps:
   a. Select B22:B23.
   b. Click the Wrap Text button in the Alignment group on the HOME tab.
2. You decide to try the *Shrink to Fit* option on the same cells to see if a better result is produced. Press Ctrl + Z or click the Undo button on the Quick Access toolbar to restore the cells back to their original state.
3. Shrink the text to fit within the cells by completing the following steps:
   a. With B22:B23 still selected, click the Alignment group dialog box launcher located in the bottom right corner of the Alignment group on the HOME tab.
   b. At the Format Cells dialog box with the Alignment tab selected, click the *Shrink to fit* check box in the *Text control* section to insert a check mark.
   c. Click OK.
   d. Deselect the range.
4. Save, print, and then close **EL2-C1-P4-Precision.xlsx**.

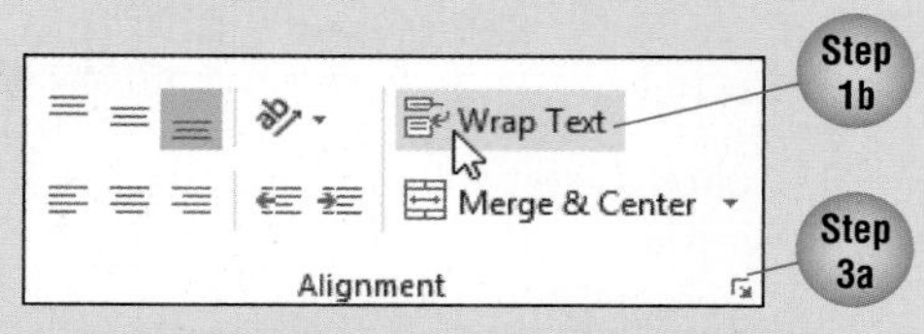

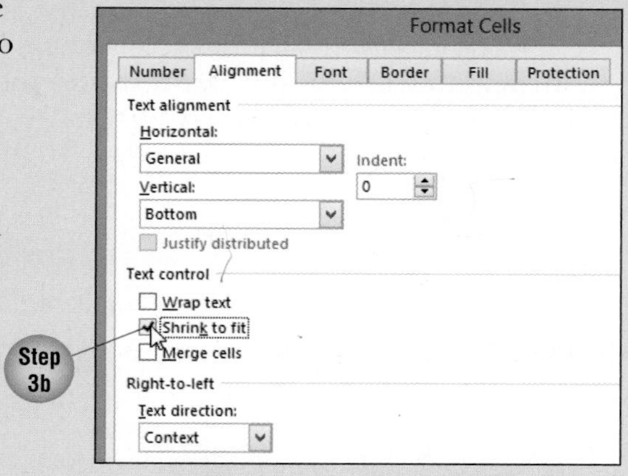

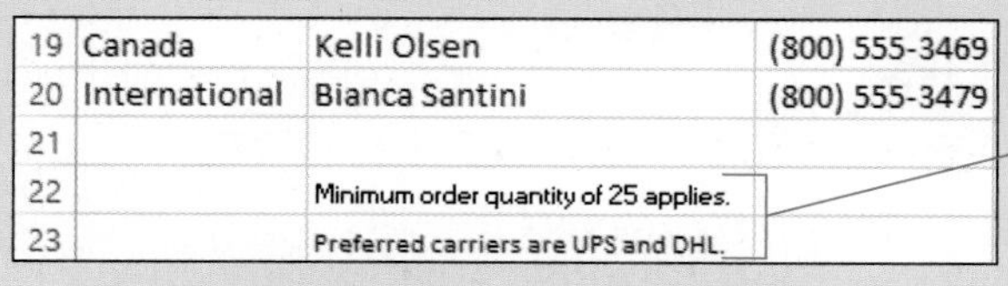

The *Shrink to fit* option is applied to B22:B23 in Steps 3b–3c.

Project 5 Convert Text Using Text Functions **2 Parts**

You will use text functions to modify a heading, convert state names to uppercase, and extract data.

Using Text Functions

Text can be formatted or modified using text functions. You can insert a text function by typing it or by clicking the Text button in the Functions group on the FORMULAS tab and then selecting a function from the drop-down list. For example, you can use the LOWER and UPPER functions to covert text from uppercase to lowercase and vice versa. Text that has incorrect capitalization can be changed to initial case using the PROPER function. New text can be substituted for existing text using the SUBSTITUTE function.

When you want to copy some of the characters in a cell, you can use text functions to extract the data. Text can be extracted from the rightmost, leftmost, or middle of a string of characters using the RIGHT, LEFT, or MID functions. These three functions, along with the TRIM function that removes extra spaces between characters, also can be used on data that has been imported or copied from another source. Table 1.2 provides more information about each text function.

Quick Steps

Use the SUBSTITUTE Function
1. Make desired cell active.
2. Type **=substitute(**.
3. Type source text cell address.
4. Type **,**.
5. Type text to be changed within quotation marks.
6. Type **,**.
7. Type replacement text within quotation marks.
8. Type **)**.
9. Press Enter.

Use the UPPER Function
1. Make desired cell active.
2. Type **=upper(**.
3. Type source cell address.
   OR
   Type text to convert within quotation marks.
4. Type **)**.
5. Press Enter.

Text

Table 1.2 Text Function Examples

Text Function	*Description*	*Example*
=PROPER(text)	Capitalizes the first letter of each word.	=PROPER("annual budget") returns *Annual Budget* in formula cell OR A3 holds the text *annual budget*; =PROPER(A3) entered in C3 causes C3 to display *Annual Budget*
=UPPER(text)	Converts text to uppercase.	=UPPER("annual budget") returns *ANNUAL BUDGET* in formula cell OR A3 holds the text *annual budget*; =UPPER(A3) entered in C3 causes C3 to display *ANNUAL BUDGET*
=LOWER(text)	Converts text to lowercase.	=LOWER("ANNUAL BUDGET") returns *annual budget* in formula cell OR A3 holds the text *ANNUAL BUDGET*; =LOWER(A3) entered in C3 causes C3 to display *annual budget*
=SUBSTITUTE(text)	Inserts new text in place of old text.	A3 holds the text *Annual Budget*; =SUBSTITUTE(A3,"Annual","2015") entered in C3 causes C3 to display *2015 Budget*

continues

Table 1.2 Text Function Examples—*Continued*

Text Function	*Description*	*Example*
=RIGHT(text,num_chars)	Extracts the requested number of characters, starting at the rightmost character.	=RIGHT("2015 Annual Budget",13) returns *Annual Budget* in formula cell OR A3 holds the text *2015 Annual Budget*; =RIGHT(C3,13) entered in C3 causes C3 to display *Annual Budget*
=LEFT(text,num_chars)	Extracts the requested number of characters, starting at the leftmost character.	=LEFT("2015 Annual Budget",4) returns *2015* in formula cell OR A3 holds the text *2015 Annual Budget*; =LEFT(C3,4) entered in C3 causes C3 to display *2015*
=MID(text,start-num, num-chars)	Extracts the requested number of characters, starting at a given position.	=MID("2015 Annual Budget",6,13) returns *Annual Budget* in formula cell OR A3 holds the text *2015 Annual Budget*; =MID(C3,6,13) entered in C3 causes C3 to display *Annual Budget*
=TRIM(text)	Removes extra spaces between words.	=TRIM("2015 Annual Budget") returns 2015 *Annual Budget* in formula cell OR A3 holds the text *2015 Annual Budget*; =TRIM(C3) entered in C3 causes C3 to display *2015 Annual Budget*

Project 5a Converting Text Using SUBSTITUTE, LOWER, and UPPER Text Functions Part 1 of 2

1. Open **USIncomeStats.xlsx**.
2. Save the workbook and name it **EL2-C1-P5-USIncomeStats**.
3. The worksheet contains 2011 median income data downloaded from the US Census Bureau. You want to estimate 2015 median income using a formula based on 2011 statistics. To begin, copy and substitute text at the top of the worksheet to create the layout for 2015 data by completing the following steps:
   a. Copy cell A1 and then click cell F1. Click the Paste Options button and then click the Keep Source Column Widths button in the *Paste* section of the drop-down gallery.

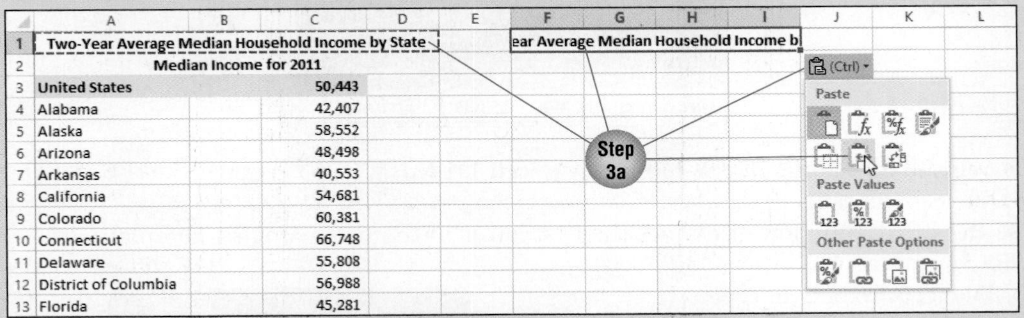

   b. Press Esc to remove the scrolling marquee from cell A1.
   c. Make cell F2 active, type =substitute(a2,"2011","2015"), and then press Enter.

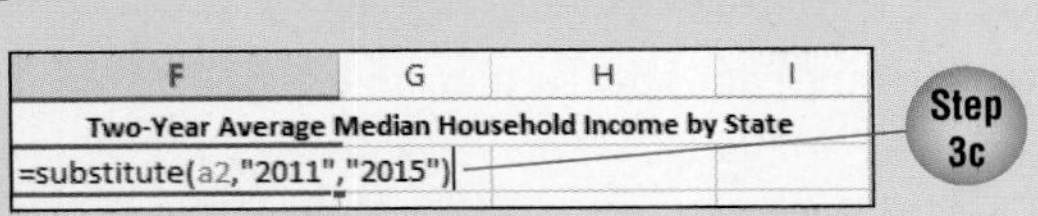

   d. Merge and center cell F2 across F2:I2 and apply bold formatting.
4. Copy cell A3 and the state names below cell A3 from column A to column F and convert the text to uppercase by completing the following steps:
   a. Make cell F3 active.
   b. Type =lower(a3) and then press Enter. Excel returns the text *united states* in cell F3. Press Ctrl + Z or click the Undo button the Quick Access toolbar to reverse this action.
   c. Type =upper(a3) and then press Enter. Excel returns the text *UNITED STATES*.

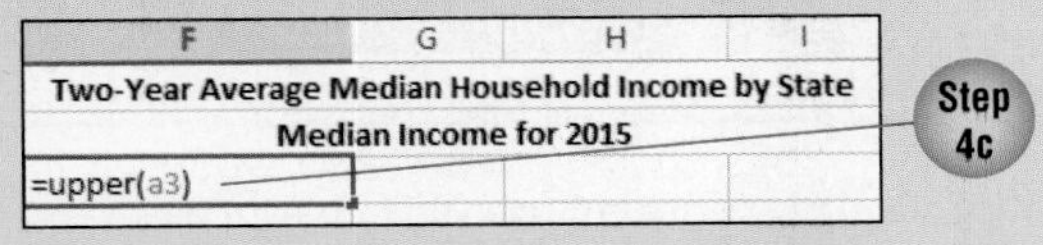

   d. Make cell F3 active and then drag the fill handle down to cell F54.
5. Enter the formula to estimate 2015 median income based on 2011 data plus 7.3% by completing the following steps:
   a. Make cell H3 active, type =c3+(c3*7.3%), and then press Enter.
   b. Select cell H3 and apply comma formatting with no places after the decimal point.
   c. Drag the fill handle in cell H3 down to cell H54.
   d. Deselect the range.
6. Select F3:H3, apply bold formatting, and then apply the Orange, Accent 6, Lighter 80% fill color (last option in second row of *Theme Colors* section). Deselect the range.
7. Save, print, and then close **EL2-C1-P5-USIncomeStats.xlsx**.

Project 5b Extracting Text Using RIGHT, LEFT, MID and TRIM Functions

1. Open **VIVCodes.xlsx**.
2. Save the workbook as **EL2-C1-P5-VivCodes**.
3. The IT director wants to create new computer user names by extracting different parts of the employees' personal information. A workbook has been created from various sources with the employees' first names, last names, and social security numbers (SSN). The director notices that the SSNs include extra spaces. Use the TRIM function to remove the extra spaces between the characters by completing the following steps:
   a. Make cell D6 active, type =trim(c6), and then press Enter.

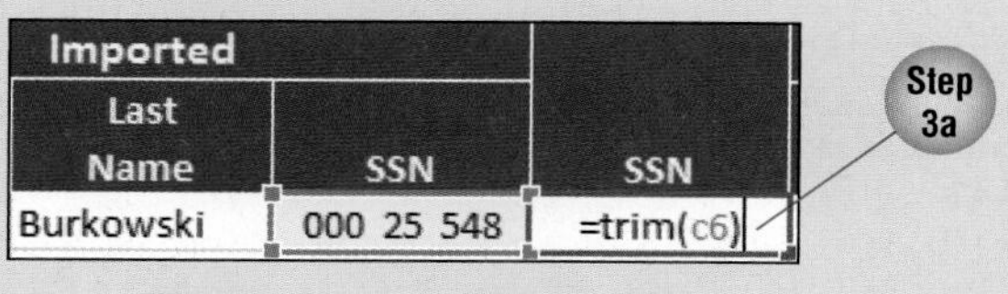

   b. Drag the fill handle in cell D6 down to cell D14.
   c. Deselect the range.
4. Use the LEFT function to extract the first letter of the first name by completing the following steps:
   a. Make cell E6 active, type =left(a6,1), and then press Enter.
   b. Drag the fill handle in cell E6 down to cell E14.
   c. Deselect the range.

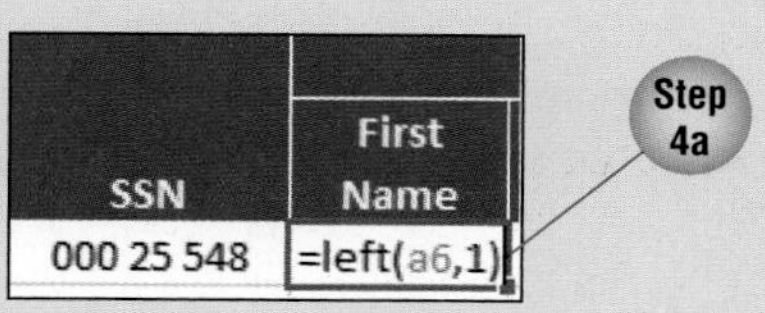

5. Use the LEFT function to extract the first four letters of the last name by completing the following steps:
   a. Make cell F6 active, type =left(b6,4), and then press Enter.
   b. Drag the fill handle in cell F6 down to cell F14.
   c. Deselect the range.
6. Extract the middle two digits of the SSN using the MID function by completing the following steps:
   a. Make cell G6 active, type =mid(d6,5,2), and then press Enter.

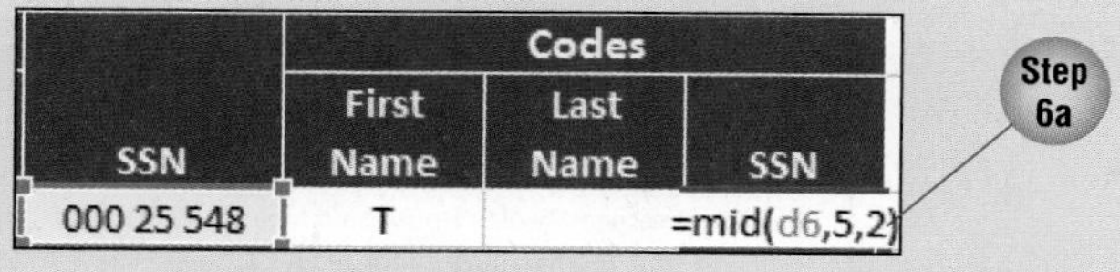

   b. Drag the fill handle in cell G6 down to cell G14.
   c. Deselect the range.
7. Use the RIGHT function to extract the date from the end of the text string in cell A2 by completing the following steps.
   a. Make cell B16 active, type =right(a2,10), and then press Enter.
   b. Deselect the range.
8. Save, print, and then close **EL2-C1-P5-VivCodes.xlsx**.

Project 6 Filter and Sort Data Based on Values, Icon Set, and Font Color

4 Parts

You will filter an insurance policy worksheet to show policies based on a range of liability limits and by number of claims, filter policies based on the number of automobiles, and filter and sort a payroll worksheet by font and cell colors.

Filtering a Worksheet Using a Custom AutoFilter

The Custom AutoFilter feature is used to display only the rows that meet specific criteria defined using the filter arrow at the top of each column. Rows that do not meet the criteria are temporarily hidden from view. At the top of each column in the selected range or table, you can click a filter arrow to display a drop-down list containing each unique field value that exists within the column. Display the Custom AutoFilter dialog box, shown in Figure 1.8, in a worksheet where you want to filter values by more than one criterion using a comparison operator. You can use the ? and * wildcard characters in a custom filter. For example, you can filter a list of products by a product number beginning with P by using *P** as the criteria.

To display the Custom AutoFilter dialog box, select the range to filter and then click the Sort & Filter button in the Editing group. Click *Filter* at the drop-down list and then deselect the range. Click the filter arrow in the column that contains the criteria. Point to *Number Filters* or *Text Filters* and then choose one of the options at the drop-down list. The type of filter and options available depend on the type of data in the column—for example, text or numbers.

Quick Steps

Filter Using a Custom AutoFilter

1. Select range.
2. Click Sort & Filter button.
3. Click *Filter*.
4. Deselect range.
5. Click filter arrow at top of desired column.
6. Point to *Number Filters*.
7. Click desired filter category.
8. Enter criteria at Custom AutoFilter dialog box.
9. Click OK.

Sort & Filter

Figure 1.8 Custom AutoFilter Dialog Box

Use the Custom AutoFilter dialog box to specify two criteria by which to filter using either an *And* or *Or* statement.

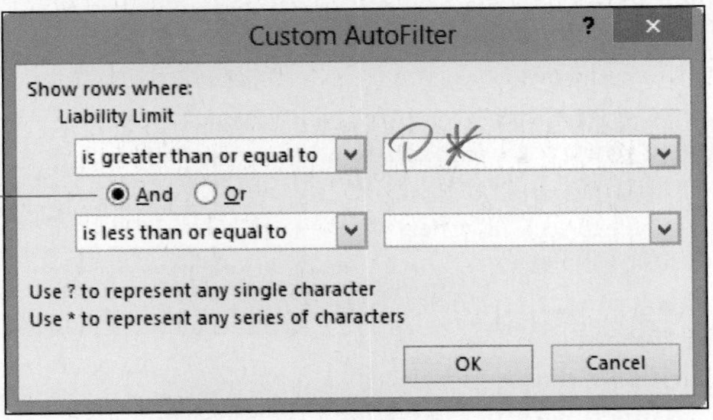

Project 6a Filtering Policy Information

1. Open **ACInsce.xlsx**.
2. Save the workbook and name it **EL2-C1-P6-ACInsce**.
3. The owner of AllClaims Insurance Brokers wants to review policies with liability limits from $500,000 to $1,000,000 that have more than one claim to determine if customers should increase their coverage. Filter the policy information to produce the list of policies that meet the owner's request by completing the following steps:
   a. Select A3:I20.
   b. Click the Sort & Filter button in the Editing group on the HOME tab.
   c. Click *Filter* at the drop-down list. A filter arrow displays at the top of each column.

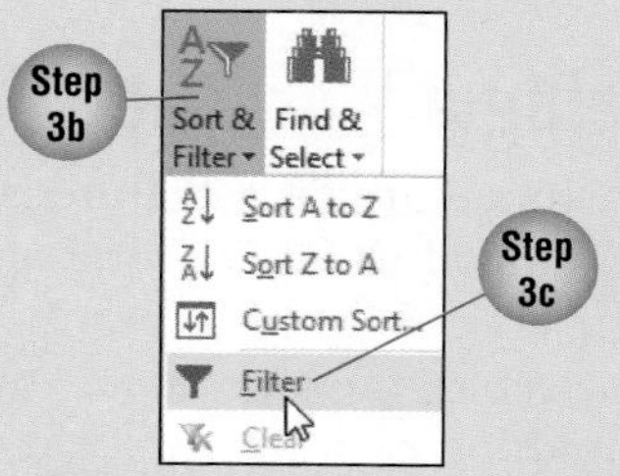

   d. Deselect the range.
   e. Click the filter arrow next to *Liability Limit* in cell E3.
   f. Point to *Number Filters* and then click *Between* at the drop-down list.

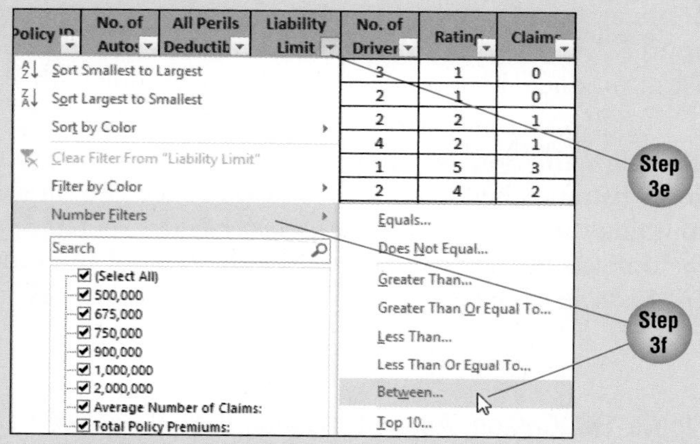

   g. At the Custom AutoFilter dialog box with the insertion point positioned in the blank text box next to *is greater than or equal to*, type 500000.
   h. Notice that *And* is the option selected between the criteria. This is correct, since the owner wants a list of policies with a liability limit greater than or equal to $500,000 *and* less than or equal to $1,000,000.
   i. Click in the blank text box next to *is less than or equal to* and type 1000000.
   j. Click OK to close the Custom AutoFilter dialog box. The range is filtered to display the rows with liability limits from $500,000 to $1,000,000.

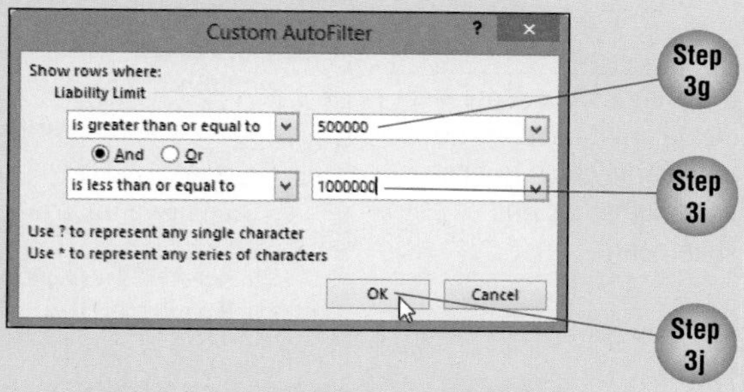

   k. Click the filter arrow next to *Claims* in cell H3.
   l. Point to *Number Filters* and then click *Greater Than* at the drop-down list.
   m. At the Custom AutoFilter dialog box with the insertion point positioned in the blank text box next to *is greater than*, type 1 and then click OK.

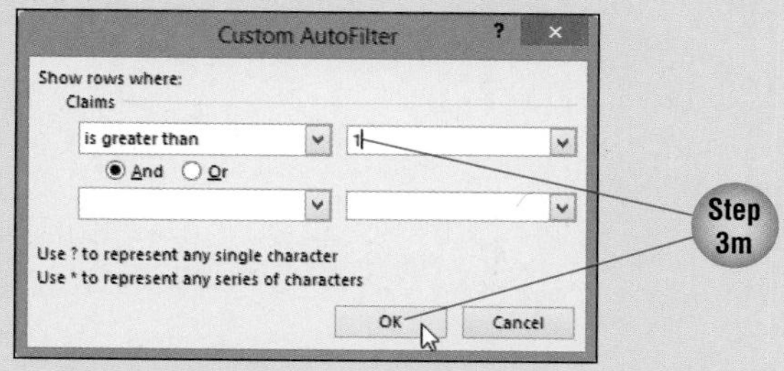

4. Print the filtered worksheet.
5. Save and then close **EL2-C1-P6-ACInsce.xlsx**.

Filtering and Sorting Data Using Conditional Formatting or Cell Attributes

A worksheet with cells that have been formatted manually or by conditional formatting to change the cell or font color can be filtered by color. In addition, a worksheet conditionally formatted using an icon set can be filtered using an icon.

To do this, select the range, click the Sort & Filter button, click *Filter*, and then deselect the range. Click the filter arrow in the column by which you want to filter and then point to *Filter by Color* at the drop-down list. Depending on the formatting that has been applied, the list contains cell colors, font colors, or icon sets. Click the desired color or icon option to filter the column.

The filter drop-down list also contains a *Sort by Color* option that you can use to sort rows within a range or table by a specified cell color, font color, or cell icon. Follow similar steps to sort by color as you would to filter by color. For example, to sort a column by font color, point to *Sort by Color* from the column's filter drop-down list and then click the desired font color. Excel sorts the column by placing cells with the specified font color at the top.

You can also sort or filter using the shortcut menu. To do this, right-click a cell that contains the color or icon by which you want to filter, point to *Filter*, and then click *Filter by Selected Cell's Color*, *Filter by Selected Cell's Font Color*, or *Filter by Selected Cell's Icon*.

Quick Steps

Filter or Sort by Color or Icon Set
1. Select range.
2. Click Sort & Filter button.
3. Click *Filter*.
4. Deselect range.
5. Click filter arrow at top of desired column.
6. Point to *Filter by Color* or *Sort by Color*.
7. Click desired color or icon.

OR
1. Right-click cell with desired color or icon.
2. Point to *Filter* or *Sort*.
3. Click desired filter or sort option.

Project 6b **Filtering by Icon Set** **Part 2 of 4**

1. Open **EL2-C1-P2-ACInsce.xlsx**.
2. Save the workbook and name it **EL2-C1-P6-ACInsce-1Auto**.
3. Filter the worksheet to display the policies that have coverage for only one automobile by completing the following steps:
   a. Select A3:I20.
   b. Click the Sort & Filter button in the Editing group on the HOME tab.
   c. Click *Filter* at the drop-down list. A filter arrow displays at the top of each column.
   d. Deselect the range.
   e. In Project 2c, you applied the Red to Black icon set to the data in column C. Note that the black circle icon represents the *1* data set. Click the filter arrow next to *No. of Autos* in cell C3.
   f. Point to *Filter by Color* at the drop-down list.
   g. Click the black circle icon in the *Filter by Cell Icon* list.
4. Print the filtered worksheet and then close **EL2-C1-P6-ACInsce-1Auto.xlsx**.

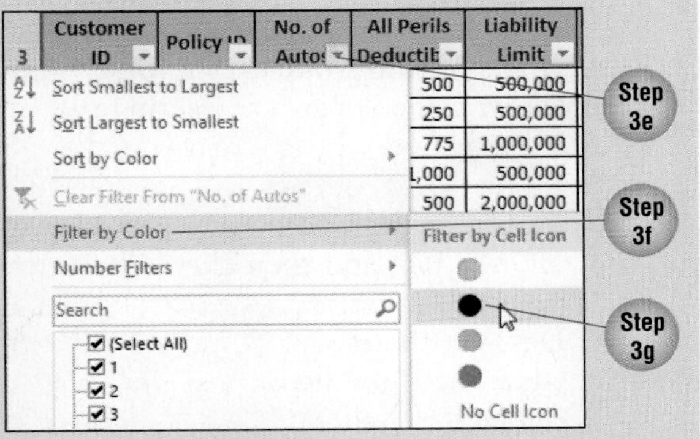

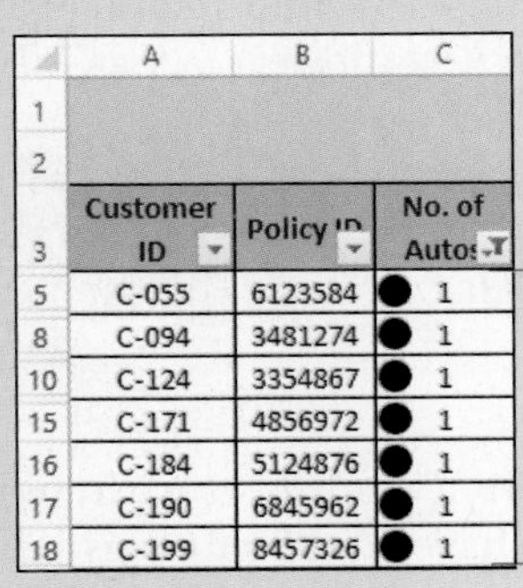

The worksheet has been filtered by the black circle icon representing the policies with one auto.

Project 6c Filtering by Font Color

Part 3 of 4

1. Open **EL2-C1-P1-VIVPay-Oct24.xlsx.**
2. Save the workbook and name it **EL2-C1-P6-VIVPay-Oct24-HighOT.**
3. The store manager wants a list of employees who worked more than five overtime hours during the pay period. You recall conditionally formatting the overtime hours by applying a red font color to cells with values greater than 5. Filter the worksheet by the conditional formatting by completing the following steps:
   a. Right-click cell K6 (or any other cell in column K with a red font color).
   b. Point to *Filter* and then click *Filter by Selected Cell's Font Color* at the shortcut menu.

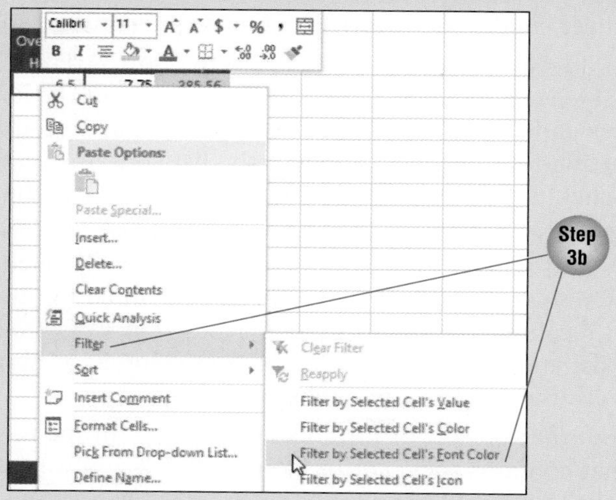

4. Print the filtered worksheet.
5. Save and then close **EL2-C1-P6-VIVPay-Oct24-HighOT.xlsx.**

Project 6d Sorting by Cell Color

Part 4 of 4

1. Open **EL2-C1-P1-VIVPay-Oct24.xlsx.**
2. Save the workbook and name it **EL2-C1-P6-VIVPay-Oct24-Sorted.**
3. Sort the payroll worksheet in descending order by cell color by completing the following steps:
   a. Select A5:M23, click the Sort & Filter button in the Editing group on the HOME tab, and then click *Filter* at the drop-down list.
   b. Deselect the range.
   c. Click the filter arrow next to *Gross Pay* in cell M5.
   d. Point to *Sort by Color* and then click the pink fill color box in the *Sort by Cell Color* section.

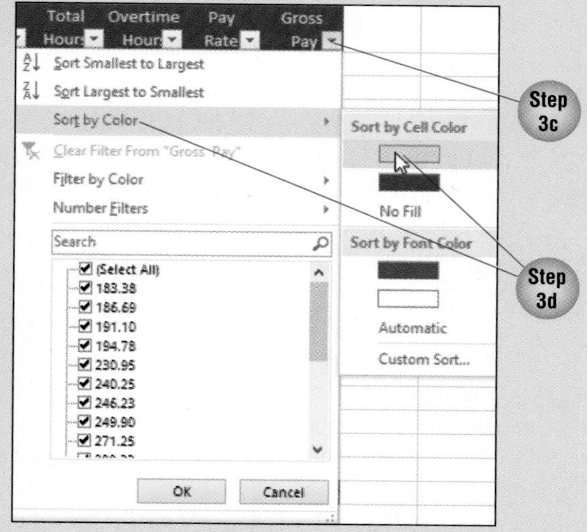

4. Print the sorted worksheet.
5. Save and then close **EL2-C1-P6-VIVPay-Oct24-Sorted.xlsx.**

In a worksheet with more than one cell or font color applied to a column, you have to define a custom sort. Click the Sort & Filter button in the Editing group on the HOME tab and then click *Custom Sort* at the drop-down list. At the Sort dialog box shown in Figure 1.9, define the color by which to sort first and

Figure 1.9 Sort Dialog Box with Four-Color Sort Defined

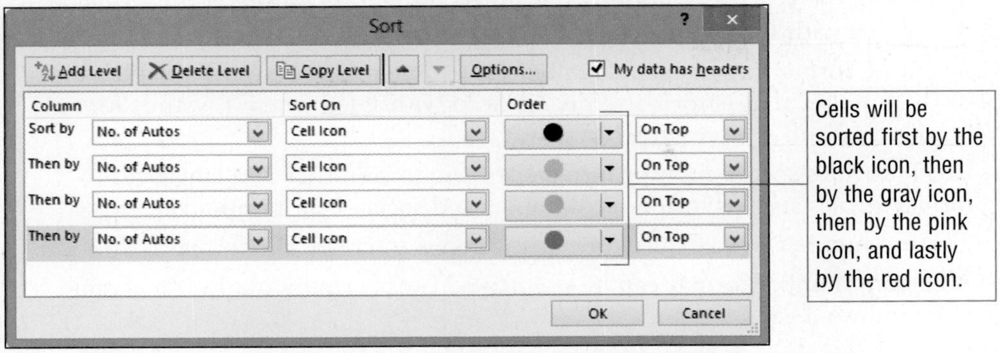

then add a level for each other color in the order in which you want the sorting to occur. The *Sort On* drop-down list at the Sort dialog box allows you to select *Values*, *Cell Color*, *Font Color*, or *Cell Icon*. Figure 1.9 contains a sort definition for a column in which four cell icons have been used.

Chapter Summary

- Conditional formatting applies format changes to cells based on a condition; cells that meet the condition have the formatting applied, and cells that do not meet the condition remain unformatted.
- Conditional formats can be based on values, dates, text entries, or duplicated values.
- Use the Quick Analysis button to quickly apply predefined conditional formats.
- Use the *Highlight Cells Rules* option at the Conditional Formatting button drop-down list to conditionally format based on a value comparison.
- Use the *Top/Bottom Rules* option at the Conditional Formatting button drop-down list to conditionally format based on the top 10 or bottom 10 percentage or average values.
- Conditional formats are based on rules that specify the criterion by which the cells are tested and the formatting attributes to apply to cells that meet the condition.
- Create your own conditional formatting rules by selecting *New Rule* at the Conditional Formatting button drop-down list.
- Edit or delete a rule at the Conditional Formatting Rules Manager dialog box.
- Conditionally format using data bars, color scales, or icon sets to add small bar charts, gradations of color, or icons to cells to make it easier to identify certain data.
- Conditionally format using a formula to apply desired formatting to the selected range of cells based on values in other cells. Excel treats any formula entered for conditional formatting as an array formula, which means you only need to add one rule for a selected range.
- An IF statement can be used to conditionally format those cells that calculate to a true result for the logical test.

- Fraction formatting converts decimal values to fractions.
- To choose the type of fraction you want to convert, open the Format Cells dialog box with the Number tab selected.
- Scientific formatting displays numbers in exponential notation, in which part of the number that is formatted is replaced with E+*n*, where E stands for "exponent" and *n* represents the power.
- Excel provides special number formats specific to countries and languages to format entries such as telephone numbers and social security numbers.
- Custom number formats use formatting codes to create the format definition.
- A custom number format can be used to add text or punctuation to a value entered into a cell.
- Long labels can be formatted to fit within a cell by wrapping the text within the cell or shrinking the font size to fit the cell.
- Convert the case of text from lowercase to uppercase or uppercase to lowercase using the UPPER and LOWER text functions.
- Replace existing text with new text using the SUBSTITUTE text function.
- Display the Custom AutoFilter dialog box to filter values by more than one criterion using a comparison operator such as greater than or equal to.
- A worksheet that has been formatted manually or by conditional formatting can be filtered by colors or icons.
- Define a custom sort if the worksheet contains more than one cell color, font color, or cell icon and you want to specify the order of the colors to sort.

Commands Review

FEATURE	RIBBON TAB, GROUP	BUTTON	KEYBOARD SHORTCUT
conditional formatting	HOME, Styles		
custom AutoFilter	HOME, Editing		Ctrl + Shift + L
custom number format	HOME, Number		Ctrl + 1
fraction formatting	HOME, Number		Ctrl + 1
scientific formatting	HOME, Number		Ctrl + 1
shrink text to fit	HOME, Alignment		
special number formatting	HOME, Number		Ctrl + 1
text functions	FORMULAS, Function Library		
wrap text	HOME, Alignment		Alt + Enter

Concepts Check Test Your Knowledge SNAP

Completion: In the space provided at the right, indicate the correct term, command, or number.

1. Point to this option at the Conditional Formatting button drop-down list to format cells based on a comparison operator such as *greater than*. 3 — high lighted cells ruls
2. To conditionally format a range using the *Above Average* condition, click this option at the Conditional Formatting button drop-down list. 3 — Top/bottom rules
3. Open this dialog box to create, edit, or delete a conditional formatting rule. 4 — conditional Formatting rules manager
4. Excel uses threshold values to classify data into three to five categories when applying conditional formatting using this option. 2 — icon sets
5. Click this option in the *Select a Rule Type* section of the New Formatting Rule dialog box to create a rule that conditionally formats cells based on the value(s) in another cell. a ______
6. Open this dialog box with this tab active to format a selected range as fractions and select the type of fraction to display. 8 ______
7. Scientific formatting is used by scientists and others who need to write very large numbers using this notation. 1 — exponent
8. The special number format options displayed in the *Type* list box are dependent on the setting in this option box. 1 — Custom
9. If you type *156.3568* in a cell with the custom number format code ###.## applied, this result will display. set of numbers — 156.36
10. Use either of these two text control options to format a long label within the existing column width. 2 to 3 words — shrink to fit
11. Use this text function to change existing text in the source cell to new text in the formula cell. 1 — Substitute
12. Open this dialog box to filter by more than one criterion using a comparison operator. 2 or 3 — new formatting rule
13. A worksheet can be filtered by a cell color that has been applied manually or by this feature. 2 — conditional formatting
14. Open this dialog box to organize cells in a worksheet by more than one color. 1 — filter

Skills Check Assess Your Performance

Assessment 1

USE CONDITIONAL AND FRACTION FORMATTING

SNAP Grade It

1. Open **RSRServRpt.xlsx**.
2. Save the workbook and name it **EL2-C1-A1-RSRServRpt**.
3. Apply the following formatting changes to the Sep worksheet:
   a. Format the values in C6:C23 as fractions using the *As quarters (2/4)* type.
   b. Format the rate codes in D6:D22 with the 3 Traffic Lights (Rimmed) icon set. (This is the first option in the right column of the *Shapes* section.)
   c. Format the parts values in F6:F22 with Light Red Fill color (sixth column, second row) for those cells with values that are equal to 0.
   d. Format the total invoice values in G6:G22 using the *Red Data Bar* option in the *Gradient Fill* section of the Data Bars side menu.
4. Save, print, and then close **EL2-C1-A1-RSRServRpt.xlsx**.

Assessment 2

APPLY CUSTOM NUMBER FORMATTING

SNAP Grade It

1. Open **EL2-C1-A1-RSRServRpt.xlsx**.
2. Save the workbook and name it **EL2-C1-A2-RSRServRpt**.
3. Create and apply the following custom number formats to the Sep worksheet:
   a. Create a custom number format that displays *hrs* one space after each value in C6:C23. ***Hint: After selecting* Custom *in the* Category *list box, click after the existing format codes in the* Type *text box and then add the required entry. (Do not delete what is already in the* Type *text box.)***
   b. Create a custom number format that displays *RSR-* in front of each work order number in B6:B22.
4. Save, print, and then close **EL2-C1-A2-RSRServRpt.xlsx**.

Assessment 3

USE CUSTOM AUTOFILTER; FILTER AND SORT BY COLOR

SNAP Grade It

1. Open **EL2-C1-A2-RSRServRpt.xlsx**.
2. Save the workbook and name it **EL2-C1-A3-RSRServRpt**.
3. Make the following changes to the Sep worksheet:
   a. Select A5:G22 and turn on the Filter feature.
   b. Using the filter arrow at the top of the *Hours Billed* column, display those invoices for which the hours billed are between 1.75 and 3.75. ***Hint: Type in the values 1.75 and 3.75. Do not select* 1 3/4 hrs *and* 3 3/4 hrs *from the drop-down lists in the Custom AutoFilter dialog box.***
4. Make the following changes to the Oct worksheet:
   a. Select A5:G22 and then turn on the Filter feature.
   b. Filter the *Parts* column by color to show only those invoices for which no parts were billed.
5. Make the following changes to the Nov worksheet:
   a. Clear the filter from the *Date* column.
   b. Filter the worksheet by the icon associated with rate code 3.

6. Make the following changes to the Dec worksheet:
   a. Remove the filter arrows from the worksheet.
   b. Make active any cell within the invoice list.
   c. Open the Sort dialog box.
   d. Define three sort levels as follows:

Sort by	*Sort On*	*Order*
rate code	cell icon	Red Traffic Light (On Top)
rate code	cell icon	Yellow Traffic Light (On Top)
rate code	cell icon	Green Traffic Light (On Top)

7. Print the workbook.
8. Save and then close **EL2-C1-A3-RSRServRpt.xlsx**.

Assessment 4 CREATE, EDIT, AND DELETE FORMATTING RULES

SNAP Grade It

1. Open **VIVPay-Oct31.xlsx**.
2. Save the workbook and name it **EL2-C1-A4-VIVPay-Oct31**.
3. Create and apply two conditional formatting rules for the values in the *Pay Rate* column as follows:
   a. Apply the Light Blue fill color (fifth column, third row) to values from 7.50 to 8.00.
   b. Apply a light green fill color (seventh column, third row) to values greater than 8.00.
4. Create a conditional formatting rule for the *Gross Pay* column that will format the values in the Dark Red font color (first option in the *Standard Colors* section) if the employee has worked overtime hours.
5. Use the Quick Analysis button to find the top 10% for the *Gross Pay* column.
6. Edit the formatting rule for *Cell Value <7.5* by applying the Light Orange fill color (tenth column, third row).
7. Use the Quick Analysis button to delete the formatting rule for *Overtime Hours*.
8. Save, print, and then close **EL2-C1-A4-VIVPay-Oct31.xlsx**.

Visual Benchmark Demonstrate Your Proficiency

FORMAT A BILLING SUMMARY

1. Open **BillingsOct5to9.xlsx**.
2. Save the workbook and name it **EL2-C1-VB-BillingsOct5to9**.
3. Format the worksheet to match the one shown in Figure 1.10 using the following information:
   - The data in the *Billing Code* column has been custom formatted to add the text *Amicus#-* in the Blue font color in front of the code number.
   - Icon sets have been used in the *Attorney Code* column and the same icon set should be applied in the *Attorney Code Table* section of the worksheet.
   - The data bars added to the values in the *Legal Fees* column have been formatted with the Turquoise, Accent 3 gradient fill. ***Hint: Select* More Rules *in the Data Bars side menu.***
   - Values below 1500.00 in the *Total Due* column have been conditionally formatted and the worksheet has been sorted by the font color used for the conditional format.
4. Save, print, and then close **EL2-C1-VB-BillingsOct5to9.xlsx**.

Figure 1.10 Visual Benchmark

	A	B	C	D	E	F	G	H	I	J
1				O'DONOVAN & SULLIVAN LAW ASSOCIATES						
2				BILLING SUMMARY						
3				OCTOBER 5 TO 9, 2015						
4	File	Client	Date	Billing Code	Attorney Code	Legal Fees	Disbursements	Total Due	Billing Code Table	
5	EP-652	10106	10/5/2015	Amicus#-3	1	1,028.50	23.75	1,052.25	Code	Area of Practice
6	EL-632	10225	10/6/2015	Amicus#-5	3	1,211.00	37.85	1,248.85	1	Corporate
7	CL-501	10341	10/7/2015	Amicus#-1	2	1,143.75	55.24	1,198.99	2	Divorce & Separation
8	IN-745	10210	10/8/2015	Amicus#-6	3	1,450.00	24.25	1,474.25	3	Wills & Estates
9	CL-412	10125	10/9/2015	Amicus#-1	2	1,143.75	38.12	1,181.87	4	Real Estate
10	IN-801	10346	10/9/2015	Amicus#-6	3	1,425.00	62.18	1,487.18	5	Employment Litigation
11	RE-501	10384	10/9/2015	Amicus#-4	4	1,237.50	34.28	1,271.78	6	Insurance Personal Injury
12	FL-325	10104	10/5/2015	Amicus#-2	1	2,273.75	95.10	2,368.85	7	Other
13	CL-412	10125	10/5/2015	Amicus#-1	2	2,493.75	55.40	2,549.15		
14	IN-745	10210	10/6/2015	Amicus#-6	3	2,425.00	65.20	2,490.20	Attorney Code Table	
15	RE-475	10285	10/6/2015	Amicus#-4	4	3,807.00	48.96	3,855.96	Code	Attorney
16	CL-521	10334	10/7/2015	Amicus#-1	2	1,518.75	27.85	1,546.60	1	Marty O'Donovan
17	PL-348	10420	10/7/2015	Amicus#-7	3	2,500.00	34.95	2,534.95	2	Toni Sullivan
18	RE-492	10425	10/7/2015	Amicus#-4	4	2,043.00	38.75	2,081.75	3	Rosa Martinez
19	EL-632	10225	10/8/2015	Amicus#-5	3	2,300.00	42.15	2,342.15	4	Kyle Williams
20	PL-512	10290	10/8/2015	Amicus#-7	3	1,620.00	65.15	1,685.15		
21	FL-385	10278	10/8/2015	Amicus#-2	1	2,040.00	85.47	2,125.47		
22	CL-450	10358	10/9/2015	Amicus#-1	2	1,762.50	55.24	1,817.74		
23	EP-685	10495	10/9/2015	Amicus#-3	3	2,375.00	94.55	2,469.55		

Case Study Apply Your Skills

Part 1

You work as a market research assistant at NuTrends Market Research. Yolanda Robertson has provided you with a workbook named **USIncomeStats.xlsx**. This workbook contains data she obtained from the US Census Bureau with the two-year average median household income by state for 2010. Open the workbook and name it **EL2-C1-CS-P1-USIncomeStats**. Yolanda wants you to format the data using colors to differentiate income levels. She has proposed the following categories for which she would like you to apply color formatting:

Average Median Income Range
Less than $45,000
Between $45,000 and $55,000
Greater than $55,000

Apply color formatting using conditional formatting for this request, since Yolanda may change these salary ranges after she reviews the data and you want to be able to edit the formatting rule if that happens. Choose colors that will be easy to distinguish from one another. Create a reference table starting in cell E3 that provides Yolanda with a legend to read the colors. For example, in cell E3, type **Less than 45,000** and in cell H3 type a sample value (such as 35,000) and then format each cell to the color that represents the formatting you applied to the rule category. Save and then print the worksheet. ***Note: If you submit your work in hard copy and do not have access to a color printer, write on the printout the color format you applied to each category***.

Part 2

Yolanda has reviewed the worksheet from Part 1 and has requested some further work. Before you begin modifying the file, you decide to keep a copy of the original file intact in case that data can be used for another purpose. Save the workbook and name it **EL2-C1-CS-P2-USIncomeStats**. You will use this workbook to make the modifications. Yolanda would like the worksheet sorted in descending order from the highest income level to the lowest. Do not include the entries in row 3 for the US average in the sort operation. After sorting the worksheet, filter the median incomes to display the top 20 states. ***Hint: You can customize the value in the Top 10 AutoFilter***. Yolanda wants to add a contact telephone list next to the top 20 state data. Create the list using the following telephone numbers and place them in a suitable location:

Yolanda (cell)	800 555 3117
Yolanda (office)	800 555 4629
Yolanda (home)	800 555 2169
Yolanda (fax)	800 555 6744

Apply the special number format for phone numbers to ensure the data is displayed consistently. Save and then print the worksheet.

Part 3

Continuing with the worksheet formatted in Part 2 of this Case Study, you decide to experiment with the filtered census data worksheet to see if formatting using color scales will highlight the spread between the highest and lowest median incomes more distinctly. Apply conditional formatting using a two-color or three-color scale to the filtered cells in column C. (Exclude the US median income at the top of the column.) Save the workbook and name it **EL2-C1-CS-P3-USIncomeStats**. Print the worksheet. ***Note: If you submit your work in hard copy and do not have access to a color printer, write on the printout the two- or three-color scale conditional formatting you applied to the filtered values in column C.***

Part 4

Yolanda is preparing a seminar for new market researchers hired at NuTrends Market Research. For background material for the training section on US Census Bureau statistics, Yolanda has asked you to research the history of the bureau. Using the Internet, go to www.census.gov/ and find the page that describes the history of the US Census Bureau. ***Hint: Explore the tabbed pages at the History link under ABOUT US at the bottom of the home page.*** In a new sheet in the same file as the median income data, type in column A five to seven interesting facts you learned about the bureau from the website. Adjust the width of column A and apply wrap text or shrink to fit formatting to improve the appearance of the sheet. Save the revised workbook and name it **EL2-C1-CS-P4-USIncomeStats**. Print the worksheet and then close the workbook.

MICROSOFT® EXCEL®

CHAPTER 2

Advanced Functions and Formulas

PERFORMANCE OBJECTIVES

Upon successful completion of Chapter 2, you will be able to:

- **Create and use named ranges in formulas**
- **Use the functions COUNTA, COUNTIF, and COUNTIFS**
- **Use the functions AVERAGEIF and AVERAGEIFS**
- **Use the functions SUMIF and SUMIFS**
- **Edit a named range**
- **Rename and delete a named range**
- **Look up data using the lookup functions VLOOKUP and HLOOKUP**
- **Analyze loan payments using PPMT**
- **Use the conditional logic functions IF, AND, and OR**

SNAP

Tutorials

2.1 Creating and Managing Range Names
2.2 Using Statistical Functions: COUNT, COUNTA, COUNTIF, and COUNTIFS
2.3 Using Statistical Functions: AVERAGEIF and AVERAGEIFS
2.4 Using Math and Trigonometry Functions: SUMIF and SUMIFS
2.5 Using Lookup Functions
2.6 Using the PPMT Function
2.7 Using Logical Functions

Excel includes numerous built-in functions grouped by function category. Thirteen categories contain preprogrammed formulas to facilitate complex calculations for worksheets containing statistical, financial, scientific, database, and other data. The Insert function dialog box assists with locating and building function formulas. The structure of a function formula begins with an equals sign (=), followed by the name of the function, and then the function argument. *Argument* is the term given to the values to be included in the calculation. The structure of the argument is dependent on the type of function being used and can include a single cell, a range, multiple ranges, or any combination of these. Model answers for this chapter's projects appear on the following pages.

Excel
EL2C2

Note: Before beginning the projects, copy to your storage medium the EL2C2 subfolder from the EL2 folder on the CD that accompanies this textbook and then make EL2C2 the active folder.

AllClaims Insurance Brokers
VEHICLE CLAIMS REPORT FOR OCTOBER 2015

Date of Claim	Policy ID	Claim No.	Auto No.	Driver No.	Rating	Deductible	Claim Estimate	Repair Shop
10/2/2015	6388569	5410	2	2	2	500.00	15,241.00	JFJ Auto
10/3/2015	4236512	5411	3	3	2	750.00	5,124.00	Logans Auto Body
10/5/2015	6974583	5412	1	1	3	1,000.00	12,451.00	Logans Auto Body
10/5/2015	2563845	5413	2	1	4	1,000.00	6,582.00	JFJ Auto
10/8/2015	2215473	5414	1	2	2	250.00	3,475.00	JFJ Auto
10/8/2015	6952384	5415	3	4	4	500.00	4,800.00	JFJ Auto
10/10/2015	4668457	5416	3	3	3	1,000.00	15,653.00	Logans Auto Body
10/10/2015	8512475	5417	4	3	5	2,000.00	18,653.00	West Collision
10/12/2015	6984563	5418	2	2	5	1,000.00	10,475.00	JFJ Auto
10/15/2015	4856972	5419	1	2	4	2,500.00	14,652.00	Logans Auto Body
10/15/2015	6845962	5420	1	1	3	500.00	4,110.00	Logans Auto Body
10/15/2015	8457326	5421	1	1	2	1,000.00	8,624.00	West Collision
10/19/2015	4968532	5422	2	1	2	250.00	2,510.00	West Collision
10/22/2015	5741356	5423	1	4	1	250.00	1,896.00	West Collision
10/22/2015	2486597	5424	1	2	3	750.00	3,841.00	JFJ Auto
10/23/2015	7134586	5425	1	2	2	500.00	6,253.00	JFJ Auto
10/24/2015	4234875	5426	2	3	4	1,000.00	5,486.00	A+ Paint & Body
10/26/2015	3894124	5427	4	1	4	2,000.00	12,986.00	JFJ Auto
10/29/2015	6952384	5428	2	3	4	500.00	2,475.00	JFJ Auto
10/30/2015	6845216	5429	3	1	2	250.00	7,684.00	A+ Paint & Body
10/31/2015	8663418	5430	2	2	1	500.00	3,486.00	A+ Paint & Body

Claim Report Statistics Summary

By Repair Shop	No. of Claims	Total Estimates
A+ Paint & Body	3	16,656
JFJ Auto	9	66,128
Logans Auto Body	5	51,990
West Collision	4	31,683
JFJ claims exceeding $5 thousand		
JFJ Auto	5	
JFJ claims for ratings greater than 3		
JFJ Auto	5	
By Rating		**Avg. Est.**
1		2,691
2		6,987
3		9,014
4		7,830
5		14,564
By Rating and Driver		
Rating 2, Driver 1		6,273
Rating 3, Driver 1		8,281

Project 1 Calculate Statistics and Sums Using Conditional Formulas
EL2-C2-P1-ACOct15VehRpt.xlsx

Precision Design and Packaging
Bulk Container Products Price List

Model Number	Description	Discount Category	List Price	Discount	Net Price
PD-1140	Gaylord with lid	A	18.67	10%	16.80
PD-2185	Premium Gaylord with lid	C	22.50	14%	19.35
PD-1150	Gaylord bottom	B	14.53	12%	12.79
PD-1155	Gaylord lid	D	5.25	16%	4.41
PD-3695	Telescoping top and bottom	A	18.54	10%	16.69
PD-3698	Telescoping bottom	A	17.65	10%	15.89
PD-3699	Telescoping top	A	17.65	10%	15.89
PD-4100	Additional lids for telescoping containers	D	9.88	16%	8.30
PD-4200	"D" 4 piece container	A	7.75	10%	6.98
PD-4415	"EO" container	A	8.25	10%	7.43
PD-5367	"EH" container	A	12.75	10%	11.48
PD-6418	"E" container	A	17.54	10%	15.79
PD-7459	Economy R.S.C.	E	8.56	20%	6.85
PD-8854	Premium R.S.C.	C	18.17	14%	15.63
PD-9101	Corrugated pads 15 x 15	E	1.10	20%	0.88
PD-9105	Corrugated pads 20 x 12	E	1.14	20%	0.91
PD-9110	Corrugated pads 24 x 18	E	1.17	20%	0.94
PD-9115	Corrugated pads 30 x 30	E	1.09	20%	0.87

Discount Table

Discount Category	Discount Percent
A	10%
B	12%
C	14%
D	16%
E	20%

NOTE: Use this price list for U.S. and Canadian orders only. Refer international customers to Bianca Santini for price quotations.

Project 2 Populate Cells by Looking Up Data
EL2-C2-P2-PrecisionPrices.xlsx

DEERING INDUSTRIES

BUILDING LOAN EXPANSION

	Victory Trust	Dominion Trust	
Interest Rate	8.15%	9.50%	annual rate
Amortization	20	15	years for repayment
Loan Amount	$ 775,000	$ 775,000	principal amount borrowed
Monthly Payment	($6,554.95)	($8,092.74)	includes principal and interest
Monthly Principal Payment (1st payment)	($1,291.40)	($1,957.32)	payment on principal for the first month of the loan
Total Loan Payments	($1,573,187.00)	($1,456,693.43)	

NOTE: Both payments are calculated based on a constant interest rate and a constant payment.

Project 3 Analyze an Expansion Project Loan
EL2-C2-P3-DExpansion.xlsx

ViewItVideo
Head Office Salaried Employees
Salary and Benefit Costs

		Full-Time/ Part-Time	Health Plan	Dental Plan	Salary	BENEFIT COSTS Pension	Health	Dental	Total Benefits	Salary + Benefits
Terri	Burkowski	FT	Family	Declined	65,000.00	3,250.00	2,100.00	-	5,350.00	70,350.00
Beatriz	Santiago	FT	Single	Single	51,500.00	2,575.00	1,380.00	1,500.00	5,455.00	56,955.00
Aram	Haji	FT	Declined	Declined	52,500.00	2,625.00	-	-	2,625.00	55,125.00
Gerri	Kinnear	PT	Family	Family	27,500.00	-	2,100.00	1,500.00	3,600.00	31,100.00
Sam	Quinn	FT	Single	Single	45,000.00	-	1,380.00	1,500.00	2,880.00	47,880.00
Andrea	Ruiz	PT	Family	Declined	22,500.00	-	2,100.00	-	2,100.00	24,600.00
Martina	Tisdale	PT	Single	Declined	28,500.00	-	1,380.00	-	1,380.00	29,880.00
Carl	Wisenberg	FT	Declined	Declined	42,500.00	-	-	-	-	42,500.00
Chen	Zhao	FT	Declined	Single	40,500.00	-	-	1,500.00	1,500.00	42,000.00
TOTAL					375,500.00	8,450.00	10,440.00	6,000.00	24,890.00	400,390.00

Project 4 Calculate Benefit Costs Using Conditional Logic
EL2-C2-P4-VIVSalCost.xlsx

Project 1 Calculate Statistics and Sums Using Conditional Formulas — 7 Parts

You will create and manage range names in an insurance claims worksheet and use the range names in statistical formulas that count, find averages, and sum based on single and multiple criteria.

Creating Name Ranges

Assigning a name to a cell or range of cells allows you to reference the source using a descriptive label, rather than the cell address or range address, when creating formulas, printing, or navigating a worksheet. Creating range names makes the task of managing complex formulas easier and helps others who may work in or edit the worksheet to understand a formula's purpose more quickly.

To demonstrate the use of range names for clarity, read the formula examples in Table 2.1. Each row provides two formulas that reference the same source cells; however, the formula on the right is easier to understand than the formula on the left. The formulas in the left column might require you to locate the source cells in the worksheet to figure out the calculation steps, whereas you will understand the formulas in the right column almost immediately.

By default, the range to which a range name applies is referenced using absolute references. Later in this chapter, when you create a lookup formula, you will take advantage of the absolute referencing of a range name when you include a group of cells in the formula that stay fixed when the formula is copied.

Create a range name by selecting a single cell or range, clicking in the Name box located to the left of the Formula bar, typing the name, and then pressing Enter. The Name box displays the active cell address or cell name when one has been defined. When creating a name for a cell or a range of cells, follow these naming rules:

- Names can be a combination of letters, numbers, underscore characters, and periods up to 255 characters.
- The first character must be a letter, underscore, or backslash (\).
- Spaces are not valid. Use underscore characters or periods to separate words.
- A valid cell address cannot become a range name.
- Range names are not case sensitive.

Quick Steps

Create a Range Name
1. Select cell(s).
2. Click in Name box.
3. Type desired range name.
4. Press Enter.

HINT

The FORMULAS tab contains a Create from Selection button in the Defined Names group that can be used to automatically create range names for a list or table. Select the list or table and click the button. Excel uses the names in the top row or left-most column as the range names.

Table 2.1 Standard Formulas and Formulas with Named Ranges

Standard Formula	*Same Formula Using Named Ranges*
=D3-D13	=Sales-Expenses
=J5*K5	=Hours*PayRate
=G10/J10	=ThisYear/LastYear
=IF(E4-B2>0,E4*D2,0)	=IF(Sales-Target>0,Sales*Bonus,0)

1. Open **ACOct15VehRpt.xlsx**.
2. Save the workbook and name it **EL2-C2-P1-ACOct15VehRpt**.
3. Assign names to ranges by completing the following steps:
   a. Select D4:D24.
   b. Click in the Name box located to the left of the Formula bar, type AutoNo, and then press Enter.
   c. Select E4:E24, click in the Name box, type DriverNo, and then press Enter.
   d. Select F4:F24, click in the Name box, type Rating, and then press Enter.
   e. Select H4:H24, click in the Name box, type ClaimEst, and then press Enter.
   f. Select I4:I24, click in the Name box, type RepShop, and then press Enter.
4. View the range names by clicking the down-pointing arrow at the right of the Name box.
5. Click *AutoNo* at the drop-down list to move the selected range to column D. One reason for creating range names is to make it easier to navigate quickly in a large worksheet.
6. Deselect the range by clicking anywhere in the worksheet.
7. Save **EL2-C2-P1-ACOct15VehRpt.xlsx**.

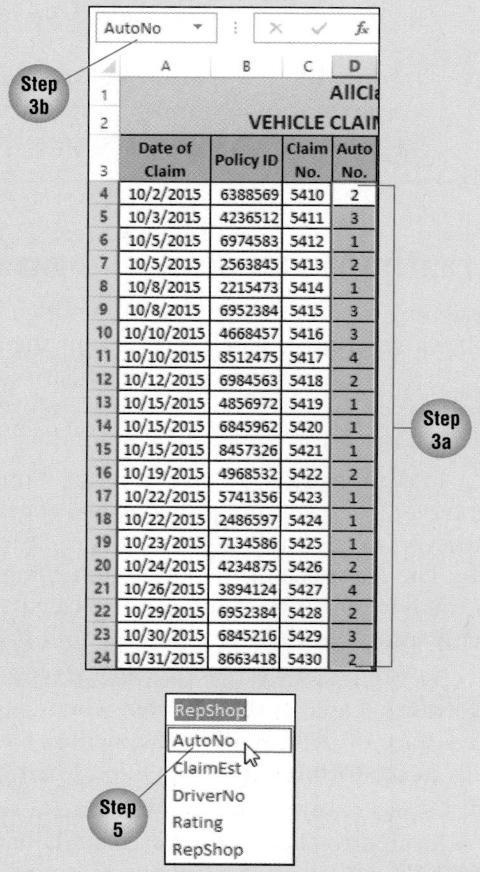

Using Statistical Functions

Commonly used statistical functions include AVERAGE, MAX, and MIN, where AVERAGE returns the arithmetic mean, MAX returns the largest value, and MIN returns the smallest value in the range. Another function used often is COUNT, which returns the number of cells that contain numbers or dates. Empty cells, text labels, or error values in the range are ignored. Excel provides additional AVERAGE and COUNT functions that are used to count text entries and find averages for a range based on a criterion.

Using the COUNTA Function

In a worksheet that requires cells containing text or a combination of text and numbers (such as *Model-2146*) to be counted, Excel provides the COUNTA function. COUNTA returns the number of cells that are not empty; therefore, this formula can be used to count a range of cells other than values. As shown in the worksheet in Figure 2.1, when the regular COUNT function is used in cell E8 to count parts in the range A2:A6, Excel returns a value of 0. However, in cell E9, when the same range is counted using COUNTA, Excel returns a value of 5.

Figure 2.1 COUNTA Example

	A	B	C	D	E
1	Part Number	Qty	Price		
2	Part#-134A	55	2.10		
3	Part#-1125	21	3.15		
4	Part#-874T	47	4.58		
5	Part#-784U	65	3.68		
6	Part#-546C	85	4.85		
7					
8	Count of column A using COUNT function:				0
9	Count of column A using COUNTA function:				5

The formula =*COUNT(A2:A6)* returns 0.

The formula =*COUNTA(A2:A6)* returns the correct result.

Using the COUNTIF and COUNTIFS Functions

Use the COUNTIF function to count cells within a range that meet a single criterion. For example, in a grades worksheet, you might use a COUNTIF function to count the number of students who achieved greater than 75%. This function uses conditional logic, in which the criterion defines a conditional test so that only those cells that meet the test are selected for action. The structure of a COUNTIF function is *=COUNTIF(range,criteria)*. For the grades worksheet example, the function to count the cells of students who achieved greater than 75% is *=COUNTIF(grades,">75")*, assuming the range name *grades* has been defined. Notice that the syntax of the argument requires the criterion to be enclosed in quotation marks. If you use the Insert Function dialog box to create a formula, Excel adds the required syntax automatically. A cell reference may also be used as the criterion. A cell reference is not enclosed in quotation marks and should only contain the exact criterion.

The COUNTIFS function is used to count cells that meet multiple criteria. The formula uses the same structure as COUNTIF with additional ranges and criteria within the argument. The structure of a COUNTIFS function is *=COUNTIFS(range1,criteria1,range2,criteria2. . .)*. Figure 2.2 illustrates a nursing education worksheet with a single criterion COUNTIF to count the number of

Figure 2.2 COUNTIF and COUNTIFS Formulas

	A	B	C	D	E	F	G	H	I	J	K
1	Department of Human Resources										
2	Full-Time Nursing Education Worksheet										
3	Employee Number	Employee Last Name	Employee First Name	Title	Unit	Extension	Years Experience	PD Current?		Nursing Educational Statistical Summary	
4	FT02001	Santos	Susan	RN	Med/Surg	36415	30	Yes		Number of RNs	16
5	FT02002	Daniels	Jasmine	RN	Med/Surg	36415	27	No		Number of LPNs	12
6	FT02003	Walden	Virgina	RN	ICU	34211	22	No			
7	FT02004	Jaffe	Paul	LPN	CSRU	36418	24	Yes		RNs who are current with PD	9
8	FT02005	Salvatore	Terry	LPN	ICU	34211	22	Yes		LPNs who are current with PD	7
9	FT02006	Mander	Kaitlynn	RN	ICU	34211	24	Yes			
10	FT02007	Friesen	Jessica	LPN	ICU	34211	20	Ye			
11	FT02008	Lavigne	Gisele	RN	CSRU	36418	20	No			
12	FT02009	Gauthier	Jacqueline	RN	PreOp	32881	19	No			
13	FT02010	Williamson	Forman	RN	CSRU	36418	19	Yes			
14	FT02011	Orlowski	William	RN	Ortho	31198	22	No			
15	FT02012	Kadri	Ahmed	LPN	Ortho	31198	21	No			
16	FT02013	El-Hamid	Lianna	LPN	Med/Surg	36415	20	No			
17	FT02014	Vezina	Ursula	LPN	Ortho	31198	20	No			
18	FT02015	Adams	Sheila	LPN	Med/Surg	36415	25				
19	FT02016	Jorgensen	Macy	RN	Med/Surg	36415	10				
20	FT02017	Pieterson	Eric	RN	ICU	34211	8				
21	FT02018	Keller	Douglas	RN	ICU	34211	10	No			
22	FT02019	Costa	Michael	RN	Ortho	31198	10	No			
23	FT02020	Li-Kee	Su-Lynn	LPN	PreOp	32881	8	No			
24	FT02021	Besterd	Mary	RN	PreOp	32881	7	Yes			

Formula =COUNTIF(Title,"RN")

Formula =COUNTIFS(Title,"RN",PDCurrent,"Yes")

Quick Steps

Create a COUNTIF Formula

1. Make desired cell active.
2. Click Insert Function button.
3. Change category to *Statistical*.
4. Select *COUNTIF*.
5. Click OK.
6. Enter range address or range name to select by in *Range* text box.
7. Enter condition expression or text in *Criteria* text box.
8. Click OK.

Create a COUNTIFS Formula

1. Make desired cell active.
2. Click Insert Function button.
3. Change category to *Statistical*.
4. Select *COUNTIFS*.
5. Click OK.
6. Enter range address or range name to select by in *Criteria_range1* text box.
7. Enter condition expression or text in *Criteria1* text box.
8. Enter range address or range name to select by in *Criteria_range2* text box.
9. Enter condition expression or text in *Criteria2* text box.
10. Continue adding criteria range expressions and criteria as needed.
11. Click OK.

fx

Insert Function

nurses (RNs) and a multiple criteria COUNTIFS to count the number of RNs who are current with their professional development (PD) activities. The formulas shown in Figure 2.2 include range names for which *Title* references the entries in column D and *PDCurrent* references the entries in column H.

Project 1b Creating COUNTIF Functions Part 2 of 7

1. With **EL2-C2-P1-ACOct15VehRpt.xlsx** open, make cell L4 active.
2. Create a COUNTIF function to count the number of claims for which A+ Paint & Body is the repair shop by completing the following steps:
   a. Click the Insert Function button in the Formula bar.
   b. At the Insert Function dialog box, click the down-pointing arrow at the right of the *Or select a category* option box and then click *Statistical* at the drop-down list. ***Note: Skip this step if* Statistical *is already selected as the category*.**
   c. Scroll down the *Select a function* list box and then click *COUNTIF.*
   d. Read the formula description below the function list box and then click OK.

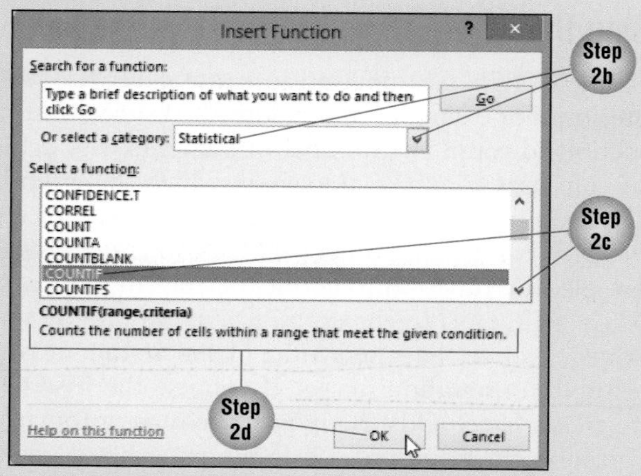

   e. At the Function Arguments dialog box with the insertion point positioned in the *Range* text box, type RepShop and then press Tab. Recall from Project 1a that you defined a range name for the entries in column I. ***Note: If the dialog box is obscuring your view of the worksheet, drag the Function Arguments dialog box title bar left or right.***
   f. With the insertion point positioned in the *Criteria* text box, type A+ Paint & Body and then press Tab. When you press Tab, Excel adds quotation marks to the criteria text.
   g. Click OK. Excel returns the value *3* in cell L4.

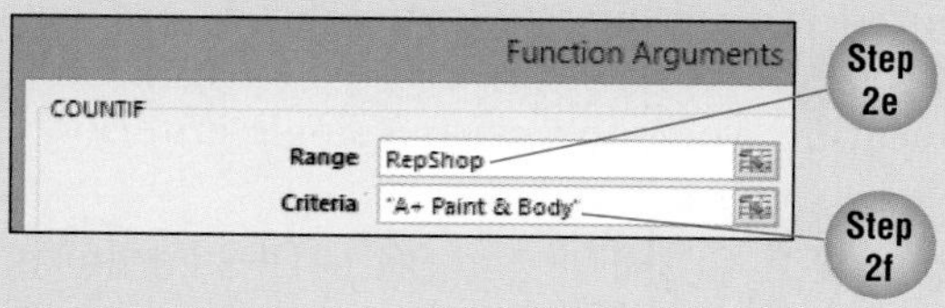

   h. Look at the formula in the Formula bar created by the Function Arguments dialog box: *=COUNTIF(RepShop,"A+ Paint & Body").*
3. Make cell L5 active. The repair shop names are located in K4:K7. Use cell K5 as the cell reference for JFJ Auto by typing the formula =countif(repshop,k5) and then press Enter. (When entering formulas, type cell references and named ranges in lowercase letters. Excel will automatically display uppercase letters once the formula has been entered.)

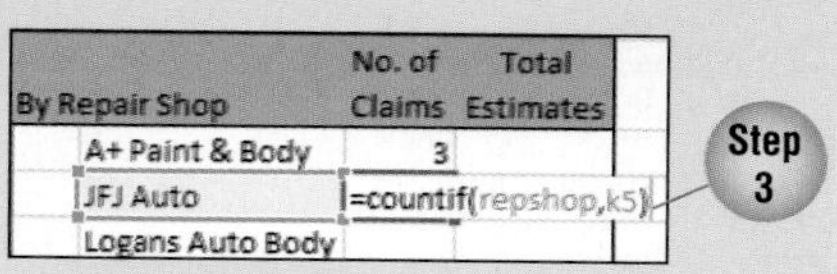

4. Use the fill handle to copy the formula in cell L5 to cells L6 through L7. When completed, the COUNTIF formulas will be as follows:
   L6: *=COUNTIF(RepShop,K6)*
   L7: *=COUNTIF(RepShop,K7)*
5. Save **EL2-C2-P1-ACOct15VehRpt.xlsx**.

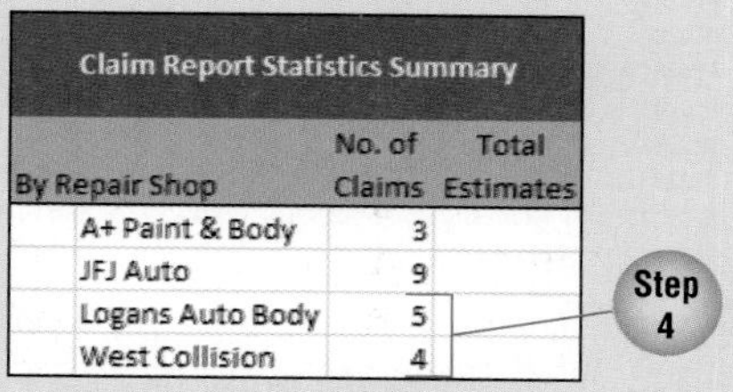

Project 1c Creating COUNTIFS Functions

Part 3 of 7

1. With **EL2-C2-P1-ACOct15VehRpt.xlsx** open, make cell L10 active.
2. Create a COUNTIFS function to count the number of claims for which the repair shop is JFJ Auto and the claims estimate is greater than $5,000 by completing the following steps:
   a. Click the Insert Function button in the Formula bar.
   b. With *Statistical* selected in the *Or select a category* option box, scroll down the *Select a function* list box and then click *COUNTIFS*.
   c. Read the formula description below the function list box and then click OK.
   d. At the Function Arguments dialog box with the insertion point positioned in the *Criteria_range1* text box, type **repshop** and then press Tab. After you press Tab, a *Criteria_range2* text box is added to the dialog box.

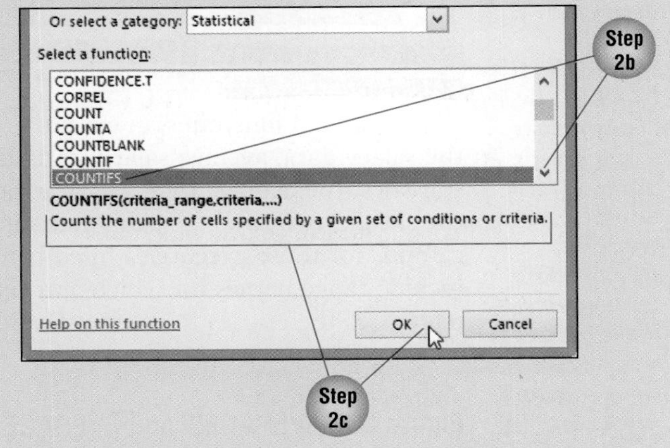

   e. With the insertion point positioned in the *Criteria1* text box, type **k10** as the cell reference for JFJ Auto and then press Tab. After you press Tab, a *Criteria2* text box is added to the dialog box.
   f. With the insertion point positioned in the *Criteria_range2* text box, type **claimest** and then press Tab. After you press Tab, a *Criteria_range3* text box is added to the dialog box.
   g. With the insertion point positioned in the *Criteria2* text box, type **>5000** and then press Tab. When you press Tab, Excel adds quotation marks to the criteria text.
   h. Click OK. Excel returns the value *5* in cell L10.

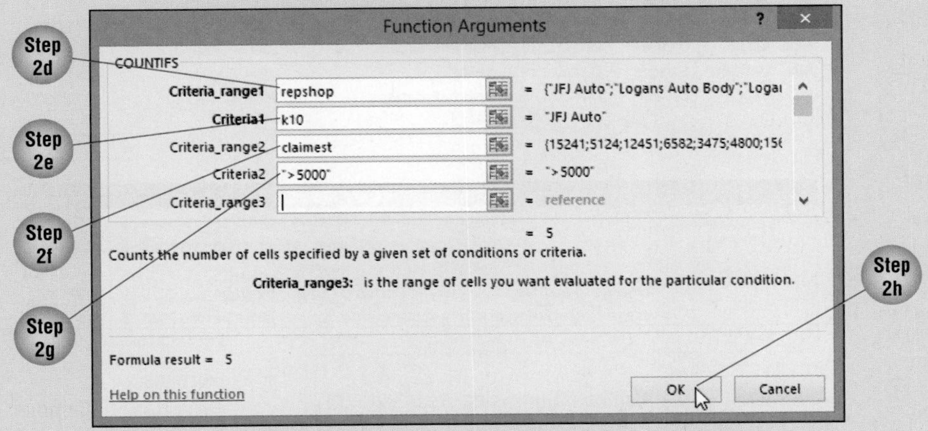

3. Look at the formula in the Formula bar created by the Function Arguments dialog box: =*COUNTIFS(RepShop*,K10,*ClaimEst*,">*5000*").
4. Enter the following COUNTIFS formula in cell L13 by using the Insert Function dialog box or by typing the formula directly into the cell: **=countifs(repshop,k13,rating,">3")**

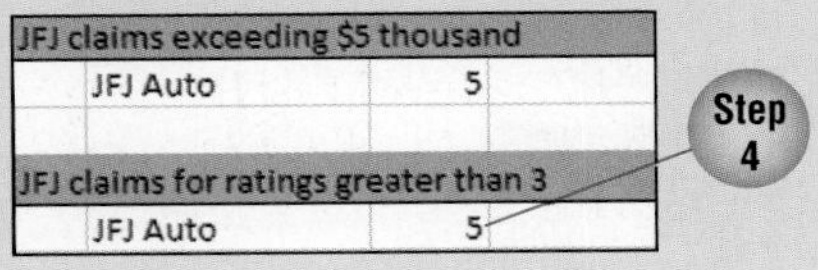

5. Save **EL2-C2-P1-ACOct15VehRpt.xlsx**.

Quick Steps

Create an AVERAGEIF Formula

1. Make desired cell active.
2. Click Insert Function button.
3. Change category to *Statistical.*
4. Select *AVERAGEIF.*
5. Click OK.
6. Enter range address or range name to select by in *Range* text box.
7. Enter condition expression or text in *Criteria* text box.
8. Enter range address or range name to average in *Average_range* text box.
9. Click OK.

Create an AVERAGEIFS Formula

1. Make desired cell active.
2. Click Insert Function button.
3. Change category to *Statistical.*
4. Select *AVERAGEIFS.*
5. Click OK.
6. Enter range address or range name to average in *Average_range* text box.
7. Enter range address or range name to select by in *Criteria_range1* text box.
8. Enter condition expression or text in *Criteria1* text box.
9. Enter range address or range name to select by in *Criteria_range2* text box.
10. Enter condition expression or text in *Criteria2* text box.
11. Continue adding criteria range expressions and criteria as needed.
12. Click OK.

Using the AVERAGEIF and AVERAGEIFS Functions

The AVERAGEIF function is used to find the arithmetic mean of the cells within a specified range that meet a single criterion. The structure of an AVERAGEIF function is *=AVERAGEIF(range,criteria,average_range),* where *range* is the cells to be tested for the criterion, *criteria* is the conditional statement used to select cells, and *average_range* is the range containing the values you want to average. The AVERAGEIFS function is used to average cells that meet multiple criteria using the formula *=AVERAGEIFS(average_range,criteria_range1,criteria1,criteria_range2,criteria2. . .).*

Figure 2.3 illustrates an executive management salary report for a hospital. Below the salary data, average salary statistics are shown. In the first two rows of salary statistics, the average total salary is calculated for each of two hospital campuses. In the second two rows of salary statistics, the average total salary is calculated for each campus for those executives hired before 2013. The formulas shown in Figure 2.3 include range names for which *Year* references the values in column E, *Campus* references the entries in column F, and *Total* references the values in column I.

Figure 2.3 AVERAGEIF and AVERAGEIFS Formulas

	A	B	C	D	E	F	G	H	I
1	Columbia River General Hospital								
2	Executive Management Salary Report								
3	For the fiscal year 2014-2015								
4				Job Title	Year Hired	Campus	Salary	Benefits	Total
5	Ms.	Michelle	Tan	Chief Executive Officer	2001	Sunnyside	$ 155,000	$ 18,400	$ 173,400
6	Mr.	Douglas	Brown	Legal Counsel	2011	Sunnyside	90,500	17,500	108,000
7	Mrs.	Lauren	Quandt	Chief Financial Officer	2014	Portland	110,750	18,400	129,150
8	Dr.	Dana	Pembroke	Medical Director	2005	Portland	101,500	14,650	116,150
9	Mrs.	Gina	Wright	Director of Nursing	2010	Portland	95,475	14,650	110,125
10	Mr.	Fernando	Ortiega	Director of Patient Care Services	2011	Sunnyside	87,750	12,675	100,425
11	Mr.	Joshua	Vitello	Director of Facilities	2008	Sunnyside	85,000	9,275	94,275
12	Miss	Carin	Ledicke	Director of Human Resources	2006	Portland	85,000	9,275	94,275
13	Mr.	William	Formet	Director of Planning	2004	Portland	85,000	9,275	94,275
14	Mr.	Paul	Unraue	Director, Community Relations	1998	Sunnyside	72,500	8,975	81,475
15									
16							$ 968,475	$133,075	$1,101,550
17									
18	Salary Statistics								
19				Average executive total salary at Portland campus			$ 108,795		
20				Average executive total salary at Sunnyside campus			$ 111,515		
21									
22				Average executive total salary at Portland campus hired before 2013			$ 103,706		
23				Average executive total salary at Sunnyside campus hired before 2013			$ 111,515		

Formula
=AVERAGEIFS(Total,Campus,"Sunnyside",Year,"<2013")

Formula
=AVERAGEIF(Campus,"Portland",Total)

Project 1d Creating AVERAGEIF Functions

Part 4 of 7

1. With **EL2-C2-P1-ACOct15VehRpt.xlsx** open, make cell M16 active.
2. Create an AVERAGEIF function to calculate the average claim estimate for those claims with a rating of 1 by completing the following steps:
   a. Click the Insert Function button in the Formula bar.
   b. With *Statistical* selected in the *Or select a category* option box, click *AVERAGEIF* in the *Select a function* list box.
   c. Read the formula description below the function list box and then click OK.
   d. At the Function Arguments dialog box with the insertion point positioned in the *Range* text box, type rating and then press Tab.
   e. With the insertion point positioned in the *Criteria* text box, type 1 and then press Tab.
   f. With the insertion point positioned in the *Average_range* text box, type claimest.
   g. Click OK. Excel returns the value *2691* in cell M16.

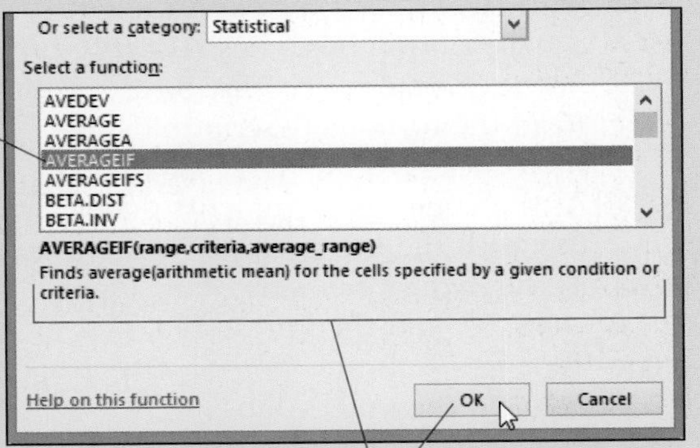

3RD argument

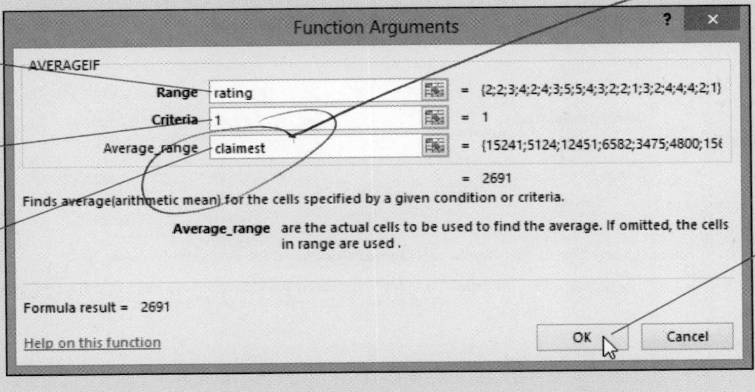

   h. Look at the formula in the Formula bar created by the Function Arguments dialog box: *=AVERAGEIF(Rating,1,ClaimEst)*.
3. Apply comma formatting with no places after the decimal point to cell M16.
4. Make cell M17 active, type the formula =averageif(rating,2,claimest), and then press Enter.
5. Apply comma formatting with no places after the decimal point to cell M17.
6. Make cell M17 active and then drag the fill handle down to M18:M20.
7. Edit the formulas in cells M18, M19, and M20 by changing the rating criterion values from *2* to *3*, *4*, and *5*, respectively. When completed, the AVERAGEIF formulas will be as follows:
   M18: *=AVERAGEIF(Rating,3,ClaimEst)*
   M19: *=AVERAGEIF(Rating,4,ClaimEst)*
   M20: *=AVERAGEIF(Rating,5,ClaimEst)*
8. Save **EL2-C2-P1-ACOct15VehRpt.xlsx**.

By Rating		Avg. Est.
	1	2,691
	2	6,987
	3	9,014
	4	7,830
	5	14,564

Step 7

Be efficient & ref cell position & not hard code the #

Project 1e Creating AVERAGEIFS Functions

1. With **EL2-C2-P1-ACOct15VehRpt.xlsx** open, make cell M22 active.
2. Create an AVERAGEIFS function to calculate the average claim estimate for those claims with a rating of 2 and a driver number of 1 by completing the following steps:
   a. Click the Insert Function button in the Formula bar.
   b. With *Statistical* selected in the *Or select a category* option box, click *AVERAGEIFS* in the *Select a function* list box.
   c. Read the formula description and then click OK.
   d. At the Function Arguments dialog box with the insertion point positioned in the *Average_range* text box, type **claimest** and then press Tab.
   e. Type **rating** in the *Criteria_range1* text box and then press Tab.
   f. Type **2** in the *Criteria1* text box and then press Tab.
   g. Type **driverno** in the *Criteria_range2* text box and then press Tab.
   h. Type **1** in the *Criteria2* text box and then click OK. Excel returns the value *6272.667* in the cell.

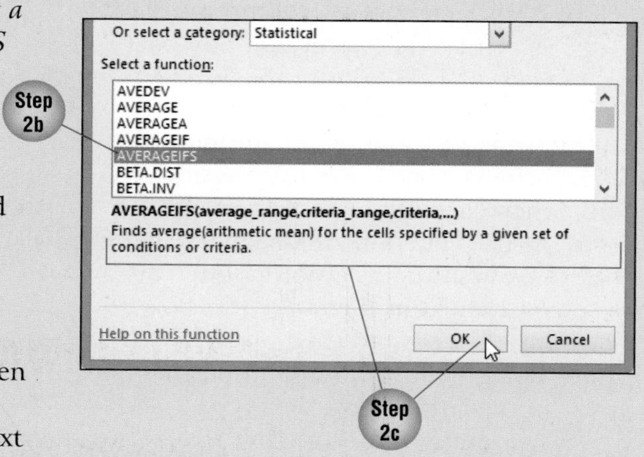

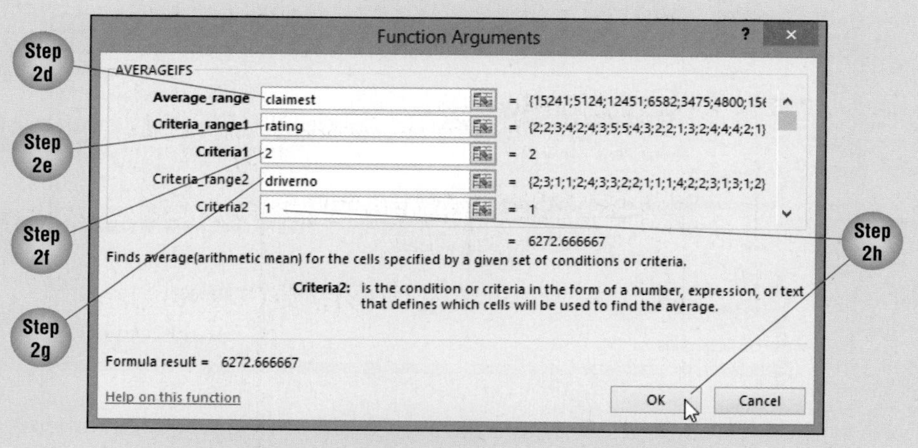

   i. Apply comma formatting with no places after the decimal point to cell M22.
3. Copy the AVERAGEIFS formula in cell M22 and paste it into cell M23.
4. Edit the formula in cell M23 to change the rating criterion from *2* to *3*. When completed, the AVERAGEIFS formula will be *=AVERAGEIFS(ClaimEst,Rating,3,DriverNo,1)*.
5. If necessary, apply comma formatting with no places after the decimal point to cell M23.
6. Save **EL2-C2-P1-ACOct15VehRpt.xlsx**.

Using Math and Trigonometry Functions: SUMIF and SUMIFS

Excel provides several math and trigonometry functions, such as ABS to return the absolute value of a number, SQRT to find the square root of a number, and RAND to return a random number between 0 and 1, to name a few. At the Insert Function dialog box, change the *Or select a category* option to *Math & Trig* and scroll down the list of available functions in the category.

Within the category of math and trigonometry functions, Excel includes SUMIF to add the cells within a range that meet a single criterion and SUMIFS to add the cells within a range that meet multiple criteria. The structure of the SUMIF formula is *=SUMIF(range,criteria,sum_range)*, where *range* is the cells to be tested for the criterion, *criteria* is the conditional statement used to select cells, and *sum_range* is the range containing the values to add. The SUMIFS function is used to add cells that meet multiple criteria using the formula *=SUMIFS(sum_range,criteria_range1,criteria1,criteria_range2,criteria2. . .)*.

Figure 2.4 provides an example of how the SUMIF and SUMIFS formulas are used in a medical clinic's standard cost worksheet for examination room supplies. At the right of the clinic supplies inventory, a SUMIF formula sums the cost for items by supplier number. A SUMIFS formula sums the cost by supplier number for items that require a minimum stock quantity of more than four. The formulas shown in Figure 2.4 include the range names *Supplier*, which references the entries in column C; *MinQty*, which references the values in column E; and *StdCost*, which references the values in column F.

Quick Steps

Create a SUMIF Formula

1. Make desired cell active.
2. Click FORMULAS tab.
3. Click Math & Trig button.
4. Scroll down and click *SUMIF*.
5. Enter range address or range name to select by in *Range* text box.
6. Enter condition expression or text in *Criteria* text box.
7. Enter range address or range name to add in *Sum_range* text box.
8. Click OK.

Math & Trig

Figure 2.4 SUMIF and SUMIFS Formulas

Formula
=SUMIF(Supplier,"101",StdCost)

	A	B	C	D	E	F	G	H	I
1	North Shore Medical Clinic								
2	Clinic Supplies Inventory Units and Price								
3	Item	Unit	Supplier Number	Price	Minimum Stock Qty	Standard Cost	Exam Room Cost Analysis		
4	Sterile powder-free synthetic gloves, size Small	per 100	101	35.95	4	143.80	Cost by Supplier		
5	Sterile powder-free synthetic gloves, size Mediu	per 100	101	35.95	8	287.60		Supplier Number 101	1,401.40
6	Sterile powder-free synthetic gloves, size Large	per 100	101	35.95	10	359.50		Supplier Number 155	364.33
7	Sterile powder-free latex gloves, size Small	per 100	101	16.25	4	65.00		Supplier Number 201	1,918.00
8	Sterile powder-free latex gloves, size Medium	per 100	101	16.25	8	130.00		Supplier Number 350	790.80
9	Sterile powder-free latex gloves, size Large	per 100	101	16.25	10	162.50			
10	Sterile powder-free vinyl gloves, size Small	per 100	101	11.50	4	46.00			
11	Sterile powder-free vinyl gloves, size Medium	per 100	101	11.50	8	92.00	Cost by Supplier with		
12	Sterile powder-free vinyl gloves, size Large	per 100	101	11.50	10	115.00	Minimum Qty over 4		
13	Disposable earloop mask	per 50	155	5.61	8	44.88		Supplier Number 101	1,146.60
14	Disposable patient gown	per dozen	155	7.90	16	126.40		Supplier Number 155	310.80
15	Disposable patient slippers	per dozen	155	4.27	16	68.32		Supplier Number 201	1,330.00
16	Cotton patient gown	per dozen	201	133.00	10	1,330.00		Supplier Number 350	659.00
17	Cotton patient robe	per dozen	201	147.00	4	588.00			
18	Disposable examination table paper	per roll	155	8.90	8	71.20			
19	Lab coat, size Small	each	350	32.95	4	131.80			
20	Lab coat, size Medium	each	350	32.95	8	263.60			
21	Lab coat, size Large	each	350	32.95	12	395.40			
22	Disposable shoe cover	per 300	155	37.75	1	37.75			
23	Disposable bouffant cap	per 100	155	7.89	2	15.78			
24	TOTAL STANDARD EXAM ROOM SUPPLIES COST:					4,474.53			

Formula
=SUMIFS(StdCost,Supplier,"350",MinQty,">4")

Project 1f Creating SUMIF Functions

Note: In Step 4, you are directed to save and print the worksheet. Check with your instructor before printing to see if you need to print two copies of the worksheets for the projects in this chapter: one as displayed and another displaying the cell formulas. Save the worksheet before displaying formulas (Ctrl + `) so that you can adjust column widths as necessary and then close without saving the changes.

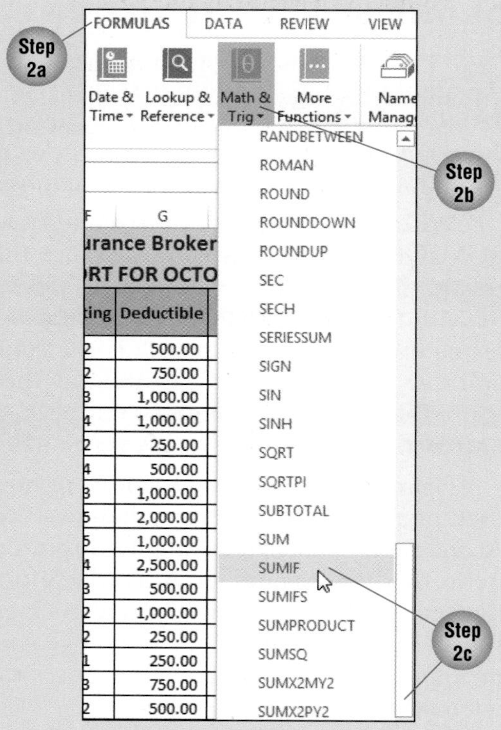

1. With **EL2-C2-P1-ACOct15VehRpt.xlsx** open, make cell M4 active.
2. Create a SUMIF function to sum the claim estimates for those claims being repaired at A+ Paint & Body by completing the following steps:
   a. Click the FORMULAS tab.
   b. Click the Math & Trig button in the Function Library group.
   c. Scroll down the drop-down list and then click *SUMIF*.
   d. At the Function Arguments dialog box with the insertion point positioned in the *Range* text box, type **repshop** and then press Tab.
   e. Designate cell K4 as the cell reference for JFJ Auto by typing **k4** in the *Criteria* text box. Press Tab.
   f. Type **claimest** in the *Sum_range* text box and then click OK. Excel returns the value *16656* in cell M4.

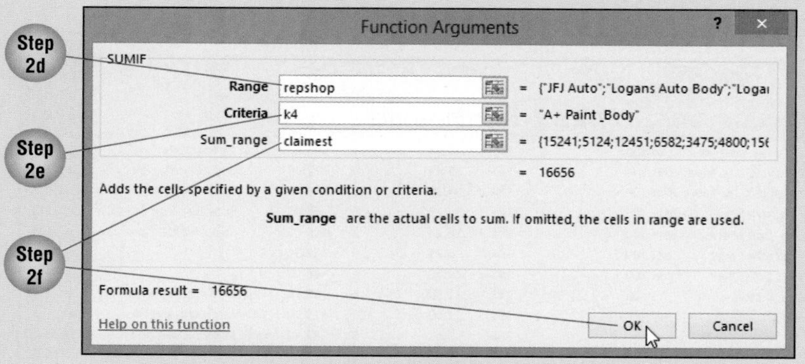

   g. Apply comma formatting with no places after the decimal point to cell M4.
3. Use the fill handle to copy the formula in cell M4 to cells M5 through M7. When completed, the SUMIF formulas will be as follows:
   M5: *=SUMIF(RepShop,K5,ClaimEst)*
   M6: *=SUMIF(RepShop,K6,ClaimEst)*
   M7: *=SUMIF(RepShop,K7,ClaimEst)*
4. Save and then print **EL2-C2-P1-ACOct15VehRpt.xlsx**.

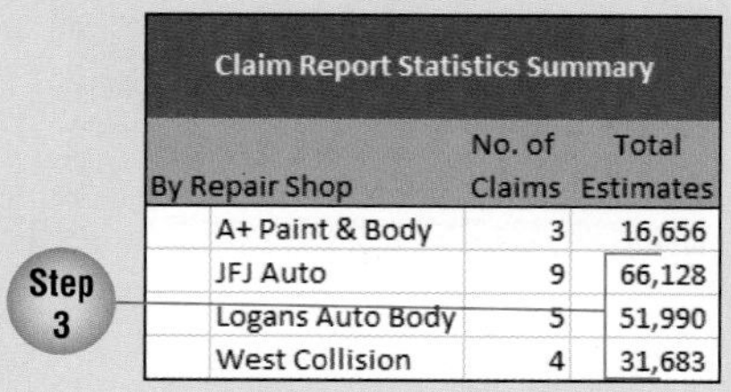

Managing Range Names

The Name Manager dialog box, which you can open by clicking the Name Manager button in the Defined Names group on the FORMULAS tab, can be used to create, edit, and delete range names. A range name can be edited by changing the name or modifying the range address associated with the name. A range name can also be deleted, but you should use extra caution when doing so. If you delete a range name used in a formula, cells that used that formula will display the error text *#NAME?* You can also use the Name Manager dialog box to add new range names to a worksheet. The Name Manager dialog box is shown in Figure 2.5.

Quick Steps

Delete a Range Name
1. Click FORMULAS tab.
2. Click Name Manager button.
3. Click desired range name.
4. Click Delete button.
5. Click OK.
6. Click Close.

Edit a Range Name
1. Click FORMULAS tab.
2. Click Name Manager button.
3. Click desired range name.
4. Click Edit button.
5. Type new range name in *Name* text box.
6. Click OK.
7. Click Close.

Name Manager

Figure 2.5 Name Manager Dialog Box

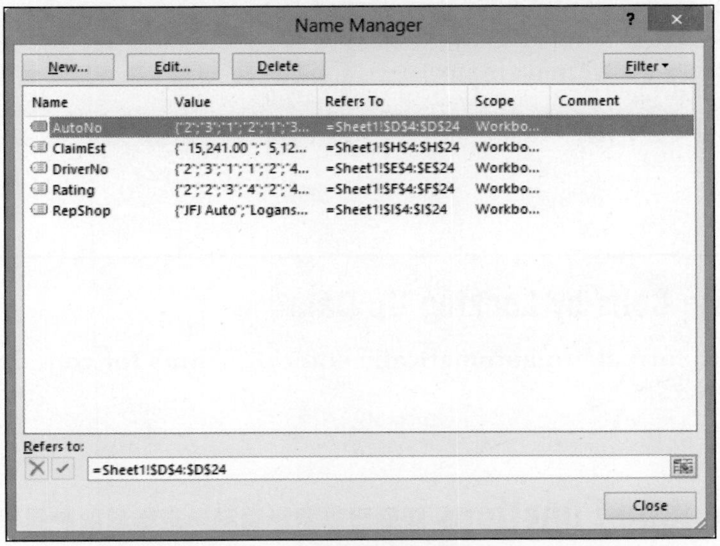

Project 1g **Editing and Deleting a Range Name** **Part 7 of 7**

1. With **EL2-C2-P1-ACOct15VehRpt.xlsx** open, click the FORMULAS tab if it is not currently active.
2. Delete the range name *AutoNo* by completing the following steps:
   a. Click the Name Manager button in the Defined Names group.
   b. At the Name Manager dialog box, with *AutoNo* already selected in the *Name* column, click the Delete button.
   c. At the Microsoft Excel message box asking you to confirm the deletion of the name *AutoNo*, click OK.

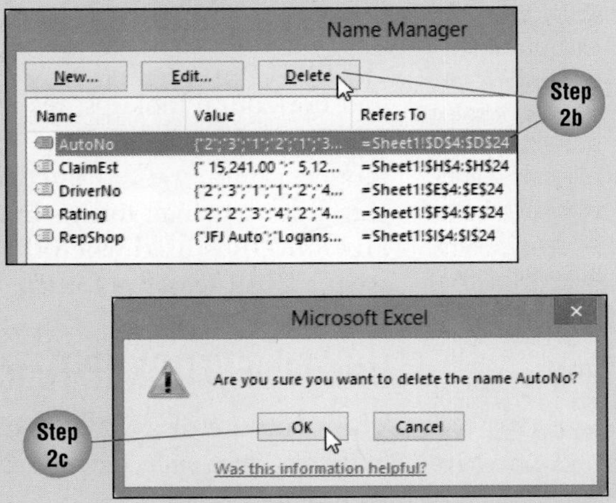

3. Edit the range name for the range named *ClaimEst* by completing the following steps:
   a. Click *ClaimEst* in the *Name* column at the Name Manager dialog box and then click the Edit button.
   b. At the Edit Name dialog box with *ClaimEst* selected in the *Name* text box, type ClaimEstimate and then click OK. Notice the new range name is now displayed in the *Name* column.
   c. Click the Close button located at the bottom right of the Name Manager dialog box.
4. Click in cell M4 and look at the formula in the Formula bar. Notice that Excel automatically changed the range name in the formula from *ClaimEst* to *ClaimEstimate*.
5. Save and then close **EL2-C2-P1-ACOct15VehRpt.xlsx**.

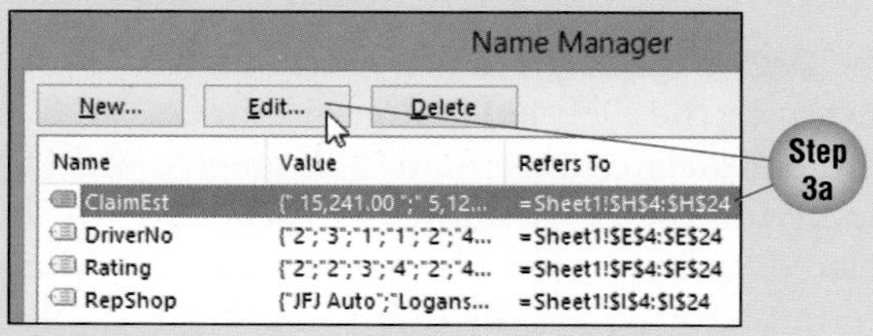

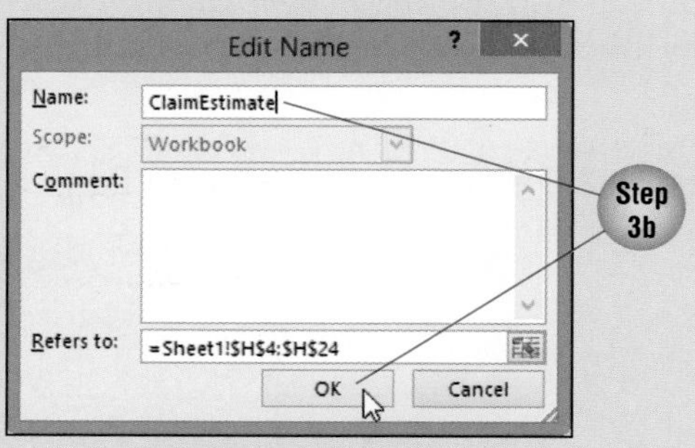

Project 2 Populate Cells by Looking Up Data — 1 Part

You will use a lookup formula to automatically enter discounts for containers and then calculate net prices.

Quick Steps

Create a VLOOKUP Formula

1. Make desired cell active.
2. Click FORMULAS tab.
3. Click Lookup & Reference button.
4. Click *VLOOKUP*.
5. Enter cell address, range name, or value in *Lookup_value* text box.
6. Enter range or range name in *Table_array* text box.
7. Type column number to return values from in *Col_index_num* text box.
8. Type false or leave blank for TRUE in *Range_lookup* text box.
9. Click OK.

Lookup & Reference

Using Lookup Functions

The Lookup & Reference functions provide formulas that can be used to look up values in a range. For example, in a grades worksheet, the final numerical score for a student can be looked up in a range of cells that contain the letter grades with a corresponding numerical score for each grade. The letter grade can be returned in the formula cell by looking up the student's score. Being able to look up a value automates data entry in large worksheets and, when used properly, can prevent inaccuracies caused by data entry errors.

Excel provides the VLOOKUP and HLOOKUP functions, which refer to vertical and horizontal lookups, respectively. The layout of the lookup range (referred to as a ***lookup table***) determines whether to use VLOOKUP or HLOOKUP. VLOOKUP is more commonly used, since most lookup tables are arranged with comparison data in columns (which means Excel searches for the lookup value in a vertical order). HLOOKUP is used when the lookup range contains comparison data in rows (which means Excel searches for the lookup value in a horizontal pattern).

Using the VLOOKUP Function

The structure of a VLOOKUP formula is =*VLOOKUP(lookup_value,table_array,col_index_num,range_lookup)*. Table 2.2 explains each section of the VLOOKUP argument.

Table 2.2 VLOOKUP Argument Parameters

Argument Parameter	*Description*
lookup_value	This is the value that you want Excel to search for in the lookup table. You can enter a value or cell reference to a value.
table_array	This is the range address or range name for the lookup table that you want Excel to search.
col_index_num	This is the column number from the lookup table that contains the data you want placed in the formula cell.
range_lookup	Enter TRUE to instruct Excel to find an exact or approximate match for the lookup value. If this parameter is left out of the formula, Excel assumes TRUE, which means if an exact match is not found, Excel returns the value for the next largest number that is less than the lookup value. For the formula to work properly, the first column of the lookup table must be sorted in ascending order. Enter FALSE to instruct Excel to return only exact matches to the lookup value.

The VLOOKUP function is easier to understand when explained using an example. In the worksheet shown in Figure 2.6, VLOOKUP is used to return the starting salary for new hires at a medical center. Each new hire is assigned a salary grid number depending on education and years of work experience. This salary grid number determines his or her starting salary. The lookup table contains the grid numbers with the corresponding starting salaries. In column E, VLOOKUP formulas automatically insert the starting salary for each new employee based on his or her grid number in column D. In the formula shown in Figure 2.6, range names have been included, where *Rating* references the values in column D and *grid* represents the lookup table in G4:H8.

Figure 2.6 VLOOKUP Example

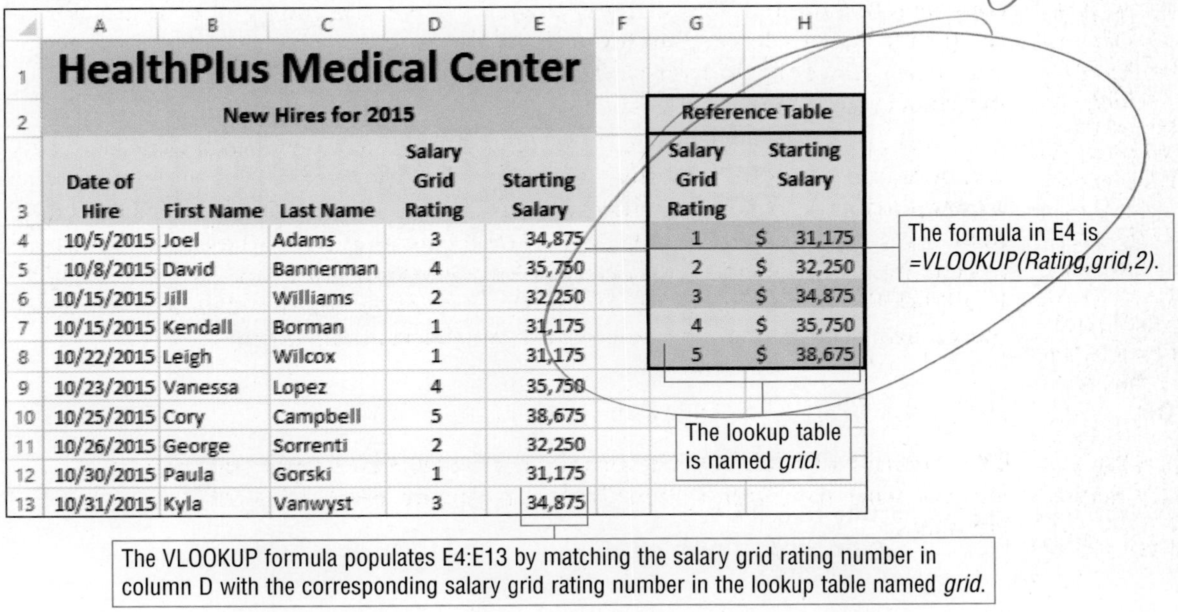

	A	B	C	D	E	F	G	H
1	HealthPlus Medical Center							
2	New Hires for 2015						Reference Table	
3	Date of Hire	First Name	Last Name	Salary Grid Rating	Starting Salary		Salary Grid Rating	Starting Salary
4	10/5/2015	Joel	Adams	3	34,875		1	$ 31,175
5	10/8/2015	David	Bannerman	4	35,750		2	$ 32,250
6	10/15/2015	Jill	Williams	2	32,250		3	$ 34,875
7	10/15/2015	Kendall	Borman	1	31,175		4	$ 35,750
8	10/22/2015	Leigh	Wilcox	1	31,175		5	$ 38,675
9	10/23/2015	Vanessa	Lopez	4	35,750			
10	10/25/2015	Cory	Campbell	5	38,675			
11	10/26/2015	George	Sorrenti	2	32,250			
12	10/30/2015	Paula	Gorski	1	31,175			
13	10/31/2015	Kyla	Vanwyst	3	34,875			

Project 2 Creating a VLOOKUP Function

Part 1 of 1

1. Open **PrecisionPrices.xlsx**.
2. Save the workbook and name it **EL2-C2-P2-PrecisionPrices**.
3. Create a VLOOKUP formula to find the correct discount values for each product by completing the following steps:
   a. Select H4:I8 and name the range *DiscTable*.
   b. Make cell E4 active and then click the FORMULAS tab.
   c. Click the Lookup & Reference button in the Function Library group.
   d. Click *VLOOKUP* at the drop-down list.
   e. If necessary, drag the Function Arguments dialog box out of the way so that you can see the first few rows of the product price list and the discount table data.
   f. With the insertion point positioned in the *Lookup_value* text box, type c4 and then press Tab. Product discounts are categorized by letter codes. To find the correct discount, you need Excel to look for the matching category letter code for the product within the first column of the discount table. Notice that the letter codes in the discount table are listed in ascending order.
   g. Type disctable in the *Table_array* text box and then press Tab. Using a range name for a reference table is a good idea, since the formula will be copied and absolute references are needed for the cells in the lookup table.
   h. Type 2 in the *Col_index_num* text box and then press Tab. You want the discount percentage in column 2 of DiscTable placed in cell E4.
   i. Type false in the *Range_lookup* text box and then click OK. By entering *false*, you are instructing Excel to return a value for exact matches only. Should a discount category be typed into a cell in column C for which no entry exists in the discount table, Excel will return *#N/A* in the formula cell, which will alert you that an error has occurred in the data entry.
4. Look at the formula in the Formula bar: *=VLOOKUP(C4,DiscTable,2,FALSE)*.

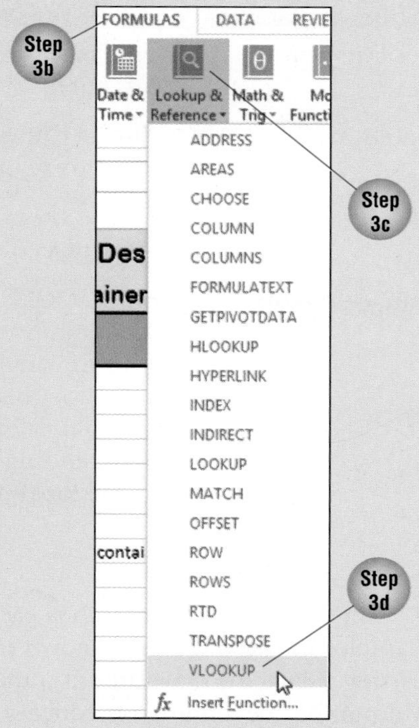

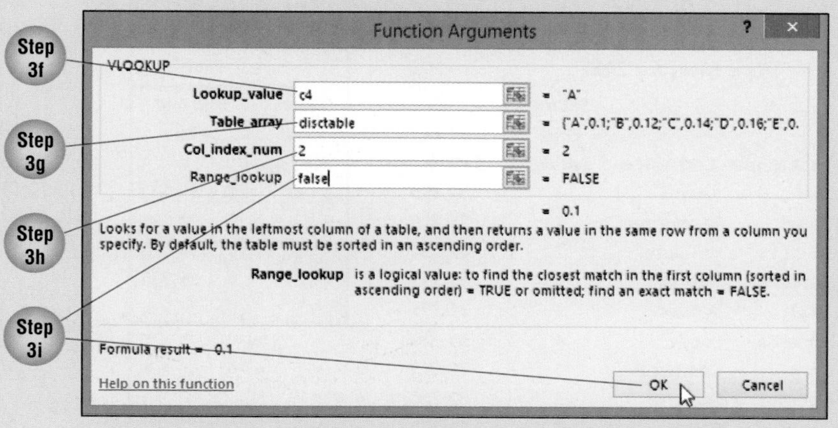

5. Apply percent formatting to cell E4.
6. Make cell F4 active, type the formula =d4-(d4*e4), and then press Enter.

7. Select E4:F4 and then drag the fill handle down to row 21.
8. Deselect the range.
9. Print the worksheet.
10. Save and then close **EL2-C2-P2-PrecisionPrices.xlsx**.

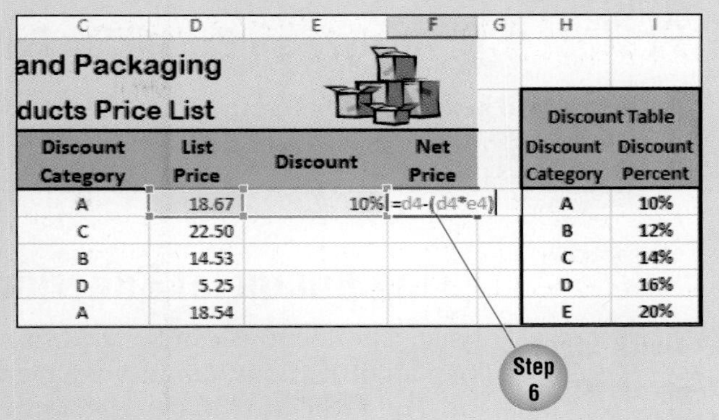

C	D	E	F	G	H	I
and Packaging						
ducts Price List					Discount Table	
Discount Category	List Price	Discount	Net Price		Discount Category	Discount Percent
A	18.67	10%	=d4-(d4*e4)		A	10%
C	22.50				B	12%
B	14.53				C	14%
D	5.25				D	16%
A	18.54				E	20%

Using the HLOOKUP Function

The HLOOKUP function uses the same argument parameters as the VLOOKUP function. Use HLOOKUP when the table in which you want to search for a comparison value is arranged horizontally, like the one shown in J3:O4 in Figure 2.7. Excel searches across the table in the first row for a matching value and then returns to the formula cell the value from the same column.

The structure of an HLOOKUP formula is *=HLOOKUP(lookup_value,table_array,row_index_num,range_lookup)*. The argument parameters are similar to the VLOOKUP parameters described in Table 2.2 on page 53. Excel searches the first row of the table for the lookup value. When a match is found, Excel returns the value from the same column in the row number specified in the *row_index_num* argument.

Figure 2.7 HLOOKUP Example

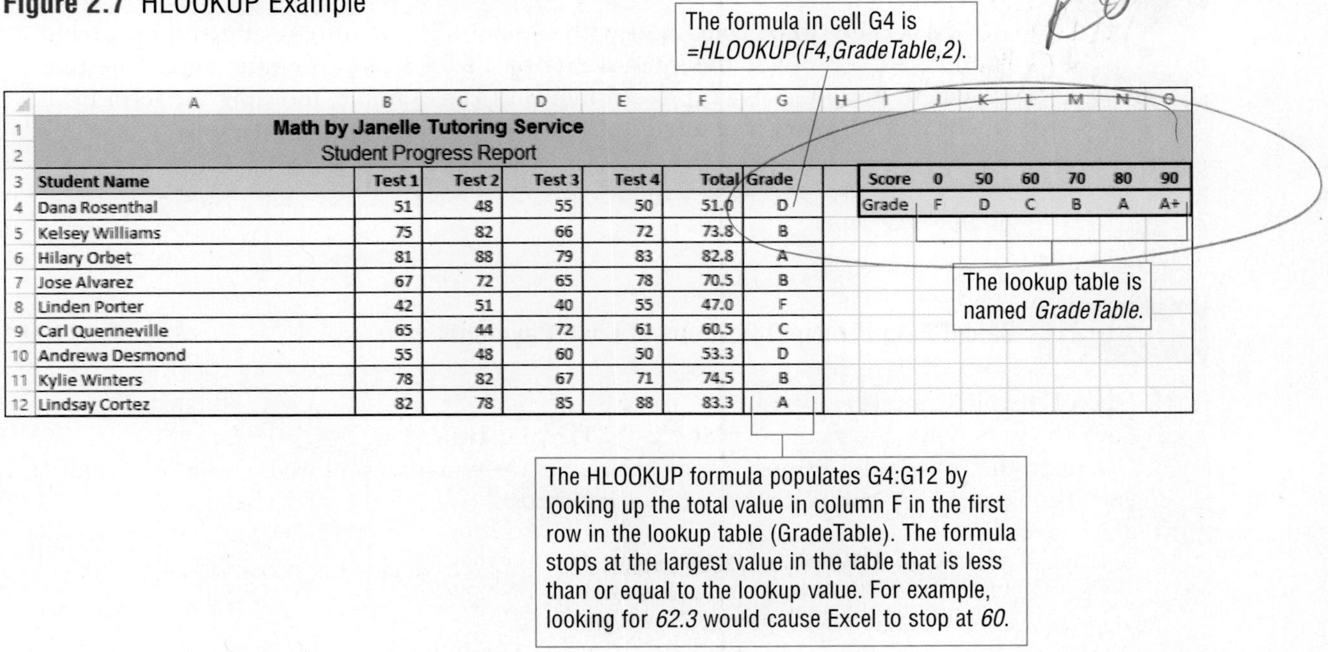

	A	B	C	D	E	F	G	H	I	J	K	L	M	N	O
1	Math by Janelle Tutoring Service														
2	Student Progress Report														
3	Student Name	Test 1	Test 2	Test 3	Test 4	Total	Grade			Score	0	50	60	70	80	90
4	Dana Rosenthal	51	48	55	50	51.0	D			Grade	F	D	C	B	A	A+
5	Kelsey Williams	75	82	66	72	73.8	B									
6	Hilary Orbet	81	88	79	83	82.8	A									
7	Jose Alvarez	67	72	65	78	70.5	B									
8	Linden Porter	42	51	40	55	47.0	F									
9	Carl Quenneville	65	44	72	61	60.5	C									
10	Andrewa Desmond	55	48	60	50	53.3	D									
11	Kylie Winters	78	82	67	71	74.5	B									
12	Lindsay Cortez	82	78	85	88	83.3	A									

Project 3 Analyze an Expansion Project Loan — 1 Part

You will use a financial function to calculate the principal portion of an expansion loan payment for two lenders.

Using Financial Functions: PPMT and IPMT

Financial functions can be used to perform a variety of financial analyses, including loan amortizations, annuity payments, investment planning, depreciation, and so on. The PMT function is used to calculate a payment for a loan based on a constant interest rate and constant payments for a set period of time. Excel provides two related financial functions: PPMT, to calculate the principal portion of the loan payment; and IPMT, to calculate the interest portion.

Knowing the principal portion of a loan payment is useful in determining the amount of the payment that is being used to reduce the principal balance owed. The difference between the loan payment and PPMT value represents the interest cost. The function returns the principal portion of a specific payment for a loan. For example, you can calculate the principal on the first payment, last payment, or any payment in between. The structure of a PPMT function is *=PPMT(rate,per,nper,pv,fv,type)*, where

- *rate* is the interest rate per period,
- *per* is the period for which you want to find the principal portion of the payment,
- *nper* is the number of payment periods,
- *pv* is the amount of money borrowed,
- *fv* is the balance at the end of the loan (if left blank, 0 is assumed), and
- *type* is either 0 (payment at end of period) or 1 (payment at beginning of period).

Make sure to be consistent with the units for the interest rate and payment periods. If you divide the interest rate by 12 for a monthly rate, make sure the payment period is also expressed monthly. For example, multiply the term by 12 if the amortization is entered in the worksheet in years.

Quick Steps

Create a PPMT Formula

1. Make desired cell active.
2. Click FORMULAS tab.
3. Click Financial button.
4. Click *PPMT.*
5. Enter value, cell address, or range name for interest rate in *Rate* text box.
6. Enter number representing payment to find principal for in *Per* text box.
7. Enter value, cell address, or range name for total number of payments in *Nper* text box.
8. Enter value, cell address, or range name for amount borrowed in *Pv* text box.
9. Click OK.

Financial

Project 3 Calculating Principal Portions of Loan Payments — Part 1 of 1

1. Open **DExpansion.xlsx**.
2. Save the workbook and name it **EL2-C2-P3-DExpansion.xlsx**.
3. Calculate the principal portions of loan payments for two loan proposals to fund a building expansion project by completing the following steps:
   a. Make cell C10 active.
   b. If necessary, click the FORMULAS tab.

c. Click the Financial button in the Function Library group.
d. Scroll down the drop-down list and then click *PPMT*.
e. If necessary, move the Function Arguments dialog box to the right side of the screen so that you can see all of the values in column C.
f. With the insertion point positioned in the *Rate* text box, type c4/12 and then press Tab. Since the interest rate is stated per annum, dividing the rate by 12 calculates the monthly rate.
g. Type 1 in the *Per* text box to calculate principal for the first loan payment and then press Tab.
h. Type c5*12 in the *Nper* text box and then press Tab. Since a loan payment is made each month, the number of payments is 12 times the amortization period.
i. Type c6 in the *Pv* text box and then click OK. *Pv* refers to present value and, in this example, means the loan amount for which the payments are being calculated. It is positive because it represents cash received by the company. Excel returns the value *-1,291.40* in cell C10. Payments are shown as negative numbers because they represent cash that is paid out. In this worksheet, negative numbers have been formatted to display in red and enclosed in parentheses.

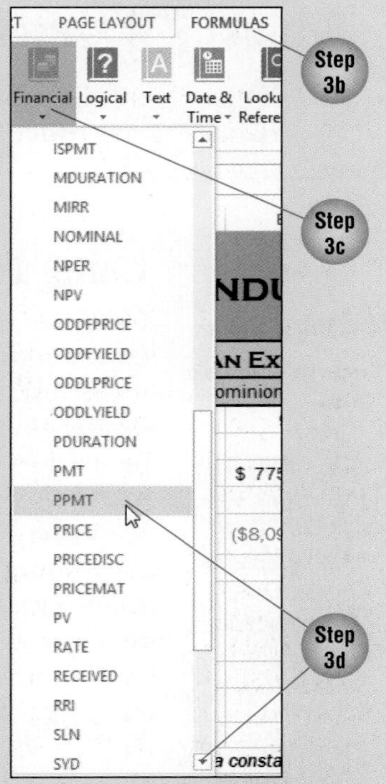

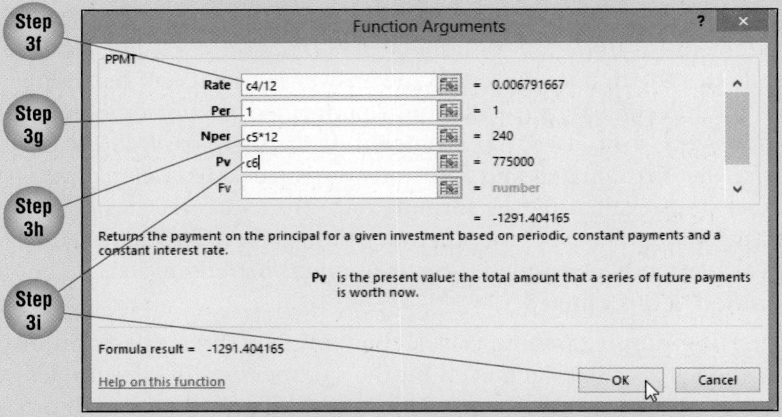

4. Copy and paste the formula from cell C10 to cell E10 and then press Esc to remove the scrolling marquee from cell C10.
5. Make cell C12 active, type =c8*12*c5, and then press Enter.
6. Copy and paste the formula from cell C12 to cell E12. Press Esc to remove the scrolling marquee from cell C12 and then AutoFit the width of column E. Notice that the loan from Dominion Trust is a better choice for Deering Industries, assuming the company can afford the higher monthly payments. Although the interest rate is higher than that for the Victory Trust loan, the shorter term means the loan will be repaid faster and at a lesser total cost.
7. Print the worksheet.
8. Save and then close **EL2-C2-P3-DExpansion.xlsx**.

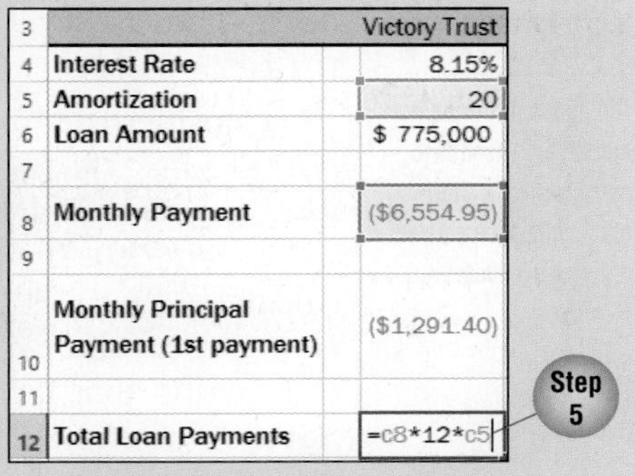

Project 4 Calculate Benefit Costs Using Conditional Logic — 2 Parts

You will create formulas to calculate the employee benefit costs for ViewItVideo using logical functions to test multiple conditions.

Using Logical Functions

Quick Steps

Create an IF Formula
1. Make desired cell active.
2. Click FORMULAS tab.
3. Click Logical button.
4. Click *IF*.
5. Type conditional test argument in *Logical_test* text box.
6. Press Tab.
7. Type argument in *Value_if_true* text box.
8. Press Tab.
9. Type argument in *Value_if_false* text box.
10. Click OK.

Logical

HINT If you type a nested IF function directly into a cell, Excel color-codes the parentheses for each IF function so you can keep track of each IF function separately.

HINT The number of right parentheses needed to end a nested IF statement equals the number of times IF appears in the formula.

Using conditional logic in a formula requires Excel to perform a calculation based on the outcome of a logical or conditional test. One calculation is performed if the test proves true and another calculation is performed if the test proves false. For example, the following is an IF formula using named ranges that could be used to calculate a salesperson's bonus if his or her sales exceed a target: *=IF(Sales>Target,Bonus,0)*. Excel first tests the value in the cell named *Sales* to see if the value is greater than the value in the cell named *Target*. If the condition proves true, Excel returns the value of the bonus in the cell named *Bonus;* if the sales are not greater than the target, the condition proves false and Excel places a *0* in the cell. The structure of the IF statement is *=IF(logical_test,value_if_true,value_if_false)*.

Creating Nested Functions

If you need Excel to perform more than two actions, create a nested IF function. A nested IF function is one IF function inside of another. The structure of a nested IF statement is *=IF(logical_test,value_if_true,IF(logical_test,value_if_true,value_if_false))*. Excel evaluates the first *logical_test*. If the answer is true, then depending on what is entered for the *value_if_true*, a calculation is performed, text or numbers are entered, or if the *value_if_true* is omitted, a 0 is entered. If the first *logical_test* is not true, then the next *logical_test* is evaluated and if the answer is true, the *value_if_true* is placed in the cell. Excel stops evaluating the formula once the *logical_test* has been answered as true. If the answer is never true, then depending on what is entered as the *value_if_false*, a calculation is performed, text or numbers are entered, or if the *value_if_false* is omitted, a 0 is entered.

For example, assume that a company has three sales commission rates based on the level of sales achieved by the salesperson. If sales are less than $40,000, the salesperson earns a 5% commission; if sales are greater than or equal to $40,000 but less than $80,000, the salesperson earns a 7% commission; and if sales are greater than or equal to $80,000, the salesperson earns a 9% commission. Since there are three possible sales commission rates, a single IF function will not work. To correctly calculate the sales commission rate, two conditional tests must be done. The last level (or in this case, the third commission rate of 9%) is used for the *value_if_false*.

Consider the following formula: *=IF(Sales<40000,Sales*5%,IF(Sales<80000,Sales*7%,Sales*9%))*. This formula includes two IF functions. In the first IF function, the conditional test is to determine if the sales value is less than $40,000 (*Sales<40000*). If the test proves true (for example, sales are $25,000), then Excel calculates the sales times 5% and returns the result in the active cell. If the test is not true, then Excel reads the next section of the argument, which is the next IF function that includes the conditional test to determine if sales are less than $80,000 (*Sales<80000*). If this second conditional test proves true, then Excel calculates the sales times 7%. If the test proves false, Excel calculates the sales times 9%. Since these are the only three possible actions, the formula ends. While up to 64 IF functions can be nested, doing that would be a very complex formula. Consider using a VLOOKUP or HLOOKUP to test different conditions.

You can nest any function inside another function. For example, in the PPMT formula you learned in the previous section, Excel returns a negative value for the principal portion of the payment. You can nest the PPMT formula inside the ABS formula to have the principal payment displayed without a negative symbol. ABS is the function used to return the absolute value of a number (that is, the number without its sign). For example, *=ABS(PPMT(C4/12,1,C5*12,C6))* displays the payment calculated in Project 3 as $1,291.40 instead of -$1,291.40.

Using the AND and OR Functions

Other logical functions offered in Excel include AND and OR. These functions use Boolean logic to construct a conditional test in a formula. Table 2.3 describes how each function works to test a statement and also provides an example of each function.

Table 2.3 AND and OR Logical Functions

Logical Function	*Description*	*Example*
AND	Excel returns *True* if all of the conditions test true. Excel returns *False* if any one of the conditions tests false.	*=AND(Sales>Target,NewClients>5)* Returns *True* if both test true. Returns *False* if Sales is greater than Target but NewClients is less than 5. Returns *False* if Sales is less than Target but NewClients is greater than 5.
OR	Excel returns *True* if any of the condition tests true. Excel returns *False* if all of the conditions test false.	*=OR(Sales>Target,NewClients>5)* Returns *True* if Sales is greater than Target or NewClients is greater than 5. Returns *False* only if Sales is not greater than Target and NewClients is not greater than 5.

Quick Steps

Create an AND Formula
1. Make desired cell active OR nest formula in IF statement *Logical_test* text box.
2. Type =and(or and(if nesting in IF statement.
3. Type first conditional test argument.
4. Type ,.
5. Type second conditional test argument.
6. Repeat Steps 4–5 for remaining conditions.
7. Type).

Create an OR Formula
1. Make desired cell active OR nest formula in IF statement *Logical_test* text box.
2. Type =or(or or(if nesting in IF statement.
3. Type first conditional test argument.
4. Type ,.
5. Type second conditional test argument.
6. Repeat Steps 4–5 for remaining conditions.
7. Type).

HINT

You can nest an AND or OR function with an IF function to test multiple conditions.

Project 4a **Calculating Pension Costs Using Nested IF and AND Functions** **Part 1 of 2**

1. Open **VIVSalCost.xlsx**.
2. Save the workbook and name it **EL2-C2-P4-VIVSalCost**.
3. ViewItVideo contributes 5% of an employee's salary into a privately managed company retirement account if the employee works full time and earns more than $45,000 a year in salary. Calculate the pension benefit costs for eligible employees by completing the following steps:
   a. Make cell H6 the active cell.
   b. Click the FORMULAS tab.

c. Click the Logical button in the Function Library group and then click *IF* at the drop-down list.

d. If necessary, drag the Function Arguments dialog box down until you can see all of row 6 in the worksheet.

e. With the insertion point positioned in the *Logical_test* text box, type and(c6="FT",g6>45000) and then press Tab. An AND function is required, since both conditions must be true for the company to contribute to the pension plan. ***Note: Excel requires quotation marks around text when it is used in a conditional test formula.***

f. Type g6*5% in the *Value_if_true* text box and then press Tab.

g. Type 0 in the *Value_if_false* text box and then click OK.

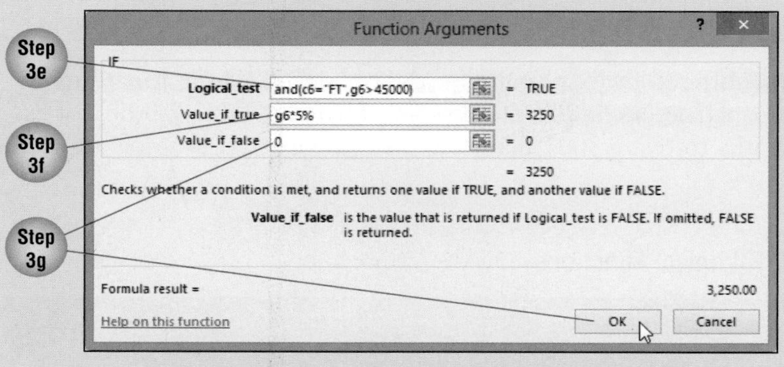

h. Look at the formula *=IF(AND(C6="FT",G6>45000),G6*5%,0)* in the Formula bar. Notice the AND function is nested within the IF function. Since both conditions for the first employee tested true, the pension cost is calculated.

i. Copy the formula in cell H6 to H7:H14. Notice that only the first three employees have pension benefit values. This is because they are the only employees who both work full time and earn over $45,000 a year in salary.

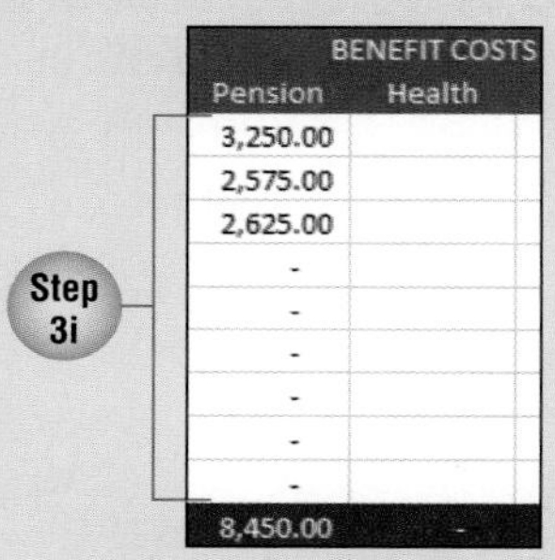

4. Save **EL2-C2-P4-VIVSalCost.xlsx**.

Project 4b Calculating Health and Dental Costs Using Nested IF and OR Functions Part 2 of 2

1. With **EL2-C2-P4-VIVSalCost.xlsx** open, make cell I6 the active cell.
2. ViewItVideo offers to pay the annual health premiums for employees not covered by any other medical plan. The company pays $2,100 per year per employee for family coverage, $1,380 per year per employee for single coverage, and $0 per year if the employee declines coverage. Calculate the cost for each employee who opted into the health plan by completing the following steps:

   a. This formula requires a nested IF statement, since the result will be *$2,180, $1,380,* or *0* depending on the contents of cell D6. (An OR statement will not work for this formula, since two different health premiums are used.) Type the formula shown below in cell I6 and then press Enter. ***Note: Recall that Excel requires the use of quotation marks around text entries within an IF function.*** =if(d6="Family",2100,if(d6="Single",1380,0))

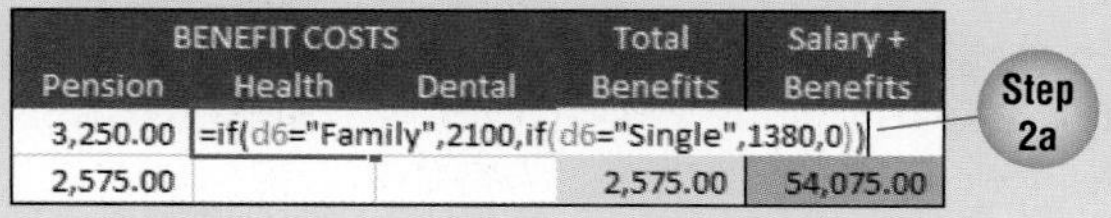

b. Copy the formula in cell I6 to I7:I14. Notice the cells in column I for which no value is entered. In column D in the corresponding row, the text *Declined* displays. Excel returned a value of 0 in column I since conditions *D6="Family"* and *D6="Single"* both proved false.

3. ViewItVideo negotiated a flat fee with its dental benefit service provider. The company pays $1,500 per year for each employee, regardless of the type of coverage. The service provider requires ViewItVideo to report each person's coverage as *Family* or *Single* for audit purposes. The dental plan is optional and some employees have declined the coverage. Calculate the cost of the dental plan by completing the following steps:
   a. Make cell J6 the active cell.
   b. If necessary, click the FORMULAS tab.
   c. Click the Logical button and then click *IF* at the drop-down list.
   d. If necessary, drag the Function Arguments dialog box down until you can see all of row 6 in the worksheet.
   e. With the insertion point positioned in the *Logical_test* text box, type or(e6="Family",e6="Single") and then press Tab. An OR function is suited to this benefit, since either condition can be true for the company to contribute to the dental plan.
   f. Type 1500 in the *Value_if_true* text box and then press Tab.
   g. Type 0 in the *Value_if_false* text box and then click OK.

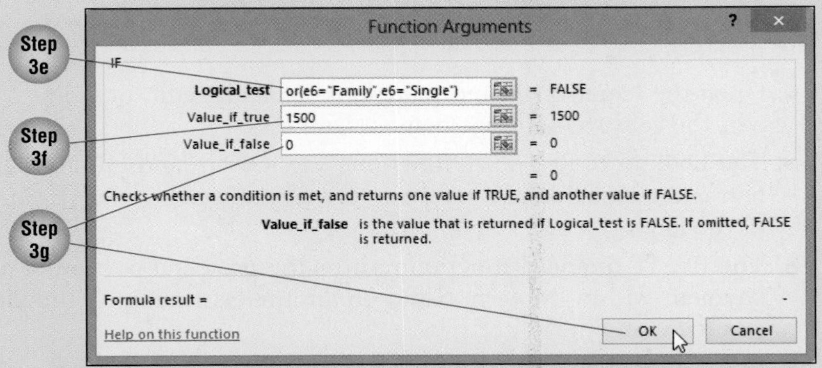

   h. Look at the formula *=IF(OR(E6="Family", E6="Single"),1500,0)* in the Formula bar. Notice that the OR function is nested within the IF function. Since cell E6 contains neither *Family* nor *Single*, the OR statement tests false and *0* is returned in cell J6.
   i. Copy the formula in cell J6 to J7:J14.

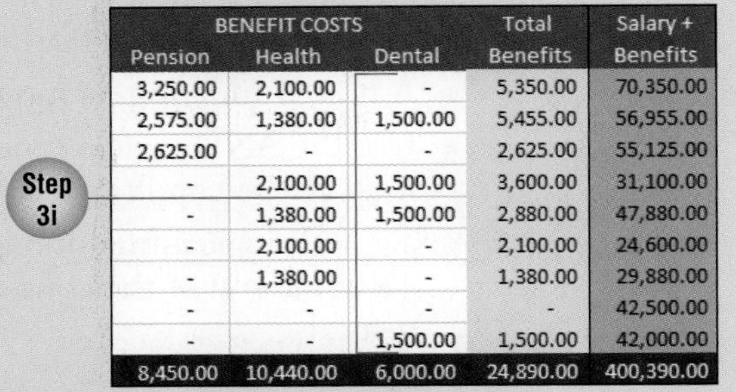

BENEFIT COSTS			Total	Salary +
Pension	Health	Dental	Benefits	Benefits
3,250.00	2,100.00	-	5,350.00	70,350.00
2,575.00	1,380.00	1,500.00	5,455.00	56,955.00
2,625.00	-	-	2,625.00	55,125.00
-	2,100.00	1,500.00	3,600.00	31,100.00
-	1,380.00	1,500.00	2,880.00	47,880.00
-	2,100.00	-	2,100.00	24,600.00
-	1,380.00	-	1,380.00	29,880.00
-	-	-	-	42,500.00
-	-	1,500.00	1,500.00	42,000.00
8,450.00	10,440.00	6,000.00	24,890.00	400,390.00

4. Save **EL2-C2-P4-VIVSalCost.xlsx**.
5. Print and then close **EL2-C2-P4-VIVSalCost.xlsx**.

In this chapter, you learned how to use a small sampling of functions from the statistical, math and trigonometry, lookup, financial, and logical categories. Excel provides more than 300 functions in 11 categories. When you need to enter a complex formula and are not sure if Excel includes a preprogrammed function, open the Insert Function dialog box, type a description of the function in the *Search for a function* text box, and then click the Go button.

Chapter Summary

- Assign names to cells or ranges to reference in formulas or navigation.
- Using range names in formulas makes it easier to understand the formulas.
- Create a range name by selecting the source range and then typing a name in the Name box.
- The COUNTA statistical function counts cells that are not blank.. Use the function to count cells containing text and a combination of text and numbers.
- The COUNTIF statistical function counts cells within a range based on a single criterion.
- The COUNTIFS statistical function counts cells within a range based on multiple criteria.
- Find the arithmetic mean of a range of cells based on a single criterion using the statistical AVERAGEIF function.
- The AVERAGEIFS statistical function finds the arithmetic mean for a range based on multiple criteria.
- The math function SUMIF adds cells within a range based on a single criterion.
- To add cells within a range based on multiple criteria, use the SUMIFS math function.
- Open the Name Manager dialog box to create, edit, or delete a range name or edit the cells that a range name references.
- The Lookup & Reference functions VLOOKUP and HLOOKUP look up data in a reference table and return in the formula cell a value from a column or row in the lookup table.
- The PPMT financial function returns the principal portion of a specified loan payment within the term based on an interest rate, total number of payments, and loan amount.
- Conditional logic in a formula performs a calculation based on the outcome of a conditional test, in which one action is performed if the test proves true and another action is performed if the test proves false.
- A nested function is one function inside another function.
- Use the AND logical function to test multiple conditions. Excel returns *TRUE* if all of the conditions test true and *FALSE* if any of the conditions test false.
- The OR logical function also tests multiple conditions. The function returns *TRUE* if any of the conditions tests true and *FALSE* if all of the conditions test false.

Commands Review

FEATURE	RIBBON TAB, GROUP	BUTTON	KEYBOARD SHORTCUT
financial functions	FORMULAS, Function Library		
Insert Function dialog box	FORMULAS, Function Library	fx	Shift + F3
logical functions	FORMULAS, Function Library		
lookup and reference functions	FORMULAS, Function Library		
math and trigonometry functions	FORMULAS, Function Library		
Name Manager dialog box	FORMULAS, Defined Names		Ctrl + F3
statistical functions accessed from More Functions button	FORMULAS, Function Library		

Concepts Check

Test Your Knowledge

Completion: In the space provided at the right, indicate the correct term, command, or number.

1. Assign a name to a selected range by typing the desired name in this box. ____________________
2. A range name can be a combination of letters, numbers, underscore characters, and this punctuation character. ____________________
3. Use this function to count cells that contain text or a combination of text and numbers. ____________________
4. Write the COUNTIF function that will count the number of cells in a range named *Sales* in which the values are greater than $50,000. ____________________
5. Use this statistical function to find the mean of a range based on two criteria. ____________________
6. SUMIF is found in this category of functions. ____________________
7. Open this dialog box to delete a range name. ____________________
8. Use this lookup function to locate a value in a reference table in which the comparison data is arranged in rows. ____________________

9. This financial function returns the principal portion of a specified loan payment. ____________

10. Access the IF function from this button in the Function Library group on the FORMULAS tab. ____________

11. This term refers to a formula in which one function is created inside another function. ____________

12. Excel's AND and OR functions use this type of logic to construct conditional tests. ____________

Skills Check Assess Your Performance

Assessment 1

CREATE RANGE NAMES AND USE THE LOOKUP FUNCTION

SNAP Grade It

Note: If you submit your work in hard copy, check with your instructor before printing assessments to see if you need to print two copies: one with numbers displayed and another with cell formulas displayed.

1. Open **RSROctLabor.xlsx**.
2. Save the workbook and name it **EL2-C2-A1-RSROctLabor**.
3. Create the following range names:

   F7:F22 *LaborCost*

   I3:J5 *RateChart*
4. Change the range name for the range named *Hr* to *Hours*.
5. In cell E7, create a VLOOKUP formula to return the correct hourly rate based on the technician code in cell D7. Use the range name *RateChart* within the formula to reference the hourly rate chart. Make sure Excel will return values for exact matches only.
6. Create or copy the following formulas:
   a. Copy the VLOOKUP formula in cell E7 and paste it into E8:E22.
   b. In cell F7, multiply the named range *Hours* by the hourly rate in cell E7.
   c. Copy the formula in cell F7 and paste it into F8:F22.
   d. Create the formula in cell F23 to sum the column.
7. Preview and then print the worksheet.
8. Save and then close **EL2-C2-A1-RSROctLabor.xlsx**.

Assessment 2

USE CONDITIONAL STATISTICAL AND MATH FUNCTIONS

SNAP Grade It

Note: For all functions in Assessment 2 with the exception of Step 3, use range names in the formulas to reference sources.

1. Open **EL2-C2-A1-RSROctLabor.xlsx**.
2. Save the workbook and name it **EL2-C2-A2-RSROctLabor**.

3. In cell I23, create a COUNTA formula to count the number of calls made in October using the dates in column A as the source range.
4. Using the range named *TechCode,* create COUNTIF formulas in the cells indicated below:
   I9: Count the number of calls made by technician 1.
   I10: Count the number of calls made by technician 2.
   I11: Count the number of calls made by technician 3.
5. Using range names where possible, in cell I14, create a COUNTIFS formula to count the number of calls made by technician 3 for which the hours logged were greater than three.
6. Using the ranges named *TechCode* and *LaborCost,* create SUMIF formulas in the cells indicated below:
   J9: Add the labor cost for calls made by technician 1.
   J10: Add the labor cost for calls made by technician 2.
   J11: Add the labor cost for calls made by technician 3.
7. Using the ranges named *TechCode, LaborCost,* and *Hours,* create a SUMIFS formula in cell J14 to add the labor cost for calls made by technician 3 (criteria 1) in which the hours logged were greater than three (criteria 2).
8. Using the named ranges *TechCode* and *LaborCost,* create AVERAGEIF formulas in the cells indicated below:
   J18: Average the labor cost for calls made by technician 1.
   J19: Average the labor cost for calls made by technician 2.
   J20: Average the labor cost for calls made by technician 3.
9. Apply comma formatting to the following cells:
   J9:J11
   J14
   J18:J20
10. Save, print, and then close **EL2-C2-A2-RSROctLabor.xlsx.**

Assessment 3

USE THE FINANCIAL FUNCTIONS PMT AND PPMT

SNAP Grade It

1. Open **PrecisionWarehouse.xlsx.**
2. Save the workbook and name it **EL2-C2-A3-PrecisionWarehouse.xlsx.**
3. Using cell references, create a PMT formula in cell D8 to calculate the monthly loan payment for a proposed loan from NewVentures Capital Inc. ***Note: The PMT payment uses the same arguments as PPMT with the exception that there is no* Per *criterion. Remember to divide the rate by 12 and multiply the nper by 12 to use monthly units.***
4. Using cell references, find the principal portion of the loan payment for the first loan payment in cell D10 and the last loan payment in cell D11 using PPMT formulas.
5. In cell D13, create a formula to calculate the total cost of the loan by multiplying the monthly loan payment times the amortization period in years times 12.
6. Print the worksheet.
7. Save and then close **EL2-C2-A3-PrecisionWarehouse.xlsx.**

Assessment 4

USE LOGICAL FUNCTIONS

SNAP Grade It

1. Open **ACPremiumReview.xlsx**.
2. Save the workbook and name it **EL2-C2-A4-ACPremiumReview.xlsx**.
3. Create the following range names:

B4:B23	*Claims*
C4:C23	*AtFault*
D4:D23	*Rating*
E4:E23	*Deductible*

4. Using the named ranges created in Step 3, create a formula in cell G4 to display the text *Yes* if the number of at-fault claims is greater than one and the current rating is greater than two. Both conditions must test true to display *Yes*; otherwise, display *No* in the cell. ***Hint: Use a nested IF and AND formula***.
5. Using the named ranges created in Step 3, create a formula in cell H4 to display the text *Yes* in the cell if either the number of claims is greater than two or the current deductible is less than $1,000.00; otherwise, display *No* in the cell. ***Hint: Use a nested IF and OR formula***.
6. Center the results in cells G4 and H4 and then copy the formulas to G5:G23 and H5:H23, respectively. Deselect the range after copying.
7. Save, print, and then close **EL2-C2-A4-ACPremiumReview.xlsx**.

Assessment 5

USE THE HLOOKUP FUNCTION

SNAP Grade It

1. Open **JTutorProgressRpt.xlsx**.
2. Save the workbook and name it **EL2-C2-A5-JTutorProgressRpt**.
3. Make ProgressComments the active worksheet and review the layout of the lookup table. Notice that the data is organized in rows, with the scores in row 1 and the grade comments in row 2.
4. Select A1:G2 and type GradeTable as the range name.
5. Deselect the range and then make StudentProgress the active worksheet.
6. Create a formula in cell G4 that will look up the student's total score in the range named *GradeTable* and return the appropriate progress comment.
7. Copy the formula in cell G4 and paste it to G5:G12. Deselect the range.
8. Save, print, and then close **EL2-C2-A5-JTutorProgressRpt.xlsx**.

Visual Benchmark Demonstrate Your Proficiency

1 USE LOOKUP, STATISTICAL, AND MATH FUNCTIONS IN A BILLING SUMMARY

1. Open **BillHrsOct5to9.xlsx**.
2. Save the workbook and name it **EL2-C2-VB1-BillHrsOct5to9**.
3. Review the worksheet shown in Figure 2.8. The gray shaded cells require formulas to complete the worksheet. Use the following information to create the required formulas. Create range names to use in all of the formulas so that the reader can easily interpret the formula:
   - In column F, create a formula to look up the attorney's hourly rate from the table located at the bottom right of the worksheet.
   - In column G, calculate the legal fees billed by multiplying the billable hours times the hourly rate.
   - In J6:J9, calculate the total legal fees billed by attorney.
   - In J13:J16, calculate the average hours billed by attorney.
4. Save, print, and then close **EL2-C2-VB1-BillHrsOct5to9.xlsx**.

Figure 2.8 Visual Benchmark 1

	A	B	C	D	E	F	G	H	I	J
1	O'DONOVAN & SULLIVAN LAW ASSOCIATES									
2	BILLING SUMMARY									
3	OCTOBER 5 TO 9, 2015									
4	File	Client	Date	Attorney Code	Billable Hours	Hourly Rate	Legal Fees	Billing Statistics		
5	FL-325	10104	10/5/2015	1	26.75	85.00	2,273.75	Total Legal Fees Billed by Attorney		
6	EP-652	10106	10/5/2015	1	12.10	85.00	1,028.50	1	Marty O'Donovan	$ 5,342.25
7	CL-412	10125	10/5/2015	2	33.25	75.00	2,493.75	2	Toni Sullivan	$ 8,062.50
8	IN-745	10210	10/6/2015	3	24.25	100.00	2,425.00	3	Rosa Martinez	$ 15,306.00
9	EL-632	10225	10/6/2015	3	12.11	100.00	1,211.00	4	Kyle Williams	$ 7,087.50
10	RE-475	10285	10/6/2015	4	42.30	90.00	3,807.00		TOTAL	$ 35,798.25
11	CL-501	10341	10/7/2015	2	15.25	75.00	1,143.75			
12	CL-521	10334	10/7/2015	2	20.25	75.00	1,518.75	Average Billable Hours by Attorney		
13	PL-348	10420	10/7/2015	3	25.00	100.00	2,500.00	1	Marty O'Donovan	$ 1,780.75
14	RE-492	10425	10/7/2015	4	22.70	90.00	2,043.00	2	Toni Sullivan	$ 1,612.50
15	EL-632	10225	10/8/2015	3	23.00	100.00	2,300.00	3	Rosa Martinez	$ 1,913.25
16	PL-512	10290	10/8/2015	3	16.20	100.00	1,620.00	4	Kyle Williams	$ 2,362.50
17	IN-745	10210	10/8/2015	3	14.50	100.00	1,450.00			
18	FL-385	10278	10/8/2015	1	24.00	85.00	2,040.00	Attorney Code Table		
19	CL-412	10125	10/9/2015	2	15.25	75.00	1,143.75	Code	Attorney	Hourly Rate
20	CL-450	10358	10/9/2015	2	23.50	75.00	1,762.50	1	Marty O'Donovan	85.00
21	IN-801	10346	10/9/2015	3	14.25	100.00	1,425.00	2	Toni Sullivan	75.00
22	EP-685	10495	10/9/2015	3	23.75	100.00	2,375.00	3	Rosa Martinez	100.00
23	RE-501	10384	10/9/2015	4	13.75	90.00	1,237.50	4	Kyle Williams	90.00

SUM(F

table

3 rows

=vlookup(D5,table,3,false)

2 USE LOOKUP AND LOGICAL FUNCTIONS TO CALCULATE CARDIOLOGY COSTS

1. Open **WPMCCardioCosts.xlsx.**
2. Save the workbook and name it **EL2-C2-VB2-WPMCCardioCosts.**
3. Range names for this worksheet have already been created for you. Spend a few moments reviewing the range names and the cells each name references to become familiar with the worksheet.
4. Review the worksheet shown in Figure 2.9 and complete the worksheet to match the one shown by creating formulas using the following information:
   - In column G, create a formula to look up the surgery fee in the table located at the bottom of the worksheet. Specify in the formula to return results for exact matches only.
   - In column H, insert the aortic or mitral valve cost if the cardiac surgery required a replacement valve; otherwise, place a 0 in the cell. ***Hint: The surgery codes for surgeries that include a replacement valve are*** **ART** ***and*** **MRT**.
   - In column I, calculate the postoperative hospital cost by multiplying the number of days the patient was in hospital by the postoperative cost per day.
   - In column J, calculate the total cost as the sum of the surgery fee, valve cost, and postoperative hospital cost.
   - Calculate the total cost for each column in row 22.
5. Format the numbers as shown in Figure 2.9.
6. Save, print, and then close **EL2-C2-VB2-WPMCCardioCosts.xlsx.**

Figure 2.9 Visual Benchmark 2

	A	B	C	D	E	F	G	H	I	J
1	Wellington Park Medical Center									
2	Division of Cardiology									
3	Adult Cardiac Surgery Costs									
4	Month:	October	Surgeon:	Novak						
5	Patient Number	Patient Last Name	Patient First Name	Surgery Code	Days in Hospital		Surgery Fee	Valve Cost	Postoperative Hospital Cost	Total Cost
6	60334124	Wagner	Sara	MRP	7		$ 5,325.00	$ -	$ 6,317.50	$ 11,642.50
7	60334567	Gonzalez	Hector	ARP	10		4,876.00	-	9,025.00	13,901.00
8	60398754	Vezina	Paula	ABP	5		4,820.00	-	4,512.50	9,332.50
9	60347821	Dowling	Jager	MRT	11		6,240.00	775.00	9,927.50	16,942.50
10	60328192	Ashman	Carl	ARP	4		4,876.00	-	3,610.00	8,486.00
11	60321349	Kaiser	Lana	ART	12		6,190.00	775.00	10,830.00	17,795.00
12	60398545	Van Bomm	Emile	ABP	7		4,820.00	-	6,317.50	11,137.50
13	60342548	Youngblood	Frank	ABP	6		4,820.00	-	5,415.00	10,235.00
14	60331569	Lorimar	Hannah	MRT	8		6,240.00	775.00	7,220.00	14,235.00
15	60247859	Peterson	Mark	ART	9		6,190.00	775.00	8,122.50	15,087.50
16	60158642	O'Connor	Terry	ABP	7		4,820.00	-	6,317.50	11,137.50
17	60458962	Jenkins	Esther	MRP	9		5,325.00	-	8,122.50	13,447.50
18	68521245	Norfolk	Leslie	ABP	8		4,820.00	-	7,220.00	12,040.00
19	63552158	Adams-Wiley	Susan	MRT	6		6,240.00	775.00	5,415.00	12,430.00
20	68451278	Estevez	Stefan	ARP	6		4,876.00	-	5,415.00	10,291.00
21										
22	Postoperative hospital cost per day:			$ 902.50		Total Cost:	$ 80,478.00	$ 3,875.00	$ 103,787.50	$ 188,140.50
23	Aortic or mitral valve cost:			$ 775.00						
24										
25		Surgery Code	Surgery Fee	Surgery Procedure						
26		ABP	4,820	Artery Bypass						
27		ARP	4,876	Aortic Valve Repair						
28		ART	6,190	Aortic Valve Replacement						
29		MRP	5,325	Mitral Valve Repair						
30		MRT	6,240	Mitral Valve Replacement						

Case Study Apply Your Skills

Part 1

Yolanda Robertson of NuTrends Market Research was pleased with your previous work and has requested that you be assigned to assist her with a new client. Yolanda is preparing a marketing plan for a franchise expansion for the owners of Pizza By Mario. The franchise was started in Michigan and has stores in Ohio, Wisconsin, and Iowa. The owners plan to double the number of locations within the next two years by expanding into neighboring states. The owners have provided a confidential franchise sales report to Yolanda in an Excel file named **PBMSales.xlsx**. Yolanda needs your help with Excel to extract some statistics and calculate franchise royalty payments. With this information, Yolanda will develop a franchise communication package for prospective franchisees. Open the workbook and save it as **EL2-C2-CS-P1-PBMSales**. Yolanda has asked for the following statistics:

- A count of the number of stores with sales greater than $500,000
- A count of the number of stores located in Michigan with sales greater than $500,000
- Average sales for the stores in Detroit, Michigan
- Average sales for the Michigan stores established prior to 2004
- Total sales for stores established prior to 2010
- Total sales for the Michigan stores established prior to 2010

Create the above formulas for Yolanda in rows 3 to 16 of columns H and I. Create range names for the data so Yolanda will be able to easily understand the formula when she reviews the worksheet. You determine the layout, labels, and other formats for the statistics section. The royalty rate and fee will be completed in Part 2. Save and print the worksheet.

Part 2

In the marketing package for new prospects, Yolanda plans to include sample sales figures and related franchise royalty payments. Pizza By Mario charges each store a royalty percentage based on its annual sales. As sales increase, the royalty percentage increases. For example, a store that sells $430,000 pays a royalty of 2% of sales, while a store that sells $765,000 pays a royalty of 5% of sales. A royalty rate table is included in the worksheet. Create a range name for the table and then create a lookup formula to insert the correct royalty percentage for each store in column F. Next, create a formula to calculate the dollar amount of the royalty payment based on the store's sales multiplied by the percentage value in column F. Format the royalty percentage and royalty fee columns appropriately. Save the revised workbook and name it **EL2-C2-CS-P2-PBMSales**. Print the worksheet.

Part 3

Help

Use the Help feature to learn about the MEDIAN and STDEV functions. Yolanda would like to calculate further statistics in a separate worksheet. Copy A2:E29 to Sheet2, keeping the source column widths. Using the sales data in column E, calculate the following statistics. (You determine the layout, labels, and other formats.)

- Average sales
- Maximum store sales
- Minimum store sales
- Median store sales
- Standard deviation of the sales data

Create a text box below the statistics and write an explanation in each box to explain what the median and standard deviation numbers mean based on what you learned by researching in Help. Print the worksheet, making sure all of the data fits on one page. Save the revised workbook and name it **EL2-C2-CS-P3-PBMSales**.

Part 4

WWW

Choose two states near Michigan, Ohio, Wisconsin, and/or Iowa and find statistics on the Internet that Yolanda can use to prepare a marketing plan for expanding Pizza By Mario into these states. Within each new state, find population and income statistics for two cities. In a new worksheet within the Pizza By Mario franchise workbook, prepare a summary of your research findings. Include the URLs of the sites from which you obtained your data in the worksheet, in case Yolanda wants to explore the links for further details. Print the worksheet, making sure all of the data fits on one page. Save the revised workbook and name it **EL2-C2-CS-P4-PBMSales**. Close the workbook.

MICROSOFT® EXCEL®

CHAPTER 3

Working with Tables and Data Features

PERFORMANCE OBJECTIVES

Upon successful completion of Chapter 3, you will be able to:

- **Create a table in a worksheet**
- **Expand a table to include new rows and columns**
- **Add a calculated column in a table**
- **Format a table by applying table styles and table style options**
- **Add a *Total* row to a table and formulas to total cells**
- **Sort and filter a table**
- **Split contents of a cell into separate columns**
- **Use Flash Fill**
- **Remove duplicate records**
- **Restrict data entry by creating validation criteria**
- **Convert a table to a normal range**
- **Create subtotals in groups of related data**
- **Group and ungroup data**

SNAP

Tutorials

3.1 Creating and Modifying Tables
3.2 Adding Rows to a Table
3.3 Formatting Data as a Table
3.4 Using the Sort Feature in Tables
3.5 Filtering a Table
3.6 Using Data Tools
3.7 Removing Duplicate Records
3.8 Validating and Restricting Data Entry
3.9 Converting a Table to a Normal Range; Subtotaling Related Data
3.10 Grouping and Ungrouping Data

A ***table*** is a range that can be managed separately from other rows and columns in a worksheet. Data in a table can be sorted, filtered, and totaled as a separate unit. A worksheet can contain more than one table, which allows multiple groups of data to be managed separately within the same workbook. In this chapter, you will learn how to use the table feature to manage a range. You will use tools such as data validation, searching for and removing duplicate records, and converting text to a table. You will also convert a table back to a normal range and use data tools such as grouping related records and calculating subtotals. Model answers for this chapter's projects appear on the following pages.

Excel
EL2C3

Note: Before beginning the projects, copy to your storage medium the EL2C3 subfolder from the EL2 folder on the CD that accompanies this textbook and then make EL2C3 the active folder.

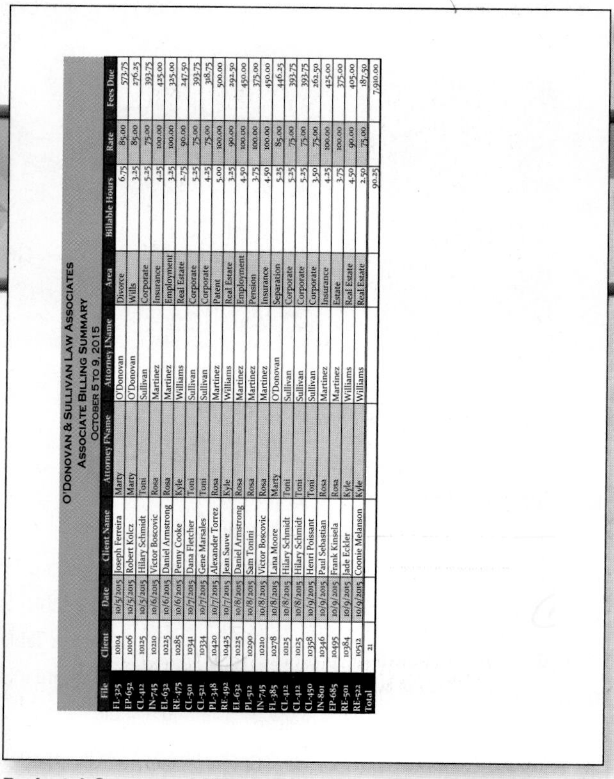

O'DONOVAN & SULLIVAN LAW ASSOCIATES
ASSOCIATE BILLING SUMMARY
OCTOBER 5 TO 9, 2015

File	Client	Date	Client Name	Attorney FName	Attorney LName	Area	Billable Hours	Rate	Fees Due
FL-325	10104	10/5/2015	Joseph Ferreira	Marty	O'Donovan	Divorce	6.75	85.00	573.75
EP-652	10106	10/5/2015	Robert Kolcz	Marty	O'Donovan	Wills	3.25	85.00	276.25
CL-412	10125	10/5/2015	Hilary Schmidt	Toni	Sullivan	Corporate	5.25	75.00	393.75
IN-745	10210	10/6/2015	Victor Boscovic	Rosa	Martinez	Insurance	4.25	100.00	425.00
EL-632	10225	10/6/2015	Daniel Armstrong	Rosa	Martinez	Employment	3.25	100.00	325.00
RE-475	10285	10/6/2015	Penny Cooke	Kyle	Williams	Real Estate	2.75	90.00	247.50
CL-501	10341	10/7/2015	Dana Fletcher	Toni	Sullivan	Corporate	5.25	75.00	393.75
CL-521	10334	10/7/2015	Gene Marsales	Toni	Sullivan	Corporate	4.25	75.00	318.75
PL-348	10420	10/7/2015	Alexander Torrez	Rosa	Martinez	Patent	5.00	100.00	500.00
RE-492	10425	10/7/2015	Jean Sauve	Kyle	Williams	Real Estate	3.25	90.00	292.50
EL-632	10225	10/8/2015	Daniel Armstrong	Rosa	Martinez	Employment	4.50	100.00	450.00
PL-512	10290	10/8/2015	Sam Tonini	Rosa	Martinez	Pension	3.75	100.00	375.00
IN-745	10210	10/8/2015	Victor Boscovic	Rosa	Martinez	Insurance	4.50	100.00	450.00
FL-385	10278	10/8/2015	Lana Moore	Marty	O'Donovan	Separation	5.25	85.00	446.25
CL-412	10125	10/8/2015	Hilary Schmidt	Toni	Sullivan	Corporate	5.25	75.00	393.75
CL-412	10125	10/8/2015	Hilary Schmidt	Toni	Sullivan	Corporate	5.25	75.00	393.75
CL-450	10358	10/9/2015	Henri Poissant	Toni	Sullivan	Corporate	3.50	75.00	262.50
IN-801	10346	10/9/2015	Paul Sebastian	Rosa	Martinez	Insurance	4.25	100.00	425.00
EP-685	10495	10/9/2015	Frank Kinsela	Rosa	Martinez	Estate	3.75	100.00	375.00
RE-501	10384	10/9/2015	Jade Eckler	Kyle	Williams	Real Estate	4.50	90.00	405.00
RE-522	10512	10/9/2015	Coonie Melanson	Kyle	Williams	Real Estate	2.50	75.00	187.50
Total	21						90.25		7,910.00

Project 1 Create and Modify a Table

Project 1c, EL2-C3-P1-BillSumOctWk1.xlsx

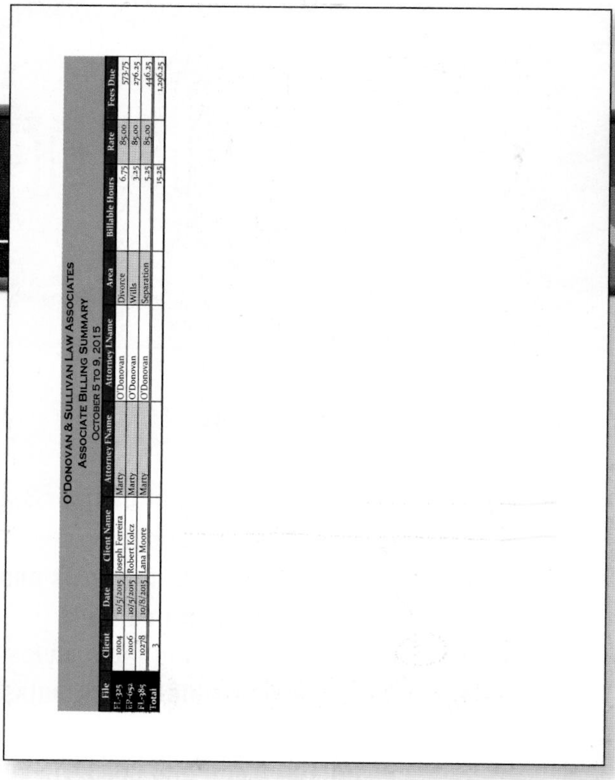

O'DONOVAN & SULLIVAN LAW ASSOCIATES
ASSOCIATE BILLING SUMMARY
OCTOBER 5 TO 9, 2015

File	Client	Date	Client Name	Attorney FName	Attorney LName	Area	Billable Hours	Rate	Fees Due
FL-325	10104	10/5/2015	Joseph Ferreira	Marty	O'Donovan	Divorce	6.75	85.00	573.75
EP-652	10106	10/5/2015	Robert Kolcz	Marty	O'Donovan	Wills	3.25	85.00	276.25
FL-385	10278	10/8/2015	Lana Moore	Marty	O'Donovan	Separation	5.25	85.00	446.25
Total	3						15.25		1,296.25

Project 1d, Step 1d, EL2-C3-P1-BillSumOctWk1.xlsx

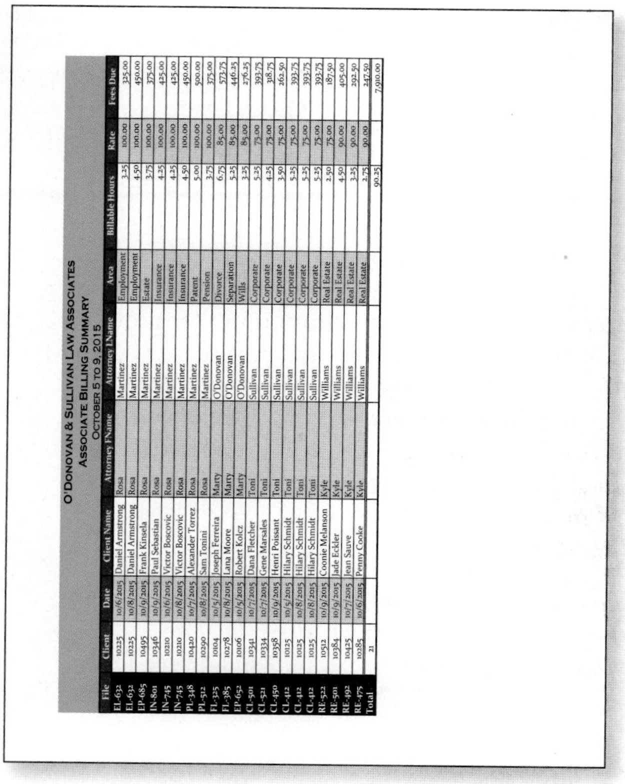

O'DONOVAN & SULLIVAN LAW ASSOCIATES
ASSOCIATE BILLING SUMMARY
OCTOBER 5 TO 9, 2015

File	Client	Date	Client Name	Attorney FName	Attorney LName	Area	Billable Hours	Rate	Fees Due
EL-632	10225	10/6/2015	Daniel Armstrong	Rosa	Martinez	Employment	3.25	100.00	325.00
EL-632	10225	10/8/2015	Daniel Armstrong	Rosa	Martinez	Employment	4.50	100.00	450.00
EP-685	10495	10/9/2015	Frank Kinsela	Rosa	Martinez	Estate	3.75	100.00	375.00
IN-801	10346	10/9/2015	Paul Sebastian	Rosa	Martinez	Insurance	4.25	100.00	425.00
IN-745	10210	10/6/2015	Victor Boscovic	Rosa	Martinez	Insurance	4.25	100.00	425.00
IN-745	10210	10/8/2015	Victor Boscovic	Rosa	Martinez	Insurance	4.50	100.00	450.00
PL-348	10420	10/7/2015	Alexander Torrez	Rosa	Martinez	Patent	5.00	100.00	500.00
PL-512	10290	10/8/2015	Sam Tonini	Rosa	Martinez	Pension	3.75	100.00	375.00
FL-325	10104	10/5/2015	Joseph Ferreira	Marty	O'Donovan	Divorce	6.75	85.00	573.75
FL-385	10278	10/8/2015	Lana Moore	Marty	O'Donovan	Separation	5.25	85.00	446.25
EP-652	10106	10/5/2015	Robert Kolcz	Marty	O'Donovan	Wills	3.25	85.00	276.25
CL-501	10341	10/7/2015	Dana Fletcher	Toni	Sullivan	Corporate	5.25	75.00	393.75
CL-521	10334	10/7/2015	Gene Marsales	Toni	Sullivan	Corporate	4.25	75.00	318.75
CL-450	10358	10/9/2015	Henri Poissant	Toni	Sullivan	Corporate	3.50	75.00	262.50
CL-412	10125	10/5/2015	Hilary Schmidt	Toni	Sullivan	Corporate	5.25	75.00	393.75
CL-412	10125	10/8/2015	Hilary Schmidt	Toni	Sullivan	Corporate	5.25	75.00	393.75
CL-412	10125	10/8/2015	Hilary Schmidt	Toni	Sullivan	Corporate	5.25	75.00	393.75
RE-522	10512	10/9/2015	Coonie Melanson	Kyle	Williams	Real Estate	2.50	75.00	187.50
RE-501	10384	10/9/2015	Jade Eckler	Kyle	Williams	Real Estate	4.50	90.00	405.00
RE-492	10425	10/7/2015	Jean Sauve	Kyle	Williams	Real Estate	3.25	90.00	292.50
RE-475	10285	10/6/2015	Penny Cooke	Kyle	Williams	Real Estate	2.75	90.00	247.50
Total	21						90.25		7,910.00

Project 1d, Step 4, EL2-C3-P1-BillSumOctWk1.xlsx

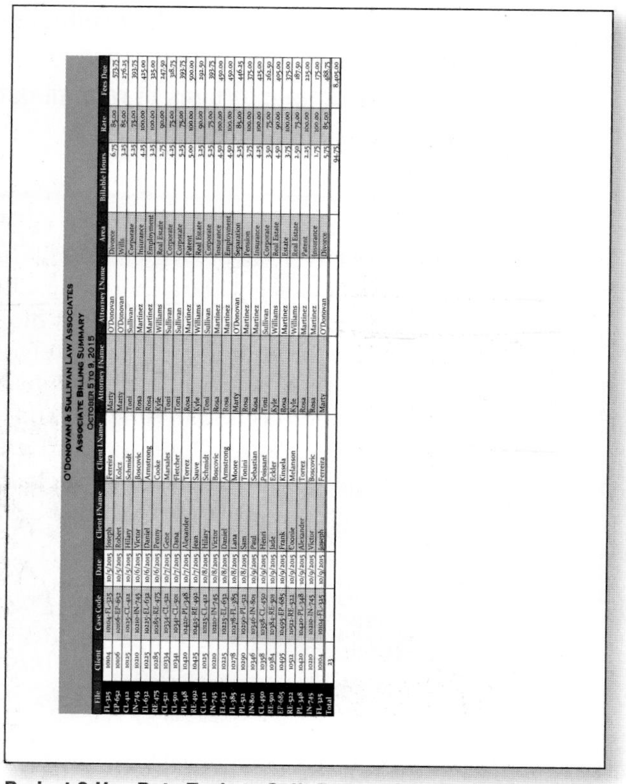

O'DONOVAN & SULLIVAN LAW ASSOCIATES
ASSOCIATE BILLING SUMMARY
OCTOBER 5 TO 9, 2015

File	Client	Case Code	Date	Client FName	Client LName	Attorney FName	Attorney LName	Area	Billable Hours	Rate	Fees Due
FL-325	10104	10104-FL-325	10/5/2015	Joseph	Ferreira	Marty	O'Donovan	Divorce	6.75	85.00	573.75
EP-652	10106	10106-EP-652	10/5/2015	Robert	Kolcz	Marty	O'Donovan	Wills	3.25	85.00	276.25
CL-412	10125	10125-CL-412	10/5/2015	Hilary	Schmidt	Toni	Sullivan	Corporate	5.25	75.00	393.75
IN-745	10210	10210-IN-745	10/6/2015	Victor	Boscovic	Rosa	Martinez	Insurance	4.25	100.00	425.00
EL-632	10225	10225-EL-632	10/6/2015	Daniel	Armstrong	Rosa	Martinez	Employment	3.25	100.00	325.00
RE-475	10285	10285-RE-475	10/6/2015	Penny	Cooke	Kyle	Williams	Real Estate	2.75	90.00	247.50
CL-521	10334	10334-CL-521	10/7/2015	Gene	Marsales	Toni	Sullivan	Corporate	4.25	75.00	318.75
CL-501	10341	10341-CL-501	10/7/2015	Dana	Fletcher	Toni	Sullivan	Corporate	5.25	75.00	393.75
PL-348	10420	10420-PL-348	10/7/2015	Alexander	Torrez	Rosa	Martinez	Patent	5.00	100.00	500.00
RE-492	10425	10425-RE-492	10/7/2015	Jean	Sauve	Kyle	Williams	Real Estate	3.25	90.00	292.50
CL-412	10125	10125-CL-412	10/8/2015	Hilary	Schmidt	Toni	Sullivan	Corporate	5.25	75.00	393.75
IN-745	10210	10210-IN-745	10/8/2015	Victor	Boscovic	Rosa	Martinez	Insurance	4.50	100.00	450.00
EL-632	10225	10225-EL-632	10/8/2015	Daniel	Armstrong	Rosa	Martinez	Employment	4.50	100.00	450.00
FL-385	10278	10278-FL-385	10/8/2015	Lana	Moore	Marty	O'Donovan	Separation	5.25	85.00	446.25
PL-512	10290	10290-PL-512	10/8/2015	Sam	Tonini	Rosa	Martinez	Pension	3.75	100.00	375.00
IN-801	10346	10346-IN-801	10/9/2015	Paul	Sebastian	Rosa	Martinez	Insurance	4.25	100.00	425.00
CL-450	10358	10358-CL-450	10/9/2015	Henri	Poissant	Toni	Sullivan	Corporate	3.50	75.00	262.50
RE-501	10384	10384-RE-501	10/9/2015	Jade	Eckler	Kyle	Williams	Real Estate	4.50	90.00	405.00
EP-685	10495	10495-EP-685	10/9/2015	Frank	Kinsela	Rosa	Martinez	Estate	3.75	100.00	375.00
RE-522	10512	10512-RE-522	10/9/2015	Coonie	Melanson	Kyle	Williams	Real Estate	2.50	75.00	187.50
PL-348	10420	10420-PL-348	10/9/2015	Alexander	Torrez	Rosa	Martinez	Patent	2.25	100.00	225.00
IN-745	10210	10210-IN-745	10/9/2015	Victor	Boscovic	Rosa	Martinez	Insurance	1.75	100.00	175.00
FL-325	10104	10104-FL-325	10/9/2015	Joseph	Ferreira	Marty	O'Donovan	Divorce	5.75	85.00	488.75
Total	23								94.75		8,405.00

Project 2 Use Data Tools to Split Data and Ensure Data Integrity

Project 2f, EL2-C3-P2-BillSumOctWk1.xlsx

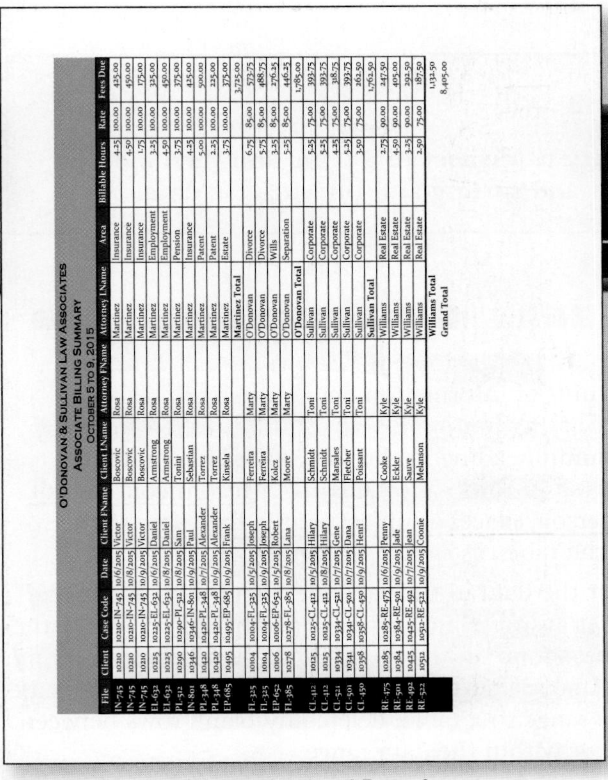

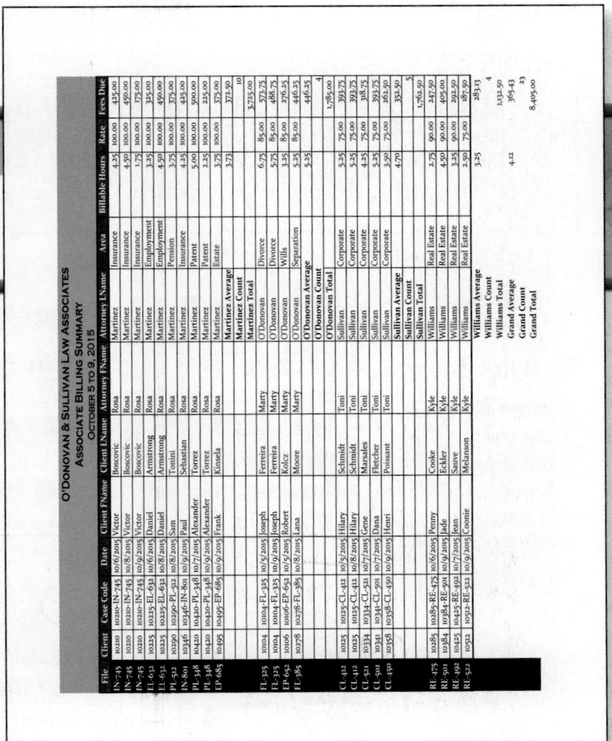

Project 3 Group and Subtotal Related Records

Project 3a, Step 6, EL2-C3-P3-BillSumOctWk1.xlsx

Project 3b, EL2-C3-P3-BillSumOctWk1-Prj3b.xlsx

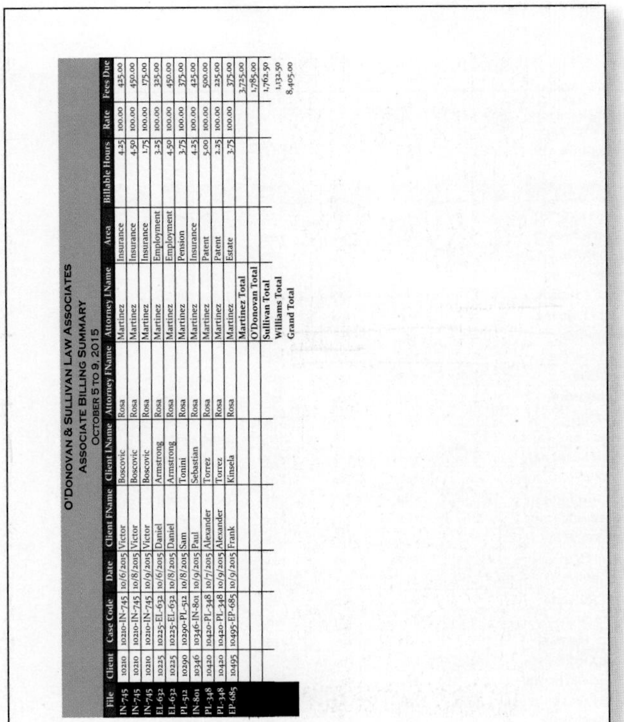

Project 3c, EL2-C3-P3-BillSumOctWk1-Prj3c.xlsx

Project 1 Create and Modify a Table — 4 Parts

You will convert data in a billing summary worksheet to a table and then modify the table by applying Table Style options and sorting and filtering the data.

Creating Tables

Quick Steps

Create a Table
1. Select range.
2. Click Quick Analysis button.
3. Click TABLES tab.
4. Click Table button.
5. Deselect range.

Table

A table in Excel is similar in structure to a database. Columns are called ***fields***. Each field is used to store a single unit of information about a person, place, or object. The first row of the table contains column headings and is called the ***field names row*** or ***header row***. Each column heading in the table should be unique. Below the field names, data is entered in rows called ***records***. A record contains all of the field values related to one person, place, or object that is the topic of the table. No blank rows exist within the table, as shown in Figure 3.1.

To create a table in Excel, enter the data in the worksheet and then define the range as a table using the Table button in the Tables group on the INSERT tab, the Format as Table button in the Styles group on the HOME tab, or the Table button on the TABLES tab in the Quick Analysis button located at the bottom right of the selected range. Before converting a range to a table, delete any blank rows between the column headings and the data or within the data range.

Figure 3.1 Worksheet with the Range Formatted as a Table

The first row of a table contains field names and is called the *header row*.

	A	B	C	D	E	F	G	H	I	J	K	L
1						ViewItVideo						
2						Classic Video Collection						
3												
4	Stock No.	Title	Year	Genre	Stock Dat	Director	Copie	VHS	DVD	Blu-ra	Category	Cost Pric
5	CV-1001	Abbott & Costello Go to Mars	1953	Comedy	9/4/2010	Charles Lamont	2	Yes	No	No	7-day rental	5.87
6	CV-1002	Miracle on 34th Street	1947	Family	9/14/2010	George Seaton	8	Yes	No	Yes	2-day rental	7.55
7	CV-1003	Moby Dick	1956	Action	10/3/2010	John Huston	3	No	Yes	No	7-day rental	8.10
8	CV-1004	Dial M for Murder	1954	Thriller	10/11/2010	Alfred Hitchcock	5	No	Yes	No	7-day rental	6.54
9	CV-1005	Breakfast at Tiffany's	1961	Comedy	10/31/2010	Blake Edwards	1	Yes	No	Yes	7-day rental	4.88
10	CV-1006	Gone with the Wind	1939	Drama	11/28/2010	Victor Fleming	4	Yes	No	Yes	7-day rental	8.22
11	CV-1007	Doctor Zhivago	1965	Drama	12/7/2010	David Lean	4	Yes	No	Yes	7-day rental	5.63
12	CV-1008	The Great Escape	1963	War	1/14/2011	John Sturges	3	Yes	No	No	2-day rental	6.15
13	CV-1009	The Odd Couple	1968	Comedy	2/14/2011	Gene Saks	4	Yes	Yes	No	2-day rental	4.95
14	CV-1010	The Sound of Music	1965	Musical	3/8/2011	Robert Wise	5	Yes	Yes	Yes	2-day rental	5.12
15	CV-1011	A Christmas Carol	1951	Family	7/17/2011	Brian Hurst	4	Yes	Yes	Yes	2-day rental	5.88
16	CV-1012	The Bridge on the River Kwai	1957	War	8/14/2011	David Lean	2	Yes	No	No	2-day rental	6.32
17	CV-1013	Cool Hand Luke	1967	Drama	10/22/2011	Stuart Rosenberg	5	Yes	Yes	Yes	2-day rental	5.42
18	CV-1014	Patton	1970	War	12/17/2011	Franklin Schaffner	3	Yes	Yes	Yes	7-day rental	6.84
19	CV-1015	Blue Hawaii	1961	Musical	1/24/2012	Norman Taurog	1	Yes	No	No	7-day rental	4.52
20	CV-1016	Psycho	1960	Horror	1/30/2012	Alfred Hitchcock	2	Yes	No	Yes	2-day rental	7.54
21	CV-1017	The Longest Day	1962	War	2/4/2012	Ken Annakin	5	Yes	Yes	No	7-day rental	6.51
22	CV-1018	To Kill a Mockingbird	1962	Drama	2/11/2012	Robert Mulligan	2	Yes	No	Yes	2-day rental	8.40
23	CV-1019	Bonnie and Clyde	1967	Drama	3/14/2013	Arthur Penn	3	Yes	Yes	Yes	2-day rental	8.95
24	CV-1020	The Maltese Falcon	1941	Drama	11/9/2013	John Huston	1	No	No	Yes	2-day rental	12.15
25	CV-1007	Doctor Zhivago	1965	Drama	12/7/2010	David Lean	4	Yes	No	Yes	7-day rental	5.63
26	CV-1022	The Wizard of Oz	1939	Musical	5/2/2014	Victor Fleming	5	Yes	Yes	Yes	7-day rental	9.56
27	CV-1023	Rear Window	1954	Thriller	8/14/2014	Alfred Hitchcock	3	Yes	Yes	Yes	7-day rental	8.55
28	CV-1004	Dial M for Murder	1954	Thriller	10/11/2010	Alfred Hitchcock	5	No	Yes	No	7-day rental	6.54
29	CV-1024	Citizen Kane	1941	Drama	6/9/2015	Orson Welles	2	No	Yes	Yes	2-day rental	9.85
30	CV-1025	Ben-Hur	1959	History	10/14/2015	William Wyler	1	No	No	Yes	7-day rental	9.85

A row in a table is called a *record*.

A column in a table contains a single unit of information for each record and is called a *field*.

Project 1a Converting a Range to a Table

Part 1 of 4

1. Open **BillSumOctWk1.xlsx**.
2. Save the workbook and name it **EL2-C3-P1-BillSumOctWk1**.
3. Convert the billing summary data to a table by completing the following steps:
   a. Select A4:I24.
   b. Click the INSERT tab.
   c. Click the Table button in the Tables group.
   d. At the Create Table dialog box with *=$A$4:$I$24* selected in the *Where is the data for your table?* text box and the *My table has headers* check box selected, click OK.
   e. Deselect the range.
4. Select columns A through I and AutoFit the column widths.
5. Save **EL2-C3-P1-BillSumOctWk1.xlsx**.

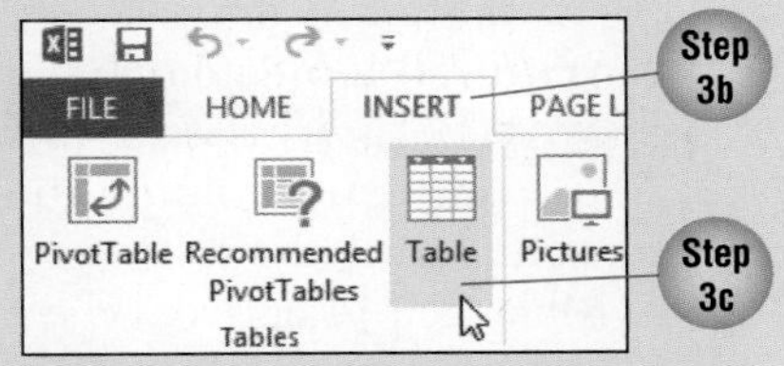

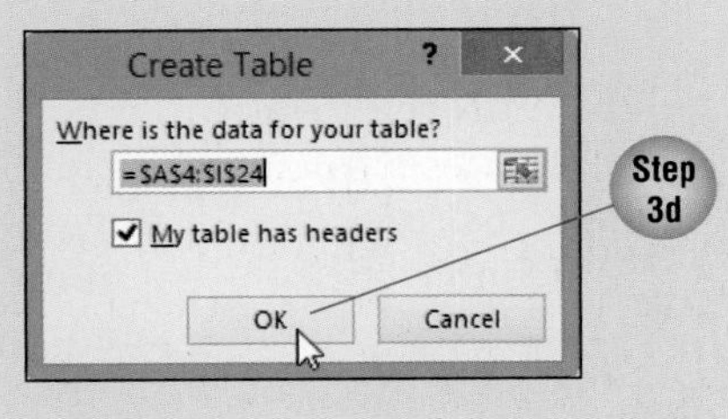

Modifying a Table

Once a table has been defined, typing new data in the row immediately below the last row of the table or in the column immediately right of the last column causes the table to automatically expand to include the new entries. Excel displays the AutoCorrect Options button when the table is expanded. Click the button to display a drop-down list with the options *Undo Table AutoExpansion* and *Stop Automatically Expanding Tables*. If you want to add data near a table without having the table expand, leave a blank column or row between the table and the new data.

Typing a formula in the first record of a new table column automatically creates a calculated column. In a calculated column, Excel copies the formula from the first cell to the remaining cells in the column as soon as you enter the formula. The AutoCorrect Options button appears when Excel converts a column to a calculated column. Click the button to display the options *Undo Calculated Column*, *Stop Automatically Creating Calculated Columns*, and *Control AutoCorrect Options*.

Quick Steps

Add Rows or Columns to a Table
Type data in first row below table or first column to right of table.

Add a Calculated Column
1. Type formula in first record in column.
2. Press Enter.

Project 1b Adding a Row and Calculated Column to a Table

Part 2 of 4

1. With **EL2-C3-P1-BillSumOctWk1.xlsx** open, add a new record to the table by completing the following steps:
   a. Make cell A25 active, type RE-522, and then press Enter. Excel automatically expands the table to include the new row and displays the AutoCorrect Options button.
   b. Make cell B25 active and then type the remainder of the record as follows. Press Tab to move from column to column in the table.

Client	10512
Date	10/9/2015
Client Name	Connie Melanson
Attorney FName	Kyle
Attorney LName	Williams

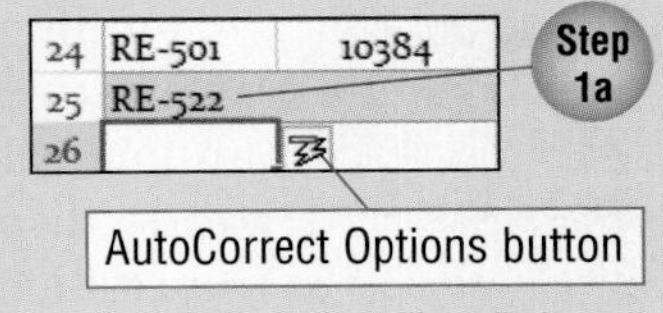

Rate	Fees Due
85.00	573.75
85.00	276.25
75.00	393.75
100.00	425.00
100.00	325.00
90.00	247.50
75.00	393.75
75.00	318.75
100.00	500.00
90.00	292.50
100.00	450.00
100.00	375.00
100.00	450.00
85.00	446.25
75.00	393.75
75.00	393.75
75.00	262.50
100.00	425.00
100.00	375.00
90.00	405.00
75.00	187.50

Step 2a

Step 2b

Area Real Estate
Billable Hours 2.5

c. With cell I25 active, type 75 and then press Enter. (If you press Tab, a new table row will be created.)

2. Add a calculated column to multiply billable hours times rate by completing the following steps:
   a. Make cell J4 active, type Fees Due, and then press Enter. Excel automatically expands the table to include the new column.
   b With cell J5 active, type =h5*i5 and then press Enter. Excel creates a calculated column and copies the formula to the rest of the rows in the table.
   c. Double-click the column J boundary to AutoFit the column.
3. Adjust the centering and fill color of the titles across the top of the table by completing the following steps:
   a. Select A1:J1 and then click the Merge & Center button in the Alignment group on the HOME tab twice.
   b. Select A2:J2 and press F4 to repeat the command to merge and center row 2 across columns A through J.
   c. Select A3:J3 and press F4 to repeat the command to merge and center row 3 across columns A through J.
4. Save **EL2-C3-P1-BillSumOctWk1.xlsx**.

Applying Table Styles and Table Style Options

Quick Steps

Change the Table Style
1. Make table cell active.
2. If necessary, click TABLE TOOLS DESIGN tab.
3. Click desired style in Table Styles gallery.

OR

1. Click More button in Table Styles gallery.
2. Click desired style at drop-down gallery.

Add a *Total* Row
1. Make table cell active.
2. If necessary, click TABLE TOOLS DESIGN tab.
3. Click *Total Row* check box.
4. Click in desired cell in *Total* row.
5. Click down-pointing arrow.
6. Click desired function.

The contextual TABLE TOOLS DESIGN tab, shown in Figure 3.2, contains options for formatting the table. Apply a different visual style to the table using the Table Styles gallery. Excel provides several table styles categorized by Light, Medium, and Dark color themes. By default, Excel bands the rows within the table, which means that even-numbered rows are formatted differently from odd-numbered rows. ***Banding*** rows or columns makes it easier to read data across a row or down a column in a large table. You can remove the banding from the rows and/or add banding to the columns. Use the *First Column* and *Last Column* check boxes in the Table Style Options group to add emphasis to the first or last column in the table by formatting them differently than the rest of the table. The *Header Row* check box is used to show or hide the column headings row in the table. New to Excel 2013, the *Filter Button* check box removes the filter arrows from the header row.

Adding a *Total* row to the table causes Excel to add the word *Total* in the leftmost cell of a new row at the bottom of the table. A Sum function is added automatically to the last numeric column in the table. Click in a cell in the *Total* row to display a down-pointing arrow that you can click to display a pop-up list from which you can select a function formula.

Figure 3.2 TABLE TOOLS DESIGN Tab

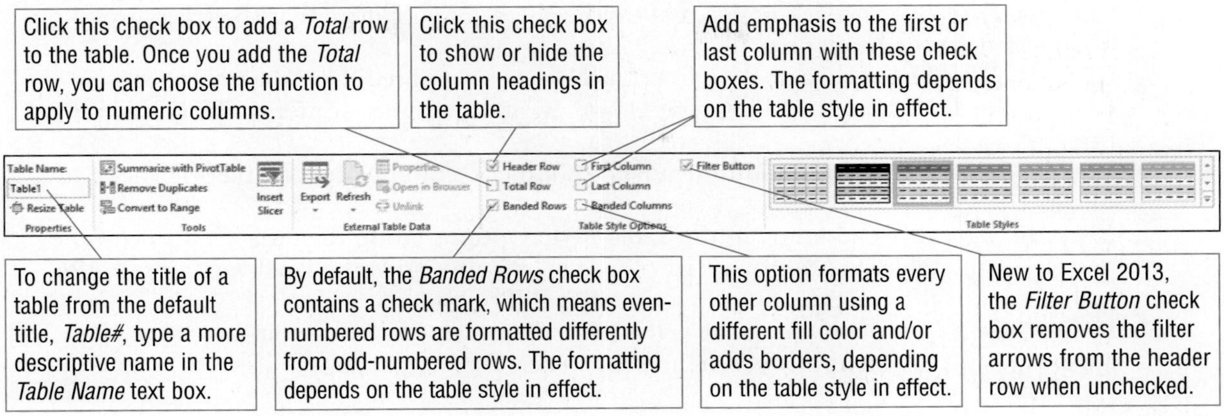

Project 1c Formatting a Table and Adding a *Total* Row — Part 3 of 4

1. With **EL2-C3-P1-BillSumOctWk1.xlsx** open, change the table style by completing the following steps:
   a. Click any cell within the table to activate the table and the contextual TABLE TOOLS DESIGN tab.
   b. Click the TABLE TOOLS DESIGN tab.
   c. Click the More button in the Table Styles gallery.
   d. Click *Table Style Medium 15* at the drop-down gallery (first column, third row in *Medium* section).

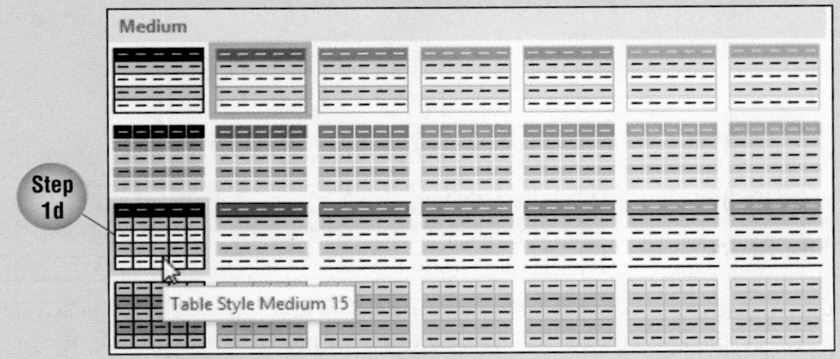

2. Change the table style options to remove the row banding, insert column banding, and emphasize the first column in the table by completing the following steps:
   a. Click the *Banded Rows* check box in the Table Style Options group on the TABLE TOOLS DESIGN tab to remove the check mark. All of the rows in the table are now formatted the same.
   b. Click the *Banded Columns* check box in the Table Style Options group to insert a check mark. Every other column in the table is now formatted differently.
   c. Click the *First Column* check box in the Table Style Options group to insert a check mark. Notice that the first column has a darker fill color and reverse font color applied.
   d. Click the *Header Row* check box in the Table Style Options group to uncheck the box. Notice that the first row of the table (the row containing the column headings) disappears and is replaced with empty cells. The row is also removed from the table range definition.

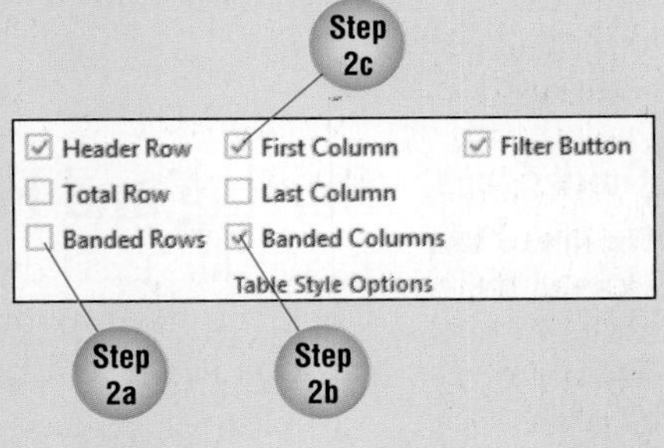

e. Click the *Header Row* check box to insert a check mark and redisplay the column headings.
f. Click the *Filter Button* check box to remove the check mark. Notice that the filter arrows disappear from the header row.
g. Click the *Filter Button* check box to insert a check mark and redisplay the filter arrows.
h. Click in the *Table Name* text box, type OctWk1, and then press Enter to define the table title.

3. Add a *Total* row and add function formulas to numeric columns by completing the following steps:
   a. Click the *Total Row* check box in the Table Style Options group to add a *Total* row to the bottom of the table. Excel formats row 26 as a *Total* row, adds the label *Total* in cell A26, and automatically creates a Sum function in cell J26.
   b. In the *Billable Hours* column, make cell H26 active, click the down-pointing arrow that appears just at the right of the cell, and then click *Sum* at the pop-up list.

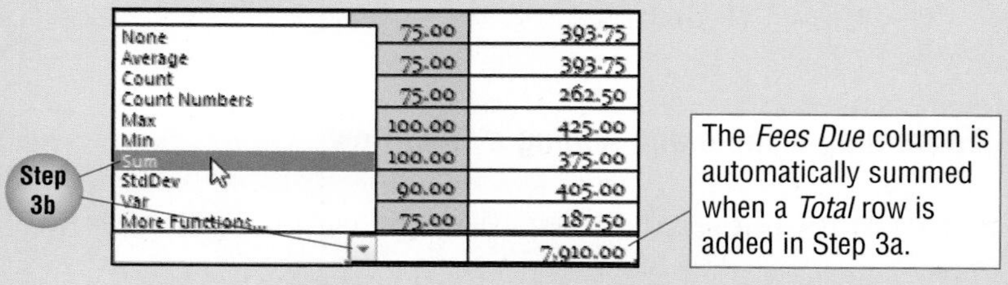

   c. Make cell B26 active, click the down-pointing arrow that appears, and then click *Count* at the pop-up list.

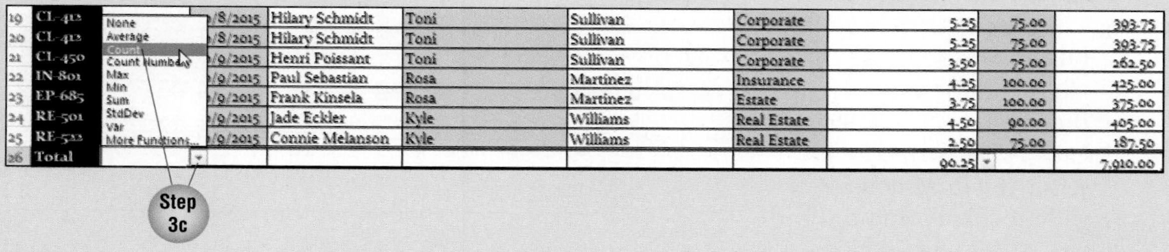

4. Click the PAGE LAYOUT tab and change *Width* to *1 page* in the Scale to Fit group.
5. Preview and then print the worksheet.
6. Save **EL2-C3-P1-BillSumOctWk1.xlsx**.

Quick Steps

Sort or Filter a Table
1. Click desired filter arrow.
2. Click desired sort or filter options.
3. Click OK.

Custom Sort a Table
1. Click Sort & Filter button.
2. Click *Custom Sort*.
3. Define sort levels.
4. Click OK.

Sorting and Filtering Tables

By default, Excel displays a filter arrow next to each label in the table header row. Click the filter arrow to display a drop-down list with the same sort and filter options you used in Chapter 1.

Project 1d Sorting and Filtering a Table

1. With **EL2-C3-P1-BillSumOctWk1.xlsx** open, filter the table by the attorney's last name to print a list of billable hours for O'Donovan by completing the following steps:
   a. Click the filter arrow located next to *Attorney LName* in cell F4.
   b. Click the *(Select All)* check box to remove the check mark.
   c. Click the *O'Donovan* check box to insert a check mark and then click OK. The table is filtered to display only those records with *O'Donovan* in the *Attorney LName* field. The Sum functions in columns H and J reflect the totals for the filtered records only.
   d. Print the filtered worksheet.

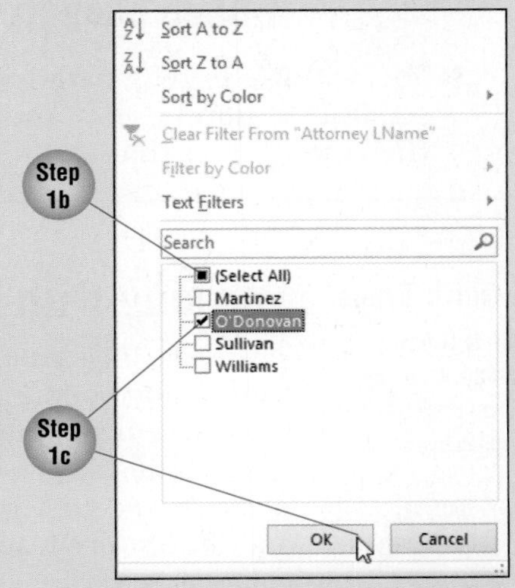

2. Redisplay all of the records by clicking the *Attorney LName* filter arrow and then clicking *Clear Filter From "Attorney LName"* at the drop-down list.
3. Use the Sort dialog box to sort the table first by the attorney's last name, then by the area of law, and then by the client name by completing the following steps:
   a. With the active cell positioned anywhere within the table, click the HOME tab.
   b. Click the Sort & Filter button in the Editing group and then click *Custom Sort* at the drop-down list.
   c. At the Sort dialog box, click the down-pointing arrow next to the *Sort by* option box in the *Column* section and then click *Attorney LName* at the drop-down list. The default options for *Sort On* and *Order* are correct, since you want to sort by the column values in ascending order.

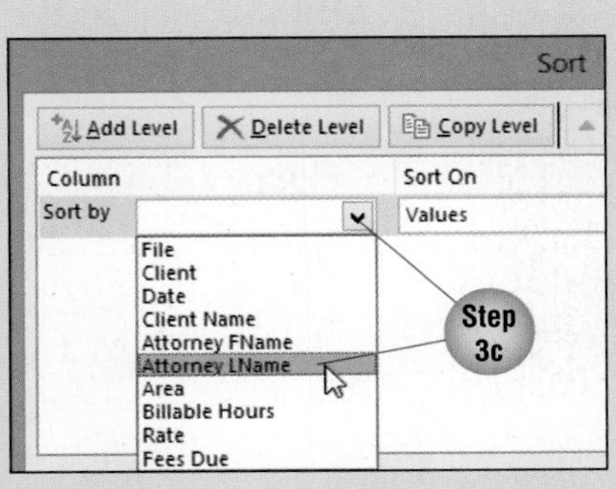

   d. Click the Add Level button.
   e. Click the down-pointing arrow next to the *Then by* option box and then click *Area* at the drop-down list.
   f. Click the Add Level button.
   g. Click the down-pointing arrow next to the second *Then by* option box and then click *Client Name* at the drop-down list.
   h. Click OK.

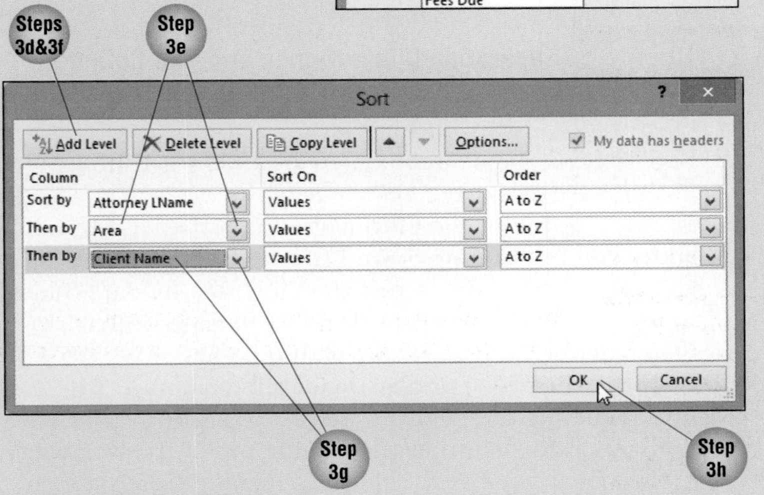

4. Print the sorted table.
5. Save and then close **EL2-C3-P1-BillSumOctWk1.xlsx**.

Project 2 Use Data Tools to Split Data and Ensure Data Integrity — 6 Parts

You will use Excel's data tools to split the client's first and last names into two separate columns, combine two columns, remove duplicate records, and restrict the type of data that can be entered into a field.

Quick Steps

Split Text into Multiple Columns

1. Insert blank column(s) next to source data.
2. Select data to be split.
3. Click DATA tab.
4. Click Text to Columns button.
5. Click Next at first dialog box.
6. Select delimiter check box for character that separates data.
7. Click Next.
8. Click Finish.
9. Deselect range.

Text to Columns

Working with Data Tools

The Data Tools group on the DATA tab, shown in Figure 3.3, includes useful features for working with data in tables. A worksheet in which more than one field has been entered into the same column can be separated into multiple columns using the Text to Columns feature. For example, a column that has first and last names in the same cell can be split so that the first name appears in one column and the last name appears in a separate column. Breaking up the data into separate columns better facilitates sorting and other data management tasks.

Before using the Text to Columns feature, insert the number of blank columns you will need to separate the data immediately to the right of the column to be split. Next, select the column to be split and then click the Text to Columns button to start the Convert Text to Columns Wizard. The wizard contains three dialog boxes to guide you through the steps of separating the data.

Figure 3.3 Data Tools Group on the DATA Tab

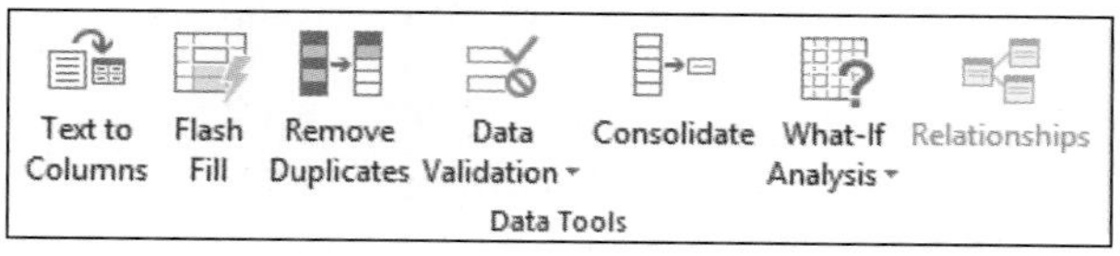

Project 2a Separating Client Names into Two Columns — Part 1 of 6

1. Open **EL2-C3-P1-BillSumOctWk1.xlsx**.
2. Save the workbook and name it **EL2-C3-P2-BillSumOctWk1**.
3. Position the active cell anywhere within the table, click the Sort & Filter button in the Editing group on the HOME tab, and then click *Clear* at the drop-down list to clear the existing sort criteria.
4. Create a custom sort to sort the table first by date (oldest to newest) and then by client (smallest to largest). Refer to Project 1d, Step 3, if you need assistance with this step.
5. Split the client first and last names in column D into two columns by completing the following steps:
   a. Right-click column letter E at the top of the worksheet area and then click *Insert* at the shortcut menu to insert a blank column between the *Client Name* and *Attorney FName* columns in the table.
   b. Select D5:D25.
   c. Click the DATA tab.
   d. Click the Text to Columns button in the Data Tools group.

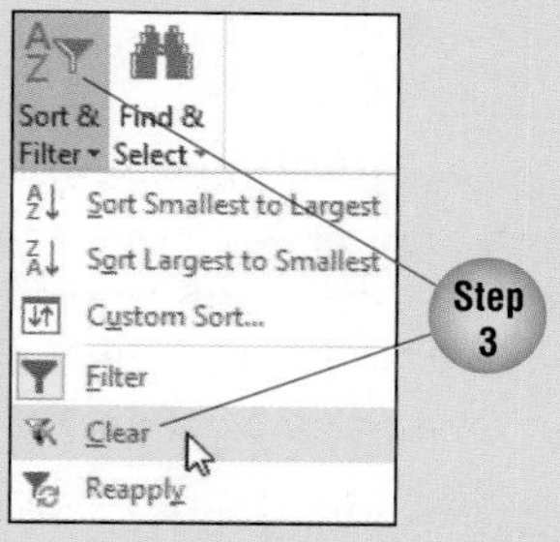

e. At the Convert Text to Columns Wizard - Step 1 of 3 dialog box, with *Delimited* selected in the *Choose the file type that best describes your data* section, click Next.

f. In the *Delimiters* section of the Convert Text to Columns Wizard - Step 2 of 3 dialog box, click the *Space* check box to insert a check mark and then click Next. The *Data preview* section of the dialog box updates after you click the *Space* check box to show the names split into two columns.

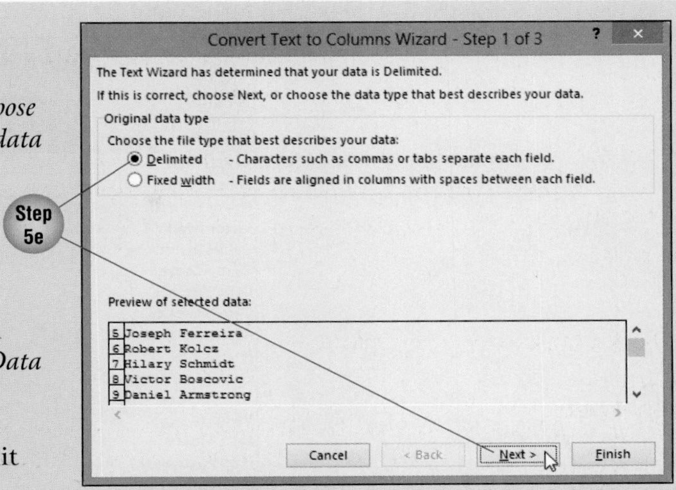

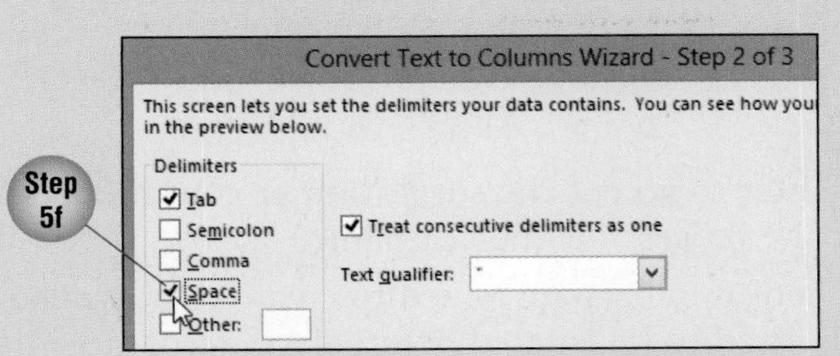

Step 6 | Step 7

Client FName	Client LName
Joseph	Ferreira
Robert	Kolcz
Hilary	Schmidt
Victor	Boscovic
Daniel	Armstrong
Penny	Cooke
Gene	Marsales
Dana	Fletcher
Alexander	Torrez
Jean	Sauve
Hilary	Schmidt
Hilary	Schmidt
Victor	Boscovic
Daniel	Armstrong
Lana	Moore
Sam	Tonini
Paul	Sebastian
Henri	Poissant
Jade	Eckler
Frank	Kinsela
Coonie	Melanson

Client first and last names are split into two columns in Steps 5a–5g.

g. Click Finish at the last Convert Text to Columns Wizard dialog box to accept the default General data format for both columns.

h. Deselect the range.

6. Make cell D4 active, change the label to *Client FName*, and then AutoFit the column width.
7. Make cell E4 active, change the label to *Client LName*, and then AutoFit the column width.
8. Save **EL2-C3-P2-BillSumOctWk1.xlsx**.

Populating Data Using Flash Fill

Flash Fill is a new feature added to Excel 2013 that extracts, joins, and inserts text, numbers, dates, and times. This feature is useful for organizing data that has been pasted or imported from other sources. You can join all or extract part of the contents of cells. Flash Fill analyzes adjacent columns while entering data, detects any patterns, and suggests how the rest of the column should be completed.

For example, in Project 2a, instead of using Text to Columns to split the client names into two columns, you could use Flash Fill. To do this, insert two new columns instead of one. Type the first name *Joseph* in column E, as shown in Figure 3.4. Press Enter and then type *R* to start the second name, *Robert*. Excel recognizes that you are taking the first word of the adjacent column D and suggests doing the same for the remaining cells in column E. Notice that the rest

Quick Steps

Extract Data Using Flash Fill

1. Insert blank column(s) next to source data.
2. Type the first record.
3. Press Enter.
4. Start typing second record.
5. When grayed-out text appears, press Enter.

Figure 3.4 Flash Fill for Project 2a

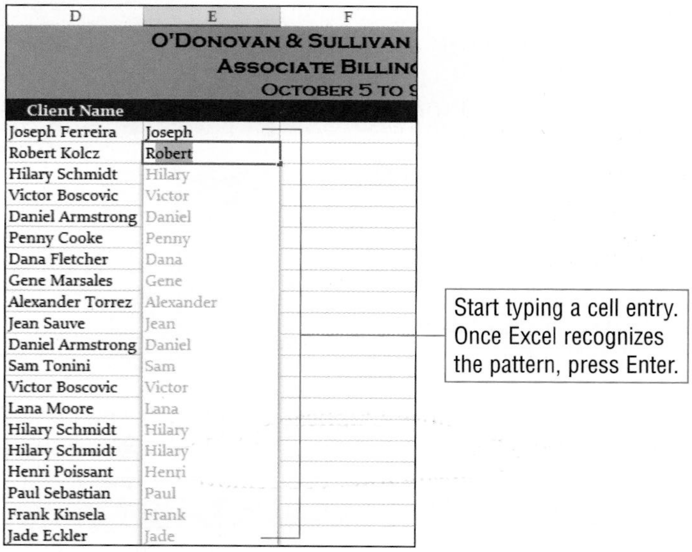

of names are grayed out. Press Enter to accept the suggestion or continue typing to reject the suggestion. Repeat the process for the last name.

In Project 2b, the file and client numbers are joined to create the case code number. A few rows of data may need to be entered before Excel recognizes the pattern. Once the pattern is established, click the Fill button in the Editing Group on the HOME tab and then choose *Flash Fill* from the drop-down menu. You can also click the Flash Fill button in the Data Tools group on the DATA Tab, press Ctrl + E, or press Enter if the grayed-out text appears.

Flash Fill

Another method to join together the content of two or more cells is to use the CONCATENATE function. You can join text, numbers, or cell references. The formula used in Project 2b, *=CONCATENATE(A5, "-",B5)*, joins the case code and the client number together with a dash. In the formula, cell references are separated by commas and any spaces or characters (text, numbers, or symbols) added directly into the formula are enclosed in quotation marks.

Removing Duplicate Records

Quick Steps

Remove Duplicate Rows

1. Select range or make cell active in table.
2. Click DATA tab.
3. Click Remove Duplicates button.
4. Select columns to compare.
5. Click OK.
6. Click OK.

Remove Duplicates

Excel can compare records within a worksheet and automatically delete duplicate rows based on the columns you select that might contain duplicate values. When you open the Remove Duplicates dialog box, shown in Figure 3.5, all columns are selected by default. If you do not want Excel to check for duplicates in every column, click the Unselect All button to remove the check marks from all of the columns, click the individual columns you want to compare, and then click OK. When you click OK, Excel automatically deletes rows containing duplicate values and, when the operation is completed, displays a message informing you of the number of rows that were removed from the worksheet or table and the number of unique values that remain.

Consider conditionally formatting duplicate values first to view the records that will be deleted. To do this, use the *Duplicate Values* option, which can be accessed by pointing to *Highlight Cells Rules* at the Conditional Formatting drop-down list. (Display the Conditional Formatting drop-down list by clicking the Conditional Formatting button in the Styles group on the HOME tab.)

Figure 3.5 Remove Duplicates Dialog Box

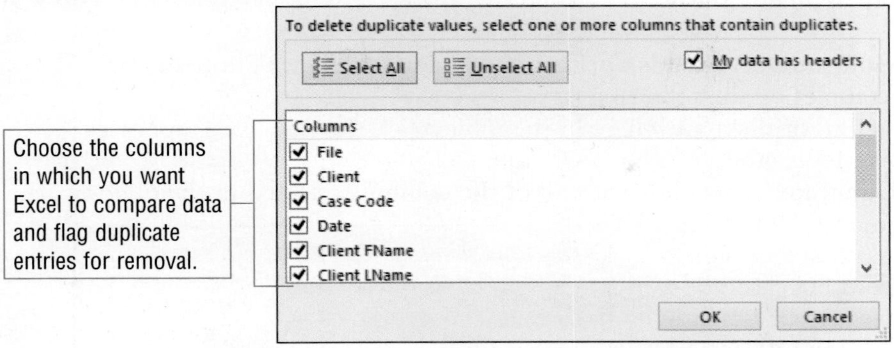

Excel includes the Remove Duplicates button in the Data Tools group on the DATA tab and in the Tools group on the TABLE TOOLS DESIGN tab. Click Undo to restore any duplicate rows you remove by mistake.

Project 2b Combining Client and File Numbers to Create Case Codes — Part 2 of 6

1. With **EL2-C3-P2-BillSumOctWk1.xlsx** open, combine the information in the *File* and *Client* columns to create the data in the *Case Code* column by completing the following steps:
   a. Insert a column between the *Client* and *Date* columns in the table. Refer to Project 2a, Step 5a, if you need assistance with this step.
   b. Change the column width to 13 characters.
   c. In cell C4, type Case Code and then press Enter.
   d. In cell C5, type =concatenate(a5,"-",b5) and then press Enter. (The case code is the file number followed by a dash and then the client number.)
2. After reviewing the data, you decide that the client number should come before the file number in the case code. Delete the column from the table by right-clicking the column letter C at the top of the worksheet area and then clicking *Delete* at the shortcut menu.
3. Combine the client and file information by completing the following steps:
   a. Insert a column between the *Client* and *Date* columns in the table, change the column width to 13 characters, and then type Case Code in cell C4. In cell C5, type 10104-FL-325 and then press Enter. (You typed the client number, a dash, and then the file number.)
   b. In cell C6, type 1. Flash Fill recognizes the sequence and suggests how to fill the rest of the column.
   c. Press Enter to accept the suggestions. If Excel does not recognize the pattern right away, continue to type the client number, a dash, and then the file number, or click the Flash Fill button in the Data Tools group on the DATA tab.
4. Save **EL2-C3-P2-BillSumOctWk1.xlsx**.

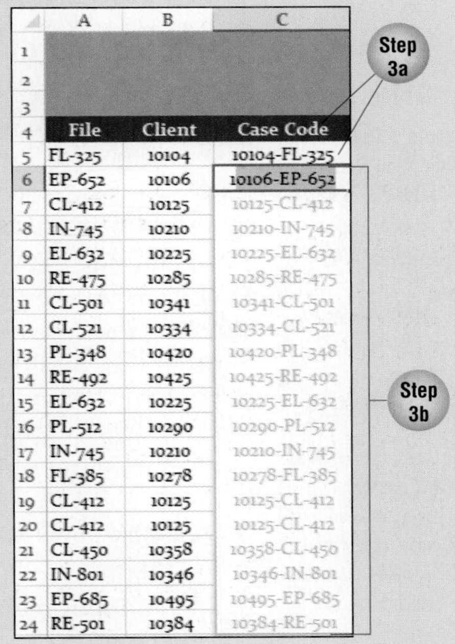

	A	B	C
1			
2			
3			
4	File	Client	Case Code
5	FL-325	10104	10104-FL-325
6	EP-652	10106	10106-EP-652
7	CL-412	10125	10125-CL-412
8	IN-745	10210	10210-IN-745
9	EL-632	10225	10225-EL-632
10	RE-475	10285	10285-RE-475
11	CL-501	10341	10341-CL-501
12	CL-521	10334	10334-CL-521
13	PL-348	10420	10420-PL-348
14	RE-492	10425	10425-RE-492
15	EL-632	10225	10225-EL-632
16	PL-512	10290	10290-PL-512
17	IN-745	10210	10210-IN-745
18	FL-385	10278	10278-FL-385
19	CL-412	10125	10125-CL-412
20	CL-412	10125	10125-CL-412
21	CL-450	10358	10358-CL-450
22	IN-801	10346	10346-IN-801
23	EP-685	10495	10495-EP-685
24	RE-501	10384	10384-RE-501

Project 2c Removing Duplicate Rows Part 3 of 6

1. With **EL2-C3-P2-BillSumOctWk1.xlsx** open, remove duplicate rows in the billing summary table by completing the following steps:
   a. With the active cell positioned anywhere in the table, click the Remove Duplicates button in the Data Tools group on the DATA tab.
   b. At the Remove Duplicates dialog box with all of the columns selected in the *Columns* list box, click the Unselect All button.
   c. The billing summary table should have only one record per case code per date, since attorneys record once per day the total hours spent on each case. A record is a duplicate if the same values exist in the two columns that store the case code number and date. Click the *Case Code* check box to insert a check mark.
   d. Click the *Date* check box to insert a check mark and then click OK.
   e. Click OK at the Microsoft Excel message box that says a duplicate value was found and removed and 20 unique values remain.

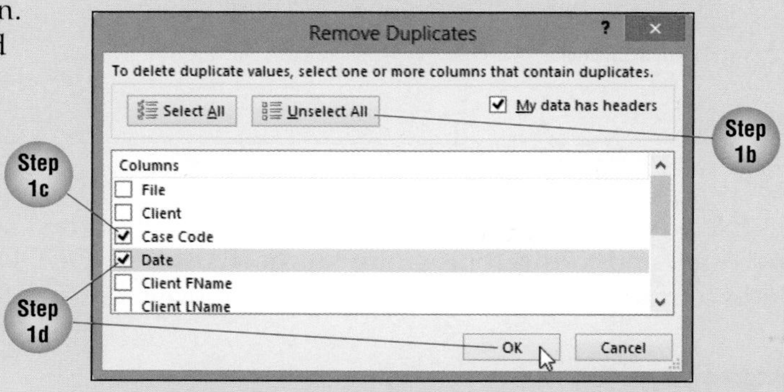

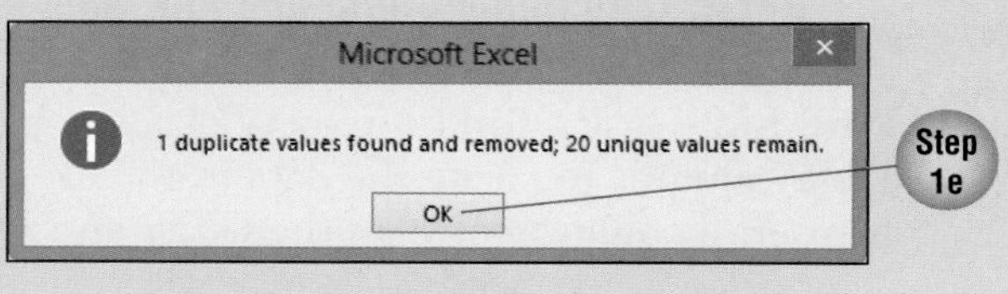

2. Scroll down the worksheet to view the total in cell L25. Compare the total with your printout from Project 1d, Step 4. Notice the total of the fees due is now *7,516.25* compared to *7,910.00* in the printout.
3. Save **EL2-C3-P2-BillSumOctWk1.xlsx**.

Validating and Restricting Data Entry

Quick Steps

Create a Data Validation Rule
1. Select desired range.
2. Click DATA tab.
3. Click Data Validation button.
4. Specify validation criteria in Settings tab.
5. Click Input Message tab.
6. Type input message title and text.
7. Click Error Alert tab.
8. Select error style.
9. Type error alert title and message text.
10. Click OK.

Data Validation

Excel's data validation feature allows you to control the type of data that is accepted for entry in a cell. You can specify the type of data that is allowed, as well as parameters that validate whether the entry is within a certain range of acceptable values, dates, times, or text lengths. You can also set up a list of values that display in a drop-down list when the cell is made active.

To do this, click the Data Validation button in the Data Tools group on the DATA tab. At the Data Validation dialog box, shown in Figure 3.6, begin by choosing the type of data you want to validate in the *Allow* option box on the Settings tab. Additional list or text boxes appear in the dialog box depending on the option chosen in the *Allow* drop-down list.

If a custom number format adds punctuation or text to the appearance of a cell, ignore the added characters when validating or restricting data entry. For example, a cell that contains the number *1234*, has the custom number format *"PD-"####*, and displays as *PD-1234* has a text length equal to 4 characters.

In addition to defining acceptable data entry parameters, you have the option to add an input message and an error alert message to the range. You define the text that appears in these messages.

Figure 3.6 Data Validation Dialog Box with Settings Tab Selected

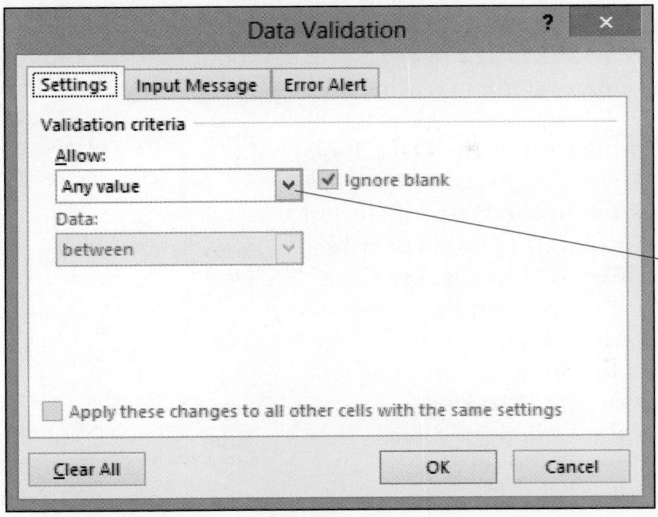

Specify the type of data you will allow to be entered into the cells in the range by specifying one of the following options: *Whole number*, *Decimal*, *List*, *Date*, *Time*, *Text length*, or *Custom*. Other parameter boxes may also appear, depending on the selection made in the *Allow* option box.

An input message displays when a cell is made active for which data validation rules apply. This kind of message is informational in nature. An error alert is a message that appears when incorrect data is entered in a cell. Three styles of error alerts are available, and a description and example of each type of alert is provided in Table 3.1. If an error alert message has not been defined, Excel displays the Stop error alert with the default error message *The value you entered is not valid. A user has restricted values that can be entered into this cell.*

Table 3.1 Data Validation Error Alert Message Styles

Error Alert Icon	*Error Alert Style*	*Description*	
	Stop	Prevents the data from being entered into the cell. The error alert message box provides three buttons to ensure new data is entered.	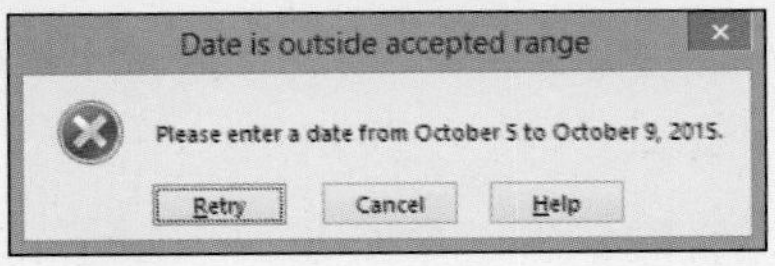
	Warning	Does not prevent the data from being entered into the cell. The error alert message box provides four buttons displayed below the prompt *Continue?*	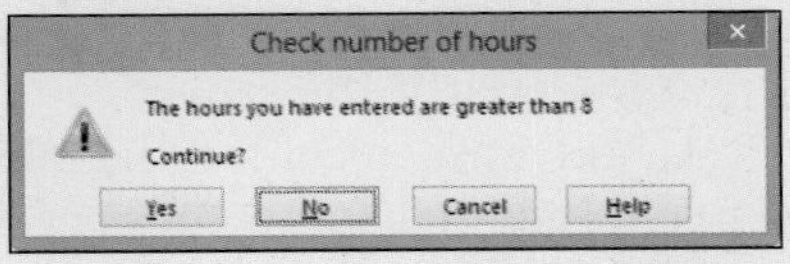
	Information	Does not prevent the data from being entered into the cell. The error alert message box provides three buttons displayed below the error message.	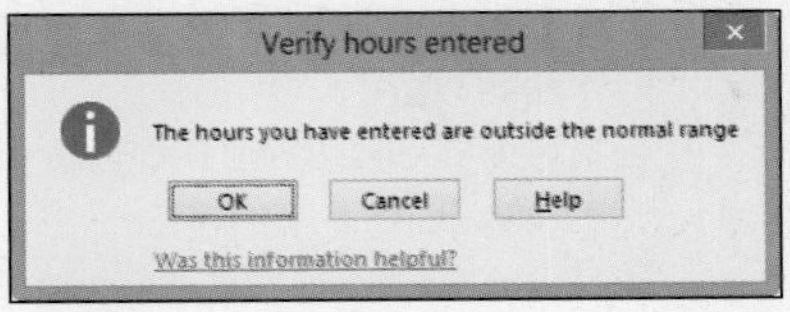

Project 2d Restricting Data Entry to Dates Within a Range

Part 4 of 6

1. With **EL2-C3-P2-BillSumOctWk1.xlsx** open, create a validation rule, input message, and error alert for dates in the billing summary worksheet by completing the following steps:
   a. Select D5:D24.
   b. Click the Data Validation button in the Data Tools group on the DATA tab.
   c. With Settings the active tab in the Data Validation dialog box, click the down-pointing arrow next to the *Allow* option box (currently displays *Any value*) and then click *Date* at the drop-down list. Validation options are dependent on the *Allow* setting. When you choose *Date*, Excel adds *Start date* and *End date* text boxes to the *Validation criteria* section.
   d. With *between* selected in the *Data* option box, click in the *Start date* text box and then type 10/5/2015.
   e. Click in the *End date* text box and then type 10/9/2015. (Since the billing summary worksheet is for the week of October 5 to 9, 2015, entering this validation criteria will ensure that only dates between the start date and end date are accepted.)
   f. Click the Input Message tab.
   g. Click in the *Title* text box and then type Billing Date.
   h. Click in the *Input message* text box and then type This worksheet is for the week of October 5 to October 9 only.
   i. Click the Error Alert tab.
   j. With *Stop* selected in the *Style* option box, click in the *Title* text box and then type Date is outside accepted range.
   k. Click in the *Error message* text box and then type Please enter a date from October 5 to October 9, 2015.
   l. Click OK. Since the range is active for which the data validation rules apply, the input message box appears.
   m. Deselect the range.

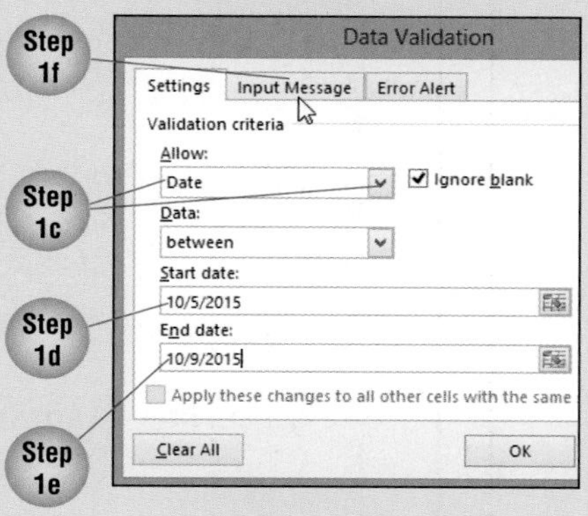

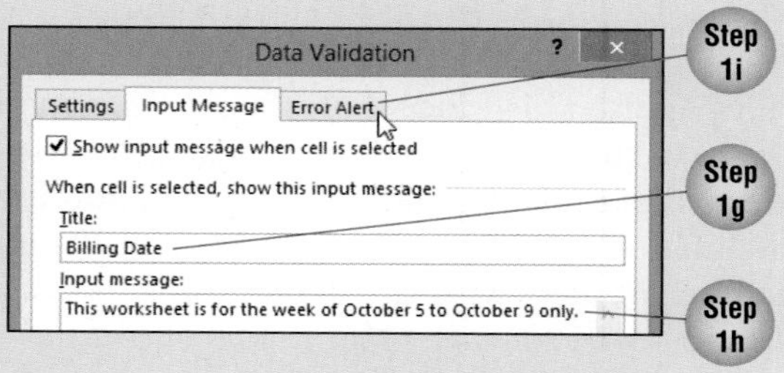

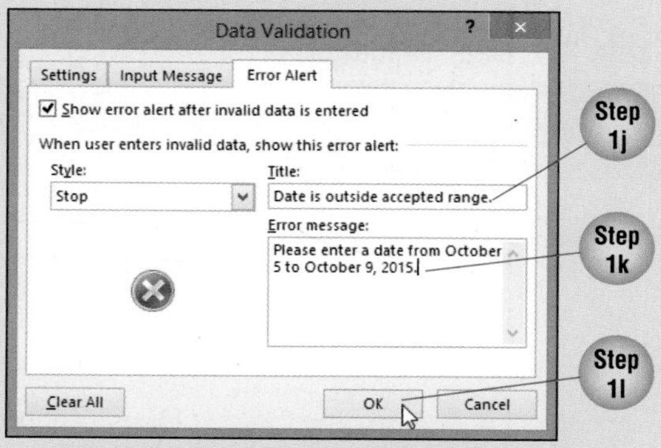

2. Add a new record to the table to test the date validation rule by completing the following steps:
   a. Right-click row number 25 and then click *Insert* at the shortcut menu to insert a new row into the table.
   b. Make cell A25 active, type PL-348, and then press Tab.
   c. Type 10420 in the *Client* column and then press Tab.
   d. Type 10420-PL-348 and then press Tab. The input message title and text appear when the *Date* column is made active.
   e. Type 10/10/2015 and then press Tab. Since the date entered is invalid, the error alert message box appears.

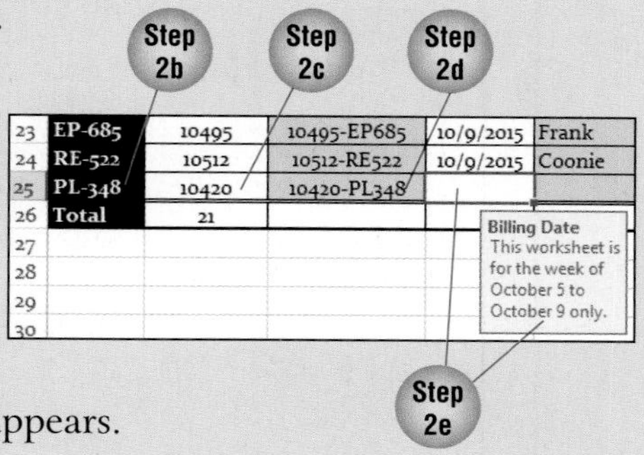

f. Click the Retry button.
g. Type 10/9/2015 and then press Tab.
h. Enter the data in the remaining fields as follows (pressing Tab to move from column to column in the table and pressing Enter after the Fees Due calculation is done):

Client FName	Alexander
Client LName	Torrez
Attorney FName	Rosa
Attorney LName	Martinez
Area	Patent
Billable Hours	2.25
Rate	100.00

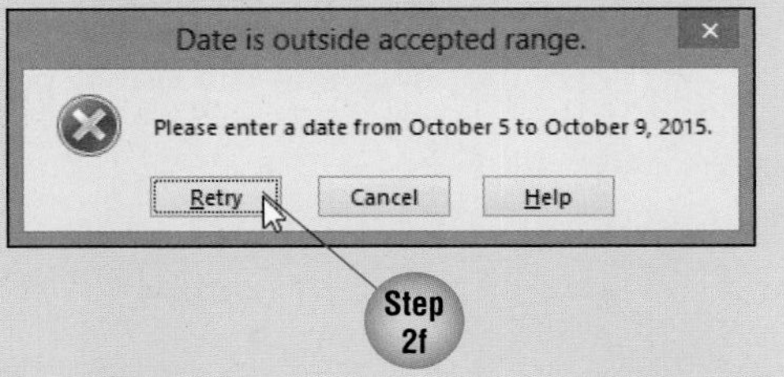

3. Save **EL2-C3-P2-BillSumOctWk1.xlsx**.

Project 2e Restricting Data Entry to Values Within a List

Part 5 of 6

1. With **EL2-C3-P2-BillSumOctWk1.xlsx** open, create a list of values that are allowed in a cell by completing the following steps:
   a. Select K5:K25.
   b. Click the Data Validation button in the Data Tools group.
   c. If necessary, click the Settings tab.
   d. Click the down-pointing arrow next to the *Allow* option box and then click *List* at the drop-down list.
   e. Click in the *Source* text box and then type 75.00,85.00,90.00,100.00.
   f. Click OK.
   g. Deselect the range.

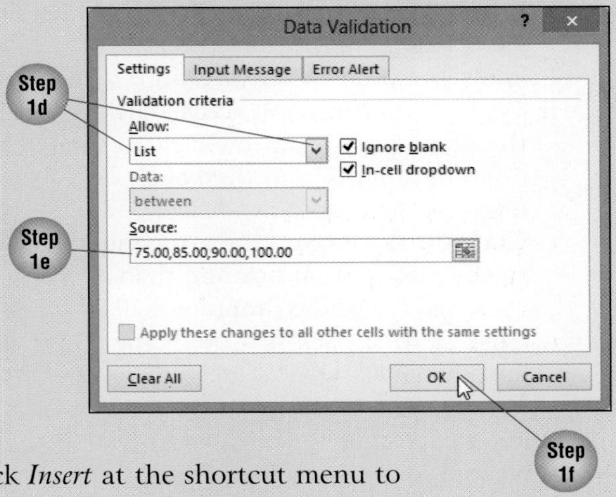

2. Add a new record to the table to test the rate validation list by completing the following steps:
   a. Right-click row number 26 and then click *Insert* at the shortcut menu to insert a new row in the table.
   b. Make cell A26 active and then type data in the fields as follows (pressing Tab to move from column to column in the table):

File	IN-745
Client	10210
Case Code	10210-IN-745
Date	10/9/2015
Client FName	Victor
Client LName	Boscovic
Attorney FName	Rosa
Attorney LName	Martinez
Area	Insurance
Billable Hours	1.75

c. At the *Rate* field, the validation list becomes active and a down-pointing arrow appears to the right of the cell. Type 125.00 and then press Tab to test the validation rule. Since no error alert message was entered, the default message appears.

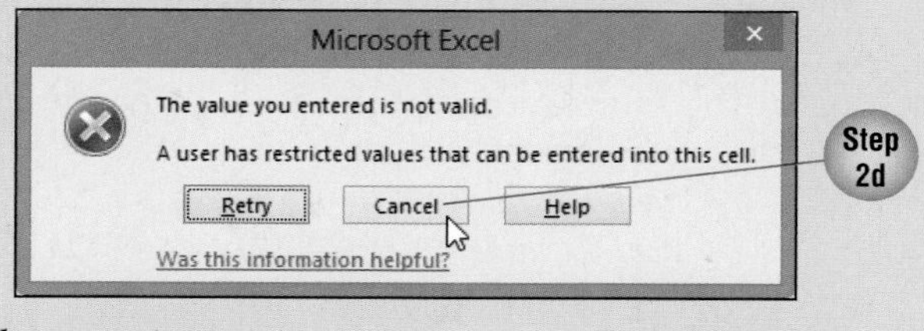

d. Click the Cancel button. The value is cleared from the field.

e. Make cell K26 the active cell, click the down-pointing arrow at the right side of the cell, click *100.00* at the drop-down list, and then press Tab.

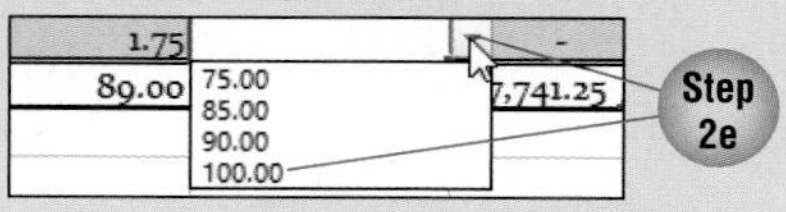

3. Save **EL2-C3-P2-BillSumOctWk1.xlsx**.

Project 2f Ensuring Data Entered Is a Specified Text Length Part 6 of 6

1. With **EL2-C3-P2-BillSumOctWk1.xlsx** open, create a validation rule to ensure that all client identification numbers are 5 characters in length (to be compatible with the firm's accounting system) by completing the following steps:
   a. Select B5:B26 and then click the Data Validation button in the Data Tools group on the DATA tab.
   b. With the Settings tab active, click the down-pointing arrow next to the *Allow* option box and then click *Text length* at the drop-down list.
   c. Click the down-pointing arrow next to the *Data* option box and then click *equal to* at the drop-down list.
   d. Click in the *Length* text box, type 5, and then click OK.
   e. Deselect the range.

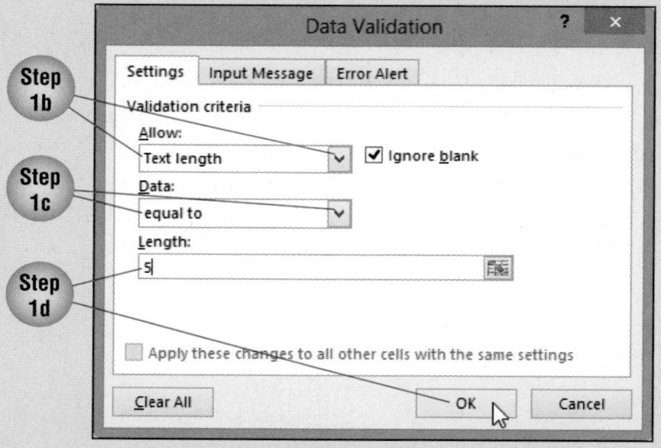

2. Add a new record to the table to test the client identification validation rule by completing the following steps:
   a. Right-click row number 27 and then click *Insert* at the shortcut menu.
   b. Make cell A27 active, type FL-325, and then press Tab.
   c. Type 1010411 in cell B27 and then press Tab. Since this value is greater than the specified number of characters allowed in the cell, the default error message appears.
   d. Click the Retry button.
   e. Delete the selected text, type 1010, and then press Tab. Since this value is less than the specified text length, the default error message appears again. (Using a Text Length validation rule ensures that all entries in the range have the same number of characters. This rule is useful to validate customer numbers, employee numbers, inventory numbers, or any other data that requires a consistent number of characters.)
   f. Click the Cancel button, type 10104, and then press Tab. Since this entry is 5 characters in length, Excel moves to the next field.

g. Enter the remaining fields as follows:

Case Code	10104-FL-325
Date	10/9/2015
Client FName	Joseph
Client LName	Ferreira
Attorney FName	Marty
Attorney LName	O'Donovan
Area	Divorce
Billable Hours	5.75
Rate	85.00

3. Save, print, and then close **EL2-C3-P2-BillSumOctWk1.xlsx**.

Project 3 Group and Subtotal Related Records — 3 Parts

You will convert the billing summary table to a normal range, sort the rows by the attorney names, and then add subtotals to display total fees due, a count of fees, and the average billable hours and fees due for each attorney.

Converting a Table to a Normal Range

A table can be converted to a normal range using the Convert to Range button in the Tools group on the TABLE TOOLS DESIGN tab. Convert a table to a range to use the Subtotal feature or if you no longer need to treat the table data as a range independent of data in the rest of the worksheet. You may want to remove some or all of the table styles before you convert the table to a range. Use the Clear button in the Table Styles gallery or click the individual options in the Table Style Options group to remove any unwanted formatting.

Quick Steps

Convert a Table to a Range
1. Make table cell active.
2. Click TABLE TOOLS DESIGN tab.
3. Click Convert to Range button.
4. Click Yes.

Create a Subtotal
1. Select range.
2. Click DATA tab.
3. Click Subtotals button.
4. Select field to group by in *At each change in* option box.
5. Select desired function in *Use function* option box.
6. Select field(s) to subtotal in *Add subtotal to* list box.
7. Click OK.
8. Deselect range.

Convert to Range

Subtotaling Related Data

A range of data with a column that has multiple rows with the same field value can be grouped and subtotals can be created for each group automatically. For example, a worksheet with multiple records with the same department name in a field can be grouped by department name and a subtotal of a numeric field can be calculated for each department. You can choose from a list of functions for the subtotal, such as Average and Sum, and you can also create multiple subtotal values for each group. Before creating subtotals, sort the data by the fields in which you want the records grouped. Make sure no blank rows exist within the range that is to be grouped and subtotaled.

Excel displays a new row with a summary total when the field value for the specified subtotal column changes content. A grand total is also automatically included at the bottom of the range. Excel displays the subtotals with buttons along the left side of the worksheet area used to show or hide the details for each group using the Outline feature. Excel can create an outline with up to eight levels.

Figure 3.7 illustrates the data you will group and subtotal in Project 3a displayed with the worksheet at level 2 of the outline. In Figure 3.8, the same worksheet is shown with two attorney groups expanded to show the detail records.

Figure 3.7 Worksheet with Subtotals by Attorney Last Name Displaying Level 2 of the Outline

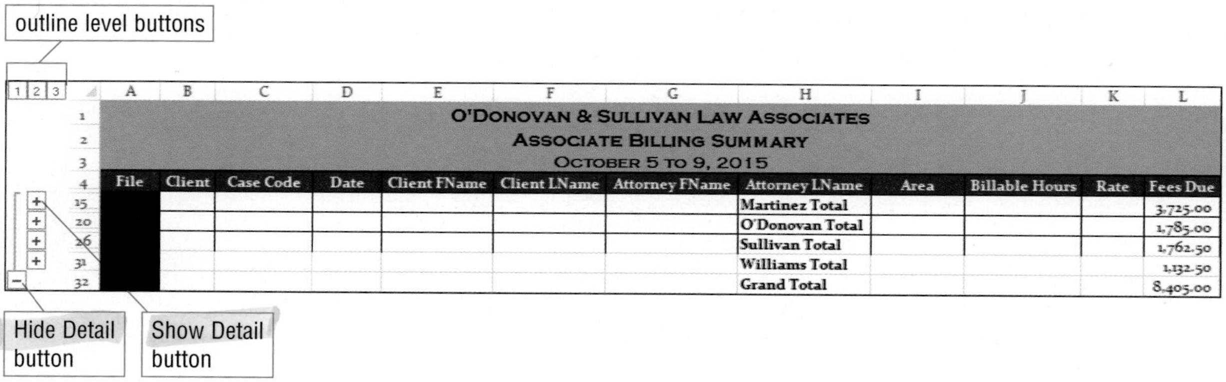

O'DONOVAN & SULLIVAN LAW ASSOCIATES
ASSOCIATE BILLING SUMMARY
OCTOBER 5 TO 9, 2015

File	Client	Case Code	Date	Client FName	Client LName	Attorney FName	Attorney LName	Area	Billable Hours	Rate	Fees Due
							Martinez Total				3,725.00
							O'Donovan Total				1,785.00
							Sullivan Total				1,762.50
							Williams Total				1,132.50
							Grand Total				8,405.00

Figure 3.8 Worksheet with Subtotals by Attorney Last Name with Martinez and Sullivan Groups Expanded

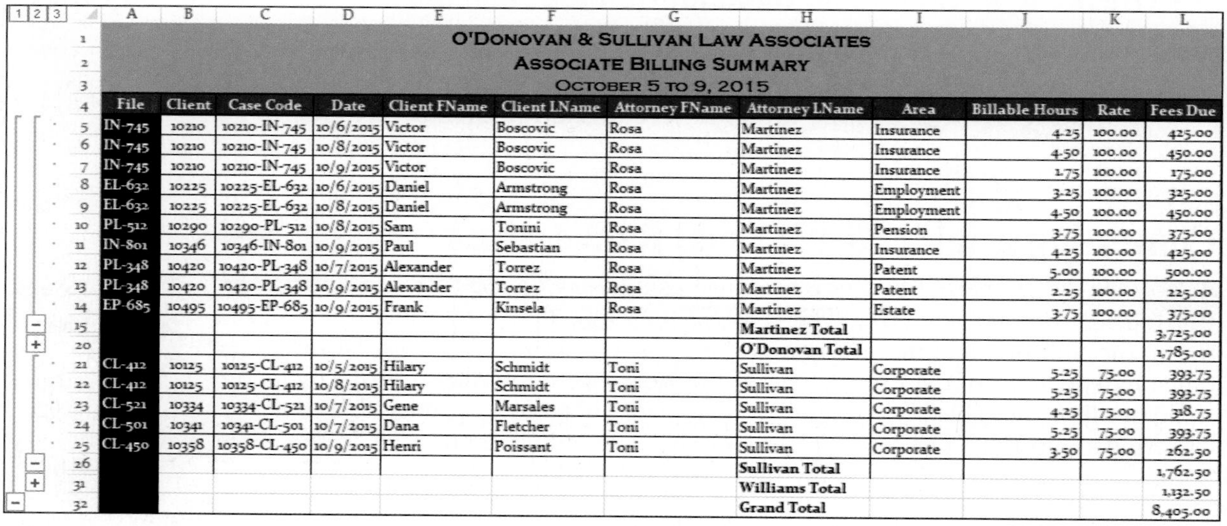

O'DONOVAN & SULLIVAN LAW ASSOCIATES
ASSOCIATE BILLING SUMMARY
OCTOBER 5 TO 9, 2015

File	Client	Case Code	Date	Client FName	Client LName	Attorney FName	Attorney LName	Area	Billable Hours	Rate	Fees Due
IN-745	10210	10210-IN-745	10/6/2015	Victor	Boscovic	Rosa	Martinez	Insurance	4.25	100.00	425.00
IN-745	10210	10210-IN-745	10/8/2015	Victor	Boscovic	Rosa	Martinez	Insurance	4.50	100.00	450.00
IN-745	10210	10210-IN-745	10/9/2015	Victor	Boscovic	Rosa	Martinez	Insurance	1.75	100.00	175.00
EL-632	10225	10225-EL-632	10/6/2015	Daniel	Armstrong	Rosa	Martinez	Employment	3.25	100.00	325.00
EL-632	10225	10225-EL-632	10/8/2015	Daniel	Armstrong	Rosa	Martinez	Employment	4.50	100.00	450.00
PL-512	10290	10290-PL-512	10/8/2015	Sam	Tonini	Rosa	Martinez	Pension	3.75	100.00	375.00
IN-801	10346	10346-IN-801	10/9/2015	Paul	Sebastian	Rosa	Martinez	Insurance	4.25	100.00	425.00
PL-348	10420	10420-PL-348	10/7/2015	Alexander	Torrez	Rosa	Martinez	Patent	5.00	100.00	500.00
PL-348	10420	10420-PL-348	10/9/2015	Alexander	Torrez	Rosa	Martinez	Patent	2.25	100.00	225.00
EP-685	10495	10495-EP-685	10/9/2015	Frank	Kinsela	Rosa	Martinez	Estate	3.75	100.00	375.00
							Martinez Total				3,725.00
							O'Donovan Total				1,785.00
CL-412	10125	10125-CL-412	10/5/2015	Hilary	Schmidt	Toni	Sullivan	Corporate	5.25	75.00	393.75
CL-412	10125	10125-CL-412	10/8/2015	Hilary	Schmidt	Toni	Sullivan	Corporate	5.25	75.00	393.75
CL-521	10334	10334-CL-521	10/7/2015	Gene	Marsales	Toni	Sullivan	Corporate	4.25	75.00	318.75
CL-501	10341	10341-CL-501	10/7/2015	Dana	Fletcher	Toni	Sullivan	Corporate	5.25	75.00	393.75
CL-450	10358	10358-CL-450	10/9/2015	Henri	Poissant	Toni	Sullivan	Corporate	3.50	75.00	262.50
							Sullivan Total				1,762.50
							Williams Total				1,132.50
							Grand Total				8,405.00

Project 3a Converting a Table to a Range and Creating Subtotals — Part 1 of 3

1. Open **EL2-C3-P2-BillSumOctWk1.xlsx**.
2. Save the workbook and name it **EL2-C3-P3-BillSumOctWk1.xlsx**.
3. Remove style options and convert the table to a normal range to group and subtotal the records by completing the following steps:
   a. Position the active cell anywhere within the table and click the TABLE TOOLS DESIGN tab.
   b. Click the *Total Row* check box in the Table Style Options group to remove the *Total* row from the table. The Subtotal feature includes a grand total automatically, so the *Total* row is no longer needed.
   c. Click the *Banded Columns* check box in the Table Style Options group to remove the banded formatting.
   d. Click the Convert to Range button in the Tools group.

e. Click Yes at the Microsoft Excel message box asking if you want to convert the table to a normal range.

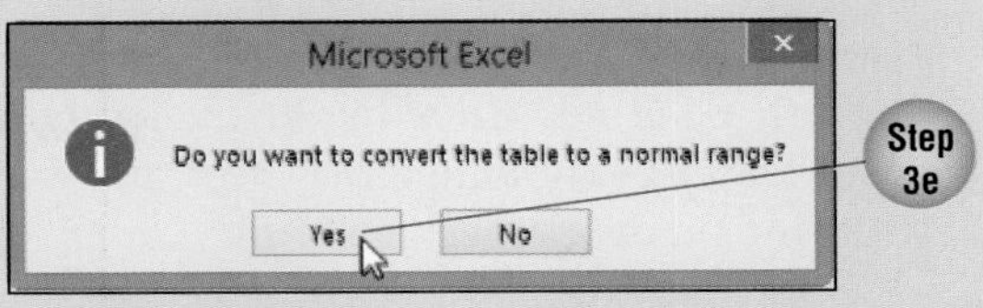

f. Select columns A through L and AutoFit the column widths.

g. Deselect the columns.

4. Sort the data by the fields you want to subtotal and group by completing the following steps:
   a. Select A4:L27.
   b. Click the Sort & Filter button in the Editing group on the HOME tab and then click *Custom Sort* at the drop-down list.
   c. At the Sort dialog box, define three levels to group and sort the records as follows:

Column	*Sort On*	*Order*
Attorney LName	Values	A to Z
Client	Values	Smallest to Largest
Date	Values	Oldest to Newest

   d. Click OK.

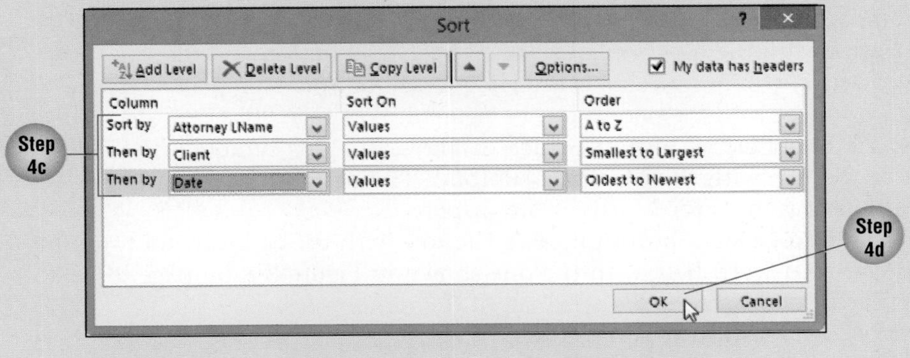

5. Create subtotals at each change in attorney last name by completing the following steps:
   a. With A4:L27 still selected, click the DATA tab.
   b. Click the Subtotal button in the Outline group.
   c. At the Subtotal dialog box, click the down-pointing arrow to the right of the *At each change in* option box (which currently displays *File*), scroll down the list, and then click *Attorney LName*.

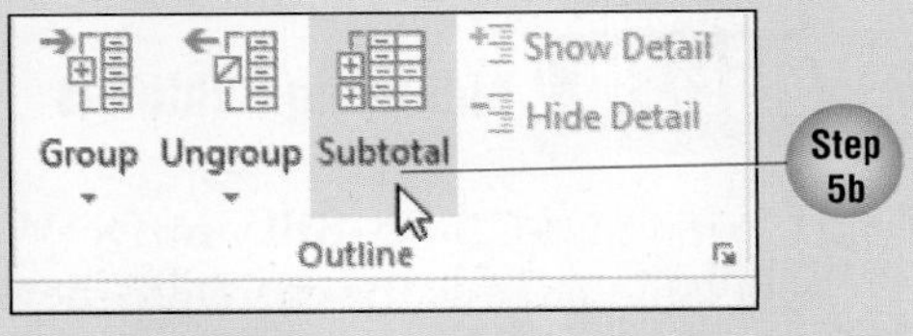

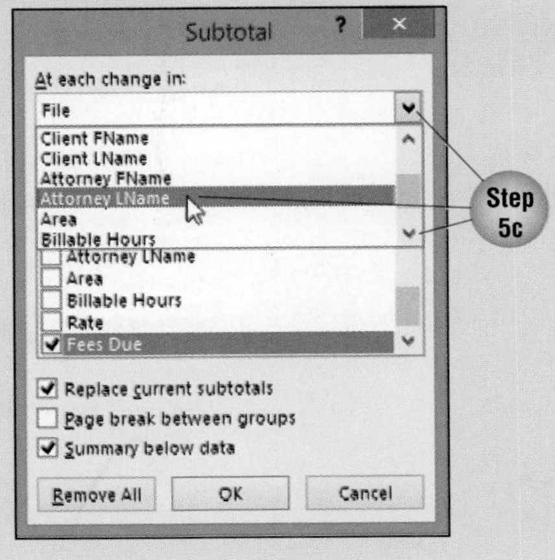

d. With *Use function* set to *Sum* and *Fees Due* selected in the *Add subtotal to* list box, click OK.
e. Deselect the range.

6. Print the worksheet.
7. Show and hide levels in the outlined worksheet by completing the following steps:
   a. Click the level 1 button located at the top left of the worksheet area below the Name text box. Excel collapses the worksheet to display only the grand total of the *Fees Due* column.

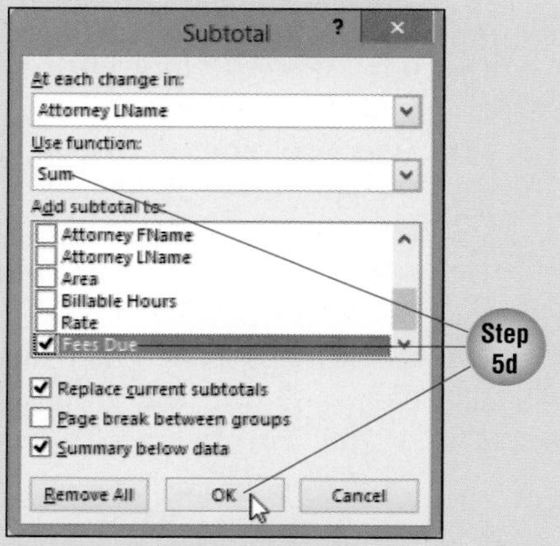

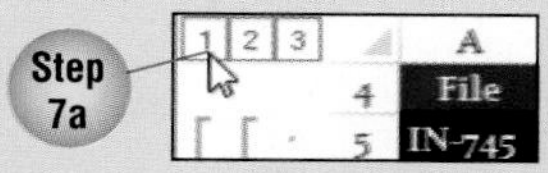

   b. Click the level 2 button to display the subtotals by attorney last name. Notice that a button with a plus symbol displays next to each subtotal in the Outline section at the left side of the worksheet area. The button with the plus symbol is the Show Detail button and the button with the minus symbol is the Hide Detail button. Compare your worksheet with the one shown in Figure 3.7 on page 90.
   c. Click the Show Detail button (which displays as a plus symbol) next to the row with the Martinez subtotal. The detail rows for the group of records for Martinez are displayed.

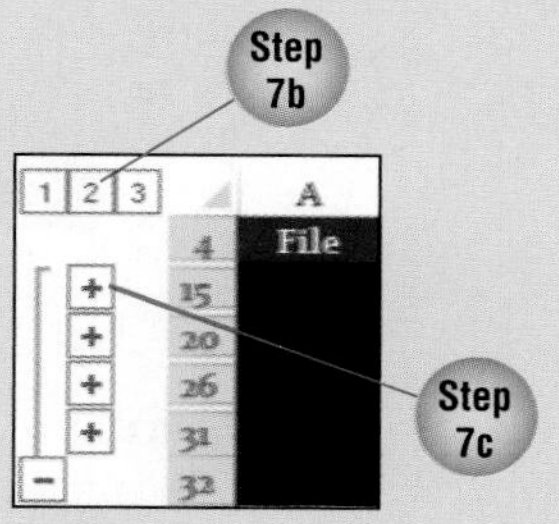

   d. Click the Show Detail button next to the row with the Sullivan subtotal.
   e. Compare your worksheet with the one shown in Figure 3.8 on page 90.
   f. Click the level 3 button to display all of the detail rows.
8. Save **EL2-C3-P3-BillSumOctWk1.xlsx**.

Project 3b Modifying Subtotals — Part 2 of 3

1. With **EL2-C3-P3-BillSumOctWk1.xlsx** open, add a subtotal to count the number of billable records for each attorney for the week by completing the following steps:
   a. Select A4:L32 and then click the Subtotal button in the Outline group on the DATA tab. The Subtotal dialog box opens with the settings used for the subtotals created in Project 3a.
   b. Click the *Replace current subtotals* check box to remove the check mark. By clearing the check box, you are instructing Excel to add another subtotal row to each group.
   c. Click the down-pointing arrow next to the *Use function* option box and then click *Count* at the drop-down list.
   d. With *Fees Due* still selected in the *Add subtotal to* list box, click OK. Excel adds a new subtotal row to each group with the count of records displayed.

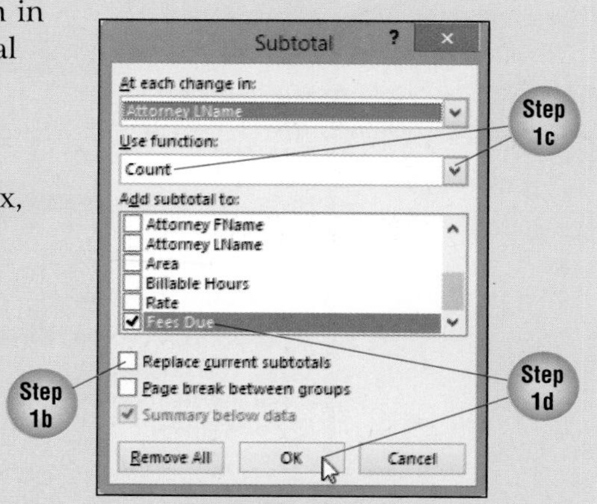

2. Add a subtotal to calculate the average billable hours and average fees due for each attorney by completing the following steps:
   a. With the data range still selected, click the Subtotal button.
   b. Click the down-pointing arrow next to the *Use function* option box and then click *Average* at the drop-down list.
   c. Click the *Billable Hours* check box in the *Add subtotal to* list box and then click OK. Excel adds a new subtotal row to each group with the average billable hours and average fees due for each attorney.

Attorney LName	Area	Billable Hours	Rate	Fees Due
Martinez	Insurance	4.25	100.00	425.00
Martinez	Insurance	4.50	100.00	450.00
Martinez	Insurance	1.75	100.00	175.00
Martinez	Employment	3.25	100.00	325.00
Martinez	Employment	4.50	100.00	450.00
Martinez	Pension	3.75	100.00	375.00
Martinez	Insurance	4.25	100.00	425.00
Martinez	Patent	5.00	100.00	500.00
Martinez	Patent	2.25	100.00	225.00
Martinez	Estate	3.75	100.00	375.00
Martinez Average		3.73		372.50
Martinez Count				10
Martinez Total				3,725.00

The averages of the *Billable Hours* and *Fees Due* columns are added to the subtotals for all attorneys in Steps 2a–2c. The data for the Martinez group is shown.

   d. Deselect the range.
3. Save the revised workbook and name it **EL2-C3-P3-BillSumOctWk1-Prj3b**.
4. Click the PAGE LAYOUT tab and scale the height of the worksheet to 1 page.
5. Print the worksheet.
6. Save and then close **EL2-C3-P3-BillSumOctWk1-Prj3b.xlsx**.

Grouping and Ungrouping Data

When a worksheet is outlined, use the Group and Ungroup buttons in the Outline group on the DATA tab to individually manage collapsing and expanding groups of records at the various levels. For example, in an outlined worksheet with detailed rows displayed, selecting a group of records and clicking the Ungroup button opens the Ungroup dialog box, shown in Figure 3.9. Clicking OK with *Rows* selected removes the group feature applied to the selection and removes the Hide Detail button so the records remain displayed at the outline level. Selecting records that have been ungrouped and clicking the Group button reattaches the group feature to the selection and redisplays the Hide Detail button.

Quick Steps

Group Data by Rows
1. Select range to be grouped within outlined worksheet.
2. Click DATA tab.
3. Click Group button.
4. Click OK.

Ungroup Data by Rows
1. Select grouped range within outlined worksheet.
2. Click DATA tab.
3. Click Ungroup button.
4. Click OK.

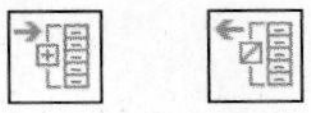

Group Ungroup

Figure 3.9 Ungroup Dialog Box

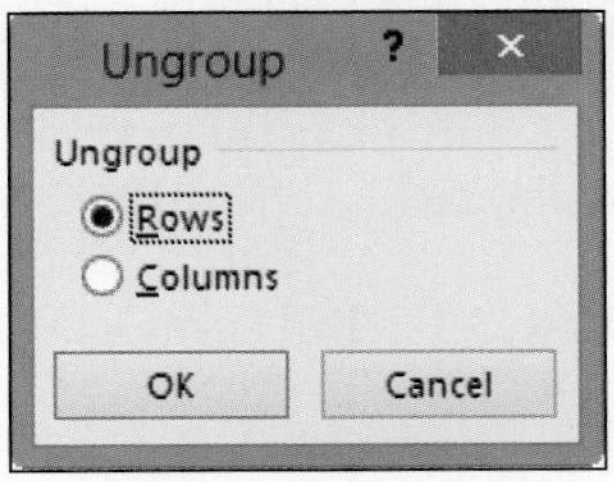

Columns can also be grouped and ungrouped. The outline section with the level numbers and Show and Hide Detail buttons displays across the top of the worksheet area. For example, in a worksheet in which two columns are used to arrive at a formula, the source columns can be grouped and the details hidden so that only the formula column with the calculated results is displayed in an outlined worksheet.

Project 3c Grouping and Ungrouping Data — Part 3 of 3

1. Open **EL2-C3-P3-BillSumOctWk1.xlsx.** Group client data within the Martinez attorney group by completing the following steps:
   a. Select A5:L7. These three rows contain billing information for client 10210.
   b. Click the Group button in the Outline group on the DATA tab. (Make sure to click the button and not the button arrow.)
   c. At the Group dialog box with *Rows* selected, click OK. Excel adds a fourth outline level to the worksheet and a Hide Detail button is added below the last row of the grouped records in the Outline section.
   d. Select A12:L13, click the Group button, and then click OK at the Group dialog box.

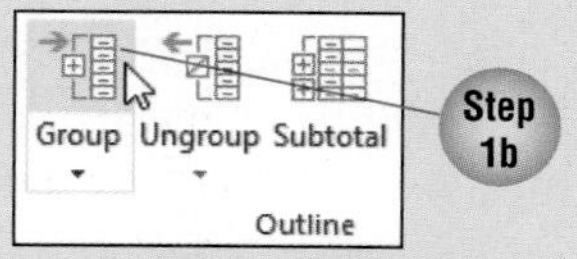

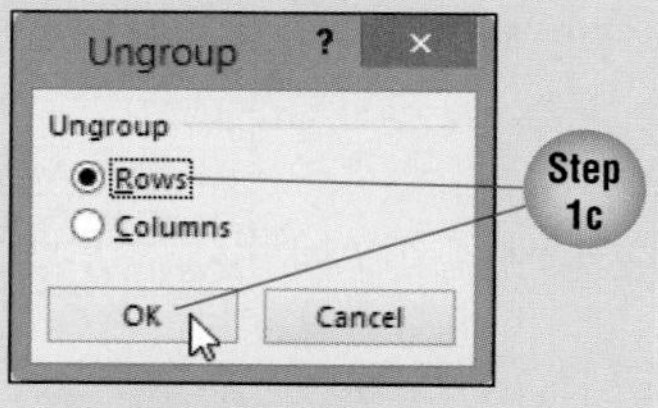

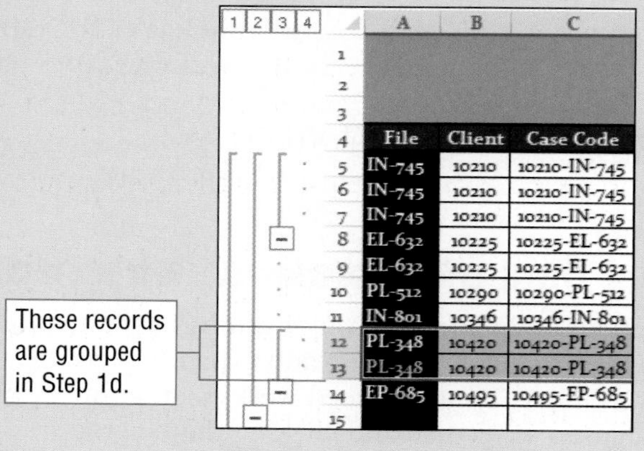

   e. Deselect the range.
2. Experiment with the Hide Detail buttons in the Martinez group by hiding the detail for client 10210 and then hiding the detail for client 10420.
3. Redisplay the detail rows by clicking the Show Detail button for each client.
4. Select A5:L7, click the Ungroup button (make sure to click the button and not the button arrow), and then click OK at the Ungroup dialog box.
5. Select A12:L13, click the Ungroup button, and then click OK at the Ungroup dialog box.
6. Select A5:L14, click the Ungroup button, and then click OK at the Ungroup dialog box. Notice that the Hide Detail button is removed for the entire Martinez group.
7. Deselect the range and then click the level 2 button at the top of the outline section. Notice that the Martinez records do not collapse like the others, since they are no longer grouped.
8. Save the revised workbook and name it **EL2-C3-P3-BillSumOctWk1-Prj3c**.
9. Print and then close **EL2-C3-P3-BillSumOctWk1-Prj3c.xlsx**.

Chapter Summary

- A table in Excel is a range of cells similar in structure to a database in which no blank rows exist and the first row of the range contains column headings.
- Define a range as a table using the Table button in the Tables group on the INSERT tab.
- Columns in a table are called *fields* and rows are called *records*.
- The first row of a table contains column headings and is called the *field names row* or *header row*.
- A table automatically expands to include data typed in a row or column immediately adjacent to a range that has been defined as a table.
- Typing a formula in the first record of a new column causes Excel to define the column as a calculated column and automatically copy the formula to the remaining rows in the table.
- The contextual TABLE TOOLS DESIGN tab contains options for formatting tables.
- The Table Styles gallery contains several options that you can use to change the visual appearance of a table.
- Banding rows or columns formats every other row or column differently to make reading a large table easier.
- You can add emphasis to the first column or last column in a table. Excel generally formats the column with a darker fill color and reverse font or bold font and borders, depending on the Table Style in effect.
- The row containing field names in a table can be shown or hidden using the *Header Row* option in the Table Style Options group.
- Adding a *Total* row to a table causes Excel to add the word *Total* in the left-most column and create a Sum function in the last numeric column in the table. You can add additional functions by clicking in the desired column in the *Total* row and selecting a function from the pop-up list.
- Excel automatically includes a filter arrow at the top of each column in a table. Use these arrows to filter and sort the table.
- A column containing text that you want to split can be separated into multiple columns using the Text to Columns button in the Data Tools group on the DATA tab. The Convert Text to Columns Wizard contains three dialog boxes to define how to split the data.
- Use Flash Fill to extract, join, and insert text, numbers, dates, and times.
- Using the Remove Duplicates dialog box, you can instruct Excel to compare records within a worksheet and automatically delete rows that are duplicated.
- Data can be validated as it is being entered into a worksheet, and invalid data can be prevented from being stored or a warning can be issued to state that data has been entered that does not conform to the restrictions.
- At the Settings tab in the Data Validation dialog box, you define the validation criteria for the cell entry. You can allow data based on values, dates, times, and text lengths or restrict the entries to values within a drop-down list.

- At the Input Message tab in the Data Validation dialog box, you can define a message that pops up when a cell for which data is restricted becomes active.
- At the Error Alert tab in the Data Validation dialog box, you can define the type of error alert to display and the content of the error message.
- Convert a table to a normal range when you want to use the Subtotal feature or no longer need to treat a range of cells independently from the rest of the worksheet.
- Sort a worksheet by the column(s) for which you want to group data for subtotals before opening the Subtotals dialog box.
- The Subtotals button is located in the Outline group on the DATA tab.
- Excel adds a subtotal automatically at each change in content for the column you specify as the subtotal field. A grand total is also automatically added to the bottom of the range.
- You can display more than one subtotal row for a group to calculate multiple functions, such as Sum and Average.
- A subtotaled range is outlined and record details can be collapsed or expanded using the level number, Hide Detail, and Show Detail buttons.
- When a worksheet is outlined, use the Group and Ungroup buttons in the Outline group on the DATA tab to manage the display of individual groups.

Commands Review

FEATURE	RIBBON TAB, GROUP	BUTTON	KEYBOARD SHORTCUT
convert table to range	TABLE TOOLS DESIGN, Tools		
convert text to table	DATA, Data Tools		
create table	INSERT, Tables		Ctrl + T
Flash Fill	HOME, Editing OR DATA, Data Tools		Ctrl + E
group data	DATA, Outline		Shift + Alt + Right Arrow key
remove duplicates	DATA, Data Tools OR TABLE TOOLS DESIGN, Tools		
sort and filter table	HOME, Editing		
subtotals	DATA, Outline		
table styles	TABLE TOOLS DESIGN, Table Styles		
Total row	TABLE TOOLS DESIGN, Table Style Options		Ctrl + Shift + T
ungroup	DATA, Outline		Shift + Alt + Left Arrow key
validate data	DATA, Data Tools		

Concepts Check Test Your Knowledge SNAP

Completion: In the space provided at the right, indicate the correct term, command, or number.

1. The first row of a table that contains the column headings is called the field names row or this row. 2 — header row
2. Typing a formula in the first record of a column in a table causes Excel to define the field as this type of column. 1 — calculated
3. Change the visual appearance of a table using this gallery in the TABLE TOOLS DESIGN tab. 2 — table Styles
4. This term describes the formatting feature in a table in which even-numbered rows are formatted differently from odd-numbered rows. 1 — banding
5. Clicking this button causes the Convert Text to Columns Wizard to appear. 3 — text to columns
6. Open this dialog box to instruct Excel to compare the entries in the columns you specify and automatically delete rows that contain repeated data. 2 — remove duplicates
7. Open this dialog box to restrict entries in a cell to those that you set up in a drop-down list. 2 — Data validation
8. This option in the *Allow* option box is used to require that data entered into a cell be a specific number of characters. 2 — text length
9. This is the default error alert style that prevents invalid data from being entered into a cell. 1 — Stop
10. The Convert to Range button is found on this tab. 3 — Table tools design
11. Prior to creating subtotals using the Subtotal button in the Outline group on the DATA tab, arrange the data in this order. 10 — by the feilds in which the records should be grouped
12. In a worksheet with subtotal rows only displayed, click this button next to a subtotal row to view the grouped rows. 2 — show detail
13. Click this button in an outlined worksheet to collapse the rows for a group. 2 — hide detail
14. In an outlined worksheet, use this button to collapse all records and display only the row with the grand total. 2 — level one
15. Clicking this button in an outlined worksheet will cause the Hide Detail button for the selected rows to be removed. 1 — ungroup

Skills Check Assess Your Performance

Assessment 1

CREATE AND FORMAT A TABLE

SNAP Grade It

1. Open **VIVClassics.xlsx**.
2. Save the workbook and name it **EL2-C3-A1-VIVClassics**.
3. Select A4:L30 and create a table using the Table Style Medium 12 table style (fifth column, second row in *Medium* section). The table has headers.
4. Add a calculated column to the table in column M by completing the following:
   a. Type **Total Cost** as the column heading in cell M4.
   b. Create a formula in the first record that multiplies the number of copies in column G times the cost price in column L. The formula will copy to the rest of the rows in the table.
5. Adjust the three rows above the table to merge and center across columns A through M and adjust all column widths to AutoFit.
6. Add banding to the columns, remove banding from the rows, and emphasize the last column in the table.
7. Add a *Total* row to the table. Add Average functions that calculate the average number of copies and the average cost price of a video. Format the average value in the *Copies* column of the *Total* row to no places after the decimal point and M5:M31 to two places after the decimal point.
8. The video *Blue Hawaii* cannot be located and the manager would like you to remove the record from the table. Delete the row in the table for the record with stock number CV-1015.
9. Save, print, and then close **EL2-C3-A1-VIVClassics.xlsx**.

Assessment 2

USE DATA TOOLS

SNAP Grade It

1. Open **EL2-C3-A1-VIVClassics.xlsx**.
2. Save the workbook and name it **EL2-C3-A2-VIVClassics**.
3. Make the following changes:
   a. Insert a new blank column to the right of the column containing the director names and change the column headings to *Director FName* and *Director LName*.
   b. Split the director names into two columns (first and last names).
4. Use the Remove Duplicates feature to find and remove any duplicate rows using *Title* as the comparison column.
5. Create the following validation rules:
   a. A custom format of "CV-"#### has been applied to the stock numbers. Create a validation rule for the *Stock No.* column that ensures all new entries are 4 characters in length. (With custom number formats, you do not include the characters between the quotation marks in the text length.)
   b. Add an input message to the column that reads **Enter the last four digits of the stock number.** Use the default error alert options.

c. The manager would like to ensure that in the future, five copies is the maximum inventory of any individual classic video in the collection. Create a validation rule that restricts entries in the *Copies* column to a number less than six. Do not add an input message and use the default Stop error alert.

d. Create a drop-down list for the *Genre* column with the entries provided. Do not enter an input message and use the default error alert settings.

6. Add the record below to the table to test the data validation rules. (Initially enter incorrect values in the *Stock No.*, *Genre*, and *Copies* columns to make sure the rule and the messages work correctly.)

Stock No.	CV-1026
Title	The Philadelphia Story
Year	1940
Genre	Comedy
Stock Date	12/12/2015
Director FName	George
Director LName	Cukor
Copies	3
VHS	No
DVD	Yes
Blu-ray	Yes
Category	7-day rental
Cost Price	10.15

7. Save, print, and then close **EL2-C3-A2-VIVClassics.xlsx**.

Assessment 3

SUBTOTAL RECORDS

SNAP Grade It

1. Open **EL2-C3-A2-VIVClassics.xlsx**.
2. Save the workbook and name it **EL2-C3-A3-VIVClassics**.
3. Remove the *Total* row and remove the emphasis from the last column in the table.
4. Convert the table to a normal range.
5. Adjust all column widths to AutoFit.
6. Sort the list first by the genre, then by the director's last name, and then by the title of the video. Use the default sort values and sort order for each level.
7. Using the Subtotal button in the Outline group on the DATA tab, add subtotals to the *Total Cost* column to calculate the sum and average total costs of videos by genre.
8. Display the worksheet at level 2 of the outline.
9. Show the details for the Comedy, Drama, and Family genres.
10. Print the worksheet.
11. Save and then close **EL2-C3-A3-VIVClassics.xlsx**.

Visual Benchmark Demonstrate Your Proficiency

1 USING TABLE AND DATA TOOLS IN A CALL LIST

1. Open **WPMCallList.xlsx**.
2. Save the workbook and name it **EL2-C3-VB1-WPMCallList**.
3. Format and apply data tools as required to duplicate the worksheet in Figure 3.10 using the following information:
   - The worksheet has *Table Style Medium 5* applied to the table range.
   - Look closely at the sorted order. The table is sorted by three levels using the fields *Designation*, *Hourly Rate*, and *Hire Date*.
   - Shift cost equals the hourly rate times 8 hours.
   - Use Flash Fill to split the names into two columns.
   - Include the *Total* row and apply the appropriate banded options.
4. Save, print, and then close **EL2-C3-VB1-WPMCallList.xlsx**.

2 USING SUBTOTALS IN A CALL LIST

1. Open **EL2-C3-VB1-WPMCallList.xlsx**.
2. Save the workbook and name it **EL2-C3-VB2-WPMCallList**.
3. Create subtotals and view the revised worksheet at the appropriate level to display as shown in Figure 3.11 on the next page.
4. Save, print, and then close **EL2-C3-VB2-WPMCallList.xlsx**.

Figure 3.10 Visual Benchmark 1

	A	B	C	D	E	F	G	H	I	J	K	L
1	Wellington Park Medical Center											
2	Nursing Division Casual Relief Call List											
3	Payroll No.	First Name	Last Name	Designation	Hire Date	Telephone	OR Exp?	Day Shift Only?	Night Shift Only?	Either Shift?	Hourly Rate	Shift Cost
4	19658	Paula	Sanderson	RN	4/28/2000	555-3485	No	No	No	Yes	38.50	**308.00**
5	38642	Tania	Ravi	RN	6/22/2002	555-6969	Yes	Yes	No	Weekends only	38.50	**308.00**
6	78452	Terry	Mason	RN	10/8/2015	555-1279	Yes	No	Yes	No	38.50	**308.00**
7	96523	Lynn	Pietre	RN	10/22/1998	555-2548	Yes	Yes	No	Weekends only	35.00	**280.00**
8	45968	David	Featherstone	RN	9/9/2001	555-5961	No	No	No	Yes	35.00	**280.00**
9	46956	Orlando	Zambian	RN	11/10/2001	555-1186	No	Yes	No	No	35.00	**280.00**
10	56983	Amanda	Sanchez	RN	4/27/1999	555-4896	Yes	No	Yes	No	33.00	**264.00**
11	68429	Rene	Quenneville	RN	8/15/2003	555-4663	Yes	Yes	No	Weekends only	22.50	**180.00**
12	69417	Denis	LaPierre	RN	8/23/2003	555-8643	No	No	Yes	No	22.50	**180.00**
13	37944	Fernando	Este	RN	7/18/2005	555-4545	No	No	No	Yes	22.50	**180.00**
14	78647	Jay	Bjorg	RN	5/14/2007	555-6598	No	No	No	Yes	22.50	**180.00**
15	95558	Sam	Vargas	RN	3/2/2009	555-4571	No	No	No	Yes	22.50	**180.00**
16	98731	Zail	Singh	RN	5/6/2011	555-3561	Yes	Yes	No	No	22.50	**180.00**
17	58612	Savana	Ruiz	RN	4/15/2012	555-8457	Yes	No	Yes	Weekends only	22.50	**180.00**
18	96721	Noreen	Kalir	RN	4/3/2009	555-1876	Yes	Yes	No	No	21.50	**172.00**
19	89367	Xiu	Zheng	LPN	4/23/2006	555-7383	Yes	Yes	No	No	18.75	**150.00**
20	14586	Alma	Fernandez	LPN	8/3/1997	555-7412	Yes	No	No	Yes	16.75	**134.00**
21	48652	Dana	Casselman	LPN	10/15/1997	555-6325	Yes	No	No	Yes	16.75	**134.00**
22	85412	Kelly	Lund	LPN	11/19/1998	555-3684	No	Yes	No	Weekends only	15.75	**126.00**
23	98364	Lana	Bourne	LPN	7/15/2008	555-9012	Yes	Yes	No	No	15.50	**124.00**
24	90467	Nadir	Abouzeen	LPN	8/12/2008	555-9023	No	No	No	Yes	14.50	**116.00**
25	68475	Kelly	O'Brien	LPN	1/20/2012	555-6344	No	Yes	No	Weekends only	13.75	**110.00**
26										**Average Hourly Rate and Shift Cost:**	**24.74**	**197.91**

Figure 3.11 Visual Benchmark 2

	A	B	C	D	E	F	G	H	I	J	K	L
1	Wellington Park Medical Center											
2	Nursing Division Casual Relief Call List											
3	Payroll No.	First Name	Last Name	Designation	Hire Date	Telephone	OR Exp?	Day Shift Only?	Night Shift Only?	Either Shift?	Hourly Rate	Shift Cost
19				**RN Average**							28.83	230.67
27				**LPN Average**							15.96	127.71
28				**Grand Average**							24.74	197.91

Case Study Apply Your Skills

Part 1

Rajiv Patel, Vice-President of NuTrends Market Research, has sent you a file named **NuTrendsMktPlans.xlsx**. The workbook contains client information for the company's first-quarter marketing plans for three marketing consultants. Rajiv would like you to improve the reporting in the file by completing the following tasks:

- Set up the data as a table sorted first by the consultant's last name and then by the marketing campaign's start date, both in ascending order. Rajiv would prefer that consultant names be split into two columns.
- Improve the formatting of the dollar values.
- Add a *Total* row to sum the columns containing dollar amounts.
- Add formatting to the titles above the table that are suited to the colors in the table style you selected.
- Make any other formatting changes you think will improve the worksheet's appearance.

Save the revised workbook and name it **EL2-C3-CS-P1-NuTrendsMktPlans**. Print the worksheet in landscape orientation with the width scaled to one page.

Part 2

Rajiv would like statistics for each consultant added to the workbook. Specifically, he would like to see the following information:

- The total marketing plan budget values being managed by each consultant, as well as the total planned expenditures by month
- The average marketing plan budget being managed by each consultant, as well as the average planned expenditures by month

Rajiv would like a printout that displays only the total and average values for each consultant, as well as the grand average and grand total. Save the revised workbook and name it **EL2-C3-CS-P2-NuTrendsMktPlans**. Print and then close the worksheet.

Part 3

In addition, Rajiv has asked that you provide another report from the file named **NuTrendsMktPlans.xlsx**. Specifically, he would like a printout of the worksheet that shows the original data at the top of the worksheet and a few blank rows below the worksheet. Rajiv would like to see the marketing plan details for Yolanda Robertson's clients that have campaigns starting after January 31, 2015.

Research in Help how to filter a range of cells using the Advanced Filter button in the Sort & Filter group on the DATA tab. Make sure you read how to copy rows that meet your filter criteria to another area of the worksheet. Using the information you have learned, open **NuTrendsMktPlans.xlsx**, insert three new rows above the worksheet, and use these rows to create the criteria range. Filter the list according to Rajiv's specifications. Rows that meet the criteria should be copied below the worksheet starting in cell A21. Add an appropriate title to describe the copied data in cell A20. Make any formatting changes you think will improve the appearance of the worksheet. Save the revised workbook and name it **EL2-C3-CS-P3-NuTrendsMktPlans**. Print the worksheet and then close the workbook.

Part 4

Rajiv is looking for information on current salary ranges for a market researcher in the United States. Use the Internet to find this information. If possible, find salary information that is specific to your state for a minimum of three cities. Find a low salary and high salary for a market researcher in each city.

Create a workbook that summarizes the results of your research. Include in the workbook the website addresses as hyperlinked cells next to items about salary range. Organize the data in the workbook as a table. Apply table formatting options so the data is attractively presented and easy to read. Add a *Total* row to the table and include an Average function to find the average salary from the three cities. Find a minimum of three and a maximum of five resources. Save the workbook and name it **EL2-C3-CS-P4-NuTrendsSalaryAnalysis**. Print the worksheet and then close the workbook.

MICROSOFT® EXCEL®

CHAPTER 4

Summarizing and Consolidating Data

PERFORMANCE OBJECTIVES

Upon successful completion of Chapter 4, you will be able to:

- **Summarize data by creating formulas with range names that reference other worksheets**
- **Modify the range assigned to a range name**
- **Summarize data by creating 3-D references**
- **Create formulas that link to cells in other worksheets or workbooks**
- **Edit a link to a source workbook**
- **Break a link to an external reference**
- **Use the Consolidate feature to summarize data in multiple worksheets**
- **Create, edit, and format a PivotTable**
- **Filter a PivotTable using Slicers**
- **Filter a PivotTable using Timelines**
- **Create and format a PivotChart**
- **Create and format Sparklines**

SNAP

Tutorials

4.1 Summarizing Data in Multiple Worksheets Using Range Names and 3-D References

4.2 Summarizing Data by Linking Ranges in Other Worksheets or Workbooks

4.3 Summarizing Data Using the Consolidate Feature

4.4 Creating a PivotTable

4.5 Filtering a PivotTable Using Slicers

4.6 Filtering a PivotTable Using a Timeline

4.7 Creating a PivotChart

4.8 Summarizing Data with Sparklines

You can summarize data by creating formulas that reference cells in other areas of the active worksheet or other worksheets within the same workbook or by linking to cells in other worksheets or workbooks. The Consolidate feature can also be used to summarize data from other worksheets or other workbooks into a master worksheet. Once the data has been summarized, consider presenting or analyzing the data by creating and formatting a PivotTable or PivotChart. Sparklines are miniature charts that are inserted into cells and allow you to see at a glance a trend or other pattern in the data. Timelines allow you to filter a PivotTable or PivotChart using a specified timeframe. In this chapter, you will learn how to summarize and filter data using a variety of methods and present visually summarized data for analysis. Model answers for this chapter's projects appear on the following pages.

Excel
EL2C4

Note: Before beginning the projects, copy to your storage medium the EL2C4 subfolder from the EL2 folder on the CD that accompanies this textbook and then make EL2C4 the active folder.

National Park Service
U.S. Department of the Interior
May 2015
Attendance Summary
Southwest Region, Zone C

Private Vehicle and Individual Entrances Only	10,460
Commercial Tour Vehicles Only	15,069
Total Attendance	25,529

National Park Service
U.S. Department of the Interior
May 2015
Attendance Summary
Southwest Region, Zone C

Private Vehicle and Individual Entrances Only	10,460
Commercial Tour Vehicles Only	15,434
Total Attendance	25,894

Project 1 Calculate Park Attendance Totals

Project 1c, EL2-C4-P1-MayEntries.xlsx

Project 1d, EL2-C4-P1-MayEntries.xlsx

NewAge Dental Services

Fee Revenue Summary

	January	February	March	Total
General Examinations	$ 3,374.47	$ 3,386.41	$ 3,510.45	$ 10,271.33
Cleanings and Fillings	9,634.98	9,016.37	7,107.42	25,758.77
Teeth Whitening	2,743.90	5,993.69	4,431.19	13,168.78
Bonding	5,835.61	7,262.00	7,420.33	20,517.94
Porcelain Veneers	5,674.21	3,685.67	3,671.52	13,031.40
Crowns and Bridges	4,977.27	10,636.33	7,119.07	22,732.67
Full and Partial Dentures	7,608.05	8,926.64	11,886.13	28,420.82
Emergency Extractions	1,301.24	1,291.32	1,515.69	4,108.25
Root Canals	3,157.20	2,488.20	6,034.21	11,679.61
Total	**$ 44,306.93**	**$ 52,686.63**	**$ 52,696.01**	**$ 149,689.57**

Project 2 Calculate Total Fees Billed by Three Dentists

EL2-C4-P2-NADQ1Fees.xlsx

Model (Multiple Items)

Sum of Sale Pric	Column Labels			
Row Labels	Clarke	Fernandez	Kazmarek	Grand Total
Central	4,470		5,224	9,694
North	1,150		8,099	9,249
South	2,499	1,150		3,649
West			1,575	1,575
Grand Total	**8,119**	**1,150**	**14,898**	**24,167**

Project 3 Analyze Fitness Equipment Sales Data in a PivotTable and PivotChart

Project 3c, EL2-C4-P3-PF1stQSales.xlsx

Manufacturer Vision

Sum of Sale Pric	**Column Labels**	
Row Labels	**West**	**Grand Total**
CrossTrainer	2,975	2,975
Stepper	1,745	1,745
Treadmill	2,250	2,250
Grand Total	**6,970**	**6,970**

Manufacturer
- Cybex
- SportArt
- TrueFit
- Vision

Region
- Central
- East
- North
- West
- South

Project 3d, EL2-C4-P3-PF1stQSales.xlsx

Model (All)

Sum of Sale Pric	Column Labels				
Row Labels	Adams	Clarke	Fernandez	Kazmarek	Grand Total
Central	975	3,595		4,074	8,644
East	4,933		1,745	3,540	10,218
North	2,250	4,775		3,150	10,175
South			3,795		3,795
West	2,975		1,745	999	5,719
Grand Total	**11,133**	**8,370**	**7,285**	**11,763**	**38,551**

Purchase Date
Feb - Mar 2015
MONTHS
2015
JAN FEB MAR APR MAY JUN JUL

Project 3e, EL2-C4-P3-PF1stQSales.xlsx

Model Answers

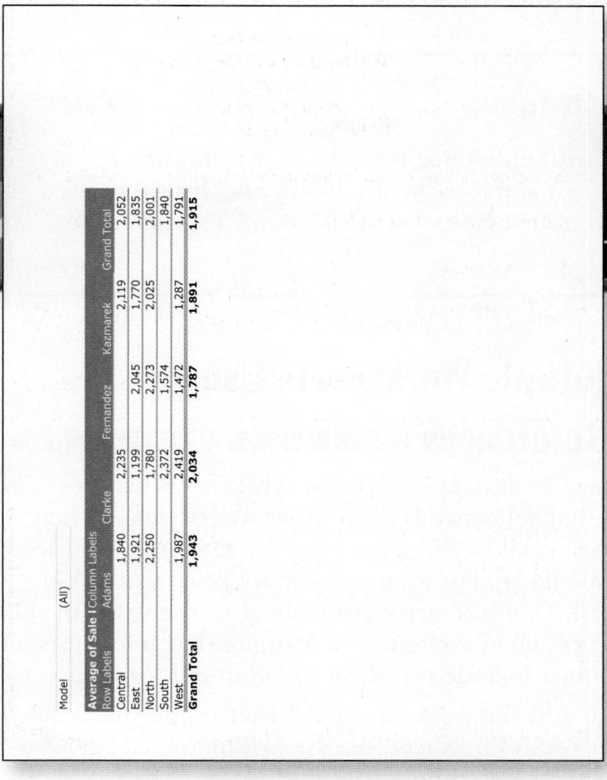

Model	(All)				
Average of Sale I	**Column Labels**				
Row Labels	Adams	Clarke	Fernandez	Kazmarek	Grand Total
Central	1,840	2,235		2,119	2,052
East	1,921	1,199	2,045	1,770	1,835
North	2,250	1,780	2,273	2,025	2,001
South		2,372	1,574		1,840
West	1,987	2,419	1,472	1,287	1,791
Grand Total	**1,943**	**2,034**	**1,787**	**1,891**	**1,915**

Project 3f, EL2-C4-P3-PFAvg1stQSales.xlsx

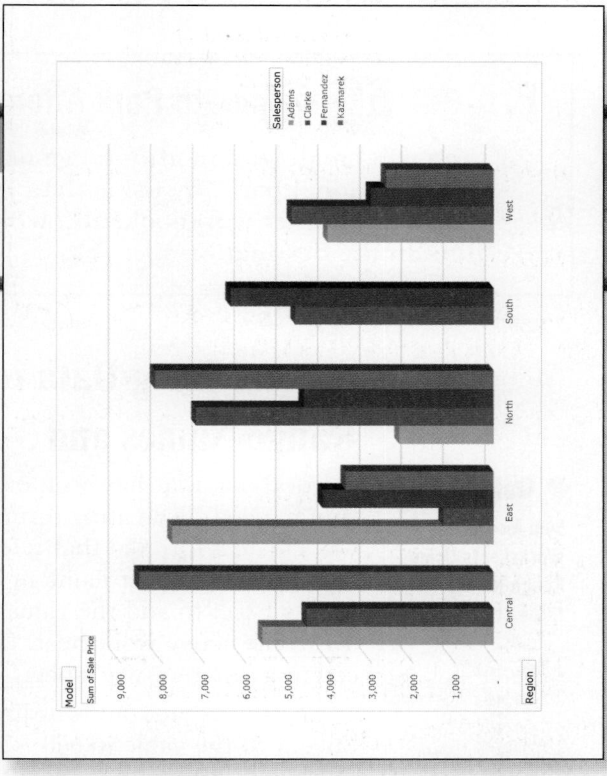

Project 3g, EL2-C4-P3-PF1stQSales.xlsx

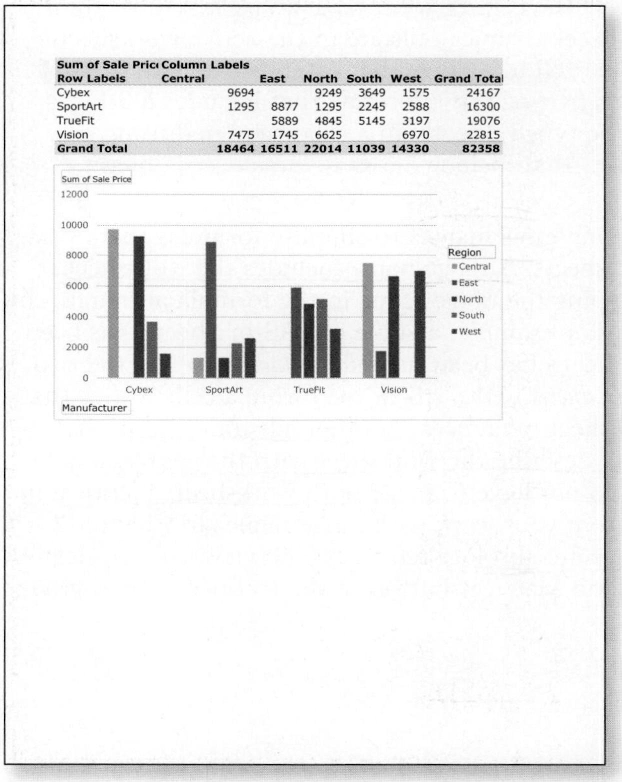

Sum of Sale Pric	**Column Labels**					
Row Labels	**Central**	**East**	**North**	**South**	**West**	**Grand Total**
Cybex	9694		9249	3649	1575	24167
SportArt	1295	8877	1295	2245	2588	16300
TrueFit		5889	4845	5145	3197	19076
Vision	7475	1745	6625		6970	22815
Grand Total	**18464**	**16511**	**22014**	**11039**	**14330**	**82358**

Project 3h, EL2-C4-P3-PFChart.xlsx

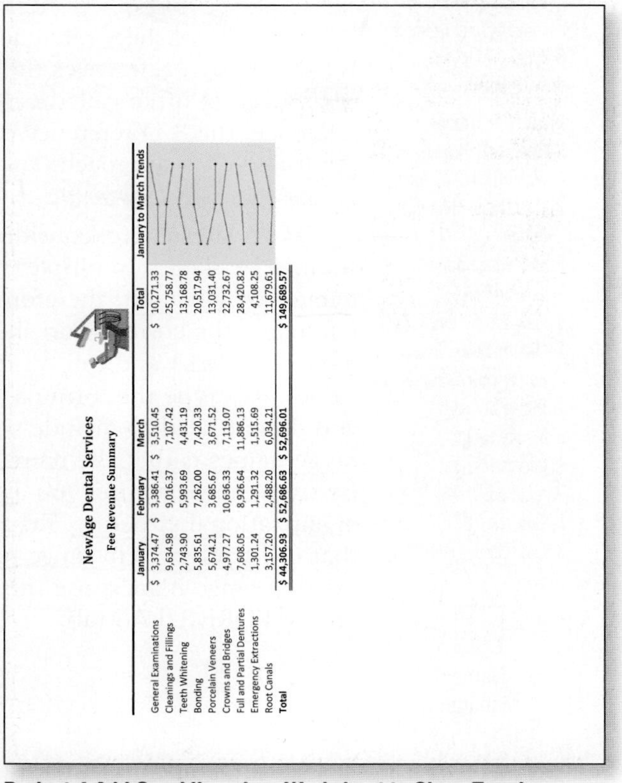

NewAge Dental Services

Fee Revenue Summary

	January	February	March	Total	January to March Trends
General Examinations	$ 3,374.47	$ 3,386.41	$ 3,510.45	$ 10,271.33	
Cleanings and Fillings	9,634.98	9,016.37	7,107.42	25,758.77	
Teeth Whitening	2,743.90	5,993.69	4,431.19	13,168.78	
Bonding	5,835.61	7,262.00	7,420.33	20,517.94	
Porcelain Veneers	5,674.21	3,685.67	3,671.52	13,031.40	
Crowns and Bridges	4,977.27	10,636.33	7,119.07	22,732.67	
Full and Partial Dentures	7,608.05	8,926.64	11,886.13	28,420.82	
Emergency Extractions	1,301.24	1,291.32	1,515.69	4,108.25	
Root Canals	3,157.20	2,488.20	6,034.21	11,679.61	
Total	**$ 44,306.93**	**$ 52,686.63**	**$ 52,696.01**	**$ 149,689.57**	

Project 4 Add Sparklines in a Worksheet to Show Trends

EL2-C4-P4-NADQ1Fees.xlsx

Project 1 Calculate Park Attendance Totals 5 Parts

You will create and modify range names and calculate total park attendance at three national parks by using data stored in separate worksheets and linking to a cell in another workbook. You will also edit a linked workbook and update the link in the destination file.

Summarizing Data in Multiple Worksheets Using Range Names and 3-D References

A workbook that has been organized with data in separate worksheets can be summarized by creating formulas that reference cells in other worksheets. When you create a formula that references a cell in the same worksheet, you do not need to include the sheet name in the reference. For example, the formula =A3+A4 causes Excel to add the value in cell A3 in the active worksheet to the value in cell A4 in the active worksheet. However, when you create a formula that references a cell in a different worksheet, you must include the sheet name in the formula.

Assume that you want Excel to add the value in cell A3 that resides in Sheet2 to the value in cell A3 that resides in Sheet3 in the workbook. To do this, you need to include the worksheet name in the formula by typing *=Sheet2!A3+Sheet3!A3* into the formula cell. This formula contains both worksheet references and cell references. The worksheet reference precedes the cell reference and is separated from the cell reference with an exclamation point. Without a worksheet reference, Excel assumes cells are in the active worksheet. A formula that references the same cell in a range that extends over two or more worksheets is often called a ***3-D reference***. For a formula that includes a 3-D reference, the 3-D reference can be typed directly in a cell or entered using a point-and-click approach. Formulas that include a 3-D reference are sometimes referred to as *3-D formulas*.

As an alternative, consider using range names to simplify formulas that summarize data in multiple worksheets. A range name includes the worksheet reference by default; therefore, typing the range name in the formula automatically references the correct worksheet. For example, assume cell A3 in Sheet2 has been named *ProductA* and cell A3 in Sheet3 has been named *ProductB*. To add the two values, you type the formula *=ProductA+ProductB* in the formula cell. Notice that you do not need to include worksheet references. Another advantage to using range names is that the name can describe the worksheet with the source data. By using range names, you also do not have to make both worksheets identical in organizational structure. Recall from your work with range names in Chapter 2 that cell references in range names are absolute references. To view, edit, or delete existing range names, use the Name Manager button in the Defined Names group on the FORMULAS tab.

Quick Steps

Sum Multiple Worksheets Using Range Names
1. Make formula cell active.
2. Type **=sum(**.
3. Type first range name.
4. Type comma **,**.
5. Type second range name.
6. Type comma **,**.
7. Continue typing range names separated by commas until finished.
8. Type **)**.
9. Press Enter.

Modify a Range Name Reference
1. Click FORMULAS tab.
2. Click Name Manager button.
3. Click range name to be modified.
4. Click Edit button.
5. Click in *Refers to* text box or click Collapse Dialog button.
6. Modify range address(es) as required.
7. Click OK.
8. Click Close.

Name Manager

Project 1a Modifying a Named Range and Summarizing Data in Multiple Worksheets

Part 1 of 5

1. Open **MayEntries.xlsx**.
2. Save the workbook and name it **EL2-C4-P1-MayEntries**.
3. Click each sheet tab and review the data. Each park has attendance data entered as a separate worksheet. In the workbook, range names have already been created. Check each range name to make sure the cell references are correct before creating the summary formula by completing the following steps:
   a. Click the down-pointing arrow next to the Name box and then click *Bryce* at the drop-down list. Notice that the BryceCanyon sheet is active and the ranges B7:B22 and E7:E21 are selected.
   b. Click the down-pointing arrow next to the Name box and then click *Grand* at the drop-down list. Notice that the GrandCanyon sheet is active and the range B7:B22 is selected. This range is missing the entries for days 17 through 31. You will correct this range in Step 4.
   c. Click the down-pointing arrow next to the Name box and then click *Mesa* at the drop-down list. Notice that the MesaVerde sheet is active and the ranges B7:B22 and E7:E21 are selected.

Step 3a

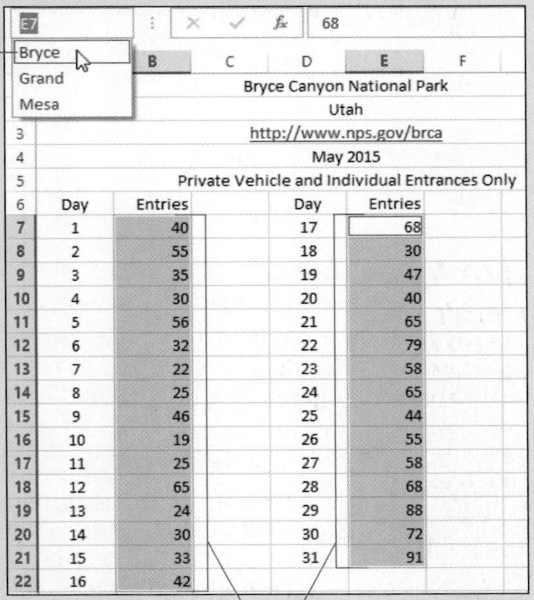

These ranges are automatically selected when you select *Bryce* from the Name box.

4. Modify the references in a named range by adding the data in column E of the GrandCanyon worksheet to the range named *Grand* by completing the following steps:
   a. Click in any cell to deselect the Mesa range.
   b. Click the FORMULAS tab.
   c. Click the Name Manager button in the Defined Names group.
   d. Click *Grand* in the *Name* list at the Name Manager dialog box.
   e. Click the Edit button.
   f. At the Edit Name dialog box, click the Collapse Dialog button located at the right of the *Refers to* text box (which currently displays *=GrandCanyon!$B$7:$B$22*).

Step 4e

Step 4d

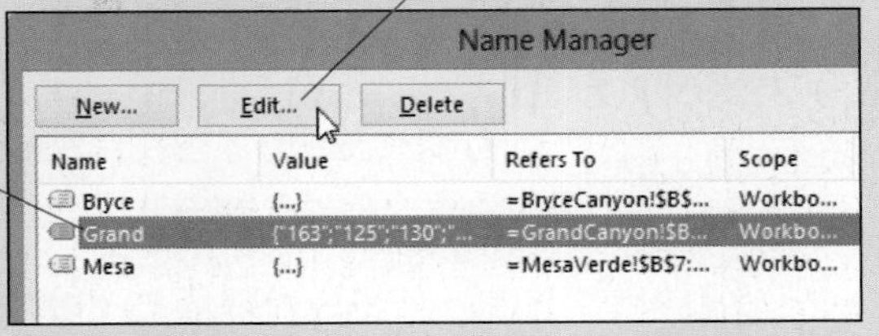

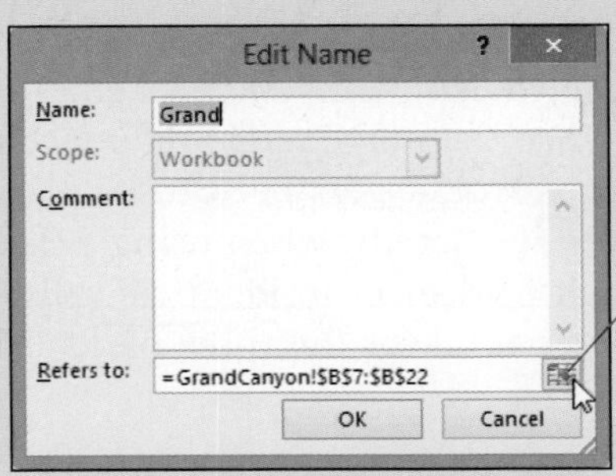

Step 4f

g. With GrandCanyon the active worksheet and the range B7:B22 selected, hold down the Ctrl key and then select E7:E21.

h. Click the Expand Dialog button to restore the Edit Name dialog box. Notice that a comma separates the nonadjacent ranges in the range name and that the cell addresses are absolute references.

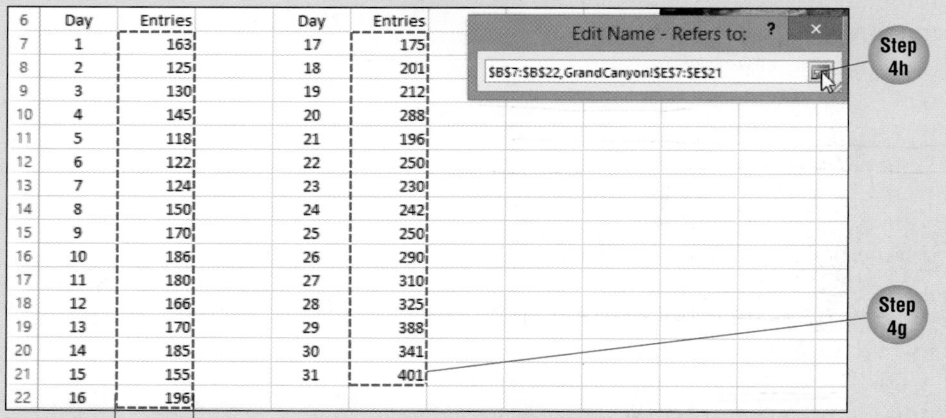

This range is automatically selected when you collapse the Edit Name dialog box.

i. Click OK to close the Edit Name dialog box.

j. Click Close to close the Name Manager dialog box.

k. Click the down-pointing arrow next to the Name box and then click *Grand* at the drop-down list to make sure the revised range name is referencing B7:B22 and E7:E21 in the GrandCanyon worksheet.

5. Create a formula to add the total attendance for May at all three parks by completing the following steps:

a. Click the AttendanceSummary tab to activate the worksheet.

b. If necessary, make cell F7 active, type =sum(bryce,grand,mesa), and then press Enter. Notice that in a Sum formula, multiple range names are separated with commas. Excel returns the result *10460* in cell F7 of the AttendanceSummary worksheet.

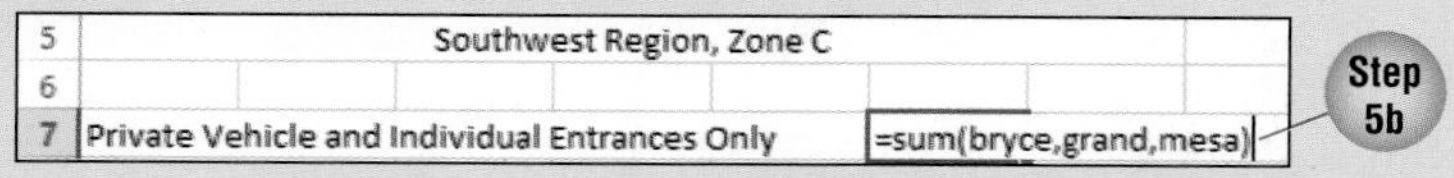

c. Apply comma formatting with no places after the decimal point to cell F7.

6. Save and then close **EL2-C4-P1-MayEntries.xlsx**.

A disadvantage to using range names emerges when several worksheets need to be summarized, since the range name reference must be created in each individual worksheet. If several worksheets need to be summed, a more efficient method is to use a 3-D reference. Generally, when using a 3-D reference, it is a good idea to set up the data in each worksheet in identical cells. In Project 1b, you will calculate the same attendance total for the three parks using a 3-D reference instead of range names.

Project 1b Summarizing Data in Multiple Worksheets Using a 3-D Reference Formula

Part 2 of 5

1. Open **MayEntries.xlsx**.
2. Save the workbook and name it **EL2-C4-P1-3D-MayEntries**.
3. Calculate the attendance total for the three parks using a point-and-click approach to creating a 3-D reference by completing the following steps:
   a. In the AttendanceSummary worksheet, make cell F7 active and then type =sum(.
   b. Click the BryceCanyon sheet tab.
   c. Hold down the Shift key and then click the MesaVerde sheet tab. (Using the Shift key while clicking a sheet tab selects all worksheets from the first sheet tab to the last sheet tab clicked.) Notice in the Formula bar that the formula reads *=sum('BryceCanyon:MesaVerde'!*
   d. With BryceCanyon the active worksheet, select B7:B22, hold down the Ctrl key, and then select E7:E21.
   e. Type) and then press Enter. Excel returns the value *10460* in cell F7 in the AttendanceSummary worksheet.
   f. Apply comma formatting with no places after the decimal point to cell F7.
4. With cell F7 the active cell, compare your formula with the one shown in Figure 4.1.
5. Save and then close **EL2-C4-P1-3D-MayEntries.xlsx**.

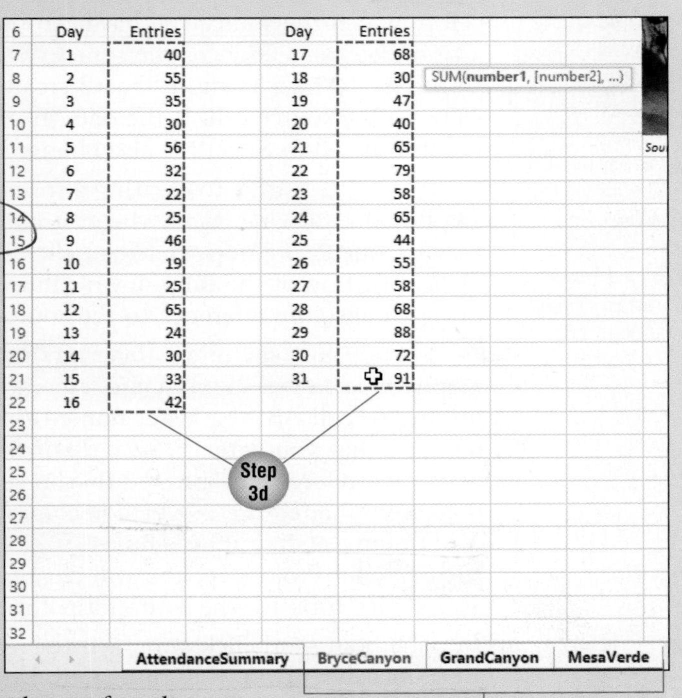

The three worksheets are grouped into the 3-D reference in Steps 3b and 3c.

Figure 4.1 3-D Formula Created in Project 1b

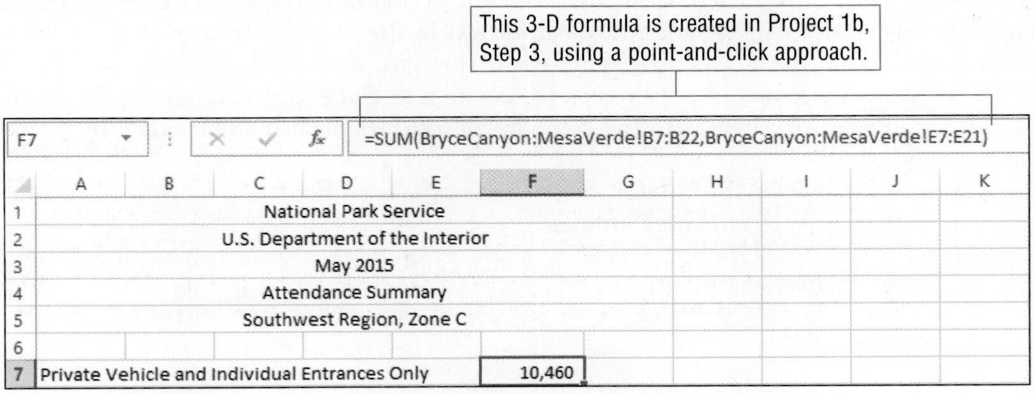

Summarizing Data by Linking to Ranges in Other Worksheets or Workbooks

Quick Steps

Create a Link to an External Reference

1. Open source workbook.
2. Open destination workbook.
3. Arrange windows as desired.
4. Make formula cell active in destination workbook.
5. Type =.
6. Click to activate source workbook.
7. Click source cell.
8. Press Enter.

Using a method similar to that used in Project 1a or Project 1b, you can summarize data in one workbook by linking to a cell, range, or range name in another worksheet or workbook. When data is linked, a change made in the source cell (the cell in which the original data is stored) is updated in any other cell to which the source cell has been linked. A link is established by creating a formula that references the source data. For example, entering the formula *=Sheet1!B10* into a cell in Sheet2 creates a link. The cell in Sheet2 displays the value in the source cell. If the data in cell B10 in Sheet1 is changed, the value in the linked cell in Sheet2 is also changed.

As an alternative to creating a formula yourself, copy the source cell to the Clipboard task pane. Make the destination cell active, click the Paste button arrow in the Clipboard group, and then click the Paste Link button in the *Other Paste Options* section of the drop-down gallery. Excel creates the link formula for you using an absolute reference to the source cell.

Linking to a cell in another workbook incorporates external references and requires that a workbook name reference be added to a formula. For example, linking to cell A3 in a sheet named *ProductA* in a workbook named *Sales* requires that you enter *=[Sales.xlsx]ProductA!A3* in the cell. Notice that the workbook reference is entered first in square brackets. The workbook in which the external reference is added becomes the ***destination workbook***. The workbook containing the data that is linked to the destination workbook is called the ***source workbook***. In Project 1c, you will create a link to an external cell containing the attendance total for the tour group entrances for the three parks.

The point-and-click approach to creating a linked external reference creates an absolute reference to the source cell. Delete the dollar symbols in the cell reference if you plan to copy the formula and need the source cell to be relative. Note that workbook and worksheet references remain absolute regardless.

Project 1c **Summarizing Data by Linking to Another Workbook** **Part 3 of 5**

1. Open **EL2-C4-P1-MayEntries.xlsx**.
2. Open **MayGroupSales.xlsx**. This workbook contains tour group attendance data for the three national parks. Tour groups are charged a flat rate entrance fee, so their attendance values represent bus capacity rather than not the actual number of patrons on each bus.
3. Click the VIEW tab, click the Arrange All button in the Window group, click *Vertical* in the *Arrange* section of the Arrange Windows dialog box, and then click OK.
4. In the worksheet you created in Project 1a, create a linked external reference to the total attendance in the worksheet with the commercial tour vehicle attendance data by completing the following steps:
   a. Click in **EL2-C4-P1-MayEntries.xlsx** to make the workbook active. Make sure the active worksheet is AttendanceSummary.
   b. Make cell A9 active, type Commercial Tour Vehicles Only, and then press Enter.
   c. Make cell F9 active and then type =.

d. Click the **MayGroupSales.xlsx** title bar to activate the workbook and then click cell F7. Notice that the formula being entered into the formula cell contains a workbook reference and a worksheet reference in front of the cell reference.
e. Press Enter.
f. Apply comma formatting with no places after the decimal point to cell F9.
g. With cell F9 active, compare your worksheet with the one shown below at the right.

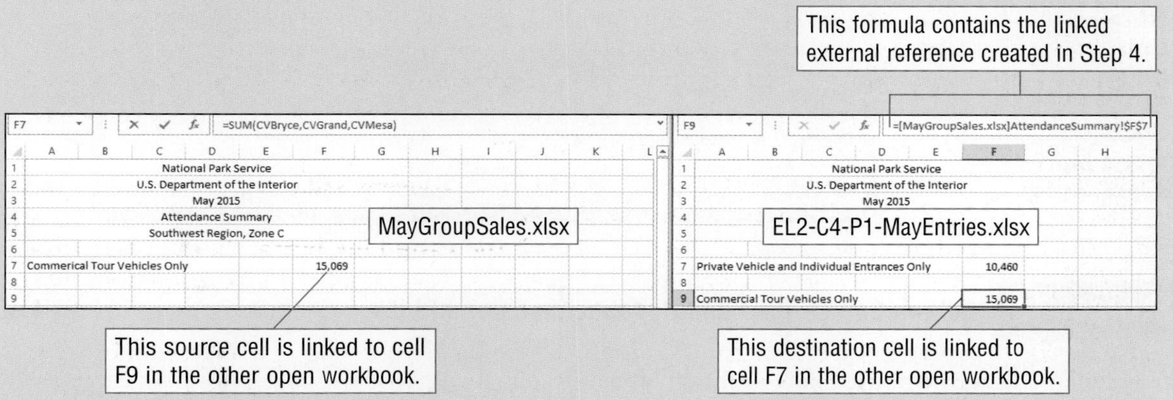

5. Click the Maximize button in the **EL2-C4-P1-MayEntries.xlsx** title bar.
6. Make cell A11 active, type **Total Attendance**, and then press Enter.
7. Make cell F11 active and then create a formula to add the values in cells F7 and F9.
8. Print the AttendanceSummary worksheet in **EL2-C4-P1-MayEntries.xlsx**. ***Note: If you submit your work in hard copy, check with your instructor to see if you need to print two copies of the worksheet, with one copy displaying cell formulas.***
9. Save and then close **EL2-C4-P1-MayEntries.xlsx**.
10. Close **MayGroupSales.xlsx**. Click Don't Save when prompted to save changes.

Maintaining External References

When you link to an external reference, Excel includes the drive and folder names in the path to the source workbook. If you move the source workbook or change the workbook name, the link will no longer work. By default, when you open a workbook with a linked external reference, automatic updates is disabled and Excel displays a security warning message in the Message bar area located above the workbook. From the message bar, you can enable the content so that links can be updated.

Links can be edited or broken at the Edit Links dialog box, shown in Figure 4.2. If more than one link is present in the workbook, begin by clicking the link to be changed in the Source list. Click the Change Source button to open the Change Source dialog box, in which you can navigate to the drive and/or folder in which the source workbook was moved or renamed. Click the Break Link button to permanently remove the linked reference and convert the linked cells to their existing values. The Undo feature does not operate to restore a link. If you break a link that you later decide you want to restore, you will have to recreate the linked formula.

Quick Steps

Edit a Link to an External Reference
1. Open destination workbook.
2. Click DATA tab.
3. Click Edit Links button.
4. Click link.
5. Click Change Source button.
6. Navigate to drive and/or folder.
7. Double-click source workbook file name.
8. Click Close button.
9. Save and close destination workbook.

Edit Links

Quick Steps

Break a Link to an External Reference

1. Open destination workbook.
2. Click DATA tab.
3. Click Edit Links button.
4. Click link.
5. Click Break Link button.
6. Click Break Links button.
7. Click Close button.
8. Save and close destination workbook.

Figure 4.2 Edit Links Dialog Box

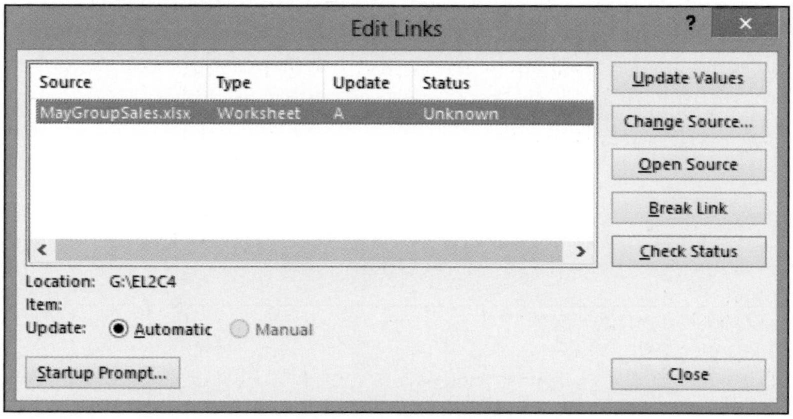

Project 1d Editing Source Data and Updating an External Link

Part 4 of 5

1. Open **MayGroupSales.xlsx** and maximize the screen.
2. Save the workbook and name it **EL2-C4-P1-Source**.
3. Edit the attendance data value at each park by completing the following steps:
   a. Click the BryceCanyon sheet tab.
   b. Make cell B8 active and then change the value from *55* to *361*.
   c. Click the GrandCanyon sheet tab.
   d. Make cell B20 active and then change the value from *275* to *240*.
   e. Click the MesaVerde sheet tab.
   f. Make cell E21 active and then change the value from *312* to *406*.
4. Click the AttendanceSummary tab. Note that the updated value in cell F7 is *15,434*.
5. Save and then close **EL2-C4-P1-Source.xlsx**.
6. Open **EL2-C4-P1-MayEntries.xlsx**. Notice the security warning that appears in the Message bar above the worksheet area with the message that automatic update of links has been disabled. Instruct Excel to allow automatic updates for this workbook, since you are sure the content is from a trusted source, by clicking the Enable Content button next to the message. ***Note: If a Security Warning dialog box appears asking if you want to make the file a trusted document, click No.***

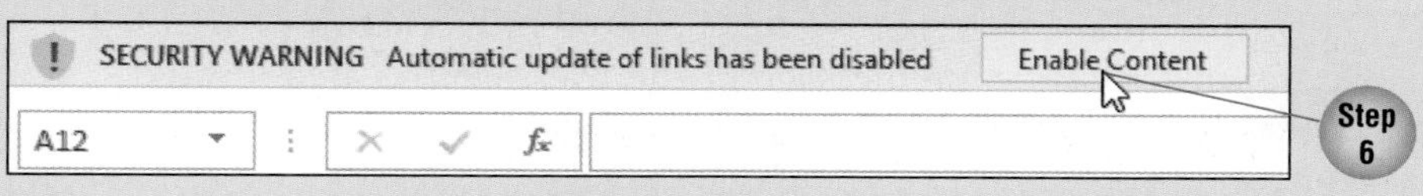

7. Edit the link to retrieve the data from the workbook you revised in Steps 2–5 by completing the following steps:
   a. Click the DATA tab.
   b. Click the Edit Links button in the Connections group.

c. At the Edit Links dialog box, click the Change Source button.
d. At the Change Source: MayGroupSales.xlsx dialog box, double-click ***EL2-C4-P1-Source.xlsx*** in the file list box. Excel returns to the Edit Links dialog box and updates the source workbook file name and path.
e. Click the Close button.

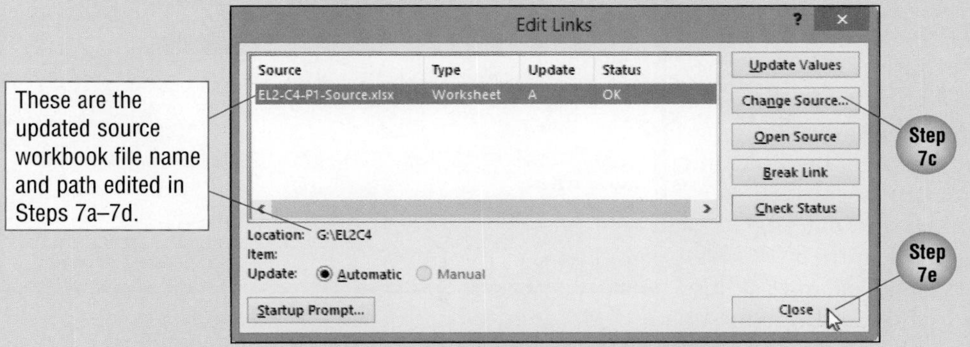

8. Click cell F9 in the AttendanceSummary worksheet to view the updated linked formula. Notice that the workbook reference in the formula is *[EL2-C4-P1-Source.xlsx]* and the drive and path are included in the formula. (Your drive and/or path may vary from the one shown.)

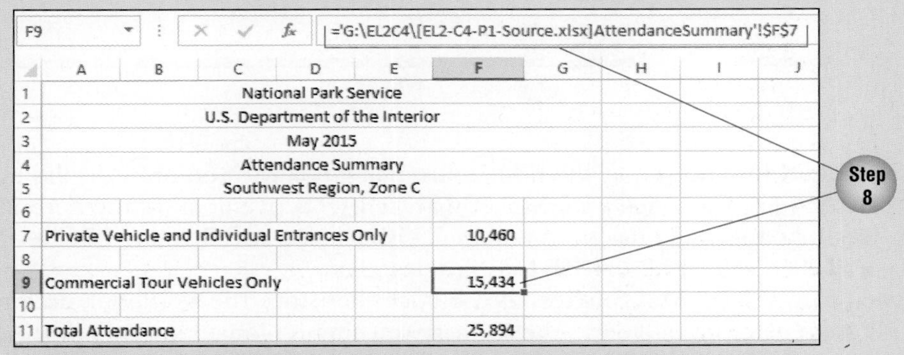

9. Print the AttendanceSummary worksheet.
10. Save and then close **EL2-C4-P1-MayEntries.xlsx**.

Project 1e Removing a Linked External Reference Part 5 of 5

1. Open **EL2-C4-P1-MayEntries.xlsx**.
2. At the Microsoft Excel message box that appears stating that the workbook contains links to other sources, read the message text and then click the Update button to update the links. ***Note: Depending on the system settings on the computer you are using, this message may not appear. Proceed to Step 3.***

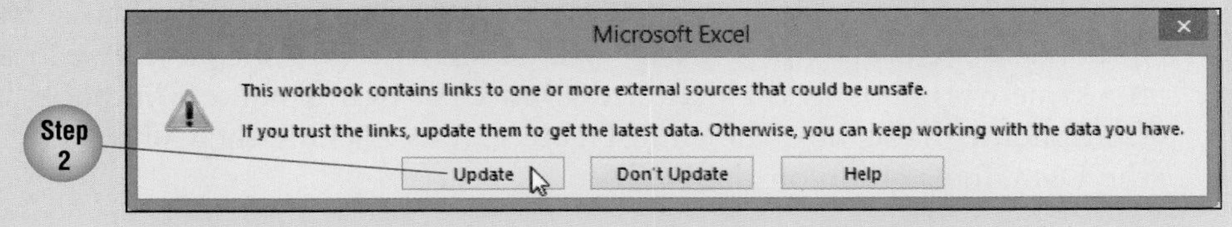

3. Remove the linked external reference to attendance values for commercial tour vehicles by completing the following steps:
   a. With the DATA tab active, click the Edit Links button in the Connections group.
   b. Click the Break Link button at the Edit Links dialog box.
   c. Click the Break Links button at the Microsoft Excel message box warning you that breaking links permanently converts formulas and external references to their existing values and asking you if you are sure you want to break the links.

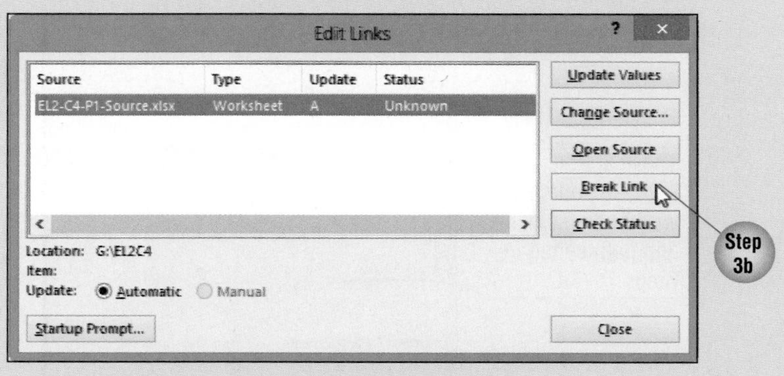

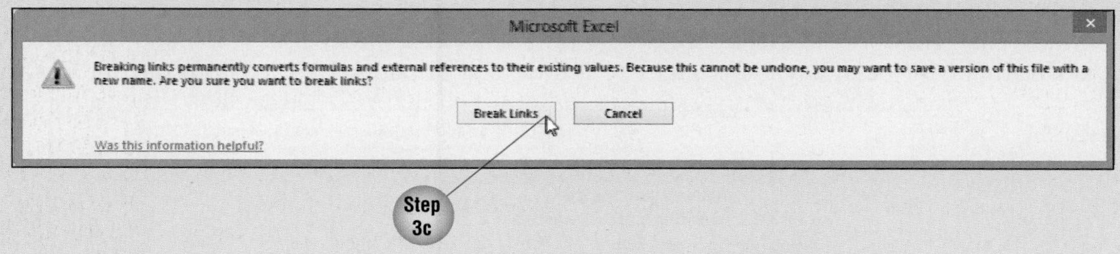

   d. Click the Close button at the Edit Links dialog box with no links displayed.
4. In the AttendanceSummary worksheet with cell F9 active, look in the Formula bar. Notice that the linked formula has been replaced with the latest cell value, *15434*.
5. Save and then close **EL2-C4-P1-MayEntries.xlsx**.
6. Reopen **EL2-C4-P1-MayEntries.xlsx**. Notice that since the workbook no longer contains a link to an external reference, the security warning no longer appears in the Message bar.
7. Close **EL2-C4-P1-MayEntries.xlsx**. Click Don't Save if prompted to save changes.

Project 2 Calculate Total Fees Billed by Three Dentists — 1 Part

You will use the Consolidate feature to summarize the total dental fees billed by treatment category for three dentists.

Summarizing Data Using the Consolidate Feature

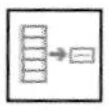

Consolidate

The Consolidate feature is another tool that can be used to summarize data from multiple worksheets into a master worksheet. The worksheets can be located in the same workbook as the master worksheet or in a separate workbook. Open the Consolidate dialog box, shown in Figure 4.3, by clicking the Consolidate button in the Data Tools group on the DATA tab.

Figure 4.3 Consolidate Dialog Box

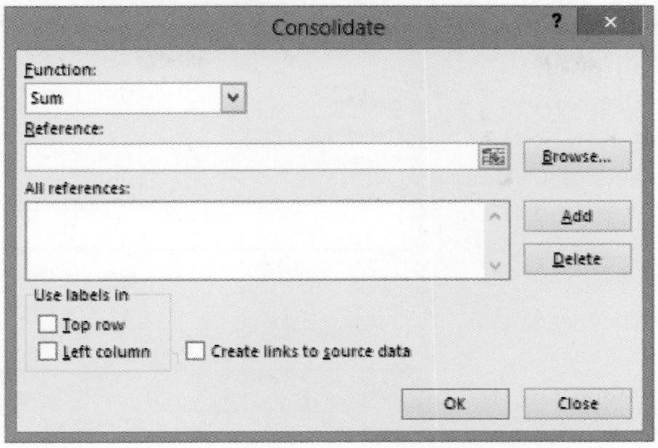

When the Consolidate dialog box opens, the Sum function is selected by default. Change to a different function, such as Count or Average, using the *Function* drop-down list. In the *Reference* text box, type the range name or use the Collapse Dialog button to navigate to the cells to be consolidated. If the cells are located in another workbook, use the Browse button to navigate to the drive and/or folder and locate the file name. Once the correct reference is inserted in the *Reference* text box, click the Add button. Continue adding references for all of the units of data to be summarized.

In the *Use labels in* section, click to insert a check mark in the *Top row* or *Left column* check boxes to indicate where the labels are located in the source ranges. Insert a check mark in the *Create links to source data* check box to instruct Excel to update the data automatically when the source ranges change. Make sure enough empty cells are available to the right of and below the active cell when you open the Consolidate dialog box, since Excel populates the rows and columns based on the size of the source data.

Quick Steps

Consolidate Data

1. Make starting cell active.
2. Click DATA tab.
3. Click Consolidate button.
4. If necessary, change function.
5. Enter first range in *Reference* text box.
6. Click Add button.
7. Enter next range in *Reference* text box.
8. Click Add button.
9. Repeat Steps 7–8 until all ranges have been added.
10. If necessary, click *Top row* and/or *Left column* check boxes.
11. If necessary, click *Create links to source data* check box.
12. Click OK.

Project 2 Summarizing Data Using the Consolidate Feature — Part 1 of 1

1. Open **NADQ1Fees.xlsx**.
2. Save the workbook and name it **EL2-C4-P2-NADQ1Fees**.
3. The workbook is organized with the first quarter's fees for each of three dentists entered in separate worksheets. Range names have been defined for each dentist's first-quarter earnings. Review the workbook structure by completing the following steps:
   a. Click the down-pointing arrow in the Name box and then click *Popovich* at the drop-down list. Excel makes the Popovich worksheet active and selects the range A2:F13.
   b. Deselect the range.
   c. Display the defined range for the range name *Vanket* and then deselect the range.
   d. Display the defined range for the range name *Jovanovic* and then deselect the range.
4. Use the Consolidate feature to total the fees billed by treatment category for each month by completing the following steps:
   a. Make FeeSummary the active worksheet.
   b. With cell A5 active, click the DATA tab.
   c. Click the Consolidate button in the Data Tools group.

d. With *Sum* selected in the *Function* option box at the Consolidate dialog box and with the insertion point positioned in the *Reference* text box, type **Popovich** and then click the Add button.
e. With the text *Popovich* selected in the *Reference* text box, type **Vanket** and then click the Add button.
f. With the text *Vanket* selected in the *Reference* text box, type **Jovanovic** and then click the Add button.
g. Click the *Top row* and *Left column* check boxes in the *Use labels in* section to insert a check mark in each check box.
h. Click OK.

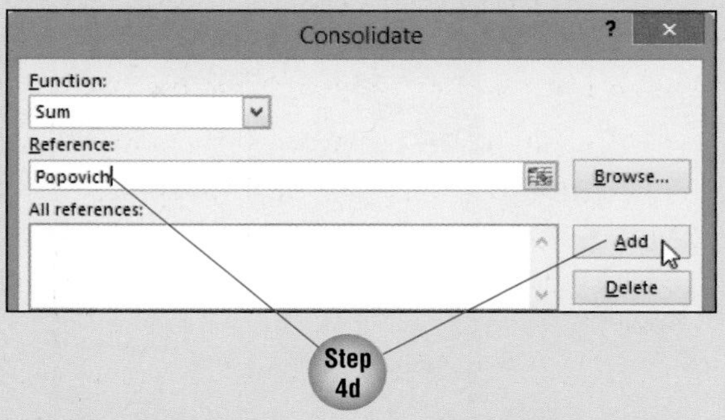

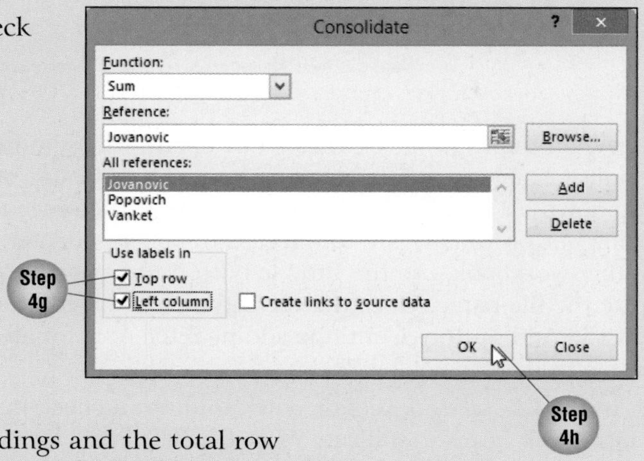

5. Deselect the consolidated range in the FeeSummary worksheet.
6. Adjust the width of each column in the FeeSummary worksheet to AutoFit.
7. Move the data in E5:E15 to F5:F15 and then AutoFit the column width.
8. Use Format Painter to apply the formatting options for the column headings and the total row from any of the three dentist worksheets to the FeeSummary worksheet.
9. Print page one of the FeeSummary worksheet.
10. Save and then close **EL2-C4-P2-NADQ1Fees.xlsx**.

Project 3 Analyze Fitness Equipment Sales Data in a PivotTable and PivotChart — 8 Parts

You will create and edit a PivotTable and PivotChart to analyze fitness equipment sales by region, product, manufacturer, and salesperson.

Quick Steps

Create a PivotTable
1. Select source range.
2. Click INSERT tab.
3. Click PivotTable button.
4. Click OK.
5. Add fields as needed using PivotTable Fields task pane.
6. Modify and/or format as desired.

PivotTable

Creating PivotTables

A ***PivotTable*** is an interactive table that organizes and summarizes data based on fields (column headings) and records (rows). A numeric column that you select is then grouped by the rows and columns category and the data is summarized using a function such as Sum, Average, or Count. PivotTables are useful management tools, since they allow you to analyze data in a variety of scenarios by filtering a row or column category and instantly seeing the change in results. The interactivity of a PivotTable allows you to examine a variety of scenarios with just a few mouse clicks. Create a PivotTable using the PivotTable button in the Tables group on the INSERT tab.

Before creating a PivotTable, examine the source data and determine the following elements:

- Which rows and columns will define how to format and group the data?
- Which numeric field contains the values that should be grouped?
- Which summary function will be applied to the values? For example, do you want to sum, average, or count?
- Do you want to be able to filter the report as a whole, as well as by columns or rows?
- Do you want the PivotTable to be beside the source data or in a new sheet?
- How many reports do you want to extract from the PivotTable by filtering fields?

HINT

Make sure that the source data contains no blank rows or columns and is structured in such a way that repeated data in columns or rows can be grouped.

Excel 2013 has a new feature called ***Recommended PivotTables***. This feature analyzes the data and creates different PivotTable previews for you to choose from. The PivotTable can then be edited and formatted further if required. (You will learn how to format a PivotTable in Project 3c.)

To have Excel analyze your data and create a PivotTable using a recommended view, select the source range, click the INSERT tab, change the source data if required, and then click the Recommended PivotTables button in the Tables group. Click a PivotTable in the left panel of the Recommended PivotTables dialog box to preview it. Click OK to insert the selected PivotTable.

Recommended PivotTables

To build a PivotTable using the PivotTable button in the Tables group on the INSERT tab, select the source range or make sure the active cell is positioned within the list range, click the INSERT tab, and then click the PivotTable button in the Tables group. At the Create PivotTable dialog box, confirm the source range

Figure 4.4 PivotTable and PivotTable Fields Task Pane Used to Define Report Layout

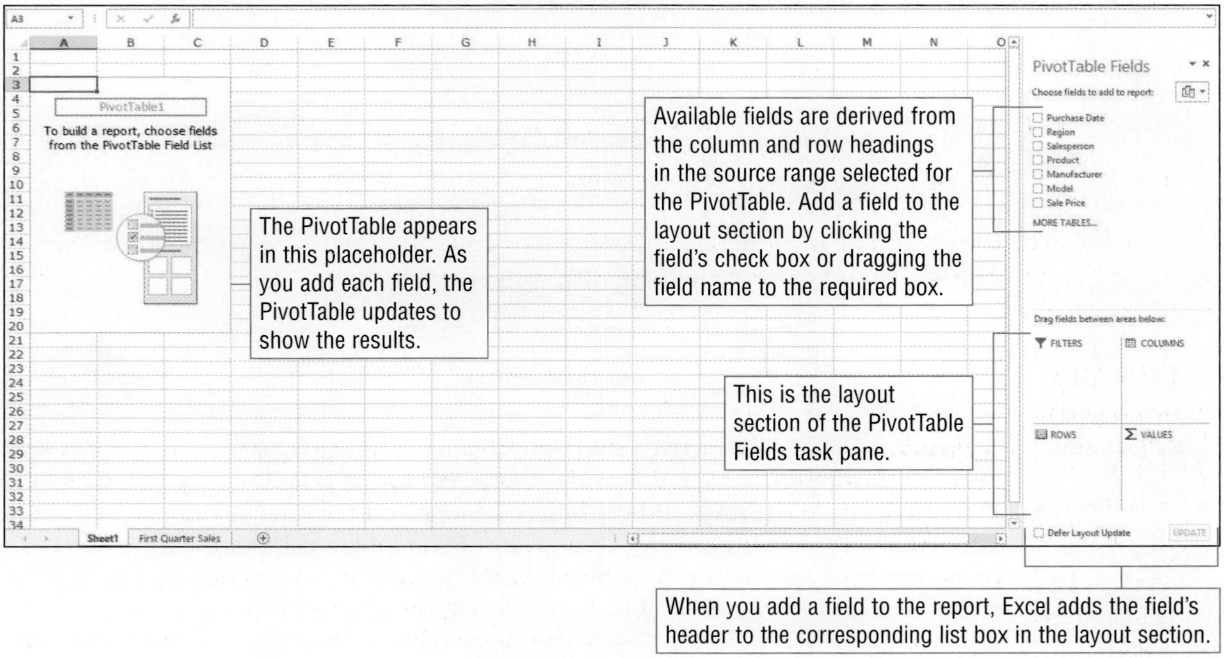

is correct and select whether to place the PivotTable in the existing worksheet or a new worksheet. Figure 4.4 presents the initial PivotTable and PivotTable Fields task pane, in which you define the report layout. Each column or row heading in the source range becomes a field in the PivotTable Fields task pane list. You can also create the initial PivotTable using the PivotTable button in the TABLES tab of the Quick Analysis button.

Build a PivotTable by selecting fields in the PivotTable Fields task pane. Click the check box next to a field to add it to the PivotTable. By default, non-numeric fields are added to the *Rows* box and numeric fields are added to the *Values* box in the layout section of the pane. Once a field has been added, you can move it to a different box by dragging the field header or clicking the field to display a shortcut menu. As you add each field, the PivotTable updates to show the results. If you do not like the results, uncheck the check box for the field to remove it from the report. Figure 4.5 displays the PivotTable you will build in Project 3b.

Project 3a Creating a PivotTable Using Recommended PivotTables — Part 1 of 8

1. Open **PF1stQSales.xlsx**.
2. Save the workbook and name it **EL2-C4-P3-PF1stQSales**.
3. Create a PivotTable to summarize the sale price by product by completing the following steps:
   a. A range has been defined to select the list data. Click the down-pointing arrow in the Name box and then click *FirstQ* at the drop-down list.
   b. Click the INSERT tab.
   c. Click the Recommended PivotTables button in the Tables group.

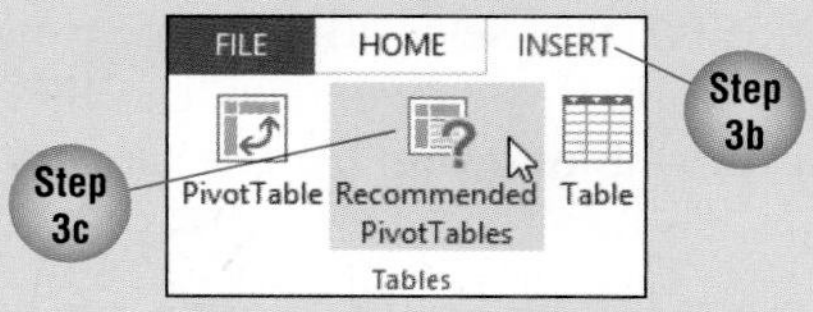

   d. Click the Change Source Data hyperlink at the bottom of the Recommended PivotTables dialog box to expand the range.

   e. At the Choose Data Source dialog box, with *FirstQuarterSales!$A$4:$G$47* entered in the *Table/Range* text box, click OK.

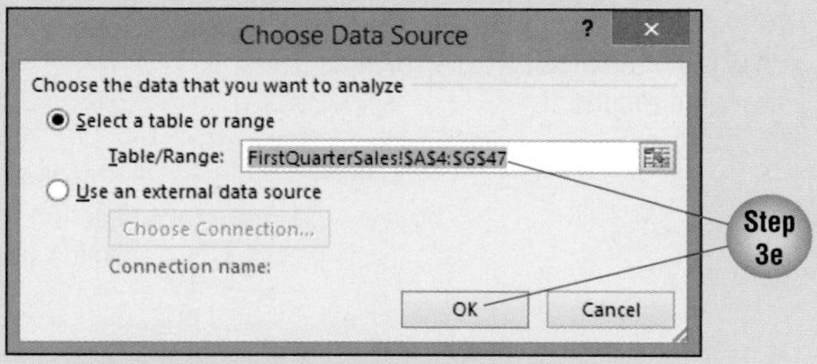

f. Click the second PivotTable scenario in the left column to select the *Sum of Sale Price by Product* PivotTable.
g. Click OK to insert the PivotTable in a new worksheet.

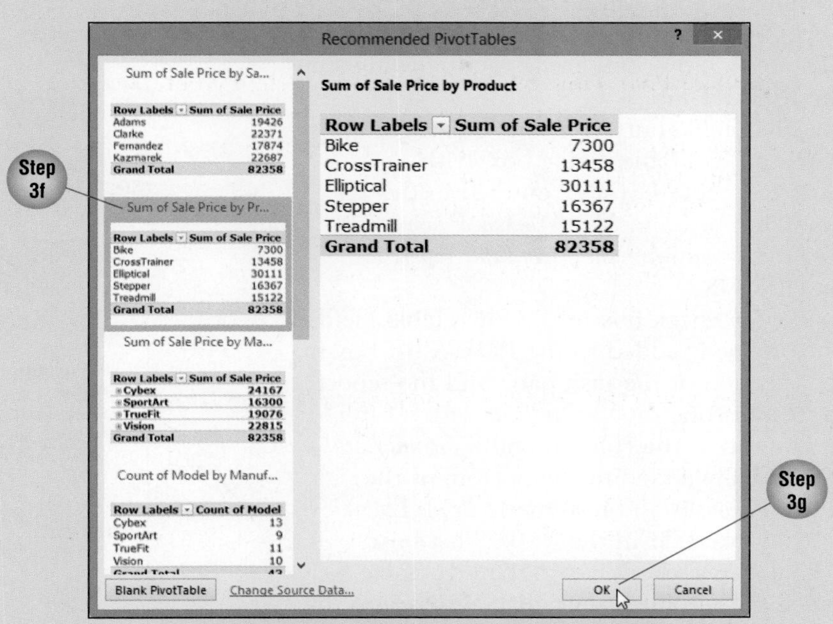

4. Apply comma formatting with no places after the decimal point to B4:B9.
5. Rename the worksheet *PriceByProduct*.
6. Save **EL2-C4-P3-PF1stQSales.xlsx**.

Figure 4.5 PivotTable for Project 3b

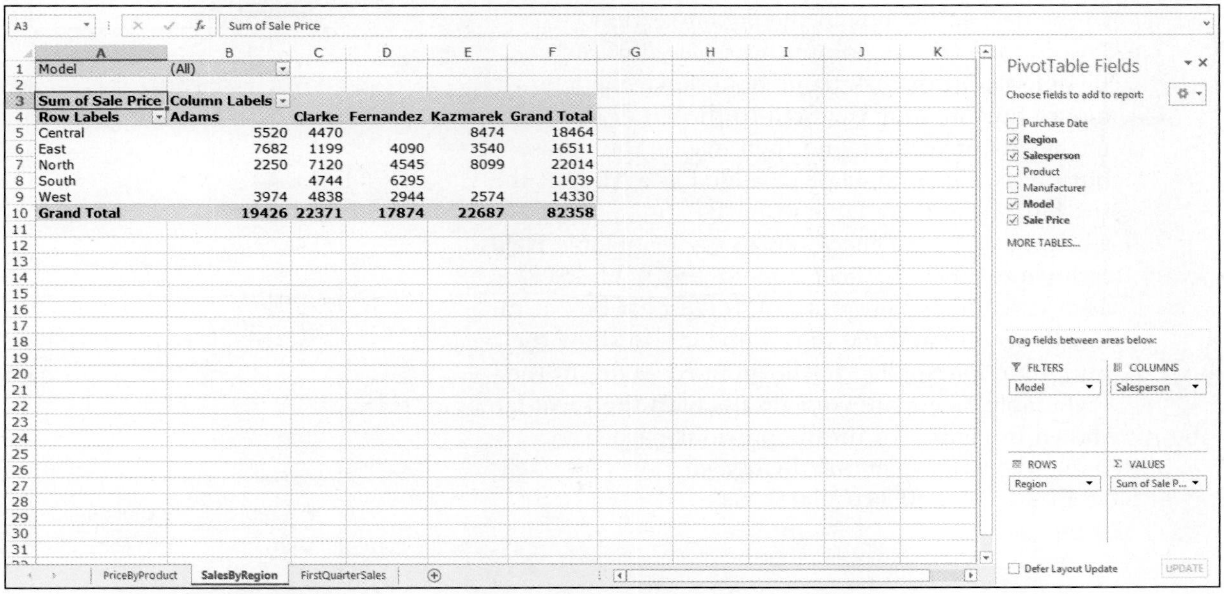

Project 3b Building a PivotTable

1. With **EL2-C4-P3-PF1stQSales.xlsx** open, make the FirstQuarterSales worksheet active. The FirstQ range should still be selected.
2. Create a PivotTable to summarize the fitness equipment sales by region and salesperson, as shown in Figure 4.5, by completing the following steps:
   a. Click the INSERT tab.
   b. Click the PivotTable button in the Tables group.
   c. At the Create PivotTable dialog box, with *FirstQuarterSales!$A$4:$G$47* entered in the *Table/Range* text box and *New Worksheet* selected for *Choose where you want the PivotTable report to be placed*, click OK.
   d. Click the *Region* check box in the PivotTable Fields task pane. *Region* is added to the *ROWS* list box in the layout section of the task pane and the report updates to show one row per region with a filter arrow at the top of the column and a *Grand Total* row automatically added to the bottom of the table. Since *Region* is a non-numeric field, Excel automatically places it in the *ROWS* list box.
   e. Click the *Salesperson* check box in the PivotTable Fields task pane. Excel automatically adds *Salesperson* to the *ROWS* list box in the layout section. (In the next step, you will correct the placement of the field to move it to the *COLUMNS* list box.)
   f. Click the *Salesperson* field header in the *ROWS* list box in the layout section and then click *Move to Column Labels* at the pop-up list. Notice that the layout of the report now displays one row per region and one column per salesperson. (In the next step, you will drag a field from the PivotTable Fields list to the desired list box in the layout section.)
   g. Position the mouse pointer over *Model* in the PivotTable Fields task pane, hold down the left mouse button, drag the field to the *FILTERS* list box in the layout section, and then release the mouse button. Notice that *Model* is added as a filter at the top left of the PivotTable in A1:B1.
   h. Click the *Sale Price* check box in the PivotTable Fields task pane. Since the field is a numeric field, Excel adds it automatically to the *VALUES* list box in the layout section and the report updates to show the Sum function applied to the grouped values in the PivotTable. Compare your results with the PivotTable shown in Figure 4.5 on the previous page.
3. Rename the worksheet *SalesByRegion*.
4. Save **EL2-C4-P3-PF1stQSales.xlsx**.

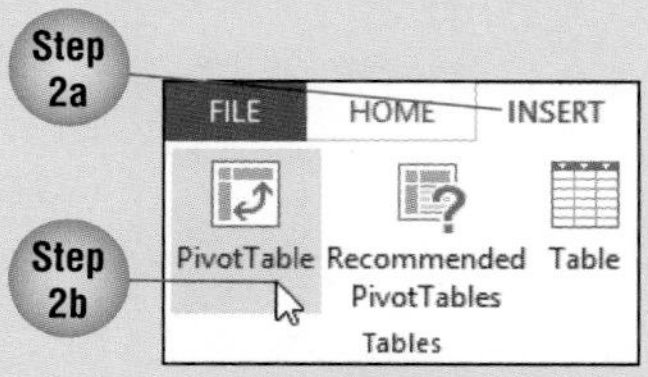

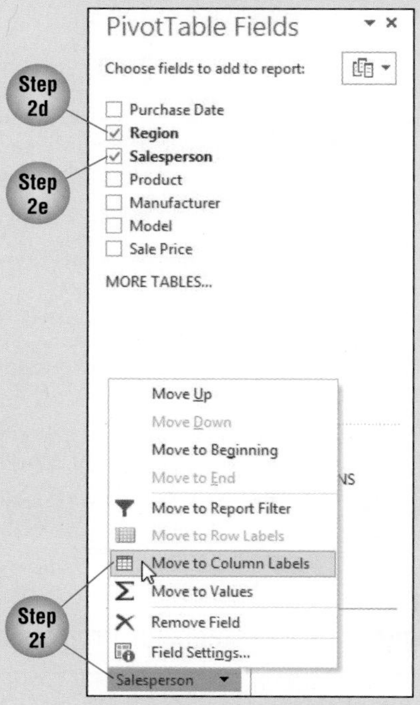

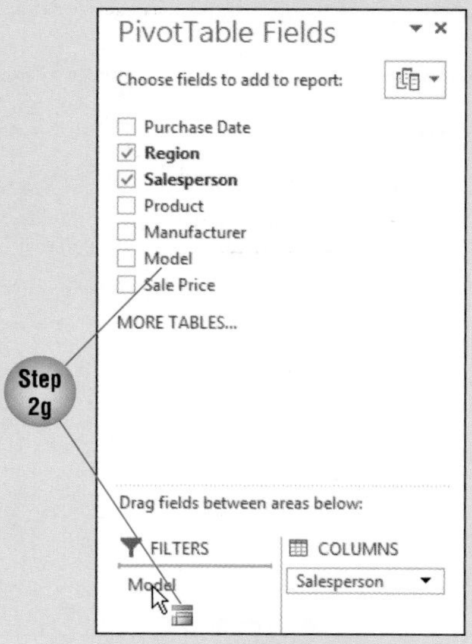

When the active cell is positioned inside a PivotTable, the contextual PIVOTTABLE TOOLS ANALYZE and PIVOTTABLE TOOLS DESIGN tabs become available. Features on the PIVOTTABLE TOOLS DESIGN tab, shown in Figure 4.6, are similar to those on the TABLE TOOLS DESIGN tab, which you learned about in Chapter 3.

Figure 4.6 PIVOTTABLE TOOLS DESIGN Tab

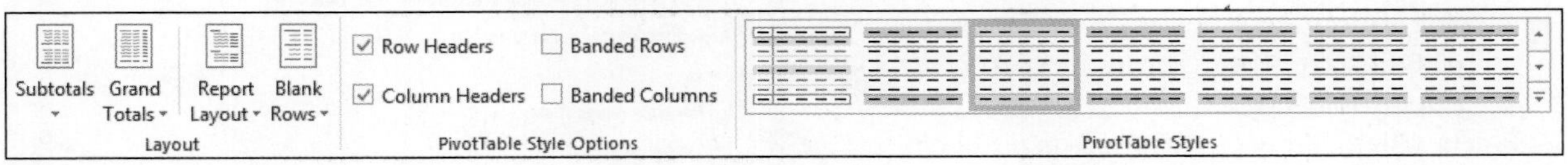

Project 3c Formatting and Filtering a PivotTable — Part 3 of 8

1. With **EL2-C4-P3-PF1stQSales.xlsx** open and the SalesByRegion worksheet active, apply formatting options to the PivotTable to improve the report's appearance by completing the following steps:
   a. With the active cell positioned in the PivotTable, click the PIVOTTABLE TOOLS DESIGN tab.
   b. Click the More button in the PivotTable Styles gallery.
   c. Click *Pivot Style Medium 2* at the drop-down gallery (first row, second column of the *Medium* section).
   d. Click the *Banded Rows* check box in the PivotTable Style Options group to insert a check mark. Excel adds border lines between rows in the PivotTable. Recall from Chapter 3 that banding rows or columns adds a fill color or border style, depending on the style that has been applied to the PivotTable.
   e. Apply comma formatting with no places after the decimal point to B5:F10.
   f. Change the column width of columns B through F to 12 characters.

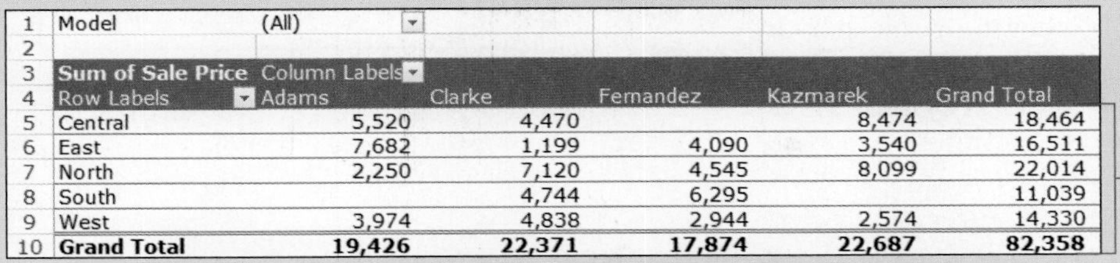

1	Model	(All)				
2						
3	Sum of Sale Price	Column Labels				
4	Row Labels	Adams	Clarke	Fernandez	Kazmarek	Grand Total
5	Central	5,520	4,470		8,474	18,464
6	East	7,682	1,199	4,090	3,540	16,511
7	North	2,250	7,120	4,545	8,099	22,014
8	South		4,744	6,295		11,039
9	West	3,974	4,838	2,944	2,574	14,330
10	Grand Total	19,426	22,371	17,874	22,687	82,358

Formatting options are applied to the PivotTable in Steps 1a-1f.

   g. To stop Excel from using AutoFit to adjust the column widths after you update cell content, right-click in the PivotTable and then click *PivotTable Options* at the shortcut menu. The PivotTable Options dialog box opens.

h. On the Layout & Format tab of the PivotTable Options dialog box, click the *Autofit column widths on update* check box to remove the check mark.
i. Click OK.

2. Filter the PivotTable to view sales for a group of model numbers by completing the following steps:
   a. Click the filter arrow next to *(All)* in cell B1.
   b. Click the *Select Multiple Items* check box to insert a check mark and turn on the display of check boxes next to all of the model numbers in the drop-down list.
   c. Click the *(All)* check box to remove the check marks next to all of the model numbers.
   d. Click the check boxes for those model numbers that begin with *CX* to insert check marks. This selects all six models from Cybex.
   e. Click OK.
   f. Print the filtered PivotTable.
   g. Click the filter arrow next to *(Multiple Items)* in cell B1, click the *(All)* check box to select all of the model numbers in the drop-down list, and then click OK.
   h. Experiment with the Column Labels and Row Labels filter arrows to filter the PivotTable by region or salesperson.
   i. Make sure all of the filters are cleared.
3. Save **EL2-C4-P3-PF1stQSales.xlsx**.

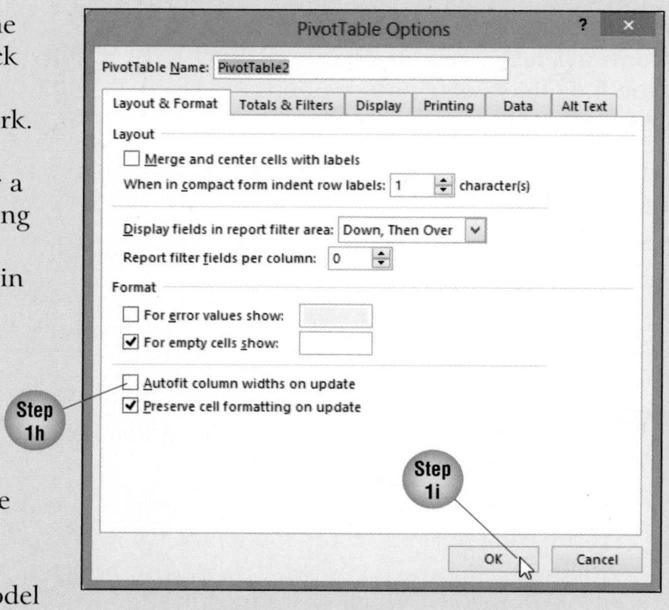

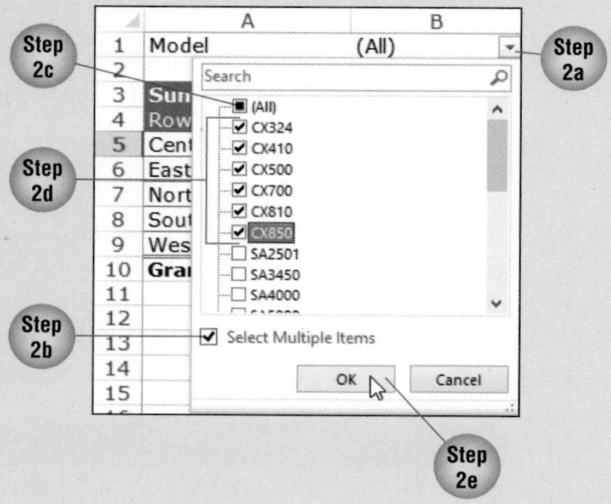

Quick Steps

Add a Slicer to a PivotTable
1. Make any cell within PivotTable active.
2. Click PIVOTTABLE TOOLS ANALYZE tab.
3. Click Insert Slicer button.
4. Click check box for desired field.
5. Click OK.

Insert Slicer

Filtering a PivotTable Using Slicers

Slicers allow you to filter a PivotTable or PivotChart without opening the FILTERS list box. When Slicers are added to a PivotTable or PivotChart, a Slicer pane containing all of the unique values for the specified field is added to the window. Click the desired option in the Slicer pane to immediately filter the PivotTable or PivotChart. You can add several Slicer panes to a PivotTable or PivotChart to filter by more than one field as needed.

To insert a Slicer pane, make any cell within the PivotTable active, click the PIVOTTABLE TOOLS ANALYZE tab, and then click the Insert Slicer button in the Filter group. Excel opens the Insert Slicers dialog box, which contains a list of the fields in the PivotTable with a check box next to each field. Click to insert a check mark in the check box for each field for which you want to add a Slicer pane and then click OK.

Project 3d Using a Slicer to Filter a PivotTable

Part 4 of 8

1. With **EL2-C4-P3-PF1stQSales.xlsx** open, make PriceByProduct the active worksheet and then display a Slicer pane for the manufacturer by completing the following steps:
   a. Make any cell active within the PivotTable.
   b. Add *Manufacturer* to the *FILTERS* list box and *Region* to the *COLUMNS* list box. (If necessary, refer to Project 3b, Steps 2e–2g for assistance.)
   c. Click the PIVOTTABLE TOOLS ANALYZE tab.
   d. Click the Insert Slicer button in the Filter group.
   e. At the Insert Slicers dialog box, click the *Manufacturer* check box to insert a check mark and then click OK. Excel inserts a Slicer pane in the worksheet with all of the manufacturer numbers.

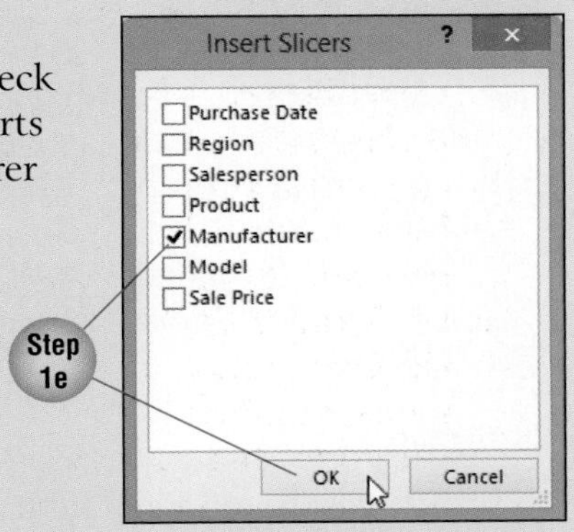

2. If necessary, position the mouse pointer at the top of the Manufacturer Slicer pane until the pointer changes to a four-headed arrow and then drag the pane to an empty location below the PivotTable.
3. Click *Vision* in the Manufacturer Slicer pane to filter the PivotTable. Excel filters the PivotTable by the Vision manufacturer. Notice that the *Manufacturer* filter arrow in cell B1 displays *Vision*.
4. Click the Clear Filter button at the top right of the Manufacturer Slicer pane to redisplay all of the data.

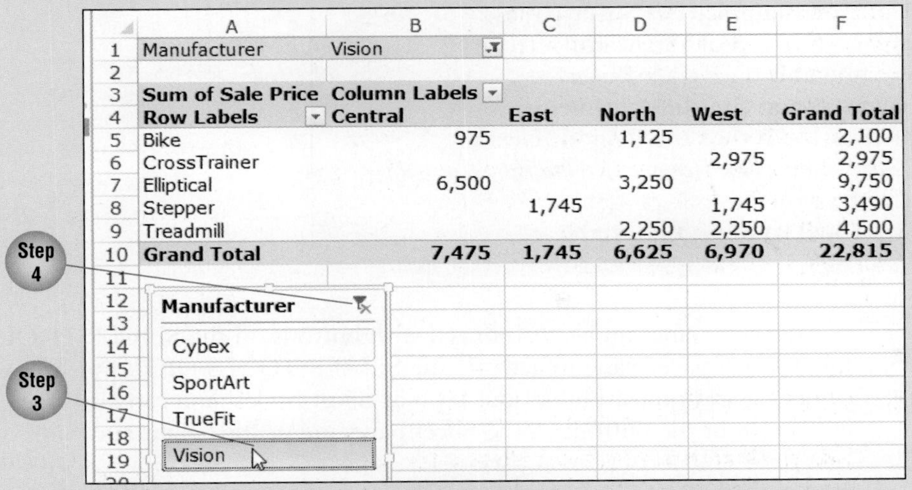

	A	B	C	D	E	F
1	Manufacturer	Vision				
2						
3	**Sum of Sale Price**	**Column Labels**				
4	**Row Labels**	**Central**	**East**	**North**	**West**	**Grand Total**
5	Bike	975		1,125		2,100
6	CrossTrainer				2,975	2,975
7	Elliptical	6,500		3,250		9,750
8	Stepper		1,745		1,745	3,490
9	Treadmill			2,250	2,250	4,500
10	**Grand Total**	**7,475**	**1,745**	**6,625**	**6,970**	**22,815**

5. Add a second Slicer pane and filter by two fields by completing the following steps:
   a. If necessary, make any cell active within the PivotTable.
   b. Click the PIVOTTABLE TOOLS ANALYZE tab and then click the Insert Slicer button.
   c. At the Insert Slicers dialog box, click the *Region* check box to insert a check mark and then click OK.
   d. Drag the Region Slicer pane so that it is positioned below the PivotTable next to the Manufacturer Slicer pane.

e. Click *West* in the Region Slicer pane to filter the PivotTable.
f. Click *Vision* in the Manufacturer Slicer pane to filter the West region sales by the Vision manufacturer.

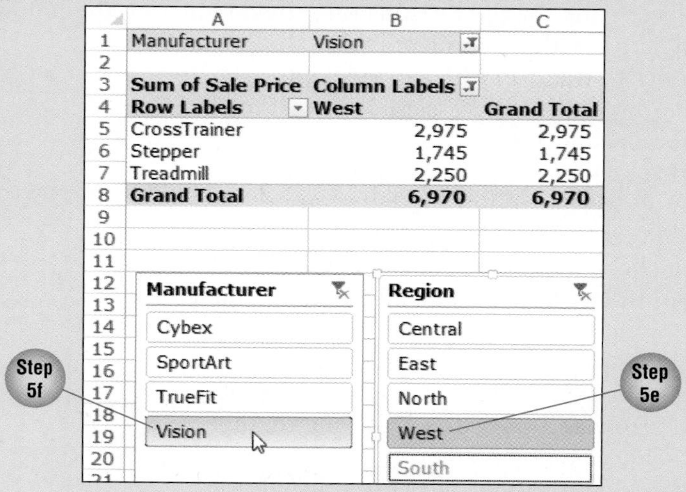

6. Print the filtered PivotTable.
7. Redisplay all of the data and remove the two Slicer panes by completing the following steps:
   a. Click the Clear Filter button at the top right of the Region Slicer pane.
   b. Click the Clear Filter button at the top right of the Manufacturer Slicer pane.
   c. Right-click the top of the Manufacturer Slicer pane and then click *Remove "Manufacturer"* at the shortcut menu.
   d. Right-click the top of the Region Slicer pane and then click *Remove "Region"* at the shortcut menu.

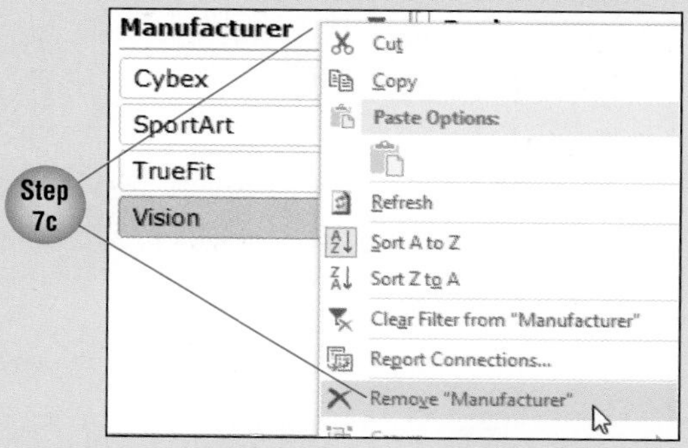

8. Save **EL2-C4-P3-PF1stQSales.xlsx**.

Quick Steps

Add a Timeline to a PivotTable

1. Make any cell within PivotTable active.
2. Click PIVOTTABLE TOOLS ANALYZE tab.
3. Click Insert Timeline button.
4. Click check box for desired field.
5. Click OK.
6. Select desired timeframe.

Insert Timeline

A Slicer pane can be customized with buttons on the SLICER TOOLS OPTIONS tab. Click a Slicer pane to activate the SLICER TOOLS OPTIONS tab. Click the tab to display customization options such as Slicer Styles. You can also change the height and width of the buttons in the Slicer pane and/or the height and width of the pane.

Filtering a PivotTable Using Timelines

Timelines is a new feature added to Excel 2013 that allows you to group and filter a PivotTable or PivotChart based on specific timeframes. A date field you select adds a Timeline pane containing a timeline slicer that you can extend or shorten to instantly filter the data by the selected date range.

To insert a timeline, make any cell within the PivotTable active, click the PIVOTTABLE TOOLS ANALYZE tab, and then click the Insert Timeline button in the Filter group. Excel opens the Insert Timelines dialog box and displays any field that contains data that has been formatted as a date, with a check box next to each field. Click to insert a check mark in the check box of any date field for which you want to add a Timeline pane and then click OK. Even though you can have more than one Timeline pane, you only filter the data using one Timeline at a time. The PivotTable will display the data for the time period you select. Use the Time Level indicator located near the upper right of the pane to change the grouping to years, quarters, months, or days.

Project 3e Using a Timeline to Filter a PivotTable — Part 5 of 8

1. With **EL2-C4-P3-PF1stQSales.xlsx** open, make the SalesByRegion worksheet active. Display one Timeline for January and then another for February and March combined by completing the following steps:
   a. Make any cell active within the PivotTable.
   b. Click the PIVOTTABLE TOOLS ANALYZE tab.
   c. Click the Insert Timeline button in the Filter group. Excel displays an Insert Timelines dialog box with all of the fields that have been formatted as dates.

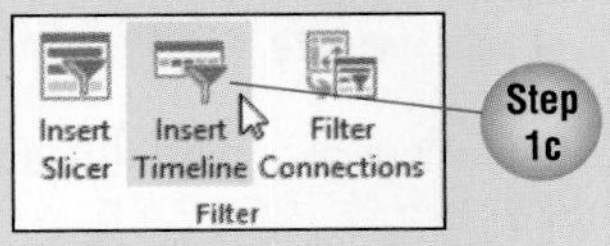

   d. Click the check box next to *Purchase Date* in the Insert Timelines dialog box to insert a check mark.
   e. Click OK. Excel inserts a Timeline pane in the worksheet. The selection label displays *All Periods* to indicate that PivotTable displays all periods.
2. If necessary, position the mouse pointer at the top of the Timeline pane until the pointer changes to a four-headed arrow and then drag the pane to an empty location below the PivotTable.
3. Using the scroll bar at the bottom of the Timeline pane, scroll to the left and then click *JAN*. Excel filters the PivotTable by January. Notice that the selection label displays *Jan 2015*.
4. Click immediately to the right of the orange box on the timeline to filter the PivotTable to include only the sales for February 2015. The selection label displays *Feb 2015*.

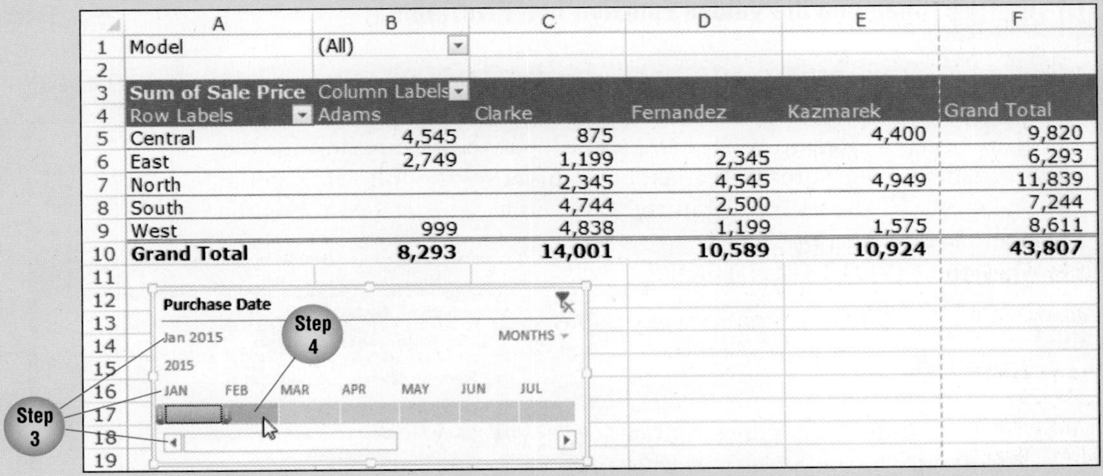

5. Click and drag the orange box to the right so that the February timeframe is extended to include March. The selection label displays *Feb - Mar 2015* to indicate that the PivotTable has been filtered to include data for February and March.

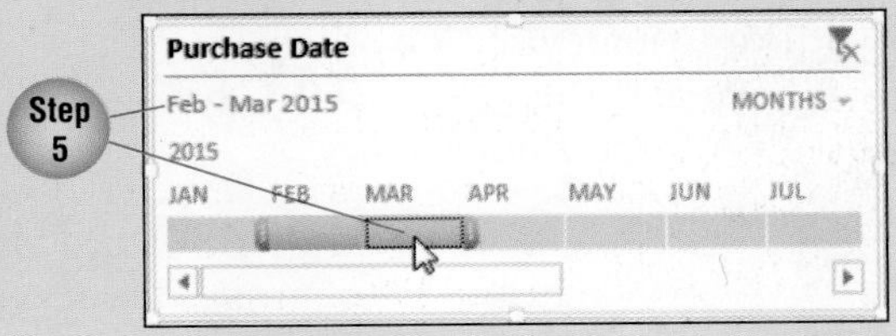

6. Change the page orientation to landscape and print the filtered PivotTable.
7. Redisplay all of the data and remove the Timeline pane by completing the following steps:
   a. Click the Clear Filter button at the top right of the Timeline pane.
   b. Right-click the top of the Timeline pane and then click *Remove Timeline* at the shortcut menu.
8. Save **EL2-C4-P3-PF1stQSales.xlsx**.

Quick Steps

Change the PivotTable Summary Function

1. Make any PivotTable cell active.
2. Click PIVOTTABLE TOOLS ANALYZE tab.
3. Click Field Settings button.
4. Click desired function.
5. Click OK.

Field Settings

You can customize the Timeline pane with buttons on the TIMELINE TOOLS OPTIONS tab. Click a Timeline pane to activate the TIMELINE TOOLS OPTIONS tab. Click the tab to display customization options such as Timeline styles. You can also change the height and width of the buttons in the Timeline pane and/or the height and width of the pane.

Changing the Summary Function

By default, Excel uses the Sum function to summarize the numeric value added to a PivotTable. To change Sum to another function, click any numeric value within the PivotTable or click the cell containing *Sum of [Fieldname]* at the top left of the PivotTable. Click the PIVOTTABLE TOOLS ANALYZE tab and then click the Field Settings button in the Active Field group. This opens the Value Field Settings dialog box, in which you can choose a function other than Sum. Alternatively, you can right-click any numeric value within the PivotTable, point to *Summarize Values By* at the shortcut menu, and then click the desired function name.

Project 3f **Changing the Values Function in a PivotTable** **Part 6 of 8**

1. With **EL2-C4-P3-PF1stQSales.xlsx** open, save the workbook and name it **EL2-C4-P3-PFAvg1stQSales.**
2. With the SalesByRegion worksheet active, change the function for the *SalePrice* field from Sum to Average by completing the following steps:
   a. Make cell A3 the active cell in the PivotTable. This cell contains the label *Sum of Sale Price*.
   b. Click the PIVOTTABLE TOOLS ANALYZE tab.
   c. Click the Field Settings button in the Active Field group.
   d. At the Value Field Settings dialog box with the Summarize Values By tab active, click *Average* in the *Summarize value field by* list box and then click OK.
3. Print the revised PivotTable.
4. Save and then close **EL2-C4-P3-PFAvg1stQSales.xlsx**.

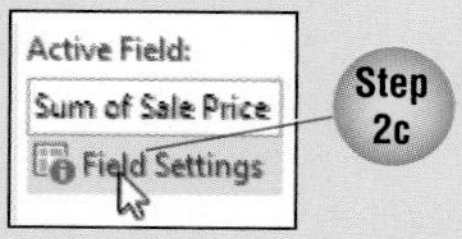

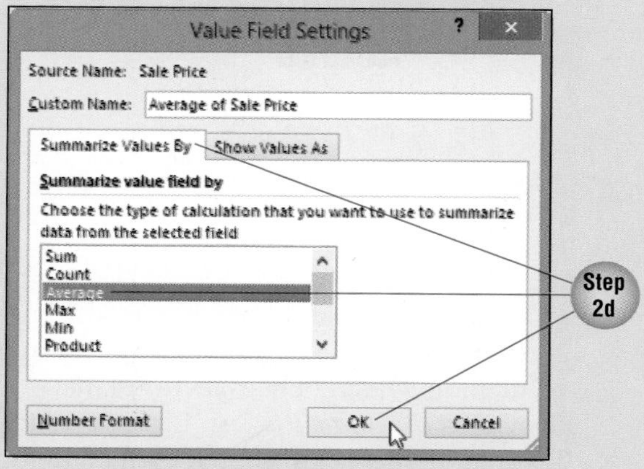

Creating PivotCharts

A ***PivotChart*** visually displays data in chart form. As with a PivotTable, you can filter the data in a PivotChart to examine various scenarios between categories. As you make changes to the PivotChart, the PivotTable associated with the PivotChart is also updated. Figure 4.7 displays the PivotChart you will create in Project 3g.

In a worksheet that already contains a PivotTable, position the active cell anywhere within the PivotTable, click the PIVOTTABLE TOOLS ANALYZE tab, and then click the PivotChart button in the Tools group to create a chart from the existing summary data. Excel displays the Insert Chart dialog box, in which you choose the type of chart to create. Once the PivotChart has been generated, the PivotTable and PivotChart become connected. Changes made to the data by filtering in one object cause the other object to update with the same filter. For example, filtering the PivotChart by an individual salesperson name causes the PivotTable to also filter by the same salesperson name.

If you open a worksheet that does not contain a pre-existing PivotTable and create a PivotChart, Excel displays a blank chart, a PivotTable placeholder, and the PivotChart Fields task pane. Build the chart using the same techniques you used to build a PivotTable. As you build a PivotChart, Excel also builds a PivotTable that is connected to the PivotChart.

Before you begin creating a PivotChart from scratch, examine the source data and determine the following:

- Which fields do you want to display along the *x* (horizontal) axis? In other words, how do you want to compare data when viewing the chart: by time period (such as months or years), by salesperson names, by department names, or by some other category?
- Which fields do you want to display in the legend? In other words, how many data series (bars in a column chart) do you want to view in the chart: one for each region, product, salesperson, department, or some other category?
- Which numeric field contains the values you want to graph in the chart?

Quick Steps

Create a PivotChart from a PivotTable
1. Make cell active within PivotTable.
2. Click PIVOTTABLE TOOLS ANALYZE tab.
3. Click PivotChart button.
4. Select desired chart type.
5. Click OK.

Create a PivotChart without an Existing PivotTable
1. Select range containing data for chart.
2. Click INSERT tab.
3. Click PivotChart button arrow.
4. Click *PivotChart*.
5. Click OK.
6. Add fields as needed in PivotTable Fields task pane to build chart.
7. Modify and/or format as required.

PivotChart

Figure 4.7 PivotChart for Project 3g

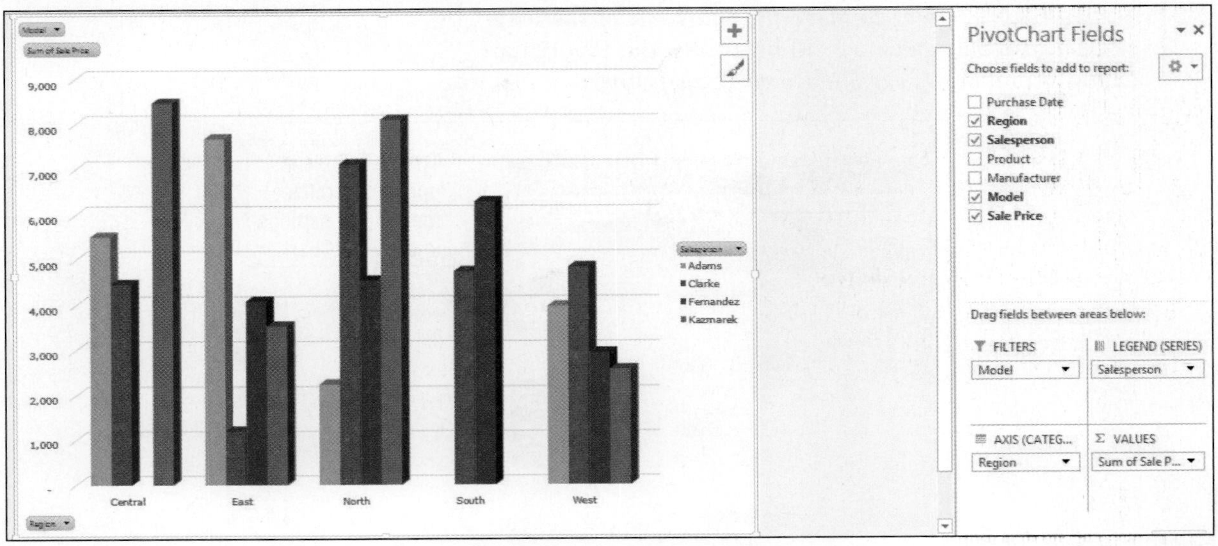

Use the Chart Elements button and the Chart Styles button located in the top right corner of the PivotChart to add or remove titles, labels, or other chart elements and apply a style or color scheme to your PivotChart. To move the chart to a new sheet, use the Move Chart button in the Actions group on the PIVOTCHART TOOLS ANALYZE tab.

Move Chart

Project 3g Creating a PivotChart

Part 7 of 8

1. Open **EL2-C4-P3-PF1stQSales.xlsx** and, if necessary, make the SalesByRegion sheet active.
2. Create a PivotChart to visually present the data in the PivotTable by completing the following steps:
   a. If necessary, click any cell within the PivotTable to activate the PivotTable contextual tabs.
   b. Click the PIVOTTABLE TOOLS ANALYZE tab.
   c. Click the PivotChart button in the Tools group.
   d. At the Insert Chart dialog box with *Column* selected in the left pane, click *3-D Clustered Column* (fourth option above preview) and then click OK.

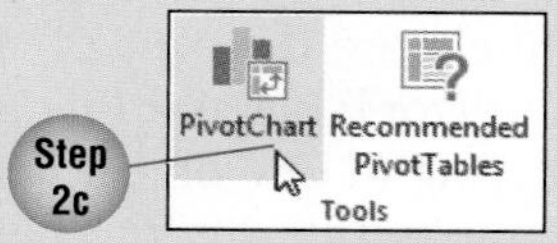

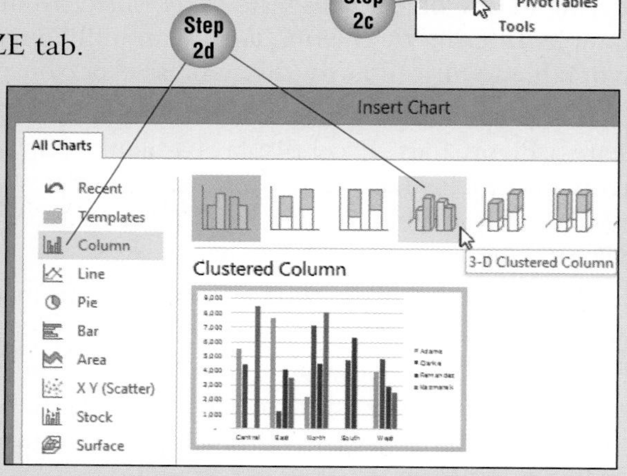

3. Filter the PivotChart to display sales for only one salesperson by completing the following steps:
   a. Click the Salesperson field button in the PivotChart. (This is the button above the salesperson names in the PivotChart legend.)
   b. Click the *(Select All)* check box to clear all of the check boxes.
   c. Click the *Kazmarek* check box to insert a check mark and then click OK.
   d. Notice the PivotTable behind the chart is also filtered to reflect the chart's display. ***Note: If the chart is obscuring your view of the PivotTable, drag the PivotChart border to move the chart out of the way.***
   e. Click the Salesperson field button in the PivotChart and then click *Clear Filter From "Salesperson"*.

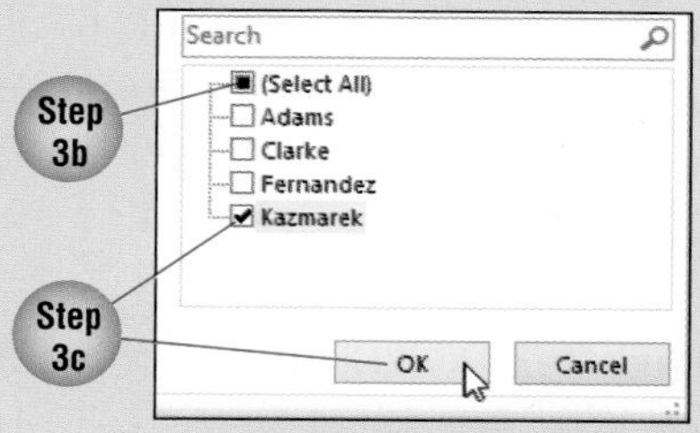

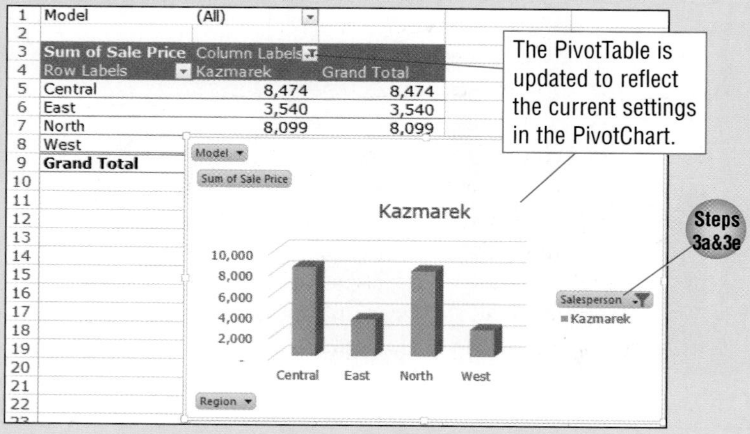

4. Move the PivotChart to a separate worksheet by completing the following steps:
   a. Click the Move Chart button in the Actions group on the PIVOTCHART TOOLS ANALYZE tab.

   b. At the Move Chart dialog box, click the *New sheet* option, type PivotChart in the *New sheet* text box, and then click OK. Excel moves the PivotChart to a separate worksheet. Compare your PivotChart with the one shown in Figure 4.7 on page 127.

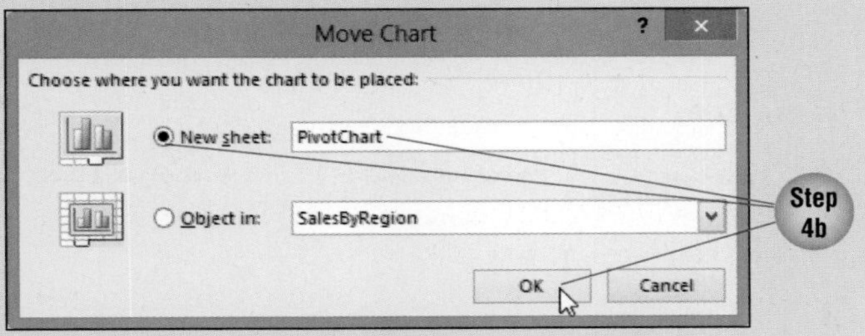

5. Print the PivotChart.
6. Save and then close **EL2-C4-P3-PF1stQSales.xlsx**.

Project 3h Creating a PivotChart from Scratch — Part 8 of 8

1. Open **PF1stQSales**.
2. Save the workbook and name it **EL2-C4-P3-PFChart**.
3. Create a PivotChart to display the sales by manufacturer by region by completing the following steps:
   a. Select the *FirstQ* named range and then click the INSERT tab.
   b. Click the PivotChart button arrow in the Charts group and then click *PivotChart* at the drop-down list.

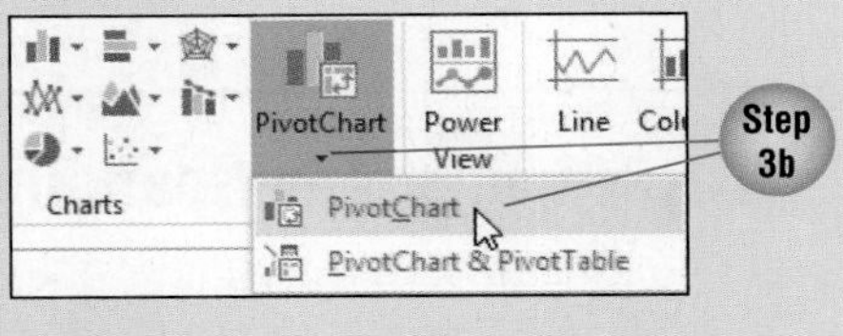

   c. At the Create PivotChart dialog box, with *FirstQuarterSales!$A$4:$G$47* entered in the *Table/Range* text box and *New Worksheet* selected in the *Choose where you want the PivotChart to be placed* section, click OK.
   d. Excel displays a blank sheet with the PivotChart Fields task pane at the right side of the window. A PivotTable placeholder and chart placeholder appear in the worksheet area. As you build the PivotChart, notice that a PivotTable is created automatically.
   e. Click the *Manufacturer* check box in the PivotChart Fields task pane. Excel adds the field to the *AXIS (CATEGORIES)* list box in the layout section.
   f. Click the *Region* check box in the PivotChart Fields task pane. Excel adds the field below *Manufacturer* in the *AXIS (CATEGORIES)* list box in the layout section.
   g. Click the *Region* field header in the *AXIS (CATEGORIES)* list box and then click *Move to Legend Fields (Series)* at the pop-up list. Excel moves the field and updates the chart and PivotTable.

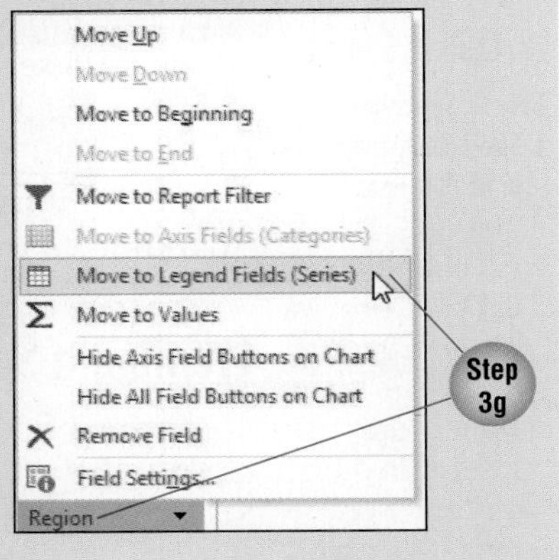

   h. Click the *Sale Price* check box in the PivotTable Fields task pane. Excel graphs the sum of the sale price values in the PivotChart and updates the PivotTable.

4. Point to the border of the PivotChart and then drag the PivotChart below the PivotTable.
5. Resize the chart to the approximate height and width of the chart shown below.
6. Experiment with the Chart Elements and Chart Styles buttons located in the upper right corner of the chart. (See Level 1, Chapter 7 for more information on these buttons.)

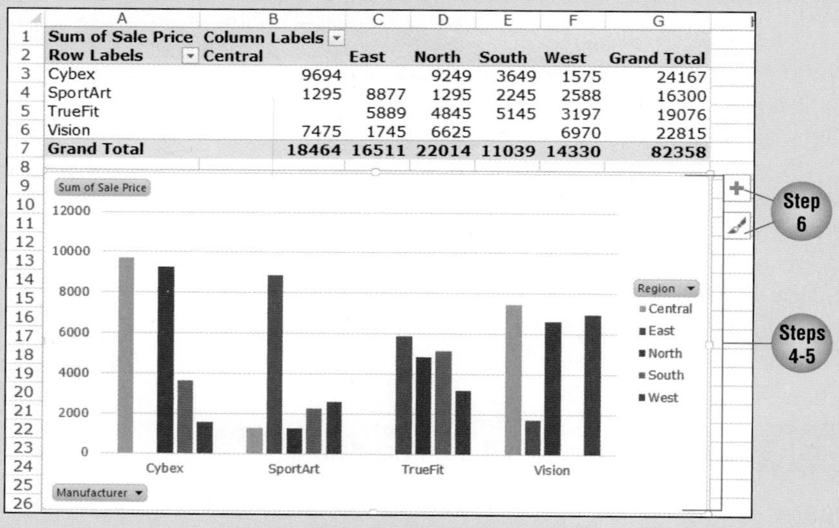

Sum of Sale Price	Column Labels					
Row Labels	Central	East	North	South	West	Grand Total
Cybex	9694		9249	3649	1575	24167
SportArt	1295	8877	1295	2245	2588	16300
TrueFit		5889	4845	5145	3197	19076
Vision	7475	1745	6625		6970	22815
Grand Total	18464	16511	22014	11039	14330	82358

7. Rename the sheet containing the PivotTable and PivotChart as *SummaryData*.
8. Print the PivotTable and PivotChart worksheet.
9. Save and then close **EL2-C4-P3-PFChart.xlsx**.

Project 4 Add Sparklines in a Worksheet to Show Trends — 2 Parts

You will add and format Sparklines to identify trends in fees for dental services over the first quarter.

Summarizing Data with Sparklines

Quick Steps

Create Sparklines
1. Select empty range in which to insert Sparklines.
2. Click INSERT tab.
3. Click Line, Column, or Win/Loss in Sparklines group.
4. Type data range address or drag to select data range in *Data Range* text box.
5. Click OK.

Sparklines are miniature charts that are embedded into the background of cells. An entire chart exists in a single cell. Since Sparklines can be placed directly next to the data set that is being represented, viewing them allows you to quickly determine if a trend or pattern exists within the data. Consider using Sparklines to show high and low values within a range, as well as trends and other patterns. Figure 4.8 illustrates the three buttons in the Sparklines group used to create Sparkline charts: Line, Column, and Win/Loss.

Creating a Sparkline

To create a Sparkline, select the empty cell range in which to insert the miniature charts, click the INSERT tab, and then click the desired Sparkline type in the Sparklines group, as shown in Figure 4.9. At the Create Sparklines dialog box, type or click the range for the cells that contain the data you wish to graph in the *Data Range* text box and then click OK.

Figure 4.8 Line, Column, and Win/Loss Sparklines Added to a Worksheet

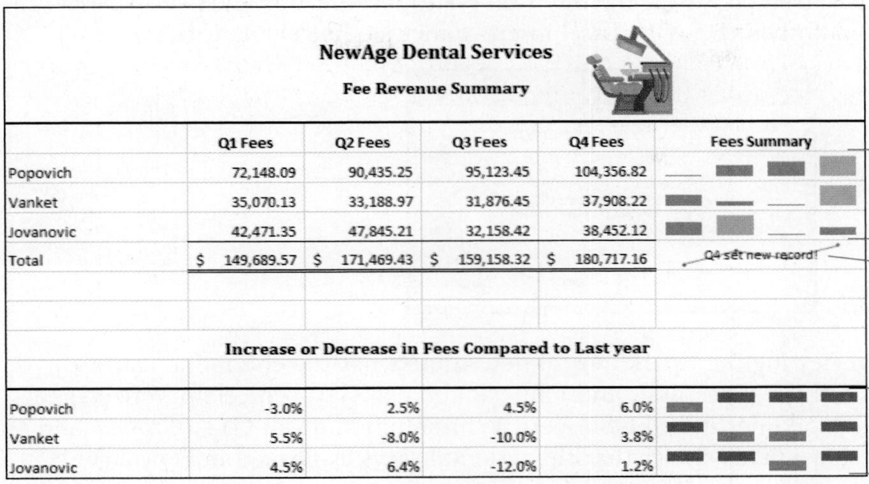

Use the Line or Column buttons to create Sparklines to show trends or patterns over a time period.

Since Sparklines are part of the cell's background, you can add text to the Sparklines cell.

Use the Win/Loss button to create Sparklines to show positive and negative values using bars. Notice that the bars are all the same height but that those quarters in which fees are lower than last year (negative percentages) show as red bars below the baseline.

Figure 4.9 Sparklines Group on the INSERT Tab

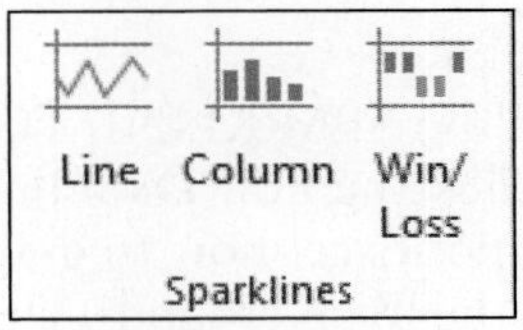

Project 4a Creating Sparklines

Part 1 of 2

1. Open **EL2-C4-P2-NADQ1Fees.xlsx**.
2. Save the workbook and name it **EL2-C4-P4-NADQ1Fees**.
3. Create a Sparkline to illustrate the trends in categories of dental service fees during the first quarter by completing the following steps:
   a. With the FeeSummary worksheet active, select G6:G14.
   b. Click the INSERT tab.
   c. Click the Line button in the Sparklines group.

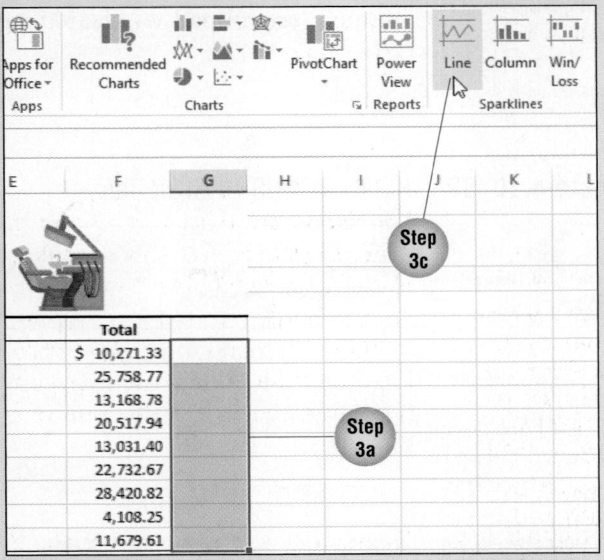

d. At the Create Sparklines dialog box with the insertion point positioned in the *Data Range* text box, type b6:d14 and then click OK. Excel inserts miniature line charts within the cells.

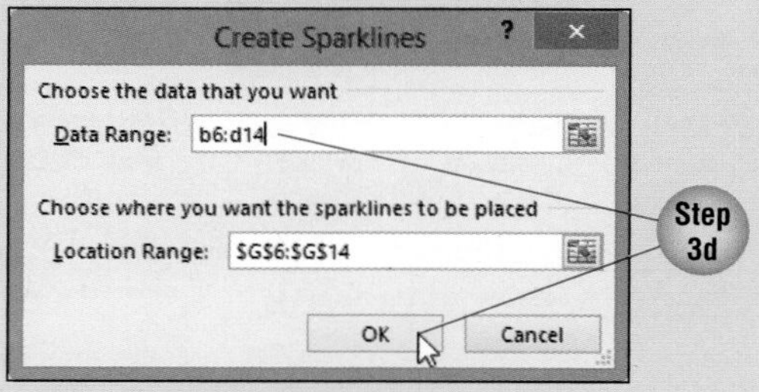

4. Spend a few moments reviewing the Sparklines to determine what the charts indicate. Notice that the lines in cell G7 (Cleanings and Fillings) and cell G10 (Porcelain Veneers) slope downward and that the lines in cell G8 (Teeth Whitening) and cell G11 (Crowns and Bridges) have a similar shape. This shows that these dental services peaked in February and are on a decline.
5. Save **EL2-C4-P4-NADQ1Fees.xlsx**.

Customizing Sparklines

Quick Steps

Customize Sparklines
1. Click in any Sparklines cell.
2. Click SPARKLINE TOOLS DESIGN tab.
3. Change chart type, show/hide points or markers, and change chart style, color, or marker color.

Activate any Sparkline cell and the SPARKLINE TOOLS DESIGN tab, shown in Figure 4.10, becomes visible. Click the Edit Data button to edit a range used to generate the Sparklines or instruct Excel how to graph hidden or empty cells in the data range. Use buttons in the Type group to change the chart type from line to column or win/loss. Click the check boxes in the Show group to show or hide data points in the chart or show markers. With options in the Style group, you can change the line and/or marker appearance. Click the Axis button in the last group to customize the horizontal or vertical axis in the charts. Sparklines can be grouped, ungrouped, or cleared with the last three buttons in the tab.

Figure 4.10 SPARKLINE TOOLS DESIGN Tab

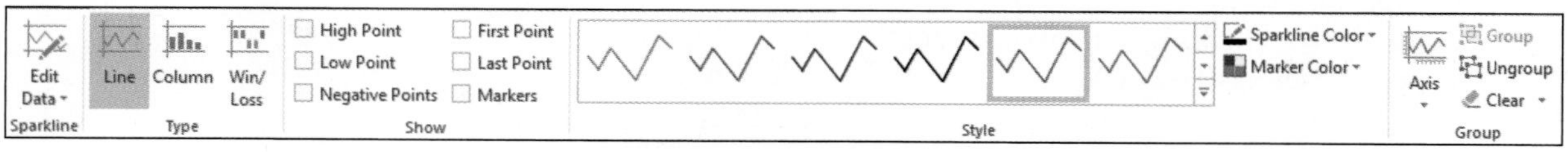

1. With **EL2-C4-P4-NADQ1Fees.xlsx** open, customize the Sparklines by completing the following steps:
   a. If necessary, click any Sparkline cell to activate the SPARKLINE TOOLS DESIGN tab.
   b. Click the SPARKLINE TOOLS DESIGN tab.
   c. Click the Sparkline Color button in the Style group and then click *Dark Red* (first option in the *Standard Colors* section) at the drop-down color palette.

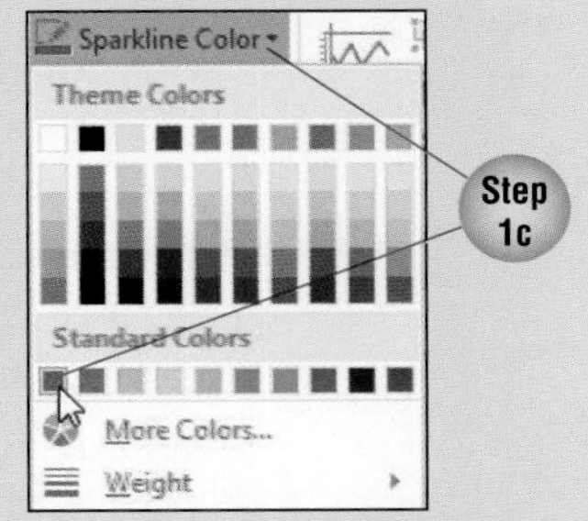

   d. Click the *High Point* check box in the Show group to insert a check mark. Excel adds a marker at the highest point on each line graph.
   e. Click the *Markers* check box in the Show group to insert a check mark. Excel adds markers to all of the other data points on each line.

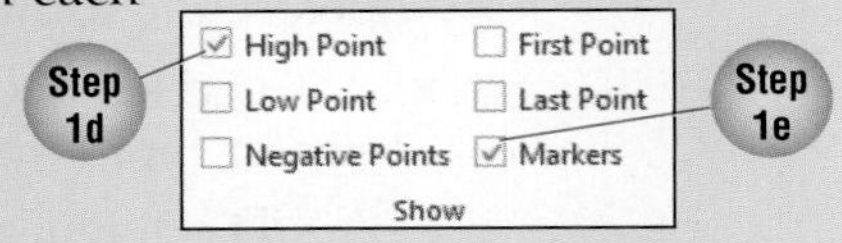

   f. Click the Marker Color button in the Style group, point to *Markers,* and then click *Black, Text 1* (first row, second column in the *Theme Colors* section) at the drop-down color palette.

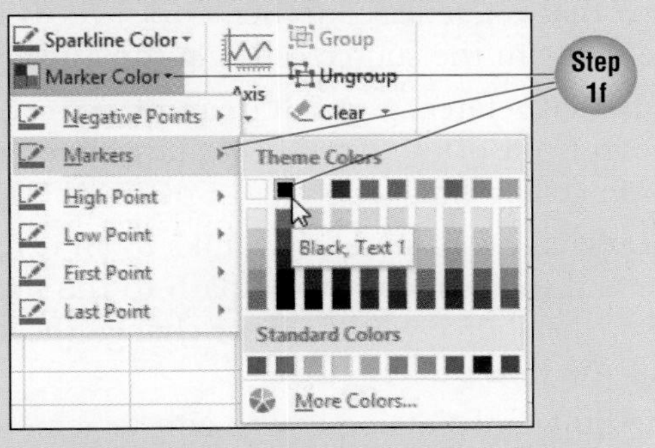

2. Improve the appearance of the Sparklines by widening the column and adding fill color by completing the following steps:
   a. Change the width of column G to 22 characters.
   b. Select G6:G14, click the HOME tab, and then apply the Blue, Accent 1, Lighter 80% fill color (second row, fifth column in the *Theme Colors* section) to the selected cells.
   c. Click in any cell to deselect the range.
3. Make cell G5 active, type January to March Trends, and then format the cell so that it has the same formatting as the other titles in row 5.
4. Change the page orientation to landscape and then print the FeeSummary worksheet.
5. Save and then close **EL2-C4-P4-NADQ1Fees.xlsx**.

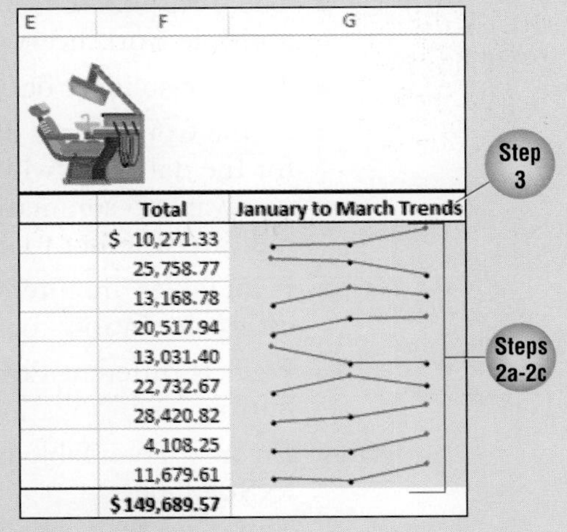

Chapter Summary

- A formula that references a cell in another worksheet within the same workbook contains a worksheet reference and cell reference separated by an exclamation point.
- Range names can be used to simplify the references to cells in another worksheet, since the worksheet reference is automatically included in the definition of the range name.
- A disadvantage to using range names to reference other worksheets emerges if several worksheets are to be summarized, since each name has to be defined before the formula can be created.
- A 3-D reference is used to summarize the same cell in a range that extends over two or more worksheets.
- A 3-D reference includes the starting worksheet name and ending worksheet name separated by a colon, similar to the method used to define a range of cells.
- A formula that references another worksheet is linked to that worksheet, so that a change made in the source cell is automatically made in the other worksheet.
- A formula that references a cell in another workbook must include a workbook reference in front of the worksheet and cell references. Workbook references are enclosed in square brackets.
- When you create a formula that links to an external reference, Excel includes the drive and folder name in the path to the source workbook. If you move the location of the source workbook or change the source workbook file name, you must edit the linked reference.
- Open the Edit Links dialog box to edit or remove a linked external reference.
- The Consolidate feature is another method you can use to summarize data in multiple worksheets or workbooks.
- The Consolidate button is located in the Data Tools group on the DATA tab.
- At the Consolidate dialog box, choose the summary function you want to use for the data that will be consolidated, add the references containing the data you want to summarize, specify the location of the labels to duplicate, and indicate whether to create a link to the source data.
- PivotTables are interactive tables that organize and summarize data based on categories in rows or columns.
- Preview different PivotTable scenarios with the Recommended PivotTables button.
- Create a PivotTable using the PivotTable button in the Tables group on the INSERT tab.
- Add fields to the PivotTable using the field name check boxes in the PivotTable Fields task pane.
- Once created, a PivotTable can be used to view a variety of scenarios by filtering the row, column, or report headings.
- Use buttons in the contextual PIVOTTABLE TOOLS ANALYZE and DESIGN tabs to format the PivotTable and/or edit the features used in the table.

- Slicers are used to filter data in a PivotTable without having to open a filter drop-down list.
- A Slicer pane contains all of the items in the designated field, so the report can be filtered with one mouse click.
- Click the Insert Slicer button in the Filter group on the PIVOTTABLE TOOLS ANALYZE tab to add a Slicer pane to a PivotTable.
- Timelines are used to group and filter data in a PivotTable using timeframes such as years, quarters, months, and days.
- Click the Insert Timeline button in the Filter group on the PIVOTTABLE TOOLS ANALYZE tab to add a Timeline pane to a PivotTable.
- A PivotChart displays the data in a PivotTable in a specified chart type.
- Filter a PivotChart using the legend or axis field buttons located on the PivotChart.
- Sparklines are miniature charts inserted into the backgrounds of cells.
- Add Sparklines to a worksheet to show trends or high or low values in a range of source data next to the data.
- To add Sparklines, select an empty range next to the source data, click the INSERT tab, and then click the desired chart type in the Sparklines group. At the Create Sparklines dialog box, type the range containing the values you want to graph or drag to select the range and then click OK.
- Sparklines can be customized using options in the SPARKLINE TOOLS DESIGN tab.

Commands Review

FEATURE	RIBBON TAB, GROUP	BUTTON	KEYBOARD SHORTCUT
Consolidate	DATA, Data Tools		
edit links	DATA, Connections		
manage range names	FORMULAS, Defined Names		Ctrl + F3
PivotChart	INSERT, Charts OR PIVOTTABLES TOOLS ANALYZE, Tools		
PivotTable	INSERT, Tables		
Slicer	INSERT, Filters		
Sparklines	INSERT, Sparklines		
Timelines	INSERT, Filters		

Concepts Check Test Your Knowledge SNAP

Completion: In the space provided at the right, indicate the correct term, command, or number.

1. This symbol separates a worksheet reference from a cell reference. exclamation point
2. This term describes a formula that references the same cell in a range that spans two or more worksheets. 3D reference
3. Assume that a workbook contains the following defined range names that reference cells in four worksheets: Qtr1, Qtr2, Qtr3, and Qtr4. Provide the formula to add the data in the four ranges. =sum(Qtr1, Qtr2, 3, 4
4. Create this formula entry for QtrlySales.xlsx to link to an external reference cell C12 in a worksheet named *Summary*. =[QtrlySales.xlsx]Sumary!C12
5. Open this dialog box to change the source of a linked external reference after moving the source workbook to another folder. edit link
6. Click this button to permanently remove a linked external reference and convert the linked cells to their existing values. break link
7. This default function is active when you open the Consolidate dialog box. sum
8. Use this button to preview different PivotTable scenarios. pivottable styles
9. Add fields to a PivotTable by clicking the field check box in this task pane. Pivottable tools design
10. The PivotTable Styles gallery is accessible from this tab. Pivottable field list
11. Insert this type of pane to filter a PivotTable with one mouse click. slicer
12. Insert this type of pane to filter a PivotTable by dates. slicer
13. Choose a function other than Sum for a PivotTable numeric field by clicking this button in the Active Group on the PIVOTTABLE TOOLS ANALYZE tab. field settings
14. The buttons to filter a PivotChart are found here.
15. This is the first step in adding Sparklines to a worksheet.
16. Click this tab to customize Sparklines. Sparkline tools design tab

Skills Check Assess Your Performance

Note: If you submit your work in hard copy, check with your instructor before completing these Assessments to see if you need to print two copies of worksheets in which you have created formulas, with one copy showing the cell formulas.

Assessment 1

SUMMARIZE DATA IN MULTIPLE WORKSHEETS USING RANGE NAMES

SNAP Grade It

1. Open **NADQ1Fees.xlsx**.
2. Save the workbook and name it **EL2-C4-A1-NADQ1Fees**.
3. The workbook contains three worksheets showing dental fees earned in January, February, and March for three dentists at a dental clinic. Create a range name in cell F13 of each worksheet to reference the total fees earned by each dentist for the quarter as follows:
   a. Type **PopovichTotal** as the name for cell F13 in the Popovich worksheet.
   b. Type **VanketTotal** as the name for cell F13 in the Vanket worksheet.
   c. Type **JovanovicTotal** as the name for cell F13 in the Jovanovic worksheet.
4. Make FeeSummary the active worksheet and then type the following label in cell A6: **Quarter 1 fees for Popovich, Vanket, and Jovanovic**.
5. Make cell F6 the active cell and create a Sum formula to add the total fees earned by each dentist using the range names created in Step 3.
6. Apply accounting formatting to cell F6 and then adjust the column width to AutoFit.
7. Print the FeeSummary worksheet.
8. Save and then close **EL2-C4-A1-NADQ1Fees.xlsx**.

Assessment 2

SUMMARIZE DATA USING LINKED EXTERNAL REFERENCES

1. Open **PFSalesSum.xlsx**.
2. Save the workbook and name it **EL2-C4-A2-PFSalesSum**.
3. Open **PFQ1.xlsx**, **PFQ2.xlsx**, **PFQ3.xlsx**, and **PFQ4.xlsx**.
4. Tile all of the open workbooks. ***Hint: Use the Arrange All button on the VIEW tab.***
5. Starting in cell B5 in **EL2-C4-A2-PFSalesSum.xlsx**, create formulas to populate the cells in column B by linking to the appropriate source cells in **PFQ1.xlsx**. ***Hint: After creating the first formula, edit the entry in cell B5 to use a relative reference to the source cell (instead of an absolute reference) so you can copy and paste the formula in cell B5 to B6:B9.***
6. Create formulas to link to the appropriate source cells for the second-, third-, and fourth-quarter sales.
7. Close the four quarterly sales workbooks. Click Don't Save when prompted to save changes.
8. Maximize **EL2-C4-A2-PFSalesSum.xlsx**.
9. Make cell B5 the active cell and break the link to **PFQ1.xlsx**.
10. Print the worksheet.
11. Save and then close **EL2-C4-A2-PFSalesSum.xlsx**.

Assessment

3 SUMMARIZE DATA USING 3-D REFERENCES

SNAP Grade It

1. Open **JuneEntries.xlsx**.
2. Save the workbook and name it **EL2-C4-A3-JuneEntries**.
3. With AttendanceSummary the active worksheet, summarize the data in the three park worksheets using 3-D references as follows:
   a. Make cell B7 the active cell and then create a 3-D formula to sum the attendance values in the three park worksheets for day 1. Copy and paste the formula into the remaining cells in column B to complete the summary to day 16.
   b. Make cell E7 the active cell and then create a 3-D formula to sum the attendance values in the three park worksheets for day 17. Copy and paste the formula into the remaining cells in column E to complete the summary to day 30.
4. Type the label Total Vehicle and Individual Entrances in cell A24 and create a Sum formula in cell E24 to compute the grand total. Apply comma formatting with no places after the decimal point.
5. Print the AttendanceSummary worksheet.
6. Save and then close **EL2-C4-A3-JuneEntries.xlsx**.

Assessment

4 SUMMARIZE DATA IN A PIVOTTABLE AND PIVOTCHART

SNAP Grade It

1. Open **BillingSummary3Q.xlsx**.
2. Save the workbook and name it **EL2-C4-A4-BillingSummary3Q**.
3. Create a PivotTable in a new worksheet as follows:
   a. Display the range named *ThirdQ* and then insert a PivotTable in a new worksheet.
   b. Add the *Attorney LName* field as rows.
   c. Add the *Area* field as columns.
   d. Sum the *Fees Due* field.
4. Apply the Pivot Style Medium 2 style to the PivotTable (second column first row in the *Medium* section).
5. Apply comma formatting with no places after the decimal point to the values. Also change the column widths of B through H to 13 characters and right-align the *Martinez, O'Donovan, Sullivan, Williams,* and *Grand Total* labels in column A.
6. Name the worksheet *PivotTable* and then do the following:
   a. In cell A1, type Associate Billing Summary. Change the font to 14-point Copperplate Gothic Bold. Merge and center the text across the PivotTable.
   b. In cell A2, type October - December 2015. Change the font to 14-point Copperplate Gothic Bold. Merge and center the text across the PivotTable.
   c. Change the orientation to landscape and print the PivotTable.
7. Create a PivotChart from the PivotTable using the 3-D Stacked Column chart type and move the chart to its own sheet named *PivotChart*.
8. Apply Style 7 to the PivotChart (seventh style in the Chart Styles gallery).
9. Filter the PivotChart by the attorney named *Martinez*.
10. Print the PivotChart.
11. Save and then close **EL2-C4-A4-BillingSummary3Q.xlsx**.

Assessment 5

FILTERING A PIVOTTABLE USING A SLICER AND TIMELINE

SNAP Grade It

1. Open **EL2-C4-A4-BillingSummary3Q.xlsx**.
2. Save the workbook and name it **EL2-C4-A5-BillingSummary3Q.xlsx**.
3. Click the PivotTable sheet to view the PivotTable.
4. Remove the filter to display all of the attorney names.
5. Insert a Slicer pane for the *Area* field and move the Slicer pane below the PivotTable.
6. Using the Slicer pane, filter the PivotTable by *Corporate*. Hold down the Shift key and then click the button for *Divorce*. (Use the Shift key to filter by multiple fields in a Slicer pane when the two fields are adjacent in the pane.)
7. Insert a Timeline pane for the *Date* field and move the Timeline pane to the right of the Slicer pane.
8. Using the Timeline pane, filter the PivotTable for Oct to Nov 2015.
9. Print the PivotTable.
10. Save and then close **EL2-C4-A5-BillingSummary3Q.xlsx**.

Assessment 6

CREATING AND CUSTOMIZING SPARKLINES

SNAP Grade It

1. Open **EL2-C4-A2-PFSalesSum.xlsx** and enable the content.
2. Save the workbook and name it **EL2-C4-A6-PFSalesSum**.
3. Select H5:H9 and insert line-type Sparklines referencing the data range B5:E9.
4. Show the high point using markers on each line.
5. Change the Sparkline color to *Dark Blue* (in *Standard Colors* section).
6. Change the width of column H to 21 characters and type the label **Region Sales by Quarter** in cell H4.
7. Change the page orientation to landscape and then print the worksheet.
8. Save and then close **EL2-C4-A6-PFSalesSum.xlsx**.

Visual Benchmark Demonstrate Your Proficiency

SUMMARIZING REAL ESTATE SALES AND COMMISSION DATA

1. Open **HROctSales.xlsx**.
2. Save the workbook and name it **EL2-C4-VB-HROctSales**.
3. Create the PivotTable shown in Figure 4.11 in a new worksheet named *PivotTable*. Apply the Pivot Style Medium 11 style and set the column widths to 18 characters.
4. Create the PivotChart shown in Figure 4.12 in a new worksheet named *PivotChart*. Use the 3-D Clustered Column chart type and apply the Style 11 style.
5. Print the PivotTable and PivotChart worksheets.
6. Save and then close **EL2-C4-VB-HROctSales.xlsx**.

Figure 4.11 Visual Benchmark PivotTable

	A	B	C	D	E
1	Hillsdale Realtors				
2	October Sales				
3	Sum of Sale Price	Column Labels			
4	Row Labels	Condominium	Single family home	Townhome	Grand Total
5	Chandler	$ 610,900	$ 325,500	$ 952,100	$ 1,888,500
6	Glendale	640,400	881,375		1,521,775
7	Mesa	275,800	846,750	165,800	1,288,350
8	Phoenix	695,000	2,148,100	174,900	3,018,000
9	**Grand Total**	**$ 2,222,100**	**$ 4,201,725**	**$ 1,292,800**	**$ 7,716,625**

Figure 4.12 Visual Benchmark PivotChart

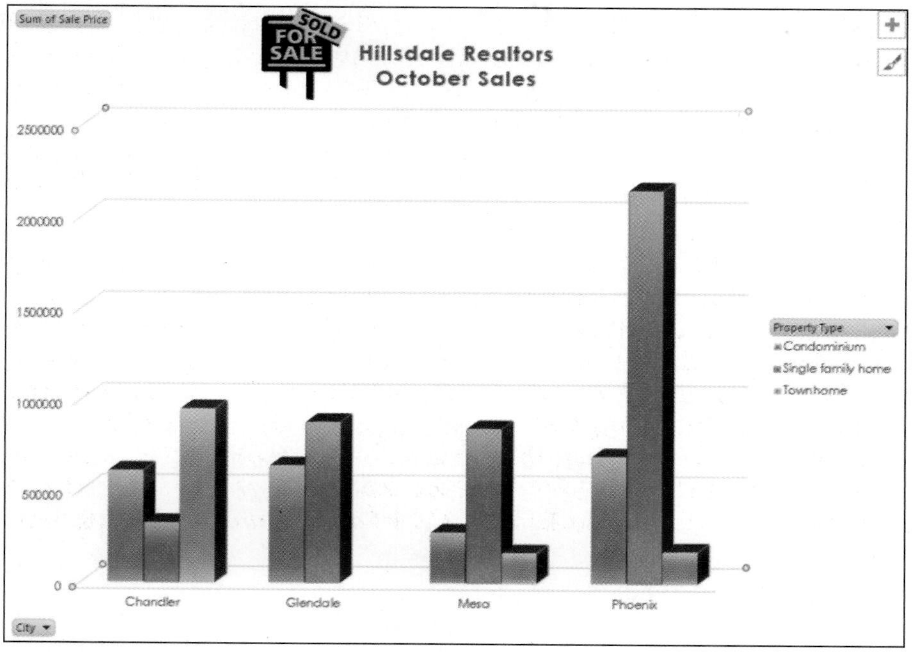

Case Study Apply Your Skills

Part 1

Yolanda Robertson of NuTrends Market Research is continuing to work on the franchise expansion plan for the owners of Pizza By Mario. Yolanda has received a new workbook from the owners with profit information by store and would like you to summarize the data. Open the workbook named **PBMSales&Profits.xlsx** and review the structure of the data. Yolanda would like to have a PivotTable that provides the average gross sales and average net income by city and state. You determine how to organize the layout of the report. ***Hint: You can add more than one numeric field to the* Values *list box***. Remove the grand totals at the right of the report so that only a grand total row appears at the bottom of the PivotTable. ***Hint: Use the Grand Totals button in the Layout group on the PIVOTTABLE TOOLS DESIGN tab***. Apply formatting options to improve the report's appearance and make sure the report prints on one page in landscape orientation. Rename the worksheet containing the report *PivotTable*. Save the revised workbook and name it **EL2-C4-CS-P1-PBMRpt**.

Part 2

Yolanda would like to have a chart that graphs the average net income data for the state of Michigan. Create a PivotChart in a new sheet named *PivotChart* and filter the chart appropriately to meet Yolanda's request. You determine the appropriate chart style and elements to include in the chart. Yolanda will use this chart at an upcoming meeting with the franchise owners and wants the chart to be of professional quality. Print the chart. Save the revised workbook and name it **EL2-C4-CS-P2-PBMRpt** and then close the workbook.

Part 3

Help

Open **EL2-C4-CS-P1-PBMRpt.xlsx**. Use the Help feature to find out how to modify a numeric field setting to show values as ranked numbers, from largest to smallest. For example, instead of displaying the average value next to the city name, you will display the city's ranking as it compares to other cities in the same state. Ranking from largest to smallest means the highest value in the state is ranked as 1. Using the information you have learned in Help, change the display of the average sales to show the values ranked from largest to smallest using *City* as the base field. Remove the *Net Income* field from the PivotTable. Remove the *Grand Total* row at the bottom of the PivotTable. Make any other formatting changes to the report that you think will improve its appearance. Print the PivotTable. Save the revised workbook and name it **EL2-C4-CS-P3-PBMRpt**.

Part 4

Yolanda would like you to do some comparison research with another pizza franchise. Use the Internet to research the sales and net income of a pizza franchise with which you are familiar. Create a new workbook that compares the total annual sales and net income values of the pizza franchise you researched with the Pizza By Mario information in **EL2-C4-CS-P1-PBMRpt.xlsx**. Provide the URL of the website from which you obtained the information about the competitor. Create a chart that presents the comparison data. Save the workbook and name it **EL2-C4-CS-P4-PizzaFranchiseComparison**. Print the comparison data and the chart. Close **EL2-C4-CS-P4-PizzaFranchiseComparison.xlsx**.

MICROSOFT® EXCEL® Performance Assessment

Access
EL2U1

Note: Before beginning assessments, copy to your storage medium the EL2U1 subfolder from the EL2 folder on the CD that accompanies this textbook and then make EL2U1 the active folder.

Assessing Proficiency

In this unit, you have learned to apply advanced formatting options, such as conditional formatting and custom number formats; perform advanced sort and filtering techniques; create functions that incorporate conditional logic, look up data, convert text, and calculate financial results; define a table and apply data management features to a table or list range; consolidate and summarize data; and present summary information in PivotTables, PivotCharts, and Sparklines.

Assessment 1 Conditionally Format and Filter a Help Desk Worksheet

1. Open **RSRHelpDesk.xlsx**.
2. Save the workbook using the name **EL2-U1-A1-RSRHelpDesk**.
3. Use the icon set from the Quick Analysis button to apply conditional formatting to the values in the *Priority* column.
4. Create a custom format for the values in the *Time Spent* column. The format should display a leading zero, two places after the decimal point, and the text *hrs* after each entry, separated by one space from the number (e.g. 2.20 hrs, 0.25 hrs, etc.).
5. Create two conditional formatting rules for the values in the *Time Spent* column as follows:
   a. For all entries in which the time spent is less than one hour, apply bold formatting and the Olive Green, Accent 3, Lighter 80% fill color (seventh column, second row).
   b. For all entries in which the time spent is more than two hours, apply the Yellow fill color (fourth column, last row).
6. Filter the worksheet by the Yellow fill color applied in the *Time Spent* column.
7. Print the filtered worksheet.
8. Clear the filter and filter arrow(s) and then print the worksheet.
9. Save and then close **EL2-U1-A1-RSRHelpDesk.xlsx**.

Assessment 2 Use Conditional Logic Formulas in a Help Desk Worksheet

1. Open **EL2-U1-A1-RSRHelpDesk.xlsx**.
2. Save the workbook using the name **EL2-U1-A2-RSRHelpDesk.xlsx**.
3. Create range names of your choosing for each of the following ranges:
   - A4:E6, which will be used in a lookup formula
   - E8:E30 in the *Operator ID* column
   - I8:I30 in the *Time Spent* column
   - J8:J30 in the *Status* column
4. In cell I4, create a COUNTA formula to count the number of help desk calls in March, using column A as the source range.
5. In cells I5 and I6, create COUNTIF formulas to count the number of active calls (I5) and number of closed calls (I6). Use range names in the formulas.
6. Create COUNTIF formulas in cells K3 through K6 to count the calls assigned to operator IDs 1, 2, 3, and 4, respectively. Use range names in the formulas.
7. Create SUMIF formulas in cells L3 through L6 to calculate the total time spent on calls assigned to operator IDs 1, 2, 3, and 4, respectively. Use range names in the formulas. Format the results to display two places after the decimal point.
8. Create AVERAGEIF formulas in cells M3 through M6 to find the average time spent on calls assigned to operator IDs 1, 2, 3, and 4, respectively. Use range names in the formulas. Format the results to display two places after the decimal point.
9. Create the HLOOKUP formula with an exact match in cell G8 to return the last name of the operator assigned to the call. Use the range name for the lookup table in the formula.
10. Create the HLOOKUP formula with an exact match in cell H8 to return the first name of the operator assigned to the call. Use the range name for the lookup table in the formula.
11. Copy the HLOOKUP formulas in G8:H8 and paste them to the remaining rows in the list.
12. Save, print, and then close **EL2-U1-A2-RSRHelpDesk.xlsx**.

Assessment 3 Use Table and Data Management Features in a Help Desk Worksheet

1. Open **EL2-U1-A2-RSRHelpDesk.xlsx**.
2. Save the workbook using the name **EL2-U1-A3-RSRHelpDesk.xlsx**.
3. Create the file number in column F using the ticket number in column B followed by a dash, the priority in column C followed by a dash, and the operator ID. ***Hint: It may take Flash Fill a few rows before it recognizes the correct sequence.***
4. Format A7:J30 as a table using the Table Style Medium 20 table style.
5. Add a calculated column to the table in column K that multiplies the time spent times 15. Use the column heading *Cost* in cell K7. Apply comma formatting with two places after the decimal point to the results.
6. Add a *Total* row to the table. Display totals for columns I and K.
7. Add emphasis to the last column in the table and band the columns instead of the rows.
8. Create a drop-down list for the *Operator ID* column that displays entries 1, 2, 3, and 4.

9. The help desk policy states that help desk operators cannot spend more than three hours on a call. Any call that requires more than three hours must be routed to the help desk manager and assigned to another group. Create a validation rule in the *Time Spent* column that prevents any value greater than 3 from being entered. Create appropriate input and error messages. ***Note: Ignore the green triangle indicator in cell I17 that specifies that the hours should be less than or equal to 3.***
10. Type the following two records in the table above the total in row 31:

Date	3/31/2015	*Date*	3/31/2015
Ticket No.	14424	*Ticket No.*	14425
Priority	2	*Priority*	2
Type of Call	Email	*Type of Call*	Password
Operator ID	3	*Operator ID*	4
File No.	14424-2-3	*File No.*	14425-2-4
Time Spent	.75	*Time Spent*	.25
Status	Active	*Status*	Closed

11. Filter the table to display only those calls with a *Closed* status.
12. Print the filtered list.
13. Filter the worksheet to display only those calls with a *Closed* status and for which the type of call was *Password*.
14. Print the filtered list.
15. Clear both filters.
16. Save, print, and then close **EL2-U1-A3-RSRHelpDesk.xlsx**.

Assessment 4 Add Subtotals and Outline a Help Desk Worksheet

1. Open **EL2-U1-A3-RSRHelpDesk.xlsx**.
2. Save the workbook using the name **EL2-U1-A4-RSRHelpDesk**.
3. Remove the *Total* row from the table.
4. Convert the table to a normal range.
5. Sort the list first by the operator's last name, then by the operator's first name, then by the call priority, and finally by the type of call—all in ascending order.
6. Add a subtotal to the list at each change in operator last name to calculate the total cost of calls by each operator.
7. Display the outlined worksheet at level 2 and then print the worksheet.
8. Display the outlined worksheet at level 3 and then print the worksheet.
9. Save and then close **EL2-U1-A4-RSRHelpDesk.xlsx**.

Assessment 5 Use Financial and Text Functions to Analyze Data for a Project

1. Open **ACLoan.xlsx**.
2. Save the workbook using the name **EL2-U1-A5-ACLoan**.
3. Create formulas to analyze the cost of the loan from Newfunds Trust and Delta Capital as follows:
   a. In cells C10 and E10, calculate the monthly loan payment from each lender.
   b. In cells C12 and E12, calculate the principal portion of each payment for the first loan payment.
   c. In cells C14 and E14, calculate the total loan payment that will be made over the life of the loan from each lender.
4. In cell E20, use the text function =PROPER to return the loan company name for the loan that represents the lowest total cost to AllClaims Insurance Brokers. ***Hint: The argument for the function will reference either cell C4 or cell E4.***

5. In cell E21, use the text function =LOWER to return the loan application number for the loan company name displayed in cell E20.
6. Save, print, and then close **EL2-U1-A5-ACLoan.xlsx**.

Assessment 6 Analyze Sales Using a PivotTable, PivotChart, and Sparklines

1. Open **PreBulkSales.xlsx**.
2. Save the workbook using the name **EL2-U1-A6-PreBulkSales**.
3. Select A4:I22 and create a PivotTable in a new worksheet as follows:
   a. Add the *Category* field as the report filter field.
   b. Add the *Distributor* field as the rows.
   c. Sum the North, South, East, and West sales values.
   d. Name the worksheet PivotTable.
4. Apply formatting options to the PivotTable to make the data easier to read and interpret.
5. Insert a Slicer for the Model and show the data for *PD-1140*, *PD-1150*, and *PD-1155*.
6. Move the Slicer pane under the PivotTable and print the PivotTable and Slicer pane on one sheet.
7. Create a PivotChart and move it to a separate sheet named PivotChart that graphs the data from the PivotTable in a 3-D Clustered Column chart.
8. Move the legend to the bottom of the chart.
9. Apply the Style 3 format to the chart.
10. Print the chart.
11. Make Sheet1 the active sheet and then create Sparklines in J5:J22 that show the North, South, East, and West sales in a line chart. Set the width of column J to 18 characters. Customize the Sparklines by changing the Sparkline color and adding data points. (You determine which data point to show and what color to make the points.) Type an appropriate label in cell J4 and add other formatting that will improve the appearance of the worksheet.
12. Save, print, and then close **EL2-U1-A6-PreBulkSales.xlsx**.

Assessment 7 Link to an External Data Source and Calculate Distributor Payments

1. Open **PreDistPymnt.xlsx**.
2. Save the workbook using the name **EL2-U1-A7-PreDistPymnt**.
3. Open **EL2-U1-A6-PreBulkSales.xlsx**.
4. Save the workbook using the name **EL2-U1-A7-PreSource**.
5. Make the PivotTable worksheet active, remove any filters, delete the Slicer pane, and then edit the PivotTable Fields so that *Sum of Total* is the only numeric field displayed in the table.
6. Save **EL2-U1-A7-PreSource.xlsx**.
7. Arrange the display of the two workbooks vertically.
8. Create linked external references starting in cell D6 in **EL2-U1-A7-PreDistPymnt.xlsx** to the appropriate source cells in the PivotTable in **EL2-U1-A7-PreSource.xlsx** so that the distributor payment worksheet displays the total sales for each distributor. ***Note: Since you are linking to a PivotTable, Excel automatically generates a GETPIVOTDATA function formula in each linked cell.***
9. Close **EL2-U1-A7-PreSource.xlsx**.
10. Maximize **EL2-U1-A7-PreDistPymnt.xlsx**.
11. Apply comma formatting with no places after the decimal point to D6:D8.

12. Precision Design and Packaging pays each distributor a percentage of sales depending on the total sales achieved. The percentage for each category of sales is shown in the following chart:

Sales	**Percentage**
Less than $600,000	1%
Greater than or equal to $600,000 but less than $1,000,000	2%
$1,000,000 and above	4%

Calculate the payment owed for the distributors in H6:H8. Perform the calculation using one of the following two methods. (Choose the method that you find easiest to understand.)

- Create a nested IF statement.
- Create a lookup table in the worksheet that contains the sale ranges and three percentage values. Next, add a column next to each distributor with a lookup formula to return the correct percentage and then calculate the payment using total sales times the percentage value.

13. Apply comma formatting with two places after the decimal point to H6:H8.
14. Type TOTALS in cell B10 and then create formulas in cells D10 and H10 to calculate the total sales and total payments, respectively. Format the totals and adjust column widths as necessary.
15. Print the worksheet. Write the GETPIVOTDATA formula for cell D6 at the bottom of the printout.
16. Break the link to the external references and convert the formulas to their existing values.
17. Save, print, and then close **EL2-U1-A7-PreDistPymnt.xlsx**.

Writing Activities

The following activities give you the opportunity to practice your writing skills along with demonstrating an understanding of some of the important Excel features you have mastered in this unit. Use appropriate word choices and correct grammar, capitalization, and punctuation when setting up new worksheets. Also make sure that labels clearly describe the data that are presented.

Activity 1 Create a Worksheet to Track Movie Rental Memberships

ViewItVideo is offering a new membership program for its frequent customers. Customers will pay an annual membership fee that entitles them to a discount on movie rentals based on their membership levels. Figure U1.1 shows the three membership levels and discounts. The manager of ViewItVideo has asked you to create a worksheet that will be used to provide a master list that includes the

Figure U1.1 Activity 1

Membership Category	Annual Fee	Discount on Movie Rentals
Gold	$45.00	15%
Silver	$30.00	12%
Classic	$20.00	10%

name of each customer participating in the membership program, the membership level for which the customer has paid, and the discount on movie rentals the customer is entitled to receive. The worksheet should provide in list format the following information:

- Date annual membership needs to be renewed
- Customer name
- Customer telephone number
- Membership level
- Annual membership fee
- Discount on movie rentals

Create a worksheet for the membership list. Use a lookup table to populate the cells containing the membership fee and discount level. Create a drop-down list for the cell containing the membership level that restricts the data entered to the three membership categories. Use a special number format for the telephone number column so that all telephone numbers include an area code and are displayed in a consistent format. Enter a minimum of five sample records to test the worksheet with your settings. The manager anticipates that approximately 35 customers will subscribe to the membership program. Format enough rows with the data features to include at least 35 memberships. Save the completed worksheet and name it **EL2-U1-Act01-VIVMemberships**. Print and then close the worksheet.

Activity 2 Create a Worksheet to Log Hours Walked in a Company Fitness Contest

Your company is sponsoring a contest this year to encourage employees to participate in a walking fitness program during the lunch hour. Participating employees in the department that logs the most miles or kilometers during the year will be awarded an expense-paid spa weekend at an exclusive luxury resort. You work in Human Resources and are in charge of keeping track of each department's walking record. Create a worksheet you can use to enter each department's total by month and summarize the data to show the total distance walked by all participating employees at the end of the year as follows:

- Four departments have signed up for the contest: Accounting, Human Resources, Purchasing, and Marketing. Create a separate worksheet for each department.
- Each department will send you a paper copy of its employees' walking log each month. You will use this source document to enter the miles or kilometers walked by day. At the end of each month, you want to calculate statistics by department to show the total distance walked, average distance walked, and number of days that employees walked during the lunch hour. When calculating the average and number of days, include only those days of which employees logged a distance. In other words, exclude from the statistics those days for which employees did not log any distance. ***Hint: Consider adding a column that contains* Yes *or* No *to record whether or not employees participated in the walking program each day to use as the criteria range.***
- Create a summary worksheet that calculates the total miles or kilometers walked by participating employees in all four departments.

Test your settings by entering at least five days of sample data in each worksheet. Save the completed workbook and name it **EL2-U1-Act02-FitProgram**. Print the entire workbook and then close the workbook.

Optional: Using the Internet or other sources, find information on the health benefits of walking. Prepare a summary of the information and include it in a memo to employees that announces the contest. The memo is to be sent from Human Resources to all departments. Save the memo and name it **EL2-U2-Act02-FitMemo**. Print the memo and then close the file.

Internet Research

Create a Worksheet to Compare Online Auction Listing Fees

You are assisting a friend who is interested in selling a few items on an auction website on the Internet. Research a minimum of two Internet auction sites to identify all of the selling and payment fees associated with selling online. For example, be sure to find out costs for the following activities involved in an auction sale:

- Listing fees (sometimes called *insertion fees*)
- Optional features that can be attached to an ad, such as reserve bid fees, picture fees, listing upgrades, and so on
- Fees paid when the item is sold based on the sale value
- Fees paid to a third party to accept credit card payments (such as PayPal)

Create a worksheet that compares the fees for each auction website you researched. Include for each site two sample transactions and calculate the total fees that would be paid:

Sample transaction 1: Item sold for $24.99
Sample transaction 2: Item sold for $49.99

- Add optional features to the listing, such as a picture and reserve bid
- Assume in both sample transactions that the buyer pays by credit card using a third-party service

Based on your analysis, decide which auction site is the best choice from a cost perspective. Apply formatting options to make the worksheet easy to read and explain your recommendation for the lower-cost auction site. Save the completed worksheet and name it **EL2-U1-Act03-AuctionAnalysis**. Print and then close the worksheet.

MICROSOFT®

EXCEL® Level 2

Unit 2 ■ Managing and Integrating Data and the Excel Environment

Chapter 5 ■ Using Data Analysis Features

Chapter 6 ■ Protecting and Sharing Workbooks

Chapter 7 ■ Automating Repetitive Tasks and Customizing Excel

Chapter 8 ■ Importing, Exporting, and Distributing Data

MICROSOFT® EXCEL®

CHAPTER 5

Using Data Analysis Features

PERFORMANCE OBJECTIVES

Upon successful completion of Chapter 5, you will be able to:

- **Switch data arranged in columns to rows and vice versa**
- **Perform a mathematical operation during a paste routine**
- **Populate a cell using Goal Seek**
- **Save and display various worksheet models using Scenario Manager**
- **Create a scenario summary report**
- **Create a one-variable data table to analyze various outcomes**
- **Create a two-variable data table to analyze various outcomes**
- **View relationships between cells in formulas**
- **Identify Excel error codes and troubleshoot a formula using formula auditing tools**
- **Circle invalid data**
- **Use the Watch Window to track a value**

SNAP

Tutorials

5.1 Pasting Data Using Paste Special Options

5.2 Using Goal Seek to Populate a Cell

5.3 Using Scenario Manager

5.4 Performing What-If Analysis Using Data Tables

5.5 Using Auditing Tools

5.6 Circling Invalid Data and Watching Formulas

Excel's Paste Special dialog box includes several options for pasting copied data. You can choose to paste attributes of a copied cell or alter the paste routine to perform a more complex operation. A variety of *what-if* analysis tools allow you to manage data to assist with decision-making and management tasks. Formula-auditing tools can be used to troubleshoot a formula or view dependencies between cells. By working through the projects in this chapter, you will learn about these tools and features available in Excel to assist with accurate data analysis. Model answers for this chapter's projects appear on the following pages.

Excel

EL2C5

Note: Before beginning the projects, copy to your storage medium the EL2C5 subfolder from the EL2 folder on the CD that accompanies this textbook and then make EL2C5 the active folder.

Precision Design and Packaging
Enterprise Resource Planning (ERP) Information System
Finance Department
Request For Proposal (RFP) No. 385-XR-78

Company	Hardware	Software	Maintenance	Service Level	Term	Total Cost
Westerveld Inc.	675,000	212,000	22,500	Same day	5	909,500
Core Solutions	625,000	250,000	23,450	Same day	5	898,450

Project 1 Analyze Data from a Request for Proposal

Project 1a, EL2-C5-P1-PreERP.xlsx

Precision Design and Packaging
Enterprise Resource Planning (ERP) Information System
Finance Department
Request For Proposal (RFP) No. 385-XR-78

Company	Hardware	Software	Maintenance	Service Level	Term	Total Cost
Westerveld Inc.	675,000	212,000	112,500	Same day	5	999,500
Kampson Ltd.	595,000	281,000	86,700	24 hours	4	962,700
Jensen Systems	615,000	267,000	103,750	24 hours	5	985,750
Core Solutions	625,000	250,000	117,250	Same day	5	992,250
NuTech Partners	596,000	292,000	105,728	Same day	4	993,728

Project 1b, EL2-C5-P1-PreERP.xlsx

Math by Janelle Tutoring Service
Student Assessment Report
Whitney Orlowicz

Assessments	100	Session
Objective test	64.5	1
Performance test	72.0	6
Problem-solving test	83.5	10
Comprehensive test	78.5	15
Final test	81.5	20
Average grade	76.0	

Project 2 Calculate a Target Test Score

EL2-C5-P2-JTutorOrlowiczRpt.xlsx

Scenario Summary

	Current Values:	LowInflation	HighInflation	OriginalForecast
Changing Cells:				
WageInc	13,016	12,010	15,224	13,016
SuppliesInc	2,255	2,150	2,765	2,255
TrainingInc	6,385	5,276	7,236	6,385
AdminIncrease	2,479	1,998	3,195	2,479
Result Cells:				
TotalNewCosts	659,786	657,085	664,071	659,786

Notes: Current Values column represents values of changing cells at time Scenario Summary Report was created. Changing cells for each scenario are highlighted in gray.

Project 3 Forecast a Budget Based on Various Inflation Rates

EL2-C5-P3-NationalBdgt.xlsx

Precision Design and Packaging
Cost Price Analysis
"E" Container Bulk Cargo Box

Factory costs per shift			Variable unit production impact on cost	
Direct materials	$ 580,000			3.21
Direct labor	880,552		425,000	3.78
Overhead	145,350		450,000	3.57
Total cost	$ 1,605,902		475,000	3.38
			500,000	3.21
Standard production	500,000	units	525,000	3.06
			550,000	2.92
Cost per unit	$ 3.21		575,000	2.79

Project 4 Compare the Impacts of Various Inputs Related to Cost and Sales Pricing

Project 4a, EL2-C5-P4-PreEBoxCost.xlsx

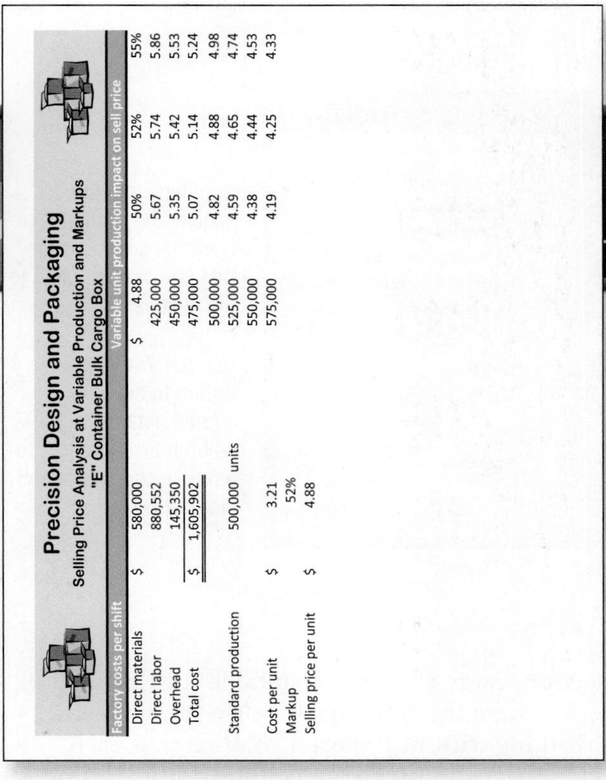

Precision Design and Packaging
Selling Price Analysis at Variable Production and Markups
"E" Container Bulk Cargo Box

Factory costs per shift			Variable unit production impact on sell price			
Direct materials	$	580,000	$ 4.88	50%	52%	55%
Direct labor		880,552	425,000	5.67	5.74	5.86
Overhead		145,350	450,000	5.35	5.42	5.53
Total cost	$	1,605,902	475,000	5.07	5.14	5.24
			500,000	4.82	4.88	4.98
Standard production		500,000 units	525,000	4.59	4.65	4.74
			550,000	4.38	4.44	4.53
Cost per unit	$	3.21	575,000	4.19	4.25	4.33
Markup		52%				
Selling price per unit	$	4.88				

Project 4b, EL2-C5-P4-PreEBoxSell.xlsx

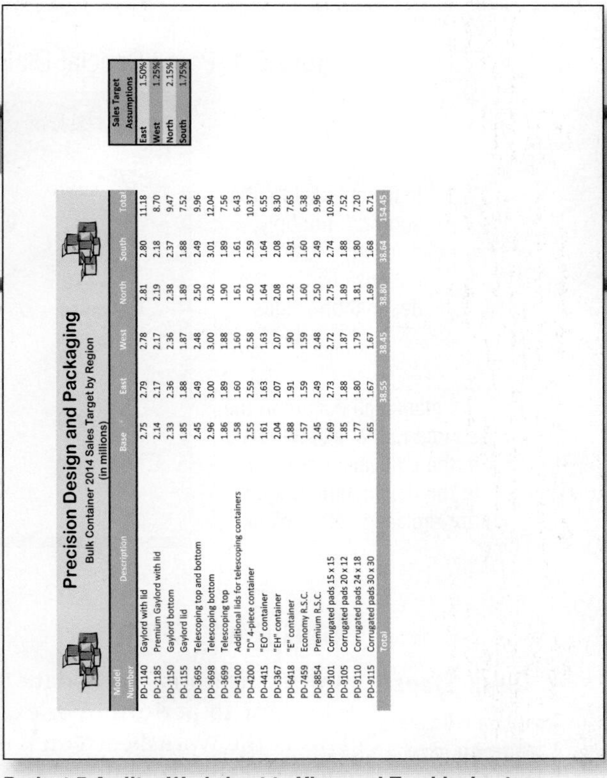

Precision Design and Packaging
Bulk Container 2014 Sales Target by Region
(in millions)

Model Number	Description	Base	East	West	North	South	Total
PD-1140	Gaylord with lid	2.75	2.79	2.78	2.81	2.80	11.18
PD-2185	Premium Gaylord with lid	2.14	2.17	2.17	2.19	2.18	8.70
PD-1150	Gaylord bottom	2.33	2.36	2.36	2.38	2.37	9.47
PD-1155	Gaylord lid	1.85	1.88	1.87	1.89	1.88	7.52
PD-3695	Telescoping top and bottom	2.45	2.49	2.48	2.50	2.49	9.96
PD-3698	Telescoping bottom	2.96	3.00	3.00	3.02	3.01	12.04
PD-3699	Telescoping top	1.86	1.89	1.88	1.90	1.89	7.56
PD-4100	Additional lids for telescoping containers	1.58	1.60	1.60	1.61	1.61	6.43
PD-4200	"D" 4-piece container	2.55	2.59	2.58	2.60	2.59	10.37
PD-4415	"EO" container	1.61	1.63	1.63	1.64	1.64	6.55
PD-5367	"EH" container	2.04	2.07	2.07	2.08	2.08	8.30
PD-6418	"E" container	1.88	1.91	1.90	1.92	1.91	7.65
PD-7459	Economy R.S.C.	1.57	1.59	1.59	1.60	1.60	6.38
PD-8854	Premium R.S.C.	2.45	2.49	2.48	2.50	2.49	9.96
PD-9101	Corrugated pads 15 x 15	2.69	2.73	2.72	2.75	2.74	10.94
PD-9105	Corrugated pads 20 x 12	1.85	1.88	1.87	1.89	1.88	7.52
PD-9110	Corrugated pads 24 x 18	1.77	1.80	1.79	1.81	1.80	7.20
PD-9115	Corrugated pads 30 x 30	1.65	1.67	1.67	1.69	1.68	6.71
	Total		38.55	38.45	38.80	38.64	154.45

Sales Target Assumptions	
East	1.50%
West	1.25%
North	2.15%
South	1.75%

Project 5 Audit a Worksheet to View and Troubleshoot Formulas Project 5c, EL2-C5-P5-PreSalesTrgt.xlsx

Project 1 Analyze Data from a Request for Proposal — 2 Parts

You will manipulate a worksheet containing vendor quotations for an enterprise resource-planning information system by copying and pasting using Paste Special options.

Pasting Data Using Paste Special Options

Paste

Clicking the Paste button arrow opens the Paste drop-down gallery. This gallery contains many options for pasting copied data and is grouped into three sections: *Paste*, *Paste Values*, and *Other Paste Options*. The Paste gallery includes a live preview of how the data will be pasted to assist you in choosing the correct paste option. Click *Paste Special* at the bottom of the Paste gallery to open the Paste Special dialog box, shown in Figure 5.1. Use options in this dialog box to paste specific attributes of the source data, perform a mathematical operation in the destination range based on values in the source range, or carry out a more complex paste sequence.

Several options in the Paste Special dialog box are also available by clicking a button at the Paste drop-down gallery. For example, if you copy a range of cells that has border formatting applied and want to paste the range without the borders, click the Paste button arrow and then click the No Borders button (first column, second row in the *Paste* section) at the drop-down gallery. This produces the same result as clicking the Paste button arrow, clicking *Paste Special* at the drop-down gallery, clicking *All except borders* in the *Paste* section of the Paste Special dialog box, and then clicking OK.

Figure 5.1 Paste Special Dialog Box

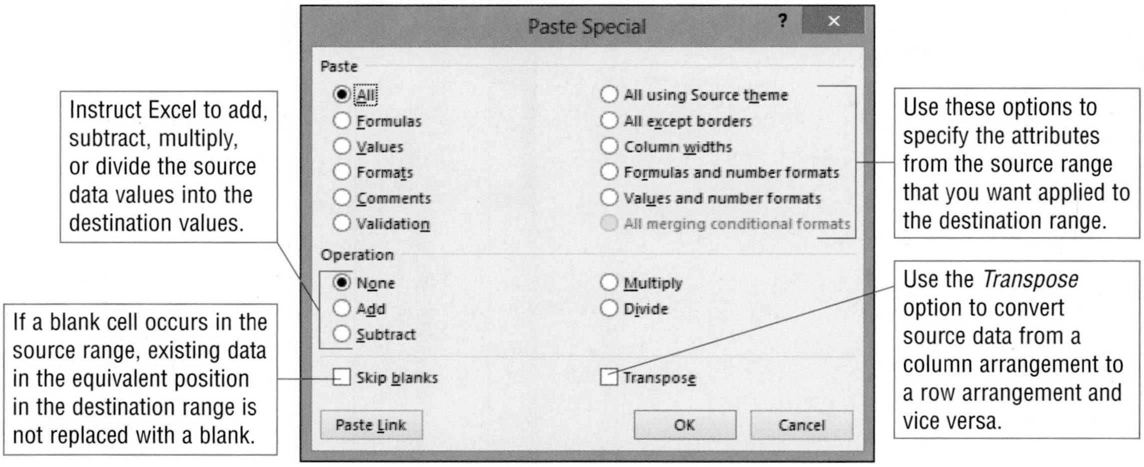

Transposing Data

Quick Steps

Transpose a Range

1. Select source range.
2. Click Copy button.
3. Click starting cell in destination range.
4. Click Paste button arrow.
5. Click Transpose button.

A worksheet may have data arranged in a way that is not suitable for the analysis you want to perform. For example, examine the worksheet shown in Figure 5.2. This is the worksheet you will be working with in Project 1. Notice that each company that submitted a proposal appears in a separate column, with the criteria for analysis (such as the cost of the hardware) arranged in rows. At first glance, this layout may seem appropriate, but consider how you will analyze this data if you want to examine only those vendors that offer a five-year contract. To use the filter feature on this data, you would need the contract term to display in a columnar format. Rearranging the data in this worksheet manually would be time consuming and risky due to the possibility of making errors during the conversion process. To avoid this, convert the columns to rows and rows to columns using the Transpose button in the Paste drop-down gallery or Paste Special dialog box.

Figure 5.2 Project 1 Worksheet

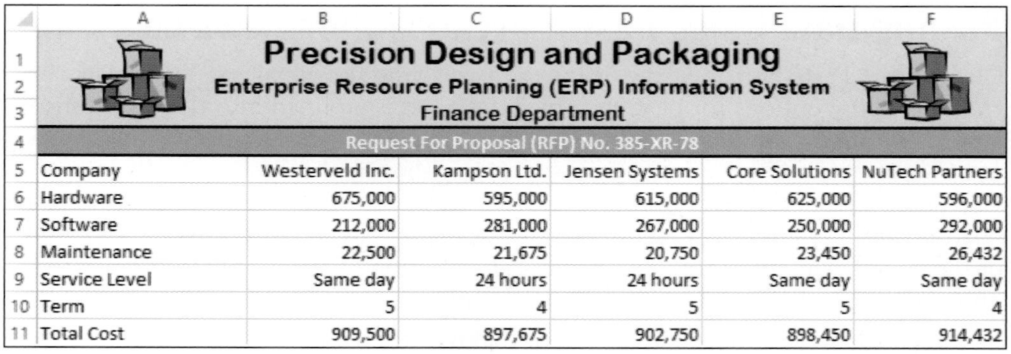

	A	B	C	D	E	F
1	Precision Design and Packaging					
2	Enterprise Resource Planning (ERP) Information System					
3	Finance Department					
4	Request For Proposal (RFP) No. 385-XR-78					
5	Company	Westerveld Inc.	Kampson Ltd.	Jensen Systems	Core Solutions	NuTech Partners
6	Hardware	675,000	595,000	615,000	625,000	596,000
7	Software	212,000	281,000	267,000	250,000	292,000
8	Maintenance	22,500	21,675	20,750	23,450	26,432
9	Service Level	Same day	24 hours	24 hours	Same day	Same day
10	Term	5	4	5	5	4
11	Total Cost	909,500	897,675	902,750	898,450	914,432

Project 1a Converting Data from Rows to Columns

Part 1 of 2

1. Open **PreERP.xlsx**.
2. Save the workbook and name it **EL2-C5-P1-PreERP**.
3. Convert the worksheet to arrange the company names in rows and criteria data in columns by completing the following steps:
   a. Select A5:F11.
   b. Click the Copy button.
   c. Click in cell A13.
   d. Click the Paste button arrow and then position the mouse over the Transpose button (second row, third column in the *Paste* section) at the drop-down gallery. A live preview shows how the copied data will be pasted. Click the Transpose button.

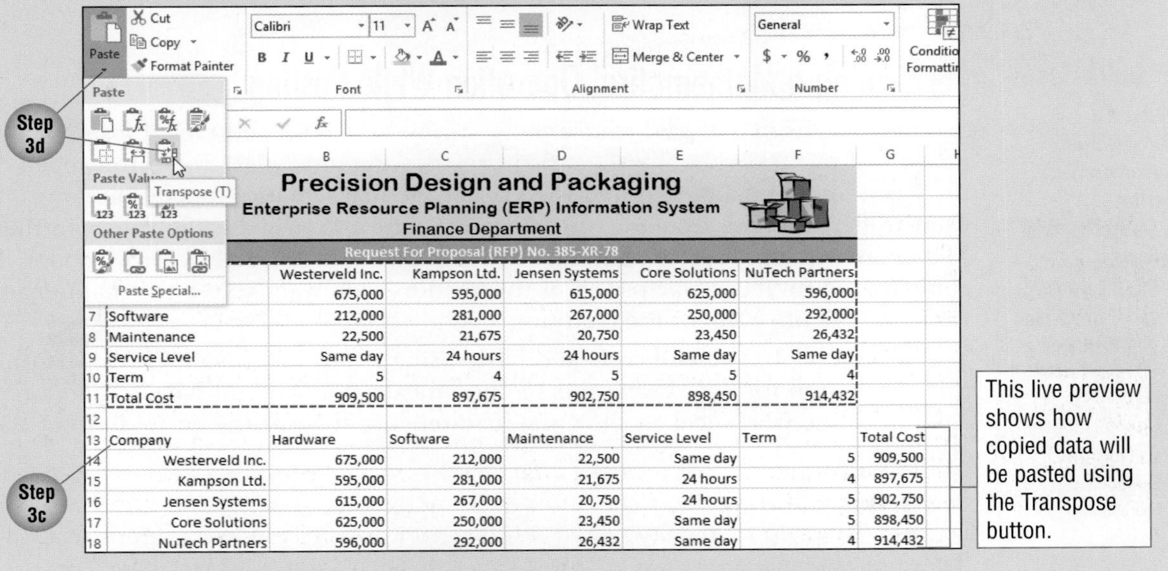

   e. Press the Esc key to remove the scrolling marquee from the source range and then click in any cell to deselect the range.
4. Delete rows 5 through 12.
5. Correct the merge and centering in rows 1 through 4 to extend the titles across columns A through G. If necessary, move or otherwise adjust the position of the clip art at the right side of the worksheet after merging and centering to column G.
6. Add a thick bottom border to cells A3 and A4.
7. Apply bold formatting and center-align the labels in A5:G5.
8. Select A5:G10, turn on the Filter feature, and then click in any cell to deselect the range.
9. Click the filter arrow in cell F5 and then filter the worksheet to display only those vendors offering a five-year contract.

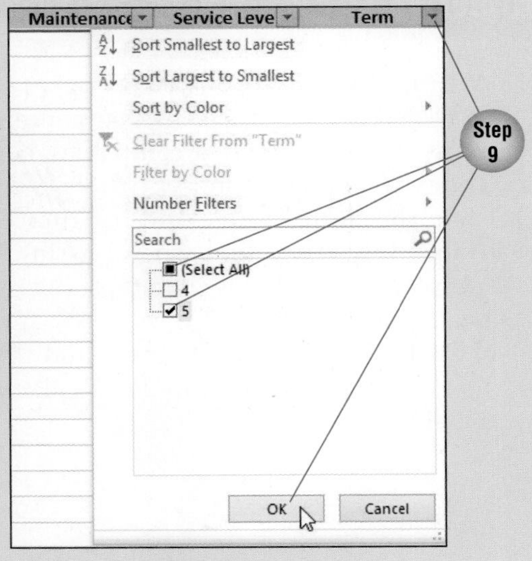

10. Click the filter arrow in cell E5 and then filter the remaining rows to display only those vendors offering same-day service.

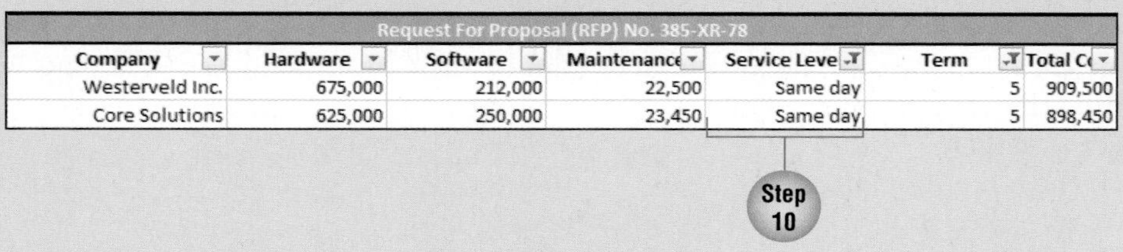

Request For Proposal (RFP) No. 385-XR-78						
Company	Hardware	Software	Maintenance	Service Level	Term	Total C(
Westerveld Inc.	675,000	212,000	22,500	Same day	5	909,500
Core Solutions	625,000	250,000	23,450	Same day	5	898,450

11. Print the filtered worksheet.
12. Turn off the Filter feature and then save **EL2-C5-P1-PreERP.xlsx**.

Quick Steps

Perform a Mathematical Operation While Pasting
1. Select source range values.
2. Click Copy button.
3. Click starting cell in destination range.
4. Click Paste button arrow.
5. Click *Paste Special*.
6. Click desired mathematical operation.
7. Click OK.

Performing a Mathematical Operation While Pasting

A range of cells in a copied source range can be added to, subtracted from, multiplied by, or divided by the cells in the destination range. To do this, open the Paste Special dialog box and then select the mathematical operation you want to perform. For example, in the worksheet for Project 1a, the values in the *Maintenance* column relate to annual maintenance fees charged by each vendor. To compare the total costs across all of the vendors, you want to see the maintenance value for the life cycle of the contract.

In Project 1b, you will copy and paste using a multiply operation to perform this calculation for you. Using this method means you will not have to add a new column to the worksheet to show the maintenance fees for the entire term of the contract.

Project 1b Multiplying the Source Cells by the Destination Cells — Part 2 of 2

1. With **EL2-C5-P1-PreERP.xlsx** open, select F6:F10. These are the cells that contain the terms for the individual companies' contracts.
2. Click the Copy button.
3. Paste the source range and instruct Excel to multiply the values when pasting by completing the following steps:
   a. Click in cell D6.
   b. Click the Paste button arrow and then click *Paste Special* at the drop-down gallery.

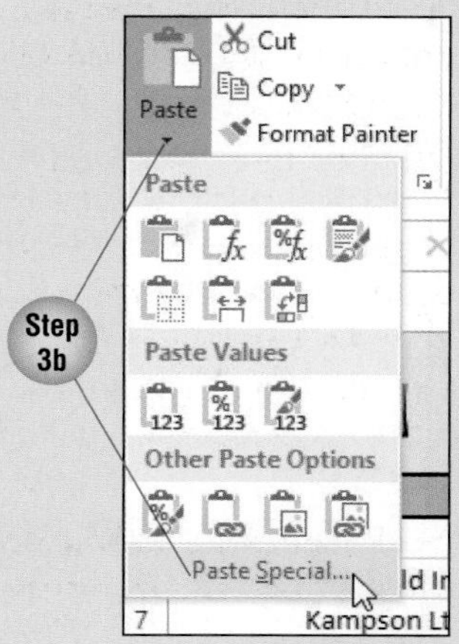

c. Click *Multiply* in the *Operation* section of the Paste Special dialog box and then click OK.
d. Press the *Esc* key to remove the scrolling marquee from the source range and then click in any cell to deselect the range.
4. Print the worksheet.
5. Save and then close **EL2-C5-P1-PreERP.xlsx**.

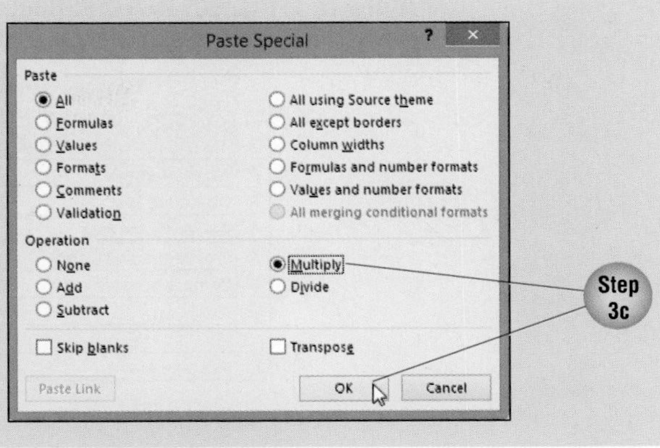

Selecting Other Paste Special Options

You can select from a variety of different options at the Paste Special dialog box. Click *Formulas* or *Values* to paste only the source formulas or displayed values, click *Formats* to paste only the formatting options from the source, and click *Validation* to paste a validation rule. Click *All using Source theme* to apply the theme from the source, click *All except borders* to paste everything but the borders from the source, and click *Column widths* to adjust the destination cells to the same column width as the source. To paste formulas or values including the number formats from the source, click the *Formulas and number formats* option or the *Values and number formats* option.

Project 2 Calculate a Target Test Score — 1 Part

Using a grades worksheet for a student, you will determine the score the student needs to earn on a final test to achieve a specified final average grade.

Using Goal Seek to Populate Cells

Goal Seek calculates a value using a target that you want to achieve in another cell that is dependent on the cell you want Goal Seek to populate. For example, the worksheet shown in Figure 5.3 shows Whitney's grades on the first four tutoring assessments. The value in cell B11 (average grade) is the average of the five values in B5:B9. Note that the final test shows a grade of 0 even though the test has not yet occurred. Once the final test grade is entered, the value in cell B11 will update to reflect the average of all five scores. Suppose Whitney wants to achieve a final average grade of 76% in her tutoring assessments. Using Goal Seek, you can determine the score she needs to earn on the final test to achieve the 76% average. In Project 2, you return a value in cell B9 that the Goal Seek feature will calculate based on the target value you will set in cell B11.

Goal Seek causes Excel to calculate in reverse: you specify the ending value and Excel figures out the input numbers that will achieve the result you want. Note that the cell in which you want Excel to calculate the target value must be referenced by a formula in the *Set cell* text box. Goal Seek is useful for any situation in which you know the result you want to achieve but are not sure what value will get you there.

Quick Steps

Use Goal Seek to Return a Value
1. Make desired cell active.
2. Click DATA tab.
3. Click What-If Analysis button.
4. Click *Goal Seek*.
5. Enter desired cell address in *Set cell* text box.
6. Enter desired target value in *To value* text box.
7. Enter dependent cell address in *By changing cell* text box.
8. Click OK.
9. Click OK or Cancel.

What-If Analysis

Figure 5.3 Project 2 Worksheet

	A	B	C
1	**Math by Janelle Tutoring Service**		
2	**Student Assessment Report**		
3	Whitney Orlowicz		
4	**Assessments**	**100**	**Session**
5	Objective test	64.5	1
6	Performance test	72.0	6
7	Problem-solving test	83.5	10
8	Comprehensive test	78.5	15
9	Final test	0.0	20
10			
11	Average grade	59.7	

Use Goal Seek to determine the value that needs to be entered for the final test to achieve the desired average grade in cell B11.

Project 2 Using Goal Seek to Return a Target Value

Part 1 of 1

1. Open **JTutorOrlowiczRpt.xlsx**.
2. Save the workbook and name it **EL2-C5-P2-JTutorOrlowiczRpt**.
3. Use Goal Seek to find the score Whitney needs to earn on the final test to achieve a 76% average grade by completing the following steps:
   a. Make cell B11 active.
   b. Click the DATA tab.
   c. Click the What-If Analysis button in the Data Tools group and then click *Goal Seek* at the drop-down list.
   d. If necessary, drag the Goal Seek dialog box to the right of the worksheet so you can see all of the values in column B.
   e. With *B11* already entered in the *Set cell* text box, click in the *To value* text box and then type 76.
   f. Press Tab and then type b9 in the *By changing cell* text box.
   g. Click OK.
   h. Click OK at the Goal Seek Status dialog box that shows Excel found a solution.

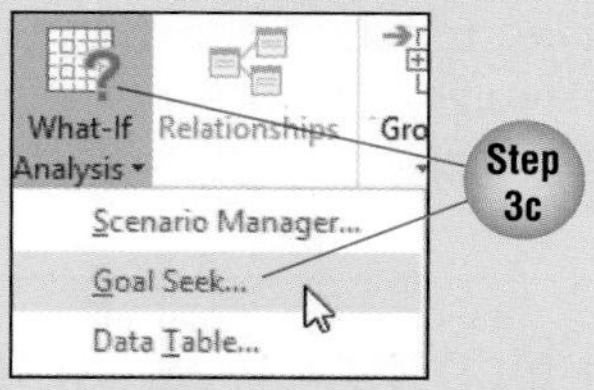

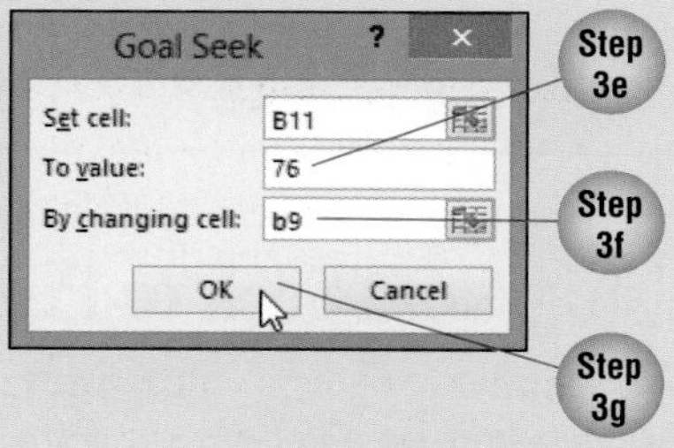

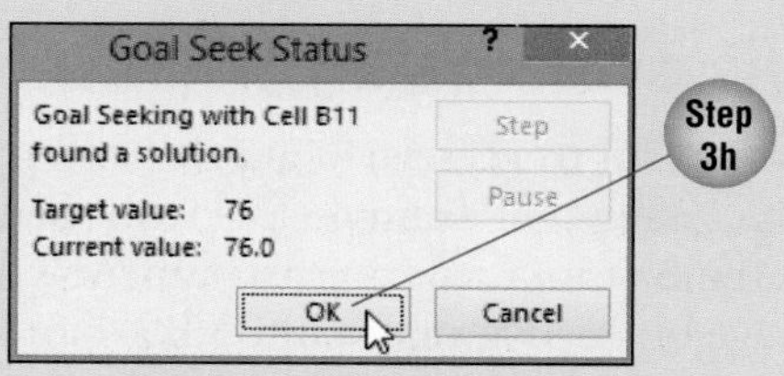

4. Notice that Excel entered the value *81.5* in cell B9. This is the score Whitney must earn to achieve a final average grade of 76%.
5. Assume that Whitney wants to achieve a final average grade of 80%. Use Goal Seek to find the score she will need to earn on the final test to accomplish the new target by completing the following steps:
   a. Click the What-If Analysis button in the Data Tools group and then click *Goal Seek* at the drop-down list.
   b. Click in the *To value* text box, type 80, and then press Tab.
   c. Type b9 in the *By changing cell* text box.
   d. Click OK.

e. Notice that the value entered in cell B9 is *101.5*. This is the score that Excel has calculated Whitney needs on the final test to earn an 80% average grade.

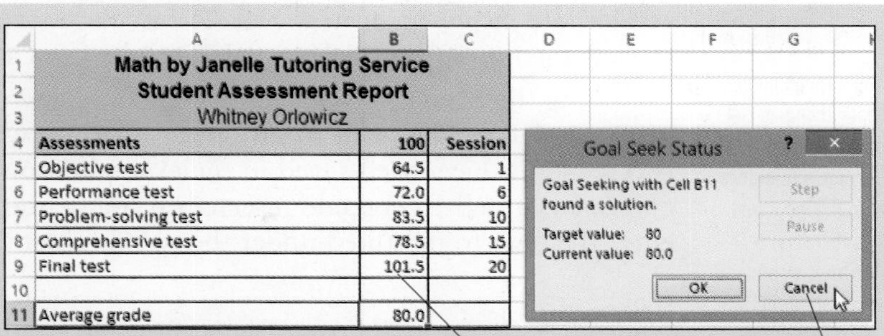

f. The final test is worth only 100, so Whitney will not be able to score 101.5. Restore the previous values in the report by clicking the Cancel button at the Goal Seek Status dialog box.

6. Save, print, and then close **EL2-C5-P2-JTutorOrlowiczRpt.xlsx**.

Project 3 Forecast a Budget Based on Various Inflation Rates — 3 Parts

You will determine how various rates of inflation impact a department's budget to determine the funding request to present to management to maintain service.

Creating Assumptions for What-If Analysis Using the Scenario Manager

The ***Scenario Manager*** allows you to store multiple sets of assumptions about data and then view how each set of assumptions affects your worksheet. You can switch the display between scenarios to test the various inputs on your worksheet model. You can also save each scenario using a descriptive name, such as *BestCase* or *WorstCase*, to indicate the type of data assumptions you have stored in it.

Examine the worksheet shown in Figure 5.4. In this worksheet, the Computing Services department budget for the next year has been calculated based on projected percentage increases for various expense items. Assume that the department manager has more than one estimate of the percentages based on different inflation rates or

Quick Steps

Add a Scenario

1. Click DATA tab.
2. Click What-If Analysis button.
3. Click *Scenario Manager*.
4. Click Add button.
5. Type name in *Scenario name* text box.
6. Type or select variable cells in *Changing cells* text box.
7. Click OK.
8. Enter value for each changing cell.
9. Click OK.
10. Click Close button.

Figure 5.4 Project 3 Worksheet

	A	B	C	D
1	National Online Marketing Inc.			
2	Computing Services Department			
3		Current budget	Projected increase	New budget
4	Wages and benefits	371,875	13,016	384,891
5	Computer supplies	150,350	2,255	152,605
6	Training and development	63,850	6,385	70,235
7	Other administrative costs	49,576	2,479	52,055
8	Total costs:	635,651		659,786

HINT
Create a range name for each changing cell. This allows you to see a descriptive reference next to the input text box, rather than a cell address, when adding a scenario.

vendor rate increases for next year. The manager can create and save various scenarios to view the impact on total costs that results from a combination of different forecasts.

Using the Scenario Manager dialog box, shown in Figure 5.5, you can create as many models as you want to save to test various what-if conditions. For example, two scenarios have been saved in the example shown in Figure 5.5: *LowInflation* and *HighInflation*. When you add a scenario, you define which cells will change and then enter the data to be stored under the scenario name.

Figure 5.5 Scenario Manager Dialog Box and Scenario Values Dialog Box

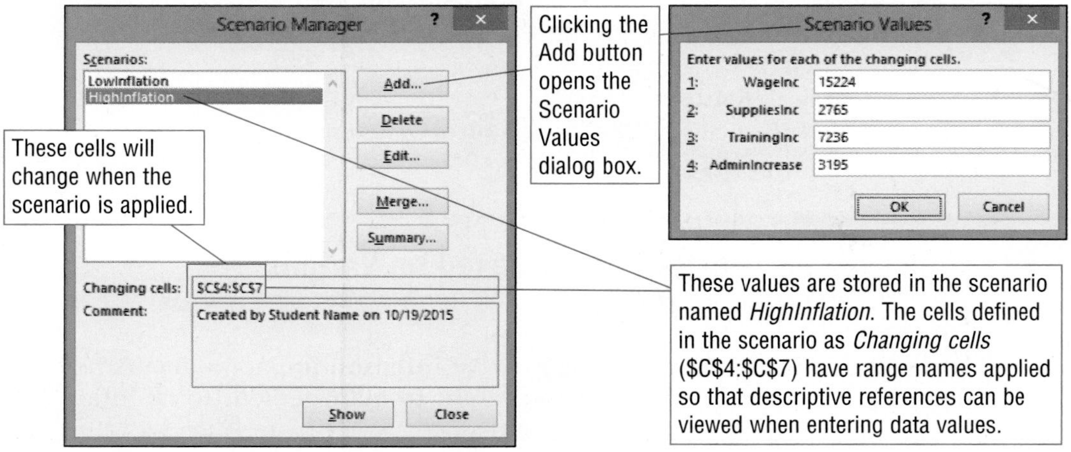

Project 3a Adding Scenarios to a Worksheet Model — Part 1 of 3

1. Open **NationalBdgt.xlsx**.
2. Save the workbook and name it **EL2-C5-P3-NationalBdgt**.
3. View the range names already created in the worksheet by clicking the down-pointing arrow at the right of the Name box and then clicking *WageInc* at the drop-down list. Cell C4 becomes active. A range name has been created for each data cell in column C so that a descriptive label displays when you add scenarios in Steps 4 and 5.
4. Add a scenario with values assuming a low inflation rate for next year by completing the following steps:
   a. Click the DATA tab.
   b. Click the What-If Analysis button in the Data Tools group and then click *Scenario Manager* at the drop-down list.
   c. Click the Add button at the Scenario Manager dialog box.
   d. At the Add Scenario dialog box with the insertion point positioned in the *Scenario name* text box, type LowInflation and then press Tab.
   e. Type c4:c7 in the *Changing cells* text box and then press Enter or click OK. (As an alternative, you can move the dialog box out of the way and select the cells that will change in the worksheet.)

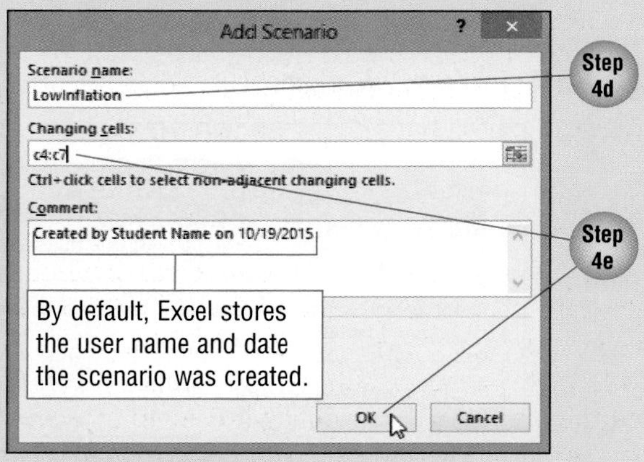

f. With the insertion point positioned in the *1: WageInc* text box, type 12010 and then press Tab.
g. Type 2150 and then press Tab.
h. Type 5276 and then press Tab.
i. Type 1998 and then press Enter or click OK.

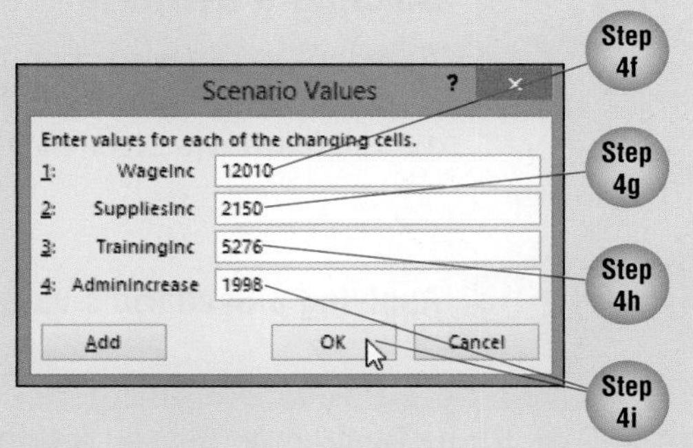

5. Add another scenario that assumes a high inflation rate to the worksheet by completing the following steps:
   a. Click the Add button at the Scenario Manager dialog box.
   b. Type HighInflation in the *Scenario name* text box and then click OK. Notice that the *Changing cells* text box already contains the range C4:C7.
   c. At the Scenario Values dialog box, type the following values into the text boxes indicated:
      1: WageInc 15224
      2: SuppliesInc 2765
      3: TrainingInc 7236
      4: AdminIncrease 3195
   d. Click OK.

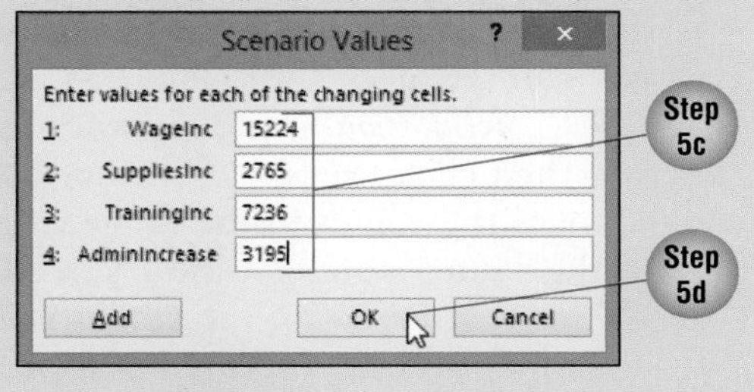

6. Add a third scenario, named *OriginalForecast*, that contains the original worksheet values by completing the following steps:
   a. Click the Add button at the Scenario Manager dialog box.
   b. Type OriginalForecast in the *Scenario name* text box and then click OK.
   c. At the Scenario Values dialog box, notice that the original values are already entered in each text box. Click OK.
7. Click the Close button to close the Scenario Manager dialog box.
8. Save **EL2-C5-P3-NationalBdgt.xlsx**.

Applying a Scenario

After you have created the various scenarios you want to save with the worksheet, you can apply the values stored in each scenario to the variable cells to view the effects on your worksheet model. To do this, open the Scenario Manager dialog box, click the name of the scenario that contains the values you want to apply to the worksheet, and then click the Show button. Generally, the first scenario you create should contain the original values in the worksheet, since Excel replaces the content of each changing cell when you show a scenario.

Quick Steps

Apply a Scenario
1. Click DATA tab.
2. Click What-If Analysis button.
3. Click *Scenario Manager* at drop-down list.
4. Click desired scenario name.
5. Click Show button.
6. Click Close button.

Editing a Scenario

You can change the values associated with a scenario by opening the Scenario Manager dialog box, clicking the name of the scenario that contains the values you want to change, and then clicking the Edit button. At the Edit Scenario dialog box, make any desired changes to the scenario name and/or changing cells and then click OK to open the Scenario Values dialog box to edit the individual value associated with each changing cell. When you have finished editing, click OK and then click Close.

Deleting a Scenario

To delete a scenario, open the Scenario Manager dialog box, click the scenario you want to remove, and then click the Delete button. Click the Close button to close the Scenario Manager dialog box.

Project 3b **Applying a Scenario's Values to a Worksheet** **Part 2 of 3**

1. With **EL2-C5-P3-NationalBdgt.xlsx** open, apply the scenario that assumes the low inflation rate by completing the following steps:
   a. With DATA as the active tab, click the What-If Analysis button and then click *Scenario Manager* at the drop-down list.
   b. If necessary, drag the Scenario Manager dialog box to the right of the worksheet so you can see all of the values in Column D.
   c. Click *LowInflation* in the *Scenarios* list box and then click the Show button. Excel changes the values in the range C4:C7 to the values stored within the scenario. Notice that based on the assumption of a low inflation rate, the total cost of the new budget shown in cell D8 is $657,085.
2. With the Scenario Manager dialog box still open, change the worksheet to display the scenario that assumes a high inflation rate by clicking *HighInflation* in the *Scenarios* list box and then clicking the Show button. Notice that in this high-inflation scenario, the total cost of the new budget is $664,071.

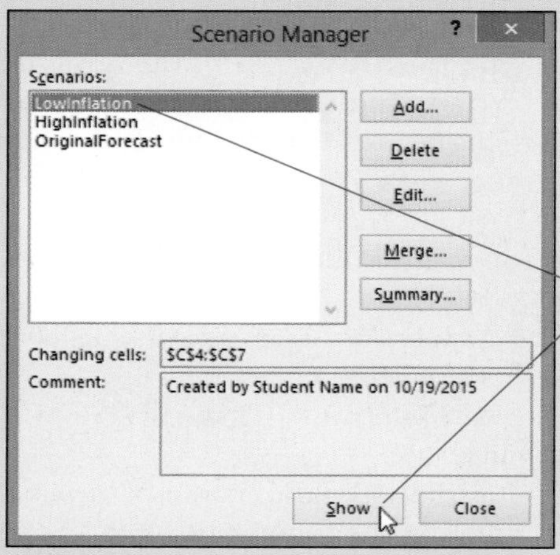

Step 1c

	A	B	C	D
1	National Online Marketing Inc.			
2	Computing Services Department			
3		Current budget	Projected increase	New budget
4	Wages and benefits	371,875	15,224	387,099
5	Computer supplies	150,350	2,765	153,115
6	Training and development	63,850	7,236	71,086
7	Other administrative costs	49,576	3,195	52,771
8	Total costs:	**635,651**		**664,071**

Excel displays the worksheet with the high inflation values applied in Step 2.

3. Show the worksheet with the data values from the *OriginalForecast* scenario.
4. Click the Close button to close the Scenario Manager dialog box.
5. Save **EL2-C5-P3-NationalBdgt.xlsx**.

Compiling a Scenario Summary Report

You can create a scenario summary report to compare scenarios side by side in a worksheet or PivotTable. At the Scenario Summary dialog box, shown in Figure 5.6, enter in the *Result cells* text box the formula cell or cells that change when you apply the data in various scenarios. Enter multiple cell addresses in this text box and use commas to separate them.

Quick Steps

Create a Scenario Summary Report
1. Click DATA tab.
2. Click What-If Analysis button.
3. Click *Scenario Manager*.
4. Click Summary button.
5. If necessary, change cell address in *Result cells* text box.
6. Click OK.

Figure 5.6 Scenario Summary Dialog Box

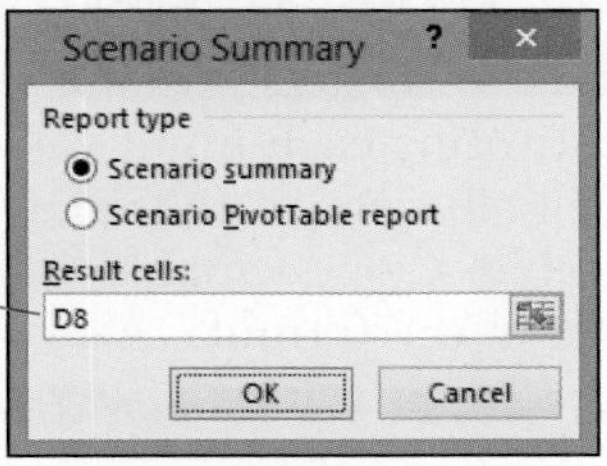

Enter the address of the cell containing the total or other formula results impacted by the changing cells in each scenario. Enter multiple results cell addresses separated by commas.

Project 3c **Generating a Scenario Summary Report** **Part 3 of 3**

1. With **EL2-C5-P3-NationalBdgt.xlsx** open, display a scenario summary report by completing the following steps:
   a. With DATA the active tab, click the What-If Analysis button and then click *Scenario Manager* at the drop-down list.
   b. Click the Summary button at the Scenario Manager dialog box.
   c. At the Scenario Summary dialog box, with the *Report type* set to *Scenario summary* and *Result cells* displaying the address *D8*, click OK.

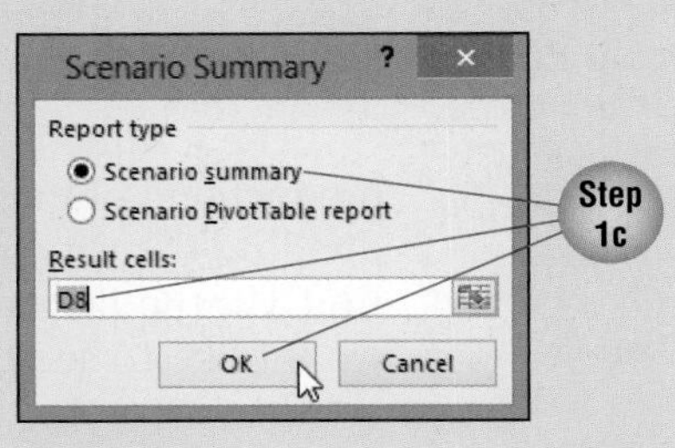

2. Examine the Scenario Summary sheet added to the workbook. It displays each changing cell with the input for each scenario. Below the Changing Cells table, Excel displays the Result Cells, providing the value that results from each scenario's input.

In Step 2, Excel displays the Scenario Summary worksheet created in Step 1.

Scenario Summary	Current Values:	LowInflation	HighInflation	OriginalForecast
Changing Cells:				
WageInc	13,016	12,010	15,224	13,016
SuppliesInc	2,255	2,150	2,765	2,255
TrainingInc	6,385	5,276	7,236	6,385
AdminIncrease	2,479	1,998	3,195	2,479
Result Cells:				
TotalNewCosts	659,786	657,085	664,071	659,786

Notes: Current Values column represents values of changing cells at time Scenario Summary Report was created. Changing cells for each scenario are highlighted in gray.

3. Print the Scenario Summary worksheet.
4. Save and then close **EL2-C5-P3-NationalBdgt.xlsx**.

Project 4 Compare the Impacts of Various Inputs Related to Cost and Sales Pricing — 2 Parts

Using one-variable and two-variable data tables, you will analyze the impact on the cost per unit and selling price per unit of a manufactured container.

Performing What-If Analysis Using Data Tables

A ***data table*** is a range of cells that contains a series of input values. Excel calculates a formula substituting each input value in the data table range and places the result in the cell adjacent to the value. You can create a one-variable or a two-variable data table. A one-variable data table calculates a formula by modifying one input value in the formula. A two-variable data table calculates a formula substituting two input values. Using data tables provides a means to analyze various outcomes in a calculation that occur as a result of changing a dependent value without creating multiple formulas.

Quick Steps

Create a One-Variable Data Table

1. Create variable data in column at right of worksheet.
2. Enter formula one row above and one cell right of variable data.
3. Select data range, including formula cell.
4. Click DATA tab.
5. Click What-If Analysis button.
6. Click *Data Table.*
7. Type cell address for variable data in source formula in *Column input cell* text box.
8. Press Enter or click OK.

Creating a One-Variable Data Table

Design a one-variable data table with the variable input data values in a series down a column or across a row. Examine the worksheet shown in Figure 5.7. Assume that management wants to calculate the effects on the cost per unit for a variety of production volumes given a standard set of costs per factory shift. The worksheet includes the total costs for direct materials, direct labor, and overhead.

The formula in cell B8 sums the three cost categories. Based on a standard production volume of 500,000 units, the cost per unit is $3.21, calculated by dividing the total cost by the production volume (cell B8 divided by cell B10). In E6:E12, the factory manager has input varying levels of production. The manager would like to see the change in the cost per unit for each level of production volume, assuming the costs remain the same. In Project 4a, you will use a data table to show the various costs. This data table will manipulate one input value—production volume—so the table is a one-variable data table.

Figure 5.7 Project 4a One-Variable Data Table

	A	B	C	D	E	F	G	H
1	Precision Design and Packaging							
2	Cost Price Analysis							
3	"E" Container Bulk Cargo Box							
4	Factory costs per shift				Variable unit production impact on cost			
5	Direct materials	$ 580,000						
6	Direct labor	880,552			425,000			
7	Overhead	145,350			450,000			
8	Total cost	$ 1,605,902			475,000			
9					500,000			
10	Standard production	500,000	units		525,000			
11					550,000			
12	Cost per unit	$ 3.21			575,000			

In this area of the worksheet, you can calculate the change in cost per unit based on varying the production volume using a data table.

Project 4a Creating a One-Variable Data Table

Part 1 of 2

1. Open **PreEBoxCost.xlsx**.
2. Save the workbook and name it **EL2-C5-P4-PreEBoxCost**.
3. Calculate the cost per unit for seven different production levels using a one-variable data table by completing the following steps:
   a. A data table requires that the formula for calculating the various outcomes be placed in the cell in the first row above and one column right of the table values. The data table values have been entered in E6:E12; therefore, make cell F5 active.
   b. The formula that calculates the cost per unit is =B8/B10. This formula has already been entered in cell B12. Link to the source formula by typing =b12 and then pressing Enter.

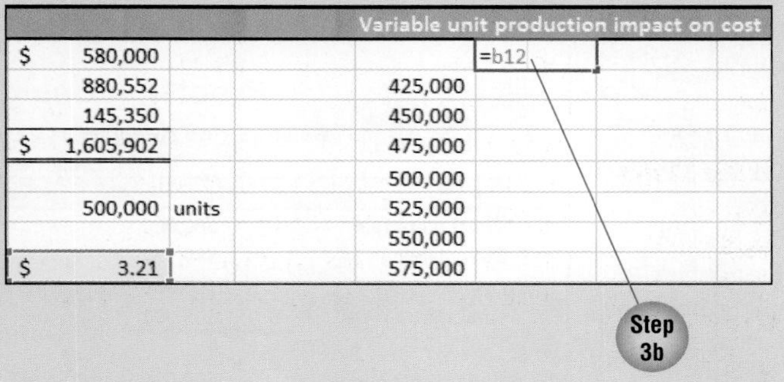

   c. Select E5:F12.
   d. Click the DATA tab.
   e. Click the What-If Analysis button and then click *Data Table* at the drop-down list.

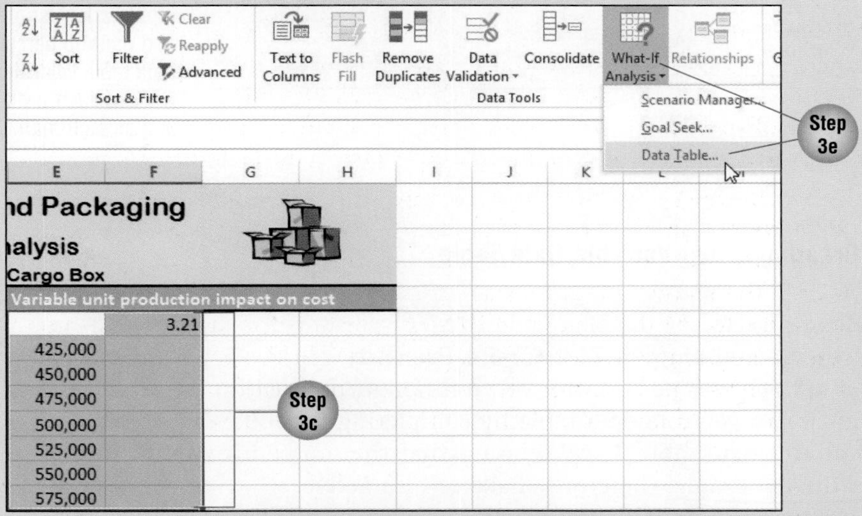

   f. At the Data Table dialog box, click in the *Column input cell* text box, type b10, and then press Enter or click OK. At the Data Table dialog box, Excel needs to know which reference in the source formula is the address for which the variable data is to be inserted. (The production volume is cell B10 in the source formula.)

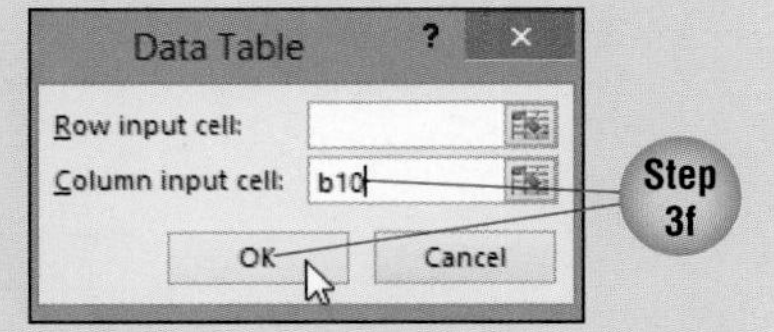

   g. Click in any cell to deselect the range.
4. Print the worksheet.
5. Save and then close **EL2-C5-P4-PreEBoxCost.xlsx**.

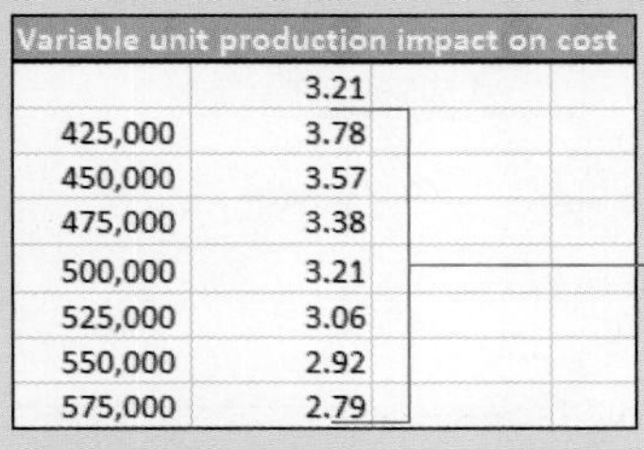

The data table calculates costs at each production volume. Notice the costs are higher at lower volumes and decrease as production volume increases.

Creating a Two-Variable Data Table

Quick Steps

Create a Two-Variable Data Table

1. Create variable data at right of worksheet with one input series in column and another in row across top of table.
2. Enter formula in top left cell of table.
3. Select data table range.
4. Click DATA tab.
5. Click What-If Analysis button.
6. Click *Data Table.*
7. Type cell address for variable data in source formula in *Row input cell* text box.
8. Press Tab.
9. Type cell address for variable data in source formula in *Column input cell* text box.
10. Press Enter or click OK.

A data table can substitute two variables in a source formula. To modify two input cells, design the data table with a column along the left containing one set of variable input values and a row along the top containing the second set of variable input values. In a two-variable data table, the source formula is placed at the top left cell in the table. In the worksheet shown in Figure 5.8, the source formula will be inserted in cell E5, which is the top left cell in the data table.

Figure 5.8 Project 4b Two-Variable Data Table

	A	B	C	D	E	F	G	H
1	Precision Design and Packaging							
2	Selling Price Analysis at Variable Production and Markups							
3	"E" Container Bulk Cargo Box							
4	Factory costs per shift				Variable unit production impact on sell price			
5	Direct materials	$ 580,000				50%	52%	55%
6	Direct labor	880,552			425,000			
7	Overhead	145,350			450,000			
8	Total cost	$ 1,605,902			475,000			
9					500,000			
10	Standard production	500,000	units		525,000			
11					550,000			
12	Cost per unit	$ 3.21			575,000			
13	Markup	52%						
14	Selling price per unit	$ 4.88						

This data table contains two input variables: production units and markup percentage. The data table will calculate a selling price at each production volume and at each markup percentage.

Project 4b Creating a Two-Variable Data Table — Part 2 of 2

1. Open **PreEBoxSell.xlsx.**
2. Save the workbook and name it **EL2-C5-P4-PreEBoxSell.**
3. Calculate the selling price per unit for seven different production levels and three different markups using a two-variable data table by completing the following steps:
   a. In a two-variable data table, Excel requires that the source formula be placed in the top left cell in the data table; therefore, make cell E5 active.
   b. Type **=b14** and press Enter. The formula that you want Excel to use to create the data table is in cell B14. The selling price per unit found in cell B14 is calculated by adding the cost per unit (cell B12) to the result of multiplying the cost per unit (cell B12) by the markup (cell B13).

			Variable unit
$ 580,000			=b14
880,552			425,000
145,350			450,000
$ 1,605,902			475,000
			500,000
500,000	units		525,000
			550,000
$ 3.21			575,000
52%			
$ 4.88			

Step 3b

c. Select E5:H12.
d. Click the DATA tab.
e. Click the What-If Analysis button and then click *Data Table* at the drop-down list.
f. At the Data Table dialog box with the insertion point positioned in the *Row input cell* text box, type **b13** and press Tab. Excel needs to know which reference in the source formula is the address relating to the variable data in the first row of the data table. (The markup value is in cell B13 in the source formula.)
g. Type **b10** in the *Column input cell* text box and then press Enter or click OK. As in Project 4a, Excel needs to know which reference relates to the production volume in the source formula.
h. Click in any cell to deselect the range.

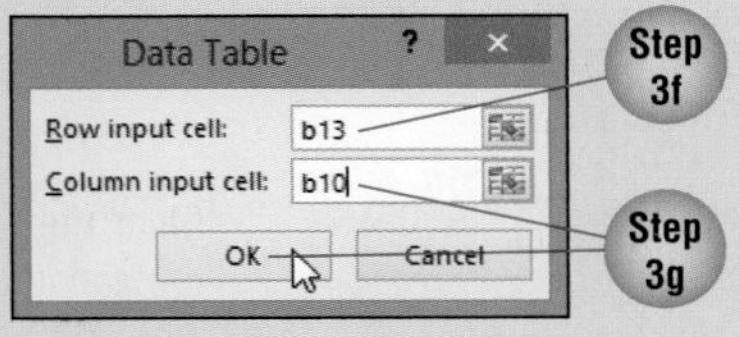

Variable unit production impact on sell price			
$ 4.88	50%	52%	55%
425,000	5.67	5.74	5.86
450,000	5.35	5.42	5.53
475,000	5.07	5.14	5.24
500,000	4.82	4.88	4.98
525,000	4.59	4.65	4.74
550,000	4.38	4.44	4.53
575,000	4.19	4.25	4.33

Selling prices are calculated by the data table at each production volume and each percentage markup.

4. Print the worksheet.
5. Save and then close **EL2-C5-P4-PreEBoxSell.xlsx**.

Project 5 Audit a Worksheet to View and Troubleshoot Formulas — 3 Parts

You will use buttons in the Formula Auditing group to view relationships between cells that comprise a formula, identify error codes in a worksheet, and troubleshoot errors using error checking tools.

Using Auditing Tools

The Formula Auditing group on the FORMULAS tab, shown in Figure 5.9, contains buttons that are useful for viewing relationships between cells in formulas. Checking a formula for accuracy can be difficult when the formula is part of a complex sequence of operations. Opening a worksheet created by someone else can also present a challenge in understanding the relationships between sets of data. When Excel displays an error message in a cell, viewing the relationships between the dependencies of cells assists with finding the source of the error.

Figure 5.9 Formula Auditing Group on FORMULAS Tab

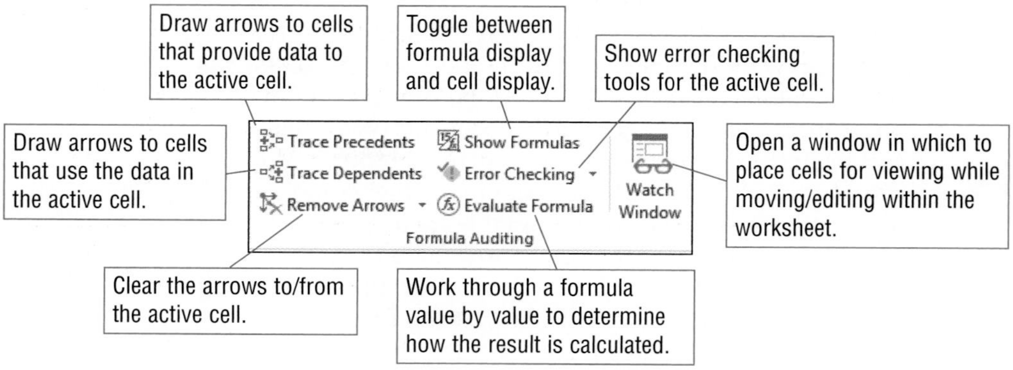

Quick Steps

Trace Precedent Cells
1. Open worksheet.
2. Make desired cell active.
3. Click FORMULAS tab.
4. Click Trace Precedents button.
5. Continue clicking until all relationships are visible.

Trace Dependent Cells
1. Open worksheet.
2. Make desired cell active.
3. Click FORMULAS tab.
4. Click Trace Dependents button.
5. Continue clicking until all relationships are visible.

Trace Dependents

Remove Arrows

Show Formulas

Tracing Precedent and Dependent Cells

Precedent cells are cells that provide data to a formula cell. For example, if cell B3 contains the formula =B1+B2, then cell B1 and cell B2 are precedent cells. ***Dependent cells*** are cells that contain a formula that refers to other cells. In the previous example, cell B3 is the dependent cell to cells B1 and B2, since cell B3 relies on the data from cells B1 and B2. Click a cell and click the Trace Precedents button to draw tracer arrows that show direct relationships to cell(s) that provide data to the active cell. Click the button a second time to show indirect relationships to cell(s) that provide data to the active cell at the next level. Continue clicking the button until no further arrows are drawn. Excel will sound a beep when you click the button if no more relationships exist.

Click a cell and click the Trace Dependents button to draw tracer arrows that show direct relationships to other cell(s) in the worksheet that use the active cell's contents. As with the Trace Precedents button, click a second time to show the next level of indirect relationships and continue clicking the button until no further tracer arrows are drawn.

Excel draws blue tracer arrows if no error is detected in the active cell and red tracer arrows if an error condition is detected within the active cell.

Project 5a **Viewing Relationships between Cells and Formulas** **Part 1 of 3**

1. Open **EL2-C5-P4-PreEBoxSell.xlsx.**
2. View relationships between cells and formulas by displaying tracer arrows between cells by completing the following steps:
   a. Make cell B8 active.
   b. Click the FORMULAS tab.
   c. Click the Trace Precedents button in the Formula Auditing group. Excel draws a blue tracer arrow that shows the cells that provide data to cell B8.
   d. Click the Remove Arrows button in the Formula Auditing group. The blue tracer arrow leading to cell B8 is cleared.
   e. Make cell B14 active.

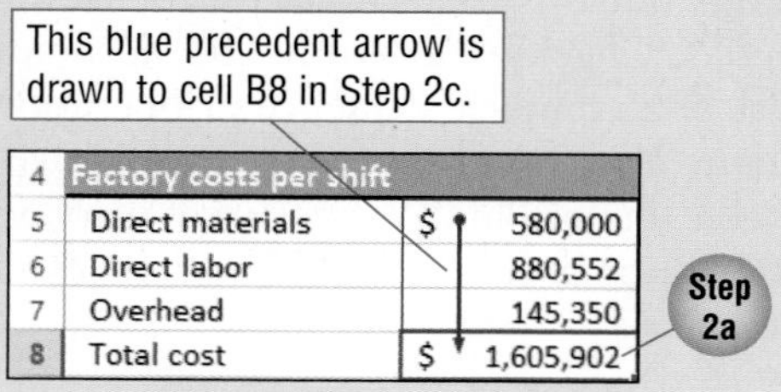

f. Click the Trace Precedents button.
g. Click the Trace Precedents button a second time to show the next level of cells that provide data to cell B14.
h. Click the Trace Dependents button to view cell(s) dependent on cell B14.

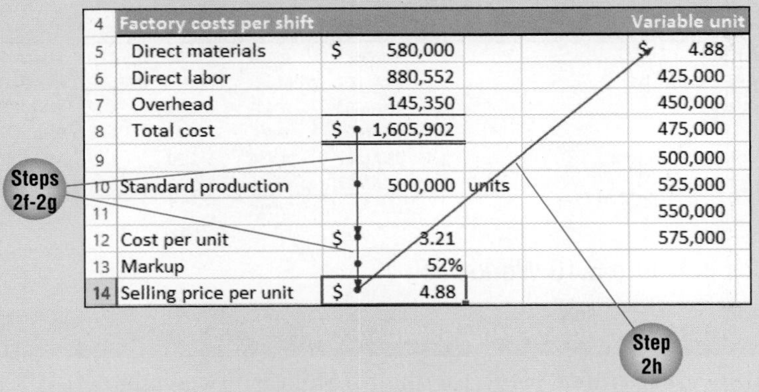

3. Click the Remove Arrows button to clear all of the arrows.
4. Click the Show Formulas button to display cell formulas. Click the Show Formulas button again to turn off the display of formulas.
5. Close **EL2-C5-P4-PreEBoxSell.xlsx**. Click Don't Save when prompted to save changes.

Troubleshooting Formulas

Formulas in Excel can contain various types of errors. Some errors are obvious because Excel displays an error message such as *#VALUE!*. Other errors can occur that do not display error messages but are incorrect because the logic is flawed. For example, you could enter a formula in a cell that Excel does not flag as an error because the syntax is correct; however, the calculation could be incorrect for the data and the situation. Logic errors are difficult to find and require that you check a worksheet by entering proof formulas or by manually checking the accuracy of each formula.

A ***proof formula*** is a formula entered outside the main worksheet area that checks key figures within the worksheet. For example, in a payroll worksheet, a proof formula to check the total net pay column could add the total net pay to the totals of all of the deduction columns. The total displayed should be equal to the total gross pay amount in the worksheet.

Excel displays an error message code in a cell that is detected to have an error. Two types of error flags can occur. A green diagonal triangle in the upper left corner of a cell indicates an error condition. Activate the cell and an error checking button displays that you can use to access error checking tools. Errors can also be indicated with text entries, such as *#NAME?*. Figure 5.10 displays a portion of the worksheet you will use in Project 5b to troubleshoot errors. Table 5.1 describes the three error codes displayed in Figure 5.10.

Quick Steps

Trace Errors
1. Click cell containing error message.
2. Click FORMULAS tab.
3. Click down-pointing arrow on Error Checking button.
4. Click *Trace Error*.

HINT

Reference errors can also occur—for instance, when the formula uses correct syntax and logic but refers to the wrong data. These errors are difficult to find and only a thorough review and test of key figures will reveal their existence.

Figure 5.10 Project 5b Partial Worksheet

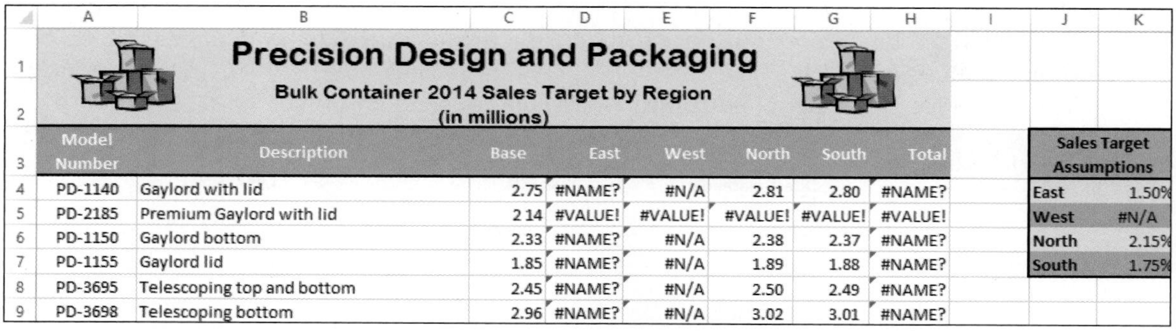

	A	B	C	D	E	F	G	H	I	J	K
1	Precision Design and Packaging										
2	Bulk Container 2014 Sales Target by Region (in millions)										
3	Model Number	Description	Base	East	West	North	South	Total		Sales Target Assumptions	
4	PD-1140	Gaylord with lid	2.75	#NAME?	#N/A	2.81	2.80	#NAME?		East	1.50%
5	PD-2185	Premium Gaylord with lid	2.14	#VALUE!	#VALUE!	#VALUE!	#VALUE!	#VALUE!		West	#N/A
6	PD-1150	Gaylord bottom	2.33	#NAME?	#N/A	2.38	2.37	#NAME?		North	2.15%
7	PD-1155	Gaylord lid	1.85	#NAME?	#N/A	1.89	1.88	#NAME?		South	1.75%
8	PD-3695	Telescoping top and bottom	2.45	#NAME?	#N/A	2.50	2.49	#NAME?			
9	PD-3698	Telescoping bottom	2.96	#NAME?	#N/A	3.02	3.01	#NAME?			

Table 5.1 Error Codes in Figure 5.10 Worksheet

Error Code	*Description of Error Condition*
#N/A	A required value for the formula is not available.
#NAME?	The formula contains an unrecognized entry.
#VALUE!	A value within the formula is of the wrong type or otherwise invalid.

Error Checking

Evaluate Formula

The Error Checking button in the Formula Auditing group can be used to assist with finding the source of an error condition in a cell by displaying the Error Checking dialog box or drawing a red tracer arrow to locate the source cell that is contributing to the error. The Evaluate Formula button can be used to work through a formula value by value to determine the position within the formula where an error exists.

Project 5b Troubleshooting Formulas — Part 2 of 3

1. Open **PreSalesTrgt.xlsx**.
2. Save the workbook and name it **EL2-C5-P5-PreSalesTrgt**.
3. Solve the #N/A error by completing the following steps:
   a. Make cell E4 active.
   b. Point to the Trace Error button that displays next to the cell and read the ScreenTip that displays below the button.
   c. Look in the Formula bar at the formula that has been entered into the cell. Notice that the formula includes a reference to a named cell. You decide to use the tracer arrows to locate the source of the named cell.

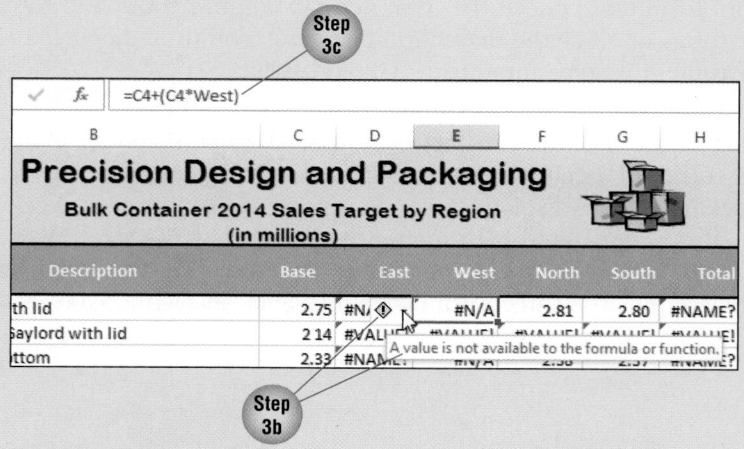

d. Click the down-pointing arrow to the right of the Error Checking button in the Formula Auditing group on the FORMULAS tab and then click *Trace Error* at the drop-down list.

e. Excel moves the active cell to K5 and draws a red tracer arrow from cell K5 to cell E4. Look in the Formula bar and notice that *#N/A* displays as the entry in cell K5. Also notice the cell name *West* displayed in the Name box. Since a value does not exist in the cell named *West*, which is cell K5, the dependent cell E4 was not able to calculate its formula.

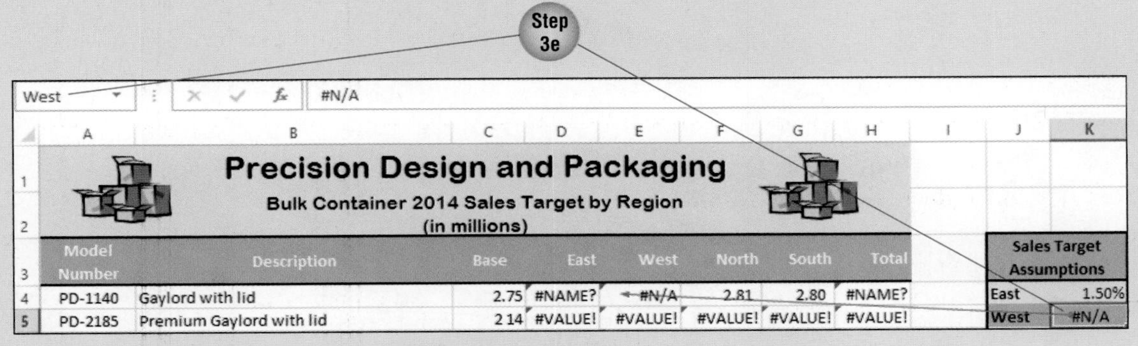

f. With cell K5 active, type 1.25% and press Enter. The red tracer arrow changes to blue now that the error is corrected and the #N/A error messages have disappeared.

g. Click the Remove Arrows button to clear the blue tracer arrow and then right-align the entry in cell K5.

4. Solve the #NAME? error by completing the following steps:

a. Make cell D4 active, point to the Trace Error button that appears, and then read the ScreenTip that appears. The message indicates that the formula contains unrecognized text.

b. Look at the entry in the Formula bar: *=C4+(C4*East)*. Notice the formula is the same as the formula you reviewed in Step 3c except that the named range is *East* instead of *West*. The formula appears to be valid.

c. Click the down-pointing arrow to the right of the Name box and view the range names in the drop-down list. Notice that a range named *East* is not in the list.

d. Click *North* at the Name box drop-down list. Cell K6 becomes the active cell. You know from this step and Step 3d that the named ranges should reference the percentage values within column K.

e. Make cell K4 active, type East in the Name box, and press Enter. The #NAME? error is resolved.

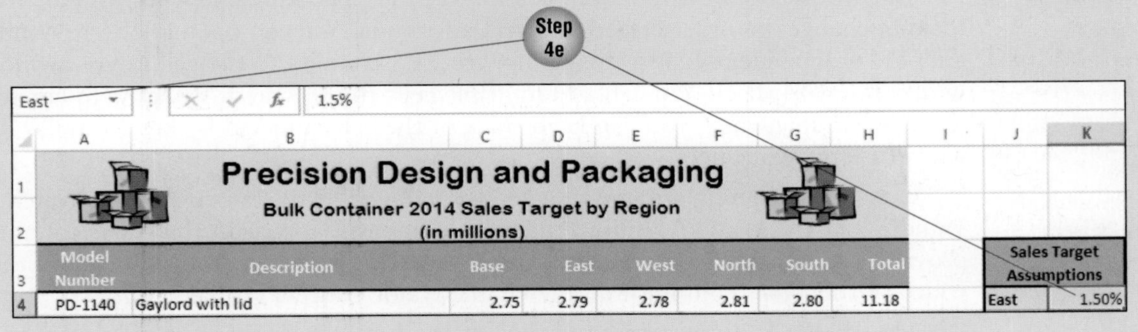

5. Solve the #VALUE! error by completing the following steps:

a. Make cell D5 active, point to the Trace Error button that appears, and then read the ScreenTip that appears. The message indicates that a value within the formula is of the wrong data type.

b. Click the Trace Precedents button in the Formula Auditing group on the FORMULAS tab to display tracer arrows showing the source cells that provide data to cell D5. Two blue arrows appear, indicating that two cells provide the source values: cells K4 and C5.
c. Make cell K4 active and look at the entry in the Formula bar: *1.5%*. This value is valid.
d. Make cell C5 active and look at the entry in the Formula bar: *2 14*. Notice there is a space instead of a decimal point between *2* and *1*.

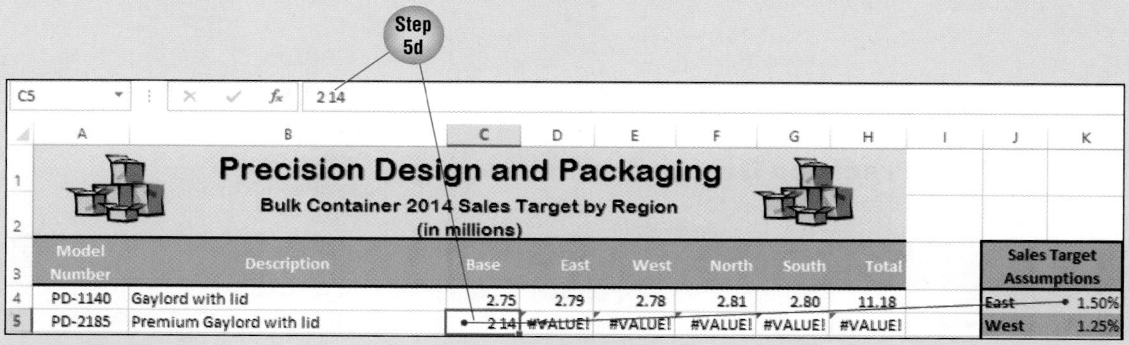

e. Click in the Formula bar and then edit the formula to delete the space between *2* and *1* and type a period (inserting a decimal point). Press Enter. The #VALUE! error is resolved.
f. Click the Remove Arrows button to clear the blue tracer arrows.

6. Save **EL2-C5-P5-PreSalesTrgt.xlsx**.

Quick Steps

Circle Invalid Data
1. Open worksheet containing validation rules.
2. Click DATA tab.
3. Click Data Validation button arrow.
4. Click *Circle Invalid Data*.

Watch a Formula Cell
1. Click FORMULAS tab.
2. Click Watch Window button.
3. Click Add Watch button.
4. Click desired cell.
5. Click Add button.

Watch Window

Data Validation

Circling Invalid Data

Recall from Chapter 3 that Data Validation is a feature used to restrict cell entries. If data validation rules are set up after data has been entered, existing values will not be tested against the new rules. In this situation, you can use the Circle Invalid Data feature, which draws red circles around the cells that do not conform to the new rule.

Watching a Formula Cell

In a large worksheet, a dependent cell may not always be visible while you are making changes to other cells that affect a formula. You can open a Watch Window and add a dependent cell to the window to view changes to the cell as you work within the worksheet. You can add multiple cells to the Watch Window to create a single window where you can keep track of the cells affected by key formulas within a large worksheet.

Consider assigning a name to a cell that you want to track using the Watch Window. At the Watch Window, the cell's name will appear in the *Name* column, providing a descriptive reference to the entry being watched. You can expand the width of the *Name* column if a range name is not entirely visible.

The Watch Window can be docked at the top, left, bottom, or right edge of the worksheet area by clicking the top edge of the window and dragging it to the desired edge of the screen. When the Watch Window is docked, Excel changes it to a Watch Window task pane.

Project 5c Circling Invalid Data and Watching a Formula Cell

Part 3 of 3

1. With **EL2-C5-P5-PreSalesTrgt.xlsx** open, view the Data Validation rule in effect for column C by completing the following steps:
   a. If necessary, make any cell containing a value in column C active.
   b. Click the DATA tab.
   c. Click the top of the Data Validation button in the Data Tools group. (Do not click the down-pointing arrow on the button.) The Data Validation dialog box opens.
   d. Review the parameters for data entry in the Settings tab. Notice the restriction is that values should be greater than or equal to 1.57.
   e. Click OK.

2. Click the Data Validation button arrow and then click *Circle Invalid Data* at the drop-down list. Three cells are circled in the worksheet: C11, C13, and C16.

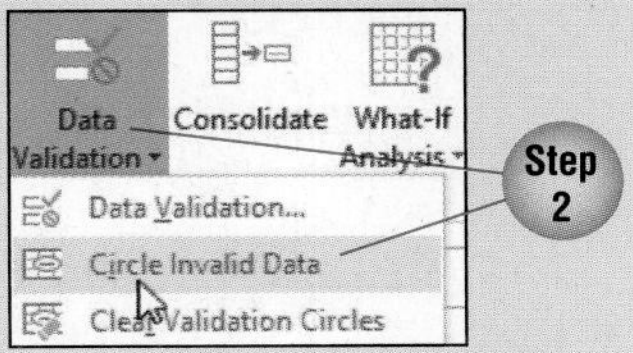

3. Watch the total in cell H22 update as you correct the invalid data by completing the following steps:
   a. Make cell H22 active and then click the FORMULAS tab.
   b. Click the Watch Window button in the Formula Auditing group. A Watch Window opens.
   c. Click the Add Watch button in the Watch Window.
   d. At the Add Watch dialog box, move the dialog box out of the way if necessary to view cell H22. Notice that cell H22 is entered by default as the watch cell. Click the Add button.

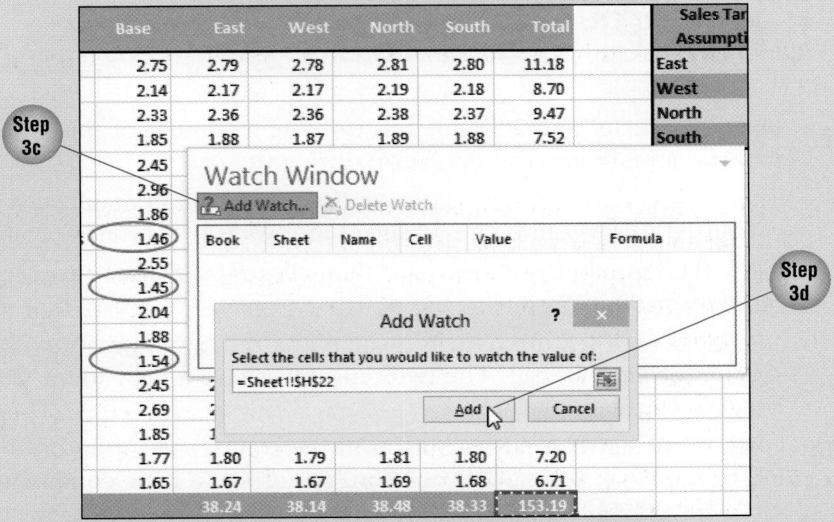

   e. Scroll up the worksheet if necessary until you can view cell C11. If necessary, drag the Watch Window to an out-of-the-way location in the worksheet.
   f. Make cell C11 active, type 1.58, and press Enter. Notice that the red circle disappears, since you have now entered a value that conforms to the validation rule. Look at the value for cell H22 in the Watch Window. The new value is *153.67*.

g. Make cell C13 the active cell, type 1.61, and then press Enter. Look at the updated value for cell H22 in the Watch Window.

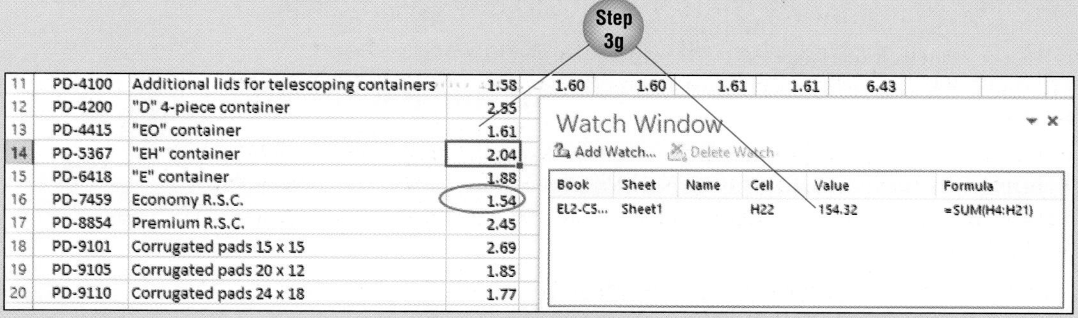

h. Make cell C16 active, type 1.57, and press Enter.

i. Click the Watch Window button in the Formula Auditing group on the FORMULAS tab to close the Watch Window.

4. Print the worksheet.
5. Save and then close **EL2-C5-P5-PreSalesTrgt.xlsx**.

Checking a worksheet for accuracy using auditing and error checking tools is an important skill to develop. Worksheets provide critical information to decision makers who rely on the validity of the data. After completing a worksheet, examine it carefully, looking for data entry mistakes, values that do not appear realistic, and other indications of potential errors that should be fixed.

Chapter Summary

- Open the Paste Special dialog box to paste attributes of the source cell(s) or perform a mathematical operation during the paste.
- Transposing data during a paste routine means that data arranged in columns is converted to rows and data arranged in rows is converted to columns.
- Click the Paste button arrow and then click *Paste Special* to access a gallery of different pasting options.
- The Goal Seek feature returns a value in a cell based on a target value you specify for another cell. The two cells must have a dependent relationship for Excel to calculate a value.
- Click the What-If Analysis button in the Data Tools group on the DATA tab to locate the Goal Seek, Scenario Manager, or Data Table command.
- Scenario Manager allows you to save multiple sets of values for key cells in a worksheet. Switch between scenarios to view the impact of changing the input cells on one of the worksheet's saved data sets.
- A scenario summary report presents the input data for each key cell in a scenario in tabular format with a results cell below each data set displaying the value if the data set is applied.

- A data table is a range of cells containing a series of input values with a calculated formula result adjacent to each input value.
- A one-variable data table modifies one input value within a formula.
- A two-variable data table modifies two input values within a formula.
- Design a one-variable data table with the input values in a columnar arrangement and the formula cell one row above and one column right of the input values.
- Design a two-variable data table with one set of input values in a columnar arrangement and the other set of input values starting in the first column right and first row above the first set of values. Add the formula cell to the top left cell within the input table.
- Buttons in the Formula Auditing group on the FORMULAS tab allow you to view relationships between cells and find and resolve errors.
- Use the Trace Precedents button to draw tracer arrows to cells that feed data into the active cell.
- Use the Trace Dependents button to draw tracer arrows to cells that use data from the active cell.
- Click the Trace Precedents or Trace Dependents button a second time to display an indirect set of relationship arrows at the next level.
- Logic errors occur when the formula is not correct for the data or situation.
- Reference errors occur when a formula points to the wrong data cell.
- Use proof formulas to test the accuracy of key figures in a worksheet. A proof formula is entered outside the main worksheet area and double-checks data within the worksheet.
- Excel displays two types of error flags in a cell in which an error has been detected.
- A green diagonal triangle in the upper left corner of the cell indicates an error is presumed. Click the active cell and use the Trace Error button to access error checking options.
- Error codes within a cell also indicate an error. For example, #NAME? means that the formula contains text that Excel cannot recognize.
- Other error codes include #VALUE!, which means a value within the formula is not valid, and #N/A, which means a value needed by the formula is not available.
- When a worksheet has data validation rules in force, data that existed before the rule was created is not tested. Use the Circle Invalid Data feature from the Data Validation button to place red circles around cells that do not test correct with the new rule.
- A Watch Window is a window that remains visible in the worksheet area while you scroll and edit other parts of a large worksheet. Add cells to the Watch Window that you want to observe while you make changes.
- After completing a worksheet, take time to examine the data carefully for data entry errors and logic errors that can impact the results.

Commands Review

FEATURE	RIBBON TAB, GROUP	BUTTON
circle invalid data	DATA, Data Tools	
data table	DATA, Data Tools	
Goal Seek dialog box	DATA, Data Tools	
Paste Special dialog box	HOME, Clipboard	
remove tracer arrow	FORMULAS, Formula Auditing	
Scenario Manager	DATA, Data Tools	
trace dependent cell	FORMULAS, Formula Auditing	
trace error	FORMULAS, Formula Auditing	
trace precedent cell	FORMULAS, Formula Auditing	
transpose	HOME, Clipboard	
Watch Window	FORMULAS, Formula Auditing	

Concepts Check

Test Your Knowledge SNAP

Completion: In the space provided at the right, indicate the correct term, command, or number.

1. This option from the Paste drop-down gallery converts columns to rows and rows to columns. transpose
2. Open this dialog box to perform a mathematical operation while pasting the copied range to the destination cells. paste special
3. Use this feature if you know the result you want to obtain but are not sure what input value you need to achieve that result. goal seek
4. This feature allows you to store various sets of data for specified cells under a name. scenario manager
5. This report compares various saved data sets side by side so you can view all of the results on one page. scenario summary
6. In a one-variable data table, the source formula is entered at this location within the data table range. one cell above and one column right of input values

7. The Data Table feature is accessed from this button. what if analysis

8. In a two-variable data table, the source formula is entered at this location within the data table range. 3 top left cell

9. Click this button to draw arrows to cells that feed data into the active cell. 2 trace precedents

10. Click this button to draw arrows to cells that use the data in the active cell. 2 trace dependents

11. Use this button in the Formula Auditing group to assist with locating the source cell that is causing an error code. \ error checking

12. This type of formula is entered outside the main worksheet area and used to check key figures within the worksheet. 2 proof formula

13. This error code indicates that a value needed by the formula to calculate the result is not available. 2 ______

14. This type of error occurs when the formula has correct syntax but is not correct for the data or situation. \ syntax error

15. Use this feature to test existing data in a worksheet that has had a new data validation rule created. 3 circle invalid data

Skills Check Assess Your Performance

Assessment

1 CONVERT COLUMNS TO ROWS, ADD SOURCE CELLS TO DESTINATION CELLS, AND FILTER

SNAP Grade It

1. Open **CRC.xlsx**.
2. Save the workbook and name it **EL2-C5-A1-CRC**.
3. Copy A4:F12, select cell A14, and paste the data so the columns become rows and vice versa.
4. Delete rows 4 through 13—the original source data rows from the worksheet.
5. Adjust the merging and centering of the title rows across the top of the worksheet. Apply bold formatting to B4:I4 and AutoFit all of the column widths.
6. Copy the values in the *Shipping* column. Paste the values into the *Total Cost* column using an Add operation so that the total cost now includes the shipping fee.
7. The values in the *Compact* column have a validation rule that you want to duplicate in the *Mid-size* and *SUV* columns. Copy the values in the *Compact* column and paste only the validation rule to the *Mid-size* and *SUV* columns.
8. Save, print, and then close **EL2-C5-A1-CRC.xlsx**.

Assessment

2 USE GOAL SEEK

SNAP Grade It

1. Open **NationalBdgt.xlsx**.
2. Save the workbook and name it **EL2-C5-A2-NationalBdgt**.
3. Make cell D8 the active cell and open the Goal Seek dialog box.
4. Find the projected increase for wages and benefits that will make the total cost of the new budget equal $655,000.
5. Accept the solution Goal Seek calculates.
6. Save, print, and then close **EL2-C5-A2-NationalBdgt.xlsx**.

Assessment

3 USE SCENARIO MANAGER

SNAP Grade It

1. Open **PreCdnTarget.xlsx**.
2. Save the workbook and name it **EL2-C5-A3-PreCdnTarget**.
3. Create scenarios to save various percentage data sets for the four regions using the following information:
   a. A scenario named *OriginalTarget* that stores the current values in K4:K7.
   b. A scenario named *LowSales* with the following values:
      East 0.20
      West 0.32
      Ontario 0.48
      Quebec 0.37
   c. A scenario named *HighSales* with the following values:
      East 0.36
      West 0.58
      Ontario 0.77
      Quebec 0.63
4. Show the LowSales scenario and then print the worksheet.
5. Create a scenario summary report displaying cell H18 as the result cell.
6. Print the Scenario Summary sheet.
7. Save and then close **EL2-C5-A3-PreCdnTarget.xlsx**.

Assessment

4 CREATE A TWO-VARIABLE DATA TABLE

SNAP Grade It

1. Open **NationalHlpDsk.xlsx**.
2. Save the workbook and name it **EL2-C5-A4-NationalHlpDsk**.
3. Create a two-variable data table that will calculate the average cost per call in the data table for each level of total call minutes logged and at each average cost per minute.
4. Save, print, and then close **EL2-C5-A4-NationalHlpDsk.xlsx**.

Assessment

5 FIND AND CORRECT FORMULA ERRORS

1. Open **NationalCapital.xlsx**.
2. Save the workbook and name it **EL2-C5-A5-NationalCapital**.
3. Make cell D19 the active cell and use the Trace Error feature to draw red tracer arrows to find the source cell creating the #N/A error.
4. The Customer Service department manager has reported that the cost of a Pix firewall is $4,720. Enter this data in the appropriate cell to correct the #N/A error.
5. Remove the tracer arrows.
6. The worksheet contains a logic error in one of the formulas. Find and correct the error.
7. Save, print, and then close **EL2-C5-A5-NationalCapital.xlsx**.

Visual Benchmark Demonstrate Your Proficiency

1 FIND THE BASE HOURLY RATE FOR DRUM LESSONS

1. Open **Lessons.xlsx**.
2. Save the workbook and name it **EL2-C5-VB1-Lessons**.
3. The current worksheet is shown in Figure 5.11 on the next page. The hourly rates in B5:B13 are linked to the cell named *BaseRate,* which is located in cell B16. Intermediate and advanced lessons have $4 and $8 added to the hourly base rate, respectively.
4. The drum teacher wants to earn $2,645.50 per month from drum lessons (instead of the current total of $2,292.00). Use the Goal Seek feature to change the base hourly rate to the required value needed to reach the drum teacher's target.
5. Save, print, and then close **EL2-C5-VB1-Lessons.xlsx**.

Figure 5.11 Visual Benchmark 1

	A	B	C	D
1	**THE DRUM STUDIO**			
2	**MONTHLY DRUM LESSON REVENUE**			
3				
4	**Class**	**Hourly Rate**	**Registered Students**	**Monthly Revenue**
5	Basic Drum Theory	18.00	10	180.00
6	Beginner Rock Drumming	18.00	15	270.00
7	Intermediate Rock Drumming	22.00	8	176.00
8	Advanced Rock Drumming	26.00	4	104.00
9	Beginner Jazz Drumming	18.00	18	324.00
10	Developing Jazz Style	22.00	10	220.00
11	Single Pedal Drum Beats	18.00	22	396.00
12	Single Pedal Drum Fills	18.00	15	270.00
13	Bass Drum Doubles	22.00	16	352.00
14	**TOTAL**			**2,292.00**
15				
16	Base hourly rate for all lessons:	18.00		

2 CREATE SCENARIOS FOR DRUM LESSON REVENUE

1. Open **Lessons.xlsx**.
2. Save the workbook and name it **EL2-C5-VB2-Lessons**.
3. The drum teacher has decided to create three models for an increase in the base hourly rate charged for drum lessons before deciding which base rate to use for next year. Examine the Scenario Summary report shown in Figure 5.12. Create three scenarios to save the hourly base rates shown: Low Rate Increase, Mid Rate Increase, and High Rate Increase.
4. Generate the Scenario Summary report to show the monthly revenue for each class at the three hourly base rates.
5. Format the report by changing the fill colors and font colors and adding the descriptive text in row 7. Use your best judgment in choosing colors that match those shown in Figure 5.12.
6. Edit the *Notes* text in cell B20 so that the sentence correctly references the highlighted color for changing cells.
7. Print the Scenario Summary worksheet.
8. Save and then close **EL2-C5-VB2-Lessons.xlsx**.

Figure 5.12 Visual Benchmark 2

	A	B	C	D	E	F	G
1							
2		**Scenario Summary**					
3				Current Values:	Low Rate Increase	Mid Rate Increase	High Rate Increase
5		Changing Cells:					
6			**BaseRate**	18.00	20.00	22.00	24.00
7		Result Cells:		***Monthly revenue for each lesson assuming no change in number of registered students***			
8			**BasicTheory**	180.00	200.00	220.00	240.00
9			**BegRock**	270.00	300.00	330.00	360.00
10			**IntRock**	176.00	192.00	208.00	224.00
11			**AdvRock**	104.00	112.00	120.00	128.00
12			**BegJazz**	324.00	360.00	396.00	432.00
13			**DevJazz**	220.00	240.00	260.00	280.00
14			**SinglePedalBeats**	396.00	440.00	484.00	528.00
15			**SinglePedalFills**	270.00	300.00	330.00	360.00
16			**BassDoubles**	352.00	384.00	416.00	448.00
17			**MonthlyRevTotal**	**2,292.00**	**2,528.00**	**2,764.00**	**3,000.00**
18		Notes: Current Values column represents values of changing cells at					
19		time Scenario Summary Report was created. Changing cells for each					
20		scenario are highlighted in green.					

Case Study Apply Your Skills

Part 1

Yolanda Robertson is continuing her work on the marketing information package for prospective new franchise owners. She has sent you a workbook named **PBMStartup.xlsx**. The workbook contains information on the estimated capital investment required to start a new franchise, along with estimated sales and profits for the first year. The workbook calculates the number of months in which a new franchisee can expect to recoup his or her investment based on estimated sales and profits for the first year. Yolanda wants you to use the What-If Analysis tools to find out the value that is needed for projected sales in year 1 to pay back the initial investment in 12 months (instead of 17). Accept the proposed solution and save the revised workbook and name it **EL2-C5-CS-P1-PBMStartup**. Print the worksheet.

Part 2

After reviewing the printout from Part 1, Yolanda is concerned that the revised sales figure is not attainable in the first year. Restore the sales for year 1 to the original value of $485,000. Yolanda has created the following three models for the startup investment worksheet:

Item	Conservative	Optimistic	Aggressive
Projected Sales	$450,000	$590,000	$615,000
Profit Percent	20%	22%	18%

Yolanda would like you to set up the worksheet to save all three of these models. ***Hint: Use a comma to separate two cell references as the changing cells***. Create a report that shows Yolanda the input variables for each model and how the model affects the number of months needed to recoup the initial investment. Save the revised workbook as **EL2-C5-CS-P2-PBMStartup**. Print the summary report. Switch to the worksheet and show the model that reduces the number of months to recoup the initial investment to the lowest value. Print the worksheet. Save **EL2-C5-CS-P2-PBMStartup**.

Part 3

Help

Show Formula
Evaluate Formula

Yolanda would like you to check all of the formulas in the worksheet to make sure they are accurate before submitting this worksheet to the client. Since you did not create this worksheet, you decide to check if there is a feature in Excel that navigates to formula cells automatically so you do not miss any calculated cells. Use the Help feature to find out how to select cells that contain formulas. Based on the information you learned in Help, select the cells within the worksheet that contain formulas and then review each formula cell in the Formula bar to ensure the formula is logically correct. ***Hint: When the formula cells are selected as a group, press the Enter key to move to the next formula cell without losing the selection***. When you are finished reviewing the formula cells, type the name of the feature you used in a blank cell below the worksheet and then print the worksheet. Save the revised workbook and name it **EL2-C5-CS-P3-PBMStartup**.

Part 4

WWW

When meeting with prospective franchise owners, Yolanda expects that individuals who do not have excellent credit ratings will find it difficult to raise the money required for the initial capital investment. Assume that the owners of Pizza by Mario are willing to finance the initial investment. Search the Internet for the current lending rate for a secured credit line at the bank at which you have an account. In a new worksheet within the workbook, document the current loan rate you found and the URL of the bank website from which you obtained the rate. Add two percentage points to the lending rate to compensate the owners for the higher risk associated with financing the startup. Create a linked cell in the new worksheet to the Total Estimated Initial Investment in Sheet1. Calculate the monthly loan payment for a term of five years. Add appropriate labels to describe the data and format the worksheet as desired to improve its appearance. Save the revised workbook and name it **EL2-C5-CS-P4-PBMStartup**. Print the loan worksheet.

MICROSOFT®

EXCEL®

CHAPTER 6

Protecting and Sharing Workbooks

PERFORMANCE OBJECTIVES

Upon successful completion of Chapter 6, you will be able to:

- **Add information to a workbook's properties**
- **Add comments containing additional information or other notes to the reader**
- **Share a workbook with other people and view other users who have the shared workbook open at the same time**
- **Edit a shared workbook and resolve conflicts with changes**
- **Print a history of changes made to a shared workbook**
- **Stop sharing a workbook**
- **Save and share a workbook using SkyDrive**
- **Protect cells within a worksheet to prevent changes**
- **Add a password to open a workbook**
- **Track changes made to a workbook**
- **Modify and resolve tracked changes**

SNAP

Tutorials

6.1 Inserting and Editing Comments
6.2 Adding Workbook Properties
6.3 Printing and Editing Comments
6.4 Sharing a Workbook
6.5 Resolving Conflicts in a Shared Workbook
6.6 Saving a Workbook to Windows SkyDrive, Inviting People to Share a Workbook, and Sending a Workbook via Email
6.7 Protecting and Unprotecting Worksheets
6.8 Protecting and Unprotecting the Structure of a Workbook
6.9 Adding Password Protection to a Workbook
6.10 Tracking Changes

In today's electronic business environment, collaborating with other people on an Excel workbook is becoming commonplace. Excel includes several features and tools that are useful for working in a collaborative environment. Adding information to a workbook's properties provides other editors with descriptive information about the nature and purpose of the workbook. Attaching a comment to a cell allows you to add explanatory information or ask questions when collaborating with others. Sharing a workbook, locking and unlocking worksheets and ranges, and tracking changes are all vital features for managing data that will be accessed by multiple individuals. By completing the projects in this chapter, you will learn how to use the collaborative tools in Excel. Model answers for this chapter's projects appear on the following page.

Excel
EL2C6

Note: Before beginning the projects, copy to your storage medium the EL2C6 subfolder from the EL2 folder on the CD that accompanies this textbook and then make EL2C6 the active folder.

Cell: C10
Comment: Student Name:
Most competitors charge 168.99 for weekend rentals of luxury vehicles.

Cell: F10
Comment: Student Name:
Last year this discount was 15%.

Project 1 Add Workbook Properties and Insert Comments

Project 1b, EL2-C6-P1-CRPricing.xlsx Comments Page

Action Number	Date	Time	Who	Change	Sheet	Range	New Value	Old Value	Action Type	Losing Action
1	3/20/2015	10:05 AM	Aaron Rubin	Cell Change	Sheet1	F5	12%	15%		
2	3/20/2015	10:05 AM	Aaron Rubin	Cell Change	Sheet1	B10	$95.99	$85.99		
3	3/20/2015	10:05 AM	Aaron Rubin	Cell Change	Sheet1	D10	$325.99	$299.99		
4	3/20/2015	10:09 AM	Chris Zajac	Cell Change	Sheet1	D10	$319.99	$325.99		

The history ends with the changes saved on 3/20/2015 at 10:09 AM.

Project 2 Sharing a Workbook

Project 2e, EL2-C6-P2-CRPricingShared.xlsx

CutRate Car Rentals
Estimated Monthly Revenue
West Region

Effective Date: May 1, 2015

Category	Weekday (Mo to Th)	Target Rentals	Target Revenue	Weekend (Fr to Su)	Target Rentals	Target Revenue	Weekly (*Min 5 days)	Target Rentals	Target Revenue	Monthly (*Min 21 days)	Target Rentals	Target Revenue
Compact	$ 35.99	362	$ **13,028**	$ 55.99	173	$ **9,686**	$ 175.99	33	$ **5,808**	$ 675.99	11	$ **7,436**
Mid-size	38.99	285	**11,112**	62.99	214	**13,480**	185.99	25	**4,650**	692.99	10	**6,930**
Full-size	40.99	175	**7,173**	65.99	75	**4,949**	215.99	30	**6,480**	775.99	8	**6,208**
Minivan	75.99	155	**11,778**	130.99	68	**8,907**	251.99	28	**7,056**	866.99	8	**6,936**
SUV	89.99	146	**13,139**	139.99	22	**3,080**	249.99	31	**7,750**	885.99	12	**10,632**
Luxury	99.99	55	**5,499**	155.99	30	**4,680**	329.99	10	**3,300**	999.99	5	**5,000**
TOTAL		Weekday:	$ **61,730**		Weekend:	$ **44,782**		Weekly:	$ **35,042**		Monthly:	$ **43,141**

TOTAL ESTIMATED MONTHLY REVENUE **$ 184,696**

**Days rented must be consecutive to qualify for weekly or monthly rate.*

TOTAL ESTIMATED MONTHLY REVENUE BY CRITERIA

Compact	$ 35,958
Mid-size	36,172
Full-size	24,810
Minivan	34,677
SUV	34,600
Luxury	18,479
TOTAL	**$184,696**

Project 4 Track and Resolve Changes Made to a Workbook

Project 4c, EL2-C6-P4-CRWestReg.xlsx

Model Answers

Project 1 Add Workbook Properties and Insert Comments 2 Parts

You will add the author's name and other descriptive information in a workbook's properties and insert comments with explanatory information.

Adding Workbook Properties

Workbook properties include information about the workbook such as the author's name, a title, a subject, a category to which the workbook is related (such as finance), and general comments about the workbook. This information can be added to the file at the Info backstage area, shown in Figure 6.1, or by using the document information panel, shown in Figure 6.2.

Some information is added to file properties automatically by Microsoft Excel. For example, Excel maintains workbook statistics such as the date the workbook was created, the date the workbook was last modified, and the name of the last person to save the workbook. Workbook properties are sometimes referred to as ***metadata***—a term used to identify descriptive information about data.

To add an author's name or other descriptive information about a workbook, click the FILE tab. Excel displays the Info backstage area with the workbook's properties displayed at the right side of the screen. By default, Excel inserts in the *Author* property box the name of the computer user (as defined when Microsoft Office is installed) when a new workbook is created. To add another author or make a change to a workbook property (such as the title), click the mouse to open the text box next to the property's name. For example, click *Add a title* next to the Title property name. A text box opens in which you can type the desired title. Click outside the text box to end the entry. Properties that do not display with the message *Add a [property]* cannot be edited. Click the Show All Properties hyperlink at the bottom of the right section in the Info backstage area to add more properties to the view.

Quick Steps

Add Information to Properties
1. Click FILE tab.
2. Click *Add a [property]* next to desired property name.
3. Type desired text.
4. Click outside property box.

Figure 6.1 Properties in the Info Backstage Area

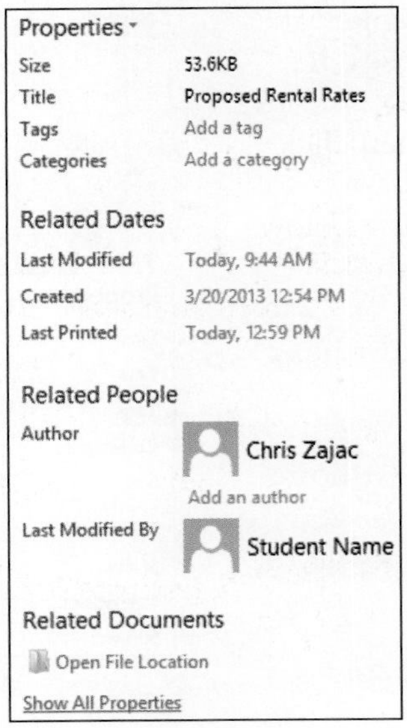

Quick Steps

Add or Edit Properties Using the Document Information Panel

1. Click FILE tab.
2. Click Properties button.
3. Click *Show Document Panel*.
4. Add or edit properties as required.
5. Close document information panel.

The document information panel, shown in Figure 6.2, displays between the ribbon and the worksheet. If you prefer to add or edit properties while viewing the worksheet, open the panel by clicking the Properties button at the top of the right section in the Info backstage area and then click *Show Document Panel* at the drop-down list.

In Chapter 8, you will learn how to strip metadata (including personal information) from a file if you do not want this information to be included when distributing a workbook outside your organization. Including personal information can be useful, however, when you are browsing a list of files. The words *Authors*, *Size*, and *Date Modified* appear in a ScreenTip when you hover the mouse pointer over a workbook name in the Open dialog box. This information helps you to select the correct file.

Figure 6.2 Document Information Panel

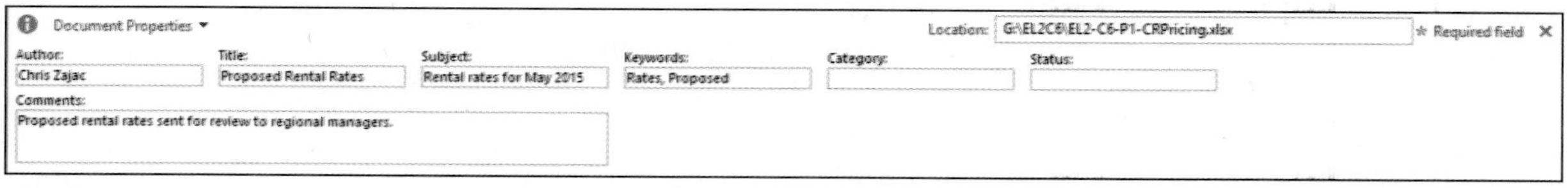

Project 1a Adding Information to Workbook Properties

Part 1 of 2

1. Open **CRPricing.xlsx**.
2. Save the workbook and name it **EL2-C6-P1-CRPricing**.
3. Add an additional author's name, as well as a title, subject, and comments to be associated with the workbook, by completing the following steps:
   a. Click the FILE tab.
   b. At the Info backstage area, click *Add an author* below the current author's name in the *Related People* section to open an *Author* text box.
   c. Type Chris Zajac. If the message *We couldn't find the person you were looking for* displays, ignore it.
   d. Click outside the *Author* text box to close it.
   e. Click *Add a title* in the *Title* text box, type Proposed Rental Rates, and then click outside the text box.
   f. Click the Show All Properties hyperlink below the *Related Documents* section to display additional properties.
   g. Click *Specify the subject* in the *Subject* text box, type Rental rates for May 2015, and then click outside the text box.
   h. Click *Add comments* in the *Comments* text box, type Proposed rental rates sent for review to regional managers. and then click outside the text box.

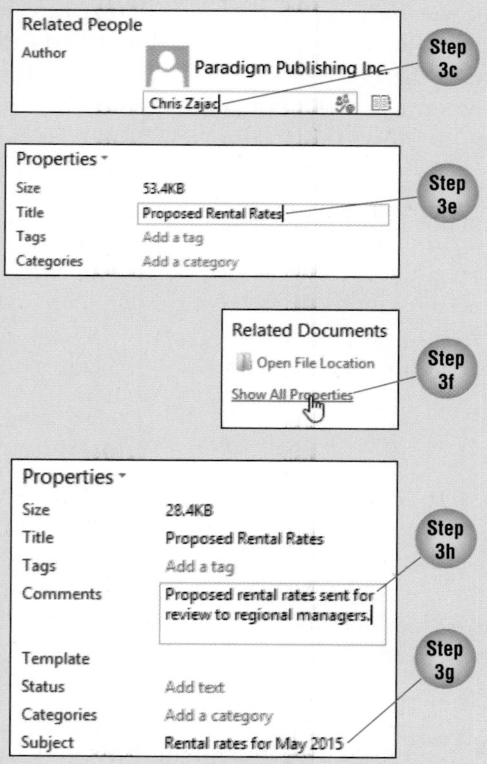

4. Right-click *Paradigm Publishing Inc.* next to the *Author* text box and then click *Remove Person* at the shortcut menu.
5. Click the Show Fewer Properties hyperlink at the bottom of the properties.
6. Compare your properties with those shown in Figure 6.1 on page 187. Some of the dates may vary.

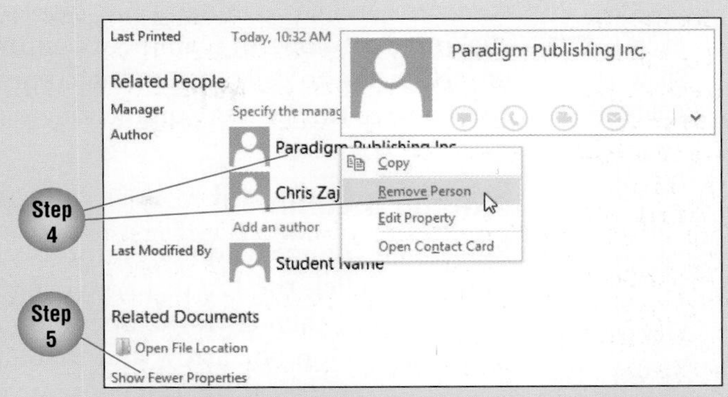

7. View the document information panel and add text to a workbook property by completing the following steps:
   a. Click the Properties button above the workbook properties and then click *Show Document Panel* at the drop-down list. The Info backstage area closes and the document information panel displays between the ribbon and the worksheet. Use this panel to view the worksheet while adding or modifying properties.

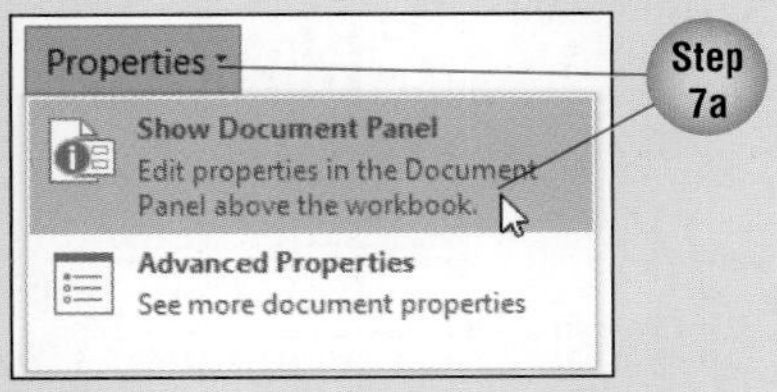

   b. Click in the *Keywords* text box, type **Rates, Proposed**, and then press Tab.
   c. Compare your document information panel with the one shown in Figure 6.2 on page 188.
   d. Click the Close button located in the top right corner of the document information panel. Be careful to click the Close button within the document information panel and not the Close button located at the top right of the ribbon.

8. Save **EL2-C6-P1-CRPricing.xlsx**.

Managing Comments

A ***comment*** is a pop-up box containing text that displays when you hover the mouse pointer over the cell to which it is attached. Use a comment to provide instructions, identify critical information, or add other explanatory information about a cell entry. Comments are also useful when you are collaborating with others to create or edit a worksheet. All of the reviewers can use comments to add feedback or pose questions about cell entries or layout.

Inserting a Comment

Insert a comment by clicking the REVIEW tab and then clicking the New Comment button in the Comments group. This displays a shaded box with the user's name inside. Type the comment text and then click in the worksheet area outside the comment box. You can also insert a comment by right-clicking a cell and then clicking *Insert Comment* at the shortcut menu.

Quick Steps

Insert a Comment
1. Make desired cell active.
2. Click REVIEW tab.
3. Click New Comment button.
4. Type comment text.
5. Click in worksheet area outside comment box.

New Comment

Viewing a Comment

A small, red, diagonal triangle appears in the upper right corner of a cell to alert the reader that a comment exists. Hover the mouse pointer over a cell containing a

Show All Comments

Next

Previous

Edit Comment

Delete

comment and the comment box displays. Turn on the display of all comments by clicking the Show All Comments button in the Comments group on the REVIEW tab. Navigate to cells containing comments by clicking the Next button or the Previous button in the Comments group on the REVIEW tab.

Printing a Comment

By default, comments do not print. If you want comments printed with the worksheet, click the PAGE LAYOUT tab, click the Page Setup group dialog box launcher, and then click the Sheet tab at the Page Setup dialog box. Click the *Comments* option box arrow and then click *At end of sheet* to print the comments on a separate page after the cell contents or *As displayed on sheet* to print the comments as they appear within the worksheet area.

Editing and Deleting a Comment

To edit a comment, click the cell containing the comment and then click the Edit Comment button in the Comments group on the REVIEW tab. (The New Comment button changes to the Edit Comment button when the active cell contains a comment.) You can also edit a comment by right-clicking the cell containing the comment and then clicking *Edit Comment* at the shortcut menu. Insert or delete text as desired and then click in the worksheet area outside the comment box.

To delete a comment, click the cell containing the comment and then click the Delete button in the Comments group. You can also delete a comment by right-clicking the cell containing the comment and then clicking *Delete Comment* at the shortcut menu.

Quick Steps

Copy and Paste Comments

1. Select source cell containing comment.
2. Click Copy button.
3. Click destination cell(s).
4. Click Paste button arrow.
5. Click *Paste Special*.
6. Click *Comments*.
7. Click OK.

Copying and Pasting Comments

A comment that has been added to a cell can be copied and pasted to one or more cells. After copying the source cell, click the destination cell and then open the Paste Special dialog box. Click *Comments* in the *Paste* section and then click OK.

Project 1b **Inserting, Editing, Pasting, Viewing, and Deleting Comments** **Part 2 of 2**

1. With **EL2-C6-P1-CRPricing.xlsx** open, insert comments by completing the following steps:
   a. Make cell C10 active.
   b. Click the REVIEW tab and then click the New Comment button in the Comments group. A tan shaded box with a green arrow pointing to cell C10 appears. The current user name is inserted in bold text at the top of the comment box followed by a colon. The insertion point is positioned at the left edge of the box on the second line.

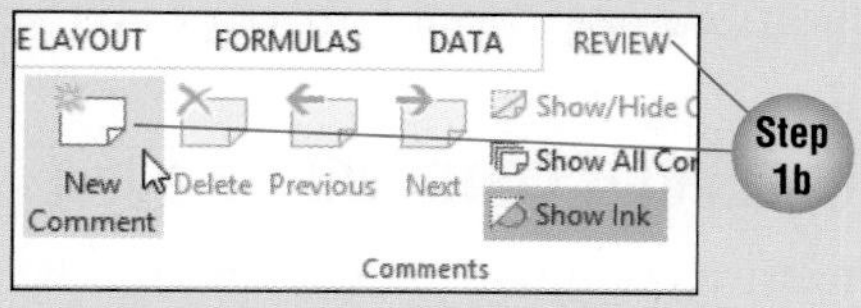

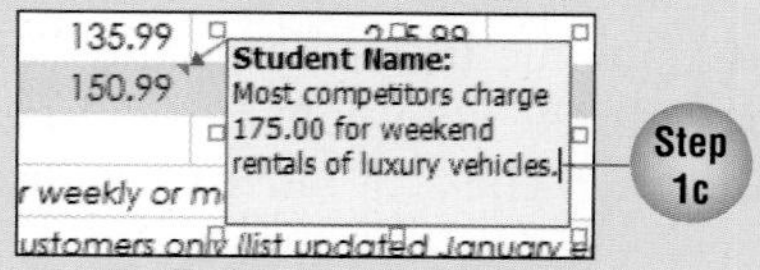

   c. Type Most competitors charge 175.00 for weekend rentals of luxury vehicles.
   d. Click in the worksheet area outside the comment box. A small, red, diagonal triangle appears in the upper right corner of cell C10, indicating a comment exists for the cell.
   e. Right-click cell F8 and then click *Insert Comment* at the shortcut menu.

f. Type **Consider reducing the discount for minivans to 18%.** and then click in the worksheet area outside the comment box.

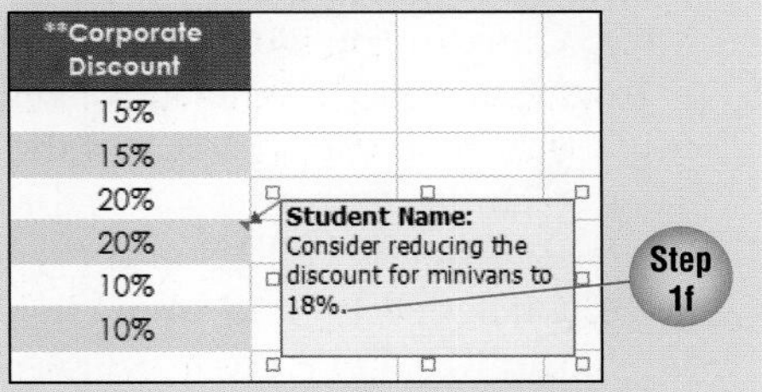

g. Right-click cell F9, click *Insert Comment* at the shortcut menu, type **Last year this discount was 12%.**, and then click in the worksheet area outside the comment box.

h. Right-click cell F9, click *Copy* at the shortcut menu, right-click cell F10, point to *Paste Special*, and then click *Paste Special* at the shortcut menu.

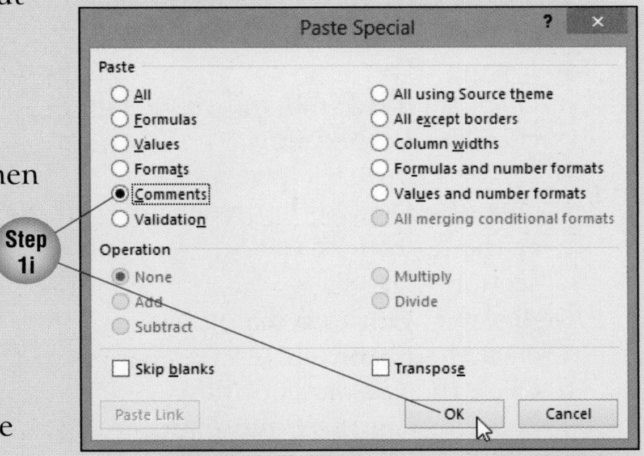

i. At the Paste Special dialog box, click the *Comments* option in the *Paste* section and then click OK.

j. Press the Esc key to remove the scrolling marquee from cell F9.

2. View comments by completing the following steps:

a. Hover the mouse pointer over cell C10. The comment box pops up and displays the comment text.

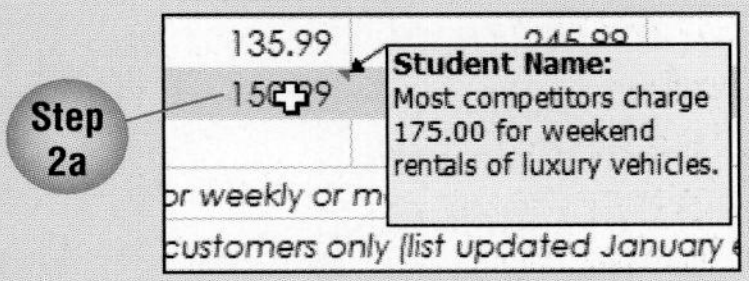

b. Hover the mouse pointer over cells F8, F9, and F10 (one after the other) to review the comments in those cells.

c. Press Ctrl + Home to make cell A1 active.

d. Click the Next button in the Comments group on the REVIEW tab. Excel displays the comment box in cell F8.

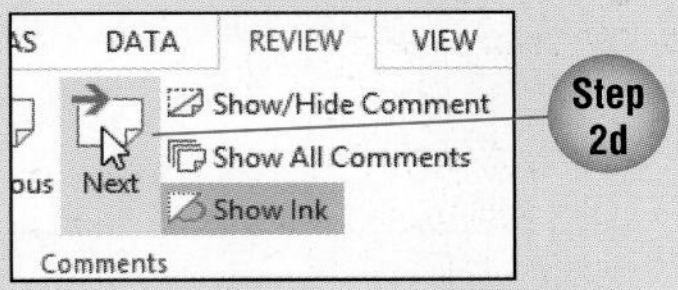

e. Click the Next button to display the comment box in cell F9.

f. Click the Next button to display the comment box in cell C10.

g. Click Next to display the comment box in cell F10. Consider using the Next button to view comments in a large worksheet to ensure you do not miss any comment cells.

h. Click the Show All Comments button in the Comments group on the REVIEW tab. All comment boxes display in the worksheet area.

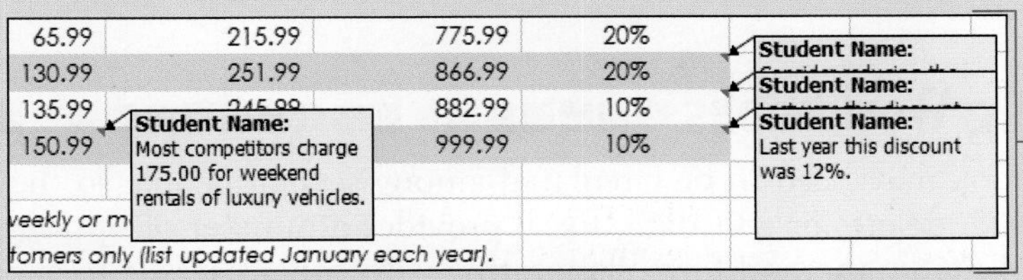

Clicking the Show All Comments button in Step 2h causes all of the comments in the worksheet to display.

i. Click the Show All Comments button again to turn off the display of all comments.

3. Edit and delete a comment by completing the following steps:

a. Right-click cell C10 and then click *Edit Comment* at the shortcut menu. The comment box pops up with the insertion point positioned at the end of the existing comment text.

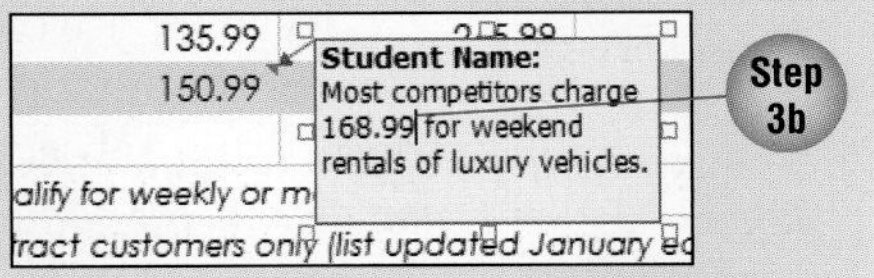

b. Change *175.00* to *168.99* by moving the insertion point and then inserting and deleting text as required.

c. Click in the worksheet area outside the comment box.
d. Make cell F10 the active cell and then click the Edit Comment button in the Comments group on the REVIEW tab.
e. Change *12%* to *15%* and then click in the worksheet area outside the comment box.
f. Right-click cell F8 and then click *Delete Comment* at the shortcut menu.
g. Click cell F9 and then click the Delete button in the Comments group on the REVIEW tab.

4. Print the comments at the end of the worksheet by completing the following steps:
   a. Click the FILE tab and then click the *Print* option.
   b. At the Print backstage area, click the Page Setup hyperlink at the bottom of the *Settings* section.
   c. At the Page Setup dialog box, click the Sheet tab.
   d. Click the *Comments* option box arrow in the *Print* section and then click *At end of sheet* to print the comments on a separate sheet at the end of the document.
   e. Click OK.

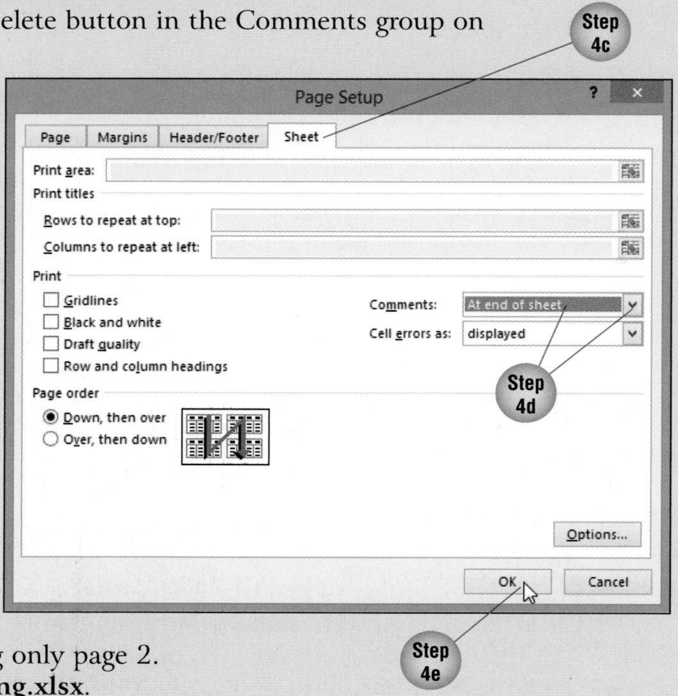

5. Print only the comments by printing only page 2.
6. Save and close **EL2-C6-P1-CRPricing.xlsx**.

Project 2 Sharing a Workbook — 7 Parts

You will share the workbook with other users for editing and viewing purposes.

Sharing Workbooks

Quick Steps

Share a Workbook
1. Open workbook.
2. Click REVIEW tab.
3. Click Share Workbook button.
4. Click *Allow changes by more than one user at the same time* check box.
5. Click OK to close Share Workbook dialog box.
6. Click OK to continue.

Share Workbook

A workbook may need to be circulated among several people so they can review, add, delete, or edit data. Excel provides a number of options for sharing workbooks. One method for collaborating with other users is to share a workbook. A shared workbook can be saved to a network folder that is accessible by other individuals who need the file. Excel tracks each person's changes and displays a prompt if two people have the file open at the same time and attempt to make changes to the same data.

To share a workbook, click the REVIEW tab and then click the Share Workbook button in the Changes group. At the Share Workbook dialog box with the Editing tab active, as shown in Figure 6.3, click the *Allow changes by more than one user at the same time* check box.

Figure 6.3 Share Workbook Dialog Box with Editing Tab Selected

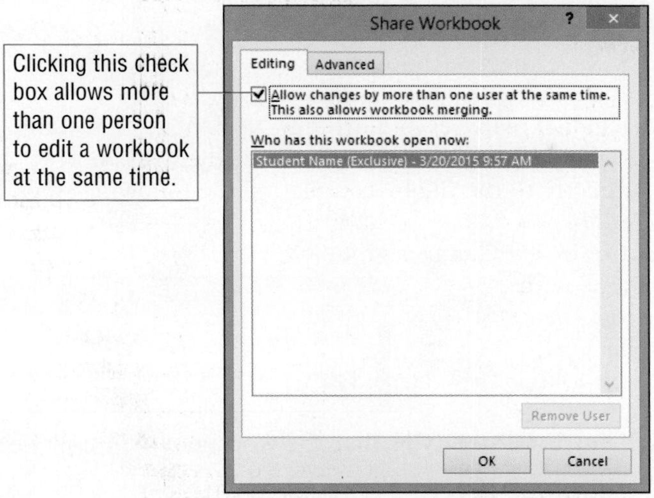

Click the Advanced tab in the Share Workbook dialog box to define the sharing options, as shown in Figure 6.4. A shared workbook should be saved to a network folder that is designated as a shared folder and is accessible to the other users. The network administrator is usually the person who creates a folder on a server designated with the read/write access rights for multiple accounts (referred to as a ***network share***) and he or she can assist you with navigating to and saving to a network share. All individuals with access to the shared network folder will have full access to the shared workbook.

One drawback of using a shared workbook is that it cannot support all of Excel's features. If you need to use a feature that is unavailable or make a changes to a feature that is not allowed, you will first need to remove shared access. In a later section, you will learn how to lock and unlock worksheets and cells for editing if you want to protect the worksheet or sections of the worksheet from changes before you share the workbook.

Quick Steps

View Other Users of a Shared Workbook

1. Open shared workbook.
2. Click REVIEW tab.
3. Click Share Workbook button.
4. Review names in *Who has this workbook open now* list box.
5. Click OK.

HINT

To instruct Excel not to display the Resolve Conflicts dialog box, open the Share Workbook dialog box, click the Advanced tab, and then select *The changes being saved win* in the *Conflicting changes between users* section.

Figure 6.4 Share Workbook Dialog Box with Advanced Tab Selected

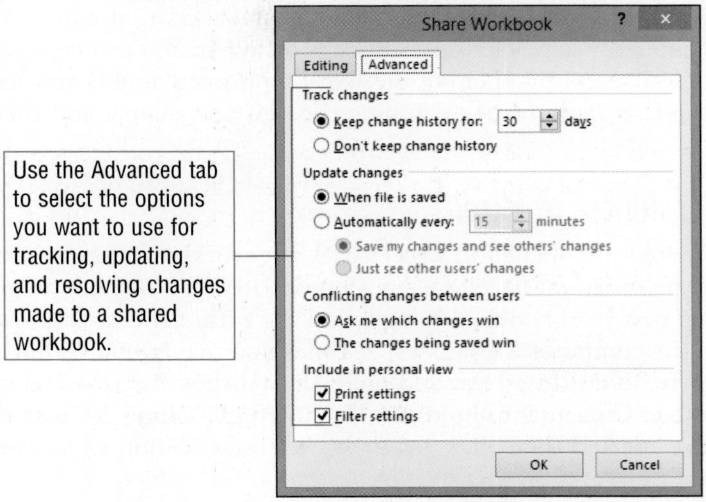

Project 2a Sharing a Workbook

1. Open **EL2-C6-P1-CRPricing.xlsx**, save the workbook and name it **EL2-C6-P2-CRPricingShared**.
2. Assume that you are Chris Zajac, regional manager of CutRate Car Rentals. You want feedback from another manager on the proposed rental rates. Share the workbook so that the other manager can make changes directly to the file by completing the following steps:
   a. If necessary, click the REVIEW tab.
   b. Click the Share Workbook button in the Changes group.
   c. At the Share Workbook dialog box with the Editing tab selected, click the *Allow changes by more than one user at the same time* check box to insert a check mark.

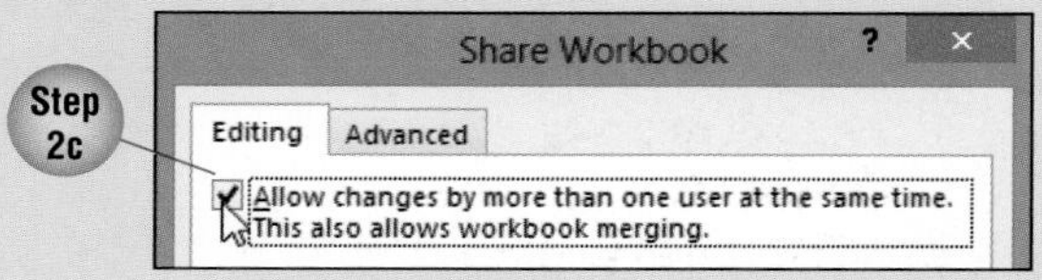

   d. Click OK.
   e. At the Microsoft Excel message box informing you that the workbook will now be saved and asking if you want to continue, click OK.

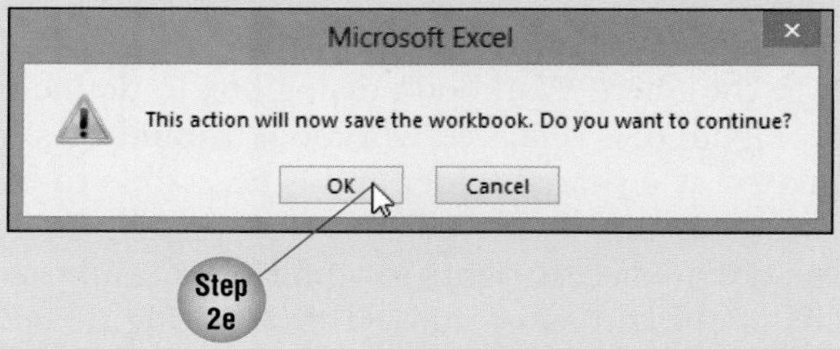

3. Notice that Excel adds *[Shared]* in the Title bar next to the workbook file name to indicate the workbook's status.

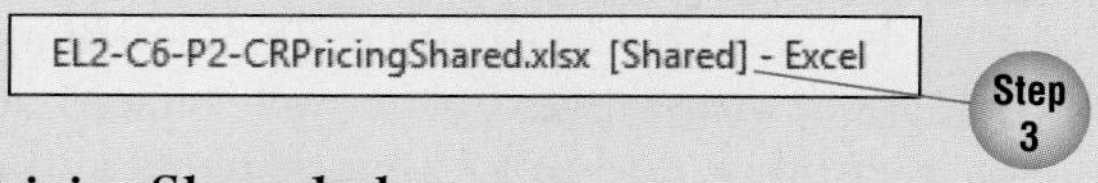

4. Close **EL2-C6-P2-CRPricingShared.xlsx**.

Quick Steps

Change the User Name
1. Click FILE tab.
2. Click *Options*.
3. Select text in *User name* text box.
4. Type new user name.
5. Click OK.

Opening Two Instances of Excel
1. Press and hold Alt.
2. Right-click Excel icon in Taskbar.
3. Click *Excel 2013*.
4. Release Alt.
5. Click Yes.

Changing the User Name

When a workbook is shared, Excel tracks the names of the users that edit it. User name information is entered when Microsoft Office is installed. You can change the user name associated with Excel by opening the Excel Options dialog box, selecting the existing text in the *User name* text box, typing the new user name, and then clicking OK.

Opening Multiple Instances of Excel

When multiple workbooks are opened in Excel 2013, the workbooks are opened in the same instance of the program. Excel does not open a new copy of the program every time you open a new workbook. Although working within the same instance of the program saves the computer's resources, at times you may prefer to have multiple instances open. To do this, press and hold Alt and then right-click the Excel icon in the Taskbar. Continue to hold Alt as you left-click *Excel 2013* at the shortcut menu. Release Alt and then click Yes to answer the question *Do you want to start a new instance of Excel?*.

Project 2b Changing the User Name and Editing a Shared Workbook — Part 2 of 7

1. At a blank Excel screen, change the user name on your computer to simulate an environment in which another manager is opening the shared workbook from a network share location by completing the following steps:
   a. Click the FILE tab.
   b. Click *Options*.
   c. At the Excel Options dialog box with *General* selected in the left pane, make a note of the existing entry in the *User name* text box in the *Personalize your copy of Microsoft Office* section, if the entry is a name other than your own. ***Note: You will restore the original user name in Project 4c.***
   d. Select the current entry in the *User name* text box, type Aaron Rubin, and then click OK.

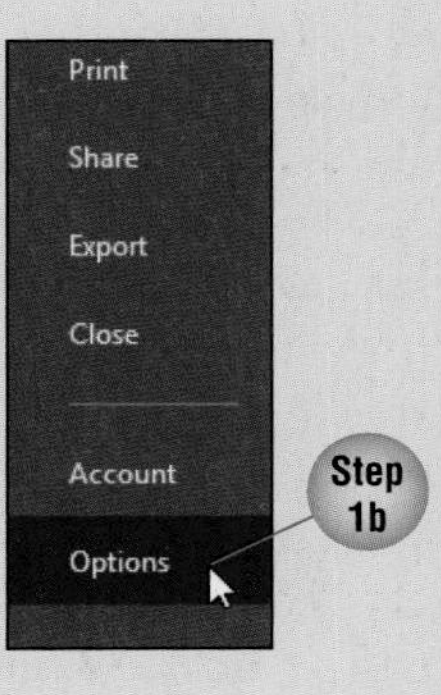

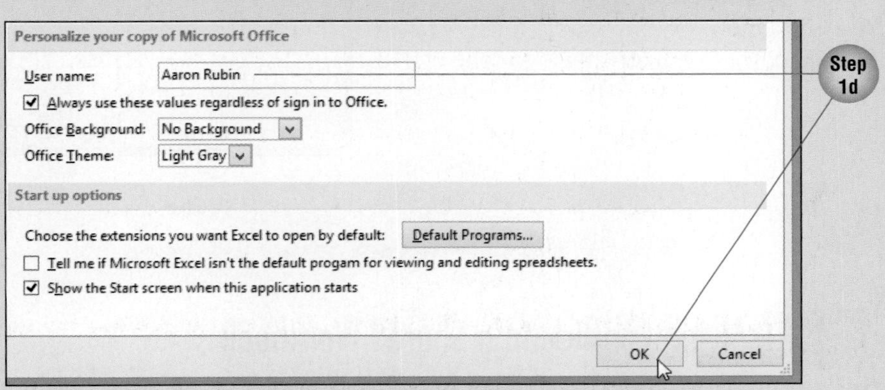

2. Open **EL2-C6-P2-CRPricingShared.xlsx**.
3. Make the following changes to the proposed rental rates:
   a. Make cell F5 active and then change the entry from *15%* to *12%*.
   b. Make cell B10 active and then change the entry from *85.99* to *95.99*.
   c. Make cell D10 active and then change the entry from *299.99* to *325.99*.
4. Save **EL2-C6-P2-CRPricingShared.xlsx**.

Project 2c Viewing Other Users of a Shared Workbook — Part 3 of 7

1. Open a new instance of Excel by completing the following steps:
   a. Press and hold Alt and then right-click the Excel icon on the Taskbar.
   b. Continue to hold Alt as you left-click *Excel 2013* at the shortcut menu.
   c. Release Alt and then click Yes to answer the question *Do you want to start a new instance of Excel?* ***Note: You are opening another copy of Excel to simulate an environment in which multiple copies of the shared workbook are open. You will also change the user name to continue the simulation using a different identity.***

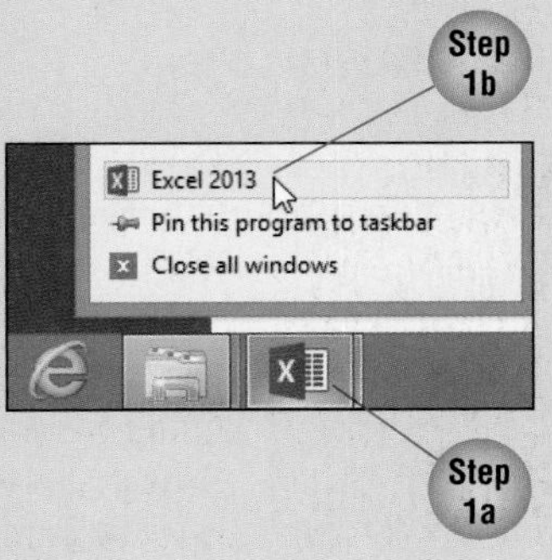

2. Click the Open Other Workbooks hyperlink at the bottom of the *Recent* section.
3. Click *Options* to open the Excel Options dialog box and then change the user name in the new copy of Excel to *Chris Zajac*. (Refer to Steps 1a–1d of Project 2b if you need assistance with this step.)
4. In the new copy of Excel, open **EL2-C6-P2-CRPricingShared.xlsx**.
5. View the names of the other users sharing the workbook by completing the following steps:
   a. Click the REVIEW tab.
   b. Click the Share Workbook button in the Changes group.
   c. At the Share Workbook dialog box with the Editing tab selected, look at the names in the *Who has this workbook open now* list box.
   d. Click OK.
6. Leave both copies of Excel open for the next project.

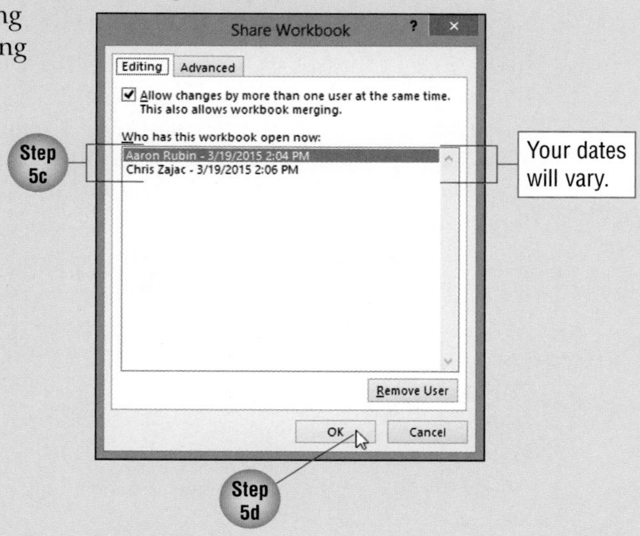

Resolving Conflicts in a Shared Workbook

Quick Steps

Resolving Conflicts in a Shared Workbook
1. Open shared workbook.
2. Make desired edits.
3. Click Save button.
4. Click Accept Mine or Accept Other button at each conflict.
5. Click OK.

When two users have copies of a shared workbook open and each user makes a change to the same cell, Excel prompts the second user to resolve the conflict by displaying the Resolve Conflicts dialog box, shown in Figure 6.5. The cell address, original entry, and revised entry are shown for each user. Click the Accept Mine button to save your revision or click the Accept Other button to remove your change and restore the cell to the entry made by the other user. Click the Accept All Mine button or Accept All Others button to avoid being prompted at each individual cell that has a conflict.

Figure 6.5 Resolve Conflicts Dialog Box

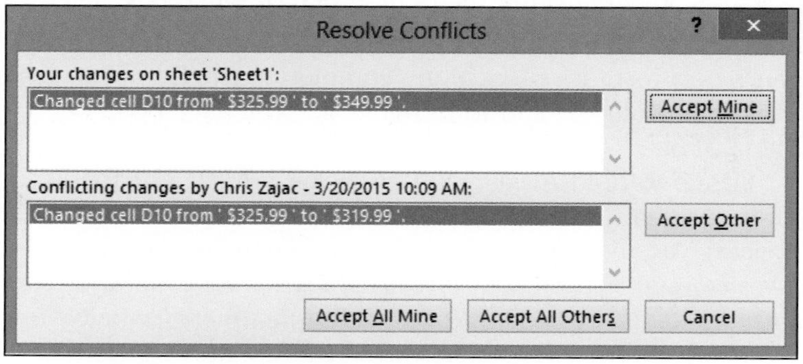

Project 2d Resolving Conflicts in a Shared Workbook

Part 4 of 7

1. With **EL2-C6-P2-CRPricingShared.xlsx** open, assume that you are Chris Zajac and that you want to make a change to a proposed rental rate that will conflict with a change made by Aaron Rubin. Complete the following steps:
   a. Make sure the second copy of Excel you opened for Project 2c, in which you viewed the users with the shared workbook open, is active.
   b. Make cell D10 the active cell and then change *325.99* to *319.99*.
   c. Save **EL2-C6-P2-CRPricingShared.xlsx**.
2. Aaron Rubin has decided to change the weekly luxury rate again. Switch to the other copy of Excel to edit the worksheet and resolve the conflict by completing the following steps:
   a. Click the Excel icon on the Taskbar and then click the other copy of the shared workbook to make it active.
   b. Make cell D10 active and change the entry to *349.99*.
   c. Click the Save button. Since this change conflicts with the change made by Chris Zajac in Step 1b, Excel prompts the second user with the Resolve Conflicts dialog box.
   d. Click the Accept Other button to restore the cell to the value entered by Chris Zajac.
   e. At the Microsoft Excel message box informing you that the workbook has been updated with changes saved by other users, click OK.

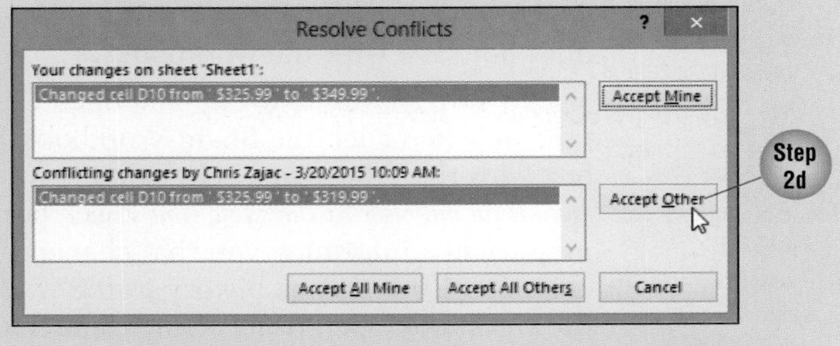

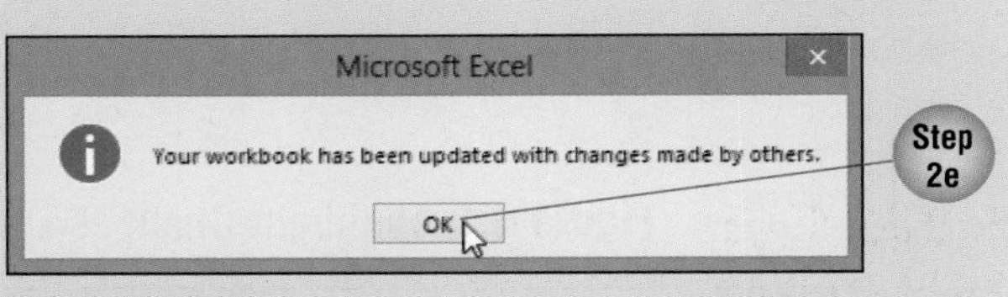

3. Notice that cell D10 is displayed with a colored border, indicating that a change has been made. Hover the mouse pointer over cell D10 to view the pop-up box with the name, date, and time the cell change was saved as well as the original and revised entries.

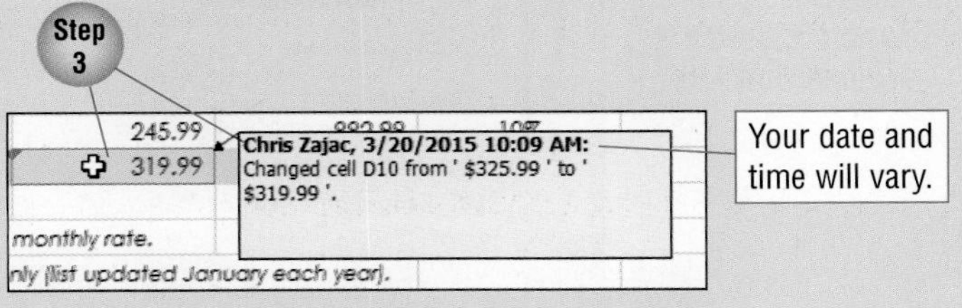

4. Exit the active copy of Excel.
5. With the other copy of Excel active, close **EL2-C6-P2-CRPricingShared.xlsx**.

Printing a History Sheet and Removing Shared Workbook Access

Quick Steps

Print a History Sheet
1. Open shared workbook.
2. Click REVIEW tab.
3. Click Track Changes button.
4. Click *Highlight Changes*.
5. Change *When* to *All*.
6. If necessary, clear *Who* check box.
7. If necessary, clear *Where* check box.
8. Click *List changes on a new sheet* check box.
9. Click OK.
10. Print history sheet.

Stop Sharing a Workbook
1. Open shared workbook.
2. Click REVIEW tab.
3. Click Share Workbook button.
4. Remove check mark from *Allow changes by more than one user at the same time* check box.
5. Click OK.
6. Click Yes.

Track Changes

HINT

Before changing the status of a shared workbook to exclusive, make sure no one else is currently editing the workbook. Once you remove shared access, users that have the file open will not be able to save their changes.

Before changing the status of a shared workbook to an exclusive workbook, consider printing the change history so you have a record of the edits made by all of the users who worked on the file.

To do this, click the REVIEW tab, click the Track Changes button, and then click *Highlight Changes* at the drop-down list. At the Highlight Changes dialog box, shown in Figure 6.6, change *When* to *All*, remove the check marks from the *Who* and *Where* check boxes, click the *List changes on a new sheet* check box to insert a check mark, and then click OK.

By default, Excel displays a colored border around each changed cell. When you rest the mouse pointer over a cell with a colored border, Excel displays in a pop-up box the cell's change history. Remove the check mark from the *Highlight changes on screen* check box if you prefer not to highlight changed cells in the worksheet. Print the history sheet before you save the document, since this sheet does not save with the workbook.

To stop sharing a workbook, open the shared workbook, click the REVIEW tab, and then click the Share Workbook button. At the Share Workbook dialog box with the Editing tab selected, remove the check mark from the *Allow changes by more than one user at the same time* check box. When you click OK, Excel displays a message box informing you that changing the workbook to exclusive status will erase all of the change history in the workbook and prevent users who might have the workbook open from saving their changes. Consider copying and pasting the cells in the history sheet to a new workbook and saving the history as a separate file, since the history sheet will be removed when the shared workbook is saved.

Figure 6.6 Highlight Changes Dialog Box

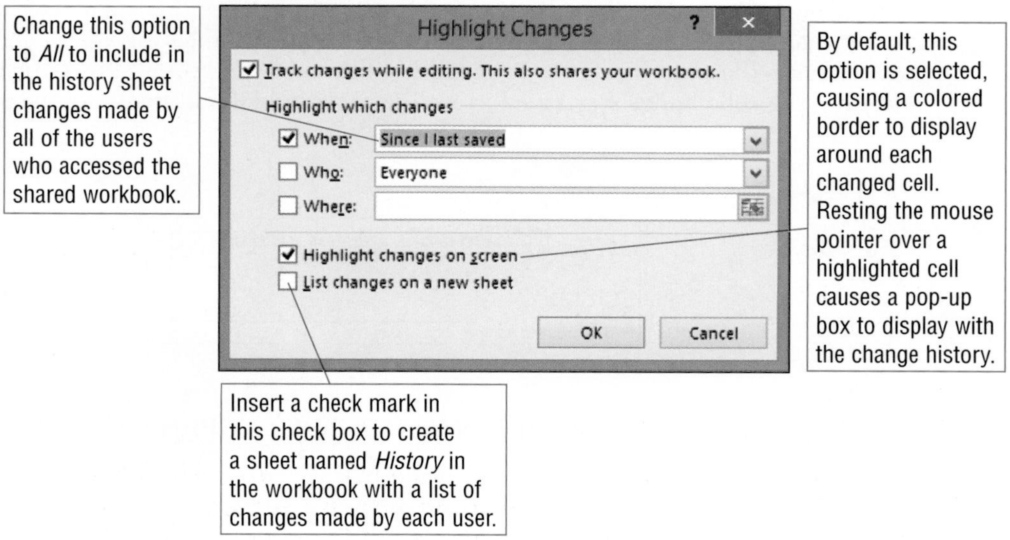

Project 2e Printing the History Sheet and Removing Shared Access to a Workbook

Part 5 of 7

1. Open **EL2-C6-P2-CRPricingShared.xlsx**.
2. Create a new sheet named *History* and print the record of changes made to the shared workbook by completing the following steps:
   a. If necessary, click the REVIEW tab.
   b. Click the Track Changes button in the Changes group and then click *Highlight Changes* at the drop-down list.
   c. At the Highlight Changes dialog box, click the *When* option box arrow and then click *All* at the drop-down list.
   d. If necessary, remove the check mark from the *Who* check box.
   e. If necessary, remove the check mark from the *Where* check box.
   f. Click the *List changes on a new sheet* check box to insert a check mark and then click OK.
   g. Print the history sheet.

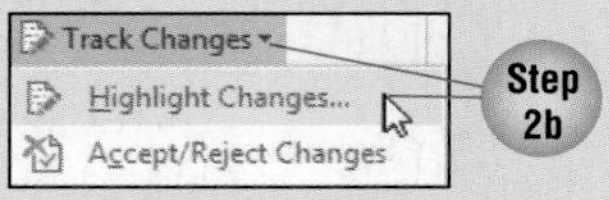

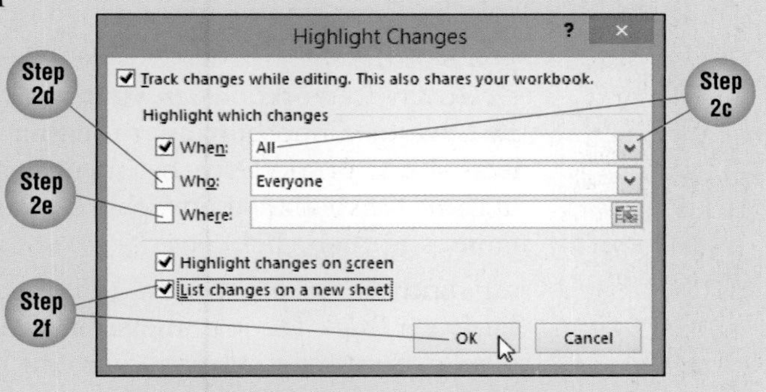

3. Stop sharing the workbook by completing the following steps:
   a. Click the Share Workbook button.
   b. Click the *Allow changes by more than one user at the same time* check box to remove the check mark.
   c. Click OK.
   d. At the Microsoft Excel message box informing you that the workbook will be removed from shared use, click Yes to make the workbook exclusive.

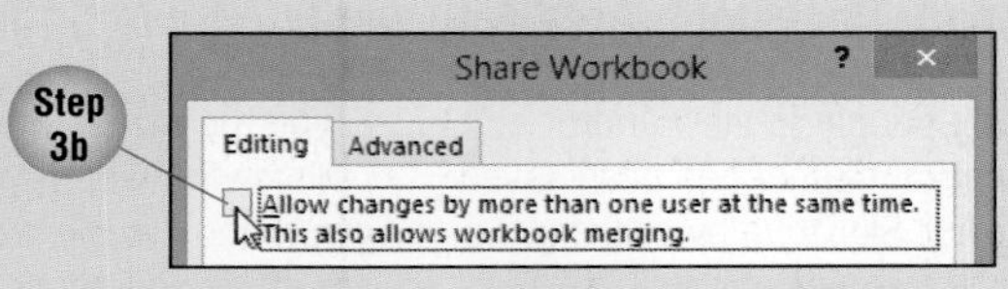

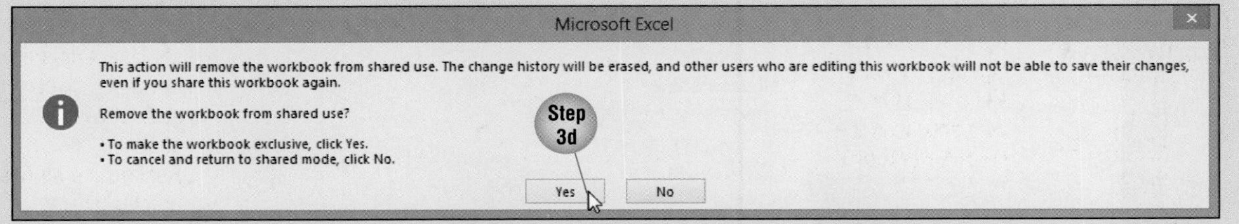

4. Close **EL2-C6-P2-CRPricingShared.xlsx**.

Sharing a Workbook on Windows SkyDrive

Another way to share workbooks is by using Windows SkyDrive. This Office 2013 feature allows you to save and share documents in a storage location on the Internet. You can save a workbook to your SkyDrive and then access the file from any other location where you have Internet access. Instructions for saving a document to your SkyDrive are provided on the next page, but SkyDrive is constantly changing, so the steps may vary.

HINT

If you have access to Microsoft SharePoint, a server application that allows you to share and collaborate on documents, you can save your workbook to a SharePoint library for others to view and/or edit.

Saving to your SkyDrive means you do not have to make a copy of the workbook on a USB drive or some other storage medium in order to edit the workbook at another location. After your workbook is saved to your SkyDrive, invite people to share your workbook with the *Invite People* option at the Share backstage area. When multiple people edit the workbook on SkyDrive, you do not need to manage multiple versions of the same file.

Quick Steps

Save a Workbook to SkyDrive
1. Open workbook.
2. Click FILE tab.
3. Click *Save As* option.
4. Click *SkyDrive* option.
5. Log in if necessary.
6. Click Browse button.
7. If necessary, select desired folder name.
8. Click Save button.

To save a workbook to SkyDrive, you need to have a Windows Live account. If you use Microsoft Hotmail or Messenger, the account you use to sign in to those applications is your Windows Live ID. If you do not already have a Windows Live user name and password, you can sign up for a free account at login.live.com by clicking the Sign up now button. SkyDrive is free and includes 25 gigabytes (GB) of storage on the SkyDrive server.

To save a workbook to your SkyDrive, click the *Share* option and then click the Save to Cloud button at the Share backstage area. At the Save As backstage area with your SkyDrive selected in the *Places* section, click the Browse button. At the Save As dialog box, choose the folder within your SkyDrive, type the file name, and then click Save.

To invite people to view and/or edit your workbook, click the *Share* option. In the *Invite People* section, shown in Figure 6.7, type the names or email addresses of people you want to view and/or edit the workbook or click the Address Book icon

Figure 6.7 Share Backstage Area with *Invite People* Option Selected

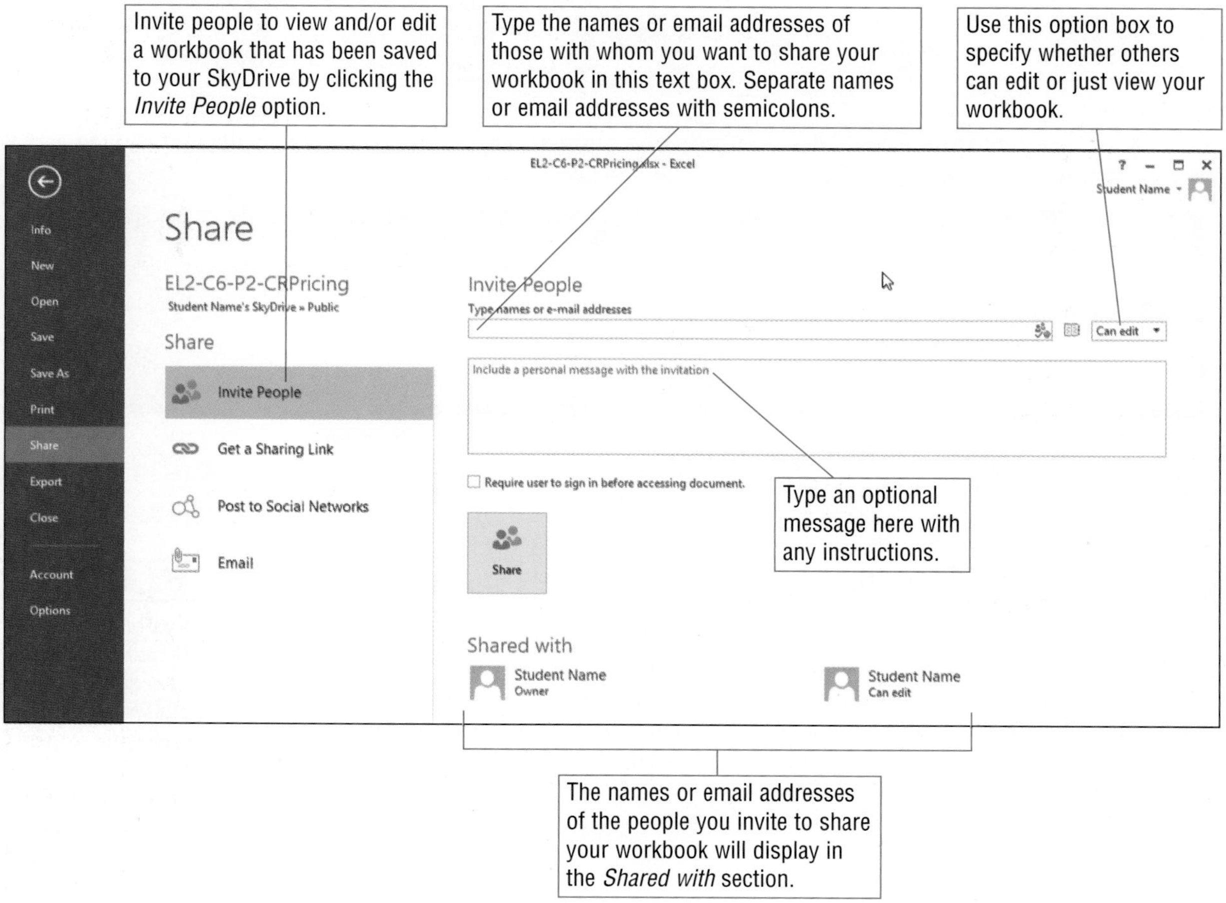

to the right of the *Type names or e-mail addresses* text box and choose people from your contacts. The option box to the right of the Address Book icon offers the options *Can edit* and *Can view*. If you want to allow people to view the workbook but do not want to allow them to make changes, ensure that you change this option from the default *Can edit* to *Can view*. You must send separate invitations if you want to invite certain people to edit and others only to view. After you type a personal message with the invitation, click the Share button. Emails are sent to the people you invited and their names or email addresses will appear in the *Shared with* section.

At the Share backstage area, you can also get a sharing link, post your workbook to your social networks, or email your workbook. Place the sharing link in a Word document or PowerPoint presentation and use it as a hyperlink to your workbook saved on SkyDrive.

To stop sharing a workbook with someone else, right-click the person's name in the *Shared with* section and then click *Remove User* at the shortcut menu. To remove the sharing link, click the Disable Link button at the Share backstage area.

Quick Steps

Share a Workbook Saved on SkyDrive

1. Click FILE tab.
2. Click *Share* option.
3. Type names or addresses.
4. Choose *Can edit* or *Can view* option.
5. Type optional message.
6. Click Share button.

Share

Project 2f Optional: Saving and Sharing a Workbook Using Windows SkyDrive

Part 6 of 7

Note: Complete this project only if you have a Windows Live ID.

1. Open **EL2-C6-P2-CRPricingShared.xlsx** and save the workbook to your SkyDrive by completing the following steps. ***Note: If you already save your work to your SkyDrive, skip to Step 2.***
   a. Click the FILE tab and then click the *Save As* option.
   b. Click *SkyDrive* at the Save As backstage area. Log in to your SkyDrive account or click the Browse button if you are already logged in. ***Note: SkyDrive is constantly changing, so these steps may vary.***

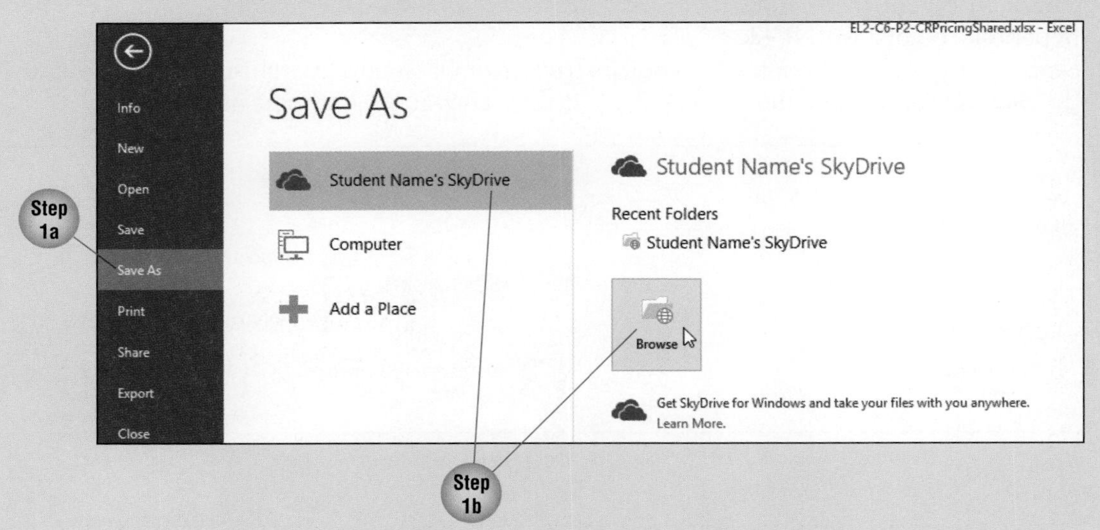

   c. Navigate to the public folder, if necessary, and then click Save.

2. To invite people to share your workbook, complete the following steps:
   a. Click the FILE tab and then click the *Share* option.
   b. At the Share backstage area, click in the *Type names or e-mail addresses* text box and then type the email address of your instructor or a classmate.
   c. Click the down-pointing arrow at the right side of the option box containing the text *Can edit* and then click *Can view*.
   d. Click in the *Include a personal message with the invitation* text box and type **Please review proposed rate changes.**
   e. Click the Share button. An email is sent to the person you invited and his or her name displays in the *Shared with* section of the Share backstage area.

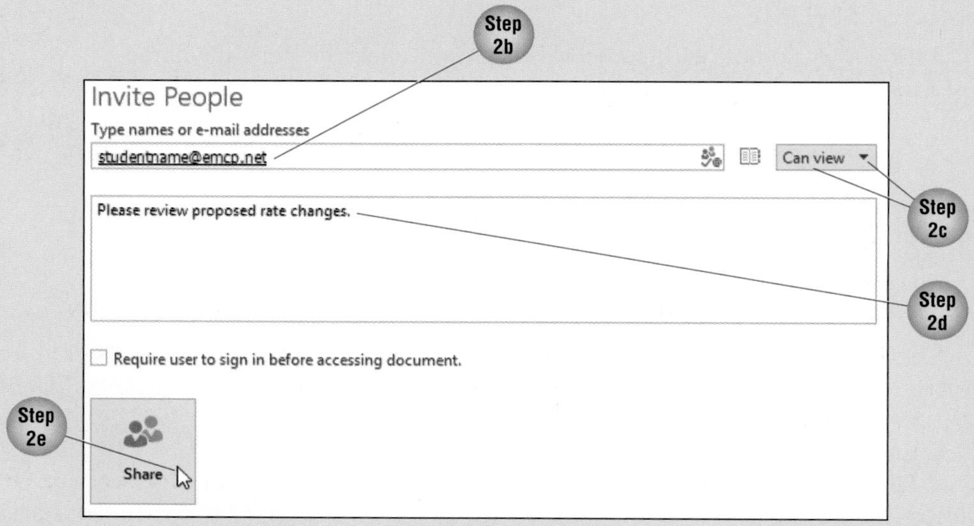

3. Check with your instructor or classmate to see if he or she received your email with the hyperlink to your workbook.
4. Stop sharing the workbook with your instructor or classmate by right-clicking the name in the *Shared with* section and then clicking *Remove User* at the shortcut menu.

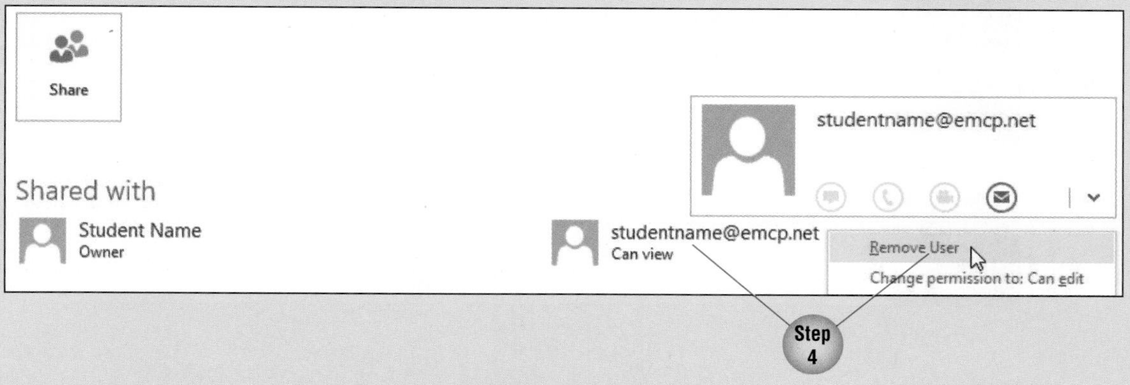

5. Save and close **EL2-C6-P2-CRPricingShared.xlsx**.

Sending a Workbook via Email

A workbook can be sent to others as a file attached to an email message. You can attach the workbook using your email program's file attachment feature or you can initiate the message using Excel. To do this, click the FILE tab and then click the Share option. At the Share backstage area with *Email* selected in the *Share* section, click the Send as Attachment button located in the *Email* section. The default email program, Microsoft Outlook, launches an email message window with the workbook file already attached and the file name inserted in the *Subject* text box. Type the recipient's email address in the *To* text box, type the message text in the message window, and then click the Send button. The message is moved to Outlook's Outbox folder and is then sent out to the recipient.

The *Email* section of the Share backstage area also contains buttons to attach the workbook to an email message as a portable document format (PDF) or as an XML paper specification (XPS) document instead of the default workbook file format. In addition to sending the workbook as an attachment, you can also send a link to the workbook in an email or send the workbook as an Internet fax.

Quick Steps

Send a Workbook via Email

1. Open workbook.
2. Click FILE tab.
3. Click *Share*.
4. Click *Email*.
5. Click Send as Attachment button.
6. Type recipient's email address in *To* text box.
7. If necessary, edit text in *Subject* text box.
8. Type message in message window.
9. Click Send.

Project 2g **Optional: Sending a Workbook via Email** **Part 7 of 7**

Note: Complete this project only if you use Microsoft Outlook as your email provider.

1. Open **CRFinalPrices.xlsx**.
2. Save the workbook and name it **EL2-C6-P2-CRFinalPrices**.
3. Send the workbook as a file attached to an email message by completing the following steps:
   a. Click the FILE tab and then click the *Share* option.
   b. Click *Email* in the *Share* section and then click the Send as Attachment button in the *Email* section.

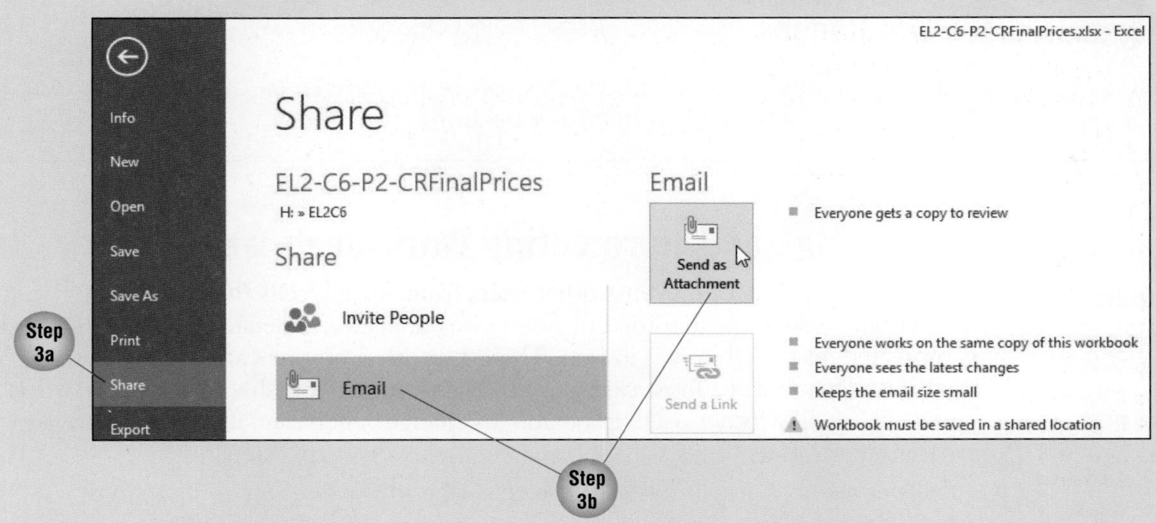

c. With the insertion point positioned in the *To* text box at the message window, type your own email address.
d. Click in the message window and then type the following text:
Here are the new rental rates that are effective May 1, 2015. Please ensure that everyone is using these rates for any rentals after April 30, 2015. Target revenues are on the second sheet.
e. Click the Send button. The message is sent and the message window closes.

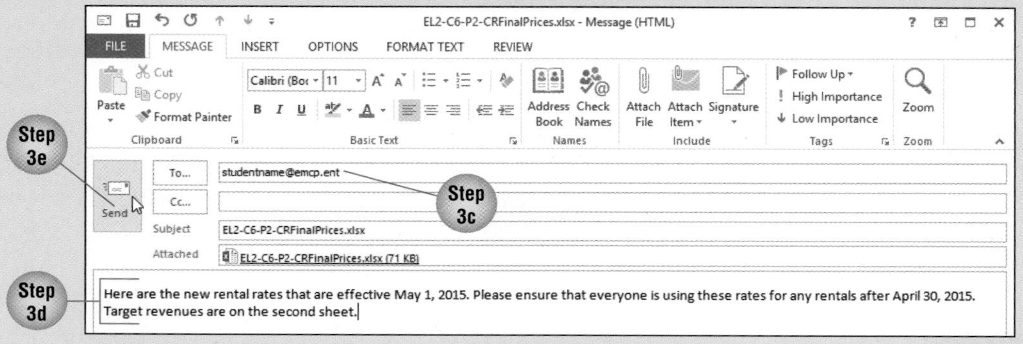

4. Open Outlook.
5. Check your inbox for the new message and then open and view the message. ***Note: Depending on your mail server, you may need to wait a few seconds for the message to be processed.***
6. Close the message and then exit Outlook.
7. Close **EL2-C6-P2-CRFinalPrices.xlsx**.

Project 3 Lock and Unlock a Workbook, Worksheet, and Ranges — 4 Parts

You will protect a worksheet, unlock ranges, prevent changes to the structure of a workbook, and add a password to open a workbook.

Protecting and Unprotecting Worksheets

Quick Steps

Protect a Worksheet
1. Open workbook.
2. Activate desired sheet.
3. Click REVIEW tab.
4. Click Protect Sheet button.
5. Type password.
6. Choose allowable actions.
7. Click OK.
8. Retype password.
9. Click OK.

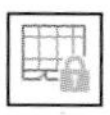
Protect Sheet

Protecting a worksheet prevents other users from editing cells that you do not want accidentally deleted or modified or otherwise changed. By default, when a worksheet is protected, each cell in it is locked. This means that no one can insert, delete, or modify the content. In most cases, some cells within a worksheet contain data that you want to allow other users to be able to change. Therefore, in a collaborative environment, protecting a worksheet generally involves two steps:

1. Clear the lock attribute on those cells that you will allow to be edited.
2. Protect the worksheet.

To clear the lock attribute for (unlock) the cells that you will allow to be modified, select the cells, click the HOME tab, and then click the Format button in the Cells group. Click *Lock Cell* in the *Protection* section of the drop-down list to turn off the lock attribute. Next, turn on worksheet protection by clicking the REVIEW tab and then clicking the Protect Sheet button in the Changes group. At the Protect Sheet dialog box, as shown in Figure 6.8, select the actions you want to allow and then click OK. You can also choose to assign a password to unprotect the sheet. Be cautious if you add a password to remove protection, since you will not be able to unprotect the worksheet if you forget the password. If necessary, write down the password and store it in a secure location.

Quick Steps

Unlock a Cell
1. Select cell(s) to be unlocked.
2. Click HOME tab.
3. Click Format button.
4. Click *Lock Cell*.
5. Deselect cell(s).

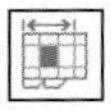

Format

Figure 6.8 Protect Sheet Dialog Box

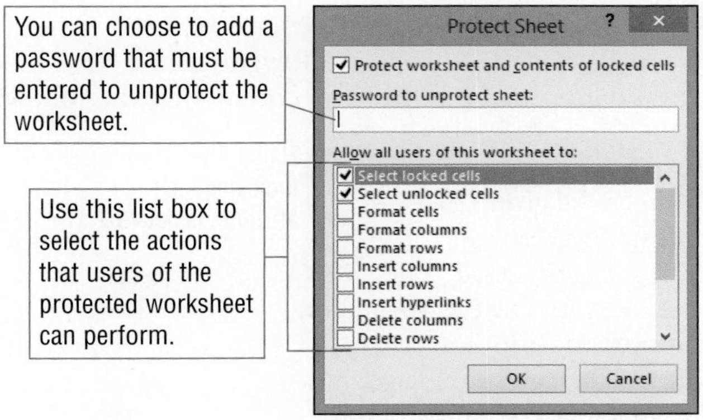

Project 3a Protecting an Entire Worksheet

Part 1 of 4

1. Open **CRFinalPrices.xlsx**.
2. Save the workbook and name it **EL2-C6-P3-CRFinalPrices**.
3. Protect the entire FinalPrices worksheet by completing the following steps:
   a. Make sure FinalPrices is the active sheet.
   b. Click the REVIEW tab.
   c. Click the Protect Sheet button in the Changes group.
   d. At the Protect Sheet dialog box with the insertion point positioned in the *Password to unprotect sheet* text box, type eL2-C6 and then click OK.
   e. At the Confirm Password dialog box with the insertion point positioned in the *Reenter password to proceed* text box, type eL2-C6 and then press Enter or click OK.
   f. Make any cell active in the FinalPrices sheet and attempt to delete the data or type new data. Since the entire worksheet is now protected, all cells are locked and Excel displays a message that the worksheet is protected. Click OK at the Microsoft Excel message indicating that you need to unprotect the sheet to modify the cell.

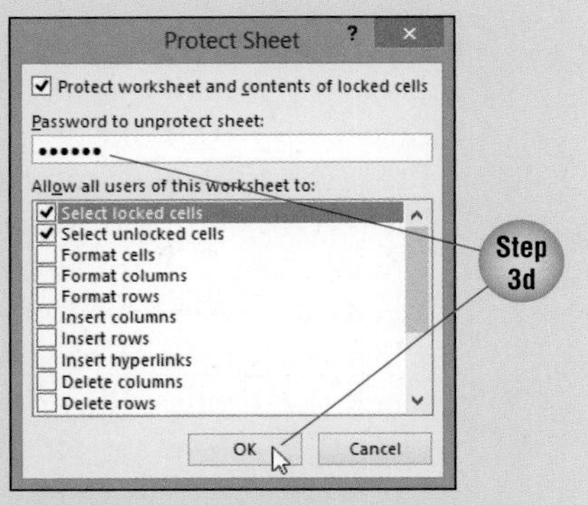

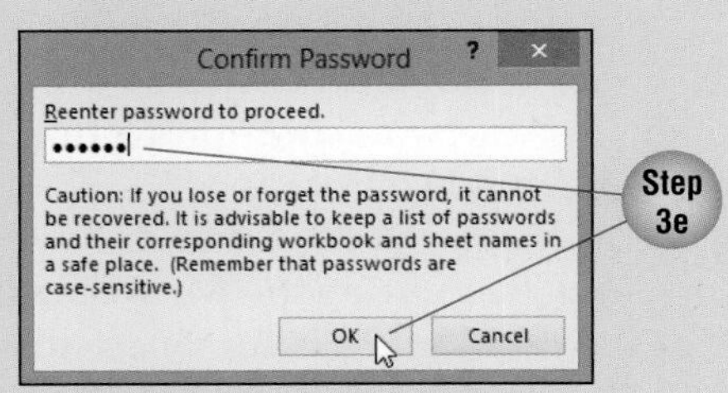

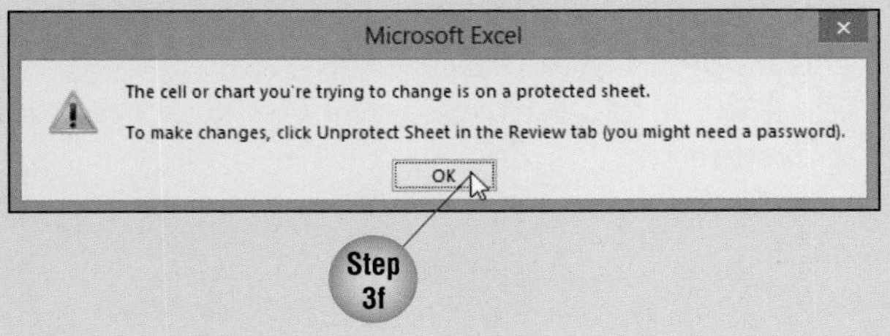

4. Notice the Protect Sheet button changes to the Unprotect Sheet button when a worksheet has been protected.
5. Save **EL2-C6-P3-CRFinalPrices.xlsx**.

Project 3b Unlocking Cells and Protecting a Worksheet — Part 2 of 4

1. With **EL2-C6-P3-CRFinalPrices.xlsx** open, make TargetRevenue the active sheet.
2. Unlock the weekday target rental data cells for editing by completing the following steps:
   a. Select C5:C10.
   b. Click the HOME tab.
   c. Click the Format button in the Cells group.
   d. At the Format button drop-down list, look at the icon next to *Lock Cell* in the *Protection* section. The highlighted icon indicates the lock attribute is turned on.

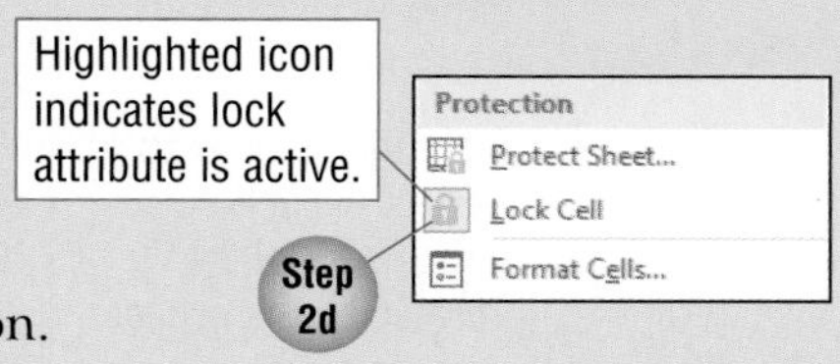

   e. Click *Lock Cell* at the Format button drop-down list to turn the lock attribute off for the selected range.
   f. Click in any cell within the range C5:C10 and then click the Format button in the Cells group. Look at the icon next to *Lock Cell* in the drop-down list. The icon is no longer highlighted, which indicates the cell is unlocked.

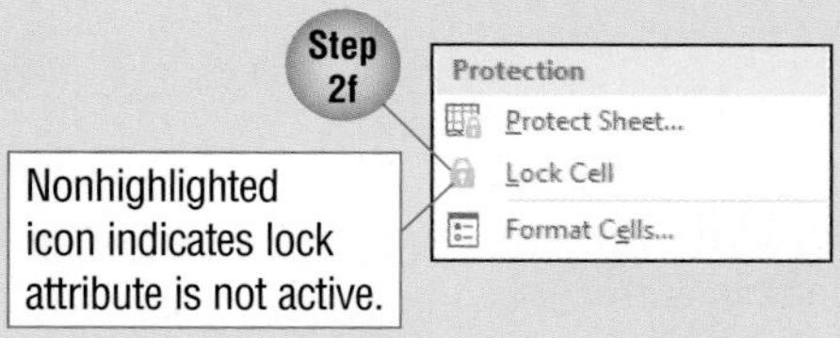

   g. Click within the worksheet area to close the drop-down list.
3. Unlock the remaining target rental ranges for editing by completing the following steps:
   a. Select F5:F10, hold down the Ctrl key, and then select I5:I10 and L5:L10.
   b. Press the F4 key to repeat the command to unlock the cells or click the Format button in the Cells group and then click *Lock Cell* at the drop-down list.
   c. Click in any cell to deselect the ranges.
4. Protect the TargetRevenue worksheet by completing the following steps:
   a. Click the REVIEW tab.
   b. Click the Protect Sheet button in the Changes group.
   c. Type eL2-C6 in the *Password to unprotect sheet* text box.
   d. Click OK.
   e. Type eL2-C6 in the *Reenter password to proceed* text box and then press Enter or click OK.
5. Save **EL2-C6-P3-CRFinalPrices.xlsx**.
6. Test the worksheet protection applied to the TargetRevenue sheet by completing the following steps:
   a. Make cell B8 active and then press the Delete key.
   b. Click OK at the Microsoft Office Excel message box that indicates the protected cell cannot be changed.
   c. Make cell C8 active and then press the Delete key. Since cell C8 is unlocked, its contents are deleted and its dependent cells are updated.
   d. Click the Undo button on the Quick Access toolbar to restore the contents of cell C8.
7. Save and then close **EL2-C6-P3-CRFinalPrices.xlsx**.

Step 6c

4	Category	Weekday (Mo to Th)	Target Rentals	Target Revenue
5	Compact	$ 36	675	$ 24,293
6	Mid-size	38.99	880	34,311
7	Full-size	40.99	425	17,421
8	Minivan	75.99		-
9	SUV	89.99	198	17,818
10	Luxury	99.99	86	8,599
11	TOTAL		Weekday:	$ 102,442

When a worksheet has protection turned on, the Protect Sheet button in the Changes group on the REVIEW tab changes to the Unprotect Sheet button. To remove worksheet protection, click the Unprotect Sheet button or click the Unprotect hyperlink in the Info backstage area in the *Protect Workbook* section. If a password was entered when the worksheet was protected, the Unprotect Sheet dialog box, shown in Figure 6.9, appears. Type the password and then press Enter or click OK.

Unprotect Sheet

Figure 6.9 Unprotect Sheet Dialog Box

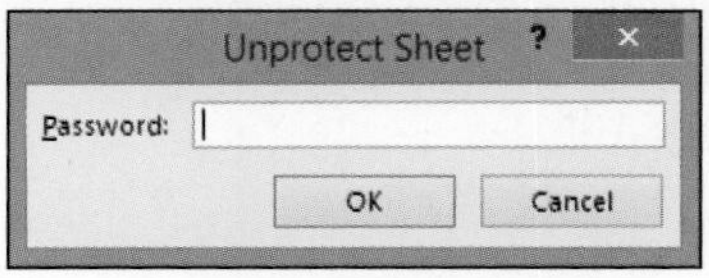

Protecting and Unprotecting the Structure of a Workbook

Use the Protect Workbook button in the Changes group on the REVIEW tab to prevent changes to the structure of a workbook, such as inserting a new sheet, deleting a sheet, or unhiding a hidden worksheet. At the Protect Structure and Windows dialog box, shown in Figure 6.10, you can also turn on protection for the workbook's windows. Click the *Windows* check box to prevent a user from resizing or changing the position of the windows in the workbook. As you did to protect a worksheet, you can enter an optional password that will protect the workbook in the future.

Quick Steps

Protect the Workbook Structure

1. Open workbook.
2. Click REVIEW tab.
3. Click Protect Workbook button.
4. Type password if desired.
5. Click OK.
6. Retype password if entered at Step 4.
7. Click OK.

Protect Workbook

Figure 6.10 Protect Structure and Windows Dialog Box

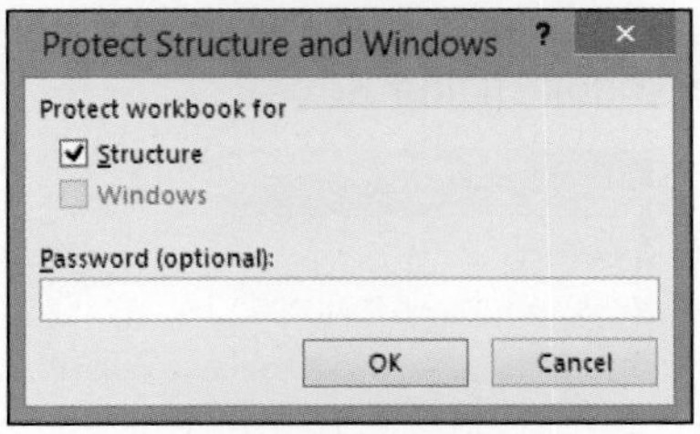

Project 3c **Protecting the Structure of a Workbook** **Part 3 of 4**

1. Open **EL2-C6-P3-CRFinalPrices.xlsx**.
2. Protect the workbook structure by completing the following steps:
   a. If necessary, click the REVIEW tab.
   b. Click the Protect Workbook button in the Changes group.
   c. At the Protect Structure and Windows dialog box with the insertion point positioned in the *Password (optional)* text box, type eL2-C6 and then press Enter or click OK.

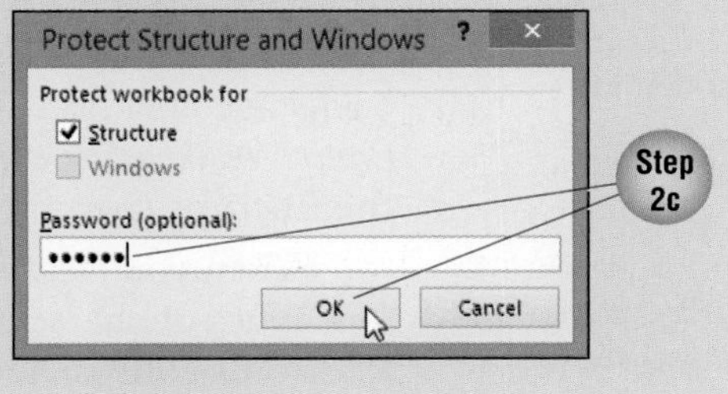

d. At the Confirm Password dialog box with the insertion point positioned in the *Reenter password to proceed* text box, type eL2-C6 and press Enter or click OK.

3. To test the workbook protection, attempt to insert a new worksheet by completing the following steps:
   a. Right-click the TargetRevenue sheet tab.
   b. Look at the shortcut menu. Notice that all of the options related to managing worksheets are dimmed, which means the options are unavailable.
   c. Click within the worksheet area to close the shortcut menu.
4. Save **EL2-C6-P3-CRFinalPrices.xlsx**.

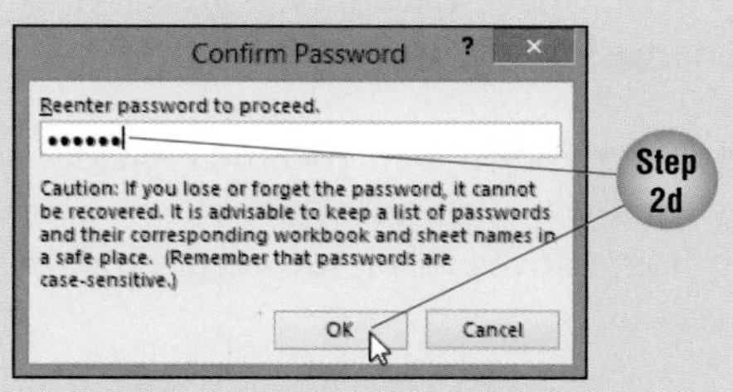

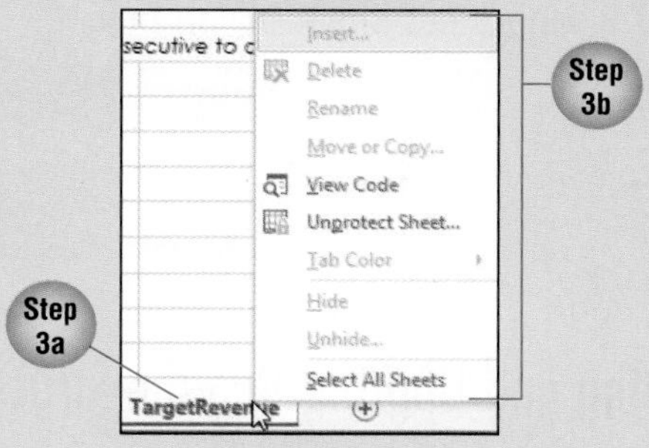

Unprotecting a Workbook

Protect Workbook

When the structure of a workbook has been protected, the Protect Workbook button in the Changes group on the REVIEW tab displays with a green, shaded background. To remove workbook protection, click the Protect Workbook button. If a password was entered when the workbook was protected, the Unprotect Workbook dialog box, shown in Figure 6.11, appears. Type the password and then press Enter or click OK.

Figure 6.11 Unprotect Workbook Dialog Box

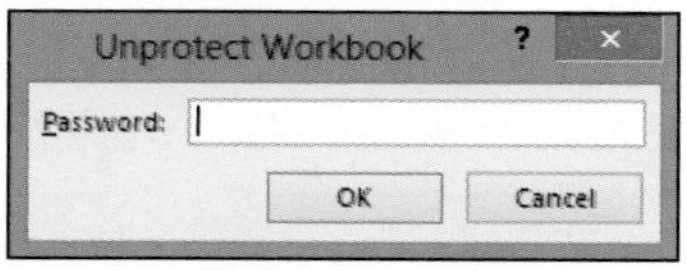

Adding and Removing a Password in a Workbook

Quick Steps

Add a Workbook Password
1. Open workbook.
2. Click FILE tab.
3. Click Protect Workbook button.
4. Click *Encrypt with Password.*
5. Type password.
6. Press Enter or click OK.
7. Retype password.
8. Press Enter or click OK.
9. Save workbook.

You can prevent unauthorized access to Excel data by requiring a password to open a workbook. The password to open a workbook is encrypted. In an ***encrypted password***, the plain text you type is converted into a scrambled format called ***ciphertext***, which prevents unauthorized users from retrieving the password. To add an encrypted password to an open workbook, click the FILE tab. At the Info backstage area, as shown in Figure 6.12, click the Protect Workbook button in *Protect Workbook* section. Click *Encrypt with Password* at the drop-down list to open the Encrypt Document dialog box, shown in Figure 6.13.

When you create a password, it is good practice to include a combination of four types of characters: uppercase letters, lowercase letters, symbols, and numbers. Passwords constructed using these elements are considered secure and more difficult to crack. Note that if you forget the password, you will not be able to open the workbook. If necessary, write down the password and store it in a secure location.

Figure 6.12 Info Backstage Area with Protect Workbook Drop-down List

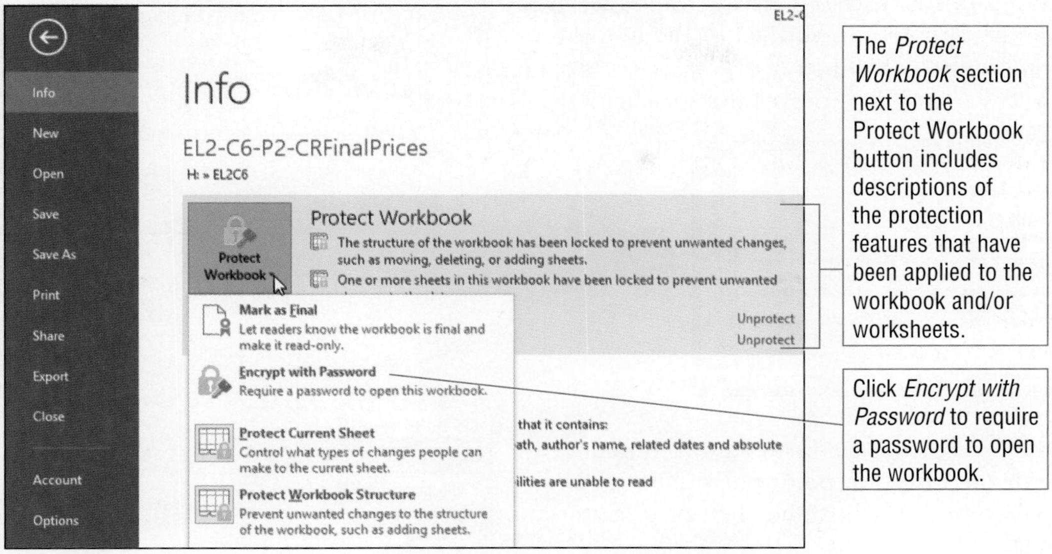

Figure 6.13 Encrypt Document Dialog Box

Project 3d Adding a Password to Open a Workbook

Part 4 of 4

1. With **EL2-C6-P3-CRFinalPrices.xlsx** open, add a password to open the workbook by completing the following steps:
   a. Click the FILE tab. The backstage area opens with the *Info* option selected.
   b. Read the information in the *Protect Workbook* section. Since this workbook has protection features already applied, the existing features are described and a hyperlink is provided to unprotect each protected worksheet. In a workbook with no pre-existing protection, the *Permissions* section displays the text *Control what types of changes people can make to this workbook.*
   c. Click the Protect Workbook button.

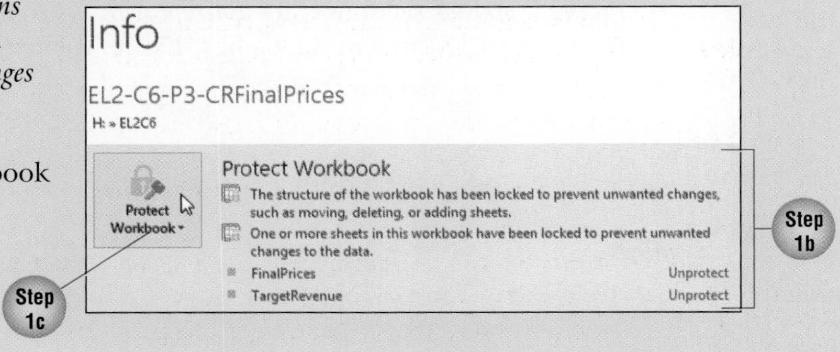

d. Click *Encrypt with Password* at the drop-down list.

e. At the Encrypt Document dialog box with the insertion point positioned in the *Password* text box, type eL2-C6 and then press Enter or click OK.

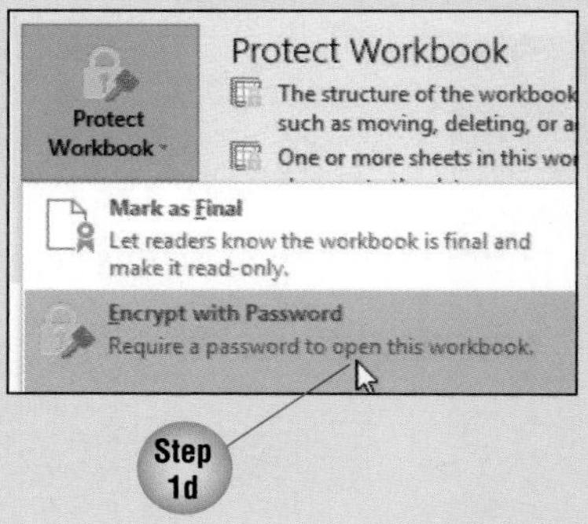

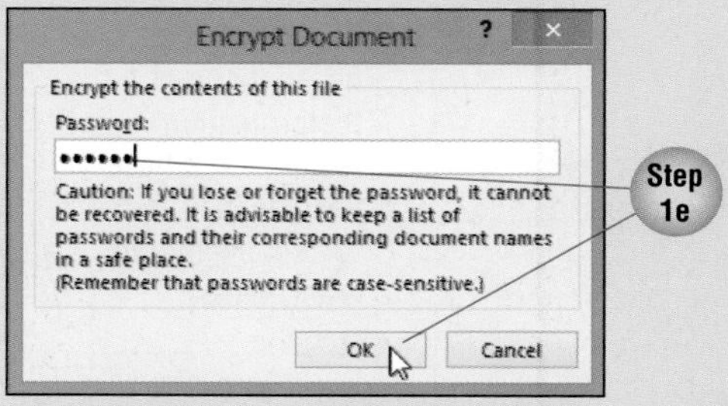

f. Type eL2-C6 at the Confirm Password dialog box with the insertion point positioned in the *Reenter password* text box and then press Enter or click OK.

g. Notice that Excel has added to the first line of the *Protect Workbook* section next to the Protect Workbook button the text *A password is required to open this workbook.*

h. Click the Back button to return to the worksheet.

2. Save and then close **EL2-C6-P3-CRFinalPrices.xlsx**.
3. Test the password security on the workbook by completing the following steps:

a. Open **EL2-C6-P3-CRFinalPrices.xlsx**.

b. At the Password dialog box with the insertion point positioned in the *Password* text box, type a password that is incorrect for the file and then press Enter.

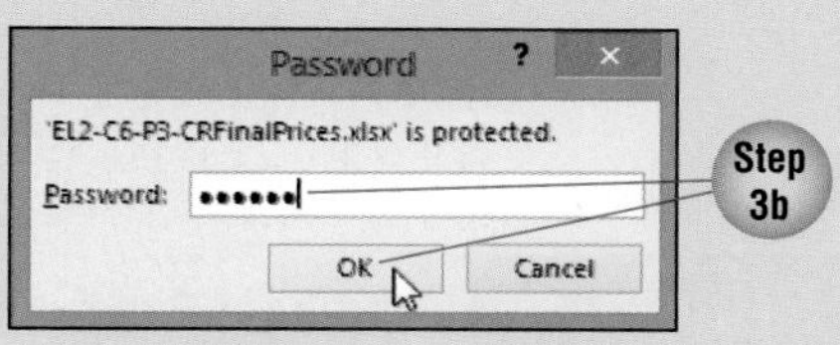

c. At the Microsoft Excel message box indicating that the password you supplied is not correct, click OK.

d. Open **EL2-C6-P3-CRFinalPrices.xlsx**.

e. Type eL2-C6 in the *Password* text box and then press Enter or click OK.

4. Close **EL2-C6-P3-CRFinalPrices.xlsx**.

To remove a password from a workbook, open the workbook using your password. At the Info backstage area, click the Protect Workbook button in the *Protect Workbook* section. Click *Encrypt with Password* at the drop-down list to open the Encrypt Document dialog box. Delete the password and then click OK.

Project 4 Track and Resolve Changes Made to a Workbook — 3 Parts

You will begin tracking changes made to a workbook, view changes made by two users, and accept and reject changes.

Tracking Changes to a Workbook

As you learned in Project 1, Excel automatically tracks changes made by individuals who share a workbook. As you saw with the history sheet in Project 2e, you can display and print a record of the changes. If a workbook is not shared, you can turn on the Track Changes feature and Excel will automatically share the workbook. To do this, click the Track Changes button in the Changes group on the REVIEW tab and then click *Highlight Changes* at the drop-down list. At the Highlight Changes dialog box, click the *Track changes while editing* check box and then click OK.

As the owner of a shared workbook, you might want to view the worksheet with all of the cells highlighted in which changes have been made to the data. Figure 6.14 displays the worksheet you will edit in Project 4 with all of the changes highlighted. As you hover the mouse pointer over a highlighted cell, a pop-up box displays the name of the person who changed the cell, along with the date, time, original entry, and revised entry.

Quick Steps

Track Changes

1. Open workbook.
2. Click REVIEW tab.
3. Click Track Changes button.
4. Click *Highlight Changes*.
5. Click *Track changes while editing* check box.
6. Click OK twice.

Highlight Changes

1. Open tracked workbook.
2. Click REVIEW tab.
3. Click Track Changes button.
4. Click *Highlight Changes*.
5. Change *When* to *Not yet reviewed*.
6. Make sure *Who* is set to *Everyone*.
7. Click OK.

Figure 6.14 Project 4 Worksheet with Changes Highlighted

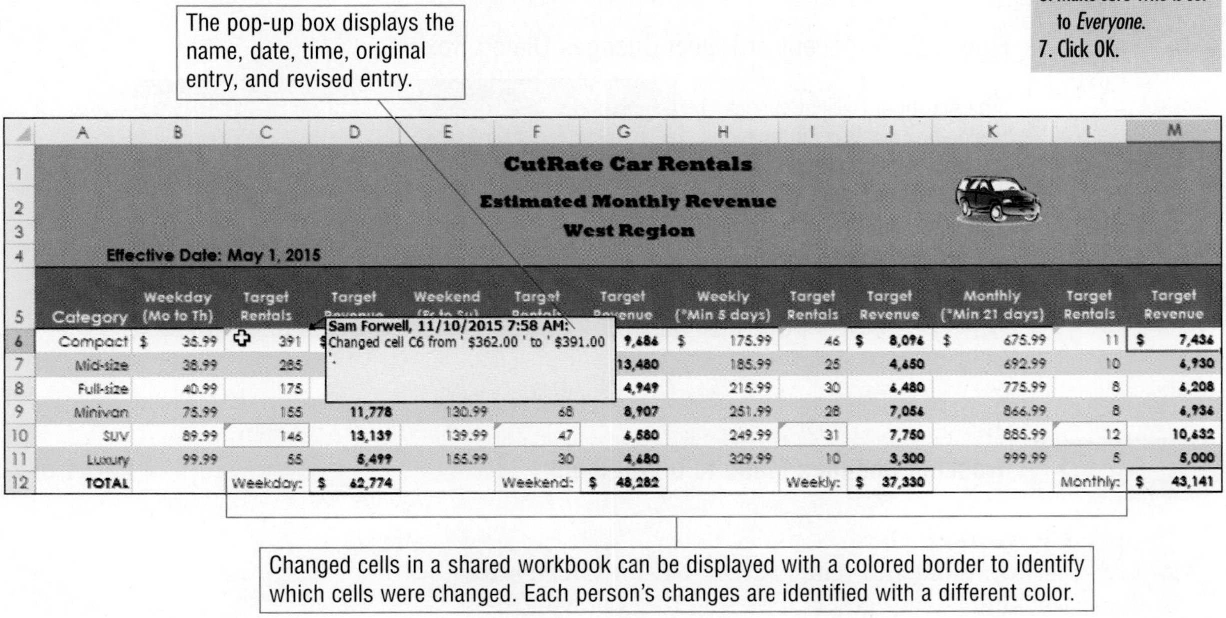

Accepting and Rejecting Tracked Changes

Quick Steps

Accept and Reject Changes
1. Open tracked workbook.
2. Click REVIEW tab.
3. Click Track Changes button.
4. Click *Accept/Reject Changes.*
5. Make sure *When* is set to *Not yet reviewed.*
6. Make sure *Who* is set to *Everyone.*
7. Click OK.
8. Click Accept or Reject button at each change.

In addition to displaying the worksheet with the changes highlighted, you can navigate to each change and accept or reject it. To do this, click the Track Changes button in the Changes group on the REVIEW tab and then click *Accept/Reject Changes* at the drop-down list. At the Select Changes to Accept or Reject dialog box, as shown in Figure 6.15, define which changes you want to review and then click OK.

Excel navigates to the first changed cell and displays the Accept or Reject Changes dialog box, shown in Figure 6.16. Review the information in the dialog box and click the Accept button or the Reject button. If you reject a change, the cell is restored to its original value. After you respond to each changed cell, the colored border is removed since the cell has been reviewed. The dialog box also includes an Accept All button and a Reject All button, which you can use to make a global review decision, if desired. Be careful when accepting and rejecting changes, since Undo is not available after you review the cells.

Figure 6.15 Select Changes to Accept or Reject Dialog Box

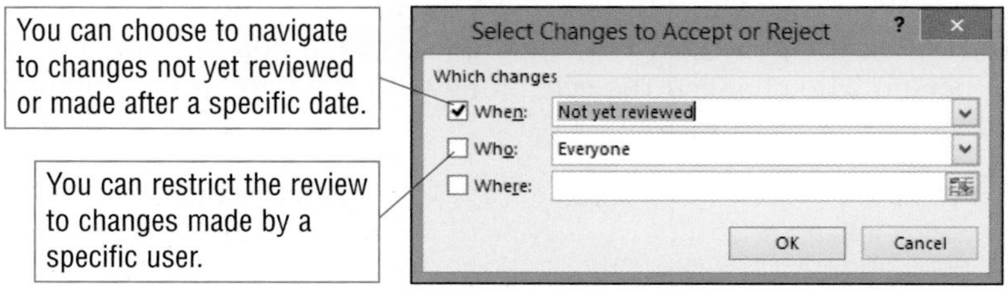

Figure 6.16 Accept or Reject Changes Dialog Box

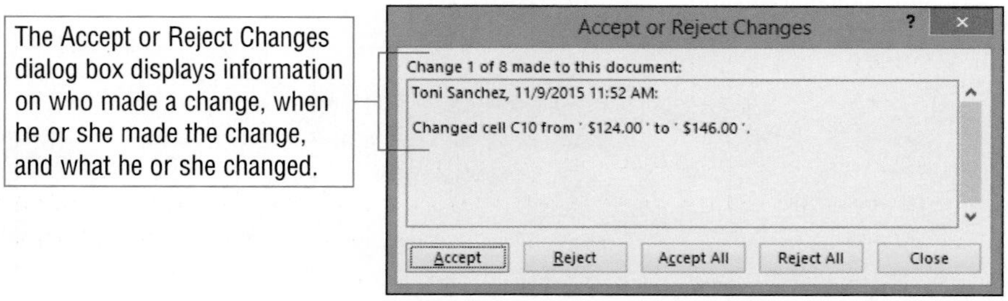

Project 4a **Tracking Changes Made to a Workbook** **Part 1 of 3**

1. Open **CRWestReg.xlsx**.
2. Save the workbook and name it **EL2-C6-P4-CRWestReg**.
3. Begin tracking changes by completing the following steps:
   a. If necessary, click the REVIEW tab.
   b. Click the Track Changes button in the Changes group.
   c. Click *Highlight Changes* at the drop-down list.

d. At the Highlight Changes dialog box, click the *Track changes while editing* check box to insert a check mark. Notice that turning on the Track Changes feature automatically shares the workbook.

e. With *When* set to *All* and *Who* set to *Everyone* by default, click OK.

f. At the Microsoft Excel message box indicating that this action will now save the workbook, click OK to continue.

4. Close **EL2-C6-P4-CRWestReg.xlsx**.

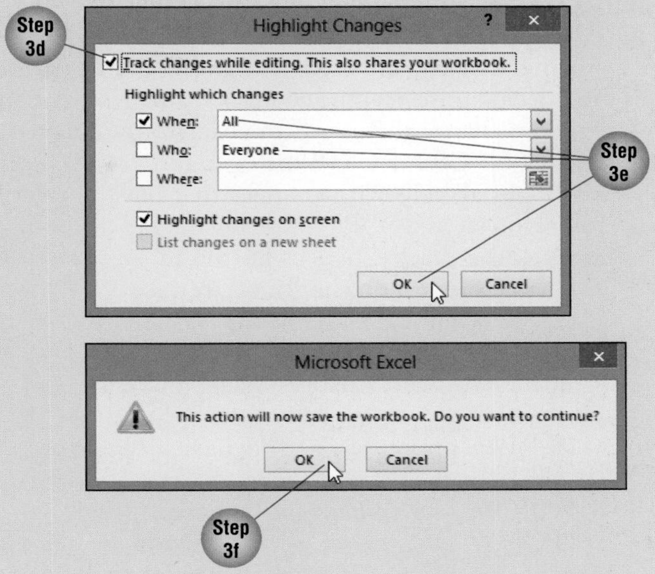

Project 4b Editing a Tracked Workbook

Part 2 of 3

1. Assume that you are Toni Sanchez, the SUV rental manager for the West region at CutRate Car Rentals. You have been asked to edit the target rental values for SUVs. At a blank Excel window, change the user name to *Toni Sanchez*. (Refer to Project 2b, Step 1 if you need assistance changing the user name.) You will return to the original user name in Project 4c.
2. Open **EL2-C6-P4-CRWestReg.xlsx**.
3. Edit the cells that contain the SUV target data as follows:

C10:	from	*124*	to	*146*
F10:	from	*22*	to	*47*
I10:	from	*22*	to	*31*
L10:	from	*8*	to	*12*

4. Save and then close **EL2-C6-P4-CRWestReg.xlsx**.
5. Assume that you are Sam Forwell, the compact rental manager for the West region at CutRate Car Rentals. You have been asked to edit the target rental values for compact cars. At a blank Excel window, change the user name to *Sam Forwell*.
6. Open **EL2-C6-P4-CRWestReg.xlsx**.
7. Edit the cells that contain the compact target data as follows:

C6:	from	*362*	to	*391*
F6:	from	*165*	to	*173*
I6:	from	*33*	to	*46*
L6:	from	*15*	to	*11*

8. Save and then close **EL2-C6-P4-CRWestReg.xlsx**.

Project 4c Highlighting and Reviewing Tracked Changes

Part 3 of 3

1. Assume that you are the operations manager for the West region at CutRate Car Rentals. You decide to review the changes made by Toni Sanchez and Sam Forwell. At a blank Excel window, change the user name back to the original user name for the computer you are using.
2. Open **EL2-C6-P4-CRWestReg.xlsx**.
3. Highlight all cells with changes that have not yet been reviewed by completing the following steps:
   a. Click the Track Changes button in the Changes group on the REVIEW tab.
   b. Click *Highlight Changes* at the drop-down list.
   c. At the Highlight Changes dialog box, click the down-pointing arrow at the right of the *When* option box and then click *Not yet reviewed* at the drop-down list.
   d. With *Who* set to *Everyone* by default, click OK.

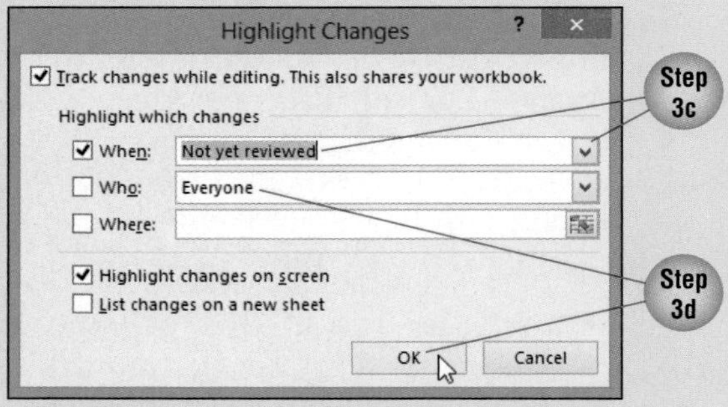

4. Accept and reject changes as you navigate through the worksheet by completing the following steps:
   a. Press Ctrl + Home to make cell A1 active.
   b. Click the Track Changes button and then click *Accept/Reject Changes* at the drop-down list.
   c. At the Select Changes to Accept or Reject dialog box with *When* set to *Not yet reviewed* and *Who* set to *Everyone*, click OK.
   d. Excel moves the active cell to cell C10, where the first change was made, and displays the Accept or Reject Changes dialog box. Click the Accept button to leave cell C10 at *$146.00*.

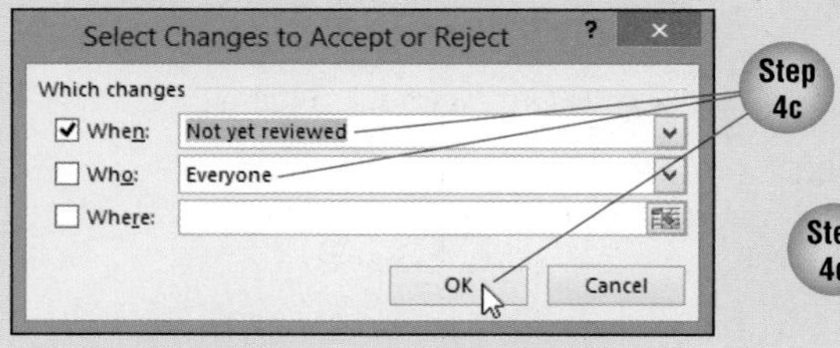

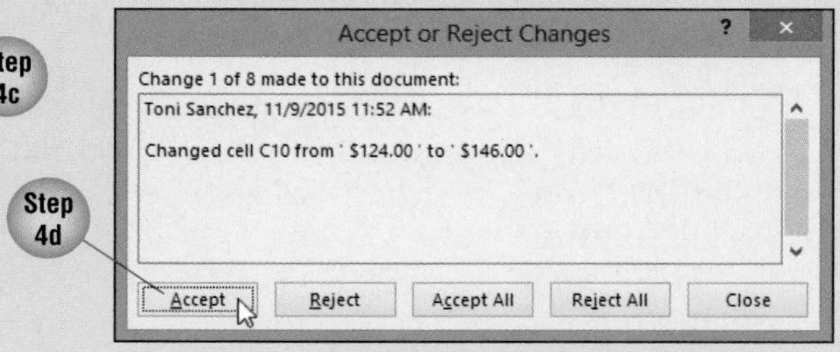

   e. Excel makes cell F10 the active cell. Click the Reject button to restore cell F10 to the original value of *$22.00*. ***Note: If necessary, drag the Accept or Reject Changes dialog box out of the way to see the cell being reviewed in the worksheet area.***

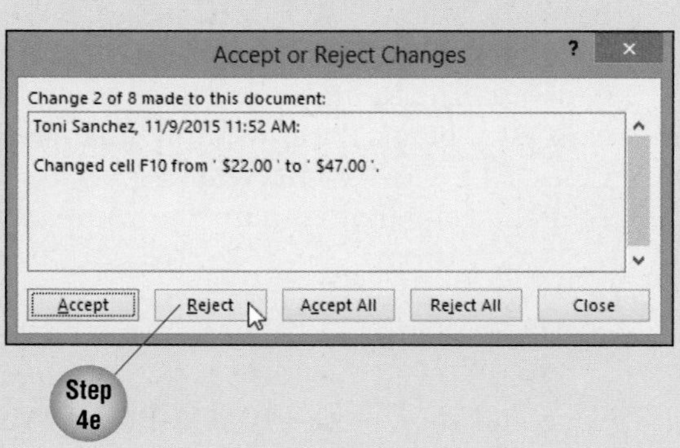

   f. Respond to the remaining changes to the cells as follows:

I10:	Accept
L10:	Accept
C6:	Reject
F6:	Accept
I6:	Reject
L6:	Accept

5. Save the worksheet.
6. Print and then close **EL2-C6-P4-CRWestReg.xlsx**.

Turning Off Track Changes

When you no longer need to track the changes made to a workbook, click the Track Changes button and then click *Highlight Changes* at the drop-down list. At the Highlight Changes dialog box, click the *Track changes while editing* check box to remove the check mark and then click OK. Excel displays the warning message that the workbook will no longer be shared and that the change history will be erased. Click Yes to complete the action.

If you have not reviewed all of the changes made to the workbook, consider printing a copy of the history sheet before turning off the Track Changes feature. (Refer to Project 2e, Step 2, for assistance with printing a history sheet.)

Excel provides several methods to share and collaborate data with other users of Excel. The method that you choose depends on factors such as the availability of a network share folder, need to protect ranges or otherwise restrict access to sensitive data, and resources available by the users who will receive the data. In Chapter 8, you will explore other features that are important to consider when distributing a workbook, such as restricting access and removing personal information.

Quick Steps

Turn Off Track Changes

1. Open tracked workbook.
2. Click REVIEW tab.
3. Click *Highlight Changes.*
4. Click *Track changes while editing check box* check box to remove check mark.
5. Click OK.
6. Click Yes.

Chapter Summary

- Workbook properties include descriptive information about the workbook, such as the author's name and the workbook title, subject, or comments.
- Workbook properties are sometimes referred to as *metadata*.
- Display the Info backstage area or open the document information panel to add information to a workbook's properties.
- Comments display text in a pop-up box when the cell pointer is hovering over a cell to which a comment has been attached.
- Comments are useful for adding explanatory notes, descriptions, or questions about a cell entry when a workbook is being created, edited, or shared with other reviewers.
- Insert, edit, view, or delete a comment using buttons in the Comments group on the REVIEW tab. Comment text can be copied and pasted to another cell using the Paste Special dialog box.
- Sharing a workbook generally involves turning on the sharing feature and saving the workbook to a folder on a networked server that is accessible to the other users who need the file.
- Use the Share Workbook button in the Changes group on the REVIEW tab to turn on the sharing feature.
- When Microsoft Office is installed, a user name is defined for the computer onto which the software has been copied. Excel automatically inserts this name in the *Author* workbook property when a new workbook is created.
- Change the user name at the Excel Options dialog box.
- View other users who have a shared workbook open at the Share Workbook dialog box.
- When a workbook is shared, Excel automatically tracks the changes made by all of the individuals who access the file.

- If two users have a shared workbook open at the same time and each one makes a change to the same cell, a Resolve Conflicts dialog box appears when the second user saves the workbook.
- At the Resolve Conflicts dialog box, the second user can choose to accept the change he or she made or restore the cell to the entry made by the last person to save the file.
- Print a history sheet to provide a detailed record of all of the changes made to a shared workbook before removing shared access to the workbook.
- When a shared workbook is changed to an exclusive workbook, all of the change history is removed from the file.
- You can save workbook to a folder in your own storage location on Windows Live SkyDrive, where you can retrieve it from any location with Internet access.
- Invite people to edit or view the workbooks that you have saved to your SkyDrive folders or SharePoint library.
- An email message with the current workbook added as a file attachment can be generated from Excel using the Share backstage area. You can attach the workbook in the default Excel (.xlsx) format, as a portable data format (PDF) document, or as an XML paper specification (XPS) document.
- You can protect an entire worksheet to prevent another person from accidentally inserting or deleting or otherwise changing data that you do not want modified.
- Protect a worksheet using the Protect Sheet button in the Changes group on the REVIEW tab.
- You can add a password that is required to unprotect a worksheet.
- Each cell in a worksheet has a lock attribute that activates when the worksheet is protected.
- To allow individual cells in a protected worksheet to be editable, select the cells and turn off the lock attribute before protecting the worksheet.
- The Protect Workbook button in the Changes group on the REVIEW tab is used to protect a workbook from a user inserting, deleting, renaming, or otherwise managing worksheets in it.
- You can prevent unauthorized access to an Excel workbook by adding an encrypted password to open and/or modify the workbook.
- At the Info backstage area, click the Protect Workbook button and then click *Encrypt with Password* to add a workbook password. Save the workbook after typing and confirming the password.
- Turn on or off the Track Changes feature or display changes in a shared workbook by opening the Highlight Changes dialog box.
- The Accept/Reject Changes feature is used to navigate to each changed cell in a worksheet and then accept or reject the revision.

Commands Review

FEATURE	RIBBON TAB, GROUP/OPTION	BUTTON	KEYBOARD SHORTCUT
accept/reject changes	REVIEW, Changes		
add comment	REVIEW, Comments		Shift + F2
add password	FILE, *Info*		
change user name	FILE, *Options*		
delete comment	REVIEW, Comments		
document information panel	FILE, *Info*	Properties ▾	
edit comment	REVIEW, Comments		
highlight changes	REVIEW, Changes		
paste copied comment	HOME, Clipboard		Ctrl + Alt + V
protect workbook	REVIEW, Changes		
protect worksheet	REVIEW, Changes		
share workbook	REVIEW, Changes		
track changes	REVIEW, Changes		
unlock cells	HOME, Format		

Concepts Check Test Your Knowledge SNAP

Completion: In the space provided at the right, indicate the correct term, command, or number.

1. Open this view to add descriptive information about a workbook, such as a title or subject heading. ____________________
2. This panel displays the workbook's properties between the ribbon and worksheet. ____________________
3. A small, red, diagonal triangle in the upper right corner of a cell indicates that this box will pop up when the mouse pointer rests on the cell. ____________________
4. Open this dialog box to turn on the feature that allows changes to be made by more than one user at the same time. ____________________
5. Change the user name for the computer that you are using by opening this dialog box. ____________________
6. When two users have the same workbook open at the same time and both make changes to the same cell, this dialog box appears when the second person saves the workbook. ____________________
7. Open this dialog box to create a history sheet, which includes a record of all of the changes made to a shared workbook. ____________________
8. Select a cell that you want to allow changes to and then click this button and menu option to unlock the cell before protecting the worksheet. ____________________
9. At this dialog box, you can add a password that is required to unprotect a worksheet. ____________________
10. Prevent users from inserting or deleting worksheets in a workbook by opening this dialog box. ____________________
11. Click this option from the Protect Workbook drop-down list at the Info backstage area view to assign a password to open a workbook. ____________________
12. Turn on this feature and Excel automatically changes the workbook to a shared workbook, if it is not already shared. ____________________
13. Excel applies this formatting to cells in a shared workbook that have been modified to make the revised cells stand out. ____________________
14. Use this feature to navigate to each changed cell in a shared workbook and decide whether to keep the change or restore the cell back to its previous value. ____________________
15. This feature is not available to restore cells to their previous values after you have finished reviewing tracked changes. ____________________

Skills Check Assess Your Performance

Assessment 1

ENTER AND DISPLAY WORKBOOK PROPERTIES AND INSERT COMMENTS

SNAP Grade It

1. Open **NationalLicenses.xlsx**.
2. Save the workbook and name it **EL2-C6-A1-NationalLicenses**.
3. Type the following text in the appropriate workbook properties:

Add an Author	Wendy Cheung
Title	MSO 2013 License Chargeback
Subject	Journal entry by department
Categories	JE supporting document
Status	Posted
Comments	Audit worksheet for Office 2013 site license with internal chargebacks

4. Remove the existing author, *Paradigm Publishing Inc.*
5. Display the document information panel.
6. Insert a screen image of the worksheet showing the document information panel in a new Microsoft Word document using Print Screen with Paste or the Screenshot feature in Word (INSERT tab, Screenshot button in Illustrations group). Type your name a few lines below the screen image.
7. Save the Microsoft Word document and name it **EL2-C6-A1-NationalLicenses.docx**.
8. Print **EL2-C6-A1-NationalLicenses.docx** and then exit Word.
9. At the Microsoft Excel worksheet, close the document information panel.
10. Make cell B8 active and insert a new comment. Type Check this quantity with Marty. The number seems high. in the comment box.
11. Make cell B14 active and insert a new comment. Type Make a note in the budget file for next year. This quantity will increase by 5. in the comment box.
12. Print the worksheet with the comments at the end of the sheet.
13. Save and close **EL2-C6-A1-NationalLicenses.xlsx**.

Assessment 2

SHARE A WORKSHEET, EDIT A SHARED WORKBOOK, AND PRINT A HISTORY SHEET

1. Open **PreMfgTargets.xlsx**.
2. Save the workbook and name it **EL2-C6-A2-PreMfgTargets**.
3. Share the workbook.
4. Change the user name to *Lorne Moir* and then edit the following cells:

C11:	from	*4,352*	to	*5520*
C18:	from	*15,241*	to	*15960*

5. Save the workbook.
6. Open a new instance of Excel. ***Note: Refer to Project 2c to open a new instance of Excel.***

7. Change the user name to *Gerri Gonzales,* open **EL2-C6-A2-PreMfgTargets.xlsx**, and then edit the following cells:

   F4: from *3,845* to *5126*

   F9: from *7,745* to *9320*
8. Save the workbook.
9. Create a history sheet with a record of the changes made to the data by all of the users.
10. Print the history sheet. ***Note: If you submit your assignment work electronically, create a copy of the history sheet in a new workbook, since the history sheet is automatically deleted when the file is saved.***
11. Save and then close both instances of **EL2-C6-A2-PreMfgTargets.xlsx**.
12. Change the user name back to the original user name for the computer you are using.

Assessment 3

REMOVE SHARED ACCESS

Grade It

1. Open **EL2-C6-A2-PreMfgTargets.xlsx**.
2. Save the workbook and name it **EL2-C6-A3-PreMfgTargets**.
3. Remove the shared access to the workbook.
4. Close **EL2-C6-A3-PreMfgTargets.xlsx**.

Assessment 4

PROTECT AN ENTIRE WORKSHEET AND ADD A PASSWORD TO A WORKBOOK

Grade It

1. Open **EL2-C6-A1-NationalLicenses.xlsx**.
2. Save the workbook and name it **EL2-C6-A4-NationalLicenses**.
3. Protect the entire worksheet using the password *eL2-A4* to unprotect.
4. Add the password *eL2-A4* to open the workbook.
5. Save and close **EL2-C6-A4-NationalLicenses.xlsx**.
6. Open **EL2-C6-A4-NationalLicenses.xlsx** and test the password to open the workbook.
7. Close **EL2-C6-A4-NationalLicenses.xlsx**.

Assessment 5

UNLOCK CELLS AND PROTECT A WORKSHEET AND PROTECT WORKBOOK STRUCTURE

Grade It

1. Open **PreMfgTargets.xlsx**.
2. Save the workbook and name it **EL2-C6-A5-PreMfgTargets**.
3. Select C4:F21 and unlock the cells.
4. Deselect the range and then protect the worksheet using the password *eL2-A5* to unprotect.
5. Rename Sheet1 as *2015MfgTargets*.
6. Protect the workbook structure to prevent users from inserting, deleting, or renaming sheets using the password *eL2-A5* to unprotect.
7. Save and then close **EL2-C6-A5-PreMfgTargets.xlsx**.

Assessment 6

TRACK CHANGES, ACCEPT/REJECT CHANGES, AND PRINT A HISTORY SHEET

1. Open **EL2-C6-A5-PreMfgTargets.xlsx**.
2. Save the workbook and name it **EL2-C6-A6-PreMfgTargets**.
3. Unprotect the workbook structure so that new sheets can be added, deleted, renamed, or copied.
4. Turn on the Track Changes feature.
5. Change the user name to *Grant Antone* and then edit the following cells:
   D4: from *3,251* to *3755*
   D17: from *5,748* to *6176*
6. Save the workbook, change the user name to *Jean Kocsis*, and then edit the following cells:
   E6: from *6,145* to *5748*
   E11: from *2,214* to *3417*
7. Save the workbook and then change the user name back to the original user name for the computer you are using.
8. Accept and Reject the changes in the cells as follows:
   D4: Accept
   D17: Reject
   E6: Reject
   E11: Accept
9. Create and print a history sheet of the changes made to the worksheet. ***Note: If you submit your assignment work electronically, create a copy of the history sheet in a new workbook, since the history sheet is automatically deleted when the file is saved.***
10. Print the 2015MfgTargets worksheet.
11. Save and then close **EL2-C6-A6-PreMfgTargets.xlsx**

Optional: Open **EL2-C6-A6-A6-PreMfgTargets.xlsx** and email the workbook to yourself. Compose an appropriate message within the message window, as if you are an employee of Precision Design and Packaging sending the file to the office manager. Open the message window from the inbox in your email program and print the message. Close the message window and exit your email program.

Visual Benchmark Demonstrate Your Proficiency

TRACK CHANGES; INSERT COMMENTS

1. Open **PawsParadise.xlsx**.
2. Save the workbook and name it **EL2-C6-VB-PawsParadise**.
3. Figure 6.17 illustrates the worksheet after the owner/operator reviewed the worksheet created by the kennel manager. While reviewing the service price list, the owner made comments and changed cells. Using Figure 6.17 and Figure 6.18, make the same changes to your copy of the worksheet, ensuring that the changes are associated with the owner's name.

4. Create and print a history sheet scaled to fit on one page. ***Note: If you submit your assignment work electronically, create a copy of the sheet in a new workbook, since the history sheet is automatically deleted when the file is saved.***
5. Print the worksheet with the changes highlighted and the comments as displayed on the worksheet.
6. Save and then close **EL2-C6-VB-PawsParadise.xlsx**.
7. Change the user name back to the original user name for the computer you are using.

Figure 6.17 Visual Benchmark Worksheet with Comments

	A	B	C	D	E
1	Paradise for Paws Kennels Inc.				
2	Owned and operated by Erin Haviland since 1998				
3	Service	Options	Price		
4	Doggie Daycare		$ 17.25	per day	
5	Doggie Walks				
6		15 minute trail walk	4.50		
7		25 minute trail walk	8.50		
8	Doggie Grooming				
9		Full groom	35.00		
10		Shampoo only	22.50		
11		Nails and ears only	15.00		
12	Doggie Boarding				
13		Indoor/outdoor suite	25.00	per day	
14		Deluxe suite	27.50	per day	
15		VIP suite	38.00	per day	

Erin Haviland:
I plan to raise this to 6.50 when I am finished with comparison data.

Erin Haviland:
I may reduce this to 12.00 once I have the groomer's new rates.

Figure 6.18 Visual Benchmark History Worksheet

	A	B	C	D	E	F	G	H	I	J	K
1	Action Number	Date	Time	Who	Change	Sheet	Range	New Value	Old Value	Action Type	Losing Action
2	1	11/11/2015	4:03 PM	Erin Haviland	Cell Change	Sheet1	C4	$17.25	$16.50		
3	2	11/11/2015	4:03 PM	Erin Haviland	Cell Change	Sheet1	C7	$8.50	$8.25		
4	3	11/11/2015	4:03 PM	Erin Haviland	Cell Change	Sheet1	C10	$22.50	$20.00		
5	4	11/11/2015	4:03 PM	Erin Haviland	Cell Change	Sheet1	C14	$27.50	$28.50		
6	5	11/11/2015	4:03 PM	Erin Haviland	Cell Change	Sheet1	B7	25 minute trail walk	30 minute trail walk		
7											
8	The history ends with the changes saved on 11/11/2015 at 4:03 PM.										

Case Study Apply Your Skills

Part 1

Yolanda Robertson of NuTrends Market Research is working with Nicola Carlucci of Pizza by Mario on a workbook with projected franchise startups for 2015. The workbook is currently in draft format in a file named **PBMNewFranchises.xlsx**. Open the workbook and save the document as **EL2-C6-CS-P1-PBMNewFranchises**. Add an appropriate title and subject to the workbook's properties and include comment text to explain that the draft workbook was created in consultation with Nicola Carlucci. Yolanda has asked for your assistance with protecting the workbook to prevent accidental data modifications or erasures when the workbook is shared with others. Yolanda and Nicola have agreed that the city, state, and store numbers should be protected; however, the month a new store is planned to open and names of prospective franchisees can change. Share the workbook. Yolanda and Nicola have agreed on the following passwords:

- Password to unprotect the worksheet is *eL2-CS1*.
- Password to open the workbook is *eL2-CS1*.

Part 2

Save the workbook and name it **EL2-C6-CS-P2-PBMNewFranchises**. Yolanda has reviewed her research files and meeting notes and would like the following changes made to the data. Make sure the user name is correct so that the following changes are associated with Yolanda:

Store 138: Franchisee is Jae-Dong Han
Store 149: Franchisee is Leslie Posno

Save the workbook. Nicola is in charge of logistics planning and has two changes to make to the months that stores are scheduled to open. Make sure the user name is correct so that the following changes are associated with Nicola:

Store 135: Open in February
Store 141: Open in December

Save the workbook and then display the worksheet with all of the changes made by Yolanda and Nicola highlighted. Create a history sheet. Print the worksheet with the cells highlighted and also print the history sheet. ***Note: If you submit your assignment work electronically, create a copy of the history sheet in a new workbook, since the history sheet is automatically deleted when the file is saved.*** Restore the worksheet to exclusive use. Close **EL2-C6-CS-P2-PBMNewFranchises.xlsx**. Change the user name back to the original user name for the computer you are using.

Part 3

Yolanda will be sending the shared workbook from Part 1 to Leonard Scriver, a colleague at the Michigan office of NuTrends Market Research. Yolanda wants Leonard to review the data and add his recommendations; however, Yolanda would prefer that Leonard save his copy using a different name so that the original shared version is not changed. Open **EL2-C6-CS-P1-PBMNewFranchises.xlsx**. Unprotect the worksheet, remove the password to open the workbook, and then save the workbook using the name **EL2-C6-CS-P3-PBM-LScriver**. Based on Leonard's experience with franchise startups, he has the following recommendations, which he prefers to show in comments within the worksheet. Make sure the user name is correct so that the comment boxes display Leonard's name:

Store 136: Opening a second store in Chicago is more likely to occur in April.

Store 144: Move this opening to June, as resources at the head office will be stretched in May.

Store 152: Try to open this franchise at the same time as store 151.

Show all comments within the worksheet and then print the worksheet, making sure the comments print as displayed. Save and then close **EL2-C6-CS-P3-PBM-LScriver.xlsx**. Change the user name back to the original user name for the computer that you are using.

Part 4

Mario Carlucci has commented that the password to open the workbook is not intuitive for him and he has had trouble remembering it. He wants to change the workbook password to something more user friendly, such as *Target14*. Yolanda and Nicola chose the passwords they have used in the workbook carefully based on their understanding of strong passwords that are difficult to crack by unauthorized users. Yolanda has asked you to assist with a training package for Mario that will educate him on strong passwords. Conduct research on the Internet to find guidelines for creating strong passwords. Based on what you have learned from your research, create a document in Microsoft Word that highlights the components of a strong password. Include a table of do's and don'ts for creating strong passwords in a user-friendly, easy-to-understand format for Mario. Finally, create a minimum of three examples that show weak passwords improved by stronger passwords. Include a suggestion for how to use the phrasing technique to create strong passwords so they are easier to remember. Save the document and name it **EL2-C6-CS-P4-PBMPasswords**. Print and then close **EL2-C6-CS-P4-PBMPasswords.docx**.

MICROSOFT® EXCEL®

CHAPTER 7

Automating Repetitive Tasks and Customizing Excel

PERFORMANCE OBJECTIVES

Upon successful completion of Chapter 7, you will be able to:

- **Record, run, and edit a macro**
- **Save a workbook containing macros as a macro-enabled workbook**
- **Create a macro that is run using a shortcut key combination**
- **Pin and unpin a frequently used file to the Recent Workbooks list**
- **Customize the display options for Excel**
- **Hide the ribbon to increase space in the work area**
- **Customize the ribbon by creating a custom tab and adding buttons**
- **Add and remove buttons for frequently used commands to the Quick Access toolbar**
- **Create and apply custom views**
- **Create and use a template**
- **Customize save options for AutoRecover files**

SNAP

Tutorials

7.1 Using Macros
7.2 Editing a Macro
7.3 Managing Macros
7.4 Pinning Workbooks to the Recent Workbooks List
7.5 Customizing the Work Area
7.6 Customizing the Ribbon
7.7 Customizing the Quick Access Toolbar
7.8 Using Custom Templates

Automating and customizing the Excel environment to accommodate your preferences can increase your efficiency. For example, create a macro when you find yourself repeating the same task frequently to save time and ensure consistency. Add a button for a frequently used command to the Quick Access toolbar to provide single-click access to the feature. Other ways to customize Excel include pinning frequently used files to the Recent Workbooks list; creating a custom template, ribbon tab, or view; and modifying display and save options. Through completing the projects in this chapter, you will learn how to effectively automate and customize the Excel environment. Model answers for this chapter's projects appear on the following page.

Excel
EL2C7

Note: Before beginning the projects, copy to your storage medium the EL2C7 subfolder from the EL2 folder on the CD that accompanies this textbook and then make EL2C7 the active folder.

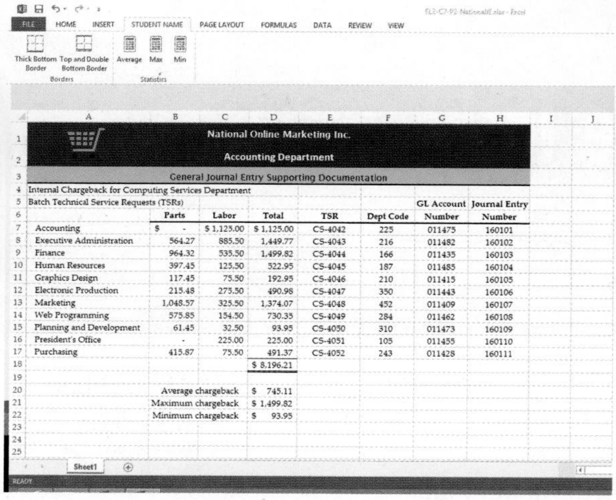

	A	B	C	D	E	F	G	H
1	National Online Marketing Inc.							
2	Accounting Department							
3	General Journal Entry Supporting Documentation							
4	Internal Chargeback for Computing Services Department							
5	Batch Technical Service Requests (TSRs)						GL Account	Journal Entry
6		Parts	Labor	Total	TSR	Dept Code	Number	Number
7	Accounting	$ -	$ 1,125.00	$ 1,125.00	CS-4042	225	011475	160101
8	Executive Administration	564.27	885.50	1,449.77	CS-4043	216	011482	160102
9	Finance	964.32	535.50	1,499.82	CS-4044	166	011435	160103
10	Human Resources	397.45	125.50	522.95	CS-4045	187	011485	160104
11	Graphics Design	117.45	75.50	192.95	CS-4046	210	011415	160105
12	Electronic Production	215.48	275.50	490.98	CS-4047	350	011443	160106
13	Marketing	1,048.57	325.50	1,374.07	CS-4048	452	011409	160107
14	Web Programming	575.85	154.50	730.35	CS-4049	284	011462	160108
15	Planning and Development	61.45	32.50	93.95	CS-4050	310	011473	160109
16	President's Office	-	225.00	225.00	CS-4051	105	011455	160110
17	Purchasing	415.87	75.50	491.37	CS-4052	243	011428	160111
18				$ 8,196.21				
19								
20		Average chargeback		$ 745.11				
21		Maximum chargeback		$ 1,499.82				
22		Minimum chargeback		$ 93.95				

Student Name

Project 2 Customize the Excel Work Environment

Project 2e, EL2-C7-P2-NationalJE.docx

National Online Marketing Inc.

Accounting Department

General Journal Entry Supporting Documentation

Internal Chargeback for Computing Services Department

Batch Technical Service Requests (TSRs)

	Parts	Labor	Total	TSR	Dept Code	GL Account Number	Journal Entry Number
Accounting	$ -	$ 1,125.00	$ 1,125.00	CS-4042	225	011475	160101
Executive Administration	564.27	885.50	1,449.77	CS-4043	216	011482	160102
Finance	964.32	535.50	1,499.82	CS-4044	166	011435	160103
Human Resources	397.45	125.50	522.95	CS-4045	187	011485	160104
Graphics Design	117.45	75.50	192.95	CS-4046	210	011415	160105
Electronic Production	215.48	275.50	490.98	CS-4047	350	011443	160106
Marketing	1,048.57	325.50	1,374.07	CS-4048	452	011409	160107
Web Programming	575.85	154.50	730.35	CS-4049	284	011462	160108
Planning and Development	61.45	32.50	93.95	CS-4050	310	011473	160109
President's Office	-	225.00	225.00	CS-4051	105	011455	160110
Purchasing	415.87	75.50	491.37	CS-4052	243	011428	160111
			$ 8,196.21				

Average chargeback $ 745.11
Maximum chargeback $ 1,499.82
Minimum chargeback $ 93.95

Project 2e, EL2-C7-P2-NationalJE.xlsx

Noranda Sportsplex

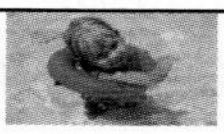

Swimming Schedule

Winter 2015

Day	Start time	End time	Pool	Activity
DAYTIME				
Monday, Wednesday	6:30	7:50	Red, Blue	Adult swim
Tuesday, Thursday, Friday	6:30	7:50	All	Leisure swim
Monday, Wednesday	8:00	8:45		
Tuesday, Thursday, Friday	8:00	8:45		
Monday, Wednesday	8:00	8:45		
Monday, Wednesday	9:00	9:45		
Monday, Wednesday	9:00	9:45		
Tuesday, Thursday, Friday	9:00	9:45		
Monday, Wednesday	10:00	11:45		
Tuesday, Thursday, Friday	10:00	11:45		
Saturday, Sunday	9:00	11:45		
Monday, Wednesday	1:00	1:45		
Tuesday, Thursday, Friday	1:00	1:45		
Monday, Wednesday	2:00	3:45		
Tuesday, Thursday, Friday	2:00	3:45		
Tuesday, Thursday, Friday	2:00	3:45		
Monday, Wednesday	2:00	3:45		
Tuesday, Thursday, Friday	2:00	3:45		
Saturday, Sunday	2:00	4:45		
EVENINGS				
Monday, Wednesday	5:00	5:45		
Tuesday, Thursday, Friday	5:00	5:45		
Monday, Wednesday	5:00	5:45		
Tuesday, Thursday, Friday	5:00	5:45		
Monday, Wednesday	6:00	6:45		
Tuesday, Thursday, Friday	6:00	6:45		
Monday, Wednesday	7:00	7:45		
Tuesday, Thursday, Friday	7:00	7:45		
Monday, Wednesday	8:00	9:45		
Tuesday, Thursday, Friday	8:00	9:45		
Monday, Wednesday	8:00	9:45		
Tuesday, Thursday	8:00	9:45		
Friday	8:00	8:45		

Project 3 Save a Workbook as a Template

Project 3b, EL2-C7-P3-SwimSchWinter2015.xlsx

Project 1 **Create Macros** **4 Parts**

You will create, edit, run, and delete macros to automate tasks, including assigning a macro to a shortcut key and storing frequently used macros in a macro workbook.

Automating Tasks Using Macros

A ***macro*** is a series of instructions stored in a sequence that can be recalled and carried out whenever the need arises. You might consider creating a macro when you find yourself repeatedly performing the same task without variation. Saving the instructions for a task in a macro not only saves time—it also ensures that the steps are performed consistently every time, which can prevent errors in data entry, formatting, or other worksheet options.

Before you record a new macro, take a few moments to plan the steps you need to perform. Also consider if the active cell location at the time the macro is run will be a factor. For example, will the first step in the macro involve making a specific cell active? If so, you can position the active cell using a shortcut key or Go To command during the recording.

To create a macro, begin by turning on the macro recorder, which opens the Record Macro dialog box, shown in Figure 7.1. Identify your macro by assigning a unique name to the steps that will be saved. A macro name must begin with a letter and can be a combination of letters, numbers, and underscore characters. A macro name cannot include spaces; use the underscore character if you want to separate words in a macro name. You also use the Record Macro dialog box, to choose the location in which to save the macro. By default, Excel saves the macro within the current workbook.

A macro can be assigned to a Ctrl shortcut key combination, which allows the user to run the macro more quickly by pressing Ctrl plus the chosen lowercase or uppercase letter. Entering a description of the macro's purpose provides information to other users who might use or edit the macro. In a macro workbook that will be shared, also consider entering the creator's name and the date into

Quick Steps

Record a Macro
1. Click VIEW tab.
2. Click Macros button arrow.
3. Click *Record Macro.*
4. Type macro name.
5. Click in *Description* text box and type description text.
6. Click OK.
7. Perform desired actions.
8. Click Stop Recording button.

Macros

HINT

When recording a macro, your mouse clicks to select tabs within the ribbon are not saved.

Figure 7.1 Record Macro Dialog Box

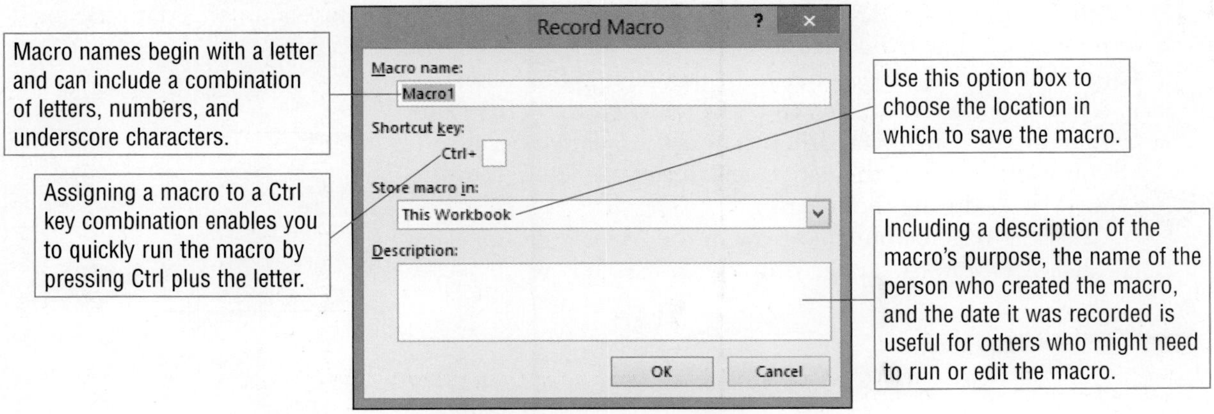

the description box for reference purposes. Click OK when you are finished identifying the macro and the recorder will begin saving the text and/or steps that you perform. Do not be concerned if you make a typing mistake or have to cancel a dialog box while recording a macro. Correct your mistakes as you go, since only the result will be saved. Once you have completed the tasks you want saved, click the Stop Recording button on the Status bar to end the recording.

Stop Recording

Saving Workbooks Containing Macros

When a macro is created in Excel, the commands are written and saved in a language called ***Microsoft Visual Basic for Applications (VBA)***. A workbook that contains a macro should be saved using the macro-enabled file format. The default format for extensible markup language (XML) files, .xlsx, cannot store the macro code. The macro recorder that you use when creating a macro converts your actions to VBA statements behind the scenes. You can view and edit the VBA code or you can create macros from scratch by using the VBA Editor in Microsoft Visual Basic for Applications. In Project 1e, you will look at the VBA statements created when the AcctgDocumentation macro was recorded and edit an instruction.

To save a new or existing workbook as a macro-enabled workbook, perform one of the following actions:

- *New workbook*. Click the Save button on the Quick Access toolbar or click the FILE tab and then click the *Save As* option. At the Save As backstage area, click the desired location in the *Places* section. Click the Browse button to display the Save As dialog box. Type the file name and then change the *Save as type* option to *Excel Macro-Enabled Workbook (*.xlsm)*. Click the Save button.
- *Existing workbook*. Click the FILE tab and then click the *Save As* option. At the Save As backstage area, click the desired location in the *Places* section. Click the Browse button to display the Save As dialog box. Type the file name and then change the *Save as type* option to *Excel Macro-Enabled Workbook (*.xlsm)*. Click the Save button.

Quick Steps

Save a Macro-Enabled Workbook

1. Click FILE tab.
2. Click *Save As*.
3. If necessary, click desired place.
4. Click Browse button.
5. Type file name in *File name* text box.
6. Click *Save as type* list arrow.
7. Click *Excel Macro-Enabled Workbook (*.xlsm)*.
8. Click Save.

Project 1a **Creating a Macro and Saving a Workbook as a Macro-Enabled Workbook** **Part 1 of 4**

1. You work in the Accounting department at a large company. The company has a documentation standard for all Excel workbooks that requires each worksheet to show the department name, author's name, creation date, and revision history. To standardize the documentation, you decide to create a macro that will insert row labels for this data. Begin by opening a new blank workbook.
2. Create the documentation macro by completing the following steps:
   a. Make cell C4 the active cell and then click the VIEW tab. (You are making a cell other than cell A1 active because you want to move the active cell to the top left cell in the worksheet during the macro.)
   b. Click the Macros button arrow in the Macros group.
   c. Click *Record Macro* at the drop-down list.

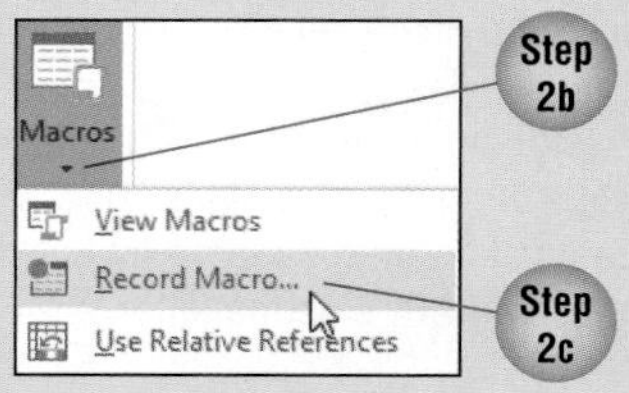

d. At the Record Macro dialog box, with the insertion point positioned in the *Macro name* text box, type AcctgDocumentation.

e. Click in the *Description* text box and then type Accounting department documentation macro. Created by [Student Name] on [Date]. Substitute your name for *[Student Name]* and the current date for *[Date]*.

f. Click OK. The macro recorder is now turned on, as indicated by the Stop Recording button in the Status bar (which displays as a white square next to *READY*).

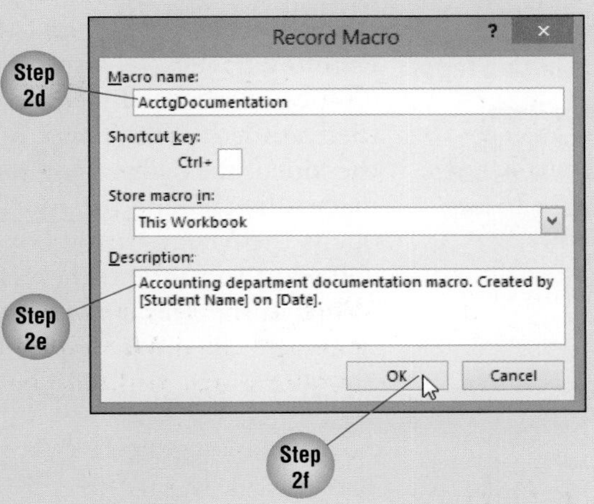

g. Press Ctrl + Home to move the active cell to cell A1. Including this command in the macro ensures that the documentation will begin at cell A1 in every workbook.

h. Type Accounting department and then press Enter.

i. With cell A2 active, type Author and then press Enter.

j. With cell A3 active, type Date created and then press Enter.

k. With cell A4 active, type Revision history and then press Enter three times to leave two blank rows before the start of the worksheet.

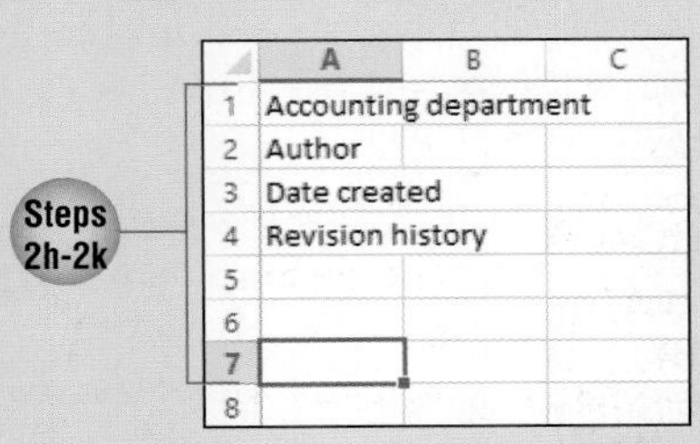

l. Click the Stop Recording button located at the left side of the Status bar, next to *READY*.

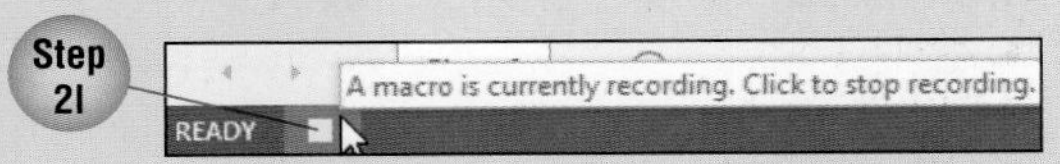

3. Save the workbook as a macro-enabled workbook by completing the following steps:
   a. Click the Save button on the Quick Access toolbar.
   b. At the Save As backstage area, click the desired location in the *Places* section and then click the Browse button.
   c. At the Save As dialog box, navigate to the EL2C7 folder in the Navigation pane and then double-click the *EL2C7* folder that displays in the Content pane.
   d. Click in the *File name* text box and then type EL2-C7-P1-Macros.
   e. Click the *Save as type* option box, scroll up or down the pop-up list, and then click *Excel Macro-Enabled Workbook (*.xlsm)*.
   f. Click the Save button.

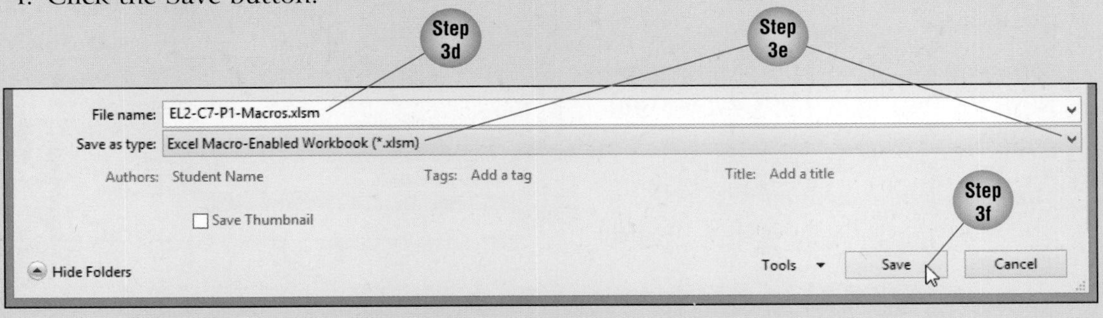

Running a Macro

Quick Steps

Run a Macro
1. Click VIEW tab.
2. Click Macros button.
3. Double-click macro name.

Running a macro is also sometimes referred to as *playing a macro*. Since a macro is a series of recorded tasks, running a macro involves instructing Excel to *play back* the recorded tasks. Think of a macro as a video you have made. When you play the video, the same thing happens every time. To run (play) a macro, view a list of macros by clicking the Macros button in the Macros group on the VIEW tab. This opens the Macro dialog box, as shown in Figure 7.2. Click the name of the macro you want to run and then click the Run button, or double-click the name of the macro in the *Macro name* list box.

Figure 7.2 Macro Dialog Box

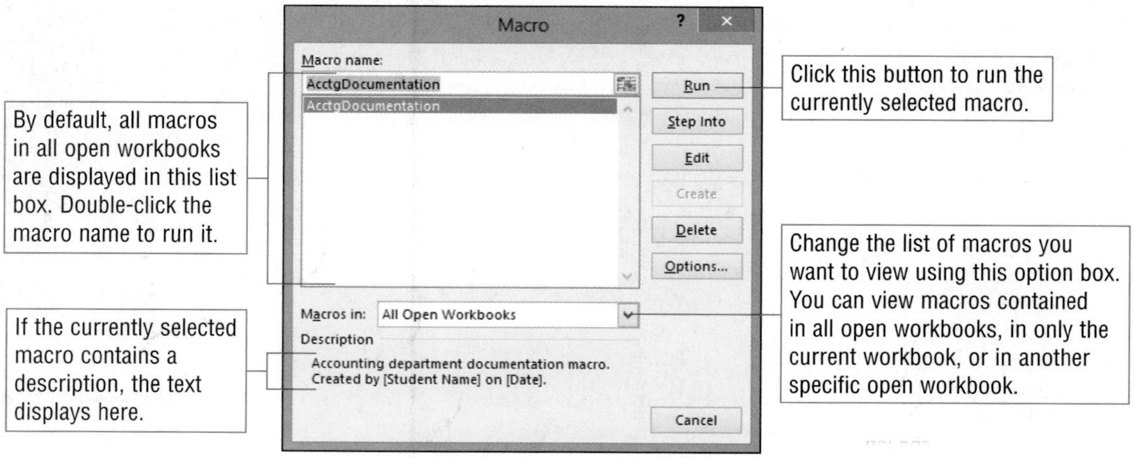

Project 1b **Running a Macro** **Part 2 of 4**

1. With **EL2-C7-P1-Macros.xlsm** open, run the AcctgDocumentation macro to test that it works correctly by completing the following steps:
   a. Select A1:A4 and press Delete to erase the cell contents.
   b. To test the Ctrl + Home command in the macro, you need to make sure cell A1 is not active when the macro begins playing. Click any cell in the worksheet other than cell A1 to deselect the range.
   c. Click the Macros button in the Macros group on the VIEW tab. Make sure to click the button and not the button arrow.
   d. At the Macro dialog box with *AcctgDocumentation* already selected in the *Macro name* list box, click the Run button.
2. Save and then close **EL2-C7-P1-Macros.xlsm**.

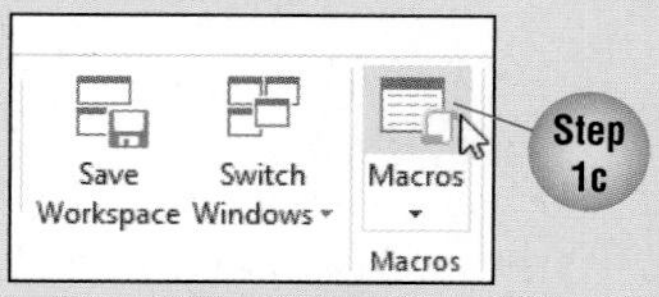

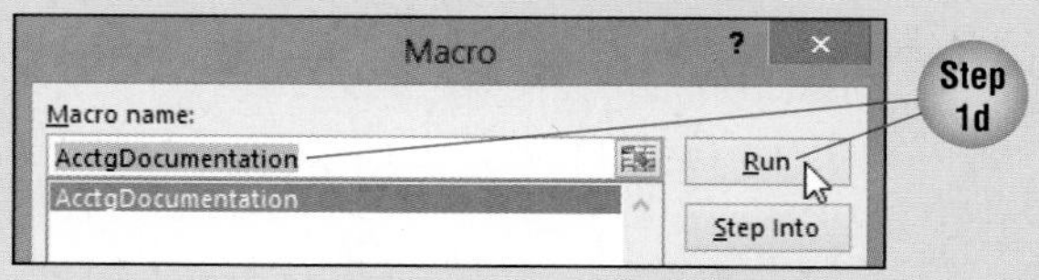

Assigning a Macro to a Shortcut Key

When recording a macro, you have the option to assign the macro to a Ctrl key combination. A macro that is assigned to a keyboard shortcut can be run without displaying the Macro dialog box. You can choose any lowercase or uppercase letter for a macro's keyboard shortcut. Excel distinguishes the case of the letter you choose when you type the letter in the *Shortcut key* text box at the Record Macro dialog box. For example, if you type an uppercase O, Excel defines the shortcut key as *Ctrl + Shift + O*, as shown in Figure 7.3.

If an Excel feature is already assigned to the key combination you choose, your macro will override the existing Excel feature. For example, pressing Ctrl + p in Excel causes the Print dialog box to appear. If you create a macro and assign it to Ctrl + p, pressing that keyboard shortcut will now run your macro instead of displaying the Print dialog box. You can view a list of Excel-assigned keyboard shortcuts in Help by typing *keyboard shortcuts* in the search box in the Excel Help window. Select *Keyboard shortcuts in Excel 2013* in the Results list.

Quick Steps

Assign a Macro to a Shortcut Key

1. Click VIEW tab.
2. Click Macros button arrow.
3. Click *Record Macro*.
4. Type macro name.
5. Click in *Shortcut key* text box.
6. Type desired letter.
7. Click in *Description* text box.
8. Type description text.
9. Click OK.
10. Perform desired actions.
11. Click Stop Recording button.

Record Macro

Figure 7.3 Record Macro Dialog Box with Shortcut Key Assigned

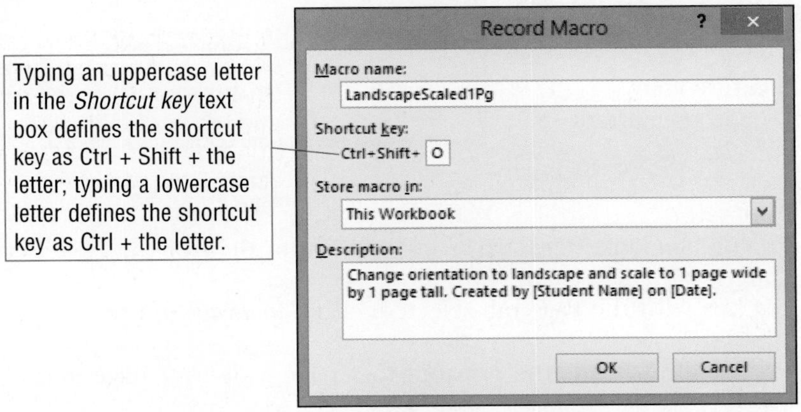

Project 1c **Creating and Running a Macro Using a Shortcut Key** **Part 3 of 4**

1. Open **EL2-C7-P1-Macros.xlsm**.
2. The default security setting when opening any workbook that contains a macro is *Disable all macros with notification*. This causes a security warning to appear in the message bar (between the ribbon and the formula bar) notifying you that macros have been disabled. Enable the macros in the workbook by clicking the Enable Content button.

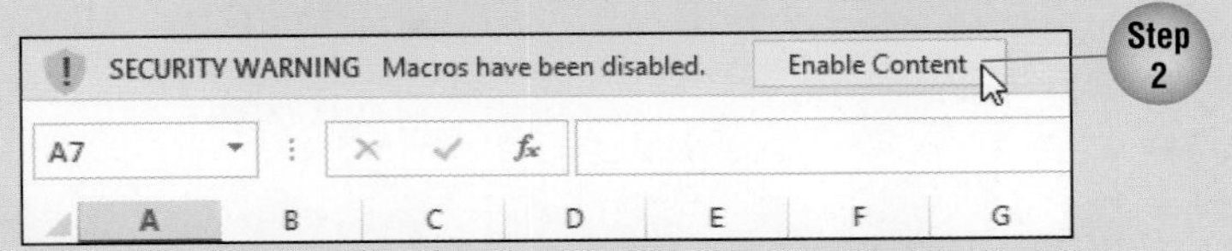

3. Create a macro that changes print options for a worksheet and assign it to a keyboard shortcut by completing the following steps:
   a. Once a macro has been recorded and stopped in an Excel session, the Stop Recording button in the Status bar changes to the Record New Macro button. Click the Record New Macro button located at the left side of the Status bar next to *READY*. If you exited Excel before starting this project, start a new macro by clicking the VIEW tab, clicking the down-pointing arrow on the Macros button, and then clicking *Record Macro*.

   b. Type LandscapeScaled1Pg in the *Macro name* text box.
   c. Click in the *Shortcut key* text box, hold down the Shift key, and then type the letter o.
   d. Click in the *Description* text box and then type Change orientation to landscape and scale to 1 page wide by 1 page tall. Created by [Student Name] on [Date]. Substitute your name for *[Student Name]* and the current date for *[Date]*.
   e. Click OK.

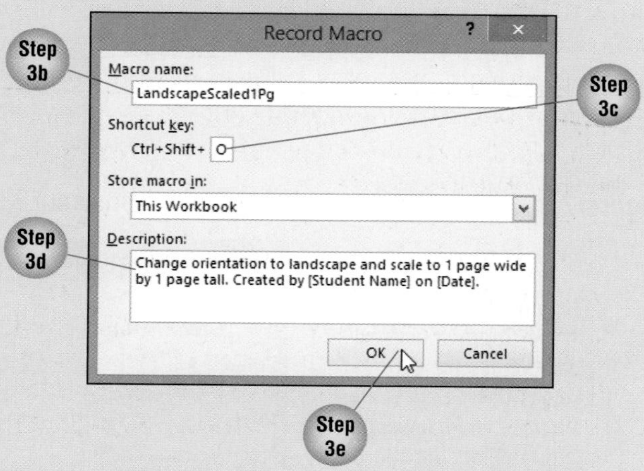

   f. Click the PAGE LAYOUT tab.
   g. Click the Page Setup dialog box launcher located at the bottom right of the Page Setup group.
   h. At the Page Setup dialog box with the Page tab selected, click *Landscape* in the *Orientation* section.
   i. Click *Fit to* in the *Scaling* section to scale the printout to 1 page wide by 1 page tall.
   j. Click OK.

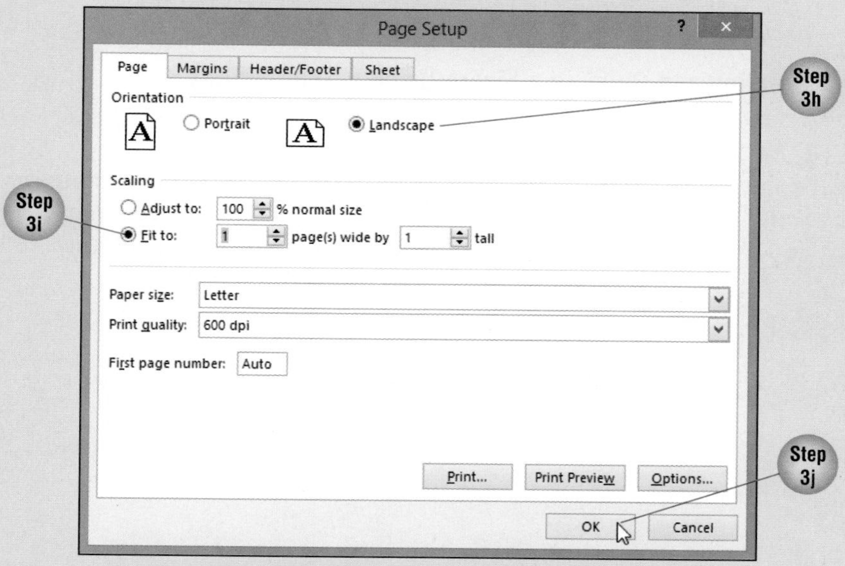

   k. Click the Stop Recording button.

4. Press Ctrl + N to open a new blank workbook.
5. Press Ctrl + Shift + o to run the LandscapeScaled1Pg macro.
6. Type your name in cell A1, press Enter, and then press Ctrl + F2 to display the worksheet in the Print backstage area. Notice in the Print Preview that the page orientation is landscape. Review the options in the Settings category. Notice that *Landscape Orientation* and *Fit Sheet on One Page* have been selected by the macro.
7. Click the Back button to return to the worksheet and then close the workbook. Click Don't Save when prompted to save changes.
8. Save **EL2-C7-P1-Macros.xlsm**.

Editing a Macro

The actions that you perform while recording a macro are stored in Visual Basic for Applications (VBA) program code. Each macro is saved as a separate module within a VBAProject for the workbook. A ***module*** can be described as a receptacle for the macro instructions. Figure 7.4 displays the window containing the VBA code module for the macro created in Project 1a.

You can use the module to edit a macro if the change you need to make is easy to decipher within the VBA statements. If you need to make several changes to a macro, or if you do not feel comfortable with the VBA code, you can re-record the macro. When you record a new macro that has the same name as an existing macro, Excel prompts you to replace the existing macro. You can then record the correct steps by overwriting the original macro.

Quick Steps

Edit a Macro
1. Open workbook containing macro.
2. Click VIEW tab.
3. Click Macros button.
4. Click desired macro name.
5. Click Edit button.
6. Make desired changes in VBA code window.
7. Click Save button.
8. Click File.
9. Click *Close and Return to Microsoft Excel.*

Figure 7.4 Microsoft Visual Basic for Applications Window for Project 1a AcctgDocumentation Macro

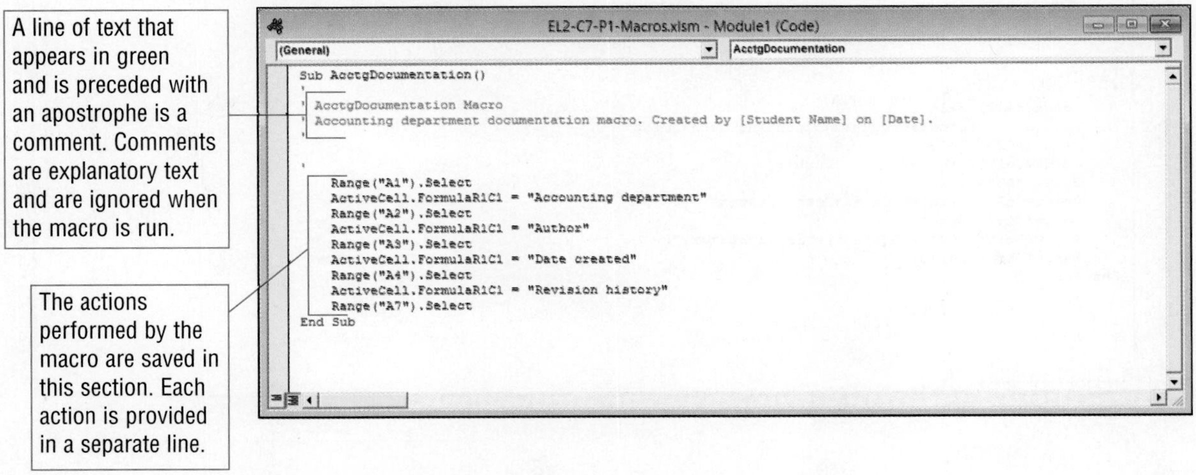

Project 1d Editing a Macro

Part 4 of 4

1. With **EL2-C7-P1-Macros.xlsm** open, edit the AcctgDocumentation macro to leave only one blank row after the last entry by completing the following steps:
   a. If necessary, click the VIEW tab.
   b. Click the Macros button in the Macros group.
   c. At the Macro dialog box with *AcctgDocumentation* already selected in the *Macro name* list box, click the Edit button. A Microsoft Visual Basic for Applications window opens with the program code displayed for EL2-C7-P1-Macros.xlsm - [Module1 (Code)].

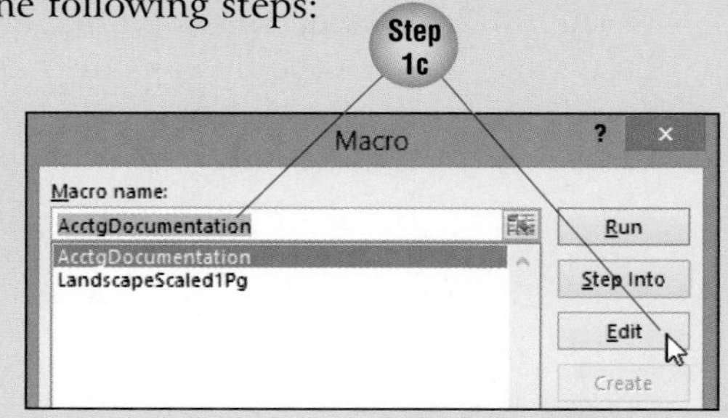

   d. Read the statements between the *Sub* and *End Sub* statements. *Sub* indicates the beginning of the procedure and *End Sub* indicates the end of the procedure. A ***procedure*** is a set of VBA statements that perform actions. The name of the procedure is placed after the opening *Sub* statement and is the macro name. Each line beginning with a single apostrophe (') is a comment. A comment is used in programming to insert explanatory text that describes the logic or purpose of a statement. Statements that begin with apostrophes are ignored when the macro is run. The commands that are executed when the macro is run are the indented lines of text below the comment lines.
   e. The last statement before *End Sub* reads *Range("A7").Select.* This is the last action in the macro and it makes cell A7 active. Notice that the entry two lines above this final action reads *Range("A4").Select.* To edit the macro to leave only one blank row, change the address in the last statement from *A7* to *A6.* To do this, position the insertion point between the *A* and the *7* and then click the left mouse button. Press Delete and then type 6.

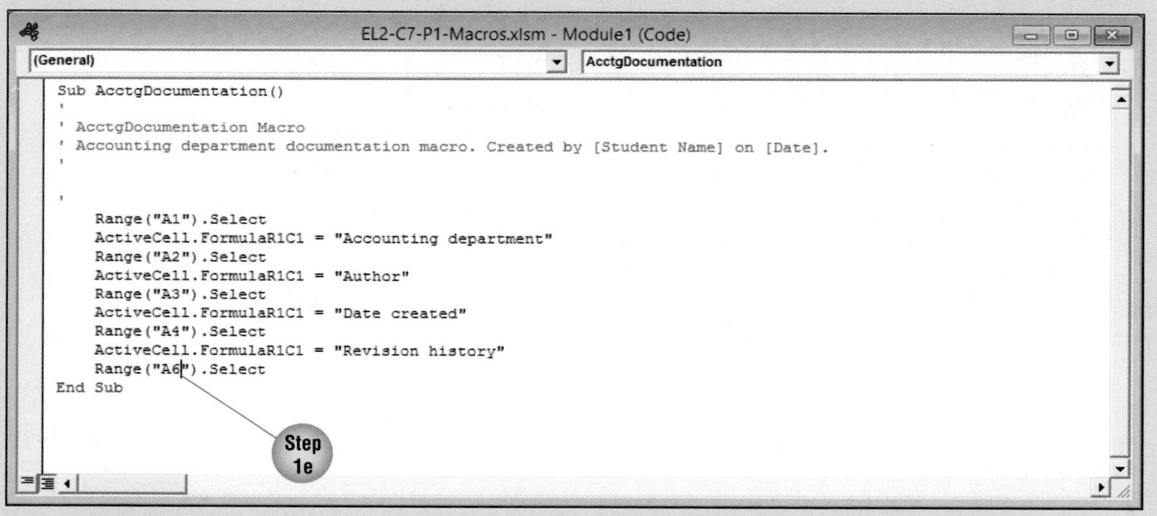

   f. Click the Save button on the toolbar.

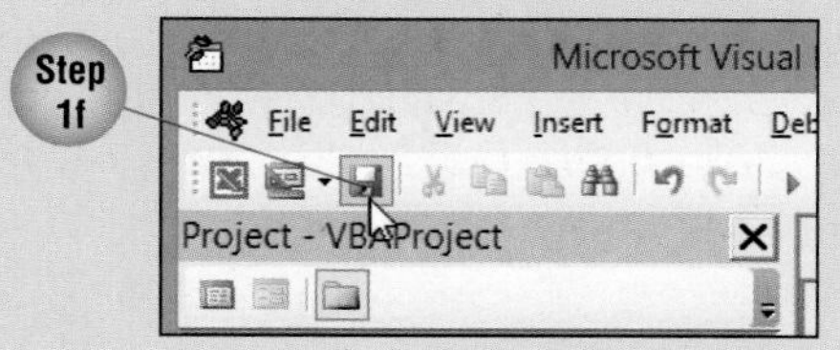

2. Click File and then click *Close and Return to Microsoft Excel*.
3. Test the edited macro to make sure only one blank row is left before the active cell by completing the following steps:
    a. Select the range A1:A4 and then press Delete.
    b. Make any cell other than cell A1 active.
    c. Click the Macros button in the Macros group on the VIEW tab. Make sure to click the button and not the button arrow.
    d. At the Macro dialog box, double-click *AcctgDocumentation* in the *Macro name* list box.
4. Save and then close **EL2-C7-P1-Macros.xlsm**.

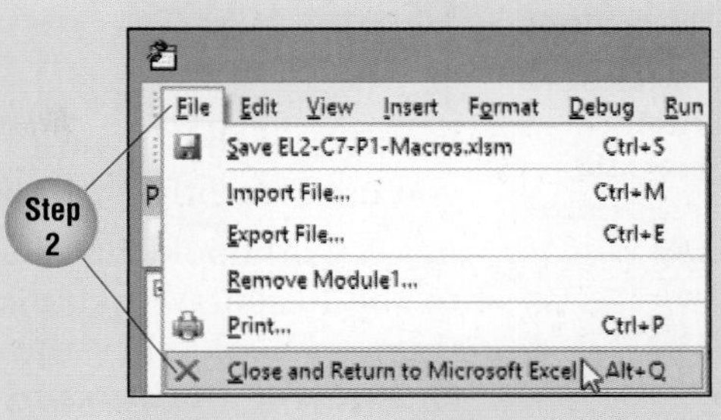

Deleting a Macro

If you no longer need a macro, you can delete it at the Macro dialog box. Open the Macro dialog box, select the macro name in the *Macro name* list box, and then click the Delete button.

Quick Steps

Delete a Macro
1. Open Macro dialog box.
2. Click macro name.
3. Click Delete button.
4. Click Yes.

Managing Macros

By default, a macro is stored within the workbook that is active when the macro is recorded. When you close the workbook, the macros within the file are no longer available. For example, if you close the EL2-C7-P1-Macros.xlsm file, the AcctgDocumentation macro you created will not be available to you in a new workbook. If you want to use the macros you have created in other workbooks, leave the workbook containing the macros open, since the Macro dialog box displays macros for all open workbooks in the *Macro name* list box by default.

Consider creating a macros workbook with a set of standard macros that you want to use in any file, similar to the macros workbook you created in Projects 1a through 1d. Open this workbook whenever you are working in Excel and the macros stored within it will be available to you for all of the files that you create or edit during an Excel session. When you create a macros workbook, you can also copy it to any other computer so that a set of standard macros can be distributed to others for their use.

Project 2 Customize the Excel Work Environment — 8 Parts

You will customize the Excel environment by pinning a frequently used workbook to the Recent Workbooks list, minimizing the ribbon to create more space in the work area, changing display options, importing and exporting custom settings for the Quick Access toolbar and ribbon, creating a custom ribbon tab, adding buttons to the Quick Access toolbar to make features more accessible, and creating custom views.

Quick Steps

Pin a Workbook to the Recent Workbooks List
1. Make sure workbook has been opened recently.
2. Click FILE tab.
3. If necessary, click *Open*.
4. Position mouse over workbook name and click pin icon.

Unpin a Workbook from the Recent Workbooks List
1. Click FILE tab.
2. If necessary, click *Open*.
3. Click down-pointing pin icon next to workbook name.

Pinning Workbooks to the Recent Workbooks List

The Recent Workbooks list at the Open backstage area displays the file names and locations of the 25 most recently opened workbooks by default. To open a workbook you used recently, click the workbook name in the Recent Workbooks list.

A workbook that you use frequently can be permanently added, or *pinned*, to the Recent Workbooks list. To do this, make sure you have recently opened the workbook, click the FILE tab, click the *Open* option, and, if necessary, click *Recent Workbooks* in the *Places* section. Hover your mouse over the desired workbook and then click the pin icon to the right of the workbook name. A workbook that is permanently pinned to the list displays with a down-pointing pin icon. Click the down-pointing pin icon to unpin a workbook from the list.

To change the number of workbooks shown in the Recent Workbooks list, open the Excel Options dialog box and then click *Advanced* in the left pane. In the *Display* section, change the number in the *Show this number of Recent Documents* text box to the desired value.

Project 2a **Pinning a Frequently Used Workbook to the Recent Workbooks List** **Part 1 of 8**

1. Open **NWinterSch.xlsx**.
2. Scroll down the worksheet to review the winter swimming schedule and then close the workbook.
3. At a blank Excel screen, pin two workbooks to the Recent Workbooks list by completing the following steps:
   a. Click the FILE tab.
   b. By default, the Open backstage area displays if no workbooks are currently open.
   c. Position your mouse over **NWinterSch.xlsx** in the Recent Workbooks list and then click the pin icon located at the right.

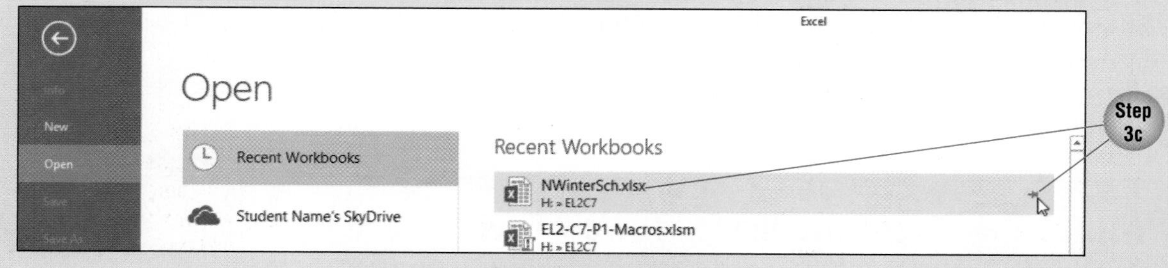

   d. Position your mouse over **EL2-C7-P1-Macros.xlsm** and then click the pin icon located at the right.
   e. Press Esc to close the backstage area.

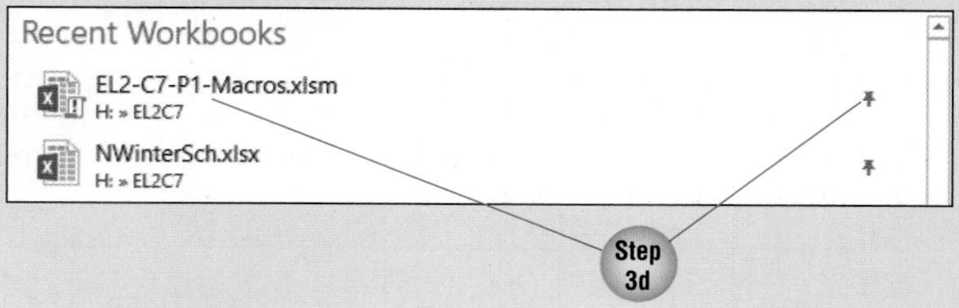

4. Click the FILE tab and then click ***EL2-C7-P1-Macros.xlsm*** in the Recent Workbooks list to open the workbook.
5. Close **EL2-C7-P1-Macros.xlsm**.
6. Unpin the two workbooks by completing the following steps:
   a. Click the FILE tab.
   b. Click the down-pointing pin icon to the right of **EL2-C7-P1-Macros.xlsm**.
   c. Click the down-pointing pin icon to the right of **NWinterSch.xlsx**.
   d. Press Esc to close the Open backstage area.

Changing Display Options to Customize the Work Area

When the default display options in Excel do not suit your needs, the Excel Options dialog box contains many options for customizing the environment. As shown in Figure 7.5, Excel groups options that affect the display by those that are global settings, those that affect the entire workbook, and those that affect only the active worksheet. Changes to workbook and/or worksheet display options are saved with the workbook.

Quick Steps

Customize Display Options
1. Click FILE tab.
2. Click *Options*.
3. Click *Advanced* in left pane.
4. Change display options as required.
5. Click OK.

Figure 7.5 Excel Options Dialog Box with Display Options Shown

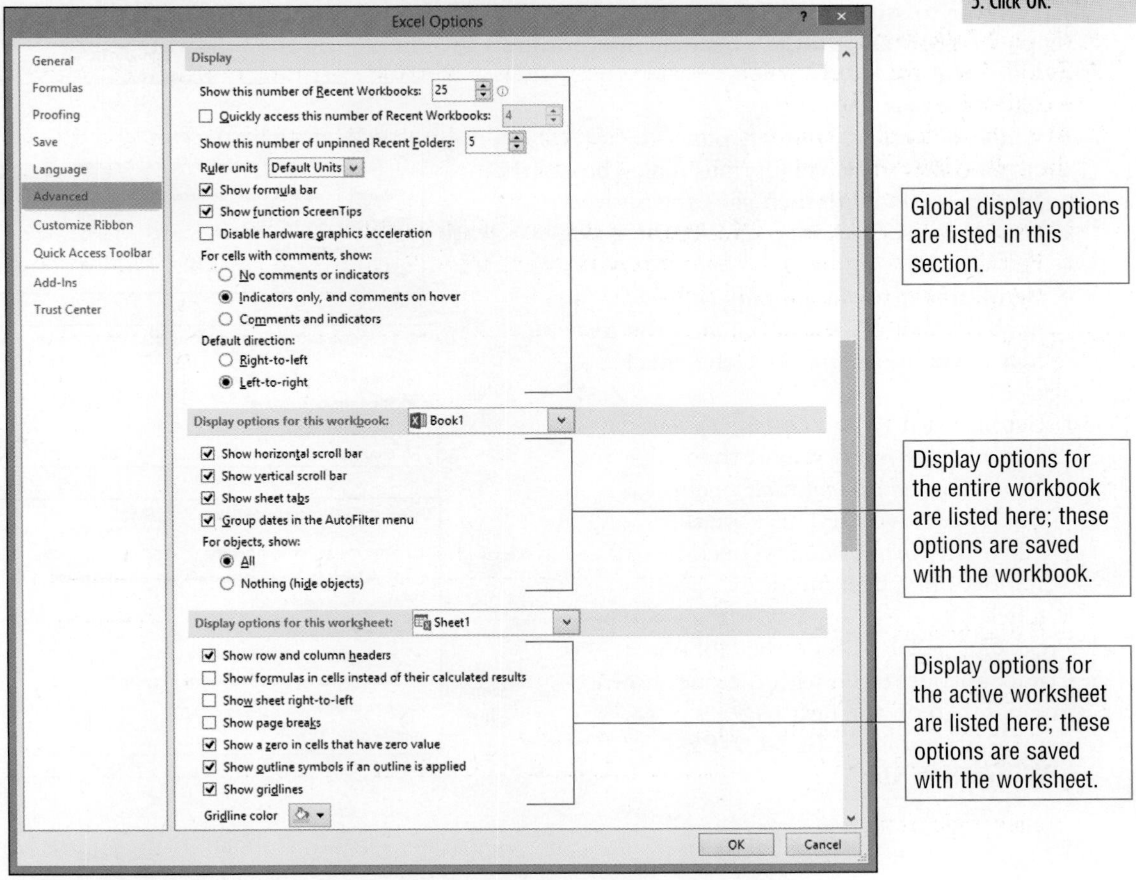

Minimizing the Ribbon

Quick Steps

Minimize the Ribbon
Press Ctrl + F1.
OR
1. Click Ribbon Display Options button.
2. Click Show Tabs.
OR
Click Collapse the Ribbon button.

Collapse the Ribbon   Ribbon Display Options

When you are working with a large worksheet, you may find it easier to work with the ribbon minimized, which creates more space within the work area. Figure 7.6 on the next page shows the worksheet you will use in Project 2b to customize the display options and minimize the ribbon.

One way to minimize the ribbon is to click the Collapse the Ribbon button. With the ribbon minimized, clicking a tab temporarily redisplays it to allow you to select a feature. After you select the feature, the ribbon returns to the minimized state. Press Ctrl + F1 or double-click the ribbon to toggle the ribbon on or off.

Another way to minimize the ribbon, new in Excel 2013, is to click the Ribbon Display Options button. This button remains in the upper right corner of the screen and allows you to quickly hide the ribbon (including the tabs), show tabs, or show just the tabs and commands.

Project 2b **Customizing Display Options and Minimizing the Ribbon** **Part 2 of 8**

1. Open **NWinterSch.xlsx**.
2. Save the workbook and name it **EL2-C7-P2-NWinterSch**.
3. Turn off the display of the Formula bar (since no formulas exist in the workbook), turn off the display of sheet tabs (since only one sheet exists in the workbook), and turn off the display of row and column headers and gridlines by completing the following steps:
   a. Click the FILE tab.
   b. Click *Options*.
   c. Click *Advanced* in the left pane.
   d. Scroll down the Excel Options dialog box to the *Display* section and then click the *Show formula bar* check box to remove the check mark.
   e. Scroll down to the *Display options for this workbook* section and then click the *Show sheet tabs* check box to remove the check mark.
   f. Scroll down to the *Display options for this worksheet* section and then click the *Show row and column headers* check box to remove the check mark.
   g. Click the *Show gridlines* check box to remove the check mark.
   h. Click OK.
4. Press Ctrl + F1 to hide the ribbon.
5. Compare your screen with the one shown in Figure 7.6 on the next page.
6. Save and then close **EL2-C7-P2-NWinterSch.xlsx**.

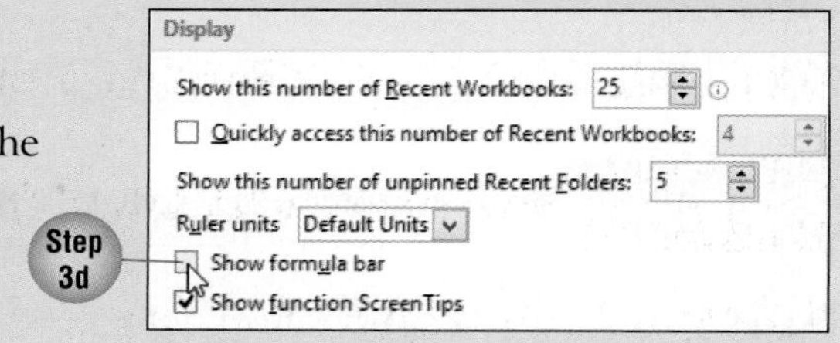

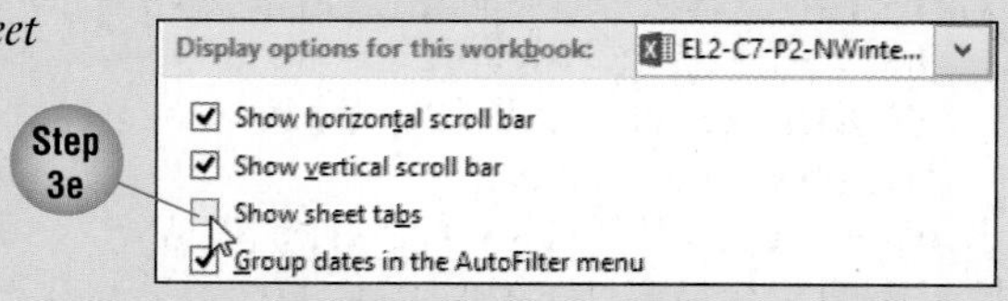

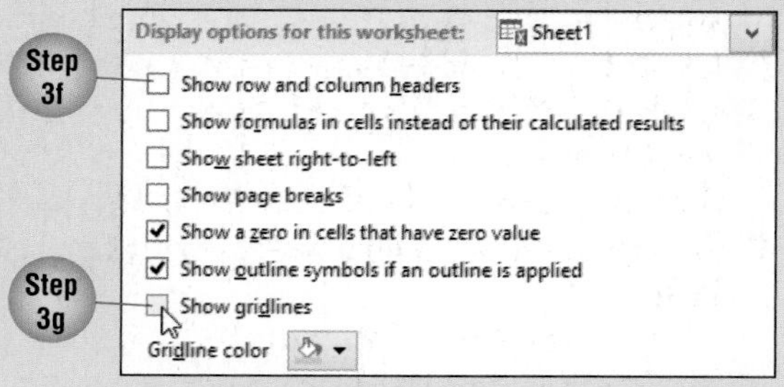

Figure 7.6 Project 2b Worksheet with Customized Display Options and Minimized Ribbon

Day	Start time	End time	Pool	Activity
DAYTIME				
Monday, Wednesday	6:30	7:50	All	Adult swim
Tuesday, Thursday, Friday	6:30	7:50	All	Moms & tots swim
Monday, Wednesday	8:00	8:45	Blue, Green	Beginner aquafit
Tuesday, Thursday, Friday	8:00	8:45	Blue, Green	Adult swim
Monday, Wednesday	8:00	8:45	Red	Deep water aquafit
Monday, Wednesday	9:00	9:45	Blue, Green	Intermediate aquafit
Monday, Wednesday	9:00	9:45	Red	Senior aquafit
Tuesday, Thursday, Friday	9:00	9:45	Red	Beginner aquafit
Monday, Wednesday	10:00	11:45	All	Leisure swim
Tuesday, Thursday, Friday	10:00	11:45	Blue, Green	Senior aquafit
Saturday, Sunday	9:00	11:45	All	Swimming lessons
Monday, Wednesday	1:00	1:45	Blue	Moms & tots swim
Tuesday, Thursday, Friday	1:00	1:45	Red, Green	Intermediate aquafit
Monday, Wednesday	2:00	3:45	All	Leisure swim
Tuesday, Thursday, Friday	2:00	3:45	Blue, Green	Private bookings
Tuesday, Thursday, Friday	2:00	3:45	Red	Diving club
Monday, Wednesday	2:00	3:45	Blue, Green	Intermediate aquafit
Tuesday, Thursday, Friday	2:00	3:45	Blue, Green	Beginner aquafit
Saturday, Sunday	2:00	4:45	All	Family swim
EVENINGS				
Monday, Wednesday	5:00	5:45	Blue, Green	Swimming lessons
Tuesday, Thursday, Friday	5:00	5:45	Blue, Green	Swimming lessons
Monday, Wednesday	5:00	5:45	Red	Beginner aquafit
Tuesday, Thursday, Friday	5:00	5:45	Red	Deep water aquafit
Monday, Wednesday	6:00	6:45	All	Swimming lessons

Project 2c Restoring Default Display Options

Part 3 of 8

1. Press Ctrl + N to open a new blank workbook.
2. Notice that the workbook and worksheet display options that were changed in Project 2b are restored to the default options. The Formula bar remains hidden (since this is a global display option) and the ribbon remains minimized (since the display of the ribbon is a toggle on/off option).
3. Open **EL2-C7-P2-NWinterSch.xlsx**.
4. Notice that the sheet tabs, row and column headers, and gridlines are hidden (since these display option settings are saved with the workbook).
5. Close **EL2-C7-P2-NWinterSch.xlsx** without saving it.
6. Click the Ribbon Display Options button next to the Minimize button in the upper right corner of the screen and then click *Show Tabs and Commands* at the drop-down list.

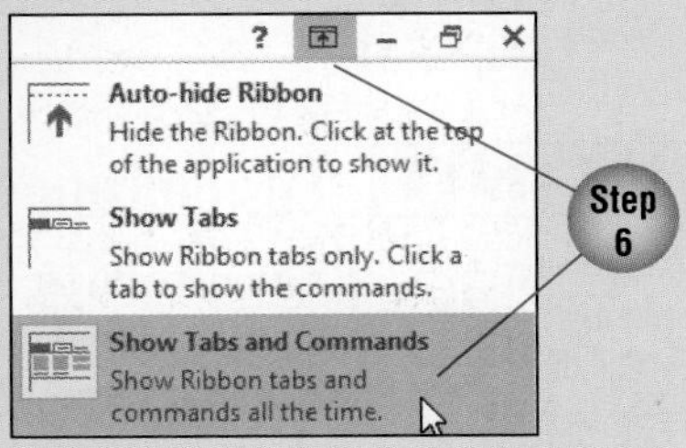

7. Redisplay the Formula bar by completing the following steps:
   a. Open the Excel Options dialog box.
   b. Click *Advanced* in the left pane.
   c. Scroll down the Excel Options dialog box to the *Display* section, click the *Show formula bar* check box to insert a check mark, and then click OK.
8. Close the workbook without saving it.

Customizing Ribbons and the Quick Access Toolbar

As you work with Excel, you may find that you prefer to access frequently used features from the Quick Access toolbar or in a new group within an existing or new ribbon. You will learn how to customize both the ribbon and the Quick Access toolbar in Projects 2e and 2f.

You or your instructor may already have taken the time to customize a ribbon or the Quick Access toolbar on the computers in your institution's computer lab. To be able to restore these customizations after you make changes in the upcoming projects, you will learn how to save (export) them in Project 2d. You will then learn how to reinstall (import) them in Project 2g.

To save your current ribbon and Quick Access toolbar settings, click the FILE tab and then click *Options*. At the Excel Options dialog box, click *Customize Ribbon* in the left pane. The dialog box will display as shown in Figure 7.7 on the next page.

Click the Import/Export button in the lower right corner of the Excel Options dialog box. Click *Export all customizations* to save the file with the custom settings. You can then use this file to reinstall the saved settings in Project 2g or install customized settings on a different computer. Click the Import/Export button and then click *Import customization file*. Locate the file and reinstall the customized settings.

Project 2d **Exporting Customizations** **Part 4 of 8**

1. Press Ctrl + N to open a new blank workbook.
2. Save the current ribbon and Quick Access toolbar settings to the desktop by completing the following steps:
   a. Click the FILE tab and then click *Options*.
   b. Click *Customize Ribbon* in the left pane of the Excel Options dialog box.
   c. Click the Import/Export button located at the bottom right of the Excel Options dialog box.
   d. Click *Export all customizations* at the drop-down list.
   e. Click *Desktop* in the *Favorites* list at the left of the File Save dialog box.
   f. Change the file name to **EL2-C7-P2-ExcelCustomizations** and then click the Save button. The file saves with the name **EL2-C7-P2-ExcelCustomizations.exportedUI**.
   g. Click OK.
   h. Close the workbook. Click Don't Save if prompted to save changes.

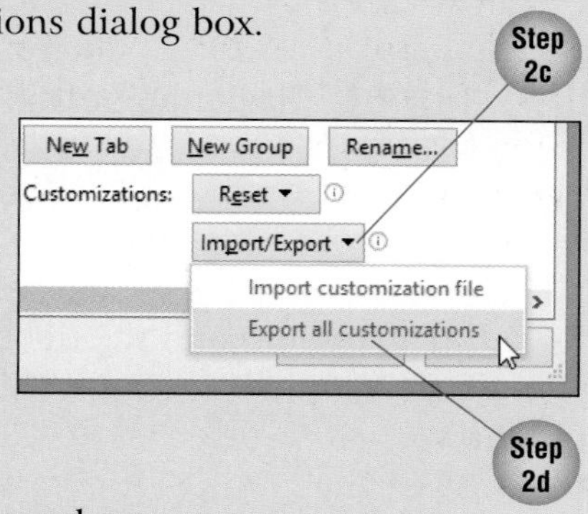

HINT

To save mouse clicks used when switching tabs and choosing options from drop-down lists, consider creating a custom tab with the buttons you use on a regular basis.

Customizing the Ribbon

To customize the ribbon by adding a new tab, group, or button, click the FILE tab and then click *Options*. At the Excel Options dialog box, click *Customize Ribbon* in the left pane. The dialog box will display as shown in Figure 7.7.

The commands shown in the left list box are dependent on the current option in the *Choose commands from* option box. Click the down-pointing arrow at the right of the current option (*Popular Commands*) to select from a variety of command lists, such as *Commands Not In the Ribbon* and *All Commands*. The tabs shown in

Figure 7.7 Excel Options Dialog Box with *Customize Ribbon* Selected

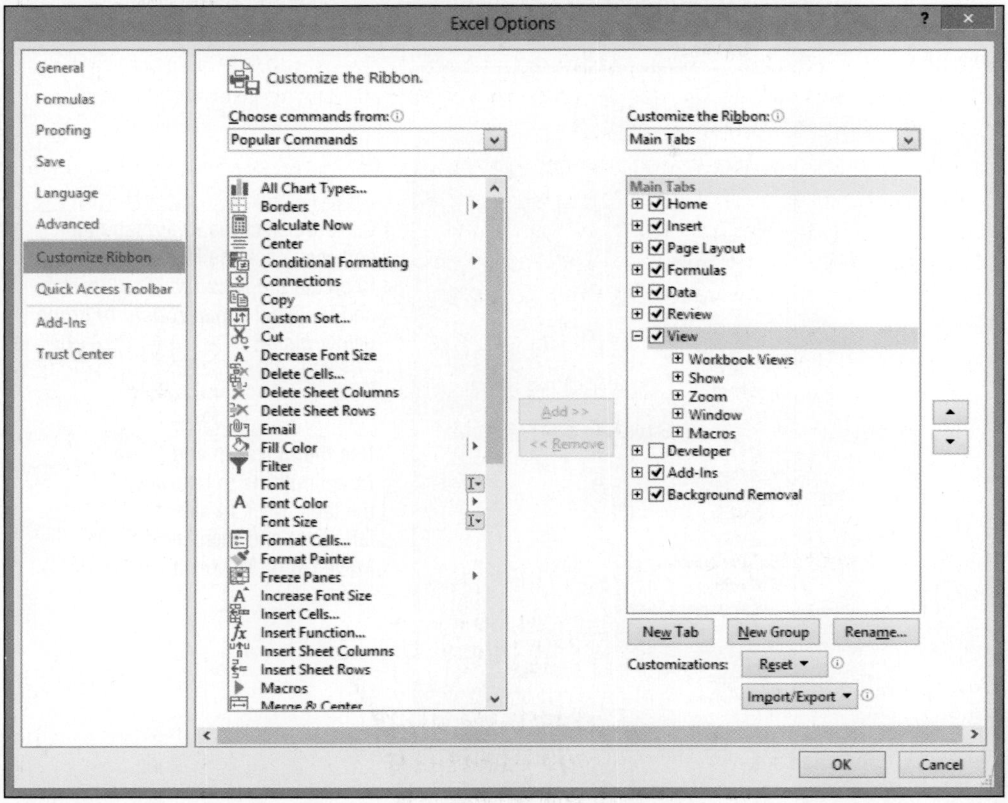

the right list box are dependent on the current option in the *Customize the Ribbon* option box. Click the down-pointing arrow at the right of the current option (*Main Tabs*) to select *All Tabs*, *Main Tabs*, or *Tool Tabs*.

You can create a new group in an existing tab and add buttons within the new group, or you can create a new tab, create a new group within the tab, and then add buttons to the new group.

Creating a New Tab

To create a new tab, in the *Main Tabs* list box, click the tab name after which you want the new tab positioned and then click the New Tab button located below the *Main Tabs* list box. This inserts a new tab in the list box along with a new group below the new tab, as shown in Figure 7.8. If you selected the wrong tab name before clicking the *New Tab* button, you can move the new tab up or down the list box by clicking *New Tab (Custom)* and then clicking the Move Up button or Move Down button at the right side of the dialog box.

Adding Buttons to a Group

Add commands to a tab by clicking the group name within the tab, clicking the desired command in the list box at the left, and then clicking the Add button that displays between the two list boxes. Remove commands in a similar manner: click the command you want to remove from the tab group and then click the Remove button that displays between the two list boxes.

Quick Steps

Create a New Tab and Group

1. Click FILE tab.
2. Click *Options*.
3. Click *Customize Ribbon* in left pane.
4. Click tab name to precede new tab.
5. Click New Tab button.

Add a New Group to an Existing Tab

1. Click FILE tab.
2. Click *Options*.
3. Click *Customize Ribbon* in left pane.
4. Click tab name on which to add new group.
5. Click New Group button.

Add Buttons to a Group

1. Click FILE tab.
2. Click *Options*.
3. Click *Customize Ribbon* in left pane.
4. Click group name in which to insert new button.
5. Change *Choose commands from* to desired command list.
6. Click desired command.
7. Click Add button.

Figure 7.8 New Tab and Group Created in the Customize Ribbon Pane at the Excel Options Dialog Box

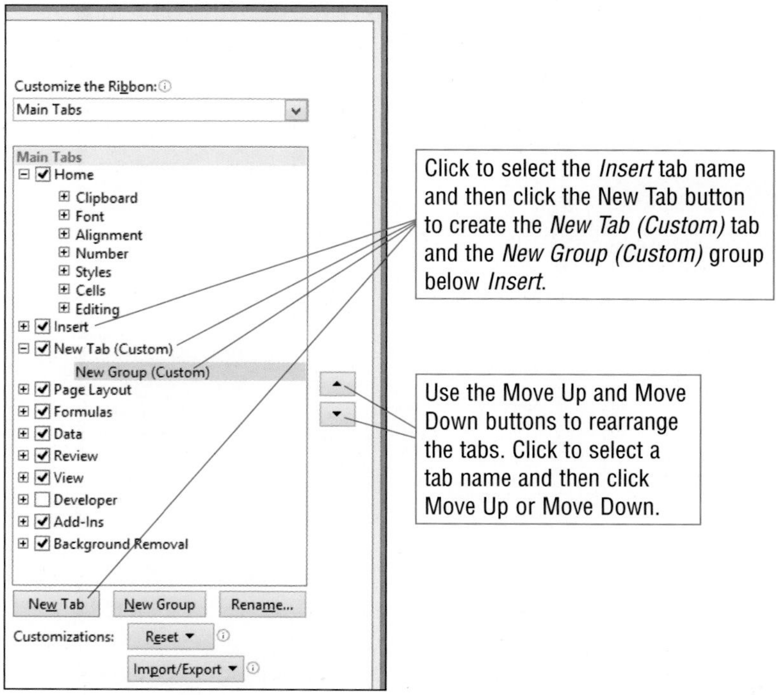

Quick Steps

Rename a Tab or Group
1. Click FILE tab.
2. Click *Options*.
3. Click *Customize Ribbon* in left pane.
4. Click tab or group to be renamed.
5. Click Rename button.
6. Type new name.
7. Press Enter or click OK.

Renaming a Tab, Group, or Command

Rename a tab by clicking the tab name in the *Main Tabs* list box and then clicking the Rename button located below the *Main Tabs* list box. At the Rename dialog box, type the desired name for the tab and then press Enter or click OK. You can also display the Rename dialog box by right-clicking the tab name and then clicking *Rename* at the shortcut menu.

Complete similar steps to rename a group or command. The Rename dialog box for a group or command name contains a *Symbol* list as well as the *Display name* text box. Type the new name for the group in the *Display name* text box and then press Enter or click OK. The symbols are useful for identifying new buttons.

Project 2e **Customizing the Ribbon** **Part 5 of 8**

1. Open **NationalJE.xlsx**.
2. Save the workbook and name it **EL2-C7-P2-NationalJE.**
3. Customize the ribbon by adding a new tab and two new groups within the tab by completing the following steps. ***Note: The ribbon will be reset to its original settings in Project 2g.***
   a. Click the FILE tab and then click *Options*.
   b. Click *Customize Ribbon* in the left pane of the Excel Options dialog box.

c. Click to select *Insert* in the *Main Tabs* list box located at the right of the dialog box.
d. Click the New Tab button located below the list box. (This inserts a new tab below the Insert tab and a new group below the new tab.)
e. With *New Group (Custom)* selected below *New Tab (Custom)*, click the New Group button that displays below the list box. (This inserts another new group on the new tab.)

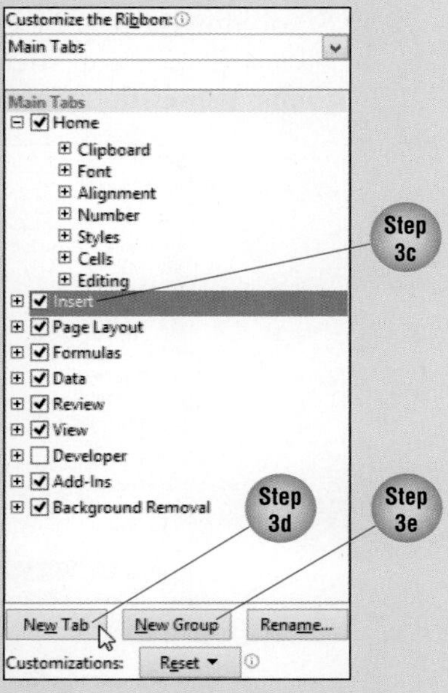

4. Rename the tab and groups by completing the following steps:
   a. Click to select *New Tab (Custom)* in the *Main Tabs* list box.
   b. Click the Rename button that displays below the list box.
   c. At the Rename dialog box, type your first and last names in all caps and then press Enter or click OK.
   d. Click to select the first *New Group (Custom)* group name that displays below the new tab.
   e. Click the Rename button.
   f. At the Rename dialog box, type **Borders** in the *Display name* text box and then press Enter or click OK. (The Rename dialog box for a group or button displays symbols in addition to the *Display name* text box. You will apply a symbol to a button in a later step.)
   g. Right-click the *New Group (Custom)* group name below *Borders (Custom)* and then click *Rename* at the shortcut menu.
   h. Type **Statistics** in the *Display name* text box at the Rename dialog box and then press Enter or click OK.

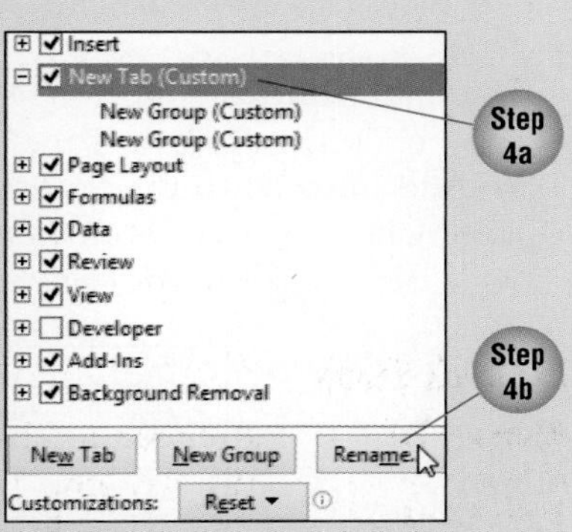

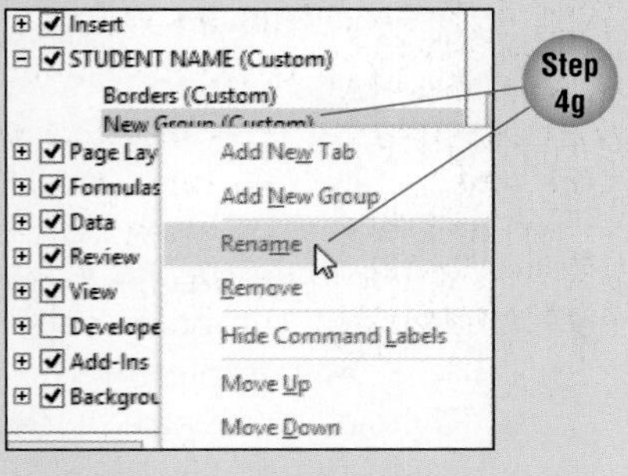

5. Add buttons to the *Borders (Custom)* group by completing the following steps:
   a. Click to select *Borders (Custom)* in the *Main Tabs* list box.
   b. Click the down-pointing arrow at the right of the *Choose commands from* option box (which currently displays *Popular Commands*) and then click *All Commands* at the drop-down list.

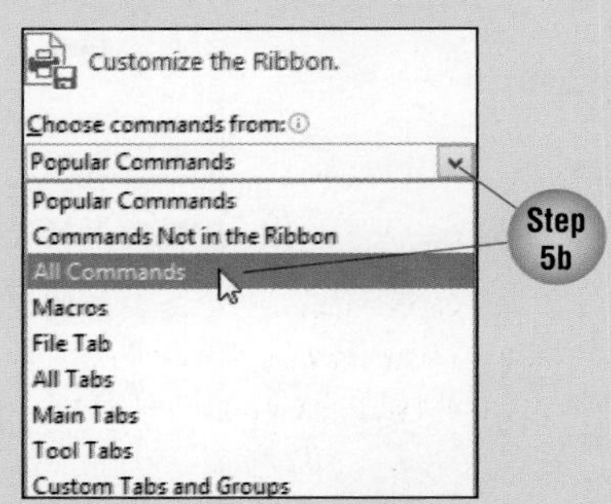

c. Scroll down the *All Commands* list box (the list displays alphabetically), click *Thick Bottom Border*, and then click the Add button located between the two list boxes. (This inserts the command below the *Borders (Custom)* group name.)

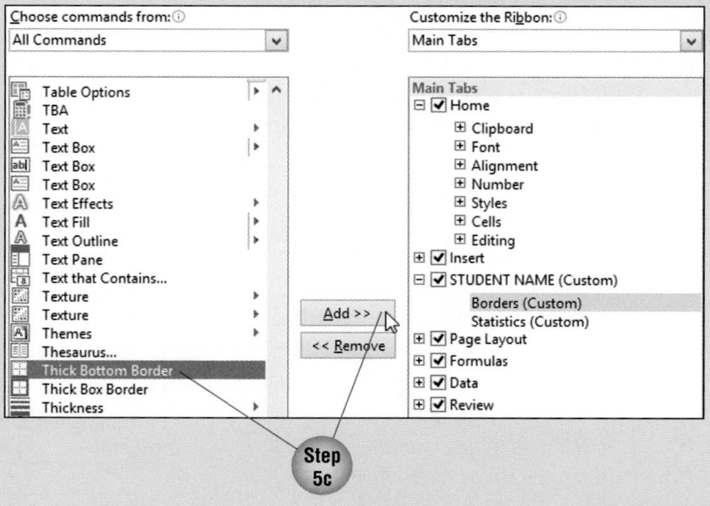

d. Scroll down the *All Commands* list box, click *Top and Double Bottom Border*, and then click the Add button.

6. Add buttons to the *Statistics (Custom)* group by completing the following steps:
   a. Click to select *Statistics (Custom)* in the *Main Tabs* list box.
   b. Scroll up the *All Commands* list box, click *Average*, and then click the Add button.

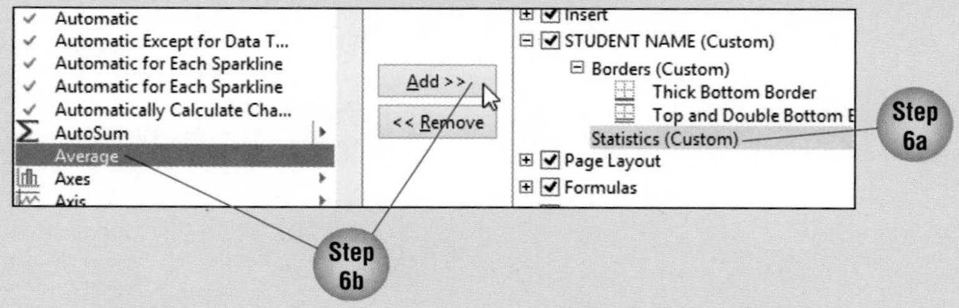

   c. Scroll down the *All Commands* list box, click *Max*, and then click the Add button.
   d. Scroll down the *All Commands* list box, click *Min*, and then click the Add button.

7. Change the symbol for the Average, Max, and Min buttons by completing the following steps:
   a. Right-click *Average* below *Statistics (Custom)* in the *Main Tabs* list box and then click *Rename* at the shortcut menu.
   b. At the Rename dialog box, click the calculator icon in the *Symbol* list box (fifth row, second column) and then click OK.
   c. Change the symbol for *Max* and *Min* to the calculator symbol by completing actions similar to those in Step 7b.

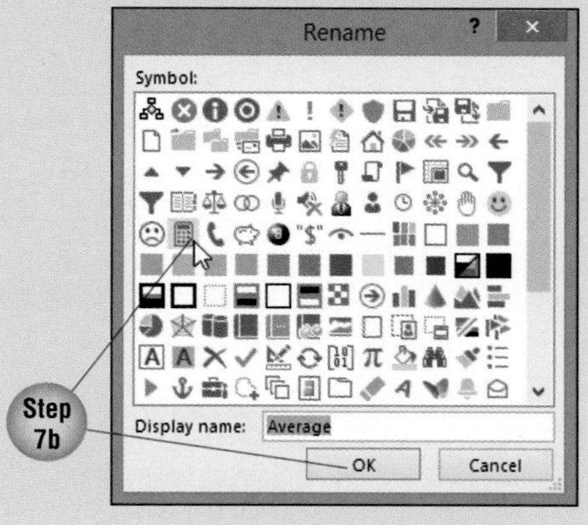

8. Click OK to close the Excel Options dialog box.
9. Use buttons in the custom tab to format and add formulas to the worksheet by completing the following steps:
   a. Make cell A3 the active cell, click the custom tab with your name, and then click the Thick Bottom Border button in the Borders group.

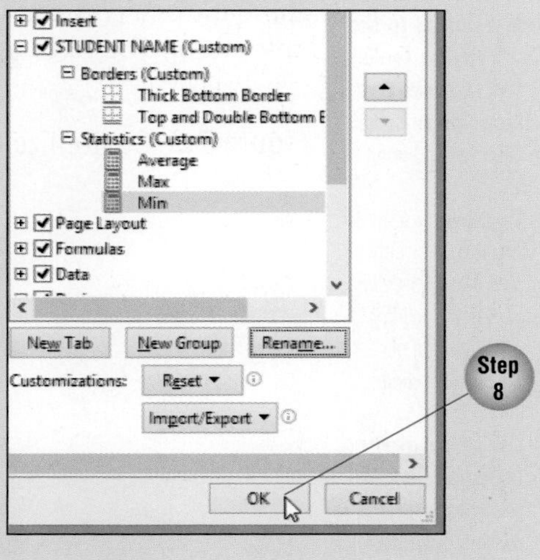

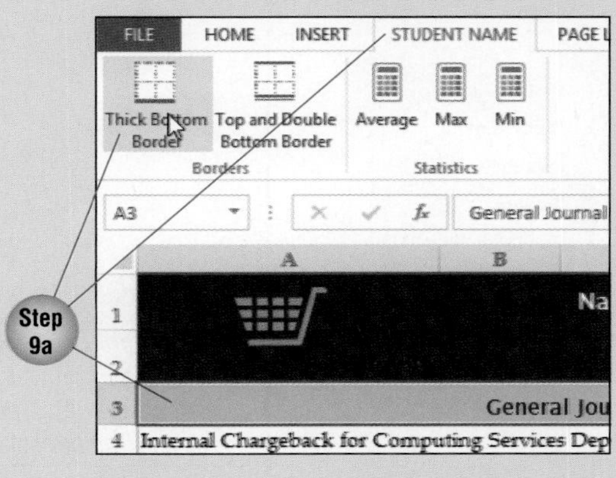

   b. Select B6:H6 and then click the Thick Bottom Border button in the Borders group.
   c. Make cell D18 the active cell and then click the Top and Double Bottom Border button in the Borders group.
   d. Make cell D20 the active cell and then click the Average button in the Statistics group.
   e. With D7:D19 selected in the formula *=AVERAGE(D7:D19)*, drag to select D7:D17 and then press Enter.
   f. With cell D21 active, click the Max button in the Statistics group, drag to select D7:D17, and then press Enter.
   g. With cell D22 active, click the Min button in the Statistics group, drag to select D7:D17, and then press Enter.
10. Save **EL2-C7-P2-NationalJE.xlsx**.
11. In a new Word document, insert a screenshot of the worksheet showing the custom tab using either Print Screen with Paste or the Screenshot feature (INSERT tab, Screenshot button in Illustrations group). Type your name a few lines below the screenshot.
12. Save the Microsoft Word document and name it **EL2-C7-P2-NationalJE**.
13. Print **EL2-C7-P2-NationalJE.docx** and then exit Word.
14. Print and then close **EL2-C7-P2-NationalJE.xlsx**.

Customizing the Quick Access Toolbar

Customize Quick Access Toolbar

Click the Customize Quick Access Toolbar button located at the right side of the Quick Access toolbar to open the Customize Quick Access Toolbar drop-down list, as shown in Figure 7.9. Click *More Commands* at the drop-down list to open the Excel Options dialog box with *Quick Access Toolbar* selected in the left pane, as shown in Figure 7.10. Change the list of commands shown in the left list box by clicking the down-pointing arrow to the right of *Choose commands from* and then clicking the desired category. Scroll down the list box to locate the command and then double-click the command name to add it to the Quick Access toolbar.

Quick Steps

Add a Button to the Quick Access Toolbar

1. Click Customize Quick Access Toolbar button.
2. Click desired button.

OR

1. Click Customize Quick Access Toolbar button.
2. Click *More Commands.*
3. Click down-pointing arrow at right of *Choose commands from.*
4. Click desired category.
5. Double-click desired command in commands list box.
6. Click OK.

Remove a Button from the Quick Access Toolbar

1. Click Customize Quick Access Toolbar button.
2. Click desired command.

OR

1. Click Customize Quick Access Toolbar button.
2. Click *More Commands.*
3. Click desired command in right list box.
4. Click Remove button.
5. Click OK.

A few less popular features in Excel are available only by adding buttons to the Quick Access toolbar. If a feature you are trying to locate is not available in any tab on the ribbon, search for it in the *All Commands* list.

Figure 7.9 Customize Quick Access Toolbar Drop-down List

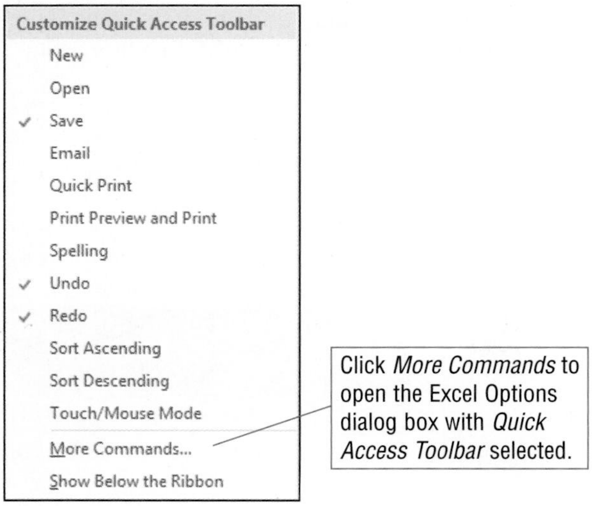

Figure 7.10 Excel Options Dialog Box with *Quick Access Toolbar* Selected

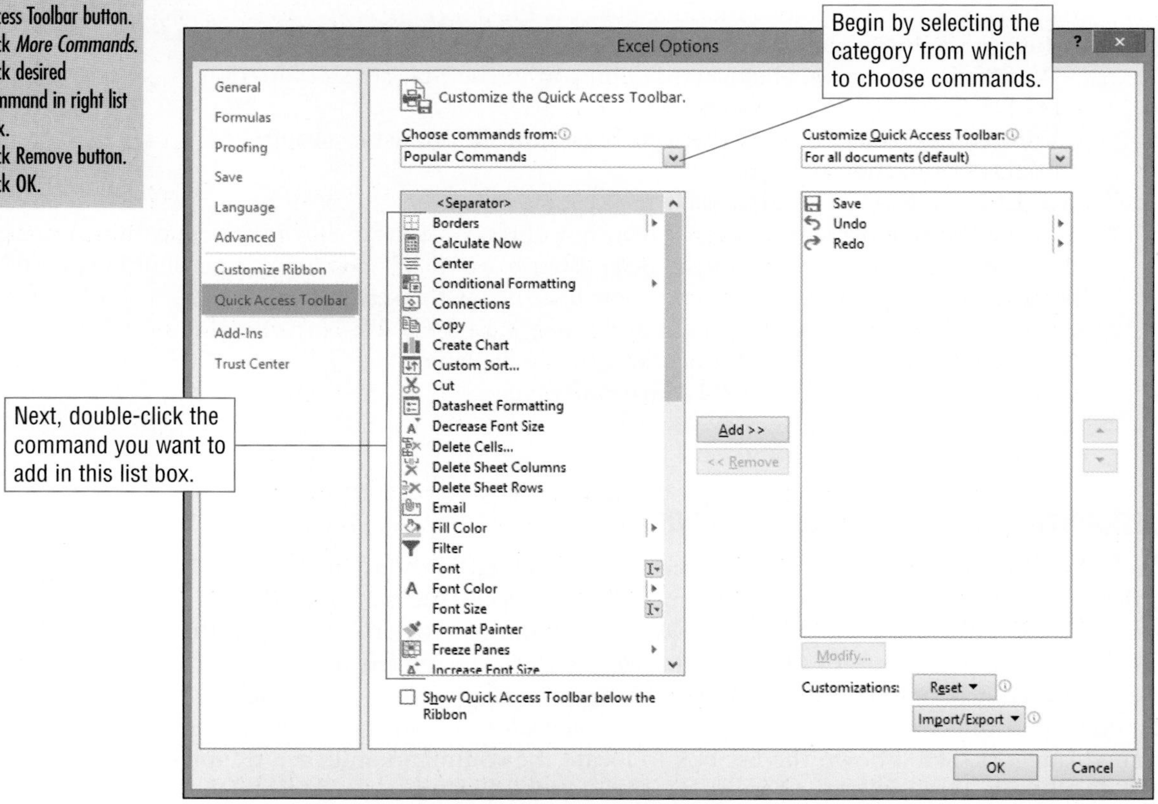

Project 2f Adding Commands to the Quick Access Toolbar Part 6 of 8

1. Press Ctrl + N to open a new blank workbook and then add the Print Preview and Print and Sort commands to the Quick Access toolbar by completing the following steps. ***Note: You will reset the Quick Access toolbar to the original settings in Project 2g.***
   a. Click the Customize Quick Access Toolbar button located at the right side of the Quick Access toolbar.
   b. Click *Print Preview and Print* at the drop-down list. The Print Preview and Print button is added to the end of the Quick Access toolbar. ***Note: Skip to Step 1d if the Print Preview and Print button is already present on your Quick Access toolbar.***
   c. Click the Customize Quick Access Toolbar button.
   d. Click *More Commands* at the drop-down list.
   e. At the Excel Options dialog box with *Quick Access Toolbar* selected in the left pane, click the *Choose commands from* option box arrow and then click *All Commands*.

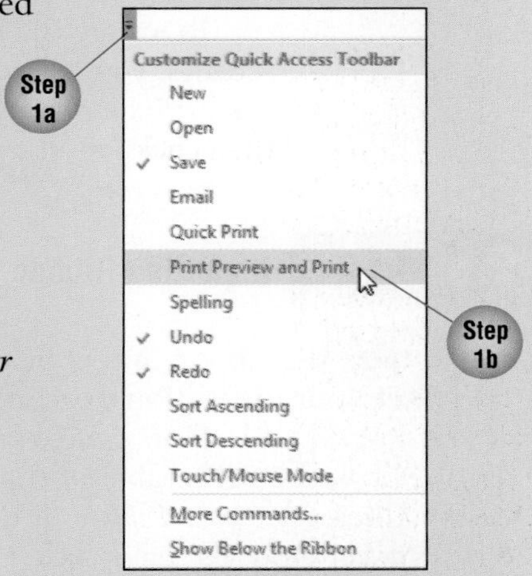

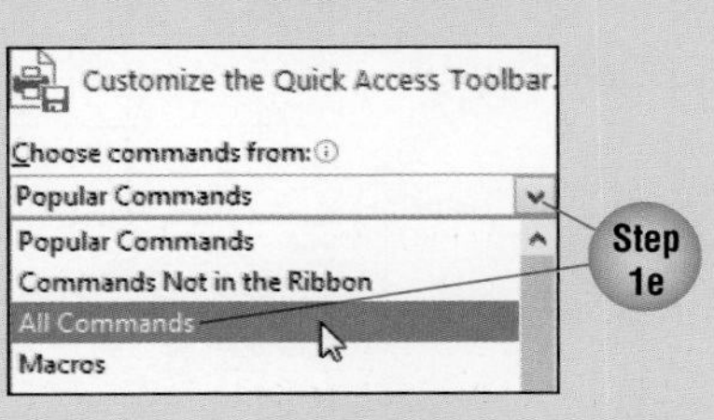

   f. Scroll down the *All Commands* list box and then double-click the second *Sort* option, which displays the ScreenTip *Data Tab | Sort & Filter | Sort.... (SortDialog)*. ***Note: The commands are organized in alphabetical order; you will need to scroll far down the list to find this option.***

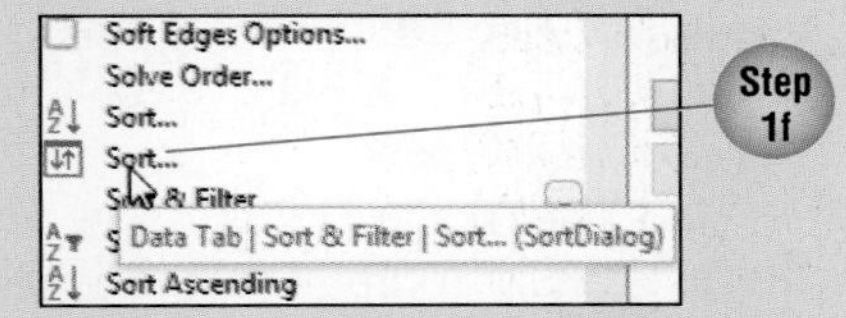

   g. Click OK. The Sort button is added to the end of the Quick Access toolbar.
2. Type your name in cell A1, press Enter, and then click the Print Preview and Print button on the Quick Access toolbar to display the Print backstage area.
3. Press Esc to close the Print backstage area.
4. Click the Sort button on the Quick Access toolbar to open the Sort dialog box.
5. Click the Cancel button at the Sort dialog box.
6. Close the workbook. Click Don't Save when prompted to save changes.

You can delete a button from the Quick Access Toolbar by clicking the Customize Quick Access Toolbar button and then clicking the command at the drop-down list. If the command is not in the drop-down list, click the *More Commands* option. At the Excel Options dialog box, click the desired command in the right list box and then click the Remove button.

Resetting the Ribbons and the Quick Access Toolbar

Restore the original ribbons and Quick Access toolbar that came with Excel 2013 by clicking the Reset button that displays below the *Main Tabs* list box in the Excel Options dialog box with *Customize Ribbon* selected. Clicking the Reset button displays two options: *Reset only selected Ribbon tab* and *Reset all customizations*. Click *Reset all customizations* to restore the ribbons and Quick Access toolbar to their original settings and then click Yes at the message box that displays *Delete all Ribbon and Quick Access Toolbar customizations for this program?* If you want to remove a tab that you previously created, right-click the tab and then click *Customize the Ribbon*. Right-click the tab in the *Main Tabs* list box and then click *Remove*.

To restore the ribbons and Quick Access toolbar to your institution's original settings, you will need to import the settings you exported in Project 2d. Click the Import/Export button in the lower right corner of the Excel Options dialog box and then click *Import customization file*. Locate the file and reinstall the customized settings.

Project 2g Importing Ribbon and Quick Access Toolbar Customizations — Part 7 of 8

1. Import the ribbon and Quick Access Toolbar customizations you saved in Project 2d to reset your institution's original settings by completing the following steps:
   a. Press Ctrl + N to open a new blank workbook.
   b. Click the FILE tab and then click *Options*.
   c. Click *Customize Ribbon* in the left pane of the Excel Options dialog box.
   d. Click the Import/Export button located at the bottom right of the Excel Options dialog box.
   e. Click *Import customization file* at the drop-down list.
   f. Click *Desktop* in the *Favorites* list at the left of the File Open dialog box.
   g. Click **EL2-C7-P2-ExcelCustomizations.exportedUI**.
   h. Click Open.
   i. Click Yes at the message asking if you want to replace all existing ribbon and Quick Access Toolbar customizations for this program.
   j. Click OK.
2. Close the workbook. Click Don't Save if prompted to save changes.

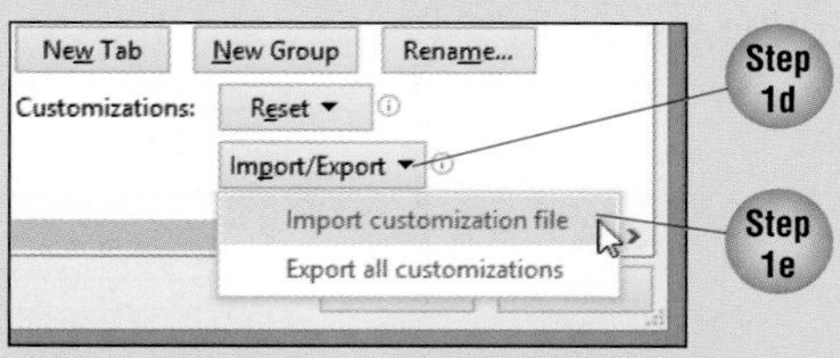

Creating and Applying a Custom View

A ***custom view*** saves display and print settings for the active worksheet. These settings can include column widths, row heights, hidden rows and/or columns, filter settings, cell selections, windows settings, page layout options, and print areas. You can create multiple custom views for the same worksheet and access stored views using the Custom Views dialog box. In Project 2h, you will create three custom views that store display settings, hidden rows, and a row height for a swimming schedule. You will switch between views to show different portions of the worksheet, such as only the daytime swimming activities.

Begin creating a custom view by applying the desired settings to the active worksheet, clicking the cell you want to be active, and displaying the rows and columns you want shown on the screen. When you are finished, click the VIEW tab, click the Custom Views button in the Workbook Views group, click the Add button, type a name for the custom view, and then click OK.

Quick Steps

Create a Custom View
1. Change display and print settings as desired.
2. Click VIEW tab.
3. Click Custom Views.
4. Click Add.
5. Type name for view.
6. Choose desired *Include in view* options.
7. Click OK.

Apply a Custom View
1. Click VIEW tab.
2. Click Custom Views.
3. Click desired view name.
4. Click Show.

Custom Views

Change a worksheet to display a custom view's settings by opening the Custom Views dialog box, selecting the desired view name in the *Views* list box, and then clicking the Show button. You can also double-click the desired view name to apply the saved display and print settings to the worksheet. If a worksheet other than the one in which the view was created is active, you will be switched to the worksheet for which the view applies.

HINT

You can only apply a custom view to the worksheet in which it was created.

Project 2h Creating and Applying Custom Views — Part 8 of 8

1. Open **EL2-C7-P2-NWinterSch.xlsx**.
2. Save the workbook, name it **EL2-C7-P2-NWinterSch-CV**, and redisplay the row and column headers in the worksheet. Refer to Project 2c if you need assistance with this step.
3. Create a custom view with display settings for all swimming sessions by completing the following steps:
   a. Select rows 4 through 37, click the Format button in the Cells group on the HOME tab, click *Row Height* at the drop-down list, type 20 in the *Row height* text box at the Row Height dialog box, and then press Enter or click OK.
   b. Press Ctrl + Home.
   c. Click the VIEW tab.
   d. Click the Custom Views button in the Workbook Views group.
   e. Click the Add button at the Custom Views dialog box.
   f. With the insertion point positioned in the *Name* text box at the Add View dialog box, type AllSessions.
   g. Make sure that the *Print settings* and *Hidden rows, columns and filter settings* check boxes contain check marks and then click OK.

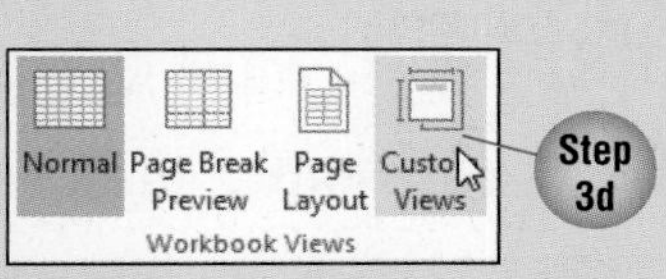

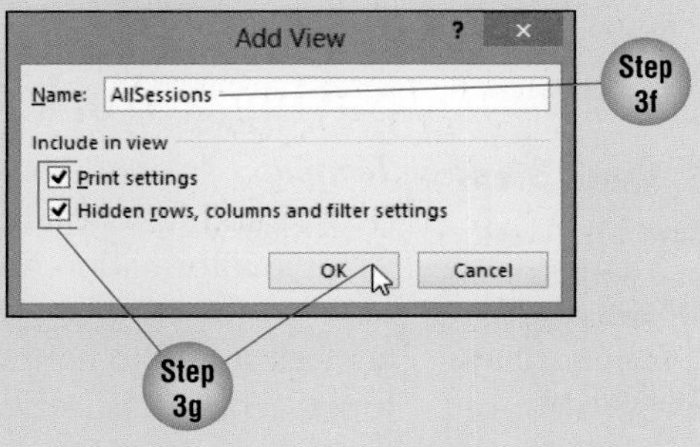

4. Create a second custom view to display the daytime swimming activities and hide the evening activities by completing the following steps:
   a. Select rows 24 through 37, click the HOME tab, click the Format button in the Cells group, point to *Hide & Unhide* in the *Visibility* section, and then click *Hide Rows*.
   b. Press Ctrl + Home.
   c. Click the VIEW tab and then click the Custom Views button in the Workbook Views group.
   d. At the Custom Views dialog box, click the Add button.
   e. At the Add View dialog box, type DaytimeSessions in the *Name* text box.
   f. Make sure that the *Print settings* and *Hidden rows, columns and filter settings* check boxes contain check marks and then click OK.

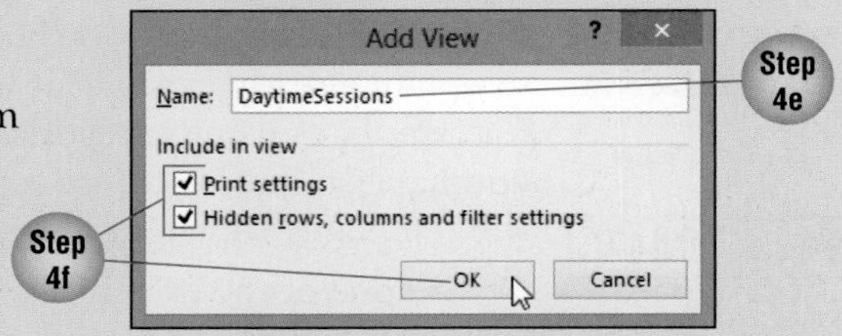

5. Click the Custom Views button in the Workbook Views group. With *AllSessions* selected in the *Views* list box, click the Show button to apply the custom view.

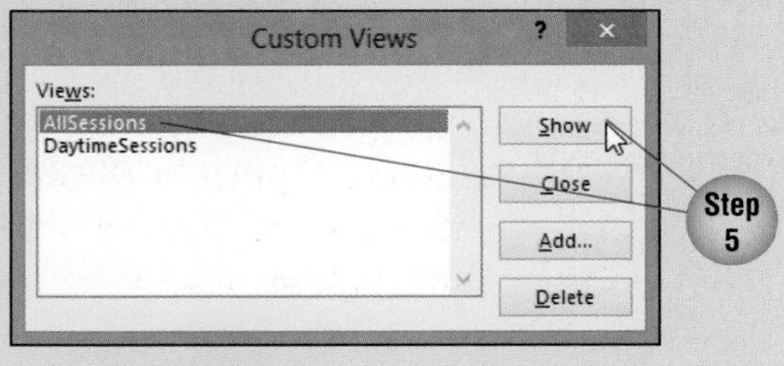

6. Create a third custom view to show only the evening swimming sessions by completing the following steps:
   a. Select rows 4 through 23 and hide the rows by completing a step similar to Step 4a.
   b. Create a custom view named *EveningSessions* by completing steps similar to Steps 4b–4f.
7. Click the Custom Views button and then double-click *DaytimeSessions* in the *Views* list box at the Custom Views dialog box.
8. Show the *EveningSessions* custom view.
9. Show the *AllSessions* custom view.
10. Save and then close **EL2-C7-P2-NWinterSch-CV.xlsx**.

HINT

Custom views cannot be created for any worksheet in which a table resides.

If you no longer need a custom view you previously created, delete it by opening the Custom Views dialog box, selecting the custom view name in the *Views* list box, and then clicking the Delete button.

Project 3 Save a Workbook as a Template — 2 Parts

You will modify an existing workbook and save the revised version as a template.

Saving a Workbook as a Template

Quick Steps

Save a Workbook as a Template
1. Open workbook.
2. Make desired changes.
3. Click FILE tab.
4. Click *Save As*.
5. Click Browse button.
6. Change *Save as type* to *Excel Template (*.xltx)*.
7. Type desired file name.
8. Click OK.

HINT

If macros exist in the template workbook, change the *Save as type* option to *Excel Macro-Enabled Template (*.xltm)*.

Templates are workbooks with standard text, formulas, and formatting. Cell entries are created and formatted for all of the data that does not change. Cells that will contain variable information have formatting applied, but are left empty since they will be filled in when the template is used to generate a worksheet. Examples of worksheets that are well suited to templates include invoices, purchase orders, time cards, and expense forms. These types of worksheets are usually filled in with the same kinds of data, but the data itself varies.

Several templates have already been created and are installed on your computer or can be installed after they are downloaded. If you want to use a template to create a worksheet, first check the New backstage area to see if a template already exists that is suited to your purpose. You can also search online for templates using categories such as *Budget*, *Invoice*, *Calendars*, and *Expenses*. Once you have selected a topic in Suggested Searches, you can either download one of the templates shown or choose another topic from the Category task pane.

If none of the existing templates meet your needs, you can create your own custom template. To do this, create a workbook that contains all of the standard data, formulas, and formatting. Leave cells empty for any information that is variable; however, format those cells as required. When you are ready to save the workbook as a template, use the Save As dialog box and change the *Save as type* option to *Excel Template (*.xltx)*. Before saving it as a template, consider protecting the worksheet by locking all of the cells except those that will hold variable data.

Project 3a Saving a Workbook as a Template Part 1 of 2

1. Open **EL2-C7-P2-NWinterSch.xlsx**.
2. Redisplay the row and column headers in the worksheet. Refer to Project 2c if you need assistance with this step.
3. Assume that you work at the Noranda Sportsplex, which publishes swimming schedules on a continual basis. The sportsplex manager never changes the days or times the pool operates, but the activities and assigned pools often change. You decide to modify this workbook and then save it as a template to be reused whenever the schedule changes. To begin, make the following changes to the worksheet:
   a. Clear the cell contents for the ranges D5:E23 and D25:E37.
   b. Make cell A2 the active cell and then delete *Winter* in *Winter Swimming Schedule* so that the subtitle reads *Swimming Schedule*.
   c. Insert a new row between rows 2 and 3 and merge and center the cells in the new row to match the subtitle. (This will be used later to enter the timeframe for the new schedule.)

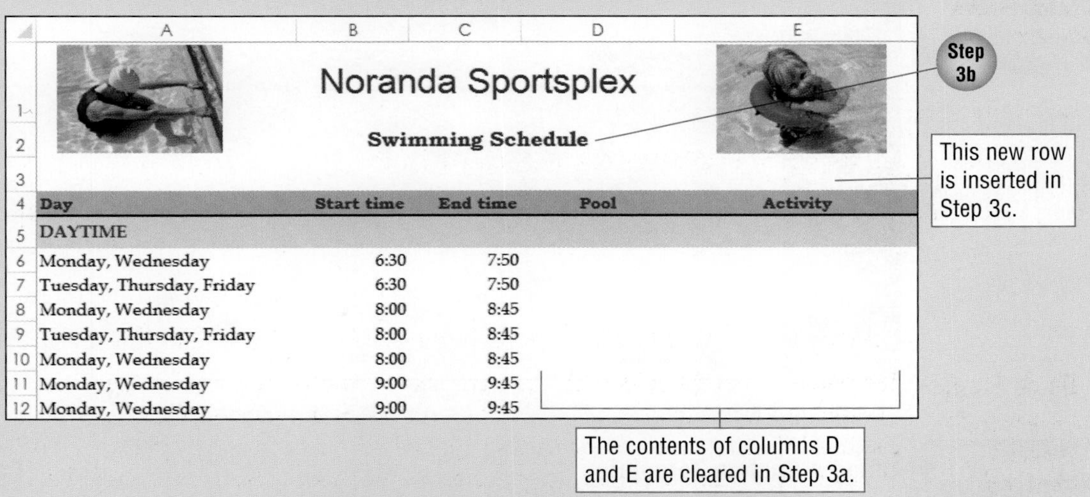

   d. Select and turn off the lock attribute for cell A3 and the ranges D6:E24 and D26:E38. Deselect the range.
   e. Protect the worksheet. Do not assign a password to unprotect.
4. Save the revised workbook as a template by completing the following steps:
   a. Click the FILE tab.
   b. Click *Save As*.
   c. Click the Browse button.
   d. Click *Save as type* and then click *Excel Template (*.xltx)* at the pop-up list.
   e. Select the current text in the *File name* text box and then type **SwimSchTemplate-StudentName**, substituting your name for *StudentName*.
   f. Click the Save button.

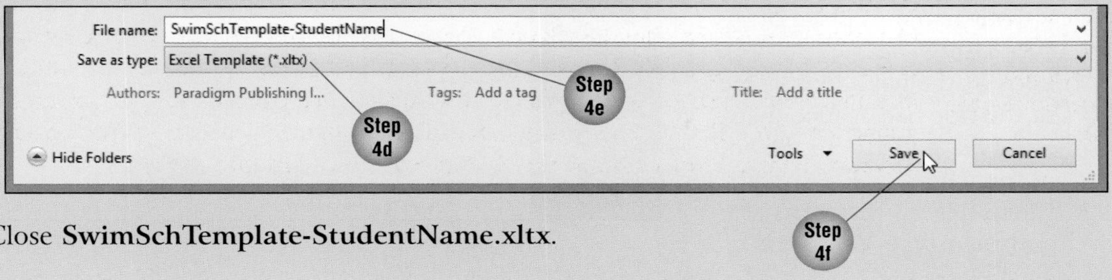

5. Close **SwimSchTemplate-StudentName.xltx**.

Using a Custom Template

Quick Steps

Use a Custom Template

1. Click FILE tab.
2. Click *New*.
3. Click *PERSONAL*.
4. Double-click desired template.

To use a template that you created yourself, click the FILE tab and then click *New*. At the New backstage area, click *PERSONAL*. This opens the PERSONAL template section, as shown in Figure 7.11. Double-click the name of the desired template to open it. A workbook (.xlsx) opens with the name of the template followed by a *1*. You can then save the document with a more descriptive name. In Project 3b you will create a new workbook using the template created in Project 3a, add information for the Winter 2015 schedule, and then save the workbook as EL2-C7-P3-SwimSchWinter2015.

HINT

By default, custom template workbook files are stored in the path [c:\Users*username*\My Documents\Custom Office Templates.

Figure 7.11 New Backstage Area

Project 3b **Using a Custom Template** **Part 2 of 2**

1. At a blank Excel screen, open the template created in Project 3a by completing the following steps:
   a. Click the FILE tab.
   b. Click *New*.
   c. At the New backstage area, click *PERSONAL*.
   d. In the PERSONAL template section, double-click *SwimSchTemplate-StudentName.xltx.* (Your template will have your name in place of *StudentName*.)
2. Look at the workbook name in the title bar. Notice that Excel has added *1* to the end of the name.
3. Make cell A3 the active cell and then type Winter 2015.

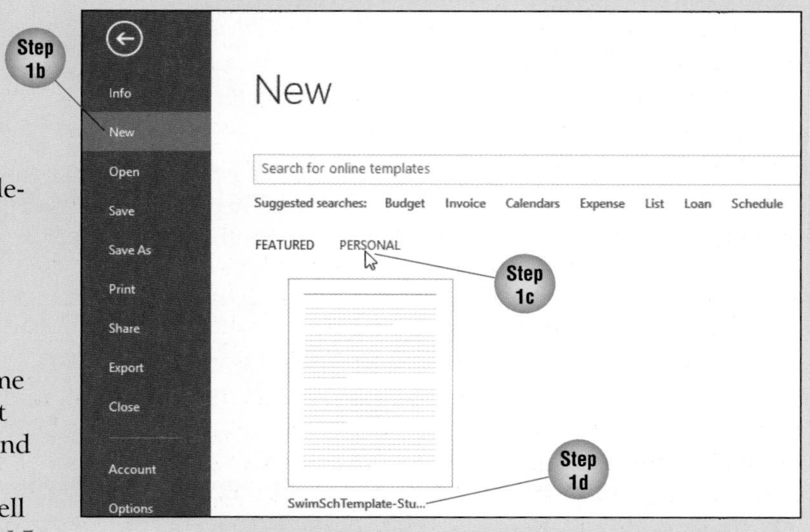

4. Enter data for the first two rows in the *Daytime* section by making up a pool name and activity for each row.
5. Click the Save button on the Quick Access toolbar.
6. Excel opens the Save As dialog box and automatically changes the *Save as type* option to *Excel Workbook (*.xlsx)*. Navigate to the EL2C7 folder on your storage medium, type EL2-C7-P3-SwimSchWinter2015 in the *File name* text box, and then click the Save button.
7. Print and then close **EL2-C7-P3-SwimSchWinter2015.xlsx**.

Deleting a Custom Template

To delete a custom template, use the Open dialog box to navigate to [c]\Users\ *username*\My Documents\Custom Office Templates. Right-click the name of the template you want to delete and then click *Delete* at the shortcut menu. Click Cancel to close the Open dialog box.

Quick Steps

Delete a Custom Template
1. Click FILE tab.
2. Click *Open*.
3. Navigate to [c:]\ Users\ *username*\My Documents\Custom Office Templates.
4. Right-click desired template name.
5. Click *Delete*.
6. Click Cancel.

Project 4 Managing Excel's Save Options — 2 Parts

You will review Excel's current save options, modify the AutoRecover options, and recover an unsaved workbook.

Customizing Save Options

The ***AutoRecover*** feature saves versions of your work at a specified time interval so that you can restore all or part of your data should you forget to save or if you experience a situation that causes Excel to close unexpectedly (such as a power outage). When you restart Excel, the opening screen displays a *Recovered* section above the Recent files list. Click the Show Recovered Files hyperlink and the Document Recovery task pane opens with a list of workbooks for which an AutoRecover file exists.

By default, Excel's AutoRecover feature is turned on and will automatically save AutoRecover information every 10 minutes. You can adjust the time interval to meet your needs. Keep in mind that data loss can still occur even with AutoRecover turned on. For example, suppose the time interval is 20 minutes and a power outage occurs. Depending on when the power outage occurred, when you restart Excel, the recovered file may not contain the last 19 minutes of work if you did not save manually.

In conjunction with AutoRecover, Excel includes the ***AutoSave*** feature, which keeps the last version of a workbook saved in a temporary file. If you close a workbook without saving or want to return to an earlier version of the file, you can recover the AutoSaved version. At the bottom of the Recent Workbooks list, click the Recover Unsaved Workbooks button to view a list of AutoSaved files.

Open the Excel Options dialog box and select *Save* in the left pane to view and/or change the AutoRecover and AutoSave options.

Quick Steps

Customize Save Options
1. Click FILE tab.
2. Click *Options*.
3. Click *Save* in left pane.
4. Change save options as desired.
5. Click OK.

HINT

Do not rely on AutoRecover and AutoSave as you work. Saving regularly to minimize data loss and protect against unforeseen events is the best practice.

Project 4a Customizing Save Options — Part 1 of 2

1. At a blank Excel screen, click the FILE tab and then click *Options* to open the Excel Options dialog box.
2. Click *Save* in the left pane of the Excel Options dialog box.
3. Take note of the current settings for *Save AutoRecover information every [ ] minutes* and *Keep the last autosaved version if I close without saving*. By default, both check boxes should be checked and the time interval should be 10 minutes; however, the settings may have been changed on the computer you are using. In that case, write down the options so that you can restore the program to its original state once you are finished.
4. If necessary, click the two check boxes to turn on the AutoRecover and AutoSave features.
5. Select the current value in the *Save AutoRecover information every [ ] minutes* text box and then type 2 to change the time interval to 2 minutes.
6. Click OK.

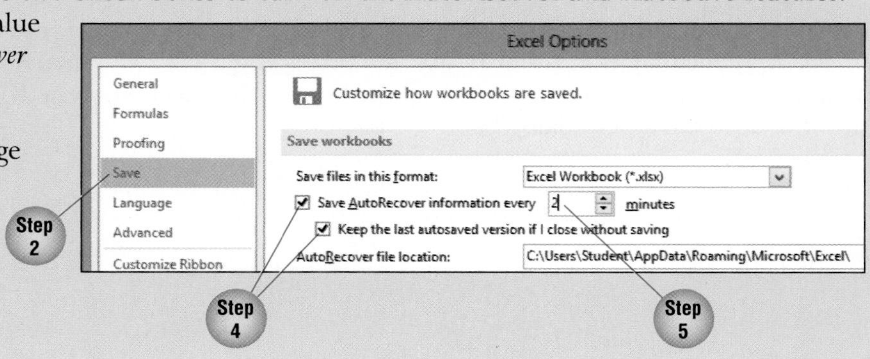

Project 4b Recovering a Workbook — Part 2 of 2

1. Open **EL2-C7-P2-NationalJE.xlsx**.
2. Save the workbook and name it **EL2-C7-P4-NationalJE**.
3. Note the system time in the bottom right corner of the screen. You will use this time to make sure that more than two minutes elapse before you interrupt the Excel session.
4. Make the following changes to the worksheet:
   a. Select A7:A17 and apply the Dark Red font color (first color in the *Standard Colors* section of the drop-down color palette).
   b. Select E7:E17 and apply the Dark Red font color.
   c. Delete rows 20 through 22 to remove the data from the workbook.

Step 4b

6		Parts	Labor	Total	TSR	Dept Code	Number	Number
7	Accounting	$ -	$ 1,125.00	$ 1,125.00	CS-4042	225	011475	160101
8	Executive Administration	564.27	885.50	1,449.77	CS-4043	216	011482	160102
9	Finance	964.32	535.50	1,499.82	CS-4044	166	011435	160103
10	Human Resources	397.45	125.50	522.95	CS-4045	187	011485	160104
11	Graphics Design	117.45	75.50	192.95	CS-4046	210	011415	160105
12	Electronic Production	215.48	275.50	490.98	CS-4047	350	011443	160106
13	Marketing	1,048.57	325.50	1,374.07	CS-4048	452	011409	160107
14	Web Programming	575.85	154.50	730.35	CS-4049	284	011462	160108
15	Planning and Development	61.45	32.50	93.95	CS-4050	310	011473	160109
16	President's Office	-	225.00	225.00	CS-4051	105	011455	160110
17	Purchasing	415.87	75.50	491.37	CS-4052	243	011428	160111
18				$ 8,196.21				
19								
20								
21								
22								

Step 4a

The data in rows 20–22 is deleted in Step 4c.

5. Make sure more than two minutes have elapsed since you checked the system time in Step 3. If necessary, wait until you are sure an AutoRecover file has been saved.
6. Press Alt + Ctrl + Delete.
7. At the Windows screen, select *Task Manager*.
8. At the Task Manager dialog box, click *Microsoft Excel (32 bit)* in the task list box and then click the End task button.
9. Close the Task Manager dialog box.
10. Restart Microsoft Excel. At the opening screen, click the Show Recovered Files hyperlink in the *Recovered* section. There are two available files: the original version of the file used in this project and the AutoRecovered version.

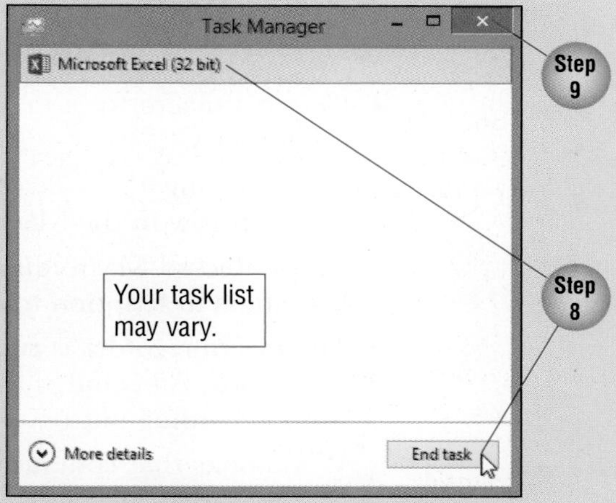

11. Point to the first file in the Document Recovery task pane. A ScreenTip displays to inform you that the first file is the AutoRecover version.
12. Point to the second file in the Document Recovery task pane. A ScreenTip displays to inform you that the second file is the original workbook.

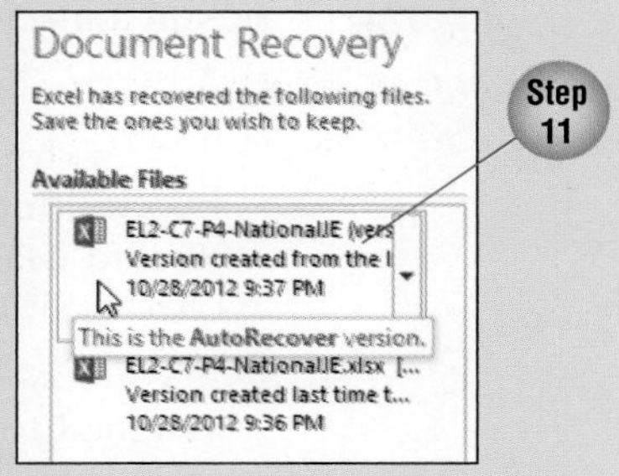

13. Click the first file in the Document Recovery task pane. Notice that the edited version of the file appears. Look at the additional information displayed next to the file name in the Title bar. Excel includes *(version 1)* and *[Autosaved]* in the file name. Notice also that the Autosaved file has the file extension *.xlsb*.

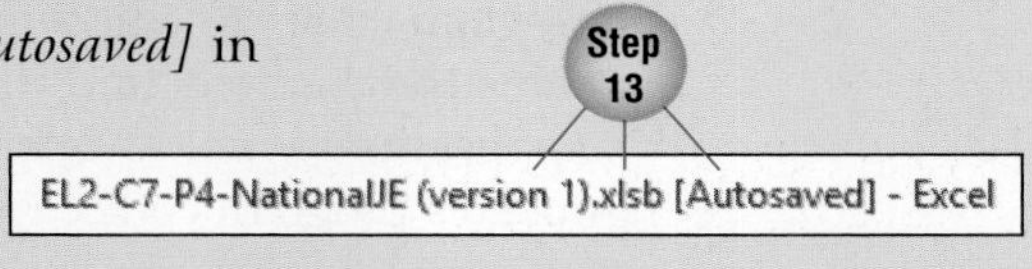

14. Click *Recovered* next to *Ready* in the task bar at the bottom of the screen to redisplay the Document Recovery task pane.
15. Click the second file in the Document Recovery task pane. Notice that the original workbook opens and the message *[Last saved by user]* is added to the file name in the Title bar.

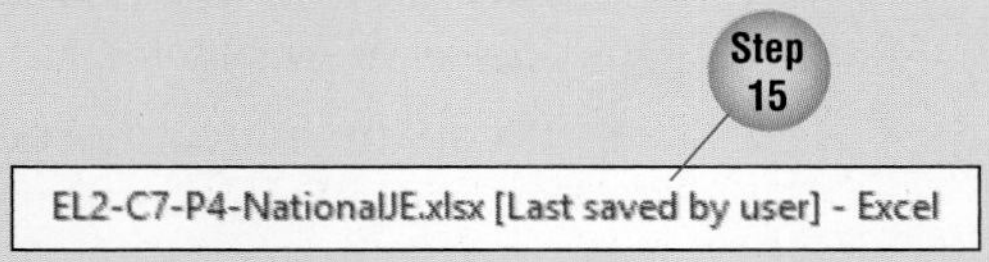

16. Close both workbooks. Click Save when prompted to save changes and then click *Save* at the Save As dialog box to accept the default name *EL2-C7-P4-NationalJE (Autosaved).xlsx*.
17. Open the Excel Options dialog box. The time interval changed back to 10 minutes when you clicked End task in Project 4b Step 8. If necessary, restore the Save options to the settings you wrote down in Project 4a. Close the Excel Options dialog box.

The Save options at the Excel Options dialog box also allow you to specify the drive and/or folder in which to store AutoRecovered files, as well as the default file location for all new workbooks.

At the Recent backstage view, click the Recover Unsaved Workbooks button at the bottom of the Recent Places pane to view a list of Autosaved files.

Chapter Summary

- Create a macro for a task that you repeat frequently and for which the steps do not vary.
- Start creating a new macro by clicking the VIEW tab, clicking the Macros button arrow in the Macros group, and then clicking *Record Macro*.
- At the Record Macro dialog box, you can assign a name, an optional shortcut key, and a description to the macro.
- The macro recorder is turned on after you click OK to close the Record Macro dialog box. All commands and keystrokes will be recorded until you click the Stop Recording button.
- Workbooks that contain macros are saved in the *Excel Macro-Enabled Workbook (*.xlsm)* file format.
- Run a macro by opening the Macro dialog box and double-clicking the macro name.
- A macro assigned to a shortcut key can be run by pressing Ctrl + the assigned letter.
- Excel differentiates the case of the letter typed in the *Shortcut key* text box at the Record Macro dialog box. An uppercase letter is assigned with the shortcut key Ctrl + Shift + the assigned letter.
- If you assign a shortcut key to a macro that is the same as a shortcut key assigned to an Excel feature, the macro overrides the Excel feature.
- The instructions for a macro are recorded in Visual Basic for Applications (VBA) program code. To edit a macro, open the Macro dialog box, click the macro name to be edited, and then click the Edit button. A Microsoft Visual Basic for Applications window opens, displaying a code module in which you can edit the macro's program code.
- After editing the macro, save the changes, click File, and then click *Close and Return to Microsoft Excel*.
- If you are not comfortable with editing a macro in VBA, you can record a new macro with the correct steps and then save it with the same name to replace the existing macro.
- Delete a macro at the Macro dialog box.
- Macros are stored in the workbook in which they are created. When you open the Macro dialog box, all macros from all open workbooks are accessible. Therefore, to use a macro stored in another workbook, you will need to open that workbook first.
- Another option for making macros accessible to other workbooks is to create a macros workbook with all of your standard macros and then open the macros workbook each time you start Excel.
- Pin a workbook that you want to make permanently available in the Recent Workbooks list at the Open backstage area.
- A pinned workbook displays with a down-pointing pin icon. Clicking the icon unpins the workbook from the list.

- Add buttons to or delete buttons from the Quick Access toolbar using the Customize Quick Access Toolbar button. To locate a feature you want to add to the Quick Access toolbar, click *More Commands* at the drop-down list to open the Excel Options dialog box with *Quick Access Toolbar* selected.
- Display options in Excel are grouped by global display options, options that affect the current workbook, and options that affect the current worksheet.
- Customized workbook and worksheet display options are saved with the file.
- Minimize the ribbon to provide more space in the work area when working with a large worksheet. Clicking a tab temporarily redisplays the ribbon to allow you to select a feature.
- You can customize the ribbon by creating a new tab, creating a new group within the new tab, and/or adding buttons within the new group.
- To customize the ribbon, open the Excel Options dialog box and then click *Customize Ribbon* in the left pane.
- Create a new ribbon tab by clicking the tab name that will precede the new tab and then clicking the New Tab button. A new group is automatically added with the new tab.
- Rename a custom tab by selecting the tab name, clicking the Rename button, typing a new name, and then pressing Enter or clicking OK. Rename a group or command using a similar process.
- Add buttons to a group by clicking the group name, selecting the desired command in the commands list box, and then clicking the Add button located between the two list boxes.
- Export and import customizations to save and restore previous settings on the ribbon(s) and Quick Access toolbar.
- A custom view saves display settings so that you can apply the saved settings to a worksheet when needed. Multiple custom views can be created for the same worksheet at the Custom Views dialog box. Open this dialog box by clicking the Custom Views button in the Workbook Views group on the VIEW tab.
- Templates are workbooks with standard text, formatting, and formulas.
- You can create a custom template from an existing workbook by selecting *Excel template (*.xltx)* in the *Save as type* option box in the Save As dialog box.
- To use a custom template, open the New backstage area, click *PERSONAL* to display the templates, and then double-click the custom template name.
- By default, Excel saves your work every 10 minutes to an AutoRecover file. If your Excel session is unexpectedly terminated or you close the file without saving, you can recover the file when you restart Excel at the Document Recovery task pane.

Commands Review

FEATURE	RIBBON TAB, GROUP/OPTIONS	BUTTON	KEYBOARD SHORTCUT
customize display options	FILE, *Options*		
customize Quick Access toolbar	FILE, *Options*		
customize ribbons	FILE, *Options*		
customize save options	FILE, *Options*		
custom views	VIEW, Workbook Views		
delete macro	VIEW, Macros		Alt + F8
edit a macro	VIEW, Macros		Alt + F8
minimize the ribbon			Ctrl + F1
record a macro	VIEW, Macros	OR	
ribbon display options			Ctrl + F1
save as a macro-enabled workbook	FILE, *Save As*		F12
use a custom template	FILE, *New*		

Concepts Check

Test Your Knowledge SNAP

Completion: In the space provided at the right, indicate the correct term, command, or number.

1. A macro name must begin with a letter and can contain a combination of letters, numbers, and this character. ____________________
2. Click this button to indicate that you have finished the tasks or keystrokes you want saved in the macro. ____________________
3. A workbook containing a macro is saved in this file format. ____________________
4. A macro can be assigned to a shortcut key that is a combination of a lowercase or uppercase letter and this key. ____________________
5. Macro instructions are stored in this program code. ____________________
6. A workbook that you use frequently can be permanently added to the Recent Workbooks list by clicking this icon next to the workbook name. ____________________

7. Display options are shown in the Excel Options dialog box with this option selected in the left pane. ________________

8. Click this button to minimize the ribbon and provide more space in the work area. ________________

9. Click this option in the left pane at the Excel Options dialog box to create a custom ribbon tab. ________________

10. Click this option at the Customize Quick Access Toolbar drop-down list to locate a feature to add to the toolbar from the commands list box. ________________

11. Click this button at the Custom Views dialog box to create a new custom view that will save the current display settings for the active worksheet. ________________

12. Change *Save as type* to this option at the Save As dialog box to save the current workbook as a standard workbook that can be opened from the New dialog box. ________________

13. This task pane opens when Excel is restarted after the previous session ended abnormally. ________________

Skills Check Assess Your Performance

Assessment 1

CREATE MACROS

SNAP Grade It

1. At a new blank workbook, create the following two macros:
   a. Create a macro named *Landscape* that changes the page orientation to landscape, sets custom margins (top = 1 inch; bottom, left, and right = 0.5 inch), and centers the worksheet horizontally. Assign the macro to the shortcut key Ctrl + Shift + Q. Enter an appropriate description that includes your name and the date the macro was created.
   b. Create a macro named *Ion* that applies the Ion theme and turns off the display of gridlines in the active worksheet. Assign the macro to the shortcut key Ctrl + t. Enter an appropriate description that includes your name and the date the macro was created.
2. Save the workbook as a macro-enabled workbook named **MyMacros-StudentName**, with your name substituted for *StudentName*.
3. Leave the **MyMacros-StudentName.xlsm** workbook open for the next assessment.

Assessment 2

RUN MACROS

SNAP Grade It

1. Open **NationalCS.xlsx**.
2. Save the workbook and name it **EL2-C7-A2-NationalCS**.
3. Press Ctrl + t to run the Ion macro.
4. Press Ctrl + Shift + Q to run the Landscape macro.
5. Save, print, and then close **EL2-C7-A2-NationalCS.xlsx**.
6. Close **MyMacros-StudentName.xlsm**.

Assessment 3

CREATE MACROS; SAVE AS A MACRO-ENABLED WORKBOOK

SNAP Grade It

1. Open **EL2-C7-A2-NationalCS.xlsx**.
2. Create the following two macros within the current workbook:
   a. Create a macro named *FormulaBarOff* that turns off the display of the Formula bar and protects the worksheet. Do not enter a password to unprotect the sheet. Assign the macro to the shortcut key Ctrl + Shift + M. Enter an appropriate description that includes your name and the date the macro was created.
   b. Create a macro named *FormulaBarOn* that turns on the display of the Formula bar and unprotects the worksheet. Assign the macro to the shortcut key Ctrl + Shift + B. Enter an appropriate description that includes your name and the date the macro was created.
3. Test each macro to make sure the shortcut key runs the correct commands.
4. Save the revised workbook as a macro-enabled workbook and name it **EL2-C7-A3-NationalCS**.
5. Close **EL2-C7-A3-NationalCS.xlsm**.

Assessment 4

PRINT MACROS

1. Open **EL2-C7-A3-NationalCS.xlsm** and enable the content.
2. Open the Macro dialog box and edit the FormulaBarOff macro.
3. At the Microsoft Visual Basic for Applications window with the insertion point blinking in the code window, click File on the Menu bar and then click *Print*. At the Print - VBAProject dialog box, click OK. ***Note: The FormulaBarOn macro code will also print, since both macros are stored within the VBAProject.***
4. Click File on the Menu bar and then click *Close and Return to Microsoft Excel*.
5. Close **EL2-C7-A3-NationalCS.xlsm**.
6. Open **MyMacros-StudentName.xlsm** and enable the content.
7. Open the Macro dialog box and edit the Landscape macro.
8. At the Microsoft Visual Basic for Applications window with the insertion point blinking in the code window, click File on the Menu bar and then click *Print*. At the Print - VBAProject dialog box, click OK. ***Note: The Ion macro code will also print, since both macros are stored within the VBAProject.***
9. Click File on the Menu bar and then click *Close and Return to Microsoft Excel*.
10. Close **MyMacros-StudentName.xlsm**.

Assessment 5

CUSTOMIZE THE EXCEL ENVIRONMENT

SNAP Grade It

1. Open **BillingsDec18.xlsx**.
2. Save the workbook and name it **EL2-C7-A5-BillingsDec18**.
3. Make the following changes to the display options:
   a. Turn off the horizontal scroll bar.
   b. Turn off sheet tabs.
   c. Turn off row and column headers.
   d. Turn off gridlines.
4. Change the current theme to the Wisp theme.
5. Freeze the first four rows in the worksheet.
6. Create a screen image of the worksheet with the modified display options and paste the image into a new Word document. Type your name a few lines below the screen image.
7. Save the Word document and name it **EL2-C7-A5-BillingsDec18**.
8. Print **EL2-C7-A5-BillingsDec18.docx** and then exit Word.
9. Save and close **EL2-C7-A5-BillingsDec18.xlsx**.

Assessment 6

CREATE CUSTOM VIEWS

1. Open **BillingsDec18.xlsx**.
2. Save the workbook and name it **EL2-C7-A6-BillingsDec18**.
3. Select A4:I23 and custom sort the cells in ascending order by attorney and then by the client's last name.
4. With A4:I23 still selected, turn on filter arrows.
5. Deselect the range and then filter the *Attorney* column to show only those rows with attorney Kyle Williams.
6. Press Ctrl + Home and create a custom view named *Williams* to save the filter settings.
7. Clear the filter in the *Attorney* column.
8. Filter the list by the attorney name *Marty O'Donovan*.
9. With cell A1 still selected, create a custom view named *O'Donovan* to save the filter settings.
10. Clear the filter in the *Attorney* column.
11. Create a custom view named *Martinez* by completing steps similar to those in Steps 8 and 9 and then clear the filter from the *Attorney* column.
12. Create a custom view named *Sullivan* by completing steps similar to those in Steps 8 and 9 and then clear the filter from the *Attorney* column.
13. Open the Custom Views dialog box. If necessary, drag the Custom Views dialog box Title bar to move the dialog box to the right of the worksheet. Create a screen image of the worksheet with the dialog box open and paste the image into a new Word document. Type your name a few lines below the screen image.
14. Save the Word document and name it **EL2-C7-A6-BillingsDec18**.
15. Print **EL2-C7-A6-BillingsDec18.docx** and then exit Word.
16. Close the Custom Views dialog box and then save and close **EL2-C7-A6-BillingsDec18.xlsx**.

Assessment

7 CREATE AND USE A TEMPLATE

SNAP Grade It

1. Open **EL2-C7-A5-BillingsDec18.xlsx** and turn on the display of row and column headers.
2. Make the following changes to the workbook:
   a. Select and delete all of the data below the column headings in row 4.
   b. Delete the text in cell A3.
   c. Edit the subtitle in cell A2 to *Associate Weekly Billing Summary*.
3. Save the revised workbook as a template named **Billings-StudentName**, with your name substituted for *StudentName*.
4. Close **Billings-StudentName.xltx**.
5. Start a new workbook based on the **Billings-StudentName.xltx** template.
6. Type **November 16 to 20, 2015** in cell A3.
7. Enter the two billings shown in Figure 7.12.
8. Save the worksheet as an Excel workbook named **EL2-C7-A7-Billings**.
9. Print and then close **EL2-C7-A7-Billings.xlsx**.
10. Copy **Billings-StudentName.xltx** from [c]\Users\username\My Documents\Custom Office Templates folder to the *EL2C7* folder on your storage medium. Close the Computer window.

Figure 7.12 Assessment 7

IN-774	10665	11/16/2015	Rankin	Jan	Maureen Myers	Insurance	4.50	100.00
EP-895	10996	11/17/2015	Knox	Velma	Rosa Martinez	Estate	3.50	100.00

Visual Benchmark Demonstrate Your Proficiency

1 CUSTOMIZE THE RIBBON

1. Create the custom tab including the groups and buttons shown in Figure 7.13. Substitute your name for *STUDENT NAME* in the tab. You can locate all of the buttons using the *All Commands* list.
2. Insert a screen image in a new Word document that shows the ribbon with the custom tab displayed in Microsoft Excel.
3. Save the Word document and name it **EL2-C7-VB1-MyRibbon**.
4. Print **EL2-C7-VB1-MyRibbon.docx** and then exit Word.
5. Remove the STUDENT NAME tab.

2 CREATE A CUSTOM TEMPLATE

1. Create a custom template that can be used to generate a sales invoice similar to the one shown in Figure 7.14. Use your best judgment to match the column widths, row heights, and color formatting. The font used in cell A1 is 36-point Footlight MT Light, and Garamond is used for the remaining cells (18-point in cell A2 and 12-point elsewhere). Substitute an appropriate clip art image if the one shown is not available on the computer you are using. (Recall that a template should contain only text, formulas, and formatting that does not change from one invoice to another.)
2. Save the workbook as a template and name it **EL2-C7-VB2-AudennitaSalesInv**.
3. Using the template, fill out a sales invoice using the data shown in Figure 7.14.
4. Save the completed invoice and name it **EL2-C7-VB2-AudennitaInvToVanderwyst**.
5. Print the invoice and then close **EL2-C7-VB2-AudennitaInvToVanderwyst.xlsx.**
6. Make a copy of the custom template at the New dialog box, saving the copy to your storage medium in the EL2C7 folder.

Figure 7.13 Visual Benchmark 1

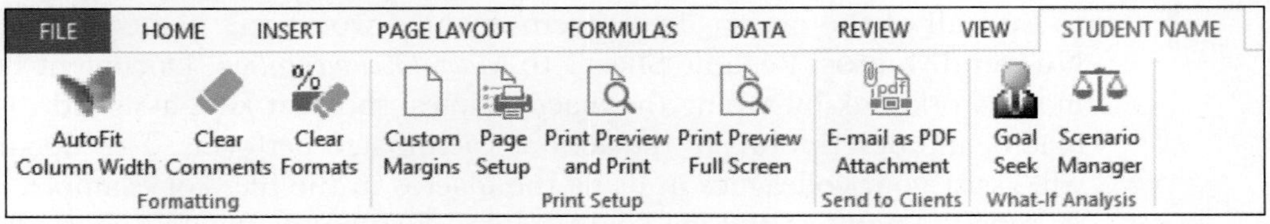

Figure 7.14 Visual Benchmark 2

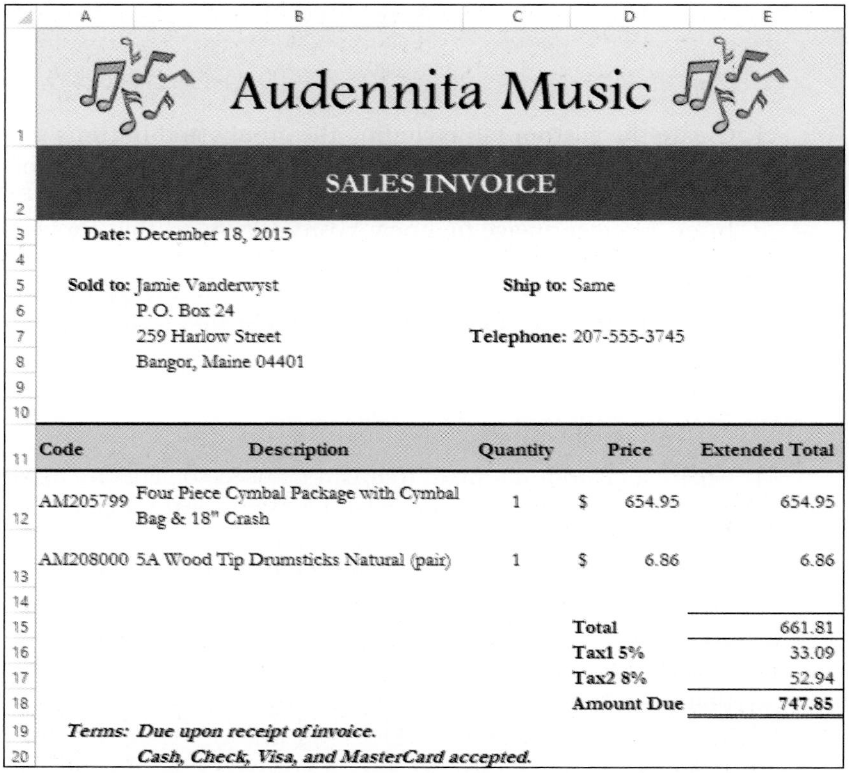

Case Study Apply Your Skills

Part 1

Yolanda Robertson of NuTrends Market Research would like you to help her become more efficient by creating macros for the frequently performed tasks in the list below. To share the macros with colleagues in the office, you decide to save all of the macros in a macro-enabled workbook named **EL2-C7-CS-P1-NuTrendMacros**. Rename Sheet1 to *MacroDocumentation*. Document the macros in the workbook by typing the macro names, shortcut keys assigned to each macro, and descriptions of the actions each macro performs. This documentation will assist your colleagues in using the macros in the file. For example, in column A, type the name of the macro; in column B, type the macro's shortcut key; and in column C, enter a description of the actions that the macro performs.

Create a separate macro for each of the following tasks. At the Record Macro dialog box, type your name and the current date in the *Description* text box for each macro.

- Apply the Organic theme and show all comments.
- Set the active column's width to 20 characters.
- Apply conditional formatting to highlight the top 10 in a selected list. Accept the default formatting options.
- Apply the Accounting format with no places after the decimal point.
- Create a footer that prints your name centered at the bottom of the worksheet.

Print the MacroDocumentation worksheet. Open the Macro dialog box and edit the first macro. At the Microsoft Visual Basic for Applications window, print the macros in the VBAProject. Close the Visual Basic for Applications window to return to the worksheet. Save **EL2-C7-CS-P1-NuTrendsMacros.xlsm**.

Part 2

Yolanda has received the file named **PBMNewFranchiseRev.xlsx** from Nicola Carlucci. She wants you to format the workbook using the macros created in Part 1. Open the workbook save it using the name **EL2-C7-CS-P2-PBMNewFranchiseRev**. Run each macro created in Part 1 using the following information:

- Set all of the column widths to 20 characters except column C.
- Run the number formatting and conditional formatting with the values in column E selected.
- Run the theme and footer macros.

Print the worksheet making sure the comments print as displayed. Save and then close **EL2-C7-CS-P2-PBMNewFranchiseRev.xlsx**. Close **EL2-C7-CS-P1-NuTrendsMacros.xlsm**.

Part 3

Help

Yolanda would like to customize the Quick Access toolbar but finds the process using the Excel Options dialog box to locate commands cumbersome. Use Excel Help to learn how to add a button to the Quick Access toolbar directly from the ribbon. Test the information you learned by adding two buttons of your choosing to the Quick Access toolbar using the ribbon. For example, add the Orientation button from the PAGE LAYOUT tab and the New Comment button from the REVIEW tab. Using Microsoft Word, compose a memo to Yolanda that describes the steps for adding a button to the Quick Access toolbar directly from the ribbon. Insert a screen image of the Quick Access toolbar in Excel that displays the buttons you added below the memo text. Save the Word memo and name it **EL2-C7-C5-P3-CustomizeQATMemo**. Print **EL2-C7-CS-P3-CustomizeQATMemo.docx** and then exit Word. Remove the two buttons you added to the Quick Access toolbar.

Part 4

Yolanda has mentioned that she sometimes sees a *Recovered* section above the *Recent* files list when she starts Excel. She has asked you to explain why this appears and what she should do when she sees it. Compose a memo to Yolanda using Microsoft Word in which you explain the AutoRecover and AutoSave features in your own words. Include an explanation that the *Recovered* section appears in the opening screen after Excel has not been properly closed and provide advice for Yolanda on how to review the files in the Document Recovery task pane to make sure she has not lost data.

MICROSOFT® EXCEL®

CHAPTER 8

Importing, Exporting, and Distributing Data

PERFORMANCE OBJECTIVES

Upon successful completion of Chapter 8, you will be able to:

- **Import data from an Access table, website, and text file**
- **Append data from an Excel worksheet to an Access table**
- **Embed and link data in an Excel worksheet to a Word document**
- **Copy and paste data in an Excel worksheet to a PowerPoint presentation**
- **Export data as a text file**
- **Scan and remove private or confidential information from a workbook**
- **Mark a workbook as final**
- **Check a workbook for features incompatible with earlier versions of Excel**
- **View Trust Center settings**
- **Save an Excel workbook as a PDF or XPS file**
- **Save an Excel worksheet as a web page**

SNAP

Tutorials

8.1 Importing Data from Access, a Text File, or a Website

8.2 Exporting Data from Excel

8.3 Copying and Pasting Worksheet Data between Programs

8.4 Copying and Pasting Worksheet Data to a Word Document

8.5 Exporting Data as a Text File

8.6 Preparing a Worksheet for Distribution

8.7 Converting a Workbook to a Different Format

8.8 Viewing Trust Center Settings

8.9 Creating a PDF/XPS Copy of a Workbook

8.10 Publishing a Worksheet as a Web Page

Exchanging data contained in one program with another by importing or exporting eliminates duplication of effort and reduces the likelihood of data errors or missed entries that would arise if the data was retyped. One of the advantages of working with a suite of programs such as Word, Excel, Access, and PowerPoint is being able to easily integrate data from one program to another. In this chapter, you will learn how to bring data into an Excel worksheet from sources external to Excel and how to export data in a worksheet for use with other programs. You will also learn to use features that allow you to send Excel data using a variety of distribution methods. Model answers for this chapter's projects appear on the following pages.

Excel
EL2C8

Note: Before beginning the projects, copy to your storage medium the EL2C8 subfolder from the EL2 folder on the CD that accompanies this textbook and then make EL2C8 the active folder.

NuTrends Market Research
US Population Estimates by State

Source: US Census Bureau

ID	State	July2011	July2010	July2009	July2008
1	Alabama	4,802,740	4,779,736	4,708,708	4,677,464
2	Alaska	722,718	710,231	698,473	688,125
3	Arizona	6,482,505	6,392,017	6,595,778	6,499,377
4	Arkansas	2,937,979	2,915,918	2,889,450	2,867,764
5	California	37,691,912	37,253,956	36,961,664	36,580,371
6	Colorado	5,116,796	5,029,196	5,024,748	4,935,213
7	Connecticut	3,580,709	3,574,097	3,518,288	3,502,932
8	Delaware	907,135	897,934	885,122	876,211
9	District of Columbia	617,996	601,723	599,657	590,074
10	Florida	19,057,542	18,801,310	18,537,969	18,423,878
11	Georgia	9,815,210	9,687,653	9,829,211	9,697,838
12	Hawaii	1,374,810	1,360,301	1,295,178	1,287,481
13	Idaho	1,584,985	1,567,582	1,545,801	1,527,506
14	Illinois	12,869,257	12,830,632	12,910,409	12,842,954
15	Indiana	6,516,922	6,483,802	6,423,113	6,388,309
16	Iowa	3,062,309	3,046,355	3,007,856	2,993,987
17	Kansas	2,871,238	2,853,118	2,818,747	2,797,375
18	Kentucky	4,369,356	4,339,367	4,314,113	4,287,931
19	Louisiana	4,574,836	4,533,372	4,492,076	4,451,513
20	Maine	1,328,188	1,328,361	1,318,301	1,319,691
21	Maryland	5,828,289	5,773,552	5,699,478	5,658,655
22	Massachusetts	6,587,536	6,547,629	6,593,587	6,543,595
23	Michigan	9,846,187	9,883,640	9,969,727	10,002,486
24	Minnesota	5,344,861	5,303,925	5,266,214	5,230,567
25	Mississippi	2,978,512	2,967,297	2,951,996	2,940,212
26	Missouri	6,010,688	5,988,927	5,987,580	5,956,335
27	Montana	998,199	989,415	974,989	968,035
28	Nebraska	1,842,641	1,826,341	1,796,619	1,781,949
29	Nevada	2,723,322	2,700,551	2,643,085	2,615,772
30	New Hampshire	1,318,194	1,316,470	1,324,575	1,321,872
31	New Jersey	8,821,155	8,791,894	8,707,739	8,663,398
32	New Mexico	2,082,224	2,059,179	2,009,671	1,986,763
33	New York	19,465,197	19,378,102	19,541,453	19,467,789
34	North Carolina	9,656,401	9,535,483	9,380,884	9,247,134
35	North Dakota	683,932	672,591	646,844	641,421
36	Ohio	11,544,951	11,536,504	11,542,645	11,528,072
37	Oklahoma	3,791,508	3,751,351	3,687,050	3,644,025
38	Oregon	3,871,859	3,831,074	3,825,657	3,782,991
39	Pennsylvania	12,742,886	12,702,379	12,604,767	12,566,368
40	Rhode Island	1,051,302	1,052,567	1,053,209	1,053,502
41	South Carolina	4,679,230	4,625,364	4,561,242	4,503,280
42	South Dakota	824,082	814,180	812,383	804,532
43	Tennessee	6,403,353	6,346,105	6,296,254	6,240,456
44	Texas	25,674,681	25,145,561	24,782,302	24,304,290
45	Utah	2,817,222	2,763,885	2,784,572	2,727,343
46	Vermont	626,431	625,741	621,760	621,049
47	Virginia	8,096,604	8,001,024	7,882,590	7,795,424
48	Washington	6,830,038	6,830,038	6,664,195	6,566,073
49	West Virginia	1,855,364	1,852,994	1,819,777	1,814,873
50	Wisconsin	5,711,767	5,686,986	5,654,774	5,627,610
51	Wyoming	568,158	563,626	544,270	532,981
52	Puerto Rico	3,706,690	3,725,789	3,967,288	3,954,553

NuTrends Market Research
Florida Geographic Data

Source US Census Bureau: State and County QuickFacts
http://quickfacts.census.gov/qfd/states/12000.html

	Business QuickFacts	Florida	USA
Private nonfarm establishments definition and source info	Private nonfarm establishments, 2010	4,911,501	7,396,628
Private nonfarm employment definition and source info	Private nonfarm employment, 2010	66,265,581	111,970,095
Private nonfarm employment, percent change definition and source info	Private nonfarm employment, percent change, 2000-2010	6.61	-1.8
Nonemployer establishments definition and source info	Nonemployer establishments, 2010	1,686,142	22,110,628
Total number of firms definition and source info	Total number of firms, 2007	2,009,589	27,092,908
Black-owned firms, percent definition and source info	Black-owned firms, percent, 2007	9.00%	7.10%
American Indian- and Alaska Native-owned firms, percent definition and source info	American Indian- and Alaska Native-owned firms, percent, 2007	0.50%	0.90%
Asian-owned firms, percent definition and source info	Asian-owned firms, percent, 2007	3.20%	5.70%
Native Hawaiian and Other Pacific Islander-owned firms, percent definition and source info	Native Hawaiian and Other Pacific Islander-owned firms, percent, 2007	0.10%	0.10%
Hispanic-owned firms, percent definition and source info	Hispanic-owned firms, percent, 2007	22.40%	8.30%
Women-owned firms, percent definition and source info	Women-owned firms, percent, 2007	28.90%	28.80%
Manufacturers shipments definition and source info	Manufacturers shipments, 2007 ($1000)	104,832,907	5,338,306,501
Merchant wholesaler sales definition and source info	Merchant wholesaler sales, 2007 ($1000)	221,641,518	4,174,286,516
Retail sales definition and source info	Retail sales, 2007 ($1000)	262,341,127	3,917,663,456
Retail sales per capita definition and source info	Retail sales per capita, 2007	$14,353	$12,990
Accommodation and food services sales definition and source info	Accommodation and food services sales, 2007 ($1000)	41,922,059	613,795,732
Building permits definition and source info	Building permits, 2011	42,360	624,061
	Geography QuickFacts	Florida	USA
Land area in square miles definition and source info	Land area in square miles, 2010	53,624.76	3,531,905.43
Persons per square mile definition and source info	Persons per square mile, 2010	350.6	87.4
definition and source info	FIPS Code	12	

Project 1 Import Data from External Sources to Excel

Project 1a, EL2-C8-P1-NuTrendsCensusData.xlsx with PopulationEstimates Worksheet

Project 1b, EL2-C8-P1-NuTrendsCensusData.xlsx with FloridaGeographicData Worksheet

Housing Unit Estimates
100 Fastest Growing Counties
Change between April 1, 2010 and July 1, 2011

Source: Population Division, US Census Bureau (HU-EST2005-06)

Rank	Geographic Area	Housing Unit Estimates		Change, 2010 to 2011	
		1-Apr-10	1-Jul-11	Number	Percent
1	Long County, GA	6,030	6,412	382	6.3
2	Fort Bend County, TX	197,031	208,696	11,665	5.9
3	Sumter County, FL	53,026	55,988	2,962	5.6
4	Rockwall County, TX	27,939	29,306	1,367	4.9
5	Matanuska-Susitna Borough, AK	41,329	43,242	1,913	4.6
6	Taney County, MO	29,255	30,605	1,350	4.6
7	Madison County, MT	6,940	7,253	313	4.5
8	Lincoln County, SD	17,875	18,665	790	4.4
9	McIntosh County, GA	9,220	9,615	395	4.3
10	Lamar County, MS	24,070	25,083	1,013	4.2
11	Campbell County, WY	18,955	19,743	788	4.2
12	Telfair County, GA	7,297	7,597	300	4.1
13	Hays County, TX	59,416	61,821	2,405	4
14	White County, GA	16,062	16,685	623	3.9
15	Dooly County, GA	6,328	6,573	245	3.9
16	Hancock County, MS	21,840	22,658	818	3.7
17	Faulkner County, AR	46,612	48,325	1,713	3.7
18	Wilson County, TX	16,765	17,377	612	3.7
19	Guadalupe County, TX	50,015	51,815	1,800	3.6
20	Hoke County, NC	18,211	18,858	647	3.6
21	Williamson County, TX	162,773	168,515	5,742	3.5
22	Columbia County, GA	48,626	50,331	1,705	3.5
23	Blanco County, TX	5,532	5,725	193	3.5
24	Parker County, TX	46,628	48,241	1,613	3.5
25	Sevier County, TN	55,917	57,804	1,887	3.4
26	Sublette County, WY	5,770	5,963	193	3.3
27	Summit County, UT	26,544	27,407	863	3.3
28	Nye County, NV	22,350	23,068	718	3.2
29	Onslow County, NC	68,226	70,366	2,140	3.1
30	Denton County, TX	256,139	264,071	7,932	3.1
31	Harrison County, MS	85,181	87,773	2,592	3
32	Limestone County, AL	34,977	36,019	1,042	3
33	Hood County, TX	24,951	25,694	743	3
34	Fredericksburg city, VA	10,467	10,777	310	3
35	Dallas County, IA	27,260	28,065	805	3
36	Franklin County, WA	24,423	25,120	697	2.9
37	Livingston Parish, LA	50,195	51,607	1,412	2.8
38	Kane County, UT	5,815	5,978	163	2.8
39	Sweetwater County, WY	18,735	19,258	523	2.8
40	Sequatchie County, TN	6,368	6,545	177	2.8

Page 1

177,650	182,513	4,863	2.7
13,313	13,671	358	2.7
9,493	9,745	252	2.7
19,303	19,813	510	2.6
125,470	128,777	3,307	2.6
38,323	39,320	997	2.6
6,678	6,850	172	2.6
13,137	13,472	335	2.6
7,161	7,343	182	2.5
17,444	17,887	443	2.5
55,186	56,576	1,390	2.5
109,442	112,189	2,747	2.5
46,963	48,141	1,178	2.5
106,772	109,440	2,668	2.5
10,379	10,637	258	2.5
73,372	75,194	1,822	2.5
32,137	32,932	795	2.5
40,321	41,308	987	2.4
24,669	25,269	600	2.4
10,464	10,717	253	2.4
22,547	23,090	543	2.4
21,011	21,513	502	2.4
67,938	69,560	1,622	2.4
30,578	31,308	730	2.4
21,114	21,616	502	2.4
5,147	5,269	122	2.4
12,928	13,233	305	2.4
17,195	17,598	403	2.3
40,757	41,702	945	2.3
41,783	42,740	957	2.3
13,291	13,593	302	2.3
13,868	14,183	315	2.3
32,687	33,429	742	2.3
12,780	13,070	290	2.3
61,938	63,343	1,405	2.3
22,730	23,242	512	2.3
189,896	194,138	4,242	2.2
94,196	96,281	2,085	2.2
14,517	14,837	320	2.2
11,413	11,663	250	2.2
93,084	95,116	2,032	2.2
26,740	27,323	583	2.2
70,099	71,622	1,523	2.2
28,212	28,820	608	2.2
113,958	116,403	2,445	2.1
300,960	307,353	6,393	2.1
5,055	5,162	107	2.1

Page 2

8,285	8,460	175	2.1
8,085	8,252	167	2.1
44,812	45,737	925	2.1
49,351	50,369	1,018	2.1
159,222	162,504	3,282	2.1
11,788	12,028	240	2
28,151	28,721	570	2
25,728	26,248	520	2
146,447	149,385	2,938	2
29,315	29,895	580	2
45,810	46,715	905	2
17,462	17,802	340	1.9
50,739	51,726	987	1.9

se reflects changes to the 2010 Census housing units from
her geographic program revisions. It does not reflect
ram. All geographic boundaries for the 2011 housing unit

t Growing Counties With 5,000 or More Housing Units in
)

Page 3

Project 1c, EL2-C8-P1-NuTrendsCensusData.xlsx with HousingUnitData Worksheet

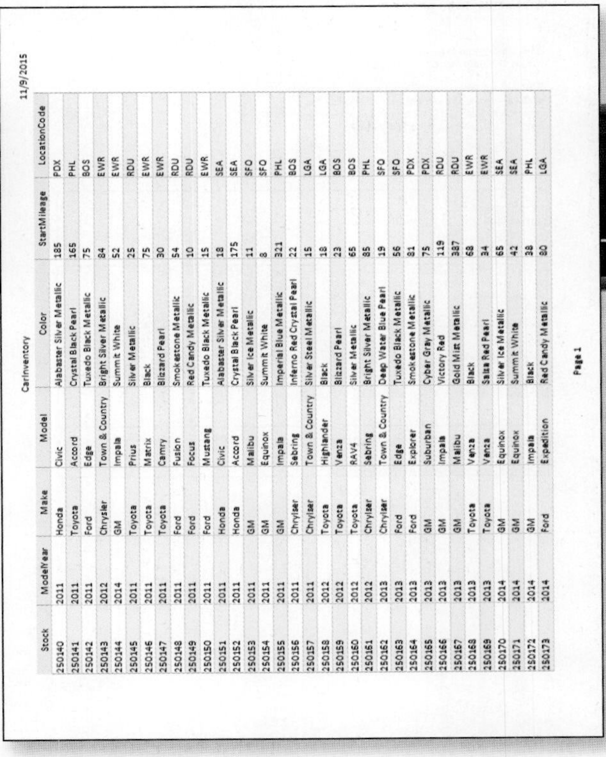

11/9/2015

CarInventory

Stock	ModelYear	Make	Model	Color	StartMileage	LocationCode
250140	2011	Honda	Civic	Alabaster Silver Metallic	185	PDX
250141	2011	Toyota	Accord	Crystal Black Pearl	165	PHL
250142	2011	Ford	Edge	Tuxedo Black Metallic	75	BOS
250143	2012	Chrysler	Town & Country	Bright Silver Metallic	84	EWR
250144	2014	GM	Impala	Summit White	52	EWR
250145	2011	Toyota	Prius	Silver Metallic	25	RDU
250146	2011	Toyota	Matrix	Black	75	EWR
250147	2011	Toyota	Camry	Blizzard Pearl	30	EWR
250148	2011	Ford	Fusion	Smokestone Metallic	54	RDU
250149	2011	Ford	Focus	Red Candy Metallic	10	RDU
250150	2011	Ford	Mustang	Tuxedo Black Metallic	15	EWR
250151	2011	Honda	Civic	Alabaster Silver Metallic	18	SEA
250152	2011	Honda	Accord	Crystal Black Pearl	175	SEA
250153	2011	GM	Malibu	Silver Ice Metallic	11	SFO
250154	2011	GM	Equinox	Summit White	8	SFO
250155	2011	GM	Impala	Imperial Blue Metallic	321	PHL
250156	2011	Chrylser	Sebring	Inferno Red Crystal Pearl	22	BOS
250157	2011	Chrylser	Town & Country	Silver Steel Metallic	15	LGA
250158	2012	Toyota	Highlander	Black	18	LGA
250159	2012	Toyota	Venza	Blizzard Pearl	23	BOS
250160	2012	Toyota	RAV4	Silver Metallic	65	BOS
250161	2012	Chrylser	Sebring	Bright Silver Metallic	85	PHL
250162	2013	Chrylser	Town & Country	Deep Water Blue Pearl	19	SFO
250163	2013	Ford	Edge	Tuxedo Black Metallic	56	SFO
250164	2013	Ford	Explorer	Smokestone Metallic	81	PDX
250165	2013	GM	Suburban	Cyber Gray Metallic	75	PDX
250166	2013	GM	Impala	Victory Red	119	RDU
250167	2013	GM	Malibu	Gold Mist Metallic	387	RDU
250168	2013	Toyota	Venza	Black	68	EWR
250169	2013	Toyota	Venza	Salsa Red Pearl	34	EWR
250170	2014	GM	Equinox	Silver Ice Metallic	65	SEA
250171	2014	GM	Equinox	Summit White	42	SEA
250172	2014	GM	Impala	Black	38	PHL
250173	2014	Ford	Expedition	Red Candy Metallic	80	LGA

Page 1

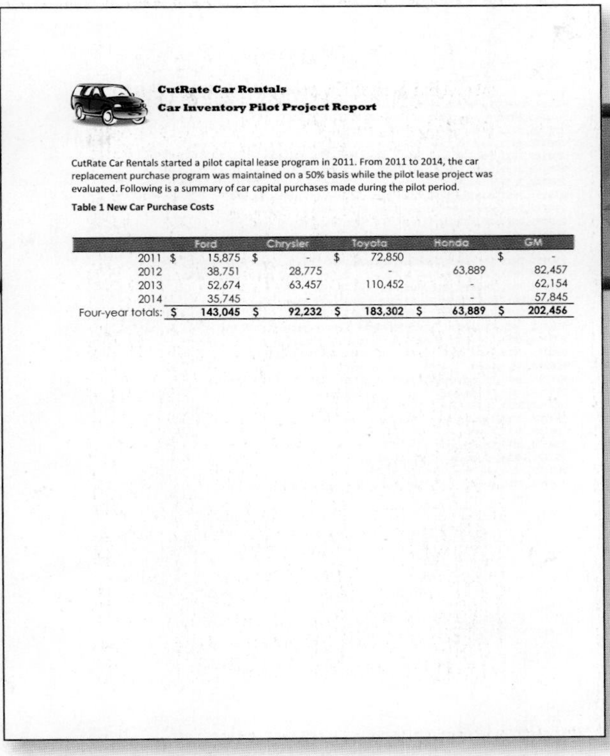

CutRate Car Rentals
Car Inventory Pilot Project Report

CutRate Car Rentals started a pilot capital lease program in 2011. From 2011 to 2014, the car replacement purchase program was maintained on a 50% basis while the pilot lease project was evaluated. Following is a summary of car capital purchases made during the pilot period.

Table 1 New Car Purchase Costs

	Ford	Chrysler	Toyota	Honda	GM
2011	$ 15,875	$ -	$ 72,850		$ -
2012	38,751	28,775	-	63,889	82,457
2013	52,674	63,457	110,452	-	62,154
2014	35,745	-		-	57,845
Four-year totals:	$ 143,045	$ 92,232	$ 183,302	$ 63,889	$ 202,456

Project 2 Export Data in Excel

Project 2a, CarInventory Datasheet from CRInventory.accdb

Project 2b, EL2-C8-P2-CRCarRpt.docx

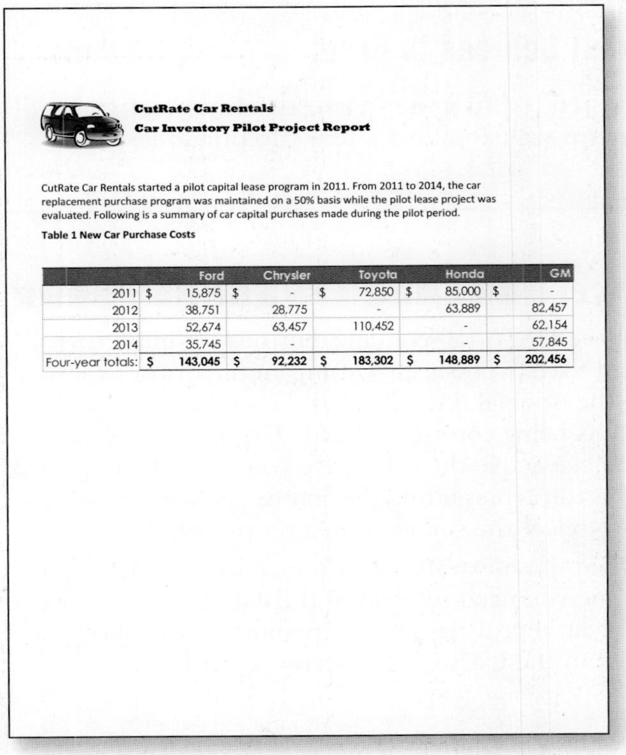

CutRate Car Rentals
Car Inventory Pilot Project Report

CutRate Car Rentals started a pilot capital lease program in 2011. From 2011 to 2014, the car replacement purchase program was maintained on a 50% basis while the pilot lease project was evaluated. Following is a summary of car capital purchases made during the pilot period.

Table 1 New Car Purchase Costs

	Ford	Chrysler	Toyota	Honda	GM
2011	$ 15,875	$ -	$ 72,850	$ 85,000	$ -
2012	38,751	28,775	-	63,889	82,457
2013	52,674	63,457	110,452	-	62,154
2014	35,745	-		-	57,845
Four-year totals:	$ 143,045	$ 92,232	$ 183,302	$ 148,889	$ 202,456

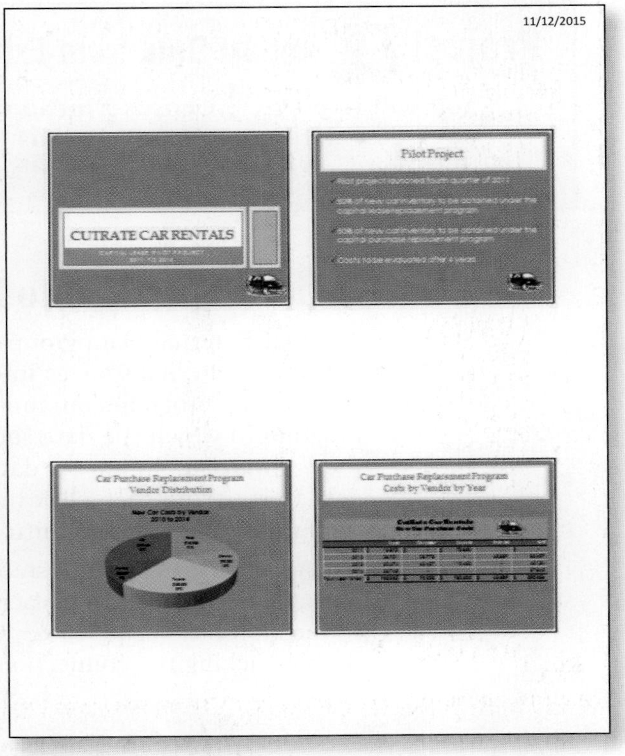

Project 2c, EL2-C8-P2-CRCarRptLinked.docx

Project 2e, EL2-C8-P2-CRCarRpt.pptx

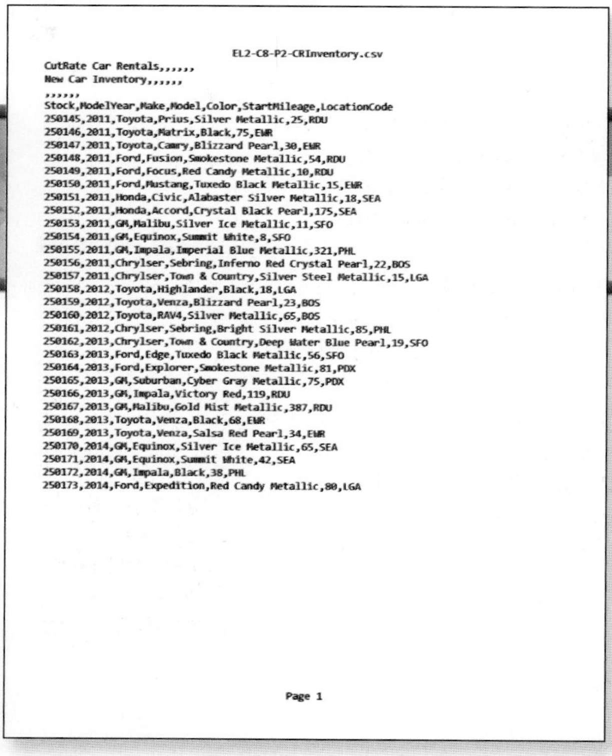
EL2-C8-P2-CRInventory.csv

```
CutRate Car Rentals,,,,,,
New Car Inventory,,,,,,
,,,,,,
Stock,ModelYear,Make,Model,Color,StartMileage,LocationCode
250145,2011,Toyota,Prius,Silver Metallic,25,RDU
250146,2011,Toyota,Matrix,Black,75,EWR
250147,2011,Toyota,Camry,Blizzard Pearl,30,EWR
250148,2011,Ford,Fusion,Smokestone Metallic,54,RDU
250149,2011,Ford,Focus,Red Candy Metallic,10,RDU
250150,2011,Ford,Mustang,Tuxedo Black Metallic,15,EWR
250151,2011,Honda,Civic,Alabaster Silver Metallic,18,SEA
250152,2011,Honda,Accord,Crystal Black Pearl,175,SEA
250153,2011,GM,Malibu,Silver Ice Metallic,11,SFO
250154,2011,GM,Equinox,Summit White,8,SFO
250155,2011,GM,Impala,Imperial Blue Metallic,321,PHL
250156,2011,Chrylser,Sebring,Inferno Red Crystal Pearl,22,BOS
250157,2011,Chrylser,Town & Country,Silver Steel Metallic,15,LGA
250158,2012,Toyota,Highlander,Black,18,LGA
250159,2012,Toyota,Venza,Blizzard Pearl,23,BOS
250160,2012,Toyota,RAV4,Silver Metallic,65,BOS
250161,2012,Chrylser,Sebring,Bright Silver Metallic,85,PHL
250162,2013,Chrylser,Town & Country,Deep Water Blue Pearl,19,SFO
250163,2013,Ford,Edge,Tuxedo Black Metallic,56,SFO
250164,2013,Ford,Explorer,Smokestone Metallic,81,PDX
250165,2013,GM,Suburban,Cyber Gray Metallic,75,PDX
250166,2013,GM,Impala,Victory Red,119,RDU
250167,2013,GM,Malibu,Gold Mist Metallic,387,RDU
250168,2013,Toyota,Venza,Black,68,EWR
250169,2013,Toyota,Venza,Salsa Red Pearl,34,EWR
250170,2014,GM,Equinox,Silver Ice Metallic,65,SEA
250171,2014,GM,Equinox,Summit White,42,SEA
250172,2014,GM,Impala,Black,38,PHL
250173,2014,Ford,Expedition,Red Candy Metallic,80,LGA
```

Page 1

Project 2f, EL2-C8-P2-CRInventory.csv

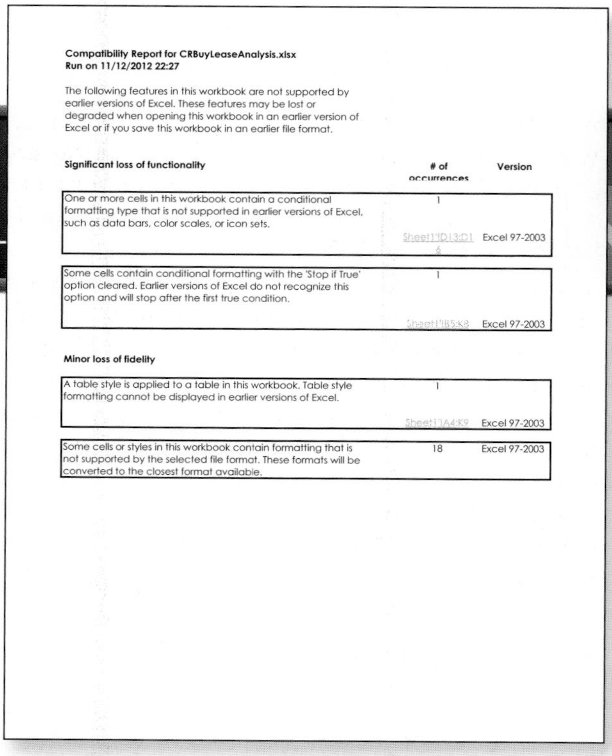
Compatibility Report for CRBuyLeaseAnalysis.xlsx
Run on 11/12/2012 22:27

The following features in this workbook are not supported by earlier versions of Excel. These features may be lost or degraded when opening this workbook in an earlier version of Excel or if you save this workbook in an earlier file format.

Significant loss of functionality	# of occurrences	Version
One or more cells in this workbook contain a conditional formatting type that is not supported in earlier versions of Excel, such as data bars, color scales, or icon sets.	1 Sheet1'!D13:D16	Excel 97-2003
Some cells contain conditional formatting with the 'Stop if True' option cleared. Earlier versions of Excel do not recognize this option and will stop after the first true condition.	1 Sheet1'!B5:K8	Excel 97-2003

Minor loss of fidelity		
A table style is applied to a table in this workbook. Table style formatting cannot be displayed in earlier versions of Excel.	1 Sheet1'!A4:K9	Excel 97-2003
Some cells or styles in this workbook contain formatting that is not supported by the selected file format. These formats will be converted to the closest format available.	18	Excel 97-2003

Project 3 Prepare a Workbook for Distribution

Project 3c, EL2-C8-P3-CRBuyLeaseAnalysisCompChk.xlsx

Project 1 Import Data from External Sources to Excel — 3 Parts

You will import US Census Bureau data related to a market research project from an Access database, the US Census Bureau website, and a text file previously downloaded from the Census Bureau.

Importing Data into Excel

The Get External Data group on the DATA tab contains buttons for importing data from external sources into an Excel worksheet. During an import or export routine, the program containing the original data is called the ***source*** and the program to which the data source is being copied, embedded, or linked is called the ***destination***. To import data, make active the cell where you want the imported data to start and then click the button representing the source application or click the From Other Sources button to select the source from a drop-down list.

A connection can be established to an external data source to avoid having to repeat the import process each time you need to analyze the data in Excel. Once a connection has been created, you can repeat the import in another worksheet by simply clicking the connection file in the Existing Connections dialog box.

Importing Data from Access

Exchanging data between Access and Excel is a seamless process since data in an Access datasheet is structured in the same row and column format as an Excel worksheet. You can import the Access data as an Excel table, PivotTable Report, or PivotChart. The imported data can be appended to an existing worksheet or placed in a new worksheet.

To import an Access table, click the DATA tab and then click the From Access button in the Get External Data group. At the Select Data Source dialog box, navigate to the drive and/or folder in which the source database resides and then double-click the Access database file name in the file list. If the source database contains more than one table, the Select Table dialog box opens so you can choose the table containing the data you want to import. If the source database contains only one table, you will not be prompted to select a table name. Once the table is identified, the Import Data dialog box appears, as shown in Figure 8.1. Choose how you want to view the data, select the location to begin the import, and then click OK.

Quick Steps

Import an Access Table

1. Make active cell at which to begin import.
2. Click DATA tab.
3. Click From Access button.
4. Navigate to drive and/or folder.
5. Double-click source database file name.
6. If necessary, click desired table name and then OK.
7. Select desired view format.
8. Click OK.

From Access

HINT

Only one table can be imported at a time. To import all of the tables in the source database, repeat the import process for each table.

Figure 8.1 Import Data Dialog Box

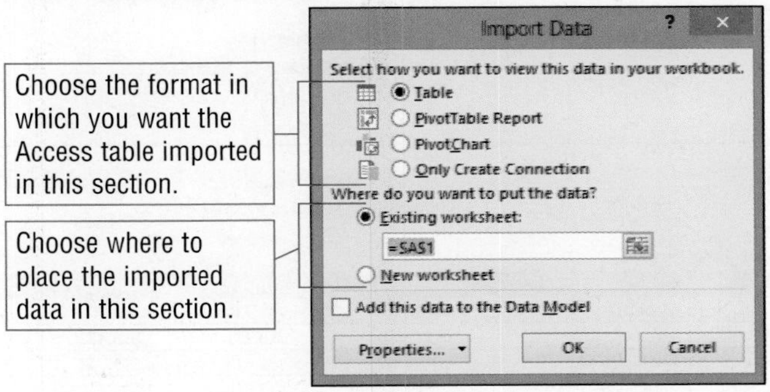

Project 1a **Importing Data from an Access Database** **Part 1 of 3**

1. Open **NuTrendsCensus.xlsx**.
2. Save the workbook and name it **EL2-C8-P1-NuTrendsCensus**.
3. Import four years of US state population estimates, which have been compiled by the US Census Bureau and stored in an Access database, and append it to an existing worksheet by completing the following steps:
   a. With PopulationEstimates the active worksheet, make cell A5 active.
   b. Click the DATA tab.
   c. Click the From Access button in the Get External Data group.
   d. At the Select Data Source dialog box, navigate to the EL2C8 folder on your storage medium and then double-click ***NuTrendsCensus.accdb***.

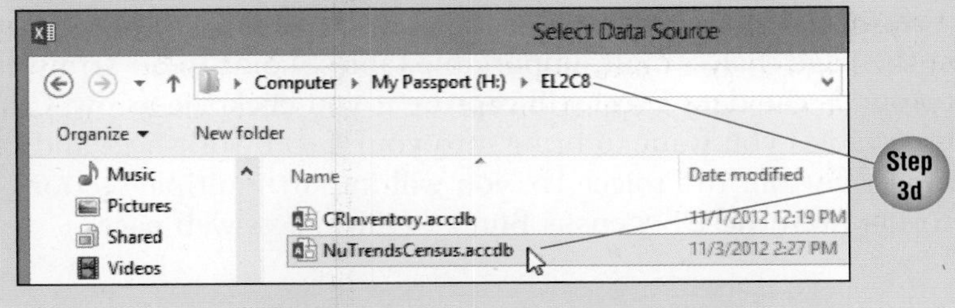

e. Since the source database contains more than one table, the Select Table dialog box appears. Click *PopByState* in the *Name* column and then click OK.

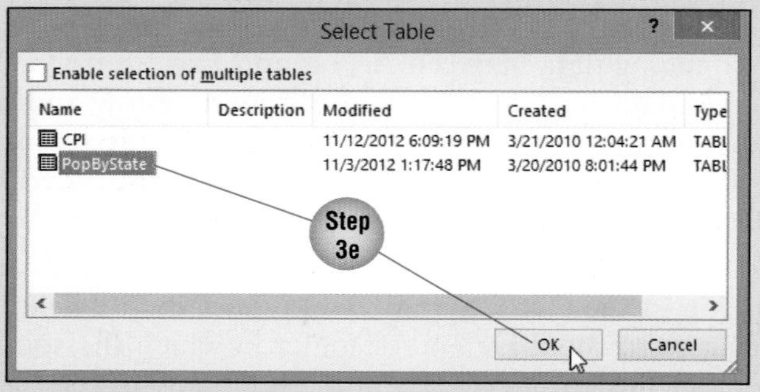

f. At the Import Data dialog box with *Table* selected in the *Select how you want to view this data in your workbook* section and the cell reference *=$A$5* in the *Existing worksheet* text box in the *Where do you want to put the data?* section, click OK.

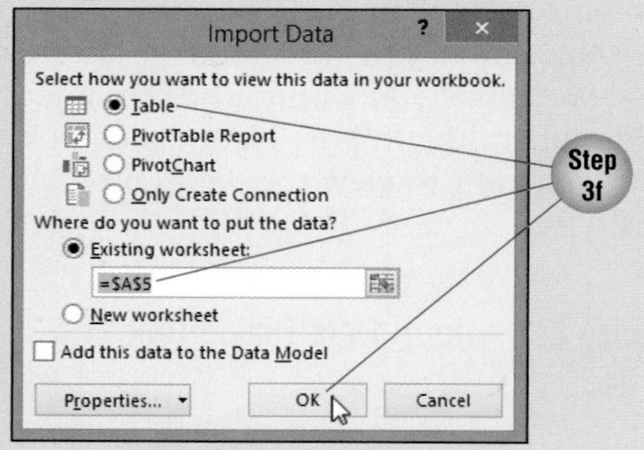

4. Scroll down the imported table data. Notice that the data is formatted as a table with filter arrows.
5. With the TABLE TOOLS DESIGN tab active, make the following changes to the worksheet:
   a. Remove the filter arrows.
   b. Change the table style to *Table Style Medium 1* (first column in the first row of the *Medium* section).
   c. Make the HOME tab active and apply comma formatting with no places after the decimal point.
   d. Adjust the widths of columns C through F to 15 characters.
   e. Center-align the labels in C5:F5.

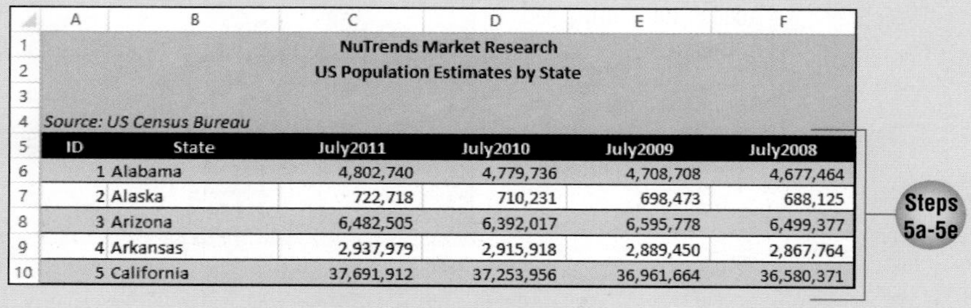

6. Print the PopulationEstimates worksheet scaled to fit one page in width and height and centered horizontally between the left and right margins.
7. Save **EL2-C8-P1-NuTrendsCensus.xlsx**.

Quick Steps

Import Data from a Website
1. Make cell active at which to begin import.
2. Click DATA tab.
3. Click From Web button.
4. Navigate to desired web page.
5. Click arrows next to tables to import.
6. Click Import button.
7. Click OK.

From Web

Importing Data from a Website

Tables in a website can be downloaded directly using the New Web Query dialog box, as shown in Figure 8.2. Make active the cell at which you want to begin the import, click the DATA tab, and then click the From Web button in the Get External Data group. Use the Address bar and web navigation buttons to go to the page containing the data you want to use in Excel. At the desired page, Excel displays black right-pointing arrows inside yellow boxes next to elements on the page that contain importable tables. Point to an arrow and a blue border surrounds the data Excel will capture if you click the arrow. Click the arrow for those tables you want to bring into your Excel worksheet and then click the Import button. In Project 1b, you will import multiple sections of data about Florida from the US Census Bureau QuickFacts web page.

Figure 8.2 New Web Query Dialog Box

Navigate to the desired website, as you would in a browser window.

Point to an arrow in a yellow box to display a blue border around a table on the web page. Click the arrow to select the table and then click the Import button to copy the data into the active cell.

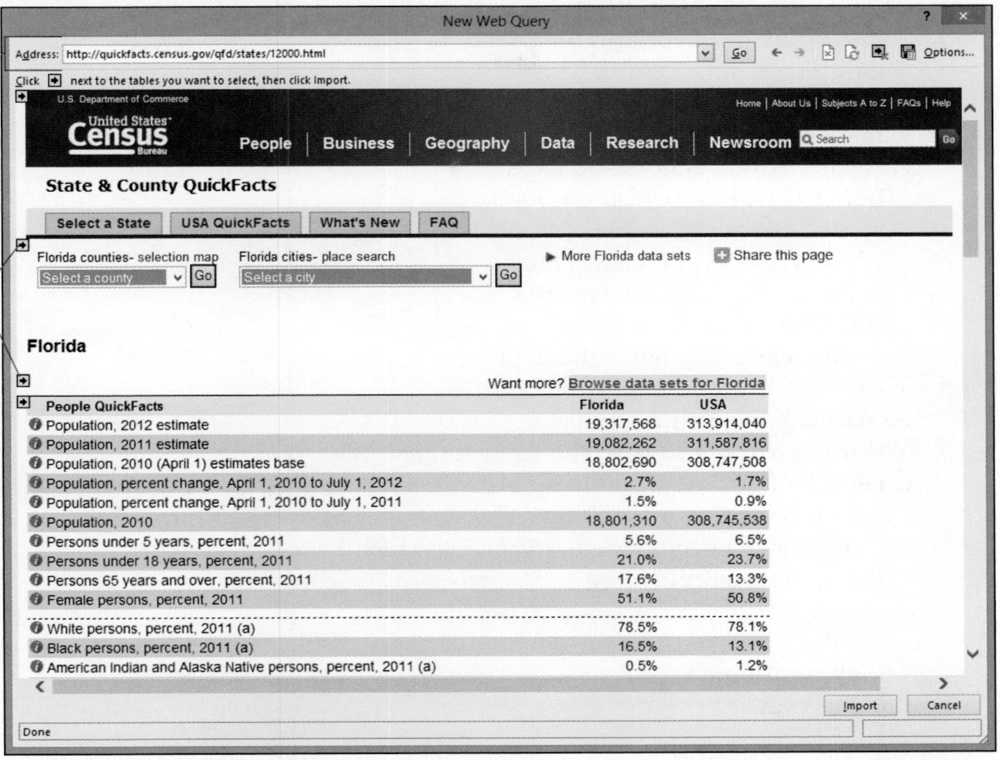

Project 1b Importing a Table from a Web Page

Part 2 of 3

1. With **EL2-C8-P1-NuTrendsCensus.xlsx** open, make FloridaGeographicData the active worksheet.
2. Import statistics related to Florida from the US Census Bureau QuickFacts web page by completing the following steps. ***Note: During any part of this project, if a Script Error dialog box displays, click Yes to continue running scripts on the page.***
   a. Make cell A6 active.
   b. Click the From Web button in the Get External Data group on the DATA tab.
   c. At the New Web Query dialog box, select the current entry in the *Address* text box, type **http://www.census.gov**, and then press Enter.
   d. Point to the Data tab located near the top of the web page and then click *Quick Facts* at the drop-down list.

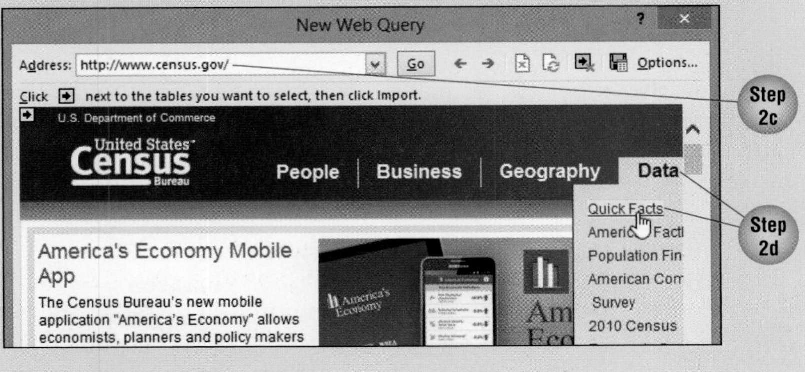

e. Resize the New Web Query dialog box until you can see the entire map of the United States.
f. Click the state of Florida in the map.
g. At the Florida QuickFacts page, notice the black right-pointing arrows inside yellow boxes along the left edge of the page. Point to one of the arrows to see the yellow box change to green and a blue border surround the data that will be imported into Excel if you click the arrow.

h. Scroll down the page to the section titled *Business QuickFacts*.
i. Click the black right-pointing arrow next to *Business QuickFacts* to select the table. The arrow changes to a check mark inside a green box when the table is selected for import.
j. Click the arrow next to *Geography QuickFacts* to select the table.
k. Click the Import button.

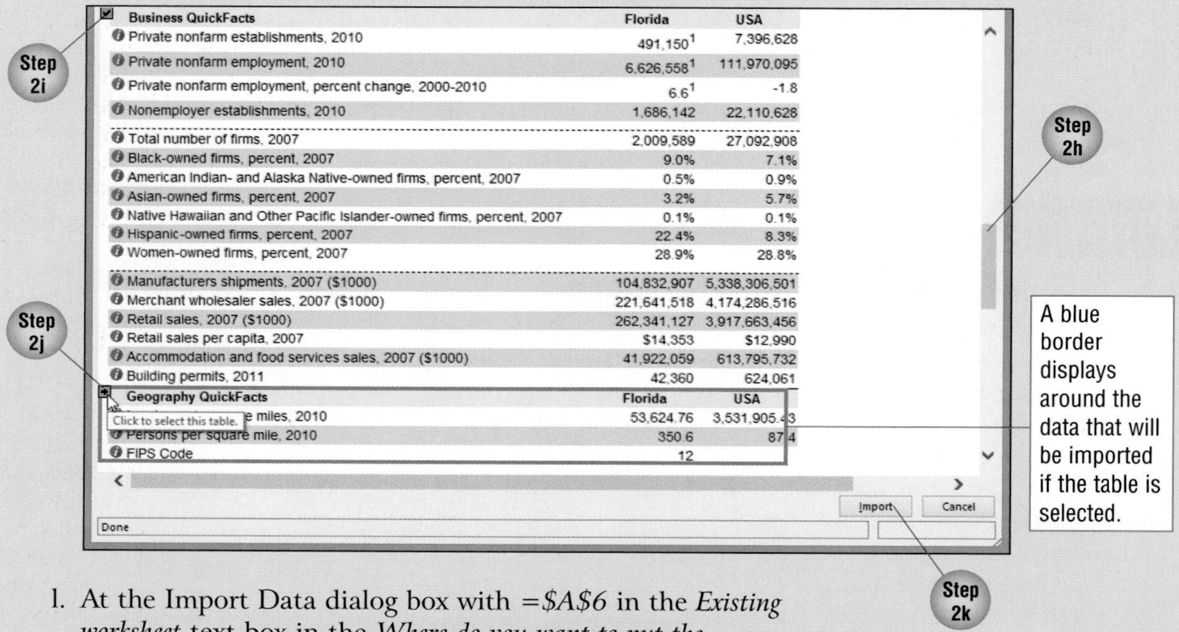

Business QuickFacts	Florida	USA
Private nonfarm establishments, 2010	491,150[1]	7,396,628
Private nonfarm employment, 2010	6,626,558[1]	111,970,095
Private nonfarm employment, percent change, 2000-2010	6.6[1]	-1.8
Nonemployer establishments, 2010	1,686,142	22,110,628
Total number of firms, 2007	2,009,589	27,092,908
Black-owned firms, percent, 2007	9.0%	7.1%
American Indian- and Alaska Native-owned firms, percent, 2007	0.5%	0.9%
Asian-owned firms, percent, 2007	3.2%	5.7%
Native Hawaiian and Other Pacific Islander-owned firms, percent, 2007	0.1%	0.1%
Hispanic-owned firms, percent, 2007	22.4%	8.3%
Women-owned firms, percent, 2007	28.9%	28.8%
Manufacturers shipments, 2007 ($1000)	104,832,907	5,338,306,501
Merchant wholesaler sales, 2007 ($1000)	221,641,518	4,174,286,516
Retail sales, 2007 ($1000)	262,341,127	3,917,663,456
Retail sales per capita, 2007	$14,353	$12,990
Accommodation and food services sales, 2007 ($1000)	41,922,059	613,795,732
Building permits, 2011	42,360	624,061

Geography QuickFacts	Florida	USA
e miles, 2010	53,624.76	3,531,905.43
Persons per square mile, 2010	350.6	87.4
FIPS Code	12	

l. At the Import Data dialog box with =$A$6 in the *Existing worksheet* text box in the *Where do you want to put the data?* section, click OK. Excel imports the data from the web page into the Excel worksheet starting in cell A6.

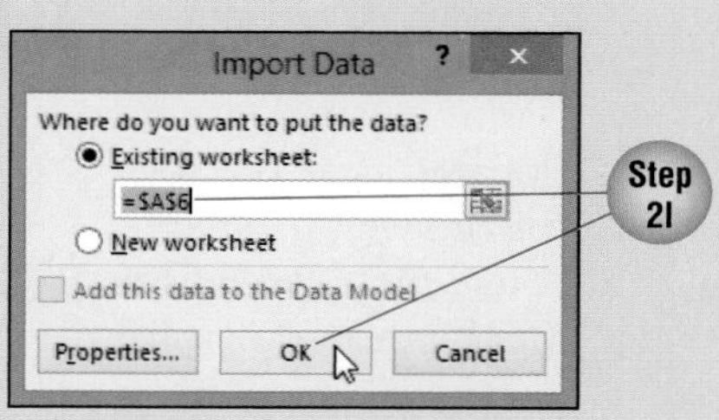

3. Make the following changes to the worksheet:
a. Decrease the width of column A to 35 characters.
b. Select the cells in column A that contain imported text, click the HOME tab, and then click the Wrap Text button in the Alignment group.

c. With the cells in column A still selected, click the Format button in the Cells group on the HOME tab and then click *AutoFit Row Height* at the drop-down list.
d. Center-align the text in the range C6:D6.
e. Change the page orientation to landscape.

4. Print the FloridaGeographicData worksheet scaled to fit on one page and centered between the left and right margins.
5. Save **EL2-C8-P1-NuTrendsCensus.xlsx**.

Importing Data from a Text File

A ***text file*** is often used to exchange data between dissimilar programs since the file format is recognized by nearly all applications. Text files contain no formatting and consist only of letters, numbers, punctuation symbols, and a few control characters. Two commonly used text file formats separate fields with either tab characters (***delimited file format***) or commas (***comma separated file format***). The text file you will use in Project 1c is shown in a Notepad window in Figure 8.3. If necessary, you can view and edit a text file in Notepad prior to importing it.

To import a text file into Excel, use the From Text button in the Get External Data group on the DATA tab and then select the source file at the Import Text File dialog box. Excel displays in the file list any file in the active folder that ends with the file extension *.prn, .txt,* or *.csv*. Once the source file is selected, Excel begins the Text Import Wizard, which guides you through the import process using three dialog boxes.

Quick Steps

Import Data from a Comma Separated Text File

1. Make active cell at which to begin import.
2. Click DATA tab.
3. Click From Text button.
4. Double-click .csv file name.
5. Click Next.
6. Click *Comma* check box.
7. Click Next.
8. Click Finish.
9. Click OK.

From Text

HINT

Most programs can export data in a text file. If you need to use data from a program that is not compatible with Excel, check the source program's export options for a text file format.

Figure 8.3 Project 1c Text File Contents

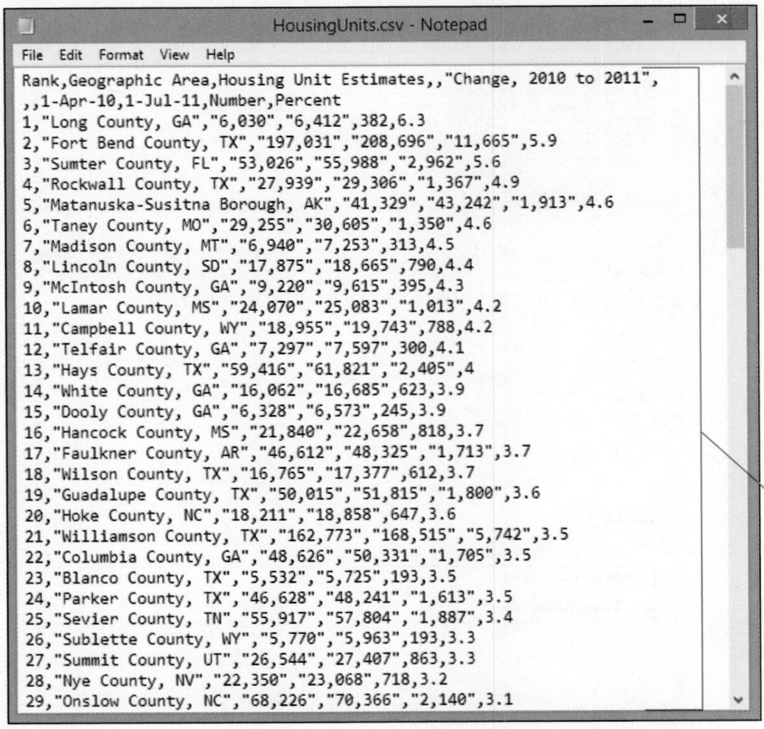


```
Rank,Geographic Area,Housing Unit Estimates,,"Change, 2010 to 2011",
,,1-Apr-10,1-Jul-11,Number,Percent
1,"Long County, GA","6,030","6,412",382,6.3
2,"Fort Bend County, TX","197,031","208,696","11,665",5.9
3,"Sumter County, FL","53,026","55,988","2,962",5.6
4,"Rockwall County, TX","27,939","29,306","1,367",4.9
5,"Matanuska-Susitna Borough, AK","41,329","43,242","1,913",4.6
6,"Taney County, MO","29,255","30,605","1,350",4.6
7,"Madison County, MT","6,940","7,253",313,4.5
8,"Lincoln County, SD","17,875","18,665",790,4.4
9,"McIntosh County, GA","9,220","9,615",395,4.3
10,"Lamar County, MS","24,070","25,083","1,013",4.2
11,"Campbell County, WY","18,955","19,743",788,4.2
12,"Telfair County, GA","7,297","7,597",300,4.1
13,"Hays County, TX","59,416","61,821","2,405",4
14,"White County, GA","16,062","16,685",623,3.9
15,"Dooly County, GA","6,328","6,573",245,3.9
16,"Hancock County, MS","21,840","22,658",818,3.7
17,"Faulkner County, AR","46,612","48,325","1,713",3.7
18,"Wilson County, TX","16,765","17,377",612,3.7
19,"Guadalupe County, TX","50,015","51,815","1,800",3.6
20,"Hoke County, NC","18,211","18,858",647,3.6
21,"Williamson County, TX","162,773","168,515","5,742",3.5
22,"Columbia County, GA","48,626","50,331","1,705",3.5
23,"Blanco County, TX","5,532","5,725",193,3.5
24,"Parker County, TX","46,628","48,241","1,613",3.5
25,"Sevier County, TN","55,917","57,804","1,887",3.4
26,"Sublette County, WY","5,770","5,963",193,3.3
27,"Summit County, UT","26,544","27,407",863,3.3
28,"Nye County, NV","22,350","23,068",718,3.2
29,"Onslow County, NC","68,226","70,366","2,140",3.1
```

Text files contain no formatting codes. In a comma separated file (.csv), commas separate the fields. During the import, Excel starts a new column at each comma. Notice also that quotes surround text data. Excel strips the quotes from the data upon importing it.

Non-native files including, but not limited to, web pages, XML files, text files and data sources can also be opened directly in Excel. To open a non-native file directly in Excel, click the FILE tab and then click the *Open* option. Click the file location and then click the Browse button to display the Open dialog box. Navigate to the specific folder and then click the *File Type* option box to display a drop down list of all the different file types that can be opened in Excel. Click the specific file type and then double-click the file name. If you are not sure of the exact file type, select *All Files (*.*)* to display all of the available files. Save the file as an Excel workbook or, if changes were made, resave it as a text file, noting that some features might be lost.

Project 1c Importing Data from a Comma Separated Text File — Part 3 of 3

1. With **EL2-C8-P1-NuTrendsCensus.xlsx** open, make HousingUnitData the active worksheet.
2. Import statistics related to the top-growing US counties based on changes in housing units, which have been downloaded from the US Census Bureau website and saved in a text file, by completing the following steps:
   a. Make cell A6 active.
   b. Click the DATA tab.
   c. Click the From Text button in the Get External Data group.
   d. At the Import Text File dialog box, double-click ***HousingUnits.csv*** in the file list.
   e. At the Text Import Wizard - Step 1 of 3 dialog box, with *Delimited* selected in the *Original data type* section, click the *My data has headers* check box to insert a check mark and then click Next. Notice that the preview window in the lower half of the dialog box displays a sample of the data in the source text file. Delimited files use commas or tabs as separators, while fixed-width files use spaces.
   f. At the Text Import Wizard - Step 2 of 3 dialog box, click the *Comma* check box in the *Delimiters* section to insert a check mark and then click Next. Notice that after you select the comma as the delimiter character, the data in the *Data preview* section updates to show the imported data arranged in columns.

Step 2e

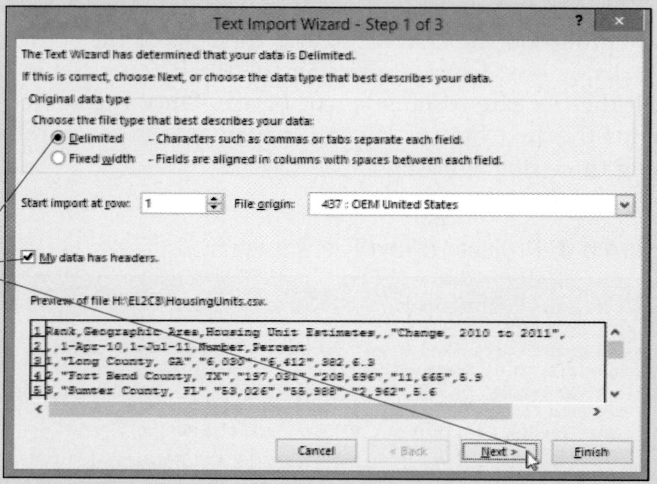

Step 2f

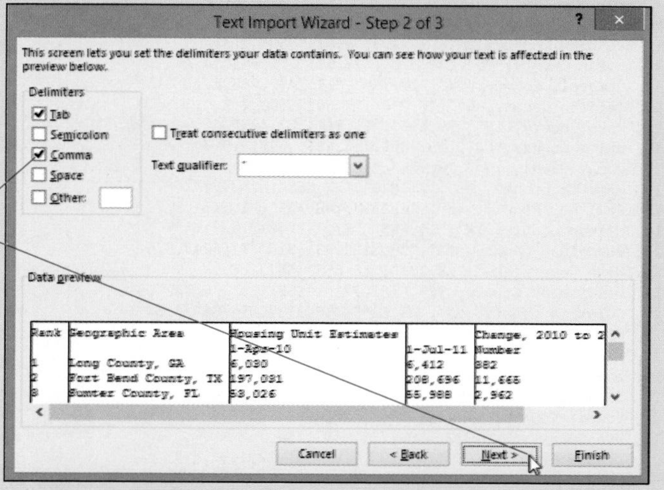

g. Click Finish at the Text Import Wizard - Step 3 of 3 dialog box to import all of the columns using the default *General* format. Formatting can be applied after the data has been imported into the worksheet.

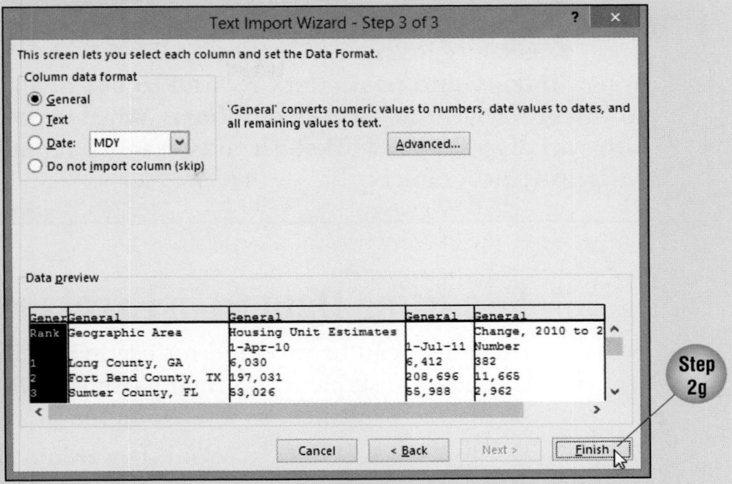

h. At the Import Data dialog box with *=$A$6* in the *Existing worksheet* text box in the *Where do you want to put the data?* section, click OK.

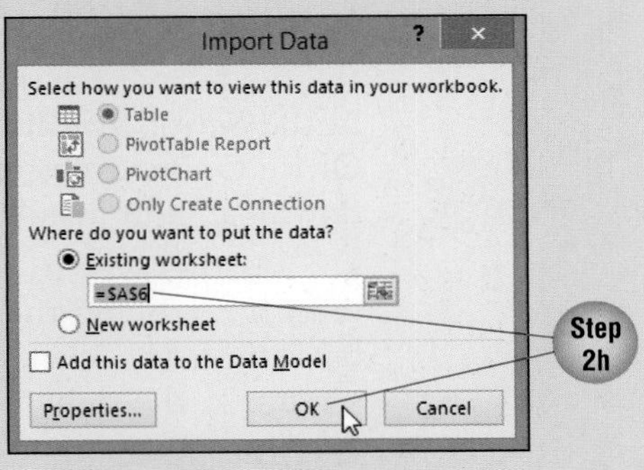

3. Scroll down the worksheet and view the imported data. The text file contained the top 100 counties in the United States ranked by change in housing units from 2010 to 2011. The number of housing units and the percent change are included for each county.
4. Make the following changes to the data:
   a. Change the width of column A to 5 characters and columns C, D, and E to 14 characters.
   b. Select C6:D6, click the HOME tab, and then click the Merge & Center button in the Alignment group.
   c. Merge and center E6:F6.
   d. Right-align the data in cell E7.
   e. Scroll to the bottom of the list. Using features in the Alignment and Cells groups on the HOME tab, adjust the notes so that they fit between columns A through F.
5. Print the HousingUnitData worksheet centered between the left and right margins.
6. Save and then close **EL2-C8-P1-NuTrendsCensus.xlsx**.
7. The workbook **EL2-C8-P1-NuTrendsCensus** required three worksheets. If you require only one worksheet in your workbook, you can open the .csv file directly in Excel by completing the following steps:
   a. Click the FILE tab and then click the *Open* option. At the Open backstage area, click your SkyDrive or *Computer* to locate your data files.
   b. Click the Browse button and then navigate to your EL2C8 folder.
   c. Click the *File Type* option box and then click *Text Files (*.prn, *.txt, *.csv)*.
   d. Double-click ***HousingUnits.csv*** in the file list.
8. Close the workbook without saving.

Project 2 Export Data in Excel — 6 Parts

You will copy and paste data related to car inventory from an Excel worksheet to integrate with an Access database, Word report, and PowerPoint presentation. You will also save a worksheet as a comma separated text file for use in a non-Microsoft program.

Exporting Data from Excel

Excel data can be exported for use in other programs by copying the cells to the Clipboard task pane and then pasting them into the destination document, or by saving the worksheet as a separate file in another file format.

To use Excel data in Word, PowerPoint, or Access, use the copy and paste method, since the programs within the Microsoft Office suite are designed for integration. To export Excel data for use in another program, open the Save As dialog box and then change the *Save as type* option to the desired file format. If the file format for the destination program that you want to use does not appear in the *Save as type* list, try copying and pasting the data or go to the Microsoft Office Online website and search for a file format converter that you can download and install.

Another way to save the current worksheet in a different file format is to click the FILE tab and then click the *Export* option at the backstage area. At the Export backstage area, click *Change File Type* in the center section. In the *Change File Type* section at the right, click the desired file format in the *Workbook File Types* or *Other File Types* section and then click the Save As button. If necessary, navigate to the desired drive and/or folder in the Save As dialog box. Type the desired file name and then click the Save button.

Quick Steps

Append Excel Data to an Access Table
1. Select cells.
2. Click Copy button.
3. Start Access.
4. Open database.
5. Open table in Datasheet view.
6. Click Paste button arrow.
7. Click *Paste Append*.
8. Click Yes.
9. Deselect pasted range.

Copying and Pasting Worksheet Data to an Access Table

Data in an Excel worksheet can be copied and pasted into an Access table datasheet, query, or form using the Clipboard task pane. To paste data into a table datasheet, make sure that the column structures in the two programs match. If the Access datasheet already contains records, you can choose to replace the existing records or append the Excel data to the end of the table. If you want to export Excel data to an Access database that does not have an existing table in which to receive the data, perform an import routine from Access. To do this, start Access, open the desired database, click the EXTERNAL DATA tab, and then click the Import Excel spreadsheet button.

Project 2a Copying and Pasting Excel Data to an Access Datasheet — Part 1 of 6

1. Open **CRInventory.xlsx**.
2. Copy and paste the rows in the Inventory worksheet to the bottom of an Access table by completing the following steps:
   a. Make sure Inventory is the active worksheet.
   b. Select A5:G33 and then click the Copy button in the Clipboard group on the HOME tab.
   c. Start Microsoft Access 2013.

d. At the Access 2013 opening screen, click the *Open Other Files* option.

e. At the Open backstage area, click the desired location in the *Places* section and then click the Browse button. At the open dialog box, navigate to the EL2C8 folder on your storage medium and then double-click ***CRInventory.accdb***. If a security warning message displays below the ribbon stating that active content has been disabled, click the Enable Content button.

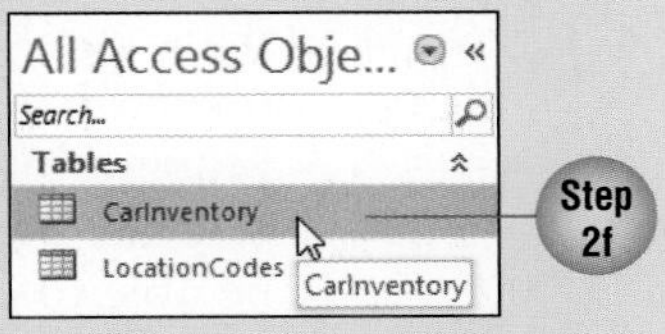

f. Double-click the object named *CarInventory* in the Tables group in the Navigation pane at the left side of the Access window. This opens the CarInventory table in Datasheet view. Notice that the structure of the columns in the datasheet is the same as in the source worksheet in Excel.

g. With the table open in Datasheet view, click the down-pointing arrow on the Paste button in the Clipboard group and then click *Paste Append* at the drop-down list.

h. At the Microsoft Access message box informing you that you are about to paste 29 records and asking if you are sure, click Yes.

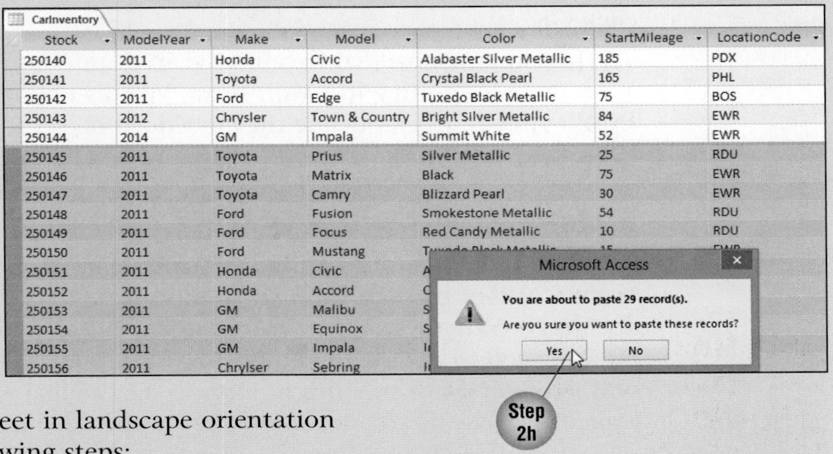

i. Click in any cell within the datasheet to deselect the pasted records.

3. Print the Access datasheet in landscape orientation by completing the following steps:

a. Click the FILE tab, click the *Print* option, and then click Print Preview.

b. Click the Landscape button in the Page Layout group on the PRINT PREVIEW tab.

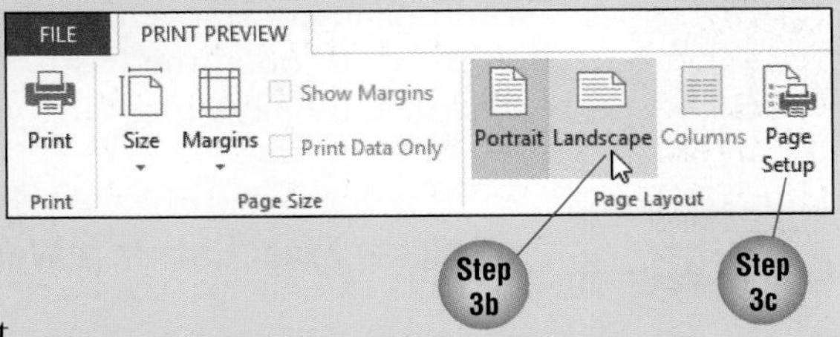

c. Click the Page Setup button in the Page Layout group.

d. At the Page Setup dialog box with the Print Options tab selected, change the top and bottom margins to 0.5 inch. The left and right margins should already be set to 1 inch. Click OK.

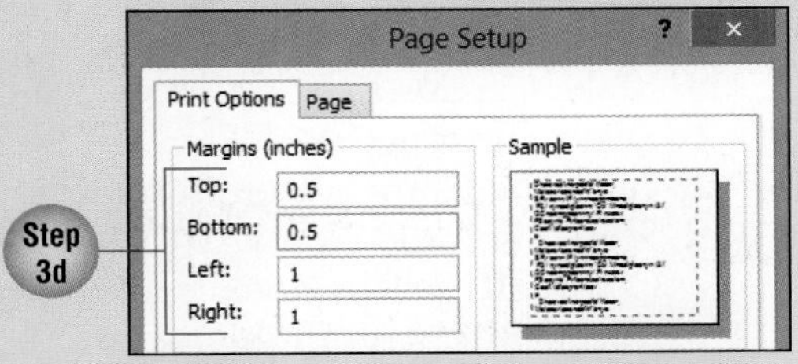

e. Click the Print button in the Print group and then click OK at the Print dialog box.

f. Click the Close Print Preview button in the Close Preview group.

4. Click the Close button in the upper right corner to close Access.

5. Click in any cell to deselect the range in the Inventory worksheet and then press Esc to remove the scrolling marquee.

6. Leave the **CRInventory.xlsx** workbook open for the next project.

Copying and Pasting Worksheet Data to a Word Document

Using a process similar to the one in Project 2a, you can copy and paste Excel data, copy and embed Excel data as an object, or copy and link Excel data as an object in a Word document. Use the copy and paste method if the data being brought into Word will not likely be updated or require editing after the source cells are pasted in the Word document. Copy and embed the data if you want to be able to edit the data in Word using Excel's editing tools and features. Copy and link the data if the information being pasted into Word will likely be changed in the future and you want the document in Word updated if the data in the source file changes.

Quick Steps

Embed Excel Data in a Word Document
1. Select cells.
2. Click Copy button.
3. Open Word document.
4. Position insertion point at desired location.
5. Click Paste button arrow.
6. Click *Paste Special*.
7. Click *Microsoft Excel Worksheet Object*.
8. Click OK.

Link Excel Data to a Word Document
1. Select cells.
2. Click Copy button.
3. Open Word document.
4. Position insertion point at desired location.
5. Click Paste button arrow.
6. Click *Paste Special*.
7. Click *Microsoft Excel Worksheet Object*.
8. Click Paste link.
9. Click OK.

Embedding Excel Data into a Word Document

To embed copied Excel data into a Word document, open the desired Word document, move the insertion point to the location at which you want to insert the copied Excel data, and then open the Paste Special dialog box. At the Paste Special dialog box, click *Microsoft Excel Worksheet Object* in the *As* list box and then click OK.

To edit an embedded Excel object in Word, double-click the embedded cells to open them for editing in a worksheet. Word's ribbon is temporarily replaced with Excel's ribbon. Click outside the embedded object to restore Word's ribbon and close the worksheet object in Word.

Linking Excel Data to a Word Document

Linking Excel data to a Word document means that the source data exists only in Excel. Word places a shortcut to the source data file name and range in the document. When you open a Word document containing one or more links, Word prompts you to update the links. Since the data resides in the Excel workbook only, be careful not to move or rename the original workbook from which you copied the cells. If you do so, the link in the document will no longer work.

To paste copied Excel data as a link in a Word document, open the desired Word document, move the insertion point to the location at which you want to link the cells, open the Paste Special dialog box, click *Microsoft Excel Worksheet Object* in the *As* list box, click *Paste link*, and then click OK.

Project 2b **Embedding Excel Data in a Word Document** **Part 2 of 6**

1. With **CRInventory.xlsx** open, copy and embed the data in the CarCosts worksheet to a Word document by completing the following steps:
   a. Make CarCosts the active worksheet.
   b. Select the range A4:F9.
   c. Click the Copy button in the Clipboard group.
   d. Start Microsoft Word 2013.
   e. Open **CRCarRpt.docx** from the EL2C8 folder on your storage medium. If a security warning displays in the message bar below the ribbon stating that the document is in Protected View, click the Enable Editing button.
   f. Save the document and name it **EL2-C8-P2-CRCarRpt**.

g. Press Ctrl + End to move the insertion point to the end of the document.
h. Click the Paste button arrow in the Clipboard group and then click *Paste Special* at the drop-down list.
i. At the Paste Special dialog box, click *Microsoft Excel Worksheet Object* in the *As* list box and then click OK.

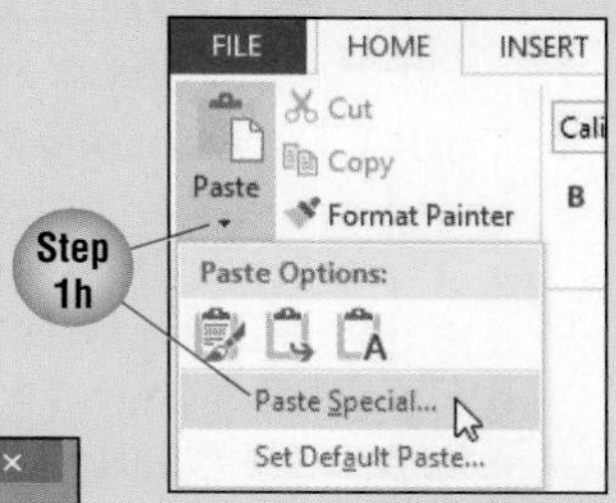

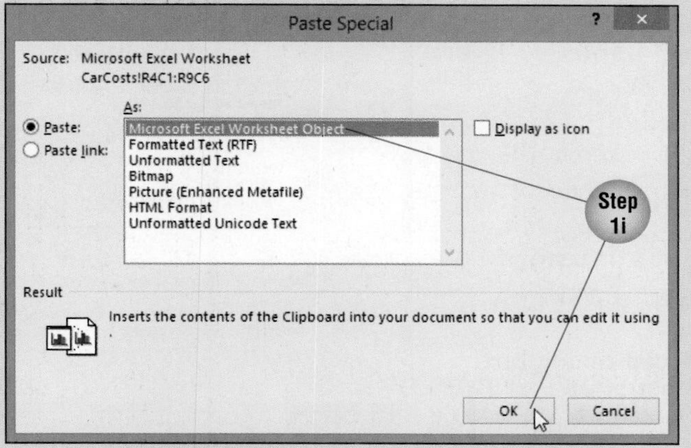

2. Save **EL2-C8-P2-CRCarRpt.docx**.
3. When you use Paste Special, the copied cells are embedded as an object in the Word document. Edit the embedded object using Excel's editing tools by completing the following steps:
   a. Double-click any cell in the embedded worksheet object. The object is surrounded with a border and Excel's column and row headers appear. Word's ribbon is temporarily replaced with Excel's ribbon.
   b. Select the range B4:F4 and then click the Center button in the Alignment group.

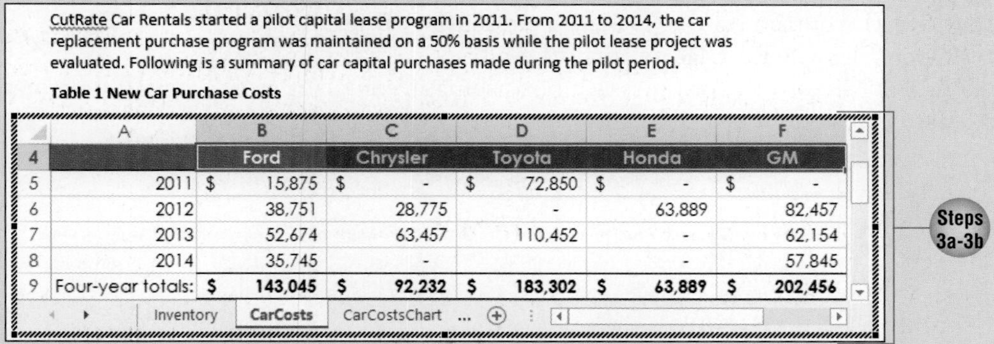

   c. Click in the document outside the embedded object to close the object and restore Word's ribbon. Excel becomes the active application.
4. Double-click Word in the Taskbar. Save and then print **EL2-C8-P2-CRCarRpt.docx**.
5. Close Word.
6. Click in any cell to deselect the range in the CarCosts worksheet and leave the **CRInventory.xlsx** workbook open for the next project.

Project 2c Linking Excel Data in a Word Document

Part 3 of 6

1. With **CRInventory.xlsx** open, copy and link the data in the CarCosts worksheet to a Word document by completing the following steps:
   a. With CarCosts the active worksheet, select the range A4:F9 and then click the Copy button.
   b. Start Microsoft Word 2013.
   c. Open **CRCarRpt.docx**.
   d. Save the document and name it **EL2-C8-P2-CRCarRptLinked**.
   e. Press Ctrl + End to move the insertion point to the end of the document.
   f. Click the Paste button arrow and then click *Paste Special* at the drop-down list.
   g. At the Paste Special dialog box, click *Microsoft Excel Worksheet Object* in the *As* list box and then click the *Paste link* option.
   h. Click OK.

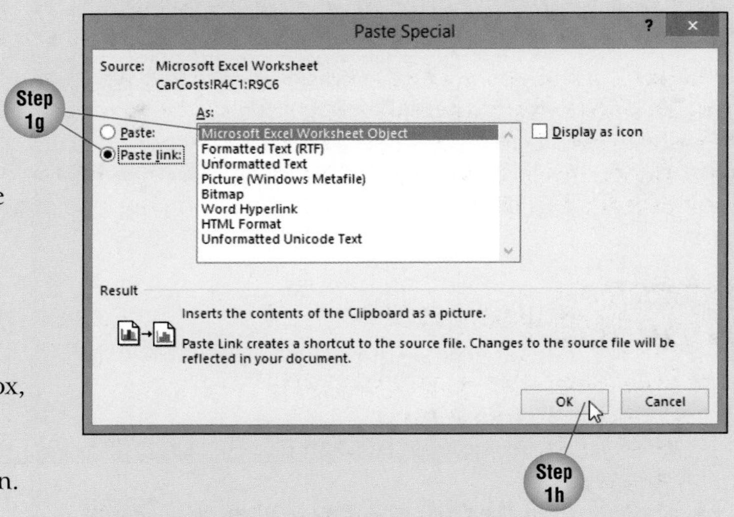

2. Save and then close **EL2-C8-P2-CRCarRptLinked.docx**. When data is linked, the data exists only in the source program. In the destination document, Word inserts a shortcut to the source range. Edit the source range and view the update to the Word document by completing the following steps:
   a. Click the button on the Taskbar representing the Excel workbook **CRInventory.xlsx**.
   b. With CarCosts the active worksheet, press Esc to remove the scrolling marquee (if necessary) and then click in any cell to deselect the copied range.
   c. Make cell E5 active, type 85000, and then press Enter.
   d. Click the button on the Taskbar representing Word.
   e. Open **EL2-C8-P2-CRCarRptLinked.docx**.
   f. At the Microsoft Word message box asking if you want to update the document with data from the linked files, click Yes.

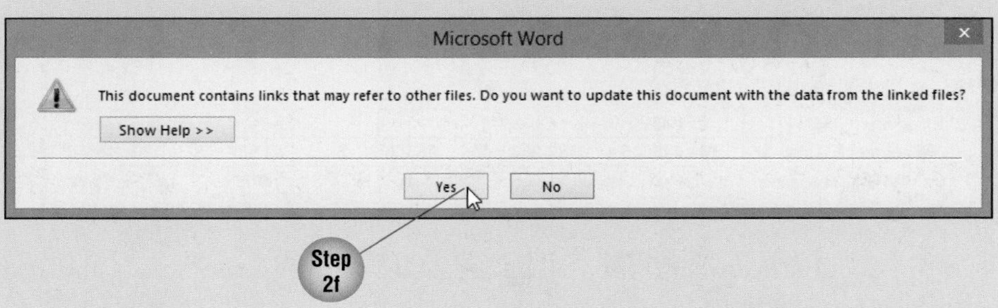

3. Notice that the data inserted in the Excel worksheet is also shown in the linked Word document.
4. Save and then print **EL2-C8-P2-CRCarRptLinked.docx**.
5. Exit Word.
6. With CarCosts the active worksheet in **CRInventory.xlsx**, delete the contents of cell E5 and leave the workbook open for a later project.

Breaking a Link to an Excel Object

If you link Excel data to a Word document and later decide you no longer need the data to be linked, you can break the connection between the source and destination files so that you are not prompted to update the object each time you open the document. Breaking the link means that the data in the Word document will no longer be connected to the data in the Excel workbook. If you make a change to the original data in Excel, the Word document will not reflect the updated information.

To break a link, open the document, right-click the linked object, point to *Linked Worksheet Object,* and then click *Links* at the shortcut menu. This opens the Links dialog box. If more than one linked object exists in the document, click the source object for the link you want to break and then click the Break Link button. At the message box that appears, click Yes to confirm you want to break the link.

Quick Steps

Break a Link to an Excel Object

1. Open document.
2. Right-click linked object.
3. Point to *Linked Worksheet Object.*
4. Click *Links.*
5. Click Break Link button.
6. Click Yes.
7. Save document.

Project 2d **Breaking a Link** **Part 4 of 6**

1. Start Word and open **EL2-C8-P2-CRCarRptLinked.docx**.
2. At the message asking if you want to update links, click No.
3. Break the link between the Excel workbook and the linked object by completing the following steps:
   a. Right-click the linked Excel worksheet object.
   b. Point to *Linked Worksheet Object* and then click *Links* at the shortcut menu.
   c. At the Links dialog box, with the linked object file name selected in the *Source file* list box, click the Break Link button.

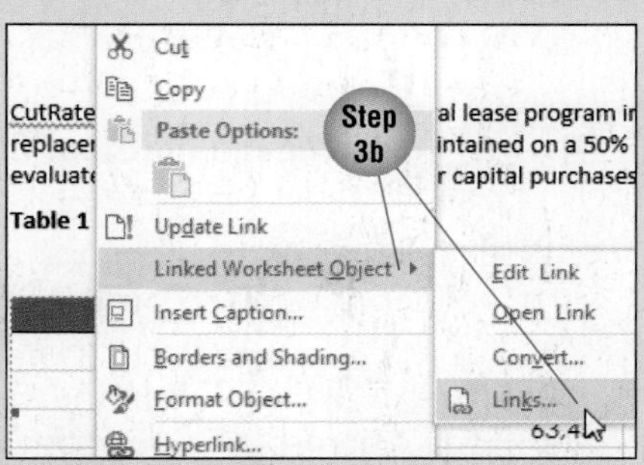

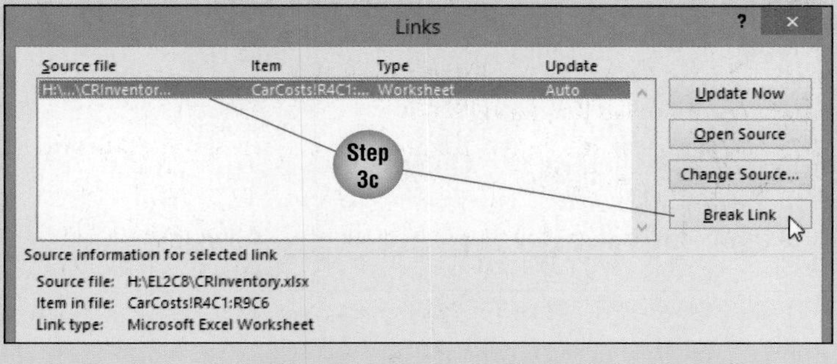

   d. At the Microsoft Word dialog box asking if you are sure you want to break the selected link, click Yes.

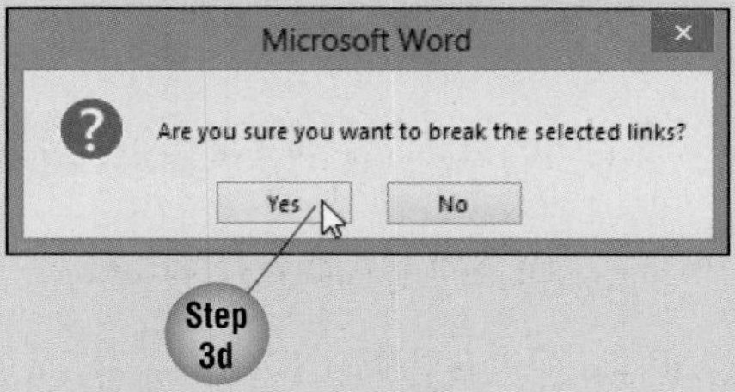

4. Save **EL2-C8-P2-CRCarRptLinked.docx** and then exit Word.

Quick Steps

Embed Excel Data in a PowerPoint Presentation

1. Select cells.
2. Click Copy button.
3. Open PowerPoint presentation.
4. Make desired slide active.
5. Click Paste button arrow.
6. Click *Paste Special.*
7. Make sure *Microsoft Excel Worksheet Object* is selected in *As* list box.
8. Click OK.

Copying and Pasting Worksheet Data to a PowerPoint Presentation

As with Word, you can copy and paste, copy and embed, or copy and link Excel data to slides in a PowerPoint presentation. Presentations often incorporate charts to visually depict numerical data in a graph format that is easy to understand. Although you can create tables and charts in a PowerPoint slide, you may prefer to use Excel for these tasks and then copy and paste the data in to PowerPoint. In the Office 2013 suite, the charting system is fully integrated within Word, Excel, and PowerPoint. A chart inserted in a Word document or PowerPoint presentation is created as an embedded object with the source data used to generate the chart stored in an Excel worksheet; the Excel worksheet with the source data becomes part of the document or presentation file.

Since the chart feature is fully integrated within Word, Excel, and PowerPoint, you can edit a chart in a PowerPoint presentation using the same techniques you learned to edit a chart in Excel. Clicking a chart in a PowerPoint slide causes the contextual CHART TOOLS DESIGN and CHART TOOLS FORMAT tabs to become active with the same groups and buttons available as in Excel. Three new buttons—Chart Elements, Chart Styles and Chart Filter—are also available for editing.

Project 2e Embedding Excel Data in a PowerPoint Presentation — Part 5 of 6

1. With **CRInventory.xlsx** open, copy and embed the chart in the CarCostsChart worksheet to a slide in a PowerPoint presentation by completing the following steps:
   a. Make CarCostsChart the active worksheet.
   b. Click the HOME tab and then click the Copy button.
   c. Start Microsoft PowerPoint 2013.
   d. Open **CRCarRpt.pptx**.
   e. Save the presentation and name it **EL2-C8-P2-CRCarRpt**.
   f. Click Slide 3 in the slide thumbnails pane.
   g. Click in the *Click to add text* placeholder and then click the Paste button in the Clipboard group. Since all charts are embedded by default, you do not need to use Paste Special.
2. Change the chart colors by clicking the Chart Styles button and then clicking the COLOR tab. Click the *Color 2* option from the *Colorful* section of the color palette.

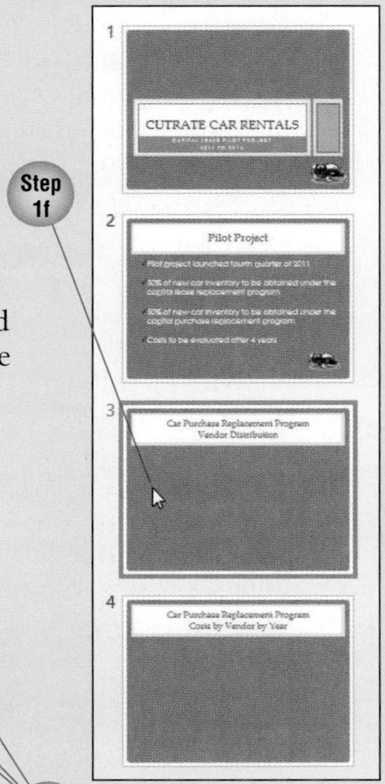

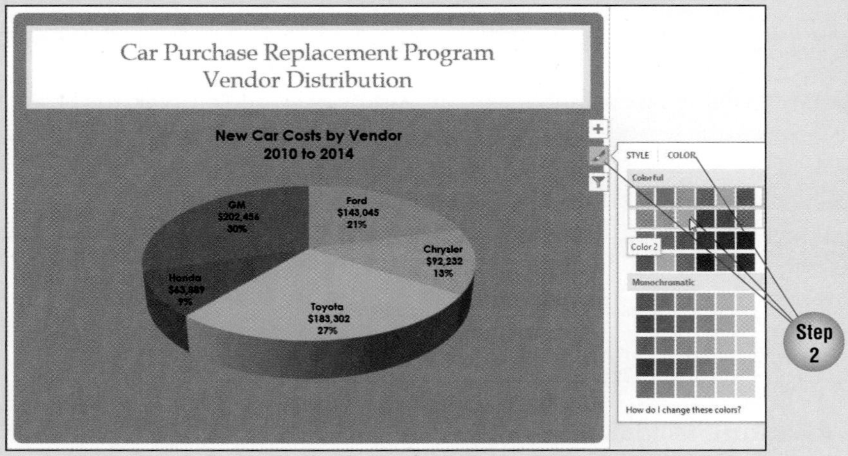

3. Copy and embed the table used to generate the chart in the CarCosts worksheet to the next slide in the PowerPoint presentation by completing the following steps:
   a. Click Slide 4 in the slide thumbnails pane.
   b. Click the button on the Taskbar representing the Excel workbook **CRInventory.xlsx**.
   c. Make CarCosts the active worksheet, select the range A1:F9, and then click the Copy button.
   d. Click the button on the Taskbar representing the PowerPoint presentation **EL2-C8-P2-CRCarRpt.pptx**.
   e. Click the Paste button arrow and then click *Paste Special* at the drop-down list.
   f. With *Microsoft Excel Worksheet Object* selected in the *As* list box, click OK.

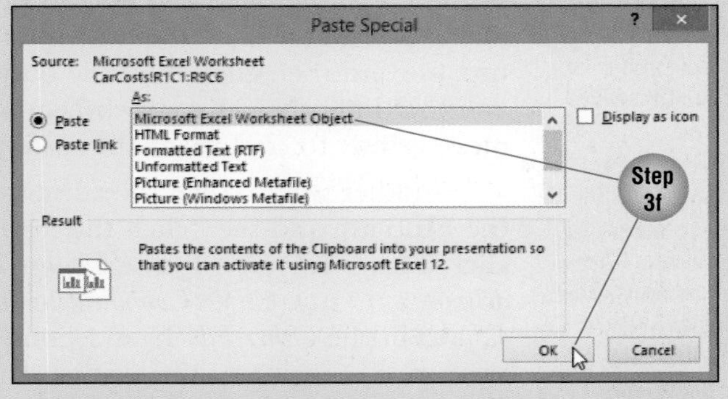

4. Resize and position the embedded table to the approximate height, width, and position shown at the right.

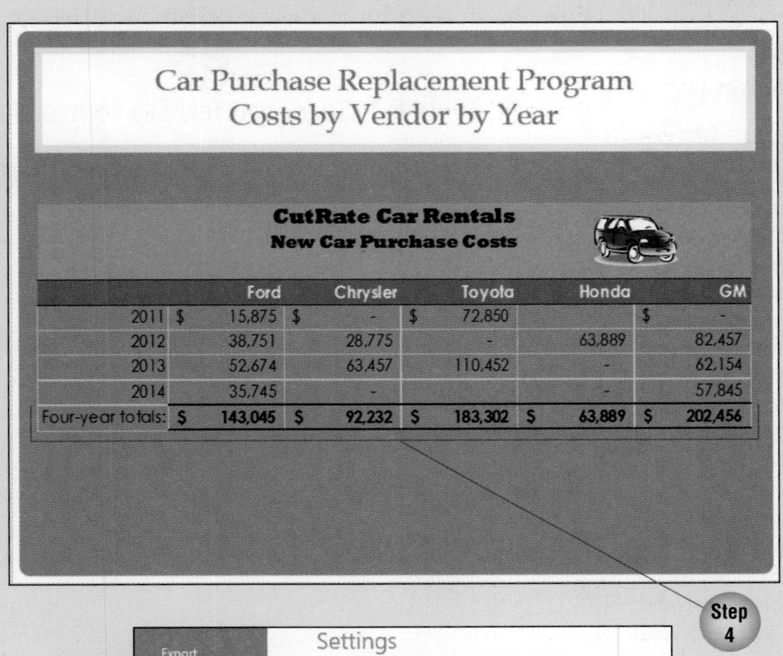

5. Click the FILE tab and then click the *Print* option. At the Print backstage area, click the button in the *Settings* category that currently reads *Full Page Slides* and then click *4 Slides Horizontal* at the drop-down list. Click the Print button.
6. Save **EL2-C8-P2-CRCarRpt.pptx** and then exit PowerPoint.
7. Press Esc to remove the scrolling marquee and then click in any cell to deselect the range in the CarCosts worksheet. Leave the **CRInventory.xlsx** workbook open for the next project.

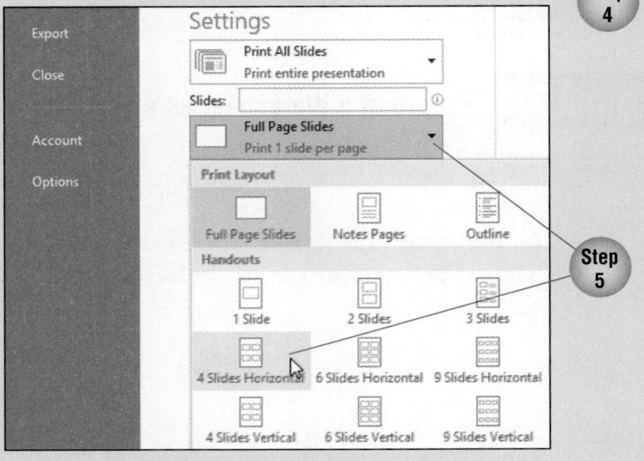

Exporting Excel Data as a Text File

Quick Steps

Export a Worksheet as a Text File

1. Make desired sheet active.
2. Click FILE tab.
3. Click *Export* option.
4. Click *Change File Type*.
5. Click desired text file type in *Other File Types* section.
6. Click Save As button.
7. If necessary, navigate to desired drive and/or folder.
8. Type file name.
9. Click Save button.
10. Click OK.
11. Click Yes.

HINT

Why are there so many text file formats? Although all systems support text files, differences occur across platforms. For example, a Macintosh computer denotes the end of a line in a text file with a carriage return character, Unix uses a linefeed character, and DOS inserts both a linefeed and a carriage return character code at the end of each line.

If you need to exchange Excel data with someone who is not able to import a Microsoft Excel worksheet or cannot copy and paste using the Clipboard task pane, you can save the data as a text file. Excel provides several text file options, including file formats suitable for computers that use the Macintosh operating system, as shown in Table 8.1. To save a worksheet as a text file, open the Save As dialog box and change the file type to the desired option. Type a file name for the text file and then click the Save button. Click OK at the message box that informs you that only the active worksheet will be saved and then click Yes at the next message box to confirm that you want to save the data as a text file.

Another way to save the current worksheet in a text file format is to click the FILE tab and then click the *Export* option. At the Export backstage area, click *Change File Type*. In the *Change File Type* section at the right, click *Text (Tab delimited) (*.txt)*, *CSV (Comma delimited) (*.csv)*, or *Formatted Text (Space delimited) (*.prn)* in the *Other File Types* section and then click the Save As button. If necessary, navigate to the desired drive and/or folder in the Save As dialog box. Type the desired file name and then click the Save button.

Table 8.1 Supported Text File Formats for Exporting

Text File Format Option	*File Extension*
text (tab delimited)	.txt
unicode text	.txt
CSV (comma delimited)	.csv
formatted text (space delimited)	.prn
text (Macintosh)	.txt
text (MS-DOS)	.txt
CSV (Macintosh)	.csv
CSV (MS-DOS)	.csv

Project 2f **Exporting a Worksheet as a Text File** **Part 6 of 6**

1. With **CRInventory.xlsx** open, export the Inventory worksheet data as a text file by completing the following steps:
   a. Make Inventory the active worksheet.
   b. Click the FILE tab and then click *Export* option.

c. Click *Change File Type* at the Export backstage area.
d. Click *CSV (Comma delimited) (*.csv)* in the *Other File Types* section.
e. Click the Save As button.

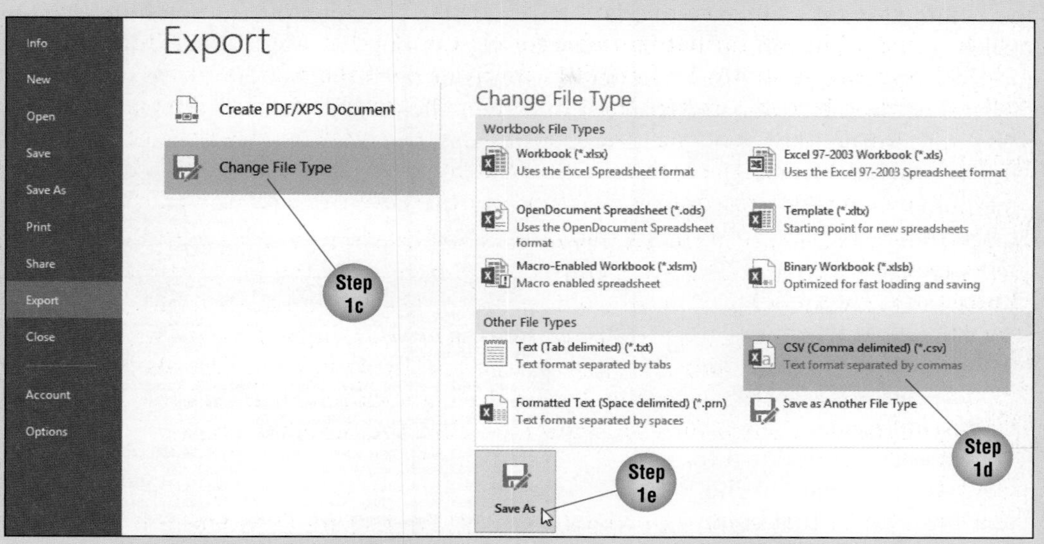

f. Type EL2-C8-P2-CRInventory in the *File name* text box.
g. Click the Save button.

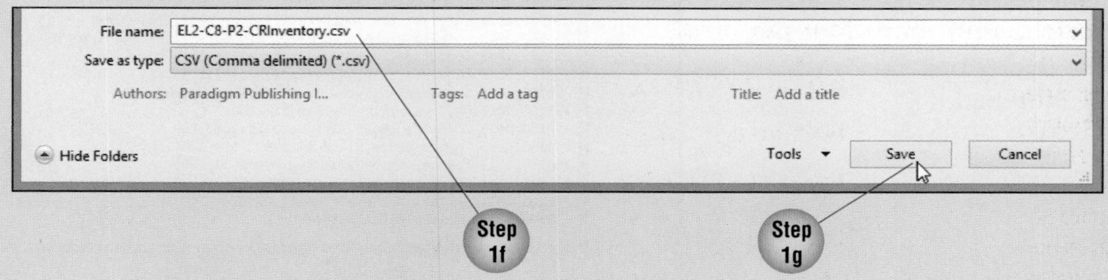

h. Click OK to save only the active sheet at the Microsoft Excel message box that informs you the selected file type does not support workbooks that contain multiple sheets.

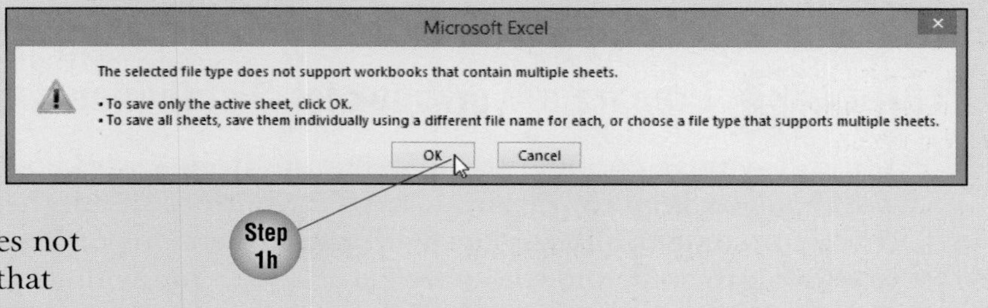

i. Click Yes to save the workbook in this format at the next message box that informs you **EL2-C8-P2-CRInventory.csv** may contain features that are not compatible with CSV (comma delimited).

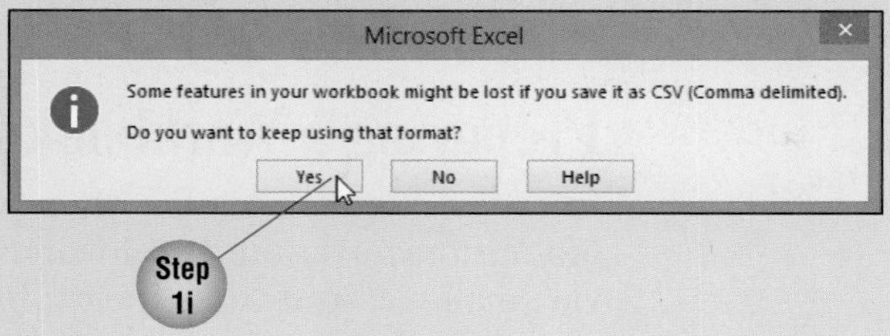

2. Close **EL2-C8-P2-CRInventory.csv**. Click Don't Save when prompted to save changes. (You do not need to save the file, because you have not made any changes since you changed the file type.)
3. Open Notepad and view the text file created in Step 1 by completing the following steps:
   a. Click the Start button. At the Start screen, start typing notepad. When *Notepad* appears in the *Apps* area, press Enter. (Depending on your operating system, these steps may vary.)
   b. Click File on the Notepad Menu bar and then click *Open*.
   c. Navigate to the EL2C8 folder on your storage medium.
   d. Click the Text Documents (*.txt) button and then click *All Files (*.*)* at the drop-down list.
   e. Double-click ***EL2-C8-P2-CRInventory.csv***.
   f. If necessary, scroll down to view all of the data in the text file. Notice that commas have been inserted between the columns' data.
4. Click File on the Notepad Menu bar and then click *Print*. Click the Print button at the Print dialog box.
5. Exit Notepad.

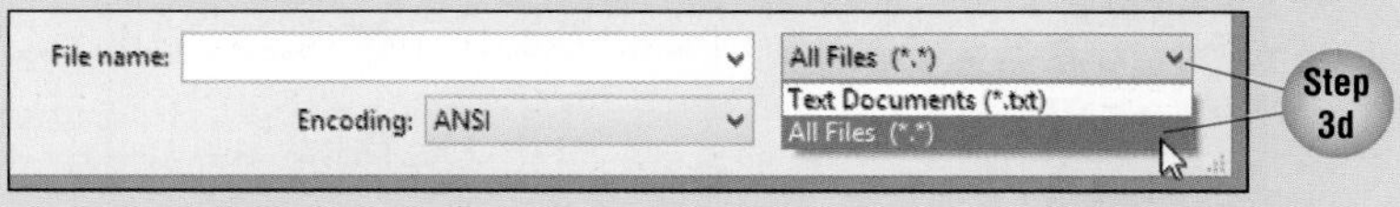

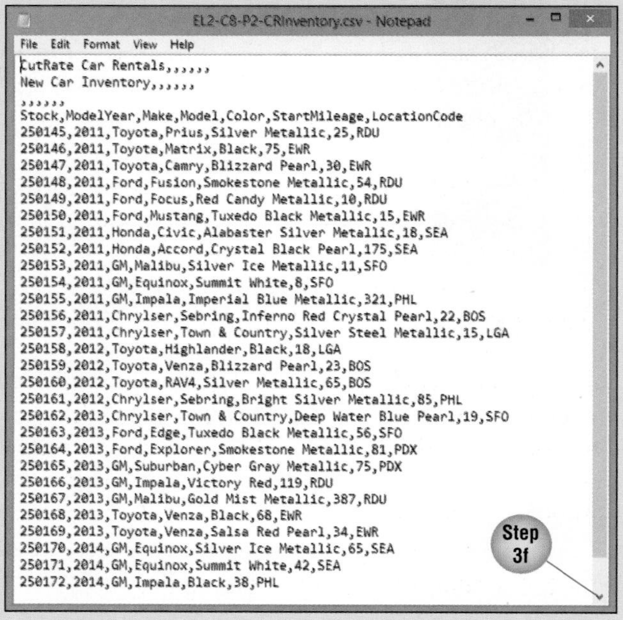

Project 3 Prepare a Workbook for Distribution — 4 Parts

You will remove confidential information from a workbook and mark the workbook as final to prepare it for distribution. In another workbook, you will check for compatibility issues with earlier versions of Excel before sending the workbook to someone who uses Excel 2003. You will also explore the default settings in the Trust Center.

Preparing a Workbook for Distribution

In today's workplace, you often work as part of a team both within and outside of your organization. Excel workbooks are frequently exchanged between workers via email message attachments; by saving to a shared network folder, a document management server, or a company website; or by other means of electronic distribution. Prior to making a workbook available for others to open, view, and edit, Excel provides several features that allow you to protect and/or maintain confidentiality.

Removing Information from a Workbook before Distributing

Before distributing a workbook electronically to others, you should consider using the ***Document Inspector*** to scan the workbook for personal data or other hidden information that you would not want others to view. Recall from Chapter 6 that a workbook's properties, sometimes referred to as ***metadata***, include information that is tracked automatically by Excel, such as the names of the individuals that accessed and edited a workbook. If a workbook will be sent electronically by email or made available on a document management server or other website, consider the implications of recipients of that workbook being able to look at some of this hidden information. Ask yourself if this information should remain confidential and, if so, remove sensitive data and/or metadata before distributing the file. To do this, click the FILE tab. At the Info backstage area, click the Check for Issues button in the *Inspect Workbook* section and then click *Inspect Document* at the drop-down list. This opens the Document Inspector dialog box shown in Figure 8.4. By default, all check boxes are selected. Clear the check boxes for those items that you do not need or want to scan for and/or remove and then click the Inspect button.

Before removing sensitive data, you can save a copy of the original file that retains all content using password protection or other security measures to limit access. In addition, you can use the Document Inspector to reveal the presence of headers, footers, hidden items, or other invisible data in a workbook of which you are not the original author.

The Document Inspector scans the workbook for the existence of any of the checked items. When completed, a dialog box like the one in Figure 8.5 appears. Excel displays check marks in the sections for which no items were found and red exclamation marks in the sections in which items were detected within the workbook. Click the Remove All button in the section that contains content you decide you want to remove. Click OK when finished and then distribute the workbook as needed.

Quick Steps

Use the Document Inspector to Remove Private Information

1. Open workbook.
2. Click FILE tab.
3. Click Check for Issues button.
4. Click *Inspect Document.*
5. Clear check boxes for those items you do not want to scan and remove.
6. Click Inspect button.
7. Click Remove All button in those sections with items you want removed.
8. Click Close button.

Inspect

Figure 8.4 Document Inspector Dialog Box

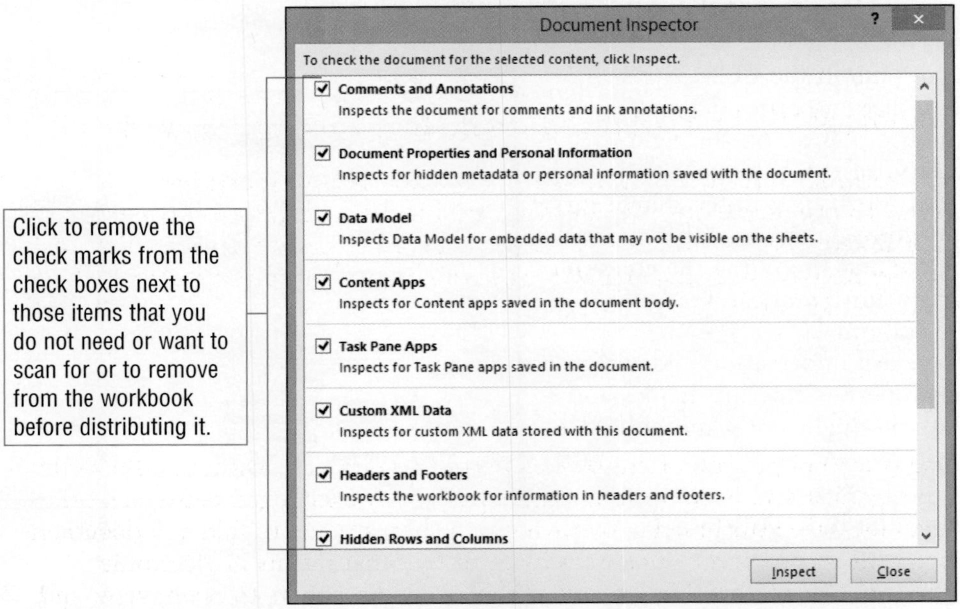

Figure 8.5 Document Inspector Dialog Box with Inspection Results Shown

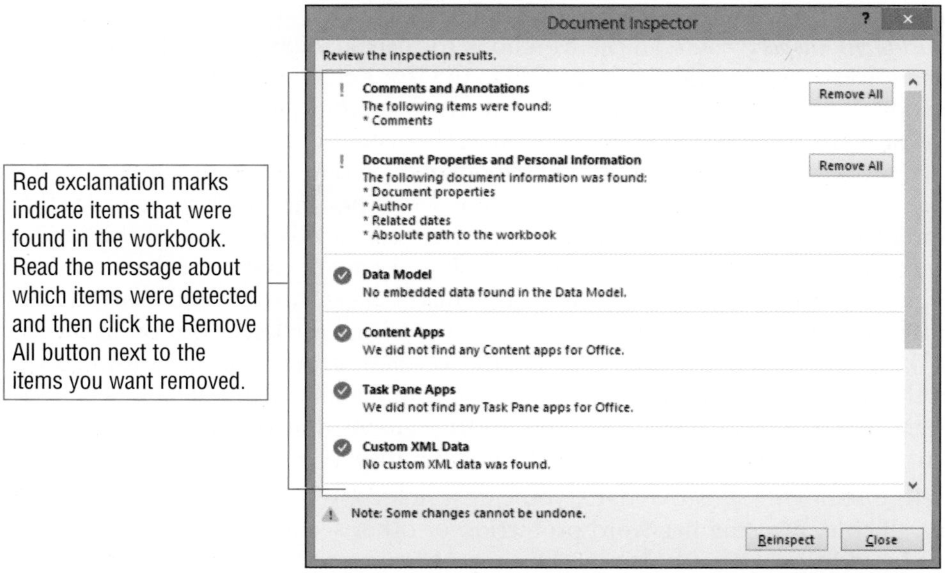

Project 3a Removing Private and Confidential Data from a Workbook Part 1 of 4

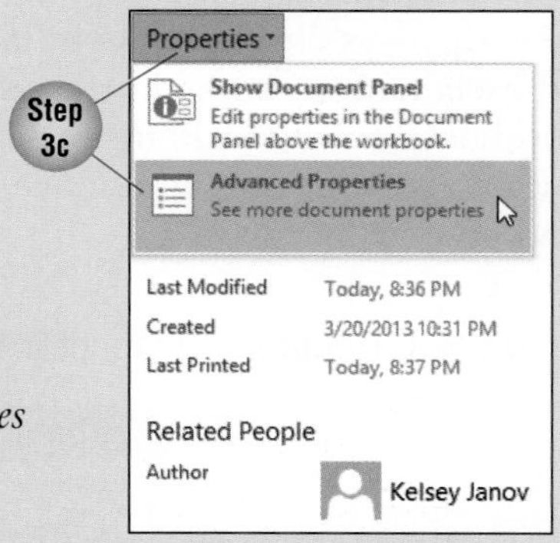

1. Open **CRPilotPrjRpt.xlsx**.
2. Save the workbook and name it **EL2-C8-P3-CRPilotPrjRpt**.
3. Examine the workbook for private and other confidential information by completing the following steps:
   a. Click the FILE tab.
   b. Read the property information in the fields in the *Properties* section located at the right side of the screen.
   c. Click the Properties button and then click *Advanced Properties* at the drop-down list.
   d. Click the Custom tab in the **EL2-C8-P3-CRPilotPrjRpt.xlsx** Properties dialog box.
   e. Position the mouse pointer on the right column boundary for the *Value* column in the *Properties* list box until the pointer changes to a left-and-right-pointing arrow with a vertical line in the middle and then drag the column width to the right until you can read all of the text in the column.
   f. Notice that the extra information added to the workbook properties contains names and other data that you might not want widely circulated.
   g. Click OK.
   h. Press Esc or click the Back button.

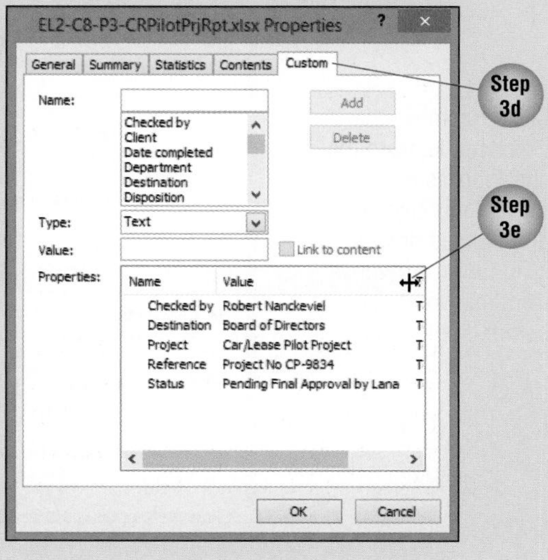

i. Click the REVIEW tab and then click the Show All Comments button in the Comments group.

j. Read the two comments displayed in the worksheet area.

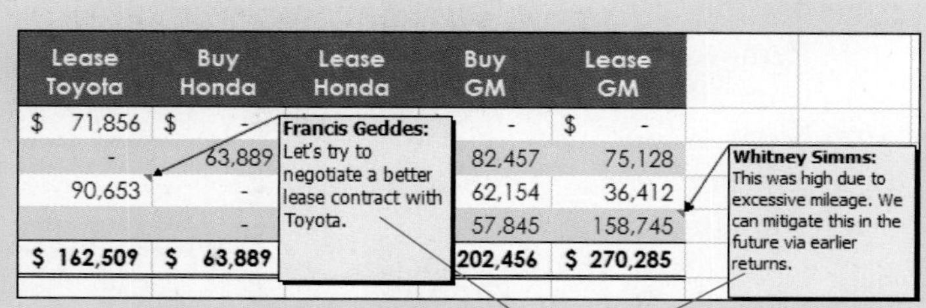

4. Use the Document Inspector to scan the workbook for other confidential information by completing the following steps:
   a. Click the FILE tab, click the Check for Issues button in the *Inspect Workbook* section at the Info backstage area, and then click *Inspect Document* at the drop-down list.
   b. At the message box indicating that the file contains changes that have not been saved, click Yes to save the file now.
   c. At the Document Inspector dialog box with all of the check boxes selected, click the Inspect button to check for all of the items.
   d. Read the messages in each section of the Document Inspector dialog box that displays with a red exclamation mark.
   e. Click the Remove All button in the *Document Properties and Personal Information* section. Excel deletes the metadata and the section now displays with a check mark indicating the information has been removed.

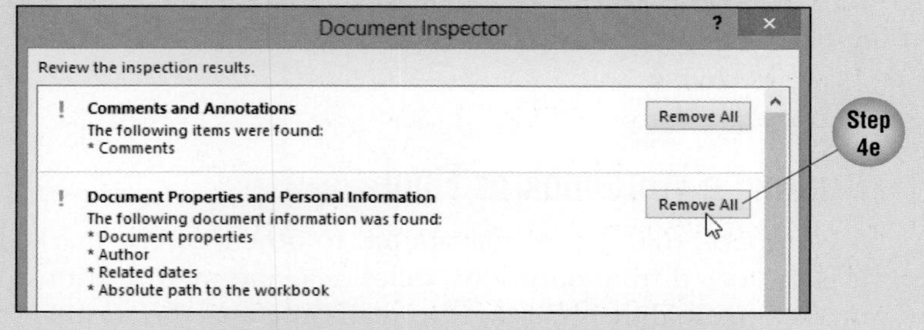

   f. Notice that the inspection results indicate that a header and three hidden rows were found. You decide to review these items before removing them. Click the Close button to close the Document Inspector dialog box.
5. Display the worksheet in Page Layout view and view the header.
6. Look at the row numbers in the worksheet area. Notice that after row 10, the next row number is 14. Select row numbers 10 and 14, right-click the selected rows, and then click *Unhide* at the shortcut menu to display rows 11 through 13.

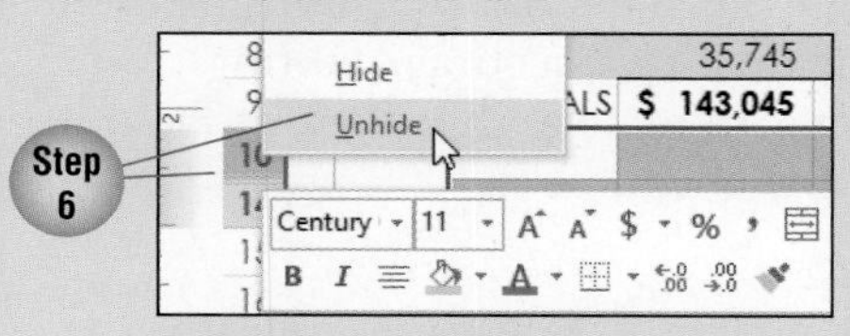

7. Click in any cell to deselect the range. Review the information in the rows that were hidden.
8. You decide that the rows that were initially hidden should remain displayed, but you want to prevent reviewers of the workbook from seeing the header and comments. Use the Document Inspector to remove these items by completing the following steps:
   a. Click the FILE tab, click the Check for Issues button, click *Inspect Document* at the drop-down list, and then click Yes to save the changes to the workbook.

b. Remove the check marks from all of the check boxes except those next to *Comments and Annotations* and *Headers and Footers*.
c. Click the Inspect button.
d. Click the Remove All button in the *Comments and Annotations* section.
e. Click the Remove All button in the *Headers and Footers* section.
f. Click the Close button.

9. Notice that the comments and header have been deleted from the worksheet. Switch back to Normal view.
10. Click the Show All Comments button in the Comments group on the REVIEW tab to turn off the feature.
11. Save and then close **EL2-C8-P3-CRPilotPrjRpt.xlsx**.

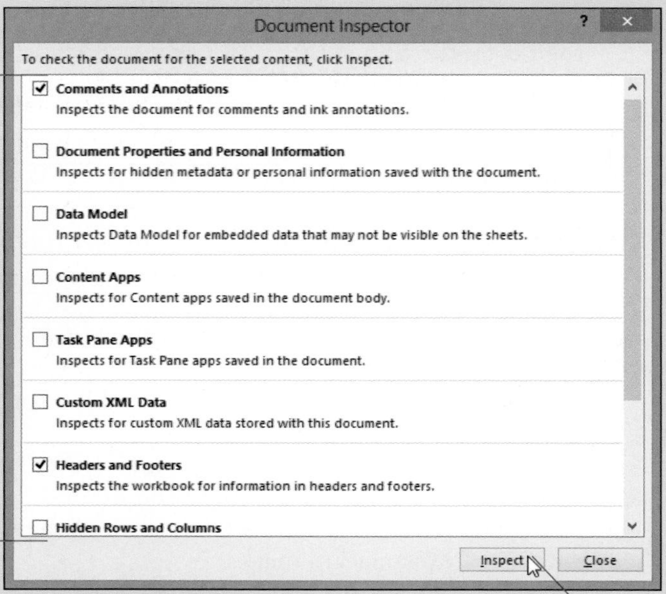

Marking a Workbook as Final

Quick Steps

Mark a Workbook as Final

1. Open workbook.
2. Click FILE tab.
3. Click Protect Workbook button.
4. Click *Mark as Final*.
5. Click OK twice.

Mark as Final

A workbook that will be distributed to others can be marked as final, which means it is protected from additions, deletions, and modifications. When a workbook is marked as final, it is changed to read-only and the status property is set to *Final*. In addition to protecting it, marking a workbook as final also serves to indicate to the recipient(s) of the workbook that you consider the content complete. To mark a workbook as final, click the FILE tab. At the Info backstage area, click the Protect Workbook button and then click *Mark as Final* at the drop-down list. (Note that marking a workbook as final should not be considered as secure as using password-protected, locked ranges.)

A workbook marked as final displays with the ribbon minimized and a message above the Formula bar that informs the reader that an author has marked the workbook as final to discourage editing. You can click the Edit Anyway button in the message bar to remove the Mark as Final feature, redisplay the ribbon, and make changes to the workbook.

Project 3b Marking a Workbook as Final

Part 2 of 4

1. Open **EL2-C8-P3-CRPilotPrjRpt.xlsx**.
2. Save the workbook and name it **EL2-C8-P3-CRPilotPrjRptFinal**.
3. Mark the workbook as final to prevent changes and set the Status property to *Final* by completing the following steps:
   a. Click the FILE tab, click the Protect Workbook button in the *Protect Workbook* section of the Info backstage area, and then click *Mark as Final*.

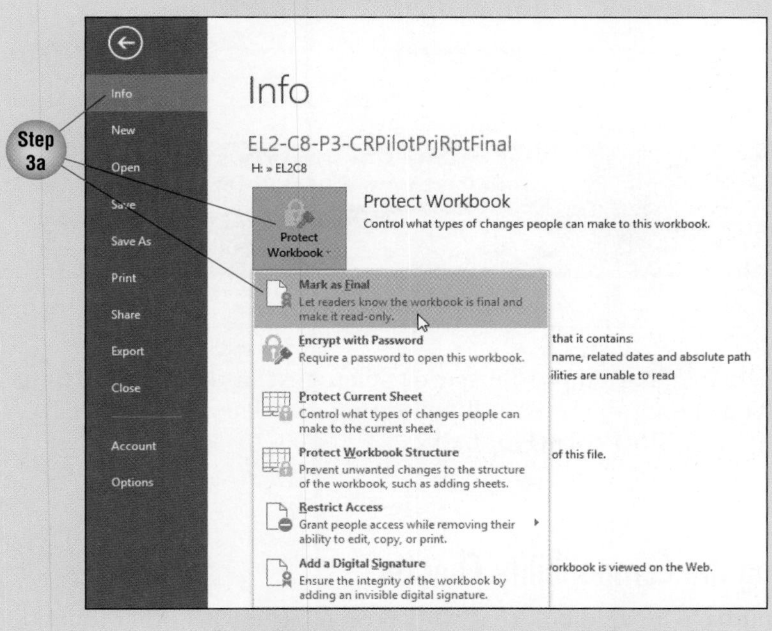

   b. Click OK at the message box that says the workbook will be marked as final and then saved.

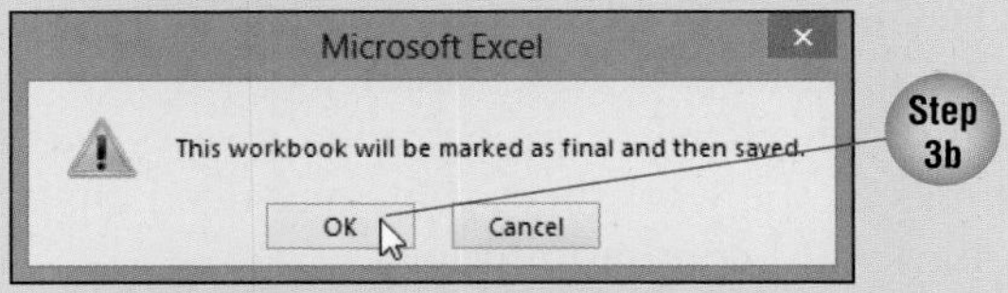

   c. Click OK at the second message box that says the workbook has been marked as final to indicate that editing is complete and this is the final version of the document. ***Note: If this message box does not appear, it has been turned off by a previous user who clicked the* Don't show this message again *check box.***

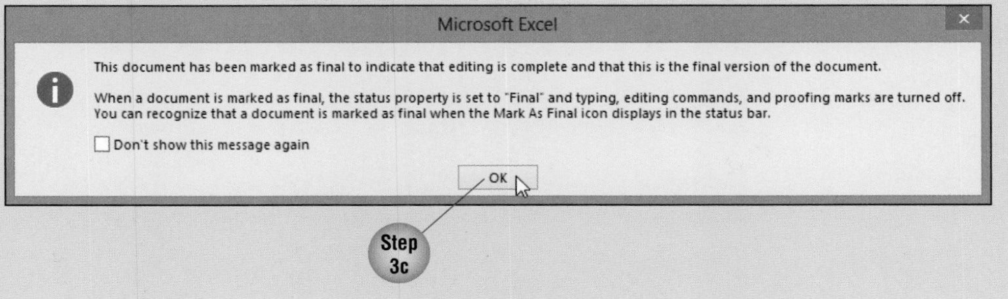

4. Click the FILE tab and notice that the *Protect Workbook* section of the Info backstage area displays in yellow and with a message indicating the workbook has been marked as final. Click the Back button and notice also the addition of *[Read-Only]* next to the file name in the Title bar.
5. The ribbon is minimized and a marked as final message displays above the Formula bar, indicating that the workbook has been marked as final to discourage editing. Additionally, a *Marked as Final* icon displays in the Status bar next to *Ready*.

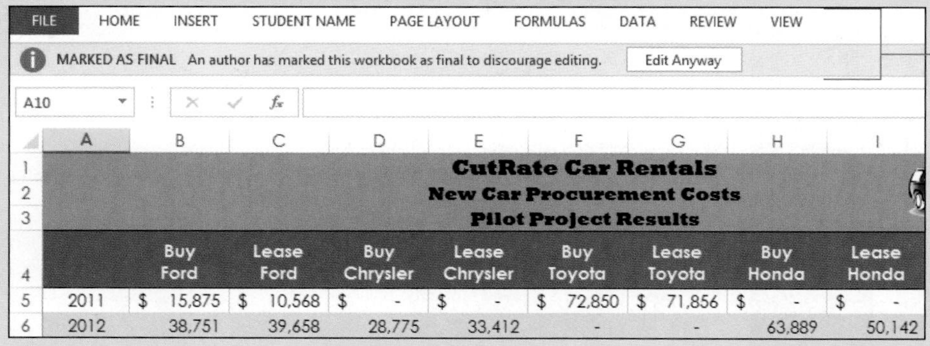

The ribbon is minimized and a marked as final message displays as described in Step 5.

6. Make any cell active and attempt to insert or delete text in the cell. Since the workbook is now read-only, you cannot open the cell for editing or delete the contents.
7. Close **EL2-C8-P3-CRPilotPrjRptFinal.xlsx**.

Using the Compatibility Checker

Quick Steps

Check a Workbook for Compatibility

1. Open workbook.
2. Click FILE tab.
3. Click Check for Issues button.
4. Click *Check Compatibility*.
5. Read information in *Summary* list box.
6. If desired, click *Copy to New Sheet* button.
OR
Click Close.

Check Compatibility

If you have a workbook that will be exchanged with other individuals who do not have Excel 2007, Excel 2010, or Excel 2013, you can save the workbook in the Excel 97-2003 file format. When you save the file in the earlier version's file format, Excel automatically does a compatibility check and prompts you with information about loss of functionality or fidelity. If you prefer, you can use the Compatibility Checker feature before you save the workbook so that you know in advance areas of the worksheet that may need changes prior to saving in order to maintain backward compatibility.

In the *Summary* list box at the Microsoft Excel - Compatibility Checker dialog box, if an issue displays a Fix hyperlink, click Fix to resolve the problem. If you want more information about a loss of functionality or fidelity, click the Help hyperlink next to the issue. To return to the worksheet with the cells selected that are problematic for earlier Excel versions, click the Find hyperlink next to the issue.

Project 3c Checking a Workbook for Compatibility with Earlier Versions of Excel — Part 3 of 4

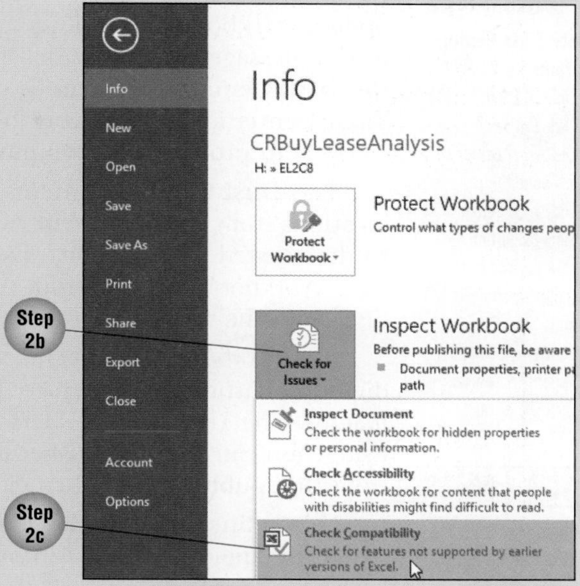

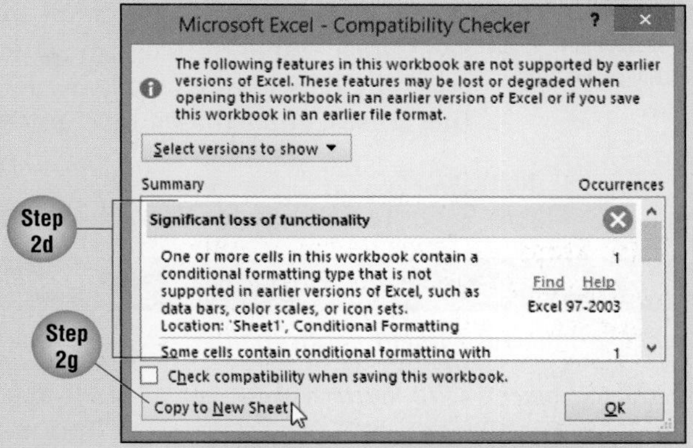

1. Open **CRBuyLeaseAnalysis.xlsx**.
2. Run the Compatibility Checker to check the workbook before you save in an earlier Excel file format by completing the following steps:
   a. Click the FILE tab.
   b. Click the Check for Issues button in the Info backstage area.
   c. Click *Check Compatibility* at the drop-down list.
   d. At the Microsoft Excel - Compatibility Checker dialog box, read the information in the *Summary* box in the *Significant loss of functionality* section.
   e. Scroll down and read the information displayed in the *Minor loss of fidelity* section.
   f. Scroll back up to the top of the *Summary* box.
   g. Click the Copy to New Sheet button.
3. At the Compatibility Report sheet, read the information in the box with the hyperlink Sheet1'!D13:D16 and then click the hyperlink. Sheet1 becomes active with the cells selected that have conditional formatting applied that is not supported in the earlier version of Excel (D13:D16).
4. Make the Compatibility Report sheet active and then print the worksheet with the worksheet scaled to *Fit Sheet on One Page*.

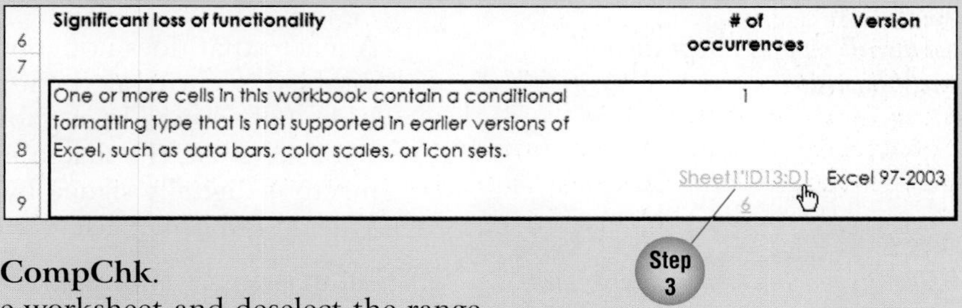

5. Save the revised workbook and name it **EL2-C8-P3-CRBuyLeaseAnalysisCompChk**.
6. Make Sheet1 the active worksheet and deselect the range.
7. To save the workbook in an earlier version of Excel, click the FILE tab, click the *Export* option, click *Change File Type*, click *Excel 97-2003 Workbook (*.xls)* in the *Workbook File Types* section, and then click the Save As button. Click the Save button at the Save As dialog box to accept the default file name. Click the Continue button at the Compatibility Checker dialog box.
8. Close **EL2-C8-P3-CRBuyLeaseAnalysisCompChk.xls**.

Viewing Trust Center Settings for Excel

Quick Steps

View Trust Center Options
1. Click FILE tab.
2. Click *Options*.
3. Click *Trust Center* in left pane.
4. Click Trust Center Settings button.
5. Click desired trust center category in left pane.
6. View and/or modify options as desired.
7. Click OK twice.

HINT

Changing the macro security setting in Excel does not affect the macro security setting in other Microsoft programs such as Word or Access.

In Excel, the Trust Center is responsible for blocking unsafe content when you open a workbook. You may recall the security warning that sometimes appears in the message bar when you open a workbook—this warning is generated by the Trust Center, and it can be closed by clicking the Enable Content button. The Trust Center also allows you to view and/or modify the security options that are in place to protect your computer from malicious content.

The Trust Center maintains a Trusted Locations list that keeps track of locations from which content can be considered trusted. When you add a location to the Trusted Locations list, Excel will treat any files opened from that location as safe. Workbooks opened from trusted locations do not cause a security warning to display in the message bar and none of their content will be blocked.

If a workbook contains macros, the Trust Center checks for a valid and current digital signature from an entity in the Trusted Publishers list before it enables the macros. The Trusted Publishers list is maintained by you on the computer you are using. You can add a publisher to the Trusted Publishers list by enabling content from that publisher and then clicking the *Trust all content from this publisher* option.

Depending on the active macro security setting, if the Trust Center cannot match the digital signature information with an entity in the Trusted Publishers list or the macro does not contain a digital signature, a security warning displays in the message bar. The default macro security setting is *Disable all macros with notification*. Table 8.2 describes the four options for macro security. In some cases, you may decide to change the default macro security setting, and you can do so at the Trust Center dialog box. You will explore the Trust Center in Project 3d.

Table 8.2 Macro Security Settings for Workbooks Not Opened from a Trusted Location

Macro Setting	*Description*
Disable all macros without notification	All macros are disabled; security alerts will not appear.
Disable all macros with notification	All macros are disabled; security alerts appear with the option to enable content if you trust the source of the file. This is the default setting.
Disable all macros except digitally signed macros	A macro that does not contain a digital signature is disabled; security alerts do not appear. If the macro is digitally signed by a publisher in your Trusted Publishers list, the macro is allowed to run. If the macro is digitally signed by a publisher not in your Trusted Publishers list, a security alert appears.
Enable all macros (not recommended, potentially dangerous code can run)	All macros are allowed; security alerts do not appear.

Project 3d Exploring Trust Center Settings Part 4 of 4

1. To explore current settings in the Trust Center, complete the following steps:
   a. Click the FILE tab and then click *Options*.
   b. Click *Trust Center* in the left pane of the Excel Options dialog box.
   c. Click the Trust Center Settings button in the *Microsoft Excel Trust Center* section.

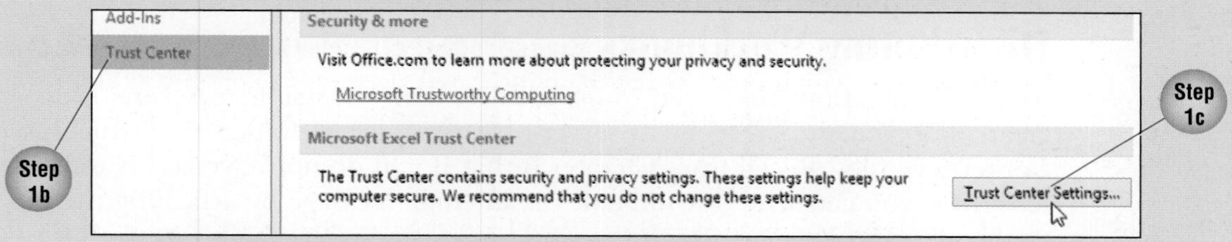

   d. At the Trust Center dialog box, click *Macro Settings* in the left pane.
   e. Review the options in the *Macro Settings* section. Note which option is active on the computer you are using. The default option is *Disable all macros with notification*. ***Note: The security setting on the computer you are using may be different than the default option. Do not change the security setting without your instructor's permission.***
   f. Click *Trusted Publishers* in the left pane. If any publishers have been added to the list on the computer you are using, their names will be shown in the list box. If the list box is empty, no trusted publishers have been added.

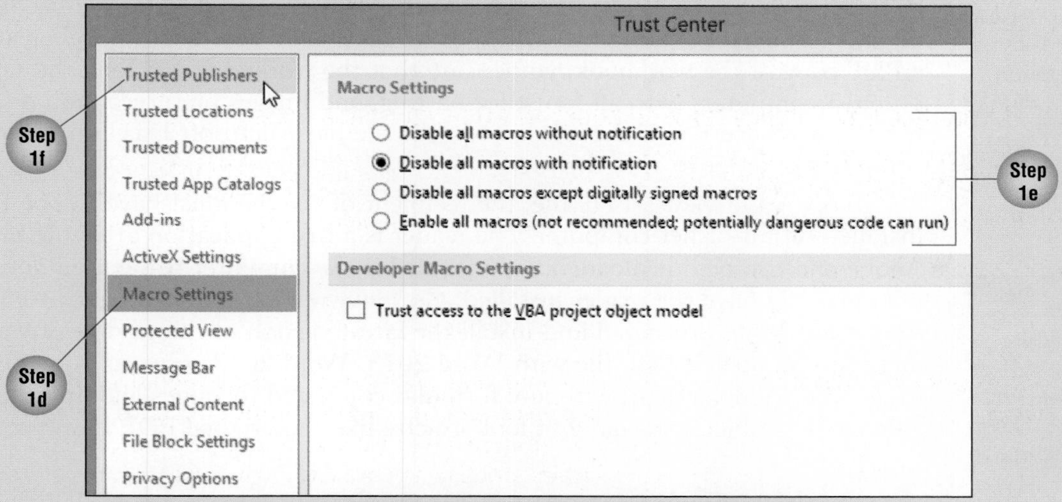

   g. Click *Trusted Locations* in the left pane. Review the paths and descriptions of any folders in the trusted locations list. By default, Excel adds the folder created upon installation that contains the templates provided by Microsoft. Additional folders that have been added by a system administrator or network administrator may also appear.
   h. Click OK to close the Trust Center dialog box.
2. Click OK to close the Excel Options dialog box.

Project 4 Distributing Workbooks — 3 Parts

You will publish a workbook as a PDF document, and an XPS document. You will also publish a worksheet as a web page.

Distributing Workbooks

Many organizations that need to make documents accessible to several users create a document management server or network share folder from which users can retrieve files. Recall from Chapter 6 that if you do not have access to these resources, you can send a workbook via an email message by attaching the file to the message. You can attach the workbook using your email program's file attachment feature or you can initiate the email attachment feature directly from Excel.

A popular method of distributing documents that travel over the Internet is to publish the workbook as a PDF or XPS document. A workbook can also be published as a web page to make the content available on the Internet.

Publishing a Workbook as a PDF Document

Quick Steps

Publish a Workbook as a PDF Document
1. Open workbook.
2. Click FILE tab.
3. Click *Export*.
4. Click Create PDF/XPS button.
5. Click Publish button.

HINT

You can publish a multi-sheet workbook as a multi-page PDF document by clicking the Options button in the Publish as PDF or XPS dialog box and then clicking *Entire workbook* in the *Publish what* section of the Options dialog box.

A PDF document is a workbook saved in a fixed-layout format known as ***portable document format***. The PDF standard was developed by Adobe and has become a popular choice for sharing files with people outside an organization. By creating a PDF copy of the workbook, you ensure that the workbook will look the same on most computers with all fonts, formatting, and images preserved. You do not need to be concerned if the recipient of the file has Microsoft Excel on his or her computer in order to read the file.

To open and view a PDF file, the recipient of the file must have Adobe Reader installed on his or her computer. The reader is a free application available from Adobe and can be downloaded and installed if the computer being used does not currently have the reader installed. Go to www.adobe.com and click Get Adobe Reader to download and install the latest version of the reader software. You can also open a PDF file with Word 2013. Word 2013 converts your PDF to an editable document, with any formulas converted to values and any charts converted to objects. It may not look exactly like the original PDF, however.

Project 4a Publishing a Workbook as a PDF Document — Part 1 of 3

1. Open **EL2-C8-P3-CRPilotPrjRpt.xlsx**.
2. Publish the workbook as a PDF document by completing the following steps:
   a. Click the FILE tab.
   b. Click the *Export* option.
   c. With *Create PDF/XPS Document* selected in the Export backstage area, click the Create PDF/XPS button.

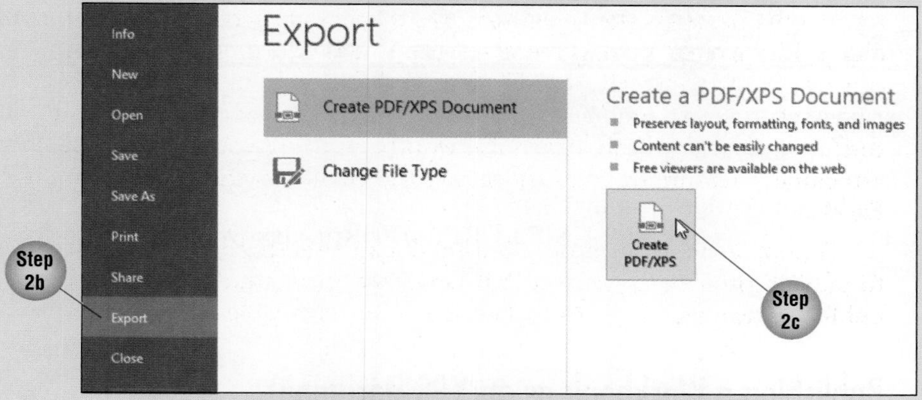

   d. Insert a check mark in the *Open file after publishing* check box at the bottom of the Publish as PDF or XPS dialog box.
   e. With *PDF(*.pdf)* in the *Save as type* text box and *EL2-C8-P3-CRPilotPrjRpt.pdf* in the *File name* text box, click the Publish button.

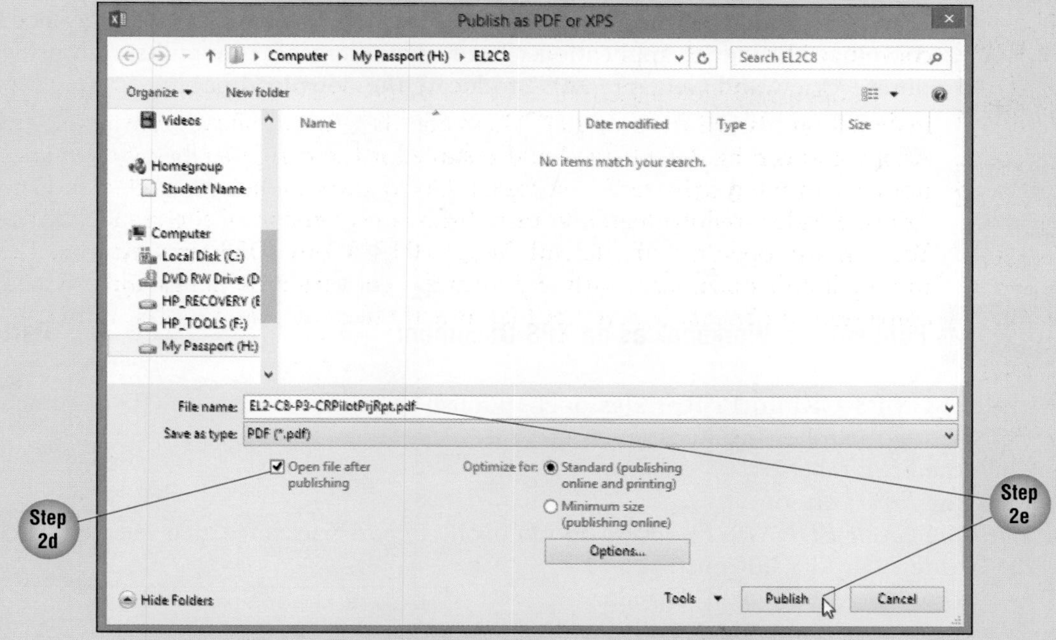

3. An Adobe Reader (or Adobe Acrobat) application window opens with the published workbook displayed. Notice that the workbook has retained all of the Excel formatting and other visual features.

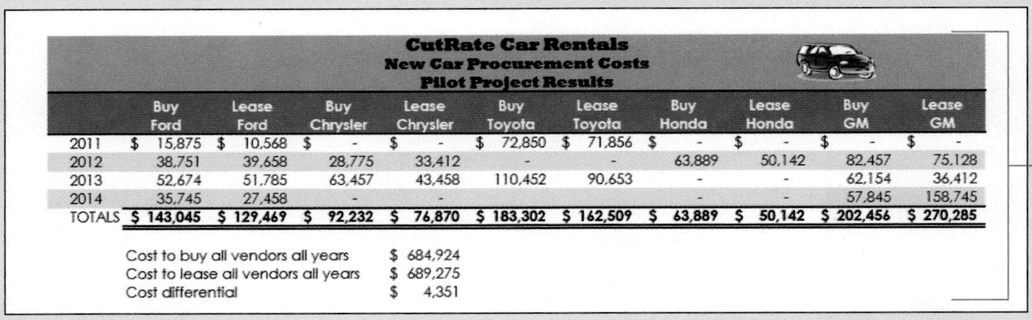

CutRate Car Rentals
New Car Procurement Costs
Pilot Project Results

	Buy Ford	Lease Ford	Buy Chrysler	Lease Chrysler	Buy Toyota	Lease Toyota	Buy Honda	Lease Honda	Buy GM	Lease GM
2011	$ 15,875	$ 10,568	$ -	$ -	$ 72,850	$ 71,856	$ -	$ -	$ -	$ -
2012	38,751	39,658	28,775	33,412	-	-	63,889	50,142	82,457	75,128
2013	52,674	51,785	63,457	43,458	110,452	90,653	-	-	62,154	36,412
2014	35,745	27,458	-	-			-	-	57,845	158,745
TOTALS	$ 143,045	$ 129,469	$ 92,232	$ 76,870	$ 183,302	$ 162,509	$ 63,889	$ 50,142	$ 202,456	$ 270,285

Cost to buy all vendors all years	$ 684,924
Cost to lease all vendors all years	$ 689,275
Cost differential	$ 4,351

Step 3

4. Close the Adobe application window.
5. Return to Excel and leave the **EL2-C8-P3-CRPilotPrjRpt.xlsx** workbook open for the next project.

Publishing a Workbook as an XPS Document

Quick Steps

Publish a Workbook as an XPS Document

1. Open workbook.
2. Click FILE tab.
3. Click *Export*.
4. Click Create PDF/XPS button.
5. Click Save as type option box.
6. Click *XPS Document (*.xps)*.
7. Click Publish button.

XPS stands for ***XML paper specification***, which is another fixed-layout format with all of the same advantages as a PDF document. XPS was developed by Microsoft with the Office 2007 suite. Similar to PDF files, which require Adobe Reader to view documents, XPS documents require the XPS viewer. The viewer is provided by Microsoft and is packaged with Windows 8, Windows 7, and Windows Vista. However, to view an XPS document using Windows XP, you may need to download the viewer application. Go to www.microsoft.com and search using the phrase "View and Generate XPS" to locate the download page.

Project 4b Publishing a Workbook as an XPS Document — Part 2 of 3

1. With **EL2-C8-P3-CRPilotPrjRpt.xlsx** open, publish the workbook as an XPS document by completing the following steps:
   a. Click the FILE tab.
   b. Click the *Export* option.
   c. With the *Create PDF/XPS Document* option in the Export backstage area selected, click the Create PDF/XPS button.
   d. At the Publish as PDF or XPS dialog box, click the *Save as type* option box located below the *File name* text box and then click *XPS Document (*.xps)* at the drop-down list.

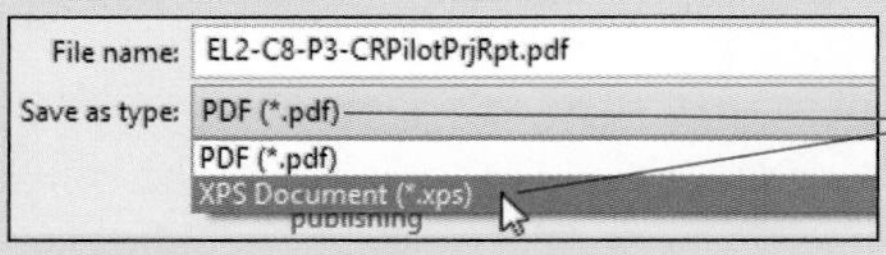

Step 1d

e. With a check mark in the *Open file after publishing* check box and *EL2-C8-P3-CRPilotPrjRpt.xps* in the *File name* text box, click the Publish button.

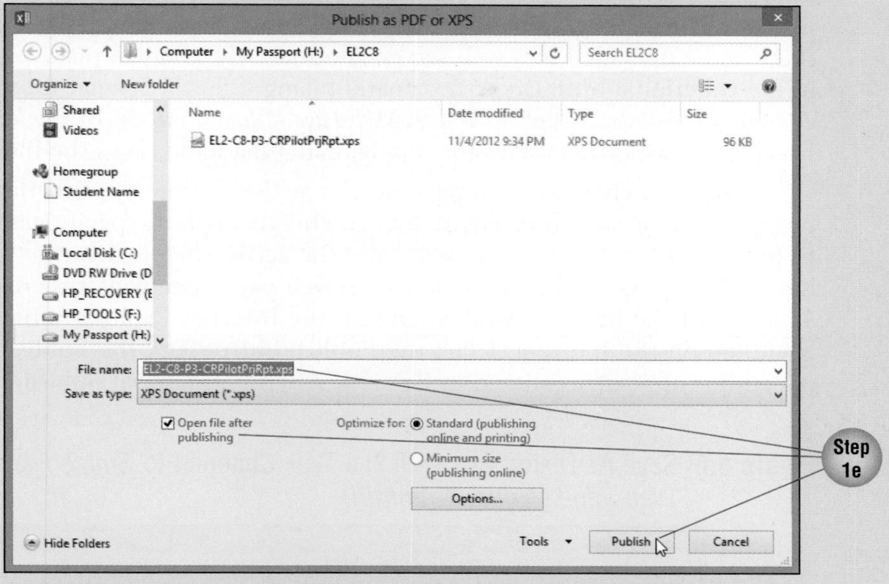

2. The XPS Viewer application window opens with the published worksheet displayed. Notice that similar to the PDF document format, the XPS document format has retained all of the Excel formatting and other visual features.
3. Close the XPS Viewer application window.

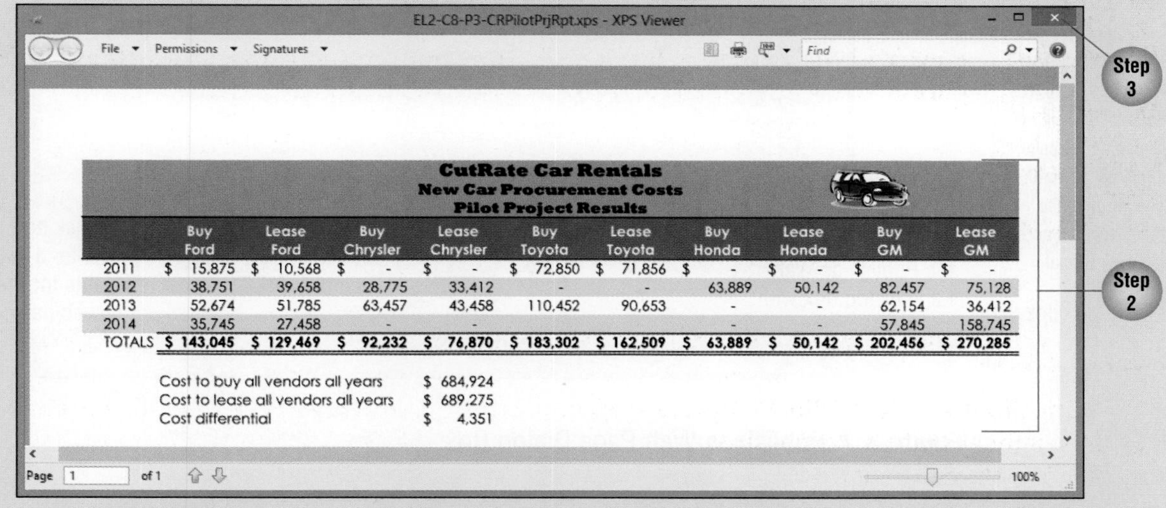

4. Leave **EL2-C8-P3-CRPilotPrjRpt.xlsx** open for the next project.

Publishing a Worksheet as a Web Page

Quick Steps

Publish a Worksheet as a Web Page

1. Open workbook.
2. Click FILE tab.
3. Click *Export.*
4. Click *Change File Types.*
5. Click *Save as Another File Type* option.
6. Click Save As button.
7. Click *Save as type* option box.
8. Click *Single File Web Page (*.mht; *.mhtml).*
9. If necessary, change the drive, folder, and/or file name.
10. Click Change Title button, type title, and then click OK.
11. Click Publish button.
12. Set desired options.
13. Click Publish.

HINT

Not all browsers support the single file (.mht) web page format. If you or others will not be viewing the page in Internet Explorer, consider using the traditional .htm or .html web page format.

You can publish a worksheet as a single web page by changing the *Save as type* option to *Single File Web Page (*.mht; *.mhtml).* In this format, all of the data in the worksheet, such as graphics and other supplemental data, is saved in a single file that can be uploaded to a web server. Alternatively, you can publish the worksheet in the traditional html (hypertext markup language) file format for web pages by changing the *Save as type* option to *Web Page (*.htm; *.html).* In the *html* option, Excel creates additional files for supplemental data and saves the files in a subfolder.

When you choose a web page option at the *Save as type* list, the Save As dialog box changes, as shown in Figure 8.6. At this dialog box, specify whether you want to publish the entire workbook or only the active sheet. Click the Change Title button if you want to add a title to the web page. The page title displays in the Title bar of the browser window and on the Internet Explorer tab when the page is viewed on the Internet. Click the Publish button and the Publish as Web Page dialog box appears as shown in Figure 8.7, with additional publishing options.

Figure 8.6 Save As Dialog Box with File Type Changed to *Single File Web Page (*.mht; *.mhtml)*

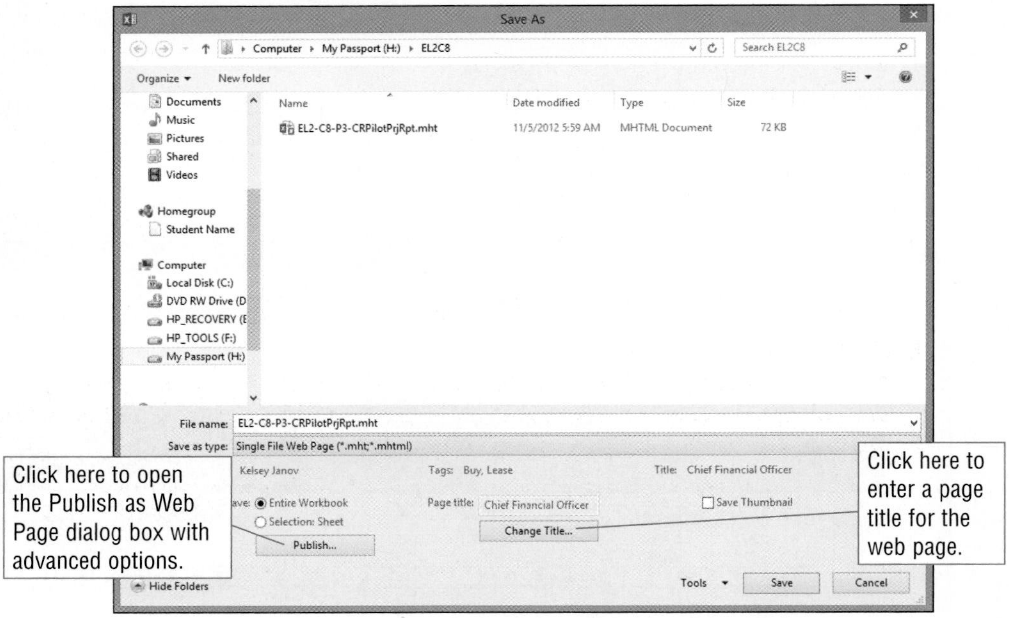

Figure 8.7 Publish as Web Page Dialog Box

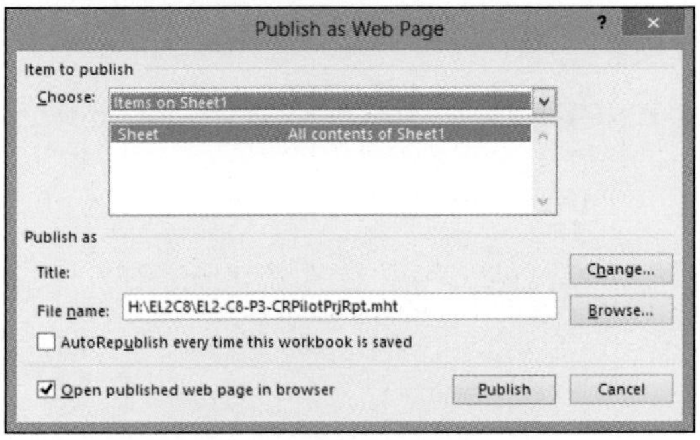

Project 4c Publishing a Worksheet as a Web Page Part 3 of 3

1. With **EL2-C8-P3-CRPilotPrjRpt.xlsx** open, publish the worksheet as a single file web page by completing the following steps:
   a. Click the FILE tab.
   b. Click the *Export* option.
   c. Click the *Change File Type* option and then click the *Save as Another File Type* option in the Other File Types section.
   d. Click the Save As button.
   e. Click the *Save as type* option box and then click *Single File Web Page (*.mht; *.mhtml)* at the pop-up list.
   f. Click the Change Title button.

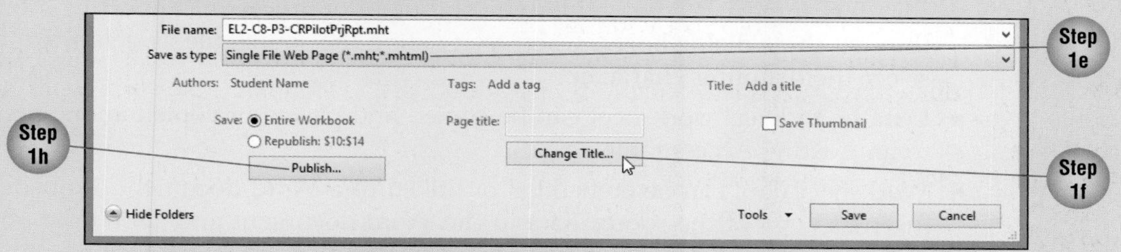

   g. At the Enter Text dialog box, type **Cut Rate Car Rentals Pilot Project Report** in the *Page title* text box and then click OK.

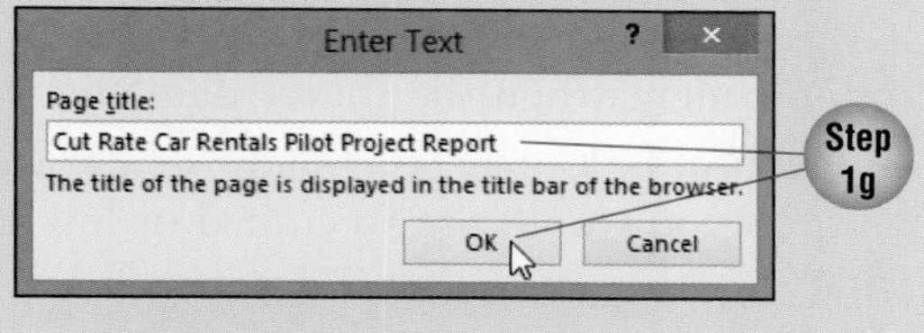

   h. Click the Publish button.
   i. At the Publish as Web Page dialog box, click the *Open published web page in browser* check box to insert a check mark and then click the Publish button. (This automatically displays the worksheet in your default web browser.)

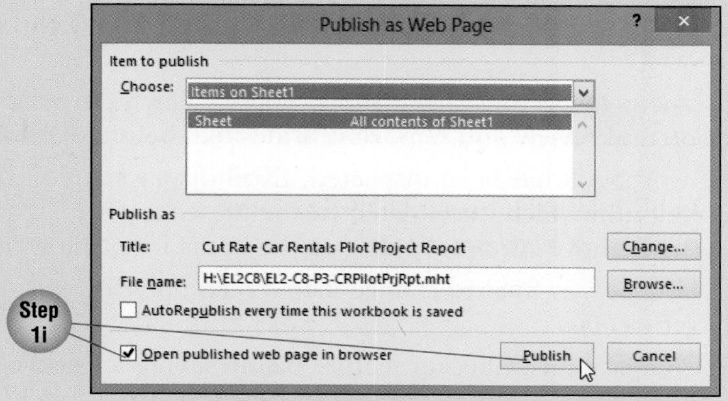

2. After viewing the web page, close the browser window.
3. Save and close **EL2-C8-P3-CRPilotPrjRpt.xlsx**.

Chapter Summary

- The Get External Data group in the DATA tab contains buttons to use for importing data into an Excel worksheet from Access, the Web, or a text file.
- Only one Access table can be imported at a time.
- Tables in a website can be imported to Excel using the New Web Query dialog box.
- Text files are often used to exchange data between different programs, since the file format is recognized by nearly all applications.
- Text files generally separate data between fields with either a tab character or a comma.
- The Text Import Wizard guides you through the process of importing a text file through three dialog boxes, where you define the source file as delimited and select the delimiter character.
- Data in an Excel worksheet can be copied and pasted or copied and appended to an existing Access table.
- Worksheet data can be embedded or linked to a Word document. Embedding inserts a copy of the source data in the Word document and allows the object to be edited using Excel's tools within the Word environment, whereas linking the object inserts a shortcut to the Excel workbook from which the source data is retrieved.
- Breaking a link involves removing the connection between the source program and destination program so that the object is no longer updated in the destination document when the source data changes.
- You can embed and link objects to slides in a PowerPoint presentation using the same techniques you would use to embed or link cells to a Word document.
- In Office 2013, the charting tools are fully integrated. A chart copied and pasted from Excel to a PowerPoint presentation or Word document is embedded by default.
- Save a worksheet as a text file by changing the file type at the Export backstage area.
- Excel includes several text file formats to accommodate differences across operating systems, which configure text files using various end of line character codes.
- The Document Inspector feature allows you to search for personal or hidden information and review and remove it, if desired, before distributing a file.
- Once the workbook has been inspected, Excel displays a red exclamation mark in each section in which Excel detected the presence of the requested item. Clicking the Remove All button deletes the items from the workbook.
- Mark a workbook as final to change it to a read-only file with the status property set to *Final*.
- Run the Compatibility Checker feature before saving a workbook in an earlier version of Excel to determine if a loss of functionality or fidelity will occur.
- The results of the compatibility check can be copied to a new worksheet for easy referencing and documentation purposes.

- A workbook can be saved in PDF or XPS format, which are fixed-layout formats that preserve all of the Excel formatting and layout features.
- Adobe Reader or Word 2013 is required to open and view a workbook saved as a PDF file.
- The XPS Viewer is included automatically with Windows Vista and Windows 7 or Windows 8.
- If necessary, Adobe Reader or the XPS Viewer application can be downloaded from the Adobe or Microsoft websites. Both readers are free.
- Open the Save As dialog box and change the *Save as type* option to either *Single File Web Page* or *Web Page* to publish the current worksheet as a web page.

Commands Review

FEATURE	RIBBON TAB, GROUP/OPTION	BUTTON, OPTION	KEYBOARD SHORTCUT
Compatibility Checker	FILE, *Info*		
copy	HOME, Clipboard		Ctrl + C
Document Inspector	FILE, *Info*		
import from Access table	DATA, Get External Data		
import from text file	DATA, Get External Data		
import from web page	DATA, Get External Data		
mark workbook as final	FILE, *Info*		
Paste Special	HOME, Clipboard	, *Paste Special*	Ctrl + Alt + V
save as	FILE, *Save As*		F12
save as PDF/XPS	FILE, *Export* OR FILE, *Save As*		
save as web page	FILE, *Export* OR *FILE, Save As*		F12

Concepts Check Test Your Knowledge

Completion: In the space provided at the right, indicate the correct term, command, or number.

1. This group on the DATA tab contains buttons for importing data from Access. ____________________
2. If the source database used to import data contains more than one table, this dialog box appears after you select the data source to allow you to choose the desired table. ____________________
3. To import tables from a web page, open this dialog box to browse to the website and click arrows next to tables on the page that you want to import. ____________________
4. These are the two commonly used delimiter characters in delimited text file formats. ____________________
5. To add to the bottom of the active Access datasheet cells that have been copied to the Clipboard task pane, click this option at the Paste button drop-down list. ____________________
6. Choosing *Microsoft Excel Worksheet Object* at the Paste Special dialog box in a Word document and then clicking OK inserts the copied cells as this type of object. ____________________
7. If the Excel data you are pasting into a Word document will likely be updated in the future and you will want the Word document to reflect the updated values, paste the data as this type of object. ____________________
8. A chart copied from Excel and pasted to a slide in a PowerPoint presentation is pasted as this type of object by default. ____________________
9. Click this option in the *Other File Types* section of the Export backstage area to select the CSV file format to export the active worksheet as a text file. ____________________
10. This feature scans the open workbook for personal and hidden information and provides you with the opportunity to review and remove the items. ____________________
11. A workbook that has been marked as final is changed to this type of workbook to prevent additions, deletions, and modifications to cells. ____________________
12. Use this feature to check the current workbook for formatting or features that are not available with versions of Excel prior to Excel 2007 and that could cause loss of functionality if saved in the earlier file format. ____________________

13. Save a workbook in either of these fixed-layout formats, which preserve Excel's formatting and layout features while allowing distribution of the file to others who may not have Excel installed on their computers. ______________

14. Click this button in the Save As dialog box once the *Save as type* option has been changed to a web page file format to type a page title. ______________

Skills Check Assess Your Performance

Assessment 1

IMPORT DATA FROM ACCESS AND A TEXT FILE

SNAP Grade It

1. Open **HRS.xlsx**.
2. Save the workbook and name it **EL2-C8-A1-HRS**.
3. Make cell A6 active in the CPIData worksheet. Import the CPI table from the Access database named ***NuTrendsCensus.accdb***.
4. Make the following changes to the worksheet:
   a. Apply the Table Style Medium 15 table style to the imported cells.
   b. Format the values in all columns *except* column A to have one place after the decimal point.
   c. Remove the filter arrows and then center the column headings.
   d. If necessary, adjust the column widths to accommodate the data.
5. Print the CPIData worksheet.
6. Make UIRateMI the active worksheet.
7. Make cell A6 active. Import the comma delimited text file named ***UIRateMI.csv***.
8. Make the following changes to the data:
   a. Change the width of column B to 8 characters.
   b. Change the width of columns C to F to 15 characters.
9. Print the UIRateMI worksheet.
10. Save and then close **EL2-C8-A1-HRS.xlsx**.

Assessment 2

LINK DATA TO A WORD DOCUMENT

1. Open **HROctSalesByDateByRep.xlsx**.
2. Save the workbook and name it **EL2-C8-A2-HROctSalesByDateByRep**.
3. With SalesByDate the active worksheet, link A3:G27 at the end of the Word document named **HROctRpt.docx**.
4. Change the margins in the Word document to *Narrow* (top, bottom, left, and right to 0.5 inch).
5. Use Save As to name the revised Word document **EL2-C8-A2-HROctRpt.docx**.
6. Switch to Excel and then press Esc to remove the scrolling marquee and then deselect the range.
7. Change the value in cell F4 to *525000*.

8. Change the value in cell F5 to *212000*.
9. Save **EL2-C8-A2-HROctSalesByDateByRep.xlsx**.
10. Switch to Word, right-click the linked object, and then click *Update Link* at the shortcut menu.
11. Print the Word document.
12. Break the link in the Word document.
13. Save **EL2-C8-A2-HROctRpt.docx** and then exit Word.
14. Save and then close **EL2-C8-A2-HROctSalesByDateByRep.xlsx**.

Assessment 3

EMBED DATA IN A POWERPOINT PRESENTATION

1. Open **HROctSalesByDateByRep.xlsx**.
2. Save the workbook and name it **EL2-C8-A3-HROctSalesByDateByRep**.
3. Make SalesByRep the active worksheet.
4. Display the worksheet at outline level 2 so that only the sales agent names, sale prices, and commissions display.
5. Create a column chart in a separate sheet to graph the sales commissions earned by each sales agent. You determine an appropriate chart style, title, and other chart elements.
6. Start PowerPoint and open **HROctRpt.pptx**.
7. Save the presentation with Save As and name it **EL2-C8-A3-HROctRpt**.
8. Embed the chart created in Step 5 on Slide 3 of the presentation. Resize the chart if necessary.
9. Print the presentation as Handouts with three slides per page.
10. Save **EL2-C8-A3-HROctRpt.pptx** and then exit PowerPoint.
11. Save and then close **EL2-C8-A3-HROctSalesByDateByRep.xlsx**.

Assessment 4

EXPORT DATA AS A TEXT FILE

1. Open **HROctSalesByDateByRep.xlsx**.
2. With SalesByDate the active worksheet, save the worksheet as a CSV (Comma delimited) (*.csv) text file named **EL2-C8-A4-HROctSalesByDateByRep**.
3. Close **EL2-C8-A4-HROctSalesByDateByRep.csv**. Click Don't Save when prompted to save changes.
4. Start Notepad and open **EL2-C8-A4-HROctSalesByDateByRep.csv**.
5. Delete the first two lines at the beginning of the file that contain the title text from the top of the worksheet. The first words in the file that should be deleted begin the heading *Hillsdale Realtors* and end with *Commission.*
6. Delete the bottom row in the file that contains the commas and the total commission value.
7. Print the document.
8. Save **EL2-C8-A4-HROctSalesByDateByRep.csv** and then exit Notepad.

Assessment 5

PREPARE A WORKBOOK FOR DISTRIBUTION

1. Open **HR2015Sales.xlsx**.
2. Save the workbook and name it **EL2-C8-A5-HR2015Sales**.
3. Display the Info backstage area and show all properties. Read the information in the *Author, Title,* and *Subject* property text boxes. Open the Properties dialog box (by clicking *Advanced Properties* from the Properties button drop-down list) and read the information in the Statistics and Custom tabs. Close the Properties dialog box. Click the Back button and click the REVIEW tab.
4. Turn on the display of all comments and then read the comments that appear.
5. Change to Page Layout view and check for a header or footer in the workbook.
6. Use the Document Inspector feature to check the workbook for private and hidden information. Leave all options selected at the Document Inspector dialog box.
7. Remove all items that display with red exclamation marks and then close the dialog box.
8. Click the REVIEW tab, turn off the Show All Comments feature, and switch to Normal view.
9. Click the FILE tab. With the Info backstage area displayed showing all properties, paste a screen image into a new Word document using the Print Screen with Paste or the Screenshot feature. Type your name a few lines below the screen image. Print the Word document and then exit Word without saving.
10. Run the Compatibility Feature to check for loss of functionality or fidelity in the workbook if saved in an earlier Excel version. Save the Summary report to a new sheet and then print the Compatibility Report sheet on one page.
11. Mark the workbook as final.
12. Close **EL2-C8-A5-HR2015Sales.xlsx**.

Assessment 6

PREPARE AND DISTRIBUTE A WORKBOOK

1. Open **HR2015Sales.xlsx**.
2. Save the workbook and name it **EL2-C8-A6-HR2015Sales**.
3. Use the Document Inspector feature to remove comments and annotations.
4. Publish the workbook as a PDF file named **EL2-C8-A6-HR2015Sales.pdf**.
5. Publish the worksheet as a single file web page named **EL2-C8-A6-HR2015Sales.mht** with a page title *Hillsdale Realtors*.
6. Save and close **EL2-C8-A6-HR2015Sales.xlsx**.
7. Display the contents of the EL2C8 folder on your storage medium. Make sure the folder is displaying file extensions. Paste a screen image of the folder's contents into a new Word document using the Print Screen with Paste or the Screenshot feature. Type your name a few lines below the screen image. Print the Word document and then exit Word without saving. Close the Computer or Documents window.

Visual Benchmark Demonstrate Your Proficiency

IMPORT, ANALYZE, AND EXPORT POPULATION DATA

1. Look at the data in the worksheet shown in Figure 8.8. Create this worksheet by importing the PopByState table from the Access database named ***NuTrendsCensus.accdb*** into a new worksheet. Once imported, the rows and columns included in the database but not shown in the figure were deleted and the filter arrows removed. The Table Style Light 2 style has been applied to the worksheet. Add the title rows at the top of the imported data and change the title in cell B4 as shown. Use your best judgment to match other formatting characteristics, such as column width, row height, number formatting, alignment, and fill color.
2. Rename the worksheet *PopulationTable* and then print it.
3. Select A4:B19 and create the chart shown in Figure 8.9 in a new sheet named *PopulationChart*. The chart has the Style 12 style applied. The *Rounded Rectangle* in the Insert Shapes group on the CHART TOOLS FORMAT tab was used to insert the source information. Use the Shape Effects button in the Shape Styles group to apply the shadow. Use your best judgment to match the other chart options and formatting with the chart shown.
4. Save the workbook and name it **EL2-C8-VB-PBMPopData**.
5. Start Microsoft Word and then open **PBMReport.docx**. Rename the workbook **EL2-C8-VB-PBMReport**. Change *Student Name* on page 1 to your name. Copy and paste the Excel chart, positioning the chart between the last two paragraphs on page 2 of the document. Make any formatting adjustments to the chart you think are necessary once the chart has been inserted. Save, print, and then close **EL2-C8-VB-PBMReport.docx**.
6. Close **EL2-C8-VB-PBMPopData.xlsx**.

Figure 8.8 Visual Benchmark PopulationTable Worksheet

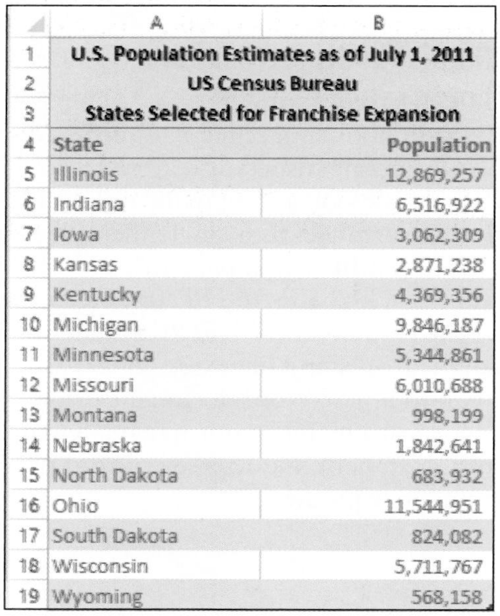

	A	B
1	**U.S. Population Estimates as of July 1, 2011**	
2	**US Census Bureau**	
3	**States Selected for Franchise Expansion**	
4	State	Population
5	Illinois	12,869,257
6	Indiana	6,516,922
7	Iowa	3,062,309
8	Kansas	2,871,238
9	Kentucky	4,369,356
10	Michigan	9,846,187
11	Minnesota	5,344,861
12	Missouri	6,010,688
13	Montana	998,199
14	Nebraska	1,842,641
15	North Dakota	683,932
16	Ohio	11,544,951
17	South Dakota	824,082
18	Wisconsin	5,711,767
19	Wyoming	568,158

Figure 8.9 Visual Benchmark PopulationChart Chart

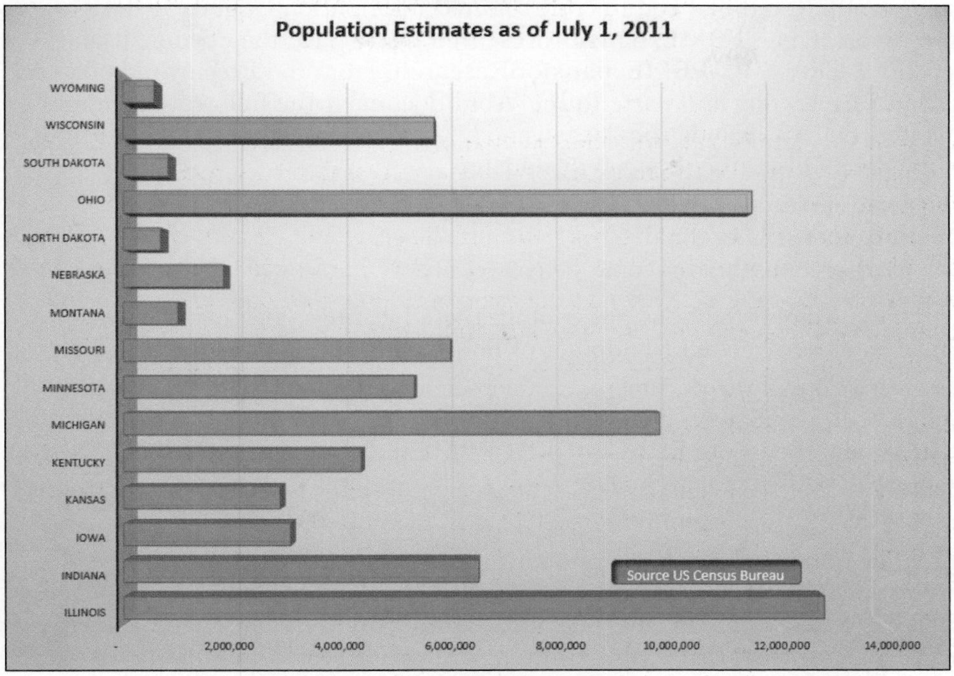

Case Study Apply Your Skills

Part 1

Yolanda Robertson of NuTrends Market Research would like new research data from the US Census Bureau for her Pizza by Mario franchise expansion project. The franchise expansion is planned for the states of Illinois, Indiana, and Kentucky. Start a new workbook and set up three worksheets named using the state names. In each sheet, using the New Web Query feature, display the web page http://quickfacts.census.gov/qfd/ and import the People Quickfacts table for the state. Once the data is imported, delete column A, which is the definitions information. Add an appropriate title, merged and centered above the imported data, and apply formatting enhancements to improve the appearance of the column headings. Save the workbook and name it **EL2-C8-CS-P1-PBMResearch**. Print all three worksheets.

Part 2

To prepare for an upcoming meeting with Mario and Nicola Carlucci of Pizza by Mario, Yolanda would like you to copy selected information from each state to a Word report. Open **PBMExpansionResearch.docx**. Save the document and name it **EL2-C8-CS-P2-PBMExpansionResearch**. From the Excel workbook you created in Part 1, copy and paste to the Word document the following data for each state. (Do not include the data in the *USA* column.) Do not embed or link, since the data will not be changed or updated.

Households
Persons per household
Median household income

If the data you imported does not contain these headings, locate and copy information closely related to number of households and income for the state.

At the bottom of the document, create a reference for the data from the US Census Bureau. Check with your instructor for the preferred format for the reference. Save, print, and then close **EL2-C8-CS-P2-PBMExpansionResearch.docx**. Close **EL2-C8-CS-P1-PBMResearch.xlsx**.

Part 3

Help

Yolanda has noticed that when she opens the workbook created in Part 1, a message appears in the message bar that says *Data connections have been disabled*. Yolanda has asked what this message means and wonders what circumstances are acceptable to click the Enable Content button. Research in Help how to manage connections to external data using the Workbook Connections dialog box. Since the data that was imported does not need to be refreshed in the future, you decide to remove the connections so that Yolanda does not see the security message in the future. Open **EL2-C8-CS-P1-PBMResearch.xlsx** and click the Enable Content button that appears in the message bar. Open the Workbook Connections dialog box and using the information you learned in Help, remove all of the connections. Save the revised workbook as **EL2-C8-CS-P3-PBMResearch** and then close the workbook.

Compose a memo to Yolanda using Microsoft Word that provides a brief explanation of why the security warning message about data connections appears when a workbook is opened that contains external content. Base the memo on the information you learned in Help, making sure that you compose the explanation using your own words. Explain that you have created a new copy of the workbook with the connections removed. Save the Word memo and name it **EL2-C8-CS-P3-DataConnectionsMemo**. Print and then close **EL2-C8-CS-P3-DataConnectionsMemo.docx** and then exit Word.

Part 4

Help

WWW

Yolanda noticed that you can save a workbook as a web page (*.htm,*.html). Research in Excel Help the different options in the Browser View Options dialog box. Next, search the Internet for at least two web-hosting providers. Using Microsoft Word, compose a memo to Yolanda that briefly explains the options in the Browser View Options dialog box in Excel, making sure you compose the explanation using your own words. Include in the memo the URLs of the two web-hosting providers you visited and add your recommendation for the provider you want to use. Save the memo and name it **EL2-C8-CS-P4-WebMemo**. Print and then close **EL2-C8-CS-P4-WebMemo.docx** and then exit Word.

UNIT 2

MICROSOFT® EXCEL® Performance Assessment

Excel
EL2U2

Note: Before beginning unit assessments, copy to your storage medium the EL2U2 subfolder from the EL2 folder on the CD that accompanies this textbook and then make EL2U2 the active folder.

Assessing Proficiency

In this unit, you learned to use features in Excel that facilitate performing what-if analysis, identifying relationships between worksheet formulas, collaborating with others by sharing and protecting workbooks, and automating repetitive tasks using macros. You also learned how to customize the Excel environment to suit your preferences and to integrate Excel data by importing from and exporting to external resources. Finally, you learned how to prepare and distribute a workbook to others by removing items that are private or confidential, marking the workbook as final, checking for features incompatible with earlier versions of Excel, and saving and sending a worksheet in various formats.

Assessment 1 Use Goal Seek and Scenario Manager to Calculate Investment Proposals

1. Open **HillsInvtPlan.xlsx**.
2. Save the workbook and name it **EL2-U2-A1-HillsInvtPlan**.
3. Use Goal Seek to find the monthly contribution amount the client must make to increase the projected value of the plan to $65,000 at the end of the term. Accept the solution Goal Seek calculates.
4. Assign the range name *AvgReturn* to cell E8.
5. Create three scenarios for changing cell E8 as follows:

Scenario name	*Interest rate*
Moderate	5.5%
Conservative	4.0%
Aggressive	12.5%

6. Apply the Aggressive scenario and then print the worksheet.
7. Change the Moderate scenario's interest rate to 8.0% and then apply the scenario.
8. Create and then print a scenario summary report.
9. Save and then close **EL2-U2-A1-HillsInvtPlan.xlsx**.

Assessment 2 Calculate Investment Outcomes for a Portfolio Using a Two-Variable Data Table

1. Open **HillsResearchInvtTbl.xlsx**.
2. Save the workbook and name it **EL2-U2-A2-HillsResearchInvtTbl**.
3. Create a two-variable data table that calculates the projected value of the investment plan at the end of the term for each monthly contribution payment and at each interest rate in the range A11:G20.
4. Apply comma formatting to the projected values in the table and adjust the column widths as necessary.
5. Make cell E8 active and display precedent arrows.
6. Make cell A11 active and display precedent arrows.
7. Remove the arrows.
8. Save, print, and then close **EL2-U2-A2-HillsResearchInvtTbl.xlsx**.

Assessment 3 Solve an Error and Check for Accuracy in Investment Commission Formulas

1. Open **HillsModPortfolio.xlsx**.
2. Save the workbook and name it **EL2-U2-A3-HillsModPortfolio**.
3. Solve the #VALUE! error in cell E19. Use formula auditing tools to help find the source cell containing the invalid entry.
4. Check the logic accuracy of the formula in cell E19 by creating proof formulas below the worksheet as follows:
   a. In row 21, calculate the amount from the customer's deposit that would be deposited into each of the six funds based on the percentages in column B. For example, in cell B21, create a formula to multiply the customer's deposit in cell B19 ($5,000.00) by the percentage recommended for investment in the DW Bond fund in cell B5 (40%). Create similar formulas for the remaining funds in C21:G21.
   b. In row 22, multiply the amount deposited to each fund by the fund's commission rate. For example, in cell B22, create a formula to multiply the value in cell B21 ($2,000.00) by the commission rate paid by the DW Bond fund in cell B17 (1.15%). Create similar formulas for the remaining funds in C22:G22.
   c. In cell B23, use the SUM function to calculate the total of the commissions for the six funds in B22:G22.
   d. Add appropriate labels next to the values created in rows 21 through 23.
5. Save, print, and then close **EL2-U2-A3-HillsModPortfolio.xlsx**.

Assessment 4 Document and Share a Workbook and Manage Changes in an Investment Portfolio Worksheet

1. Open **EL2-U2-A3-HillsModPortfolio.xlsx**.
2. Save the workbook and name it **EL2-U2-A4-HillsModPortfolio**.
3. Type the following data into the workbook properties. ***Note: If any of the properties currently contains text, replace it with the entries indicated below.***

Author	Logan Whitmore
Title	Recommended Moderate Portfolio
Comments	Proposed moderate fund
Subject	Moderate Investment Allocation

4. In a new Word document, paste a screenshot of the Info backstage area with all properties visible. Type your name a few lines below the image, print the document, and then close Word without saving.
5. Click the REVIEW tab and then share the workbook.
6. Change the user name to *Carey Winters* and then edit the cells as follows:
   B7: from *10%* to *15%*
   B8: from *15%* to *10%*
7. Save **EL2-U2-A4-HillsModPortfolio.xlsx**.
8. Change the user name to *Jodi VanKemenade* and then edit the cells as follows:
   D17: from *2.15%* to *2.32%*
   E17: from *2.35%* to *2.19%*
9. Save **EL2-U2-A4-HillsModPortfolio.xlsx**.
10. Create and then print a History sheet. ***Note: If you are to submit your assignment electronically, create a copy of the History worksheet in a new workbook named EL2-U2-A4-HillsModPortfolioHistory.***
11. Change the user name back to the original name on the computer you are using.
12. Accept and reject changes made to the cells in the ModeratePortfolio worksheet as follows:
    B7: Reject
    B8: Reject
    D17: Accept
    E17: Reject
13. Save, print, and then close **EL2-U2-A4-HillsModPortfolio.xlsx**.

Assessment 5 Insert Comments and Protect a Confidential Investment Portfolio Workbook

1. Open **EL2-U2-A4-HillsModPortfolio.xlsx**.
2. Save the workbook and name it **EL2-U2-A5-HillsModPortfolio.xlsx**.
3. Remove the shared access to the workbook.
4. Hide rows 20 through 23.
5. Make cell B17 the active cell and insert a comment. Type **Commission rate to be renegotiated in 2015** in the comment box.
6. Copy the comment in cell B17 and paste it to cells D17 and G17. Press the Esc key to remove the scrolling marquee from cell B17.
7. Edit the comment in cell G17 to change the year from *2015* to *2016*.
8. Protect the worksheet to only allow editing in cell B19. Assign the password *eL2-U2* to unprotect the worksheet.
9. Encrypt the workbook with the password *eL2-U2*.
10. Save and close **EL2-U2-A5-HillsModPortfolio.xlsx**.
11. Test the security features added to the workbook by opening **EL2-U2-A5-HillsModPortfolio.xlsx** using the password created in Step 9. Try to change one of the values in the range B5:B10 and in the range B17:G17.
12. Make cell B19 active and then change the value to *10000*.
13. Display all of the comments in the worksheet and then print the worksheet with the comments displayed and with the worksheet scaled to fit on one page.
14. Save and then close **EL2-U2-A5-HillsModPortfolio.xlsx**.

Assessment 6 Automate and Customize an Investment Portfolio Workbook

1. Open **EL2-U2-A5-HillsModPortfolio.xlsx**.
2. Unprotect the worksheet, turn off the display of all comments, and then delete the comments in cells B17, D17, and G17.
3. Display the Custom Views dialog box. When a workbook has been shared, Excel automatically creates a custom view (with the label *Personal View*) for each person who accessed the file and for the original worksheet state before sharing was enabled. Delete all of the custom views in the dialog box and then add a new custom view named *ModeratePortfolioOriginalView*.
4. Create two macros to be stored in the active workbook as follows:
   a. Create a macro named *CustomDisplay* that applies the Metropolitan theme and turns off the display of gridlines and row and column headers in the current worksheet. Assign the macro to the shortcut key Ctrl + Shift + T. Enter an appropriate description that includes your name and the date the macro was created.
   b. Create a macro named *CustomHeader* that prints the text *Private and Confidential* at the left margin in the header. Assign the macro to the shortcut key Ctrl + Shift + H. Enter an appropriate description that includes your name and the date the macro was created.
5. Test the macros by opening **EL2-U2-A1-HillsInvtPlan.xlsx**. Make InvestmentPlanProposal the active worksheet and then run the two macros created in Step 4. View the worksheet in the Print backstage area. Close the Print backstage area and then close **EL2-U2-A1-HillsInvtPlan.xlsx** without saving the changes.
6. Print the VBA program code for the two macros and then close the Microsoft Visual Basic for Applications window and return to Excel.
7. Create a custom view named *ModeratePortfolioTemplateView*.
8. Save the revised workbook as a macro-enabled workbook named **EL2-U2-A6-HillsModPortfolio.xlsm** and remove the password to open the workbook.
9. Print the worksheet.
10. Display the Custom Views dialog box. Paste a screenshot of the worksheet with the Custom Views dialog box open into a new Word document. Type your name a few lines below the image, print the document, and then exit Word without saving.
11. Close the Custom Views dialog box and then close **EL2-U2-A6-HillsModPortfolio.xlsm**.

Assessment 7 Create and Use an Investment Planner Template

1. Open **EL2-U2-A2-HillsResearchInvtTbl.xlsx**.
2. Make the following changes to the worksheet:
   a. Change the label in cell A3 to *Investment Planner*.
   b. Change the font color of cell A11 to white. This will make the cell appear to be empty. (You want to disguise the entry in this cell because you think displaying the value at the top left of the data table will confuse Hillsdale customers.)
   c. Clear the contents of E5:E7.
   d. Protect the worksheet so that editing is allowed only in E5:E7. Assign the password *eL2-U2* to unprotect the worksheet.
3. Save the revised workbook as a template named **HillsInvPlan-StudentName** with your name substituted for *StudentName*.

4. Close **HillsInvPlan-StudentName.xltx**.
5. Start a new workbook based on the **HillsInvPlan-StudentName.xltx** template.
6. Type the following information in the appropriate cells:

Monthly contribution:	-475
Number of years to invest:	5
Forecasted annual interest rate:	4.75%

7. Save the workbook as an Excel workbook named **EL2-U2-A7-HillsInvPlan**.
8. Print and then close **EL2-U2-A7-HillsInvPlan.xlsx**.
9. Copy the template created in this assessment to the EL2U2 folder on your storage medium.

Assessment 8 Export a Chart and Prepare and Distribute an Investment Portfolio Worksheet

1. Open **EL2-U2-A6-HillsModPortfolio.xlsm**. If a security warning appears, enable the content.
2. Start Microsoft PowerPoint 2013 and then open **HillsPortfolios.pptx**.
3. Save the presentation and name it **EL2-U2-A8-HillsPortfolios**.
4. Copy the pie chart from the Excel worksheet to Slide 7 in the PowerPoint presentation.
5. Resize the chart on the slide and edit the legend if necessary to make the chart consistent with the other charts in the presentation.
6. Print the PowerPoint presentation as a handout with nine slides printed horizontally on the page.
7. Save **EL2-U2-A8-HillsPortfolios.pptx** and then exit PowerPoint.
8. Deselect the chart in the Excel worksheet.
9. Inspect the document, leaving all items checked at the Document Inspector dialog box.
10. Remove all items that display with red exclamation marks and then close the dialog box.
11. Change the file type to a workbook with an .xlsx file extension and name it **EL2-U2-A8-HillsModPortfolio**. Click Yes at the message stating that the file cannot be saved with the VB Project. Click OK at the privacy warning message box.
12. Mark the workbook as final. Click OK if the privacy warning message box reappears.
13. Send the workbook to yourself as an XPS document in an email initiated from Excel. Include an appropriate message in the message window, assuming you work for Hillsdale Financial Services and are sending the portfolio file to a potential client. Open the message window from the inbox in your email program and print the message. Close the message window and exit your email program.
14. Display the Info backstage area and make sure all properties are visible. Take a screenshot and paste it into a new Word document. Type your name a few lines below the image, print the document, and then exit Word without saving.
15. Close **EL2-U2-A8-HillsModPortfolio.xlsx**.

Writing Activities

The following activities give you the opportunity to practice your writing skills while demonstrating an understanding of some of the important Excel features you have mastered in this unit. Use appropriate word choices and correct grammar, capitalization, and punctuation when setting up new worksheets. Labels should clearly describe the data that is presented.

Create a Computer Maintenance Template

The Computing Services department of National Online Marketing Inc. wants to create a computer maintenance template for Help Desk employees to complete electronically and save to a document management server. This system will make it easy for a technician to check the status of any employee's computer from any location within the company. Help Desk employees perform the following computer maintenance tasks at each computer twice annually:

- Delete temporary Internet files
- Delete temporary document files that begin with a tilde (~)
- Update hardware drivers
- Reconfirm all serial numbers and asset records
- Have employee change password
- Check that automatic updates for the operating system are active
- Check that automatic updates for virus protection are active
- Confirm that automatic backup to the computing services server is active
- Confirm that the employee is archiving all email messages
- Clean the computer's screen, keyboard, and system unit

In a new workbook, create a template that can be used to complete the maintenance form electronically. The template should include information that identifies the workstation by asset ID number, the department in which the computer is located, the name of the employee using the computer, the name of the technician that performs the maintenance, and the date the maintenance is performed. In addition, include a column next to each task with a drop-down list containing these options: *Completed*, *Not Completed*, and *Not Applicable*. Next to this column, include a column in which the technician can type notes. At the bottom of the template, include a text box and type the following message inside it:

> **Save using the file naming standard CM-StationID##-yourinitials, where ## is the asset ID. Example: CM-StationID56-JW**

Protect the worksheet, leaving unlocked the cells that the technician will fill in as he or she completes a maintenance visit. Do not include a password for unprotecting the sheet. Save the template and name it **NationalCMForm-StudentName** with your name substituted for *StudentName*. Start a new workbook based on the custom template. To test the template's organization and layout, fill out a form as if you are a technician working on your own computer. Save the completed form as an Excel workbook named **EL2-U2-Act1-NationalCMForm**. Print the form scaled to fit on one page. Copy the **NationalCMForm-StudentName.xltx** template file to your storage medium.

Internet Research

Apply What-If Analysis to a Planned Move

Following graduation, you plan to move out of the state/province for a few years to live on your own. Create a new workbook to use as you plan this move to develop a budget for expenses in the first year. Research typical rents for apartments in the city in which you want to find your first job. Estimate other living costs in the city including transportation, food, entertainment, clothes, telephone, cable/satellite, cell phone, Internet, and so on. Calculate total living costs for an entire year. Next, research annual starting salaries for your chosen field of study in the same area. Estimate the take-home pay at approximately 70% of the annual salary you decide to use. Using the take-home pay and the total living costs for the year, calculate whether you will have enough money to cover your expenses.

Next, assume you want to save money to go on a vacation at the end of the year. Use Goal Seek to find the take-home pay you need to earn to have $2,000 left over at the end of the year. Accept the solution that Goal Seek provides and then create two scenarios in the worksheet, as follows:

- A scenario named *LowestValues,* in which you adjust each value down to the lowest amount you think is reasonable
- A scenario named *HighestValues,* in which you adjust each value up to the highest amount you think is reasonable

Apply each scenario and watch the impact on the amount left over at the end of the year. Display the worksheet in the *HighestValues* scenario and then create a scenario summary report. Print the worksheet, applying print options as necessary to minimize the pages required. Print the scenario summary report. Save the workbook as **EL2-U2-Act2-MyFirstYearBudget**. Close **EL2-U2-Act2-MyFirstYearBudget.xlsx**.

Research and Compare Smartphones

You work for an independent marketing consultant who travels frequently in North America and Europe for work. The consultant, Lindsay Somers, would like to purchase a smartphone. While traveling, Lindsay will use the smartphone for conference calls, sending email, web browsing, text messaging, and modifying PowerPoint presentations, Word documents, and Excel worksheets. Using the Internet, research the latest smartphones from three different manufacturers. Prepare a worksheet that compares the three smartphones, organizing the information so the main features are shown along the left side of the page by category and each phone's specifications for those features are set in columns. At the bottom of each column, provide the hyperlink to the phone's specifications on the Web. Based on your perception of the best value, select one of the phones as your recommendation and use a comment box in the worksheet to note the phone you think Lindsay should select. In the comment box, provide a brief explanation of why you chose this phone. Make sure comments are displayed in the worksheet. Save the worksheet and name it **EL2-U2-Act3-Smartphones**. Publish the worksheet as a single file web page, accepting the default file name and changing the page title to *Smartphone Feature and Price Comparison*. Print the web page from the Internet Explorer window. Close Internet Explorer and then close **EL2-U2-Act3-Smartphones.xlsx**.

Job Study

Prepare a Wages Budget and Link the Budget to a Word Document

You work at a small, independent, long-term care facility named Gardenview Place Long-Term Care. As assistant to the business manager, you are helping with the preparation of next year's hourly wages budget. Create a worksheet to estimate next year's hourly wage expenses using the average wage costs in Table U2.1 and the following information about hourly paid workers:

- The facility runs three 8-hour shifts, 7 days per week, 52 weeks per year: 6 a.m. to 2 p.m., 2 p.m. to 10 p.m., and 10 p.m. to 6 a.m.
- Each shift requires two registered nurses, four licensed practical nurses, and two health-care aid workers.
- On each shift, one of the registered nurses is designated as the charge nurse and is paid a premium of 15% his or her regular hourly rate.
- The shifts from 6 a.m. to 2 p.m. and 2 p.m. to 10 p.m. require one custodian; the shift from 10 p.m. to 6 a.m. requires two custodians.
- Each shift requires the services of an on-call physician and on-call pharmacist. Budget for the physician and pharmacist at 4 hours per shift.
- Add 14% to each shift's total wage costs to cover the estimated costs of benefits such as vacation pay, holiday pay, and medical care coverage plans for all workers *except* the on-call physician and on-call pharmacist, who do not receive these benefits.

Make use of colors, themes, and table features to make the budget calculations workbook easy to read. Save the workbook and name it **EL2-U2-JS-GardenviewWageBdgt**. Print the worksheet, adjusting print options as necessary to minimize the pages required. Create a chart in a separate sheet to show the total hourly wages budget by worker category. You determine the chart type and chart options to use in presenting the information.

Start Word and open the document named **GardenviewOpBdgt.docx**. Change the year on the title page to the current year. Change the name and date at the bottom of the title page to your name and the current date. Link the chart created in the Excel worksheet to the end of the Word document. Save the revised document as **EL2-U2-JS-GardenviewOpBdgt**. Print and then close **EL2-U2-JS-GardenviewOpBdgt.docx**. Deselect the chart and close it.

Table U2.1 Average Hourly Wage Rates

Wage Category	*Average Wage Rate*
registered nurse	29.64
licensed practical nurse	18.63
health-care aid worker	14.05
custodian	10.96
on-call physician	66.00
on-call pharmacist	48.00

Index

A

ABS function, 59
absolute reference, range name and, 41
Accept All button, 212
Accept or Reject Changes dialog box, 212
Access
  copying and pasting worksheet data to, 278–279
  importing data from, 271–272
Adobe Reader, 298
Alignment group, 22
AND logical function, 59–61
argument, in function formula, 39
array formula, 15
* (asterisk), in custom filter, 27
auditing tools, 169–176
  circling invalid data, 174–176
  tracing precedent and dependent cells, 170
  troubleshooting formulas, 171–174
  viewing relationships between cells and formulas, 170–171
  watching formula cell, 174–176
Author property, 187–188
AutoCorrect Options button, 75–76
AutoFilter, filtering worksheet using custom, 27–28
automating tasks using macros, 227–235
AutoRecover feature, 253–255
AutoSave feature, 253–255
AVERAGE function, 42
AVERAGEIF function, 46–47
AVERAGEIFS function, 46, 48

B

banding rows, 76
Break Link button, 111, 283

C

calculated column, adding to table, 75–76
cells
  dependent cells, 170
  filtering and sorting by attributes of, 29–31
  formatting
    based on Top/Bottom Rules list, 7–8
    based on value comparison, 7
    new formatting rule, 8–10
  precedent cells, 170
  unlocking, 204–206
  viewing relationships between cells and formulas, 170–171
  watching formula cell, 174–176
  wrapping and shrinking text to fit within, 22
Change Source button, 111
Change Source dialog box, 111
Chart Elements button, 128
Chart Styles button, 128
ciphertext, 208
Clear Format button, 11
Clipboard task pane, 278
col_index_num, 53
Collapse the Ribbon button, 238
color
  filtering by font color, 30
  sorting by cell color, 30
[color] in custom number format code, 20
color scales, conditional formatting using, 14
Column button, 130, 131
columns
  adding calculated column to table, 75–76
  banding, 76
  converting data from rows to columns, 156–158–158
  converting text to, 80–81
  Flash Fill feature, 81–82
  removing duplicate records, 82–84
commands
  adding to quick Access toolbar, 247
  renaming, 242
comma separated file format, 275
comments
  copying, 190–191
  defined, 189
  editing and deleting, 190–191
  inserting, 189–192
  pasting, 190–191
  printing, 190–191
  viewing, 189–190
compatibility checker, 294–295
Compatibility Checker button, 294
CONCATENATE function, 82
conditional formatting, 6–16
  color scales in, 14
  create and apply new formatting rule, 8–10
  data bars in, 14
  defined, 6
  drop-down list, 6–7
  editing and deleting rules, 10–12
  filtering and sorting using, 29–31
  format cell based on Top/Bottom Rules list, 7–8
  format cell based on value comparison, 7
  formulas in, 15–16
  icon set for applying, 12–13
  Quick Analysis button, 6–7
Conditional Formatting button, 6
Conditional Formatting Rules Manager, 10–11
conditional test, 43, 58
Consolidate button, 114
Consolidate dialog box, 115
Consolidate feature, summarizing data using, 103, 114–116
Convert Text to Columns Wizard, 80–81
Convert to Range button, 89

copying
to Access, 278–279
comments, 190–191
to PowerPoint, 284–285
to Word, 280–282
COUNTA function, 42–43
COUNT function, 42
COUNTIF function, 43–44
COUNTIFS function, 43, 45
Create Sparklines dialog box, 130, 131
.csv file format, 286
Custom AutoFilter, filtering worksheet using, 27–28
Custom AutoFilter dialog box, 27–28
Customize Quick Access Toolbar button, 245
customizing
creating and applying custom view, 248–250
display options, 237–238
macros, 227–235
pinning workbooks to Recent Workbooks list, 236–237
Quick Access toolbar, 245–248
ribbon, 238–245
save options, 253–255
Sparklines, 132–133
custom number format, creating, 20–22
Custom Sort, 30–31
custom view, creating and applying, 248–250
Custom View button, 248
Custom View dialog box, 248, 249

D

data
circling invalid data, 174–176
converting, from rows to columns, 157–158
Data Tools group, 80–89
exporting, 278–288
to Access, 278–279
breaking link to Excel object, 283
to PowerPoint, 284–285
as text file, 286–288
to Word, 280–282
filtering and sorting, using conditional formatting or cell attributes, 29–31
Flash Fill, 81–82
Goal Seek to find target value, 159–161
grouping and ungrouping, 93–94
importing, 270–277
from Access, 271–272
from text file, 275–277
from website, 272–275
maintaining external references for, 111–113
pasting using Paste Special options, 155–159
PivotCharts, 127–130
PivotTables, 116–126
restricting data entry, 86–89
source, 270
subtotaling related data, 89–93
summarizing
with consolidate feature, 114–116
linking to ranges in other worksheets/workbooks, 110–111
in multiple worksheets using range names and 3-D references, 106–109
with Sparklines, 130–133
transposing, 156–158
validating data entry, 84–89
what-if analysis
with data tables, 166–169
with Scenario Manager, 161–165
data bars, conditional formatting using, 14
DATA tab, 80, 83, 270, 271
data table
defined, 166
one-variable data table, 166–167
two-variable data table, 168–169
Data Tools group, 80–89
converting text to columns, 80–81
overview, 80
populating data using Flash Fill, 81–82
removing duplicate records, 82–84
validating and restricting data entry, 84–89
data validation
circling invalid data, 174–176
ensuring data entered in specified text length, 88–89
error alert message, 85
input message, 84–85
restricting data entry to dates within range, 86–87
restricting data entry to values within list, 87–88
Data Validation button, 84, 174
Data Validation dialog box, 84–85
Defined Names group, 51, 106
Delete button, 190
deleting
comments, 190–191
conditional formatting rules, 10–12
custom template, 253
macro, 235
range name, 51–52
Scenario Manager, 164
delimited file format, 275
dependent cell, tracing, 170
destination, 270
destination workbook, 110
Disable Link button, 201
display options
customizing, 237–238
restoring default, 239
distributing workbooks/worksheets
compatibility checker, 294–295
marking as final, 292–294
preparation for, 289–295
publishing as PDF document, 298–300
publishing as web page, 302–303
publishing as XPS document, 300–301

removing information before, 289–292
document information panel, 187, 188
Document Inspector, 289–292

E

Edit Anyway button, 292
Edit Comment button, 190
editing
comments, 190–191
conditional formatting rules, 10–12
macro, 233–235
range name, 51–52
Scenario Manager, 163
source data, 111–113
tracked workbook, 213
Edit Links button, 111
Edit Links dialog box, 111–112
Edit the Rule Description section, 8–9
email, sending workbook by, 203–204
embedding Excel data
in PowerPoint presentation, 284–285
in Word document, 280–281
Encrypt Document dialog box, 208, 209
encrypted passwords, 208
error alert messages, 85
Error Checking button, 172
errors
error codes, 171–172
logic errors, 171
troubleshooting formulas, 171–174
Evaluate Formula button, 172
Existing Connections dialog box, 270
exponential notation, 16–17
exporting data, 278–288
breaking link to Excel object, 283
copying and pasting worksheet data to
Access, 278–279
PowerPoint, 284–285
Word, 280–282
as text file, 286–288
EXTERNAL DATA tab, 278
external reference
editing source data and updating external link, 111–113
point-and-click approach to creating, 110
removing, 113–114

F

field names row, 74
fields, defined, 74
Field Settings button, 126
files
comma separated file format, 275
delimited file format, 275
importing data from text file, 275–277
FILE tab, 187
filtering
by font color, 30
by icon set, 29
PivotTables
overview, 121–122
using Slicers, 122–124
using Timelines, 124–126
tables, 78–79
using conditional formatting or cell attributes, 29–31
worksheet using Custom AutoFilter, 27–28
Financial button, 56, 57
financial functions, 56–57
IPMT function, 56
PMT function, 56
PPMT function, 56–57
Flash Fill, populating data using, 81–82
folder, shared, 193
Format as Table button, 74
Format button, 204, 205
Format Cells dialog box, 16–17, 18–19
formatting
conditional, 6–16
custom number formats, 20–22
filtering and sorting using conditional formatting, 29–31
fraction, 16–18
PivotTables, 121–122
scientific, 16–18
special number, 18–19
table, 76–78
with text functions, 23–26
Formula Auditing group, 169–176
circling invalid data, 174–176
tracing precedent and dependent cells, 170
troubleshooting formulas, 171–174
viewing relationships between cells and formulas, 170–171
watching formula cell, 174–176
formulas
array formula, 15
auditing tools for, 169–176
conditional formatting using, 15–16
one-variable data table, 166–167
proof formula, 171
range names for, 41–42, 51–52
referencing cell in separate worksheet, 106–109
standard, 41
3-D formulas, 106
two-variable data table, 168–169
viewing relationships between cells and formulas, 170–171
FORMULAS tab, 23, 51, 106, 169
fraction formatting, 16–18
From Access button, 271
From Other Sources button, 270
From Text button, 275
From Web button, 272
function formula
argument in, 39
creating range name, 41–42
editing and deleting range name, 51–52
standard, 41
structure of, 39

functions
changing in PivotTable, 126
financial functions, 56–57
logical functions, 58–61
Lookup & Reference functions, 52–55
math and trigonometry functions, 49–50
nested functions, 58–59
search for, 61
statistical functions, 42–48
Sum function, 76, 115
text functions, 23–26

G

Get External Data group, 270, 271
Goal Seek, 159–161
Gradient Fill section, 14
group
adding button to, 241
renaming, 242
Group button, 93–94

H

header row, 74
formatting, 76
Hide Detail button, 90, 93–94
Highlight Changes dialog box, 198
HLOOKUP function, 52, 55
HOME tab, 204

I

icon set
conditional formatting using, 12–13
filtering by, 29
IF function, nested, 58–59
IF statement
conditional formatting using, 15–16
structure of, 58
Import Data dialog box, 271
importing data, 270–277
from Access, 271–272
from text file, 275–277
from website, 272–275
Import Text File dialog box, 275
Info backstage area, 187
Information error alert message, 85
input message, 84–85
Insert Comment, 189
Insert Function button, 43, 44
inserting comments, 189–192
Insert Slicer button, 122
INSERT tab, 116, 130
Insert Timeline button, 124
Inspect button, 289
Invite People option, 200–201
IPMT function, 56

K

keyboard shortcut, creating and assigning macro to, 231–233

L

LEFT text function, 24, 26
Line button, 130, 131
linking Excel data to Word document, 280, 282
breaking link, 283
Links dialog box, 283
loan payments, calculating principal portion of, 56–57
Logical button, 58
logical functions, 58–61
AND functions, 59–61
IF function, 58–59
nested functions, 58–59
OR functions, 59–61
logic errors, 171
Lookup & Reference button, 52
Lookup & Reference functions, 52–55
HLOOKUP function, 52, 55
VLOOKUP function, 52–55
lookup table, 52
lookup_value, 53
LOWER text function, 23, 25

M

Macro dialog box, 230
macros, 227–235
assigning to shortcut key, 231–233
creating, 227–229
defined, 227
deleting, 235
editing, 233–235
macro-enabled workbook creation, 235
naming, 227
playing, 230
running, 230
saving workbooks containing, 228–229
Macros button, 227
marking workbook as final, 292–294
mathematical operations, performing while pasting, 158–159
math functions, 49–50
Math & Trig button, 49, 50
MAX function, 42
metadata
defined, 187
removing, 289–292
Microsoft Visual Basic for Applications (VBA), 228
MID text function, 24, 26
MIN function, 42
minimizing the ribbon, 238–239
module, 233
Move Chart button, 128
Move Down button, 241, 242
Move Up button, 241, 242

N

#N/A error, 171, 172
Name box, 41, 42
#NAME? error, 171, 172
Name Manager button, 51, 106, 107
Name Manager dialog box, 51
nested functions, 58–59
network share, 193
New Comment button, 189
New Formatting Rule dialog box, 8–10, 15
New Tab button, 241
New Web Query dialog box, 272, 273
Next button, 190
Notepad, 275
Number Format button, 16
number formats
custom, 20–22
special, 18–19

O

one-variable data table, 166–167
Options dialog box, 240–242
OR logical function, 59–61
Outline feature, 89–90
Outline group, 90, 93

P

PAGE LAYOUT tab, 190
password
  adding and removing to workbook, 208–210
  elements of good password, 208
  encrypted, 208
  to unprotect worksheet, 205
Paste button, 155
Paste Special dialog box, 155–156, 158, 190, 280
Paste Special options
  converting data from rows to columns, 157–158
  performing mathematical operations while pasting, 158–159
  selecting other, 159
  transposing data, 156–158
pasting
  to Access, 278–279
  comments, 190–191
  to PowerPoint, 284–285
  using Paste Special options, 155–159
  to Word, 280–282
PDF document, publishing workbook as, 298–300
pensions costs, calculating using nested IF and AND functions, 59–60
personal information, removing from workbook before publishing, 289–292
pinning workbooks to Recent Workbooks list, 236–237
PivotChart button, 127
PivotCharts, 127–130
  creating, 127–130
  creating using PivotTable, 127–129
  defined, 127
  overview of, 127–128
  from scratch, 129–130
PivotTable button, 116, 117
PivotTables, 116–126
  changing Sum function in, 126
  creating with PivotTable button, 117–118, 120
  defined, 116
  filtering
    overview, 121–122
    using Slicers, 122–124
    using Timelines, 124–126
  formatting, 121–122
  making PivotChart from, 127–129
  overview, 116–118
  Recommended PivotTables, 117–119
PIVOTTABLE TOOLS ANALYZE tab, 121, 122, 127
PIVOTTABLE TOOLS DESIGN tab, 121
playing a macro, 230
PMT function, 56
portable document format (PDF), 298–300
(pound symbol), in custom number format code, 20
PowerPoint
  copying and pasting worksheet data to, 284–285
  embedding Excel data in, 284–285
PPMT function, 56–57
precedent cell, tracing, 170
Previous button, 190
principal portion of loan payment, 56–57
printing
  change history of shared workbook, 198–199
  comments, 190–191
proof formula, 171
PROPER text function, 23
properties, adding to workbook, 187–189
Properties button, 188
protecting
  workbook, 207–208
  worksheets, 204–207
Protect Sheet button, 204
Protect Sheet dialog box, 205
Protect Structure and Windows dialog box, 207
Protect Workbook button, 207, 208
Publish as Web Page dialog box, 302

Q

? (question mark)
  in custom filter, 27
  in custom number format code, 20
Quick Access toolbar
  adding commands to, 247
  customizing, 245–248
  importing customizations to, 248
  removing buttons from, 247
  resetting to original setting, 247–248
Quick Analysis button, 6–7

R

range
  converting table to normal range, 89
  converting table to range and creating subtotals, 90–92
  converting to table, 74–75
  restricting data entry to dates within range, 86–87
range_lookup, 53
range name
  creating, 41
  deleting, 51–52
  editing, 51–52
  Name Manager to modify, 106–108
  summarize data in multiple worksheets using, 106–108
Recent Workbooks list, pinning workbook to, 236–237
Recommended PivotTables, 117–119
Recommended PivotTables button, 117
Record Macro button, 231
Record Macro dialog box, 227, 231

records
  defined, 74
  removing duplicate, 82–84
recovering workbook, 254–255
references
  3-D reference, 106
  worksheet reference, 106
Reject All button, 212
Remove Arrow button, 170
Remove Duplicates dialog box, 82, 83
Remove Duplicates button, 82–83
Rename button, 242
Reset button, 247–248
Resolve Conflicts dialog box, 196
REVIEW tab, 189, 190, 192, 204
ribbon
  adding buttons to a group, 241
  creating a new tab, 241–242
  customizing, 240–245
  importing customizations, 248
  minimizing, 238–239
  renaming tab, group, or command on, 242
  resetting, 247–248
Ribbon Display Options button, 238
RIGHT text function, 24, 26
rows
  adding to table, 75–76
  banding, 76
  converting data from rows to columns, 156–158–158
  header row formatting, 76
  removing duplicate, 82–84
  Total row, adding, 76–78
Run button, 230

S

Save As dialog box, 286, 302
Save As option, 228, 278
Save button, 228
saving
  AutoRecover and AutoSave, 253
  customizing save options, 253–255
  workbook as template, 250–253
  workbooks containing macros, 228–229
Scenario Manager
  adding to worksheet, 162–163
  applying, 163
  creating assumptions for what-if analysis, 161–165
  deleting, 164
  editing, 163
  generating scenario summary report, 165
Scenario Manager dialog box, 162
Scenario Summary dialog box, 165
Scenario Values dialog box, 162
scientific formatting, 16–18
security setting, Trust Center settings, 296–297
Select a Rule Type section, 8–9, 15
Select Changes to Accept or Reject dialog box, 212
Select Data Source dialog box, 271
Select Table dialog box, 271, 272
; (semicolon), in custom number format code, 20
Share backstage area, 200–201
shared network folder, 193
shared workbooks, 192–194
  changing user name, 194, 195
  opening multiple instances of Excel, 194
  overview of, 193–194
  printing history sheet, 198–199
  removing shared workbook access, 198–199
  resolving conflicts in, 196–197
  sending by email, 203–204
  viewing other users of, 195–196
  on Windows SkyDrive, 199–202
Share Workbook button, 192
Share Workbook dialog box, 192–194, 198
shortcut key, creating and assigning macro to, 231–233
Show All Comments button, 190
Show Detail button, 90, 94
Show Formulas button, 170
shrinking text to fit, 22
SkyDrive, sharing workbook on, 199–202
Slicer pane, 122, 123
Slicers, filtering PivotTable using, 122–124
SLICER TOOLS OPTIONS tab, 124
Sort Dialog Box, 30–31
Sort & Filter button, 27, 29
sorting
  by cell color, 30
  custom sort, 30–31
  tables, 78–79
  using conditional formatting or cell attributes, 29–31
source data, 270
  editing and updating external link, 111–113
source workbook, 110
Sparklines
  creating, 130–132
  customizing, 132–133
  defined, 130
SPARKLINE TOOLS DESIGN tab, 132
special number format, 18–19
standard formula, 41
statistical functions, 42–48
  AVERAGE function, 42
  AVERAGEIF function, 46–47
  AVERAGEIFS function, 46, 48
  COUNTA function, 42–43
  COUNT function, 42
  COUNTIF function, 43–44
  COUNTIFS function, 43, 45
  MAX function, 42
  MIN function, 42
Stop error alert message, 85
Stop Recording button, 228

SUBSTITUTE text function, 23, 25
subtotals
  converting table to range and creating subtotals, 90–92
  modifying, 92–93
  overview, 89
Sum function, 76, 115
  changing in PivotTable, 126
SUMIF function, 49–50
SUMIFS function, 49
summarizing data
  with consolidate feature, 114–116
  by linking to ranges in other worksheets/workbooks, 110–111
  in multiple worksheets using range names and 3-D references, 106–109
  with Sparklines, 130–133

T

tab
  creating new, 241
  renaming, 242
table
  copying and pasting data from Access to, 278–279
  importing
    from Access, 271–272
    from website, 272–275
table_array, 53
Table button, 74
tables
  adding row and calculated column to, 75–76
  automatic expansion of, 75
  banding rows and columns in, 76
  converting range to table, 74–75
  converting table to range and creating subtotals, 90–92
  converting to normal range, 89
  creating, 74–75
  defined, 71
  field names row in, 74
  fields in, 74
  filtering, 78–79
  formatting and adding *Total* row to, 77–78
  header row in, 74
  modifying, 75–76
  PivotTables, 116–126
  records in, 74
  sorting, 78–79
  style options for, 76–77
  subtotaling related data, 89–93
Table Styles gallery, 76
TABLE TOOLS DESIGN tab, 76–77, 83, 89
target value, using Goal Seek to find, 159–161
template
  deleting custom, 253
  saving workbook as, 250–251
  using custom, 252–253
text
  converting to columns, 80–81
  wrapping and shrinking to fit in cells, 22
Text button, 23
text file
  exporting worksheets as, 286–288
  importing data from, 275–277
text functions, 23–26
Text Import Wizard, 275–277
"text" in custom number format code, 20
text #NAME? error message, 51
Text to Columns button, 80
3-D formulas, 106
3-D references
  defined, 106
  summarize data in multiple worksheet using, 106–109
Time Level indicator, 125
Timelines, filtering PivotTables using, 124–126
TIMELINE TOOLS OPTIONS tab, 126
Title property, 187–188
Top/Bottom Rules list, formatting cell based on, 7–8
Total row, 76–78
Trace Dependents button, 170
Track Changes, 211–215
  accepting and rejecting changes, 212
  editing using, 213
  highlighting and reviewing changes, 214
  turning off, 215
Track Changes button, 198, 211
Transpose button, 156
transposing data, 156–158
trigonometry functions, 49–50
TRIM text function, 24, 26
troubleshooting formulas, 171–174
Trust Center settings, 296–297
Trusted Locations list, 296–297
Trusted Publishers, 296
two-variable data table, 168–169

U

Undo feature, 111
Ungroup button, 93–94
Ungroup dialog box, 93
unicode text, 286
Unprotected Sheet dialog box, 207
unprotecting
  workbook, 207–208
  worksheet, 204–207
Unprotect Sheet button, 207
UPPER text function, 23, 25
user name, changing, 194, 195

V

value comparison, formatting cells based on, 7
#VALUE! error, 171, 172
Value Field Setting dialog box, 126
viewing comments, 189–190
Visual Basic for Applications (VBA), 228, 233
VLOOKUP function, 52–55

W

Warning error alert message, 85
Watch Window button, 174
website
  importing data from, 272–275
  publishing worksheet as web page, 302–303
what-if analysis
  creating assumptions with Scenario Manager, 161–165
  with data tables, 166–169
wildcard characters, in custom filter, 27
Windows Live account, 200
Windows SkyDrive, sharing workbooks on, 199–202
Win/Loss button, 130, 131
Word document
  breaking link to Excel worksheet, 283
  copying and pasting worksheet data to, 280–281
  embedding Excel data into, 280–281
  linking Excel data to, 280, 282
workbooks
  changing user name, 194, 195
  creating macro-enabled workbook, 235
  destination, 110
  distributing, 298–303
    compatibility checker, 294–295
    marking as final, 292–294
    preparing for, 289–295
    publishing as PDF document, 298–300
    publishing as XPS document, 300–301
    removing information before, 289–292
  opening multiple instances of Excel, 194
  passwords, adding and removing, 208–210
  pinning to Recent Workbooks list, 236–237
  properties, adding, 187–189
  protecting and unprotecting, 207–208
  recovering, 254–255
  saving as template, 250–253
  saving containing macros, 228–229
  sending by email, 203–204
  sharing, 192–194
    changing user name, 194, 195
    opening multiple instances of Excel, 194
    overview of, 193–194
    printing history sheet, 198–199
    removing shared workbook access, 198–199
    resolving conflicts in, 196–197
    sending by email, 203–204
    viewing other users of, 195–196
    on Windows SkyDrive, 199–202
  source, 110
  summarizing data by linking to ranges in another workbook or worksheet, 110–111
  tracking changes, 211–215
    accepting and rejecting changes, 212
    editing, 213
    highlighting and reviewing changes, 214
    turning off, 215
worksheets
  comments, managing, 189–192
  custom view for, 248–250
  distributing, as web page, 302–303
  exporting, 278–288
    breaking link to Excel object, 283
    copying and pasting worksheet data to
      Access, 278–279
      PowerPoint, 284–285
      Word, 280–282
    as text file, 286–288
  filtering, using Custom AutoFilter, 27–28
  importing data, 270–277
    from Access, 271–272
    from text file, 275–277
    from website, 272–275
  protecting and unprotecting, 204–207
  summarizing data
    Consolidate feature, 114–116
    by linking ranges in another workbook, 110–111
    in multiple worksheets using range names and 3-D references, 106–109
  worksheet reference, 106
wrapping text, 22
Wrap Text button, 22

X–Z

XML paper specification, 300
XPS document, publishing workbook as, 300–301
0 (zero), in custom number format code, 20